Fodor's Fourth Edition

South America

D1301898

The complete guide, thoroughly up-to-date

Packed with details that will make your trip

The must-see sights, off and on the beaten path

What to see, what to skip

Vacation itineraries, walking tours, day trips

Smart lodging and dining options

Essential local dos and taboos

Transportation tips

Key contacts, savvy travel advice

When to go, what to pack

Clear, accurate, easy-to-use maps

Fodor's Travel Publications • New York, Toronto, London, Sydney, Auckland
www.fodors.com

Fodor's South America

EDITORS: Melisse Gelula, Natasha Lesser, Laura M. Kidder, and Holly S. Smith

Editorial Contributors: Eddy Ancinas, Karen Bressler, Karla Brunet, Deb Carroll, Shane Christensen, Joyce Dalton, Mary Dempsey, Mick Elmore, Marilene Felinto B. de Lima, Wilma Felinto B. de Lima, Joan Gonzalez, Amy Karafin, Christina Knight, Kristen Masick, Chelsea Mauldin, Corey Nettles, Charles Runnette, Tom Samiljan, Carlos Henrique Severo, Robert P. Walzer, Brad Weiss

Production Editorial: Melissa Klurman, Rebecca Zeiler

Maps: David Lindroth, *cartographer;* Rebecca Baer and Bob Blake, *map editors*

Design: Fabrizio La Rocca, *creative director;* Guido Caroti, *art director;* Jolie Novak, *photo editor*

Cover Design: Pentagram

Production/Manufacturing: Mike Costa

Cover Photograph: Ric Ergenbright/Corbis

Copyright

Fourth Edition

ISBN 0–679–00441–6

ISSN 0362–0220

Special Sales

Fodor's Travel Publications are available at special discounts for bulk purchases for sales promotions or premiums. Special editions, including personalized covers, excerpts of existing guides, and corporate imprints, can be created in large quantities for special needs. For more information, contact your local bookseller or write to Special Markets, Fodor's Travel Publications, 201 East 50th Street, New York, NY 10022. Inquiries from Canada should be directed to your local Canadian bookseller or sent to Random House of Canada, Ltd., Marketing Department, 2775 Matheson Boulevard East, Mississauga, Ontario L4W 4P7. Inquiries from the United Kingdom should be sent to Fodor's Travel Publications, 20 Vauxhall Bridge Road, London SW1V 2SA, England.

PRINTED IN THE UNITED STATES OF AMERICA

10 9 8 7 6 5 4 3 2 1

Important Tip

Although all prices, opening times, and other details in this book are based on information supplied to us at press time, changes occur all the time in the travel world, and Fodor's cannot accept responsibility for facts that become outdated or for inadvertent errors or omissions. So **always confirm information when it matters,** especially if you're making a detour to visit a specific place.

CONTENTS

Contents

Maps

ON THE ROAD WITH FODOR'S

The trips you take this year and next are going to be significant trips, if only because they'll be your first in the new millennium. Acutely aware of that fact, we've pulled out all stops in preparing *Fodor's South America*. To guide you in putting together your South American experience, we've created multiday itineraries and neighborhood walks. And to direct you to the places that are truly worth your time and money in these important years, we've rallied the team of endearingly picky know-it-alls we're pleased to call our writers. Having seen all corners of the regions they cover for us, they're real experts. If you knew them, you'd poll them for tips yourself.

Eddy Ancinas, who contributed to Argentina's Patagonia section, met an Argentine ski racer at the 1960 Winter Olympics in Squaw Valley, California. After they were married in 1962, they crossed the Andes from Chile to Mendoza by train, and then drove south to Bariloche, where they lived for six months before traveling to Patagonia. Since then, Eddy has imported sweaters from Peru and Bolivia; led ski and horseback trips in Peru, Argentina, and Chile; and written about travel in those countries.

New York–based **Karen Bressler** rolled up her veteran travel writer's sleeves and helped to fact-check and fine-tune the Salvador section of Brazil. Karen has written for *Condé Nast Traveler, Bridal Guide, Honeymoon, Elegant Bride,* and *Recommend* magazines and is a correspondent for Condé Nast's on-line travel publication, www.concierge.com.

Shane Christensen, who updated the Ecuador chapter, the Minas Gerais section of the Brazil chapter, and Smart Travel Tips has traveled extensively in South America and has previously written about Argentina and Paraguay for Fodor's. He's based in Washington, D.C., where he's the bureau chief for On the Road, Inc.

Joyce Dalton has explored exotic destinations from Argentina and Albania to Zaire and Zanzibar. Her travel stories and photos have appeared in various trade and consumer publications. Joyce won a journalistic excellence award for her coverage of the World Dracula Congress held in Romania in 1995.

Mary A. Dempsey was bitten by the travel bug 15 years ago while working at a newspaper in Venezuela. Two more years writing from Peru and a newspaper stint in Puerto Rico solidified her wanderlust. Mary, who worked on the Rio section of Brazil, has written articles about South America and the Caribbean for such publications as the *Los Angeles Times, Condé Nast Traveler,* and *Travel & Leisure.*

Bangkok-based journalist **Mick Elmore** once lived in Colombia, where he studied in Bogotá, traversed the countryside, and even worked on a coffee *finca* (plantation). On his trip back for Fodor's, Mick scouted the best places from which to sip the brew that was once his livelihood. In addition to this assignment, Mick revised the Java and Sumatra chapters of *Fodor's Southeast Asia.*

The Brazil chapter's Salvador writer, **Marilene Felinto B. de Lima,** is a São Paulo–based freelancer who works for the city's large daily newspaper, *Folha.* She was assisted by her sister, Wilma.

Peru and Bolivia updater **Joan Gonzalez** started her career on newspapers in Ohio. Her involvement with South America began with a job as a flight attendant for Pan Am. She presently works as a freelancer, writing for travel-industry publications and publishing newsletters and newspapers for airlines and tourist boards.

After graduating from Boston University with a degree in international studies, **Kristen Masick** set off for Latin America. She ended up living in Buenos Aires for two years, managing press relations for the Embassy of Nigeria. While there, she also covered Buenos Aires for Fodor's, doing particularly in-depth research on the restaurants, bars, and nightclubs.

A 2½-month, 5-country trek provided **Chelsea Mauldin** with a wealth of South American travel experience, which she shared in the chapters on Argentina, Bolivia, Brazil, Chile, and Peru as well Smart Travel Tips. Before becoming an Internet consultant, she was the editor of Fodor's Web site and numerous Fodor's books—including previous editions of this guide.

Corey Nettles caught the travel bug while living in Germany as a high-school exchange student. Subsequent stints in France and traveling abroad—from Cuba and Chile to Russia and Azerbaijan—have fueled her passion to learn about different cultures. In addition to updating the Venezuela chapter of this book, Corey has written for Fodor's about Spain, England, and Ireland.

The son of an airline executive, **Charles Runnette** traveled to many a place before settling in New York. He has been a writer/editor for *New York Magazine,* Microsoft's Sidewalk, and the *New York Times* Electronic Media. He also developed the Travel channel for StarMedia.com, the AOL of Latin America. Charles updated the Chile chapter.

New York City–based journalist **Tom Samiljan,** who updated the Paraguay and Uruguay chapters, has lived in Ecuador, France, Spain, and the Netherlands. He writes for *Rolling Stone, Elle, TV Guide, Travel & Leisure* and *Time Out New York* and is currently an associate editor at Wenner Media.

The Brazil chapter's São Paulo section writer **Carlos Henrique Severo** is a journalist who has put his talents to work on the Internet since 1995. He was assisted by **Karla Brunet,** a designer and photographer who studied art for four years in San Francisco, CA. Both Carlos and Karla live in São Paulo.

Robert P. Walzer is a journalist who has spent most of the past decade living and working in the Caribbean and Latin America. After returning to his native New York from a year in Milan, he couldn't pass up the chance to visit the world's southernmost post office in Ushuaia while contributing to Argentina's Patagonia section.

Fluent in both Spanish and Portuguese, English-teacher, translator, and intrepid traveler **Brad Weiss** put his language skills to work on the Litoral section of Argentina and the Amazon section of Brazil. Brad lives in São Paulo where he works for the financial newspaper *Gazeta Mercantil* and is a weekend tour guide.

We'd also like to thank Continental Airline, particularly Thomas Anderson; Carlos Paredes Mora and the staff at the Cormetur office in Mérida; Stela Maris Dallari of the Brazilian Consulate in New York; the Latin American Reservation Service; Luis Enrique Costa R. at the Museum of Modern Art in Caracas; Meg Pearson; Rony Pollak; Mary Lamberti of Pro-Brazil, Inc.; Natalia Zapatero and Mario Brito of RioTur; Rosario Rozas; Maria Taraboulos, Kreps & Adams, and the Inter-Continental hotels; Franz Orthmann Testa; Elisabeth Lajtonyi Trenkmann; Tom Dovidas at Varig Airlines; and John Benus, Director of the Venezuelan Tourism Association.

Don't Forget to Write

Keeping a travel guide fresh and up-to-date is a big job. So we love your feedback—positive and negative—and follow up on all suggestions. Contact the South America editor at editors@fodors.com or c/o Fodor's, 201 East 50th Street, New York, New York 10022. And have a wonderful trip!

Karen Cure
Editorial Director

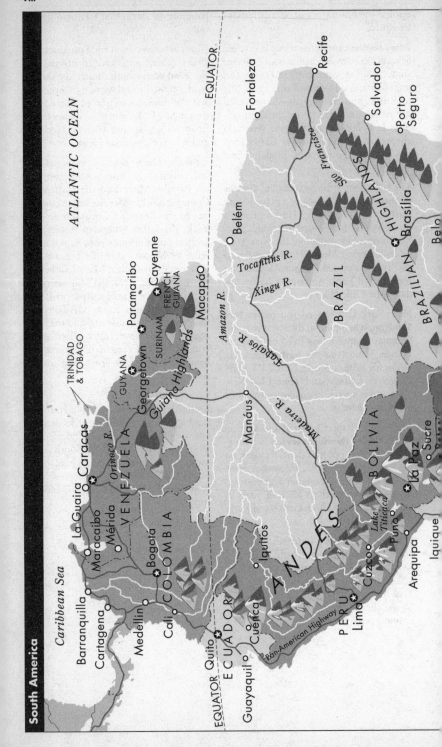

South America

ATLANTIC OCEAN

Caribbean Sea

Recife
Fortaleza
Salvador
Porto Seguro
São Francisco
HIGHLANDS
Brasília
Belo

Belém
Tocantins R.
Xingu R.
BRAZIL
Amazon R.
BRAZILIAN
Tapajós R.

Cayenne
FRENCH GUIANA
Macapáo
Paramaribo
SURINAM
Guiana Highlands
TRINIDAD & TOBAGO
GUYANA
Georgetown
Manáus
Madeira R.
La Paz
BOLIVIA
Sucre

Caracas
La Guaira
Orinoco R.
VENEZUELA
Maracaibo
Mérida
Barranquilla
Cartagena
Bogotá
COLOMBIA
Medellín
Cali
Iquitos
ANDES
Lake Titicaca
Puno
Iquique

Quito
ECUADOR
Cuenca
Guayaquil
EQUATOR
Cuzco
PERU
Lima
Pan-American Highway
Arequipa
Iquique

EQUATOR

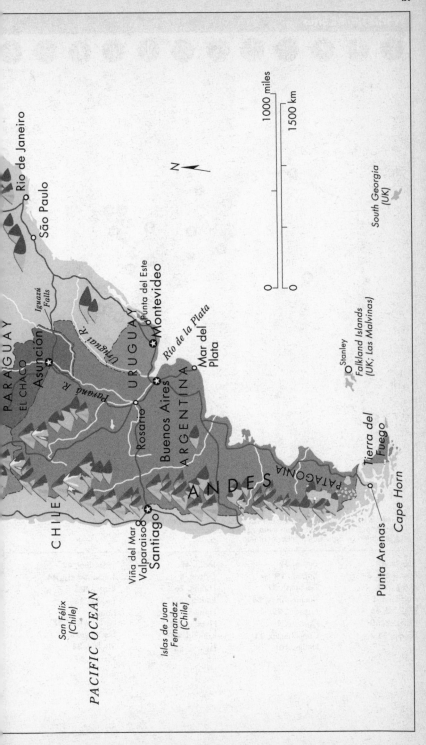

World Time Zones

Numbers below vertical bands relate each zone to Greenwich Mean Time (0 hrs.).
Local times frequently differ from these general indications,
as indicated by light-face numbers on map.

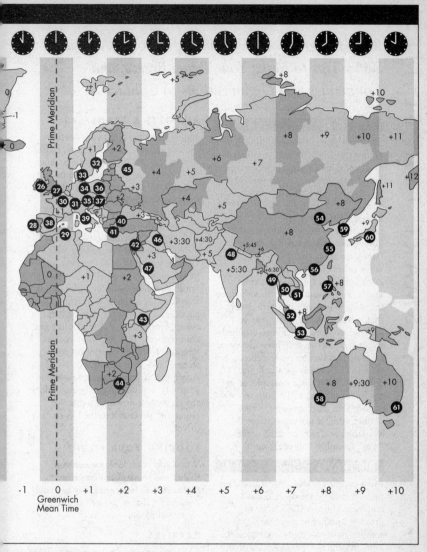

SMART TRAVEL TIPS A TO Z

*Basic Information on Traveling in South America,
Savvy Tips to Make Your Trip a Breeze, and
Companies and Organizations to Contact*

ADDRESSES

The most common street terms in
Spanish are *calle* (street), *avenida*
(avenue), and *bulevar* (boulevard); the
latter two terms are often abbreviated
(as *Av.* and *Bul.*), calle is either
spelled out or, in some countries,
dropped entirely so that the street is
referred to by proper name only. In
Portuguese *avenida* and *travessa*
(lane) are abbreviated (as *Av.* and *Tr.*)
while other common terms such as
estrada (highway) and *rua* (street)
aren't. Street numbering doesn't enjoy
the wide popularity in South America
that it has achieved elsewhere. In
some of this guide's listings, establishments have necessarily been identified
by the street they're on and their
nearest cross street—Calle Bolívar
and Av. Valdivia, for example, or in
the Spanish form, Calle Bolívar y Av.
Valdivia. In extreme cases, where
neither address nor cross street is
available, you may find the notation
"s/n," meaning "no street number."

AIR TRAVEL

Most people choose a flight based on
price. Yet there are other issues to
consider. Major airlines offer the
greatest number of departures;
smaller airlines—including regional,
low-cost and no-frill airlines—usually
have a more limited number of flights
daily. Major airlines have frequent-
flyer partners that allow you to credit
mileage earned on one airline to your
account with another. Low-cost
airlines offer a definite price advantage and fewer restrictions, such as
advance-purchase requirements.
Safety-wise, low-cost carriers as a
group have a good history, but **check
the safety record before booking** any
low-cost carrier; call the Federal
Aviation Administration's Consumer
Hot line (☞ Airline Complaints,
below).

AIRPORTS & TRANSFERS

Major gateways to South America
include Buenos Aires, Caracas, Lima,
Quito, Rio de Janeiro, Santiago, and
São Paulo. Dallas, Houston, Los
Angeles, Miami, and New York are
major gateways for flights to South
America from the United States. For
details on the major airports, *see*
Arriving and Departing By Plane in
individual country A to Z sections.
Getting to and from the airport won't
be the most pleasant aspect of your
South American journey. Subway
transit to the airports is nearly nonexistent, and bus service, while often
cheap, tends to require a serious time
commitment. Taxi fares to city centers vary from the reasonable to a
steep $20–$35 in Brazil and
Argentina. If you're concerned about
your city destination not being understood, write it down on a piece of
paper and present it to the bus or taxi
driver.

BOOKING YOUR FLIGHT

When you book **look for nonstop
flights** and **remember that "direct"
flights stop at least once.** Try to avoid
connecting flights, which require a
change of plane.

CARRIERS

The foremost North American carrier
is American Airlines, which has
service from Dallas, Miami, and New
York to all the countries covered in
this book. Continental flies from
Houston to Bogotá, Caracas,
Guayaquil, Lima, Quito, Rio, Santiago, and São Paulo. Another good bet
is United, which flies from Chicago,
Miami, and New York to Buenos
Aires, Caracas, Lima, Montevideo,
Rio, Santiago, and São Paulo. Although none of the Canadian airlines
fly to South American destinations,
Canadian Airlines has a service partnership with American and Air
Canada has one with United.

Many South American carriers offer service from North America to, and often, between South American hubs (for details, ☞ *below*). Note, however, that at press time, the economic crisis that hit Asia so hard was beginning to hit South America as well. One casualty was Peru's national carrier, Aeroperu, which had indefinitely cancelled all service. The crisis may well have affected other carriers, so be sure to check on the service they offer.

From the United Kingdom, you can take American or United from London Heathrow and fly to South America via Miami or New York. British Airways has service from London Gatwick to Bogotá, Buenos Aires, Caracas, Rio, Santiago, and São Paulo. From London, you can fly Aerolineas Argentina to Buenos Aires via Madrid. LanChile offers service from London to Santiago via Frankfurt (connection on British Airways). Varig has direct flights from London to both Rio and São Paulo.

From Sydney, you can fly Qantas to Buenos Aires. All flights stop in Auckland before proceeding on to South America. (Flights on Monday and Saturday proceed to Auckland, where you must change planes for an Aerolineas flight to Argentina; flights departing on Friday and Sunday are all on Qantas through to Buenos Aires.) From Auckland, Air New Zealand offers flights to major Brazilian cities through their partnership with Varig. Direct flights to Los Angeles, where you transfer to Varig, depart from Auckland once or twice a day.

➤ NORTH AMERICAN AIRLINES: **Air Canada** (☎ 800/776–3000 or 800/361–8620 in Canada), **American Airlines** (☎ 800/433–7300 in North America), **Canadian Airlines** (☎ 800/663–0290 in Canada or 800/426–7000 in the U.S.), **Continental Airlines** (☎ 800/231–0856 in North America), **United Airlines** (☎ 800/538–2929).

➤ SOUTH AMERICAN AIRLINES: **Aces** (☎ 800/846–2237) to such major Colombian cities as Bogotá, Cali, and Medellín; **Aerolineas Argentinas** (☎ 800/333–0276) to Buenos Aires with connections to cities throughout Argentina as well as to Asuncíon, Bogotá, Caracas, Lima, Montevideo, Rio, Santiago, and São Paulo; **Avensa** (☎ 800/428–3672) to Caracas with connections to Canaima, Maracaibo, Porlamar, and Mérida; **Avianca** (☎ 800/284–2622) to Barranquilla, Bogotá, Cali, Cartagena, Medellín, and Pereira; **LAB** (☎ 800/327–7407) to all major Bolivian cities with connections to Asuncíon, Buenos Aires, Belo Horizonte, Manaus, Montevideo, Rio, Santiago, and São Paulo; **LanChile** (☎ 800/735–5526) to Santiago and Lima with connections to destinations throughout South America; **Saeta** (☎ 800/827–2382) to Guayaquil and Quito with connections to Bogotá, Caracas, Lima, and Santiago; **Transbrasil** (☎ 800/872–3153) to São Paulo with connections to Belém, Belo Horizonte, Brasília, Fortaleza, Manaus, Recife, Rio, and Salvador; **Varig** (☎ 800/468–2744) to Fortaleza, Lima, Manaus, Rio, São Paulo and with connections to Bogotá, Buenos Aires, Caracas, La Paz, Montevideo, and Santiago; **Vasp** (☎ 800/732–8277) to Recife and São Paulo with connections to Brasília, Manaus, Rio, and Salvador.

➤ FROM THE U.K.: **Aerolineas Argentina** (☎ 020/7494–1075), **American Airlines** (☎ 0345/789–789), **British Airways** (☎ 0345/222–111), **LanChile** (☎ 129/359–6606), **United Airlines** (☎ 0845/844–4777), **Varig** (☎ 020/7287–3131).

➤ FROM AUSTRALIA AND NEW ZEALAND: **Air New Zealand** (☎ 0396/703–700 in Australia or 0800/737–000 in New Zealand), **Qantas**(☎ 13–13–13 in Australia or 0800/808–767 in New Zealand).

CHECK-IN & BOARDING

Assuming that not everyone with a ticket will show up, airlines routinely overbook planes. When that happens, airlines ask for volunteers to give up their seats. In return these volunteers usually get a certificate for a free flight and are rebooked on the next flight out. If there aren't enough volunteers, the airline must choose who will be denied boarding. The first to get bumped are passengers who checked in late and those flying on discounted tickets, so **get to the gate and check in as early as possible,** especially during peak periods.

Always **bring a government-issued photo I.D. to the airport—even in your own nation.** You may be asked to show it before you can check in. **Be prepared to show your passport when leaving any South American country and to pay hefty airport taxes.** Fees on international flights from Brazil, for example, can run as high as $40; even domestic flights may incur $10 in additional charges. Although some countries accept dollars, you should **plan to pay taxes with local currency.**

CUTTING COSTS

The least-expensive airfares to South America must usually be purchased in advance and are non-refundable. It's smart to **call a number of airlines, and when you're quoted a good price, book it on the spot**—the same fare may not be available the next day. Always **check different routings** and **look into using different airports.** International flights are also sensitive to the season: try to **fly in the off season** for the cheapest fares. Travel agents, especially low-fare specialists (☞ Discounts & Deals, *below*), are helpful.

Consolidators are another good source. They buy tickets for scheduled international flights at reduced rates from the airlines, then sell them at prices that beat the best fare available directly from the airlines, usually without restrictions. Sometimes you can even get your money back if you need to return the ticket. Carefully read the fine print detailing penalties for changes and cancellations, and **confirm your consolidator reservation with the airline.** It can be hard to find a consolidator who does South American ticketing, but one good bet is the Seattle-based company, Around the World.

Look into discount passes. Country carriers, such as Varig in Brazil, often have passes that make flying to several destinations within one country affordable. The MERCOSUR (Southern Common Market) pass—which covers Argentina, Brazil, Chile, Paraguay, and Uruguay—can save you money, but it has very tricky requirements. You must already have a round-trip ticket to and from South America; you must visit at least two countries; and you're limited to two stops in any country, excepting your inbound flight, outbound flight, and a stop at Iguaçu/Iguazú Falls. A maximum of eight flight segments are covered by the pass (nine with the falls), and flights must occur over a minimum of 7 days and a maximum of 30 days. If your itinerary can accommodate these restrictions, you're eligible for fares ranging from around $250 to $900. The cost is based on the number of miles flown, from a minimum of 1,200 to 7,200-plus. Refunds and changes are permitted, with some restrictions.

It's very difficult to get reliable information about the MERCOSUR pass from the participating airlines, which include the flag carriers of each of the nations involved. A better bet is to contact a travel agent who specializes in open-jaw or round-the-world tickets, and even then, be patient.

➤ CONSOLIDATORS: **Around the World** (☎ 206/223–3600), **Cheap Tickets** (☎ 800/377–1000), **Up & Away Travel** (☎ 212/889–2345), **Discount Airline Ticket Service** (☎ 800/576–1600), **Unitravel** (☎ 800/325–2222), **United States Air Consolidators Association** (☎ 916/441–4166), **World Travel Network** (☎ 800/409–6753).

ENJOYING THE FLIGHT

For more legroom **request an emergency-aisle seat.** Don't sit in the row in front of the emergency aisle or in front of a bulkhead, where seats may not recline. If you have dietary concerns, **ask for special meals when booking.** These can be vegetarian, low-cholesterol, or kosher, for example. On long flights, try to maintain a normal routine, to help fight jet lag. At night **get some sleep.** By day **eat light meals, drink water** (not alcohol), and **move around the cabin** to stretch your legs.

Some carriers have prohibited smoking throughout their systems; others allow smoking only on certain routes or even certain departures from that route, so **contact your carrier regarding its smoking policy.**

International travel between the Americas is a bit less wearing than to Europe or the Orient because there's far less jet lag. New York, for instance, is in the same time zone as Lima. If you have a choice between day or night flights—and those to Rio de Janeiro and Buenos Aires always depart after dark—**take a night plane if you sleep well while flying.** Especially en route to the Andean countries, you will have lovely sunrises over the mountains. Southbound, the best views are usually out windows on the plane's left side.

FLYING TIMES

The major North American departure points for South American flights are New York (8½ hours to Rio, 11 hours to Buenos Aires, 4 hours to Caracas) and Miami (7 hours to Rio, 8 hours to Buenos Aires, 3½ hours to Caracas). If you're traveling from Canada and connecting in the United States the Toronto–New York flight is just over an hour; that to Miami is 3 hours. If you're connecting in the U.S. from London it's about 6 hours to New York and 9 hours to Miami. Note that flight times may vary according to the size of the plane. Flights within South America can be as long as 6 hours (Buenos Aires–Caracas) and as short as 2 hours (Buenos Aires–Santiago).

HOW TO COMPLAIN

If your baggage goes astray or your flight goes awry, complain right away. Most carriers require that you **file a claim immediately.**

➤ AIRLINE COMPLAINTS: U.S. Department of Transportation **Aviation Consumer Protection Division** (✉ C-75, Room 4107, Washington, DC 20590, ☎ 202/366–2220), **Federal Aviation Administration Consumer Hot line** (☎ 800/322–7873).

RECONFIRMING

Always **reconfirm your flights,** even if you have a ticket and a reservation. This is particularly true for travel within South America, where flights tend to operate at full capacity— usually with passengers who have a great deal of baggage to process before departure.

BIKE TRAVEL

Riding a bike will put you face to face with the people and landscapes of South America. However, the rugged terrain and varying road conditions pose considerable challenges. **Consider a mountain bike,** since basic touring bikes are too fragile for off-road treks. Many tour operators within South America offer bike trips—sometimes including equipment rental—that range in length from a half-day to several days. Always remember to **lock your bike when you make stops,** and **avoid riding in congested urban areas,** where it's difficult (and dangerous) enough getting around by car let alone by bike.

BIKES IN FLIGHT

Most airlines accommodate bikes as luggage, provided they are dismantled and boxed. For bike boxes, often free at bike shops, you'll pay about $5 (at least $100 for bike bags) from airlines. International travelers can sometimes substitute a bike for a piece of checked luggage at no charge; otherwise, the cost is about $100. Domestic and Canadian airlines charge $25–$50.

BOAT & FERRY TRAVEL

Many boats and ferries—too many to list here—travel to islands just off the coastlines and to destinations along inland waterways. Details on such service are discussed where applicable—both in general text and in the various A to Z sections—throughout this guide.

BUS TRAVEL

Buses are the primary means of transportation for most South Americans, and buses run regularly almost anywhere there are roads—and some places where there aren't. Accordingly, bus-travel options are much greater than in most Northern Hemisphere countries. In particular, Brazil, Chile, and Venezuela have good service. In Bolivia, Ecuador, and Peru, badly built or washed-out roads can cause delays—but the views are spectacular. Note that the U.S. State Department strongly warns against traveling between Colombian cities by bus due to the risk of theft, druggings, violence, and kidnapping—in fact it forbids bus travel for U.S. government employees. If you must take the bus, opt for a first-class bus (variously called *pullman, metropolitano, de lujo,* or *directo*) or a deluxe bus with

THE GOLD GUIDE / SMART TRAVEL TIPS

THE GOLD GUIDE / SMART TRAVEL TIPS

air-conditioning (called *thermo* or *climatizado*), which only run between Bogotá, Medellín, Cali, and the Caribbean coast. Don't accept food or gum from other travelers, and be absolutely self-protective and discreet.

Without doubt, the low cost of bus travel is its greatest advantage; its greatest drawback is the time you need to cover the distances involved and, in some countries, allow for delays due to faulty equipment or poor road conditions. When traveling by bus, **pack light and dress comfortably** and be sure to **keep a close watch on your belongings.**

CLASSES

Various classes of service are offered, with each increase in price buying plusher seats and more leg room. Tickets often include assigned seat numbers. If you're over 5′10″ buy the most expensive ticket available and try for front-row seats; otherwise, be prepared for knee pain.

Bathrooms, air-conditioning, and in-bus movies or music are common amenities. Chile, on the extreme end of the scale, offers business-class-style sleeper buses with all of the above, plus pillows, blankets, and a bow-tied attendant who serves surprisingly palatable meals. Even in cash-strapped countries, the buses are generally modern and clean; you should, however, be prepared to relieve yourself by the side of the road. Food stops are usually made en route, though it's a good idea to bring snacks and water. An additional top layer of clothing comes in handy if it gets cold, or it can serve as a pillow.

FARES

Bus fares are substantially cheaper than in North America or Europe. Even in Chile and Brazil, you'll usually pay no more than $2 per hour of travel (some ritzy sleeper buses are more). Competing bus companies serve all major and many minor routes, so it can really pay to shop around. Always speak to the counter clerk, as cut-throat inter-company competition may mean fares are cheaper than the official price posted on the fare board.

PAYING AND RESERVATIONS

Tickets are sold at bus-company offices and at city bus terminals. Note that in larger cities there may be different terminals for buses to different destinations, and some small towns may not have a terminal at all (instead you'll be picked up and dropped off at the bus line's office, invariably in a central location). **Expect to pay with cash** as credit cards aren't accepted everywhere. Note that reservations for advance-ticket purchases aren't necessary except for trips to resort areas during high season—particularly on weekends—or during major holidays (Christmas, Carnival, etc.) and school-break periods. You should **arrive at bus stations extra early for travel during peak seasons.**

BUSINESS HOURS

For details on hours and holidays, *see* Opening and Closing times *in* the country A to Z sections at the end of each chapter.

CAMERAS & PHOTOGRAPHY

South America, with its majestic landscapes and varied cityscapes, is a photographer's dream. Latin Americans seem amenable to having picture-taking tourists in their midst, but you should always **ask permission before taking pictures in churches or of individuals.** If you're bashful about approaching total strangers, **make a point of photographing people with whom you interact:** your waiter, your desk clerk, the vendor selling you crafts. Even better, have a traveling companion or a passerby photograph you *with* them.

To avoid the blurriness caused by hand shake, **buy a mini tripod**—they're available in sizes as small as 6 inches. **Get a small beanbag to support your camera on uneven surfaces.** If you'll be visiting the Andes, **get a skylight (81B or 81C) or polarizing filter to minimize haze and light problems.** The higher the altitude, the greater the proportion of ultraviolet rays. Light meters don't read these rays and consequently, except for close-ups or full-frame portraits where the reading is taken directly off the subject, photos may be overexposed. These filters may also help with the glare caused by white adobe buildings, sandy beaches, and so on. **Bring high-speed film to compensate for low light under the tree canopy on jungle trips. Invest in a telephoto lens to photograph wildlife**: even standard zoom lenses of the 35–88 range won't capture a satisfying amount of detail.

Casual photographers should **consider using inexpensive disposable cameras** to reduce the risks inherent in traveling with sophisticated equipment. One-use cameras with panoramic or underwater functions can be nice supplements to a standard camera and its gear.

➤ PHOTO HELP: **Kodak Information Center** (☎ 800/242–2424). *Kodak Guide to Shooting Great Travel Pictures,* available in bookstores or from Fodor's Travel Publications (☎ 800/533–6478; $16.50 plus $4 shipping).

EQUIPMENT PRECAUTIONS

Always **keep your film and tape out of the sun** and on jungle trips **keep your equipment in resealable plastic bags to protect it from the dampness.** As petty crime is a problem throughout South America, particularly in the cities, **keep a close eye on your gear. Carry an extra supply of batteries,** and **be prepared to turn on your camera or camcorder** to prove to security personnel that the device is real. Always **ask for hand inspection of film,** which becomes clouded after successive exposures to airport X-ray machines, and **keep videotapes away from metal detectors.**

FILM

Bring your own film. In many countries, film is expensive and frequently stored in hot conditions. In general, Kodak film seems to maintain better color saturation at high altitudes and in low light than Fuji film. Plan on shooting a minimum of one 36-exposure roll per week of travel. If you don't want the hassle of keeping a shot log, **make a quick note whenever you start a new roll**—it will make identifying your photos much easier when you get home.

CAR RENTAL

In cities, driving is chaotic at best, mortally dangerous at worst; in the countryside, the usually rough roads, lack of clearly marked signs, and language differences are discouraging (☞ Car Travel, *below*). Further, wherever you go, the cost of renting is steep. All that said, many seasoned travelers like to drive in South America, and certain areas are most enjoyable when explored on your own in a car: in Venezuela, Margarita Island and the mountains of Mérida; in Chile, the central valley around Santiago, its nearby ski areas, and the Lake District; in Brazil, Minas Gerais State with all its historic Gold Towns; in Peru, Ica and the Nazca plain on the road from Lima.

Always **give the rental car a once-over** to make sure that the headlights, jack, and tires (including the spare) are in working condition.

CUTTING COSTS

Fly/drive packages are rare in South America. To make arrangements before you leave home, **book through a travel agent who will shop around.** Although international car-rental agencies have better service and maintenance track records than local firms (they also provide better breakdown assistance), your best bet at getting a good rate is to **rent on arrival, particularly from smaller, local companies.** Only reserve ahead (and check that a confirmed reservation guarantees you a car) if you plan to rent during a holiday period.

Consider hiring a car and driver through your hotel concierge, or make a deal with a taxi driver for some extended sightseeing at a longer-term rate. Often, drivers charge a set hourly rate, regardless of the distance traveled. You'll have to pay cash, but you'll often spend less than you would for a rental car.

Look into wholesalers, companies that do not own fleets but rent in bulk from those that do and often offer better rates than traditional car-rental operations. Payment must be made before you leave home.

➤ LOCAL AGENCIES: For information on agencies and details on costs, *see* the A to Z sections throughout the individual country chapters.

➤ Major Agencies: **Alamo** (☎ 800/522–9696; 020/8759–6200 in the U.K.), **Avis** (☎ 800/331–1084; 800/879–2847 in Canada; 02/9353–9000 in Australia; 09/525–1982 in New Zealand), **Budget** (☎ 800/527–0700; 0144/227–6266 in the U.K.), **Dollar** (☎ 800/800–6000; 020/8897–0811 in the U.K., where it is known as Eurodollar; 02/9223–1444 in Australia), **Hertz** (☎ 800/654–3001; 800/263–0600 in Canada; 0990/90–60–90 in the U.K.; 02/9669–2444 in Australia; 03/358–6777 in New Zealand), **National InterRent** (☎ 800/227–3876; 0345/222525 in the U.K., where it is known as Europcar InterRent).

➤ Wholesalers: **Auto Europe** (☎ 207/842–2000 or 800/223–5555), **Kemwel Holiday Autos** (☎ 914/825–3000 or 800/678–0678).

INSURANCE

When driving a rented car you're generally responsible for any damage to or loss of the vehicle as well as for any property damage or personal injury that you may cause. Before you rent **see what coverage your personal auto-insurance policy and credit cards already provide.**

REQUIREMENTS & RESTRICTIONS

In South America your own driver's license is acceptable. An International Driver's Permit, available from most national automobile associations, is a good idea. Minimum driving ages vary from country to country.

SURCHARGES

Before you pick up a car in one city and leave it in another **ask about drop-off charges or one-way service fees,** which can be substantial. Note, too, that some rental agencies charge extra if you return the car before the time specified in your contract. To avoid a hefty refueling fee **fill the tank just before you turn in the car,** but be aware that gas stations near the rental outlet may overcharge.

CAR TRAVEL

Driving in South America can be difficult. In general, road conditions outside the big cities are poor and heavily affected by weather; paved highways are manageable, but dirt

roads are all you'll find in many places. Within cities and on major highways, signs—where they exist—are often confusing. For these reasons, you may find it easier to rely on taxis and buses for short distances and on planes for longer journeys.

Some common-sense rules of the road: before you set out **establish an itinerary** and **ask about gas stations.** Be sure to **plan your daily driving distance conservatively** and **don't drive after dark.** Always **obey speed limits and traffic regulations.** And above all, **if you get a traffic ticket, don't argue**—and plan to spend longer than you want settling it. For more specific information on conditions, emergencies, gasoline and the like, *see* Getting Around By Car *in* the country A to Z section at the end of each chapter.

AUTO CLUBS

➤ In Australia: **Australian Automobile Association** (☎ 02/6247–7311).

➤ In Canada: **Canadian Automobile Association** (CAA, ☎ 613/247–0117).

➤ In New Zealand: **New Zealand Automobile Association** (☎ 09/377–4660).

➤ In the U.K.: **Automobile Association** (AA, ☎ 0990/500–600), **Royal Automobile Club** (RAC, ☎ 0990/722–722 for membership; 0345/121–345 for insurance).

➤ In the U.S.: **American Automobile Association** (☎ 800/564–6222).

CHILDREN IN SOUTH AMERICA

South Americans love children, and having yours along may prove to be your special ticket to meeting the locals. Children are welcomed in hotels and in restaurants, especially on weekends, when South American families go out for lunch in droves.

Let older children join in on planning as you outline your trip. **Scout your library** for picture books, storybooks, and maps about places you'll be going. Try to **explain the concept of foreign language;** some kids, who may have just learned to talk, are thrown when they can't understand strangers and strangers can't understand them. On sightseeing days try to **schedule activities of special interest to your children.** If you're renting a car don't forget to **arrange for a car seat** when you reserve.

FLYING

If your children are two or older **ask about children's airfares.** As a rule, infants under two not occupying a seat fly at greatly reduced fares or even for free. When booking **confirm carry-on allowances** if you're traveling with infants. In general, for babies charged 10% of the adult fare, you're allowed one carry-on bag and a collapsible stroller; if the flight is full the stroller may have to be checked or you may be limited to less.

Experts agree that it's a good idea to use safety seats aloft for children weighing less than 40 pounds. Airlines set their own policies: U.S. carriers usually require that the child be ticketed, even if he or she is young enough to ride free, since the seats must be strapped into regular seats. Do **check your airline's policy about using safety seats during takeoff and landing.** And since safety seats aren't allowed just everywhere in the plane, get your seat assignments early.

When reserving, **request children's meals or a freestanding bassinet** if you need them. But note that bulkhead seats, where you must sit to use the bassinet, may lack an overhead bin or storage space on the floor.

PRECAUTIONS

Children must have all their inoculations up to date before leaving home. Make sure that health precautions, such as what to drink and eat, are applied to the whole family. Not cramming too much into each day will keep the whole family healthier while on the road.

LODGING

Most hotels in South America allow children under a certain age to stay in their parents' room at no extra charge, but others charge for them as extra adults. Be sure to **find out the cutoff age for children's discounts.**

SIGHTS & ATTRACTIONS

Places that are especially good for children are indicated by a rubber duckie icon in the margin.

SUPPLIES & EQUIPMENT

Pack things to keep your children busy while traveling. For children of reading age, **bring books from home;** locally, literature for kids in English is hard to find.

COMPUTERS ON THE ROAD

If you're traveling with a laptop, carry a spare battery, a universal adapter plug, and a converter if your computer isn't dual voltage. **Ask about electrical surges** before plugging in your computer. **Keep your disks out of the sun** and **avoid excessive heat for both your computer and disks.** In many Latin American countries, carrying a laptop computer signals wealth and could make you a target for thieves; **conceal your laptop in a generic bag, and keep it close to you at all times.** Note that South America's luxury hotels typically offer business centers with computers.

CONCIERGES

Concierges, found in many urban hotels, can help you with theater tickets and dinner reservations: a good one with connections—which are always key in South America—may be able to get you seats for a hot show or prime-time dinner reservations at the restaurant of the moment. You can also turn to your hotel's concierge for help with travel arrangements, sightseeing plans, services ranging from aromatherapy to zipper repair, and emergencies. **Always tip** a concierge who has been of assistance.

CONSUMER PROTECTION

Whenever shopping or buying travel services in South America, **pay with a major credit card** so you can cancel payment or get reimbursed if there's a problem. If you're doing business with a particular company for the first time, **contact your local Better Business Bureau and the attorney general's offices** in your state and the company's home state as well. Have any complaints been filed? Finally, if you're buying a package or tour,

SMART TRAVEL TIPS / THE GOLD GUIDE

always **consider travel insurance** that includes default coverage (☞ Insurance, *below*).

➤ LOCAL BBBs: **Council of Better Business Bureaus** (✉ 4200 Wilson Blvd., Suite 800, Arlington, VA 22203, ☎ 703/276–0100, FAX 703/525–8277).

CRUISING

For information on cruise lines with itineraries that include South American destinations, *see* Cruises *in* Chapter 2.

CUSTOMS & DUTIES

When shopping, **keep receipts** for all purchases. Upon reentering the country, **be ready to show customs officials what you've bought.** If you feel a duty is incorrect or object to the way your clearance was handled, note the inspector's badge number and ask to see a supervisor. If the problem isn't resolved, write to the appropriate authorities, beginning with the director at your point of entry.

IN SOUTH AMERICA

For individual country customs information *see* Customs and Duties *in* the A to Z section at the end of each chapter.

IN AUSTRALIA

Australia residents who are 18 or older may bring home $A400 worth of souvenirs and gifts (including jewelry), 250 cigarettes or 250 grams of tobacco, and 1,125 ml of alcohol (including wine, beer, and spirits). Residents under 18 may bring back $A200 worth of goods. Prohibited items include meat products. Seeds, plants, and fruits need to be declared upon arrival.

➤ INFORMATION: **Australian Customs Service** (Regional Director, ✉ Box 8, Sydney, NSW 2001, ☎ 02/9213–2000, FAX 02/9213–4000).

IN CANADA

Canadian residents who have been out of Canada for at least seven days may bring home C$500 worth of goods duty-free. If you've been away less than seven days but more than 48 hours, the duty-free allowance drops to C$200; if your trip lasts 24–48 hours, the allowance is C$50. You may not pool allowances with family members. Goods claimed under the C$500 exemption may follow you by mail; those claimed under the lesser exemptions must accompany you. Alcohol and tobacco products may be included in the seven-day and 48-hour exemptions but not in the 24-hour exemption. If you meet the age requirements of the province or territory through which you reenter Canada, you may bring in, duty-free, 1.14 liters (40 imperial ounces) of wine or liquor *or* 24 12-ounce cans or bottles of beer or ale. If you are 16 or older you may bring in, duty-free, 200 cigarettes and 50 cigars. Check ahead of time with Revenue Canada or the Department of Agriculture for policies regarding meat products, seeds, plants, and fruits.

You may send an unlimited number of gifts worth up to C$60 each duty-free to Canada. Label the package UNSOLICITED GIFT—VALUE UNDER $60. Alcohol and tobacco are excluded.

➤ INFORMATION: **Revenue Canada** (✉ 2265 St. Laurent Blvd. S, Ottawa, Ontario K1G 4K3, ☎ 613/993–0534; 800/461–9999 in Canada).

IN NEW ZEALAND

Homeward-bound residents 17 or older may bring back $700 worth of souvenirs and gifts. Your duty-free allowance also includes 4.5 liters of wine or beer; one 1,125-ml bottle of spirits; and either 200 cigarettes, 250 grams of tobacco, 50 cigars, or a combination of the three up to 250 grams. Prohibited items include meat products, seeds, plants, and fruits.

➤ INFORMATION: **New Zealand Customs** (Custom House, ✉ 50 Anzac Ave., Box 29, Auckland, ☎ 09/359–6655, FAX 09/359–6732).

IN THE U.K.

From countries outside the EU, including those in South America, you may bring home, duty-free, 200 cigarettes or 50 cigars; 1 liter of spirits or 2 liters of fortified or sparkling wine or liqueurs; 2 liters of still table wine; 60 ml of perfume; 250 ml of toilet water; plus £136 worth of other goods, including gifts and souvenirs. If returning from outside the EU, prohibited items include meat products, seeds, plants, and fruits.

➤ INFORMATION: **HM Customs and Excise** (✉ Dorset House, Stamford St., Bromley Kent BR1 1XX, ☎ 020/7202–4227).

IN THE U.S.

U.S. residents who have been out of the country for at least 48 hours (and who have not used the $400 allowance or any part of it in the past 30 days) may bring home $400 worth of foreign goods duty-free.

U.S. residents 21 and older may bring back 1 liter of alcohol duty-free. In addition, regardless of your age, you are allowed 200 cigarettes and 100 non-Cuban cigars. Antiques, which the U.S. Customs Service defines as objects more than 100 years old, enter duty-free, as do original works of art done entirely by hand, including paintings, drawings, and sculptures.

You may also send packages home duty-free: up to $200 worth of goods for personal use, with a limit of one parcel per addressee per day (and no alcohol or tobacco products or perfume worth more than $5); label the package PERSONAL USE and attach a list of its contents and their retail value. Do not label the package UNSOLICITED GIFT or your duty-free exemption will drop to $100. Mailed items do not affect your duty-free allowance on your return.

➤ INFORMATION: **U.S. Customs Service** (inquiries, ✉ 1300 Pennsylvania Ave. NW, Washington, DC 20229, ☎ 202/927–6724; complaints, ✉ Office of Regulations and Rulings, 1300 Pennsylvania Ave. NW, Washington, DC 20229; registration of equipment, ✉ Registration Information, 1300 Pennsylvania Ave. NW, Washington, DC 20229, ☎ 202/927–0540).

DINING

The restaurants (all of which are indicated by a ✗) that we list are the cream of the crop in each price category. Properties indicated by a ✗🏠 are lodging establishments whose restaurant warrants a special trip. For details on food and drink, mealtimes, paying, and tipping, *see* Dining *in*

Pleasures and Pastimes at the start of each chapter as well as the country A to Z sections at the end of each chapter. Price categories are as follows:

CATEGORY	COST*
$$$$	over $35
$$$	$25–$35
$$	$15–$25
$	$5–$15
¢	under $5

per person for an appetizer, entrée, and dessert, excluding tax, tip, and beverages

RESERVATIONS & DRESS

Reservations are always a good idea: we mention them only when they're essential or aren't accepted. Book as far ahead as you can, and reconfirm as soon as you arrive. We mention dress only when men are required to wear a jacket or a jacket and tie.

DISABILITIES & ACCESSIBILITY

Although international chain hotels in large cities have some suitable rooms and it's easy to hire private cars and drivers for excursions, South America isn't very well equipped to handle travelers with disabilities. There are few ramps and curb cuts, and it takes effort and planning to negotiate cobbled city streets, get around museums and other buildings, and explore the countryside. City centers such as Rio de Janeiro, Buenos Aires, Santiago, and Caracas are the most comfortable to visit.

LODGING

When discussing accessibility with an operator or reservations agent **ask hard questions.** Are there any stairs, inside *or* out? Are there grab bars next to the toilet *and* in the shower/tub? How wide is the doorway to the room? To the bathroom? For the most extensive facilities meeting the latest legal specifications **opt for newer accommodations.**

➤ COMPLAINTS: **Aviation Consumer Protection Division** (☞ Air Travel, *above*) for airline-related problems, **Civil Rights Office** (✉ U.S. Department of Transportation, Departmental Office of Civil Rights, S-30, 400 7th St. SW, Room 10215, Washington, DC 20590, ☎ 202/366–4648, FAX 202/366–9371) for problems with surface transportation, **Disability**

THE GOLD GUIDE / SMART TRAVEL TIPS

Rights Section (✉ U.S. Department of Justice, Civil Rights Division, Box 66738, Washington, DC 20035-6738, ☎ 202/514–0301; 800/514–0301; 202/514–0301 TTY; 800/514–0301 TTY, FAX 202/307–1198) for general complaints.

TRAVEL AGENCIES

In the United States, although the Americans with Disabilities Act requires that travel firms serve the needs of all travelers, some agencies specialize in working with people with disabilities.

➤ TRAVELERS WITH MOBILITY PROBLEMS: **Access Adventures** (✉ 206 Chestnut Ridge Rd., Rochester, NY 14624, ☎ 716/889–9096), run by a former physical-rehabilitation counselor; **CareVacations** (✉ 5-5110 50th Ave., Leduc, Alberta T9E 6V4, ☎ 780/986–6404 or 877/478–7827, FAX 780/986–8332) has group tours and is especially helpful with cruise vacations; **Flying Wheels Travel** (✉ 143 W. Bridge St., Box 382, Owatonna, MN 55060, ☎ 507/451–5005 or 800/535–6790, FAX 507/451–1685); **Hinsdale Travel Service** (✉ 201 E. Ogden Ave., Suite 100, Hinsdale, IL 60521, ☎ 630/325–1335, FAX 630/325–1342).

DISCOUNTS & DEALS

Be a smart shopper and **compare all your options** before making decisions. A plane ticket bought with a promotional coupon from travel clubs, coupon books, and direct-mail offers may not be cheaper than the least expensive fare from a discount ticket agency. And always keep in mind that what you get is just as important as what you save.

DISCOUNT RESERVATIONS

To save money **look into discount-reservations services** with toll-free numbers, which use their buying power to get a better price on hotels, airline tickets, even car rentals. When booking a room, always **call the hotel's local toll-free number** (if one is available) rather than the central reservations number—you'll often get a better price. Always ask about special packages or corporate rates.

When shopping for the best deal on hotels and car rentals **look for guaranteed exchange rates,** which protect you against a falling dollar. With your rate locked in, you won't pay more, even if the price goes up in the local currency.

➤ AIRLINE TICKETS: ☎ **800/FLY–4–LESS.**

➤ HOTEL ROOMS: **Steigenberger Reservation Service** (☎ 800/223–5652).

PACKAGE DEALS

Don't confuse packages and guided tours. When you buy a package, you travel on your own, just as though you had planned the trip yourself. Fly/drive packages, which combine airfare and car rental, are often a good deal.

ECOTOURISM

For details on trips that put you in touch with the great outdoors, *see* Chapter 2, Adventure and Learning Vacations.

ELECTRICITY

Unlike the United States and Canada—which have a 110- to 120-volt standard—the current in Argentina, Chile, Paraguay, Peru, Uruguay, and the urban areas of Brazil is 220 volts to 240 volts, 50 cycles alternating current (AC). Ecuador, Colombia, Venezuela, and rural Brazil use currents of 110 volts, 60 cycles alternating current. To use 110/120-volt equipment in a 220/240 country, bring a converter. Also, many wall outlets in South America take Continental-type plugs, with two round prongs. To accommodate U.S.-style flat-prong plugs, you'll need an adapter. **Consider buying a universal adapter;** the Swiss-Army-knife of adapters, a universal has several types of plugs in one handy unit.

If your appliances are dual-voltage—as many laptops are these days—you'll need only an adapter. Don't use 110-volt outlets, marked FOR SHAVERS ONLY, for high-wattage appliances such as blow-dryers.

EMBASSIES & CONSULATES

For information on Australian, Canadian, New Zealand, U.K., and U.S.

embassies and consulates in South America, *see* the individual country A to Z section at the end of each chapter.

➤ EMBASSIES IN AUSTRALIA: **Argentina** (✉ Box 262, Woden, ACT 2606, ☎ 616/282–4855), **Brazil** (✉ Box 1540, Canberra, ACT 2601, ☎ 616/273–2372), **Chile** (✉ Box 69, Monaco Crescent, ACT 2603, ☎ 616/286–2430), **Colombia** (✉ 101 Northbourne Ave., 2nd floor, Turner, ACT 2601, ☎ 616/258–2027), **Peru** (✉ Box 106, Red Hill, ACT 2606, ☎ 616/290–0922), **Uruguay** (✉ MLC Tower, Suite 107, 1st floor, Woden ACT 2601, ☎ 616/282–4418), **Venezuela** (✉ MLC Tower, Suite 106, Woden, ACT 2606, ☎ 616/282–4827).

➤ EMBASSIES IN CANADA: **Argentina** (✉ 90 Sparks St., Suite 620, Ottawa, Ontario, K1P 5B4, ☎ 613/236–2351), **Bolivia** (✉ 130 Albert St., Suite 504, Ottawa, Ontario, K1P 5G4, ☎ 613/236–5730), **Brazil** (✉ 450 Wilbrod St., Ottawa, Ontario, K1P 6M8, ☎ 613/237–1090), **Chile** (✉ 151 Slater St., Suite 605, Ottawa, Ontario, K1P 5A9, ☎ 613/235–4402), **Colombia** (✉ 360 Albert St., Suite 1002, Ottawa, Ontario K1R 7X7, ☎ 613/230–3760), **Ecuador** (✉ 50 O'Connor St., Suite 1311, Ottawa, Ontario, K1P 6L2, ☎ 613/563–8206), **Paraguay** (✉ 151 Slater St., Suite 401, Ottawa, Ontario, K1P5H3, ☎ 613/567–1283), **Peru** (✉ 170 Laurier Ave. West, Suite 1007, Ottawa, Ontario, K1P 5V5, ☎ 613/238–1777), **Uruguay** (✉ 130 Albert St., Suite 1905, Ottawa, Ontario, K1P 5G4, ☎ 613/234–2727), **Venezuela** (✉ 32 Range Rd., Ottawa, Ontario, K1N 8J4, ☎ 613/235–5151).

➤ EMBASSIES IN NEW ZEALAND: **Chile** (✉ 1-3 Willeston St., 7th floor, Wellington, ☎ 644/472–5180), **Peru** (✉ 35–37 Victoria St., 3rd floor, Wellington, ☎ 644/725–171).

➤ EMBASSIES IN THE U.K.: **Argentina** (✉ 53 Hans Place, London, SW1X OLA, ☎ 020/7584–6494), **Bolivia** (✉ 106 Eaton Sq., London, SW1W 9AD, ☎ 020/7235–1286), **Brazil** (✉ 32 Green St., London, W1Y 4AT, ☎ 020/7499–0877), **Chile** (✉ 12 Devonshire St., London, W1N 2DS, ☎ 020/7580–6392), **Colombia** (✉ Flat 3A, 3 Hans Crescent, London, SW1X OLR, ☎ 020/7589–9177),

Ecuador (✉ Flat 3B, 3 Hans Crescent, London, SW1X OLS, ☎ 020/7584–1367), **Paraguay** (✉ Braemar Lodge, Cornwall Gardens, London, SW7 4AQ, ☎ 020/7937–1253), **Peru** (✉ 52 Sloane St., London, SW1X 9SP, ☎ 020/7235–1917), **Uruguay** (✉ 2nd floor, 140 Brompton Rd., London, SW3 1HY, ☎ 020/7584–8192), **Venezuela** (✉ 1 Cromwell Rd., London SW7 2HR, ☎ 020/7584–4206).

➤ EMBASSIES IN THE U.S: **Argentina** (✉ 1600 New Hampshire Ave. NW, Washington, DC 20009, ☎ 202/939–6400), **Bolivia** (✉ 3014 Massachusetts Ave. NW, Washington, DC 20008, ☎ 202/483–4410), **Brazil** (✉ 3006 Massachusetts Ave. NW, Washington, DC 20008, ☎ 202/745–2700), **Chile** (✉ 1732 Massachusetts Ave. NW, Washington, DC 20036, ☎ 202/785–1746, ext. 145), **Colombia** (✉ 2118 Leroy Place NW, Washington, DC 20008, ☎ 202/387–8338), **Ecuador** (✉ 2535 15th St. NW, Washington, DC 20009, ☎ 202/234–7200), **Paraguay** (✉ 2400 Massachusetts Ave. NW, Washington, DC 20008, ☎ 202/483–6960), **Peru** (✉ 1700 Massachusetts Avenue NW, Washington, DC 20036, ☎ 202/833–9860), **Uruguay** (✉ 1918 F St. NW, Washington, DC 20006, ☎ 202/331–1313), **Venezuela** (✉ 1099 30th St. NW, Washington, DC 20007, ☎ 202/342–2214).

GAY & LESBIAN TRAVEL

Brazil is South America's most popular destination for gay and lesbian travelers, and major cities such as Rio, São Paulo, and Salvador have numerous gay bars, organizations, and publications. Argentines hold a liberal attitude toward homosexuality, and Buenos Aires enjoys an active gay scene. In Uruguay and Venezuela, gay rights are increasingly discussed, with gay communities in Montevideo and Caracas leading the way. Outside these destinations, however, gay and lesbian travel can be difficult due to conservative political and religious norms. In Ecuador, Peru, and Chile, for example, gay acts are illegal and public attitudes toward homosexuality are generally negative. Police harassment in these countries occasionally occurs.

➤ GAY- AND LESBIAN-FRIENDLY TRAVEL AGENCIES: **Different Roads Travel** (⊠ 8383 Wilshire Blvd., Suite 902, Beverly Hills, CA 90211, ☎ 323/651–5557 or 800/429–8747, ℻ 323/651–3678); **Kennedy Travel** (⊠ 314 Jericho Turnpike, Floral Park, NY 11001, ☎ 516/352–4888 or 800/237–7433, ℻ 516/354–8849); **Now Voyager** (⊠ 4406 18th St., San Francisco, CA 94114, ☎ 415/626–1169 or 800/255–6951, ℻ 415/626–8626); **Skylink Travel and Tour** (⊠ 1006 Mendocino Ave., Santa Rosa, CA 95401, ☎ 707/546–9888 or 800/225–5759, ℻ 707/546–9891), serving lesbian travelers.

➤ GAY- AND LESBIAN-TRAVEL WEB SITES: www.planetout.com/travel, www.gay.com

HEALTH

ALTITUDE SICKNESS

Soroche, or altitude sickness—which causes shortness of breath, nausea, and splitting headaches—may be a problem when you visit Andean countries. The best way to prevent it is to ascend slowly. Spend a few nights at 6,000–9,000 feet before you head higher. If you must fly straight in, plan on doing next to nothing for your first few days. If you begin to feel ill, the traditional Bolivian remedy is herbal tea made from coca leaves. Over-the-counter analgesics and napping also help. If symptoms persist, return to lower elevations. Note that if you have high blood pressure and/or a history of heart trouble, check with your doctor before traveling to such heights as those at Cuzco in Peru and La Paz in Bolivia (both above 11,000 feet) and Quito in Ecuador (above 9,000 feet).

DIVERS' ALERT

Scuba divers take note: **Do not fly within 24 hours of scuba diving.** Neophyte divers should have a complete physical exam before undertaking a dive. If you have travel insurance, **make sure your policy applies to scuba-related injuries,** as not all companies provide this coverage.

FOOD & DRINK

In South America the major health risk is Montezuma's Revenge, or traveler's diarrhea, caused by eating contaminated fruit or vegetables or drinking contaminated water. So **watch what you eat.** Stay away from ice, uncooked food, and unpasteurized milk and milk products, and **drink only bottled water** or water that has been boiled for at least 20 minutes, even when you're brushing your teeth.

MEDICAL PLANS

No one plans to get sick while traveling, but it happens, so **consider signing up with a medical-assistance company.** Members get doctor referrals, emergency evacuation or repatriation, hot lines for medical consultation, cash for emergencies, and other assistance.

➤ MEDICAL-ASSISTANCE COMPANY: **AEA International SOS** (⊠ 8 Neshaminy Interplex, Suite 207, Trevose, PA 19053, ☎ 215/245–4707 or 800/523–6586, ℻ 215/244–9617; ⊠ 12 Chemin Riantbosson, 1217 Meyrin 1, Geneva, ☎ 4122/785–6464, ℻ 4122/785–6424; ⊠ 331 N. Bridge Rd., 17-00, Odeon Towers, Singapore 188720, ☎ 65/338–7800, ℻ 65/338–7611).

OVER-THE-COUNTER REMEDIES

Mild cases of diarrhea may respond to Imodium (known generically as loperamide), Pepto-Bismol (not as strong), and Lomotil, which can be purchased over the counter. Paregoric, another antidiarrheal agent, doesn't require a doctor's prescription in South America.

Drink plenty of purified water or tea—chamomile (*camomila* in both languages) is a good folk remedy. In severe cases, rehydrate yourself with a salt-sugar solution (½ teaspoon salt, *sal* in both languages, and 4 tablespoons sugar, *açúcar* in Portuguese and *azucar* in Spanish) per quart of water (*agua* in both languages).

SHOTS & MEDICATIONS

All travelers should have up-to-date tetanus boosters, and a hepatitis A inoculation can prevent one of the most common intestinal infections. If you're heading to tropical regions (including parts of Bolivia, Brazil, Colombia, Ecuador, French Guiana,

Guyana, Paraguay, Peru, Suriname, and Venezuela) you should get yellow fever shots. Children traveling to South America should have current inoculations against measles, mumps, rubella, and polio.

According to the Centers for Disease Control (CDC) there's a limited risk of cholera, typhoid, malaria, hepatitis B, dengue, and chagas. While a few of these you could catch anywhere, most are restricted to jungle areas. If you plan to visit remote regions or stay for more than six weeks, **check with the CDC's International Travelers Hot Line.**

In areas with malaria and dengue, which are both carried by mosquitoes, take mosquito nets, wear clothing that covers the body, apply repellent containing DEET, and use a spray against flying insects in living and sleeping areas. The hot line recommends chloroquine (analen) as an antimalarial agent; no vaccine exists against dengue.

➤ HEALTH WARNINGS: **National Centers for Disease Control** (CDC, National Center for Infectious Diseases, Division of Quarantine, Traveler's Health Section, ✉ 1600 Clifton Rd. NE, M/S E-03, Atlanta, GA 30333, ☎ 888/232–3228, FAX 888/232–3299).

INSURANCE

The most useful travel insurance plan is a comprehensive policy that includes coverage for trip cancellation and interruption, default, trip delay, and medical expenses (with a waiver for preexisting conditions).

Without insurance you'll lose all or most of your money if you cancel your trip, regardless of the reason. Default insurance covers you if your tour operator, airline, or cruise line goes out of business. Trip-delay covers expenses that arise because of bad weather or mechanical delays. Study the fine print when comparing policies.

If you're traveling internationally, a key component of travel insurance is coverage for medical bills incurred if you get sick on the road. Such expenses aren't generally covered by Medicare or private policies. U.K. residents can buy a travel-insurance policy valid for most vacations taken during the year in which it's purchased (but check pre-existing-condition coverage). British and Australian citizens need extra medical coverage when traveling overseas.

Always **buy travel policies directly from the insurance company**; if you buy it from a cruise line, airline, or tour operator that goes out of business you probably won't be covered for the agency or operator's default, a major risk. Before you make any purchase **review your existing health and home-owner's policies** to find what they cover away from home.

➤ TRAVEL INSURERS: In the U.S. **Access America** (✉ 6600 W. Broad St., Richmond, VA 23230, ☎ 804/285–3300 or 800/284–8300) and **Travel Guard International** (✉ 1145 Clark St., Stevens Point, WI 54481, ☎ 715/345–0505 or 800/826–1300). In Canada **Voyager Insurance** (✉ 44 Peel Center Dr., Brampton, Ontario L6T 4M8, ☎ 905/791–8700; 800/668–4342 in Canada).

➤ INSURANCE INFORMATION: In the U.K. the **Association of British Insurers** (✉ 51–55 Gresham St., London EC2V 7HQ, ☎ 020/7600–3333, FAX 020/7696–8999). In Australia the **Insurance Council of Australia** (☎ 03/9614–1077, FAX 03/9614–7924).

LANGUAGE & ETIQUETTE

In Brazil, the language is Portuguese; Spanish is spoken in all other countries covered in this guide. (Note that in French Guiana, or Cayenne, French is spoken; in Guyana it's English; and in Suriname it's Dutch). In some rural areas, indigenous Indian languages are spoken. As in many places throughout the world, you're more likely to find English-speaking locals in major cities than in small towns or the countryside.

Attitudes range from the strict Catholicism of a country like Ecuador to the anything-goes outlook of Brazil. In general, however, Latin Americans lean toward conservative dress and quiet behavior. Except in beach cities, men typically don't wear shorts and women don't wear short skirts. People dress nicely to enter churches, and hats are frowned upon during mass.

The conservative dress belies the warmth and friendliness of most all Latin Americans. Don't be afraid to smile in the streets, ask for directions, or strike up a conversation with a local (be aware, however, that a Latin American may give you false directions before admitting that he or she doesn't know where to point you). The slower pace of life across the continent reflects an unwavering appreciation of family and friendship; knowing this will help you understand why things may take a little longer to get done.

LANGUAGES FOR TRAVELERS

A phrase book and language-tape set can help get you started.

➤ PHRASE BOOKS & LANGUAGE-TAPE SETS: *Fodor's Spanish for Travelers* (☎ 800/733–3000 in the U.S.; 800/668–4247 in Canada; $7 for phrase book, $16.95 for audio set).

LODGING

It's always good to **look at any room before accepting it;** expense is no guarantee of charm or cleanliness, and accommodations can vary dramatically within one hotel. Many older hotels in Spanish-speaking South America have rooms with charming Old World–style balconies; ask if there's a room *con balcon* when checking in.

Be sure to check the shower: An unfortunate number of South American hotels have electric-powered shower heads, rather than central hot-water heaters. In theory, you can adjust both the water's heat and its pressure. In practice, if you want hot water, you have to turn the water pressure down; if you want pressure, expect a brisk rinse. Careful! Don't adjust the power when you're under the water—you can get a little shock.

If you ask for a double room, you'll get a room for two people, but you're not guaranteed a double mattress. If you'd like to avoid twin beds, you'll have to **ask for a *cama matrimonial* in Spanish or *cama de casal* in Portuguese** (no wedding ring seems to be required).

The lodgings (all indicated with 🏨) that we list are the cream of the crop in each price category. We always list the facilities that are available—but we don't specify whether they cost extra: When pricing accommodations, always ask what's included and what costs extra. All hotels listed have private bath unless otherwise noted. Properties indicated by ✗🏨 are lodging establishments whose restaurant warrants a special trip.

Assume that hotels operate on the European Plan (**EP,** with no meals) unless we specify that they're all-inclusive (including all meals and most activities) or use the Breakfast Plan (**BP,** with a full breakfast daily), Continental Plan (**CP,** with a Continental breakfast daily), or Modified American Plan (**MAP,** with breakfast and dinner daily). For country-specific lodging information, *see* Lodging *in* Pleasures and Pastimes at the start of each chapter. Price categories are as follows:

CATEGORY	COST*
$$$$	over $150
$$$	$100–$150
$$	$50–$100
$	$25–$50
¢	under $25

for a double room in high season, excluding taxes

APARTMENT & VILLA RENTALS

If you want a home base that's roomy enough for a family and comes with cooking facilities **consider a furnished rental.** These can save you money, especially if you're traveling with a group. Home-exchange directories sometimes list rentals as well as exchanges.

➤ INTERNATIONAL AGENT: **Hideaways International** (✉ 767 Islington St., Portsmouth, NH 03801, ☎ 603/430–4433 or 800/843–4433, FAX 603/430–4444; membership $99).

HOME EXCHANGES

If you'd like to exchange your home for someone else's **join a home-exchange organization,** which will send you its updated listings of available exchanges for a year and will include your own listing in at least one of them. It's up to you to make specific arrangements.

➤ EXCHANGE CLUBS: **HomeLink International** (✉ Box 650, Key West, FL 33041, ☎ 305/294–7766 or 800/638–3841, FAX 305/294–1448; $93 per year), **Intervac U.S.** (✉ Box 590504, San Francisco, CA 94159, ☎ 800/756–4663, FAX 415/435–7440; $83 for catalogs).

HOSTELS

No matter what your age you can **save on lodging costs by staying at hostels.** In some 5,000 locations in more than 70 countries around the world, Hostelling International (HI), the umbrella group for a number of national youth-hostel associations, offers single-sex, dorm-style beds and, at many hostels, couples rooms and family accommodations. Membership in any HI national hostel association, open to travelers of all ages, allows you to stay in HI-affiliated hostels at member rates (one-year membership is about $25 for adults; hostels run about $10–$25 per night). Members also have priority if the hostel is full; they're eligible for discounts around the world, even on rail and bus travel in some countries.

➤ ORGANIZATIONS: **Australian Youth Hostel Association** (✉ 10 Mallett St., Camperdown, NSW 2050, ☎ 02/9565–1699, FAX 02/9565–1325), **Hostelling International—American Youth Hostels** (✉ 733 15th St. NW, Suite 840, Washington, DC 20005, ☎ 202/783–6161, FAX 202/783–6171), **Hostelling International—Canada** (✉ 400–205 Catherine St., Ottawa, Ontario K2P 1C3, ☎ 613/237–7884, FAX 613/237–7868), **Youth Hostel Association of England and Wales** (✉ Trevelyan House, 8 St. Stephen's Hill, St. Albans, Hertfordshire AL1 2DY, ☎ 01727/855215 or 01727/845047, FAX 01727/844126), **Youth Hostels Association of New Zealand** (✉ Box 436, Christchurch, ☎ 03/379–9970, FAX 03/365–4476). Membership in the U.S. $25, in Canada C$26.75, in the U.K. £9.30, in Australia $44, in New Zealand $24.

MAIL & SHIPPING

For details on mail service, postal rates, and overnight services, *see* the A to Z sections throughout each chapter.

MONEY MATTERS

Due to the relative instability of some South American currencies and the fact that admission prices tend to change constantly, we don't usually list admission prices in the local currency or in dollars. The word "admission" appears where an entry fee is charged and the word "free" where one is not. Occasionally, we cite sample prices for cab fares and sports-equipment rental; these are cited in U.S. dollars based on exchange rates at press time. For information on service charges, taxes, and tipping *see* the country A to Z sections at the end of each chapter.

ATMS

ATMs are widely available, and you can get cash with a Cirrus- or Plus-linked debit card or with a major credit card. Some bank machines in Argentina and Bolivia even offer a choice of local or U.S. currencies.

The bank networks aren't evenly dispersed. American Express ATMs are limited to major cities. MasterCard and Cirrus seem to be more common in the southern cone countries, while almost all ATMs in Brazil and Peru accept Visa or Plus cards only. To be on the safe side, carry a variety of cards. Note also that if your PIN is more than four digits long and/or uses letters instead of numbers, it might not work in some countries. Check with your bank or with Cirrus or Plus for details. Also, for your card to work on some ATMs, you may need to hit a screen command that roughly translates to "foreign client."

➤ ATM LOCATIONS: **MasterCard Cirrus** (☎ 800/424–7787, www.mastercard.com/atm). **Visa Plus** (☎ 800/843–7587; www.visa.com/atm).

CREDIT CARDS

Throughout this guide, the following abbreviations are used: **AE**, American Express; **DC**, Diner's Club; **MC**, MasterCard; and **V**, Visa.

CURRENCY EXCHANGE

For the most favorable rates, **change money through banks.** Although ATM transaction fees may be higher

SMART TRAVEL TIPS / THE GOLD GUIDE

abroad than at home, ATM rates are excellent because they're based on wholesale rates offered only by major banks. You won't do as well at exchange booths in airports or rail and bus stations, in hotels, in restaurants, or in stores. To avoid lines at airport exchange booths and ATMs, **get a bit of local currency before you leave home.**

Plan ahead, since it's often hard to change large amounts of money at hotels on weekends, even in capital cities. If you're heading for rural areas, you may not be able to change currency at all, so don't leave the city without adequate amounts of local currency, in small denominations.

For costly items use your credit card whenever possible—you'll come out ahead, whether the exchange rate at which your purchase is calculated is the one in effect the day the vendor's bank abroad processes the charge or the one prevailing on the day the charge company's service center processes it at home.

➤ EXCHANGE SERVICES: **International Currency Express** (☎ 888/842–0880 on East Coast; 888/278–6628 on West Coast), **Thomas Cook Currency Services** (☎ 800/287–7362 for telephone orders and retail locations).

TRAVELER'S CHECKS

Do you need traveler's checks? It depends on where you're headed. If you're going to rural areas and small towns, go with cash; traveler's checks are best used in cities. Lost or stolen checks can usually be replaced within 24 hours. To ensure a speedy refund, buy your own traveler's checks—don't let someone else pay for them: irregularities like this can cause delays. The person who bought the checks should make the call to request a refund.

PACKING

If there's a rule for dressing in South America, it's this: **Dress more conservatively in countries on the west coast than those on the east.** Colombia is conservative, Venezuela isn't. Argentines are very clothes conscious, but don't demand high-style fashion of you. In the Andean countries avoid

wearing short shorts or halter tops. Women traveling to Brazil can bring their most risque outfits—and be prepared for no one to even notice. If you're doing business in South America, you'll need the same attire you would wear in U.S. and European cities: for men, suits and ties; for women, suits for day wear and cocktail dresses or other suitable dinner clothes.

For sightseeing and leisure, casual clothing and good walking shoes are both desirable and appropriate, and most cities don't require very formal clothes, even for evenings. For beach vacations, you'll need lightweight sportswear, a bathing suit, a sun hat, and sunscreen. Travel in rain forest areas will require long-sleeve shirts, long pants, socks, sneakers, a hat, a light waterproof jacket, a bathing suit, and insect repellent. Light colors are best, since mosquitoes avoid them. You can never have too many large resealable plastic bags (bring a whole box), which are ideal for storing film, protecting things from rain and damp, quarantining stinky socks, and more.

If you're visiting Patagonian areas in the south or high altitudes areas, bring a jacket and sweater, or plan to acquire one of the hand-knit sweaters or ponchos crowding the marketplaces. Evening temperatures in Cuzco, La Paz, or Quito are rarely above the 50s. Southern cities, such as Buenos Aires and Santiago, also become cool during the South American winter (May–Sept.).

Other useful items include a screwtop water bottle that you can fill with bottled water, a money pouch, a travel flashlight and extra batteries, a Swiss Army knife with a bottle opener, a medical kit, binoculars, and a pocket calculator to help with currency conversions. A sarong or light cotton blanket can have many uses: beach towel, picnic blanket, and cushion for hard seats, among other things.

In your carry-on luggage **bring an extra pair of eyeglasses or contact lenses and enough of any medication you take to last the entire trip.** You may also want your doctor to write a spare prescription using the drug's generic name, since brand names may vary from country to country. In luggage to be checked, **never pack prescription drugs or valuables.** To avoid customs delays, carry medications in their original packaging. And don't forget to copy down and **carry addresses of offices that handle refunds of lost traveler's checks and overseas contacts that help with lost credit cards.**

CHECKING LUGGAGE

How many carry-on bags you can bring with you is up to the airline. Most allow two, but not always, so make sure that everything you carry aboard will fit under your seat, and get to the gate early. If you have a seat at the back of the plane, you'll probably board first, while the overhead bins are still empty.

If you're flying internationally, note that baggage allowances may be determined not by piece but by weight— generally 88 pounds (40 kilograms) in first class, 66 pounds (30 kilograms) in business class, and 44 pounds (20 kilograms) in economy.

Airline liability for baggage is limited to $1,250 per person on flights within the United States. On international flights it amounts to $9.07 per pound or $20 per kilogram for checked baggage (roughly $640 per 70-pound bag) and $400 per passenger for unchecked baggage. You can buy additional coverage at check-in for about $10 per $1,000 of coverage, but it excludes a rather extensive list of items, shown on your airline ticket.

Before departure **itemize your bags' contents** and their worth, and label the bags with your name, address, and phone number. (If you use your home address, cover it so that potential thieves can't see it readily.) Inside each bag **pack a copy of your itinerary.** At check-in **make sure that each bag is correctly tagged** with the destination airport's three-letter code. If your bags arrive damaged or fail to arrive at all, file a written report with the airline before leaving the airport.

PASSPORTS & VISAS

Before traveling, **make two photocopies of your passport's data page** (one for someone at home and another for you, carried separately from your passport). While sightseeing in South America it's best to carry the copy of your passport and leave the original in your hotel's safe. If you lose your passport promptly call the nearest embassy or consulate and the local police.

ENTERING SOUTH AMERICA

For details on passport and visa requirements, *see* the country A to Z section at the end of each chapter.

PASSPORT OFFICES

The best time to apply for a passport or to renew is during the fall and winter. Before any trip, check your passport's expiration date, and, if necessary, renew it as soon as possible.

➤ AUSTRALIAN CITIZENS: **Australian Passport Office** (☎ 131–232).

➤ CANADIAN CITIZENS: **Passport Office** (☎ 819/994–3500 or 800/567–6868).

➤ NEW ZEALAND CITIZENS: **New Zealand Passport Office** (☎ 04/494–0700 for information on how to apply; 04/474–8000 or 0800/225–050 in New Zealand for information on applications already submitted).

➤ U.K. CITIZENS: **London Passport Office** (☎ 0990/210–410 for fees and documentation requirements and to request an emergency passport).

➤ U.S. CITIZENS: **National Passport Information Center** (☎ 900/225–5674; calls are 35¢ per minute for automated service, $1.05 per minute for operator service).

SAFETY

Although there has been a real effort to crack down on tourist-related crime throughout South America, petty street thievery is still prevalent in urban areas, especially in places around tourist hotels, restaurants, and discos. **Avoid flashing money around.** To safeguard your funds, **lock traveler's checks and cash in a hotel safe,** except for what you need to carry each day. Money (and important documents) that you do carry are best tucked into a money belt or carried in the inside pockets of your clothing. Wear the simplest of time-pieces and **do not wear any jewelry you aren't willing to lose**—stories of travelers having chains and even earrings yanked off them aren't uncommon. **Keep cameras in a secure camera bag,** preferably one with a chain or wire embedded in the strap. Always **remain alert for pickpockets,** particularly in market areas, and **don't walk alone at night in the big cities.**

TRAVEL ADVISORIES

South America has had its share of political struggle and drug-related strife. Before heading to a particular country, **get the latest travel warnings and advisories.** The U.S. State Department has a 24-hour hot line, a "fax on demand" (just dial the number and follow the instructions) number, and a Web site.

At press time, Colombia was the only South American country listed on the state department's travel warning list, due to violence by narcotraffickers, guerillas, paramilitary groups, and other criminal activities. Tourists should exercise extreme caution when visiting Colombia and be sure to contact the state department before-hand for up-to-the-minute restrictions and advisories.

In Bolivia civil unrest associated with antinarcotics activities in the Capare region between Santa Cruz and Cochabamba presents risks for travel-ers to those areas. The U.S. Embassy advises against travel to Ecuador's northern province of Sucumbios and areas of Carachi Province on the Colombian border. Extra caution should also be taken in Guayaquil, especially at the airport and along the dock areas where crime is rampant. In Peru, the U.S. Embassy still restricts the travel of U.S. Government em-ployees in several areas, where terror-ist groups and narcotics traffickers resort to violence.

➤ U.S. GOVERNMENT ADVISORIES: **U.S. Department of State** (✉ Overseas Citizens Services Office, Room 4811 N.S., 2201 C St. NW, Washington, DC 20520; ☎ 202/647–5225 for interactive hot line; 301/946–4400 for computer bulletin board; FAX 202/647–3000 for interactive hot line; www.travel.state.gov.); enclose a self-addressed, stamped, business-size envelope.

WOMEN IN SOUTH AMERICA

Women, especially those with light hair, can expect many pointed looks and the occasional hiss or catcall, integral aspects of the "machismo" culture. Outright come-ons or grab-bing aren't common, however.

SENIOR-CITIZEN TRAVEL

There's no reason that active, well-traveled senior citizens shouldn't visit South America, whether on an inde-pendent (but prebooked) vacation, an escorted tour, or an adventure vaca-tion. Before you leave home, however, determine what medical services your health insurance will cover outside the United States; note that Medicare doesn't provide for payment of hospi-tal and medical services outside the United States. If you need additional travel insurance, buy it (☞ Insurance, *above*).

The continent is full of good hotels and competent ground operators who will meet your flights and organize your sightseeing. To qualify for age-related discounts **mention your senior-citizen status up front** when booking hotel reservations (not when checking out) and before you're seated in restaurants (not when paying the bill). When renting a car **ask about promo-tional car-rental discounts,** which can be cheaper than senior-citizen rates.

➤ ADVENTURE TRAVEL: **Overseas Adventure Travel** (✉ Grand Circle Corporation, 625 Mt. Auburn St., Cambridge, MA 02138, ☎ 617/876–0533 or 800/221–0814, FAX 617/876–0826).

➤ EDUCATIONAL PROGRAMS: **Elderhos-tel** (✉ 75 Federal St., 3rd floor, Boston, MA 02110, ☎ 877/426–8056, FAX 877/426–2166), **Smithso-nian Study Tours** (✉ 1100 Jefferson Dr., SW, Washington, DC, 20560-0702, ☎ 202/357–4700, FAX 202/633–9250).

STUDENTS IN SOUTH
AMERICA

Although airfares to and within the continent are high, you can take buses to most South American destinations for mere dollars, and you can usually find safe, comfortable (if sparse), affordable accommodations for a fraction of what it might cost back home. Youth hostels exist in Argentina, Brazil, Chile, Colombia, Ecuador, and Peru, and backpacking is popular throughout the continent. Most South American cities also have vibrant student populations.

➤ STUDENT IDs & SERVICES: **Council on International Educational Exchange** (CIEE, ✉ 205 E. 42nd St., 14th floor, New York, NY 10017, ☎ 212/822–2600 or 888/268–6245, FAX 212/822–2699) for mail orders only, in the U.S. **Travel Cuts** (✉ 187 College St., Toronto, Ontario M5T 1P7, ☎ 416/979–2406 or 800/667–2887) in Canada.

TELEPHONES & THE INTERNET

When dialing a number from abroad, drop the initial 0 from the local area code. For details on country codes, directory and operator assistance, local and long-distance calls, phone cards, pay phones, and phone offices *see* the A to Z section at the end of each country chapter.

Internet access is surprisingly widespread. In addition to full-fledged cybercafés, look for machines set up in phone offices. Rates range from $1 to $10 an hour. Dial-up speeds are equally variable; just don't expect to find a T1. Brazil's connection rate is particularly sluggish.

LONG-DISTANCE SERVICES

AT&T, MCI, and Sprint access codes make calling long distance relatively convenient, but you may find the local access number blocked in many hotel rooms. First ask the hotel operator to connect you. If the hotel operator balks ask for an international operator, or dial the international operator yourself. One way to improve your odds of getting connected to your long-distance carrier is to travel with more than one company's calling card (a hotel may block Sprint, for example, but not MCI). If all else fails call from a pay phone.

➤ ACCESS CODES: **AT&T ADirect** (☎ 800/225–5288), **MCI Worldcom** (☎ 800/444–4444), **Sprint Express** (☎ 800/793–1153).

TIME

South America covers three time zones. New York, Caracas, Quito, and Santiago share a time zone. Lima is an hour behind New York; Brasília, Buenos Aires, Montevideo, and Rio are an hour ahead. Note that Brazil and Chile observe daylight saving time from October–March.

TOURS & PACKAGES

On a prepackaged tour or independent vacation everything is prearranged so you'll spend less time planning—and often get it all at a good price.

BOOKING WITH AN AGENT

Travel agents are excellent resources. But it's a good idea to collect brochures from several agencies because some agents' suggestions may be influenced by relationships with tour and package firms that reward them for volume sales. If you have a special interest **find an agent with expertise in that area**; ASTA (☞ Travel Agencies, *below*) has a database of specialists worldwide.

Make sure your travel agent knows the accommodations and other services of the place they're recommending. Ask about the hotel's location, room size, beds, and whether it has a pool, room service, or programs for children, if you care about these. Has your agent been there in person or sent others whom you can contact?

Do some homework on your own, too: Local tourism boards can provide information about lesser-known and small-niche operators, some of which may sell only direct.

BUYER BEWARE

Each year consumers are stranded or lose their money when tour operators—even large ones with excellent reputations—go out of business. So **check out the operator.** Ask several travel agents about its reputation, and try to **book with a company that has a consumer-protection program.**

(Look for information in the company's brochure.) In the United States, members of the National Tour Association and United States Tour Operators Association are required to set aside funds to cover your payments and travel arrangements in case the company defaults. It's also a good idea to choose a company that participates in the American Society of Travel Agent's Tour Operator Program (TOP); ASTA will act as mediator in any disputes between you and your tour operator.

Remember that the more your package or tour includes the better you can predict the ultimate cost of your vacation. Make sure you know exactly what is covered, and **beware of hidden costs.** Are taxes, tips, and transfers included? Entertainment and excursions? These can add up.

➤ TOUR-OPERATOR RECOMMENDATIONS: **American Society of Travel Agents (ASTA;** ☞ Travel Agencies, *below*), **National Tour Association (NTA;** ✉ 546 E. Main St., Lexington, KY 40508, ☎ 606/226–4444 or 800/682–8886), **United States Tour Operators Association (USTOA;** ✉ 342 Madison Ave., Suite 1522, New York, NY 10173, ☎ 212/599–6599 or 800/468–7862, ℻ 212/599–6744).

TRAIN TRAVEL

In most South American countries, trains don't play an important role in the transportation system. (Venezuela, for example, has no rail service at all, the result of its oil economy and the low cost of gasoline.) Still, there are high points. One country to see at least in part by rail is Paraguay, where some lines are operated with steam locomotives dating from the 19th century. In Peru, take the three-hour run to Machu Picchu from Cuzco and the all-day ride from Cuzco to Puno on Lake Titicaca. In Ecuador, a worthwhile trip is the dawn-to-dusk run through the Andes down the Avenue of the Volcanoes between Quito and Riobamba.

Chile has a good rail system that runs south from the capital through the Lake District. Take the overnight trip from Santiago to Temuco, a route using sleeper cars that are atmospher-

ically appointed in faded velvet and veneered woods. Argentina's rail system was built by the British. The most popular routes are all from Buenos Aires—the all-day or all-night ride to Bariloche is recommended. The latter two countries have sleeping and dining cars, the others, few facilities at all.

Ticket prices are low. Usually there are two classes of travel. Plan to **buy your train tickets three days ahead,** two weeks in summer months, and **arrive at the station well before departure time.** There are no rail passes except in Argentina (whose passes are difficult to obtain in the United States), and there's no way of reserving seats before you leave home.

TRAVEL AGENCIES

A good travel agent puts your needs first. Look for an agency that has been in business at least five years, emphasizes customer service, and has someone on staff who specializes in your destination. In addition **make sure the agency belongs to a professional trade organization.** The American Society of Travel Agents (ASTA), with 27,000 agents in some 170 countries, is the largest and most influential in the field. Operating under the motto "Integrity in Travel," it maintains and enforces a strict code of ethics and will step in to help mediate any agent-client disputes if necessary. ASTA also maintains a Web site that includes a directory of agents. If a travel agency is also acting as your tour operator, *see* Buyer Beware *in* Tours & Packages, *above.*

➤ LOCAL AGENT REFERRALS: **ASTA** (☎ 800/965–2782 24-hr hot line, ℻ 703/684–8319, www.astanet.com), **Association of British Travel Agents** (✉ 68–271 Newman St., London W1P 4AH, ☎ 020/7637–2444, ℻ 020/7637–0713), **Association of Canadian Travel Agents** (✉ 1729 Bank St., Suite 201, Ottawa, Ontario K1V 7Z5, ☎ 613/521–0474, ℻ 613/521–0805), **Australian Federation of Travel Agents** (✉ Level 3, 309 Pitt St., Sydney 2000, ☎ 02/9264–3299, ℻ 02/9264–1085), **Travel Agents' Association of New Zealand** (✉ Box 1888, Wellington 10033, ☎ 04/499–0104, ℻ 04/499–0786).

VISITOR INFORMATION

Most South American countries offer very little basic travel information. Few countries have tourist offices overseas, though there are a few travel sections in some embassies and consulates (and some cultural attachés will mail brochures and the like). Often your best bets are the airlines and tour operators with programs to South America (☞ Air Travel and Tour Operators, above).

➤ ARGENTINA: **Argentina Government Tourist Office** (✉ 12 W. 56th St., New York, NY 10019, ☎ 212/603–0443; ✉ 5055 Wilshire Blvd., Los Angeles, CA 90036, ☎ 323/930–0681; ✉ 2655 Le Jeune Rd., Miami, FL 33134, ☎ 305/442–1366).

➤ BOLIVIA: **Embassy of Bolivia** (☞ Embassies & Consulates, above).

➤ BRAZIL: **Consulate General of Brazil and Trade Bureau** (✉ 1185 Ave. of the Americas, 21st Floor, New York, NY 10036, ☎ 212/827–0976), for general travel and business information on Brazil; **Pro-Brazil, Inc.** (✉ 554 5th Ave., 4th floor, New York, NY 10036, ☎ 212/997–4070), for information on the states of Bahia, Rio de Janeiro, and São Paulo; **Riotur** (✉ 3601 Aviation Blvd., Suite 2100, Manhattan Beach, CA 90266, ☎ 310/643–2638; ✉ 201 E. 12th St., Suite 509, New York, NY 10003, ☎ 212/375–0801), for information on the city of Rio.

➤ CHILE: **Embassy of Chile** (☞ Embassies & Consulates, above).

➤ COLOMBIA: **Embassy of Colombia** (☞ Embassies & Consulates, above).

➤ ECUADOR: **Embassy of Ecuador** (☞ Embassies & Consulates, above).

➤ PARAGUAY: **Embassy of Paraguay** (☞ Embassies & Consulates, above).

➤ PERU: **Embassy of Peru** (☞ Embassies & Consulates, above).

➤ URUGUAY: **Uruguayan Tourism Office** (✉ 1077 Ponce de Leon Blvd., Coral Gables, FL 33134, ☎ FAX 305/443–7431).

➤ VENEZUELA: **Embassy of Venezuela** (☞ Embassies & Consulates, above), **Venezuelan Tourism Association**

(✉ Box 3010, Sausalito, CA 94966, ☎ 415/331–0100).

WEB SITES

Do **check out the World Wide Web** when you're planning. You'll find everything from up-to-date weather forecasts to virtual tours of famous cities. Fodor's Web site, www.fodors.com, is a great place to start your online travels.

For South American countries, "decentralized" best describes not only tourist boards but also Web sites. It's as rare to find one main, official tourism site for many of the countries as it is to find a national tourist board with an overseas office. Further, existing national sites aren't always comprehensive. **Be prepared to really surf.** For good information, you may have to **search by region, state/province, or city**—and hope that at least one of them has a comprehensive official site of its own. **Don't rule out foreign-language sites;** some have links to sites that present information in more than one language, including English.

On Portuguese- or Spanish-language sites, watch for the name of the country, region, state, or city in which you have an interest. The search terms for "look," "find," and "get" are olhar/achar, buscar, and pegar in Portuguese, and mirar and buscar in Spanish. "Next" and "last" (as in "next/last 10") are próximo and último/anterior in both Portuguese and Spanish. Keep an eye out for such words as (where the words are different, Portuguese is provided first, followed by Spanish): turismo (tourism), turístico (tourist-related), hoteis/hoteles (hotels), restaurantes (restaurants), governo/gobierno (government), estado (state), província/provincia (province), cidade/ciudad (city).

The following sites are good places to start a search (unless otherwise noted, these sites have information in English): www.bolivia.com (some tourism information on Bolivia); www.embratur.gov.br (official Brazilian tourist board site); www.consuladobrasilny.org (the consular Web site in New York, with details about other consulates, travel information, and links to other sites);

www.gochile.cl or www.chilnet.cl (tourist and business information on Chile); www.winesofchile.com (site for true oenophiles); www.colombia.com (business and tourism information on Colombia); www.colostate.edu (Colorado State University's site with information on Colombia courtesy of the Latin American Student Organization); www.ecuador.org (Ecuador Embassy's official site); www.paraguay.com (with travel information on Paraguay, including maps and city-specific information on where to eat and sleep and what to see); www.peru.com (Spanish-language business, tourism, and news site on Peru with links to English-language sites); www.peru-explorer.com (with Peruvian geography and cultural history as well as travel facts and photos); www.turismo.gub.uy (the Uruguay Ministry of Tourism's site); www.embavenez-us.org (the Venezuelan Embassy's site, with news and travel and economic information).

WHEN TO GO

Two factors should guide your travel planning: the climate in a particular country and an event or activity that interests you.

CLIMATE

Because of the great variety of latitudes, altitudes, and climatic zones on the continent, you'll encounter many different kinds of weather in any given month. The highland areas of the Andes Mountains—which run north to south down the west coast of South America from Colombia through Ecuador, Peru, Bolivia, Chile, and Argentina—are at their most accessible and most comfortable in the dry season, May–October. July–September is the time to ski in Chile

and Argentina or to cruise south to Antarctica.

An entirely different climate reigns in the Amazon Basin, whose tropical and subtropical rain forests spread in a broad west–east band from the headwaters in Ecuador and Peru across the northern third of Brazil. May–September, the Andean dry season, is the nonrainy season here—that is, it's simply less rainy than at any other time. Contrary to what you may expect, you may prefer the rainy season for an Amazon River trip; the waters are higher then and boats can venture farther upriver into the tributaries.

Certain ocean regions—the Atlantic coast from Brazil all the way down to the famous resort of Punta del Este in Uruguay, as well as the Caribbean shore of Venezuela—are at their hottest and most crowded during North America's winter, December–March. The sea moderates temperatures in most of South America's cities year-round, even as far south as Buenos Aires. The Pacific coast is bordered mostly by a strip of desert, whose climate is always hospitable. Southern Chile is fjord country, perfect for cruising from November to March.

Weather-wise, May is probably the best month to visit South America. From then through June you can expect both good weather and off-season prices. These months, as well as September and October, are also relatively uncrowded.

➤ FORECASTS: **Weather Channel Connection** (☎ 900/932–8437), 95¢ per minute from a Touch-Tone phone.

1 DESTINATION: SOUTH AMERICA

A CONTINENT OF TREASURES

FOR EVERYONE FROM bird-watchers to beach bums, South America is the perfect destination. Increasing numbers of restless vacationers are being drawn by the continent's fascinating contrasts, its bustling metropolises, and its dramatic landscapes. Often those who visit are dreamers, escapists, lovers of the unusual. Those who visit often do so with great expectations and few prejudices.

In many cosmopolitan cities, smartly dressed socialites brush shoulders with women clad in traditional costumes that have changed little since the colonial conquests. Centuries-old churches with dazzling baroque facades stand in the shadow of sleek skyscrapers. In rural areas, shiny new Volvos and BMWs share dusty streets with lumbering oxcarts and men on horseback. Dry gives way to wet as the rainy season begins suddenly, and cold becomes hot within minutes of leaving the highlands for a coastal destination. Throughout the continent, nature's splendors are often rivaled by man-made pre-Columbian and colonial treasures.

Any number of appetites can be satisfied on the same vacation. In Rio, for example, you can spend the afternoon touring the historic Palácio Catete after a splendid morning of sunbathing on the beach at Ipanema or hiking through the lush Floresta da Tijuca that surrounds the Corcovado stature. In Buenos Aires, you can pass the day at one of the all-season horse-racing tracks, followed by an excellent dinner (accompanied by a superb Argentine wine) and a night of tango in La Boca, the city's picturesque waterfront district. Such diversity means that there's something, somewhere, for everyone, on any budget, to see, do, and treasure in South America.

A Short History

Christopher Columbus didn't actually set foot on the continent until his third voyage, in 1498, when he reached the mouth of the Orinoco River in what is now Venezuela. Both Spain and Portugal were eager to develop overseas empires at that time, so it didn't take long for them to send others to explore and colonize this new territory. In 1531, Francisco Pizarro sailed south from Panama with some 180 men and 27 horses. He landed in Peru, and by 1533 he had conquered the entire Inca empire, doing in South America what Cortés had done more easily in Mexico. One of Pizarro's officers, Pedro de Valdivia, conquered northern Chile and founded Santiago in 1541, giving Spain control of the west coast of the continent from Panama to central Chile.

The Portuguese, meanwhile, were busy on the east coast laying claim to Brazil. Unlike the situation in the rest of South America, however, the colonization of Brazil was gradual and relatively peaceful. While Spanish conquistadors were seeking the gold of legendary El Dorado, wood was the first natural resource exploited by the Portuguese. Then came sugar, which gave rise to vast plantations along the coast—and to the importation of millions of African slaves to do the backbreaking labor. Afterward came gold and diamonds, first opening up the land in the interior. Coffee followed, and with it the appearance of planters on the red earth of southeastern Brazil.

Many Spaniards and Portuguese came here to make a quick fortune and return to Europe as soon as possible. Their expeditions, however, often included farmers and craftsmen who wished to begin life anew in the Americas. What these settlers encountered instead was an oppressive feudal system that evolved apace with such glittering colonial cities as Lima, Quito, and Ouro Prêto. For three centuries colonists labored under European rule, but between 1808 and 1823 the New World empires built by Spain and Portugal began to crumble—often due to political and economic factors similar to those that had precipitated the revolution in Britain's 13 North American colonies.

Although each country had its own revolutionary heroes, two men stand out as leaders in South America's struggle for independence. The first is Venezuelan general Simón Bolívar, a man of tremendous vision, whose courageous battles freed Bolivia, Colombia, Ecuador, Peru, and Venezuela. The second is José de San Martín, the Argentine general who helped win independence for Chile and (along with Bolívar) Peru. Brazil won its independence from Portugal in 1822 without bloodshed and changed from colony to monarchy to republic fairly easily.

Inspired by the American and French revolutions, eager patriots in the Southern Hemisphere established republican governments. Unfortunately, the new nations were ill-prepared for self-government. Most lacked the broad popular base necessary to enforce their fragile constitutions. A disheartening number of civil wars, coups d'état, and upheavals have shaken South America's nations since they gained independence. Down through the centuries since Pizarro, the real power in the Southern Hemisphere has always been vested in its charismatic leaders, rather than in well-intentioned but weak legislatures. Things do change, however, and recent elections have brought democratic rule (albeit fragile in some cases) to the entire region.

WHAT'S WHERE

The profusion of countries and cities might make selecting one destination—or even two or three—seem impossible. The truth is, however, that the Andes split the continent rather conveniently into two very distinct regions, so making sense of the whole thing is only half as hard. (There are actually three ranges that make up South America's great, jagged spine; they vary between 322 and 644 km, or 200 and 400 mi, in width and average some 4,000 m, or 13,000 ft, in height.) West of this monumental chain of peaks, nature is at its finest—from the highlands of Ecuador, Peru, and Bolivia to the gemlike lakes of southern Chile. East of the Andes, the marvels are no less alluring. Some of the world's largest and most exciting cities are found here—Rio de Janeiro, São Paulo, and Buenos Aires—along with the incomparable Atlantic coastline.

Argentina

Romantic notions of handsome gauchos and seductive tango dancers have given Argentina a mystique, but these images tell only half the story. Stroll through Buenos Aires's classy Recoleta district with its upscale boutiques, sit down to tea in an elegant *confitería,* or attend an opera at the world-famous Teatro Colón, and you'll see that *porteños* (residents of Buenos Aires) are educated, sophisticated, and urbane. Their city never seems to sleep. Dinner is often taken at midnight, and the streets are still full of people when you leave the restaurant at 2 AM.

Away from the capital, the pace is slower, the people more open, and the culture easier to appreciate. North of Buenos Aires are the stunning Iguazú Falls—in all, some 300 separate waterfalls that thunder over a 2½-mi-wide precipice on the border of Brazil, Argentina, and Paraguay. In Patagonia to the south, you'll find the ski resort of Bariloche; Glaciers National Park, whose icy sights will take your breath away; and the famous Tierra del Fuego National Park at the very tip of the country.

Bolivia

Visitors are often giddy upon arrival in La Paz, perhaps with relief at having landed safely at the world's highest commercial airport, set just above the world's highest capital city at over 3,700 m (12,000 ft). More likely, though, it's *soroche,* a dizziness caused by the lack of oxygen at high altitudes. But even after you've taken your coco-leaf tea and headache pill and are steady on your feet, you may find that Bolivia has an otherworldly appeal.

Not to be missed here are the ruins of Tiahuanaco, a short ride from La Paz across the barren but strangely beautiful altiplano, the vast plateau that lies between two ranges of the Andes. Although the ruins are shrouded in mystery, some researchers believe Tiahuanaco was a cradle of civilization some 7,000 years ago. The indigenous Aymaras still farm the islands and shores of Lake Titicaca—the highest navigable lake in the world and the legendary birthplace of the Inca empire. To the Aymaras, this lake and its islands are mystical and sacred. Hydrofoils and hovercrafts ply the waters, passing traditional gondola-shape boats made of *totora* reeds.

Brazil

Portuguese-speaking Brazil is the fifth-largest country in the world and has an oversized vitality to match. Its high-energy attitude can be seen everywhere—in highways, dams, industrial complexes, and even in the capital city of Brasília, which was constructed from scratch in the wilderness in an effort to promote development of the nation's vast interior.

To most visitors, Brazil is Rio de Janeiro, famous for its spectacular bay-side setting, fabulous beaches, skimpy string bikinis, and riotous Carnaval (Carnival). But Brazil goes far beyond Rio's beaches and hedonistic pleasures. Skyscrapers, stock markets, and agribusiness set the pace in the megalopolis of São Paulo. Baroque art beautifies the colonial cities of Minas Gerais State. A unique Afro-Brazilian culture thrives in tropical Salvador, capital of Bahia State. And there's the amazing Amazon, the name given to both the legendary 6,440-km-long (4,000-mi-long) river and the 750,000,000-acre expanse of trackless jungle, menacing wildlife, and merciless heat through which the river flows.

Chile

This 4,267-km-long (2,650-mi-long) ribbon of a country averages only 177 km (110 mi) in width. From north to south it cuts across five ranges of soil and climate, producing a variety of exceptional scenic attractions. In the north, you'll find the Atacama Desert, so dry that in some areas no rain has ever been recorded. Next come the copper mines and rich nitrate deposits, followed by the fertile central valley that's home to Santiago, the capital. The beautiful lake and forest region is below this, with outstanding fishing and skiing. Finally, in the extreme south lies cold, forbidding, windswept Tierra del Fuego.

Known for its award-winning wines and excellent seafood, Chile is also justly famous for the resort city of Viña del Mar, with its wide, white, sandy beaches and year-round casino overlooking the Pacific Ocean. Jet-set skiers from the United States and Europe often prefer the championship slopes at Portillo and Valle Nevado, outside Santiago, and Las Lenas, in Argentina, where they can schuss during summer months when snows melt in the Northern Hemisphere. Huge, mysterious *moai* statues await those looking for a different type of adventure on Chile's remote Easter Island.

Colombia

Colombia is the continent's only country to have both Pacific and Caribbean coasts. It also comprises the northern end of the Andes, which means the altitudes and climates range from chilly mountaintops to sultry coastal lowlands. As a result, Colombia has diverse plant and animal life. The country's major cities sit at different altitudes and with each altitude comes a different attitude. As you move from one region to the next, you'll notice changes in the music, cuisine, and dialect—creating the potpourri that's responsible for much of Colombia's charm. Bogotá, the sprawling capital, sits at 2,650 m (8,700 ft) and has a formal air that's reminiscent of Spain. The atmosphere grows more relaxed and informal, however, if you descend 610 m (2,000 ft) to Medellín, a small but vibrant community whose mild climate has earned it the name "city of eternal spring." Another 457 m (1,500 ft) lower is Cali, an attractive city at the end of a fertile valley, next to which is the beautifully restored colonial town of Popayán. The historical port of Cartagena is one of the best-preserved colonial cities in the Americas; it's also a lively, colorful town with strong Afro-Caribbean influence.

Ecuador

A patchwork of highland and jungle, this tiny nation claims some of the hemisphere's most impressive landscapes. A living quilt of terraced green plots covers the lower slopes of cloud-capped volcanoes, where corn grows twice as tall as the sturdy peasant farmers. Quito, the capital, lies at the foot of mighty Mt. Pichincha. The city has outstanding examples of Spanish colonial architecture and winding cobblestone streets. Just 24 km (15 mi) outside the city, you can have your picture taken as you straddle the equator at a monument indicating the dividing line between the Northern and Southern hemispheres.

Cuenca, a beautifully preserved colonial city, offers both architectural charm and an outstanding market. The coastal region and its bustling port of Guayaquil also have much to offer, and the most memorable way to get here from Quito is by rail. When in operation, the train maneuvers—on narrow-gauge tracks—up and down mountain passes via a series of switchbacks to the steamy lowlands. Guayaquil also serves as a departure point for planes and ships to the enchanting Galápagos Islands, home of the remarkable wildlife that sparked Darwin's theories of evolution.

Paraguay

In this unspoiled land, time and tradition have stood still for generations. Paraguay may be short on extravagant facilities, but it's long on charm and authenticity. Asuncíon is a provincial capital whose pleasures are simple: a stroll through the Botanical Gardens; a leisurely lunch at an outdoor café; or an afternoon of shopping for *ñandutí,* the country's unique, intricate, spiderweb lace. In the countryside, motorcycles and pop music compete with oxcarts and traditional *polca* music in the hearts and minds of the rural people. The country's original inhabitants were the Guaraní, and high rates of intermarriage between Europeans and the indigenous peoples led to much cultural blending. Mission ruins near Encarnacíon are an impressive reminder of the Guaraní legacy. Here, the Jesuits converted the native population and organized a unique communal society. Several of the lovely missions, abandoned when the Jesuits were expelled in 1767, are being restored.

Peru

Peru contains a wealth of history in its borders. Cuzco, once the capital of the Inca empire, is one of the hemisphere's most interesting cities. Although the Spaniards tried to superimpose their culture on the conquered Inca, they succeeded only in penetrating the surface. Symbolically, when a 1953 earthquake struck, it felled much of the convent of Santo Domingo, which had been built over the ruins of the sacred Temple of the Sun. The inner Inca walls that were revealed withstood the devastating quake.

The three-hour trip by rail from Cuzco to Machu Picchu and all of its marvels is exhilarating. Thought by many to have been the last refuge of the Incas, Machu Picchu was never discovered by the Spaniards. The maze of temples, houses, terraces, and stairways lay abandoned in lofty solitude until Hiram Bingham, later a U.S. senator, stumbled upon the city in 1911. If the gems of Peru's Inca past are locked away on the altiplano, then its capital, Lima, is the safekeeper of colonial treasures. Perhaps no other city in the Americas enjoyed such power and prestige during the height of the colonial era. For an entirely different side of Peru, you can visit Iquitos, where the sounds of the Amazon jungle are ever present.

Uruguay

Gently rolling hills and grasslands are the hallmarks of Uruguay, one of South America's smallest countries. Ninety percent of the land is used for grazing, and Uruguayans are justifiably proud of their fine beef cattle. A visit to an *estancia* (ranch) is an excellent way to experience both the scenery and the people—well-educated yet unpretentious, industrious yet relaxed, they're the most remarkable aspect of Uruguay. Another culture exists along the coasts. The country's beaches are among the best in the southern part of the continent; without even leaving Montevideo, Uruguay's gracious capital, you can sample more than half a dozen of them. The most fashionable beach, however, is 137 km (85 mi) to the east at Punta del Este, a haven for well-heeled foreign visitors. Often called the Riviera of South America, this resort is also a popular site for international conferences and movie festivals.

Venezuela

Just a few hours from the eastern United States, Venezuela is perhaps the continent's most accessible destination for North American travelers. Caracas, the capital, is a futuristic blend of glass office buildings and space-age apartments built on the heels of the oil boom. What it lacks in colonial charm, Caracas makes up for in its selection of world-class restaurants, art galleries, and night spots.

Venezuela enjoys South America's longest Caribbean coast, with stretches of pristine white sand lapped by warm turquoise waters. Margarita Island is a Caribbean destination popular with sun-seeking Europeans. In the Andean region, the world's longest and highest cable car carries you to the foot of glacier-topped Pico Bolivar. The *llanos,* vast savannas that cover the central part of the country, are home to colorful wildlife. In the southeast, huge table-top mountains called *tepuis* tower over the high elevation grasslands of Canaima, a national park the size of Belgium. Here, the Angel Falls plummet more than 807 m (2,647 ft) in a bizarre landscape of black lagoons, pink sand beaches, and unique plant life.

NEW AND NOTEWORTHY

Argentina

Patagonia, it seems, is being invaded by the rich and famous. When CNN founder Ted Turner and his wife Jane Fonda bought the 11,000-acre La Primavera (Springtime) Ranch on Lago Traful near Bariloche, a few local eyebrows were raised. "There isn't a more beautiful place in the world," he told a Buenos Aires newspaper. Photos of President Clinton and President Menem, smiling under a blue sky with Lago Nahuel Huapi in the background, would confirm this. Hungarian financier George Soros also succumbed to Patagonia's charms, buying the Llao Llao Hotel near Bariloche plus another million acres of wilderness. French movie actor Christopher Lambert and American Sylvester Stallone have both made offers on lakefront land and ranches. Argentines have mixed feelings about this gringo invasion; some express concern over the future ownership of what they consider their heritage.

Bolivia

After years of inadequate lodging facilities, Bolivia has experienced a boom in hotel construction, including the privatization of the former government-owned chain and a subsequent rush to renovate. In addition, numerous historic buildings throughout the country have been turned into exotic accommodations for adventurous travelers.

Brazil

City, state, and federal governments have been pumping out new, improved brochures and maps. And just in time, too, as the real has weakened, resulting in a favorable rate of exchange for North American and European travelers. The president of Brazil, forward-thinking Fernando Henrique Cardoso, was reelected in 1998. He avoided draconian economic measures and a 35% currency devaluation until the day after the election. Then, new taxes and budget cuts were announced, recession settled in, and unemployment soared. Still, Brazilians hope he'll continue his crusade against political corruption and his slow but constant efforts to stimulate economic development.

Chile

The democratization of Chile, which began with the 1990 end of military rule, has continued. Tensions with the military ran high after General Augusto Pinochet's 1999 arrest in Britain for alleged human-rights violations—and Chile's civilian government's failure to get him released. The ongoing foreign investigations of abuses committed during Pinochet's 1973–90 rule have left the country divided. Meanwhile, Chile is realizing the moneymaking potential of tourism. Catering to a culture of respect towards nature, the ecotourist infrastructure is slowly creeping southward, bumping heads with an incessant Chilean willingness to allow multinationals to extract, cut down, bottle up, and export their precious natural resources.

Colombia

Two popular luxury hotels, both in restored colonial convents, are captivating visitors who would otherwise opt for the comforts of international chains. The historical ascetic appeal of Santa Clara and Santa Teresa in Cartagena's Ciudad Amurallada (Old City) is joined by a simple, modern decadence (no colonial convent ever had a roof-top pool like that at the Santa Teresa). In Bogotá, Casa San Isidro turns out the country's best French seafood with white-glove service from its glamorous hillside location.

After decades of civil war, however, residual violence and economic instability make Colombia a troubled travel destination. Guerrilla terrorism has resulted in the death of kidnapped Americans; at press time the prospect of peace between rebel groups and the government was slim. You're advised to exercise extreme caution when traveling in and around Colombia. Bus travel or renting a car for travel between cities isn't recommended.

Ecuador

Travelers have long headed to the highlands and Galápagos Islands, but Ecuador has a third region—all too often ignored—that holds an ecological and cultural treasure trove: the Amazon. Rapidly becoming popular as a tourist destination, Ecuador's piece of the Amazon Basin, known locally as El Oriente, is home to eight different indigenous cultures and all the wildlife one would expect to see in the jungles of Brazil or Peru.

Paraguay

Widespread corruption and smuggling (especially in the tri-border area around Ciudad de Este) continue to create instability and undermine the rule of law. But for visitors, Paraguay is safe and remains the path less traveled, a welcome change from heavily touristed destinations.

Peru

Peru is once again considered a safe tourist destination, especially since the capture of the last two heads of the terrorist group that once held the country hostage. Foreign investment has also increased, new hotels have opened, roads have been improved, and central Lima's Plaza Mayor (renamed from Plaza de Armas, to rid it of its military association) has been revitalized. The north coast is drawing more visitors with new archaeological discoveries and greater access to remote pre-Inca ruins such as the impressive Kuelap site.

Uruguay

A new spirit has overtaken this most relaxed of countries. A slew of young entrepreneurs have begun a period of development and investment. The country has also begun to capitalize on its tourist potential, with new world-class hotels. In the capital, better street lighting and the opening of an array of restaurants and nightclubs have given the city a vibrant nightlife.

Venezuela

Populist president Hugo Chavez was elected in 1998. At press time, he was pushing for constitutional reform and the possible dissolution of the legislature and the supreme court. Although he's viewed as a nationalistic strongman, he doesn't seem to be pushing his stated mission of greater wealth distribution to the point of disrupting market forces or scaring off foreign investors. Although critics contend that Chavez's goal is dictatorship, the ongoing political changes in this long-democratic nation shouldn't affect the average visitor. On a lighter note, trips to the Andes, the Llanos, and many of the country's national parks are becoming easier to arrange. In the last couple years more foreign visitors have been discovering Venezuela's natural beauty.

PLEASURES AND PASTIMES

Archaeology

The mysteries of ancient ruins such as the silent, windswept stones and temples at Tiahuanaco, near La Paz in Bolivia, and the majestic remains of Inca civilizations never fail to tantalize. Peru alone has a wealth of pre-Columbian sites that would take weeks, if not months or years, to fully explore. Almost everything in the country is worth seeing, but the especially exceptional sights include Machu Picchu, the fortresses of Pisac and Ollantaytambo, and the Coricancha. If you have more time, visit the Nazca lines, gigantic, mysterious "drawings" in the desert; the Chimú city of Chán Chán, outside Trujillo; and the Moche tomb of the warrior priest at Sipán. In Colombia, you can visit la Ciudad Perdida (the Lost City), near the Caribbean coast, or the intricately decorated tombs of Tierradentro and mysterious megaliths of San Agustín, near Cali. In Ecuador, there are Inca and pre-Inca ruins at Ingapirca, two hours north of Cuenca.

Dining

Culinary partisans may argue over whether exotic Afro-Brazilian concoctions, delicious Peruvian and Chilean seafood dishes, or sinfully succulent Argentine and Uruguayan meats should claim the title of South America's most delicious regional foods. For most visitors, however, the entire continent is a diner's delight. For details on the cuisine in each country, *see* Dining *in* Pleasures and Pastimes at the start of each chapter.

Festivals

It's fun to be in many countries—particularly Brazil and the Caribbean countries—during Carnaval, the week before Ash Wednesday, which usually falls in February or March. In strongly Catholic South America, dozens of saints days are marked by processions and other festivities; Holy Week, the week of Easter, and Corpus Christi, eight Sundays later, are particularly important. In the Andean countries, the time between harvest and the next planting (June to November) sees many folkloric festivals, usually village events. (*See* Festivals and Seasonal Events *in* the country A to Z section at the end of each chapter for more information on specific festivals of note.)

Natural Wonders

Volcanoes, some still active, run the length of the Andes; at their feet lie everything from the desolate, windswept desert and dunes of Peru's Paracas National Reserve to the turquoise lakes and burbling hot springs of Chile's lake district. The 30,000-year-old Perito Moreno Glacier broods in Argentina's Glacier National Park, while spires of ice slide off the San Rafael Glacier, south of Puerto Montt in Chile. A mighty roar fills the air as the raging waters of Iguazú Falls—higher and wider than Niagara—plunge over basalt cliffs where Argentina, Paraguay, and Brazil meet. Angel Falls crash nearly two-thirds of a mile down a cliff in a corner of Venezuela so remote that it was unknown to the world until 1937.

Sports enthusiasts will appreciate the thrills of white-water rafting in Peruvian jungles, bone-fishing along Venezuela's coast, downhill skiing in the Argentine and Chilean Andes, and hiking and climbing in the pristine mountain fastness of the Chilean lake district. Sun worshipers, those most dedicated of hedonists, can mingle with the beautiful people on glittering beaches in posh Punta del Este, Viña del Mar, or Margarita Island.

Photography

Few vacation spots provide better subjects—from landscapes and cityscapes to wildlife and people—for photographers. It's hard to imagine colors more brilliant, light more intense, or textures more complex than those that meet the eye at every glance: the perfectly shaped cones of Ecuador's volcanoes, the colonial splendor of Lima's churches, and the riot of fishing skiffs plying Reloncavi Sound in southern Chile.

Shopping

Savvy shoppers can spend all day at chic boutiques brimming with good buys in Brazilian gemstones, Colombian emeralds, Argentine leather, or Uruguayan furs. Handicrafts lovers will marvel at the Paraguayan lace, Peruvian textiles, or fine Panama hats (from Ecuador, no less) sold in bustling *mercados*, the New World's answer to the chaotic bazaar.

Wildlife

You can come nose to nose with sea lions and giant tortoises in the Galápagos Islands or spot the pterodactyl-like hoatzin on Venezuela's vast savannas. In Argentina, see whales and elephant seals frolic at Península Valdés and attend the annual gathering of the Magellanic penguin clan on the beaches at Punta Tombo. Flamingos, llama-like guanacos, and foxes inhabit Chile's Torres del Paine National Park.

FODOR'S CHOICE

Flavors

Argentina

★ **Cabaña las Lilas, Buenos Aires.** The best beef in the city, a well-stocked wine cellar, and impeccable service attract statesmen and movie stars to this establishment. *$$$$*

★ **El Patacón, Bariloche (Patagonia).** Dishes prepared with fresh herbs, berries, vegetables, game, and fish; stunning lake views; and a gaucho-style decor made this the restaurant of choice for President Clinton and Argentine President Menem in 1998. *$$$*

★ **Ideal, Buenos Aires.** At this charming, slightly tattered, café—a real classic—you can get a tango lesson with your coffee. *$*

Bolivia

★ **Pig & Whistle, La Paz.** Although the decor evokes a cozy British pub, you'll find Indian and Southeast Asian dishes and, on weekends, soothing live music of varying types. *$*

★ **Sujna Wasi, Copacabana.** This small restaurant with a big menu and great prices serves breakfast, lunch, and dinner and features vegetarian dishes, seafood, soups, homemade pizzas, and a complete bar. *¢–$*

Brazil

★ **Le Coq d'Or, Ouro Prêto (Minas Gerais).** Here the executive chef (who trained at the prestigious Cordon Bleu in Paris) brings French inspiration to Brazilian cuisine. *$$$$*

☆ **Famiglia Mancini, São Paulo.** The atmosphere here is jovial, the decor unique, and the Italian food delicious. *$$$*

☆ **Porcão, Rio de Janeiro.** This restaurant embodies the boisterous churrascaria experience: harried waiters zip among tables, slicing sizzling chunks of tender grilled beef, pork, and chicken onto the plates of hungry diners. *$$$*

☆ **Lá em Casa, Belém (Amazon).** The outstanding interpretations of indigenous Amazon dishes have given this restaurant an international renown. *$$*

☆ **Canto da Paixada, Manaus (Amazon).** This restaurant's popularity stems from its masterful preparation of river fish, the staple of the Amazon. *$$*

Chile

☆ **Aquí Está Coco, Santiago.** The best fish and shellfish in Santiago are served up in comfortable surroundings decorated with flotsam and jetsam from Chilean shores. *$$$$*

☆ **Balzac, Puerto Montt.** Seafood dishes with a French flare are the specialty here. The owner's endearing father—a rich source of local Chilote history—sits downstairs and makes everyone feel at home. *$$$*

☆ **El Remezón, Punta Arenas.** The homey atmosphere, perfect pisco sours, and delicious seafood make this place stand out. *$$$*

☆ **Restorán Don Peyo, Santiago.** The hot sauce and the garlic and avocado spreads in themselves warrant a visit, but the beef dishes are what keep this out-of-the-way Chilean restaurant on the map. *$*

Colombia

☆ **Casa San Isidro, Bogotá.** You travel by cable car to this French seafood restaurant perched well above Bogotá. *$$$$*

☆ **La Vitrola, Cartagena.** An original menu and relaxed atmosphere make this friendly restaurant in the historic walled city one of Cartagena's most popular. *$$$*

☆ **El Hato Viejo, Medellín.** Large portions of grilled meat and fresh seafood have made this second-story restaurant in the heart of town a local hangout. *$$*

☆ **Restaurante SEAP, Bogotá.** Housed in a colonial mansion in the Candelaria district, this elegant restaurant is the perfect place to enjoy a typical Colombian lunch. *$$*

Ecuador

☆ **Trattoria da Enrico, Guayaquil.** Set in a former home on a quiet street in Guayaquil's Urdesa district, the Trattoria serves what may be the country's best Italian cuisine. *$$$*

☆ **La Querencia, Quito.** Though the city views and private gardens provide plenty of ambience, La Querencia is best known for its superb Ecuadoran cuisine. *$$*

☆ **Raymipampa, Cuenca.** Conveniently located next to the cathedral, this popular spot serves a large selection of Ecuadoran and foreign dishes in a pleasant atmosphere. *¢–$*

☆ **La Canoa Manabita, Quito.** This simple eatery in the Mariscal district serves exquisite Ecuadoran seafood lunches at remarkably low prices. *¢*

Paraguay

☆ **Peter's Restaurant en Casapueblo, Asunción.** Renowned Argentine chef Gato Dumas prepares unique international entrées in this modern Mediterranean restaurant. *$$–$$$*

☆ **La Paraguayita, Asunción.** Paraguayan steaks are turned on the grill while you sit beneath jacaranda trees at this terraced eatery. *$$*

Peru

☆ **La Costa Verde, Lima.** Both the setting—overlooking the Pacific—and the food are great here. The menu is international, but the local seafood is highly recommended, as is the Sunday buffet. *$$$$*

☆ **La Posada del Puente, Arequipa.** International and local specialties are featured at this elegant restaurant overlooking the Chili River, making it the perfect spot for a candlelight dinner. *$$*

☆ **Pucara, Cuzco.** Cuzco's best restaurant for regional specialties is always packed with locals, and offers a tasty, economical fixed-price lunch special. *$*

Uruguay

☆ **La Bourgogne, Punta del Este.** The food at this splendid restaurant is served by impeccably clad waiters and is prepared with only the finest and freshest ingredients. *$$$$*

★ **La Proa, Montevideo.** This restaurant might offer what the proprietor, Darwin, refers to as the best in "refined" cooking, but most people come for the outstanding *parillada* (grilled meats). $$

Venezuela

★ **Bahia, Porlamar.** Here you can savor fresh seafood dishes while enjoying the lovely beach view and the strolling musicians. $$

★ **El Oso Polar, Mérida.** Located on the outskirts of town, this ordinary looking restaurant offers truly innovative dishes. $$

★ **Tarzilandia, Caracas.** At the Caracas landmark the exotic Venezuelan dishes are as much a part of the experience as the garden's lush vegetation, parrots, tree frogs, and turtles. $$

Comforts

Argentina

★ **Alvear Palace Hotel, Buenos Aires.** Conceived as a luxury apartment building in 1932, this traditional hotel in the fashionable Recoleta district is close to the museums and good restaurants. $$$$

★ **Park Hyatt, Buenos Aires.** The city's most luxurious hotel has a million-dollar art collection and beautiful rooms and suites. $$$$

★ **Sheraton Internacional Iguazú, Iguazú National Park.** Guests at this five-star hotel can have breakfast or a drink on spacious balconies that overlook the stunning falls, which are directly visible from half the rooms. $$$$

Bolivia

★ **Gran Hotel Paris, La Paz.** This turn-of-the-century hotel in La Paz's oldest plaza was remodeled in 1996. Six Louis XVI–style suites have balconies overlooking the Plaza Murillo. $$–$$$

★ **Inca Utama Hotel & Spa, Huatajata.** On Lake Titicaca, this hotel offers comfortable rooms and a spa with such soothing treatments as mud or salt baths. $$–$$$

★ **Hostal de su Merced, Sucre.** Built in a renovated 17th-century home, this hostel has a colorful wooden ceiling that replicates those in the country's baroque Jesuit churches and an upper-floor terrace with excellent views. $

★ **Hotel–Galeria Virgen del Rosario, La Paz.** Located right in the middle of the market area, this budget hotel has many surprising amenities as well as a light, cheery restaurant. $

Brazil

★ **Copacabana Palace, Rio de Janeiro.** The Palace was built in 1923 for the visiting King of Belgium, and has attracted royals, movie stars, and other VIPs ever since. Recent restorations have given it a renewed sparkle. $$$$

★ **Inter-Continental, São Paulo.** Attentive service and well-appointed guest rooms and public areas are just some of the things that make this a top-notch hotel. $$$$

★ **Solar da Ponte, Tiradentes.** Long included among Brazil's finest small hotels, the Solar has the spirit of a house in the country, complete with sprawling lawns and gardens. $$$$

★ **Tropical, Manaus.** The only major resort in the Amazon has verdant gardens all around and a privileged location overlooking the Rio Negro. $$$$

Chile

★ **Hotel Antumalal, Pucón.** Along the entryway of this 1950s, lake-district gem are pictures of many famous guests—Queen Elizabeth, King Leopold of Belgium, and Jimmy Stewart, among them. $$$$

★ **Hotel Salto Chico–Explora, Torres del Paine National Park.** There's no better base for exploring the national park than this world-famous ecohotel. No expense has been spared to bring you the finest of creature comforts. $$$$

★ **Sheraton Santiago and San Cristóbal Tower, Santiago.** Such amenities as a business center, 24-hour butler service, and a purifier that treats all the water make this the best establishment in the capital. $$$$

★ **Hotel Continental, Temuco.** Chile's oldest hotel (founded in 1890) has hosted such Chilean personalities as Pablo Neruda and Salvador Allende. $

Colombia

★ **Santa Clara, Cartagena.** This elegant hotel in a restored colonial convent, with its verdant courtyard and ocean views, provides one of Colombia's most charming lodging experiences. $$$$

★ **Santa Teresa, Cartagena.** The city's second hotel occupying a meticulously renovated and decorated former convent is another monument to fine lodging. $$$$

★ **Hostería de la Candelaria, Bogotá.** This friendly lodge occupies two restored colonial houses in the heart of the historic Candelaria district. $$

★ **Hotel Monasterio, Popayán.** The spacious rooms in this 18th-century Franciscan monastery surround an attractive courtyard and have large balconies overlooking the lush grounds. $$

Ecuador

★ **Hostería Cusín, Imbabura Province.** Built in the 17th century, this quiet hacienda is furnished with antiques and surrounded by gardens; it also serves as the perfect base for horseback excursions. $$$

★ **Luna Runtún, Baños.** Set on the slopes of the Tungurahua Volcano, this colonial-style hotel features breathtaking views, Continental cuisine, and various outdoor activities. $$$

★ **Apart-Hotel Antinea, Quito.** A friendly, family-run inn on a shady side street in Quito's Mariscal district, Antinea has a small selection of comfortable hotel rooms and spacious apartments, which open onto patios and gardens. $–$$

★ **Posada del Sol, Cuenca.** Occupying a 19th-century building in the heart of town, this inexpensive place has carpeted rooms and a small, covered courtyard where a complimentary Continental breakfast is served. ¢

Paraguay

★ **Sabe Center Hotel, Asunción.** Asunción's newest and most lavish hotel is considerably nicer than the city's alternatives. $$$

★ **Centu Cué, Villa Florida.** This isolated lodge has bungalows and a restaurant on the banks of the Tebicuary, one of South America's most beautiful rivers. $$

Peru

★ **Machu Picchu Pueblo Hotel, Aguas Calientes.** In this semitropical paradise, the stone bungalows have cathedral ceilings, exposed beams, flagstone floors, and cartwheel headboards, creating an atmosphere of rustic elegance. $$$–$$$$

★ **Explornapo Camp, Iquitos.** This rustic lodge deep in the Amazon rain forest offers access to a canopy walkway 34 m (110 ft) above ground in the jungle rafters. $$

★ **Hotel Mossone, Huacachina.** Set in a century-old mansion, the Mossone has an interior garden patio and dining on a veranda that overlooks the Huacachina lagoon. $$

★ **Posada del Inca, Sacred Valley of the Incas.** The colonial-style guest rooms at this 300-year-old former convent have balconies that overlook the gardens or the terraced hillsides. $$

★ **La Casa de Melgar, Arequipa.** This family-owned, colonial hostel has double rooms and suites with the original *sillar* ceilings and old cookstoves. Staying here is like traveling back in time. $

Uruguay

★ **La Posta del Cangrejo, La Barra de Maldonado.** Mediterranean styling and an informal approach to luxury complement the impeccably decorated guest rooms here; the staff is warm, accommodating, and proud of their hotel. $$$$

★ **Hostería del Lago, Montevideo.** This white-stucco, Spanish-colonial hotel has a relaxed atmosphere, a lakefront beach, and a multilingual staff. $$$–$$$$

Venezuela

★ **Cumanagoto Hesperia, Cumaná.** Exquisite attention to detail and style set this beachside resort above even the most luxurious hotels in Venezuela. $$$$

★ **Estancia San Francisco, El Valle.** This deluxe mountain retreat pampers you with rustic, yet elegant, suites and a restaurant with superb food. $$$$

★ **Hotel Avila, Caracas.** Surrounded by gardens and bedecked with flowers and vines, this hotel is a haven from the urban hurly-burly. $$$$

★ **Hotel Belensate, Mérida.** Spacious rooms, lush gardens, and a gorgeous swimming pool make you feel truly pampered here. $$$

★ **Miragua Village, Playa El Agua.** At this Margarita Island hotel, thatched roofs, white-washed walls, and bamboo furnishings lend an appropriately Caribbean air. $$

Markets and Crafts

Argentina

⭐ **Plaza Dorrego, Buenos Aires.** On Sunday, the plaza comes alive with the bustling San Telmo Antiques Fair, a magnet for both Porteño and tourist.

Bolivia

⭐ **Calle Sagárnaga, La Paz.** A thousand voices clamor for everything from llama fetuses to coca leaves to colorful alpaca sweaters on this famous old street.

⭐ **Sunday market, Tarabuco.** This colorful handicrafts and produce market in a small town near Sucre is a fascinating insight into the local culture.

Brazil

⭐ **Mercado Modelo, Salvador.** Local foodstuffs, lace, fossils, gemstones, African-print clothing, and regional musical instruments are peddled at this daily crafts market.

⭐ **Ver-o-Peso, Belém.** This daily market is stocked with everything from Amazon fish to good-luck charms and medicinal roots and herbs.

Chile

⭐ **Los Graneros del Alba, Santiago.** Hats, sweaters, lamps, antiques, and wicker items are sold daily at this market beside the Iglesia los Domínicos.

Colombia

⭐ **Las Bovedas, Cartagena.** A series of large arched vaults in the northwest corner of the walled city holds about two dozen crafts shops.

⭐ **Tuesday market, Silvia.** Colombia's biggest indigenous market may not compare to those of Ecuador, Peru, and Bolivia, but it's well worth checking out if you're in Cali or Popayán.

Ecuador

⭐ **Saturday market, Otavalo.** Ecuador's biggest tourist market is held alongside the traditional weekly market of this highland town, so you can shop for sweaters, jewelry, bags, and rugs, or simply watch the bartering over vegetables and ponchos.

Paraguay

⭐ **Ao P'oí Raity, Asunción.** Excellent ñandutí lacework and *ao p'oí* embroidery are sold here.

⭐ **Constancio Sanabria, Luque.** Paraguayan harps and guitars are made and sold in this workshop just outside Asunción.

Peru

⭐ **Sunday market, Pisac.** In the Cuzco area, this is the place for Andean demon masks and weavings.

⭐ **Town market, Chiclayo.** Everything you could want or need for your favorite *bruja* (witch) and *curandero* (magical healer) is on hand at this market on the North Coast.

Uruguay

⭐ **Feria Tristán Narvaja, Montevideo.** The premier Sunday attraction, this market sprawls along Calle Tristán Narvaja and spills onto cross streets.

Venezuela

⭐ **Mercado Principal, Mérida.** You can buy flowers, food, clothing, souvenirs—you name it—sold in the more than 400 stalls of this market.

Museums and Masterpieces

Argentina

⭐ **Museo Histórico Nacional, Buenos Aires.** The official history of Argentina is on display in a stately, if decaying, old mansion; exhibits cover the country's past from the 16th century to the beginning of this century.

⭐ **Museo Nacional de Bellas Artes, Buenos Aires.** Argentina's only major art museum is housed in a building that was once the capital's waterworks. The collection includes several major Impressionist paintings and an overview of 19th- and 20th-century Argentine art.

Bolivia

⭐ **Casa de Moneda, Potosí.** This massive, block-long mint was once used to forge coins from silver mined in nearby Cerro Rico.

⭐ **Museo Archeologico, Cochabamba.** The museum houses one of the most comprehensive displays of pre-Columbian pottery, silver and gold work, and textiles outside of La Paz.

⭐ **Museo National del Arte, La Paz.** Set in a baroque, 18th-century mansion, the country's premier museum displays a wide range of Bolivian and international art.

Brazil

⭐ **Museu de Arte Naif do Brasil, Rio de Janeiro.** Works by the best naive artists from Brazil and around the world fill the walls of a beautiful colonial mansion.

⭐ **Museu de Arte de São Paulo.** Dazzling works by the likes of Vincent Van Gogh, Pierre-Auguste Renoir, and Edgar Degas are housed in this striking building.

⭐ **Museu Emílio Goeldi, Belém.** In a research facility founded by a naturalist and a group of intellectuals in 1866 you'll find an extensive collection of Indian artifacts; the grounds contain many examples of Amazon plant and animal life.

Chile

⭐ **The *maoi*, Easter Island.** Massive, stone-carved figures, some more than 60 ft tall, the *maoi* represent the island's Polynesian pantheon of ancestral deities.

⭐ **Museo Precolumbino, Santiago.** Enjoy an extraordinary collection of artifacts and artwork of Central and South America's indigenous peoples, housed in a beautifully restored colonial building.

⭐ **Museo Regional de Magallanes, Punta Arenas.** Carrara marble hearths, English bath fixtures, and cordovan leather walls complete the furnishings of this mansion, which dates from the city's pre–Panama Canal age of splendor.

⭐ **La Sebastiana, Valparaíso.** Washed in sky-blue and pink "so that the walls might begin to dance," the three floors of Pablo Neruda's third house are crammed with odds and ends from the poet's past.

Colombia

⭐ **Museo de Arte Religioso, Bogotá.** The gem-encrusted Tulua and Lechuga processional crosses are the highlights in this extensive collection of religious art.

⭐ **Museo de Oro, Bogotá.** This modern building houses the world's largest collection of pre-Columbian gold artifacts.

⭐ **Palacio de la Inquisición, Cartagena.** This former headquarters of the Spanish Inquisition for much of South America displays the implements of torture used by those protectors of the faith.

Ecuador

⭐ **Museo Arqueológico Weilbauer, Quito.** Located in a colonial building in Quito's new city, this museum has an impressive collection of pre-Columbian ceramics and other artifacts.

⭐ **Museo del Banco Central, Quito.** Several floors of exhibits in the modern Casa de la Cultura range from pre-Columbian artifacts to colonial religious art.

Paraguay

⭐ **Museo de San Ignacio, San Ignacio.** Paraguay's first Jesuit mission is now a museum of wood carvings; look for the figure of St. Paul with Garaní faces at his feet.

Peru

⭐ **Museo Brúning, Lambayeque.** The Bruning displays ancient, pre-Incan artifacts from the Chiclayo area, including the fascinating remains from the tomb of the Lord of Sipán.

⭐ **Museo de Oro, Lima.** The gold museum, considered one of the finest in South America, displays a massive collection of ancient gold artifacts discovered in Peru.

⭐ **Museo Nacional de Antropología y Arqueología, Lima.** This museum's collection of anthropological artifacts from throughout Peru includes Chavín obelisks and Paracas weavings.

⭐ **Museo Rafael Larco Herrera, Lima.** The museum houses an impressive collection of pre-Columbian ceramics, including a large collection of erotic sculptures.

⭐ **Museo Regional, Ica.** A visit to this museum provides an excellent overview of the area's ancient cultures, with fine displays of Paracas weavings and Nazca ceramic sculptures.

Uruguay

⭐ **Museo del Gaucho y la Moneda, Montevideo.** Set in a lavish 19th-century mansion, this museum contains displays on coins and on gaucho life.

Venezuela

⭐ **Museo Sacro de Caracas.** Beautiful religious statues and costumes are displayed in this colonial sacristy and ecclesiastical prison.

Natural Wonders and Outdoor Adventures

Argentina

⭐ **Cataratas del Iguazú.** At a bend in a river, on the border with Brazil and Paraguay, Iguazú Falls extend for almost 3 km (1½ mi) and are made up of some 275 (more in the rainy season) cascades that plunge more than 200 ft.

Parque Nacional los Glaciares. Extending along the Chilean border for 350 km (217 mi), the park is 40% covered with ice fields branching off into 47 major glaciers that feed two lakes.

Parque Nacional Tierra del Fuego. The spirit of the farthest corner of the world takes hold in this park when the light at sundown casts the landscape—backed by snowcapped mountains and fronted by still channel waters—in a subdued, sensual tone.

Bolivia

⭐ **Cerro Rico, Potosí.** Descend into the dank, sweaty bowels of this silver mine, to experience a little of the harsh conditions of one of the ancient professions, mining.

⭐ **Madidi National Park.** This park is home to more than 1,000 species of birds, monkeys, and other wildlife. The only way to reach it is on a five-hour trip by motorized dugout canoe along the Rio Tuichi River.

⭐ **Salar de Uyuni.** Visit the world's biggest and highest desert of salt near Potosí, where you'll find red and green mineral-tinted lagoons and an island with towering cacti.

Brazil

⭐ **The Amazon.** Sleep in a hammock under the stars aboard a double-decker commercial boat on the river.

Chile

⭐ **Horseback Riding, Maipo Canyon.** Journey on horseback into the canyon from San Alfonso.

⭐ **Trekking, Huerquehue National Park.** Hike through Araucaria Pines with Villarrica Volcano as a looming chaperon.

⭐ **White-water rafting, Lake District.** Shoot rapids in the rivers around Pucón.

Colombia

⭐ **Parque Nacional Tayrona.** Stretching from the Caribbean coast all the way up to the snowcapped mountains, this vast park east of Santa Marta protects palm-fringed beaches, coral reefs, tropical forests, and pre-Columbian ruins.

⭐ **Puracé National Park.** Nature lovers and hikers will want to visit this highland park southeast of Cali, with its volcanoes, waterfalls, hot springs, and exotic wildlife.

⭐ **Snorkeling and Diving, the Caribbean.** Whether you're a certified diver or a die-hard snorkeler, be sure to explore the marine wonders around the archipelago of the Islas del Rosario, near Cartagena, and around the islands of San Andrés and Providencia.

Ecuador

⭐ **Galápagos Islands.** One of the planet's great natural wonders, the islands not only provide close contact with an array of marine and island-bound wildlife, they also provide a unique perspective on Darwin's theory of evolution.

⭐ **Horseback Excursions, the Highlands.** One-day or overnight horseback excursions are available throughout the Ecuadoran highlands, offering an unforgettable way to experience the country's spectacular Andean scenery.

⭐ **Machalilla National Park.** This 136,850-acre park northwest of Guayaquil protects patches of endangered tropical dry forests, stretches of spectacular coastline, and the offshore island of Isla de la Plata, a 3,000-acre seabird sanctuary where whales are often sighted from July through October.

Paraguay

⭐ **Tebicuary River.** Fish for the salmonlike dorado from a launch on the river, whose banks are home to monkeys, capybaras, and the occasional alligator.

Peru

⭐ **Inca Trail.** Hike where the Incas once did on the 50 km (31 mi) of rugged mountain trail leading to the ruins of Machu Picchu, and camp at the entrance.

Venezuela

★ **Angel Falls and Canaima National Park.** Here tepuis rise above a high grassland filled with bizarre plants and punctuated by black rivers and powerful yellow waterfalls, including the mighty Angel Falls themselves.

★ **Los Llanos.** See spectacular gatherings of wildlife during the dry season (December to May) when capybaras, egrets, spoonbills, scarlet ibis, and caimans crowd shrinking pools of water, and anteaters, foxes, and deer range across this open savanna.

★ **Los Roques.** This archipelago and national park offers some of the most incredible snorkeling, diving, and bone-fishing in the Caribbean.

Spiritual Sights

Argentina

★ **Cementario de La Recoleta, Buenos Aires.** The beautiful mausoleums of the country's most famous people, including Evita herself, are in this cemetery.

Bolivia

★ **Jesuit Missions of the Chiquitania.** These restored baroque churches are in the jungle near Santa Cruz.

★ **Iglesia de San Francisco, La Paz.** The facade of this 16th-century church is elaborately adorned, making it one of the continent's finest examples of Spanish colonial architecture.

Brazil

★ **Igreja Bom Jesus do Matosinho, Congonhas do Campo, Minas Gerais.** Aleijadinho's life-size soapstone sculptures of the Old Testament prophets are incredibly moving.

★ **Igreja de São Francisco, Salvador.** The ornately carved interior of this 18th-century baroque masterpiece is completely awash with shimmering gold leaf.

Chile

★ **Cementerio General, Santiago.** Resting spot of Salvador Allende, Santiago's General Cemetery provides insight into traditional Chilean society.

★ **Cementerio Punta Arenas.** Pay homage to the remains of Tierra del Fuego's last Selk'nam native.

Colombia

★ **Cerro de la Popa, Cartagena.** This colonial monastery on a hill southeast of the walled city affords the best view in Cartagena and has a small museum and a chapel.

★ **Iglesia Museo Santa Clara, Bogotá.** The interior of this 17th-century church features dazzling frescoes and wall reliefs—the work of nuns who were once cloistered there.

★ **Iglesia San Francisco, Popayán.** The bright interior of this colonial city's most important church is filled with gilded wooden altars.

Ecuador

★ **Catedral de la Inmaculada, Cuenca.** The city's large, new redbrick cathedral has marble pillars, a gilded altar, and lovely stained-glass windows.

★ **La Compañía de Jesús, Quito.** The sculpted stone facade of this church is impressive, but its gilded interior is even more so.

★ **La Iglesia de San Francisco, Quito.** Established by Franciscan monks in 1536, this church has an extraordinary interior of intricately sculpted, gilded, and painted wood.

Peru

★ **Catedral, Cuzco.** This baroque cathedral, located where there once was an ancient Inca palace, is considered one of the most splendid churches in the Americas.

★ **Coricancha, Cuzco.** When a 1953 earthquake crumbled the interior walls of the convent of Santo Domingo, the interior walls of the ancient Inca Temple of the Sun were revealed underneath.

★ **Convento de Santa Catalina, Arequipa.** In the late 1500s, 400 Dominican nuns and their servants walled themselves off from the rest of the city in this complex, a maze of streets and structures where 20 nuns still reside.

Venezuela

★ **Iglesia de San Francisco, Caracas.** Gilded altarpieces make this a lovely example of colonial architecture.

2 ADVENTURE AND LEARNING VACATIONS

There's a new demand for soft—and not so soft—adventure travel, and South America offers it all. Explore the Amazon by riverboat or from a jungle lodge; trek, ski, or climb the Andes; raft some of the world's most challenging rivers or kayak over peaceful lakes; fish for peacock bass or saber-toothed payara; or join a research project in a national park or indigenous village.

Updated by
Joyce Dalton

SOUTH AMERICA PRESENTS A HOST OF VACATION possibilities beyond the usual tourist agenda of hotels and museums. Tour operators are responding to the ever-increasing interest in sports-centered and off-the-beaten-path travel. The number of adventure-oriented operators and variety of programs are also significantly growing. Although more remote regions still require roughing it, others—such as the Amazon—offer a wide range of comfort levels, making it all the more important to choose your trip carefully. Despite the potential delays, inconveniences, and risks of venturing into South America's hinterlands, the safety record of established tour operators is excellent. For the fit and adventurous, who pack a sense of wonder and curiosity along with the bug spray, special-interest vacations lead to experiences and memories that are, in a word, special.

For additional information about a specific destination, contact the country's tourist office (which is often attached to the embassy) or the **South American Explorers Club** (⌂ 126 Indian Creek Rd., Ithaca, NY 14850, ☎ 607/277–0488 or 800/274–0568, ℻ 607/277–6122, www.samexplo.org). The Explorers Club also has offices in Quito, Ecuador, and in Lima, Peru.

Choosing Your Vacation

With hundreds of tour operators selling adventure and special-interest vacations to South America, there are several factors to keep in mind when deciding which company and package will best meet your traveling needs.

How strenuous a vacation do you want? Adventure vacations commonly are split into "soft" and "hard" adventures. A hard adventure is physically challenging. While most trips do not demand technical skills or athletic ability, some require pre-trip training and a doctor's approval. A soft adventure emphasizes the destination itself, rather than the means of travel. A day's activity might include easy rafting or trekking, but you usually can count on a hot shower and warm bed at night. A little honesty goes a long way—make sure you know your own comfort needs and level of physical fitness before signing on to climb a glacier or navigate wild rapids.

Where is the tour company based and how comprehensive is its operation? Some operators have both an office in the United States and a base in South America; others contract with a local firm to provide services on-site. The former can result in lower costs since you aren't paying for an intermediary's markup. Due to their greater buying power, larger companies sometimes can offer better prices and more frequent departures. Many factors affect price and the roughest trip could well be the most expensive.

How untrodden do you want your itinerary? Although most of the trips detailed below sound exotic, many companies utilize the same riverboats and lodges (usually the most comfortable ones), so you won't exactly be living like Indiana Jones. Other operators take small groups into less-touristed regions where the wildlife and the locals are less accustomed to the clicking of cameras. Such trips typically involve camping or more spartan facilities.

For more helpful hints on selecting a travel company, *see* Tour Operators *in* Smart Travel Tips.

Tour Operators

Below are the addresses of the adventure and special-interest tour operators mentioned in this chapter. They were chosen on the basis of their reputation for quality and the originality of their itineraries. Operators of adventure tours are usually the first to introduce travelers to great new destinations, forging ahead before luxury hotels and air-conditioned coaches tempt less hardy visitors. Suriname and Guyana are spots yet to be discovered by all but the most intrepid travelers. Although their emerging tourist infrastructures don't yet merit coverage in this book's main chapters, both countries offer the adventurous traveler natural beauty, historical sites, and cultures who welcome visitors.

Abercrombie & Kent: ✉ 1520 Kensington Rd., Suite 212, Oak Brook, IL 60523, ☎ 630/954–2944 or 800/323–7308, ℻ 630/954–3324, www.abercrombiekent.com.

Above the Clouds Trekking: ✉ Box 398, Worcester, MA 01602, ☎ 508/799–4499 or 800/233–4499, ℻ 508/797–4779, www.gorp.com/abv-clds.htm.

Adventure Associates: ✉ 13150 Coit Rd., Suite 110, Dallas, TX 75240, ☎ 972/907–0414 or 800/527–2500, ℻ 972/783–1286, www.ecuadorable.com.

Adventure Center: ✉ 1311 63rd St., Suite 200, Emeryville, CA 94608, ☎ 510/654–1879 or 800/227–8747, ℻ 510/654–4200, www.adventure-center.com.

Adventures on Skis: ✉ 815 North Rd., Westfield, MA 01085, ☎ 413/568–2855 or 800/628–9655, ℻ 413/562–3621, www.advonskis.com.

Amazon Tours and Cruises: ✉ 8700 W. Flagler St., Suite 190, Miami, FL 33174, ☎ 305/227–2266 or 800/423–2791, ℻ 305/227–1880, Amazoncruz@aol.com.

American Alpine Institute: ✉ 1515 12th St., Bellingham, WA 98225, ☎ 360/671–1505, ℻ 360/734–8890, www.aai.cc.

American Wilderness Experience: ✉ Box 1486, Boulder, CO 80306, ☎ 303/444–2622 or 800/444–0099, ℻ 303/444–3999, www.awetrips.com.

Amizade, Ltd.: ✉ 7612 N. Rogers Ave., Chicago, IL 60626, ☎ 773/973–3719, ℻ 773/973–3731, www.amizade.org.

Backroads: ✉ 801 Cedar St., Berkeley, CA 94710, ☎ 510/527–1555 or 800/462–2848, ℻ 510/527–1444, www.backroads.com.

Brazil Nuts: ✉ 1854 Trade Center Way, Suite 101B, Naples, FL 34109, ☎ 941/593–0266 or 800/553–9959, ℻ 941/593–0267, www.com.brazilnuts.com.

Clipper Cruise Line: ✉ 7711 Bonhomme Ave., St. Louis, MO, 63105, ☎ 314/727–2929 or 800/325–0010, ℻ 314/727–6576, www.clippercruise.com.

Close-Up Expeditions: ✉ 858 56th St., Oakland, CA 94608, ☎ 510/654–1548 or 800/457–9553, ℻ 510/654–3043, qcuephotog@aol.com.

Country Walkers: ✉ Box 180, Waterbury, VT 05676-0180, ☎ 802/244–1387 or 800/464–9255, ℻ 802/244–5661, www.countrywalkers.com.

Dragoman, Encounter, Explore: These London-based companies are represented in the United States by Adventure Center (☞ *above*).

Earthquest Adventure Travel: ✉ 1335 N. Northlake Way, Suite 101, Seattle, WA 98103, ☎ 206/675–9585 or 800/542–7111, ℻ 206/545–8339, www.earthquestadventure.com.

Earth River Expeditions: ✉ 180 Towpath Rd., Accord, NY 12404, ☎ 914/626–2665 or 800/643–2784, ℻ 914/626–4423, www.earthriver.com.

Earthwatch: ✉ Box 9104, 680 Mount Auburn St., Watertown, MA 02471, ☎ 617/926–8200 or 800/776–0188, FAX 617/926–8532, www.earthwatch.org.

Ecosummer Expeditions: ✉ 5640 Hollybridge Way, Unit 130, Richmond, BC V7C 4N3 Canada, ☎ 604/214–7484 or 800/465–8884, FAX 604/214–7485, www.ecosummer.com.

Equitours : ✉ Box 807, Dubois, WY 82513, ☎ 307/455–3363 or 800/545–0019, FAX 307/455–2354, www.ridingtours.com.

Exodus, Travelbag Adventures: These companies, based in Great Britain, are represented in North America by G.A.P. Adventures (☞ *below*).

Explorers Travel Group: ✉ 1 Main St., Suite 304, Eatontown, NJ 07724, ☎ 732/542–9006 or 800/631–5650, FAX 732/542–9420, explorers@monmouth.co.

Far Horizons: ✉ Box 91900, Albuquerque, NM 87199, ☎ 505/343–9400 or 800/552–4575, FAX 505/343–8076, www.farhorizon.com.

Field Guides, Inc.: ✉ Box 160723, Austin, TX 78716, ☎ 512/327–4953 or 800/728–4953, FAX 512/327–9231, www.fieldguides.com.

Fishing International: ✉ Box 2132, Santa Rosa, CA 95405, ☎ 707/542–4242 or 800/950–4242, FAX 707/526–3474, www.fishinginternational.com.

Focus Tours: ✉ 403 Moya Rd., Santa Fe, NM 87505, ☎ 505/466–4688, FAX 505/466–4689, www.FocusTours.com.

4th Dimension Tours: ✉ 7101 S.W. 99th Ave., Suite 106, Miami, FL 33173, ☎ 305/279–0014 or 800/343–0020, FAX 305/273–9777, www.4thdimension.com.

Frontiers: ✉ Box 959, 305 Logan Rd., Wexford, PA 15090, ☎ 724/935–1577 or 800/245–1950, FAX 724/935–5388, www.Frontierstrvl.com.

Galápagos Network: ✉ 7200 Corporate Center Dr., Suite 510, Miami, FL 33126, ☎ 305/592–2294 or 800/633–7972, FAX 305/592–6394, www.ecoventura.com.

G.A.P. Adventures: ✉ 266 Dupont St., Toronto, Ontario M5R 1V7 Canada, ☎ 416/922–8899 or 800/465–5600, FAX 416/922–0822, www.gap.ca.

Geo Expeditions: ✉ 67 Linoberg St., Sonora, CA 95370, ☎ 209/532–0152 or 800/351–5041, FAX 209/532–1979, www.geoexpeditions.com.

Geographic Expeditions: ✉ 2627 Lombard St., San Francisco, CA 94123, ☎ 415/922–0448 or 800/777–8183, FAX 415/346–5535, www.geoex.com.

Hanns Ebensten Travel (gay male–oriented): ✉ 513 Fleming St., Key West, FL 33040, ☎ 305/294–8174, FAX 305/292–9665.

Himalayan Travel: ✉ 110 Prospect St., Stamford, CT 06901, ☎ 203/359–3711 or 800/225–2380, FAX 203/359–3669, www.gorp.com/himtravel.htm.

Inca Floats: ✉ 1311 63rd St., Emeryville, CA 94608, ☎ 510/420–1550, FAX 510/420–0947 www.incafloats.com.

International Adventure Travel: ✉ 2 Toronto St., Suite 302, Toronto, Ontario M5C 2B6 Canada, ☎ 416/461–6667 or 888/805–0061, FAX 416/461–0488, www.bikehike.com.

International Expeditions: ✉ One Environs Park, Helena, AL 35080, ☎ 205/428–1700 or 800/633–4734, FAX 205/428–1714, www.ietravel.com.

Joseph Van Os Photo Safaris: ✉ Box 655, Vashon Island, WA 98070, ☎ 206/463–5383, FAX 206/463–5484, www.photosafaris.com.

Journeys International: ✉ 107 April Dr., Suite 3, Ann Arbor, MI 48103, ☎ 313/665–4407 or 800/255–8735, FAX 313/665–2945, www.journeys-intl.com.

Ladatco Tours: ⊠ 2220 Coral Way, Miami, FL 33145, ☎ 305/854–8422 or 800/327–6162, FAX 800/327–6162, www.ladatco.com.

Lindblad Special Expeditions: ⊠ 720 5th Ave., New York, NY 10019, ☎ 212/765–7740 or 800/762–0003, FAX 212/265–3770, www.expeditions.com.

Lost World Adventures: ⊠ 112 Church St., Decatur, GA 30030, ☎ 404/373–5820 or 800/999–0558, FAX 404/377–1902, www.lostworldadventures.com.

Marine Expeditions: ⊠ 890 Yonge St., Toronto, Ontario MW4 3P4 Canada, ☎ 416/964–9069 or 800/263–9147, FAX 416/964–2366, www.marineex.com.

Maxim Tours: ⊠ 50 Cutler St., Morristown, NJ 07960, ☎ 973/984–9068 or 800/655–0222, FAX 973/984–5383, www.maximtours.com.

Mountain Travel-Sobek: ⊠ 6420 Fairmount Ave., El Cerrito, CA 94530, ☎ 510/527–8100 or 800/227–2384, FAX 510/525–7710, www.mtsobek.com.

Myths and Mountains: ⊠ 976 Tee Ct., Incline Village, NV 89451, ☎ 702/832–5454 or 800/670–6984, FAX 702/832–4454, www.mythsandmountains.com.

Natural Habitat Adventures: ⊠ 2945 Center Green Ct., Boulder, CO 80301, ☎ 303/449–3711 or 800/543–8917, FAX 303/449–3712, www.nathab.com.

Nature Expeditions International: ⊠ 6400 E. El Dorado Center, Suite 210, Tucson, AZ 85715, ☎ 520/721–6712 or 800/869–0639, FAX 520/721–6719, www.naturexp.com.

Naturequest: ⊠ 30872 S. Coast Hwy., Suite 185, Laguna Beach, CA 92561, ☎ 949/499–9561 or 800/369–3033, FAX 949/499–0812, www.naturequesttours.com.

Oceanic Society Expeditions: ⊠ Fort Mason Center, Bldg. E, San Francisco, CA 94123, ☎ 415/441–1106 or 800/326–7491, FAX 415/474–3395, www.oceanic-society.org.

Overseas Adventure Travel: ⊠ 625 Mt. Auburn St., Cambridge, MA 02138, ☎ 617/876–0533 or 800/955–1925, FAX 617/876–0455, www.oattravel.com.

Quark Expeditions: ⊠ 980 Post Rd., Darien, CT 06820, ☎ 203/656–0499 or 800/356–5699, FAX 203/655–6623, www.quark-expeditions.com.

Quest Global Angling Adventures: ⊠ 3595 Canton Hwy., Suite C11, Marietta, GA 30066, ☎ 770/971–8586 or 888/891–3474, FAX 770/517–0018, www.fishquest.com.

Rod and Reel Adventures: ⊠ 566 Thomson La., Copperopolis, CA 95228, ☎ 209/785–0444 or 800/356–6982, FAX 209/785–0447, www.rodandreeladv.com.

ROW (Remote Odysseys Worldwide): ⊠ Box 579, Coeur d'Alene, ID 83816, ☎ 208/765–0841 or 800/451–6034, FAX 208/667–6506, www.rowinc.com.

Safaricentre: ⊠ 3201 N. Sepulveda Blvd., Manhattan Beach, CA 90266, ☎ 310/546–4411 or 800/223–6046, FAX 310/546–3188, www.safaricentre.com.

Society Expeditions: ⊠ 2001 Western Ave., Suite 300, Seattle, WA 98121, ☎ 206/728–9400 or 800/548–8669, FAX 206/728–2301, www.societyexpeditions.com.

South American Expeditions: ⊠ 9921 Cabanas Ave., Tujunga, CA 91042, ☎ FAX 818/352–8289 or 800/884–7474, www.sangama.com.

Southwind Adventures: ⊠ Box 621057, Littleton, CO 80162, ☎ 303/972–0701 or 800/377–9463, FAX 303/972–0708, www.southwindadventures.com.

Swallows and Amazons: ⊠ Box 771, Eastham, MA 02642, ☎ 508/255–1886, FAX 508/240–0345, www.overlookinn.com/swallows.html.

Tara Tours: ✉ 6595 N.W. 36th St., Suite 306, Miami Springs, FL 33166, ☎ 305/871–1246 or 800/327–0080, ℻ 305/871–0417, www.taratours.com.

Tours International: ✉ 12750 Briar Forest Dr., Suite 603, Houston, TX 77077, ☎ 281/293–0809 or 800/247–7965, ℻ 281/589–0870, www.toursinternational.com.

Travcoa: ✉ 2350 S.E. Bristol St., Newport Beach, CA 92660, ☎ 949/476–2800 or 800/992–2003, 800/992–2004 in California, ℻ 949/476–2538, www.travcoa.com.

Tropical Adventures : ✉ Box 4337, Seattle, WA 98104, ☎ 206/441–3483 or 888/250–1799, ℻ 206/441–5431, www.divetropical.com.

Tucan: This Australia-based company is represented in the United States by Himalayan Travel (☞ *above*).

Tumbaco-Quasar Náutica: ✉ 7855 N.W. 12th St., Suite 221, Miami, FL 33126, ☎ 305/599–9008 or 800/247–2925, ℻ 305/592–7060, www.quasarnauticatumbaco.com.

University Research Expeditions Program: ✉ University of California, 1 Shields Ave., Davis, CA 95616, ☎ 530/752–0692, ℻ 530/752–0681, www.mipberkeley.edu/urep.

Victor Emanuel Nature Tours: ✉ Box 33008, Austin, TX 78764, ☎ 512/328–5221 or 800/328–8368, ℻ 512/328–2919, www.ventbird.com.

Wilderness Travel: ✉ 1102 9th St., Berkeley, CA 94710, ☎ 510/558–2488 or 800/368–2794, ℻ 510/558–2489, www.wildernesstravel.com.

Wildland Adventures: ✉ 3516 N.E. 155th St., Seattle, WA 98155, ☎ 206/365–0686 or 800/345–4453, ℻ 206/363–6615, www.wildland.com.

Zegrahm & Eco Expeditions: ✉ 1414 Dexter Ave. N, No. 327, Seattle, WA 98109, ☎ 206/285–4000 or 800/628–8747, ℻ 206/285–5037, www.zeco.com.

CRUISES

Antarctica Cruises

Season: November–February.

Location: Most cruises depart from Ushuaia in Tierra del Fuego, Argentina.

Cost: From $3,495 for 13 days from New York or Miami.

Tour Operators: Abercrombie & Kent; Clipper Cruise Line; Geographic Expeditions; International Expeditions; Lindblad Special Expeditions; Marine Expeditions; Mountain Travel-Sobek; Quark Expeditions; Society Expeditions; Zegrahm & Eco Expeditions.

From Ushuaia, the world's southernmost town, you'll sail for two days through Drake Passage to reach the Great White Continent. Accompanied by naturalists and Antarctic experts, you'll travel ashore in small crafts called zodiacs to view thousands of penguins, nesting seabirds, and spectacular landscapes. Some cruises visit research stations on the Antarctic Peninsula, and many combine Antarctica with the Falkland, South Orkney, and South Georgia islands. Expedition vessels range from luxury ships with ice-hardened hulls to Russian polar-research ships that have been refitted for cruise passengers. Two world-class icebreakers are among the vessels used by Quark Expeditions. They can travel to more remote reaches and carry helicopters for aerial viewing.

The International Association of Antarctica Tour Operators (IAATO; ☎ 212/460–8715, www.iaato.org) was founded in 1991 to promote and practice safe and environmentally responsible travel to Antarctica. IAATO is a good source of information, including suggested readings.

Ocean Cruises

Season: December–March.

Locations: The most common cruise itineraries to South America, sometimes known as "Caribazon" sailings, combine Caribbean ports of call with a navigation of the Amazon River. The grandest of all is a circumnavigation of South America, which takes in most of the major ports in about 50 days. You can sign on for the whole cruise or sail on single or multiple segments. Popular ports are Caracas, Belém, Fortaleza, Salvador, Rio de Janeiro, Montevideo, Tierra del Fuego, and Puerto Montt. Many expedition ships headed for Antarctica (☞ *above*) depart from ports in Chile or Argentina. For cruises of the Galápagos Islands, *see* Natural History *below* and The Galápagos Islands *in* Chapter 8.

Cost: From about $500 to thousands of dollars depending on ship, cabin category, and itinerary.

Tour Operators: For an ocean-and-Amazon cruise, contact **Abercrombie & Kent** (☏ 800/323–7308), **Clipper Cruise Line** (☏ 800/325–0010), **Crystal Cruises** (☏ 800/446–6620), **Radisson Seven Seas Cruises** (☏ 800/477–7500), **Seabourn Cruise Line** (☏ 800/929–9595), or **Silversea Cruises** (☏ 800/722–6655). For a cruise that calls at multiple South American ports, contact **Holland America Line** (☏ 800/426–0327), **Lindblad Special Expeditions** (☏ 800/762–0003), **Orient Lines** (☏ 800/333–7300), **Radisson Seven Seas Cruises** (☏ 800/477–7500), or **Silversea Cruises** (☏ 800/722–6655). You also can sail on a passenger-freighter from **Ivaran Lines** (☏ 800/451–1639). For more information on itineraries and cruise lines that sail in South American waters, see *Fodor's Cruises and Ports of Call.*

Patagonia Coastal and Lake Cruises

Cruising the southern tip of South America encompasses some of the most spectacular scenery the world has to offer. Fjords, glaciers, lagoons, lakes, narrow channels, waterfalls, forested shorelines, fishing villages, penguins, and other wildlife all vie as photo subjects. While many itineraries include a boating excursion of one or two days, the companies listed below offer six or more nights aboard ship.

Argentina and Chile

Season: October–April.

Locations: Beagle Channel; Chiloe Archipelago, Chile; Puerto Montt, Chile; Punta Arenas, Chile; Ushuaia, Argentina.

Cost: From $1,122 for eight days from Punta Arenas.

Tour Operators: 4th Dimension; Ladatco; Safaricentre; Tara Tours.

Cruise the continent's southern tip aboard the *M/V Terra Australis,* a 100-passenger vessel sailing from Punta Arenas. All cabins have private bathrooms, telephones, and individual heating/air-conditioning units. Ladatco offers a 19-day trip that spends eight days in the Falkland Islands following the cruise. In addition to their itineraries in the extreme south, 4th Dimension and Safaricentre feature seven-day cruises that begin and end in Puerto Montt. The vessels *M/V Skorpios I, II,* and *III* carry from 74 to 160 passengers in heated/air-conditioned cabins with private baths.

River Cruises

Spanning 4,200 mi, the Amazon is the largest river in the world. From its source in southern Peru, the river also encompasses parts of

Brazil, Ecuador, Colombia, and Bolivia. The Amazon and its more than 1,000 tributaries nourish the last great wooded wilderness of its kind on earth, a natural laboratory with thousands of species of birds, mammals, and plants. Whatever your style of travel, there's a boat plying the river to suit your needs. Sleep in a hammock on the deck of a thatch-roofed riverboat or in the air-conditioned suite of an upscale operator's private ship.

Bolivia

Season: Year-round.
Locations: Mamoré, Ibaré, and Secure rivers.
Cost: From $475 for five days from Trinidad.
Tour Operator: Safaricentre.

Following a city tour of Trinidad, board the *Reina de Enín* for a four-night cruise. By day, make stops along the route for sightseeing, hiking, horseback riding, fishing, swimming, and water sports.

Brazil

Season: Year-round.
Locations: Belém; Manaus; Río Negro; various Amazon tributaries.
Cost: From $858 for six days from Manaus.
Tour Operators: Abercrombie & Kent; Brazil Nuts; Clipper Cruise Line; Explorers Travel Group; Journeys International; Marine Expeditions; Nature Expeditions International; Tara Tours; Travcoa.

The choices for Amazon cruises in Brazil are vast. Most of the above operators, who cover the territory from Belém to Manaus, have a variety of itineraries that last from 3 to 19 days, with comfort levels that range from hammocks to luxurious wood-paneled cabins. Along the way, visit indigenous villages, explore tributaries by small boats, and learn about the local flora and fauna.

Ecuador

Season: Year-round.
Locations: Aguarico and Cuyabeno rivers.
Cost: From $325 for three days from Lago Agrio.
Tour Operators: Adventure Associates; Earthquest; Safaricentre; Tours International.

From your base aboard the comfortable *Flotel Orellana,* enjoy such highlights as forest walks among gigantic Amazonian trees, bird-watching, visits to Cofan indigenous communities, dugout trips, and night caiman searches. The *Orellana* sleeps 48 people in double and four-berth cabins with private facilities. Multilingual naturalists lead excursions. For the truly adventurous, Earthquest also offers an eight-day dugout canoe exploration of a historical Indian hunting preserve. Camp under thatched-roof shelters or sleep in hammocks.

Peru

Season: March–December.
Locations: Iquitos to Tabatinga; various Amazon tributaries.
Cost: From $599 for five days from Iquitos.
Tour Operators: Abercrombie & Kent; Amazon Tours and Cruises; Ecosummer Expeditions; Explorers Travel Group; 4th Dimension; Hanns Ebensten Travel; International Expeditions; Journeys International; Nature Expeditions International; Tara Tours.

Peru vies with Brazil as a destination for Amazon cruises. A typical itinerary begins in Iquitos and travels to *Tres Fronteras,* where Peru, Brazil, and Colombia meet. Along the way, there's time for jungle hikes and visits to river towns and indigenous communities. Most boats carry from 16 to 42 passengers. Ecosummer cruises the Madre de Dios

River, while Amazon Tours and Cruises' camping trip along the Napo and Tacha Curaray rivers includes travel by boat and floatplane.

LEARNING VACATIONS

Cultural Tours

For some travelers, a quick look at many sights is the goal, while others prefer to immerse themselves in a country's culture. This could mean a serious focus on the archaeological remains of great civilizations, the present-day lives and customs of indigenous groups, or the legacy of cultural expression found in local art and crafts.

Argentina
Season: Year-round.
Location: Buenos Aires.
Cost: $680 for five days from Buenos Aires.
Tour Operator: Maxim Tours.

Learn the tango, the dance that Buenos Aires made famous. Join a workshop, led by a professional dancer, where most other students will be locals. Discover the distinction between traditional and modern tango. Price includes one private and three group lessons, an evening at a tango ballroom, accommodation, transfers, and a city tour.

Bolivia
Season: June–October.
Locations: Lake Titicaca; Potosí; Samaipata; Tiahuanaco.
Cost: From $1,550 for 10 days from La Paz.
Tour Operator: Far Horizons; Myths and Mountains.

Visit artisans in their homes and workshops on a Myths and Mountains trip timed to coincide with the famed San Bartolome festival in Potosí. Other programs offered by this company explore the remains of the Tiahuanaco civilization, which arose 2,700 years before the Incas, and study the secrets of Kallawaya medicine men. Far Horizons' 14-day journey spends three days as guests of the Tiahuanaco Archaeological Project, living in an Aymara household, before moving on to a number of other archaeological sites around the country.

Brazil
Season: Year-round.
Location: Amazon.
Cost: From $2,050 for 11 days from Manaus.
Tour Operator: Swallows and Amazons.

Although Brazil prohibits visits to Indian reservations, travelers with an interest in indigenous cultures can learn about the Yanomamo people on 11- or 15-day itineraries. Using small boats, travel along the Río Negro and the Cauburis, visiting small Yanomamo communities that are not part of a reservation and spending several days with the people of one village.

Chile and Easter Island
Season: Year-round.
Locations: Atacama Desert; Chiloe; Easter Island.
Cost: From $1,560 for five days from Santiago.
Tour Operators: Far Horizons; 4th Dimension; Hanns Ebensten Travel; Ladatco; Maxim Tours; Myths and Mountains; Nature Expeditions International; Tara Tours; Tours International.

Despite its remote location in the Pacific Ocean 3,680 km (2,300 mi) west of Chile, windswept Easter Island continues to draw hundreds of visitors each year to its unique open-air archaeological museum. Nearly 1,000 stone statues, or *moai*, stand gazing with brooding eyes over the island's gently rolling hills. The operators listed above spend from four to nine days on this intriguing island. For other cultural journeys, you can explore Chile's long wine-making history with Myths and Mountains, or discover the northern Atacama Desert, home to archaeological sites and numerous ancient petroglyphs, with Far Horizons and Ladatco.

Colombia

Season: Year-round.
Locations: Bogotá; San Agustín; Villa de Leyva.
Cost: From $1,100 for 14 days from Bogotá.
Tour Operators: Explorers Travel Group; Safaricentre; Tours International.

Although little is known of the people who once inhabited San Agustín, its huge stone statues (500 excavated to date) have fueled speculation. San Agustín is a collection of several dozen sites scattered over a wide area. Most trips combine several days here with visits to Villa de Leyva and Bogotá, including its world-acclaimed Gold Museum.

Ecuador

Season: Year-round.
Locations: Throughout Ecuador.
Cost: From $1,550 for 11 days from Quito.
Tour Operators: Far Horizons; Myths and Mountains; Safaricentre.

With Myths and Mountains, you can hike and sail in parts of the country rarely visited by tourists, learning about local culture along the way. On the company's other itineraries, you can meet artisans and visit their homes and workshops, or join a native of southern Ecuador for a unique journey through the region he knows best. Far Horizons offers a 17-day trip visiting markets, pyramids, and other historical sites, during which you will raft on the Río Napo and spend three nights with a local family. Shamanism is the focus of Safaricentre's program, which visits Colorado, Otavalo, and Shuar indigenous communities.

Peru

Season: Year-round.
Locations: Amazon; Cuzco area; Lake Titicaca; Sipan.
Cost: From $1,698 for eight days from Miami.
Tour Operators: Far Horizons; Geo Expeditions; Myths and Mountains; South American Expeditions; Tours International.

In Sipan archaeologists unearthed a sealed, pre-Inca tomb in 1988 to find treasures of pure gold: ornate headdresses and masks, exquisite jewelry, and intricately sculpted figures. Sipan is featured on tours run by most of the companies listed above. In addition, Far Horizons has an archaeological expedition to study Inca, Moche, and Chimor cultures; Myths and Mountains' programs center on handicrafts or visits to remote Inca sites to learn about ancient ceremonies and rituals. South American Expeditions offers various itineraries focusing on shamanism (Amazon region), yoga (Andes), and artists (Amazon).

Scientific Research Trips

Whether your interests lie in preserving the earth's dwindling resources, improving the lives of people in developing nations, or searching for clues to the past at archaeological sites, joining a research expedition team contributes labor and money to such projects. Participants should be interested in learning, enjoy working as a team, and have the flexibility and sense of humor needed to meet the challenges of a research expedition.

Argentina

Season: July.
Locations: Río Riachuelo.
Cost: $1,395 for 10 days from Corrientes.
Tour Operator: Earthwatch.

Black howler monkeys, whose cries can travel 5 km (3 mi) through the rain forest, are the focus of this Earthwatch, one of the few to study the population and group structure of this species. Fieldwork includes observing the monkeys' social behavior for up to 12 hours straight. Other days, you'll conduct a demographic survey and assist in capturing selected monkeys for weighing and other tests.

Bolivia

Season: July–August.
Locations: Andes; Beni Biosphere Reserve.
Cost: From $1,645 for 15 days from Beni.
Tour Operators: Amizade; Earthwatch.

Earthwatch's team will study a few of Beni's 499 bird species to determine how they use the savanna and how they respond to the increased grazing and burning of their environment. Amizade participants and Bolivian volunteers will renovate a nursing home in Cochabama, as well as create rental units and shops so that the home can generate income to become self-sufficient.

Brazil

Season: January–September.
Locations: Amazon; Desengaño State Park; São Paulo state.
Cost: From $1,595 for 15 days from Cumbica.
Tour Operators: Amizade; Earthwatch.

Join other Amizade volunteers and Brazilian students in constructing a self-sustaining silk-screen workshop where Amazonian street children can learn a viable skill. Earthwatch's two nature projects investigate the vulnerability of fruit-eaters, such as peccaries, to forest fragmentation and study stingless bees' pollination of some 650 orchid species to measure forest fragment health.

Ecuador

Season: December–January, March–August.
Locations: Bilsa Reserve; Cayambe; Colonche Mountains.
Cost: From $1,395 for 14 days from Quito.
Tour Operator: Earthwatch.

Amid the mountain rain-forest of northern Ecuador, study butterfly defense tactics to learn about predator–prey relationships. You'll hike several kilometers a day on steep, muddy trails and live in rustic accommodations. Ecuador claims more than 50% of South America's bird species, and you can participate in surveys to determine their whereabouts in the Loma Alta Ecological Reserve. Or, you can join an archeological dig in the Guayllabamba valley to determine how the Caranqui evolved from a homogenous hunter–gatherer society into a chiefdom with defined social roles.

Peru

Season: May–December.
Locations: Amazon; Arequipa; Chicama Valley; Lake Titicaca; Manu Biosphere Reserve.
Cost: From $1,435 for 14 days from Trujillo.
Tour Operators: Earthwatch; Oceanic Society Expeditions; University Research Expeditions Program.

The Oceanic Society's Peruvian research trip studies the Amazon's *bufeos colorados*, the largest river dolphin. Identify individual dolphins, record their behaviors and vocalizations, and plot locations from a base aboard a 76-ft motor vessel. With UREP, work with archaeologists studying the Moche civilization in the Chicama Valley; field activities involve trowel and brush work, drawing maps, and photographing the site. Another program joins excavations on the shores of Lake Titicaca to determine how ancient societies coexisted. At famed Manu Reserve, Earthwatch observes Andean hummingbirds to learn how these tiny creatures survive change and harsh environments. A second study helps scholars and photographers organize, digitize, print, and catalog thousands of vintage glass negatives, which comprise a valuable collection of Peruvian images in urgent need of conservation.

Suriname
Season: March–July.
Location: Galibi Nature Reserve.
Cost: $1,890 for eight days from Miami.
Tour Operator: Oceanic Society Expeditions.

In cooperation with the Suriname Foundation for Nature Preservation, this trip conducts a sea turtle research and monitoring program at a new research facility. Assist wardens and researchers in monitoring the nesting activities of leatherback, green, and olive ridley turtles and in collecting biological data. In addition, learn about the cultural traditions and crafts of local Amerindian communities that are cooperating with the sea turtle effort.

Uruguay
Season: October, February.
Location: Colonia del Sacramento.
Cost: $1,695 for 13 days from Montevideo.
Tour Operator: Earthwatch.

Team members assist a Uruguayan archaeologist in determining the daily activities and social changes of the country's first settlement along the Río de la Plata. Working alongside Uruguayan volunteers, you wash, label, draw, and catalog artifacts unearthed. Accommodations are in a modern hotel.

Venezuela
Season: January–April.
Location: Hato Piñero.
Cost: $1,595 for 14 days from Caracas.
Tour Operator: Earthwatch.

Join an American anthropologist in learning how wedge-capped capuchin monkeys balance the advantages and drawbacks of group life. The study also evaluates how such factors as age, sex, status, and troop size affect primate foraging. Live at a comfortable ranch science center.

THE OUTDOORS

Amazon Jungle Camping and Lodges

Because the Amazon River provides easy and natural access to the jungle, it is a great starting point for camping and lodge excursions. Transportation is provided by thatch-roof motorboats, riverboats (☞ River Cruises, *above*), and canoes. Accommodations range from camps with sleeping hammocks to comfortable lodges with or without private baths. Such expeditions can be tremendously rewarding for adventurers who want to see the deep rain forest and its inhabitants at close range.

Numerous Amazon itineraries are available, so study several companies' brochures to choose the trip that is best for you.

Bolivia
Season: Year-round.
Location: Madidi National Park.
Cost: From $595 for seven days from La Paz.
Tour Operator: G.A.P. Adventures.

By motorized canoe and on foot, make your way to Chalalan Ecolodge on the shores of Lake Chalalan in the midst of the Bolivian Amazon. From this comfortable base, take day hikes, led by a naturalist, through the tropical rain forest to learn about plant and animal life. Time is allotted for swimming, canoeing, and lazing hours away in a hammock.

Brazil
Season: Year-round.
Location: Ariaú; Cristalino Forest Reserve; Lake Juma; Lake Puraquequara; Manaus, Río Negro.
Cost: From $925 for six days from Manaus.
Tour Operators: Amazon Tours and Cruises; Brazil Nuts; Explorers Travel Group; Naturequest; Safaricentre; Southwind Adventures; Swallows and Amazons.

Most jungle adventures begin with a boat trip up the Río Negro, the main Amazon tributary that flows from Manaus. Some trips are based at Ariaú Jungle Towers, where four-story accommodations, linked by catwalks, stand atop stilts. Other programs combine cruises with jungle lodge stays, while the adventurous can opt for itineraries featuring camping. Trips range from 3 to 15 days. All include jungle walks, usually led by a naturalist.

Colombia
Season: Year-round.
Locations: Amacayacu National Park; Leticia; Río Yavari.
Cost: From $950 for four days from Leticia.
Tour Operators: Amazon Tours and Cruises; Tours International.

Leticia is in the heart of the Amazon, at Colombia's border with Peru and Brazil. From Leticia, set off for Yavari Lodge, located on the river of the same name. Some 2,000 species of fish, 1,500 of birds, including 120 varieties of hummingbirds, and numerous butterflies inhabit this area. The anaconda, world's largest snake, and Victoria Regia, the largest water lily, also are found here.

Ecuador
Season: Year-round.
Locations: Amazon Basin.
Cost: From $790 for four days from Quito.
Tour Operators: Adventure Associates; Ecosummer Expeditions; Galápagos Network; G.A.P. Adventures; International Expeditions; Lost World Adventures; Myths and Mountains; Safaricentre.

Scientists estimate that the Ecuadorean Amazon is home to some 1,450 species of birds and as many as 20,000 varieties of plants. Operators use several comfortable lodges, including Sacha Jungle Lodge, a cluster of cabanas nestled deep in the rain forest; Kapawi, a pioneering example in both ecotourism and benefit-sharing with the region's indigenous Achuar people; La Selva Lodge, overlooking Lago Garzacocha (Heron Lake); Cuyabeno Jungle Lodge, on Lake Cuyabeno; and Iripari Lodge, which is surrounded by towering trees. From any of these bases you will take guided nature walks and visit indigenous communities.

Peru

Season: March–December.

Locations: Amazon Center for Environmental Education and Research; Curaray and Napo rivers; Manu National Park.

Cost: From $1,375 for eight days from Iquitos.

Tour Operators: Amazon Tours and Cruises; Explorers Travel Group; International Expeditions; Nature Expeditions International; Naturequest; Oceanic Society Expeditions; Southwind Adventures; Tours International; Wildland Adventures; Zegrahm & Eco Expeditions.

In Peru's Amazon Basin, Manu National Park is one of the most undisturbed, biologically rich regions on the continent. Several operators package Manu with a stay at Explorama Lodge and at the Amazon Center for Environmental Education and Research (ACEER), where an elevated canopy walkway allows observations from 40 m (120 ft) above the forest floor. Naturequest offers a canoeing, hiking, and camping journey, while Amazon Tours and Cruises features explorations from the company's Amazon Jungle Camp.

Venezuela

Season: Year-round.

Locations: Caura; Coro Coro; Manapiare and Orinoco rivers.

Cost: From $525 for four days from Caracas.

Tour Operators: Lost World Adventures; Safaricentre; Tours International.

With Lost World Adventures, explore the rain forest around the Coro Coro and Manapiare rivers. Learn about the Piaroa Indians' culture as well as the region's natural riches. Safaricentre offers three- and four-day programs along the Orinoco River, where nights are spent in hammocks protected by mosquito nets. With Tours International, camp along the Caura River and explore the area by foot and canoe.

Bird-Watching Tours

When selecting a bird-watching tour, one expert suggests asking the following questions: What are the guide's qualifications? What equipment is used? (In addition to binoculars, this should include a high-powered telescope, a tape recorder with a microphone to record and play back bird calls—a way of attracting birds, and a spotlight for night viewing.) What species might be seen? How is the operator protecting habitats in which he or she operates?

Argentina

Season: October–December.

Locations: Chaco; La Pampa; Patagonia.

Cost: From $3,075 for 14 days from Buenos Aires.

Tour Operators: Field Guides; Focus Tours; Victor Emanuel Nature Tours.

More than 1,000 species of birds inhabit Argentina, and each of the operators listed above offers birding programs covering both the northern and southern regions of this vast country. Depending on the itinerary, expect to see such diverse species as the red-tailed comet, Andean condor, crested gallito, snowy sheathbill, and hooded grebe. Punta Tambo, in the south, is home to a colony of about one million Magellanic penguins.

Bolivia

Season: Year-round.

Locations: Serrantía de Siberia; Noel Kempff Mercado Park; Beni.

Cost: From $3,195 for 16 days from Santa Cruz.

Tour Operators: Field Guides; Focus Tours; Victor Emanuel Nature Tours.

Due to the country's varied geography, Bolivia has some 40% of South America's bird species; in the Beni region, one group recorded 213 species in a single day. Manakins, guans, eagles, macaws, toucans, and hummingbirds are but a hint of the bird life found in Noel Kempff Mercado Park. At elevations reaching 3,000 m (9,900 ft), the cloud forest of Serrantía de Siberia is home to many Andean birds.

Brazil

Season: Year-round.
Locations: Pantanal; Northeast; Southeast; Itatiaia and Chapada National Parks; Amazon Basin.
Cost: From $1,650 for seven days from Manaus.
Tour Operators: Field Guides; Focus Tours; Swallows and Amazons; Victor Emanuel Nature Tours.

Bird habitats range from coastal rain forest and wet pampas to cloud forest and plateau grassland. The northeast boasts some of the least-known species in the New World, while the southeast claims more than 160 endemic species. The Pantanal, a vast area of seasonally flooded grassland, is home to the hyacinth macaw, bare-faced curassow, epaulet oriole, and nacunda nighthawk, among others.

Chile

Season: October–December.
Locations: Atacama Desert; Chiloe Island; Patagonia.
Cost: From $1,159 for five days from Arica.
Tour Operators: Field Guides; Focus Tours; Tours International.

From the Atacama Desert in the north to the glaciers of Patagonia, Chile offers a comfortable infrastructure, scenic vistas, and an impressive variety of bird life, including many endemic species. Visitors might spot the Magellanic plover, moustached turca, Patagonian tyrant, puna teal, and Andean avocet.

Ecuador

Season: Year-round.
Locations: Amazon Basin; Andes; Galápagos Islands; Mindo Cloud Forest.
Cost: From $1,500 for seven days from Quito.
Tour Operators: Adventure Associates; Field Guides; Safaricentre; Victor Emanuel Nature Tours.

Ecuador's bird habitats include steaming Amazonian rain forests, Andean slopes, cloud forests, and the páramo grasses and marshes. Each region is home to its own variety of birds, including sword-billed and giant hummingbirds, quetzals, Andean cock-of-the-rocks, bearded guans, and plate-billed mountain toucans.

Guyana

Season: January.
Locations: Iwokrama Forest Reserve; Pakaraima Mountains; Rupununi Savanna.
Cost: $3,950 for 16 days from Georgetown.
Tour Operator: Field Guides.

English-speaking Guyana is just beginning to develop a tourist infrastructure, which is good news for birders. This tour utilizes four remote but comfortable lodges and a small research center as bases for explorations ranging from the coast to Mount Roraima. Participants could see 20 species of parrots, rare white-winged potoos, bearded tachuris, and various Guianan shield specialties.

Peru
Season: Year-round.
Locations: Bosque Unchog; Manu National Park; Tambopata-Candamo Reserve; Tumbes National Forest.
Cost: From $1,200 for six days from Cuzco.
Tour Operators: Field Guides; Journeys International; Victor Emanuel Nature Tours.

Peruvian birding itineraries range from the Amazon to the Andes and feature such sighting coups as the manu antbird, horned screamer, black-necked red-cotinga, golden-backed mountain tanager, and the lyre-tailed nightjar. Some trips involve camping or stays at clean, simple lodges. At Tambopata, hundreds of macaws, parrots, and parakeets flock to clay licks.

Suriname
Season: November–December.
Locations: Brownsberg Nature Reserve; Río Coppename; Raleigh Falls; Voltzberg Reserve.
Cost: $3,100 for 14 days from Paramaribo.
Tour Operator: Victor Emanuel Nature Tours.

Although Suriname has a good nature reserve system, it remains one of South America's lesser-known destinations. Those willing to accept rustic accommodations in some areas are rewarded with good chances of seeing harpy eagles, spix's guans, arrowhead piculets, and pale-bellied mourners. Suriname boasts the largest display site ever found of the Guianan cock-of-the-rock; more than 50 males have been reported.

Venezuela
Season: January–June.
Locations: The Llanos; Amazonas; Yacambu and Henri Pittier National Parks; Río Caura; Cordillera de la Costa Central.
Cost: From $2,300 for nine days from Caracas.
Tour Operators: Field Guides; Tours International; Victor Emanuel Nature Tours.

Venezuela is a well-known birding destination and itineraries are offered to most parts of this accessible nation. Depending on the program selected, birders might spot the harpy eagle, Orinocan saltator, fiery-capped manakin, velvet-browed brilliant, crested quetzal, or agami heron.

Natural History

Many adventure vacations provide insight into the importance and fragility of South America's ecological treasures. The itineraries mentioned below focus on a specific aspect of the ecosystem or on a region not typically explored by other intrepid travelers. The physical adventure becomes secondary to the learning experience.

Argentina and Chile
Season: October–March.
Locations: Atacama Desert, Chile; Iguazú Falls, Argentina; Patagonia; Tierra del Fuego; Valdés Peninsula, Argentina.
Cost: From $2,075 for nine days from Buenos Aires.
Tour Operators: Focus Tours; Geo Expeditions; Journeys International; Marine Expeditions; Naturequest; Oceanic Society Expeditions; Safaricentre; Southwind Adventures.

Argentina and Chile abound in ecotourism experiences, from the tropical forests around Iguazú Falls to the Atacama Desert, to the Antarctic environment of their southern extremes. Although most itineraries combine the two countries, others offer an in-depth focus on one. Accommodations range from comfortable lodges to rustic camps.

Bolivia

Season: Year-round.
Locations: Uyuni Salt Flats; Tororo National Park.
Cost: From $545 for three days from Potosí.
Tour Operators: Focus Tours; Safaricentre.

Focus Tours offers a small-group trip to remote Tororo National Park, a region termed a "naturalist's treasure." Discover dinosaur tracks and bones, and explore Umajalanta Cave from your base in a minister's home. From a camp base, Safaricentre visits Bolivia's famed salt flats, plus the Red and Green Lagoons, noted for flamingos, geysers, and boiling mud. Both trips involve rough travel.

Brazil

Season: Year-round.
Locations: Pantanal; Atlantic forest reserves.
Cost: From $788 for four days from Rio.
Tour Operators Brazil Nuts; Focus Tours; 4th Dimension; Naturequest; Safaricentre; Southwind Adventures; Tours International.

The Pantanal, the world's largest wetlands, is an ideal place for wildlife observation. Travelers will see colorful tropical birds, caimans, anteaters, howler monkeys, capybaras (the world's largest rodents), and possibly jaguars. Accommodations include lodges and houseboats. Focus Tours also has trips to two Atlantic forest reserves known for orchids, birds, and primates.

Ecuador

Season: Year-round.
Locations: Galápagos Islands.
Cost: From $2,195 for 11 days from Quito.
Tour Operators: Abercrombie & Kent; Galápagos Network; Geo Expeditions; Inca Floats; International Expeditions; Lindblad Special Expeditions; Mountain Travel-Sobek; Natural Habitat Adventures; Travcoa; Wilderness Travel.

The Galápagos Islands comprise a rare showcase of evolution. In fact, two-thirds of the birds and most reptiles on this barren, volcanic archipelago are found nowhere else. To protect the fragile environment, Ecuador limits ship size to 90 passengers, but most vessels are smaller. Many tour companies offer Galápagos cruises; the above operators were chosen for the intensity of their programs and the number of departures.

Guyana

Season: April–October.
Locations: Kaieteur Falls; Nappi Village; Shell Beach.
Cost: $1,195 for 15 days from Georgetown, Guyana.
Tour Operator: G.A.P. Adventures.

Though little known to tourists, Guyana claims some of Earth's best preserved tropical forests. Discover wildlife and indigenous cultures of the rain forest along the Río Pomeroon and at Nappi Village, where Conservation International is encouraging a small ecotourism initiative. Accommodations include several lodges, as well as camping in rustic conditions.

Paraguay

Season: Year-round.
Locations: Chaco; Paraguayan Pantanal.
Cost: From $1,050 for five days from Asunción.
Tour Operators: Ladatco; Safaricentre.

Travelers might opt to combine two short trips (four days in the Chaco and five in the Pantanal) offered by Safaricentre. Both focus on wildlife observation. The Pantanal program involves some camping. Ladatco's 12-day itinerary combines three days of eco-activities at Chaco Lodge with time in Asunción and at Iguazú Falls (Brazilian side).

Peru

Season: March–December.
Locations: Tambopata.
Cost: From $1,495 for seven days from Lima.
Tour Operators: International Expeditions; Southwind Adventures; Wildland Adventures.

The Tambopata-Candamo Reserve covers 3.7 million acres and is primarily known for its Macaw Research Center, where a huge clay lick attracts hundreds of birds. Nature walks led by naturalists also check out such inhabitants as otters, peccaries, ocelots, monkeys, and the occasional jaguar.

Suriname

Season: March.
Locations: Brownsberg Nature Park; Galibi Sea Turtle Reserve; Raleigh Falls Nature Reserve.
Cost: $2,090 for 12 days from Miami.
Tour Operator: Oceanic Society Expeditions.

Suriname's beaches are sites for three endangered species of nesting sea turtles. The Oceanic Society has research facilities here and works with the Suriname Nature Foundation to monitor the turtles. Expedition members will learn about these creatures, which can weigh up to 1,000 pounds, before moving on to tropical forests, home to exotic birds, river otters, and seven species of monkeys.

Venezuela

Season: November–April.
Locations: Amazonas; Andes; Gran Sabana; Llanos.
Cost: From $600 for four days from San Fernando.
Tour Operators: Lost World Adventures; Safaricentre; Southwind Adventures.

Among Lost World Adventures' Venezuela packages is a four-day Llanos exploration. More than 300 species of birds plus numerous mammals and reptiles live here. Southwind Adventures' nature-oriented itinerary visits several distinct regions and includes day hikes and canoe trips, while Safaricentre's 12-day journey travels from the Amazon to the Andes, always with a focus on nature.

Overland Safaris

There is no surer way to immerse yourself in a number of cultures and landscapes than by an overland trip in a special vehicle designed to cross the toughest desert, jungle, and mountain areas. On such an adventure you journey far from the beaten path to explore a South America seldom seen by tourists. Camping is the most common way to spend the night, though lodges, inns, and hotels also are utilized. You'll be expected to help with pitching tents, cooking, and—if necessary—pulling the vehicle out of a ditch. The camaraderie that evolves often sparks long-term friendships. Flexibility and adaptability are key.

Season: Year-round.
Locations: Throughout South America.

Cost: From $47 per day, depending on location, trip length, and mode of transport. International airfare and a "kitty" for such expenses as camp food and park entrance fees are extra.
Tour Operators: Dragoman, Encounter, Explore; Encounter; G.A.P. Adventures; Tucan.

These companies specialize in overland expeditions utilizing trucks, local buses, and occasional trains or boats. Trips range from 16 to 182 days. The longer of these journeys comprise consecutive segments, and travelers combine as many segments as they wish. G.A.P. Adventures' 105-day itinerary, for example, travels through Venezuela, Colombia, Ecuador, Peru, Bolivia, Chile, Argentina, Uruguay, and Brazil. Participants choose from nine segments, or the entire trip.

Photo Safaris

A distinctive feature of photo tours is the amount of time spent at each place visited. Whether the subject is wildlife, a waterfall, or a person in traditional dress, participants learn to focus (both minds and cameras) on the scene before them. The tours listed below are led by professional photographers who offer instruction and hands-on tips.

Brazil
Season: May–September.
Location: Pantanal.
Cost: From $4,595 for 15 days.
Tour Operator: Close-Up Expeditions; Joseph Van Os Photo Safaris.

The Pantanal, Earth's largest freshwater wetland, is considered one of the most photographically evocative places on the continent. From small boats and by vehicles, tour participants photograph jabirus (the world's largest stork), caimans, capybaras, howler monkeys, giant anteaters, numerous birds, and perhaps, the elusive jaguar.

Ecuador
Season: November.
Locations: Galápagos.
Cost: $6,595 for 13 days from Miami.
Tour Operator: Joseph Van Os Photo Safaris.

One of the world's best locations for nature photography, the Galápagos Islands, 600 mi west of mainland Ecuador, are home to tortoises, iguanas, sea lions, fur seals, penguins, and numerous exotic bird species. Each island differs from the others, and this trip visits several not included on less intensive programs. Shooting sessions take place each morning and afternoon, allowing time for snorkeling. A luxurious motor yacht is home to 12 photographers and two leaders.

Venezuela
Season: November.
Locations: Throughout Venezuela.
Cost: $3,850 for 16 days from Caracas.
Tour Operator: Close-Up Expeditions.

From the Andes to the Río Orinoco and the Llanos to the Caribbean coast, this expedition is led by one of Venezuela's foremost nature photographers. Angel Falls, palm-lined beaches, colorful mountain villages, and the 300-plus bird species of the Llanos are among the highlights. Several nights are spent at a jungle lodge and on Margarita Island.

SPORTS

Bicycling

Argentina and Chile

Season: October–March.
Locations: Lake District; Torres del Paine and Huerquehue National Parks, Chile.
Cost: From $3,298 for 11 days of inn-to-inn mountain biking from Puerto Montt.
Tour Operators: Backroads; Southwind Adventures.

Excursions follow a moderately challenging route around the waters and valleys of the Lake District, a region of glacier-clad peaks and volcanic cones. All itineraries visit two or more national parks and feature comfortable to luxurious inns. Programs might include some hiking and rafting.

Ecuador

Season: July–February.
Location: Cotopaxi National Park; Intag Cloud-Forest Reserve; Lake San Pablo; Otavalo Valley.
Cost: From $4,198 for 11 days from Quito.
Tour Operators: Backroads; Southwind Adventures.

These journeys through the rolling hills of northern Ecuador, past volcanoes and glaciers, are rated moderate, though elevations reach 3,353 m (11,000 ft). The region is dotted with small, colonial-style villages and ecological reserves. Southwind Adventures features guided nature hikes at Intag Cloud-Forest Reserve, while Backroads' bike/hike trip includes a five-day cruise in the Galápagos Islands.

Peru

Season: April–October.
Location: Amazon; Andes; Cuzco vicinity.
Cost: From $3,098 for eight days from Cuzco.
Tour Operator: Backroads; Safaricentre; Southwind Adventures.

Cycling through the Sacred Valley of the Incas and beside the Río Urubamba, trip participants explore Quechua hamlets and markets, as well as ancient ruins. Safaricentre's and Backroads' itineraries include several days at Amazon camps or lodges; Southwind Adventures' cyclists spend seven nights in hotels and three camping. Journeys feature moderate to strenuous mountain-bike touring.

Venezuela

Season: Year-round; November–May recommended.
Location: Andes.
Cost: From $660 for four days from Caracas.
Tour Operator: Lost World Adventures; Safaricentre.

Ride through tropical cloud forests, the *páramo* (highlands), and across unpaved passes leading to secluded lakes and villages. Overnight at hotels or inns while support vehicles tote your gear. Expect moderate to strenuous biking at elevations above 1,524 m (5,000 ft).

Fishing

Argentina and Chile

Season: September–May.
Locations: Tierra del Fuego; Patagonia; Río Grande, Argentina.
Cost: From $2,850 for seven days from Coyhaique, Chile.

Tour Operators: Earthquest; Fishing International; Frontiers; Quest Global Angling Adventures; Rod & Reel Adventures.

For anglers, Argentina and Chile are the southern hemisphere's Alaska, offering world-class brown- and rainbow-trout fishing in clear streams. An added bonus is the availability of landlocked salmon and golden dorado. Bilingual fishing guides accompany groups, and accommodations are generally in private lodges.

Brazil
Season: July–March.
Locations: Amazon; Commandatuba Island.
Cost: From $2,300 for five days of fishing from Vitoria.
Tour Operators: Fishing International; Frontiers; Quest Global Angling Adventures; Rod & Reel Adventures.

Some 20 species, including pirapitinga, pirarucú, jancundá, matrincha, and arapá inhabit the Amazon. But it is the legendary peacock bass, described as the "ultimate adversary," that most lures anglers. Mobile safari camps allow fishermen to reach obscure, unpopulated watersheds, or you can opt for an air-conditioned stateroom aboard the *Amazon Queen*. Commandatuba Island has offshore fishing for the likes of blue marlin, sailfish, wahoo, tuna, and barracuda. Accommodations are at a deluxe resort.

Ecuador
Season: October–March.
Locations: Salinas.
Cost: From $1,245 for three days from Guayaquil.
Tour Operator: Fishing International.

For striped, blue, and black marlin, the seas off Salinas, 2½ hours from Guayaquil, are hard to beat. In fact, where weight and numbers are concerned, this could well be the world's best area for striped marlin. Catches average 120 to 150 pounds. Comfortable, oceanfront hotels and boats of various sizes, manned by Ecuadoran crews, are utilized.

Venezuela
Season: Year-round.
Locations: Amazonas; La Guaira Bank; Lake Guri; Los Roques; Río Chico; Ventuari River.
Cost: From $795 for four days from Caracas.
Tour Operators: Fishing International; Lost World Adventures; Quest Global Angling Adventures; Rod &Reel Adventures.

Venezuela has gained an enviable reputation for both saltwater and freshwater fishing. Los Roques archipelago, a short flight from Caracas, offers exciting bonefishing, while Guri Lake and the Amazon region are top places for peacock bass. Río Chico is known for tarpon and snook, and Río Ventuari is home to the fierce payara, described as the up-and-coming sportfish. From La Guaira, on the outskirts of Caracas, enjoy prime offshore fishing for the likes of marlin, sailfish, and swordfish.

Horseback Riding

Season: November–April.
Location: Northern Patagonia.
Cost: $240 per night from San Martin de los Andes.
Tour Operator: Equitours.

Few countries have a greater equestrian tradition than Argentina. Equitours gives riders a taste of the country's gaucho culture at a 15,000-

acre *estancia* (cattle ranch). Ride over vast grasslands and through basalt canyons surrounded by the Andes. Equitours' nine-day program includes several days exploring the beech forests of Lanin National Park and camping at the foot of Lanin Volcano.

Chile

Season: January–March.
Location: Southern Patagonia.
Cost: $2,330 for 10 days from Punta Arenas.
Tour Operator: Equitours.

This trip traverses famed valleys, lakes, forests, rivers, waterfalls, and towering mountains of Torres del Paine National Park. After rides of five to six hours per day, participants camp beside lakes, rivers, and other scenic spots.

Ecuador

Season: Year-round.
Location: Imbabura Province.
Cost: $1,700 for eight days from Quito.
Tour Operator: Equitours.

A two-hour drive from Quito takes participants to Hacienda Zuleta, base for daily rides across grasslands, pine forests, and into the mountains. Visits are made to Inca pyramids, the famous Otavalo market, and Cotacachi, known for leather products. This trip involves slow to moderate riding, four to six hours per day.

Venezuela

Season: Year-round; November–May recommended.
Location: The Andes; Margarita Island.
Cost: From $600 for four days from Caracas.
Tour Operator: American Wilderness Experience; Lost World Adventures; Safaricentre.

Lost World Adventures and Safaricentre offer four- and five-day rides through the páramo, where elevations vary between 1,524 and 3,600 m (5,000 and 12,000 ft). Remote mountain villages are visited and two nights are spent camping. Members of American Wilderness Experience's seven-day trip need bathing suits as well as boots, as they canter along the beaches of Margarita Island and visit fishing villages.

Mountaineering

Argentina and Chile

Season: December–March.
Locations: Fitzroy and Cerro Torre area, Argentina; Mt. Aconcagua, Argentina; Torres del Paine National Park, Chile.
Cost: From $2,460 for 14 days from Puenta Arenas.
Tour Operators: American Alpine Institute; Southwind Adventures.

At 6,960 m (22,835 ft), Argentina's Mt. Aconcagua is the highest peak outside Asia. Although ascent via the Polish Glacier is not extremely technical, it demands solid alpine climbing skills. Both Southwind and AAI have Aconcagua expeditions. The latter company also offers a 14-day trip to Argentina's Fitzroy and Cerro, at the edge of the Patagonian Ice Cap, which involves trekking and alpine climbing; its Chile program treks the Torres del Paine range, ascends Cerro Blanco Sur and Cerro Almirante, and attempts an unclimbed peak.

Bolivia

Season: May–October.
Locations: Cordillera Real.

Cost: From $1,625 for 11 days from La Paz.
Tour Operators: American Alpine Institute; Southwind Adventures.

Bolivia's 160-km-long (100-mi-long) Cordillera Real has some of the continent's finest and most varied alpine climbing. Twenty-two peaks 5,791 m (19,000 ft) or higher make this Bolivia's largest glacier complex. At 6,462 m (21,201 ft), Illimani is the range's highest peak. Climbers confront large crevasses and a 40- to 45-degree glacial face; snow bridges and ice ramps are utilized. In addition to Illimani, American Alpine Institute offers ascents of 6,430-m (21,095-ft) Ancohuma and 6,362-m (20,873-ft) Illampu, plus programs for beginning mountaineering instruction and advanced ice-climbing techniques. Southwind Adventures' 11-day itinerary includes a four-day acclimatization trek and a summit bid on Huayna Potosí.

Ecuador
Season: July–February.
Location: Antisana; Cayambe; Chimborazo; Cotopaxi; El Altar; Illiniza Sur.
Cost: From $1,580 for 10 days from Quito.
Tour Operators: American Alpine Institute; Earthquest; Southwind Adventures.

The American Alpine Institute leads climbs on six of the Andes' finest peaks, including 6,310-m (20,703-ft) Chimborazo and 5,897-m (19,348-ft) Cotopaxi (the world's highest active volcano) to Illiniza Sur at 5,263 m (17,268 ft). Although acclimatization is vital, high altitude experience is not a prerequisite for Illiniza. Southwind Adventures' ascent of Cotopaxi is preceded by a three-day warm-up trek to the foot of El Altar. Earthquest offers challenging programs for all levels of skill.

Peru
Season: May–September.
Locations: Alpamayo; Huascarán.
Cost: From $2,865 for 18 days from Lima.
Tour Operators: American Alpine Institute; Southwind Adventures.

With more than 60 glaciered peaks above 5,639 m (18,500 ft), the Peruvian Andes beckon climbers. Following a five-day acclimatization trek along the Santa Cruz gorge and a warm-up climb on Mt. Pisco, Southwind Adventures heads up the south summit of Huascarán. American Alpine Institute's participants acclimatize on Nevado Pisco Oeste before ascending Huascará Sur. That challenge met, an attempt is made on seldom-climbed Huascará Norte. This company also has an expedition to Alpamayo. Expect a sustained 60 degree climb; altitude experience and snow and ice skills are necessary.

Skiing

Perhaps one of the greatest advantages to skiing in South America is that when everyone back home is soaking up the sun, you can get in your season of summer downhill.

Argentina and Chile
Season: June–October.
Locations: Bariloche, Chatelco, and Las Leñas, Argentina; Portillo, Termas de Chillan, and Valle Nevado, Chile.
Cost: From $976 for eight days from Buenos Aires, including meals, tax, and lift tickets.
Tour Operators: Adventures on Skis; 4th Dimension; Lost World Adventures; Tours International.

In the heart of the Chilean Andes (but only an hour's drive from Santiago), Valle Nevado has more than 64 km (40 mi) of groomed runs. Near the base of Mt. Aconcagua, the highest mountain in the western hemisphere, lies Portillo resort, with views across the waters of Laguna del Inca. Termas de Chillan offers South America's longest trail—13 km (8 mi)—and a network of forest tracks for cross country skiers.

Argentina has the legendary Bariloche, an alpine-type resort town on the shores of Lake Nahuel Huapí. The ski mountain, Cerro Catedral (Cathedral Hill), is 13 km (8 mi) from town. Known as Little Switzerland, Bariloche offers restaurants, a casino, and plenty of nightlife. For 56 km (35 mi) of downhill trails and a vertical drop of 1,219 m (4,000 ft), try the slopes of Las Leñas, where several Olympic ski teams train. Situated near a glacial lake, Chapelco boasts steep chutes, forest skiing, and off-piste touring opportunities.

Snorkeling, Diving, and Sailing

Ecuador
Season: Year-round; August–November suggested.
Locations: Galápagos Islands.
Cost: From $2,100 for an eight-day diving cruise.
Tour Operators: Tumbaco Quasar Náutica; Tropical Adventures.

Most Galápagos cruises offer time to snorkel among the sea lions. (☞ See Natural History section, *above*.) The two companies mentioned here have cruises designed for serious divers. Various islands are visited, with time each day for two to four dives plus wildlife viewing. Twelve- to 18-passenger yachts are specifically equipped for diving trips. Cold waters, strong currents, and surges make the Galápagos suitable for experienced divers only.

Venezuela
Season: Year-round.
Locations: Coche Island; Los Roques Archipelago.
Cost: From $595 for three days with scuba surcharge of $83 per day.
Tour Operators: Lost World Adventures; Safaricentre; Tropical Adventures.

Less than an hour by air from Caracas, the 350 small islands that make up Los Roques Archipelago offer white sand beaches and crystal waters for snorkeling and diving. Lost World Adventures and Safaricentre have two- and three-day packages, overnighting at guest houses or on sailing vessels. Tropical Adventures has a seven-day diving trip aboard an 85-ft yacht. Day trips from Caracas may also be arranged.

Trekking

In recent years, trekking holidays have soared in popularity, and few destinations can match South America's magnificent setting for such travel. In addition to scenic splendor, the Andes also have a vast network of roads constructed centuries ago by the Incas, which today lead hikers to ancient ruins, spectacular mountain peaks, and traditional communities. Trekking usually refers to an organized tour led by qualified local guides. Camping is part of the experience, although in most cases, cooks prepare meals and pack animals tote equipment. Some treks utilize inns and small hotels, with little or no camping.

Argentina and Chile
Season: November–March; Salta trek year-round.
Locations: Patagonia; Salta, Argentina.
Cost: From $1,395 for nine days from Buenos Aires.

Tour Operators: Above the Clouds Trekking; Backroads; Earthquest; Ecosummer Expeditions; Geographic Expeditions; Mountain Travel-Sobek; Naturequest; Southwind Adventures; Wilderness Travel; Wildland Adventures.

Southern Argentina and Chile, commonly referred to as Patagonia, may be the most-trekked region in South America. While some itineraries focus on a single country, most combine the two. Highlights include treks in Torres del Paine or Glacier National Park and over the Patagonian Ice Cap. For the latter, crampons are attached to hiking boots. Trips range from eight to 23 days of moderate to vigorous trekking. Wildland Adventures also offers a nine-day "Salta Trek through Silent Valleys" program. Participants experience a variety of ecological zones and visit remote Andean villages. Daily hikes in this relatively unexplored region average five to seven hours over rugged terrain at high altitude.

Bolivia
Season: April–October.
Location: Cordillera Apolobamba; Cordillera Real.
Cost: From $1,995 for 17 days from La Paz.
Tour Operators: Above the Clouds Trekking; Myths and Mountains; Naturequest; Southwind Adventures.

La Paz, the highest capital city in the world, is the place to acclimatize before heading to even higher ground. Southwind Adventures has a 16-day llama trek with eight nights of camping, while Above the Clouds' "Apolobamba" program explores an untraveled region where participants cross passes, some over 4,877 m (16,000 ft), on almost a daily basis. With Myths and Mountains, hike to the mountain homeland of Kallawaya medicine men and join them in the search for healing herbs. Naturequest offers itineraries of varied lengths where trekking may be combined with whitewater rafting.

Brazil
Season: Year-round.
Locations: Amazon.
Cost: From $1,100 for seven days from Manaus.
Tour Operators: Explorers Travel Group; Swallows and Amazons.

For a firsthand jungle experience, join a trek where days are spent hiking an average of six hours through thick vegetation. In the evening, fall asleep—perhaps in a hammock—serenaded by resident wildlife. Itineraries start in Manaus, traveling into the jungle by riverboat.

Colombia
Season: December–February, July–August.
Locations: Caribbean; Sierra Nevada de Santa Marta.
Cost: $2,020 for 17 days from Bogotá.
Tour Operator: Travelbag Adventures.

The highlight of Travelbag's "Trek to the Lost City" program is a five-day hike through splendid mountain scenery to isolated Ciudad Perdida, a center of Tairona culture in the 6th century. Time also is spent in Bogotá, the colonial town of Villa de Leyva, Cartagena, and Santa Marta. The latter two are situated on the Caribbean.

Ecuador
Season: Year-round.
Locations: Amazon; Andes; Otavalo area.
Cost: From $1,245 for seven days from Quito.
Tour Operators: Adventure Associates; Backroads; Country Walkers; Earthquest; Journeys International; Safaricentre; Southwind Adventures.

The Andes cross Ecuador from north to south in two ranges. Between them lies the fertile Central Valley, along the so-called Avenue of Volcanoes, one of the largest concentrations of volcanoes in the world. Some trekking routes lead to glacier-clad peaks, while others explore the unspoiled Amazon rain forest. Accommodations range from rustic camps to comfortable inns. A few packages include time in the Galápagos.

Peru
Season: March–October.
Locations: Colca Canyon; Cordilleras Blanca; Vilcabamba and Vilcanota; Huayhuash; Inca Trail.
Cost: From $925 for nine days from Lima.
Tour Operators: American Wilderness Experience; Earthquest; Exodus; Geographic Expeditions; Journeys International; Mountain Travel-Sobek; Safaricentre; Southwind Adventures; Wilderness Travel; Wildland Adventures.

From the ancient Inca capital of Cuzco to the lost city of Machu Picchu, the 45-km (28-mi) Inca Trail rivals Patagonia as South America's most popular trekking route. Requiring moderate to strenuous hiking, the trail leads past indigenous communities and Inca ruins. Other trekking programs vary in trip length, areas covered, and degree of physical challenge. Elevations can reach 5,300 m (17,384 ft). Some companies offer treks through Colca Canyon, thought to be the world's deepest, or hikes on Lake Titicaca's Isla del Sol. On most trips, the majority of nights are spent camping.

Venezuela
Season: October–May.
Locations: Angel Falls; Mt. Auyán-tepuí; Mt. Roraima.
Cost: From $1,025 for eight days from Puerto Ordaz.
Tour Operators: Earthquest; Lost World Adventures; Mountain Travel-Sobek; Safaricentre; Southwind Adventures; Travelbag; Wilderness Travel.

Sir Arthur Conan Doyle's "Lost World" can be found in the Gran Sabana, with its more than 100 flat-top mountains soaring above tropical forests. The summits have their origins in some of the oldest rock formations on earth. The region's premiere attractions are Mt. Roraima and Angel Falls, which cascades more than 914 m (3,000 ft) from the summit of Mt. Auyán-tepuí. Most operators combine a visit to the falls with a mountain trek. Depending on the itinerary, expect moderate to strenuous trekking and a combination of camping, lodges, and hotels.

White-Water Rafting and Kayaking

Alternately exhilarating and relaxing, white-water rafting and kayaking provide a pace and perspective all their own. You don't have to be an expert paddler to enjoy many river adventures, but you should be a strong swimmer. Rivers are rated from Class I to Class V according to how difficult they are to navigate, and South America has some of the wildest commercially rafted rivers in the world. Generally speaking, Class I to III rapids are rolling to rollicking and suitable for beginners, while many Class IV and V rapids are potentially dangerous and strictly for the experienced.

Bolivia
Season: May–October.
Locations: Amazon basin; Lake Titicaca.
Cost: From $595 for six days from La Paz.
Tour Operator: Naturequest.

Some call Bolivia the country that has everything—except hordes of tourists. Naturequest offers three kayaking adventures, ranging from 6 to 10 days, in this intriguing nation. All explore the hidden bays, cliffs, and traces of past civilizations at Lake Titicaca's Island of the Sun. Situated 3,810 m (12,500 ft) above sea level, Titicaca is the world's highest navigable lake. One itinerary combines Titicaca with time in the Amazon, paddling along the Ibare and Mamore rivers. Trips are considered moderately strenuous and require a degree of physical fitness, though kayaking experience is not necessary.

Brazil

Season: Year-round.
Location: Amazon.
Cost: From $1,200 for seven days from Manaus.
Tour Operator: Swallows and Amazons.

Paddling local wooden canoes, explore the Anavilhanas Archipelago (the second largest group of river islands in the world) and the rain forest that lines the banks of the Río Negro. Continue along smaller tributaries such as the Arara, Jaraqui, and Tucuman. View monkeys, iguanas, river dolphins, and alligators and visit with local river people. Seven- and 10-day canoeing and camping trips are offered.

Chile

Season: December–March.
Locations: Río Bío-Bío, Class IV–V; Río Futaleufú, Class IV; Tierra del Fuego, Class III.
Cost: From $1,450 for 10 days from Santiago.
Tour Operators: Earthquest; Earth River Expeditions; Ecosummer Expeditions; Myths and Mountains; Naturequest; Wilderness Travel; Wildland Adventures.

Chile boasts both scenic fjords for kayaking and challenging rivers for white-water rafting. Kayaking adventures explore the fishing villages, glaciers, hot springs, and marine wildlife of Tierra del Fuego. Some trips combine paddling with trekking. For the experienced rafter, Chile's Bío-Bío and Futaleufú rivers offer challenges aplenty. The Futaleufú's sheer-walled Inferno Canyon claims such well-named rapids as Infierno and Purgatorio. Earth River's program includes a Challenge Cirque with rock climbs, as well as harness and zip line traverses of the Zeta Rapids. Rafters eager to experience the legendary Bío-Bío may be in for a disappointment: A second dam is under consideration. At press time, construction plans were not finalized and several companies still operated Bío-Bío trips.

Ecuador

Season: November–March, July–August.
Locations: Galápagos; Río Upano, Class III–IV.
Cost: From $1,995 for 11 days from Quito.
Tour Operator: Earth River Expeditions; Mountain Travel-Sobek; ROW; Tumbaco Quasar Náutica.

Since 1992, when ROW made the first descent of the Upano, the river's whitewater rapids have become synonymous with world-class rafting. Flowing through an immense rain forest, the rapids are described as "big volume" rides. Spectacular waterfalls drop hundreds of feet into the river. Participants learn about the fragile ecosystem and visit Shuar Indian communities. Quasar Náutica pioneered kayaking adventures in the Galápagos Islands and carries kayaks aboard all its yachts.

Peru

Season: Year-round; June–September suggested.
Locations: Amazon; Río Apurímac, Class IV–V; Colca Canyon, Class V; Río Tambopata, Class III–IV.
Cost: From $2,500 for 12 days from Lima.
Tour Operator: Earthquest; Earth River Expeditions; Mountain Travel-Sobek; Naturequest; Tours International.

Descending the Tambopata to the nature reserve of the same name, rafters experience the excitement of moderate to difficult rapids. Camps are set up along the river. The Apurimac cuts through spectacular gorges and canyons under towering Andean peaks. Some programs combine rafting with a trek along the Inca Trail to Machu Picchu. For serious rafters in excellent physical condition, a Río Colca adventure negotiates one of the deepest and most inaccessible river canyons in the world. Kayaking along Amazonian tributaries allows participants to visit local villages and to view wildlife, including pink river dolphins, manatees, and blue macaws.

Venezuela

Season: June.
Location: Angel Falls; Akanan; Carrao and Churun rivers.
Cost: $2,695 for 16 days from Caracas.
Tour Operator: Wilderness Travel.

Following a six-day Roraima summit trek, embark in dugout canoes for a six-day expedition to Angel Falls, Earth's highest waterfall. Travel along blackwater rivers with easy rapids and sleep in hammocks at Indian river camps. Spend two days at the falls observing the phenomenon from a series of lookout points.

3 ARGENTINA

Cosmopolitan Buenos Aires has hundreds of theaters and tango halls, dozens of parks, and myriad restaurants—all providing diversion for a population in perpetual motion. Away from the capital city's constant commotion, the pace is slower, the people are more open, and the scenery— ranging from the snowy heights of the Andes to the thundering flow of Iguazú Falls—is spectacular.

MOST TRAVELERS THINK THEY'VE STUMBLED ON a long-lost European country when they get to Argentina. Most Argentines, too, are convinced they're more European than South American. A quick look at the people walking down the avenues of any Argentine city confirms the impression. There are more Italian surnames than Spanish and the largest colony of Yugoslavs outside of their fractured homeland. There are tens of thousands of descendants of Jewish immigrants from Eastern Europe, and communities of British, French, and German families enjoy cultural and financial clout far beyond their insignificant numbers.

But in spite of the symbiosis with Europe, the country has had a chaotic past, politically and economically. The pitfalls of Argentine politics weren't inappropriately characterized in the musical *Evita:* "Truth is stranger than fiction" is a maxim confirmed by the musical-chairs–like process that has placed both soldiers and civilians in the country's presidency. Further, Argentina is a me-first society that considers government a thorn in its side and whose citizens avoid paying taxes with the finesse of bullfighters. As a community, it's totally chaotic, but as individuals, Argentines are generous and delightful, full of life, and eager to explain the intricacies of their complex society. They're also philosophers, anxious to justify their often enviable existence. Friendship is a time-consuming priority, and family connections are strong. Argentines work longer hours than New Yorkers—just not so efficiently—and rival Madrileños at dining until dawn.

Argentina's vast territory stretches more than 5,000 km (3,000 mi) from north to south and encompasses everything from snow-covered mountains to subtropical jungle. In the north, in the sultry province of Misiones, nature is raucous and rampant; here the spectacular Iguazú Falls flow amid foliage that is rain-forest–thick. In the pampas, or plains, of central Argentina, the countryside recalls the American West: Gauchos herd the cattle that provide Argentina with the beef it consumes in massive quantities. In the west, the Andean backbone Argentina shares with Chile attracts climbers to Mt. Aconcagua, the Southern Hemisphere's highest peak, and draws skiers to Bariloche and other resorts. Patagonia, in the south, is like no other place on earth. Monumental glaciers tumble into mountain lakes, depositing icebergs like meringue on a floating island. Penguins troop along beaches like invading forces, whales hang out with several yards of their tails emerging from the sea, and at the tip of Patagonia, South America slips into Beagle Channel in Tierra del Fuego.

Pleasures and Pastimes

Dining

Most Argentine dishes are stolen from other cultures and called international. Of course, this is the world's beef capital, and steak dishes tend to crowd the menu. Argentina's one true cuisine is the *parrillada*, or barbecue (to confuse matters, *a* barbecue—i.e. the event—is called an *asado*). Other than that, Argentine food tends toward the bland, since few sauces and spices are used. For price categories, *see* Dining *in* Smart Travel Tips A to Z.

SPECIALTIES

Beef, or *bife*, as they say in Argentine Spanish, is still the staple of the country's diet. Once a major export, cattle traditionally have outnumbered people two to one in Argentina. Gauchos spend their lifetimes in the saddle eating exclusively the range-fed native cattle they raise. Some 50 million cattle—Angus, Hereford, and a dozen other

Argentina

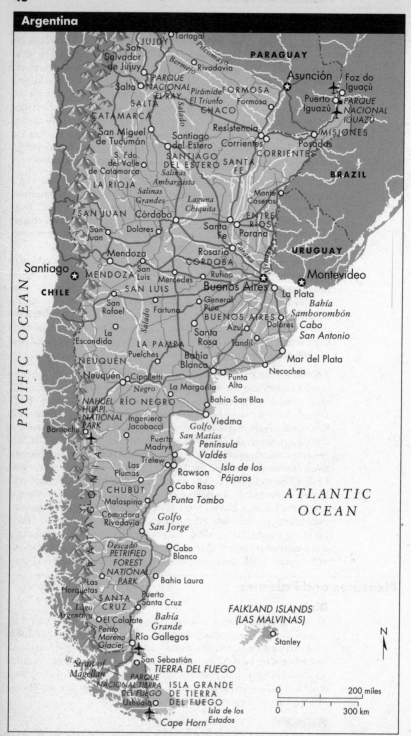

breeds—thrive on the pampas grasses, which are so nutritious that there's no need for grain supplements.

Nothing can duplicate the indescribable flavor of a lean, tender, 3-inch-thick steak grilled over coals of a log from the *quebracho* tree, an ax-breaking hardwood. Many different cuts of a steer are grilled on the *parrilla* (grill) at an asado, as a barbecue is called here. Steaks can be accompanied by *picante* (hot) sauce, although Argentines traditionally prefer theirs straight. (Picante doesn't burn like Mexican chiles or Indian curries.) If you ask for *chimichurri,* chefs will serve a picante sauce prepared with garlic, olive oil, vinegar, and cilantro. Bife *de chorizo* is a basic strip sirloin, but three times the size; bife *de lomo* can be a 3-inch-high fillet. Often a half portion is more than enough. *Jugoso* means rare, but Argentines like their meat well-done, so it is hard to get a *parrillero* to prepare a steak so that it's red when sliced.

Adventurous meat eaters will want to have their steak served sizzling on a miniature grill, the parrillada, whose hot coals keep the cuts warm at the table. The mixed grill includes blood sausage, short ribs, and various internal and external organs like intestines and udder. A typical beef hors d'oeuvre consists of thin slices of *matambre,* made by laying out boiled eggs, chunks of ham, and hearts of palm on flank steak, rolling it into a loaf, soaking it in a marinade, and baking it. Beef is also traditionally served in the form of a breaded cutlet wrapped in ham and cheese and sometimes served with a tomato sauce. The simple version is referred to as a Milanesa, while the kind with ham, cheese, and sauce is a Milanesa Napolitana.

Italian cuisines, particularly those of Naples and Sicily, are found throughout Argentina. Buenos Aires has the most concentrated immigrant influence, with Jewish delicatessens and British, French, and Asian restaurants (especially good for high tea) to name a few. While staying in Ushuaia in Tierra del Fuego, try tidbits of *corderito al asador* (roasted baby lamb) right off the spit. This dish is the tasty mainstay of Patagonian cuisine, as are hot potato salads; *centolla,* the large crab trapped off the town's shores; and gigantic *mejillones* (mussels), often 5 inches long.

Most Argentine desserts are made with one principal ingredient: *dulce de leche,* a sticky sweet made of milk boiled with sugar, a pinch of soda, and a few drops of vanilla. The thick, brownish cream is spread on breakfast toast and baked in cakes, meringues, and tarts, and is often eaten alone by the spoonful. Mixed with bits of chocolate, it's a favorite flavor in ice cream shops. Argentines have been known to travel with several pots of it when they go abroad.

WINE

Given the high consumption of beef rather than fish, Argentines understandably drink *vino tinto* (red wine). For those who prefer *vino blanco* (white wine), try vintages from Mendoza and from lesser known wineries farther north: La Rioja and Salta. Here the Torrontés grape thrives and produces a dry white with an overwhelming, unforgettable bouquet that has been a consistent prizewinner in German and French competitions. A popular summer cooler is *clericot,* a white version of sangria, made with strawberries, peaches, oranges, or whatever fruits are in season or appeal to a particular bartender.

Lodging

Amenities in most nice hotels—private baths, 24-hour room service, air-conditioning, cable TV, dry cleaning—are above average. In the less expensive establishments you may not have as many amenities, but you'll still find charm, cleanliness, and hospitality. Rooms that have a private bath may only have a shower. In all but the most upscale hotels, you may be asked to leave your key at the reception desk whenever you leave, and many hotels have a curfew, so if you arrive after the reception desk closes, you may not be able to get your key. Most hotels in all categories offer breakfast, whether or not there's a full restaurant in the hotel.

In smaller towns you'll find *residenciales,* which can be either family-run pensions or bed-and-breakfasts. *Estancias* are another option; these are working ranches where you can stay as a guest. Campgrounds usually have running water, electricity, and bathroom facilities. Provincial tourist offices have lists of campgrounds in their regions.

Note that *albergues transitorios* (temporary lodgings) is the euphemism name for drive-in hotels, which are generally used for romantic trysts. Very common in this country where people often live with their parents until marriage, they're easily recognizable by their hourly rates and purple and orange exterior lights. Real motels can be found through the Automovil Club Argentino (☞ Getting Around by Car *in* Argentina A to Z, *below*). For price categories, *see* Lodging *in* Smart Travel Tips A to Z.

Exploring Argentina

Buenos Aires is the political, economic, and cultural capital of Argentina and the gateway to the rest of the country. The Iguazú Falls lie roughly 1,300 km (800 mi) to the city's northeast on the border with Paraguay and Brazil. The pampas—vast plains of cattle ranches and home of the gauchos—extends south from the Federal Capital. Below the pampas is Patagonia, the rough and largely uninhabited territory that extends south to Tierra del Fuego and consumes a third of Argentina. It's divided into two regions: the Atlantic, with an incomparable variety of marine life including whales, sea elephants, and penguins, and the Andes, with frozen lakes, glaciers, and thousand-year-old forests.

Great Itineraries

A trip to Argentina should begin in Buenos Aires, where you'll develop a strong sense of the peoples' character and their culture. You could spend your entire trip here—strolling the wide, tree-lined boulevards, visiting the numerous boutiques and cafés, touring the city's unique districts with their churches and museums, and immersing yourself in the rich nightlife. Iguazú Falls are perhaps the most spectacular in the world, and the dive into nature for a few days may come as a welcome change after the crowded, noisy city. If you're searching for even greater serenity, immense Patagonia with its silent snow-capped mountains and breathtaking glaciers beckons—but you'll need at least a week to cover its great distances.

IF YOU HAVE 5 DAYS

Narrow your visit to **Buenos Aires,** which has more than enough to keep you happily occupied. Try walking the tours listed below, which are divided into charming districts. In many ways, this is a city that comes alive at night—so be sure to enjoy the restaurant, theater, tango, and café scene.

IF YOU HAVE 7 DAYS

Spend a couple of days in **Buenos Aires,** and then travel to **Iguazú Falls,** a 1½-hour flight from the capital and one of the most amazing sights on earth. You'll need at least two days to see the best waterfalls, but three or four would be better.

IF YOU HAVE 10 DAYS

Visit **Buenos Aires** for two or three days and then head to **Patagonia.** Spend at least a week and focus on either the Atlantic Coast or the Andes region.

BUENOS AIRES

Updated by
Kristen Masick

Buenos Aires, the ninth largest city in the world and the hub of the southern cone, is a sprawling megalopolis that rises from the Río de la Plata
and stretches more than 200 sq km (75 sq mi) to the surrounding pampas, the fertile Argentine plains. It's the political, economic, and cultural capital of Argentina and the gateway to the rest of the country.

Buenos Aires has 47 *barrios* (neighborhoods)—each with its own character and its own story to tell. Most residents have lived in the same
barrio their entire lives and feel much more of an affinity to their neighborhood than to the city as a whole. Block after block of tidy high-
rise apartment buildings are interspersed with 19th-century houses.
Neighborhoods such as Palermo, La Recoleta, and Belgrano feel more
like Paris, with wide boulevards lined with palatial mansions, luxury
high-rises, and spacious parks. Flowers are sold at colorful corner
kiosks, the smell of freshly baked bread wafts from well-stocked bakeries, terrace cafés can be found on every block, and pedestrians carry
themselves with a fashionable reserve. Other neighborhoods, such as
San Telmo and La Boca, have a distinctly working-class Italian feel.
Many have compared the Plaza de Mayo, principally the Avenida de
Mayo, to Budapest; and the Galerías Pacífico, a shopping mall in the
center of the city, was built to look like Galleria Vittorio Emanuele in
Milan.

Buenos Aires locals are referred to as *Porteños* because many of them
originally arrived by boat from Europe and started out in the city's port
area, La Boca. Porteños are thinkers. They enjoy philosophical discussions and psychoanalysis (as proven by the large number of psy-
choanalysts per capita—in fact, the most of any city in the world). They
seem perpetually confused about their national identity—South American or European?—and are often concerned about how outsiders per-
ceive them. Many are also deeply image-conscious, and go to great lengths
to be beautiful.

Buenos Aires has no Eiffel Tower, no internationally renowned museums, no must-see sights that clearly identify it as a world-class city. Rather,
it provides a series of small interactions that have intense Latin spirit—
a flirtatious glance, a heartfelt chat, a juicy steak, a beautiful tango—
which combine to create a vibrant and unforgettable urban experience.

Exploring Buenos Aires

You're best off exploring one neighborhood at a time by foot and taking public transportation—bus or *subte* (subway). Streets are basically
laid out in a grid, though a few transverse the grid at 45-degree angles; these are helpfully called *diagonal*. *Avenidas* are two-way avenues
(at most hours of the day), and *calles* are generally one way. Each city
block is exactly 100 meters long, and addresses are based on the building's measured position on the street, not by street number (for instance,
180 Calle Florida is 100 meters, or one block, from 80 Calle Florida).

*Numbers in the text correspond to numbers in the margin and on the
Buenos Aires Exploring map.*

San Telmo

The appealing if a bit run-down neighborhood of San Telmo, halfway
between midtown Buenos Aires and the south end of the city, is comparable to New York's Greenwich Village. Its cobblestone streets are
rich with early 19th-century colonial mansions, once inhabited by
upper-class Spaniards. Over the years the mansions have been converted
into multifamily housing for the immigrants (particularly Italians)

who began moving here in the late 19th century. For the past 20 years these old houses have been transformed into shops, art galleries, restaurants, and bars. The neighborhood is a cradle of Buenos Aires history and culture. Neighborhood highlights include the Sunday flea market, the antiques shops along Calle Defensa, and the tango bars that come to life nightly. To reach San Telmo from anywhere in the city, take Line E to the Independencia stop; from here it's an eight-block walk down Calle Estados Unidos to Calle Defensa.

A GOOD WALK

Plaza Dorrego ①, at the corner of Calles Defensa and Humberto Primo, is the focal point of San Telmo and the home of the Sunday flea market. Marking the southern edge of San Telmo are the gardens of the **Parque Lezama** ②; the Lezama home is now the **Museo Histórico Nacional** ③. Overlooking the park are the onion-shape domes of the **Iglesia Ortodoxa Rusa** ④. Continue north from the park along Calle Defensa. The street leads past many of the city's best art spaces, including the **Fundación del Rotary Club** ⑤ and the **Museo de Arte Moderno** ⑥. San Telmo's antiques shopping district begins at the corner of Calle Defensa and Avenida San Juan. Close to the corner of the Plaza Dorrego, on Calle Humberto Primo, stands a small chapel, **Nuestra Señora del Carmen** ⑦. The adjoining cloister, which later became a hospice and then a women's prison, is now the **Museo Penitenciario Antonio Balve** ⑧. A few relics of the colonial period are still found on Calle Carlos Calvo, just off Calle Defensa, including the **Pasaje Giuffra** ⑨ along with its neighbor, the **Pasaje de la Defensa** ⑩, and **La Casa de Esteban de Luca** ⑪. Continuing along Calle Defensa, take a right on Calle Independencia to reach the **Viejo Almacén** ⑫.

TIMING AND PRECAUTIONS

If possible, visit San Telmo on a Sunday, when the market on Plaza Dorrego bustles with life. A few hours will give you plenty of time to see the sights, but you could easily spend a full day exploring the side streets and shops. Exercise caution when walking here—especially at night. Violent crime is rare, but unemployment in San Telmo and its neighboring barrios, combined with the knowledge that foreign tourists will always hit the area for at least one tango show, has led to more instances of pickpocketing and muggings.

SIGHTS TO SEE

⑪ **La Casa de Esteban de Luca.** This old home, now a typical Argentine restaurant, was declared a National Historic Monument in 1941. It belonged to Esteban de Luca, a distinguished poet and soldier who wrote Argentina's first national anthem. It's a great place to stop for a bite, taking in a bit of history with your Argentine wine. ⊠ *Defensa 1000,* ☎ *11/4361–4338.*

⑤ **Fundación del Rotary Club.** The Rotary Club Foundation, housed in a fine postcolonial house with an enclosed courtyard, puts on monthly shows by contemporary Argentine and international artists and hosts concerts. ⊠ *Defensa 1344,* ☎ *11/4361–5485.* 🎫 *Free.* ☉ *Weekdays after 4 (call for exact concert times), Sat. 8–8.*

④ **Iglesia Ortodoxa Rusa.** The Russian Orthodox Church with its sky blue dome was hastily built in the late 1910s by the eclectic Danish architect Alejandro Cristophersen for the congregation of Russians who had settled in the city. The property, strangely, still belongs to Russia. ⊠ *Av. Brasil 315.* ☉ *Sat. 6 PM–8:30 PM, Sun. 10 AM–12:30 PM.*

⑥ **Museo de Arte Moderno.** This old cigarette factory with a classical brick facade has been transformed into the Museum of Modern Art. It holds temporary shows by local painters and sculptors and permanent exhibits of prominent international contemporary artists. It's often possible to meet the artists here—in lectures or just hanging out at the gallery—discussing their own works and those of others. ⊠ *Av. San Juan 350,* ☎ *11/4361–1121.* ⊡ *Admission; free on Wed.* ☉ *Tues.– Fri. 10–8, weekends and holidays 11–8.*

★ ❸ **Museo Histórico Nacional.** The Lezama family home, an example of a stately but decaying old mansion, is now the National Historical Museum. The focus is on the official history of Argentina from the 16th century to the beginning of the 1900s. Most prominently displayed are memorabilia relating to General José de San Martín and his campaigns in 1810 during the War of Independence against Spain. The jewel of the museum is the collection of paintings by Cándido López, a forceful precursor of contemporary primitive painting. López, who lost an arm in the Paraguayan War of the 1870s, which Paraguay fought against Argentina and Brazil, learned to paint with his left hand and produced an exciting series of war scenes on a scale that would have captivated Cecil B. DeMille. ⊠ *Defensa 1600,* ☎ *11/4307–1182.* ⊡ *Free.* ☉ *Feb.–Dec., Tues.–Sun. noon–6.*

❽ **Museo Penitenciario Antonio Balve.** The modest Antonio Balve Penitentiary Museum has mementos of early 20th-century prison life. Behind the museum's large courtyard is **Nuestra Señora del Carmen** (☞ *below*). Next door is an even larger church, the **Parroquia de San Pedro González Telmo** (San González Telmo Parish Church). ⊠ *Humberto Primero 378.* ⊡ *Admission.* ☉ *Weekdays 10–noon and 2–5; Sun. noon–6.*

❼ **Nuestra Señora del Carmen.** This chapel behind the Museo Penitenciario Antonio Balve's (☞ *above*) large courtyard dates from the Jesuit period. Next door is the **Parroquia de San Pedro González Telmo** (San González Telmo Parish Church), which was abandoned halfway through its construction by the Jesuits in 1767, when the order was expelled from Argentina, and was not completed until 1858. The cloisters and the domed chapel to the left, designed by Father Andrés Blanqui in 1738, are the only remnants of the original structure. ⊠ *Humberto Primero 378.*

❷ **Parque Lezama.** Enormous magnolia, palm, cedar, and elm trees fill the sloping hillside in Lezama Park, and winding paths lead down to the river. The land fell into the hands of an English family in the 1840s, who sold it to George Ridgely Horne, an American businessman, who in turn sold it in 1858 to Gregorio Lezama, an entrepreneur. Lezama decorated the gardens of his luxurious estate with life-size statues and enormous urns. At the end of the last century, his widow donated the property to the city, and it has since become a popular spot for family picnics on weekends. On Sunday an arts and crafts market takes place. ⊠ *Brasil and Paseo Colón.* ⊡ *Free.* ☉ *Daily, dawn–dusk.*

❿ **Pasaje de la Defensa.** Defense Alley gives you an idea of what Buenos Aires looked like 200 years ago. ⊠ *Off of Calle Defensa.*

❾ **Pasaje Giuffra.** A glimpse down the short Giuffra Alley, which runs toward the river, gives you a sense of what the city looked like two centuries ago. ⊠ *Off of Calle Defensa.*

★ ❶ **Plaza Dorrego.** On weekdays Dorrego Square is a peaceful haven for chess-playing pensioners, who sit at outdoor tables shaded by stately old trees. On Sunday from 10 to 5 the plaza comes alive with the bustling **San Telmo Antiques Fair.** Often you'll find a young couple dancing frenzied tangos on one corner to the music of veteran tango musicians playing violins and *bandoneons* (the local version of the accordion).

Buenos Aires Exploring

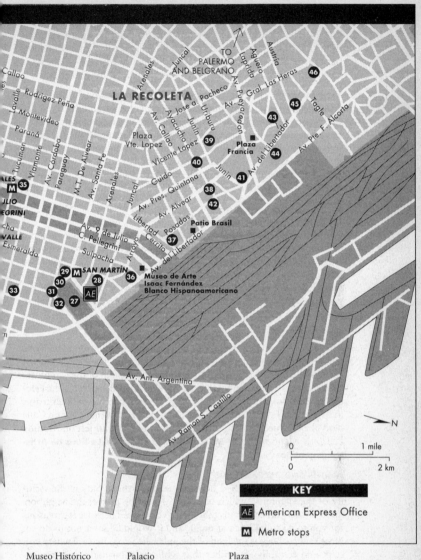

KEY

AE American Express Office

M Metro stops

The fair provides a great opportunity to buy tango memorabilia, leather goods, high-quality silver, and a wide variety of Argentine knickknacks. The buildings surrounding the plaza provide a sampling of the architectural styles—Spanish colonial, French classical, and lots of ornately decorated masonry done by Italian craftsmen—that gained a significant presence in the city in the 19th and 20th centuries.

⑫ **Viejo Almacén.** This popular nightspot for tango (☞ Nightlife and the Arts, *below*) is another fine example of colonial architecture. The building dates from 1798, during which time it was a general store (Almacén de Campaña). After a stint as a hospital in the 1800s, the building was purchased by Paula Kravnic, the daughter of a Russian immigrant, who transformed it into a tango bar at the turn of the century. The bar gained even greater popularity when it was purchased, in 1969, by Argentine tango sensation Eduardo Rivero. ✉ *Av. Independencia.*

La Boca

The vibrant working-class neighborhood of La Boca is the southern neighbor of San Telmo. The first port of Buenos Aires, it has seen many waves of immigrants pass through its borders. The most significant and lasting group were Italians from Genoa, who arrived between 1880 and 1930. Still known as the Little Italy of Argentina, La Boca is the perfect place to find an authentic and inexpensive pizza or an impromptu tango lesson in the street.

A GOOD WALK

Your entire experience in La Boca will probably center around the **Calle Museo Caminito** ⑬, an outdoor art market and museum right off Avenida Pedro de Mendoza. Once you reach the end of the Caminito, turn right on Calle Garibaldi. Four blocks down the street is the **Estadio de Boca Juniors** ⑭, home to one of the most popular soccer teams in Argentina. Take a right on Calle Brandsen and another right on Calle del Valle Iberlucea to return to the Caminito. To your left on Avenida Pedro de Mendoza is the **Museo de Bellas Artes de La Boca de Artistas Argentinos** ⑮.

TIMING AND PRECAUTIONS

You really only need 1½–2 hours to see everything. Stay in the vicinity of the Caminito, which is well patrolled by police; the neighborhood borders other barrios that aren't very safe. There are few reasons for you to go to La Boca at night, and it would be safer not to do so. Note that La Boca is the land of the unleashed dog: Beware where you step, and certainly remember that while neighborhood dogs are accustomed to people, they may not react kindly to being petted.

SIGHTS TO SEE

★ ⑬ **Calle Museo Caminito.** The Caminito is a colorful pedestrians-only street that since 1959 has functioned as an open-air museum and art market. It's only about a block and a half long, but you can find numerous quality souvenirs, sculptures, and free open-air tango demonstrations. Walking along the Caminito, notice the distinctive, rather hastily constructed architecture, which is often painted in vibrant colors to cover shoddy materials. ✉ *Av. Pedro de Mendoza and Calle Palos.* 🎫 *Free.* ☉ *Daily 10–6.*

⑭ **Estadio de Boca Juniors.** The Boca Juniors are one of Argentina's most popular soccer teams and, as such, are the proud owners of this very distinctive stadium. If you have the chance to visit the stadium on a game day, be prepared for crowds, pandemonium, and street parties—and never wear red and white, the colors of River Plate, the rival team! ✉ *Brandsen 805.*

⑮ **Museo de Bellas Artes de La Boca de Artistas Argentinos.** La Boca Fine Arts Museum of Argentine Artists is worth a visit, as it provides a good overview of Argentine artistic history. It closes in summer for renovation and to set up new exhibits, so it's wise to call ahead to see if it's open. ✉ *Av. Pedro de Mendoza 1835,* ☎ *11/4301–1080.* 🎫 *Free.* ☉ *Weekdays 8–6, weekends 10–5.*

Plaza de Mayo

In a well-known scene in the musical *Evita*, Eva Perón stands on a picturesque balcony and waves to the Argentine masses assembled on a square below. She is supposed to be here, at the Plaza de Mayo. The political and historical center of Buenos Aires, the square is home to the presidential palace and other governmental buildings. It has survived wars, floods, and political upheaval; on every corner you see evidence of its history. Its attractions are principally architectural—the cathedral, where you may catch sight of visiting dignitaries (as well as Argentina's president) at Sunday services, and some well-preserved remnants of Spanish colonial architecture.

A GOOD WALK

Get your bearings at the **Plaza de Mayo** ⑯. At the eastern end of the square, the Casa de Gobierno, better known as the **Casa Rosada** ⑰, dominates the view toward the river. At the far western end of Avenida de Mayo is Argentina's parliament, the **Congreso** ⑱. All along Avenida de Mayo are sidewalk cafés and interesting buildings. Across Avenida Rivadavía is the **Banco de la Nación Argentina** ⑲. On the next block is the **Catedral Metropolitana** ⑳. Continue to the plaza's west side to see the **Cabildo** ㉑. Leaving the plaza, walk one block on Diaganol Sur to reach **La Manzana de las Luces** ㉒ and the Colegio Nacional. Next to the school is Buenos Aires's oldest church, the **Parroquia de San Ignacio** ㉓. Continue east on Calle Alsina to the **Museo de la Ciudad** ㉔, which has exhibits on the history of Buenos Aires. Across Calle Defensa is the **Basilica y Convento de San Francisco** ㉕, a colonial-era church, and the smaller Capilla San Roque, to its left. Another of the city's oldest churches, **Santo Domingo** ㉖, is two blocks south on Calle Defensa.

TIMING AND PRECAUTIONS

This walk will take about two hours, though you could easily spend a full day exploring all the sights in the area. Avoid hailing a taxi in front of a bank (people will think you've just taken out money and may rob your cab); instead, hail one in front of a local coffee shop. On weekends the streets are deserted, so pay close attention to your belongings, especially when walking alone.

SIGHTS TO SEE

⑲ **Banco de la Nación Argentina.** The imposing National Bank of Argentina was designed in 1940 in monumental neoclassical style by architect Alejandro Bustillo, who designed most of the city's government buildings in the 1930s and 1940s. ✉ *At corner of Reconquista and Rivadavía.*

㉕ **Basilica y Convento de San Francisco.** Originally built in 1754, the Bavarian baroque facade of the Convent and Basilica of St. Francis was added in 1911, and the interior was lavishly refurbished after the church was looted and burned in 1955 in the turmoil just before Perón's government fell. Inside, an archive of 20,000 books remains. ✉ *Defensa and Alsina,* ☎ *11/4331–0625.* 🎫 *Free.*

㉑ **Cabildo.** The Town Council building is considered one of Argentina's national shrines. In May 1810 patriotic citizens gathered here to vote against Spanish rule. The original building dates from 1765 but has been the product of successive renovations, the latest of which was in 1948. Inside is a small museum, but the building alone is worth the trip. After visiting this monument, you can't help but notice how many places in the city are named Cabildo. ⊠ *Bolívar 65,* ☎ *11/4334–1782.* ☜ *Free.* ☉ *Tues.–Fri. 12:30–7, Sun. 3–7; guided tours at 3 and 5.*

⑰ Casa Rosada. The Casa de Gobierno (Government Palace), better known as the Pink House, is the government headquarters (the president doesn't live here, though). The elite Grenadiers Regiment keeps close guard over the pale pink house. The first-floor balcony on the building's northern wing is used by the country's leaders to address the enormous crowds that gather below. This is where Evita came to rally the workers and where Madonna sang her rendition of "Don't Cry for Me Argentina" (the ugly window air-conditioning units were taken out for the movie). In back, on the basement level, the brick walls of the **Taylor Customs House**—which dates from the 1850s—have been partially uncovered after being buried for half a century, when the Plaza Colón was built. The site can be seen from the outside or as part of a visit to the adjoining **Museo de la Casa Rosada,** a museum containing presidential memorabilia. You may find it interesting that unlike a White House tour, the tour of the Casa Rosada Museum is relatively unsupervised, leading you to wonder just a little about security issues. ⊠ *Hipólito Yrigoyen 211,* ☎ *11/4343–3051 or 11/4374–9841 for guided tours.* ☜ *Free; charge for guided tours.* ☉ *Mon.–Tues. and Thurs.–Fri. 10–6; Sun. 2–6; guided tours at 4.*

⑳ Catedral Metropolitana. The first building on this site was an adobe ranch house, which disappeared in 1593. Since then the land has been continually in use. But it wasn't until 1822 that the Neoclassical facade of the Metropolitan Cathedral was begun (the building itself predates the facade by a century). The remains of General José de San Martín, known as the Argentine Liberator for his role in the War of Independence against Spain, are buried here in a marble mausoleum carved by the French sculptor Carrière Belleuse. The tomb is permanently guarded by soldiers of the Grenadier Regiment, a troop created and trained by San Martín in 1811. ⊠ *At Rivadavía and San Martín,* ☎ *11/4331–2845.* ☜ *Free.* ☉ *Guided tour weekdays 1:30, Sat. 10:30 and 11:15.*

⑱ Congreso. Built in 1906, the exterior was modeled after the U.S. Congress building. The building is surrounded by an attractive park, and is considered Kilometer 0 for every Argentine highway. ⊠ *Plaza del Congreso.* ☉ *Not open to the public.*

㉒ La Manzana de las Luces. The Block of Bright Lights was constructed in the early 1800s on property that originally belonged to the Jesuits, who were expelled in 1767. Home to a succession of schools, the area is famous as the breeding ground for Argentina's *intelligentsía* and it houses Argentina's most famous school. The bulky Neoclassical building on the site, where the San Ignacio school once stood, is now home to the **Colegio Nacional,** the country's leading public high school. You can take a guided tour of La Manzana de las Luces and the surrounding area; though infrequent and conducted in Spanish, these tours are worthwhile (call to verify the times listed below, as tour times change frequently). Going on a tour is your only chance to view the cavernous, historic tunnels that run under La Manzana. The tours follow various routes: Circuit B brings you to the tunnels and nearby churches; Circuit C takes you to the tunnels and the old State Representatives room; Circuit D takes you through the Colegio Nacional; and Circuit E takes you to the tunnels and past historic local homes. ⊠ *Perú 272,* ☎ *11/4342–6973.* ☜ *Admission.* ☉ *Guided tours on weekends between 3 and 6:30 PM.*

㉔ Museo de la Ciudad. The Municipal Museum houses temporary exhibitions both whimsical and probing about many aspects of domestic and public life in Buenos Aires in times past. On the ground floor, for instance, is the **Farmacia La Estrella** (Star Pharmacy), a quaint survivor from the 19th century. ⊠ *Calle Alsina 412,* ☎ *11/4331–9855 or 11/4343–2123.* 🎟 *Admission.* ⊙ *Weekdays 11–7, Sun. 3–7.*

㉓ **Parroquia de San Ignacio.** Started in 1713, St. Ignatius Church is the only church from that era to have a baroque facade. Behind it, a neo-classical facade dating from 1863 hides the old colonial building that headquartered the administrators of the Jesuits' vast land holdings in northeastern Argentina and Paraguay. In 1780 the city's first Facultad de Medicina (Medical School) was established here, and in the early 19th century was home to the Universidad de Buenos Aires (University of Buenos Aires). The tunnels underneath the building, which crisscrossed the colonial town and were used either by the military or by smugglers, depending on which version you believe, can still be visited by guided tour (☞ La Manzana de las Luces, *above*). ⊠ *Bolívar 225,* ☎ *11/4331–2458.* 🎟 *Free.* ⊙ *Tours on weekends at 3:30 and 5.*

★ ⑯ **Plaza de Mayo.** The two-block-long May Square has been the stage for many important events, including the uprising against Spain on May 25, 1810, in memory of which the square was given its name. The present layout dates from 1912, when the obelisk known as the **Pirámide de Mayo** was placed in the center; it was erected in 1811 to celebrate the first anniversary of the Revolution of May. A bronze equestrian statue of General Manuel Belgrano, cast in 1873, stands at the east end of the plaza. The tradition of staging celebrations and protests in this central plaza continues to this day. It's here that the Madres de la Plaza de Mayo (Mothers of Plaza de Mayo), the mothers of young *desaparecidos,* young people who were "disappeared" during the military government's reign from 1976 to 1983, still hold their Thursday-afternoon marches, which attracted international attention in the late 1970s.

㉖ **Santo Domingo.** Built in the 1750s, this convent is dedicated to Our Lady of the Rosary. On display in the chapel are four banners captured in 1806 from fleeing British troops—after their unsuccessful attempt to invade the then-Spanish colony—and two flags taken from the Spanish armies during the War of Independence. On one of the bell towers, bullet craters—testimony to the battle with British soldiers—are reminders of the conflict. The remains of General Manuel Belgrano, a hero of the War of Independence, rest in the courtyard's central mausoleum, guarded by marble angels. ⊠ *Defensa 422,* ☎ *11/4331–1668.* 🎟 *Free.*

El Centro

Your first glimpse of El Centro will most likely be en route from the airport. But be sure to return: Walking around the city center, dominated by a giant obelisk and the never-sleeping Avenida Corrientes, gives you a good feel for cosmopolitan Buenos Aires and its passionate Latin spirit. From the packed pedestrians-only Calle Florida and Calle Lavalle to the urban calm of Plaza San Martín, this is the social and business center of Argentina.

Every subway line goes through El Centro, though the most logical stop is Estación 9 de Julio (alternately known as Estación Carlos Pelligrini), which puts you right at the obelisk. The area is also accessible from Estación Plaza San Martín and Estación Lavalle.

A GOOD WALK

Start your walk on **Plaza San Martín** ㉗. On one side of the park is the **Palacio San Martín** ㉘ and on another, the **Círculo Militar** ㉙. Across Calle Marcelo T. de Alvear from the Círculo, behind the sixth-floor windows of the corner apartment at No. 994 Calle Maipú, are the rooms where Jorge Luis Borges lived and worked. Also right here are the **Edificio Ka-**

vanagh ⑳ and the landmark **Marriott Plaza Hotel** ㉛. The **Galería Ruth Benzacar** ㉜, with good contemporary art exhibits, forms the entrance to Calle Florida, down a set of stairs. Take this crowded pedestrians-only shopping street south to the **Galerías Pacífico** ㉝, one of the city's nicest shopping centers. Continue along Calle Florida to Avenida Corrientes, the "street that never sleeps"; it's lined with theaters and cinemas and bustles with activity day and night. Turn right (west) and walk toward the giant **Obelisco** ㉞. The **Teatro Colón** ㉟ is two blocks north of the obelisk on vast Avenida 9 de Julio.

TIMING AND PRECAUTIONS
Set aside a full day to explore El Centro. It's an easy area to navigate on foot, though summer heat and crowds may leave you begging for air-conditioning. On weekdays it's packed, on Saturday it's relatively calm, and by Sunday it's nearly deserted. (Many stores and most restaurants have limited hours on weekends.) In January most businesses (including banks) in El Centro close, though some may have limited hours. Although Calle Lavalle is a shopping and commercial center, it's also home to many of the city's adult entertainment establishments; take care when visiting the area at night.

SIGHTS TO SEE
㉙ **Circulo Militar** (Military Circle). A monument to the nobler historic pursuits of the Argentine armed forces, the Officers' Club was built by French architect Louis Sortais in 1902 in the heavily ornamental French style of the period. The **Museo Nacional de Armas** (National Arms Museum), in the basement, is packed with military memorabilia. ⊠ *Av. Santa Fe 750,* ☎ *11/4311–1071.* ⊡ *Free.* ⊘ *Mar.–Dec., Tues.–Fri. 2–7, Sat. 11–5, Sun. 1–6.*

㉚ **Edificio Kavanagh.** The soaring Kavanagh apartment building was constructed in the 1930s in the then-popular rationalist style by a displaced New Yorker. It's still one of the nicest-looking apartment buildings in the city. ⊠ *On San Martín, a few doors down from Plaza San Martín.*

㉜ **Galería Ruth Benzacar.** This well-designed gallery has monthly shows of significant modern Argentine artists. If you want a stimulating overview of contemporary Argentine art, ask to see the vast collection of paintings in the basement. ⊠ *Florida 1000,* ☎ *11/4313–8480.* ⊡ *Free.* ⊘ *Mon.–Sat. 9:30–8.*

㉝ **Galerías Pacífico.** The former headquarters of the Buenos Aires–Pacific Railway, the building was designed during Buenos Aires's turn-of-the-century golden age as a copy of Milan's Gallerie Vittorio Emanuele. In 1992 it was turned into a glossy, multilevel American-style shopping mall. In an earlier renovation a large skylighted dome was added, and five leading Argentine artists were commissioned to paint murals (☞ *Shopping, below*). ⊠ *Florida 753.*

㉛ **Marriott Plaza Hotel.** In 1908 local financier Ernesto Tornquist commissioned German architect Alfred Zucker to build the Plaza Hotel, a building that—like its namesake in New York City—still maintains its glow. ⊠ *Plaza San Martín.*

㉞ **Obelisco.** This enormous 221½-ft-tall obelisk is one of the city's most prominent landmarks; it was built in 1936 as part of a major public-works program. If you're in Buenos Aires during an election or a major soccer match, you'll witness crowds of Porteños surrounding the obelisk, voicing their opinions about the day's events. ⊠ *Av. 9 de Julio and Corrientes.*

㉘ **Palacio San Martín.** Once the residence of the Anchorena family, the San Martín Palace has been the Ministry of Foreign Affairs since 1936. The ornate building, designed in 1909 by Alejandro Cristophersen in grandiose French neoclassical style, is an example of the turn-of-the-century opulence of Buenos Aires. ⊠ *Arenales 800.* ⊘ *Not open to public.*

OFF THE BEATEN PATH

MUSEO DE ARTE HISPANOAMERICANO ISAAC FERNÁNDEZ BLANCO – Built as the residence of the architect Martín Noel in the late 18th century in an eclectic post–Spanish colonial style, it's now home to the Isaac Fernández Blanco Hispanic-American Art Museum. The extensive collection of colonial silver, wood carvings, and paintings gives you a sense of the wealth and the quality of craftsmanship in colonial South America. The overgrown, almost junglelike garden provides an awesome background for the outdoor theatrical performances mounted here during the summer. ⊠ *Suipacha 1422,* ☎ *11/4327–0228.* ⊠ *Admission.* ⊘ *Feb.– Dec., Tues.–Sun. 2–8.*

㉗ **Plaza San Martín.** Once a field in a muddy suburb at the northern end of the city next to the steep riverbank, San Martín Square gradually evolved into its present state. At one time populated by vagrants and marginal members of the rough-and-tumble colonial society, the area around the square was transformed in the late 1800s into the site of some of the most sumptuous town houses in Buenos Aires. The imposing bronze equestrian monument to General José de San Martín, created in 1862 by French artist Louis Daumas, dominates the park. French landscape architect Charles Thays designed the plaza in the 19th century, using a mix of traditional local and exotic imported trees. To get a feel for real life in Buenos Aires, plan a visit to Plaza San Martín during a weekday lunch hour and relax in the crowded park while you watch business deals being hashed out and young lovers sneaking a kiss.

NEED A BREAK?

Wouldn't now be the perfect time for a great glass of Argentine wine in a cool, hidden grotto? Then head to **Tancat** (⊠ Paraguay 645, ☎ 11/ 4312–5442), a dark, friendly establishment where you'll most likely end up sitting at the bar as there's only one table. The menu consists of whatever the chef decides to cook that day, but the food is always good.

★ ㉟ **Teatro Colón.** This opera house opened in 1908 and has hosted the likes of Maria Callas, Arturo Toscanini, Igor Stravinsky, Enrico Caruso, and Luciano Pavarotti. Argentines proudly claim that the theater has the best acoustics in the world, and few would argue. The Italianate building with French decoration is the result of a joint effort by several successive turn-of-the-century architects. The seven-tier theater has a central chandelier with a sprawling diameter of 21 ft. Yet because there are only 2,500 seats, many of which are held by season-ticket holders, the lines stretch around the block when an international celebrity is starring. A fascinating guided tour of the theater and museum provides a glimpse at the building's inner workshops, 45 ft below the street. The international season runs from April to November. ⊠ *Toscanini 1180,* ☎ *11/4382–6632.* ⊠ *Admission.* ⊘ *Jan.–Mar., tours hourly weekdays 10–5; fewer tours in winter.*

La Recoleta

La Recoleta, an elegant district northwest of downtown, is packed with boutiques, cafés, handsome old apartment buildings, plazas, museums, and cultural centers. Once a neighborhood where nobody wanted to live, today La Recoleta is one of Buenos Aires's most sought-after districts. About 25 years ago a few brave entrepreneurs decided to take advantage of its low rents, opening some of the city's best restaurants. Upscale, European-style boutiques followed, and then members of Argentina's high society began moving here as well. Part of La Recoleta is now closed to traffic, and street-side cafés dot the area. Here people-watching is a highly developed art form, practiced predominantly by the perennially tanned and trim.

A GOOD WALK

Begin your walk on **Plazoleta Carlos Pelligrini** ㊱. On one side is the **Alzaga Unzué** ㊲. Follow elegant Avenida Alvear, lined with some of the best in French-style architecture and boutiques and the beautiful **Alvear Palace Hotel** ㊳. Continue along Alvear to the **Cementerio de La Recoleta** ㊴. Bordering the cemetery is the **Basílica del Pilar** ㊵. Just down the block from the basilica is the **Centro Cultural La Recoleta** ㊶, where art shows and performances are held. Below the cultural center is the Design Center (☞ Shopping, *below*), a mall filled entirely with home-furnishings stores. To your right, at the bottom of the hill, is the yellow **Palais de Glace–Salas Nacionales de Cultura** ㊷, which hosts temporary exhibits. From here walk west along Avenida del Libertador, past Plaza Francia and **Plaza Mitre** ㊸ to reach the **Museo Nacional de Bellas Artes** ㊹, the city's major art museum, the **Biblioteca Nacional** ㊺, a modern library, and the **Museo Nacional de Arte Decorativo** ㊻, a decorative arts museum.

TIMING AND PRECAUTIONS

Count on at least half a day to explore La Recoleta, though you could easily spend a morning or afternoon in the cemetery or art museum alone. In general, this is one of the city's safest areas and can be visited day and night.

SIGHTS TO SEE

㊳ **Alvear Palace Hotel.** The city's most traditional, old-world hotel opened its doors in 1932. It remains a principal gathering place for the Porteño elite. The elegant lobby is a great spot to stop for tea or a drink (☞ Lodging, *below*). ✉ *Av. Alvear 1891,* ☎ *11/4808–2100 or 11/4804–7777.*

㊲ **Alzaga Unzué.** This French Renaissance–style house built in the late 19th century was saved from demolition by a group of local conservationists in the Perón era. Now a part of the Park Hyatt Hotel (☞ Lodging, *below*), the tower of the hotel rises from what was once the garden, and the old house is now called La Mansion. ✉ *Posadas 1086.*

㊵ **Basílica del Pilar.** In 1732 Franciscan monks built the Basilica of the Pillar and its cloister, which are fine examples of early colonial baroque. The principal altar is made of engraved silver from Peru. Today the church is a popular place for weddings, and you can sometimes see the elegantly dressed guests mingling with the craftspeople who hold a weekend fair on the slopes of the adjoining park. ✉ *Junin 1898,* ☎ *11/4803–6793.* 🎟 *Free.* ☉ *Weekdays 7:30–1 and 4–8:30, weekends 1–6.*

㊺ **Biblioteca Nacional.** It took three decades to build the National Library, which was finally inaugurated in 1991. The eccentric modern building was the result of a design competition won by Argentine architects Clorindo Testa and Francisco Bullrich. ✉ *Aguero 2502,* ☎ *11/4806–6155.* 🎟 *Free.* ☉ *Mon.–Sat. 10–7.*

★ ㊴ **Cementerio de La Recoleta.** As you enter the tall, ominous gates of the vast, 13½-acre La Recoleta Cemetery, you can feel history around you. You may sense the wealth as well, since this is the costliest bit of land in all of Argentina, and it contains the elaborate mausoleums of a veritable who's who of Argentine history: presidents, political leaders, soldiers, authors, and other heroes. The cemetery also functions as a mini-tour of art, sculpture, and architecture. Mausoleums were built to resemble chapels, Greek temples, pyramids, and scaled-down versions of family homes. In some you need to go inside to see what's special; for a small tip you can get a caretaker to open one of the multifloor mausoleums for a peek inside. The embalmed body of Eva Duarte de Perón rests here in the Duarte family tomb. To find Evita, from the entrance walk straight to the first major crossway and turn left; walk straight until a mausoleum stands in your way; walk around it on the right and then turn right; continue three rows down and turn left (or, just follow the tourists who pay tribute at her tomb). Look, too, for the flowers placed on the tomb and the epitaph in Spanish that reads "Don't Cry for Me." Also, look for is the statue of Luis Angel Firpo, the world heavyweight boxing champion known as the Bull of the Pampas. There's no map of the cemetery, so be prepared to walk in circles. ⊠ *Entrance on Junin.* ⊙ *Daily 10–5.*

㊶ Centro Cultural La Recoleta. On weekends this cultural center attracts thousands of visitors to its exhibits, concerts, and performances. It's also a resource for other arts events happening around the city. ⊠ *Junin 1930,* ☎ *11/4803–1041.* ▧ *Free.* ⊙ *Tues.–Sat. after 2 (call for specific hrs), all day Sun.*

★ ㊻ Museo Nacional de Arte Decorativo. The National Museum of Decorative Art is in a magnificent French classical landmark building (it's worth the price of admission just to enter this breathtaking structure). It houses a fascinating collection of furnishings and home decor; most was donated by Argentina's leading families. Also here is the **Museo de Arte Oriental** (Museum of Eastern Art), which has art and articles from places such as India and the Middle East. The museum café is great for a snack. ⊠ *Av. del Libertador 1902,* ☎ *11/4801–8248.* ▧ *Admission.* ⊙ *Weekdays 2–8, weekends 11–7.*

★ ㊹ Museo Nacional de Bellas Artes. Buenos Aires's only major art museum, the National Museum of Fine Arts is housed in a building that was once the city's waterworks. The museum's collection includes several major Impressionist paintings and an overview of 19th- and 20th-century Argentine art. The highlight is a room dedicated to Paraguayan War scenes painted by a soldier, Cándido López, whose work is also in the Museo Histórico Nacional (☞ San Telmo, *above*). The new wing has a selection of contemporary Argentine art and temporary exhibits. ⊠ *Av. del Libertador 1473,* ☎ *11/4803–0802 for a tour.* ▧ *Free.* ⊙ *Tues.–Sun. 12:30–7:30.*

㊷ Palais de Glace–Salas Nacionales de Cultura. Always worth checking out are the changing exhibits, ranging from fine art to ponchos to national foods, at the Mirror Palace–National Cultural Exhibition Halls. The banner outside will tell you what's going on. ⊠ *Posadas 1725,* ☎ *11/4805–4354.* ▧ *Admission.* ⊙ *Weekdays 1–8, weekends 3–8.*

㊸ Plaza Mitre. A large equestrian statue of General Bartolomé Mitre, the military hero and former president, dominates this square on Avenida del Libertador between Calle Luis Agote and Calle Aguero. The site, which was once at the edge of the river, provides a perspective on the surrounding parks.

㊱ Plazoleta Carlos Pellegrini. Carlos Pellegrini Square is surrounded by a cluster of mansions, which were once residences of the country's large landowning families and are now apartment buildings.

Palermo

Palermo, a district of parks and lakes surrounded by quiet streets and elegant mansions, offers a peaceful escape from the rush of downtown

Buenos Aires. Families flock to the parks on weekends to picnic, suntan, bicycle, rollerblade, and jog. Palermo is also home to the polo field and the horse racetrack and is thus the center of horse culture in Buenos Aires. One of the city's largest barrios, Palermo has many distinct sub-neighborhoods: Palermo Viejo has classic Spanish-style architecture; Las Cañitas is a trendy place to go out at night; and Palermo Chico is an elegant residential area. Some of the most expensive real estate in Argentina is found along Avenida del Libertador, which cuts Palermo down the middle. Don't let Palermo's daytime tranquillity fool you: it has some of the city's best nightlife, with neighborhood bars and discos that rock to Latin beats. The Estación Plaza Italia, on Line D, takes you to the zoo and the botanical gardens in Palermo.

A GOOD WALK

Some of the city's biggest parks are found in this neighborhood around the **Plaza Italia,** at the intersection of Avenida Sarmiento, Calle Santa Fe, and Calle Las Heras: the **Jardín Botánico,** the **Jardín Zoológico,** and the **Sociedad Rural Argentina,** the city's fairgrounds. Palermo's largest park, the **Parque Tres de Febrero,** is farther down Avenida Sarmiento. Essentially a part of the park, though technically freestanding, the **Paseo del Rosedal** is abloom, in season, with all kinds of roses. Deeper into the park is the **Jardín Japonés,** a lovely Japanese garden, and the **Planetario Galileo Galilei,** the planetarium.

TIMING AND PRECAUTIONS

An even-paced ramble through Palermo should take no more than two hours, though you could easily spend an entire afternoon at the zoo, the Japanese Garden, and the Botanical Garden. If you're up for shopping, visit Alto Palermo (☞ Shopping, *below*), one of the city's nicer shopping centers (at the Bulnes stop on the D line), and the neighboring boutiques along Avenida Santa Fe.

SIGHTS TO SEE

Jardín Botánico. The Botanical Garden is a welcome, unexpected oasis in the city. Enclosed by large wrought-iron gates, it's hard to imagine the beauty inside until you enter. Modeled after an 18th-century French garden, the long, winding paths and hidden statues conjure up images of the gardens at Versailles. ⊠ *Av. Santa Fe 3817,* ☎ *11/4831–2951.* ☜ *Free.* ⊙ *Dawn–dusk.*

NEED A BREAK?	Near the Botanical Garden and steps away from the Palermo Polo field is **La Cátedra** (⊠ at Cerviño and Sinclair, ☎ 11/4777–4601), a perfect spot for lunch or a drink. In good weather you can eat outdoors.

★ **Jardín Japonés.** This unexpected haven, run by the Japanese Cultural Society, is a fine Japanese garden. It has streams, bridges, and fishponds (you can buy food to feed the already well-fed fish). The garden is particularly beautiful at sunset. ⊠ *Avs. Casares and Adolfo Berro,* ☎ *11/4804–4922.* ☜ *Admission.* ⊙ *Dawn–dusk.*

☀ **Jardín Zoológico.** The Buenos Aires zoo, where you'll find indigenous monkeys, birds, and many other animals, is a popular weekend destination for families. The animals aren't always kept in cages according to species type, so be prepared to see some interesting and unexpected cage mates. At the entrance to the zoo you can get a horse-drawn carriage to take you through the zoo and the Botanical Garden. ⊠ *República de la India 2900,* ☎ *11/4806–7412.* ☜ *Admission.*

☀ **Parque Tres de Febrero.** Palermo's main park, just north of Calle Sarmiento, has 1,000 acres of woods, lakes, and walking trails. Paddle boats can be rented for use on the small lakes, and joggers, bikers, and rollerbladers all compete for the right of way on the miles of paved lanes. It's packed on weekends, with cars parked on the grass and soccer balls flying everywhere. Drinks and snacks are available at one of the park's cafés as well as along Avenida del Libertador.

NEED A BREAK?	Have a snack or coffee in the café of the **Museo Renault** (✉ Av. Figueroa Alcorta 3399, ☎ 11/4802–9626), about a 10-minute walk from the Parque Tres de Febrero.

★ **Paseo del Rosedal.** The Rose Garden is a picturesque park full of fountains, statues of literati, and roses. On a Saturday in spring you're practically guaranteed to see a wedding here. ✉ *Av. del Libertador and Paseo de la Infanta.*

Planetario Galileo Galilei. The Galileo Galilei Planetarium, on the western side of the Parque Tres de Febrero, presents weekend-afternoon astronomy shows. ✉ *Sarmiento and Belisario Roldán,* ☎ 11/4771–6629.

Plaza Italia. This busy square at the intersection of Calle Santa Fe, Calle Las Heras, and Calle Sarmiento is a landmark in the area and a good place to meet. On weekends there's a crafts fair. ✉ *At Santa Fe and Thames.*

⟳ **Sociedad Rural Argentina** (Rural Society of Argentina). Exhibitions relating to agriculture and cattle raising are often held at the fairgrounds here. The biggest is the annual monthlong (usually in August) **Exposición Rural** (Rural Exposition), where you can see livestock such as cows and horses, gaucho shows, and expert horse performances. ☎ 11/4774–1072.

Belgrano

Primarily a residential area, this fashionable, quiet district is home to beautiful mansions, luxury high-rises, and well-kept cobblestone streets leading off bustling Avenida Cabildo. To reach Belgrano, take Line D to Estación Virrey del Piño.

A GOOD WALK

Head first to the **Museo de Arte Española Enrique Larreta** for a taste of Spanish colonial art. Then cross the street to the **Museo Histórico Sarmiento,** a shrine to independence from Spain. From here walk across the small **Plaza Manuel Belgrano** to reach the **Parroquia de Nuestra Señora de la Inmaculada Concepción.** After visiting the church, take a break at one of the many cafés nearby. Two blocks along Calle Juramento from the church, across busy Avenida Cabildo, is the **Mercado,** an open-air food market; it's worth the seemingly treacherous avenue crossing to experience this traditional market. Go in the other direction on Calle Juramento and take a right on Calle Tres de Febrero, a fancy residential street, to reach the **Museo Nacional del Hombre,** an anthropology museum.

TIMING AND PRECAUTIONS

This walk can be done in 2–3 hours. If you want to see all the museums, it's best to visit in the afternoon, when they're all open. The atmospheric cafés around the church serve patrons 24 hours a day. Belgrano is very safe as it's patrolled around the clock by private security and city police; there's rarely any crime, except for the occasional purse snatching.

SIGHTS TO SEE

Mercado. This open-air local market is a treasure trove of everything you'd expect to find—cheese, fresh vegetables, and local meat—as well as a few surprises. Vendors bring their wares straight from local farms, and bartering and bargaining is common. ⊠ *Juramento and Ciudad de la Paz.* ⊙ *Daily 5 PM–11 PM.*

★ **Museo de Arte Española Enrique Larreta.** Once the beautiful home and gardens of a Spanish governor, the building now houses the Enrique Larreta Museum of Spanish Art, home to one of Argentina's best collections of colonial art. ⊠ *Juramento 2291,* ☎ *11/4783–2640.* ☒ *Admission; Tues. free.* ⊙ *Mon.–Tues. and Fri. 2–7:45, weekends 3–7:45.*

Museo Histórico Sarmiento. The charming, colonial-style Sarmiento Historical Museum gives you yet another opportunity to learn about the history of Argentina through all kinds of art and artifacts. *Cuba 2079,* ☎ *11/4783–7555.* ☒ *Admission.* ⊙ *Tues.–Fri. and Sun. 3–8. Guided tours are available in Spanish at 4 PM Sun.*

Museo Nacional del Hombre. It won't take you long to visit the Museum of the History of Man museum, where human development is explained from a Latin-American perspective. ⊠ *Tres de Febrero 1370–8,* ☎ *11/4782–7251.* ☒ *Free.* ⊙ *Weekdays 10–6.*

Parroquia de Nuestra Señora de la Inmaculada Concepción. The beautiful, brightly colored Our Lady of the Immaculate Conception Church was modeled after Rome's Pantheon. ⊠ *Vuelta de Obligado 2042,* ☎ *11/4783–8008,* ⊙ *Mon.–Sat. 7:30–noon and 4–8:30, Sun. 7:30–1:30 and 4–9:15.*

Plaza Manuel Belgrano. This square, named after General Belgrano, the War of Independence hero, is the site of a bustling art fair on weekends. During the week it's a simple city plaza, with a little playground filled with families and schoolchildren.

Dining

All kinds of international fare is available in Buenos Aires, but most common are parrillas—restaurants serving grilled meat. These vary from upscale eateries to local spots. Different cuts of beef are available, as are chicken, sausage, and grilled cheese (*provoleta*). Meat dishes are generally accompanied by french fries and salad. Many restaurants also serve pasta (often homemade).

Cafés are a big part of Buenos Aires culture, and those in good locations are always busy, from breakfast to long after dinner. Some, called *confiterías,* have a wider selection of food—open-face sandwiches, grilled ham and cheese, "triples" (three-decker clubs filled with ham, cheese, tomatoes, olives, eggs, and onion), sandwiches made on *medias lunas* (croissants), salads, and desserts.

American

$ ✕ **Big Momma.** Argentina's version of a deli has a little bit of everything you'd expect (except pickles), such as made-to-order sandwiches, hot pastrami, bagels and lox, and even knishes. ⊠ *At Migueletes and Matienzo, Palermo,* ☎ *11/4772–0926. AE, DC, MC, V.*

Argentine

$$$$ ✕ **Cabaña las Lilas.** Presidents, movie stars, and Porteños come here
★ for the best meat in Buenos Aires. In fact, the restaurant has its own *estancia* (ranch) where it raises cattle for its grilled lomito and *cuadrillo* (beef cheeks). The wine cellar is well stocked with superb Argentine wines (try the Catena Zapata). Service is impeccable. If you have to wait long for a table, as you undoubtedly will, enjoy a glass of champagne in the cigar bar. ⊠ *Av. Dávila 516, Puerto Madero,* ☎ *11/4313–1336. AE, DC, V.*

$$$$ ✕ **Harper's.** A fashionable lunch and dinner spot, Harper's is popular with a cross section of locals—from yuppies to businesspeople to neighborhood folks. They come here to enjoy tender steak and a hearty plate of pasta as well as a traditional favorite, *cordero del diablo* (a tangy lamb dish). Paintings by local artists hang on the walls. ⊠ *R. M. Ortíz 1763, La Recoleta,* ☎ *11/4801–7140. AE, MC, V.*

$$$ ✕ **Las Nazarenas.** Across the street from the Sheraton, in a two-story Spanish colonial–style building with wrought-iron sconces and potted ferns, this parrilla is a favorite lunch stop for businesspeople. Meat is the order of the day, whether grilled steaks, brochettes, or *chivito* (kid). For an appetizer, order the matambre, the grilled provolone cheese sprinkled with oregano, or the delicious empanadas. ⊠ *Reconquista 1132, El Centro,* ☎ *11/4312–5559. AE, DC, MC, V. Subte: Estación San Martín.*

$$$ ✕ **Novecento.** This bistro has an American theme—New York City street
★ signs hang on the walls and the menu is in English and Spanish (in fact, there's also a Novecento in New York City's Soho). Yet the food, atmosphere, and crowd are all chic Porteño. The candlelit tables are close together, which makes for intimate seating. The beef salad, a pyramid of alternating layers of green salad, steak, and french fries, is especially good. In summer there's outdoor dining. ⊠ *Báez 199, Palermo,* ☎ *11/4778–1900. V. Subte: Estación Palermo.*

$$$ ✕ **Río Alba.** Stacked wine bottles, hanging hams, and sports-related memorabilia form the backdrop to such dishes as grilled tuna, salmon, and trout; or try the juicy, lean pork with lemon slices and shoestring potatoes. Right by the American Embassy, it's a noisy hangout for American expats. ⊠ *Cerviño 4499, Palermo,* ☎ *11/4773–9508. AE, DC, MC, V. Subte: Estación Palermo.*

$$$ ✕ **Tierra de los Cocineros.** An unusual mix of Argentine fare like
★ *lomito* (a cut of beef similar to filet mignon, often served thinly sliced as a sandwich) and *ñoquis* (gnocchi) and international dishes like pad thai and curry chicken are available at this bright, modern restaurant. It's extremely popular with a business-lunch crowd, so it can take a while to get a table at midday. ⊠ *Juncal 810, El Centro,* ☎ *11/4393–2010. AE, DC, MC, V. Closed Sun. Subte: Estación Plaza San Martín.*

$$–$$$ ✕ **Calle de los Angeles.** The name of this restaurant, Street of the Angels, accurately depicts the decor (made to look like you're outside on the street) in this fun but somewhat touristy spot. Tables line both walls of the long, narrow dining room, a winding brick path runs down the middle, and tree branches hang overhead, which makes you feel as if you are dining alfresco somewhere in Spain. But the food is well-prepared and artfully served Argentine parrilla. ⊠ *Chile 318, Plaza de Mayo,* ☎ *11/4361–8822. No credit cards.*

$$–$$$ ✕ **Club del Vino.** With its wine cellar, wine museum, and wine boutique, this is paradise if you love wine. The prix fixe wine taster's menu includes *milanesa* (a very traditional Argentine dish of pounded meat, breaded and fried) with sweet potatoes and flan, accompanied by merlot, Malbec, and cabernet. ⊠ *Cabrera 4737, Palermo,* ☎ *11/4833–0048. AE, DC, MC, V. ☉ No lunch. Subte: Estación Palermo.*

$$ ✕ **Munich Recoleta.** This jam-packed place has been a favorite gath-
★ ering spot for almost 40 years. The basic fare consists of great steak, creamed spinach, and shoestring potatoes, all served quickly and in generous portions. The lively atmosphere attracts young and old alike. Arrive early if you don't want to wait. ⊠ *R. M. Ortíz 1879, La Recoleta,* ☎ *11/4804–3981. Reservations not accepted. No credit cards.*

$$ ✕ **El Palacio de la Papa Frita.** A good place for a quick meal before or after a movie, this family establishment is always packed. There's lots of good, solid food—everything from chicken salad to spaghetti to grilled steak and fries. ⊠ *Lavalle 735, El Centro,* ☎ *11/4393–5849. AE, DC, MC, V. Subte: Estación Lavalle.*

$–$$ ✕ **Melo.** In Barrio Norte, a neighborhood bordering El Centro and La
★   Recoleta, Melo serves up traditional steaks, salads, and pastas. Portions are huge—usually big enough for two, and the friendly atmosphere
makes up for the sparse decor. Particularly good is the brochette of meat
and vegetables. ⊠ *Pachero de Melo, El Centro,* ☎ *11/4801–4251. No
credit cards.*

$–$$ ✕ **El Obrero.** When the rock band U2 played in Buenos Aires in 1998,
they asked to be taken to the most traditional Argentine restaurant in
the city—and this is where they were brought. A bustling hole-in-the-
wall, it serves consistently good steaks, sweetbreads, sausages, and grilled
chicken. The stark walls and cheap (even by Argentine standards)
wine make it clear that you're not in a jacket-and-tie kind of place,
but the food is cheap, fast, and always enjoyable. Note: Some cab drivers may not want to take you to the area around this restaurant; also
you should expect a wait. ⊠ *Augustín R. Caffarena 64, La Boca,* ☎
11/4363–9912. No credit cards. Closed Jan.

$–$$ ✕ **Pippo.** This is the place to go for *estofado* (a traditional meat sauce)
and pasta as well as lomito and french fries. The food is inexpensive,
the atmosphere is relaxed, and you're allowed to linger over your food
as long as you like. ⊠ *Paraná 356, El Centro,* ☎ *11/4374–6365. No
credit cards. No dinner Sun. Subte: Estación Tribunales.*

$ ✕ **Ña Serapia.** Tasty tamales and *locro* (a stew of hard corn, cooked
slowly over days) and inexpensive wine make this a perfect quick stop
in Palermo. The place is small, and the atmosphere is no-frills, but the
food is consistently good. It's also one of the few restaurants with an
Argentine menu that doesn't focus specifically on grilled meat. ⊠ *Av.
Las Heras 3357, Palermo,* ☎ *11/4801–5307. No credit cards.*

$ ✕ **La Querencia.** This country-style restaurant serves various types of
empanadas and tamales as well as rich local soups and stews such as
the traditional locro. Seating is on stools, but you can also carry out.
There are two locations in El Centro. ⊠ *Esmeralda 1392,* ☎ *11/
4822–4644. Subte: Estación San Martín;* ⊠ *Junin 1304,* ☎ *11/4393–
3202. Subte: Estación Facultad de Medicina. No credit cards. Closed
Sun.*

$ ✕ **El Sanjuanino.** Empanadas and other traditional fare from the Andes
are made at this long-established spot. Though you can get a quick bite
here, it's primarily a takeout place. ⊠ *Posadas 1515, La Recoleta,* ☎
11/4804–2909. No credit cards. Closed Mon.

Asian

$$$ ✕ **Lotus neo Thai.** At this enchanting Thai restaurant, colorful flower
lamps reach for the ceiling, and glowing candles bob in carefully placed
bowls. Excellent dishes include red curried beef in coconut milk with
pumpkin and basil leaves, fried coconut shrimp with sweet and sour
tamarind sauce, and stir-fried rice vermicelli with minced shrimp,
chicken, and pork. The fruit drinks are delicious but can make your
bill add up. ⊠ *Ortega y Gasset 1782, Palermo,* ☎ *11/4771–4449. AE,
MC. No lunch. Subte: Estación Palermo.*

$$–$$$ ✕ **Tao Tao.** Porteños come from all over the city for the locally influ-
★   enced Japanese and Chinese fare at Tao Tao. It's also not uncommon
to see ambassadors and visiting dignitaries from Asian countries here.
The surroundings are formal Chinese; the multilingual staff is excel-
lent. As an appetizer, sample the crunchy *empanaditas* (an Argentine
version of spring rolls), and for a main dish, opt for the lobster rice or
the Japanese salad. ⊠ *Av. Cabildo 1418, Belgrano,* ☎ *11/4783–5806.
Reservations essential on Sat. AE, V. Closed Mon. Subte: Estación Jose
Hernandez/Virrey del Piño.*

$ ✕ **Sensu.** Eat in or take out your food at this Japanese restaurant. The
food is good—especially the salmon (there are also shrimp, beef, and

chicken dishes, though no sushi)—and the mixed vegetables that come with every dish are a welcome change from the solitary steak plates served in most Argentine restaurants. ⊠ *Florida 528, El Centro,* ☎ *11/4393–9595. No credit cards.*

Cafés

$ ╳ **La Biela.** This La Recoleta café is a popular local spot for sipping espressos, gossiping, and people-watching. Although there are tables inside, where the decor is Paris-inspired, the outdoor tables are the place to be in warm weather. ⊠ *At Quintana and Junin, La Recoleta. V.*

$ ╳ **Florida Garden.** Sit elbow to elbow along the 20-ft bar or in the sitting room upstairs, and enjoy afternoon tea or some of the richest hot chocolate in the city. ⊠ *Florida 889, near the Plaza San Martín, El Centro,* ☎ *11/4312–7902. No credit cards. Subte: Estación Plaza San Martín.*

$ ╳ **Gran Café Tortoni.** Dating from 1858, this confitería is the oldest in
★ town. Its wooden tables, original artwork, and decorated ceilings are reminiscent of a faded, glorious past. Carlos Gardel, one of Argentina's most famous tango stars, writer José Luis Borges, Argentinian presidents, and many visiting dignitaries and intellectuals have had coffee here. On weekends nights there's a tango show (reservations essential). ⊠ *Near Plaza de Mayo at Av. de Mayo 829, El Centro,* ☎ *11/4342– 4328. AE, MC, V. Subte: Estación Avenida de Mayo.*

$ ╳ **Ideal.** Charming and a little bit tattered, this café makes you feel
★ like you've gone back in time. Not only can you come here for coffee, but you can also take beginning tango lessons and see experts perform on Tuesday and Friday nights. Some of the 1998 film *The Tango Lesson* was shot here. Unlike the Gran Café Tortoni (☞ *above*), it's fairly easy to get a table here; just beware the grouchy waiters who pretend not to understand tourists. ⊠ *Suipacha 384, near corner of Av. Corrientes, El Centro,* ☎ *11/4326–0521. AE, MC, V. Subte: Estación 9 de Julio.*

$ ╳ **Petit Paris Café.** The crystal chandeliers and marble tabletops make this place feel especially like a Parisian café. A variety of coffees are served, as are tasty salads and sandwiches. ⊠ *Av. Santa Fe 774, El Centro,* ☎ *11/4312–5885. AE. Subte: Estación Plaza San Martín.*

English

$$$ ╳ **Alexander.** Come here for the food, not the decor. The rack of lamb—not a common sight on Argentine menus—melts in the mouth, and the purées of vegetables such as sweet potato, squash, and pumpkin are delicious. Lunch is usually very busy. ⊠ *San Martín 774, El Centro,* ☎ *11/4311–2878. Reservations essential. AE, DC, MC, V. Closed Sun. Subte: Estación Plaza San Martín.*

$$$ ╳ **Down Town Matias.** Tucked behind the Plaza Hotel on the ground floor of a modern high-rise, this restaurant serves such typical English fare as lamb stew and chicken pie in a chummy, publike atmosphere. ⊠ *San Martín 979, El Centro,* ☎ *11/4312–9844. AE, DC, MC, V. Subte: Estación Plaza San Martín.*

French

$$$$ ╳ **Catalinas.** Superb seafood and game dishes await you at this French
★ restaurant that resembles a country inn. The lobster tail on fresh eggs, with caviar and cream, and the *pejerrey* (a small freshwater fish) stuffed with king-crab mousse are particularly savory. The dining room is packed wall to wall with businesspeople at lunch, but it draws a more varied crowd at night. Several fixed-price menus make this gourmet's delight easier on the pocket, but beware—Catalinas's wines and desserts can double the price of your meal. ⊠ *Reconquista 875, El Centro,* ☎ *11/4313–0182. Reservations essential. Jacket and tie. AE, DC, MC, V. Closed Sun. Subte: Estación Florida.*

Buenos Aires Dining and Lodging

Dining

Alexander, **13**
La Biela, **25**
Big Momma, **33**
Bonpler, **8**
Cabaña las Lilas, **19**
Calle de los Angeles, **2**
Catalinas, **18**
Club del Vino, **31**
Club Vasco Francés, **4**

Down Town Matías, **15**
Filo, **16**
Florida Garden, **14**
La Fornarina, **39**
Gran Café Tortoni, **7**
Harper's, **28**
Ideal, **11**
Katmandu, **41**
Ligure, **22**
Lotus neo Thai, **37**

Melo, **29**
Memorabilia, **12**
Morelia, **35**
Munich Recoleta, **26**
Ña Serapia, **34**
Las Nazarenas, **17**
Novecento, **32**
El Obrero, **1**
El Palacio de la Papa Frita, **10**
Petit Paris Café, **23**

Pippo, **5**
Pizza Cero, **36**
La Querencia, **20**
Río Alba, **30**
San Babila, **27**
El Sanjuanino, **24**
Sensu, **9**
Taberna Baska, **3**
Tao Tao, **38**
Tierra de los Cocineros, **21**

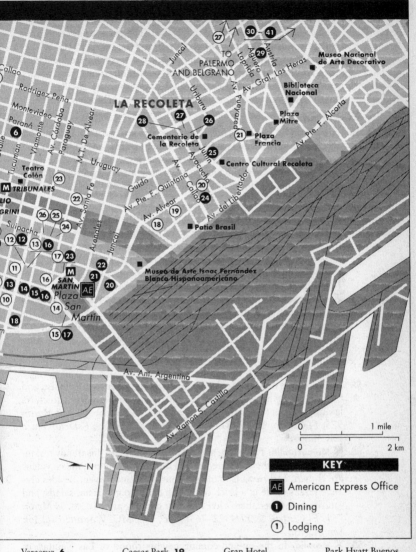

$$ ✕ **Ligure.** French cuisine adapted to Argentine tastes is the specialty here. You can get dishes like thistles *au gratin* as well as the more standard steak *au poivre* with brandy sauce. The dessert pancakes are a must. ✉ *Juncal 855, El Centro,* ☎ *11/4394–8226. AE, MC, V.*

$ ✕ **Bonpler.** If you're looking for a quick meal, come here for Argentine-style French fast food (seating is available): Salads, sandwiches, croissants, muffins, and coffee. ✉ *Florida 481, at Lavalle,* ☎ *11/ 4325–9900. No credit cards. Closed Sun. Subte: Estación Florida.*

Indian

$$$–$$$$ ✕ **Katmandu.** This cozy, off-the-beaten-path spot north of Palermo has eclectic Hindu art and two floors of Indian wares. The Indian food—especially the curries and breads—is some of the best in Buenos Aires. The crowd is primarily made up of expats living in Argentina and yuppie Porteños. ✉ *Cordoba 3547, Palermo,* ☎ *11/4963–1122. AE, DC, MC, V. Closed Sun.*

Italian

$$$–$$$$ ✕ **San Babila.** This trattoria is one of the city's most popular Italian restaurants. *Pappardelle al pesto* (butterfly pasta in a pesto sauce) and *tortelloni di zucca* (oversize tortellini with pumpkin filling) are good bets, and the fixed-price menus give you more options. ✉ *R. M. Ortíz 1815, La Recoleta,* ☎ *11/4802–8981. AE, DC, MC, V.*

$$$ ✕ **La Fornarina.** This cozy basement eatery in the heart of the fash-
★ ionable Belgrano district is worth the $8 cab ride from El Centro. The homemade pastas and desserts are excellent. Traditional Argentine cuisine is also available. ✉ *Vuelta de Obligado, Belgrano,* ☎ *11/4783–4904. AE, DC, MC, V. Subte: Estación Juramento.*

Pizza

$$ ✕ **Filo.** Come here for the flat-bread pizza, the extensive drink list, and
★ the great party atmosphere. It's definitely not the place for a quiet, relaxing meal, as the popular bar is packed all the time. ✉ *San Martín 975, El Centro,* ☎ *11/4311–0312. AE, MC, V. Subte: Estación Plaza San Martín.*

$$ ✕ **Memorabilia.** The young and fashionable flock to this trendy restaurant-bar where the walls are painted orange and yellow, music videos are shown, and pizza is made in a purple-painted oven. Besides creative pizzas made in a brick oven, you can also get pasta, salads, and sandwiches. Often there's live music or dancing after 10 PM. ✉ *Maipú 761, El Centro,* ☎ *11/4322–7630. AE, DC, MC, V. Subte: Estación San Martín.*

$$ ✕ **Morelia.** In the up-and-coming neighborhood of Las Cañitas, in Palermo, is one of the best places in the city serving pizza cooked on a grill. After your meal, head across the street to one of the many trendy bars in the area. ✉ *Báez 260, Palermo,* ☎ *11/4772–0329. AE, DC, MC, V. No lunch. Subte: Estación Palermo.*

$$ ✕ **Pizza Cero.** New Age music, outdoor tables, and a dining room filled with fresh plants and flowers set the tone at this popular, upscale pizza parlor. The pizzas have crisp crusts and mozzarella cheese with an array of toppings, including eggplant, ham, and pineapple. Tasty salads and empanadas are also available. ✉ *Cerviño 3701, Palermo,* ☎ *11/4803–3449. V.*

Spanish

$$$ ✕ **Veracruz.** This old-fashioned restaurant has carefully prepared Spanish-style seafood dishes served by staid, seasoned waiters. Especially delicious is the *cazuela* (seafood stew with clams, shrimp, octopus, scallops, and lobster). ✉ *Uruguay 538, El Centro,* ☎ *11/4371–1413. MC, V. Closed Sun.*

$$ ✗ **Club Vasco Francés.** In an old racquet club, this spacious, spruced-up dining room is one of the few places in Buenos Aires where you can get frogs' legs. Seafood is flown in from Spain especially for homesick Basque diners. ⊠ *Moreno 1370, El Centro,* ☎ *11/4383–5021. AE, V. Closed Sun.*

$$ ✗ **Taberna Baska.** Old-world decor and efficient service are hallmarks of this busy, no-nonsense Spanish restaurant. Try such dishes as *chiripones en su tinta* (a variety of squid in ink). ⊠ *Chile 980, Plaza de Mayo,* ☎ *11/4334–0903. AE, DC, MC, V. Closed Mon. No dinner Sun.*

Vegetarian

$ ✗ **Yin-Yang.** Yin-Yang caters to health-conscious vegetarians with a well-balanced menu of large, tasty plates of brown rice, fresh vegetables, tofu, and vegetable tarts. There are two locations: one in El Centro and one in Belgrano. ⊠ *Paraguay 858,* ☎ *11/4311–7798. No credit cards. Subte: Estación 9 de Julio;* ⊠ *Echeverría 2444,* ☎ *11/4783–1546. DC, MC, V. Closed Sun. Subte: Estación Juramento (under construction and scheduled to have opened by January 2000).*

Lodging

Some the city's more expensive hotels were built for the 1978 World Cup, while others opened at the turn of the century or even before. With the exception of the top luxury hotels, most establishments have a small, family-run feel, with all the charming quirks that that entails. Most rooms have a bidet, but not every room has a television. In many of the smaller hotels, you can't make a direct-dial long-distance call from your room. Don't expect to see such amenities as ice makers or vending machines.

$$$$ 🏨 **Alvear Palace Hotel.** Built in 1932 as a luxury apartment building,
★ the Alvear has since become the city's most elegant hotel and is often the site of receptions for visiting diplomats and dignitaries. Rooms are done in French Empire–style, in regal burgundy and deep blue, and have large windows, silk drapes, and feather beds. The hotel is convenient to many museums and good restaurants. The hotel's own La Bourgogne may well be Argentina's only truly gourmet restaurant. The fare tends toward the Continental; the dress toward jacket and tie (reservations are essential). ⊠ *Av. Alvear 1891, La Recoleta 1129,* ☎ *11/4808–2100 or 11/4804–7777, 800/448–8355 in the U.S.,* ℻ *11/4804–0034. 100 rooms, 100 suites. Restaurant, coffee shop, lobby lounge, piano bar, tea shop, indoor pool, health club, concierge, business services, meeting rooms. AE, DC, MC, V.*

$$$$ 🏨 **Caesar Park.** Opposite Patio Bullrich, this Westin-operated hotel is near La Recoleta and Plaza San Martín. The lavish, spacious rooms have tasteful fabrics, period furniture, marble bathrooms, and good light, though they're a bit generic when compared with other historic hotels. Upper floors have a panoramic view of the river. If you're staying at the hotel, you have access (for a fee) to a nearby 18-hole golf course. The on-site Midori Japanese restaurant and sushi bar is brightly lighted, modern, and clean (reservations are essential). ⊠ *Posadas 1232, La Recoleta 1011,* ☎ *11/4819–1100, 800/228–3000 in the U.S.,* ℻ *11/4819–1120. 172 rooms, 20 suites. 3 restaurants, bar, in-room modem lines, room service, indoor pool, beauty salon, health club, business services, meeting rooms. AE, DC, MC, V.*

$$$$ 🏨 **Claridge.** The public rooms of this stylish hotel, with their wood paneling and high ceiling, have a distinctly British feel. There's an Anglo-Argentine clientele to match. Rooms are done in shades of blue, with dark wood furnishings with bronze fittings. The health club and pool

are nice pluses. ⊠ *Tucumán 535, El Centro 1049,* ☎ *11/4314–7700, 800/223–5652 in the U.S.,* ℻ *11/4314–8022. 155 rooms, 6 suites. Restaurant, bar, room service, pool, health club, concierge, business services, meeting rooms. AE, DC, MC, V.*

$$$$ 🏨 **El Conquistador.** This hotel, near Plaza San Martín, is popular with businesspeople. The wood paneling in the public rooms and the small art gallery in the lobby lend a cozy touch, and the cheerful restaurant serves breakfast and snacks. Large windows, flowered bedspreads, and light pink carpets brighten rooms. ⊠ *Suipacha 948, El Centro 1008,* ☎ *11/4328–3012,* ℻ *11/4328–3252. 130 rooms, 14 suites. Restaurant, piano bar, massage, sauna, exercise room. AE, DC, MC, V. Subte: Estación San Martín.*

$$$$ 🏨 **Crillon.** Right across from Plaza San Martín, the Crillon was built in classic French style in 1948 and remodeled in 1995. Front rooms have beautiful views and are large and luminous. The lobby is stately and sedate, which may explain why this establishment appeals to provincial governors and the well-to-do from the interior. ⊠ *Av. Santa Fe 796, El Centro 1059,* ☎ *11/4310–2000, 0800/84448,* ℻ *11/4310–2020. 84 rooms, 12 suites. Restaurant, bar, in-room safes, room service, concierge, business services, meeting room. AE, DC, MC, V. Subte: Estación Plaza San Martín.*

$$$$ 🏨 **Inter-Continental.** One of Buenos Aires's newest luxury hotels, the Inter-Continental was designed with Argentina of the 1930s in mind. The elegant lobby, with marble, leather, bronze, and wood, leads to an outdoor terrace with a fountain. Rooms are adorned with large black armoires, marble-top nightstands, sleeper chairs, and black-and-white photos of Buenos Aires. The hotel's location in Monserrat, just above El Centro, is a mixed blessing—the neighborhood is quiet, but there's not much to do nearby. ⊠ *Moreno 809, El Centro 1091,* ☎ *11/4340–7100,* ℻ *11/4340–7119. 315 rooms and suites. Restaurant, 2 bars, room service, indoor pool, health club, concierge, business services, meeting rooms, parking. AE, DC, MC, V.*

$$$$ 🏨 **Libertador Kempinski.** This European-style hotel near the banking district serves as the base for many visiting businesspeople. The lobby, with its marble floor, has a bar and is a good spot to rendezvous. Standard rooms are classic but petite; the pastel-shaded deluxe rooms have walk-in closets, marble baths, and mahogany furnishings. The third floor La Pergola restaurant serves mouthwatering Continental fare; reservations and a jacket and tie are de rigueur. ⊠ *Av. Córdoba 690, El Centro 1054,* ☎ *11/4322–8800,* ℻ *11/4322–9703. 197 rooms, 6 suites. Restaurant, bar, coffee shop, room service, indoor-outdoor pool, health club, concierge, meeting rooms, travel services. AE, DC, MC, V.*

$$$$ 🏨 **Marriott Plaza Hotel.** One of the city's grandest hotels is across from
★   Plaza San Martín. Marriott has poured millions into the hotel since it was purchased in 1994. Crystal chandeliers and Persian carpets decorate the public rooms—the president of Argentina likes to entertain visiting dignitaries here. Some rooms have great bay windows overlooking the park; all are spacious and elegantly appointed. The Plaza Hotel Grill is favored by executives and politicians for its extensive wine list and Continental menu (dress up and make reservations). ⊠ *Florida 1005, El Centro, 1005,* ☎ *11/4318–3000, 800/228–9290 in the U.S.,* ℻ *11/4318–3008. 274 rooms, 38 suites. 2 restaurants, bar, café, in-room safes, room service, pool, health club, concierge, business services, meeting rooms. AE, DC, MC, V. Subte: Estación San Martín.*

$$$$ 🏨 **Park Hyatt Buenos Aires.** On the edge of La Recoleta, the luxuri-
★   ous Park Hyatt has a 13-floor marble tower and an adjacent turn-of-the-century mansion, with private butler service for its handsome suites. This is where Madonna stayed for two months during the filming of *Evita.* In addition to its million-dollar art collection, the hotel

houses a beautiful Roman-style pool, health club, and landscaped garden. Guest rooms are the largest of any Buenos Aires hotel, and outstanding service ensures many repeat visitors (when you check in, the hotel staff sits down with you to determine your needs). ⊠ *Posadas 1086, La Recoleta 1011, ☎ 11/4326–1234, 800/233–1234 in the U.S.,* ꜰꜰ *11/4326–3736. 116 rooms, 50 suites. Restaurant, bar, coffee shop, room service, pool, health club, concierge, business services, meeting rooms. AE, DC, MC, V.*

$$$$ 🏨 **Sheraton Buenos Aires Hotel.** The headquarters of Sheraton's South American division, this huge hotel at the bottom of Plaza San Martín has a broad range of facilities. The standard-looking rooms have views of either the Río de la Plata or the British Clock Tower and park at Retiro. It's especially popular with American businesspeople and tour groups. In late 1996 the separate Park Tower, part of Sheraton's Luxury Group, was built next door with spacious, expensive rooms that have cellular phones, entertainment centers, and 24-hour butler service. ⊠ *San Martín 1225, El Centro 1104, ☎ 11/4318–9000, 800/325–3535 in the U.S.,* ꜰꜰ *11/4318–9353. 603 rooms, 29 suites. 4 restaurants, bar, coffee shop, pool, 2 tennis courts, health club, concierge, business services, meeting rooms, car rental, parking (fee). AE, DC, MC, V. Subte: Estación Retiro.*

$$$–$$$$ 🏨 **Plaza Francia.** The best-situated small hotel in town, the Plaza Francia overlooks the park of the same name. Rooms are large and have a French feel, with overstuffed pillows, head rolls, and crisp white curtains. Ask for one with a park view, though if traffic noise bothers you, get an inside room. ⊠ *Pasaje E. Schiaffino 2189, La Recoleta 1129, ☎* ꜰꜰ *11/4804–9631. 36 rooms, 14 suites. Room service. AE, DC, MC, V.*

$$$ 🏨 **De las Américas.** In this modern residential hotel just off the shopping stretch of Avenida Santa Fe, the sunken lobby is drearily decorated. But rooms are comfortable and larger than you'd expect. The clientele consists mainly of South American tour groups and visitors from the provinces. ⊠ *Libertad 1020, El Centro 1012, ☎ 11/4816–3432,* ꜰꜰ *11/4816–0418. 150 rooms, 15 suites. Coffee shop, room service. AE, DC, MC, V. Subte: Estación Tribunales (close, but probably not close enough if you're carrying bags).*

$$$ 🏨 **Bisonte Hotel.** This hotel, on a popular shopping street, has a small, marble-floor lobby and an upstairs coffee shop overlooking a tree-lined square. Rooms are small, and the decor is on the stiff side, however. Breakfast is included in the rates. ⊠ *Paraguay 1207, El Centro 1057, ☎ 11/4816–5770,* ꜰꜰ *11/4816–5775. 87 rooms. Coffee shop, business services. AE, DC, MC, V. Subte: Estación 9 de Julio.*

$$$ 🏨 **Bisonte Palace Hotel.** This brightly lighted version of its sister establishment, the Bisonte Hotel (☞ *above*), is centrally located and popular with business travelers. Decor is standard—modern and comfortable—and you're well taken care of, though the atmosphere is a bit cold and formal. Because it's on a busy corner, rooms higher up are better bets for peace and quiet. Breakfast is included in the rate. ⊠ *M. T. de Alvear 902, El Centro 1058, ☎ 11/4328–4751,* ꜰꜰ *11/4328–6476. 62 rooms. Coffee shop, room service. AE, DC, MC, V. Subte: Estación San Martín.*

$$$ 🏨 **Buenos Aires Bauen Hotel.** With its theater, auditorium, tango shows, and city tours, the Bauen is a beehive of activity. It's near the intersection of two noisy avenues lined with lively restaurants, cafés, movie houses, and theaters, so avoid the lower floors if you think you'll be bothered by the noise. ⊠ *Av. Callao 360, El Centro 1022, ☎ 11/4370–1600, 800/448–8355 in the U.S.,* ꜰꜰ *11/4372–0315. 226 rooms, 28 suites. Restaurant, bar, coffee shop, refrigerators, room service, pool, barbershop, beauty salon, convention center. AE, DC, MC, V. Subte: Estación Callao.*

$$$ 🏨 **Carsson.** A long, mirrored corridor leads to the lobby, far from the sound of downtown traffic. An English atmosphere pervades—rooms have staid stripes of green and deep red and Louis XIV–style furniture and are larger than the average Buenos Aires hotel room; ask for one off the busy street. Service is first rate. ⊠ *Viamonte 650, El Centro 1053,* ☎ *11/4322–3551,* 𝖥𝖠𝖷 *11/4322–0158. 108 rooms, 9 suites. Bar, coffee shop, in-room safes, room service, nursery, laundry service, business services, meeting rooms, parking (fee). AE, DC, MC, V. Subte: Estación Lavalle.*

$$$ 🏨 **Posta Carretas.** This modern and very comfortable property has the atmosphere of a mountain inn. Wood paneling abounds, creating a coziness that contrasts with the bustle outside. Some of the brightly decorated rooms have hot tubs. ⊠ *Esmeralda 726, El Centro 1007,* ☎ *11/4322–8534,* 𝖥𝖠𝖷 *11/4326–2277. 40 rooms, 11 suites. Bar, room service, pool, sauna, exercise room, business services. AE, DC, MC, V. Subte: Estación San Martín.*

$$$ 🏨 **Regente Palace.** The winding brass staircase, numerous mirrors, and neon lights in the lobby make you feel like you've entered a '70s casino or a Burt Reynolds movie. Yet rooms are pleasant if small and are decorated with black wood furniture and bedspreads and curtains in beige and rose. It's near Plaza San Martín on a block with several cafés and trendy shops. ⊠ *Suipacha 964, El Centro 1008,* ☎ *11/4328–6800,* 𝖥𝖠𝖷 *11/4328–7460. 150 rooms, 6 suites. Restaurant, snack bar. AE, DC, MC, V. Subte: Estación San Martín.*

$$ 🏨 **Castelar Hotel.** Rooms have that rather institutional style associated with a business hotel; yet they're comfortable, and the lobby is small and inviting. The hotel spa has a Turkish-style bath—a rarity in Buenos Aires. It's an ideal place if you plan to focus on the Plaza de Mayo area. Breakfast is included in the rates. ⊠ *Av. de Mayo 1152, El Centro 1085,* ☎ *11/4383–5000,* 𝖥𝖠𝖷 *11/4383–8388. 50 rooms. Bar, snack bar, spa, exercise room, laundry service and dry cleaning, meeting rooms. AE, MC, V. Subte: Estación Avenida de Mayo.*

$$ 🏨 **Constitución Palace Hotel.** This hotel is near La Boca and San Telmo in the neighborhood of Constitución (you need to use caution in this area at night). Rooms are stark but you can't beat the price; breakfast is included in the rates. If you're planning any trips out of town, this hotel is right next to one of the city's main train stations, Constitución. ⊠ *Lima 1697, San Telmo, 1138,* ☎ *11/4305–9010,* 𝖥𝖠𝖷 *11/4305–9015. 150 rooms. Bar, room service, in-room modem lines, laundry, meeting rooms. AE, DC, MC, V. Subte: Estación Constitución.*

$$ 🏨 **Gran Hotel Dora.** A cozy lobby with a small bar greets you at this old-fashioned hotel. Rooms are comfortable, elegant, and decorated in Louis XVI style. It caters primarily to Europeans and Argentines who want a Continental atmosphere. ⊠ *Maipú 963, El Centro 1006,* ☎ *11/4312–7391,* 𝖥𝖠𝖷 *11/4313–8134. 96 rooms. Bar, snack bar, meeting rooms. AE, DC, MC, V. Subte: Estación San Martín.*

$$ 🏨 **Hotel Alpino.** This hotel has functional if uninteresting rooms. The Parque Zoológico and the Jardín Botánico are within easy walking distance. Breakfast is included in the rates. ⊠ *Cabello 3318, Palermo 1425,* ☎ *11/4802–5151,* 𝖥𝖠𝖷 *11/4802–5151. 35 rooms. Bar, in-room safes, parking. AE, DC, MC, V. Subte: Estación Plaza Italia.*

$$ 🏨 **Hotel Salles.** This quiet, central establishment is one of the few family-oriented hotels in the heart of the theater district. Rooms are adequate, the decor businesslike and institutional; personal service is a focus. ⊠ *Cerrito 208, El Centro 1010,* ☎ *11/4382–3962,* 𝖥𝖠𝖷 *11/4382–0754. 80 rooms, 5 suites. Coffee shop. AE, DC, MC, V. Subte: Estación 9 de Julio.*

$$ 🏨 **Lancaster.** The countess who decorated this traditional and central
★   hotel made good use of her family heirlooms—old family portraits, marble pillars, and a 200-year-old clock grace the lobby. All rooms have

antique mahogany furniture, and some have views of the port of Buenos Aires. ☒ *Av. Córdoba 405, El Centro 1054,* ☎ *11/4312–4061,* FAX *11/ 4311–3021. 88 rooms, 16 suites. Restaurant, bar, room service, meeting rooms. AE, DC, MC, V. Subte: Estación Leandro N. Alem.*

$ 🏨 **Gran Hotel Atlantic.** If you're looking for inexpensive if basic rooms and friendly (though not very quick) service, this is the place for you. ☒ *Castelli 45, El Centro 1031,* ☎ *11/4951–0081,* FAX *11/4951–0081. Bar, room service, parking. AE, DC, MC, V. Subte: Estación Plaza de Miserre.*

$ 🏨 **Gran Hotel Hispano.** The Spanish colonial architecture and small but charming rooms with flower motifs give this hotel a traditional yet friendly feel. Guests are primarily from neighboring Latin American countries. ☒ *Av. de Mayo 861, El Centro 1084,* ☎ *11/4345–2020,* FAX *11/4345–5266. 60 rooms. Bar, breakfast room, ice cream parlor, laundry. AE, DC, MC, V. Subte: Estación Piedras.*

$ 🏨 **Gran Hotel Orly.** Off Calle Florida, the Orly draws Brazilian tourists and visitors from the interior. Although the entrance is impressive, rooms are plain and small and have noisy air-conditioners. The old-timer reception staff seems to be frozen in the previous century. But you can't beat it if you're looking for a clean, basic, inexpensive place to sleep. ☒ *Paraguay 474, El Centro 1057,* ☎ *11/4312–5344,* FAX *11/4312–5344. 168 rooms, 8 suites. Bar, coffee shop. AE, DC, MC, V. Subte: Estación Facultad de Medicina.*

Nightlife and The Arts

Listings of events can be found daily in the English-language *Buenos Aires Herald* as well as in the more comprehensive Friday edition. If you read Spanish, check out the more complete weekend section in the Friday edition of *La Nación*.

The Arts

Except for some international short-run performances, tickets to most events are surprisingly easy to get at box offices and various ticket outlets. **Ticketmaster** (☎ 11/4326–9903) sells tickets for events at the Colón, Luna Park, Teatro Globo, and the Teatro Municipal San Martín, and accepts MasterCard and Visa for phone purchases. **Ticketron** (☎ 11/4321–9700) has tickets to the same venues as Ticketmaster as well as to local theaters and music halls. **Musimundo,** a record store with several branches throughout the city (there's one in every mall), sells tickets for concerts. Note that theaters take a summer vacation (January–February). Men usually wear jackets and ties to theater performances, and women also dress accordingly.

CLASSICAL MUSIC, THEATER, AND DANCE

Pavarotti has said that there's only one thing wrong with the **Teatro Colón** (☒ Tucumán 1111, ☎ 11/4382–4784): the acoustics are so good, every mistake can be heard. An ever-changing stream of imported opera talent bolsters the well-regarded local company. The National Symphony and the National Ballet are also headquartered at this theater. Publicly supported theater, mime, puppet shows, and dance (including world-class contemporary dance) are performed on the three stages of the municipal theater complex, **Teatro San Martín** (☒ Av. Corrientes 1530, ☎ 11/4374–8611 or 11/4331–7553).

When you think dance in Buenos Aires, you think of the tango—and it is the capital of that most passionate of dances. But Porteños also gather in droves on weekends to dance to the pulsating beats of samba and salsa. **Salsón** (☒ Av. Alvarez Thomas 1166, ☎ 11/4637–6970), which is *the* place for salsa in Buenos Aires, has salsa lessons on Wednesday and Friday nights at 9 PM. Head to **Sudaca** (☒ Sarmiento

1752, ☎ 11/4371–0802) for a quick samba lesson. **La Trastienda** (✉ at Balcarce and Belgrano, ☎ 11/4434–2760) is a large dance hall hosting salsa classes and energetic crowds; it also occasionally doubles as a performance space for tango shows.

First-run Hollywood movies, Argentine films, and Italian comedies are shown at the more than 50 theaters in the downtown area alone. Most of these are along two parallel streets, Avenida Corrientes and Calle Lavalle. The *Herald* has daily listings. The names of the films are generally given in Spanish, but English-language films are shown undubbed, with Spanish subtitles. Seats are assigned at movie theaters: When purchasing tickets, you can choose your seat. Ushers, who expect a one-peso tip, show you to your seats if a movie has already begun or if the theater is particularly crowded. Tickets are usually around $7.50, but the first show of the day is half price, and all cinemas are half price all day Wednesday. The following theaters show Argentine and Hollywood films: **Belgrano Multiplex** (✉ at Obligado and Mendoza, ☎ 11/4781–8183) and **Paseo Alcorta** (✉ at F. Alcorta and Salguero, ☎ 11/4806–5665).

Nightlife

It's good to begin with a basic understanding of the Argentine idea of nightlife: A date at 7 PM is considered an afternoon coffee break; theater performances start at 9 PM or 9:30 PM; the last movie begins after midnight; and nightclubs don't begin filling up until 2 AM. Tango, too, gets going after midnight and never seems to stop. Note that the subte closes at 10 PM, so if you go out late, either count on taking a taxi home or waiting until 5 AM for the subte to start running again.

Ave Porco (✉ Av. Corrientes 1980, El Centro, ☎ 11/4953–7129), in the theater district, has a little bit of everything—a techno dance room, an upstairs lounge, and a back patio.

Buenos Aires News (✉ Infanta Isabel, Palermo, ☎ 11/4778–1500) is one of the city's trendiest nightspots—you might even see a model or rock star.

La Cigale (✉ 25 de Mayo 722, El Centro, ☎ 11/4813–8275) has a large bar to lean up to and good music.

El Divino (✉ Cecilia Grierson 225, Puerto Madero, ☎ 11/4315–2791), in a space that was built to resemble the Sydney Opera House, appeals to an affluent, fashionable set.

Dorrego (✉ Defensa 1098, San Telmo, ☎ 11/4361–0141) was once a general store; it's now the place (best in the afternoon) to down Quilmes beers and peanuts.

Druid In (✉ Reconquista 1040, El Centro, ☎ 11/4312–3688) offers a little Irish-bar atmosphere and some Guinness.

Dunn (✉ San Martín 986, El Centro) is a small bar where electronic music is the soundtrack of choice.

Gallery (✉ Azcuénaga 1771, Palermo, ☎ 11/4807–1652) draws a young crowd with live salsa bands and frozen margaritas; the restaurant, which opens at 8:30, serves rather bland Tex-Mex dishes.

Hard Rock Café (✉ in La Recoleta Design Center, Av. Pueyrredón 2501, La Recoleta, ☎ 11/4807–7625), like its counterparts around the world, serves typical American drinks and snacks; on weekends an irritatingly high cover is charged.

El Living (✉ Marcelo T. de Alvear 1540, Palermo, ☎ 11/4811–4730) is a trendy disco and bar with lounge chairs and great drinks.

Morocco (✉ Hipólito Yrigoyen 851, El Centro, ☎ 11/4342–6046) is the kind of spot where you never know when you'll see an impromptu drag show.

La Morocha (✉ Av. Dorrego 3307, Palermo, ☎ 11/4778–0050), the city's most popular disco, is closed January–March, when a branch of it opens at the beach in Uruguay.

Mundo Bizarro (✉ Guatemala 4802, Palermo, ☎ 11/4773–1967) is a cool bar with a hip crowd.

Nero (✉ Marcelo T. de Alvear 538, Palermo, ☎ 11/4313–3458) has a minimalist appeal.

New York City (✉ Av. Alvarez Thomas 1391, Belgrano, ☎ 11/4555–5559), decorated to look like a spot in downtown Manhattan, is primarily filled with people in their teens and early twenties.

Open Plaza Junior (✉ Av. F. Alcorta, Costanera, ☎ 11/4782–7204), which caters to a very fashionable crowd, has a sprawling bar, pool tables, a disco, a restaurant, and a shark tank.

Sedon (✉ at 25 de Mayo and Córdoba, El Centro, ☎ 11/4361–0141) serves up quick tango lessons as well as beer.

Shamrock (✉ Rodríguez Peña 1220, El Centro, ☎ 11/4812–3584) is an Irish-style bar where an English-speaking expat crowd is often found; happy hour is 6–9 PM.

The Spot (✉ Ayacucho 1261, La Recoleta, ☎ 11/4811–8955) is a cocktail bar with a daily happy hour.

Tequila (✉ Costanera Norte and La Pampa, Costanera, ☎ 11/4788–0438) is one of the most happening bars in the city; expect a line out the door.

Tobaggo Cigar and Arts Café (✉ Alvarez Thomas 138, Belgrano, ☎ 11/4553–5530) is all about cigar culture (and hosts events).

Gay and Lesbian Bars and Clubs

Angels (✉ Viamonte 2168, El Centro) has several dance floors and attracts a primarily gay and transvestite clientele.

Bunker (✉ Anchorena 1170), an old standard, draws a gay and mixed crowd.

Confusión (✉ Av. Scalabrini Ortíz 1721, El Centro) hosts techno dance parties until dawn for a gay, lesbian, and transvestite crowd.

Teleny (✉ Juncal 2479) has good drinks and live drag shows.

JAZZ CLUBS

Café Tortoni (✉ Av. de Mayo 825, ☎ 11/4342–4328) has jazz on weekends.

Gazelle Jazz Club (✉ Estados Unidos 465, San Telmo, ☎ 11/4361–4685) is the place to see local and foreign groups.

The Jazz Club (✉ La Plaza Complex, Av. Corrientes 1660) often has jazz concerts in the evening and serves good drinks and snacks.

Notorious (✉ Av. Callao 966, ☎ 11/4813–6888) has jazz shows several times per week, and when there isn't live music, you can play music on your table's CD player.

Patio Bullrich (✉ Av. del Libertador 750) frequently has evening jazz performances.

Salo (✉ Arroyo 1167) plays jazz and blues in a dark, Paris-like setting.

Outdoor Activities and Sports

Participant Sports

ATHLETIC CLUBS

Athletic clubs in Buenos Aires are not only gyms with weightlifting equipment, aerobics classes, and pools, but they're also places to participate in organized sports. **Club de Amigos** (✉ Av. Alcorta, ☎ 11/4801–1213) has pickup soccer games and tennis lessons as well as a gym and a pool. **Coconor** (✉ Rafael Obligado and Salguero, ☎ 11/4788–5995) is the closest that Buenos Aires comes to a beach club: For $25 per day you can mix and mingle at this sports club with a pool operated by Club

Med. **Punta Carrasco** (⊠ Costanera Norte and Sarmiento, ☎ 11/4807–1010) is a sports complex with a swimming pool, tennis courts, organized sports, and lots of people-watching.

BICYCLING AND RUNNING

It's unusual to see people running on the streets; jogging and biking are usually confined to parks like the Parque Tres de Febrero in Palermo (there's usually a stand in the park where you can rent bikes). For an enclosed, bikers-only atmosphere at a nominal admission charge, head to the **Velodromo** (⊠ Av. Tornquist).

GOLF

Cancha Municipal de Golf (⊠ Tornquist and Olleros, ☎ 11/4772–7261 or 11/4772–7576) is a public golf course that's 10 minutes from downtown in Palermo. **Costa Salguero** (⊠ Rafael Obligado and Salguero, ☎ 11/4804–2444) is a complete sports and health complex, with a focus on golf. For more information call the **Asociación Argentina de Golf** (Argentine Golf Association, ⊠ Av. Corrientes 538, 11th and 12th floors, ☎ 11/4394–2743). The plush **Miraflores Country Club** (⊠ Ruta Panamericana, Km 35½, ☎ 3327/454–800), in the suburb of Garín (follow signs on the highway to the town of Pilar), is open to nonmembers on Tuesday, Saturday, and Sunday, for a $30 greens fee.

SPA

Buenos Aires's **Colmegña Spa** (⊠ Sarmiento 839, ☎ 11/4326–1257) is as relaxing as it gets. For $99 you can have a full day at the spa, including a Turkish bath, body peel, massage, hairdo, and lunch. An appointment is essential; it's open Tuesday–Saturday 11–8.

TENNIS

There are public tennis courts at the **Buenos Aires Lawn Tennis Club** (⊠ Av. Olleros 1510, ☎ 11/4772–9227). You can make arrangements through the executive offices at the **Sheraton** (⊠ San Martín 1225, ☎ 11/4318–9309) to play on the hotel's tennis courts for $15 per hour.

Spectator Sports

CRICKET

Cricket is played at the suburban **Hurlingham Club** (⊠ Av. J. A. Roca 1411, ☎ 11/4665–0401) and other Anglo-Argentine enclaves. Check the *Herald* for information.

HORSE RACING

Historians consider the strong Thoroughbreds from Argentina one of the factors that favored the British in the South African Boer War. Argentines on spending binges brought, and occasionally still bring, the best stock in the world home to breed, and swift Argentine horses are prized throughout the world. There are two main tracks in Buenos Aires; check the *Buenos Aires Herald* for schedules. Generally, races take place on Wednesday and Saturday at **Hipódromo de San Isidro** (⊠ Av. Márquez 504, ☎ 11/4743–4010), in the historic suburb of San Isidro. Closer to downtown, in Palermo, is the dirt track at the traditional **Hipódromo Argentino** (⊠ Av. del Libertador 4000, ☎ 11/4777–9009).

POLO

Argentine polo has been compared to a performance of the Bolshoi Ballet in its heyday—a strenuous display of stunning athletic showmanship. At the **Canchas Nacionales** (National Fields), on Avenida Dorrego in the barrio of Palermo in Buenos Aires, sold-out crowds cheer on national heroes. There are two seasons: March–May and September–December. Tickets can be purchased in advance through ticket agencies (☞ Nightlife and the Arts, *above*) or on the day of the event; general admission is about $7. The best teams compete in the Argentine Open

Championships in November. For match information contact the **Asociación Argentina de Polo** (✉ H. Yrigoyen 636, 1st floor, Apt. A, ☎ 11/4331–4646).

SOCCER

Soccer matches are held year-round. To avoid being jostled by zealous fans it's best to pay for a seat (around $40–$60) rather than opting for the often chaotic and frequently dangerous (but cheaper) standing-room section. Passions run especially high when La Boca's Boca Juniors take on their arch-rivals, River Plate, from the upper-crust district of Belgrano. Major games are played at the **Estadio Boca Juniors** (✉ Brandsen 805). Tickets can be purchased at the stadium before the game.

Shopping

There was a time not so long ago when Argentine families went to Miami to purchase quality goods. But the situation has changed with the lifting of trade bans and items are becoming much more widely available. Unfortunately, clothing made in Argentina is generally not that well constructed, though this is improving as well.

Areas

Downtown **Avenida Santa Fe** is great for browsing: lining it are hundreds of little boutiques and bustling cafés. It's a good place to find fashionable, reasonably priced clothes. Crowded, pedestrians-only **Calle Florida,** the main downtown shopping street, is lined with McDonald's, persistent vendors, and stores of all kinds. The street is also home to the city's best bookstores. The closer you get to Plaza San Martín, the better the offerings.

With its designer boutiques and expensive stores concentrated on Avenida Alvear and Calle Quintana, **La Recoleta** is the finest area to shop in the city. Many of the old homes in **San Telmo** have been converted into antiques shops. One—an elaborate Italianate house built in the 1850s that once belonged to the Ezeiza family—was transformed at the turn of the century into a tenement for immigrants and now houses several dozen antiques vendors.

Centers and Malls

Abasto (✉ Av. Corrientes 3200) is a shopping mall, with the usual clothing stores and restaurants, in a renovated old marketplace, which is modernized inside but has the original facade.

Alto Palermo (✉ Corner of Av. Santa Fe and Av. Colonel Diaz, subte: Line D to Estación Bulnes) has three floors of clothes shops, cafés, and toy and book stores right on the bustling Avenida Santa Fe.

Galerías Pacífico (Pacífico Shopping Center; ✉ Florida 753, at Av. Córdoba) is in the former headquarters of the Buenos Aires–Pacific Railway, a building designed during Buenos Aires's turn-of-the-century golden age in the style of Milan's Gallerie Vittorio Emanuele. In 1992 it was transformed into a glossy, multilevel shopping center—one of the finer places to shop and/or have a quick lunch on busy Calle Florida.

Paseo Alcorta (✉ at Av. Alcorta and Salguero), in Palermo, has chic Argentine clothing stores for men and women, as well as internationally known stores like Christian Dior and Yves St. Laurent, a four-screen movie theater, and a food court.

Patio Bullrich (✉ Av. del Libertador 740), near the Park Hyatt, has some of the finest and priciest shops in town as well as a six-screen movie theater. This multilevel mall was once the headquarters for the Bullrich family's auction house, Buenos Aires's most renowned auctioneers. The basement held hundreds of head of cattle during auctions, and the upper floors were dedicated to selling paintings, furniture, and antiques. If you look carefully at the walls on the upper level, you can still see stucco heads of steers emerging in relief. The auction house now functions next door under the name of Posadas (☞ Art and Antiques, *below*).

Solar de la Abadía (⊠ Marie Luis Campos and Arcos) is a great place to pick up souvenirs, buy trendy clothes, or have a snack. As it's on the border of Belgrano and the Cañitas section of Palermo, it's also a good place to begin or end a walk around the area. It's about a 10-minue walk from the Museo Nacional del Hombre, and about 20 minutes from Plaza Belgrano.

Markets

Many of the city's markets are open all day Saturday and Sunday, though none really gets going until the early afternoon. Feel free to bargain: often it works. The markets all carry basically the same types of goods, but if there's one not to miss, it's the San Telmo Market: ongoing entertainment, such as tango dancing, keeps the atmosphere particularly energetic.

Belgrano Square (⊠ Juramento and Vuelta de Obligado, subte: Line D to end). **Recoleta Feria** (⊠ Av. Libertador and Av. Pueyrredón). **San Telmo** (⊠ Plaza Dorrego). **Vuelta de Rocha handicraft market** (⊠ Av. Pedro de Mendoza and Caminito Palos).

Specialty Shops

ART AND ANTIQUES

Posadas (⊠ Posadas 1227, ☎ 11/4327–025 or 11/4815–3573), the city's largest auction house has furnishings and artwork from many local estates.

BOOKSTORES

El Atheneo (⊠ Florida 340, ☎ 11/4340–4325) is perhaps the most famous bookstore, and sells a wide selection of works by Argentine authors, and classics and best-sellers in English, as well as beautiful souvenir coffee table books depicting the tango and scenes from Argentina.

CLOTHING

European designer shops are mostly concentrated along Avenida Alvear and Calle Quintana. Chain stores selling trendy (and often very skimpy) clothing are found all over Buenos Aires. Most of these stores are in malls (☞ Shopping Malls, *above*) as well as along Avenida Santa Fe 800–1500 in the Plaza San Martín area and along Avenida Cabildo 1600–2200 in Belgrano. **Chocolate** has good quality women's clothes that appeal to a twenty-something crowd. **Ona Saez** sells both men's and women's casual and trendy nightclub clothing. **Paula Cahan D'Anvers** sells more conservative, though very small, women's clothing for casual occasions and work. **Via Vai** is a great place for separates, like that sundress or sweater you may have forgotten to pack. **Vitamina** is aimed at younger shoppers.

HANDICRAFTS

Mercado de las Luces (⊠ Peru and Alsina, subte: Line E to Estación Bolívar) sells all kinds of handmade souvenirs; note that many are overpriced (the same items can sometimes be purchased for less in the outdoor markets in Belgrano and San Telmo). **Patio del Cabildo** (⊠ Av. de Mayo and Bolívar), a crafts store in the Cabildo Museum, sells traditional souvenirs and artwork; it's only open Thursday and Friday 11–8.

JEWELRY

Antonio Belgiorno (⊠ Av. Santa Fe 1347, ☎ 11/4811–1117) is a top silversmith who creates beautiful, quality silver pieces. Decorated sculptures of birds in flight from **Cousino** (⊠ Paraguay 631, 3rd floor, Suite A, ☎ 11/4312–2336; ⊠ in Sheraton Hotel) are exhibited in the National

Museum of Decorative Arts. **Guthman** (✉ Viamonte 597, ☎ 11/4312–2471) has an acclaimed selection of jewelry. Internationally renowned **H. Stern** (✉ in Sheraton, Plaza, Hyatt, Inter-Continental, and Alvear Palace hotels; ☞ Lodging, *above*) is a good place for fine Argentine jewelry.

LEATHER

Casa López (✉ M. T. de Alvear 640, ☎ 11/4311–3044) carries jackets and bags. Polo equipment and saddles can be found at **H. Merlo** (✉ Juncal 743). **La Martina** (✉ Paraguay 661, ☎ 11/4311–5963) carries furnishings for the discriminating equestrian. **Murillo 666** (✉ Murillo 666, ☎ 11/4855–2024 has a wide selection of women's bags and jackets at good prices. For briefcases and other leather bags, try **Pullman** (✉ In the Galerías Pacífico, ☎ 11/4325–4111). **Rossi y Caruso** (✉ Av. Santa Fe 1601, ☎ 11/4811–1538) has the best in riding equipment as well as handbags, clothing, shoes, and boots; King Juan Carlos of Spain and many other celebrities are customers here.

SHEEPSKIN AND WOOL

IKS (✉ Alisa Moro de Justo 2040, 1st floor, ☎ 11/4311–4747) is a factory outlet for sweaters. **Silvia y Mario** (✉ M. T. de Alvear 550), another downtown outlet, stocks a huge selection of cashmere and very elegant two-piece knit dresses. Sheepskin jackets at **Ciudad de Cuero** (✉ Florida 940) would make the Marlboro man leap off his mount to purchase a winter's supply.

SHOES

For men's loafers, **Guido** (✉ Florida 704) is Argentina's favorite. For men's and women's shoes that look great and last forever, try **López Taibo** (✉ Av. Corrientes 350, ☎ 11/4328–2132). Shoes and boots can be found at **Rossi y Caruso** (✉ Av. Santa Fe 1601, ☎ 11/4811–1538).

Buenos Aires A to Z

Arriving and Departing

BY AIRPLANE

Most international flights land at **Ezeiza Airport** (☎ 11/4480–0217), 34 km (21 mi) and 45 minutes from downtown Buenos Aires. Domestic flights within Argentina generally depart from the **Aeroparque Jorge Newbury** (☎ 11/4773–9805), in Belgrano.

Between the Airports and Downtown. The ride to downtown in a regular taxi costs at least $35 (from Ezeiza) and $10 from the Aeroparque. At Ezeiza Airport, you can by tickets for *remises* (taxis in which the price for a ride is prearranged) from the well-marked transportation counter. City buses ($2) operate on a regular schedule, but the ride from Ezeiza takes close to two hours, and there's a baggage limit of two bags. **Manuel Tienda León** (✉ Santa Fe 790, ☎ 11/4383–4454) provides regular, 24-hour airport van and minibus service ($15) to all downtown hotels. It's a reliable service that's nearly as fast as a taxi, but costs about half the price.

BY BUS

Most long-distance and international buses arrive at and depart from the **Estación Terminal de Omnibus** (✉ Av. Ramos Mejía 1680, ☎ 11/4310–0700). The more than 60 bus companies here are arranged in order of destinations served, not by name. In general, a few different companies serving the same destination will be clumped together, which makes it easy to compare times and prices.

BY CAR

Avenida General Paz completely encircles Buenos Aires. If you're entering the city from the north, chances are you will be on the Ruta

Panamericana, one of the country's newest and nicest highways. Autopista 25 de Mayo leads out of the city center toward the airport. R2, which is often under construction, goes between Buenos Aires and the beach resorts in and around Mar del Plata.

Hydrofoils and ferries cross the Río de la Plata between Buenos Aires and Uruguay several times a day. Boats often sell out quickly, so book tickets a few days in advance at the dock or ticket sales office by phone (with a credit card). The most popular company, with the most frequent car and passenger service, is **Buquebus** (⊠ Av. Córdoba and Av. Madero; ⊠ in Patio Bullrich shopping mall, ☎ 11/4317–1001). It serves Colonia, Montevideo, Piriápolis, and Punta del Este Uruguay. The 2½-hour ride between Buenos Aires and Montevideo costs about $110 (round-trip) for tourist class and $140 for first class. There's also a cheaper and slower (and less environmentally sound) ferry between Buenos Aires and Colonia, which costs about $55 round-trip. **Ferry Lineas Argentina** (⊠ Florida 780, ☎ 11/4314–5100) serves the Buenos Aires–Uruguay route on a smaller scale with fewer boats per day.

Getting Around

BY BUS

Colectivos (local buses) run all over the city. Routes are marked on blue signs at bus stops, and the fare is required in exact change. Fares are based on destination—the minimum fare is 65¢, and the typical ride through the city is about 70¢. There's also a more comfortable and expensive bus called the *diferencial,* which is climate controlled and on which you are assured a seat; it costs about $2 for an average city ride and runs less frequently.

As you board the bus, tell the driver your destination, and he'll advise you of the fare. Drop it into the machine next to the driver and take the ticket (keep it throughout your journey as it can be collected any time). City buses run all night, but with far less frequency (sometimes only once every hour) after midnight.

BY CAR

Porteños drive with verve and a general disdain for traffic rules. A more convenient and comfortable option is to have your travel agent or hotel arrange for a car with a driver (known as a *remise*). This service costs about $20–$25 per hour, sometimes with a three-hour minimum and an additional charge per kilometer if you drive outside the city limits. The following companies arrange remise service: **Mitre Remises** (⊠ General Roca 1510, Vincente Lopez, ☎ 11/4796–2829 or 11/4794–7228); **Movicar** (☎ 11/4815–1585); **Remises Plaza de Mayo** (⊠ Azopardo 523, ☎ 11/4331–4705); **Remise Rioja** (⊠ Olivos 2286, ☎ 11/4794–4677 or 11/4794–7228); and **Remises Universal** (⊠ 25 de Mayo 611, 4th floor, ☎ 11/4315–6555).

If you prefer to try your hand at dealing with Buenos Aires road rage by being your own driver, you can rent a car at tourist-friendly **Annie Millet** (⊠ Paraguay 1122, ☎ 11/4816–8001). **Avis** (⊠ Ezeiza Airport, ☎ 11/4480–9387; ⊠ Jorge Newberry Airport, ☎ 11/4776–3003; ⊠ Cerrito 1527, ☎ 11/4326–5542; ☎ 800/4445–6284). **Budget** (⊠ Av. Santa Fe 11527, ☎ 11/4311–9870). **Primer Mundo** (⊠ Av. Libertador 6553, ☎ 11/4787–2140) is smaller than Annie Millet but offers excellent service and better prices. **Thrifty** (⊠ Leandro N. Alem 699, ☎ 11/4315–0777).

Parking has been privatized in Buenos Aires, so ticket-happy entrepreneurs are busy putting yellow-metal boots on the front wheels of cars that stand too long at a meter and towing violators off to nearby parking lots. Fines start at $75. There are a few public underground parking garages and numerous private garages. They cost $2–$3 for the first hour and are typically $1.50 per hour thereafter. Most malls have garages, which are usually free or give you a reduced rate with a purchase.

BY SUBTE

Though not comprehensive, Buenos Aires's subway system, the subte, is excellent. It's the oldest in South America, dating from 1913, and many of its stations are decorated with historic scenes of the city or murals by contemporary artists. At press time, tokens cost about 50¢, but discussions are under way to raise the price. One token is valid for any length trip on the subway. The subway is closed between 10 PM and 5 AM.

The system's five lines all basically start service in El Centro and then fan out. Line A, the oldest and most historic, runs from Plaza de Mayo to Primera Junta. Line B goes from Línea Alem, which is in the financial district of El Centro, to Federico Lacroze. Line C connects the two major train stations, Retiro and Constitución, making stops along the way in El Centro. Line D runs from Catedral on Plaza de Mayo to Jose Hernández, in Belgrano. Line E goes from Bolívar, a few blocks from Plaza de Mayo, to Plaza de los Virreyes. A new line, to be called Line H, which would wrap around the city, should be in place by 2002.

BY TAXI

Taxis are everywhere in Buenos Aires, so you should never have a problem getting one on the street. Cabs are generally independently owned and operated, and as such, their owners are always on the lookout for business. They are usually safe, but keep in mind that robberies of taxis do occur, especially in areas known to have banks, so be aware. If you don't like the look of a cab, or don't feel comfortable with the driver, do not get in the car. Another cab will be along in a matter of seconds.

Note that hailing a cab involves holding your arm out in a perpendicular fashion, as if you were pointing to something across the street. The traditional New York manner of hailing a cab, with the hand raised up in the air, will flag down a bus in Buenos Aires. Meters start at $1.20 and increase in small increments per ¼ kilometer. In the central downtown area, fares are about $2–$4; out to Recoleta will cost you $5–$6; San Telmo $4–$6; and Belgrano $8. **City Taxi** (☎ 11/4585–5544) has yellow-roofed, metered cabs.

BY TRAIN

Six private commuter rail lines serve the city and its suburbs. Trains run every 5–10 minutes during rush hour, with far fewer trains off-peak. Buy your tickets—from an attendant or a machine—before boarding. Fares, based on the point of departure and the destination, range from 40¢ for a journey of a few stops to $2 for a trip to the end of the line. Some lines have the more expensive diferencial trains, which are temperature controlled and on which you're assured a seat. These cost roughly four times as much as regular trains and run far more infrequently. Once on board any train, a uniformed ticket collector may ask you to show your ticket. If you don't have one, you'll have to pay an on-the-spot fine of $3.50–$6.50.

Following are the six commuter train lines and the stations from which they arrive and depart in Buenos Aires. **Línea Belgrano** (✉ Estación Retiro, Av. Ramos Mejía 1430, ☎ 11/4317–4407). **Línea Mitre** (✉ Estación Retiro, Av. Ramos Mejía 1398, across from Sheraton Hotel, ☎ 11/4317–4445). **Línea Roca** (✉ Estación Constitución, Av. Brasil 1138, ☎ 11/4304–0038). **Línea San Martín** (✉ Estación Retiro, Av. Ramos Mejía 1552, ☎ 11/4317–4445). **Línea Sarmiento** (✉ Estación Once, Bartolomé Mitre 2815, ☎ 11/4861–0043). **Línea Urquiza** (✉ Estación Lacroze, Av. Federico Lacroze 4181, ☎ 11/4553–0044).

Contacts and Resources

BANKS AND CURRENCY EXCHANGE

Although U.S. dollars are frequently accepted throughout Buenos Aires, it's always handy to have pesos with you. There's a currency exchange desk at the Ezeiza Airport, right near the exit to the parking lot. Currency can also be exchanged at any of the locations listed below. Most banks are open weekdays 10–3. **America** (⊠ Sarmiento 501, ☎ 11/4393–0054). **Baires** (⊠ San Martín 215, ☎ 11/4325–8547). **Banco Piano** (⊠ San Martín 347, ☎ 11/4394–2463). **Chase Manhattan Bank** (⊠ Arenales 707, 5th floor, ☎ 11/4319–2400). **Citibank** (⊠ Bartolome Mitre 502, ☎ 11/4329–1000). **Forex Cambio** (⊠ Marcelo T. de Alvear 540, ☎ 11/4312–7729). **Republic National Bank of New York** (⊠ Bartolome Mitre 343, ☎ 11/4349–1600. **Western Union** (⊠ Av. Cordoba 917, ☎ 11/4322–7774).

EMBASSIES

Australia (⊠ Villanueva 1400, ☎ 11/4777–6580). **Canada** (⊠ Tagle 2828, ☎ 11/4805–3032). **United Kingdom** (⊠ Luis Agote 2412, ☎ 11/4803–6021). **United States** (⊠ Colombia 4300, ☎ 11/4777–4533).

EMERGENCIES

Ambulance (☎ 107). **Fire** (☎ 1100). **Hospital** (British Hospital, ⊠ Perdriel 74, ☎ 11/4304–1081). **Police** (☎ 101 or 11/4383–1111).

There's a **pharmacy** (*farmacia*) on nearly every block in Buenos Aires. Your hotel will be able to guide you to the nearest one. Local pharmacies take turns staying open 24 hours; so at any time of day, you can go to the pharmacy nearest your hotel, and if it's closed, there will be a sign indicating what pharmacy is open.

ENGLISH-LANGUAGE MEDIA

The best source of information in English is the *Buenos Aires Herald*. It can be purchased at any kiosk throughout the city, for $1 on weekdays and for $1.50 on Sunday. Most bookstores sell an overpriced and very limited selection of English-language material.

HEALTH AND SAFETY

Violent crime is rare and at any time of night, you'll see young children and old ladies strolling about. Police consistently patrol areas where tourists are likely to be. That said, keep in mind that Buenos Aires is a big city and take precautions: Pickpocketing and robberies aren't uncommon. Go out at night in pairs or, better yet, in groups. Most fresh foods are well washed with city water, which is potable.

TELEPHONES, INTERNET, AND MAIL

Public phones are found on nearly every block and usually operate with a phone card, which can be purchased at any kiosk. To make a long-distance call from a pay phone, go to a Telecentro, which are found throughout the city and have private booths and fax services. (Note that you still need a local phone card to make a long-distance call, even if you have your own calling card.)

If your hotel doesn't have Internet access, try a Telefonica or Telecom phone office. Internet cafés aren't common. Two to try are **Cyber Express** (⊠ Florida 482, ☎ 11/4325–0935) and **Dos H's Bar** (⊠ Viamonte 636, ☎ 11/4326–0878).

Post offices are typically open weekdays 9–6 and Saturday 9–1. Stamps are available at kiosks, but most people go directly to the post office and stand in line to mail a letter, which seems to drastically reduce lost mail. International Express services take 3–5 days to reach the United States from Argentina. Services available include: **DHL** (⊠ Moreno 631, ☎ 11/4347–0600); **Federal Express** (⊠ Maipu 753, ☎ 11/4630–0300); and **UPS** (⊠ Bernardo de Yrigoyen 974, ☎ 11/4307–2174).

TOUR OPERATORS AND TRAVEL AGENTS
Buenos Aires Tours (✉ Lavalle 1444, ☎ 11/4371–2304 or 11/4371–2390) organizes extensive bus tours of the city and can help you plan travel all over the country. **Cauces Tours** (✉ Maipu 995, ☎ 11/4314–9001) arranges bus tours of the city and neighboring suburbs and also arranges travel throughout Argentina.

VISITOR INFORMATION
Information kiosks run by the city along Calle Florida, have English-speaking personnel and city maps, but few brochures. A great place to get friendly tourist advice and tons of brochures, maps, and even vacation-planning tips is at the information counter on the second floor of the Galerías Pacífico shopping center (☞ Shopping, *above*).

You can get information over the phone, on weekdays, 9–5, from the **Dirección de Turismo del Gobierno de la Ciudad de Buenos Aires** (Tourist Department of the City of Buenos Aires; ☎ 15/4763612). The **Secretaria de Turismo de la Nación** (✉ Av. Santa Fe 883, ☎ 11/4312–2232 or 11/4312–5550), the national tourism office, runs a telephone information service, which is toll free from any point in Argentina, 24 hours a day.

CATARATAS DEL IGUAZÚ

Updated by
Brad Weiss

The Cataratas del Iguazú (Iguazú Falls)—1,357 km (814 mi) northeast of Buenos Aires—are one of the wildest wonders of the world, with nature on the rampage in a unique show of sound and fury. The grandeur of this Cinemascopic sheet of white water cascading in constant cymbal-banging cacophony makes Niagara Falls and Victoria Falls seem sedate. At a bend in the Río Iguazú (Iguazú River), on the border with Brazil, the falls extend for almost 3 km (1½ mi) in a 270-degree arch. Iguazú is made up of some 275 separate cascades—in the rainy season there are as many as 350—that plunge more than 200 ft onto the rocks below. The tropical sun and the omnipresent moisture make the jungle around the falls grow at a pace that produces a towering pine tree in two decades instead of the seven it takes in, say, Scandinavia. By the falls and along the roadside, rainbows and butterflies are set off against vast walls of red earth, which is so ubiquitous that eventually even peso bills long in circulation in the area turn red from exposure to the stuff.

Allow at least two full days to see this magnificent sight, and be sure to see it from both the Argentine and Brazilian sides. The Brazilians are blessed with the best panoramic view, an awesome vantage point that suffers only from the sound of the gnatlike helicopters that erupt out of the lawn of the Hotel das Cataratas (☞ Dining and Lodging, *below*) right in front of the falls. (Unfortunately, most indigenous macaws and toucans have abandoned the area to escape the whine of the helicopters' engines.)

The Argentine side offers the better close-up experience of the falls, with excellent hiking paths, catwalks that approach the falls, a sandy beach to relax on, and places to bathe in the froth of the Río Iguazú. Local travel agencies and tour operators offer trips that will take you to both sides. If you want to set your own pace, you can tour the Argentine side and then take a taxi or one of the regularly scheduled buses across the International Bridge, officially called the Ponte Presidente Tancredo Neves, to Brazil. (Note that if you're a Canadian, U.K., or U.S. citizen crossing into Brazil from Argentina or Paraguay, you don't need a visa for a short visit to the falls. You must, however, pay an entry fee and have your passport stamped. Always keep your passport handy as immigration authorities keep the region under close watch.)

Many people find the small Argentine town of Puerto Iguazú a good base. The town, 17 km (10 mi) southeast of the falls, originated as a port for shipping wood from the region. It was in the early 20th century that Victoria Aguirre, a high-society Porteña, funded the building of a road that extends to Cataratas de Iguazú to make it easier for people to visit the falls. You may find Puerto Iguazú preferable to its Brazilian neighbor, Foz de Iguaçu, because it's considerably more tranquil and safe (when you go to the Brazilian side, leave your valuables in the hotel and be on the alert; crime is more frequent there).

The best way to immerse yourself in the falls is to wander the many access paths, which are a combination of bridges, ramps, stone staircases, and wooden catwalks set in a forest of ferns, begonias, orchids, and tropical trees. The catwalks over the water put you right in the middle of the action, so be ready to get doused by the rising spray. (Be sure to bring rain gear—or buy it from vendors along the trails on the Brazilian side.) If tropical heat and humidity hamper your style, plan to visit between April and October, though the falls are thrilling year-round. Be aware, however, that the river can get so high in April and May that access to certain catwalks is impossible.

Argentine Side

The falls on the Argentine side are in the **Parque Nacional Iguazú** (Iguazú National Park), which was founded in 1934 and declared a World Heritage Site in 1984. The park's **Centro de Informes** (Information Center, ☎ 3757/420180), in what was the park's original hotel, makes a good first stop. Useful maps are posted on the walls, and the rangers are friendly, multilingual, and helpful. They preside over a small observation point and museum that have local fauna and exhibits related to the area's history. In an adjoining room are slide shows on Argentina's national park program. On the nights of a full moon, rangers lead groups from the visitor center for a free night walk through the upper trails. The sensation of passing through the forest at night is eerie and exciting. The roar of the falls drowns out the sounds of the jungle and what was all bright green, red, and blue in the daytime takes on luminous hues of phosphorescent whites. The snack bar in the visitor center has tables on the lawn, and the restaurant, El Fortín—across from the parking lot—has an all-you-can-eat barbecue and sandwiches.

The **Circuito Inferior** (Lower Circuit) is an approximately 1-km-long (½-mi-long) looped trail that consists of a metal catwalk with protected promontories that offer some of the best views of the falls. On this route you cross the small, peripheral **Salto Alvar Núñez**, falls named for the Spanish conquistador Alvar Núñez Cabeza de Vaca, who accidentally stumbled onto the spectacle in the 16th century; the **Peñon de Bella Vista** (Rock of the Beautiful View); and the **Salto Lanusse** (Lanusse Falls), those farthest from the Garganta del Diablo (Devil's Throat), the tallest cataract (☞ *below*). In the distance on the right are the impressive **Salto Dos and Salto Tres Mosqueteros** (Two and Three Musketeers Falls).

Halfway along this circuit you get a panoramic peek at what is to come. Through the foliage you can see the gigantic curtain of water in the distance. The trail leads along the lower side of the **Brazo San Martín**, a branch of the river that makes a wide loop to the south. This tributary pushes to get back to the river's main course, opening up dozens of minor and a few major waterfalls along a face of rock that measures almost a mile. On the back side of the circuit—that is, where the trail loops around and starts heading back to your starting point—the **Salto Ramírez** (Ramírez Falls); the **Salto Chico** (Small Falls); and the **Salto Dos Hermanos** (Two Brothers Falls) appear directly before you, opposite the bridge. This section of your circuit, about 1 km (½ mi) long, offers the most exciting panoramic view of the Garganta del Diablo, the **Salto Bossetti** (Bossetti Falls), and the Salto Dos Hermanos. Allow about two hours to walk this circuit. There's no way to get lost on the catwalk, but you can hire English-speaking guides at the visitor center.

At the vantage point opposite the Salto Bossetti, a trail leads along the edge of the river to a small pier, where sturdy little boats take you across a branch of the river to **Isla San Martín** (San Martín Island). This free boat service operates all day, except when the river is too high. On the island a steep climb up a rustic 160-step stairway leads to a circular trail opening onto three spectacular panoramas of the **Salto San Martín** (San Martín Falls), the **Garganta del Diablo**, and the **Salto Ventana** (Window Falls). If you want to just sit and watch 1,300 cubic yards of water splash below you every second, this is the place to do it. From the southernmost point you see **Salto Escondido** (Hidden Falls), and from the easternmost point, a breathtaking panorama of the falls on the Brazilian side: **Salto Santa María, Salto Floriano,** and **Salto Deodoro.** Few people make the effort to cross the river to Isla San Martín and do this climb, so you can often enjoy the show in solitary splendor. The island has a small beach near the point where the boats land; you can stretch out on the sand to dry out from the mist. Allow about an hour for the trip to Isla San Martín from the vantage point opposite the Salto Bossetti. Unless you climb up the stairway on Isla San Martín, you'll probably find the hike very easy; no special footwear is necessary.

The **Circuito Superior** (Upper Circuit)—not a circuit at all but a path about 3,000 ft long—borders the ridge on the south side of the river, along the top of the falls. The trail leads across the rapid waters of the **Brazo San Martín,** a branch of the river, providing great views of **Dos Hermanos, Bossetti, Chico,** and **Ramírez.** The most powerful waterfall rising in front of you at the end is **San Martín,** the park's widest. From the catwalk you look out upon a seemingly endless stretch of waterfalls whose white foams of fury don't subside until they're well down river. You can also see Isla San Martín and the Brazilian side, with the pink walls of the Hotel das Cataratas peeking through the foliage. Count on about an hour and a half to walk this fairly easy circuit; arrows on the path point you in the right direction.

The tallest and most renowned waterfall, evocatively named the **Garganta del Diablo** (Devil's Throat), is a breathtaking spectacle as it furiously spills over the precipice and plummets over 230 ft. The force of the water is so great that rising mist prevents you from seeing the bottom; as you stand and watch the river fall off into space, the awesome roar below is your only confirmation that the water has reached its destination. Expect to get wet. The best viewing point is from the 1,000-ft-long catwalk that crosses over the river and leads right up to the gorge. To get to the catwalk, you need to take a boat from **Puerto Canoas,** a settlement 4 km (2½ mi) up the river from the visitor center. The five-minute boat trip runs several times each hour and costs $4 round-trip. Puerto Canoas has a basic campground with no facilities, 1 km (½ mi) farther on the banks of the Río Nandú (Nandú River), along with a restaurant and bar open for lunch only. The hourly bus from Puerto Iguazú to the national park ends its route at Puerto Canoas, and taxis are available at the visitor center ($10 round-trip with a wait). The whole excursion takes about two hours.

Add to your outings to the different panoramic points overlooking the falls with a hike in the jungle. The **Sendero Macuco** (Macuco Trail), which extends 4 km (2½ mi) into the jungle, ending at the **Salto Arrechea** (Arrechea Falls) farther downriver from the main falls, is maintained by the **Centro de Investigaciones Ecológicas Subtropicales** (Center for Subtropical Ecological Investigation, ☎ 3757/420180). The trail is very carefully marked, and descriptive signs in Spanish explain the jungle's flora and fauna. The closest you'll get to a wild animal is likely to be a paw print in the dirt, though you may glimpse a monkey. You can turn back at any point, or continue on to the refreshing view of the river and the Salto Arrechea. The best time to hear animal calls and to avoid the heat is either early in the morning or just before sunset. The battalions of butterflies, also best seen in the early morning or late afternoon, can be marvelous, and the intricate glistening cobwebs crisscrossing the trail are a treat in the dawn light. Plan on spending about three hours for the whole trip.

Brazilian Side

On the Brazilian side, the falls, known in Portuguese as the Foz do Iguaçu, can be seen from the **Parque Nacional Foz do Iguaçu,** Brazil's national park. The park is 25 km (16 mi) along a paved highway southwest of downtown Foz do Iguaçu, the nearest town to the falls on the Brazilian side. The **park entrance** (✉ Km 17, Rodovia das Cataratas, ☎ 045/5238383) is the best place to get information; it's open daily 7 AM–6 PM, and the entrance fee is roughly $3. Much of the park's 457,000 acres is protected rain forest—off limits to visitors and home to the last viable populations of panthers as well as rare flora such as bromeliads and orchids. The falls are 11 km (7 mi) from the park entrance. The luxurious, historic Hotel das Cataratas (☞ Dining and Lodging, *below*) is near the trailhead. Public parking is allowed on the highway shoulder and in a small lot near the hotel. The path to the falls is 2 km (1 mi) long, and its walkways, bridges, and stone staircases lead through the rain forest to concrete and wooden catwalks that take you to the falls. Highlights of the Brazilian side of the falls include first the **Salto Santa Maria,** from which catwalks branch off to the **Salto Deodoro** and **Salto Floriano,** where you'll be doused by the spray. The end of the catwalk puts you right in the heart of the spectacle at **Garganta do Diabo** (Devil's Throat in Portuguese), from a different perspective than the Argentine side. Back on the last section of the main trail, there's a building with facilities, including a panoramic elevator; it's open daily 8:30–6, and there's a very small fee. A balcony brings you close to the far left of **Salto Deodoro.** The trail ends at the road some 35 ft above.

Dining and Lodging

$$$ ✕ **Zaragoza.** In a quiet neighborhood on a tree-lined street in Brazil's Foz do Iguaçu, this cozy restaurant is owned by Paquito, a Spanish immigrant. The fare includes a great paella, the house specialty, as well as several delicious fish options. The surubí merits a try. ✉ *Rua Quintino Bocaiúva 882, Foz do Iguaçu, Brazil,* ☎ *045/5743084. AE, V.*

  $ ✕ **El Charo.** This restaurant is in a shabby old house that looks like it
  ★   could easily be blown down with a huff and a puff: All the paintings are tilted, the roof is sinking, and the cowhide on the seats is faded. Nevertheless, this is one of the town's most popular restaurants because of its consistently delicious and inexpensive parilladas, as well as its pasta and grilled fish. Note that napkins come only by request. ✉ *Av. Córdoba 106, Puerto Iguazú,* ☎ *3757/421529. No credit cards.*

  $ ✕ **Jardín Iguazú.** Close to the bus terminal, this restaurant serves a wide variety of tasty food and is open 24 hours a day. At lunch and at odd hours, when everything else is closed, there's a good fixed-price menu, which for about $4 provides an empanada, a salad, a main dish with pasta and meat, and a beverage. The place is all rather shiny, with highly polished stones on the floor and a stage (used for live music in the evenings) speckled with silver chips. ⊠ *Av. Misiones and Córdoba, Puerto Iguazú,* ☎ *3757/423200. AE, MC, V.*

$$$$ ☆ 🏨 **Hotel das Cataratas.** Not only is this stately hotel on the Brazilian side in the national park (with wonderful views of the falls), but it also provides the more traditional comforts—large rooms, terraces, hammocks—of a colonial-style establishment. This pink building is surrounded by galleries and gardens; its main section has been declared a Brazilian national heritage sight. The restaurant serves traditional Brazilian fare. ⊠ *Km 25, Rodovia das Cataratas 85850–970, Brazil,* ☎ *045/5232266 or 0800/452266,* ℻ *045/5741688. 200 rooms. 2 restaurants, bar, coffee shop, pool, 2 tennis courts, shops. AE, DC, MC, V.*

$$$$ ☆ 🏨 **Sheraton Internacional Iguazú.** Half the rooms in this luxury hotel have direct views of the falls, so be sure to reserve one well in advance (they are about 30% more expensive). Floor-to-ceiling windows reveal the inspiring scene to the lobby, restaurants, bars, and even the pool. The spacious balconies are ideal for breakfast or a drink; and the Garganta del Diablo restaurant serves what may be the area's finest dinners. Rooms are large and comfortable, though they have the same furnishings as when the hotel opened in 1979. But major changes are expected for the near future because the hotel has recently come under Sheraton management. ⊠ *Parque Nacional Iguazú 3372,* ☎ *3757/491800,* ℻ *3757/421600. 180 rooms, 4 suites. 2 restaurants, 2 bars, air-conditioning, minibars, room service, pool, sauna, 3 tennis courts, biking, laundry, meeting rooms. AE, DC, MC, V.*

$$$ ☆ 🏨 **Hotel Cataratas.** Though this redbrick hotel with green window sills and white awnings isn't especially attractive from the outside, inside is a different story. The classy lobby and ample guest rooms are tastefully decorated with the finest materials and furnishings. Ask for a master double, which is the same price but slightly nicer than the standard double. The hotel also has beautiful grounds and excellent facilities, including an enormous pool, sauna, exercise room, and courts for tennis, paddleball, and volleyball. The high-quality restaurant, serving international cuisine, has an à la carte menu and a fixed-price buffet (dinner only). ⊠ *R12, Km 4, Puerto Iguazú 3370,* ☎ *3757/421100,* ℻ *3757/421090. 80 rooms, 2 suites. Restaurant, bar, air-conditioning, in-room safes, minibars, room service, pool, massage, sauna, tennis court, exercise room, volleyball. AE, DC, MC, V.*

$$–$$$ 🏨 **Hotel Esturion.** This slightly aged hotel has gardens behind and sweeping views of the river. It also has a very helpful staff. Rooms show some signs of wear and tear, though they are spacious and have all the modern amenities you would expect at a luxury hotel; many have balconies with nice views of the river. The restaurant is sometimes the subject of complaints, especially from those whose package deal provides only a few choices at meals. ⊠ *Av. Fronteras 650, Puerto Iguazú 3370,* ☎ *3757/420020 or 3757/420161, 800/338–2288 in the U.S.,* ℻ *3757/420414. 114 rooms, 4 suites, 4 apartments. Restaurant, coffee shop, air-conditioning, in-room safes, minibars, pool, massage, sauna, 2 tennis courts, exercise room, dance club. AE, DC, MC, V.*

$ 🏨 **Los Helechos.** It's such a bargain that this hotel doesn't need to discount its rooms in the off-season. It's also convenient to the center of town and two blocks from the bus terminal. Rooms are simple, clean, and comfortable; half have air-conditioning and television ($10 more). ⊠ *Paulino Amarante 76, Puerto Iguazú, 3370,* ☎ ℻ *3757/420338. 54 rooms. Restaurant, bar, pool, laundry. AE, DC, MC, V.*

Nightlife

Puerto Iguazú is very quiet at night—more happens on the Brazilian side. But on weekends Puerto Iguazú's **Blanco Paraiso** (⊠ Aguirre 262, ☎

3757/422534) has live music. At **Lautaro Play's** (⊠ Av. Brasil 49, ☎ 3757/423386), you can have a drink, go dancing, or play pool. Another option is to try your luck at the fancy, European-style casino in the **Iguazú Grand Hotel Resort & Casino** (⊠ R12, Km 1,640, ☎ 3757/498050).

Shopping

In Puerto Iguazú, numerous souvenir shops line the main strip, **Avenida Aguirre,** and the surrounding blocks. All carry similar items, such as yerba maté gourds, semiprecious stones, baskets, and weavings.

Cataratas del Iguazú A to Z

Arriving and Departing

BY AIRPLANE

Argentina and Brazil each has an airport at Iguazú. The Argentine airport is 20 km (12 mi) southeast of Puerto Iguazú, Argentina; the Brazilian airport is 11 km (7 mi) from Foz do Iguaçu and 17 km (10½ mi) from the national park. **Austral** (⊠ Av. Victoria Aguirre 295, Puerto Iguazú, ☎ 3757/420849 or 3757/420168) flies three times daily between Buenos Aires and the Argentine airport near Iguazú; the trip takes an hour and a half. **LAPA** (☎ 3757/420390) also flies to and from Buenos Aires and is usually cheaper. Normal rates are $200 each way, but promotional rates, called *banderas negativas,* are sometimes available if you reserve ahead.

The Brazilian airlines—**Transbrasil** (☎ 0455/742029 in Argentina; 041/381–1579 or 041/322–5655 in Brazil), **Varig** (☎ 0455/741424 in Argentina; 041/381–1600 or 041/322–1343 in Brazil), and **Vasp** (☎ 0455/742999 in Argentina; 041/382–0345 or 041/221–7422 in Brazil)— have offices in Foz do Iguaçu and offer connecting flights all over Brazil.

Airport Transfers: The **Colectivo Aeropuerto** (☎ 3757/420298) shuttle has service to hotels in Puerto Iguazú for $3. To get from the hotel to the airport, call two hours before your departure, and the shuttle will pick you up. Taxis from the Argentine airport to Puerto Iguazú cost $18. Cabs from the Brazilian airport to Foz do Iguaçu are $12; the 45-minute regular bus ride, about 40¢.

BY BUS

Organized tours to Puerto Iguazú and the Cataratas de Iguazú by bus can be arranged through most Buenos Aires travel agencies. **Via Bariloche** (☎ 3757/421917) has the quickest and most comfortable service between Puerto Iguazú and Buenos Aires; the trip takes 16 hours, costs about $70, and includes meals. **Expreso Singer** (⊠ Perito Moreno 150, ☎ 3757/422891) takes 21 hours and costs $40. The **Puerto Iguazú Terminal de Omnibus** (⊠ Av. Cordoba and Misiones, ☎ 3757/ 423006) is in the center of town. Foz do Iguaçu's **Terminal Rodoviário** (⊠ Av. Costa e Silva s/n, ☎ 045/522–3633) is 4 km (2½ mi) northeast of downtown.

BY CAR

Puerto Iguazú is a two-day, 1,363-km (818-mi) drive from Buenos Aires on R12 and R14 (it's quickest to take R14 to Posadas, then R12 to the Cataratas). The roads are paved and rarely crowded.

Getting Around

BY CAR

In Puerto Iguazú cars are available from **Leader Rent a Car** (⊠ Eppens 30, ☎ 3757/423220). In Foz do Iguaçu, you can try **Avis** (⊠ Km 10, Rodovia das Cataratas, ☎ 045/523–1510) or **Localiza** (⊠ Km 10, Rodovia das Cataratas, ☎ 045/523–4800; ⊠ Av. Juscelino Kubitschek 2878, ☎ 045/522–1608).

BY TAXI

Taxis (*remises*) are generally inexpensive; the fare is based on the number of blocks traveled, though you can also negotiate with the drivers for set-price day trips. Taxis can be hailed, but it's generally easier to call one. In Puerto Iguazú, one of the biggest taxi companies is **Remisse Union** (☎ 3757/421328). In Foz do Iguaçu try the **radio-taxi service** (☎ 045/523–4800).

Contacts and Resources

BANKS AND CURRENCY EXCHANGE

ATMs linked to the Cirrus system are found throughout the region. Dollars and pesos are used interchangeably in Puerto Iguazú; to exchange other currencies, but not traveler's checks, go to **Argecâm** (⊠ Av. Victoria Aguirre 562, ☎ 3757/420273), open Monday–Saturday 8–7. For other banking needs in Puerto Iguazú, try **Banco Misiones** (⊠ Av. Victoria Aguirre, ☎ 3757/420212), open weekdays 7–1; it has ATMs.

In Foz do Iguaçu, try **Banco do Brasil** (Av. Brasil 1377, ☎ 045/523–2288) or **Omegatur Turismo e Câmbio** (Av. Juscelino Kubitschek 245, ☎ 045/572–2837).

CONSULATE

If you're a citizen of Canada, the United Kingdom, or the United States, you need only pay a small fee and get your passport stamped for quick trips across the border to the Brazilian side of the falls. If, however, you plan to continue on in Brazil, you'll need a tourist visa. In Puerto Iguazú, the **Brazilian consulate** (⊠ Av. Guaraní 70, ☎ 3757/421348) is open weekdays 8–11:30. It may take a couple of days to get your visa, so do it ahead of time.

EMERGENCIES

Ambulance: For ambulances call the hospital directly. **Fire:** ☎ 3757/420885 in Puerto Iguazú. **Hospitals: Hospital Internacional** (⊠ Av. Brasil 1637, Foz do Iguaçu, Brazil, ☎ 045/523–1404). **Hospital Samic** (⊠ Av. Victoria Aguirre 131, Puerto Iguazú, ☎ 3757/420626). **Pharmacies: Farmacia Bravo** (⊠ Av. Victoria Aguirre 423, Puerto Iguazú, ☎ 3757/420479), open 24 hours. **FarmaRede** (⊠ Av. Brasil 46, Foz do Iguaçu, Brazil, ☎ 045/523–1929). **Police:** ☎ 3757/421224 in Puerto Iguazú, 190 in Foz do Iguaçu, Brazil.

TELEPHONES, THE INTERNET, AND MAIL

Card-operated public phones are easy to find. Cards can be purchased in many shops and kiosks. You can make long-distance calls, send faxes, and mail letters at the **Correo and Telecentro** (⊠ Av. Victoria Aguirre 254, ☎ 3757/422454; open daily 7 AM–midnight). **Intercom Iguazú** (⊠ Av. Victoria Aguirre 240, ☎ 3757/423180), open Monday–Saturday 8–1 and 4–10, has Internet access.

On the Brazilian side, you can make phone calls and mail letters at the **Posto Telefônico TELEPAR** (Rua E. Barros s/n, Centro, Foz do Iguaçu, Brazil, ☎ 045/523–2449) and the **Correios** (Praça Getúlio Vargas 72, Foz do Iguaçu, Brazil, ☎ 045/574–2381).

TOUR OPERATORS AND TRAVEL AGENTS

Two of the most reliable Puerto Iguazú tour operators are: **Aguas Grandes** (⊠ Mariano Moreno 58, ☎ 3757/421240) and **IGR** (⊠ Bompland 110, ☎ 3757/420239). **Iguazú Explorer** (⊠ In Sheraton Internacional Iguazú Hotel, ☎ 3757/421600) has four trips to the jungle and falls. The best is the Gran Aventura, which includes a truck ride through the forest and a boat ride to San Martín, Bossetti, and the Salto Tres Mosqueteros (be ready to get soaked). Another tour takes you to Garganta del Diablo. Park ranger Daniel Somay organizes personalized Jeep tours through his **Explorador Expediciones** (☎ 3757/421632) in Puerto Iguazú. Bring binoculars to see the birds.

Reliable companies in Brazil include **Golden Foz Turismo** (✉ Rua Tarobá 557, Centro, Foz do Iguaçu, Brazil, ☎ 045/523–2121); **Macuco Boat Safari** (✉ Km 21, Rodovia das Cataratas, Foz do Iguaçu, Brazil, ☎ 045/574–4244); and **Helisul Táxi Aéreo** (✉ Km 16.5, Rodovia das Cataratas, Foz do Iguaçu, Brazil, ☎ 045/523–1190), which arranges helicopter tours of the falls; the shortest flight (10 min) costs $50 per person.

VISITOR INFORMATION

The **Cataratas de Iguazú** (✉ Visitor center at park entrance, ☎ 3757/420180) is open daily 7 AM–8 PM. The tourist board in **Puerto Iguazú** (✉ Av. Victoria Aguirre 311, ☎ 3757/420800) has hours daily 7–1 and 2–8. On the Brazilian side you can contact **FozTur** (✉ Rua Alm. Barroso 1300, Foz do Iguaçu, Brazil, ☎ 045/574–2196 or 041/1516 [24-hr hotline]).

PATAGONIA

Updated by
Eddy Ancinas
and Robert P.
Walzer

Patagonia, the vast territory that covers the southern half of Argentina and Chile, is a state of mind that has possessed travelers and writers since the first sailing ships touched its gale-swept shores centuries ago. Brilliantly publicized by Charles Darwin after his cruises on the *Beagle* in the 1830s, by Reverend Lucas Bridges at the turn of the century in his inspiring *Uttermost Part of the Earth,* and brought back to a human scale by British writer Bruce Chatwin's more recent *In Patagonia,* the region—like the Amazon—attracts polemic attention. Briefly an empire under the aegis of an ambitious Frenchman, Patagonia is too vast and complex to get to know in a single visit.

It's a land for romantic adventurers whose idea of a good time includes an ample dose of physical discomfort and unexpected challenges. You can't rent a camper and circle this vast territory in a week. Tackling Patagonia means hit-and-run plane trips into desolate, windswept airports. (It was here that Antoine de Saint-Exupéry got his start as a commercial pilot, struggling to keep his tiny aircraft and its brave passengers from blowing off the runway before takeoff.) Comfortable accommodations are available near the three major visited areas: Bariloche, the Atlantic coast around Glacier National Park, and Tierra del Fuego. Getting from one place to the other, however, is still a time- and energy-consuming struggle involving dawn flights, poor connections, and unpredictable weather conditions that stymie the best-laid plans. In addition, tourists are often seen as a cash crop to be fleeced, like the sheep whose wool used to be the region's major money producer. Given these conditions, it's recommended that you arrange your Patagonian adventure in advance; vacations ranging from skiing packages to bird-watching tours are available from numerous operators (☞ Chapter 2).

Bariloche

In 1620, the Governor of Chile sent Captain Juan Fernández and his troops across the Andes in search of the *Enchanted City of the Caesars,* a mythological city alleged to be somewhere in Patagonia. The Jesuits established a mission on the shores of the lake, near what is now Isla Huemúl. Until the 1720s they attempted to convert the Tehuelches, who were very warlike and ultimately massacred the missionaries, including the missions' founder, Father Mascardi. No Europeans again visited the area until the next century, when Captain Cox arrived by boat from Chile in 1870, and later in 1876 *perito* (expert) Francisco

Moreno led an expedition from the Atlantic, thus becoming the first explorer to arrive from the East.

Most of the indigenous people of the area were brutally massacred during the infamous Campaña del Desierto (Desert Campaign, 1879–1883). Settlers then felt safe to colonize and a fort (called Chacabuco) was built at the mouth of the Río Limay in 1883. Many were German farmers immigrating from Chile, such as Karl Wiederhold, who built the first house in Bariloche in 1895. Swiss, German, Scandinavian, and northern Italians found a rugged and relatively unexplored land similar to their Alpine homelands. They skied and climbed the mountains, fished in nearby lakes and streams, and built chalets in town and along the shore of Lago Nahuel Huapi.

Bariloche's first tourists stayed in a hotel by belonging to Carlos Wiederhold called La Cuchara Sucia (the Dirty Spoon). By 1924 tourists traveled two days from Buenos Aires by train, then drove 560 km (350 mi) on dirt roads. The railway finally reached Bariloche in 1934, and by 1938 people from all over the world came to ski on the slopes at nearby Cerro Catedral (☞ *below*).

These days Bariloche has all the comforts and conveniences of a resort town, and is the gateway to the recreational and scenic splendors of the northern lake district. Though planes, buses, trains, boats, and tour groups arrive daily, once you're away from town, you can generally find a spot where you seem to be the only person in the world. The best way to escape into the stunning wilderness of clear blue lakes, misty lagoons, rivers, waterfalls, mountain glaciers, forests, and flower-filled meadows is by mountain biking, horseback riding, or hiking. Or by going fishing in one of the 40 nearby lakes and countless streams. It's possible to get around on your own with a rented car or to go on a planned excursion with a local tour company (☞ Tour Operators and Travel Agents *in* Patagonia A to Z, *below*).

For information on mountain climbing, trails, *refugios* (refuges or mountain cabins), and campgrounds, visit the **Intendencia de Parques Nacionales** at the Civic Center (✉ Av. San Martín 24, Bariloche, ☎ 2944/23111). Another source of information on local activities, excursions, lodging, and private and public campgrounds is the **Oficina Municipal de Turismo** (☞ Visitor Information *in* Patagonia A to Z, below) in the Civic Center. Alejandro Bustillo, the architect who designed the rustic, grey-green stone-and-log buildings of the Civic Center also designed the Llao Llao Hotel (☞ Dining and Lodging, *below*). His Andean-Swiss style is recognizable, too, in lodges and buildings throughout the lake district. The spacious square in front of the Civic Center, with an equestrian statue of General Roca (1843–1914) and a wide-angle view of the lake, is a good place to begin exploring the town. Note that the Civic Center is Km 0 for measuring points from Bariloche.

The **Museo de la Patagonia** (Patagonia Museum) tells the social and geological history of northern Patagonia through displays of Indian and gaucho artifacts and exhibits on regional flora and fauna. The history of the Mapuche and the Conquista del Desierto (Conquest of the Desert) are also explained in detail. ✉ *In Centro Cívico, next to the arch over Bartolomé Mitre,* ☎ *2944/422309.* 🎫 *Admission.* ☉ *Weekdays, 10–12:30 and 2–7, Sat. 10–1.*

The **Parque Nacional Nahuel Huapi,** created in 1943, is Argentina's oldest national park, and **Lago Nahuel Huapi** is the sapphire in its crown. The park extends over 2 million acres along the eastern side of the Andes in the provinces of Neuquén and Río Negro, on the frontier with Chile. It contains the highest concentration of lakes in Argentina. The biggest is Lago Nahuel Huapi, a 897-sq-km (557-sq-mi) body of water, whose seven long arms (the longest is 96 km [60 ft] long, 12 km [7 mi] wide) reach deep into forests of *coihué* (a native beech tree), *cyprés*, and *lenga* trees. Intensely blue across its vast expanse and aqua green in its shallow bays, the lake meanders into distant lagoons and misty inlets where the mountains, covered with vegetation at their base, rise straight up out of the water to lofty heights. Participating in every water sport invented and tours to islands and other extraordinarily beautiful spots can be arranged through local tour offices, outfitters, and hotels (☞ Outdoor Activities and Sports, *below*). Throughout the park are also information offices where you can get help in exploring the miles of mountain and woodland trails, lakes, rivers, and streams.

The most popular excursion on Lago Nahuel Huapi is by boat to **Isla Victoria** (Victoria Island), the largest in the lake. A grove of redwoods transplanted from California thrives in the middle of the island. After a walk on trails that lead to enchanting views of emerald bays and still lagoons, the boat crosses to the tip of the **Quitruihué Peninsula** for a visit to the **Parque Nacional los Arrayanes** (☞ Villa La Angostura, *below*).

The renowned ski area at **Cerro Catedral** (Mt. Cathedral) is 46 km (28½ mi) west of town on Avenida Ezequiel Bustillo (R237); turn left at Km 8½ just past Playa Bonita. The mountain was named for the Gothic-looking spires that crown its peaks. Though skiing is the main activity here (☞ Outdoor Activities and Sports, *below*), the view from the top of the chairlift at 6,600 ft is spectacular any time of year. Looking northwest, the intense blue of Lago Nahuel Huapi meanders around islands into invisible bays and disappears beneath mountains and volcanoes miles away.

You can reach the summit of **Cerro Otto** (Mt. Otto; 4,608 ft), another fine ski area, by hiking, mountain-biking, or driving 8 km (5 mi) up a gravel road from Bariloche. Hiking to the top of the mountain takes you through a forest of lenga trees to Argentina's first ski area at Piedras Blancas. Here Herbert Tutzauer, Bariloche's first ski instructor, won the first ski race by climbing the mountain, then skiing down it through the forest in one hour and 30 minutes. Or you can take the **Teleférico Cerro Otto** (✉ Av. de Los Pioneros), 5 km (3 mi) west of town; a free shuttle bus leaves from the corner of Mitre and Villegas, and Perito Moreno and Independencia; the ride to the top takes about 12 minutes. At the top, a revolving cafeteria with a 360-degree panorama takes in Mt. Tronador, lakes in every direction, and Bariloche. In winter, skis and sleds are available for rent at the cafeteria. In summer, hiking and mountain biking are the main activities. For a real thrill, try soaring out over the lake with the condors in a paraplane. For information on schedules and sled or ski rentals, call ☎ 2944/41031.

A visit to **Monte Tronador** (Mt. Thunderer) requires an all day outing of 170 km (105 mi) round trip from Bariloche. The 12,000-ft extinct volcano, the highest mountain in the northern lake district, sits astride the frontier with Chile, with one peak on either side. Take R258 south along the shore of **Lago Gutiérrez**; from here you can see Cerro Catedral. The road continues along the shore of **Lago Masacardi**. Between the two lakes the road crosses from the Atlantic to the Pacific watershed. At Km 35, turn off onto a road marked TRONADOR AND PAMPA LINDA and continue along the shore of Lago Mascardi, passing a village of the same name. Just beyond the village, the road forks and you continue on a gravel road, R254. Near the bridge the road branches left to **Lago Hess** and **Cascada Los Alerces** (☞ *below*)—a detour you might want to take on your way out. Bearing right after crossing Los Rápidos Bridge, the road narrows to one direction only: It's important to remember this when you set out in the morning, as you can only go up the road before 2 PM and down it after 4 PM. The lake ends in a narrow arm (Brazo Tronador), at the lovely Hotel Tronador, which has a dock for tours arriving by boat. The road then follows the **Río Manso** (Manso River) to **Pampa Linda**, which has a lodge, restaurant, park ranger's office, campsites, and the trailhead for the climb up to the **Refugio Otto Meiling** at the snow line. Guided horseback rides are organized at the lodge. The road ends 7 km (4 mi) beyond Pampa Linda in a parking lot that was once at the tip of the now receding **Glaciar Negro** (Black Glacier). As the glacier flows down from the mountain, the dirt and black sediment of its lateral moraines is ground up and covers the ice. At first glance, it's hard to imagine the tons of ice that lie beneath its black cap. The detour to **Cascada Los Alerces** (Los Alerces Falls), 17 km (10 mi) from the turnoff at the bridge, follows the wild Río Manso, where it branches off to yet another lake, **Lago Hess**. At this junction you find a campground, refuge, restaurant, and a trailhead for the 1,000-ft climb to the falls. The path through dense vegetation over wooden bridges crossing the rushing river as it spills over steep rocky cliffs is a grand finale to a day of viewing nature at its most powerful and beautiful. For more information about excursions to and activities on Mt. Tronador, ☞ Outdoor Activities and Sports, *below,* and ☞ Tour Operators and Travel Agents *in* Patagonia A to Z, *below.*

Another excursion from Bariloche is the **Circuito Chico** (Small Circuit), a half-day, 70-km (43½-mi) scenic trip along the west shore of Lago Nahuel Huapi. You can do it by car, tour bus, or mountain bike. First head west on Avenida Bustillo (R237) toward Península Llao Llao. At Km 20, you can take a brief side trip to the **Península San Pedro**, an 11-km-long (7-mi-long) appendage running parallel to the coastal road; this dirt road passes some fine homes set back in the woods. At the **Ahumadero Familia Weiss** (Weiss Family Smokehouse), along the way, you can buy smoked fish and game. Back on the main road, continue west to **Puerto Pañuelo** (Km 25½) in a little bay on the right; it's the embarkation point for lake excursions and for the boat crossing to Chile. Across from the port, a long driveway leads up a knoll to the Hotel Llao Llao (☞ Dining and Lodging, *below*), which is worth a visit even if you're not staying there. The Circuito Chico now follows R77 to Bahía Lopez, winding along the lake's edge through a forest of ghostly, leafless lenga trees. After crossing the bridge that links **Lago Moreno** (Lake Moreno) and Lago Nahuel Huapi at Bahía Lopez, the road crosses the Arroyo Lopez (Lopez Creek). Here you can stop for a hike up to a waterfall and then climb above Lago Moreno to **Punto Panoramico**, a scenic overlook well worth a photo stop. Just before you cross Lago Moreno, an unmarked dirt road off to the right leads to the rustic village of **Colonia Suiza**, a good spot to stop for tea or lunch. After passing **Laguna El Trebol** (a small lake on your left), R77 joins R237 from Bariloche.

The **Circuito Grande** (Large Circuit), a more ambitious excursion, which is particularly lovely in spring or fall, covers 250 km (155 mi). Along the way there are plenty of spots to stop and enjoy the view, have a picnic lunch, or even stay overnight. Leaving Bariloche on R237, follow the **Río Limay** into the **Valle Encantado** (Enchanted Valley), with its magical red-rock formations. Before crossing the bridge at **Confluéncia** (where the Río Traful joins the Limay), turn left onto R65 to Lago Traful. Five km (3 mi) beyond the turnoff, on a dirt road heading toward Cuyín Manzano, are some astounding formations. As you follow the shore of Lago Traful, a sign indicates a *mirador* (lookout) on a high rock promontory, which you can climb up to on wooden stairs. At **Villa Traful** (☞ *below*), you can buy picnic supplies. In Villa Traful, stop for a break at Ñancu-Lahuen, a teahouse and restaurant with a luscious garden; it's also a good place to get travel and fishing information. From here the road dives into a dense forest until it comes to the intersection with the Seven Lakes Circuit (☞ *below*); turn left, following the shore of **Lago Correntoso** to the paved road down to the bay at **Villa La Angostura** (☞ *below*).

The **Circuito de los Siete Lagos** (Seven Lakes Circuit) is an all-day trip of 360 km (223½ mi) round-trip, which could be extended to include an overnight in San Martín de los Andes. Drive north on R237 for 21 km (13 mi), and turn left on R231 to **Villa La Angostura**, 65 km (40 mi) from Bariloche. About 11 km (7 mi) farther along the same road is the Seven Lakes Road (R234), which branches right, and along the way passes **Lago Correntoso, Lago Espejo, Lago Villarino, Lago Falkner,** and **Lago Hermoso.** After lunch or tea or an overnight in **San Martín de los Andes** (☞ *below*), head south to Bariloche on the dirt road over Paso Cordoba, passing **Lago Meliquina** on the way. At Confluéncia, the road joins R237, following the Río Limay through Valle Encantado to Bariloche.

A longer, less traveled, all-day boat excursion to **Puerto Blest** leaves from Puerto Pañulo on the Península Llao Llao (accessible by bus, auto, or tour). The boat heads west along the shore of Lago Nahuel Huapi to Brazo Blest, a 1-km-long (¾-mi-long) fjordlike arm of the lake. Along the way, waterfalls plunge down the face of high rock walls. A Valdivian rainforest of coihués, cypress, lengas, and *arrayanes* (myrtle) covers the canyon walls. After the boat docks at Puerto Blest, a bus transports you over a short pass to Puerto Alegre on **Laguna Frías** (Cold Lagoon), where a launch waits to ferry you across the frosty green water to **Puerto Fríos** on the other side. Mt. Tronador towers like a great white sentinel. The launch returns to the dock at Puerto Alegre, where you can return by foot or by bus to Puerto Blest. A trail through the forest and up 600 steps to **Cascada Los Cántaros** (Singing Waterfalls) is worth the effort. After lunch in **Puerto Blest** at its venerable old hotel, the boat returns to Bariloche. Note: this is the first leg of the Cruce a Chile por Los Lagos (☞ *below*).

★ The **Cruce a Chile por Los Lagos** (Chile Lake Crossing) is a unique excursion by land and lakes that began in the 1930s when ox carts used to haul people. These days you can do this tour in one day or two. Follow the itinerary above, stopping for lunch in **Puerto Blest** and then continuing on to **Puerto Fríos** on **Laguna Frías.** After docking at Puerto Fríos and clearing Argentine customs, another bus climbs through a lush rainforest over a pass, then descends to **Peulla,** where Chilean customs is cleared (bring your passport). A little farther on is a comfortable lodge by **Lago Todos los Santos.** Early the next morning a catamaran sets out across the lake, providing views of the volcanoes **Putiagudo** (which lost its *punto* in an earthquake) and **Osorno.** The boat trip ends at the port of Petrohué. Another (and final) bus skirts **Lago Llanquihue,** stopping for a visit at the rockbound Petrohué waterfalls, passing through the town of **Puerto Varas** (famous for its roses) and arriving, at last, at the Chilean port town of Puerto Montt. Catedral Turismo (☞ Tour Operators and Travel Agencies *in* Patagonia A to Z, *below*) specializes in this trip and can arrange a one-day return by bus to Bariloche.

Dining and Lodging

If you don't have a car, it's better to stay in town. But if you're looking for more serenity, stay at one of the family-run *residenciales* (pensions), country inns, or resort hotels outside town. Addresses for out-of-town dining and lodging are measured in kilometers from the Civic Center, and signposts along the road denote these distances. The most crowded time of the year is during school vacations (July and January). August is best for skiing; February, the height of summer; May, for fall colors. Of the many fine restaurants, most are casual and open noon–3 for lunch and 8–midnight for dinner.

$$$ ✕ **La Marmite.** If there's a Euro-Argentine cuisine, this is it: wild boar
★ in wine with local mushrooms served with cabbage and elderberry jam; and venison, trout, and lamb prepared with equal imagination. Argentina's famous malbecs or cabernets are the perfect companion for this international fare. ⊠ *Mitre 329,* ☎ *2944/423685. AE, DC, MC, V. No lunch Sun.*

$$$ ✕ **El Patacón.** On a bluff overlooking the lake, this restaurant, con-
★ structed of local stone and wood, hosted President Clinton and Argentine President Menem when they visited Bariloche in 1998. The ranch-style interior displays gaucho tools, local art, and weavings. Leather and sheepskin furniture creates a warm atmosphere. An organic garden with fresh herbs, berries, and vegetables enhances the menu of meats, game, and fish. ⊠ *Av. Bustillo, Km 7,* ☎ *2944/442898. AE, DC, MC, V.*

$$ ✕ **El Boliche de Alberto.** This popular lunch spot serves typical Argentine cuisine with a Patagonian accent. Just point at a slab of beef, chicken, or lamb and have it grilled per your instructions (if you don't speak enough Spanish, there's always pasta). Sausages, empanadas, and chimichurri sauce accompany all of the above. ⊠ *Villegas 347,* ☎ *2944/ 431433. AE, DC, MC, V.*

$$ ✕ **El Boliche Viejo.** Next to the Río Limay, under the *alamos* (poplars), is this 100-year-old tin-and-wood structure that was once part of the Jones Ranch. In its rustic atmosphere, enjoy quintessential meat-and-potato dishes served from a giant grill. ⊠ *R237, Km 17 (18 km [11 mi] north of town),* ☎ *2944/425977. DC, MC, V.*

$$ ✕ **Jauja.** Big, friendly, and casual, this spot is a favorite with locals and families for its variety of meats, fish, and game dishes. Good salads and fresh vegetables are always available, as are pasta dishes. The nonsmoking section is a plus. ⊠ *Quaglia 366,* ☎ *2944/422952. AE, DC, MC, V.*

$$$$ ✕⊡ **Hotel Edelweiss.** Three blocks from the Civic Center, and walk-
★ ing distance from tour offices, restaurants, and shops, is this excellent medium-size hotel. Fresh flowers from the owner's nursery are arranged throughout. The modern, spacious rooms and suites have lake views from their bay windows. Breakfast includes eggs, bacon, sausages, fresh fruits, and juices—unusual in this country of *medias lunas* (croissants) and coffee. Both lunch and dinner consist of good salads, grilled fish, fowl, game, and beef prepared with fresh vegetables and tasty sauces. Most ski and tour buses, whether arranged through the hotel or other travel agencies, pick up passengers at this hotel. ⊠ *Av. San Martín 202,* ☎ *2944/426165,* FAX *2944/425655. 94 rooms, 6 suites. Restaurant, bar, in-room safes, indoor pool, beauty salon, massage, sauna, exercise room, meeting rooms, travel services, parking. CP. AE, DC, MC, V.*

$$$$ ✕⊡ **Llao Llao Hotel & Resort.** This masterpiece by architect Alejandro Bustillo sits on a grassy knoll surrounded by three lakes with a backdrop of sheer rock cliffs and snow-covered mountains. Local wood— alerce, cypress, and hemlock—has been used for the walls, and wicker furniture upholstered with native weavings makes the lobby feel like an elegant hunting lodge. Along the 100-yard hallway, paintings by local artists are displayed between fine boutiques. Activities abound: children's supervised play activities, tango and salsa lessons, a full spa program, tennis courts, a superb 18-hole golf course ($25 fee for guests), windsurfing, mountain-bike rentals, and walking tours around the peninsula. ⊠ *Av. Ezequiel Bustillo, Km 25 (25 km [15½ mi] west of Bariloche),* ☎ *2944/448530,* FAX *2944/445781. 162 rooms, 8 suites. Restaurant, bar, café, piano bar, in-room safes, minibars, no-smoking*

rooms, indoor pool, beauty salon, hot tub, massage, sauna, spa, 18-hole golf course, tennis courts, aerobics, archery, exercise room, paddle tennis, dock, windsurfing, boating, skiing, children's programs, convention center, meeting rooms, travel services. AE, DC, MC, V.

$$$$ 🏨 **El Casco.** Outside town, just off the busy road to Llao Llao, El Casco is tucked away behind carefully tended gardens and trees. A fine view of Isla Huemul and the lake brightens every room, each decorated with different antiques. In the oldest part of the original house, the three-room apartment has a private entrance and a sitting room with a fireplace. ✉ Av. Ezequiel Bustillo, Km 11 8400 (11 km [7 mi] west of Bariloche), ☎ 🏧 2944/461032 or 2944/461088. 23 rooms, 1 apartment. Restaurant, bar, café, beauty salon, massage, sauna, dock. AE, DC, MC, V.

$$$$ 🏨 **Hotel Nevada.** Right in the middle of town, this traditional hotel is a favorite of business travelers and tourists. Rooms are well above street-noise level, and although the hotel is old, rooms are well furnished in a pleasant mountain style. Breakfast, snacks, and tea are served in the bar/café. The business center with fax and Internet access is a rare amenity in this recreation-minded town. ✉ Rolando 250, 8400, ☎ 2944/422778, 🏧 2944/427914. 74 rooms, 14 suites. Bar, café, sauna, business services, parking. CP. AE, DC, MC, V.

$$$$ 🏨 **Hotel Tunquelen.** Surrounded by 20 acres of woods and gardens, this châteaulike hotel outside Bariloche is visible from the lake, but not from the busy road to Llao Llao. An uninterrupted view across the water to distant peaks—even from the indoor pool—has a tranquilizing effect. From the minute you step into the lobby/living room, sink into the soft cushions in front of the fireplace, and look out on the lake, you feel at home. Rooms are neat, with whitewashed stucco and native wood, and open onto the garden or overlook the lake. A downstairs dining room serves breakfast and dinner, and cocktails are served in the garden, weather permitting. ✉ Av. Bustillo, 8400 (22 km [13 mi] west of Bariloche on the road to Llao Llao), ☎ 🏧 2944/48400 or 2944/48600. 31 rooms, 1 suite, 8 apartments. Restaurant, piano bar, indoor pool, tennis court, paddle tennis, beach, boating, meeting rooms, travel services. AE, DC, MC, V.

$$$–$$$$ 🏨 **Hotel Catedral.** The handsome stone and wood Hotel Catedral sits on a hill just beyond the tram building across the road from the Cerro Catedral ski area. Its dining room windows frame a perfect postcard view of the lake and surrounding mountains. Rooms are furnished with simple, white fabrics and solid wood furnishings; the apartments are done in quiet earth tones and modern furnishings. In winter, Argentines and Brazilians book well in advance. ✉ Cerro Catedral ski area; mailing address in Buenos Aires: Av. Cordóba 1345, ☎ 11/4816–8811 in Buenos Aires. 60 rooms. 2 restaurants, bar, pool, 2 tennis courts, sauna, shops, travel services. AE, DC, MC, V. Closed Apr.–May and Oct.–Nov.

$$ 🏨 **Casita Suiza.** Swiss-owned and -operated since 1961, this charming downtown chalet exudes old-world hospitality. Rooms are immaculate, and rates include a hearty breakfast with homemade wheat bread, jams, and juices. In summer and spring the street-side terrace explodes with blossoming pansies and violets. ✉ Quaglia 342, 8400, ☎ 🏧 0944/23775 or 0944/26111. 13 rooms. Restaurant, bar, laundry service. CP. AE, DC, MC, V.

$$ 🏨 **Patagonia Sur.** This tall, slender seven-story structure is Bariloche's newest hotel; it's high on a hill overlooking the town and the lake, just five blocks from town. The view of the church spire, rooftops, and blue lake make the climb up the stairway from town worth the effort. Inside and out it's thoroughly clean and modern, from the new softly upholstered chairs in the lobby to the sparsely furnished rooms—an appropriate treatment, as the view dominates the decor. ✉ Elfleín

340, 8400, ☎ *2944/422995,* FAX *2944/424329. 55 rooms. Café, parking. CP. AE, DC, MC, V.*

$ ⌘ **Quime Quipan.** This congenial wood and white-stucco *hostería* (inn) is surrounded by a garden in a quiet neighborhood within walking distance of the Civic Center. Rooms are small, simple, and tidy. ⊠ *Av. Los Pioneros, Km 1, 8400 (1 km [¾ mi] west of downtown),* ☎ FAX *2944/425423. 18 rooms, 1 apartment. Dining room, snack bar, parking. CP. DC, MC, V.*

Nightlife and the Arts

Three of the town's most popular *discotecas* (discos) are all on the same street, Avenida J. M. de Rosas. All open at 10 PM and cost about $10–$20 plus the purchase of a drink. Whole families—from children to grandparents—go to discos, though on Saturday night only people 25 years and older are admitted. The clubs are especially busy during school holidays and ski season. Try **Cerebro** (⊠ 405 Av. J. M. de Rosas, ☎ 2944/424965); **El Grisu** (⊠ 574 Av. J. M. de Rosas, ☎ 2944/422269); and **Rocket** (⊠ 424 Av. J. M. de Rosas, ☎ 2944/420549 day and 2944/431940 night). Around the corner from the Avenida J. M. de Rosas strip of clubs is the **Casino Española** (⊠ España 476, ☎ 2944/424421); it's open 10 PM–4 AM.

Outdoor Activities and Sports

FISHING

Lago Nahuel Huapi and the Gutiérrez, Masacardi, Correntoso, and Traful lakes are just a few of the many in the northern Lake District that attract fishing fanatics from all over the world. If you're seeking the perfect pool or secret stream for fly-fishing, you may have to do some hiking, particularly along the banks of the Chimehuín, Limáy, Traful, and Correntoso rivers. Fishing lodges offer rustic comfort in beautiful settings; boats, guides, and plenty of fishing tales are usually included. Make reservations well in advance of fishing season, which runs November 15–April 15.

Fishing licenses allowing you to catch brown trout, rainbow trout, perch, brook trout, and *salar sebago* (landlocked) salmon are easy to get at Bariloche's **Direcciones Provinciales de Pesca** (⊠ Elfleín 10, ☎ 2944/425160), in the Nahuel Huapi National Park office (☞ *above*) and at most tackle shops. Boats can be rented at **Charlie Lake Rent-A-Boat** (⊠ Av. Ezequiel Bustillo, Km 16.6, ☎ FAX 2944/448562). For information about fly-fishing, contact the following guides: Oscar Baruzzi at **Baruzzi Deportes** (⊠ Urquiza 250, ☎ 2944/424922); **Martín Pescador** (⊠ Rolando 257, ☎ 2944/422275); or **Ricardo Almeijeiras** (⊠ Quinchahuala 200, ☎ FAX 2944/441944).

MOUNTAIN BIKING

The entire Nahuel Huapi National Park is ripe for mountain-biking. Whether you're a beginner or an expert, you can find a trail to suit your ability. All of the following rent bikes and organize tours: **Adventure World** (⊠ Quaglia 262, Local 23, ☎ FAX 2944/427264); **La Bolsa del Deporte** (⊠ Elfleín 385, ☎ FAX 2944/423529); **Cumbres Patagonia** (⊠ Villegas 222, ☎ 2944/4232646); and **Dirty Bikes** (⊠ Vice Almirante O'Conner 681, ☎ FAX 2944/425616).

WHITE-WATER RAFTING

With all the interconnected lakes and rivers in the national park, there's something for everyone—from your basic family float down the swift-flowing, scenic Río Limay, to a wild and exciting ride down Río Manso (Class II), which takes you 16 km (10 mi) in three hours. If you're really adventurous, you can take the Manso all the way to Chile (Class IV) through spectacular scenery. Some tour companies organize a trip down the Manso with return by horseback and a cookout at a ranch. Both **Adventure World** and **Cumbres Patagonia** (☞ Mountain Biking, *above*) arrange white-water rafting trips along the Manso. Cumbres Patagonia also arranges trips along the Río Limay, as does **Bariloche Rafting** (⊠ Mitre 86, Room 5, ☎ 2944/424854).

Shopping

Ahumadero Familia Weiss (⊠ Palacios 401) makes pâtés and cheeses. You can't avoid the chocolate shops on both sides of Calle B. Mitre: **Abuela Goya** (⊠ Mitre 258), **Del Turista** (⊠ Mitre 239), and **Fenoglio** (⊠ Mitre and Rolando). Items for the discerning equestrian or modern gaucho—belts, jackets, boots, bags, and jewelry—are artfully displayed at **Cardon** (⊠ Villegas 216). **Cerámica Bariloche** (⊠ Mitre 112) has been creating fine ceramics inspired by colorful local flora and fauna for 50 years. **Cultura Libros** (⊠ Elfleín 78) has books in English and coffee-table books with superb photos of Patagonia. **El Establo** (⊠ Mitre 22) sells gaucho knives, maté gourds, leather clothing, and silver accessories. **Fitzroy** (⊠ Mitre 18) has a good selection of ponchos, Mapuche blankets, and gaucho articles.

Río Gallegos

The administrative and commercial capital of Santa Cruz Province and perhaps the windiest town in the world (from September to November), Río Gallegos was founded in 1885 and served as a port for coal shipments from Río Túrbio (Túrbio River), on the Chilean border. Wool and sheepskins were its only other economic factors. Now, as the gateway city to southern Patagonia and the Parque Nacional los Glaciares (☞ *below*), tourism presents a new commodity. A desk at the airport has information on all the tourist attractions in the area, and the helpful attendants can make suggestions and hotel reservations.

If you're into dinosaurs, the **Museo Regional Provincial Padre Manuel Jesus Molina** (Provincial Museum) has exhibits of reconstructed skeletons excavated at sites in Patagonia. Exhibits on biology, geology, history, paleontology, and Tehuelche ethnology are displayed in different sections of the museum. ⊠ *Ramon y Cajal 51,* ☎ *2966/423290.* ☉ *Weekdays 10–5, weekends 11–7.*

Dining and Lodging

$$ ✕ **El Horreo.** A well-heeled clientele begins to fill this rather classy Spanish-looking restaurant around 10:30 PM. Complimentary Pisco sours (a delicious drink of Pisco brandy from Chile, whirred in a blender with lemon, egg whites, and sugar) begin your repast. It's hard to beat the local spring lamb, the steaks, or the mountain trout, crab, and seafood cooked a variety of ways—grilled or in homemade sauces. Service is slow but attentive. ⊠ *Av. Roca 862,* ☎ *2966/426462. MC, V.*

$ ✕ **Trattoria Diaz.** This big, open, family-style café in the center of town has been serving grilled lamb and beef, homemade pastas, seafood, and fish since 1932. ⊠ *Av. Roca 1157,* ☎ *2966/420203. DC, MC, V.*

$$$ ▥ **Costa Rio.** Flags flutter above the entrance to this modern white-brick "apt-hotel" (hotel with apartments, similar to small condominiums) on a quiet side street. For business travelers and families in town for an extended stay, having a room with chairs, sofas, and tables makes this slightly expensive hotel (for this region) worth the extra money. A kitchenette and eating area offer an alternative to going out for every meal. All rooms are carpeted and have comfortable, contemporary furnishings. ⊠ *Av. San Martín 673, 9400,* ☎ ℻ *2966/ 423412. 54 apartments. Café, kitchenettes, minibars, laundry service and dry cleaning, baby-sitting, parking. AE, DC, MC, V.*

$$ ☎ **Hotel Santa Cruz.** This hotel looks old, but rooms are comfortable though they have no frills. Intimate seating areas, plants, and a friendly staff make the lobby bar a pleasant retreat on a windy day. Avoid rooms on the Avenida Roca side, as they can be noisy. ⊠ *Av. Roca 701, 9400,* ☎ *2966/420601,* 𝐅𝐀𝐗 *2966/420603. 53 rooms, 1 suite. Restaurant, sauna, parking. AE, DC, MC, V.*

El Calafate and the Parque Nacional los Glaciares

Founded in 1927 as a frontier town, El Calafate is the base for all excursions to the Parque Nacional los Glaciares (Glaciers National Park), which was created in 1937. Because of its location on the southern shore of Lago Argentino, the town enjoys a microclimate much milder than the rest of southern Patagonia. During the long summer days between December and February (when the sun sets around 10 PM), thousands of visitors come to see the glaciers and fill the hotels and restaurants. October, November, and March are less crowded, less expensive periods to visit. March through May is the rainy season, followed by cold winter weather through September.

Getting here may seem like a daunting task, but the experience of seeing the glaciers more than compensates for any difficulties you may encounter. Every year airlines and tour companies are making it easier. From Río Gallegos, the trip can take up to six hours by land across desolate plains filled with more sheep than you can count in a lifetime of sleepless nights. But the journey is occasionally enlivened by the sight of *ñandú* (rheas), llamalike guanacos, silver-gray foxes, and fleet-footed hares the size of small deer. A shorter option is a 45-minute flight from Río Gallegos to El Calafate on Kaiken Airlines.

Avenida del Libertador San Martín (known as Libertador or San Martín) is the only paved street with sidewalks; along it are shops selling sportswear, camping and fishing equipment, souvenirs, and food (☞ Shopping, *below*). A staircase in the middle of San Martín ascends to Avenida Julio Roca, where you'll find the bus terminal and a very busy tourist office. You can also get information at the **national park office** (⊠ Av. Libertador 1302, ☎ 2902/491005), open weekdays 7–2.

Approximately 1.5 million acres of the *hielo Continental* (Continental ice cap), which spreads its icy mantle from the Pacific Ocean across Chile and the Andes into Argentina and covers an area of approximately 21,700 sq km (8,400 sq mi), are contained in the **Parque Nacional los Glaciares,** a UNESCO World Heritage Site. Extending along the Chilean border for 350 km (217 mi), the park is 40% covered with ice fields that branch off into 47 major glaciers that feed two lakes—the 15,000-year-old **Lago Argentino** (Argentine Lake, the largest body of water in Argentina) in the southern end of the park and **Lago Viedma** at the northern end near **Monte Fitzroy** (Fitzroy Mountain Range), which rises 11,138 ft. Visits to the park are usually by tour, though you could rent a car and go on your own. Plan on a minimum of three days to see the glaciers and enjoy the town—more if you plan to visit El Chaitén, Cueva de los Manos (Cave of the Hands), or the lakes.

★ One of the few glaciers in the world still growing after 3,000 years, the **Glaciar Moreno** (Moreno Glacier), 80 km (50 mi) and a two-hour drive on R11 from El Calafate, is generally the first destination in the national park. After entering the park, the road winds through hills, until suddenly the startling sight of the glacier, descending like a long white tongue for 80 km (50 mi) through distant mountains, abruptly ends in a translucent blue wall, 3 km (2 mi) wide and 165 ft high. A viewing area, wrapped around the point of the **Península de Magallanes,** allows you to wander back and forth, looking across the **Canal de los Tempanos** (Iceberg Channel). Here you listen and wait for the cracking sound—when tons of ice break away and fall with a thunderous crash into Lago Argentino—nature's number one ice show. Sometimes water even splashes onlookers across the channel! As the glacier creeps across this narrow channel and meets the land on the other side, an ice dam builds up between **Brazo Rico** on the left and the rest of the lake on the right. As the pressure on the dam increases, everyone waits for the day it will rupture. The last time was in 1986, when the whole thing collapsed in a thunderous finale that lasted hours and could be heard in El Calafate. Videos of this event are still sold locally.

Glaciar Upsala (Upsala Glacier), the largest glacier in South America, is 60 km (37 mi) long and 10 km (6 mi) wide. Accessible only by boat, daily cruises depart from **Puerto Banderas** (40 km west of El Calafate via R11) for a 2½-hour trip. Along the way, the boats dodge floating islands of ice as they maneuver as close as they dare to the wall of ice rising up from the aqua-green water of Lago Argentino. The seven glaciers that feed the lake deposit their debris into the runoff, causing the water to cloud with minerals ground to fine powder by the glacier's moraine (the accumulation of earth and stones left by the glacier). Condors and black-chested buzzard eagles build their nests in the rocky cliffs above the lake. When the boat stops for lunch at **Onelli Bay,** you can walk behind the restaurant into a wild landscape of small glaciers and milky rivers carrying chunks of ice from four glaciers into Lago Onelli (Onelli Lake).

For a jaw-dropping view of the Glaciar Viedma (Viedma Glacier) and **Monte Fitzroy,** drive north 213 km (123 mi) to the northern limits of the park. The Fitzroy range is visible for hundreds of miles (weather permitting); the Tehuelche called it *Chaltén* (Mountains of Smoke), which is the name of the village of **Chaltén,** a hiking mecca, at the base of the range. From this little town, founded in 1985, you can do many great hikes to lakes, glaciers, and stunning viewpoints. Expert mountaineers from every corner of the globe come to Chaltén to plan their ascent of **Cerro Torre,** that most illusive peak; sometimes they camp for weeks (even months) at Laguna Torre, waiting for the wind to die down, the rain to stop, or the clouds to disperse so that they can climb. For maps, hiking, and lodging information, contact the **Comisión de Fomento** (⊠ Av. M. de M. Güemes 25, Chaltén, ☎ FAX 2962/ 493011) or the **national park office** (⊠ before you cross the bridge to town over Río Fitzroy, ☎ FAX 2962/93004). To reach this area, drive east from El Calafate on R11 (toward Río Gallegos) until it meets R40 (35 km); then take R40 north (a dirt road), crossing Río Santa Cruz and Río La Leona, which connects with Lago Viedma. At this point, stop and look at **Viedma Glacier** descending into the lake, with the Fitzroy massif towering on the horizon. The **Laguna del Desierto** (Lake of the Desert), a lovely lake surrounded by forest, is 37 km (23 mi) north of Chaltén on R23, a dirt road. The **Posada Lago del Desierto** (☎ FAX 2962/ 93010) has a restaurant and a few rooms in a small lodge as well as cabins without hot water or indoor bathrooms.

Dining and Lodging

$$ ✕ **Michelangelo.** This 22-year-old establishment won a gold medal for "International Gastronomy" in 1995. The low wooden ceilings, white stucco walls, and wooden floors create a friendly dining-hall atmosphere. Sizzling steaks prepared with a variety of sauces, grilled chicken and fish, homemade pasta, and lamb cooked in tarragon and mustard sauce are some of the local specialties. ⊠ *Moyano 1020,* ☎ *2902/ 491045. AE, DC, MC, V.*

$ ✕ **La Cocina.** This casual café on the main shopping street serves great food made with cheese—quiches, crepes, pastas, and hamburgers. Homemade ice cream and delicious cakes make a good snack any time of the day. ✉ *Av. Libertador 1245,* ☎ *2902/491758. MC.* ☾ *Closed 2–7:30.*

$$$$ ✕▥ **Hosteria los Notros.** Forty km (25 mi) west of El Calafate on the road (R11) to the Moreno Glacier, this simple wooden structure clinging to the mountainside looks across at the astounding mass of ice. Rooms are large, with simple country furnishings, gold and terracotta walls, and the glacier framed in every window; some also have fireplaces. A short stroll through the garden, over a bridge spanning a canyon with a waterfall, connects rooms to the main lodge. Appetizers and wine are served in full view of sunset (or moonrise) over the glacier, followed by dinner featuring roast beef, venison, wild boar, and trout—all enhanced by fresh vegetables and homegrown herbs. An in-house coordinator arranges tours with multilingual guides and box lunches. ✉ *Reservations in Buenos Aires: Arenales 1457, 7th floor,* ☎ *11/48143934 in Buenos Aires, 2902/491437 in El Calafate,* ℻ *11/ 48157645 in Buenos Aires, 2902/491816 in El Calafate. 20 rooms. Restaurant, bar, room service, travel services, airport shuttle. AE, DC, MC, V. Closed June–Aug.*

$$$$ ✕▥ **Hotel Kau-yatun.** A short drive from town, this former ranch house at the foot of the mountains exemplifies traditional Patagonian hospitality. The large living room, with picture windows looking out on a spacious lawn, is pleasantly cluttered with books, games, and magazines. Comfortable furniture, a well-stocked bar, and an open fireplace encourage mingling. Guest rooms vary in size, shape, and decor, but mostly follow the casual ranch theme, with flowery curtains and simple furnishings. Country cuisine—meat, pasta, and vegetables—are served in the dining room, and more exotic fare—trout, venison, and wild boar—are available at *La Brida.* On weekends, in the *quincho* (combination kitchen/grill/dining room), steaks and *chorizos* (sausages) sizzle on a large open grill, while lamb or beef cooks gaucho style on an *asador* (a skewer stuck in the ground to cook meat over hot coals). Folk music and dancing provide entertainment. ✉ *Estancia 25 de Mayo,* ☎ *2902/491059,* ℻ *2902/491045. 45 rooms. Restaurant, bar, shops. AE, MC, V.*

$$$$ ✕▥ **Posada los Alamos.** Surrounded by tall, leafy alamo trees and constructed of brick and dark *quebracho* (ironwood), this attractive country manor house is a model of tasteful luxury. The rich tones of wood, leather, and handwoven fabrics in the lobby, bar, and sitting areas; the plush comforters and chairs in every room; and a staff ready with helpful suggestions make this a top-notch hotel. Lovingly tended gardens surround the building and line a walkway through the woods to the shore of Lago Argentino. ✉ *Moyano 1355,* ☎ *2902/491144,* ℻ *2902/ 491186. 140 rooms, 4 suites. Restaurant, 2 bars, 3-hole golf course, tennis court, shops, travel services. AE, MC, V. Closed June–Aug.*

$$$ ▥ **Michelangelo.** This very reasonably priced hotel is two blocks from the town center and next to the restaurant of the same name (☞ *above*). Bright red and yellow native flowers line the front of the low log and stucco building with its distinctive A-frames over rooms, restaurant, and lobby. A fine collection of local photographs are displayed on the walls next to a sunken lobby, where a banquette covered with flower print cushions, and easy chairs surround the fireplace. Some rooms have beamed ceilings, and all are simply furnished with floral prints. ✉ *Moyano 1020, 9405,* ☎ *2902/491045,* ℻ *2902/ 491058. 20 rooms. Restaurant, café. AE, MC, V. Closed June–Aug.*

$$$ ▥ **El Quijote.** Sun shining through picture windows onto polished slate floors and high beams gives this modern hotel, on a quiet side street

in town, a light and airy feel. The carpeted rooms with plain white walls and wood furniture provide peaceful comfort. It's right next to El Molino restaurant and a few blocks from the main street. ✉ *Gregores 1155, 9405,* ☎ *2902/491017,* FAX *2902/491103. 80 rooms. Bar, café, travel services. AE, DC, MC, V.*

Outdoor Activities and Sports

HIKING

Short excursions to and along Lago Argentino, in the hills south and west of town, or to some rather overrated caves with restored paintings, 8 km (5 mi) east of town at Punta Gualichó, are the hiking options close to El Calafate. El Chaltén, the village in the northern part of the park, is a good base for many excellent hikes to lakes and glaciers and up mountain peaks like **Cerro Torre.** On the way to Lago del Desierto, the 5 km (3 mi) hike to **Chorillo del Salto** (Trickling Falls) is a good warm-up walk. The six-hour hike to the base camp for Cerro Torre at **Laguna Torre** guarantees (weather permitting) dramatic views of torres Standhart, Adelas, Grande, and Solo. The eight-hour hike to the base camp for **Monte Fitzroy** passes Laguna Capri, which mirrors the granite tower framed by ghostly lenga trees. Other hikes to and around Lago del Desierto are described in brochures and maps obtainable at the tourist office in El Chaltén (☞ *above*) or at the tourist office or national park office in El Calafate (☞ *above*).

HORSEBACK RIDING

Short rides along Lago Argentino, day trips to the caves of Gualichó, and weeklong camping excursions into the mountains can all be arranged in El Calafate by **Gustavo Holzman** (✉ J.A. Roca 2035, ☎ 2902/491203) or through the tourist office and some hotels in El Calafate. In Chaltén, most of the hiking trails can also be done on horseback, as mountaineering equipment is transported to base camps in this manner. Make arrangements through local outfitters and guides: **Rodolfo Guerra** (✉ northwest of town at the Fitzroy trailhead, ☎ 2962/493020); and **Thomás Fernandez** (✉ Lago del Desierto, ☎ 2962/493009).

ICE TREKKING

A two hour minitrek on the Moreno Glacier involves transfer from El Calafate to Brazo Rico by bus and a short lake-crossing to a dock and refugio, where you set off into the woods with a guide through the treacherous terrain. Crampons, provided, are attached over hiking boots and the climb commences. The entire outing lasts about five hours. Most hotels arrange minitreks as does **Hielo y Aventura** (✉ Av. Libertador 935, ☎ FAX 2902/491053), which also organizes much longer, more difficult trips of 8 hours to a week to other glaciers.

MOUNTAIN BIKING

Opportunities for mountain biking are numerous, including along the dirt roads and mountain paths that lead to the lakes, glaciers, and ranches. Rent bikes and get information at **Alquiler de Bicicletas** (✉ Av. Libertador and Cmte. Espora, ☎ 2902/491496).

Ushuaia and the Tierra del Fuego

Ushuaia—which at 55 degrees latitude south is closer to the South Pole (2,480 mi) than to Argentina's northern border with Bolivia (2,540 mi)—is the capital and tourism base for Tierra del Fuego, an island at the southernmost tip of Argentina. Although its physical beauty is tough to match, Tierra del Fuego's historical allure is based more on its mythic past than on reality. The island was inhabited for 6,000 years by Yamana, Haush, Selk'nam, and Alakaluf Indians. But in the late

19th century, after vanquishing the Indians in northern Patagonia, the Argentine Republic was eager to populate Patagonia to bolster its territorial claims in the face of European and Chilean territorial ambitions. An Anglican mission had already been established in Ushuaia in 1871, and Argentina had seen Great Britain claim the Falklands, a natural Argentine territory. Thus, in 1902 Argentina moved to initiate an Ushuaian penal colony, establishing the permanent settlement of its most southern territories and, by implication, everything in between.

At first, only political prisoners were sent to Ushuaia. But later, fearful of losing Tierra del Fuego to its rivals, the Argentine state sent increased numbers of more dangerous criminals. When the prison closed in 1947, Ushuaia had a population of about 3,000, mainly former inmates and prison staff. Another population boom occurred after Argentina's 1978 industrial incentives law, which attracted electronics manufacturers like Philco and Grundig to Ushuaia. In recent years many of these television and home-appliance factories have shut down because they weren't able to compete in the global marketplace. But the children those boom times produced now roam Ushuaia's streets.

Today the Indians of Darwin's "missing link" theory are long gone—wiped out by disease and indifference brought by settlers—and the 45,000 residents of Ushuaia are hitching their star to tourism. Ushuaia feels a bit like a frontier boom town, with noisy, smelly, circa-1970s cars clogging the streets, and restaurants and hotels opening on once-empty lots. In the late '90s the local government completed an airport that has the capacity to handle direct flights from abroad and finished a deep-water pier that welcomes cruise ships stopping for provisions in Ushuaia on their way to the Antarctic. Unpaved portions of R3, the last stretch of the Panamerican Highway, which connects Alaska to Tierra del Fuego, are finally, albeit slowly, being paved.

The town of Ushuaia itself can be called picturesque at best. Parts of it resemble an oversize mining camp awaiting the next strike. Wooden shacks, precariously mounted on upright piers and ready for speedy displacement to a different site, look like entrants in a contest for most original log cabin. A chaotic and contradictory urban landscape includes a handful of luxury hotels amid some of the world's most unusual public housing projects—one monstrous, corrugated-tin development has a highway running right through it. Town planning has never been a strong point in Ushuaia; instead, irregular rows of homes sprout with the haphazardness of mushrooms in a moist field.

And yet, as you stand on the banks of the Canal del Beagle (Beagle Channel) near Ushuaia, as Captain Robert Fitzroy—the captain who was sent by the English government in 1832 to survey Patagonia, including Tierra del Fuego—must have done so long ago, the spirit of the farthest corner of the world takes hold. What stands out is the light: At sundown it casts the landscape in a subdued, sensual tone; everything feels closer, softer, more human in dimension despite the vastness of the setting. The snowcapped mountains of Chile reflect the illumination of the setting sun back onto a stream rolling into the channel, as nearby peaks echo their image—on a windless day—in the still waters.

Above the city, the last mountains of the Andean Cordillera rise, and just south and west of Ushuaia they finally vanish into the often stormy sea. Snow dots the peaks with white well into summer. Nature is the principal attraction here, with trekking, fishing, horseback riding, and sailing among the most rewarding activities, especially in the Parque Nacional Tierra del Fuego (Tierra del Fuego National Park). In winter, when most international tourists stay home to enjoy their own summer, the adventurous have the place to themselves for cross-country and downhill skiing, dog sledding, and snowmobiling across the powdery dunes. In an effort to attract more tourists in winter (presently summer is the busiest season), the government built a new ski resort, Cerro Castor, and began actively promoting winter sports.

The **Antigua Casa Beben** (Old Beben House), built in 1913, is one of Ushuaia's original houses. It was initially a branch office of Banco Nacion, then a house owned by the Croatian Beben family, and was finally moved to its current location and restored in 1994. It's now a cultural center where art exhibitions are mounted. ⊠ *Maipú and Pluschow.* ⊠ *Free.*

Rainy days are a reality in Ushuaia, but two museums give you an avenue for urban exploration and a glimpse into Tierra del Fuego's fascinating past. Part of the original penal colony, the Presidio was built to house political prisoners, street orphans, and a variety of other social undesirables from the north. Today it houses the **Museo Marítimo** (Maritime Museum), within Ushuaia's naval base, with exhibits on the town's extinct indigenous population, Tierra del Fuego's navigational past, Antarctic explorations, and life and times in an Argentine penitentiary. You can enter cell blocks and read the fascinating stories of the prisoners who lived in them while gazing upon their eerily lifelike effigies. Well-presented tours, in English and Spanish, are conducted at 5 PM daily. ⊠ *Gobernador Paz and Yaganes,* ☏ *2901/437481.* ⊠ *Admission.* ☉ *Daily 10–3 and 5–8.*

At the **Museo del Fin del Mundo** (End of the World Museum), you can see a scarily large stuffed condor, among other native birds, indigenous items, maritime instruments, and such seafaring-related artifacts as an impressive mermaid figurehead taken from the bowsprit of a galleon. In addition, there are photographs and histories of El Presidio's original inmates, such as Simon Radowitzky, a Russian immigrant anarchist who received a life sentence for killing an Argentine police colonel. The museum also has the best existing library and bookstore devoted to Tierra del Fuego as well as a snack bar. ⊠ *Maipú 173 and Rivadavía,* ☏ *2901/421863.* ⊠ *Admission.* ☉ *Daily 10–3 and 5–8.*

The **Tren del Fin del Mundo** (Train of the End of the World) takes you to the Parque Nacional Tierra del Fuego (☞ *below*), 12 km (7½ mi) away. The train ride is a simulation of the trip on which El Presidio prisoners were taken into the forest to chop wood. Though it's pricey at $30, the 2¼-hour ride is a pleasant trip in which a good deal of Ushuaia history is detailed. Try to get on the more quaint and realistic steam train rather than the smelly diesel one. ⊠ *Train departs from a stop near the entrance to the national park,* ☏ *2901/431600.*

For a trip along the **Canal del Beagle,** contact tour operators in Ushuaia (☞ Tour Operators and Travel Agencies *in* Patagonia A to Z, *below*). On the tour you can get a startling close-up view of all kinds of sea mammals and birds on **Sea Lion's Island** and near **Les Eclaireurs Lighthouse.**

One good excursion in the area is to picturesque **Lago Escondido** (Hidden Lake) and Lago Fagnano (Fagnano Lake). On the way you pass through deciduous beech-wood forest and past beavers' dams, peat bogs, and glaciers. The lakes have campsites and fishing and are good spots for a picnic or a hike. A rougher, more unconventional tour of the lake area goes to **Monte Olivia** (Mt. Olivia), the tallest mountain along the Canal del Beagle, rising 4,455 ft above sea level. You also pass the **Five Brothers Mountains** and go through the **Garibaldi Pass,** which begins at the Rancho Hambre, climbs into the mountain range, and ends with a spectacular view of Lago Escondido. From here you continue on to Lago Fagnano through picturesque countryside past sawmills and lumberyards. To do this trip in a four-wheel-drive vehicle with an excellent bilingual guide, contact Canal Fun & Nature; for a more conventional tour in a comfortable bus with a bilingual guide and lunch at Valle de los Huskies, try All Patagonia (☞ Tour Operators and Travel Agencies *in* Patagonia A to Z, *below*).

Estancia Harberton (Harberton Ranch) consists of 50,000 acres of coastal marshland and wooded hillsides. The property was a late-19th-century gift from the Argentine government to Reverend Thomas Bridges, officially considered the Father of Tierra del Fuego. Today the ranch is managed by Bridges's great-grandson, Thomas Goodall, and his American wife, Natalie, a scientist who has cooperated with the National Geographic Society on conservation projects; most people visit as part of organized tours (☞ Patagonia A to Z, *below*), but you'll be welcome if you stray by yourself onto the couple's spread. They serve up a solid and tasty tea in their home, the oldest building on the island. For safety reasons, exploration of the ranch can only be done through a guide. Lodging is not available, but you can arrange to dine at the ranch by calling ahead for a reservation (☎ 2901/422742). Most tours reach the estancia by boat, offering a rare opportunity to explore the **Isla Martillo** penguin colony, in addition to a sea lion refuge on **Isla de los Lobos** (Island of the Wolves) along the way.

If you've never butted heads with a glacier, the mountain range just above Ushuaia is home to the **Glaciar Martial.** Named after Frenchman Luis F. Martial, a 19th-century scientist who wandered this way aboard the warship *Romanche* to observe the passing of planet Venus, the glacier is reached via a panoramic ski lift. Take the Camino al Glaciar (Glacier Road) 7 km (4½ mi) out of town until you reach the Glaciar Martial ski lodge (☞ Outdoor Activities and Sports, *below*). A 15-minute skyline ride brings you to the beginning of a 1-km (½-mi) trail that winds its way over lichen and shale straight up into the mountain. After a strenuous 30-minute hike, you can cool your heels in one of the many gurgling, icy rivulets that cascade down water-worn shale shoots, or enjoy a picnic while you wait for an early sunset. When the sun drops behind the glacier's jagged crown of peaks, brilliant rays beam over the mountain's crest, spilling a halo of gold-flecked light on the glacier, valley, and channel below. Moments like these are why this land is so magical. However, temperatures drop dramatically after sunset, so come prepared with warm clothing.

The pristine **Parque Nacional Tierra del Fuego,** 12 km (7½ mi) west of Ushuaia, offers you a chance to wander through peat bogs, stumble upon hidden lakes, trek through native *canelo*, lenga, and wild cherry forests, and experience the wonders of Tierra del Fuego's rich flora and fauna. Visits to the park, tucked up against the Chilean border, are commonly arranged through tour companies. Trips range from bus tours to horseback riding to more adventurous excursions, such as canoe trips across Lapataia Bay. Another way to get to the park is to take the Tren del Fin del Mundo (☞ *above*). Or you could take a bus run by **Transporte Kaupen** (☎ 2901/434015) or several other private bus companies (☞ Getting Around by Bus *in* Patagonia A to Z, *below*); the Transporte Kaupen buses travel through the park, making several stops within it; so you can get off the bus, explore the park, and then wait for the next bus to come by or trek to the next stop. Yet one more option is to drive to the park on R3 (take it until it ends and you see the last sign on the Panamerican Highway, which starts at Alaska and ends here). Trail and camping information is available at the park entrance ranger station or at the tourist office. A nice excursion in the park is by boat from lovely **Ensenada Bay** to **Isla Redonda** (Redonda Island), a wildlife refuge where you can follow a footpath to the western side and see a wonderful view of the Canal del Beagle. While on Isla Redonda, you can send a postcard and get your passport stamped at the world's southernmost post office. Tours are run by **Isla Verde**, represented by Yishka Turismo y Aventuras (☞ Tour Operators and Travel Agencies *in* Patagonia A to Z, *below*).

Dining and Lodging

Dotting the perimeter of the park are five free campgrounds, none of which has much more than a spot to pitch a tent and a fire pit. Call the **park office** (☎ 0800/231476) or consult the ranger station at the park entrance for more information. **Camping Lago Roca** (✉ Lago Roca, 20 km [12 mi] from Ushuaia, ☎ no phone), also within the park, charges $5 a day and has bathrooms, hot showers, and a small market. Of all the campgrounds in the area, **Camping Río Pipo** is the closest to Ushuaia (it's 10 km [6 mi] away).

$$ ✕ **Café Ideal.** This casual local hangout has become popular by serving good, light food and providing solid service. Try the homemade pastas, the local trout, or the pizza. It's also open all day long, unlike most Argentine restaurants. And come weekend summer evenings, the place gets funky with live music performed by local groups. ✉ *Av. San Martín 393,* ☎ *2901/437860. AE, DC, MC, V.*

$$ ✕ **La Estancia.** For lamb and other typical Patagonian meats, try this restaurant in the center of town. Sit by the glass wall to see the chef artfully coordinate the flames, the cooking, and the cutting of tender pieces of lamb and parrilla-styled meats. Don't be bashful about requesting more lamb if you're still hungry; there's no extra charge. ✉ *Av. San Martín 253,* ☎ *2901/421241. AE, DC, MC, V.*

$$ ✕ **Hotel Albatros.** Your best bet is the weekday, fixed-price menu, which includes appetizer, main course, and dessert; at other times it's much more expensive and it always costs more if you order à la carte. The food is reasonably well prepared, including such dishes as steak, ravioli with red sauce, baked chicken with french fries, and hake with mashed potatoes. Best of all, tables overlook the Canal del Beagle with the Isla Navarino in the distance. The restaurant only gets crowded when tour groups are staying at the hotel (☞ *below*). ✉ *Av. Maipú 505,* ☎ *2901/430003. AE, DC, MC, V.*

$$$$ 🛏 **Hotel y Resort Las Hayas.** In the wooded foothills of the Andes, this massive hotel serves as a lordly lookout over the town and the channel below. Not a single detail has been left out in the meticulous design and decor, making it one of Argentina's finest hotels. From the Portuguese linen to the oak furnishings and fabric-padded walls, luxurious amenities abound. A suspended glass bridge connects the hotel to a complete health spa, where you can bathe in a heated indoor pool or rekindle your hiker's spirit with aromatherapy or a lymphatic massage. The hotel is outside the town center, but frequent shuttle buses can take you there. ✉ *Camino Luis Martial, Km 3, 9410,* ☎ *2901/430710, 1/4499808 in Buenos Aires,* 🖷 *2901/430710 or 2901/430719. 102 rooms, 8 suites. Restaurant, bar, coffee shop, in-room safes, indoor pool, hot tub, massage, sauna, golf privileges, health club, squash, laundry service, convention center, meeting rooms, travel services. AE, DC, MC, V.*

$$$ 🛏 **Hotel Albatros.** The best part about this hotel is the view from the restaurant and bar; aside from that, services are solid but unremarkable. Originally constructed of lenga, a local hardwood, the Albatros burned to the ground in 1982 and was rebuilt of wood but without the same charm. Rooms are clean and standard issue: reasonably comfortable beds, plain wood furniture, and TVs; some have views of the

dock and channel. ✉ *Av. Maipú 505, 9410,* ☎ *2901/430003,* ℻ *2901/430666. 73 rooms, 4 suites. Restaurant, bar, café, minibars, laundry service, travel services. AE, DC, MC, V.*

$$ 🏨 **Hostería Petrel.** At this small, isolated lodge along the shores of Lago Escondido, fishing, hiking, and relaxing are the order of the day; the hotel can arrange for guides. Its oversize restaurant serves tour buses stopping on their way to visit Escondido and Fagnano lakes. Ask for one of the upstairs rooms if you'd like a pleasant balcony over the lake, or for a lower room if you'd prefer a large Jacuzzi but no balcony. ✉ *R3, Km 3,086, 9410 (50 km [31 mi] from Ushuaia),* ☎ ℻ *2901/433569. 9 rooms. Restaurant, snack bar. No credit cards.*

$$ 🏨 **La Posada.** This family-run hotel in the middle of town is a decent, lower-cost alternative to the bigger, more costly hotels. It has rooms facing the mountains on one side and the bay and mountains on the other; all have telephones and TVs. The owners are eager to please: With their own minivan, they'll pick you up at the airport and take you on excursions to nearby sites (for an additional fee). ✉ *Av. San Martín 1299, 9410,* ☎ ℻ *2901/454901 or 2901/433330. 17 rooms. Breakfast room. AE, MC, V (10% discount if you pay with cash).*

Nightlife and the Arts

Ushuaia has a lively nightlife scene in summer, with its casino, discos, and cozy cafés where you can have coffee or a beer. The biggest and most popular disco is **Kronos. Barney's** is a more intimate dance club. Try your luck at the only full-fledged casino, **Casino Club S.A.** (✉ Av. San Martín 638), where roulette minimums are $2 and blackjack table minimums are $5; there's a $3 entrance fee in the evening. **El Pueblo** (✉ Av. Gobernador Campo and Av. Rivadavía) has free, live folk music Wednesday–Sunday.

Outdoor Activities and Sports

FISHING

The rivers of Tierra del Fuego are home to a variety of trophy-size freshwater trout—including browns, rainbows, and brooks—making the area a sportsperson's paradise. Both fly and spin casting are available. The fishing season runs November 1–March 31; fees range from $10 a day to $40 for a month. Fishing expeditions are organized by the following companies: **Asociación de Caza y Pesca** (✉ Av. Maipú 822, ☎ 2901/423168); **Rumbo Sur** (✉ Av. San Martín 342, ☎ 2901/422441 or 2901/223085); and **Yishka Viajes y Aventuras** (✉ Gobernador Godoy 115, Piso 1, Oficína 7, ☎ 2901/431230).

MOUNTAIN BIKING

Good mountain bikes normally cost about $5 an hour and $15–$20 for a full day. They can be rented at **D. T. T. Cycles Sport** (✉ Av. San Martín 1258); **Firpo** (✉ Sebastian El Cano 176, ☎ 2901/24424); or **Seven Deportes** (✉ Av. San Martín and Av. 9 de Julio). Guided bicycle tours (including rides through the national park), for about $50 a day, are organized by **All Patagonia** (✉ Fadul 26, ☎ 2901/430725); **Licatur** (✉ Av. San Martín 880, ☎ 2901/22337); **Pretour** (✉ Tekenika 119, ☎ 2901/422150); and **Rumbo Sur** (✉ Av. San Martín 342, ☎ 2901/422441).

SKIING

Ushuaia is the cross-country skiing center of South America, thanks to enthusiastic Club Andino members who took to the sport in the 1980s and made the forested hills of a high valley about 20 minutes from town a favorite destination for skiers. From Hostería Tierra Mayor and Hostería Los Cotorras, two places where you can ride in dog-pulled sleds, rent skis, go cross-country skiing, get lessons, and eat; contact the tourist office for more information. **Glaciar Martial Ski Lodge** (☎ 2901/2433712), open year-round Tuesday–Sunday 10–7, functions as a cross-country ski center from June to October. Skis can also be rented in town, as can snowmobiles.

For downhill skiers, Club Andino has bulldozed a couple of short, flat runs directly above Ushuaia. A new downhill ski area, **Cerro Castor,** 26 km (16 mi) northeast of Ushuaia on R3 has 15 trails and four high-speed ski lifts. More than half the trails are at an intermediate level, a fifth are for beginners, and another few are for experts. You can rent skis and snowboards and take ski lessons here.

Shopping

El Globo (✉ Av. San Martín 991) carries an array of antique Patagonian furnishings and paintings, maritime antiquities, wood carvings, and picture frames. For typical regional chocolates, head for **Laguna Negra** (✉ Av. San Martín 513); or **Ushuaia** (✉ Av. San Martín 785). **Mascaras Aborigenes Fueguinas** (✉ Piedrabuena 25) has masks made from local lenga—copies of aboriginal masks used for the *hain* ceremony, in which adolescents were initiated into sexual life. **Temaukel** (✉ Av. San Martín 1051) sells some interesting local artisan goods. **Tierra de Humos** (✉ Av. San Martín 861) and **Ushuaia Drugstore** (✉ Av. San Martín 638) have leather and ceramic handicrafts, postcards, T-shirts, and Patagonian jams.

Patagonia A to Z

Arriving and Departing

BY AIRPLANE

Aerolíneas Argentinas (☎ 11/4317–3000 or 11/4340–7800 in Buenos Aires; ☎ 2944/422425 in Bariloche; ☎ 2966/422020 in Río Gallegos), the country's major airline, flies from Buenos Aires to Bariloche, Río Gallegos, and Ushuaia. **Kaiken** (☎ contact Almafuerte Travel in Buenos Aires, 11/4331–0191 or 11/4331–0191; ☎ 2944/420251 in Bariloche; ☎ 2966/442062 in Río Gallegos; ☎ 2901/432963 in Ushuaia) flies between Buenos Aires and Bariloche, Río Gallegos, and Ushuaia; request the *banda negativa* fare for cheaper tickets sold subject to availability.

In summer, **LADE** (☎ 11/4361–7071 or 11/4361–7174 in Buenos Aires; ☎ 2944/423562 in Bariloche), the Air Force transport line, flies from Buenos Aires to Bariloche. **Lapas Líneas Aereas** (☎ 11/4819–5272 or 11/4819–6200 in Buenos Aires; 2944/423714 in Bariloche) flies between Buenos Aires, Bariloche, and Ushuaia.

BY BOAT

Traveling between Bariloche and Puerto Montt, Chile, by boat is one of the most popular excursions in Argentina. It requires three lake crossings and various buses and can be done in a day or overnight (☞ Bariloche, *above*). Travel agents and tour operators in Bariloche and Buenos Aires can arrange this trip and many foreign tour companies include it in their itineraries (☞ Tour Operators and Travel Agents, *below*).

BY BUS

Bariloche's Terminal de Omnibus (Bus Station; ✉ Av. 12 de Octubre, ☎ 2944/432860) is in the Estacíon de Ferrocarril General Roca (Railroad Station) east of town, where all bus companies have offices. The following bus companies run comfortable and reliable overnight buses between Buenos Aires and Bariloche (22 hrs): **Chevallier** (✉ Moreno 107, Bariloche, ☎ 2944/423090 in Bariloche, 11/4314–0111 or 11/4314–5555 in Buenos Aires); **El Valle** (✉ Mitre 321, Bariloche, ☎ 2944/429012 in Bariloche, 11/4313–3749 in Buenos Aires); and **Via Bariloche** (✉ Av. 12 de Octubre 1884, Bariloche, ☎ 2944/422217 in Bariloche, 11/4663–8899 in Buenos Aires). Buses also depart daily from Bariloche for Chile (Osorno, Puerto Montt, Valdivia, and Santiago) via the Puyehue Pass; contact **Tas–Choapa** (✉ Bariloche Bus Terminal, ☎ 0944/26663 in Bariloche, 562/6970062 in Santiago).

The following bus companies connect Buenos Aires to Río Gallegos and El Calafate: **Don Otto** (Mitre 161, ☎ 2944/323269); **Interlagos** (✉ Av. San Martín 1175, El Calafate, ☎ 0902/91018; ☎ 0966/22614 in Río Gallegos); **El Pingüino** (☎ 11/4315–4438 in Buenos Aires); and **TAC** (☎ 11/4313–3627 or 11/4313–3632 in Buenos Aires). In summer, **Bus Sur** (☎ FAX 5661/411325); and **Turismo Zaahj** (☎ 5661/412260) make the five-hour run from Puerto Natales, Chile, to El Calafate.

You'll probably want to fly to Ushuaia, but direct bus service between Buenos Aires and Chile and Ushuaia exist. **Trans los Carlos** (✉ Av. San Martín 880, Ushuaia, ☎ 0901/22337) and **Turismo Ghisoni** (✉ Lautaro Navarro 975, Punta Arenas, ☎ 5661/223205) make the 12-hour run to and from Punta Arenas, Chile.

BY CAR

Driving to any of the towns in Patagonia from Buenos Aires is a long haul (2–3 days) along interminable stretches without motels, gas stations, or restaurants. Fuel in Argentina is expensive and if you break down in the hinterlands, it's unlikely that you'll find anyone who speaks much English. Note, too, that places on the map may just be estancias and when you arrive all you may find is a gate and a road leading off to the horizon. But roads are paved all the way to Bariloche, and if you're a more adventurous traveler driving exposes you to the heart of the country. To get to Bariloche from Buenos Aires: Take R5 to Santa Rosa (615 km/382 mi), then R35 to General Acha (107 km/66 mi), then R20 to Colonia 25 de Mayo, then R151 to Neuquen (438 km/272 mi), and then R237 to Bariloche (449 km/279 mi).

Driving to Río Gallegos (2,504 km/1,555 mi from Buenos Aires) is even more daunting, more isolated, and more monotonous. The most sensible solution is to fly and rent a car at your destination. Roads between towns and sights in both the northern and southern Lake Districts are mostly paved, and if not, generally kept in good condition.

Getting Around

BY BUS

To travel from Bariloche south contact **Don Otto** (✉ Mitre 161, ☎ 2944/323269); **Andesmar** (✉ Palacios 246, ☎ 2944/422140 or 2944/430211 at the bus terminal); and **TAC** (✉ Villegas 147, ☎ 2944/432521), which also has service to the north.

In Río Gallegos, **Pinguino** (✉ Zapiola 445, ☎ 2966/423338) has daily service to El Calafate (✉ Terminal de Omnibus, Julio Roca 1004, ☎ 2902/491273).

BY CAR

A number of international rental agencies can be found in Patagonia's major cities and tourist centers: **Avis** (☎ 11/4326–5542 in Buenos Aires); **Budget** (☎ 11/4313–9870 in Buenos Aires; ✉ Mitre 106, Bariloche, ☎ 2944/422482); **Dollar** (☎ 11/4315–8800 in Buenos Aires; ✉ Av. San Martín 491, inside the Hotel Panamericano, Bariloche, ☎ 2944/430358); and **Hertz** (☎ 11/4312–1317 in Buenos Aires).

Local chains include: **Ai-Ansa International** (✉ Av. San Martín 235, across from Edelweiss Hotel, Bariloche, ☎ 2944/422582); **Duma** (✉ Belgrano and Rosales, Ushuaia, ☎ 2901/231914); **Localiza** (☎ 11/4816–3999 or 11/4815–6303 in Buenos Aires; ✉ Av. Julio Roca, El Calafate, ☎ 2966/491446; ✉ Sarmiento 237, Río Gallegos, ☎ 2966/42441; ✉ Av. San Martín 1222, Ushuaia, ☎ 2901/230739); **Rent-A-Car** (✉ Belgrano and Ameghino, Ushuaia, ☏ 2901/230757); and **Visita Rent-a-Car** (✉ Maipú, Ushuaia, ☏ 2901/235181).

BY TAXI

Since taking a taxi doesn't cost much and drivers know their way around, arranging tours or quick trips by taxi to sights near Bariloche, Calafate, or other locales makes sense. In Bariloche, there are taxi stands at the Civic Center and at calles Mitre and Villegas. In other towns, taxis line up at the airport, the bus terminal, and at main intersections. Your hotel can also call a taxi for you.

Hiring a *remise* (car with driver) costs about the same as a taxi, but is bigger and the rate is set before you depart on your trip. In Bariloche: **Remises Auto Jet** (✉ España 11, ☏ 2944/422408); and **Remises Bariloche** (✉ Villegas 282, ☏ 2944/430222). In Río Gallegos: **Centenario** (✉ Maipú 285, ☏ 2966/422320).

Contacts and Resources

BANKS AND CURRENCY EXCHANGE

Hardly anyone changes dollars to pesos these days since the rate is equal; in fact, you often get change in both. In smaller towns, pesos are preferred. Torn or marked dollars may not be accepted. Banks are open 10–4 in most towns.

In Bariloche, ATMs (Banelco, Link, Cirrus) can be found at **Banco Frances** (✉ Av. San Martín 336, ☏ 2944/430325); and **Banco Quilmes** (✉ Mitre 433, ☏ 2944/423675). In Río Gallegos, try **Bancos de Galicia, Nazionale de Lavoro,** and **Hipotecario Nacional** (✉ all on Fagnano off of Av. Roca) or **Banco de Santa Cruz** (✉ Roca and Errázuri), which changes travelers' checks. In El Calafete, look for **Provincia de Santa Cruz** (✉ Av. Libertador 1285, ☏ 2902/491168).

EMERGENCIES

Ambulance: ☏ 107. **Coast Guard:** ☏ 106. **Fire:** ☏ 100. **Forest Fire:** ☏ 103. **Hospitals: Hospital Ramon Carillo** (✉ Moreno 601, Bariloche, ☏ 2944/42117 or 426119); **Hospital Municipal** (✉ Av. Roca 1487, El Calafate, ☏ 2902/491001); **Hospital Regional** (✉ José Ingeniero 98, Río Gallegos, ☏ 2966/420025 in emergencies, ☏ FAX 2966/420641).

Pharmacies: Del Centro (✉ Rolando 699, Bariloche, ☏ 2944/424422); **De Miguel** (✉ Mitre 130, Bariloche, ☏ 2944/423025); and **Elustondo** (✉ Mitre 379, Bariloche, ☏ 2944/422847). **Police (Local)** (☏ 2944/422992 in Bariloche; ☏ 2966/420287 in Río Gallego). **Police (Regional):** ☏ 101.

HEALTH AND SAFETY

The water in Bariloche and throughout Patagonia is generally safe. But if you're susceptible to intestinal disturbances, it's best to stick to bottled water, which is available in stores, restaurants, and at some kiosks. *Tabanas* (horse flies) are pests around horses and in the woods in summer; horse-fly repellent is more effective than general bug spray; bring enough for yourself and the horse. Car break-ins and purse snatching is on the rise late at night, so take precautions.

TELEPHONES, THE INTERNET, AND MAIL

Local calls can be made from *telecabinas* (phone booths) with a phone card purchased at kiosks. Numerous *locutorios* (telephone offices) are found in all towns. They're easy to use: An attendant sends you to a booth where you can call all over the country or the world, and then pay one bill when you leave.

In Bariloche, **Locutorio Quaglia** (✉ Quaglia 220, ☏ FAX 2944/426128) has fax, Internet, E-mail, and Western Union services; it's open daily 7:30 AM–1 AM. **Mas** (✉ Moreno 724, in front of the hospital, ☏ 2944/

428414), in Bariloche, has fax and photocopy services; it's open daily 7 AM–4 AM. **Cyber Club Bariloche** (✉ Galería del Sol, Location 54, 340 Mitre, ☎ 2944/421418), in Bariloche, has Internet and E-mail access; it's open Monday–Saturday 9:30–9:30. In Ushuaia, you can make calls and access the Internet at **Locutorio Cabo de Hornos** (✉ Av. 25 de Mayo 112) and **Locutorio Fin del Mundo** (✉ Av. San Martín 957).

Bariloche (✉ in the Centro Civico) is open daily 8–8; stamps can also be purchased at kiosks around town. **El Calafate** (✉ Av. Libertador 1122). **Río Gallegos** (✉ Avs. Julio Roca and San Martín).

TOUR OPERATORS AND TRAVEL AGENCIES
For a comprehensive tour of Patagonia, contact **Gador Viajes** (✉ Tucumán 941, Buenos Aires, ☎ 11/43229806).

In Bariloche contact **Alunco** (✉ Moreno 187, Piso 1, Bariloche, ☎ 2944/422283; ✉ Maipú 812, Piso 4, Buenos Aires, ☎ 11/43149076) or **Catedral Turismo** (✉ Mitre 399, Bariloche, ☎ 2944/425443).

In Río Gallegos contact, **Interlagos Turismo** (✉ Fagnano 35, Río Gallegos, ☎ 2966/422614), or **Tur Aike Turismo** (✉ Zapiola 63, Río Gallegos, ☎ FAX 2966/424503 or 2966/422436) organizes tours in and around Río Gallegos.

In El Calafate, good operations include **Cal Tur** (✉ Av. Libertador 1080, ☎ FAX 2966/491368); **E.V.T. Fitzroy Expeditions** (✉ Av. San Martín, ☎ 2962/493017); **Gustavo Holzman** (✉ J.A. Roca 2035, El Calafate, ☎ 2902/491203), who arranges horseback riding trips; **Hielo y Aventura** (✉ Av. Libertador 935, ☎ FAX 2902/491053); or **Interlagos Turismo** (✉ Av. Libertador 1175, ☎ 2902/491179).

Tour operators in Ushuaia include **All Patagonia** (☎ 2901/437025); **Antartur** (✉ Maipú 237, ☎ 2901/23240); **Licatur** (✉ Av. San Martín 880, ☎ 2901/22337); **Linéa B** (☎ 2901/441139); **Rumbo Sur** (✉ Av. San Martín 342, ☎ 2901/21139); **Tiempo Libre** (✉ Av. San Martín 863, ☎ 2901/31374); **Tolkeyén** (✉ Tekenika 119, ☎ 2901/22150 or 2901/32920); and **Yishka Turismo y Aventuras** (✉ Av. San Martín 1295, ☎ 2901/431230 or 2901/431535).

VISITOR INFORMATION
Provincial tourism boards include the following. **Santa Cruz Tourism Institute** (✉ Av. Roca 863, Río Gallegos, 9400, ☎ 2966/422702 or 2966/437447). **Tierra del Fuego Tourism Institute** (✉ Av. Maipú 505, Ushuaia, 9410, ☎ 2901/421423). **Tourism Secretariat of Río Negro** (✉ Gallardo 121, Viedma, 8500, ☎ 2920/422150, 2920/424615, or 2920/430996).

Local tourist offices (*Direcciónes de Turismo*) are generally easy to find, open all day and often into the evening, and helpful. **Bariloche** (✉ in the Civic Center, east end of Bartolomé Mitre, ☎ 2944/423022). **El Calafate** (✉ Terminal de Omnibus, Julio A. Roca 1004, ☎ FAX 2902/49090). **Río Gallegos** (✉ Av. Roca 1551, ☎ FAX 2966/42595). **Ushuaia** (✉ Av. San Martín 674, ☎ 2901/432000 or 0800/3331476).

ARGENTINA A TO Z

Arriving and Departing

By Airplane
Buenos Aires, out of its Ezeiza International Airport (34 km/21 mi from downtown), is served by a variety of foreign airlines, as well as domestic airlines that run international routes. If your national airline doesn't fly directly into Buenos Aires, it's often possible to fly into Brazil, and take a 2–3 hour flight on Aerolineas Argentinas into Ezeiza.

Aerolíneas Argentinas (☎ 11/4340–3777 in Buenos Aires, ☎ 800/333–0276 in U.S.). **Alitalia Italian Airlines** (☎ 11/4310–9999 in Buenos Aires). **American Airlines** (☎ 11/4480–0366 in Buenos Aires, ☎ 800/433–7300 in U.S.). **British Airways** (☎ 0345/222–111 in Buenos Aires). **Iberia Spanish Airlines** (☎ 11/4327–2739 in Buenos Aires). **KLM (Holland)** (☎ 11/4480–9470 in Buenos Aires). **LanChile** (☎ 11/4312–8161 in Buenos Aires, ☎ 800/735–5526 in U.S.). **United Airlines** (☎ 11/4316–0777 in Buenos Aires, ☎ 800/538–2929 in U.S.). **Varig Brasil** (☎ 11/4342–4420 in Buenos Aires, ☎ 800/468–2744 in U.S.). **Virgin Atlantic** (☎ 01293/747–747 in Buenos Aires).

FLYING TIMES

Flying times to Buenos Aires are 11–12 hours from New York and 8½ hours from Miami. Flights from Los Angeles are often routed through either Lima, Bogotá, or Miami.

Getting Around

By Airplane

Flights from Buenos Aires to other points within Argentina depart from **Aeroparque Jorge Newbury,** which is a 15-minute cab ride from downtown and more than 60 km (38 mi) from the international airport.

All medium-size and large cities in Argentina are served by **Aerolíneas Argentinas** (☎ 11/4340–3777, 800/333–0276 in U.S.) and **Austral** (☎ 11/4317–3605). **LAPA** (☎ 11/4912–1008) also provides regional service. Schedules are greatly reduced in the winter to tourist destinations.

By Boat

There's frequent ferry service between Argentina and Uruguay; the best boats are run by **Buquebus** (⊠ Av. Córdoba and Av. Madero; ⊠ in Patio Bullrich shopping mall, ☎ 11/4317–1001). Some cruise lines have itineraries that include Argentina (☞ Chapter 2).

By Bus

Regular, dependable bus service links Buenos Aires with all the provinces and with neighboring countries. On *comun* buses, the cheaper option, you'll usually get a seat, but it may not be that comfortable and there may not be air-conditioning or heating. **Diferencial** buses, only marginally more expensive, usually have reclining seats (some even have *coche-camas,* bed-like seats), an attendant, and snacks. To get between neighboring towns, you can often take a local city bus.

Buenos Aires's **Estación Terminal de Omnibus** (⊠ Av. Ramos Mejía 1680, Buenos Aires, ☎ 11/4310–0700) is the main gateway for long-distance bus travel. Over 60 bus companies are housed in the station; different companies serving the same destination are clumped together, making it easy to compare times and prices. You can buy tickets at the terminal right up until the bus departs. Prices depend on the company and destination, and aren't always cheaper than flying (a round-trip ticket to Paraguay, 18 hours each way, costs about $170; a roundtrip airfare for the same route can be found for the same price); compare prices.

By Car

The **Automovil Club Argentino** (ACA, ⊠ Av. del Libertador 1850, Buenos Aires, ☎ 11/4802–6061) operates gas stations, motels, and campgrounds; provides tow trucks and mechanics in case of a breakdown; and gives out maps and expert advice (sometimes in English) to help you plan your itinerary. Automobile Association of America (AAA) members can use the consulting services without charge, with proof of membership.

GASOLINE

Gas stations are easy to find in cities and along the highway outside of major cities. Farther along the highway and in rural areas, locating a station is hit or miss; don't let your tank get too low. Gas is expensive (at least $1 per liter, or about $4 per gallon). There are no regulations on leaded versus unleaded gas, and most consumers choose the cheaper, leaded option. Many vehicles also use diesel.

RENTALS

Renting a car in Argentina is expensive ($95 per day for a medium-size car, $475–$600 per week); be sure to ask about special rates as prices can be negotiated. All cities and most tourist areas have rental agencies. Another option is to hire (perhaps, through your hotel) a *remise,* a car with a driver, especially for day outings. Remises usually end up being cheaper than taxis for long rides, and at least marginally less expensive for rides within cities. You have to pay cash.

ROAD CONDITIONS

Around cities, you'll find ultramodern multilane highways. Gradually these highways become narrower routes, and then country roads. Many rural routes aren't divided and aren't in very good condition. Tolls come frequently and can be steep (on the 5-hour drive between Buenos Aires and Mar del Plata the toll is $13). Night driving can be hazardous, as highways and routes typically cut through the center of towns. Cattle often get onto the roads, and trucks seldom have all their lights working.

RULES OF THE ROAD

Plan your daily driving distances conservatively, don't drive after dark, ask about gas stations before you leave. Obey speed limits and traffic regulations; if you do get a traffic ticket, don't argue. In the not so distant past, Argentina was a military state, and the police are still treated as though they wield quite a bit of power. Although you'll see Argentines offering cash on the spot to avoid getting a written ticket, this isn't a good idea.

Turning left on avenues is prohibited unless there's a traffic-light arrow showing that it's okay. Note that lights aren't always observed, so proceed with care. Also note that traffic lights not only turn yellow when they're about to turn red, but also right before turning green. In Buenos Aires, give everyone else on the road priority, especially aggressive taxi drivers who think they're race-car drivers. In towns and cities, a 40 kph (25 mph) speed limit applies on streets, and a 60-kph limit is in effect on avenues. On expressways the limit is 120 kph (75 mph), and on other roads and highways out of town it's 80 kph (50 mph). Seat belts are required by law.

Contacts and Resources

Customs and Duties

If you come directly to Buenos Aires by air or sea, customs officials usually wave you through without any inspection. International airports have introduced a customs system for those with "nothing to declare," which has streamlined the arrival process. Bus passengers usually have their suitcases opened. Personal items and professional equipment are admitted free of duty, provided they've been used. You're supposed to declare your computer and pay a tax on it; if you're going to be in Argentina on an extended stay and plan to get Internet access for your laptop or hook up your cellular phone, declare them both at customs as you enter the country—you'll need to produce either the document from customs or a receipt to get service. Fishing gear presents no problems. Up to 2 liters of alcoholic beverages, 400 cigarettes, and 50 cigars are admitted duty-free. Note that you must pay a $20 departure tax upon leaving the country, payable in pesos or dollars.

Dining
MEALTIMES
Breakfast is usually served until 10 AM; lunch runs from 12:30 to 2:30; dinner is from 9 PM to midnight. A few restaurants in major cities stay open all night, or at least well into the morning, catering to after-the-ater and nightclub crowds.

DRESS
Jacket and tie are suggested for evening dining at more formal restaurants in the top price category, but casual chic or informal dress is accepted in most restaurants.

Emergencies
Ambulance: ☎ 107. **Fire:** ☎ 1100. **Police:** ☎ 101.

Health and Safety
ALTITUDE SICKNESS
Soroche, or altitude sickness, which results in shortness of breath and headaches, may be a problem when you visit the Andes. To remedy any discomfort, walk slowly, eat lightly, and drink plenty of fluids (avoid alcohol). If you have high blood pressure and a history of heart trouble, check with your doctor before traveling to high Andes elevations.

CRIME
Buenos Aires is quite safe; in some neighborhoods it's not uncommon to see young children and little old ladies strolling around at night. Police constantly patrol tourist areas, and violent crime is rare. Smaller towns and villages in Argentina are even safer, so much so that you may find yourself in a room in a small country inn where the door doesn't have a lock. That said, keep in mind that there are terrible incidents and crazy people everywhere, and Argentina is no exception. Follow local advice on whether or not it's safe to walk at night and where. At all times, keep documents, money, and credit cards hidden in a money belt or in zipped pockets. Passports, tickets, and other valuables are best left in hotel safes. Don't carry valuables swinging from your shoulder or hanging around your neck, and avoid wearing jewelry you aren't willing to lose. Always remain alert for pickpockets.

FOOD AND DRINK
Drinking tap water and eating uncooked greens is considered safe in Buenos Aires, but most visitors stick with bottled water. You have a greater chance of running into contamination outside of metropolitan Buenos Aires. Each year there are several hundred cases of cholera in the northern part of the country, mostly in the indigenous communities near the Bolivian border; your best protection is to avoid eating raw seafood.

Language
Argentines speak Spanish (commonly referred to as Castellano). There are a few important differences between Argentine Spanish and that of the rest of Latin America. For example, the informal *tu* form is replaced by *vos* (with some different conjugations). Also, the double L found in words like *pollo* is pronounced with a J-sound rather than a Y-sound. English replaced French as the country's second language in the 1960s, although most people still have a very limited knowledge of it. Luckily, many hotels, restaurants, and shops employ someone who speaks English.

Mail

POSTAL RATES AND DELIVERY

When delivery is normal and there are no strikes or postal vacations, mail takes 6–15 days to get from Buenos Aires to the United States and 10–15 days to the United Kingdom. Put postcards in envelopes and they will arrive more quickly. An international airmail letter costs about $1. Letters and packages sent by international courier take 3–5 days for all destinations, and the cost can be steep ($28 for a 3-day letter to the United States). Companies include **DHL** (⊠ Moreno 631, Buenos Aires, ☎ 11/4347–0600) and **Federal Express** (⊠ Maipu 753, Buenos Aires, ☎ 11/4630–0300).

RECEIVING MAIL

You can receive mail at Buenos Aires's **Correo Central** (Central Post Office, ⊠ Sarmiento 151, 1st Floor, ☎ 11/4311–5030 or 11/4311–5040). Letters should be addressed to Lista/Poste Restante, Correo Central, 1000 Buenos Aires, Argentina. Cardholders can have mail sent to **American Express** (⊠ c/o American Express, Arenales 707, 1061 Buenos Aires, Argentina, ☎ 11/4312–0900).

Money and Expenses

CHANGING MONEY

The Argentine peso is pegged to the U.S. dollar. Dollars are readily accepted by cabs, hotels, and most restaurants throughout Buenos Aires and other large cities; places that accept dollars will post a sign saying so. Be sure that bills aren't torn or dirty; dollars in poor condition won't be accepted. In rural areas, dollars are less likely to be accepted, so you'll want to have pesos. You may not be able to change currency in rural areas at all, so don't leave the city without adequate amounts of pesos in small denominations.

You can change money at your hotel, at banks, or at *casas de cambio* (money changers), which offer competitive variations on rates. (Pesos can also be obtained by making a purchase in dollars and requesting the change in pesos.) Exchange fees are better at banks, but not significantly so—and there are lines. Plan ahead, since it's often hard to change large amounts of money at hotels on weekends, even in cities. ATMs are getting easier to find, especially in Buenos Aires, Cordóba, Mar del Plata, and other major cities and resort towns. At press time, 1 U.S. dollar equaled 1 peso, 1 Canadian dollar equaled roughly .70 pesos, and 1 pound sterling equaled roughly 1.65 pesos.

CURRENCY

One peso (P) equals 100 centavos. Peso notes are in denominations of 100, 50, 20, 10, 5, and 2. Coins are in denominations of P1, and 50, 25, 10, 5, and 1 centavos.

FORMS OF PAYMENT

The long period of price stability has also meant a boom in the acceptance of credit cards (although there are often good discounts to be found for using cash). Visa is the most readily accepted card. Larger stores in downtown areas catering to foreign visitors will occasionally accept payment by a personal check drawn on a major U.S. bank, or traveler's checks. Smaller shops and restaurants are leery of traveler's checks, but most do accept major credit cards.

TAXES AND TIPPING

Keep your receipts: The 21% VAT tax, added to almost every purchase you'll make, is entirely refundable for purchases of more than $200. When you depart, plan enough time to visit the return desk at the airport to obtain your refund. Tax on rooms in hotels is also 21%

Add a 10%–15% *propina* (tip) in bars and restaurants; 10% is enough in a casual café or if the bill runs high. Argentines round off a taxi fare, but there's no need to tip cab drivers, although a few of the cabbies who hang around hotels popular with North Americans seem to expect it. Hotel porters should be tipped at least $1. Give doormen and movie ushers about $1 and beauty- and barbershop personnel about 5%.

WHAT IT WILL COST

The most sumptuous dinners, particularly in French restaurants, can run as high as $100 per person with wine and tip. But a thick slab of rare, wood-grilled sirloin with salad, potatoes, a house wine, and an espresso will cost around $20 at steak houses in Buenos Aires and less in the hinterlands. When ordering drinks, ask for Argentine liquors or you'll be paying for the tremendous import fees (a bottle of Chivas Regal costs $75–$100 in shops). Simply ask for *"whiskey nacional, por favor"* or *"vodka nacional."*

Sample Prices: A cup of coffee in a café, $2.50 (with milk, $3). A bottle of soda, $1. A taxi ride in central Buenos Aires, $4–$8. A tango show with a couple of drinks, about $60. A double room in a moderately priced, well-situated hotel, including taxes, $100–$130.

Opening and Closing Times

Bank hours are 10–3. **Shops** in Buenos Aires are open weekdays 10–7 or 8, Saturday 9–1, and later and on Sunday in the malls. Smaller shops outside the capital close for a lunch/siesta break from approximately 1 to 2:30, when they open again until 7:30 PM. Most **museums** are open only five days a week, generally from Tuesday to Saturday, though sometimes from Wednesday to Sunday. **Post offices** are open weekdays 8–6, Saturday 8–1. The ubiquitous **telecentro** offices, where you can make a long-distance call or send a fax, are open from 7:30 AM–midnight.

NATIONAL HOLIDAYS

New Year's Day (Jan. 1); Holy Thursday and Good Friday (Apr. 20–21, 2000; Apr. 12–13, 2001); Labor Day (May 1); Anniversary of the 1810 Revolution (May 25); National Sovereignty Day (June 10); Flag Day (June 20); Independence Day (July 9); Anniversary of San Martín's Death (Aug. 17); Columbus Day (Oct. 9); Immaculate Conception (Dec. 8); and Christmas (Dec. 25).

Passports and Visas

U.S., Canadian, and British citizens do not need a visa for visits of up to 90 days. Upon entering Argentina, you'll receive a tourist visa stamp on your passport. The fine for overstaying your tourist visa is $50, payable upon departure at the airport. If you do overstay your visa, plan to arrive at the airport several hours in advance of your flight to have ample time to take care of the fine.

Students in Argentina

YOUTH HOSTELS

Argentina's **Youth Hostel Association** (⊠ Talcahuano 214, 2nd Floor, Buenos Aires, ☎ 11/4372–1001) can provide you with information on hostels around the country. The **Buenos Aires Hostel** (⊠ Av. Brasil 675, ☎ 11/4362–9133) is open 24 hours a day, seven days a week.

Telephones

To call Argentina from overseas, dial the country code, 54, and then the area code, omitting the first 0. The area code for Buenos Aires is 11, and all numbers in the city are preceded by 4. Thus, to dial the local Buenos Aires number 4343–0423 from the United States, dial 011–54–11/4343–0423.

Despite the privatization of ENTEL, the formerly government-run telephone company, service at times can still be erratic. Phone numbers are often changed and a common phone greeting is *equivocado* (wrong number). The best bet is to get operator assistance or to have the operator at your hotel put your calls through.

DIRECTORY ASSISTANCE AND OPERATOR INFO

Information: ☎ 110. **International calls:** ☎ 19. **International operator:** ☎ 000. **Time:** ☎ 113.

INTERNATIONAL CALLS

Many hotels have direct-dial international lines in the rooms and all have international dialing access from the lobby (hotels, however, may add a significant service fee on top of the cost of the call). Be prepared for a hollow sound or even an echo of your own voice for the first minute or so of an international call; this resonance typically goes away after the first few sentences of a conversation.

LOCAL AND LONG-DISTANCE CALLS

Public phones are found on nearly every block and usually operate with a telephone card, which can be purchased at any kiosk. Simply slide the card in, wait for the reading of how many minutes you have remaining, and dial the number. Some public phones are coin operated and a very rare public phone is still operated by an old phone token. One card unit buys two or three minutes of time, depending on whether you are calling at prime time (8–8) or otherwise. Hotels will charge you a per minute rate that can be quite high, even for local calls. To make a long-distance call from a pay phone, go to a telecentro, which has private booths and fax services. Though it's possible to make a long distance call from a pay phone, you'll still need a local phone card to access a line, even if you plan to use a calling card.

U.S. ACCESS CODES

AT&T, MCI, and Sprint have direct-calling programs that allow you to call collect or charge calls from abroad to your calling card. Many hotels will charge a fee to access these numbers. **AT&T** (☎ 0800/54–288). **MCI** ☎ 0800/555–1002 or 0800/222–6249). **Sprint** (☎ 0800/51–003).

Visitor Information

Argentina National Tourist Council (✉ 12 W. 56th St., New York, NY 10019, ☎ 212/603–0443; ✉ 5055 Wilshire Blvd., Los Angeles, CA 90036, ☎ 213/930–0681; ✉ 2655 Le Jeune Rd., Miami, FL 33134, ☎ 305/442–1366).

When to Go

Because of the great variety of latitudes, altitudes, and climatic zones in Argentina, you're likely to encounter many different climates during any given month. The most important thing to remember is the most obvious—when it's summer in the Northern Hemisphere, it's winter in Argentina, and vice versa. Winter in Argentina stretches from July to October and summer goes from December to March. The sea moderates temperatures in most of Argentina's cities year-round. Winter can be chilly and rainy, although average winter temperatures are usually above freezing in the coastal cities (it hasn't snowed in Buenos Aires in over 100 years). If you can handle the heat (January–February temperatures usually range in the high 90s to low 100s 35°C–40°C), Buenos Aires can be wonderful in summer, which peaks in January. During this month, many businesses shut down or have reduced hours (this includes banks, but not American Express). Most banks and government offices open up again in February, but it's still school vacation, so many stores remain closed. If you have an aversion to large crowds, avoid visiting popular resort areas in January and February and in July, when they become overcrowded again due to school holidays.

Spring and fall are excellent times to visit Argentina. It's usually warm enough (over 50°F) for just a light jacket and it's right before or after the crowded, expensive tourist season. The best time to visit Iguazú Falls is August–October, when temperatures are lower and the spring coloring is at its brightest. Rain falls all year, dropping about 205 centimeters (80 inches) annually. Resort towns such as Bariloche stay open all year. Summer temperatures can get up into the high 70s (about 25°C), but most of the year, the range is from the 30s to the 60s (0°C–20°C). The Patagonia coast is on the infamous latitude that sailors call the "Roaring Forties," with southern seas that batter Patagonia throughout the year. Thirty-mph winds are common, and 100-mph gales are not unusual. Summer daytime temperatures reach the low 80s (about 28°C), but can drop suddenly to the 50s (10°C–15°C). Winters hover near the freezing mark. Most travelers visit Tierra del Fuego in summer, when temperatures range from the 40s to the 60s (5°C–20°C). Fragments of glaciers cave into southern lakes with a rumble throughout the thaw from October to the end of April, which is the best time to enjoy the show.

CLIMATE

The following are the average daily maximum and minimum temperatures for Buenos Aires.

Jan.	85F	29C	May	64F	18C	Sept.	64F	18C
	63	17		47	8		46	8
Feb.	83F	28C	June	57F	14C	Oct.	69F	21C
	63	17		41	5		50	10
Mar.	79F	26C	July	57F	14C	Nov.	76F	24C
	60	16		42	6		56	13
Apr.	72F	22C	Aug.	60F	16C	Dec.	82F	28C
	53	12		43	6		61	16

The following are the average daily maximum and minimum temperatures for Bariloche.

Jan.	70F	21C	May	50F	10C	Sept.	50F	10C
	46	6		36	2		34	1
Feb.	70F	21C	June	45F	7C	Oct.	52F	11C
	46	8		34	1		37	3
Mar.	64F	18C	July	43F	6C	Nov.	61F	16C
	43	6		32	0		41	5
Apr.	57F	14C	Aug.	46F	8C	Dec.	64F	18C
	39	4		32	0		45	7

FESTIVALS AND SEASONAL EVENTS

The **National Folklore Festival,** which features costumes, dancing, and rodeos, runs for two weeks in Cosquín (province of Córdoba), starting on January 15. **Carnival** is celebrated on weekends during February and early March, although on a considerably smaller scale than in neighboring Brazil. **Vendimia,** the wine harvest in Mendoza, happens during the first week of March. The northern city of Salta celebrates **Semana Salta** (Salta Week), a gaucho festival of note, in June. The gauchos are in their full cowboy regalia, barbecue perfumes the air, and hooves pound in furious displays of horsemanship. Buenos Aires hosts a major **livestock exhibition,** the Exposicion de Ganaderia, known as the *Rural* in July and early August—great to see, since the Argentines take their cows seriously. December 8 is the **Festival of Our Lady of Lujan,** patron saint of the republic.

4   BOLIVIA

Bolivia has a tangible otherworldliness that stays with you long after a trip is over, an impression—created by high peaks, impenetrable lakes, mysterious ruins, thin air, and a stately population—that only deepens its appeal.

LANDLOCKED AND SOFT-SPOKEN, BOLIVIA is perhaps the least discovered—and certainly the least talked about—country in South America. But anonymity has a few distinct advantages. Although it is larger than Texas and California combined, Bolivia has fewer inhabitants than New York City. And with most of its 6.8 million people concentrated in a handful of urban centers such as La Paz, Santa Cruz, Cochabamba, and Sucre, there's little to detract from the country's sometimes brooding, sometimes austere, but always captivating landscapes.

Updated by
Joan Gonzalez

Bolivia contains every type of geologically classified land—from tropical lowlands to parched desert to rugged Andean plains. Although generally considered an Andean nation, nearly two-thirds of the country sweats it out in the steamy Amazon Basin, remote, overlooked, and as inhospitable as it is soul-stirring. On Bolivia's wildest frontier, indigenous tribes live as they have for centuries, unimpressed, it seems, by the displays of the modern world. In the provinces of Beni and Santa Cruz, near the border of Brazil, tribes are still known to attack riverbank villages with bows and arrows.

Beyond these tropical lowlands, just west of Cochabamba and Santa Cruz, the Andes rise sharply to form the backbone of South America's Pacific coast. This two-prong mountain range shelters between its eastern and western peaks a rambling, high-altitude plain. Known as the altiplano, this bleak, treeless plateau, about 136 km (85 mi) wide and 832 km (520 mi) long, comprises 30% of Bolivia's landmass and supports more than half the country's population. For centuries the Aymara people have clung to the hostile land, harvesting small crops of potatoes and beans or fishing the deep-blue waters of Lake Titicaca, the world's highest navigable lake, which forms Bolivia's western border with Peru.

Perched on the edge of the altiplano is La Paz, the capital, which overlooks the barren plateau at an altitude of 3,579 m (11,811 ft). If you fly into La Paz's 3,939-m- (13,000-ft-) high El Alto airstrip, the plateau breaks without warning and reveals below a deep, jagged valley covered with adobe and brick homes clinging to the hillsides. At dusk, as the sun sets on the bare flatlands that surround La Paz, a reddish glow envelops the city's greatest landmark, 6,363-m (21,000-ft) Mt. Illimani—a breathtaking backdrop to the world's highest capital.

From its earliest days, Bolivia's fortunes have risen and fallen with its mineral wealth. Centuries ago it was the Inca and Aymara who dug deep for precious silver. In the 17th century, Spain's colonization of South America was fueled largely by the vast amounts of silver hidden deep in the bowels of Cerro Rico, the "Rich Hill" that towers over Potosí, in southern Bolivia. Cerro Rico's rich lode, first discovered in 1545, quickly brought conquerors, colonists, and prospectors to what was at the time the greatest mining operation in the New World. During the 17th and 18th centuries, Potosí, the most populous city in the Americas, was transformed with grand colonial mansions, stately baroque churches, and thick-walled fortresses. For the Spanish, "*vale un Potosí*" ("worth a Potosí") became a favorite description for untold wealth. However, there's an old saying that says it all: "Bolivia had the cow, but the other countries got the milk." Some 8 million Quechua Indians died in the mines, as they were often forced to stay inside the airless, deep black tunnels for as long as six months.

But as the silver mines in Cerro Rico were exhausted, modern Bolivia began to take shape. Spanish aristocrats fled north to Sucre, Cochabamba, and La Paz, leaving Bolivia's eastern and northern ex-

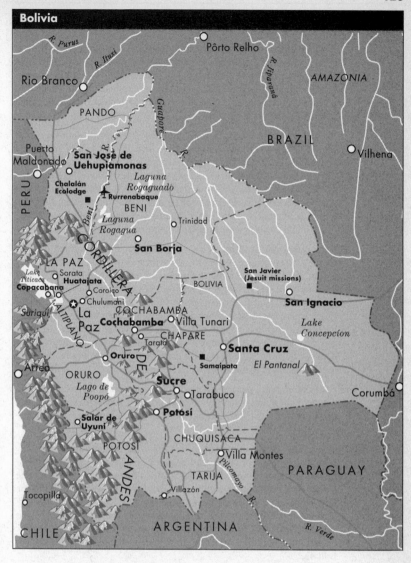

Bolivia

tremes to the Aymara and the Quechua-speaking Inca. Today Bolivia remains equally divided between the old and new worlds: more than 50% of its people are direct descendants of the Aymara and Inca, while the other half are a mix of mestizo and *criollo,* people of Spanish ancestry born in the Americas.

Bolivia was named in honor of its liberator, Simon Bolívar, who proclaimed the country's independence from Spain in 1825; until then, it had been simply called Upper Peru. Centuries of Spanish conquest left their mark here, particularly on the cities of Sucre and Potosí, where ebullient baroque cathedrals crowd the narrow streets. But modern Bolivia remains a land of indigenous farmers, ranchers, and artisans. On the windswept Andean plateau, you will still see local weavers toting their red-cheek children and crafts to weekly markets. By the time the sun has risen, the brightly dressed Aymara are in place, ready to offer a wide variety of textiles and ponchos, not to mention vegetables, fruits, live pigs, and medicinal herbs.

Pleasures and Pastimes

Dining

Bolivian cuisine is healthful, wholesome, and satisfying. Soups are excellent and make a complete meal in themselves, as they are loaded with meat, potatoes, vegetables, and the vitamin-rich, ricelike grain, *quinua*. Fresh trout from Lake Titicaca is fried, stuffed, steamed, grilled, spiced, or sauced. Another excellent, delicate fish from the lake is *pejerrey*, which is especially good in *ceviche*.

In the highlands, where carbohydrates are the dietary mainstay, look for *chuño* and *tunta*, two kinds of freeze-dried potatoes that are soaked overnight and boiled, then used to accompany main dishes. Other traditional highland fare includes *timpu* (lamb stew), *conecho cuis* (roast guinea pig), and *asado de llama* (llama steak). A traditional dish is *pique macho*, beef grilled with hot peppers, chopped tomatoes, and onions, which is often served with fried potatoes and gravy or with *sajta de pollo* (chicken stew with peppers and onions).

Each major city still has its own brewery, generally founded by Germans, who emigrated here at the same time as they came to the United States. Try *Paceña* in La Paz or *Sureña* in Sucre. *Concepción* is the local wine and *Singani* the local liquor from the wine-producing vineyards around Tarija, near the Argentine border. Singani is used to make Pisco Sours; locals sometimes mix it with Sprite or lemonade to similar effect. *Chicha* is a grain alcohol made by chewing maize, spitting out the resulting mash, adding water, and allowing the mixture to brew. The sweet, rather cloudy result is drunk mainly in the lowland valleys in and around Cochabamba.

Prices quoted are per person and include appetizer, main course, and dessert but exclude alcoholic beverages, tax, service charge, and tip. For price categories *see* Dining *in* Smart Travel Tips A to Z.

Lodging

The quality of accommodations is improving throughout Bolivia, especially in the major cities. Choices here range from luxury establishments to clean, comfortable, and affordable standard hotels. The Bolivian tourist board rates hotels on a one- to five-star basis, but some hotels have two pricing systems—one for Bolivians and one for foreigners. Still, even if you fall into the latter category, good clean rooms can be found for $25 or less, particularly away from the cities. Do not be afraid to ask to see the room in advance—it's common practice in Bolivia.

Prices quoted are for a double room and include tax and service charge. For price categories, *see* Lodging *in* Smart Travel Tips A to Z.

History

Everywhere in Bolivia you'll stumble across reminders of the country's long and eventful history, from the ancient stone ruins outside of La Paz to the centuries-old silver mines in Potosí to the lovely city of Sucre, a repository of Spanish colonial architecture. Bolivians are proud of their history, and you'll find them willing to share what they know with anyone eager to learn.

Shopping

Bolivia's rich selection of crafts includes silver jewelry, musical instruments such as the *quena* (Inca flute) and *charango* (mandolin), woven rugs, embroidery—plus sweaters, gloves, scarves, and ponchos made from alpaca, llama, or vicuña wool. Crafts shops are usually grouped together (in La Paz, for instance, most can be found on Calle Sagárnaga). It is always worth looking for cooperative crafts shops outside the capital, however. These sell traditional textiles made in rural areas, especially in the provinces of Chuquisaca and Potosí. The traditional shawls, hats, and skirts worn by highland women are sold in local markets and certain shopping districts in La Paz, but shopkeepers sometimes refuse to sell traditional garments to foreigners.

Due to the low level of tourism, tourist-oriented goods tend to be realistically priced, and although bargaining is expected, many sellers will drop their prices only by small amounts, typically 5% to 10%.

Exploring Bolivia

Bolivia is most noted for the Andes, which take up a large chunk of the west, and, to a lesser extent, the vast jungle regions of Amazonia that extend from the Andes' boundary all the way east into Brazil. But Bolivia has a surprisingly varied series of ecosystems within those two major regions. Mountain areas vary from cool and dry (as in the high-altitude cities of La Paz and Potosí), to temperate (the cities of Cochabamba and Sucre), to warm and pleasant almost year-round (in the fertile, grape-growing lands near the southern city of Tarija). Jungle areas also vary: from humid and wet, as in Santa Cruz, to the more temperate climates in the northwest province of Pando. In the northeast province of Beni, encompassing the city of Trinidad, the wet, jungle climate is occasionally broken by cold spells, called *surazos*.

Great Itineraries

IF YOU HAVE 3–5 DAYS

If you have a limited amount of time to visit Bolivia, divide it between **La Paz** and **Lake Titicaca.** Arrive in La Paz—and remember, unless you're arriving from another high-altitude destination, you'll need a full day to adjust to the thin air. On the second day, take a city tour in the morning and visit the outdoor markets, then see the Valley of the Moon in the afternoon. Visit the Tiwanacu ruins on your third day, then spend your final two days at Lake Titicaca, where you can explore Copacabana, the Sun and Moon Islands, and the Inca Utama Cultural complex.

IF YOU HAVE 7 DAYS

Follow the above itinerary, then fly to the colonial town of **Sucre,** where the altitude is lower and the climate warmer. Spend the first day touring the town, and make a visit to the market in nearby **Tarabuco** if you're there on a Sunday. On the next day, travel to the colonial mining town of **Potosí** and spend the night before flying back to La Paz.

IF YOU HAVE 14 DAYS

Follow the seven-day itinerary, but upon return to La Paz head for **Santa Cruz,** from where you can visit the Amazon. Many jungle trips and river cruises on the Río Ibaré and Río Mamoré depart from the city—you can even skip La Paz and spend your entire vacation in this region, as most international flights stop here before landing in the capital. A minimum of five days is needed to fully experience the rain forest's beauty.

LA PAZ

Set in a lunarlike landscape of great—if rather stark—beauty, La Paz is nestled in a bowl-shape valley that ranges in altitude from 3,015 to 3,615 m (9,951 to 11,930 ft), an elevation so high that even the locals walk slowly. Nearly half of the city's 1.5 million residents live in poorly constructed adobe and brick homes on a plateau, devoid of all greenery, in the "El Alto" section, as well as in the valleys that encircle the settlement. In downtown La Paz the feeling is more cosmopolitan, as buses, taxis, businesspeople, and Aymara Indians share the city's cobblestone streets.

Exploring La Paz

Crossing the downtown area is the busy, tree-lined thoroughfare called El Prado for half its length, and Avenida Mariscal Santa Cruz after that. Downhill and away from the city center, El Prado splits into two major one-way streets, Avenida 6 de Agosto and Avenida Arce. These lead to the residential areas of San Jorge and Sopocachi, which holds most of La Paz's best bars and restaurants.

Numbers in white bullets in the text correspond to numbers in black bullets in the margins and on the La Paz map.

A Good Walk

Begin your walk at the heart of downtown La Paz, the broad **Plaza San Francisco** ①. Flanking the plaza is the impressive **Iglesia de San Francisco** ②. Adjacent to the church you'll find the extremely steep **Calle Sagárnaga.** Continue along this road and turn right at **Calle Max Paredes.** Back at Plaza San Francisco, walk down Avenida Mariscal Santa Cruz and take a left at Calle Ayacucho. Keep walking uphill until you reach Plaza Murillo and La Paz's **Catedral** ③; adjacent to the cathedral is the **Palacio de Gobierno** ④. Just ahead, in nearby Plaza Murillo, you'll discover the **Museo Nacional del Arte** ⑤, housed in a stunning baroque mansion. From Plaza Murillo continue on Calle Comercio and turn right up Calle Genaro Sanjinés. Ahead you'll see the **Teatro Municipal** ⑥ and, a few doors down, the **Museo Nacional de Etnografía y Folklore** ⑦. Stroll up **Calle Jaén,** home to four important museums. Next, walk up the city's main avenue, **El Prado,** for three blocks until you come to **Avenida Ecuador.** From here, take a taxi, or turn left and walk along Avenida Ecuador (which becomes a small side street) until you reach the beautiful little **Parque Montículo** ⑧. Finally, continue along the main road, Calle Victor Sanjinés, and you will soon reach Plaza España, a pleasant residential square.

TIMING

Because La Paz is so compact, visiting the city's main sights would seem easy; however, add time for climbing the hills and taking frequent breaks to assuage the effects of the altitude. You'll need two days for a thorough exploration, but a selection of the main sights could be toured in a day. There is less traffic to contend with on weekends, but museums are closed Saturday afternoons, Sundays, and during weekday lunch hours.

SIGHTS TO SEE

Avenida Ecuador. In the heart of the Sopocachi district—where it intersects Calle Fernando Guachalla in the lower part of the city—is the site of the vast indoor Sopocachi market, worth seeing for its colorful displays of fresh produce and flowers. Note: Do not take photos of Indian women tending their stalls without first requesting permission.

Calle Jaén. One of the city's few remaining colonial streets, Calle Jaén houses four excellent museums: The **Museo Costumbrista** (⊠ Calle Jaén at Calle Sucre, ☎ 02/378478), dedicated to the political and cultural history of La Paz; the **Museo de Metales Preciosos** (⊠ Calle Jaén 777, ☎ 02/371470), which has an extensive collection of pre-Columbian gold and silver artifacts, as well as Inca and pre-Inca ceramics; the **Museo Pedro Domingo Murillo** (⊠ Calle Jaén 79, ☎ 02/375273), with exhibits of masks, herbal medicines, and weavings housed in a restored colonial mansion; and the **Museo de Litoral** (⊠ Calle Jaén 789, ☎ 02/

371222), a repository for artifacts connected with the 1879 War of the Pacific, when Bolivia lost its Pacific ports to Chile. ⊠ *Admission.* ☉ *Tues.–Fri. 9:30 –12:30 and 3–7, weekends 10–12:30.*

Calle Max Paredes. In this area you'll find whole streets filled with peddlers hawking shawls, hats, and clothing, as well as traditional medicines. Tucked into alleys and courtyards are *tambos* (thatch-roof structures) where oranges, bananas, and coca leaves are sold. The latter are officially illegal but are chewed by farmers and miners (and tourists) to ward off hunger and the effects of the altitude.

Calle Sagárnaga. This area has crafts shops and street vendors selling more weavings, jewelry, carvings, clothing, and silverware. The street is also lined with inexpensive pensions and hotels, as well as the famous Peña Naira.

❸ **Catedral.** The cathedral was built in 1835 in a severe neoclassical style, with a sober facade and imposing bronze doors. ⊠ *Plaza Murillo.* ☜ *Free.* ☉ *Mon.–Sat. 7–9 AM and 6–8, Sun. 7–noon and 6–8.*

El Prado. The city's main avenue is a colorful blur of trees, flowers, and monuments. The street is often clogged with pedestrians and vendors, especially on weekends, and many of La Paz's luxury hotels are found here, rising high above the old colonial-style homes with their elaborate latticework and balustrades.

★ ❷ **Iglesia de San Francisco.** Built in 1549 and considered one of the finest examples of Spanish colonial architecture in South America, the carved facade of the Church of San Francisco is adorned with birds of prey, ghoulish masks, pine cones, and parrots—a combination of Spanish and Indian motifs created by local artisans who borrowed heavily from the baroque style of 16th- and 17th-century Spain. Indian weddings sometimes spill out onto the plaza on Saturdays. Craft stalls line the church wall; most days you'll find colorful weavings and handmade Bolivian musical instruments. ⊠ *El Prado at Calle Sagárnaga.*

★ ❺ **Museo Nacional del Arte.** Housed in a baroque mansion commissioned by a Spanish noble in 1775, the National Art Museum holds three stories of paintings and sculpture. The first floor is devoted to contemporary Bolivian and foreign artists; the second, to the master of Andean colonial art, Melchor Pérez Holguín, and his disciples; and the third, to a permanent collection of Bolivian artists. ⊠ *Plaza Murillo at Calle Comercio,* ☎ *02/371177.* ☜ *Admission.* ☉ *Tues.–Fri. 9– 12:30 and 3–7, weekends 10–1.*

❼ **Museo Nacional de Etnografía y Folklore.** Housed in an ornate 18th-century building, the National Ethnography and Folklore Museum exhibits feathers, masks, and weavings. It also has permanent displays on the Ayoreos, who live in the Amazon region, and the Chipayas, who come from the surrounding altiplano. ⊠ *Calle Ingavi 916,* ☎ *02/358559.* ☜ *Admission.* ☉ *Tues.–Fri. 9 –12:30 and 3–7, weekends 9–1.*

❹ **Palacio de Gobierno.** The Presidential Palace, which is closed to the public, was guarded by tanks and machine gun–toting soldiers until 1982, when the constitutional government was restored following a 1979 coup and three years of military rule. In front of the palace is a statue of former president Gualberto Villarroel. In 1946 a mob attacked the building and forcibly brought Villarroel to the square, where he was hanged from a lamppost; a nearby statue commemorates the event. Diagonally across from the palace is Bolivia's congress building, **El Congreso,** which has a visitor's gallery. ⊠ *Plaza Murillo.* ☜ *Free.* ☉ *Weekdays 9–noon and 2:30–5.*

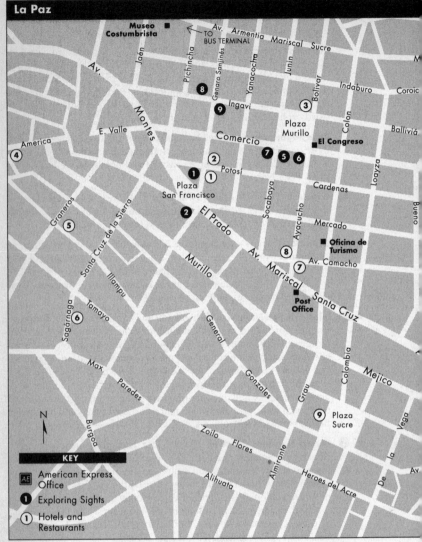

La Paz

Exploring
Catedral, **3**
Iglesia de
San Francisco, **2**
Museo Nacional del
Arte, **5**
Museo Nacional de
Etnografía y
Folklore, **7**

Palacio
de Gobierno, **4**
Parque Montículo, **8**
Plaza
San Francisco, **1**
Teatro Municipal, **6**

Dining
Aransaya, **12**
Café La Paz, **7**
Currasquería El
Gaucho, **8**
Pig & Whistle, **10**
Pizzeria Morello, **19**

Lodging
Gran Hotel Paris, **3**
Hotel Galeria, **5**
Hotel Gloria, **2**
Hotel Max Inn, **9**
Hotel Plaza, **11**
Hotel Presidente, **1**
Hotel Sagárnaga, **6**

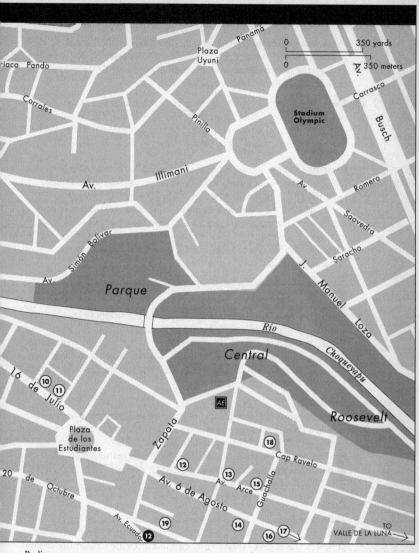

Radisson
Plaza Hotel, **12**
Residencial
Rosario, **4**

❽ **Parque Montículo.** Served by a small church, the park has breathtaking views of Mt. Illimani, especially fine during a blazing altiplano sunset.

❶ **Plaza San Francisco.** On this broad plaza, Indian sellers hawk all sorts of crafts, as well as more prosaic goods such as cassette tapes, watches, and electrical items. Numerous shoe-shine boys also ply their trade with persistence; a shine should cost less than 15¢.

❻ **Teatro Municipal.** A handsome building both inside and out as a result of an extensive 1994 restoration, the Municipal Theater regularly stages traditional dance and music as well as classical music performances and opera. ⊠ *Calle Genaro Sanjinés 629,* ☎ *02/375275.*

OFF THE
BEATEN PATH

VALLE DE LA LUNA – Erosion has shaped the Valley of the Moon into jagged peaks and canyons, forming an eerie, surrealistic landscape. From the bridge at **Barrio Aranjuez**, it's a 10-minute uphill walk to the cactus garden, the only patch of green in the area, and about 15 minutes more to the maze of pinnacles and crevasses that gives this unusual landscape its name. The valley is about 10 km (6 mi) from La Paz, in the canyon of the Río Choqueyapu, and it is included in most city tours. You can also hire a taxi or ride microbus 11 to Barrio Aranjuez.

Dining

La Paz restaurants are becoming increasingly cosmopolitan, with cuisine that includes Chinese, French, German, Italian, Japanese, and Swiss, in addition to traditional Bolivian fare. Avenida Arce, Plaza Abaroa, and the residential Sopocachi district have the widest selection of restaurants in La Paz, while the area around Calle Sagárnaga generally harbors the least expensive.

Bolivian

$$–$$$ ✕ **Aransaya.** This restaurant's location on the penthouse floor of the Radisson Plaza Hotel provides diners with spectacular panoramic views of the city and surrounding mountains. The modern decor and food presentation are exquisite, and the menu features both international dishes and regional specialties. ⊠ *Av. Arce 2177,* ☎ *02/316161. AE, MC, V. No lunch Sun.*

Cafés

$ ✕ **Café La Paz.** This old café, opposite the main post office, is a popular hangout with many La Paz politicians, journalists, and expatriates. Try the potent espresso and cappuccino, *café helado* (ice-cream coffee), and elaborate pastries, including *empanada de manzana* (apple tart). ⊠ *Calle Ayacucho at Av. Camacho,* ☎ *02/350292. No credit cards.*

International

$ ✕ **Churrasquería El Gaucho.** This Argentine-style steak house serves slabs of tender, grilled steak and kabobs on a wood plank, with a variety of delicious sauces and salad. ⊠ *Av. 20 de Octubre 2041,* ☎ *02/ 359125. AE, MC, V.*

$ ✕ **Pig & Whistle.** A short walk south from the university is this replica
★ of a cozy, turn-of-the-century British pub. Authentic Indian and Southeast Asian dishes are served in the evening. Low-key live music, performed on weekends, ranges from light classical to bossa nova to jazz. ⊠ *Calle Goitia 155, off Av. Arce,* ☎ *no phone. No credit cards. Closed Sun.*

Italian

$ ✕ **Pizzeria Morello.** This is possibly the best pizzeria in La Paz, where you can order what's hot from the oven or design your own pizza from the voluminous list of toppings. Many Paceños use Morello's prompt takeout and delivery services. ⌧ *Av. Arce 2132,* ☎ *02/372973. AE, MC, V.*

Lodging

Although the number of hotels in La Paz is growing, rooms are often booked solid during holidays and festivals. Make reservations in advance whenever possible. The city's mid-range to luxury hotels are the best value in terms of friendly service and modern amenities, and some of the less expensive pensions are improving their service and facilities to compete for customers. Rock-bottom hotels tend to be located in the crafts and market areas near Calle Sagárnaga.

$$$–$$$$ 🏨 **Hotel Plaza.** The rooms and rooftop restaurant/bar of this recently renovated luxury business hotel command excellent views of La Paz and the Andes. Ask for a room facing Mt. Illimani; it will have the best views and less street noise. ⌧ *Av. 16 de Julio 1789,* ☎ *02/378311, 800/ 442–2955 in the U.S.,* FAX *02/378318. 175 rooms, 10 suites. 2 restaurants, 2 bars, indoor pool, hot tub, sauna. AE, MC, V.*

$$$–$$$$ 🏨 **Hotel Presidente.** This modern but worn hotel has an excellent downtown location and comfortable, plain rooms; most face the street, but noise is minimal on the upper floors. The restaurant has inexpensive buffet lunches and stunning views of the city. ⌧ *Calle Potosí 920,* ☎ *02/367193,* FAX *02/354013. 101 rooms, 18 suites. 2 restaurants, 2 bars, indoor pool, sauna, exercise room, dance club. AE, MC, V.*

$$$–$$$$ 🏨 **Radisson Plaza Hotel.** The focus is on simple elegance and excellent service at this modern, high-rise business hotel. Upper-floor rooms have excellent views of the city and surrounding mountains. The rooftop restaurant, Aransaya ($$), offers spectacular views, elegant decor, and fine international dining at reasonable prices. ⌧ *Av. Arce 2177,* ☎ *02/316161, 800/777–7800 in the U.S.,* FAX *02/316302. 239 rooms, 7 suites. 2 restaurants, bar, café, indoor pool, beauty salon, hot tub, massage, sauna, exercise room, shops. AE, MC, V.*

$$–$$$ 🏨 **Gran Hotel Paris.** Built in 1911 on the Plaza Murillo, the Gran is
★ one of Bolivia's most charming hotels. All rooms are deluxe, and six suites—restored in Louis XVI style—have balconies that overlook the plaza. Though historic in ambience, with traditional afternoon teas accompanied by live music, the hotel has all the modern business amenities. Rates include an American breakfast buffet. ⌧ *Plaza Murillo,* ☎ *02/319170,* FAX *02/362547. 41 rooms, 6 suites. Restaurant, bar, café. AE, MC, V.*

$$ 🏨 **Hotel Gloria.** The clean, friendly Gloria has a certain retro charm. The hotel also has an inexpensive rooftop restaurant ($) and an excellent location, one block from Plaza San Francisco. ⌧ *Calle Potosí 909,* ☎ *02/370010,* FAX *02/391489. 79 rooms. Restaurant, bar, café. AE, MC, V.*

$–$$ 🏨 **Hotel Max Inn.** Centrally located on Plaza Sucre, the Max Inn offers bright, reasonably priced rooms with pastel accents. It is in one of the more attractive buildings in this section of town. ⌧ *Plaza Sucre 1494,* ☎ *02/374391,* FAX *02/341720. 50 rooms, 5 suites. Restaurant. AE, MC, V.*

$ 🏨 **Hotel Sagárnaga.** This quiet hotel is on a steep, cobblestone street near the Witches Market. Its advantages are reasonable prices, a central location, and an on-site travel agency. Folkloric Peñas (music and dance groups) perform every Wednesday and Sunday from 8–10 PM. ⌧ *Calle Sagárnaga 326,* ☎ *02/350252,* FAX *02/360831. 56 rooms. Restaurant, travel services. AE, MC, V.*

$ 🏨 **Residencial Rosario.** The charming, Spanish-style decor and serene atmosphere make this hotel a popular option with budget travelers. Rooms, with showers only, are clean and bright; those along the sunny inner courtyard provide the perfect place to relax. ⊠ *Calle Illampu 704,* ☎ *02/316156,* FAX *02/375532. 40 rooms. Restaurant, travel services. AE, MC, V.*

Nightlife and the Arts

The Arts

The tourist office (☞ Visitor Information *in* La Paz A to Z, *below*) can fill you in on local festivals and special events. For concert and cinema listings pick up a copy of *Última Hora, La Razón,* or *El Diario,* the main Spanish-language daily newspapers, and the English-language *Bolivian Times,* which comes out weekly on Fridays.

FILM

The **Cinemateca Boliviana** (⊠ Calle Pichincha at Calle Indabura, ☎ 02/325346), an art theater, regularly shows foreign and even a few Bolivian films.

GALLERIES

The **Galería Emusa** (⊠ Av. 16 de Julio 1607, ☎ 02/375042), centrally located on El Prado, hosts rotating exhibits of Bolivian sculpture and art. **Arte Unico** (⊠ Av. Arce 2895, ☎ 02/329238) mounts varied exhibits.

THEATER AND MUSIC

The **Teatro Municipal** (⊠ Calle Genaro Sanjinés 629, ☎ 02/375275) stages folk events and traditional music and dance concerts.

Nightlife

BARS

Calle Belisario Salinas has the largest selection of bars, which fill up around 10:30 PM. Popular with professional Bolivians, **Caras y Caretas** often features live bands. The **Café Montmartre** is a popular singles hangout with live music on weekends and delicious crepes for the hungry. Also look for **Panyco,** owned by a Frenchman who knows how to attract trendy Paceños with offbeat decorations and live music. Away from Calle Belisario Salinas, the **Andromeda** (⊠ Av. Arce at Calle Aspiazu) hosts live music. **Hotels Plaza, Presidente,** and **Radisson** (☞ Lodging, *above*) have rooftop bars worth a visit, if only for the stunning views. The intimate **Matheus** (⊠ Calle Guachalla at Av. 6 de Agosto, ☎ 02/324376) has a well-stocked bar and the occasional live band. The atmospheric **Pig & Whistle** (☞ Dining, *above*) restaurant has live music most nights.

NIGHTCLUBS

Forum (⊠ Calle Víctor Sanjinés 2908, ☎ 02/325762) is a large club two blocks from Plaza España mainly frequented by the under-thirty set. Trendy **Socavón** (⊠ Av. 20 de Octubre near Calle Guachalla, ☎ 02/353998) draws younger Paceños and foreigners with live dance music most nights.

PEÑAS

Peñas are nightclubs that showcase Bolivian folkloric music and dance. The energetic live performances are popular with tourists and Paceños alike and usually include dinner in the price—from $8 to $20 per person. Popular peñas are **Casa del Corregidor** (⊠ Calle Murillo 1040, ☎ 02/363633), **Los Escudos** (⊠ Av. Mariscal Santa Cruz, Edificio Club de la Paz, ☎ 02/322028), and **Peña Naira** (⊠ Calle Sagárnaga 161, ☎ 02/350530).

Outdoor Activities and Sports

Soccer

Bolivians would be lost without their weekly soccer fix; even the poorest, most remote villages have a playing field, which, since it's usually on the only flat piece of ground in town, often doubles as a grazing ground for sheep and cows. La Paz itself has two teams: Bolívar and The Strongest. Both strut their stuff in the **Estadio Hernando Siles** (⊠ Plaza de los Monolitos, ☎ 02/357342), in the Miraflores district.

Volleyball

Three major teams—San Antonio, Litoral, and Universidad—compete regularly in the **Coliseo Julio Borelli** (⊠ Calle México, ☎ 02/320224), in the San Pedro district.

Skiing

Chacaltaya, a primitive ski resort, is 35 km (22 mi) from La Paz. At a height of 5,136 m (17,150 ft), it's recommended only for people who have had at least a week to adjust to the altitude and are expert skiers. The season is from December to April. The resort has a very basic ski lift and ski rentals are available on-site. La Paz tour and travel agencies offer one-day trips that include a stop at an Indian cemetery along the way for about $18 per person (not including rentals, which cost another $10 per day). In addition, ski rentals and visits can be arranged through **Club Andino** (⊠ Calle México 1638, ☎ 02/324682), a local ski club.

Shopping

In La Paz you'll find everything from roughly made silver plates to sophisticated jewelry, from woven-rope sandals to sweaters made of the softest alpaca and angora wools. Prices are reasonable by North American standards, although good quality, as always, does not come cheaply.

Areas

Calle Sagárnaga is a good place to begin shopping, as the small streets that lead off to the right and left harbor a variety of crafts stores. For Aymara embroidered shawls, try the market area around **Calle Santa Cruz de la Sierra** and **Calle Max Paredes.** Prices start at $15 and peak at more than $200 for vicuña wool shawls. *Polleras,* the traditional skirts worn by local Indians, are priced between $50 and $100; bowler hats worn by the Indian women start at around $20.

Centers and Malls

Two of the three main shopping malls in the city center are on Calle Potosí near Calle Ayacucho; the better one is the glass-pyramid–capped **Shopping Norte,** which has a variety of small restaurants that serve good-value *almuerzos* (set lunches) on the top floor. The third, known as the **Handal Center,** is on Avenida Mariscal Santa Cruz, just down from Plaza San Francisco. Each shopping center carries a wide selection of jeans, T-shirts, shoes, and sports equipment.

Specialty Shops

Before you begin bargain hunting for alpaca sweaters, visit one of the better stores mentioned below to get an idea of what real quality feels like. High-quality hand-knit designs are around $100, though you may cheer yourself with the fact that they can sell for three times that amount at home. The shops along Calle Sagárnaga offer the gamut of quality in alpaca sweaters and are a good place to compare quality and price.

For high-quality alpaca knitwear with ethnic designs, try **Artesanías Sorata** (⊠ Calle Linares 862, ☎ 02/317701), **Asarti** (⊠ Radisson Plaza Hotel, Av. Arce 2177, ☎ 02/329726), or **Casa Fisher** (⊠ Av. Mariscal, Handal Center, ☎ 02/392946). One of the best places in town to buy high-quality, reasonably priced *chompas*, colorful jackets made with traditional alpaca textiles, is **Coral** (⊠ Calle Linares 836, ☎ 02/342599).

Side Trips from La Paz

Tiwanacu

Located on a treeless plain, just over an hour's drive west of La Paz, Tiwanaku is Bolivia's most important archaeological site. Partial excavations have revealed the remains of five different cities, one built on top of the other. Most impressive is La Puerta del Sol (Gate of the Sun), an imposing stone fixture believed to be a solar calendar built by a civilization that mysteriously surfaced around 600 BC and disappeared around AD 1200. The gate is part of an elaborate observatory and courtyard that contain monoliths and a subterranean temple. Although the site lacks the splendor of Peru's Machu Picchu, it does provide a glimpse into the ancestry of the Aymara, the last people to be conquered by the Inca before the Spanish came. The descendants of the Aymara still farm the ingeniously constructed terraces built nearby by their ancestors.

Take a warm sweater or poncho, as the area is frequently windy and cold. Facilities at the site are limited and it is best to book a half-day tour through a tour operator as there are no guides. If you decide to take a local bus (90 min., about $1.) be sure to ask about the return schedule; you wouldn't want to get stuck here.

Oruro

The main reason for going to this former mining town 225 km (140 mi) southeast of La Paz is the *Diablada* parade of the elaborately costumed dancing devils, which takes place during Carnival festivities the Saturday before Ash Wednesday. Although Saturday is the big day, Carnival lasts for a week, during which more than 25,000 dancers in 48 folk groups dance through the streets. Public buses make the 3-hour trip for under $3, but the city is crowded at Carnival and advance reservations a must; it's best to make arrangements through a travel agency in La Paz.

Los Yungas

Within easy reach of La Paz, Los Yungas ("The Valleys") is a semitropical paradise where the snow-covered Andes tower above waterfalls and valleys. The drive here is an experience in itself: Dropping in altitude by some 2,982 m (9,840 ft) in just under 80 km (50 mi), the poorly maintained, mostly single-lane highway is one of the most scenic and hair-raising in South America.

Your first glimpse of small **Coroico** will be unforgettable, particularly after three hours of tortuous hairpin bends. Set in steep, undulating hills overrun with citrus and banana trees, coffee trees, and coca bushes, Coroico is a resort town for Paceños, who flock here on the weekends. **America Tours** (☞ Tour Operators and Travel Agents *in* La Paz, *below*) organizes bicycle adventures for those who desire the challenge of biking the "World's Most Dangerous Road." You can also rent horses from **Ranch Beni** for about $5 an hour.

El Viejo Molino, a 30-minute walk from Coroico on the road to Caranavi, is one of the best hotels in the area (☎ 0811/6004, 02/361076 for reservations). You can linger over a plate of grilled steak in the excellent restaurant or ponder intense valley views from one of the clean, spacious bedrooms that rent from $50 per night. The most popular restaurant in Coroico is **La Casa** (⊠ Calle Kennedy, ☎ no phone), which specializes in meat and cheese fondues for about $6 per person. La Casa also has a handful of clean, simple rooms priced at less than $5 per night. A Coroico lodging option is the **Hotel Coroico** (✉ Coroico, ☎ 02/370010, ℻ 02/391489), a resort perched high above the valley with wonderful river views. Amenities include a pool, tennis court, and other recreational facilities.

Chulumani, in southern Los Yungas, is surrounded by waterfalls and has a year-round tropical climate. Here, you'll get an authentic glimpse of traditional life in a small town in the Andes. The main resort-style hotel is the **San Bartolomé Plaza Resort** (☎ 02/316161), a 30-minute walk downhill from the main square, which has rooms for around $55. Activities include tennis, horseback riding, and nature tours.

La Paz A to Z

Arriving and Departing

BY AIRPLANE

All international and domestic flights to La Paz arrive at **El Alto Airport** (☎ 02/810122), situated high above the city on the altiplano, 12 km (7 mi) from downtown. **Lloyd Aéreo Boliviano (LAB)** (✉ Av. Camacho 1456, ☎ 02/367710 or 0800–3001) and **AeroSur** (✉ Av. 16 de Julio 1616, ☎ 02/369292, 0800–3030 toll-free in Bolivia) regularly fly to most major cities in Bolivia, including Sucre, Santa Cruz, and Cochabamba.

Some La Paz hotels run their own shuttle buses to and from the airport; check with the hotel when you make your reservation. Taxis are the quickest alternative. The current going rate for the 30- to 45-minute journey is around B35 ($7.50), but fix a price with the driver before you get in. There is also service to downtown in minibuses parked just outside the airport. Cost is approximately $1; a taxi to your hotel will cost $1–$2 more.

BY BUS

All buses to La Paz arrive at the **Terminal de Buses** (✉ Av. Perú, ☎ 02/367275). You can travel almost anywhere in Bolivia from here, though you should reserve your seat at least a day in advance for the very long and tedious rides to Sucre, Potosí, and Santa Cruz. You can also cross the Chilean border and travel through the magnificent Parque Nacional Lauca on a bus heading west for the port town of Arica. For details on these journeys, contact **Expreso Mopar** (☎ 02/377443), **Trans Copacabana** (☎ 02/377894), or **Trans El Dorado** (☎ 02/359153), which have agents at the bus terminal. For up-to-date bus schedules, departure points, and recommendations on reliable companies, go to a La Paz travel agency.

BY TRAIN

La Paz is served by a single railway station, the **Estación Central de Ferrocarriles** (✉ Plaza Kennedy, ☎ 02/373069). The only rail destinations from La Paz are Sucre, Potosí, Villazón, a handful of towns along the Argentine frontier, and Arica on the coast of Chile. Although these journeys tend to be arduous, uncomfortable, and unreliable, a Chilean company that recently purchased some of Bolivia's railroads said that dependable passenger service will be operating in three to four years.

Getting Around

BY BUS

La Paz is served by a comprehensive network of *colectivos* (buses), which run daily from 6:30 AM to 10 PM. There is a flat fare of roughly 17¢ per person in the city center, payable to the driver upon entry. Slightly more expensive (B1) are *micros,* 12-seat minivans that travel the same bus routes, only more quickly. Micros and colectivos are very crowded, but are safe for tourists and stop everywhere. Listen carefully, as destinations are shouted out as the vehicles roll through the city—or ask a local to help you hail the right one.

To reach Los Yungas from La Paz, the private bus companies **Transporte 20 de Octubre** (⊠ Calle Yanacachi 1434, ☎ 02/317391) and **Veloz del Norte** (⊠ Av. de las Américas 283, ☎ 02/311753) make the three- to four-hour trip to Coroico and Chulumani for approximately $8.

BY CAR
You would have to be crazy to even think of driving in La Paz: Streets are a maze of steep hills and traffic is horrific. Before renting a car to drive outside the city, inquire about the road conditions around your proposed destination. Most roads are unpaved and in less than perfect condition; many also have hairpin curves all the way. If you can, hire a driver so that you can enjoy the scenery without frazzling your nerves.

EBA TRANSTUR (⊠ Calle Carlos Medinacelly 1120, ☎ 02/361423) has good deals on cars and larger vehicles with drivers. Other possibilities include **IMBEX** (⊠ Av. Montes 522, ☎ 02/316895) and **The Travelers** (⊠ Av. Arce 227, ☎ 02/316161), the latter of which also rents cellular phones (minimum of 24 hrs) for $5 a day, plus 2 Bs per 20 minutes. Depending on the vehicle, car rentals run from $21 to $50 per day, and from 21¢ to 50¢ per km, plus gasoline.

BY TAXI AND TRUFI
Shared taxis, easily identifiable from the taxi sign lodged in the windshield, are cheap and plentiful; expect to pay less than 50¢ for trips within the city center. Newer-looking **Radio Taxis** (☎ 02/413838), identified by the illuminated sign perched on the roof, are not shared and cost slightly more, but prices are fixed at $1–$2 depending on the length of your journey within the city. Radio Taxis are the safest option for tourists.

Contacts and Resources
BANKS AND CURRENCY EXCHANGE
Reliable banks, all of which have 24-hour ATMs, include **Banco La Paz** (⊠ Av. 16 de Julio), **Banco Mercantil** (⊠ Av. Ballaivian Esq., Calle 9), **Banco Nacional** (⊠ Av. Camacho, Esq. Colon and ⊠ Av. Garcia Lanza Esq. Calle 14), and **Provincia de San Cruz** (⊠ Av. Arce 2177).

Money exchange houses (*casas de cambio*) abound throughout the city, particularly around Avenidas Ayacucho, Camacho, Colón, and Mariscal Santa Cruz. Most are open the same hours as regular shops: 9–noon and 3–6, as well as some evenings. You should get better rates here than at the banks, and both cash and major traveler's checks are accepted. You may be approached by individual money changers on the street offering about the same rates, and although they are generally honest, it's best to go with the certified exchange houses. Your hotel will probably be able to change cash and traveler's checks as well, albeit for a higher fee. Wherever you go, make sure to ask for some small change to use in the markets, and make sure you receive clean, whole bills, as some vendors won't accept currency that is marked or torn.

EMERGENCIES
General emergency: ☎ 110.

ENGLISH-LANGUAGE BOOKSTORES
Other than the weekly *Bolivian Times* newspaper, publications in English are few here, and quite expensive. However, you will probably be able to find international newspapers at most large city newsstands and hotel shops. The main La Paz papers are *La Razon, La Prensa,* and *El Diario*.

TELEPHONES, THE INTERNET, MAIL

You can make local and international calls from the main **ENTEL** office (✉ Calle Ayacucho 267), which is open daily from 7:30 AM–10:30 PM. Connections aren't always reliable, though, so calling often requires some patience. Larger hotels often have business service offices with computers and Internet access; some allow non-guests to use such amenities for a fee. The main **post office** (✉ Av. Mariscal Santa Cruz, at Calle Oruro) is open weekdays from 8:30–8 and Saturdays from 9–7. Here you can pick up post restante mail, which is held for three months.

TOUR OPERATORS AND TRAVEL AGENTS

The following companies offer guided, English-language tours of La Paz and various trips throughout the country: **America Tours** (✉ Av. 16 de Julio 1490, ☎ 02/374204), **Crillon Tours** (✉ Av. Camacho 1223, ☎ 02/374566), **Diana Tours** (✉ Calle Sagárnaga 328, ☎ 02/350252), **Freman Tours** (✉ Calle Pedro Salazar 537, ☎ 02/417062), **Magri Turismo** (✉ Av. 16 de Julio 1490, 5th Floor, ☎ 02/360616), and **Turismo Balsa** (✉ Av. 16 de Julio 1650, ☎ FAX 02/354049).

VISITOR INFORMATION

Oficina de Turismo (✉ Edificio Mariscal Ballivián, 18th Floor, Calle Mercado, ☎ 02/367463 or 02/367464).

LAKE TITICACA

Lake Titicaca, which covers an area of 7,988 sq km (3,474 sq mi) and is shared by Bolivia and Peru, is fed by the melting snows from the Andes. It is considered sacred by the Aymara campesinos who live on its shores and islands, as it was by the Tiwanaku and Inca civilizations who inhabited the area as early as 1300 BC. At an altitude of 3,789 m (12,506 ft), it is the world's highest navigable lake, two bodies of water joined at the narrow *Estrecho de Tiquina* (Straits of Tiquina). The smaller section of the lake—freshwater Lago Huiñaymarca—is the easiest to reach from La Paz; for a sight of the largest section—brackish Lago Chuciuto—you need to include Copacabana on your itinerary. Either way, the lakes' still waters reflect an equal measure of high-altitude sun and cloudless blue sky, in addition to the palette of browns injected by the sunbaked hills that encircle Lake Titicaca.

Beyond the bumpy profile of islands with names like Suriki, del Sol, and de la Luna, each with a smattering of Inca ruins in varying states of decay, the horizon-wide panorama encompasses fishing vessels and tourist launches headed for port. On the lakeshore the scene may include Aymara Indians who have come to tend a crop of potatoes and beans or to fish for trout from their small wooden boats. The islands are covered with thousands of man-made terraces, many of which have been farmed since pre-Inca times. According to legend, Isla del Sol (Island of the Sun) is the birthplace of life in the Andes, and also where the Inca Empire was founded when Manco Kapac and Mama Ojillo, son and daughter of the Sun God Inti, came down to earth to improve the life of the Altiplano people.

An archaeological project started on Sun Island in 1994 uncovered settlements over 3,000 years old. There are unrestored archaeological sites on both the Isla del Sol and Isla de la Luna, as well as small villages of Aymara campesinos, who use the ancient farming terraces to grow potatoes, quinua, fava beans, and corn. Those Aymara who live on the islands on the Bolivian side of the lake are descendants of the aboriginal inhabitants of the altiplano, not of the Quechua-speaking Incas.

On the lake, the **Andean Roots Cultural Complex** includes the Altiplano Museum, which depicts the history and culture from pre-Columbian to colonial and modern times. Headsets and guide tapes in several languages are available, so the displays can be enjoyed at your own pace. A re-created Andean Eco Village is now home to the Limachi Brothers of Isla del Suriqui (☞ *below*), who built the reed rafts used by Thor Heyerdahl on his expeditions. The Kallaway Museum commemorates the Kallawayas, the doctors of the Andes who still travel from village to village carrying natural medicines on their shoulders and who developed and used penicillin, streptomycin, and quinine long before modern doctors. The observatory, which is equipped with a powerful telescope donated by NASA, has a roll-back roof that provides a perfect opportunity for star-gazing over the lake.

Huatajata

85 km (53 mi) from La Paz.

This popular weekend escape for Paceños is a regular stop on the guided tour circuit. Huatajata is a practical base for exploring the area; however, it lacks lakefront walking paths. For picnics, try the tree-lined waterfront at **Chúa**, the village beyond Huatajata.

Dining and Lodging

$$–$$$ ✕🔲 **Hotel Lake Titicaca.** Coming from La Paz, you'll see this well-equipped but slightly dated complex on the lakeshore a few minutes before Huatajata. The sweeping views of the lake almost justify the inflated prices. ✉ *Midway between Huarina and Huatajata,* ☎ *02/ 356931,* 📠 *02/351792 for reservations. 24 rooms. Restaurant, bar, sauna, racquetball, boating, recreation room. AE, MC, V.*

$$–$$$ ✕🔲 **Inca Utama Hotel & Spa.** This well-maintained hotel has tremen-
★ dous views over the lake and is the site of the Andean Culture Complex. Two restaurants, one inside the hotel and another out over the water, serve local and international fare and feature evening entertainment. Heated rooms have electric blankets for extra comfort. Hydrofoils depart daily from the hotel to the islands and Copacabana. Crillon Tours (☞ Tour Operators and Travel Agents *in* La Paz, *above*) handles hotel and hydrofoil reservations. ✉ *Huatajata,* ☎ *811/5050,* 📠 *02/391039. 65 rooms. Restaurant, bar, spa, health club, meeting rooms. AE, MC, V.*

Suriqui

Offshore from Huatajata.

In 1970, when Norwegian explorer Thor Heyerdahl wanted to sail from Morocco to South America in a reed-and-wood boat to prove that South American cultures could have made contact with Europe long before the age of Columbus, he commissioned local artisans on Suriqui to build his vessel, the *Ra II*. And he had the confidence to do it: In 1947, Heyerdahl had sailed from Peru to Polynesia in the balsa wood *Kon-Tiki* to test his theory that the first Polynesians came from South America, describing his journey in his book named after the boat. Today, the *Ra II* is on display in Oslo, Norway, and the Limachi brothers, who built it are now living at the Inca Utama cultural complex. Paulino Esteban, who assisted in the construction, maintains a souvenir shop and museum close to the main pier.

Copacabana

164 km (103 mi) northwest of La Paz.

From Huatajata the road continues to Tiquina, where you can see the handful of patrol boats that make up Bolivia's navy (Bolivia was left landlocked after Chile seized 256 km/160 mi of coast in 1879). In Tiquina, vehicles are loaded onto rafts and taken across the Strait of Tiquina to San Pedro. From unmemorable San Pedro it's a 90-minute drive to Copacabana, a pleasant, touristy town that fronts Lago Chucuito from the shelter of a protected bay. Copacabana is the main stopping point for those headed to Peru, and it provides easy access to the surrounding countryside and lake islands. A flat trek along the lake is possible for about 11 km (7 mi). Kayaks are also available for rent.

During Holy Week, throngs of young Paceños walk to Copacabana from the capital to pay homage to the miracle-working Black Virgin of Copacabana; the candlelight procession on Good Friday is especially spectacular. In town, the highlights of the **Catedral,** built between 1610 and 1619, are the majestic gilded altar and the striking sculpture of the Black Virgin carved by the Inca Tito Yupanqui in 1592. If you see decorated cars lined up in front of the Cathedral, the owners are waiting to have them blessed.

Dining and Lodging

¢–$ ✕ **Sujna Wasi.** This small, Spanish-owned restaurant features an ex-
★ cellent menu with many vegetarian dishes and nightly specials. The small bar, fireplace, and art hanging along the walls provide a cozy atmosphere. In addition to food, the restaurant has a side room with books, maps, and travel information. ⊠ *Gral Gonzalo Jauregeu,* ☎ *no phone. No credit cards.*

$–$$ ✕▥ **Hotel Rosario Del Lago.** This is one of the nicest hotels in Copacabana, just a few blocks up from the main plaza and right on the lake. Its clean, homey atmosphere and colonial-style rooms create a relaxing ambience. All quarters, including a large suite that sleeps six, have excellent views of the lake. ⊠ *Rigoberto Paredes Y Av. Costanera,* ☎ *0862/2140, 02/451341 in La Paz,* ℻ *02/451991. 31 rooms, 1 suite. Restaurant. AE, MC, V.*

$ ✕▥ **Copacabana Palace.** Renovated in 1997, this somewhat plain hotel still has clean, comfortable rooms with simple decor; many have lake views. ⊠ *Copacabana; reservations: Hotel La Gloria, La Paz,* ☎ *02/ 370010,* ℻ *02/391489. Restaurant, bar, recreation room. AE, MC, V.*

$ ✕▥ **Hotel Playa Azul.** Located on one of the main tourist streets, recent renovations have given the Playa Azul a cozy dining room lit with gas fires. Groups frequently stop here for the tasty lunches. Most of the comfortable, simple bedrooms overlook a small courtyard. ⊠ *Av. 6 de Agosto,* ☎ *0862/2228.* ℻ *0862/2227. Restaurant, bar. MC, V.*

$ ▥ **Ambassador Hotel.** This hotel near the lake has special student rates and is aligned with a youth hostel. Although the renovated rooms are somewhat small, you can't beat the view of the lake from the rooftop restaurant. ⊠ *Calle Jauregui, Plaza Sucre,* ☎ *0862/2216,* ℻ *02/243382. 42 rooms. Restaurant. No credit cards.*

Isla del Sol and Isla de la Luna

12 km (7 ½ mi) north of Copacabana.

The nearest Bolivia gets to the Mediterranean, Isla del Sol has beautiful coves with white sandy beaches and lies just offshore of Copacabana in the serene Lago Chucuito. This is the largest of Lake Titicaca's islands, and many tourists make brief stops at the small port of *Yumani,* where steep Inca steps and a sacred spring and fountain are located. Few, however, actually spend time on the island—and they miss out on a rewarding experience.

Old Inca stone paths and farming terraces cover Isla del Sol, and Aymara campesinos can be seen planting and harvesting crops. Days can be spent following the paths that crisscross the island, visiting Tiwanaku and Inca ruins or relaxing in a sandy cove. Visit the **Palacio de Pilkokaina** ruins, and, on the northwest corner, a strange rock formation said to be the birthplace of the sun and moon. In the late afternoon, climb to the top of the ridge to enjoy the panorama of a setting sun and the colors that play on the snowcapped peaks of the Andes.

En route to Isla del Sol, hydrofoils usually stop at **Isla de la Luna,** where the ruins of *Iñacuy* date back to the Inca conquest. Here, you'll find an ancient convent, *Ajlla Wasi* (house of the chosen women), a place of worship for women chosen to accompany the Inca and establish alliances with other ethnic leaders. Stone steps lead up to the unrestored ruins.

Lodging

$$ ⊞ **La Posada del Inca.** This beautifully restored colonial hacienda on Isla del Sol is furnished in a natural, rustic style. Rooms have spectacular views of the lake, and the restaurant serves meals in a family-style atmosphere. As the hotel is located atop a hill, a mule-drawn rickshaw provides transportation for those who would rather not make the climb. ⊠ ☎ 02/374566, ℻ 02/391039. 12 rooms. AE, MC, V.

¢ ⊞ **Inca Sama Albergue.** Follow a stone path up from the ruins of Palacio de Pilkokaina and you'll see this basic lodge, where three rooms hold up to 20 guests. Bathrooms are located outside the lodge, and simple meals are served alfresco. What the hotel lacks in comfort, though, it makes up for in splendid views. ⊠ ☎ 0862/2228, ℻ 0862/2227. 3 rooms with 20 beds. No credit cards.

Sorata

45 km (28 mi) north of Huatajata via Huarina and Warisata.

Sorata lies nearly 8,200 ft above sea level in a tropical valley at the foot of **Mt. Illampu.** This is a starting point for experienced hikers to climb the snowcapped mountain or to make the arduous, week-long trek along the **Camino del Oro** (Trail of Gold) to the gold-mining cooperatives.

Dining and Lodging

$–$$ ✕⊞ **Hotel Ex-Prefectural Sorata.** A sparkling new renovation makes the most of this hotel's charming outdoor garden and lovely views across the valley. The Bolivian restaurant specializes in traditional dishes. Coming from La Paz, the hotel is on the main highway less than 1 km (½ mi) from Sorata's central square. ⊠ ☎ 02/722846 *for reservations,* ☎ ℻ 0811/5201. *Restaurant. AE, MC, V.*

Lake Titicaca A to Z

Arriving and Departing

BY BOAT

There is no direct boat service between Peru and Bolivia, but you can travel by bus and catamaran or by bus and hydrofoil between La Paz and the Peruvian port of Puno, with brief stops in Copacabana. Make arrangements for the four- to five-hour ride through a travel agency based in La Paz or Puno.

BY BUS

Minibuses run regularly from the gates of the El Viejo Cementerio in La Paz to destinations along the lakeshore, including Batallas, Huatajata, and Tiquina. One-way prices to Huatajata are about $1. Private buses collect passengers from their hotel at 8 AM and charge roughly $10 roundtrip to Copacabana (4 hours) and $15 to Sorata (6 hours); in La Paz, contact **Combi Tours** or **Diana Tours** (☞ Tour Operators *in* La Paz, *above*) or **Turibus** (✉ Calle Illampu, Residencial Rosario, ☎ 02/325348 or 02/369542, ℻ 02/375532).

BY CAR

From La Paz take El Alto Highway northwest. After the toll booths—keep your receipt to show on your return—follow signs for Batallas, Río Seco, Huatajata, and Tiquina. The road is paved between La Paz and Tiquina, and barring heavy traffic it takes less than two hours to drive. Be very careful about leaving your car unattended, particularly in Copacabana.

A car or light truck with a capacity for seven persons can be rented (without guide) from **EBA Transtur** (☎ 02/361423) in La Paz for about $55 for a half day or $110 for a full day, including a driver, fuel, and toll. Small boats and bicycles can also be rented.

Contacts and Resources

BANKS AND CURRENCY EXCHANGE

You won't need much cash here, for there aren't many places to spend it, but do bring enough to cover local shopping, area tours, meals, and tips for guides. Most hotels will change U.S. dollars; some will change traveler's checks as well, but don't count on it. There are a few casas de cambio at Copacabana's main plaza.

EMERGENCIES

General emergency: ☎ 110.

TOUR OPERATORS

The best all-around Lake Titicaca experience is with **Crillon Tours** (☞ Tour Operators *in* La Paz, *above*), a company that has been operating on the lake for 40 years. Crillon runs daily hydrofoil trips between Huatajata harbor and many of the islands, with connecting bus service from La Paz or to Puno in Peru. **Magri Turismo** (☞ Tour Operators *in* La Paz, *above*) and **Explore Bolivia** (☎ 303/708–8810 in the U.S.) organize treks from Sorata to Mt. Illampu. **Diana Tours** and **Turismo Balsa** (☞ Tour Operators *in* La Paz, *above*) offer tours around the Lake Titicaca region.

VISITOR INFORMATION

In the center of Copacabana's main plaza, the **tourist information booth** (✉ Av. Abaroa, at Av. José Mejía, ⊘ 10–2 and 4–8) is the place to find information about things to do in the area.

CENTRAL BOLIVIA

Central Bolivia stretches from Cochabamba, nestled in the eastern foothills of the Andes, to the lowland city of Santa Cruz, perched on the edge of the Amazon Basin. Climates range from mild and sunny in Cochabamba to hot and humid in Santa Cruz, with heavy rainfall throughout the region between October and March.

The two main cities, Cochabamba and Santa Cruz, are just a bit south of Bolivia's center—but here ends all similarity. Cochabamba, the country's third-largest city, is in a fertile valley in the foothills of the Andes. It produces a large share of the country's fruit, vegetables, and meat and dairy products, and is often referred to as the "Bread Basket of Bolivia." At an altitude of 2,545 m (8,400 ft), it is also the "City of Eternal Spring," with continually mild, sunny days.

Hot and humid Santa Cruz, Bolivia's second largest city, is on the fringe of the Amazon basin. At just 407 m (1,365 ft) above sea level, it is a major entry point for international flights. In addition to agriculture, its economy is fueled by lumber, gas and oil. Downtown, with its covered sidewalks, looks a little like a movie set of an old frontier town. The rainy season here is between October and March.

Cochabamba

400 km (250 mi) southeast of La Paz.

With a population of more than 400,000, Cochabamba has the feel of a city that has grown much too quickly. Sights are scattered between the apartment-lined Río Rocha and **Plaza 14 de Septiembre,** a 25-minute walk southwest, where bougainvillea, magnolias, and jacarandas bloom. A statue of Christ watches over the city, his arms outstretched, and at 32 m (108 ft) is slightly taller than the statue on top of Corcovado in Río de Janiero. Flanking the square is the **Cathedral,** which was built in 1571 and took 154 years to complete, and towers over the old men and street vendors who sometimes congregate in the plaza at dusk.

One block southeast from the square is the **Templo de San Francisco,** a colonial masterpiece built in 1581 but thoroughly recast in 1782 and again in 1926. Inside the Temple of San Francisco are elaborately carved wooden galleries and a striking gold-leaf altar. ⊠ *Calle 25 de Mayo,* ☎ *no phone.* ☜ *Free.* ⊙ *Daily 7–11:30 AM and 5–8.*

★ Cochabamba's excellent **Museo Arqueológico** is one of the more comprehensive and interesting historical sites outside of La Paz. On display in the Museum of Archaeology are pre-Columbian pottery, silver and gold work, and strikingly patterned, handwoven Indian textiles. Hour-long English-language tours can be arranged for a small fee. ⊠ *Calle 25 de Mayo 145,* ☎ *no phone.* ☜ *Admission.* ⊙ *Weekdays 9– noon and 3–7, Sat. 9–1.*

Plaza Colón, at the eastern foot of Calle 25 de Mayo, marks the start of **El Prado** (sometimes called Avenida Ballivián), a shop- and bar-lined avenue that stretches north to the Río Rocha. Cross the river and hail a taxi for the five-minute trip to **Palacio Portales,** which was built but never occupied by Simón Patino, a local tin baron who amassed one of the world's largest fortunes. The mansion, furniture, and 10-acre gardens reflect French Renaissance style. Chambers on the upper floor contain reproductions of the Sistine Chapel. It is now a cultural and educational center. ⊠ *Av. Potosí 1450,* ☎ *042/43137.* ☜ *Admission.* ⊙ *Weekdays 5–6 PM, Sat. 10–11 AM, Sun. 11–noon.*

For a good view of Cochabamba, take a taxi from the city center to **Cerro Coronilla** (Coronilla Hill, also called San Sebastían Hill), on the city's outskirts. At the top is a monument honoring women and children who died during Bolivia's protracted War of Independence, which ended in 1825.

Tarata, a well-preserved colonial village 25 km (15 mi) southeast of Cochabamba, has a busy open-air market on Thursdays. For views of Tarata, consider the 15-minute uphill walk to the **Iglesia de San Pedro.** Although the nearby **Convento de San Francisco** is currently being restored, as are many of the finer old buildings around town, a visit is highly recommended. In Cochabamba, buses for Tarata depart from Avenida Barrientos, at the corner of Avenida 6 de Agosto. Alternatively, **Fremen Travel** in La Paz (⊠ Plaza Abaroa, Calle Pedro, ☎ 02/327073) offers weekly tours of Tarata and the nearby village of Hayculi, famous for its pottery and ceramics.

Dining and Lodging

$　✕ **Buffalo Rodizzio.** This Argentine-style eatery has an excellent salad
★　bar, all the meat you can eat carved at your table by waiters dressed

as *gauchos*, and great views of the city. Reserve a table on Sundays, which are usually packed. ⊠ *Calle Oquendo N 0654, Edificio Torres Sofer,* ☎ *042/51597. AE, MC, V.*

$ ✕ **Casa de Campo.** Informal and lively, the Casa de Campo features traditional Bolivian specialties—mostly grilled meats and a perfectly fiery *picante mixto* (grilled chicken and beef tongue)—served on a shaded outdoor patio. ⊠ *Av. Aniceto Padilla,* ☎ *042/43937. No credit cards.*

$ ✕ **Chifa Lai Lai.** All Chinese restaurants in Bolivia are called Chifa. This one has excellent food, cheap wines, and the kind of service usually found only in much more expensive places. Try the Ecuadoran shrimp dishes. ⊠ *Av. Aniceto Padilla 129,* ☎ *042/40469. MC, V.*

$ ✕ **Quinta Guadalquivir.** Parrots in cages and a small but beautifully laid-out garden create the mood at this popular outdoor eating venue; its shady trees mean it's a pleasant place to eat lunch, too. Dishes are a mix of traditional and more international stock-in-trade. ⊠ *Calle J. Bautista 370, Cala Cala district,* ☎ *042/43491. AE, MC, V.*

¢ ✕ **La Cantonata.** Come to this high-quality spot for pizza and pasta at very reasonable prices. ⊠ *Calle España at Calle Mayor Rocha,* ☎ *no phone. No credit cards.*

$$–$$$ ▥ **Hotel Portales.** Cochabamba's most luxurious address has lush gardens, numerous recreation facilities, and extremely well-equipped rooms with air-conditioning, TVs, and phones. Plan on a short taxi ride to reach the center of town. ⊠ *Av. Panda 1271,* ☎ *042/85444,* FAX *042/42071. 98 rooms, 8 suites. 2 restaurants, piano bar, 2 pools, beauty salon, exercise room. AE, MC, V.*

$$ ▥ **Gran Hotel Cochabamba.** Most of the hotel's simple, comfortable rooms—all with TV and phone—overlook the plant-filled courtyard. The adjoining Restaurante Carillón serves an excellent pique macho, as well as surubí. ⊠ *Plaza Ubaldo Anze,* ☎ *042/82551,* FAX *042/82558. 43 rooms, 5 suites. Restaurant, bar, pool, tennis court. AE, MC, V.*

$$ ▥ **Hotel Aranjuez.** Located in a nice residential area in front of Pala-
★ cio Simón Patiño, this elegant hotel is noted for its lovely terraces and gardens. Rooms are spacious and comfortable. A live jazz band plays in the lobby bar most weekends. ⊠ *Av. Buenos Aires E-563,* ☎ *042/ 80076,* FAX *042/40158. 30 rooms, 25 with bath, 3 suites. Restaurant, bar, pool. AE, MC, V.*

$ ▥ **Hotel Uni.** Budget-minded travelers will appreciate the Uni's central location, one block from the main square, and its simple, clean rooms, all of which have a phone and a TV. Ask for an upper-floor room away from noisy Avenida Heroínas. ⊠ *Calle Baptista S 0111,* ☎ FAX *042/35065. 43 rooms, 5 suites. Restaurant, bar, travel services. AE, MC, V.*

Shopping

Cochabamba is well known for its high-quality alpaca sweaters, knitwear, and leather, but don't expect prices to be much lower than in La Paz. Some of the better-quality (and more expensive) knitwear shops include **Asarti** (⊠ Calle México and Av. Ballivián, ☎ 042/ 50455), **Casa Fisher** (⊠ Calle Ramorán Rivero 0204, ☎ 042/84549), **Fotrama** (⊠ Av. Bolívar 0439, ☎ 042/22980), and **Amerindia** (⊠ Av. San Martín 6064). Also visit **Tipay** (⊠ Calle Jordán E 0732, ☎ 042/ 51303), a clothing cooperative of local women who sell handmade knits and crochets in alpaca and pima cotton. The local market, **La Cancha**, open daily on Avenida Aroma, is a good place to browse for less expensive crafts.

El Chapare

160 km (100 mi) northeast of Cochabamba.

Travel the 500 km (250 mi) between Cochabamba and Santa Cruz on the Nuevo Camino highway through the lowlands and you're in a section of Bolivia known as the Chapare, a sparsely populated region of low-lying mountains and thickening jungle. The few communities that survive here tend to earn a living by harvesting coca. The village of **Villa Tunari** (☞ Dining and Lodging, *below*) is well equipped to deal with overnight visitors.

Dining and Lodging

$ ✕🏨 **El Puente.** The secluded El Puente is in a thick forest a few km outside Villa Tunari, at the end of a rough, pebble-strewn path accessed from the Nuevo Camino. Trails cutting into the undergrowth lead to a nearby river with clear, swimmable pools. All rooms have private showers and toilets. Reservations are recommended and should be made through Fremen Travel in La Paz (☞ Cochabamba, *above*). The on-site restaurant serves hearty, simple food. ⊠ *Villa Tunari,* ☎ *042/59392,* ℻ *042/59686 for reservations. Restaurant, bar. AE, MC, V.*

$ ✕🏨 **Hotel Las Palmas.** The centrally located Las Palmas offers a range of modern comforts, including private showers and toilets. The hotel restaurant features a menu of grilled chicken and pique macho, as well as some forest game and river fish. ⊠ *Av. Integración, Villa Tunari,* ☎ *0411/4103. Restaurant, pool. No credit cards.*

Santa Cruz

900 km (560 mi) southeast of La Paz.

Santa Cruz is a lively lowland city whose sprawling industrial districts are connected by a series of ring roads. Twenty years ago oxen pulled carts through the mud streets of Santa Cruz; today, well-dressed businesspeople dodge taxis and street sellers as they maneuver between modern downtown office buildings—a sure sign that Santa Cruz and its more than 700,000 inhabitants have been dramatically transformed in recent years. Apart from its main square, **Plaza 24 de Septiembre,** Santa Cruz has little to offer in terms of sights, museums, or architecture. However, it's a good jumping off point for visiting Samaipata, pre-Inca ruins, and the Jesuit Missions.

Interesting sights include the **Basílica Menor de San Lorenzo,** built between 1845 and 1915 on the ruins of a 17th-century cathedral. Inside the imposing but architecturally uninspired church, the **Museo Histórico de la Catedral** (Cathedral Historical Museum) exhibits colonial-era religious objects, paintings, and sculptures. ⊠ *Plaza 24 de Septiembre,* ☎ *03/327381.* 🎟 *Admission.* ☉ *Tues. and Thurs. 10–noon and 4–6, Sun. 10–noon and 6–8.*

The adjacent **Casa de la Cultura** (House of Culture) hosts art exhibitions, recitals, and concerts, in addition to a permanent exhibit of local Indian crafts. ⊠ *Plaza 24 de Septiembre,* ☎ *03/340270.* 🎟 *Free.* ☉ *Daily 9–noon and 3–6.*

At the **Zoológico Municipal,** considered one of the finest zoos in South America, you'll see llamas and alpacas, flamingos, owls, snakes, bears, and a collection of native species that includes jaguars, tapirs, and toucans. The animals are well cared for and displayed in settings that approach natural. Taxis will take you from the main square to the zoo for approximately $1.50. ⊠ *Anillo Interno at Radial 26,* ☎ *03/429939.* 🎟 *Admission.* ☉ *Daily 9–6.*

OFF THE
BEATEN PATH

MADIDI NATIONAL PARK – The Chalalan Ecolodge in Madidi National Park offers a chance to experience Bolivia's Amazon. The Ecolodge, owned and operated by the Quechua-Tacana community of San Jose de Uchupiamonas, immerses guests into a culture that has lived in the tropical rain forest for 300 years. The project is supported by Conservation International (CI), a U.S. organization set up to assist indigenous communities with projects that will help them become self sustaining while at the same time conserving their culture and environment. While you're here, be on the lookout for hundreds of species of birds, troops of monkeys, herds of wild peccary, and the elusive jaguar, all of whom live in the area. Thatch-roof cabins with balconies face Chalalan Lake; four-night packages run $138–$273. Contact **America Tours** (☞ Tour Operators and Travel Agents in La Paz, *above*) for details on park trips and lodge stays.

Dining and Lodging

$ ✕ **Victory.** This bar and restaurant serves tasty Italian pastas and pizzas, but most diners gather on the balcony to sip cold beer, play cards or chess, and watch the action below. ⊠ *Calle Junín at Calle 21 de Mayo, Galería Casco Viejo,* ☎ *03/322935. MC, V.*

$$ ✕ 🏨 **Gran Hotel Santa Cruz.** The family-owned Santa Cruz has air-conditioning, cable television, and a handy downtown location. Rooms have the feel of a comfortable den, and those that overlook the pool have small private balconies. The restaurant ($$) serves very good international cuisine. ⊠ *Calle Pari 59,* ☎ *03/348811,* 🖷 *03/324194. 40 rooms, 12 suites. Restaurant, 2 bars, cafeteria, pool, exercise room. AE, MC, V.*

$$$–$$$$ 🏨 **Hotel Los Tajibos.** This resort hotel on the edge of the city features a teardrop-shape pool surrounded by a sprawling lawn. Value packages are available through Bolivian travel agencies or the hotel. ⊠ *Av. San Martín 455,* ☎ *03/421000,* 🖷 *03/426994. 185 rooms, 6 suites. Restaurant, café, pool, exercise room, shops, convention center. AE, MC, V.*

¢ 🏨 **Hotel Viru Viru.** This downtown hotel offers clean, modern rooms with air-conditioning at reasonable prices. All rooms overlook the courtyard swimming pool. ⊠ *Calle Junín 338,* ☎ *03/335298,* 🖷 *03/ 367500. 44 rooms. Café, pool. No credit cards.*

Shopping

Crafts stands and shops are scattered around the main square. The goods are more typical of La Paz than of the lowlands, and don't expect any real bargains. **Artecampo** (⊠ Calle Monseñor Salvatierra 407, ☎ 03/ 341843) is a cooperative crafts shop with a colorful selection of handmade hammocks and crewelwork cushion covers made from locally grown cotton, mobiles, ceramics, and intricate hand-painted woodwork.

Side Trips from Santa Cruz

Jesuit Missions of the Chiquitania

Local travel agencies organize trips by bus or aerotaxis to the Jesuit Missions of the Chiquitania. These restored wooden chapels, beautifully carved in baroque style, are located deep in the rain forest. **Flota Chiquitano** (⊠ Santa Cruz bus terminal, Av. Irala at Av. Cañota, ☎ 03/360320) organizes tours that visit one mission per day. Hotels are available in each area—check with a Santa Cruz travel agency for reservations.

Central Bolivia A to Z

Arriving and Departing

BY AIRPLANE

International flights on LAB and American Airlines stop at Santa Cruz before continuing on to La Paz. LAB and AeroSur also fly daily from La Paz and Sucre to Cochabamba's **Aeropuerto Jorge Wilsterman** (☎ 042/26548) and Santa Cruz's **Aeropuerto Viru-Viru** (☎ 03/44411). The airport is a 16-km (10-mi) taxi ride ($6.50) from downtown; buses headed for downtown Santa Cruz depart every 20 minutes from the airport ($1), and you can then take a taxi to your hotel for $1–$2. Cochabamba's airport is a 10-km (6-mi) taxi ride ($4) from downtown.

BY BUS

Depending on breakdowns and the state of the road, it takes about seven hours to travel by bus between La Paz and Cochabamba; roughly 20 hours between La Paz and Santa Cruz. One-way tickets for either journey cost between $10 and $15. **Trans Copacabana** (☎ 02/377894) and **Expreso Mopar** (☎ 02/377443) depart from La Paz for both Cochabamba and Santa Cruz several times daily (consult a travel agency for current schedules and departure points). To avoid standing in the aisle for 20 hours, book tickets at least one day in advance.

BY CAR

It takes nearly five hours to drive between La Paz and Cochabamba. From La Paz drive in the direction of Oruro until you reach the village of Caracollo, some 190 km (118 mi) south of La Paz and one of the few villages en route with a gas pump. Beyond Caracollo is a poorly signposted, left-hand turn for Cochabamba. The drive between Cochabamba and Santa Cruz takes 10 hours on the Nuevo Camino and is recommended only for four-wheel-drive vehicles. You can break the trip into almost equal parts by staying overnight at Villa Tunari in the Chapare.

In Cochabamba you can rent a car for a minimum of $50 per day from **Barrons Rent-a-Car** (✉ Calle Sucre E 727, ☎ 042/22774 or 042/23819) or **Toyota Rent-a-Car** (✉ Av. Libertador Bolívar 1567, ☎ 042/85703).

In Santa Cruz contact **AB Rent-a-Car** (✉ Av. Alemana, Segundo Anillo, ☎ 03/420160), **Barrons** (✉ Av. Cristóbal de Mendoza 286, ☎ 03/333886), or **IMBEX** (✉ Calle Monseñor Peña 320, ☎ 03/533603).

Getting Around

Buses are the main mode of travel in the region. The **Santa Cruz terminal** (✉ Av. Cañoto, at Av. Irala) is the place to catch a ride to Cochabamba (10–12 hours) and Sucre (18 hours). Buses to Samiapata depart from the Santa Cruz terminal at 2 PM.

Contacts and Resources

BANKS AND CURRENCY EXCHANGE

You can change money and make other banking transactions at **Banco de La Paz** (✉ Supermercado Reyes, Av. 26 Febrero, Nor 517), **Banco Mercantil** (✉ Supermercado Hipermaxi, Av. Banzer), and **Banco Nacional** (✉ Av. Monser), all of which have 24-hour ATMs. There are several casas de cambio around the main plaza; most exchange both cash and traveler's checks. Independent money changers also regularly stroll through the plaza and the bus terminal.

In Cochabamba, you can change money at **Banco La Paz** (✉ Av. Oquendo NRO, N-0684 and ✉ Plaza 14 de Septiembre), **Banco Mercantil** (✉ Av. Ayacucho S/N and ✉ Calle Calama S/N), and **Banco Nacional** (✉ Av. America NRO, E-0402), all of which have 24-hour ATMs.

EMERGENCIES

General emergency: ☎ 110.

ENGLISH-LANGUAGE BOOKSTORES

There are some English-language publications available in the bookstores, newsstands, and larger hotel shops of Santa Cruz. Otherwise, you're best off borrowing from or swapping with other travelers.

TELEPHONES, THE INTERNET, MAIL

To make local and international calls without high hotel fees, try the **ENTEL** office (✉ Calle Warnes, between Av. René Moreno and Av.

Chuquisaca). To check E-mail and browse the world wide web, try **Café Internet** (⊠ Calle Sucre 673, ☎ 5913/352161) in Santa Cruz, which is open Monday–Saturday 9–9 and Sunday 3–9. You can mail packages and pick up post restante mail from the **post office** (⊠ Calle Junín), near the main plaza.

TOUR OPERATORS

Magri Turismo (⊠ Ingavi 14, ☎ 03/344559) in Santa Cruz offers three- and five-day Jesuit Mission trips, as well as tours of Samaipata.

VISITOR INFORMATION

Cochabamba: Oficina de Turismo (⊠ Calle General Achá and Pasaje Zenteno A., 1 block west of main plaza, ☎ 042/23364); **Fremen Travel** (⊠ Calle Piloto 591, ☎ 042/59392, ℻ 042/59686).

Santa Cruz: Oficina de Turismo (⊠ Edificio Ex-Cordecruz, 1st Floor, Calles Omar Chávez O and Ana Barba, ☎ 03/368900); **Tajibos Tours** (⊠ Hotel Los Tajibos, Av. San Martín 455, ☎ ℻ 03/429046); **Umpex Travel** (⊠ Calle René Moreno 226, ☎ 03/336001, ℻ 03/330785).

SOUTHERN BOLIVIA

Sucre

740 km (460 mi) southeast of La Paz.

Without question, Sucre is Bolivia's most beautiful city. Founded in 1540 by the Marqués de Campo Redondo, it has a population of more than 160,000 and is called *La Ciudad Blanca* (the White City)—by government edict, all downtown buildings must be whitewashed each year. Sucre was also the country's original capital, but the main government functions were taken to La Paz in the late 1800s, leaving the city as only the constitutional capital and home of the supreme court. In the course of its existence, Sucre has had four names: Charcas (Indian), La Plata (because it was close to a mineral-rich mountain), Chukuisaca (meaning "Time of Indians"), and, finally, Sucre, after the second president, who was from Venezuela.

Sucre is the home of the second oldest university in South America, **Universidad de San Francisco Xavier,** which was founded in 1624, and it has a university ambience. Students are often seen along the benches in beautiful Bolivar Park, and they pack the trendy downtown cafés and bars in the evenings. Here the climate is mild and the roads uncongested, making it a pleasant place to stay for a few days while taking side trips to the Tarabuco Sunday market or Potosí. In 1992 this lovely city—with its churches, colonial mansions, cobblestone streets, and broad plazas—was declared a "Patrimonio Histórico y Cultural de la Humanidad" by UNESCO.

Exploring Sucre

SIGHTS TO SEE

Casa de la Libertad (House of Liberty). Bolivia's formal document of Independence was signed in the House of Liberty, a former Jesuit chapel, where it is now on display. A small museum displays historical documents and artifacts related to Bolivia's turbulent struggle for independence, as well as Argentina's first flag. ⊠ *Plaza 25 de Mayo,* ☎ *064/24200.* 🎟 *Admission.* ☉ *Weekdays 9–noon and 2:30–5, Sat. 9:30–11:40.*

Catedral Metropolitana and Museum. Started in 1559, this baroque and neoclassical Cathedral is famous for its priceless statue of the Virgin of Guadalupe, which is adorned with diamonds, gold, emeralds, and pearls donated during the 17th century by mining barons. ⊠ *Plaza 25 de Mayo.* 🎫 *Free.* ⊙ *Mon.–Fri. 10–noon and 3–5, Sat. 10–noon.*

Museo Charcas. The most popular exhibits at the Charcas Museum are mummified bodies discovered in the 1960s; museum curators believe the centuries-old mummies were entombed as human sacrifices. Also featured are galleries of colonial painting and textiles. ⊠ *Calle Bolívar 698,* ☎ *064/23285.* 🎫 *Admission.* ⊙ *Weekdays 8:30–noon and 3–6, Sat. 8:30–noon.*

Museo y Convento de la Recoleta. Founded in 1601 by Franciscan monks, the Museum and Convent of the Retreat displays colonial religious works in a setting of serene courtyards and gardens. Equally noteworthy is the restored chapel with its intricately carved choir seats. ⊠ *Plaza Pedro Anzures,* ☎ *064/21860.* 🎫 *Admission.* ⊙ *Weekdays 9–11:30 and 3–5:30.*

Museo y Convento de Santa Clara. Founded in 1639, the Museum and Convent of Santa Clara houses a magnificently hand-painted organ from the 17th century along with devotional paintings and colonial statuary. Also on display are works by colonial painter Melchor Pérez Holguín and his Italian mentor, Bernardo Bitti. Visit the chapel, where the sisters who died here were buried under a special floor. ⊠ *Calle Calvo 212,* ☎ *no phone.* 🎫 *Admission.* ⊙ *Weekdays 9–noon and 3–6, Sat. 9–noon.*

Museo Textil Etnográfico. Housed in a former mansion, the role of the Textile and Ethnographic Museum is to preserve the 4,000 year-old weavings and tapestries of the Andean world. A display of costumes features regional fiesta garb and hand-loom demonstrations. ⊠ *Calle San Alberto 413,* ☎ *064/53841.* 🎫 *Admission.* ⊙ *Sept.–June, Mon.–Fri. 8:30–noon and 2:30–6, Sat. 9:30–noon; July and August, Mon.–Sat. 8:30–noon and 2:30–6.*

Plaza Anzures. This beautiful residential square at the foot of Cerro Churuquella provides panoramas of Sucre's red-tiled roofs and whitewashed homes.

Plaza 25 de Mayo. In Sucre's city center, ice-cream vendors and shoeshine boys leisurely ply their wares throughout the tree-lined plaza. Waiting taxis can take you on brief city tours for less than $5 per hour, but there's little in Sucre that's not within walking distance of the main plaza.

Parque Bolívar. This beautiful park covers several city blocks northwest of the main Plaza, with the imposing Supreme Court Justice building at one end.

OFF THE
BEATEN PATH
TARABUCO – If you are in Sucre over a weekend, take a full-day excursion to the famous Tarabuco Sunday market, held every week except during Carnival, Easter, and national holidays. On the first Sunday after March 12, Tarabuco also hosts one of South America's liveliest traditional festivals, the Pujilay, which celebrates the victory of the Indians over the Spanish in 1816. Tarabuco is 64 km (40 mi) east of Sucre along a half paved, half dirt road. Buses ($3) leave from the corner of Avenida Las Americas and Avenida Manco Kapac beginning at 6:30 AM.

Dining
Sucre's large student population supports many inexpensive restaurants. Around the main plaza, many offer a "Meal of the Day" for $2–$3. If you're not accustomed to spicy food, avoid dishes prefaced with the words *ají* or *picante*.

$-$$ ✕ **El Huerto.** Vegetarians can indulge in all sorts of pastas and meat-
★ free lasagnas at El Huerto, located near the municipal park, while adventurous carnivores should try a traditional Bolivian entrée such as
picante de lengua. The open-air patio, although chilly at night, is a fine
place to linger over a long meal. ⊠ *Ladislao Cabrera 86,* ☎ *064/51538.*
No credit cards.

$ ✕ **Alliance Française la Taverna.** The traditional French menu includes
coq au vin, ratatouille, and dessert crepes. Seating is available indoors
or outside in the courtyard. ⊠ *Calle Aniceto Arce 35,* ☎ *064/53599.*
No credit cards.

$ ✕ **Bibliocafé.** The dinner menu—mostly pastas and grilled meats—may
be small, but most people come for postdinner coffee and dessert. Crepes
stuffed with banana and smothered in chocolate sauce are a divine option. ⊠ *Calle Nicolás Ortiz 30,* ☎ *no phone. No credit cards. No lunch.*

¢ ✕ **Penco Penquitos.** For mere pocket change, nibble at an impressive selection of fresh pastries, from eclairs to empanadas, at this tea house near
the university. ⊠ *Calle Estudiantes 66,* ☎ *064/43946. No credit cards.*

Lodging

Rather than large chain hotels, Sucre has many small hotels and hostels, all of which are comfortable, clean, and friendly. Most include breakfast, but be sure to ask.

$$ ▥ **Hotel Mendez Roca.** A short walk from the plaza, this pleasant
hotel has colonial decor and modern amenities. Discounts are often
available, so feel free to ask. ⊠ *Calle Francisco Argandoña 24,* ☎ *064/*
54282, ℻ *064/55472. 20 rooms. Restaurant. MC, V.*

$ ▥ **Hostal de su Merced.** From the colonial antique furniture to the col-
★ orful wood ceiling in the lobby, a reproduction of the original painted
by a Jesuit priest, this family-owned hotel—built as a private home in
the late 17th century—is a gem. Rooms are airy and bright, with large
beds, and the rooftop sundeck provides excellent views of the entire
city. ⊠ *Calle Azurduy 16,* ☎ ℻ *064/42706. 14 rooms, 2 suites.*
Restaurant. MC, V.

$ ▥ **Hostal Sucre.** The colonial-style Sucre, just two blocks from the main
square, is built around two inner courtyards, which keeps noise to a
pleasant minimum. An on-site restaurant serves light meals and snacks.
⊠ *Calle Bustillos 113,* ☎ *064/51411,* ℻ *064/52677. 30 rooms.*
Restaurant, travel services. AE, MC, V.

Shopping

The ASUR gift shop at the **Caserón de Capellenía** (⊠ Calle San Al-
berto 413, ☎ 064/53841) has an excellent selection of local weavings,
and the cooperative ensures that the majority of profits go directly to
the weavers rather than to middlepersons. For a touch of local flavor,
the market at **Calle Ravelo** and **Calle Junín** sells produce and house-
hold items.

Potosí

574 km (356 mi) southeast of La Paz.

Potosí is Bolivia's most interesting city, and it has a dual personality.
The city itself, with its winding and narrow cobblestone streets, has
many beautiful colonial buildings, museums, restaurants, and hotels,
so it's enjoyable to just sit in the park and people watch. However, with
the Cerro Rico silver mines hovering over the city, it's also difficult to
put the past atrocities and present misery of the mines out of mind.

Silver, tin, and zinc from Cerro Rico, the mountain that towers over
Potosí, once made fortunes for mineral barons and sustained the Span-
ish Empire for years—while enslavement caused early death for some

8 million indigenous workers. In 1650, with a population of 160,000, Potosí was the largest and one of the most elegant cities in the Americas. Today, the wrong set of circumstances has created conditions that have turned Potosí into one of Bolivia's poorest cities. The "Hill" is no longer "Rich." Mining methods are outdated and a continuing global mining crisis has caused a serious drop in the market. The combination of transportation difficulties, an inhospitable terrain—Potosí sits on a windy plain at 4,076 m (13,452 ft) above sea level—and the lack of skilled workers are hardly inducements for prosperity.

The one industry that is offering hope, however, is tourism. A combination of an historic, though tragic past (a tour of the mine gives visitors a small sense of it), the Spanish government's decision to give something back by helping with restoration, and the upgrading of hotels and restaurants is bringing more visitors to one of Bolivia's most interesting cities.

Exploring Potosí

The *only* way to get around Potosí is to walk. The cobblestone streets are narrow, as are the sidewalks, and pedestrian traffic can be more of a problem than cars—particularly during lunch time and after school and work hours. To visit the museums and historic buildings, you will need a guide; however, since English-speaking guides aren't always available, it's best to arrange a tour through a travel agency (☞ Tour Operators and Travel Agents, *below*).

SIGHTS TO SEE

★ **Casa de Moneda.** The original Royal Mint was built in 1572 on Plaza Regocijo and now, painted in a beautiful shade of deep orange, houses the Superior Court of Justice. Off the Plaza on Calle Ayacucho is the "new" mint, which opened in 1773 and cost the equivalent of $10 million in silver. This massive stone building, where coins were once forged with Cerro Rico silver, is Bolivia's largest and most treasured museum. On display are laminating and minting machines, an extensive coin collection, furniture, and paintings, including works by Bolivia's celebrated 20th-century artist, Cecilio Guzmán de Rojas. A guard accompanies all tours to unlock and lock each room as it's visited. The building is cool, so wear warm clothing. ⊠ *Calle Ayacucho,* ☎ FAX 062/22777. ☑ *Admission.* ◷ *Tues.–Sat. 9–noon and 2–6:30, Sat. and Sun. 9–1.*

★ **Cerro Rico.** Five thousand mining tunnels crisscross Cerro Rico, the "Rich Hill" that helped fill Spain's imperial coffers until the reserves were exhausted in the early 19th century. Today tin is the primary extract, though on the barren mountainside, independent miners still sift for silver in the remnants of ancient excavations. If you're accustomed to the altitude and not affected by confined spaces, consider a tour through one of the active cooperative mines. Along with hundreds of local miners, you'll descend into the dark, humid tunnels where it's common to work almost naked because of the intense heat. Conditions are shocking in these noisy, muddy shafts, and tours are not recommended for anyone with a weak stomach. Although hard hats, raincoats, boots, and carbide lamps are provided, be sure to wear your dirtiest clothes.

Churches. Many of Potosí's churches have erratic opening times, so check with the tourist office for current schedules. You can arrange special visits to **Iglesia San Agustín** (⊠ Calle Bolívar), **Iglesia San Martín** (⊠ Calle Hoyos), and **Iglesia Jerusalén** (⊠ Plaza del Estudiante). Potosí's most spectacular church is the **Iglesia San Lorenzo** (⊠ Calle Bustillos), which has some of the finest examples of baroque carvings in South America—elaborate combinations of mythical figures and indigenous designs carved in high relief on the stone facade.

Convento y Museo de Santa Teresa. The Convent and Museum of Saint Theresa displays a strange mix of religious artifacts. In one room are sharp iron instruments once used to inflict pain on penitent nuns, as well as a blouse embroidered with wire mesh and prongs meant to prick the flesh. Other rooms contain works by renowned colonial painters such as Melchor Pérez Holguín. ⊠ *Calle Chicas,* ☎ *064/23847.* 🖭 *Admission.* ⊙ *Weekdays 9–noon and 2–5:30.*

Dining and Lodging

There are no large hotels in Potosí, but the hostels have been upgrading their services and there are many small, clean places to stay. If your room doesn't have a heater, be sure to ask for one because Potosí is cold at night.

$ ✕ **El Mesón.** With its international menu and central location opposite the cathedral, El Mesón bills itself as Potosí's most exclusive restaurant. Dishes served in the quiet dining room include traditional Potosino fare and international standards such as lasagna. ⊠ *Calle Tarija at Calle Linares,* ☎ *062/23087. MC, V.*

$ ✕ **Sky Room.** You'll have a fine view of central Potosí from this rooftop restaurant. The menu features traditional local dishes such as *pichanga* (offal served with salad). Less adventurous diners may want to try a grilled chicken entrée. The restaurant also serves breakfast. ⊠ *Edificio Matilde, 3rd Floor, Calle Bolívar 701,* ☎ *062/26345. MC, V.*

¢ ✕ **Cherry's.** At this delightful coffee shop you can sip mugs of coffee
★ or maté de coca while you ponder the delicious selection of cakes and strudels. ⊠ *Calle Padilla 8,* ☎ *062/22969. No credit cards.*

$ 🏠 **Hostal Colonial.** This whitewashed, stone-flagged, vaguely colonial-looking low-rise is just two blocks from the main square. Many rooms overlook the hotel's two airy courtyards; all have a TV and a phone. Ask to see one of the rooms in the back, which are more modern and spacious. ⊠ *Calle Hoyos 8,* ☎ *062/24265,* 🖷 *062/27164. 20 rooms. Dining room. MC, V.*

$ 🏠 **Hotel Claudia.** More practical than refined, the Claudia matches well-equipped rooms—all have phone and TV—with other features rarely found in Potosí: an on-site restaurant, bar, and terrace. ⊠ *Av. El Maestro 322,* ☎ *062/22242,* 🖷 *062/24005. 22 rooms. Restaurant, bar. MC, V.*

¢ 🏠 **Hostal Carlos.** Though still one of the better budget lodgings in town, the hostel's somewhat cold, bare rooms are more functional than cozy, and the toilets and showers are shared. Breakfast is served on an enclosed balcony. ⊠ *Calle Linares 42,* ☎ 🖷 *062/25151. 12 rooms with shared bath. No credit cards.*

Shopping

Despite Potosí's rich mineral wealth, don't expect bargains on hand-crafted silver jewelry. Brass and low-grade silver jewelry and silver coins, however, can be found at an outdoor market between Calle Oruro and Calle Bustillos. Another market on Calle Bolívar sells fresh tropical fruits and produce, while one on the corner of Calle Sucre and Calle Modesto Omiste, four blocks from the Church of San Lorenzo, has locally produced crafts.

OFF THE
BEATEN PATH

SALAR DE UYUNI – One of Bolivia's most spectacular sites, the Salar de Uyuni is the world's largest (at 4,632 sq mi) and highest (11,976 ft) desert of salt, and its vast, white, cracked expanse must be seen to be believed. The area is noted for a wide variety of birds, a series of eerie, translucent lagoons tinted green and red due to high copper and sulfur contents, and, in the middle of the flats, **La Isla de Pescado** (Fish Island), with its 8-m- (27-ft-) high cacti. Once part of a prehistoric salt lake covering most of southwestern Bolivia, the enormous flats are 3,629 m (11,976 ft) in elevation.

Located 219 km (136 mi) and five hours over rough road southwest of Potosí, the flats are best visited on a travel agency tour, as breakdowns here can be dangerous. The site is remote and cold, with nightly temperatures falling to -25°C (-13°F). The dry months of May to December are the best time to visit, but whenever you go, take sunblock, sunglasses, and warm clothing. If you'd like to stay overnight, try the 12-room **Hotel Palacio de Sal**—built entirely of salt, including the furniture and mattresses—where guests can relax in the sauna, a small salt pool, or play on a 9-hole golf course. Packages can be arranged through **Sin Fronteras** or **Hidalgo Tours** (☞ Tour Operators and Travel Agents in Southern Bolivia A to Z, below).

Southern Bolivia A to Z

Arriving and Departing

BY AIRPLANE

LAB (⊠ Calle Bustillos 121, ☎ 064/52666) and **AeroSur** (⊠ Calle Arenales 31, ☎ 064/54895) have daily flights between Sucre's airport (☎ 064/31655) and most major cities throughout Bolivia.

Potosí has a small airstrip near town and is serviced mainly by Aerotaxis, with no regular schedules.

BY BUS

Buses leave La Paz daily between 6 PM and 8:15 PM for Sucre (via Potosí); the 19-hour trip costs less than $15. To reserve space on the five-hour ride between Sucre and Potosí, go to Sucre's **Terminal de Buses** (⊠ Calle Ostria Gutiérrez, ☎ 06/422029), from which buses depart approximately every hour until 5 PM. Buses to other destinations also depart from here.

BY CAR

From La Paz, take the main highway south to Oruro and look for signs for Potosí (12 hours) or Sucre (18 hours) near the village of Machacamarca. The road is paved from the capital to Oruro; after that, expect rough going.

Getting Around

Although the roads aren't in the best condition, a car is still the most convenient method of travel in this region. Morning buses and minibuses, as well as late-afternoon buses, ply the route between Sucre and Potosí daily (5 hours). A weekly train also runs between the two cities (6 hours).

Contacts and Resources

BANKS AND CURRENCY EXCHANGE

Sucre's **Banco La Paz** (⊠ Calle San Alberto Esq. ESPA #A 105) has a 24-hour ATM. Also in Sucre, you'll find casas de cambio and roving money changers around the market and along Avenida Hernando Siles, which runs behind it. Your best bet in Potosí is along Calle Bolívar and Calle Sucre. In both places, cash fetches a better rate than traveler's checks.

EMERGENCIES

General emergency: ☎ 110.

TELEPHONES AND MAIL

Sucre's **ENTEL** office (⊠ Calle España), one of the more reliable places to make calls, is three blocks northeast of the main plaza. Potosí also has an **ENTEL** office (⊠ Plaza Aniceto Arce) where you can make calls.

As for mail and post restante pick-ups, you'll find Sucre's main **post office** (⊠ Av. Argentina 50) a half-block from the plaza; there is also a general **post office** branch (⊠ Av. Lanza 13) in Potosí.

TOUR OPERATORS AND TRAVEL AGENTS

Candelaria Tours (⊠ Calle Audiencia 1, ☎ 064/61661) organizes Sunday and full weekend tours to Tarabuco; the latter include a stay at the family hacienda. **Sin Fronteras** (⊠ Calle Bustilos 1092, ☎ FAX 062/24058) and **Hidalgo Tours** (⊠ Av. Bolívar at Av. Junín, ☎ 25186) organize tours of Potosí. **Sin Fronteras, Hidalgo Tours** (⊠ Bolívar Esq. Junín, ☎ 62/25186), and **Andes Braulio Expeditions, Raul Braulio Mamai Israel** (⊠ Alonso de Ibañez, ☎ FAX 62/25175) organize tours of Cerro Rico. **Fremen Tours** (☎ 02/414069) can arrange wine tours around Tarija. **America Tours** (☞ Tour Operators and Travel Agents *in* La Paz, *above*) organizes packages to Madidi National Park and Chalalan Ecolodge.

VISITOR INFORMATION

Sucre Oficina de Turismo (⊠ Calle San Alberto 413, ☎ 064/55983). **Potosi Oficina de Turismo** (⊠ Cámara de Minería, 2nd Floor, Calle Quijarro, ☎ 062/25288). **Tarija Oficina de Turismo** (⊠ Calle General Trigo ☎ 066/2594).

BOLIVIA A TO Z

Arriving and Departing

By Airplane

The main U.S. carrier that serves Bolivia is **American Airlines** (⊠ Plaza Venezuela 1440, La Paz, ☎ 02/351360). Bolivia's **Lloyd Aéreo Boliviano (LAB)** (⊠ Av. Camacho 1456, La Paz, ☎ 800/327–7407 in the U.S., 0800–3001 toll-free in Bolivia) operates daily between Miami and La Paz. **Aeroperu** (☎ 800/777–7717) also serves the country.

By Boat

Bolivia is crisscrossed by navigable rivers served by supply ships, which often accept passengers for a small, negotiable fee. The only international arrivals by boat are from the Peruvian port of Puno on Lake Titicaca, and are usually a bus/hydrofoil or bus/catamaran combination. Travel agency packages usually include stops at the Isla del Sol and Isla de la Luna. The cost is approximately $250 per person.

By Bus

A variety of private bus companies connect Bolivia's major cities—two of the best are **Expreso Mopar** and **Trans Copacabana.** Because of the often poor state of road surfaces, bus journeys do not always make sense for travelers with limited time: The La Paz–Santa Cruz trip, for example, can take more than 24 hours. Crowds can be a problem on some routes, but if you can get a seat, it's likely to be fairly comfortable.

Getting Around

By Airplane

Lloyd Aéreo Boliviano (LAB, ⊠ Av. Camacho 1456, La Paz, ☎ 02/371020, 08003001 toll-free in Bolivia) and **AeroSur** (⊠ Av. 16 de Julio, Edificio Petrolero, ☎ 02/375152, 0800–3030 toll-free in Bolivia, FAX 02/390457) fly between all the major cities in the country. **AeroExpress,** a division of AeroSur, also operates flights to some of the smaller cities. One-way prices for flights range from $60 to $150. Domestic flights can be heavily booked, so *always* reconfirm your reservation and arrive at the airport an hour in advance. If you do not reconfirm, your reservation will be canceled.

LAB and **AeroSur** offer 30-day passes that allow travel to four major destinations for approximately $160. There are some stipulations on cities (Potosí is not included) and routes (passengers cannot backtrack). Pass destinations include Trinidad, Santa Cruz, Tarija, Sucre, Cochabamba, and La Paz.

By Boat

Bolivia is crisscrossed by navigable rivers served by supply ships, which often accept passengers for a negotiable fee. In addition, some travel agencies, especially those that deal in adventure tours, offer trips in the country's jungle regions by boat.

By Bus

Traveling by bus around Bolivia is the economical way to go and the service is generally good; however, it's best to book your trip through a travel agency rather than at the city terminal. An agency can advise you on schedules, costs, which companies are best for which routes, and how long journeys will take. They will also tell you which companies have more comfortable seats.

By Car

EMERGENCY ASSISTANCE

There is no national roadside automobile service, though Bolivians will often stop and offer help in the case of a breakdown.

GASOLINE

The national oil company, **YPFB,** maintains service stations on most major roads. Opening times vary, though a number operate 24 hours. Away from the main roads, GASOLINA (gasoline) signs alert you to private homes where fuel is sold (make sure they filter the gasoline for impurities when they fill your tank). Unleaded gasoline is still a novelty in Bolivia. The price of gasoline is approximately $1.70 per gallon.

RENTAL AGENCIES

Renting can be an expensive business in Bolivia, particularly because you really need a four-wheel-drive vehicle. The rate for a four-wheel-drive vehicle is $300–$700 per week, including 700 km (435 mi) free, depending on whether you rent a small Suzuki or a top-of-the-line Toyota or Mitsubishi. Compact cars cost $150–$250 per week, a fee that also includes 700 km (435 mi) free. The minimum age for most car rentals in Bolivia is 25. You need a passport, driver's license (some rental companies require an International Driver's License), and a credit card.

ROAD CONDITIONS

Bolivia's paved-road network is very limited, and conditions have been so bad that professional drivers have held brief strikes in protest. During rainy season, roads are often impassable and in rural areas there are few roadside facilities.

RULES OF THE ROAD

Bolivia's drunk-driving laws are rarely enforced, so exercise caution when driving at night or on small mountain roads.

Contacts and Resources

Customs and Duties

ON ARRIVAL

Bags are usually checked on arrival at La Paz's El Alto airport. Visitors are allowed to import 400 cigarettes and three bottles of wine or

2 liters of spirits. There is no limit on the amount of foreign currency you can bring into the country. For certain electronic goods—video cameras and personal computers, for example—you should carry your receipt or proof of purchase unless the items show obvious signs of wear. Do not attempt to import or export contraband drugs of any kind—penalties are severe.

ON DEPARTURE

At the airport all passengers must pay a departure tax—$20 for international flights, $2 for domestic flights—at an easily identifiable booth marked IMPUESTOS.

Electricity

Bolivia's electric current is 110/220 volts AC in La Paz and 220 volts AC in the rest of the country. You will need adapters for two-pronged outlets, which are used for both types of current.

Embassies and Consulates

American (⊠ Av. Arce 2780, Casilla 425, La Paz, ☎ 02/430251, FAX 02/433900). **British** (⊠ Av. Acre 2732–2754, Casilla, La Paz, ☎ 02/433424, FAX 02/431073). **Canadian** (⊠ Av. 20 de Octubre 2475, Plaza Abaroa, La Paz, ☎ 02/431215, FAX 02/432330).

Health and Safety

FOOD AND DRINK

To play it absolutely safe, do not drink tap water and pass up ice cubes in your drinks. Never eat food from street vendors and take the U.S. government's Centers for Disease Control's advice: "Boil it, cook it, peel it, or forget it."

OTHER PRECAUTIONS

Crime is not a major problem in Bolivia. In larger cities such as La Paz, Cochabamba, Sucre, and Santa Cruz, however, petty theft—from pickpocketing to bag slashing—is on the rise. Avoid displays of money and be aware of your surroundings at all times, especially in busy plazas and markets, or if you travel on crowded city buses. It's also advisable to carry a copy of your passport instead of the actual document and only as much cash as necessary when in the city, especially in market areas.

As for health precautions, always check with your doctor several weeks in advance about recommended vaccinations. At present no shots or vaccination certificates are required for entering Bolivia unless you are coming from an area known to be infected. As precautionary measures, if you'll be spending a lot of time in very remote areas off the tourist circuits, consider getting typhoid, hepatitis A and B, yellow fever, and tetanus vaccinations. If you're headed for the Amazon region, you'll need antimalarial prophylactics: pills, coils, and nets.

Due to the high altitude in La Paz, upon arrival you may suffer from *soroche* (altitude sickness). Avoid alcohol, drink lots of (bottled) water, and rest for at least a half day—then walk slowly. Usually all you'll notice is a slight tightness across your forehead and breathlessness, which will disappear by the second day. If you feel really sick and symptoms persist, consult a doctor, especially if you have a history of high blood pressure. Locals recommend several cups of mate de coca, an herbal (and completely legal) tea made from coca leaves; it helps stimulate your kidneys, the organs responsible for assisting altitude adjustment.

Bring sun block—the high altitudes may be cool, but the sun can burn, particularly when reflected off water, such as at Lake Titicaca. Finally, don't pet the cute llamas or alpacas, as they can hurl burning spit wads that can be particularly devastating to the eyes. Also, don't stand too close behind these animals, as they can throw a sharp kick.

Language, Culture, and Etiquette

Spanish is the main language in the cities and lowlands, and travelers find Bolivian Spanish to be one of the easiest on the continent to understand. Quechua and Aymara are spoken by the highlanders, who may or may not understand Spanish. Hotel staff usually have some knowledge of English, French, or German.

Mail

Most cities and towns have at least one post office, which is generally open weekdays 8–7:30, Saturdays 9–6, and Sundays 9–noon.

POSTAL RATES

International airmail letters and postcards cost 67¢ to the United States and 76¢ to Europe, and arrive within 5–10 days. International packages to the United States and Europe cost $26 and $37 per 2 kilos (4½ pounds), respectively.

RECEIVING MAIL

Mail can be sent to you in major cities in care of Poste Restante, Correo Central. If a "Casilla" number is given, it should be included in the address. You will need your passport to retrieve mail from the central post office.

Money Matters

CURRENCY

The unit of currency is the boliviano (B), which can be divided into 100 centavos. Bolivianos come in bills of 5, 10, 20, 50, 100, and 200. Coins come in denominations of 10, 20, and 50 centavos and 1 and 2 bolivianos. At press time, the exchange rate was Bs 5.68 to the U.S. dollar and Bs 7.7 to the pound sterling. Bolivians frequently refer to their currency as *pesos*.

Dollars are easily exchanged in hotels, banks, and the numerous casas de cambio along the street. Visa is the credit card of choice throughout Bolivia, but MasterCard is also usually accepted and American Express less so. Credit cards are accepted in many hotels and restaurants, but never in small villages or outside major urban centers. Traveler's checks are not popular, but are accepted in banks, often at slightly inferior rates. ATMs are popping up in the larger cities. U.S. dollars (but not British pounds) are widely accepted, though the bills must be in perfect condition with no torn edges.

SERVICE CHARGES, TAXES, AND TIPPING

Throughout Bolivia, a 13% value-added tax (IVA) is added to hotel and restaurant bills and to most store-bought purchases. In restaurants, a tip of 5%–10% is expected unless the service is really dismal. Also note that some establishments add a cover charge to your bill—from 10¢ to $2 per person—whether you eat a full meal or simply stop in for a cup of coffee. Taxi drivers do not expect tips unless you hire them for the day, in which case 10% is appropriate. Airport porters expect $1 per baggage cart they handle. At the airport all passengers must pay a departure tax—$20 for international flights, $2 for domestic flights—at an easily identifiable booth marked IMPUESTOS.

WHAT IT WILL COST

Because the boliviano is a relatively stable currency, Bolivia remains one of the least expensive countries in South America for travelers. A basic meal at a basic restaurant should cost no more than $5, and even at the most elegant restaurants you can eat well for less than $10. Moderate hotels cost $30–$50 for a double room, which often includes breakfast. The most expensive luxury hotels are more pricey, at $120–$150 per night for a double.

Sample costs: Cup of coffee, 50¢; bottle of beer, $1; soft drink, 50¢; bottle of house wine, $5; sandwich, $2; 1-mile taxi ride, $2; city bus ride, 25¢; museum entrance, $1.

Opening and Closing Times

A pending law that eliminates the long lunch closing for offices may soon change the way cities—particularly La Paz—conduct business. Presently, **banks** are open weekdays 9–11:30 and 2:30–5, **museums** are generally open Tuesday–Friday 9–noon and 3–7, and **shops** are usually open Monday–Saturday 9–noon and 3–8. There are a number of local carnivals and feast days when shops may be closed; check with local tourist offices for more details.

NATIONAL HOLIDAYS

New Year's Day (Jan. 1); Shrove Tuesday and the preceding Monday (variable, Feb. and March); Good Friday (April 24, 2000, April 15, 2001); Labor Day (May 1); Corpus Christi (variable, June); Independence Day (Aug. 6); All Saints' Day (Nov. 2); Christmas (Dec. 25).

Passports and Visas

U.S. and British citizens need only a valid passport for stays of up to 30 days. Canadian citizens additionally require a tourist visa, available for C$20 from the **Consulate of Bolivia** (⊠ 130 Albert St., Suite 504, Ottawa, Ontario K1P 5G4, ☎ 613/236–8237).

Telephones

CALLS TO BOLIVIA

The international code for Bolivia is 591.

LOCAL CALLS

Pay phones are operated by using either coins or phone cards (*tarjetas telefónicas*) purchasable at **ENTEL** (Bolivian Phone Company) offices, or where indicated. After you insert a coin or card and enter the number, the phone will tell you how much credit you have.

LONG-DISTANCE AND INTERNATIONAL CALLS

Long-distance and international calls can be made from ENTEL offices, found in all towns and cities. Collect and direct-dial calls can be made from ENTEL offices or by calling ☎ 35–67–00, which connects you with a Bolivian international operator who will ask for the city and number you wish to reach, then, up to 20 minutes later, call you back after the connection has been made. You will need to dial 00 to make an international call from within the country. The least expensive way to make international calls is through **AT&T** (☎ 0800–1111), **MCI** (☎ 0800–2222), or **Sprint** (☎ 0800–3333).

Visitor Information

Bolivian Tourist Information Office (⊠ 9745 Queens Blvd., Suite 600, Rego Park, NY 11374, ☎ 718/897–7956 or 800/205–4842, ☎ 718/275–3943).

When to Go

With its extremes of terrain, altitude, and climate, Bolivia offers the perfect environment for every traveler. Rainy season is November to March, when heavy downpours—particularly in the lowlands—make many roads virtually impassable. In the highlands, it may only rain for an hour or two, but the season brings dark, cloudy skies. If you plan to travel by bus or car, it's best to go between April and October.

CLIMATE

In high-altitude La Paz and around Lake Titicaca, the weather can get very chilly, particularly at night, while in the lowland city of Santa Cruz and the central El Chapare the climate is tropical—hot and humid.

Cochabamba, the "City of Eternal Spring," enjoys a Mediterranean climate year-round.

The following are the average monthly maximum and minimum temperatures for La Paz.

Jan.	64F	18C	May	66F	19C	Sept.	62F	17C
	43	6		35	2		38	3
Feb.	64F	18C	June	60F	16C	Oct.	65F	18C
	43	6		36	2		40	4
Mar.	64F	18C	July	61F	16C	Nov.	67F	20C
	43	6		34	1		42	6
Apr.	66F	19C	Aug.	62F	17C	Dec.	64F	18C
	40	4		35	2		43	6

FESTIVALS AND SEASONAL EVENTS

The **Feria de Alicitas** (Alicitas Fair) takes place in La Paz for two weeks beginning January 24. The **Festival of the Virgin of Candalaria (Candlemas)** takes place in Copacabana on Lake Titicaca in February. Also in February, all of Bolivia celebrates **Carnival,** a weeklong binge that includes street dancing, music, and parades; the ultimate expression of this centuries-old tradition is held in the mining town of Oruro, where brass bands and dance troupes from all over the country converge and the highly charged, wildly costumed performers parade through the streets. **Pujilay,** a colorful festival commemorating the 1816 victory by local Tarabucans over the Spanish, is celebrated the week after Carnival in the village of Tarabuco, near Sucre. **Good Friday** celebrations—which feature candlelit religious processions by masked supplicants—are particularly lively in La Paz and Copacabana.

Festivals of the Cross take place around Lake Titicaca in early May. On June 24, the **Fiesta de San Juan** (Feast of St. John the Baptist) in La Paz features fires and fireworks at dusk to mark the passing of mid-winter and to fend off the cold. From August 5–8, the **Festival of the Black Virgin** takes place in Copacabana. Tarija holds the *Fiesta de San Rogue* on the first Sunday of September, and the city's flower festival is on the second Sunday of October, when the image of the *Virgen del Rosario* is carried through the streets accompanied by a showering of flower petals. **El Día de Todos los Santos** (All Saints' Day) and **El Día de los Muertos** (All Souls' Day), also called the **Day of the Dead,** are marked all around Lake Titicaca on November 1 and 2.

5 BRAZIL

Brazil covers more than half of South America and has a raw energy and diversity to match its size. From São Paulo, a city that makes New York look small, and Rio with its spell-binding coastal scenery, to the thriving Afro-Brazilian culture of Salvador and the trackless jungles of the Amazon, Brazil seems to defy scale itself.

BRAZIL—WHICH MANY NATIVES CONSIDER a continent in its own right—is larger than the continental United States, four times the size of Mexico, and
more than twice as large as India. Occupying most of the eastern half
of South America, it borders on all of the other nations of the continent, with the exception of Chile and Ecuador. Its population of 163
million is almost equal to that of the continent's other nations combined, making it South America's true colossus.

Brazil is also a land well versed in extremes. Its continuous, 7,700-km
(4,800-mi) coast offers a seemingly infinite variety of beaches. Styles
range from the urban setting of Rio's Copacabana and Ipanema to isolated, unspoiled treasures along the northeastern coast. Brazil's Portuguese colonizers concentrated on the coastal regions, avoiding the
inland areas with rare exceptions—a preference that has dictated national life to this day. In the 1960s, the government moved the capital
from Rio to inland Brasília in an effort to overcome the "beach complex," but three decades later, the majority of the population remains
concentrated along a narrow coastal strip.

By contrast the Amazon jungle, which covers 40 percent of the nation's
land mass, has a population of only about 16 million—less than the
city of São Paulo alone. Twenty percent of the world's freshwater reserves are found here, and the area is responsible for more than 30%
of the earth's oxygen and is home to two-thirds of the world's existing species. Brazil's other hinterland regions are as sparsely populated
as they are diverse. The northeast contains the rugged sertão, a region
that frequently suffers droughts; the central-west is the site of the immense *cerrado* (savanna) area; still farther west are the enormous Pantanal Wetlands—an enormous swamp.

The country is also a melting pot of races and cultures. Beginning with
its Portuguese colonizers, Brazil has drawn waves of immigrants from
around the globe, including the forced immigration of over fifteen million Africans. The result is the ethnic mix of modern-day Brazil—Italian and German communities in the south, prosperous Japanese and
Korean colonies in the state of São Paulo, a thriving Afro-Brazilian culture in Bahia, and remnants of Indian cultures in the north. Brazilians
are white, tan, gold, black, brown, red, and seemingly all shades in between. Yet the various groups are united by a common language and
a cultural heritage distinct from that of the remainder of South America. Brazilians speak Portuguese, not Spanish, and unlike all their
neighbors, they were never a Spanish colony.

The variety of cultures, beliefs, and topographies make this warm nation a showcase of diversity. An array of nature's bounty—from passion fruit and papaya to giant river fish and coastal crabs—has inspired
chefs from all over the world to come and try their hands in Brazilian
restaurants (adding lightness and zest to the country's already exquisite
cuisine). Spas—with bubbling mineral water and soothing hot springs—
all over the land offer the best that both nature and technology can
offer. Whether you travel to the Amazon rain forest, the mountain towns
of Minas Gerais, the urban jungle of São Paulo, or the immense central plateau surrounding Brasília, you'll plunge into an exotic mix of
colors, rhythms, and pastimes.

Pleasures and Pastimes

Carnaval

Carnaval (Carnival) is the biggest party of the year. In some areas, events begin right after Reveillon (New Year's) and continue beyond the four main days of celebration (just before the start of Lent) with smaller feasts and festivities. At Carnaval's peak, businesses close throughout the country as Brazilians don costumes—from the elaborate to the barely there—and take to the streets singing and dancing. These four explosive days of color see formal parades as well as spontaneous street parties fueled by flatbed trucks that carry bands from neighborhood to neighborhood.

Dining

Indian, African, and Portuguese traditions have simmered for centuries to produce Brazil's savory cuisine. Pre-Columbian cultures cultivated dozens of edible plants that have since become world staples: cocoa, vanilla, potatoes, corn, manioc, peppers, squash, beans, tomatoes, avocados, bananas, pineapples, papayas. The Portuguese transplanted their national tastes and traditional recipes, adapting them to the foodstuffs found in the New World. It took the catalyst of African culture, however, to really turn out a national cuisine. The slaves introduced their cooking techniques and ingredients, including coconut milk, *dendê* (palm) oil, cashew nuts, and fiery hot spices.

Brazilian adaptations of Portuguese specialties include *caldeiradas* (fish stews), *cozidos* (beef stews), and *bacalhau* (salt cod cooked in sauces or grilled). *Salgados* (literally "salteds") are appetizers or snacks served in sit-down restaurants as well as stand-up *lanchonetes* (luncheonettes); *doces* (sweets) are, as their name suggests, desserts; many are direct descendents of the egg-based custards and puddings of Portugal and France. Although regional specialties abound, a typical Brazilian meal consists of *arroz* (rice) and *feijão preto* (black beans); beef, chicken, or fish; and, of course, some kind of doce. From such basic fare comes the national dish, the *feijoada* (a stew of black beans, sausage, pork, and beef), which is often served with arroz; shredded kale; orange slices; and manioc flour—called *farofa* if it is coarsely ground, *farinha* if finely ground—that has been fried with onions, oil, and egg.

Dried meats form the basis for many dishes in the interior and the northeast; the latter is also known for its seafood dishes and its generous amount of seasonings—some very hot. Pork is used heavily in dishes from Minas Gerais. From the south comes the *churrasco* (barbecue), made with marinated meats that are grilled or roasted over coals. *Churrascarias* (restaurants specializing in barbecue) serve their delicacies à la carte or in a manner known as *rodizio* (with the meats continuously brought to your table until you tell the waiters you've had enough).

The national drink is the *caipirinha,* made with crushed ice, lime juice, suga2, and *cachaça* (also called *pinga*; a strong sugarcane liquor). *Batchidas* are made with cachaça, crushed ice, fruit juice of one kind or another, and, sometimes, sweetened condensed milk. Be sure to try the carbonated soft drink *guaraná,* made from the Amazonian fruit of the same name. Coffee is served black and strong with sugar or sweetener in demitasse cups and is called *cafezinho* (little coffee). *Cafe com leite* (coffee with milk) is generally served only with breakfast.

Only at the top restaurants do Brazilians dress up, and men seldom wear jackets and ties. Mealtimes vary according to locale. In Rio and São Paulo, lunch in a restaurant usually starts at around 1 and often lasts until 3. Dinner is always eaten after 8 and in many cases not until 10. In Minas Gerais, the northeast, and smaller towns in general, din-

Brazil

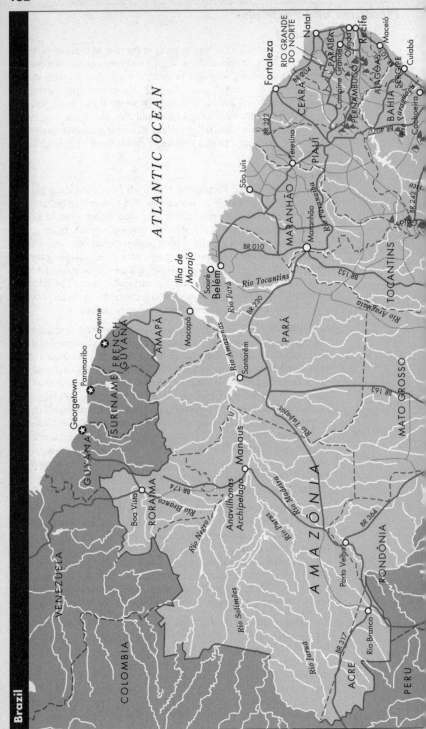

ATLANTIC OCEAN

Natal
RIO GRANDE
DO NORTE
Recife
Olinda
PARAÍBA
Campina Grande
PERNAMBUCO
Maceió
ALAGOAS
Fortaleza
CEARÁ
BR 304
SERGIPE
Cuiabá
BAHIA
Juazeiro
BR 407
Teresina
PIAUÍ
Cachoeira
Rio Parnaíba
BR 222
São Luís
MARANHÃO
Goiás
BR 153
Maranhão
BR 010
TOCANTINS
Souré
Belém
Rio Tocantins
Rio Pará
Ilha de
Marajó
BR 230
Cayenne
FRENCH
GUYANA
Paramaribo
AMAPÁ
Macapá
Rio Amazonas
Santarém
PARÁ
Rio Araguaia
Georgetown
SURINAME
Rio Tapajós
MATO GROSSO
BR 163
GUYANA
Boa Vista
RORAIMA
Rio Branco
BR 174
Rio Negro
Manaus
Anavilhanas
Archipelago
Rio Madeira
VENEZUELA
Rio Purus
A M A Z Ô N I A
BR 364
RONDÔNIA
Porto Velho
COLOMBIA
Rio Solimões
Rio Juruá
ACRE
BR 317
Rio Branco
PERU

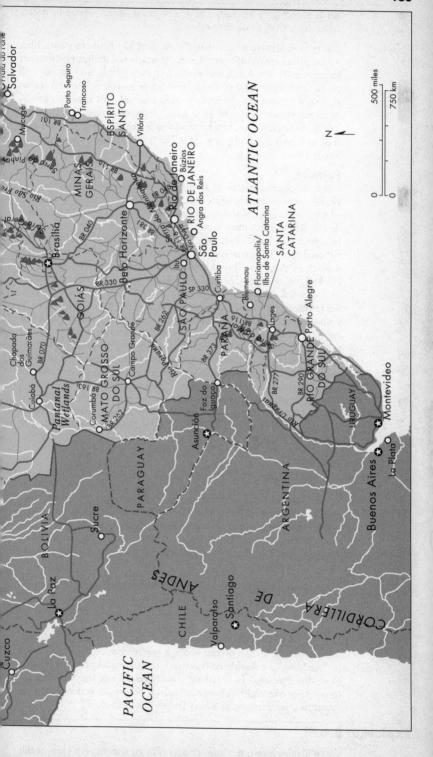

ner and lunch are eaten earlier. In general, breakfast isn't served by restaurants other than those in hotels.

Rio is as expensive as any world-class city; São Paulo more so. Elsewhere prices are significantly lower. At lunch and dinner, portions are large; often a single dish will easily feed two people, and no one will be the least surprised if you order one entrée and two plates. Note that some restaurants automatically bring a *couberto* (an appetizer course of such items as bread, cheese or pâté, olives, quail eggs, and the like). You'll be charged extra for this, and you're perfectly within your rights to send it back if you don't want it. For price categories, *see* Dining *in* Smart Travel Tips A to Z.

Futebol

South Americans in general are passionate about *futebol* (soccer), but Brazilians are virtually hysterical about it. Here the game is the stuff of myth and legend, with top players treated in a manner befitting minor deities. The world's most famous player, Pele, is Brazilian, and though he retired nearly 20 years ago, he's still revered by all Brazilians as a national hero. The game is played literally everywhere; wherever there's a patch of grass you'll find boys (and, increasingly, girls) young and old kicking, dribbling, or juggling a ball with a skill that's sometimes inspirational. In Brazil, the *o jogo bonito* (the beautiful game) is considered an art form, and matches are treated—both by players and fans—with the same gravity and admiration that you might reserve for a fine ballet. The best players possess the quality known as *jinga,* which translates roughly as a feline, almost swaggering grace. However, the professional game, although avidly followed throughout the country, suffers from chronic lack of funding; many of the best players leave to display their superlative skills abroad. Nevertheless, the national team, a repeat World Cup title holder, is one of the world's best. If you want to see the Brazilians at their passionate best (and, alas, sometimes worst), try to attend a game, particularly between the bigger teams of Rio or São Paulo.

Lodging

Variety is the catchword in Brazil, where you can stay in world-class urban high-rises, "flat" (apartment) hotels, quaint *pousadas* (inns), or rustic *fazendas* (ranches/farms) and jungle lodges. Just remember, however, that top prices aren't always indicators of deluxe accommodations. Embratur, the national tourism agency, has a rating system that often seems to merely take into consideration the amenities offered by a hotel without evaluating such vital intangibles as the quality of service and the upkeep.

Make reservations for stays in high-end establishments well in advance, particularly if you're planning a trip during peak season or special events. (Unless you're part of a tour, reservations in the best hotels must be made at least a year ahead for stays during Carnaval.) If possible, before you take a room in an inexpensive or moderate establishment, ask to see it. If you want a quieter room, a better view, or a *cama de casal* (a "wedding" or double bed) instead of two singles, be sure to ask. Note that "motels" in Brazil are usually rented out for the hour, afternoon, or overnight. A pousada is always more advisable. For price categories, *see* Lodging *in* Smart Travel Tips A to Z.

Exploring Brazil

When planning your trip, don't underestimate the country's size or the travel times. Determine your interests up front, and pick your destinations accordingly. Beaches, fun, and sun are the calling cards of Rio and Salvador. São Paulo is a huge, bustling city, full of activity day and night. Belo Horizonte, the capital of Minas Gerais State and the country's third-largest city, is a good base from which to explore the historical towns of Ouro Prêto, Tiradentes, and others. Similarly, use Manaus and Belém as hubs for trips into the Amazon.

Great Itineraries

IF YOU HAVE 5–7 DAYS

Choose one destination and fully explore it. Let your interests guide you. **São Paulo** offers lots of fine arts, fine dining, and fine nightlife. **Salvador** is perfect for beach lovers and Afro-Brazilian culture aficionados. **Rio** has its famous beaches as well as chic shops and many colonial sights. For those with more refined historical interests, the small, 18th-century "Gold Towns" of **Minas Gerais,** especially **Ouro Prêto** and **Tiradentes,** promise a unique vacation.

IF YOU HAVE 10–14 DAYS

If you have 10 days, you could fly to **Rio,** stay a few days, then fly to **Belo Horizonte.** From here, tour Minas Gerais' fascinating colonial towns of **Ouro Prêto** and **Tiradentes.** Another option is to spend some time in **São Paulo** and then catch a plane west to visit the phenomenal **Iguaçu Falls,** on the border of Argentina (where they're spelled "Iguazú") and Paraguay (☞ Chapter 3). With 14 days, you can visit the Amazon. Fly into **Manaus,** spend a few nights in a jungle lodge and continue to **Belém** for a couple days of in-town sightseeing.

IF YOU HAVE 21 DAYS

With 21 days you can easily combine more than one city and take in some bucolic sights as well. Consider visiting **Rio, São Paulo,** and either **Iguacú** or **Minas Gerais.** Another option would be to explore **Salvador, Belém,** and/or **Manaus.**

RIO DE JANEIRO

Updated by
Mary A.
Dempsey

Rio was named—or misnamed—by the crew of a Portuguese ship that arrived in what is now the city on January 1, 1502. (Portuguese navigator Gonçalo Coelho as well as Amerigo Vespucci and Gaspar de Lemos—all members of the expedition—are alternatively credited with discovering the city.) Thinking they had found the mouth of a river, instead of the bay that became known as the Baía de Guanabara (Guanabara Bay), they dubbed the spot Rio de Janeiro (January River). Sixty-five years later, on the feast of St. Sebastian, the city was founded with the official name of São Sebastião do Rio de Janeiro.

In 1763, Brazil's colonial capital was moved to Rio from Salvador and, in 1889 when the country became independent, Rio was declared the capital of the Republic of Brazil. It held this title until 1960 when the federal government was moved to Brasília.

Today, this pulsating city is synonymous with the girl from Ipanema, the dramatic Pão d'Açucar (Sugarloaf) Mountain, and the wild and outrageous Carnaval (Carnival) celebrations. But Rio is also a city of stunning architecture, good museums, and marvelous food; it's a teeming metropolis where the very rich and the very poor live in uneasy proximity and where enthusiasm is boundless—and contagious.

As you leave the airport and head to your hotel, you'll be tossed onto a massive, chaotic, not-so-scenic urban roadway. But, by the time you reach breezy, sunny Avenida Atlântica—flanked on one side by white beach and azure sea, and on the other by the pleasure-palace hotels that testify to the city's eternal lure—your heart will leap with expectation. Now you're truly in Rio, where the 10 million wicked angels and shimmering devils known as *cariocas* dwell.

The term "carioca" comes from the country's early history, when it meant "white man's house" and was used to describe a Portuguese trading station. Today the word defines more than birthplace, race, or residence: It represents an ethos of pride, a sensuality, and a passion for life. Much of the carioca verve comes from the sheer physical splendor of a city blessed with seemingly endless beaches and sculpted promontories.

Prepare to have your senses engaged and your inhibitions untied. You'll be seduced by a host of images: the joyous bustle of vendors at Sunday's Feira Hippie (Hippie Fair); the tipsy babble at sidewalk cafés as patrons sip their last glass of icy beer under the stars; the blanket of lights beneath Pão d'Açucar; the bikers, joggers, strollers, and power walkers who parade along the beach each morning. Borrow the carioca spirit for your stay; you may find yourself reluctant to give it back.

Exploring Rio de Janeiro

Cariocas divide their city into three sections: Zona Norte (North Zone), Zona Sul (South Zone), and the "downtown" area that separates them, called Centro. Except for some museums, churches, and historical sights, most of the tourism activity is in the beach- and hotel-laden Zona Sul. To sense the carioca spirit, spend a day on Copacabana and walk from the Avenida Atlântica to Ipanema. The western extension of Ipanema, Leblon, is an affluent, intimate community flush with good, small restaurants and bars (sadly, the water is polluted). The more distant southern beaches, beginning with São Conrado and extending past Barra da Tijuca to Grumari, become richer in natural beauty and increasingly isolated.

Although Rio's settlement dates back nearly 500 years, it's in every respect a modern city. Most of the historic structures have fallen victim to the wrecking ball, though a few churches and villas are still tucked in and around Centro. As these colonial vestiges are far flung, consider seeing them on an organized walking or bus tour. However, you can use the metrô (and comfortable walking shoes) to explore on your own. The bus is another option; just be sure to know where you're going and memorize some key phrases in Portuguese as bus drivers don't speak English. Police have put a dent in the crime, but as in any large city, be discreet and aware.

Centro and Environs

What locals generally refer to as Centro is a sprawling collection of several districts that contain the city's oldest neighborhoods, churches, and most enchanting cafés. Rio's beaches, broad boulevards, and modern architecture may be impressive, but its colonial structures and old narrow streets and alleyways in leafy inland neighborhoods are no less so.

Numbers in white bullets in the text correspond to numbers in black bullets in the margins and on the Rio Centro and Environs map.

A GOOD TOUR (OR TWO)

Start at the **Mosteiro de São Bento** ① for your first taste of Brazilian baroque architecture. From here, move south into the heart of Centro. At the beginning of Avenida Presidente Vargas you'll find the solid **Igreja de Nossa Senhora da Candelária** ②. From this church walk south along Avenida 1 de Março, crossing it and heading west to a network of narrow lanes and alleys highlighted by the **Beco do Comércio** ③, a pedestrian street. After wandering this area, return to Avenida 1 de Março and walk southeast to the Praça 15 de Novembro, a square that's dominated by the **Paço Imperial** ④. A few blocks away is the large **Museu Histórico Nacional** ⑤.

From the Museu Histórico Nacional, follow Rua Santa Luzia southeast to Avenida Rio Branco, Centro's main thoroughfare. North one block is the Victorian **Biblioteca Nacional** ⑥, and one block up from it is the French neoclassical **Museu Nacional de Belas Artes** ⑦. In the middle of the next block up, and across Rio Branco, you'll find the **Teatro Municipal** ⑧ and its elegant café. Continue north on Rio Branco and turn left on Avenida Almirante Barroso. A short walk northwest brings you to the Largo da Carioca, a large square near the Carioca metrô stop. Atop a low hill overlooking it are the **Igreja de São Francisco da Penitência** ⑨ and the **Convento do Santo Antônio** ⑩. The architecturally striking (or absurd, depending on your viewpoint) **Catedral de São Sebastião do Rio de Janeiro** ⑪ is just south of here (off Avenida República do Chile), as is the station where you can take a *bonde* (trolley) over the **Aqueduto da Carioca** ⑫ and along charming Rua Joaquim Murtinho into Santa Teresa. This eccentric neighborhood is famed for its cobblestone streets and its popular **Museu Chácara do Céu** ⑬, whose works are displayed in a magnificent former home with beautiful city views.

TIMING AND PRECAUTIONS

Although you can follow this tour in a day if you set out early, you might want to break it up into two days or be selective about which museums you fully explore. You can also mix some of the southernmost sights in with those (the Aterro do Flamengo, Museu de Arte Moderna, or Monumento aos Pracinhas) in the Flamengo, Botafogo, and Pão d'Açucar tour (☞ *below*). However you organize your day, you'll need plenty of energy to get everything in. Leave your camera at your hotel if you're planning to use public transportation. Wear no jewelry, and keep your cash in a money belt or safe pocket.

SIGHTS TO SEE

⑫ **Aqueduto da Carioca.** The imposing Carioca Aqueduct, with its 42 massive stone arches, was built between 1744 and 1750 to carry water from the Rio Carioca in the hillside neighborhood of Santa Teresa to Centro. In 1896 the city transportation company converted the then-abandoned aqueduct to a viaduct, laying trolley tracks along it. Since then, Rio's distinctive trolley cars (called "bondes" because they were financed by foreign bonds) have carried people between Santa Teresa and Centro. (Guard your belongings particularly closely when you ride the open-sided bondes; the fare is about 50¢.) *Metrô: Carioca or Cinelândia.*

③ **Beco do Comércio.** A network of narrow streets and alleys is the setting for this pedestrian thoroughfare. The area is flanked by restored 18th-century homes, now converted to offices. The best known is the Edifício Telles de Menezes. A famous arch, the Arco dos Telles, links this area with Praça 15 de Novembro. ⊠ *Praça 15 de Novembro No. 34, Centro. Metrô: Uruguaiana.*

⑥ **Biblioteca Nacional.** Corinthian columns flank the neoclassical National Library (built between 1905 and 1908), the first such establishment in Latin America. Its original archives were brought to Brazil by King João VI in 1808. Today it contains roughly 13 million books, including two 15th-century bibles; New Testaments from the 11th and 12th centuries; first-edition Mozart scores as well as scores by Carlos Gomes (who adapted the José de Alencar novel about Brazil's Indians, *O Guarani*, into an opera of the same name); books that belonged to the Empress Teresa Christina; and many other manuscripts, prints, and drawings. Tours aren't available in English, but the devoted staff of docents will work something out to accommodate English-speaking book lovers. ⊠ *Av. Rio*

Rio Centro and Environs

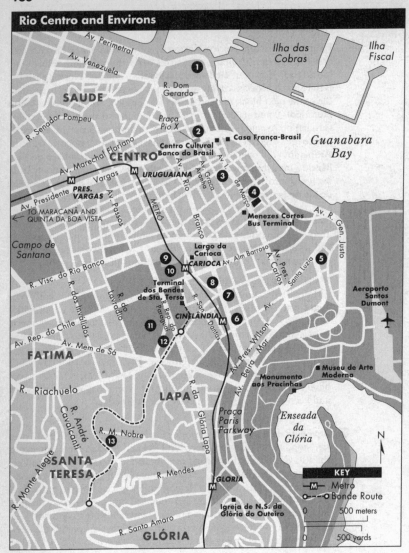

Branco 219, ☎ *021/262–8255.* 🎫 *Admission.* ⊙ *Weekdays 9–8, Sat. 9–3. Tours: Weekdays at 11, 1, 3, and 5. Metrô: Cinelândia.*

⑪ Catedral de São Sebastião do Rio de Janeiro. The exterior of this metropolitan cathedral (circa 1960), which looks like a concrete bee-hive, can be off-putting. (The daring modern design stands in sharp contrast to the baroque style of other churches.) But don't judge until you've stepped inside. Outstanding stained-glass windows transform the interior—which is 96 m (315 ft) in diameter and 80 m (263 ft) high—into a warm, yet serious, place of worship that accommodates up to 20,000 people. An 8½-ton granite rock lends considerable weight to the concept of an altar. ⊠ *Av. República do Chile 245,* ☎ *021/240–2869.* 🎫 *Free.* ⊙ *Daily 7–5:30. Metrô: Carioca or Cinelândia.*

⑩ Convento do Santo Antônio. The Convent of St. Anthony was com-pleted in 1780, but some parts date from 1615, making it one of Rio's oldest structures. (At press time, the convent was being thoroughly re-stored.) Its baroque interior contains priceless colonial art—including wood carvings and wall paintings—and the sacristy is covered with *azule-jos* (Portuguese tiles). Note that the church has no bell tower: its bells hang from a double arch on the monastery ceiling. An exterior mau-soleum contains the tombs of the offspring of Dom Pedro I and Dom Pedro II. ⊠ *Largo da Carioca 5,* ☎ *021/262–0129.* 🎫 *Free.* ⊙ *Week-days 2–5. Metrô: Carioca.*

❷ Igreja de Nossa Senhora da Candelária. The classic symmetry of Can-delária's white dome and bell towers casts an unexpected air of san-ity over the chaos of downtown traffic. The church, which supports 630 tons of stonework on its foundation, was built on the site of a chapel founded in 1610 by Antônio de Palma after he survived a shipwreck; paintings in the present dome tell his tale. Construction on the church in its present state began in 1775, and although it was formally dedi-cated by the emperor in 1811, work on the dome wasn't completed until 1877. The sculpted bronze doors were exhibited at the 1889 world's fair in Paris. ⊠ *Praça Pio X,* ☎ *021/233–2324.* 🎫 *Free.* ⊙ *Weekdays 7:30–noon and 1–4:30, weekends 8–1. Metrô: Uruguaiana.*

❾ Igreja de São Francisco da Penitência. The church was completed in 1737, nearly four decades after it was started. Today it's famed for its wooden sculptures and its rich gold-leaf interior. The nave contains a painting of St. Francis, the patron of the church—reportedly the first painting in Brazil done in perspective. ⊠ *Largo da Carioca 5,* ☎ *021/262–0197.* ⊙ *By appointment. Metrô: Carioca.*

❶ Mosteiro de São Bento. Just a glimpse of this church's main altar will fill you with awe. Layer upon layer of curvaceous wood carvings—coated in gold—create a sense of movement. Spiral columns whirl upward to capitals topped by cherubs so chubby and angels so purposeful that they seem almost animated. Although the Benedictines arrived in 1586, they didn't begin work on this church and monastery until 1617. It was completed in 1641, but such artisans as Mestre Valentim (who de-signed the silver chandeliers) continued to add details almost through to the 19th century. On some Sundays, mass here is accompanied by Gregorian chant. ⊠ *Rua Dom Gerardo 32,* ☎ *021/291–7122.* 🎫 *Free.* ⊙ *Weekdays 8–11 and 2:30–5:30.*

★ **⑬ Museu Chácara do Céu.** With its cobblestone streets and bohemian atmo-sphere, Santa Teresa is a delightfully eccentric neighborhood. Gabled Victorian mansions sit beside alpine-style chalets as well as more pro-saic dwellings—many hanging at unbelievable angles from the flower-encrusted hills. Set here, too, is the quaintly named Museum of the Small Farm of the Sky whose outstanding collection of mostly modern works were left—along with the hilltop house that contains it—by one of Rio's greatest arts patrons, Raymundo de Castro Maya. Included are originals by such 20th-century masters as Pablo Picasso, Georges Braque, Salvador Dalí, Edgar Degas, Henri Matisse, Amedeo Modigliani, and Claude Monet. The Brazilian holdings include priceless 17th- and 18th-century maps and works by leading modernists. The grounds afford fine views of the aqueduct, Centro, and the bay. ⊠ *Rua Murtinho Nobre 93,* ☎ *021/507–1932.* ☜ *Free.* ☉ *Wed.–Mon. noon–5.*

| NEED A BREAK? | Santa Teresa's has attracted artists, musicians, and intellectuals to its eclectic slopes. Their hangout is **Bar do Arnaudo** (⊠ Rua Almirante Alexandrino 316-B, ☎ 021/252-7246), which is always full. |

❺ Museu Histórico Nacional. The building that houses the National History Museum dates from 1762, though some sections—such as the battlements—were erected as early as 1603. It seems appropriate that this colonial structure should exhibit relics that document Brazil's history. Among its treasures are rare papers, Latin American coins, carriages, cannons, and religious art. ⊠ *Praça Marechal Ancora,* ☎ *021/550–9266.* ☜ *Free.* ☉ *Tues.–Fri. 10–5:30, weekends 2–6. Metrô: Carioca or Cinelândia.*

❼ Museu Nacional de Belas Artes. Works by Brazil's leading 19th- and 20th-century artists fill the space at the National Museum of Fine Arts. Although the most notable canvases are those by the country's best-known modernist, Cândido Portinari, be on the lookout for such gems as Leandro Joaquim's heart-warming, 18th-century painting of Rio. (At once primitive and classical, the small oval canvas seems a window on a time when fishermen still cast nets in the waters below the landmark Igreja de Nossa Senhora da Glória do Outeiro.) After wandering the picture galleries, consider touring the extensive collections of folk and African art. ⊠ *Av. Rio Branco 199,* ☎ *021/240–0068.* ☜ *Free.* ☉ *Tues.–Fri. 10–6, weekends 2–6. Metrô: Carioca or Cinelândia.*

❹ Paço Imperial. This two-story colonial building is notable for its thick stone walls and entrance, and its courtyard paved with huge stone slabs. It was built in 1743, and for the next 60 years it was the headquarters for Brazil's captains (viceroys), appointed by the Portuguese court in Lisbon. When King João VI arrived, he made it his royal palace. After Brazil's declaration of independence, the emperors Pedro I and II called the palace home. When the monarchy was overthrown, the building became Rio's central post office. Restoration work in the 1980s transformed it into a cultural center and concert hall. The third floor has a restaurant and a ground-floor shop sells stationery and CDs. The square, **Praça 15 de Novembro,** on which the palace is set has witnessed some of Brazil's most significant historical moments. Known in colonial days as Largo do Paço, it was here that two emperors were crowned, slavery was abolished, and Emperor Pedro II was deposed. Its modern name refers to the date of the declaration of the Republic of Brazil: November 15, 1889. ⊠ *Praça 15 de Novembro 48, Centro,* ☎ *021/533–4407.* ☜ *Free.* ☉ *Tues.–Sun. noon–6:30.*

❽ Teatro Municipal. Carrara marble, stunning mosaics, glittering chandeliers, bronze and onyx statues, gilded mirrors, German stained-glass windows, brazilwood inlay floors, and murals by Brazilian artists Eliseu Visconti and Rodolfo Amoedo make the Municipal Theater opulent, indeed. Opened in 1909, it's reportedly a scaled-down version of the Paris Opera House. The main entrance and first two galleries are particularly ornate. As you climb to the upper floors, the decor becomes more ascetic—a reflection of a time when different classes entered through different doors and sat in separate sections. The theater seats 2,357—with outstanding sightlines—for its dance performances and classical music concerts. Tours are available by appointment. ⊠ *Praça Floriano 210,* ☎ *021/297–4411. Metrô: Cinelândia or Carioca.*

NEED A BREAK?	Elegance joins good food in the lower level of the Teatro Municipal at the charming **Café do Teatro** (⊠ Praça Floriano 210, ☎ 021/297–4411). Have a light lunch (weekdays 11–3) or coffee and a pastry (served at lunch and during evening performances) as you drink in the atmosphere. Taking center stage is the Assyrian motif, replete with columns and wall mosaics that look like something out of a Cecil B. DeMille epic. The bar resembles a sarcophagus, and two sphinxes flank the sunken dining area. Note that this is one of the few cafés where you may be turned away if you're dressed too shabbily.

Flamengo, Botafogo, and Pão d'Açucar

These neighborhoods and their most famous peak—Pão d'Açucar—are like a bridge between the southern beach districts and Centro. Several highways intersect here, making it a hub for drives to Corcovado, Copacabana, Barra, or Centro. The metrô also travels through the area. Although the districts are largely residential, you'll find Rio Sul, one of the city's most popular shopping centers, as well as good museums and fabulous public spaces.

The eponymous beach at Flamengo no longer draws swimmers (its gentle waters look appealing but are polluted; the people you see here are sunning, not swimming). A marina sits on a bay at one end of the beach, which is connected via a busy boulevard to the smaller beach (also polluted) at Botafogo. This neighborhood is home to the city's yacht club, and when Rio was Brazil's capital, it was also the site of the city's glittering embassy row. The embassies were long ago transferred to Brasília, but the mansions that housed them remain. Among Botafogo's more interesting mansion- and tree-lined streets are Mariana, Sorocaba, Matriz, and Visconde de Silva.

Botafogo faces tiny sheltered Urca, which is separated by Pão d'Açucar from a small patch of yellow sand called Vermelha. This beach is, in turn, blocked by the Urubu and Leme mountains from the 1-km (½-mi) Leme Beach at the start of the Zona Sul (☞ *below*).

Numbers in white bullets in the text correspond to numbers in black bullets in the margins and on the Rio de Janeiro map.

A GOOD TOUR

Start at the northern end of the lovely, landscaped **Aterro do Flamengo** and the **Museu de Arte Moderna (MAM)** ⑭. Nearby is the **Monumento aos Pracinhas** ⑮, which honors the dead of World War II. Wander south along the Aterro before hopping a cab and heading inland to the hilltop **Igreja de Nossa Senhora da Glória do Outeiro** ⑯. From the church, walk south along Rua da Glória da Lapa (or get on the metrô at the Glória station and take it one stop to the Catete terminal). At the corner of the Rua da Catete you'll find the **Palácio Catete** ⑰. From here you can either return to the Aterro by cab and walk south to the **Museu Carmen Miranda** ⑱ or you can take the metrô to the Botafogo stop and the nearby **Casa Rui Barbosa** ⑲. Finish the tour by riding the cable car up the **Pão d'Açucar** ⑳ for panoramic views of the bay and the neighborhoods you've just explored.

TIMING AND PRECAUTIONS

This tour takes a full day and involves a lot of walking and time outdoors. You can shorten the itinerary by taking a cab to sights off the

172

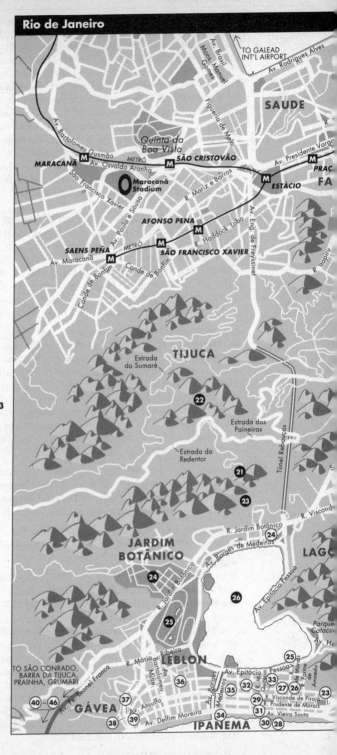

Rio de Janeiro

Aterro do Flamengo and/or from one end of the Aterro to the other. As always, keep your money and other valuables out of sight while strolling.

SIGHTS TO SEE

Aterro do Flamengo. This waterfront park flanks Baía de Guanabara from the Glória neighborhood to Flamengo. It gets its name from its location atop an *aterro* (landfill), and was designed by landscape architect Roberto Burle Marx. Paths used for jogging, walking, and biking wind through it, and there are also playgrounds and public tennis and basketball courts. On weekends the freeway beside the park is closed to traffic, and the entire area becomes one enormous public space.

⑲ Casa Rui Barbosa. Slightly inland from the Aterro is a museum in what was once the house of the 19th-century Brazilian statesmen and scholar, Rui Barbosa (a liberal from Bahia State, Barbosa drafted one of Brazil's early constitutions). The pink mansion dates from 1849 and contains memorabilia of Barbosa's life, including his 1913 car and an extensive library that's often consulted by scholars from around the world. ⊠ *Rua São Clemente 134, Botafogo,* ☎ *021/537–0036.* 🖃 *Admission.* ⊙ *Tues.–Fri. 9–4, weekends 2–5. Metrô: Botafogo.*

⑯ Igreja de Nossa Senhora da Glória do Outeiro. Set atop a hill, the baroque Glória Church is visible from many spots in the city, making it a landmark that's truly cherished by the cariocas. Its location was a strategic point in the city's early days. Estácio da Sá took this hill from the French in the 1560s and then went on to expand the first settlement and found a city for the Portuguese. The church, which wasn't built here until 1739, is notable for its octagonal floor plan, large dome, ornamental stonework, and vivid tile work. ⊠ *Praça Nossa Senhora da Glória 135, Glória,* ☎ *021/557–4600.* 🖃 *Free.* ⊙ *Tues.–Fri. 9–noon and 1–5, weekends 9–noon. Tours by appointment 1st Sun. of the month. Metrô: Glória.*

⑮ Monumento aos Pracinhas. The Monument to the Brazilian Dead of World War II (the nation sided with the Allies during the conflict) is actually a museum and monument combined. It houses military uniforms, medals, stamps, and documents belonging to soldiers in World War II. Two soaring columns flank the tomb of an unknown soldier. The first Sunday of each month, Brazil's armed forces undertake a colorful changing of the guard here. ⊠ *Parque Brigadeiro Eduardo Gomes, Flamengo,* ☎ *021/240–1283.* 🖃 *Free.* ⊙ *Tues.–Sun. 10–4. Metrô: Cinelândia.*

⑭ Museu de Arte Moderna (MAM). Set in a striking concrete and glass building, the Modern Art Museum has a collection of some 1,700 works by artists from Brazil and elsewhere. It also hosts significant special exhibitions, and its wildly popular cinema shows a broad range of films. ⊠ *Av. Infante Dom Henrique 85, Flamengo,* ☎ *021/210–2188.* 🖃 *Free.* ⊙ *Tues.–Sun. noon–6. Metrô: Cinelândia.*

⑱ Museu Carmen Miranda. This tribute to the Brazilian bombshell is in a circular building that resembles a concrete spaceship (its door even opens upward rather than outward). On display are some of the elaborate costumes and incredibly high platform shoes worn by the actress, who was viewed as a national icon by some and as a traitor to true Brazilian culture by others. Hollywood photos of Miranda, who was only 46 when she died of a heart attack in 1955, show her in her trademark turban and jewelry. You'll also find her records, movie posters, and such memorabilia as the silver hand-held mirror she was clutching when she died. ⊠ *Av. Rui Barbosa 560, Flamengo,* ☎ *021/551–2597.* 🖃 *Free.* ⊙ *Tues.–Fri. 11–5, weekends 10–4. Metrô: Flamengo.*

Flamengo contains some of Rio's better small restaurants. For authentic Brazilian fare, the bohemian community heads to **Lamas** (⊠ Rua Marques de Abrantes 18, ☎ 021/556–0799).

★ ⑰ **Palácio Catete.** Once the villa of a German baron, the elegant 19th-century granite-and-marble Catete Palace became the presidential residence after the 1889 coup overthrew the monarchy and established the Republic of Brazil. Eighteen presidents lived here.

You can gaze at the palace's gleaming parquet floors and intricate bas-relief ceilings as you wander through its **Museu da República** (Museum of the Republic). The permanent—and frank—exhibits include a shroud-draped view of the bedroom where President Getúlio Vargas committed suicide in 1954 after the military threatened to overthrow his government, presidential memorabilia, and furniture and paintings that date from the proclamation of the republic to the end of Brazil's military regime in 1985. A small contemporary art gallery and theater also operate within the museum. ⊠ *Rua do Catete 153, Catete,* ☎ *021/ 225–4302.* ⬛ *Admission; free on Wed.* ☉ *Tues.–Sun. noon–5, weekends 2–6. Metrô: Catete.*

★ ⑳ **Pão d'Açúcar.** This soaring 1,300-ft granite block at the mouth of Baía de Guanabara was originally called *pau-nh-acugua* (high, pointed peak) by the Tupi Indians. To the Portuguese the phrase was similar to their *pão de açúcar,* or "sugarloaf," and the rock's shape reminded them of the conical loaves in which refined sugar was sold. Italian-made bubble cars holding 75 passengers each move up the mountain in two stages. The first stop is at Morro da Urca, a smaller mountain (705 ft high); the second is at the summit of Pão d'Açúcar itself. The trip to each level takes three minutes. In high season, long lines often form for the cable-car; the rest of the year, the wait is seldom more than 30 minutes. ⊠ *Between Urca and Praia Vermelha.* ⬛ *Admission.* ☉ *Daily 8 AM–10 PM.*

Zona Sul

Rio is home to 23 *praias* (beaches), an almost continuous 73-km (45-mi) ribbon of sand. All are public and are served by buses and taxis. At intervals along the beaches at Copacabana and Ipanema are small *postes* with washrooms, showers, and changing rooms that can be used for a small fee. Kiosks manned by police also pepper the avenues running parallel to the beach, and crime has dropped dramatically as a result.

A GOOD BEACH STRATEGY

Although the circuit starts to the northeast at the beaches of Flamengo, Botafogo, Urca, and Vermelha, the waters off their shores are often polluted. The best sands are farther south. Leme, which is popular with senior citizens, runs into the city's grande dame, **Copacabana.** Its 3-km (2-mi) stretch is lined by a sidewalk whose swirling pattern was designed by Roberto Burle Marx. You'll also find outdoor cafés, high-rise hotels, and juice kiosks. At the end, cut around via small Arpoador—a beach favored by surfers—or Avenida Francisco Otaviano to **Ipanema.** Note that the final leg of this beach, called Leblon, is polluted; swimming here isn't recommended.

Beyond Ipanema and Leblon, mountains again form a natural wall separating you from the next beach, little Vidigal. Still more mountains block it from **São Conrado,** a beach where hang gliders land after leaping from a nearby peak. A highway through a mountain tunnel forms the link between São Conrado and the long, spectacular **Barra da Tijuca.** Its waters are clean and cool, and its far end, known as Recreio dos Bandeirantes, was home to a small fishing village until the late 1960s.

Beyond are **Prainha,** whose rough seas make it popular with surfers, and the lovely **Grumari,** whose copper sands are often packed. Just before Prainha, you can take a slight detour to visit the **Museu Casa do Pontal,** Brazil's largest folk-art museum. It's worth continuing down the hill beyond Grumari to the **Sítio Roberto Burle Marx,** for an in-depth look at one of Brazil's greatest artists.

City buses and small green minivans pick you up and drop you off wherever you request along the shore. If you're brave enough to drive, the city has established small, affordable parking lots (look for attendants in green and yellow vests) along waterfront avenues. There are several organized tours that take in the beaches, and agents at Turismo Clássico (☞ Tour Operators and Travel Agents *in* Rio de Janeiro A to Z, *below*) can arrange for drivers and/or guides.

TIMING AND PRECAUTIONS

Although you can tour the shoreline in several hours, consider spending a full day just wandering from Copacabana to Ipanema or sunbathing on Barra da Tijuca. Remember that Rio's beaches aren't just about sunning and swimming, they're also about volleyball games, strolling, biking, and people-watching.

Don't shun the beaches because of reports of crime, but *do* take precautions. Leave jewelry, passports, and large sums of cash at your hotel; avoid wandering alone and at night; and be alert when groups of friendly youths engage you in conversation. (Sometimes they're trying to distract you while one of their cohorts snatches your belongings.) The biggest danger is the sun. From 10 to 3, its rays are merciless making heavy-duty sunscreen, hats, cover-ups, and plenty of liquids essential. (You can also rent a beach umbrella from a vendor or your hotel.) Hawkers stroll the beaches with beverages—take advantage of their services. Lifeguard stations are found once every kilometer.

SIGHTS TO SEE

★ **Barra da Tijuca.** Cariocas consider the beach here to be Rio's best, and the 18-km-long (11-mi-long) sweep of sand and jostling waves certainly is dramatic. Pollution isn't a problem and, in many places, neither are crowds. Barra's water is also cooler and its breezes more refreshing than those at other beaches. However, the waves can be strong in spots, and this attracts surfers, windsurfers, and jet-skiers; swim with caution. The beach is set slightly below a sidewalk, where cafés and restaurants beckon. Condos have also sprung up here, and the city's largest shopping centers and supermarkets have made inland Barra their home.

At the far end of Barra's beachfront avenue, Sernambetiba, is **Recreio dos Bandeirantes,** a 1-km (½-mi) stretch of sand anchored by a huge rock, which creates a small protected cove. Its quiet seclusion makes it popular with families. The calm, pollution-free water, with no waves or currents, is good for bathing, but don't try to swim around the rock— it's bigger than it looks.

Copacabana. Maddening traffic, noise, packed apartment blocks, and a world-famous beach—this is Copacabana, a Manhattan with bikinis. A walk along the neighborhood's classic crescent is a must. Here you'll see the essence of Rio beach culture, a cradle-to-grave lifestyle that begins with toddlers accompanying their parents to the water and ends with graying seniors walking hand in hand along the sidewalk. It's here, too, that athletic men play volleyball using only their feet and heads, not their hands. As evidenced by all the goal nets, soccer is also popular. (Copacabana hosts the world beach soccer championships every January and February.) You can swim here, although pollution levels and a strong undertow can sometimes be discouraging.

At the Pão d'Açúcar end is **Leme,** really no more than a natural extension of Copacabana. A rock formation juts into the water here, forming a quiet cove that's less crowded than the rest of the beach. Along a sidewalk, at the side of the mountain overlooking Leme, anglers stand elbow-to-elbow with their lines dangling into the sea.

Copacabana's privileged live on beachfront **Avenida Atlântica,** famed for its wide mosaic sidewalks, hotels, and cafés. On weekends, two of the avenue's lanes are closed to traffic and are taken over by joggers, roller bladers, cyclists, and pedestrians. Two blocks inland from and parallel to the beach is **Avenida Nossa Senhora de Copacabana,** the main commercial street, with shops, restaurants, and sidewalks crowded with the colorful characters that give Copacabana its flavor.

Ipanema. As you stroll along this beach, you'll catch a cross section of the city's residents, each favoring a particular stretch. There's an area dominated by families; a spot near Copacabana, known as **Arpoador,** that tantalizes surfers; and even a strand favored by the gay community. Ipanema, nearby Leblon (off whose shores the waters are too polluted for swimming), and the blocks surrounding Lagoa Rodrigo de Freitas are part of Rio's money belt. For a close-up look at the posh apartment buildings, stroll down beachfront **Avenida Vieira Souto** and its extension, **Avenida Delfim Moreira,** or drive around the lagoon on **Avenida Epitácio Pessoa.** The tree-lined streets between Ipanema Beach and the lagoon are as peaceful as they are attractive. The boutiques along **Rua Garcia D'Avila** make window shopping a sophisticated endeavor. Other chic areas near the beach include **Praça Nossa Senhora da Paz,** which is lined with wonderful restaurants and bars; **Rua Vinícius de Morais;** and **Rua Farme de Amoedo.**

NEED A BREAK?	Have you ever wondered if there really *was* a girl from Ipanema? The song was inspired by schoolgirl Heloisa Pinheiro, who caught the fancy of songwriter Antônio Carlos (a.k.a. Tom) Jobim and his pal lyricist Vinícius de Morais as she walked past the two bohemians sitting in their favorite bar. They then penned one of the century's classics. That was in 1962, and today the bar has been renamed **Bar Garota de Ipanema** (✉ Rua Vinícius de Morais 49-A, Ipanema, ☎ 021/267–8787).
OFF THE BEATEN PATH	**MUSEU CASA DO PONTAL –** If you're heading toward Prainha or beyond to Grumari, consider taking a detour to Brazil's largest folk-art museum. One room houses a wonderful mechanical sculpture that represents all of the escolas de samba that march in the Carnaval parades. Another mechanical "scene" depicts a circus in action. This private collection is owned by a French expatriate, Jacques Van De Beuque, who has been collecting Brazilian treasures—including religious pieces—since he arrived in the country in 1946. ✉ *Estrada do Pontal 3295, Grumari,* ☎ *021/490–3278 or 021/539–4914.* 🎟 *Admission.* ⊙ *Tues.–Sun. 9–5.*

★ **Prainha and Grumari.** The length of two football fields, Prainha is a vest-pocket beach favored by surfers, who take charge of it on weekends. Set about 35 minutes west of Ipanema on a road that hugs the coast, you need a car to get here. The swimming is good, but watch out for surfboards. About 5 minutes farther down the road is Grumari, a beach that seems an incarnation of paradise. What it lacks in amenities (you'll find only a couple groupings of thatch-roof huts selling drinks and snacks) it makes up for in natural beauty: the glorious red sands of its quiet cove are backed by low, lush hills. On weekdays, especially in the off season, these beaches are almost empty; on weekends, particularly in peak season, the road to and from them is so crowded that it almost becomes a parking lot.

From Grumari, the road climbs up through dense forest, emerging atop a hill above the vast Guaratiba flatlands. Here you'll find the **Restaurante Pont de Grumari,** an eatery that's famed for grilling fish to perfection. With its shady setting, glorious vistas, and live music performances (samba, bossa nova, jazz) it's the perfect lunch spot (open daily 11:30–7) after a morning on the beach and before an afternoon at the Sítio Roberto Burle Marx or the Museu Casa do Pontal. ⊠ *Estrada do Grumari 710, Grumari,* ☎ *021/410–1434. AE, DC, MC, V.*

São Conrado. In Leblon, at the end of Ipanema where the imposing Dois Irmãos Mountain stands, Avenida Niemeyer snakes along rugged cliffs that offer spectacular sea views on the left. The road returns to sea level again in São Conrado, a natural amphitheater surrounded by forested mountains and the ocean. Development of what is now a mostly residential area began in the late '60s with an eye on Rio's high society. A short stretch along its beach includes the condominiums of a former president, the ex-wife of another former president, an ex-governor of Rio de Janeiro State, and a one-time Central Bank president. In the middle of the small valley is the exclusive Gávea Golf and Country Club. The far end of São Conrado is marked by the towering **Pedra da Gávea,** a huge flattop granite block. Next to it is Pedra Bonita, the mountain from which the gliders depart. (Although this beach was the city's most popular a few years ago, contaminated water has discouraged swimmers.)

Ironically, though, the neighborhood is surrounded by shantytowns. Much of the high ground has been taken over by Rio's largest favela, **Rocinha,** where an estimated 200,000 people live. This precarious city within a city seems poised to slide down the hill. It, and others like it, are the result of Rio's chronic housing problem coupled with the refusal by many of the city's poor to live in distant working-class neighborhoods. Though the favelas are dangerous for the uninitiated, they have their own internal order, and their tremendous expansion has even upper-class cariocas referring to them not as slums but as neighborhoods. Notice that the favelas enjoy prime vistas, and most of the structures in them are constructed of brick.

SÍTIO ROBERTO BURLE MARX – Beyond Grumari the road winds through mangrove swamps and tropical forest. It's an apt setting for the plantation-turned-museum where Brazil's famous landscape designer, Roberto Burle Marx, is memorialized. Marx, the mind behind Rio's mosaic beachfront walkways and the Aterro do Flamengo, was said to have "painted with plants" and was the first designer to use Brazilian flora in his projects. More than 3,500 species—including some discovered by and named for Marx as well as many on the endangered list—flourish at this 100-acre estate. Here he grouped his plants not only according to their soil and light needs but also according to their shape and texture. Marx also liked to mix modern things with old ones—a recurring theme throughout the property. The results are both whimsical and elegant. In 1985 he bequeathed the farm to the Brazilian government, though he remained here until his death in 1994. His house is now a cultural center full of his belongings, including collections of folk art. The grounds also contain his large, ultramodern studio (he was a painter, too) and a small, restored, colonial chapel dedicated to St. Anthony. *Estrada da Barra de Guaratiba 2019, Guaratiba,* ☎ *021/410–1412 or 021/410–1171.* 🎫 *Admission.* ☉ *Daily 9–4. Tours by appointment.*

The Lush Inland

Beyond the sand and sea in the Zona Sul are lush parks and gardens as well as marvelous museums, seductive architecture, and tantalizing restaurants. You can't say you've seen Rio until you've taken in the view from Corcovado and then strolled through its forested areas or beside its inland lagoon—hanging out just like a true carioca.

Numbers in white bullets in the text correspond to numbers in black bullets in the margins and on the Rio de Janeiro map.

A GOOD TOUR

Head first to the imposing **Corcovado** ㉑ and its hallmark Cristo Redentor statue. As you slide up the side of the steep mountain in the train, you'll pass through the lush forested area known as **Floresta da Tijuca** ㉒. (If you want to explore the forest more, you'll need to hire a cab or join a tour that offers both Corcovado and Floresta da Tijuca.) Back down the hill and at the train station again, stroll downhill a short distance to the **Museu de Arte Naïf do Brasil** ㉓, which houses a renowned collection of "naive" art from around the world. The same street leads uphill to the delightful colonial square called Largo do Boticário—a good place to rest your feet. From here, grab a taxi and journey west to the inviting **Jardim Botânico** ㉔, across from which is the **Jóque Clube** ㉕. The botanical gardens are walking distance to the **Lagoa Rodrigo de Freitas** ㉖, the giant saltwater lagoon that serves as one of the city's playgrounds—for children and adults alike.

TIMING AND PRECAUTIONS

You can see these sights in a day if you start early. Try to visit Corcovado on a clear day, as clouds often obscure the Christ statue on its summit. You can join an organized tour or hire a cabbie to take you out for the day (public transportation doesn't conveniently reach these sights). The security is good at Corcovado and Floresta da Tijuca, so you can usually carry your camera without worry. At the Jardim Botânico and the Lagoa Rodrigo de Freitas, however, be alert. Throughout this tour, keep valuables in a money belt or somewhere else out of sight.

SIGHTS TO SEE

★ ㉑ **Corcovado.** There's an eternal argument about which view is better, that from Pão d'Açucar or that from here. Corcovado has two advantages: At 2,300 ft it's nearly twice as high as and offers an excellent view of Pão d'Açucar itself. The sheer 1,000-ft granite face of Corcovado (the name means "hunchback" and refers to the mountain's shape) has always been a difficult undertaking for climbers. There are two ways to reach the top: by cogwheel train (originally built in 1885) or by winding road. The train provides delightful views of Ipanema and Leblon (from an absurd angle of ascent) as well as a close look at the thick vegetation and the butterflies and birds it attracts. (You may wonder what those oblong medicine balls hanging from the trees are, the ones that look like spiked watermelons tied to ropes. They're *jaca*, or jack fruit.) Trains leave the **Cosme Velho station** every 20 minutes, daily 8:30–6:30, for the steep, 5-km (3-mi), 20-minute ascent. Late-afternoon trains are the most popular; on weekends be prepared for a long wait. ✉ *Rua Cosme Velho 513, Cosme Velho,* ☎ *021/558–1329.* 🎟 *Admission.*

Whether you arrive by train, tour bus, or car, there's a climb up steep staircases to the summit, where the statue and viewpoints are (there are no elevators or ramps for wheelchairs). You'll pass little cafés and shops selling film and souvenirs along the way. Once at the top, all of Rio stretches out before you.

It wasn't until 1921, the centennial of Brazil's independence from Portugal, that someone had the idea of placing a statue atop Corcovado.

A team of French artisans headed by sculptor Paul Landowski was assigned the task of erecting a statue of Christ with his arms apart as if embracing the city. (Nowadays, mischievous cariocas say Christ is getting ready to clap for his favorite escola de samba.) It took 10 years, but on October 12, 1931, the **Cristo Redentor** (Christ the Redeemer) was inaugurated. The sleek, modern, figure rises more than 100 ft atop a 20-ft pedestal and weighs 700 tons. A powerful lighting system transforms it into a dramatic icon in the evenings.

㉒ Floresta da Tijuca. Surrounding Corcovado is the dense, tropical Tijuca Forest. Once part of a Brazilian nobleman's estate, it's studded with exotic trees and thick jungle vines and has a delightful waterfall, the **Cascatinha de Taunay.** About 200 yards beyond the waterfall is the small pink and purple **Capela Mayrink** (Mayrink Chapel), with painted panels by the 20th-century Brazilian artist, Cândido Portinari. From several points along this national park's 96 km (60 mi) of narrow, winding roads the views are breathtaking. Some of the most spectacular are from **Dona Marta,** on the way up Corcovado; the **Emperor's Table,** supposedly the site where Brazil's last emperor, Pedro II, took his court for picnics; and, farther down the road, the **Chinese View,** an area where Portuguese King João VI allegedly located the first Chinese settlers who came to Brazil in the early 19th century to develop tea plantations. A great way to see the forest is by Jeep; you can arrange tours through a number of Rio agencies (☞ Tour Operators and Travel Agents *in* Rio de Janeiro A to Z, *below*). *Entrance at Praça Afonso Viseu 561, Tijuca,* ☎ *021/492–2253.* ⊡ *Admission.* ⊙ *Daily 7–7.*

㉔ Jardim Botânico. The 340-acre Botanical Garden contains more than 5,000 species of tropical and subtropical plants and trees, including 900 varieties of palms (some more than a century old) and more than 140 species of birds. The cool (its temperature is usually a good 10° lower than on the street), shady garden was created by Portuguese King João VI in 1808, during his exile in Brazil. In 1842 the garden gained its most impressive adornment, the **Avenue of the Royal Palms,** an 800-yard-long double row of 134 soaring royal palms. Elsewhere in the gardens, the **Casa dos Pilões,** an old gunpowder factory, has been restored and displays objects that pertained to both the nobility and to their slaves. Also on the grounds are a library, a small café, and a gift shop that sells souvenirs with ecological themes (the shop is a product of the Earth Summit that was held in Rio in 1992). ⊠ *Rua Jardim Botânico 1008,* ☎ *021/294–6012.* ⊡ *Admission.* ⊙ *Daily 8–5.*

NEED A
BREAK?
Cool off with some homemade ice cream featuring a tropical twist. The flavors at **Mil Frutas Sorvetes** (⊠ Rua J. J. Seabra, Jardim Botânico, ☎ 021/511–2550) are concocted using such local fruits as *acerola* and *jaca*.

㉕ Jóque Clube. The Jockey Club's landmark racetrack is hard to miss owing to its opulent Louis XV style. In addition to horse races, the complex is used for shows and receptions. Its El Turf nightclub is popular on weekends. ⊠ *Praça Santos Dumont 31, Gávea,* ☎ *021/512–9988.*

㉖ Lagoa Rodrigo de Freitas. Under the watchful gaze of the Cristo Redentor, active Rio residents congregate in the park that encircles this saltwater lagoon. The many facilities here include playgrounds, a roller skating rink, and tennis courts; on weekends, you can rent paddleboats. Take advantage of the new food kiosks (each one offers a different type of cuisine—everything from Japanese to Italian to Middle Eastern). There are frequently lakeshore music performances in the evenings. While exploring the area, look for the **Parque da Catacumba,** a pleasant statue-filled park off the western edge of Avenida Epitácio Pessoa, the road around the lagoon.

★ ㉓ **Museu de Arte Naïf do Brasil.** More than 8,000 naive works by Brazil's best artists (as well as works by other self-taught painters from around the world) grace the walls of this lovely colonial mansion that was once the studio of painter Eliseu Visconti. The pieces in what is reputedly the world's largest and most complete collection of primitive paintings date from the 15th century through contemporary times. Don't miss the colorful, colossal (7×4 m/23×13 ft) canvas that depicts the city of Rio; it reportedly took five years to complete. This museum sprang from a collection started decades ago by a jewelry designer who later created a foundation to oversee the art. A small gift shop sells postcards, T-shirts, and other items. ⊠ *Rua Cosme Velho 561, Tijuca,* ☎ *021/ 205–8612 or 021/205–8547.* ⊠ *Admission.* ☉ *Tues.–Fri. 10–6, weekends noon–6.*

Dining

Meat lovers will be mesmerized by the succulent offerings in Rio's churrascarias, especially those that serve *rodízio*-style (the meat is brought to your table on skewers continuously—until you can eat no more). Hotel restaurants often offer feijoada on Saturday (sometimes Friday, too). Vegetarians will appreciate the abundance of seafood restaurants and salad bars, where you pay for your greens by the kilo. (Note that it's perfectly safe to eat fresh produce in clean, upscale places; avoid shellfish in all but the best restaurants.)

Popular places seat customers until well after midnight on weekends, when the normal closing hour is 2 AM. Cariocas love to linger in barchoperias that also serve food (☞ Bars, Choperias, and Lounges *in* Nightlife and the Arts, *below*), and such establishments abound. Most of them serve dishes in the $–$$ range, and portions are large enough for two people to share. Take note that some restaurants don't accept credit cards, many are closed on Monday, and dress is almost always casual.

Brazilian

$$$ ✕ **Casa da Feijoada.** Brazil's savory national dish is the specialty here,
★ where huge pots of the meat and stew concoction simmer every day. The restaurant does a superb job with desserts as well, whipping up a lovely selection of traditional sweets. Note that this restaurant has joined up with the famous Mangueira Escola de Samba to present weekly feijoada-samba and feijoada-pagode shows at the Centro Cultural de Mangueira (⊠ Rua Frederico Silva 85, Centro). The cost is about $13 per person. Call the restaurant for details. ⊠ *Rua Prudente de Morais 10, Ipanema,* ☎ *021/267–4994 or 021/247–2776. AE, DC, MC, V.*

$$$ ✕ **Geraes.** On a cobbled street near Praça 15, this airy restaurant is a
★ cool respite from Centro's hot, busy boulevards. Its cavernous space has a contemporary feel that's offset with such rustic touches as grand archways, tile floors, and white-washed stone walls. *Mineiro* (from Minas Gerais) dishes bubble in large black pots on the buffet table. Waiters dart efficiently between well-spaced tables, taking orders for drinks or items from the à la carte menu. Be sure to try the *feijão tropeiro* (brown beans, bacon, and manioc) with your *lingüiça* (Minas pork sausage). For dessert, have some fruit and the very mild, white *queijo do Minas* (Minas cheese). Although Geraes serves only lunch, you can stop by for drinks and live music 6 PM–midnight Wednesday–Friday. ⊠ *Rua do Ouvidor 26-28, Centro,* ☎ *021/242–8610 or 021/224–6480. AE, DC, MC, V. No dinner.*

$$$ ✕ **Mariu's.** This highly regarded churrascaria serves more than a dozen types of sizzling meats. Its popularity sparked the opening of a second restaurant in Leme. Reservations are a good idea. ⊠ *Rua Francisco Otaviano 96, Ipanema,* ☎ *021/521–0500. DC, MC, V.* ⊠ *Av. Atlântica 290–A, Leme,* ☎ *021/542–2393. DC, MC, V.*

$$$ ✕ **Porcão.** Waiters at these quintessential rodízio-style churrascarias fly
★ up and down between rows of wooden, linen-draped tables wielding giant skewers laden with sizzling barbecued beef, pork, and chicken. All the branches resonate with the good humor that seems to accompany this slightly primitive form of eating. Save room if you can: The papaya creme pudding topped by a bit of cassis shouldn't be missed. ⊠ *Rua Barão da Torre 218, Ipanema,* ☎ *021/522–0999. Reservations not accepted. AE, DC, MC, V.* ⊠ *Av. Armando Lombardi 591, Barra da Tijuca,* ☎ *021/ 492–2001. Reservations not accepted. AE, DC, MC, V.*

$$ ✕ **Baby Beef Paes Mendonça.** This traditional churrascaria occupies a top spot among the city's grills. Its huge rooms, seating a total of 600, are packed seven nights a week—an impressive testimony to the quality of the charbroiled meats served here. Portions are equally impressive. ⊠ *Av. das Américas 1510, Barra da Tijuca,* ☎ *021/494–2187. AE, DC, MC, V.*

$$ ✕ **Barra Grill.** Informal and popular, this steak house serves some of the best meat in town and is a favorite stop after a long day at the beach. ⊠ *Av. Ministro Ivan Lins 314, Barra da Tijuca,* ☎ *021/493–6060. Reservations not accepted. AE, DC, MC, V.*

$ ✕ **Terra Brasilis.** Large windows overlooking a tree-lined street, cool white ceramic tile, and stucco walls painted buttercup yellow and celery green give this "weigh-and-pay" restaurant a cheery atmosphere. You simply help yourself to the Brazilian buffet (including a good selection of salads) and head to a counter where your plate is weighed. It works out to about $8 a kilo, but it's really hard to eat that much ($2.75–$5.50 is average for a main course, $1–$2 for dessert; drinks are extra). And, yes, they do take the plate's weight into account. ⊠ *Rua Humberto de Campos 699, Leblon,* ☎ *021/274–4702. AE, DC, MC, V. No dinner.*

Eclectic

$$$$ ✕ **Mostarda.** Elegant and understated, this restaurant overlooking the
★ lagoon has great food, indoor and outdoor seating, and a chic club upstairs that opens after midnight. It's best to go with a Brazilian so that he or she can explain the menu's carioca puns to you. (A Ricardo, for example, is a cocktail of champagne and minced fresh fruits, but it's also what husbands say their wives have when the women have taken a lover.) Good salads and interesting entrées are often seasoned with mustard (hence, the restaurant's name), and there's an array of mustards on the table for real fanatics. The wine list includes an ample South American selection. ⊠ *Av. Epitacio Pessoa 980/990, Lagoa,* ☎ *021/ 523–1747 or 021/523–1629. AE, V.*

$$$ ✕ **Alho & Óleo.** On Ipanema's Praça Nossa Senhora da Paz, this restau-
★ rant features an eclectic menu with a hint of Italy. Interesting fowl dishes include partridge with dates and grilled duck with apricots; the arugula salad with eggplant, mushrooms, and sea bass is also recommended. Homemade pasta dishes include a farfalle with seafood and artichokes. ⊠ *Rua Barao da Torre 348, Ipanema,* ☎ *021/523–2703. AE.*

$ ✕ **Garfo Livre.** The by-the-kilo buffets at this eatery two blocks from the beach give economical eating a new twist. As you enter, you're given a card on which the items you select are marked. Grab a plate, help yourself to the buffet—which has many Middle Eastern dishes—get your plate weighed, and then pay on your way out. The salad bar has a large selection that includes beans, hummus, and steamed and raw veggies. Commuters come here on weeknights beginning at 7—trading rush hour for happy hour. ⊠ *Av. Nossa Senhora de Copacabana 1003, Copacabana,* ☎ *021/522–1041. AE, DC, MC, V.*

French

$$$$ ✕ **Troisgros.** Many consider this Rio's finest restaurant, though Claude
★ Troisgros himself has left and Chef Antônio Costa is now at the helm. The menu is famed for nouvelle cuisine relying entirely on Brazilian ingredients. Every dish—from the crab or lobster flan to the chicken, fish, or duck prepared with exotic herbs and sauces—is pure pleasure, and always exceptionally light. The dessert menu is headed by a to-die-for passion-fruit mousse. ⊠ *Rua Custódio Serrão 62, Jardim Botânico,* ☎ *021/537–8582. Reservations essential. AE, DC.*

Italian

$$$$ ✕ **Margutta.** The pasta, fish, and risottos are all top drawer and al-
★ ways fresh. A good wine list complements the cuisine. ⊠ *Av. Henrique Dumont 62, Ipanema,* ☎ *021/259–3887 or 021/259–3718. AE, DC, V. No lunch weekdays.*

$ ✕ **La Mole.** This popular chain of Italian restaurants is a good budget bet for lunch or dinner. For the prices, the food is surprisingly good—particularly the lasagna, fettuccine, and gnocchi dishes—and the servings are hearty. ⊠ *Rua Dias Ferreira 147, Leblon,* ☎ *021/294–0699. Reservations not accepted. No credit cards.* ⊠ *Av. Nossa Senhora de Copacabana 552, Copacabana,* ☎ *021/235–3366. Reservations not accepted. No credit cards.* ⊠ *Praia de Botafogo 228, Botafogo,* ☎ *021/ 553–2467. Reservations not accepted. No credit cards. Metrô: Flamengo.* ⊠ *Av. Armando Lombardi 175, Barra da Tijuca,* ☎ *021/494–2625. Reservations not accepted. No credit cards.*

Portuguese

$$$$ ✕ **Antiquarius.** This much-loved establishment is as famous for its flaw-
★ less—and award-winning—rendering of Portuguese classics as for its high prices. Wander through the antiques shop at the restaurant before settling in at a table. A recommended dish is the *cozido*, a stew with a multitude of ingredients, including bananas. The *cataplana*, a seafood stew with rice, is also marvelous, and the *perna de cordeiro* (leg of lamb) is the most requested dish on the menu. The wine list impresses even Portuguese gourmands. ⊠ *Rua Aristides Epínola 19, Leblon,* ☎ *021/294–1049. Reservations essential. DC.*

Seafood

$$$$ ✕ **Satyricon.** This Italian seafood restaurant is rumored to have been
★ Madonna's favorite. The *bacalhau* (fish baked in rock salt) is a specialty, and the sushi and sashimi are well loved. It's expensive, but it has some of the best seafood in town. ⊠ *Rua Barão da Torre 192, Ipanema,* ☎ *021/521–0627. DC, MC, V.*

$$$ ✕ **Quatro Sete Meia.** Internationally renowned, this restaurant is one
★ hour by car west of Copacabana, at the end of a highway that offers stunning coastal views. Simplicity is the soul of the restaurant—whose name in Portuguese is its street number—and the village in which it's set. There are only 11 tables: 5 indoors and 6 in a garden at water's edge. The menu carries seven delicious options, including *moquecas* (seafood stews), grilled seafood, and curries. ⊠ *Rua Barros de Alarcão 476, Pedra da Guaratiba,* ☎ *021/395–2716. Reservations essential. No credit cards. Closed Mon.–Tues. No dinner Wed.–Thurs.*

$$$ ✕ **Shirley.** Homemade Spanish seafood casseroles and soups are the
★ draw at this traditional Copacabana restaurant tucked onto a shady street. Try the *zarzuela*, a seafood soup, or *cazuela*, a fish fillet with white wine sauce. Don't be turned off by the simple decor (a few paintings hung on wood-paneled walls): The food is terrific. ⊠ *Rua*

Gustavo Sampaio 610, Leme, ☎ *021/275–1398. Reservations not accepted. No credit cards.*

Vegetarian

$$ ✕ **Celeiro.** What may be Rio's sole organic restaurant is always full. The buffet offers about 40 salads as well as a broad selection of pastas. ⊠ *Rua Dias Ferreira 199, Leblon,* ☎ *021/274–7843. No dinner.*

Lodging

Rio's largest concentration of hotels is in Copacabana and Ipanema. Copacabana hotels are close to the action (and the metrô), but the neighborhood is noisier than Ipanema (which is itself noisier than São Conrado and Barra da Tijuca).

Expect to pay a premium for a room with a view. Many hotels include breakfast in the rate, but the quality varies from a full buffet to a hard roll with butter. Note that air-conditioning is standard in most hotels, as are room safes. Room service is available in all $$$–$$$$ establishments; in $$–$$$$ hotels, you'll find concierges or, at the very least, reception personnel who perform concierge duties.

$$$$ 🏨 **Caesar Park.** This beachfront hotel has established itself as a favorite
★ of business travelers, celebrities, and heads of state, who appreciate its impeccable service. To assist business guests, the hotel provides secretarial services, as well as fax machines and laptops for in-room use. The Caesar Park is home to the elegant Tiberius restaurant, and is also the site of a good Saturday feijoada. ⊠ *Av. Vieira Souto 460, Ipanema 22120,* ☎ *021/525–2525 or 800/223–6800 in the U.S.,* ℻ *021/521–6000. 186 rooms, 32 suites. Restaurant, bar, pool, beauty salon, massage, sauna, exercise room, baby-sitting, laundry service, business services, meeting rooms. AE, DC, MC, V.*

$$$$ 🏨 **Copacabana Palace.** Built in 1923 for the visiting King of Belgium,
★ this was the first luxury hotel in South America. To this day, it retains more soul and elegance than any other Rio hotel. Igor Stravinsky, Marlene Dietrich, Orson Wells, Eva Peron (who reportedly showed up with 100 suitcases in tow), Robert DeNiro, and Princess Di are just a few of the luminaries who have stayed here. It also served as the set for much of the 1933 Fred Astaire and Ginger Rogers film *Flying Down to Rio.* A recent face-lift restored its facade and left the individually decorated guest rooms with such luxurious touches as inlaid agate and mahogany and a computer, fax, and modem facilities. The Copa also has a rooftop tennis court, Rio's largest hotel pool, and the elegant Cipriani restaurant. The Saturday feijoada is a social event bar none except for, perhaps, the gala Carnaval ball held here each year. ⊠ *Av. Atlântica 1702, Copacabana 22021,* ☎ *021/548–7070 or 800/237–1236 in the U.S.,* ℻ *021/235–7330. 122 rooms, 102 suites. 2 restaurants, 2 bars, in-room modem lines, pool, sauna, tennis court, health club, theater, business services, meeting rooms. AE, DC, MC, V. Metrô: Cardeal Arcoverde.*

$$$$ 🏨 **Inter-Continental Rio.** One of the city's only resorts, a member of the respected Inter-Continental chain, is in São Conrado, next to the Gávea Golf and Country Club and on its own slice of beachfront. Attractions include a cocktail lounge, a discotheque, the Monseigneur French restaurant and the Alfredo Italian restaurant, business facilities, and golf privileges. Every room has an original tapestry done by a Brazilian artist and a balcony overlooking the ocean. The nearby mall is much less crowded than those with more central locations. ⊠ *Av. Prefeito Mendes de Morais 222, São Conrado 22600,* ☎ *021/322–2200 or 800/327–0200 in the U.S.,* ℻ *021/322–5500. 391 rooms, 20 cabanas, 53 suites. 5 restaurants, 2 bars, piano bar, 3 pools, beauty*

salon, sauna, golf privileges, 3 tennis courts, health club, shops, dance club, nightclub, business services, convention center, travel services, car rental. AE, DC, MC, V.

$$$$ 🏨 **Le Meridien.** Of the leading Copacabana hotels, the 37-story French-owned Meridien is the closest to Centro, making it a favorite of business travelers. Rooms are done in pastel tones with dark wood furniture. If you have work to do, the hotel has a complete executive center. Afterward, relax over a meal in Le Saint Honoré restaurant and then head for the jazz bar, which books some of the best acts in town. ⊠ *Av. Atlântica 1020, Copacabana 22012,* ☎ *021/275–9922,* FAX *021/275–9922. 443 rooms, 53 suites. 3 restaurants, bar, pool, beauty salon, sauna, business services. AE, DC, MC, V.*

$$$$ 🏨 **Rio Othon Palace.** The flagship of the Brazilian Othon chain, this 30-story hotel is a Copacabana landmark. The high point, literally, is the rooftop pool-bar and sundeck, offering a prime view of Copacabana's distinctive black-and-white sidewalk mosaic. The hotel has an Executive Floor, with secretarial support, fax machines, and computer hookups. ⊠ *Av. Atlântica 3264, Copacabana 22070,* ☎ *021/522–1522,* FAX *021/522–1697. 554 rooms, 30 suites. 2 restaurants, 2 bars, pool, sauna, health club, nightclub, business services. AE, DC, MC, V.*

$$$$ 🏨 **Sheraton Rio Hotel & Towers.** Built so that it dominates Vidigal, between Leblon and São Conrado, this is the only hotel in Rio with its own private beach (it's set on a bluff above the water and has a stairway down to the sand). Guest rooms are decorated in pastels, and all have beach views. Four floors in a section called The Towers are reserved for business travelers, who receive separate check-in service and have access to a private lounge, a business center, a buffet breakfast, and around-the-clock butler service. The landscaping out by the pools is fabulous, and though the hotel isn't long on intimacy, the beach views are sublime. Be prepared for numerous taxi rides from this prime, though isolated, location. ⊠ *Av. Niemeyer 121, Vidigal 22450,* ☎ *021/274–1122 or 800/325–3589 in the U.S.,* FAX *021/239–5643. 561 rooms, 22 suites. 4 restaurants, 2 bars, 3 pools, sauna, 3 tennis courts, exercise room, shops, nightclub, business services, meeting rooms, travel services, car rental. AE, DC, MC, V.*

$$$$ 🏨 **Sofitel Rio Palace.** Anchoring one end of Copacabana Beach, this hotel has been given a top-to-bottom face-lift (and new management) and is, once again, one of the best on the strip. The building's H-shape gives all rooms views of the sea, the mountains, or both; all rooms have balconies. One of the pools here gets the morning sun, the other afternoon rays. The rooftop bar areas are always lively. ⊠ *Av. Atlântica 4240, Copacabana 22070,* ☎ *021/525–1232 or 800/763–4835 in the U.S.,* FAX *021/525–1200. 388 rooms, 12 suites. 2 restaurants, 2 bars, tea shop, 2 pools, sauna, health club, shops, nightclub, business services, convention center. AE, DC, MC, V.*

$$$ 🏨 **Everest Rio.** With standard service but one of Rio's finest rooftop views (a postcard shot of Corcovado and the lagoon), this hotel is in the heart of Ipanema's shopping and dining district, a block from the beach. Back rooms offer sea views. ⊠ *Rua Prudente de Morais 1117, Ipanema 22420,* ☎ *021/523–2282,* FAX *021/521–3198. 156 rooms, 11 suites. Restaurant, bar, pool, sauna, business services. AE, DC, MC, V.*

$$$ 🏨 **Excelsior.** This hotel, part of the Windsor chain, may have been built in the 1950s but its look is sleek and contemporary—from the sparkling marble lobby to the guest room closets paneled in gleaming *jacarandá* (Brazilian redwood). Service here is top rate. The expansive breakfast buffet—free for guests—is served in the hotel's window-banked restaurant facing the avenue and beach. (The equally elaborate lunch or dinner buffets cost roughly $10.) The rooftop bar–pool area offers a gentle escape from the hustle and bustle. Ask for a room with a water

view. ✉ *Av. Atlântica 1800, Copacabana 22000,* ☎ *021/257–1950 or 800/44–UTELL in the U.S.,* ℻ *021/257–1850. 230 rooms. Restaurant, 2 bars, pool, health club, meeting rooms. AE, DC, MC, V. Metrô: Cardeal Arcoverde.*

$$$ 🏨 **Guanabara Palace Hotel.** Another member of the Windsor chain, the recently renovated Guanabara is one of the only solid hotel choices right in Centro. Rooms are of a reasonable size and are tastefully done in brown and beige tones. Like its sister hotel, the Excelsior (☞ *above*), the restaurant serves elaborate buffet meals, and breakfast is included in the rate. The contemporary rooftop pool area, with its stunning views of Guanabara Bay, absolutely gleams thanks to its pristine white tiles, white trellises, and white patio furnishings. ✉ *Av. Presidente Vargas 392, Centro 22071,* ☎ *021/518–0333,* ℻ *021/516–1582. 326 rooms. Restaurant, bar, minibars, room service, pool, sauna, health club, business services, meeting rooms, parking. AE, DC, MC, V. Metrô: Uruguaiana.*

$$$ 🏨 **Miramar Palace.** The beachfront Miramar is a strange mix of old and new. Rooms are among the largest in Rio, and public areas are dominated by classic touches, from the Carrara marble floor of the lobby to the spectacular glass chandeliers that light the two restaurants. The hotel's 16th-floor bar is notable for its unobstructed view of the entire sweep of Copacabana; after 6 PM live Brazilian music adds a touch of romance. ✉ *Av. Atlântica 3668, Copacabana 22010,* ☎ *021/521–1122,* ℻ *021/521–3294. 133 rooms, 11 suites. 2 restaurants, 2 bars, coffee shop, tea shop. AE, DC, MC, V.*

$$ 🏨 **Atlântico Copacabana.** The large lobby—with its marble walls, red carpeting, black leather furniture, and mirrors—will look modern to some, pretentious to others. Guest rooms are slightly larger than average. The Atlântico is in a residential area four blocks from the beach. ✉ *Rua Sigueira Campos 90, Copacabana 20000,* ☎ *021/548–0011,* ℻ *021/235–7941. 97 rooms, 18 suites. Restaurant, 3 bars, pool, beauty salon, sauna. AE, DC, MC, V. Metrô: Cardeal Arcoverde.*

$$ 🏨 **Copa D'Or.** Rio's largest non-beachfront hotel has an excellent reputation owing to its service and amenities. Businesspeople are well served because of the hotel's location on a thoroughfare to Centro. Sun worshipers will appreciate the free transportation to Copacabana Beach, five blocks away. ✉ *Rua Figueiredo Magalhães 875, Copacabana 22060,* ☎ *021/235–6610,* ℻ *021/235–6664. 195 rooms, 20 suites. Restaurant, 2 bars, pool, sauna, health club, convention center. AE, DC, MC, V.*

$$ 🏨 **Debret.** This former apartment building scores points for keeping its prices moderate despite having a beachfront location. The decor honors Brazil's past: the lobby has baroque statues and prints depicting colonial scenes, and the rooms are furnished in dark, heavy wood. The hotel has a loyal following among diplomats and businesspeople who are more interested in functionality and low prices than elegance. ✉ *Av. Atlântica 3564, Copacabana 22041,* ☎ *021/522–0132,* ℻ *021/521–0899. 90 rooms, 10 suites. Restaurant, bar. AE, DC, MC, V.*

$$ 🏨 **Glória.** A grande dame of Rio's hotels, this classic was built in 1922 and is full of French antiques. What makes it a draw for business travelers (it's a five-minute cab ride from Centro) may discourage sun worshipers (it's a slightly longer cab ride from the beaches). ✉ *Rua do Russel 632, Glória 22210,* ☎ *021/205–7272,* ℻ *021/555–7282. 596 rooms, 20 suites. 4 restaurants, 3 bars, 2 pools, sauna, exercise room, meeting rooms. AE, DC, MC, V. Metrô: Glória*

$$ 🏨 **Grandville Ouro Verde.** For three decades, folks have favored this hotel for its efficient, personalized service. The tasteful Brazilian colonial decor and dark wood furniture are in step with the emphasis on quality and graciousness. All front rooms face the beach; those in the back on the 6th to 12th floors have a view of Corcovado. ✉ *Av. Atlântica 1456, Copacabana, 22041,* ☎ *021/543–4123,* FAX *021/542– 4597. 61 rooms, 5 suites. Restaurant, bar, library. AE, DC, MC, V.*

$$ ⌂ **Praia Ipanema.** This hotel isn't deluxe, but it has a great location and a view of the sea from all of its rooms. You can take in the dramatic beach view from the pool area on the roof of this 15-story building. You can also catch a breeze from your private balcony (every room has one). ✉ *Av. Vieira Souto 706, Ipanema, 22420,* ☎ *021/239–9932,* FAX *021/239–6889. 105 rooms. Bar, pool, beach. AE, DC, MC, V.*

$$ ⌂ **Royalty Copacabana.** Among the draws here are the moderate prices and a good location; set three blocks from the beach, it's convenient for beachgoers yet removed enough to satisfy those looking for peace and quiet. The back rooms from the third floor up are the quietest and have mountain views; front rooms face the sea. ✉ *Rua Tonelero 154, Copacabana, 22030,* ☎ *021/548–5699,* FAX *021/255– 1999. 130 rooms, 13 suites. Restaurant, bar, pool, sauna, exercise room. AE, DC, MC, V. Metrô: Cardeal Arcoverde.*

$$ ⌂ **Sol Ipanema.** Another of Rio's crop of tall, slender hotels, this one has a great location, anchoring the eastern end of Ipanema Beach. All rooms have motel-style beige carpets and drapes and light-color furniture; deluxe front rooms have panoramic beach views, while back rooms, which are the same size, have views of the lagoon and Corcovado from the eighth floor up. ✉ *Av. Vieira Souto 320, Ipanema 22420,* ☎ *021/523–0095,* FAX *021/247–8484. 66 rooms, 12 suites. Restaurant, bar, pool. AE, DC, MC, V.*

$ ⌂ **Arpoador Inn.** This pocket-size hotel occupies the stretch of sand known as Arpoador. Here surfers ride the waves and pedestrians rule the roadway—a traffic-free street allows direct beach access. The hotel is simple but comfortable. At sunset the view from the rocks that mark the end of the beach is considered one of Rio's most beautiful. The spectacle is visible from the hotel's back rooms; avoid the front rooms, which are on the noisy side. ✉ *Rua Francisco Otaviano 177, Ipanema 22080,* ☎ *021/523–6090,* FAX *021/511–5094. 46 rooms, 2 suites. Restaurant, bar. AE, DC, MC, V.*

$ ⌂ **Ipanema Inn.** This small, no-frills hotel was built for those who want to stay in Ipanema but who have no interest in paying the high prices of a beachfront hotel. Just a half block from the beach, it's convenient not only for sun-worshipers but also for those seeking to explore Ipanema's varied nightlife. ✉ *Rua Maria Quitéria 27, Ipanema 22410,* ☎ *021/523–6092,* FAX *021/511–5094. 56 rooms. Bar. AE, DC, MC, V.*

$ ⌂ **Toledo.** Although it has few amenities, the Toledo goes the extra mile to make the best of what it does have. The staff is friendly, the service is efficient, and the location—on a quiet back street of Copacabana, a block from the beach—isn't bad either. Back rooms from the 9th to the 14th floors have sea views and sliding floor-to-ceiling windows. ✉ *Rua Domingos Ferreira 71, Copacabana 22050,* ☎ *021/522–0443,* FAX *021/287–7640. 87 rooms, 8 suites. Bar, coffee shop. DC, MC, V.*

$ ⌂ **Vermont.** This hotel is clean, reliable, and just two blocks from the beach—a good choice for budget travelers. Its only drawback is its location on the main street of Ipanema, which means incessant noise during the day (it tends to quiet down at night after the shops close). ✉ *Rua Visconde de Pirajá 254, Ipanema, 22410,* ☎ *021/522–0057,* FAX *021/267–7046. 54 rooms. Bar. AE, DC, MC, V.*

Nightlife and the Arts

To find out what's going on around town, pick up the bilingual *Rio Guia,* published by Riotur, the city's tourist board. Another good publication is *Este Mês no Rio/This Month in Rio.*

Nightlife

Nightlife options range from samba shows shamelessly aimed at visitors, to sultry dance halls called *forrós*, a rhythmic music style that originated in Brazil's northeast during World War II. One of the happiest mediums is *música popular brasileira* (MPB), the generic term for popular Brazilian music, which ranges from pop to jazz. Note that establishments in this carefree city often have carefree hours; call ahead. Bars and lounges often ask for a nominal cover in the form of either a drink minimum or a music charge. Although cabarets and nightclubs often serve food, their main attraction is live music. Upon entry to some dance clubs you're given a card and each successive drink is marked on it. You pay on departure for what you've consumed.

BARS, CHOPERIAS, AND LOUNGES

Bar Bofetada (⊠ Rua Farme de Amoedo 87/87A, Ipanema, ☎ 021/522–9526 or 021/523–3992) has two floors: downstairs the tables flow out onto the street; upstairs large windows open to the sky and afford a good view of the action below. The young, energetic crowd downs chopp and caipirinhas and delicious seafood (the owners are Portuguese) or meat platters large enough to share.

Bar Garota de Ipanema (⊠ Rua Vinícius de Morais 39, Ipanema, ☎ 021/267–5757) is the choperia where regulars Tom Jobim and Vinícius de Morais, authors of *The Girl from Ipanema,* sat and longingly watched the song's heroine head for the beach. (See if you can guess where they usually sat. Hint: it's a table for two near a door.)

Barril 1800 (⊠ Av. Antônio Carlos Jobim 110, Ipanema, ☎ 021/287–0085) is an unpretentious beachfront choperia—an Ipanema landmark usually jammed with people—in which to grab an icy beer or cocktail and a snack before an evening at nearby Jazzmania (☞ *below*).

Cervantes (⊠ Av. Prado Júnior 335, Copacabana, ☎ 021/275–6174) is a great place for sandwiches after a movie. The chopp goes well with the meat and pineapple combo dishes for which Cervantes is famous.

Chico's Bar (⊠ Av. Epitácio Pessoa 1560, Lagoa, ☎ 021/523–3514) is owned by Rio nightspot entrepreneur Chico Recarey. Both the bar and the adjoining restaurant, Castelo da Lagoa, are big with affluent carioca singles and couples.

Hipódromo (⊠ Praça Santos Dumont, Gávea, near the Jóque Clube, ☎ 021/294–0095) has good chopp, honest food, and many young, happy people.

Jazzmania (⊠ Av. Rainha Elizabeth 769, Ipanema, ☎ 021/227–2447) is one of the better jazz clubs in town. If you arrive before nightfall, you get a superb view of Ipanema Beach at sunset.

Mistura Fina (⊠ Av. Borges de Medeiros 3207, Lagoa Rodrigo de Freitas, Lagoa, ☎ 021/537–2844) combines fine jazz with excellent food and is open from midnight to 3 AM.

CABARETS AND NIGHTCLUBS

Barbarela's (⊠ Av. Princesa Isabel 165, Copacabana) offers the best of the many burlesque, striptease, and sex shows along Avenida Princesa Isabel near the Meridien. It has a reputation for extremely beautiful women.

Canecão (⊠ Av. Venceslau Brás 215, Botafogo, ☎ 021/543–1241) is the city's largest nightclub. It seats up to 5,000 people at the tiny tables in its cavernous space, making it the logical place for some of the biggest names on the international music scene to hold concerts. Reserve a table up front.

Plataforma (⊠ Rua Adalberto Ferreira 32, Leblon, ☎ 021/274–4022) holds the most spectacular of Rio's samba shows, with elaborate costumes and a variety of Brazilian musical numbers including samba and

rhumba. A two-hour show costs about $38.50, drinks not included. Downstairs is a hangout for many local luminaries and entertainers. Upstairs you can eat at Plataforma's famed barbecue restaurant.
Vinícius (⊠ Rua Vinícius de Morais 39, Ipanema, ☎ 021/287–1497). You may rightly associate sultry bossa nova with Brazil, but it's increasingly hard to find venues that offer it. This club is one. Along with nightly live samba, jazz, popular music, or bossa nova, this club has a good kitchen.

CYBERCAFÉ

El Turf Cyber Bar (⊠ Av. Lauro Müller 116, Loja D91, Botafogo, ☎ 021/541–1006) has plenty of terminals, snacks, and a zippy connection—making it the best place to get your E-mail while in Rio. You'll pay about $6 per hour and access is available daily from noon until the last customer leaves. El Turf is in an entertainment complex at the very top of the Rio Sul shopping center (☞ Shopping, *below*).

DANCE CLUBS

Asa Branca (⊠ Av. Mem de Sá 17, Lapa, ☎ 021/252–4428) is Chico Recarey's large nightclub, where the decor combines modern, geometric designs with old-fashioned fixtures. Big bands and popular Brazilian musicians keep the crowd moving till dawn.
Biblo's Bar (⊠ Av. Epitácio Pessoa 1484, Lagoa, ☎ 021/521–2645) is *the* place for live music and dancing, particularly if you're single.
El Turf (⊠ Praça Santos Dumont 31, Gávea, ☎ 021/274–1444) is a hot spot with a cool location in the Jóque Clube. Its large space often fills up with the young and the beautiful, and it's open late.
Estudantina (⊠ Praça Tiradentes 79, Centro, ☎ 021/232–1149) was opened as a dance hall in 1932 and has become an eternally popular nightclub. On weekends, it packs in as many as 1,500 people.
Hippopotamus (⊠ Rua Barão da Torre 354, Ipanema, ☎ 021/247–0351) is one of Rio's exclusive (and expensive) discos, requiring membership (available to guests of the better hotels) and a stiff cover to get in. The disco is often closed for private parties, so be sure to call.
Le Maxim's (⊠ 116 Rua Lauro Muller, Botafogo, ☎ 021/541–9342), in the Rio Sul shopping center, has emerged as one of the top nightspots for professional cariocas. The city's movers and shakers are frequently seen hitting the dance floor here; many stay right until closing at 4 AM.
Sôbre as Ondas (⊠ Av. Atlântica 3432, Copacabana, ☎ 021/521–1296) overlooks Copacabana Beach. You can dance to live music, usually MPB or samba, and dine at the Terraço Atlântico restaurant downstairs.

GAY AND LESBIAN CLUBS

Rio is a relatively gay-friendly city; the community even has its own gala during Carnaval. **Style Travel** sometimes has information on local happenings (☞ Gay and Lesbian Information *in* Rio de Janeiro A to Z). **Le Boy** (⊠ Rua Paul Pompeia 94, Copacabana, ☎ 021/521–0367) is a gay disco that draws an upscale crowd. **Barra Gaiviota** (⊠ Rua Rodolfo de Amoedo 343) is reportedly popular with lesbians.

"Baixos Gay," the Botafogo neighborhood around Rua Visconde Silva and Rua Real Grandeza, has the city's highest concentration of lesbian and gay bars and cafés. Try **Queen Victoria** (⊠ Rua Visconde Silva 30, ☎ 021/530–5332), a small pub with a sushi restaurant upstairs. Extremely popular with both women and men, it's often packed on weekends and every night past 11 PM. Across the street from Queen Victoria, **Acesso** is the best women's dance bar around; drink and dance all night for a small cover. **Tamino** (⊠ Rua Arnaldo Quintela 26, ☎ 021/295–1849) is a cozy, romantic bar-restaurant with live acoustic music.

The Arts

Tickets to performing arts events are inexpensive by international standards and may be purchased at the theater, cultural center, or concert hall box offices. Dress is generally smart casual, although the conservative upper crust still likes to dress elegantly for the Teatro Municipal. Just don't wear valuable jewelry or carry lots of cash.

Rio has an avid film-going public and a well regarded film industry. (You may catch a flick here that later hits the international movie circuit.) Films are screened in small *cineclubes,* or state-of-the-art movie theaters (many in shopping malls). Foreign movies are shown in their original language with Portuguese subtitles (only children's films are dubbed). After dark, exercise caution in Cinelândia, where there's a large concentration of theaters.

VENUES

Centro Cultural Banco do Brasil (⊠ Rua 1 de Março 66, Centro, ☎ 021/216–0237 or 021/216–0626). This six-story domed building with marble floors was constructed in 1888 and was once the headquarters of the Bank of Brasil. In the late 1980s it was transformed into a cultural center where art exhibitions and music recitals are held. The state-of-the-art complex features a library, two theaters, four video rooms, an auditorium, and a permanent display of Brazilian currency. Its gift shop is full of stunning coffee-table-type tomes on art and history—some of which are in English. It's open Tuesday–Sunday 10–8.

Fundacão Casa França–Brasil (⊠ Rua Visconde de Itaboraí 78, Centro, ☎ 021/253–5366). This center, just steps away from Banco do Brasil Cultural Center, links France and Brazil in a cultural and artistic exchange. The interior of what was once a customs house has been completely restored, leaving an elegant, neoclassical space of gracious columns and arcades. Exhibits have included everything from photography and painting to displays on Carnaval and Brazil's environment. Musical shows (Gilberto Gil was a recent performer), poetry readings, and lectures round out the events. The center's hours are Tuesday–Sunday 10–8.

Metropolitan (⊠ Av. Ayrton Senna 3000, Barra da Tijuca, ☎ 021/385–0516 for tickets or 021/285–3773 for schedules). When this posh performance center opened in the Via Parque shopping complex, its premiere was marked with a concert by Diana Ross. Although shows by top-name performers are certainly one of its mainstays, the 4,500-seat venue also hosts theatrical and dance performances.

Teatro Dulcina (⊠ Rua Alcindo Guanabara 17, Centro, ☎ 021/240–4879) is a 600-seat theater that features classical opera and concerts.

Teatro Municipal (Praça Floriano, Centro, ☎ 021/297–4411). The city's main performing arts venue hosts dance, opera (an opera company puts on superb productions and often attracts international divas as guest artists), and theater events year-round, although the season officially runs from April to December. The theater's symphony orchestra has a very good reputation and includes many 19th- and 20th-century works in its program. The theater also has its own ballet company and is the site of an international ballet festival during April and May.

Teatro Paço Imperial (⊠ Praça 15 de Novembro 48, Centro, ☎ 021/533–4407), like the Teatro Municipal, features a varied schedule of theatrical, musical, and dance performances.

Outdoor Activities and Sports

Participant Sports

BICYCLING AND RUNNING

Bikers and runners share the boulevards along the beach and, for cooler and quieter outings, the path around Lagoa Rodrigo de Freitas.

On weekends many cariocas also bike or run along the stretch of Floresta da Tijuca road that becomes pedestrian-only. Although hotels can arrange bike rentals, it's just as easy to rent from stands along beachfront avenues or the road ringing the lagoon. Rates are about $7 for two hours. You're usually asked to show identification and give your hotel name and room number, but deposits are seldom required. (Note that helmets aren't usually available, so bring your own.)

BOATING AND SAILING

Captain's Yacht Charters (⊠ Rua Conde de Lages 44, Glória, ☎ 021/224–0313) charters all types of crewed vessels for any length of time. You can arrange an afternoon of water-skiing with a speedboat or a weekend aboard a yacht.

GOLF

Three golf courses are open to non-members (greens fees run as much as $50): the 18-hole **Gávea Golf Club** (⊠ Estrada da Gávea 800, São Conrado, ☎ 021/322–4141); the three-par, six-hole greens at **Golden Green Golf Club** (⊠ Av. Canal de Marapendi 2901, Barra da Tijuca, ☎ 021/433–3950); and the 27-hole **Itanhanga Golf Club** (⊠ Estrada da Barra, Barra da Tijuca, ☎ 021/494–2507).

HANG GLIDING

Superfly (⊠ Estrada das Canoas 1476, Casa 2, São Conrado, ☎ 021/332–2286) offers hang-gliding classes and tandem flights with instructors. To prove that you really made the leap, you can arrange to have your photo taken while airborne. The cost is about $80.

TENNIS

City tennis courts and clubs that allow visitors to play include **Akxe Club** (⊠ Av. Canal de Marapendi 2900, Barra da Tijuca, ☎ 021/325–3232) and **Rio Sport Center** (⊠ Av. Ayrton Senna 2541, Barra da Tijuca, ☎ 021/325–6644; ⊠ Rua Visconde de Pirajá 161, Ipanema, ☎ 021/267–4192). Court time runs from $10 to $25 an hour; you can also rent equipment and arrange lessons.

Spectator Sports

AUTO RACING

Brazilian race car drivers rank among the world's best and frequently compete in international events. In Rio, you'll get a taste of the speed if you watch the checkered flag drop on competitions in the Formula I Grand Prix circuit named after one of the country's most famous racers, Emerson Fittipaldi. The racetrack is the **Autodromo Internacional Nelson Piquet** (⊠ Av. Embaixador Abelardo Bueno, Jacarepagua, ☎ 021/441–2158).

FUTEBOL

You can watch a match at the world's largest soccer stadium, the 178,000-seat (with standing room for another 42,000) **Estádio Maracanã** (⊠ Rua Prof. Eurico Rabelo, Maracanã, ☎ 021/264–9962). The fans are half the spectacle. During the season the top game is played each Sunday at around 5 PM. The three most popular teams are Flamengo, Fluminense, and Vasco da Gama. Play between any of them is soccer at its finest.

HORSE RACING

Races are held year-round in the **Jóque Clube** (⊠ Praça Santos Dumont 31, Gávea, ☎ 021/512–9988) beginning Monday and Thursday at 7 PM and weekends at noon. The big event of the year, the Brazilian Derby, is held the first Sunday of August.

Shopping

From sophisticated jewelry and Euro-style clothes to teeny tangas and funky tie-dyed dresses, the selection in Rio is broad. Ipanema is the city's most fashionable shopping district. Its many exclusive boutiques are in arcades, the majority of which are along Rua Visconde de Pirajá. In Copacabana you'll find souvenir shops, bookstores, and branches of some of Rio's better shops along Avenida Nossa Senhora de Copacabana.

Centers and Malls

Barra Shopping (⊠ Av. das Américas 4666, Barra da Tijuca, ☎ 021/431–9922) is one of South America's largest complexes. Although it's slightly out of the way, shoppers from all over town head for this large mall, which features a medical center, eight movie theaters, and a bowling alley as well as shops.

Rio Off Price Shopping (⊠ Rua General Severiano 97, Botafogo, ☎ 021/542–5693), just down the street from the Rio Sul shopping center (☞ *below*), is a mall whose prices are 20% lower than normal. The complex has snack bars and two movie theaters.

Rio Sul (⊠ Av. Lauro Müller 116, Botafogo, ☎ 021/295–1332) is one of the city's most popular retail complexes, with more than 400 shops. The shopping is sophisticated, and the food court is endless.

São Conrado Fashion Mall (⊠ Estrada da Gávea 899, São Conrado, ☎ 021/322–0300) sells a wide array of international and domestic fashions, and is Rio's most appealing mall as it's the least crowded and has an abundance of natural light.

Shopping Center Cassino Atlântico (⊠ Av. Nossa Senhora de Copacabana, Copacabana, ☎ 021/247–8709), adjoining the Rio Palace hotel, is dominated by antiques shops, jewelry stores, art galleries, and souvenir outlets.

Shopping Center da Gávea (⊠ Rua Marquês de São Vicente 52, Gávea, ☎ 021/274–9896) has a small but select mix of fashionable clothing and leather goods stores. It also has several top art galleries, of which the best are Ana Maria Niemeyer, Beco da Arte, Borghese, Bronze, Paulo Klabin, Saramenha, and Toulouse.

Via Parque (⊠ Av. Ayrton Senna 3000, Barra da Tijuca, ☎ 021/385–0100) is a 230-store complex popular for its outlets and ample parking (nearly 2,000 spaces). In addition to movie theaters and fast-food restaurants, the mall is home to the Metropolitan Theater.

Markets

The **Feira Hippie** is a colorful handicraft street fair held every Sunday 9–6 in Ipanema's Praça General Osório. Offerings run the gamut from jewelry and hand-painted dresses and T-shirts to paintings and wood carvings, leather bags and sandals, rag dolls, knickknacks, and even furniture. A handful of booths sell samba percussion instruments.

In the evenings and on weekends along the median of **Avenida Atlântica**, artisans spread out their wares. Here you will find paintings, carvings, handicrafts, sequined dresses, and hammocks from the northeast.

Specialty Shops

ART

Cohn Edelstein (⊠ Rua Jangadeira 14B, Ipanema, ☎ 021/523–0549; Rua Barão da Torre 185A, Ipanema, ☎ 021/287–9933) is an internationally respected contemporary art gallery showing Brazilian works.
Bonino (⊠ Rua Barata Ribeiro 578, Copacabana, ☎ 021/294–7810) is the most traditional, best known, and most visited of Rio's art galleries. It has been around for some 30 years.

Rio Design Center (✉ Av. Ataulfo de Paiva 270, Leblon, ☎ 021/274–7893) contains several galleries, including Borghese, Beco da Arte, Montesanti, Museum, and Way.

BEACHWEAR

Blueman (✉ Rio Sul, Av. Lauro Müller 116, Botafogo, ☎ 021/220–4898), a bikini shop with many mall locations in addition to the Rio Sul branch, carries the bikinis that virtually define Brazil in much of North America's imagination. Tangas are said to have been invented in Ipanema—and they don't take up much room in your luggage.

Bum Bum (✉ Rua Vinícius de Morais 130, Ipanema, ☎ 021/521–1229) is the market leader in beachwear with locations in Rio Sul and Barra Shopping in addition to its Ipanema branch.

Salinas (✉ Forum de Ipanema, Visconde de Pirajá 351, Ipanema) is another très chic bikini designer and the label de rigueur with the fashionable in Búzios and other resort areas.

CDS

Toca do Vinícius (✉ Rua Vinícius de Morais 129, Ipanema, ☎ 021/247–5227) bills itself as a "cultural space and bossa nova salon." The shop, though tiny, does indeed seem like a gathering place for bossa-nova aficionados from around the world. (If you're one of them, there's a good chance you'll leave the shop with an E-mail address for at least one new pal.) Amid the atmosphere of bonhomie, you'll find books (few in English), sheet music, and T-shirts as well as CDs.

CLOTHING

Alice Tapalos (✉ Forum de Ipanema, Visconde de Pirajá 351, Ipanema, ☎ 021/247–2594) carries DKNY and other well-known sportswear in its Ipanema, São Conrado Fashion Mall, and Barra Shopping locations.

Ar Livre (✉ Av. Nossa Senhora de Copacabana 900, Copacabana, ☎ 021/549–8994) has an exceptional selection of good quality T-shirts and beachwear at appealing prices.

Krishna (✉ Rio Sul, Av. Lauro Müller 116, Botafogo, ☎ 021/542–2443; ✉ São Conrado Fashion Mall, Estrada da Gávea 899, São Conrado, ☎ 021/322–0437) specializes in classic, feminine dresses and separates—many in fine linens, cottons, and silks.

Mesbla (✉ Rua do Passeio 42/56, Centro, ☎ 021/534–7720), Rio's largest chain department store, focuses on mostly casual fashions for men, women, and children. But it also has a wide selection of toys, records, cosmetics, musical instruments, and sporting goods.

HANDICRAFTS

Casa do Pequeno Empresario (✉ Rua Real Grandeza 293, Botafogo, ☎ 021/286–9464) is an exposition center for hand-crafted items made of everything from porcelain to wood and papier-mâché to clay.

Folclore (✉ Rua Visconde de Pirajá 490, Ipanema, ☎ 021/259–7442). At H. Stern world headquarters (☞ *below*), this handicraft shop bursts with naive paintings, costume jewelry, leather and ceramic crafts, and birds and flowers carved from stone. Quality is high but take note: some items have been imported from other South American nations.

JEWELRY

Amsterdam-Sauer (✉ Rua Visconde de Pirajá 484, Ipanema, ☎ 021/512–9878) is one of Rio's top names (with top prices) in jewelry. Jules Roger Sauer, the founder of these stores (with branches in Brazil, the United States, and the Caribbean), is particularly known for his fascination with emeralds. The on-site gemstone museum (☎ 021/239–8045) is open Monday–Friday 10–5 and Saturday 9:30–1 (tour reservations are a good idea).

H. Stern (⊠ Rua Visconde de Pirajá 490, Ipanema, ☎ 021/259–7442). Hans Stern started his empire in 1945 with an initial investment of about $200. Today his interests include mining and production operations as well as 170 stores in Europe, the Americas, and the Middle East. His award-winning designers create truly unique and contemporary pieces (the inventory runs to about 300,000 items). At H. Stern world headquarters you can see exhibits of rare stones, and watch craftspeople transform rough stones into sparkling jewels. There's also a museum you can tour (by appointment only). If you feel the prices are too high in the upstairs salons, there are shops downstairs that sell more affordable pieces as well as folkloric items.

LEATHER GOODS

Formosinho (⊠ Av. Nossa Senhora de Copacabana 582, Copacabana, ☎ 021/287–8998) sells men's and women's shoes at low, wholesale prices. In addition to its Copacabana location, it has three other stores along Ipanema's Rua Visconde de Pirajá.

Frankie Amaury (⊠ Shopping Center da Gávea, Rua Marquês de São Vicente 52, Gávea, ☎ 021/294–8895) is *the* name in leather clothing.

Mariazinha (⊠ Forum de Ipanema, Praça Nossa Senhora da Paztel, Ipanema, ☎ 021/541–6695) carries fashionable footwear.

Nazaré (⊠ Shopping Center da Gávea, Rua Marquês de São Vicente 52, Gávea, ☎ 021/294–9849) has bags and fine women's shoes.

Rio de Janeiro A to Z

Arriving and Departing

BY AIRPLANE

All international flights and most domestic flights arrive and depart from the **Aeroporto Internacional Galeão** (☎ 021/398–6060). The airport is about 45 minutes northwest of the beach area and most of Rio's hotels. **Aeroporto Santos Dumont** (☎ 021/524–7070), 20 minutes from the beaches and within walking distance of Centro, serves the Rio–São Paulo air shuttle and a few air-taxi firms.

International carriers include: **Aerolineas Argentinas** (☎ 021/398–3520 or 021/224–4931), **American Airlines** (☎ 021/398–4053 or 021/210–3126), **British Airways** (☎ 021/398–3888 or 021/221–0922), **Canadian Airlines** (☎ 021/398–3604 or 021/220–5343), **Delta** (☎ 021/398–3492 or 021/507–7262), and **United** (☎ 021/398–4050 or 021/532–1212).

Several domestic carriers serve international and Brazilian destinations: **Transbrasil** (☎ 021/398–5485 or 021/297–4477), **Varig** (☎ 021/534–0333 or 021/217–4591), and **VASP** (☎ 021/292–2112 or 021/462–3363). **Nordeste/RioSul** (☎ 021/507–4488 or 021/524–9387) covers domestic routes.

From the Airports into Town. Special airport taxis have booths in the arrival areas of both airports. Fares to all parts of Rio are posted at the booths, and you pay in advance (about $35–$50). Also trustworthy are the white radio taxis parked in the same areas; these charge an average of 20% less. Three reliable special taxi firms are **Transcoopass** (☎ 021/560–4888), **Cootramo** (☎ 021/560–5442), and **Coopertramo** (☎ 021/560–2022).

Air-conditioned *frescão* buses run by **Empresa Real** (☎ 021/290–5665 or 021/270–7041) park curbside outside customs at Galeão and outside the main door at Santos Dumont; for less than $3 they make the hour-long trip into the city, following the beachfront drives and stopping at all hotels along the way. If your hotel is inland, the driver will let you off at the nearest corner. Buses leave from the airport every half-hour from 5:20 AM to 11 PM.

BY BUS

Long-distance buses leave from the **Rodoviária Novo Rio station** (⊠ Av. Francisco Bicalho 1, São Cristóvão, ☎ 021/291–5151), near the port. Any local bus marked RODOVIÁRIA will take you to the station. You can buy tickets at the depot or, for some destinations, from travel agents. Buses also leave from the more conveniently located **Menezes Cortes terminal** (⊠ Rua São José 35, Centro, ☎ 021/533–7577), near Praça 15 de Novembro.

BY CAR

Driving in from São Paulo (429 km/266 mi on BR 116), you enter Rio via Avenida Brasil, which runs into Centro's beachside drive, the Avenida Infante Dom Henrique. This runs along Rio's Baía de Guanabara and passes through the Copacabana Tunnel to Copacabana Beach. Here the beachside Avenida Atlântica continues into Ipanema and Leblon along Avenidas Antônio Carlos Jobim (Ipanema) and Delfim Moreira (Leblon). From Galeão, take the Airport Expressway (known as the Linha Vermelha, or Red Line) to the beach area.

Getting Around

BY BUS

Local buses are inexpensive and can take you anywhere you want to go. (Route maps aren't available, but the tourist office has lists of routes to the most popular sights.) Crime has dropped significantly in the last few years; if you're discreet, you shouldn't have any problems. Just don't wear expensive watches or jewelry, carry a camera or a map in hand, or talk boisterously in English. It's also wise to avoid buses during rush hour. You enter buses at the rear, where you pay an attendant, and pass through a turnstile, then exit at the front. Have your fare in hand when you board to avoid flashing bills or wallets. Be aware that bus drivers speak no English, and they drive like maniacs.

The more upscale frescão buses run between the beaches, downtown, and Rio's two airports. Also recommended are the *jardineira* buses, open-sided vehicles (they look like old-fashioned streetcars) that follow the beach drive from Copacabana to São Conrado as well as beyond to Barra da Tijuca. White posts along the street mark jardineira stops. Green minivans also run back and forth along beachfront avenues, stopping to pick up and drop off people wherever they're flagged. (Fares start at about $2.)

BY CAR

The carioca style of driving is passionate to the point of abandon, traffic jams are common, the streets aren't well marked, and red lights are often more decorative than functional. If you do choose to drive, exercise extreme caution, wear seat belts at all times, and keep the doors locked.

Car rentals can be arranged through hotels or agencies and cost about $80–$100 a day for standard models. Agencies include **Hertz** (⊠ Av. Princesa Isabel 334, Copacabana, ☎ 021/275–7440) and **Unidas** (⊠ Av. Princesa Isabel 350, Copacabana, ☎ 021/275–8299). Both also have desks at the international and domestic airports.

Turismo Clássico Travel(☞ Tour Operators and Travel Agents, *below*), one of the country's most reliable travel and transport agencies, can arrange for a driver, with or without an English-speaking guide.

BY METRÔ

Rio's subway system, the **metrô** (☎ 021/292–6116 or 021/255–5552) is clean, safe, and efficient—a delight to use—but it's not comprehensive. Reaching sights distant from metrô stations can be a challenge. Plan your tours accordingly; tourism offices and some metrô stations have maps.

Trains run daily from 6 AM to 11 PM along two lines: Linha 1 runs north from the Cardeal Arcoverde stop in Copacabana, parallel to the coast and into downtown, then west to its terminus at Saens Pena station; Linha 2 starts four stops before Saens Pena at Estacio and heads northwest to Rio's edge at the Pavuna station. A single metrô ticket costs R$1. Combination metrô-bus tickets allow you to take special buses to and from the Botafogo station: The M-21 runs to Leblon via Jardim Botânico and Jóque; the M-22 goes to Leblon by way of Túnel Velho, Copacabana, and Ipanema.

BY TAXI

Yellow taxis have meters that start at a set price and have two rates: "1" for before and "2" for after 8 PM. The "2" rate also applies to Sundays and holidays, the month of December, the neighborhoods of São Conrado and Barra da Tijuca, and when climbing steep hills. Drivers are required to post a chart noting the current fares on the inside of the left rear window. Carioca cabbies are, by and large, wonderful people, but there are exceptions. Remain alert and trust your instincts; a few drivers have taken non-natives for a ride.

Radio taxis and several companies that routinely serve hotels (and whose drivers often speak English) are also options. Radio cabs charge 30% more than other taxis but are reliable and, usually, air-conditioned. Other cabs working with the hotels will also charge more, normally a fixed fee that you should agree upon before you leave. Reliable radio cab companies include **Centro de Taxis** (☎ 021/593–2598), **Coopacarioca** (☎ 021/253–3847), and **Coopatur** (☎ 021/290–1009).

Contacts and Resources

BANKS AND CURRENCY EXCHANGE

The Banco do Brasil branch at Galeão offers good exchange rates, but it won't provide credit-card advances. *Casas do cambio* (exchange houses) are found all over the city, especially along the beaches. Many change money without charging a service fee. Automatic-teller machines (ATMs) throughout town dispense reais.

CONSULATES

Australia (✉ Av. Nilo Pecanha 50, Centro, ☎ 021/240–2294), **Canada** (✉ Rua Lauro Müller 116, Room 1104, Botafogo, ☎ 021/542–7593), **United Kingdom** (✉ Praia do Flamengo 284, 2nd Floor, Flamengo, ☎ 021/553–6850), **United States** (✉ Av. Presidente Wilson 147, Centro, ☎ 021/292–7117).

EMERGENCIES

Ambulance and fire: ☎ 193. **Clinics: Cardio Plus**(✉ Rua Visconde de Pirajá 330, Ipanema, ☎ 021/521–4899), **Galdino Campos Cardio Copa Medical Clinic**(✉ Av. Nossa Senhora de Copacabana 492, Copacabana, ☎ 021/548–9966), and **Medtur** (✉ Av. Nossa Senhora de Copacabana 647, Copacabana, ☎ 021/235–3339). **Dentist: Policlinica Barata Ribeiro**(✉ Rua Barata Ribeiro 51, Copacabana, ☎ 021/275–4697). **Pharmacies:** Round the clock pharmacies include **Drogario Pacheco** (✉ Av. Nossa Senhora de Copacabana 534, Copacabana, ☎ 021/548–1525) and **Farmacia do Leme** (✉ Av. Prado Junior 237, Leme, ☎ 021/275–3847). **Police:** ☎ 190. **Tourism Police** (✉ Av. Afranio de Melo Franco, Leblon, ☎ 021/511–5112).

ENGLISH-LANGUAGE BOOKSTORES

Bookstores that carry some English-language publications include
Livraria Argumento (⊠ Rua Dias Ferreria 417, Leblon, ☎ 021/239–
5294), **Livraria Kosmos** (⊠ Rua do Rosario 155, Centro, ☎ 021/224–
8616), and **Sodiler** (⊠ Aeroporto Internacional Galeão, ☎ 021/393–
9511; ⊠ Aeroporto Santos Dumont, ☎ 021/393–4377).

GAY AND LESBIAN INFORMATION

Style Travel (Rua Visconde de Piraja 433, 6th floor, Ipanema, ☎ 021/
522–0709, FAX 021/522–0617), an offshoot of the established Brasil Plus
travel agency, is a great source of information on gay and lesbian lodging, tour, and nightlife options in the area. *Sui Generes* is Rio's gay
and lesbian glossy magazine. It's available at most newsstands and lists
local arts, music, and style events. *Entre Nós* and *O Grito* are Rio's gay
newspapers. All of these publications are in Portuguese.

HEALTH AND SAFETY

Avoid tap water (note that ice in restaurants and bars is safe as it's usually made from bottled water), and take care not to soak up too much
sun. Despite its reputation, crime in Rio is no more dangerous these
days than any large city. Most crimes occur in crowded public areas:
beaches, busy sidewalks, intersections, and city buses. Pickpockets, usually children, work in groups. One will distract you while another grabs
a wallet, bag, or camera. Another tactic is for people to approach your
car at intersections. Always keep doors locked and windows partially
closed. Leave valuables in your hotel safe, don't wear expensive jewelry or watches, and keep cameras out of sight. Walking alone at night
on the beach isn't a good idea; neither is getting involved with drugs.
Penalties for possession are severe, and dealers are the worst of the worst.

TELEPHONES, THE INTERNET, AND MAIL

Rio's area code is 021. There are public phones on corners throughout the city. They work with cards that you can buy in a variety of denominations at newsstands, banks, and some shops. (Some phones also
work with credit cards.) For long-distance calls, there are phone offices at the main bus terminal, Galeão, downtown at Praça Tiradentes
41, and in Copacabana at Avenida Nossa Senhora de Copacabana 540.
To make international calls through the operator, dial 000111. For operator-assisted long-distance within Brazil, dial 101; information is 102.

The staff at many hotels can arrange Internet access for guests. In addition, you can head to the cybercafé, **El Turf Cyber Bar** (☞ Nightlife
and the Arts, *above*) or **CompRio** (⊠ Rua da Assembléia 10, basement
level, ☎ 021/533–4372), a computer store in the same Centro building as Turisrio. Here you'll find a few computers (note that they're on
the slow side) that are available for about $6 an hour weekdays 9–6.

The **main post office** (⊠ Av. Presidente Vargas 3077, ☎ 021/503–8222)
is in Centro but there are branches all over the city, including one at
Galeão and several on Avenida Nossa Senhora de Copacabana in Copacabana and Rua Viscondes de Pirajá in Ipanema. Most branches are
open weekdays 8–5 and Saturday 8–noon.

TOUR OPERATORS AND TRAVEL AGENTS

You can ride around the Floresta da Tijuca and Corcovado, Angra dos
Reis, or Teresópolis in renovated World War II Jeeps (1942 Dodge Com-
manders, Willys F-75's, and others) with the well-organized **Atlantic
Forest Jeep Tours** (☎ FAX 021/495–9827 or ☎ 021/494–4761). Guides
speak English, French, German, and Spanish. The company also offers a range of ecological tours, including some on horseback. The superb guides at **Gray Line** (☎ 021/512–9919) speak your language. In

addition to a variety of city tours the company also offers trips outside town and tours by helicopter.

Ecology and Culture Tours (☎ 021/522–1620) offers hiking and Jeep tours of Tijuca, Pão d'Açucar, Santa Teresa, and various beaches. Guides speak English, and morning and afternoon excursions are available. **Favela Tour** (☎ 021/322–2727) offers a fascinating half-day tour of two favelas. The company's English-speaking guides can also be contracted for other outings.

Qualitours (☎ 021/232–9710) will take you and yours in a Jeep around old Rio, the favelas, Corcovado, Floresta da Tijuca, and Prainha and Grumari. They can explain everything in English, Hungarian, French, or German. **Turismo Clássico Travel** (✉ Av. Nossa Senhora de Copacabana 1059, Suite 805, Copacabana, ☎ 021/287–3390) arranges guided tours for English-speaking visitors, and often works with film crews. They also plan more extensive tours around Brazil.

VISITOR INFORMATION

The Rio de Janeiro city tourism department, **Riotur** (✉ Rua da Assembléia 10, near Praça 15 de Novembro, Centro, ☎ 021/217–7575) has an **information booth** (☎ 021/541–7522) at Avenida Princesa Isabel 183 in Copacabana; it's open 8–5 daily. There are also city tourism desks at the airports and the Novo Rio bus terminal. The Rio de Janeiro state tourism board, **Turisrio** (✉ Rua da Assembléia 10, 7th and 8th floors, Centro, ☎ 021/531–1922), is open weekdays 9–6.

SÃO PAULO

Updated by
Carlos
Henrique
Severo and
Karla Brunet

Crowded buses grind through streets spouting black smoke, endless stands of skyscrapers block the horizon, and the din of traffic deafens the ear. But native *paulistanos* (inhabitants of São Paulo city; inhabitants of São Paulo State are called *paulistas*) love this megalopolis of 17 million. São Paulo now sprawls across 7,951 square km (3,070 square mi), 1,502 square km (580 square mi) of which make up the city proper. The largest city in South America makes New York City look small.

The draw is the dynamism of the immigrants who have been coming since the late 19th century, when São Paulo became a major coffee producer. The possibilities for work and investment attracted people from throughout Brazil as well as from Italy, Portugal, Spain, Germany, and Japan. By 1895, 70,000 of the city's 130,000 residents were immigrants. Their efforts transformed São Paulo from a sleepy Jesuit mission post into a dynamic financial and cultural hub. Avenida Paulista was once the site of many a coffee baron's mansion. Money flowed from these private domains into civic and cultural institutions. The arts began to flourish, and by the 1920s, São Paulo was already claiming its place as the country's cultural capital.

Today, like many major European or American hubs, São Paulo struggles to meet its citizens' transportation and housing needs, and goods and services are expensive. Yet, even as the smog reddens your eyes, you'll see that there's much to explore here. As a city committed to making dreams come true, São Paulo offers top-rate nightlife and dining and thriving cultural and arts scenes.

Exploring São Paulo

Each neighborhood seems a testament to a different period of the city's history. The largely pedestrian-only hilltop and valley areas, particularly Vale do Anhangabaú, are where São Paulo's first inhabitants—Jesuit missionaries and treasure-hunting pioneers—lived. Later these areas became Centro (downtown district), a financial and cultural center that's still home to the stock exchange and many banks. It's now the focus of revitalization efforts.

The Bela Vista and Bixiga (really, a subdivision of Bela Vista) neighborhoods, near Centro, are home to many theaters and bars. In the 19th century, many families who made fortunes from coffee built whimsical mansions on the ridge-top Avenida Paulista. Beginning in the post–World War II industrial boom, these homes gave way to skyscrapers. Many of the city's best hotels are also on or near this avenue.

To the west you'll find the tall buildings of Avenida Brigadeiro Faria Lima, the stylish homes of the Jardins neighborhood, and the Shopping Center Iguatemi, just off the banks of the Rio Pinheiros. Large-scale construction of corporate headquarters continues just south of here, between the Marginal Pinheiros Beltway and the Avenida Engenheiro Luís Carlos Berrini, not far from the luxurious Shopping Center Morumbi.

Centro

Even though São Paulo's downtown district is considered dangerous, it's one of the few places with a historical flavor. Here you can explore the areas where the city began and see examples of architecture, some of it beautifully restored, from the 19th century.

Numbers in white bullets in the text correspond to numbers in black bullets in the margins and on the São Paulo Centro map.

A GOOD TOUR

The **Edifício Copan** ①, designed by the great Oscar Niemeyer, seems an appropriate place to begin a tour. Farther up Avenida Ipiranga is the city's tallest building, the **Edifício Itália** ② (you might want to return here at the end of the day for a terrific view of the city). Continue north along the avenue to the **Praça da República** ③. From here, cross Ipiranga and walk down the pedestrian-only Rua Barão de Itapetininga, with its many shops and street vendors. Follow it to the neo-baroque **Teatro Municipal** ④ in the Praça Ramos de Azevedo facing the Mappin department store. Head east across the square to the Viaduto do Chá, a monumental overpass above the Valé do Anhangabaú—the heart of São Paulo. At the end of this viaduct, turn right onto Rua Líbero Badaró and follow it to the baroque **Igreja de São Francisco de Assis** ⑤. A short walk from here along Rua Benjamin Constant will bring you to the **Praça da Sé** ⑥, the city's most central spot and the site of the Catedral Metropolitana da Sé.

From the metro station at the cathedral, you can take the *metrô* (subway) west to the Barra Funda station and the **Memorial da América Latina,** or you can head north out of Praça da Sé and follow Rua Roberto Simonsen to the **Solar da Marquesa de Santos** ⑦, the city's only surviving late-19th-century residence. Nearby is the **Pátio do Colégio** ⑧. From here, walk north along Rua Boa Vista; turn left onto Rua Anchieta and then left onto Rua 15 de Novembro. Number 275, on the left, houses **BOVESPA** ⑨, the São Paulo Stock Exchange. Near the end of Rua 15 de Novembro, at Rua João Brícola 24, stands the 36-floor **Edifício BANESPA** ⑩. To the northwest of here is the **Edifício Martinelli** ⑪. Walk two blocks up on Rua São Bento to the **Basílica de São Bento** ⑫, a church constructed in the beginning of the 20th century. Near it is Café Girondino, a good spot for a break. From the basilica, you can take a train north from the São Bento station to the Luz stop and the **Pinacoteca do Estado** ⑬, the state gallery. On Avenida Tiradentes walk north to the **Museu de Arte Sacra** ⑭ and its religious art.

This route requires at least five hours on foot and use of the metrô. An early start will allow you to be more leisurely should one sight pique your interest more than another. If you're planning to take taxis or hire a driver, bear in mind that traffic jams are common.

Being a tourist in Centro is a bit hazardous. If you keep a low profile and speak at least some Spanish (if not Portuguese) you'll most likely avoid problems. Otherwise you might feel more comfortable touring with a guide (☞ Travel Agents and Tour Operators *in* São Paulo A to Z, *below*). Whatever you do, leave your Rolex back at the hotel.

SIGHTS TO SEE

⑫ **Basílica de São Bento.** This church, constructed between 1910 and 1922, was designed by German architect Richard Berndl. Its enormous organ has some 600 pipes. ⊠ *Largo de São Bento*, ☎ *011/228–3633*. 🎫 *Free.* ☉ *Mon., Wed., and Fri. 5–1 and 2–7:45; Thurs. 2–7:45; Sat. 6–1 and 3–7:30; Sun. 5–1 and 3–6. Metrô: São Bento.*

⑨ **BOVESPA.** The busy São Paulo Stock Exchange is a hub for the foreign investment Brazil has attracted in its efforts to privatize state-owned companies. If you leave an ID with the guard at the front desk, you can go up to the mezzanine and watch the hurly-burly; computer terminals in the observation gallery carry the latest stock quotes as well as general information in various languages. BOVESPA offers tours in English, but only to representatives of foreign investment institutions. (If you fit this description, you can make arrangements in advance by faxing the Superintendência Executiva de Desenvolvimento at FAX 011/239–4981.) ⊠ *Rua 15 de Novembro 275*, ☎ *011/233–2000 ext. 516.* 🎫 *Free.* ☉ *Weekdays 9–noon and 2–6. Metrô: São Bento.*

NEED A BREAK?

Café Girondino is frequented by BOVESPA traders from happy hour until midnight. The bar serves good draft beer and sandwiches. Pictures on the wall depict Centro in its early days. ⊠ *Rua Boa Vista 365*, ☎ *011/ 229–4574. Metrô: São Bento.*

⑩ **Edifício BANESPA.** The 36-floor BANESPA Building was constructed in 1947 and modeled after New York's Empire State Building. If you can't fit tea or drinks at the top of the Edifício Itália (☞ *below*) into your Centro tour, this structure offers a no-frills chance for a panoramic look at the city. A radio traffic reporter squints through the smog every morning from here. ⊠ *Praça Antônio Prado*, ☎ *no phone.* 🎫 *Free.* ☉ *Weekdays 9–6. Metrô: São Bento.*

❶ **Edifício Copan.** The serpentine Copan Building, an apartment and office block, was designed by renowned Brazilian architect Oscar Niemeyer, who went on to design much of Brasília, the nation's capital. It has the clean, white, undulating curves characteristic of his work. Although many Brazilians prefer colonial architecture, all take pride in Niemeyer's international reputation. The Copan was constructed in 1950, and its 1,850 apartments house about 4,500 people. If you want to shop in the first-floor stores, be sure to do so before dark when the area is overrun by prostitutes and transvestites. ⊠ *Av. Ipiranga at Av. Consolação*, ☎ *no phone. Metrô: Anhangabaú.*

★ ❷ **Edifício Itália.** The view of South America's largest city from the top of the Itália Building is astounding. To get to it, you'll have to patronize the bar or dining room of the Terraço Itália restaurant on the 41st floor. As the restaurant is expensive (and isn't one of the city's best), afternoon tea or a drink is the quickest, least expensive option. Tea is

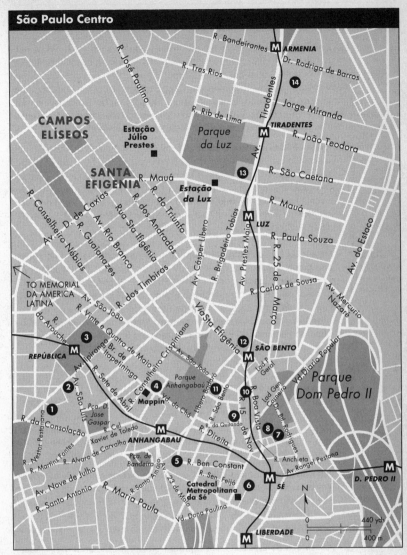

São Paulo Centro

Basilica de São
Bento, **12**

BOVESPA, **9**

Edifício
BANESPA, **10**

Edifício Copan, **1**

Edifício Itália, **2**

Edifício
Martinelli, **11**

Igreja de São
Francisco de Assis, **5**

Museu de Arte
Sacra, **14**

Pátio do Colégio, **8**

Pinacoteca do
Estado, **13**

Praça da
República, **3**

Praça da Sé, **6**

Solar da Marquesa de
Santos, **7**

Teatro Municipal, **4**

served 3–5:30, and the bar opens at 6. ☒ *Av. Ipiranga 336,* ☎ *011/ 257–6566 (restaurant). Metrô: Anhangabaú.*

⑪ **Edifício Martinelli.** Note the whimsical penthouse atop the Martinelli Building, the city's first skyscraper, which was built in 1929 by Italian immigrant-turned-count Giuseppe Martinelli. The rooftop is open weekdays 10:30–4. You need to get permission from the building manager on the ground floor and leave a photo ID at the front desk to take the elevator to the 34th floor and walk up two more flights. ☒ *Avenida São João 35,* ☎ *no phone.* ☒ *Free. Metrô: São Bento.*

⑤ **Igreja de São Francisco de Assis.** The baroque St. Francis of Assisi Church is actually two churches by the same name, one run by Catholic clergy, and the other by lay brothers. One of the city's best-preserved Portuguese colonial buildings, it was built from 1647 to 1790. ☒ *Largo São Francisco 133,* ☎ *011/606–0081.* ☒ *Free.* ☉ *Daily 7 AM–8 PM; lay brothers' church weekdays 7–11:30 and 1–8, weekends 7 AM–10 AM. Metrô: Sé or Anhangabaú.*

OFF THE
BEATEN PATH

MEMORIAL DA AMÉRICA LATINA – The Latin American Memorial consists of a group of buildings designed by Oscar Niemeyer. The Pavilhão da Criatividade Popular (Popular Creativity Pavilion) has a permanent exhibition of Latin American handicrafts and a model showing all the countries in Latin America. The Salão de Atos building shows the panel *Tiradentes,* about an independence hero from Minas Gerais, painted by Cândido Portinari in 1949 and installed here in 1989. ☒ *Av. Auro Soares de Moura Andrade 664,* ☎ *011/3823–9611.* ☒ *Free.* ☉ *Tues.–Sun. 9–6. Metrô: Barra Funda.*

⑭ **Museu de Arte Sacra.** The Museum of Sacred Art is a must-see if you can't get to Bahia during your stay in Brazil. It houses an extremely interesting collection of wooden and terra-cotta masks, jewelry, and liturgical objects that date from the 17th century through today. Don't miss the on-site convent, founded in 1774. ☒ *Av. Tiradentes 676,* ☎ *011/227–7694.* ☒ *Admission.* ☉ *Tues.–Sun. 9–6. Metrô: Luz.*

⑧ **Pátio do Colégio.** The College Courtyard is where, in 1554, São Paulo was founded by the Jesuits José de Anchieta and Manoel da Nóbrega. The church here was constructed in 1896 in the same style as the chapel built by the Jesuits. ☒ *Pátio do Colégio 84,* ☎ *011/3105–6899.* ☉ *Church: Mon.–Sat. 8:15 AM–midnight, Sun. mass 10 AM. Metrô: Sé.*

⑬ **Pinacoteca do Estado.** The building that houses the State Art Gallery was constructed in 1905 and renovated in 1998. In the permanent collection you can see the work of famous Brazilian artists such as Tarsila do Amaral (whose work consists of colorful somewhat abstract portraits), Anita Malfatti (a painter influenced by fauvism and German expressionism), Cândido Portinari (whose oil paintings have social and historical themes), Emiliano Di Cavalcanti (a multimedia artist whose illustrations, oil paintings, and engravings are influenced by cubism and contain Afro-Brazilian and urban themes), and Lasar Segall (an expressionist painter). ☒ *Praça da Luz 2,* ☎ *011/227– 6329.* ☒ *Admission.* ☉ *Tues.–Sun. 10–6. Metrô: Luz.*

③ **Praça da República.** The large, central Republic Square is the site of a huge street fair—with arts and crafts, semiprecious stones, food, and often live music—on Sunday. Some artisans display their work here all week long, so it's worth a peek anytime. *Metrô: República.*

⑥ **Praça da Sé.** The large, busy Cathedral Square, under which the city's two major metrô lines cross, is where migrants from Brazil's poor northeast often come to enjoy their music and to sell and buy such regional items as medicinal herbs. It's also the central hangout for São Paulo's street children and the focus of periodic (and controversial) police sweeps to get them off the street. The square and most of the historic area and financial district to its north have been set aside for pedestrians, official vehicles, and public transportation only.

❼ Solar da Marquesa de Santos. This 18th-century manor house was bought by Marquesa dos Santos in 1843. It now contains a museum that hosts temporary exhibitions. ⊠ *Rua Roberto Simonsen 136,* ☏ *011/3106–2218.* 🎟 *Free.* ◷ *Tues.–Sun. 9–5. Metrô: Sé.*

❹ Teatro Municipal. Inspired by the Paris Opéra, the Municipal Theater was built between 1903 and 1911 with art nouveau elements. *Hamlet* was the first play presented here, and it went on to host such luminaries as Isadora Duncan in 1916 and Anna Pavlova in 1919. Unfortunately, the fully restored auditorium, resplendent with gold leaf, moss-green velvet, marble, and mirrors, is only open to those attending cultural events (☞ Nightlife and the Arts, *below*), but sometimes you can walk in for a quick look at the vestibule. ⊠ *Praça Ramos de Azevedo,* ☏ *011/223–3022. Metrô: Anhangabaú.*

Liberdade

At the beginning of the 20th century, a group of Japanese arrived to work as contract farm laborers in São Paulo State. During the next five decades, roughly a quarter of a million of their countrymen followed, forming what is now the largest Japanese colony outside Japan. Distinguished today by a large number of college graduates and successful businesspeople, professionals, and politicians, the colony has made important contributions to Brazilian agriculture and the seafood industry. The Liberdade neighborhood, which is south of Praça da Sé behind the cathedral and whose entrance is marked by a series of red porticoes, is home to many first-, second-, and third-generation Nippo-Brazilians. Here, clustered around Avenida Liberdade, you'll find shops with everything from imported bubble gum to miniature robots to Kabuki face paint. The Sunday street fair here holds many surprises.

Numbers in white bullets in the text correspond to numbers in black bullets in the margins and on the São Paulo map.

A GOOD TOUR

From the **Praça Liberdade** ⑮, by the Liberdade metrô station, walk south along Rua Galvão Bueno. About six blocks from the square is the intriguing **Museu da Imigração Japonesa** ⑯.

TIMING AND PRECAUTIONS

The best time to visit Liberdade is on Sunday during the street fair, when you'll find tents that sell Asian food, crafts, and souvenirs. This tour takes about two hours—a little longer if you linger in the museum. Don't take this tour at night.

SIGHTS TO SEE

⑯ Museu da Imigração Japonesa. The Museum of Japanese Immigration has two floors of exhibits about Nippo-Brazilian culture and farm life and Japanese contributions to Brazilian horticulture. (They're credited with introducing the persimmon, the azalea, the tangerine, and the kiwi, among other things, to Brazil.) Call ahead to arrange for an English-language tour. ⊠ *Rua São Joaquim 381,* ☏ *011/279–5465.* 🎟 *Admission.* ◷ *Tues.–Sun. 1:30–5:30. Metrô: São Joaquim.*

⑮ Praça Liberdade. On Sunday morning Liberdade hosts a sprawling Asian food and crafts fair, where the free and easy Brazilian ethnic mix is in plain view; you'll see, for example, Afro-Brazilians dressed in colorful kimonos hawking grilled shrimp on a stick. Liberdade also hosts sev-

204

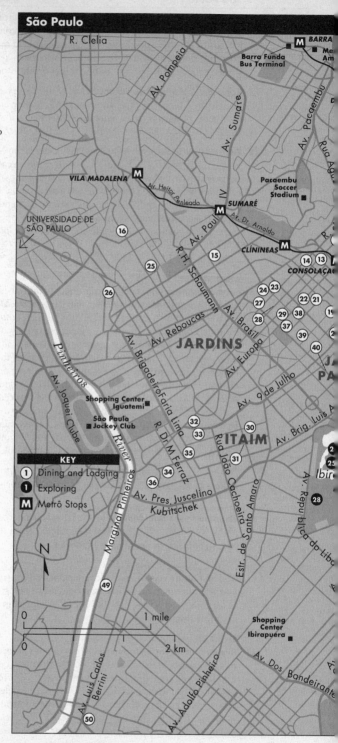

São Paulo

KEY
1 Dining and Lodging
1 Exploring
M Metrô Stops

eral ethnic celebrations, such as April's Hanamatsuri, commemorating Buddha's birth. *Metrô: Liberdade.*

Avenida Paulista and Bixiga

Money once poured into and out of the coffee barons' mansions that lined Avenida Paulista, making it, in a sense, São Paulo's financial hub. So it is today, though instead of mansions you'll find many major banks. Like the barons before them, many of these financial institutions greatly support the arts. Numerous places have changing exhibitions—often free—in the Paulista neighborhood. Nearby Bixiga, São Paulo's Little Italy, is full of restaurants.

A GOOD TOUR

Begin the tour at the **Museu de Arte de São Paulo (MASP)** ⑰, which has Brazil's best collection of fine art. Across the street is **Parque Trianon** ⑱, where many businesspeople eat lunch. Leaving the park, veer right onto Avenida Paulista and head for the **Centro Cultural FIESP** ⑲, which frequently has art and theatrical presentations. Farther down Paulista is the **Espaço Cultural Citibank** ⑳, a gallery with temporary exhibitions. Continue a few more blocks along Paulista to the **Instituto Cultural Itaú** ㉑, a great place to see contemporary Brazilian art. In the next block is the **Casa das Rosas** ㉒ with yet another noteworthy gallery. From here you can hop a bus or a taxi to the **Museu Memória do Bixiga** ㉓ with its displays on Italian immigration.

TIMING AND PRECAUTIONS

This tour takes about five hours, including a visit to MASP and the Museu do Bixiga. Busy, well-lit Avenida Paulista may well be the safest place in the city. Even so, stay alert, particularly in Parque Trianon.

SIGHTS TO SEE

㉒ **Casa das Rosas.** The House of the Roses, a French-style mansion, seems out of place next to the skyscrapers of Paulista. It was built in 1935 by famous paulistano architect Ramos de Azevedo for one of his daughters. The building was home to the same family until 1986, when it was made an official municipal landmark. It was opened as a cultural center—with changing fine-arts exhibitions and multimedia displays by up-and-coming artists—in 1991, and it's one of the avenue's few remaining early 20th-century buildings. ⊠ *Av. Paulista 37,* ☎ *011/ 251–5271.* 🎟 *Admission.* ⏱ *Tues.–Sun. 2–8. Metrô: Brigadeiro.*

⑲ **Centro Cultural FIESP.** The cultural center of São Paulo State's Federation of Industry has a theater, a library of art books, and temporary art exhibits. ⊠ *Av. Paulista 1313,* ☎ *011/253–5877.* 🎟 *Free.* ⏱ *Tues.– Sun. 9–7. Metrô: Trianon.*

⑳ **Espaço Cultural Citibank.** Citibank's cultural space hosts temporary exhibitions of Brazilian art. ⊠ *Av. Paulista 1111,* ☎ *011/576–2744.* 🎟 *Free.* ⏱ *weekdays 9–7, weekends 10–5. Metrô: Trianon.*

㉑ **Instituto Cultural Itaú.** Maintained by Itaú, one of Brazil's largest private banks, this cultural institute has art shows as well as lectures, workshops, and films. Its library specializes in works on Brazilian art and culture. ⊠ *Av. Paulista 149,* ☎ *011/238–1700.* 🎟 *Free.* ⏱ *Tues.–Sun. 10–7. Metrô: Brigadeiro.*

NEED A BREAK? | Before heading to the Museu Memória do Bixiga, try a *baurú* at **Ponto Chic** (a block east of Instituto Cultural Itaú and across Avenida Paulista). The restaurant claims to have invented this sandwich, which is made with roast beef, tomato, cucumber, and steam-heated mozzarella. ⊠ *Praça Osvaldo Cruz 26,* ☎ *011/289–1480. AE, DC, MC, V.* ⏱ *10 AM–4 AM. Metrô: Paraíso.*

★ ⑰ **Museu de Arte de São Paulo (MASP).** A striking low-rise elevated on two massive concrete pillars 256 ft apart, the São Paulo Museum of Art contains the city's premier collection of fine arts. The highlights include dazzling works by Hieronymous Bosch, Vincent Van Gogh, Pierre-Auguste Renoir, Edgar Degas, and others. Lasar Segall and Cândido Portinari are two of the many Brazilian artists represented in the collection. The huge open area beneath the museum is often used for cultural events and is the site of a Sunday antiques fair (☞ Shopping, below). ⊠ Av. Paulista 1578, ☎ 011/251–5644. 🎫 Admission. ☉ Tues.– Sun. 11–6. Metrô: Trianon.

㉓ **Museu Memória do Bixiga.** This museum, established in 1980, contains objects that belonged to Italian immigrants who lived in the Bixiga neighborhood. On Saturday and Sunday, you can extend your tour to include the **Feira do Bixiga**, at Praça Dom Orione, where handicrafts, antiques, and furniture are sold. ⊠ Rua dos Ingleses 118, ☎ 011/285– 5009. 🎫 Free. ☉ Wed.–Sun. 2–5.

⑱ **Parque Trianon.** The park was originally created in 1892 as a showcase for local vegetation. In 1968, Roberto Burle-Marx (the Brazilian landscaper famed for Rio's mosaic-tile beachfront sidewalks) renovated it and incorporated new trees. You can escape the noise of the street and admire the flora while seated on one of the benches that are sculpted to look like chairs. ⊠ Rua Peixoto Gomide 949, ☎ 011/289– 2160. 🎫 Free. ☉ Daily 6–6. Metrô: Trianon.

Parque Ibirapuera

Only 15 minutes by taxi from downtown, Ibirapuera is São Paulo's answer to New York's Central Park, although it's slightly less than half the size and gets infinitely more crowded on sunny weekends. In the 1950s the land, which originally contained the municipal nurseries, was chosen as the site of a public park to honor the city's 400th anniversary. Oscar Niemeyer was called in to head the architects assigned to the project. The park was inaugurated in 1954, and some of the pavilions used for the opening festivities still sit amid its 395 acres. You'll also find jogging and biking paths, a lake, and rolling lawns.

A GOOD WALK

Enter at Gate 9 and walk around the lake to the starry sights at the **Planetário** ㉔. As you exit the planetarium, veer left for a walk to the **Pavilhão Japonês** ㉕. From here, turn left and follow the path to the Marquise do Ibirapuera, a structure that connects several buildings, including the **Museu de Arte Moderna (MAM)** ㉖ and the **Pavilhão da Bienal** ㉗, which houses the park branch of the Museu de Arte Contemporânea. When you exit the compound, walk toward Gate 7 and the **Viveiro Manequinho Lopes** ㉘, with its many species of Brazilian trees.

TIMING AND PRECAUTIONS

The park deserves a whole day though you can probably do this tour in one afternoon. Avoid the park on Sunday, when it gets really crowded, and after sundown.

SIGHTS TO SEE

㉖ **Museu de Arte Moderna (MAM).** The permanent collection of the Museum of Modern Art includes 2,600 paintings, sculptures (some in a sculpture garden out front), and drawings from the Brazilian modernist movement, which began in the 1920s, when artists were developing a new form of expression influenced by the city's rapid industrial growth. The museum also hosts temporary exhibits that feature the works of new local artists and has a library with more than 20,000 books, photographs, videotapes, and CD-ROMs. In a 1982 renovation, Brazilian architect Lina Bo Bardi gave the building a wall of glass, creating a giant window that beckons you to peek at what's inside. The café here is a good place for a break. ⊠ *Gate 10,* ☎ *011/573–9932.* 🖭 *Admission (free on Tues.).* ⊙ *Tues.–Wed. noon–6, Thurs. noon–10, Fri.–Sat. 10–8, Sun. and holidays 10–6.*

㉗ Pavilhão da Bienal. From October through November in every even-numbered year, this pavilion hosts the Bienal (Biennial) art exhibition, which draws more than 250 artists from more than 60 countries. The first such event was held in 1951 in Parque Trianon (☞ *above*) and drew artists from 21 countries. It was moved to this Oscar Niemeyer–designed building—with its large open spaces and floors connected by circular slopes—after Ibirapuera Park's 1954 inauguration. The pavilion also houses a branch of the **Museu de Arte Contemporânea** (MAC; Museum of Contemporary Art) whose main branch is at the Universidade de São Paulo, west of Centro. Exhibits are created from the museum's total collection of 5,400 works by such European artists as Pablo Picasso, Amedeo Modigliani, Wassily Kandinsky, Joan Miró, and Henri Matisse. Look also for the works of Brazilian artists such as Anita Malfatti, Tarsila do Amaral, Cândido Portinari, and Emiliano Di Cavalcanti. ⊠ *Gate 10,* ☎ *011/573–5255.* 🖭 *Museum: Admission (free on Tues.).* ⊙ *Museum: Tues.–Wed. noon–6, Thurs. noon–10, Fri.–Sat. 10–8, Sun. and holidays 10–6.*

㉕ Pavilhão Japonês. An exact replica of the Katsura Imperial Palace in Kyoto, Japan, the Japanese Pavilion is also one of the structures built for the park's inauguration. It was designed by University of Tokyo professor Sutemi Horiguti and built in Japan. It took four months to reassemble here, beside the man-made lake and amid the Japanese-style garden. In the main building you'll find displays of samurai clothes, 11th-century sculptures, and pottery and sculpture from several dynasties. Rooms used for traditional tea ceremonies are upstairs. ⊠ *Gate 10,* ☎ *011/573–6453.* 🖭 *Admission.* ⊙ *Weekends and holidays 10–5.*

㉔ Planetário. Paulistanos love the planetarium and frequently fill the 350 seats under its 48-ft-high dome. Here you can see a projection of the 8,900 stars and 5 planets (Mercury, Venus, Mars, Jupiter, and Saturn) that are clearly visible in the Southern Hemisphere. Shows last 50 minutes and always depict the night sky just as it is on the evening of your visit. Be sure to buy tickets at least 15 minutes before the session. ⊠ *Gate 10, Av. Pedro Álvares Cabral,* ☎ *011/575–5206.* 🖭 *Admission.* ⊙ *Weekends and holidays, projections at 3:30 and 5:30.*

㉘ Viveiro Manequinho Lopes. The Manequinho Lopes Nursery is where most of the plants and trees used by the city around São Paulo are nurtured. The original was built in the '20s; the current version was designed by Roberto Burle Marx. Here you'll find specimens of such Brazilian trees as *ipê, pau-jacaré,* and *pau-brasil,* the tree after which the country was named (the red dye it produced was greatly valued by the Europeans). The **Bosque da Leitura** (Reading Forest) has a stand that provides books and magazines (all in Portuguese, though) as well as chairs so people can read among the trees. ⊠ *Enter park from Av. República do Líbano,* ☎ *no phone.* ⊙ *Daily 5–5.*

Beaches

São Paulo rests on a plateau 72 km (46 mi) inland. If you can avoid traffic, getaways are fairly quick on the parallel Imigrantes (BR 160) or Anchieta (BR 150) highways, each of which becomes one way on weekends and holidays. Although the port of Santos (near the Cubatão Industrial Park) has *praias* (beaches) in and around it, the cleanest and best beaches are along what is known as the North Shore. Here, mountains and bits of Atlantic rain forest hug numerous small, sandy coves. On weekdays when school is in session, the beaches here are gloriously deserted. Buses run along the coast from São Paulo's Jabaquara terminal near the Congonhas Airport, and there are once-daily trains from the Estação da Luz to Santos and the sands along the North Shore. Beaches often don't have bathrooms or phones right on the sands, nor do they have beach umbrellas or chairs for rent. They do, however, generally have restaurants nearby or at least vendors selling sandwiches, soft drinks, and beer.

Barra do Sahy. Families with young children favor this small, quiet beach 165 km (102 mi) north of the city on the Rio–Santos Highway. Its narrow strip of sand (with a bay and a river on one side and rocks on the other) is steep but smooth, and the water is clean and very calm. Area restaurants serve basic fish dishes with rice and salad.

Camburi. The young and the restless flock here to sunbathe, surf, and party. At the center of this beach, just north of Barra do Sahy (☞ *above*), is a cluster of cafés, ice cream shops, and bars.

Maresias. Some of the North Shore's most beautiful houses line either side of the Rio–Santos road (SP 055) on the approach to Maresias. The beach itself is also nice with its 4-km (2½-mi) stretch of white sand and its clean, green waters that are good swimming and surfing. Like Camburi (☞ *above*), just 12 km (7 mi) south, Maresias is popular with a young crowd.

Ubatuba. Many of the more than 30 beaches around Ubatuba are truly beautiful enough to merit the 229-km (148-mi) drive north along the Carvalho Pinto and Oswaldo Cruz highways. For isolation and peace, try Prumirim Beach, which can only be reached by boat; for a little more action try the centrally located Praia Grande, with its many kiosks.

Dining

São Paulo's social life centers on dining out, and there are a great many establishments from which to choose, particularly in the Jardins district. You'll find Japanese, Spanish, Italian, and Portuguese restaurants as well as top-quality French and Indian spots. There are innumerable *churrascarias* (places that serve a seemingly endless stream of barbecued meats). As in other Brazilian cities, many restaurants serve feijoada on Wednesday and Saturday.

São Paulo restaurants frequently change their credit card policies, sometimes adding a surcharge for their use or not accepting them at all. Though most places don't generally require jacket and tie, people tend to dress up; establishments in the $$ to $$$$ categories expect you to look tidy and elegant (no shorts or muddy or torn jeans).

Brazilian

$$$ ✕ **Baby Beef Rubaiyat.** Galician Belarmino Iglesias was once an employee at this restaurant; today he owns it, and he and his son run it. The meat they serve is from their ranch in Mato Grosso do Sul State. The buffet features charcoal-grilled items—from baby boar (upon request at least two hours in advance) and steak to chicken and salmon—and a salad bar with all sorts of options. Wednesday and Saturday see a feijoada; on Friday the emphasis is on seafood. ⊠ *Alameda Santos 86, Paraíso,* ☎ *011/289–6366. V. No dinner Sun. Metrô: Paraíso.*

$$$ ✕ **Bargaço.** This place has long been considered the best Bahian restaurant in Salvador. If you can't make it to the northeast, be sure to have a meal in the São Paulo branch. Seafood is the calling card. ⊠ *Rua Oscar Freire 1189, Cerqueira César,* ☎ *011/853–5058. AE, DC, MC, V. Metrô: Consolação.*

$$$ ✕ **Dona Lucinha.** Mineiro dishes—from the Minas Gerais State—are the specialties at this modest eatery with plain wooden tables. The classic cuisine is served buffet style, with more than 50 stone pots holding such dishes as *feijão tropeiro* (beans with manioc flour). Save room for a dessert of ambrosia. ⊠ *Av. Chibaras 399, Moema,* ☎ *011/549–2050. AE, DC, MC, V.* ⊠ *Rua Bela Cintra 2325, Jardins,* ☎ *011/282–3797. AE, DC, MC, V.*

$$$ ✕ **Esplanada Grill.** The beautiful people hang out in the bar of this highly
★   regarded churrascaria. The thinly sliced *picanha* steak (similar to rump steak) is excellent; it goes well with a house salad (hearts of palm and shredded, fried potatoes), onion rings, and creamed spinach. The restaurant's rendition of the traditional *pão de queijo* (cheese bread) is just right. ⊠ *Rua Haddock Lobo 1682, Jardins,* ☎ *011/881–3199. V.*

$$ ✕ **Consulado Mineiro.** During and after the Saturday crafts and antiques fair in Praça Benedito Calixto, it may take an hour to get a table at this homey restaurant set in a house. Among the traditional mineiro dishes are the *mandioca com carne de sol* (cassava with salted meat) appetizer and the *tutu* (pork loin with beans, pasta, cabbage, and rice) entrée. ⊠ *Rua Praça Benedito Calixto 74, Pinheiros,* ☎ *011/3064–3882. AE, DC, MC, V. Closed Mon.*

$ ✕ **Frevo.** Paulistanos of all ilks and ages flock to this Jardins luncheonette for its beirute sandwiches, draft beer, and fruit juices in flavors such as *acerola* (Antilles cherry), passion fruit, and papaya. ⊠ *Rua Oscar Freire 603, Jardins,* ☎ *011/282–3434. No credit cards.*

$ ✕ **Sujinho–Bisteca d'Ouro.** The modest Sujinho serves churrasco without any frills. It's the perfect place for those who simply want to eat an honest, gorgeous piece of meat. ⊠ *Rua da Consolação 2078, Cerqueira César,* ☎ *011/231–5207. No credit cards. Metrô: Consolação.*

Eclectic

$$$$ ✕ **La Tambouille.** This Italo-French restaurant with a partially enclosed garden isn't just a place to be seen; many believe it also has the best food in town. Among chef André Fernandes's recommended dishes are the linguini with fresh mussels and prawn sauce and the filet mignon *rosini* (served with foie gras and risotto with saffron). ⊠ *Av. Nove de Julho 5925, Jardim Europa,* ☎ *011/883–6276. AE, V.*

$$ ✕ **Bar des Arts.** A great place for lunch or drinks (it's a favorite with businesspeople), the Bar des Arts is set in a charming arcade near a flower shop, a wine shop, and a water fountain. You'll find both a buffet and à la carte options at lunch. ⊠ *Rua Pedro Humberto 9, at Rua Horacio Lafer, Itaim Bibi,* ☎ *011/829–7828. AE. Closed Mon.*

$$ ✕ **Mestiço.** If you like to eat a late dinner, come here. Tribal masks peer
★   down at you from the walls of the large, modern dining room. Consider the Thai *huan-hin* (chicken with shiitake in ginger sauce and rice) followed by a dessert of lemon ice cream with *baba de moça* (a syrup made with egg whites and sugar). ⊠ *Rua Fernando de Albuquerque 277, Consolação,* ☎ *011/256–3165. AE, V. Metrô: Consolação.*

$$ ✕ **Spot.** The closest thing to a chic diner as you'll find in São Paulo is just one door up from MASP (☞ Exploring, *above*). The salads and the pasta dishes are good bets; come early, though, as it gets crowded after 10 PM. ⊠ *Alameda Rocha Azevedo 72, Cerqueira César,* ☎ *011/283–0946. AE, V. Metrô: Consolação.*

French

$$$$ ✕ **Le Coq Hardy.** This award-winning restaurant has two chefs: one is a veteran of the top French kitchens in Brazil and the other spent many years cooking in France. The grilled foie gras and mango, the escargots with mushrooms in an anise and wine sauce, and the roast duck are all highly recommended. ⊠ *Rua Jerônimo da Veiga 461, Itaim Bibi,* ☎ *011/852–3344. AE, DC, MC, V.*

$$$$ ✕ **Laurent.** Chef Laurent Suadeau is famous for his use of Brazilian ingredients to create French nouvelle cuisine. Businesspeople from Avenida Paulista appreciate the fine decor and inexpensive (compared with dinner), but still superb, lunch menu. Specialties include the broccoli crepes with a cashew curry and the *bacalhau* (codfish) rolled in spinach leaves. ⊠ *Alameda Jaú 1606, Jardins,* ☎ *011/853–5573. AE, MC, V. No lunch Sat. Closed Sun.*

$$$ ✕ **La Casserole.** Facing a little Centro flower market, this charming bistro has been around for generations. Surrounded by cozy wood-paneled walls decorated with eclectic posters, you can dine on such delights as *gigot d'agneau aux soissons* (roast leg of lamb in its own juices, served with white beans) and cherry strudel. ⊠ *Largo do Arouche 346, Centro,* ☎ *011/220–6283. AE, DC, MC, V. Closed Mon. No lunch Sat.*

$$ ✕ **La Tartine.** This small restaurant has movie posters on its walls and
★ simple but comfortable furniture. The menu changes daily. On Saturday night you'll find the classic coq au vin; on Friday the option is a Moroccan couscous. ⊠ *Rua Fernando de Albuquerque 267, Consolação,* ☎ *011/259–2090. V. Closed Sun.–Mon. Metrô: Consolação.*

Indian

$$$$ ✕ **Ganesh.** Many consider this the best Indian eatery in town. The traditional menu includes curries and tandoori dishes. The decor is all Indian artwork and tapestries. ⊠ *Morumbi Shopping Center, Av. Roque Petroni Jr. 1089, Morumbi,* ☎ *011/240–6768. AE, DC, MC, V.*

Italian

$$$$ ✕ **Fasano.** A family-owned, northern Italian classic, this restaurant is as famous for its superior cuisine as for its exorbitant prices. Ever pay $29 for cream of asparagus soup? How about $49 for a green salad appetizer with foie gras? Here's your chance. Although the decor—marble, mahogany, and mirrors—has seen better days, if you're intent on experiencing the best of the best, this place is a must. ⊠ *Rua Haddock Lobo 1644, Jardins,* ☎ *011/852–4000. AE, DC, MC, V. No lunch Sat., no dinner Sun.*

$$$$ ✕ **Massimo.** Just off Avenida Paulista, this is the city's prime spot for lunchtime deal-making over such refined Italian pleasures as leg of lamb with leeks or gnocchi with shrimp, tomato, and pesto sauce. Owner Massimo Ferrari, a hefty man in shirtsleeves and suspenders, keeps the best tables on standby for VIPs. ⊠ *Alameda Santos 1826, Jardins,* ☎ *011/284–0311. No credit cards. Metrô: Trianon.*

$$$$ ✕ **La Vecchia Cucina.** Chef Sergio Arno changed the face of the city's Italian restaurants with his *nuova cucina*, exemplified by such dishes as frog risotto and duck ravioli with watercress sauce. Well-to-do patrons feast either in the ocher-color dining room decorated with Italian engravings and fresh flowers or in the glassed-in garden gazebo. ⊠ *Rua Pedroso Alvarenga 1088, Itaim Bibi,* ☎ *011/3060–9822. AE, DC, MC, V. No lunch Sat., no dinner Sun.*

$$$ ✕ **Famiglia Mancini.** A huge provolone cheese is the first thing you see
★ at this warm, cheerful restaurant. An incredible buffet with cheeses, olives, sausages, and much more is the perfect place to find a tasty appetizer. The menu has many terrific pasta options, such as the cannelloni with palm hearts and a four-cheese sauce. ⊠ *Rua Avanhandava 81, Centro,* ☎ *011/256–4320. AE, DC, MC, V. Metrô: Anhangabaú.*

$$$ ✕ **Lellis Trattoria.** Photos of famous patrons (mostly Brazilian actors) hang on the walls, and the doors and bar are made of metal, giving the typical Italian cantina a sophisticated twist. Salmon fillet *marinatta* (in white sauce with potatoes, raisins, and rice) is the best choice on the menu at this spin-off of Gigetto (☞ *below*). ⊠ *Rua Bela Cintra 1849, Jardim Paulista,* ☎ *011/3064–2727. AE, DC, MC, V.*

$$$ ✕ **Santo Colomba.** This Italian restaurant near the Paulista hotels isn't inexpensive, but some say that for the money, you won't find better in the city. It was originally built in Rio de Janeiro's Jóque Clube (Jockey Club) before being brought lock, stock, and barrel (or rather wooden walls, French tiles, and carved wooden bar) to its current São Paulo location. You can feast on pasta with shrimp, squid, tomato, and garlic while listening to live piano music. ✉ *Alameda Lorena 1165, Jardins,* ☎ *011/3061–3588. AE, DC, MC, V.*

$$ ✕ **Gigetto.** The walls here are adorned with theater posters, a tribute to the actors who dine here after performing at the theater. The modest decor, however, is offset by the elaborate menu's more than 200 delicious options. Try the cappelletti *à romanesca* (with chopped ham, peas, mushrooms, and white cream sauce). ✉ *Rua Avanhandava 63, Centro,* ☎ *011/256–9804. AE, DC, MC, V. Metrô: Anhangabaú.*

$$ ✕ **Jardim di Napoli.** Appropriately enough, just about everywhere you look in this restaurant you'll see the white, green, and red of the Italian flag. People come for the unmatchable *polpettone alla parmigiana,* a huge meatball with mozzarella and tomato sauce. There are also many other meat dishes as well as pasta selections and pizza. ✉ *Rua Doutor Martinico Prado 463, Higienópolis,* ☎ *011/3666–3022. No credit cards.*

$$ ✕ **Mamma Mia.** The waiters can't seem to bring you enough food at this eatery, which is known for its grilled chicken. You can also have a salad and pasta dishes. ✉ *Av. Moema 41, Moema,* ☎ *011/572–5100. AE, DC, MC, V.*

$$ ✕ **Ritz.** Here an animated crowd chatters as contemporary pop music plays in the background. Although each day sees a different special, one of the most popular dishes is the *bife à milanesa* (a breaded beef) with creamed spinach and french fries. ✉ *Alameda Franca 1088, Cerqueira César,* ☎ *011/280–6808. AE, V. Metrô: Consolação.*

Japanese

$$$ ✕ **Komazushi.** Real sushi connoisseurs will appreciate Komazushi. Although master chef Takatomo Hachinohe died in 1998, Jun Sakamoto, the new sushiman in charge, is maintaining the high standards set by his predecessor. The seats at the bar are reserved for customers known to order expensive options. ✉ *Rua São Carlos do Pinhal 241, Bela Vista,* ☎ *011/287–1820. No credit cards. Closed Mon. Metrô: Trianon.*

$$$ ✕ **Nagayama.** Low key, trustworthy, and well loved, both Nagayama locations consistently serve excellent sushi and sashimi. The chefs like to experiment with unusual recipes (and unusual names), such as the California *uramaki* Philadelphia (rice, cream cheese, grilled salmon, roe, cucumber, and spring onions). ✉ *Rua Bandeira Paulista 369, Itaim Bibi,* ☎ *011/3064–8937. AE, DC, MC.* ✉ *Rua da Consolação 3397, Cerqueira César,* ☎ *011/3064–0110. AE, DC, MC.*

$$$ ✕ **Roppongi.** This sushi bar is more about fun than about sushi itself, and fun it does quite well. The nightly clientele includes artists, models, and politicians. There's a private dining area and exit for the fatally chic and amenities for patrons with mobility problems. California rolls are your favorite? Roppongi makes them with mango instead of avocado. For those not fond of raw fish, steaks, pastas, and other international dishes are available. Whatever you order, be sure to refresh yourself with at least one frozen sake before you leave. ✉ *Rua Jorge Coelho 128, Itaim Bibi,* ☎ *011/883–6991. V.*

Lebanese

$$$ ✕ **Arábia.** For more than 10 years Arábia has been serving traditional Lebanese cuisine in a beautiful, high-ceilinged location. Simple dishes such as hummus and stuffed grape leaves are executed with aplomb.

The lamb melts in your mouth with astonishing speed. The "executive" lunch includes one cold dish, one meat dish, a drink, and dessert—all at a (relatively) reasonable price. Don't miss the rose syrup for dessert; it comes over a pistachio delight that may leave you in tears. ⊠ *Rua Haddock Lobo 1397, Jardins,* ☎ *011/3061–2203. AE, D.*

$ ✕ **Almanara.** Part of a chain of Lebanese semi-fast-food outlets, Al-
★ manara is perfect for a quick lunch of hummus, tabbouleh, grilled chicken, and rice. There's also a full-blown restaurant on the premises that serves Lebanese specialties *rodízio*-style (you get a taste of everything until you can ingest no more). ⊠ *Rua Oscar Freire 523, Jardins,* ☎ *011/853–6916. AE, DC, MC, V.*

Pan-Asian

$$$ ✕ **Danang.** This stunningly beautiful restaurant—a huge map of Thailand covers one wall, and a coconut tree grows in the middle of the room—serves a chic, creative mix of Asian cuisines, including Vietnamese, Thai, and Japanese. A recommended dish is *kaeng kung* (prawns with broccoli and other vegetables in a curry-and-coconut-milk sauce). ⊠ *Rua Salvador Cardoso 20, Itaim Bibi,* ☎ *011/829–4758. DC, MC, V. No lunch Mon.–Sat. No dinner Sun.*

$$$ ✕ **Oriental.** Here, high ceilings and tile floors convey a sense of space while candles flickering on tables keep things intimate. With such sophisticated dishes as shark fin soup, this newcomer is already considered the best restaurant of its kind. You'll also find less exotic dishes such as marinated chicken thighs. ⊠ *Rua José Maria Lisboa 1000, Jardim Paulista,* ☎ *011/3060–9495. No credit cards. Closed Sun.*

Pizza

$$ ✕ **Oficina de Pizzas.** Both branches of this restaurant look like something designed by the Spanish artist Gaudí, but the pizzas couldn't be more Italian and straightforward. Try a pie with mozzarella and toasted garlic. ⊠ *Rua Purpurina 517, Vila Madalena,* ☎ *011/816–3749. DC, MC, V.* ⊠ *Rua Inácio Pereira da Rocha 15, Vila Madalena,* ☎ *011/ 813–8399. DC, MC, V.*

$$ ✕ **Piola.** Part of a chain started in Italy, this restaurant serves good pasta dishes as well as pizza. It's frequented by young people who seem to match the trendy decoration perfectly. ⊠ *Rua Oscar Freire 512, Jardins,* ☎ *011/3064–6570. AE, DC, MC, V.*

$$ ✕ **Pizzaria Camelo.** Though it's neither fancy nor beautiful, the wide-variety of thin-crust pies served here has kept paulistanos enthralled for ages. The *chopp* (draft beer) is great, too. Avoid Sunday nights unless you want to wait an hour for a table. ⊠ *Rua Pamplona 1873, Cerqueira César,* ☎ *011/887–8764. No credit cards.*

$$ ✕ **Speranza.** One of the most traditional pizzerias in São Paulo is famous for its margherita pie. The crunchy *pão de linguiça* (sausage bread) appetizers have a fine reputation as well. ⊠ *Rua 13 de Maio 1004, Bela Vista,* ☎ *011/573–1229. DC, MC, V.*

$$ ✕ **I Vitelloni.** The pizza with arugula, mozzarella, sun-dried tomatoes, and roasted garlic was invented here and copied by pizzerias all over town. The place is small, but the service is great. ⊠ *Rua Conde Sílvio Álvares Penteado 31, Pinheiros,* ☎ *011/813–1588. No credit cards.*

Lodging

São Paulo's hotels are almost exclusively geared to business travelers, both homegrown and foreign. For this reason, most are in the Avenida Paulista area, with a few in the Marginal Pinheiros and charming Jardins neighborhoods. Many hotels offer discounts of 20%–40% for cash payment or weekend stays. Few include breakfast in the room rate. São Paulo hosts many international conventions, so it's wise to make reservations well ahead of your arrival. For information about youth hostels, contact the **Associação Paulista de Albergues da Juventude** (✉ Rua 7 de Abril 386, 01320-040, ☎ 011/258–0388). The association sells a book ($2.50) that lists hostels throughout Brazil.

$$$$ ★ 🏨 **Gran Meliá São Paulo.** The Meliá is in the same building as São Paulo's world trade center and the D&D Decoração & Design Center with its many shops. Off the large marble lobby is a bar whose comfortable leather chairs are perfect for unwinding after a day of meetings or shopping. Guest rooms have king-size beds, two phone lines, living rooms with sofas, and small tables that are the perfect places to set up your laptop. The apartment floors have such special amenities as pass-key access and bathroom faucets that can be programmed to record whatever water-temperature you prefer. ✉ *Av. das Nações Unidas 12559, Brooklin 04578-905,* ☎ *011/3043–8000 or 0800/15–5555,* 📠 *011/3043–8001. 300 suites. Restaurant, bar, in-room modem lines, in-room safes, room service, indoor pool, beauty salon, massage, sauna, tennis court, exercise room, paddle tennis, business services, meeting rooms. AE, DC, MC, V.*

$$$$ ★ 🏨 **Inter-Continental São Paulo.** This exquisite hotel is by far the most attractive of the city's top-tier establishments. Service is attentive, and both the private and public areas are well appointed. Creams and pastels, marble, and unique design elements come together with seamless sophistication and elegance. ✉ *Av. Santos 1123, Jardins 01419-001,* ☎ *011/3179–2600,* 📠 *011/3179–2666. 160 rooms, 33 suites. Restaurant, bar, room service, pool, massage, sauna, health club, business services, helipad. AE, DC, MC, V. Metrô: Trianon.*

$$$$ 🏨 **Maksoud Plaza.** Ronald Reagan *almost* stayed here on a 1982 presidential visit, but the Secret Service thought the soaring atrium lobby— with its panoramic elevators, fountains, greenery, and shops—posed a security risk. The staff provides professional service, the hotel's restaurants aren't bad, and the in-house theater and the Maksoud 150 nightclub offer entertainment. ✉ *Alameda Campinas 1250, Jardins 01404-900,* ☎ *011/251–2233,* 📠 *011/253–4544. 416 rooms, 99 suites. 6 restaurants, 3 bars, room service, indoor pool, health club, nightclub, theater, business services. AE, DC, MC, V. Metrô: Trianon.*

$$$$ 🏨 **Renaissance São Paulo.** A stay at this Jardins hotel, a block from Avenida Paulista, puts you close to both shops and businesses. From the street, it has the appeal of a roll of tinfoil, but its interior is graceful and elegant. There are six Renaissance Club floors of 57 suites that include a buffet breakfast, evening hors d'oeuvres, butler service, express check-in and check-out, and fax machines. If you want to arrive in style, the hotel's helipad is key. ✉ *Alameda Santos 2247, Jardins 01419-002,* ☎ *011/3069–2233 or 800/468–3571 in the U.S.,* 📠 *011/3064–3344. 452 rooms, 100 suites. 3 restaurants, 3 bars, room service, pool, massage, health club, squash, shops, business services, travel services, helipad, parking (fee). AE, DC, MC, V. Metrô: Consolação.*

$$$$ ★ 🏨 **Sheraton Mofarrej Hotel & Towers.** Just behind Avenida Paulista and next to Parque Trianon, the Mofarrej is part of Sheraton's A-class Luxury Collection hotels. Rooms are done in elegant light hues, and the four floors that have butler service offer other amenities that will make you feel all the more at home. Rooms on the west side overlook the park. ✉ *Alameda Santos 1437, Jardins 01419-905,* ☎ *011/253–5544 or 0800/11–6000,* 📠 *011/289–8670. 2 restaurants, 2 bars, room service, indoor and outdoor pools, massage, sauna, exercise room, business services, convention center. AE, DC, MC, V. Metrô: Trianon.*

$$$ 🏨 **Grande Hotel Ca' D'Oro.** Owned and run by a northern Italian family for more than 40 years, this Old World–style hotel near Centro has bar-side fireplaces, lots of wood and Persian carpeting, a great variety of room decor (all along classic European lines), ultrapersonalized service, and the beloved Ca' D'Oro restaurant. All these amenities attract many repeat customers, including quite a few Brazilian bigwigs. ⊠ *Rua Augusta 129, Cerqueira César 01303-001,* ☎ *011/236–4300,* ℻ *011/236–4311. 240 rooms, 50 suites. Restaurants, 2 bars, room service, indoor and outdoor pools, sauna, exercise room. AE, DC, MC, V. Metrô: Consolação.*

$$ 🏨 **Bourbon.** Both guests and furnishings are well cared for in this small hotel near the Largo do Arouche, a charming downtown district. A brass-accented basement bar features live piano music. The lobby has upholstered print sofas, an abstract handcrafted black and white wall hanging, and granite flooring. Rooms are done in beige and blue and have marvelously large, sunlit bathrooms. ⊠ *Av. Vieira de Carvalho 99, Centro 01210-010,* ☎ *011/250–0244,* ℻ *011/221–4076. 123 rooms. Restaurant, bar, sauna. AE, DC, MC, V. Metrô: República.*

$$ 🏨 **La Guardia.** If you don't need to be surrounded by luxury, consider this simple, affordable (compared to many São Paulo establishments) hotel. Rooms are small but comfortable and have thick carpets and marble-top tables. The environment is friendly, and the service is good. ⊠ *Rua Peixoto Gomide 154, Cerqueira César 01409-000,* ☎ *011/255–0600,* ℻ *011/258–7398. 28 rooms, 14 suites. Restaurant, free parking. AE, DC, MC, V. Metrô: Consolação.*

$$ 🏨 **Ville Hotel.** Located in the lively Higienópolis neighborhood of apartment buildings, bars, and bookstores abutting Mackenzie University, this hotel costs about $70 a night. The small lobby features a black and pink granite floor, recessed lighting, and leather sofas; rooms are done in pastels with brown carpeting. ⊠ *Rua Dona Veridiana 643, Higienópolis 01238-010,* ☎ *011/257–5288,* ☎ ℻ *011/239–1871. 54 rooms. Restaurant, meeting room. AE, DC, MC, V.*

Nightlife and the Arts

Nightlife

São Paulo is a city beset by trends, so clubs and bars come and go at a dizzying pace. Though these were all thriving spots at press time, it's best to check with hotel concierges and paulistanos you meet to confirm that a place is still open before heading out on the town.

BARS

Balcão. The word for "balcony" in Portuguese is *balcão*, and true to its name, this place has a sprawling one. If you'd like a little food to accompany your drinks and conversation, try the delicious sandwich with sun-dried tomatoes and mozzarella. ⊠ *Rua Doutor Melo Alves 150, Jardim Paulista,* ☎ *011/280–4630. Metrô: Consolação.*

Barnaldo Lucrécia. Live *música popular brasileira* (MPB; popular Brazilian music) is often a draw here. The crowd is intense, though jovial. ⊠ *Rua Abílio Soares 207, Paraíso,* ☎ *011/885–3425. Metrô: Paraíso.*

Elias. This place is a hangout for fans of the Palmeiras soccer team, whose stadium is just a few blocks away. If you want something to eat, the carpaccio is undoubtedly the best choice on the menu. ⊠ *Rua Cayowaá 70, Perdizes,* ☎ *011/864–4722.*

Empanadas. Most patrons stop here for a beer en route to another Vila Madalena bar. It's a good place to "warm up" for an evening out with a quick drink and a bite to eat. The empanadas are particularly appealing. ⊠ *Rua Wisard 489, Vila Madalena,* ☎ *011/210–2116.*

Frangó. Because it's set in the Freguesia do Ó neighborhood, a stop here makes you feel as if you've been transported to a small town. In addition to a pleasant location, Frangó also offers 90 varieties of beer, including the Brazilian export beer, Xingu. Its rich molasses-like flavor nicely complements the bar's unforgettable *bolinhos de frango com*

queijo (chicken balls with cheese). ⊠ *Largo da Matriz de Nossa Senhora do Ó 168, Freguesia do Ó,* ☎ *011/875–7818 or 011/875–9281.*
Pirajá. The pictures of Rio de Janeiro on the walls here will make you think fondly of Ipanema. The action starts at happy hour after 6 PM. ⊠ *Av. Brigadeiro Faria Lima 64, Pinheiros,* ☎ *011/815–6881.*

BRAZILIAN CLUBS

Café Soçaite. This is one of the most popular spots for MPB, especially with singles. ⊠ *Rua 13 de Maio 48, Bixiga,* ☎ *011/259–6562.*
Sem Eira Nem Beira. The decor here is inspired by Brazilian bars circa 1940. Previously called Vou Vivendo, the club is famous for its live MPB performances on Friday and Saturday. ⊠ *Rua Elvira Ferraz 966, Itaim Bibi,* ☎ *011/820–6963.*

CYBERCAFÉS

Banca Henrique Schaumann. At this newsstand-bar you'll find eight computers connected Monday–Wednesday 7 AM–1 AM and 24 hours Thursday and through Sunday. Access costs about $4 an hour. ⊠ *Av. Henrique Schaumann 159, Pinheiros,* ☎ *011/3063–3292.*
Coffee & Book at Saraiva Megastore. This store sells CDs and books and has a café as well as five computers. You can log on Monday–Saturday 10–10 and Sunday 2–8; the cost is $5 for the first half-hour and $4 for each additional 30 minutes. ⊠ *Shopping Eldorado, Av. Rebouças 3970, Pinheiros,* ☎ *011/870–5999.*

DANCE CLUBS

Avenida Club. Some nights are dedicated to Caribbean rhythms, others to MPB. Regardless, the large, wooden dance floor—one of the finest in town—attracts a crowd of thirtysomethings. ⊠ *Pedroso de Morais 1036, Pinheiros,* ☎ *011/814–7383.*
Brancaleone. Even if you've always been told that you move to the beat of a different drum, you'll find a suitable rhythm here. Each night brings a new beat, including disco, rock, funk, soul, Brazilian pop, and forró. You can take a break on the patio; refreshments include food as well as drink. ⊠ *Rua Luis Murat 298, Jardim América,* ☎ *011/870–8873.*
Carioca Club. *Carioca* is the word for a person or thing from Rio de Janeiro, and this place has the decor of old-style Rio clubs. Its large dance floor attracts an eclectic mix of college students, couples, and professional dancers who move to samba, *axé* (a type of music from Bahia), and pagode. ⊠ *Rua Cardeal Arcoverde 2899, Pinheiros,* ☎ *011/212–3782.*
Clube B.A.S.E. In the '60s this was a bathhouse, but now it hosts hot dance parties from 9 until the wee hours. Three bars and an enormous dance floor reverberate to a mix of everything from Jimi Hendrix to cutting-edge dance hits. For $6 per half-hour, you can also log onto one of eight computers here Tuesday–Friday after 10 PM and Saturday after 11 PM. ⊠ *Av. Brigadeiro Luís Antônio 1137, Bela Vista,* ☎ *011/ 605–3162.*
Dado Bier. With a dance floor, a microbrewery, a restaurant, a sushi bar, and a gift shop, this place has something for everyone. No wonder you often have to wait in line to get in. ⊠ *Av. Juscelino Kubitschek 1203, Itaim Bibi,* ☎ *011/866–2310.*
Dolores Dolores. DJs spin funk, soul, and hip hop tunes for a crowd in its twenties and thirties. Wednesday and Friday nights are the most popular, and people really do fill up the floor only after the witching hour. ⊠ *Rua Fidalga 254, Vila Madalena,* ☎ *011/212–6519.*
Kashmir. If you feel it has been too long since your last magic carpet ride, head for the exclusive Kashmir, one of the longest-lived clubs in town. The decor features pillows to sit on, walls draped in exotic textiles, and indoor and outdoor spaces. There's a belly-dancing show after

10 PM Tuesday through Saturday. ✉ *Rua Fiandeiras 696, Vila Olímpia,* ☎ *011/820–0113.*

KVA. Live or recorded forró is played here every night. There are three stages, two dance floors, and one coffee shop. ✉ *Rua Cardeal Arcoverde 2958, Pinheiros,* ☎ *011/870–2153.*

Lov.e Club & Lounge. The interior design makes you feel like you're in a set from an *Austin Powers* movie. Before 2 AM the music isn't too loud, and you can sit and talk on the '50s-style sofas. Then techno effects keep people on the small dance floor until sunrise. ✉ *Rua Pequetita 189, Vila Olímpia,* ☎ *011/3044–1613.*

Moinho Santo Antonio. With a capacity of about 5,000, this has to be one of the planet's largest nightclubs. In a converted mill far from the center of town, the Moinho (as it's called) has a sushi bar, an Italian restaurant, a juice bar, outdoor and indoor dancing, bungee jumping (from a crane), and a magnificent lighting system. ✉ *Rua Borges de Figueiredo 510, Moóca,* ☎ *011/291–3522.*

The Pool. Ever wish you could fully cool off during a hot night of dancing? Well, this place has a 26-ft-long pool where you can do just that. The club will provide you with a swimsuit, but you can't wear it back on the dance floor. DJs play house music. ✉ *Rua Teodoro Sampaio 1109, Pinheiros,* ☎ *011/881–6604.*

GAY AND LESBIAN CLUBS

Disco Fever. This place is frequented mostly by men between the ages of 18 and 35, and there's room for 1,200 of them. Bodybuilders in swim trunks dance on stages while DJ Mauro Borges and others play '70s and house music until the last patron leaves. ✉ *Av. Ibirapuera 1911, Moema,* ☎ *011/539–5910.*

A Lôca. Here you'll find a large dance floor, a video room, and two bars. A mixed gay and lesbian crowd often dances till dawn and then has breakfast in the club. ✉ *Rua Frei Caneca 916, Cerqueira César,* ☎ *011/3120–2055. Metrô: Consolação.*

Massivo. This fabulous underground disco and club welcomes gay, lesbian, and straight patrons. ✉ *Rua Alameda Itu 1548, Jardins,* ☎ *011/ 883–7505. Metrô: Consolação.*

Nostro 2000. One of São Paulo's oldest gay discos has transvestite and strip shows and an "anything goes" atmosphere. ✉ *Rua da Consolação 2554,* ☎ *011/259–2945. Metrô: Consolação.*

Jazz Clubs

All of Jazz. People come to this small place to actually *listen* to very good jazz and bossa nova. Local musicians jam here weekly. Call ahead to book a table on weekends. ✉ *Rua João Cachoeira 1366, Vila Olímpia,* ☎ *011/829–1345.*

Blue Night. At this traditional jazz, blues, and soul venue, the audience drinks beer and whiskey and eats french fries with Parmesan cheese. ✉ *Av. São Gabriel 558,* ☎ *011/884–9356.*

Bourbon Street. With a name right out of New Orleans, one of the world's coolest jazz towns, it's no wonder this is where the best jazz and blues bands play. ✉ *Rua Dos Chanés 127, Moema,* ☎ *011/5561–1643.*

Café Piu Piu. Although this establishment is best known for jazz, it also hosts groups that play rock, bossa nova, and even tango. ✉ *Rua 13 de Maio 134, Bixiga,* ☎ *011/258–8066.*

Piratininga. The tiny, round tables at this small bar-restaurant are perfect for a quiet rendezvous. The live jazz and MPB music add to the romance. ✉ *Rua Wizard 149, Vila Madalena,* ☎ *011/210–9775.*

Sanja Jazz Bar. A few tables (arrive early to get a seat) in an old town house are the setting for live jazz, rock, and blues performances. ✉ *Rua Frei Caneca 304, Consolação,* ☎ *011/255–2942.*

The Arts

The world's top orchestras, opera and dance companies, and other troupes always include São Paulo in their South American tours. Listings of events appear in the "Veja São Paulo" insert of the newsweekly *Veja*. The arts sections of the dailies *Folha de São Paulo* and *O Estado de São Paulo* also have listings and reviews. In addition, *Folha* publishes a weekly guide on Fridays called "Guia da Folha."

In addition to theater box offices, tickets for many events are available at booths throughout the city, including **Show Ticket at Shopping Center Morumbi** (⊠ Av. Brigadeiro Faria Lima 1191, 3rd floor, ☎ 011/212–7623), open Monday–Saturday 10–10 and Sunday 2–8. Some theaters deliver tickets for a surcharge, as will **Fun by Phone** (☎ 011/867–8687) and **Lucas Shows** (☎ 011/858–5783).

CLASSICAL MUSIC, DANCE, AND THEATER

The city is home to both a state and a municipal orchestra, though both suffer from a chronic lack of funds. São Paulo's theater district, in the bohemian Bela Vista neighborhood, has dozens of theaters dedicated mostly to plays in Portuguese. São Paulo has a world-class contemporary dance company, the **Ballet Stagium** (☎ 011/852–3451), and a contemporary music ensemble, **Grupo Novo Horizonte** (☎ 011/256–9766), neither of which have permanent homes. The following performance venues host events of all kinds.

Sala São Luiz. This new venue hosts chamber music performances. ⊠ *Av. Juscelino Kubitschek 1830, Itaim Bibi,* ☎ *011/827–4111.*

Teatro da Cultura Artística. Its fine acoustics make this theater perfect for classical music performances. It also hosts dance recitals and plays. ⊠ *Rua Nestor Pestana 196, Cerqueira César,* ☎ *011/258–3616.*

Teatro Municipal. Most of São Paulo's serious music, ballet, and opera is performed in the intimate gilt and moss-green-velvet surroundings of this classic theater. There are lyrical performances on Monday at 8:30 and concerts on Wednesday at 12:30. A local cultural organization, the Mozarteum Brasileira Associação Cultural, holds classical music concerts here, which include performances by visiting artists, April–October. ⊠ *Praça Ramos de Azevedo, Centro,* ☎ *011/222–8698. Metrô: Anhangabaú.*

Via Funchal. With a capacity of more than 3,000 people, this is the site of many large international shows. ⊠ *Rua Funchal 65, Vila Olímpia,* ☎ *011/866–2300 or 011/822–6855.*

ESCOLAS DE SAMBA

From December to February, many *escolas de samba* (samba "schools"; groups that perform during Carnaval) open their rehearsals to the public. The drummers get in sync with the singers, and everyone learns the lyrics to each year's songs. One of the most popular such rehearsals is that of **Rosas de Ouro** (⊠ Av. Cel. Euclides Machado 1066, Freguesia do Ó, ☎ 011/266–0608 or 011/857–4555).

Outdoor Activities and Sports

Participant Sports

BICYCLING

Parque Ibirapuera has places that rent bicycles for about $8 an hour and a special bike path. There are also bike lanes on Avenida Sumaré and Avenida Pedroso de Morais. **Night Biker's Club** (⊠ Rua Pacheco de Miranda 141, Jardim Paulista, ☎ 011/887–4773) has bike tours in the city at night. **Sampa Bikers** (⊠ Alameda dos Anapurus 1580, Moema, ☎ 011/9990–0083 or 011/5183–9477) offers tours inside the city and biking side trips outside town; costs start at about $90.

GOLF

The greens fee at the 18-hole **Clube de Campo** (⊠ Praça Rockford 28, Vila Represa, ☎ 011/5929–3111) is $50. It's open Monday–Tuesday and Thursday–Friday 7–7. The **Golf School** (⊠ Av. Guido Caloi 2160, Santo Amaro, ☎ 011/5515–3372) is a driving range that offers 30-minute classes for $20; $10 gets you 100 balls.

TENNIS

Tênis Coach (⊠ Rua Dr. Francisco Tomás de Carvalho, 940, Morumbi) rents courts and gives classes to people of all ages. Court fees at **Play Tênis** (⊠ Leopoldo Couto de Magalhães Jr. 1097, Itaim Bibi, ☎ 011/820–7446) are $35 an hour, but they don't rent rackets.

Spectator Sports

AUTO RACING

São Paulo hosts a Formula I race every March, bringing this city of 4.5 million cars to heights of spontaneous combustion, especially when a Brazilian driver wins. The race is held at **Autódromo de Interlagos** (⊠ Av. Senador Teotônio Vilela 315, Interlagos, ☎ 011/521–9911), which also hosts other kinds of races on weekends. For ticket information on the Formula I race contact the **Confederação Brasileira de Automobilismo** (⊠ Rua da Glória 290, 8th Floor, Rio de Janeiro, RJ 20241-180, ☎ 021/221–4895).

FUTEBOL

Futebol (soccer) has always been a Brazilian passion. The nation's love affair with the sport became even stronger after Brazil won the 1994 World Cup and reached the finals during the 1998 World Cup. São Paulo has several well-funded teams with some of the country's best players. The five main teams—São Paulo, Palmeiras, Portuguesa, Corinthians, and Juventus—even attract fans from other states. The two biggest stadiums are **Morumbi** (⊠ Praça Roberto Gomes Pedrosa, ☎ 011/842–3377) and the municipally run **Pacaembu** (⊠ Praça Charles Miller, ☎ 011/256–9111). Note that covered seats offer the best protection not only from the elements but also from rowdy spectators.

HORSE RACING

Thoroughbreds race at the **São Paulo Jockey Club** (⊠ Rua Lineu de Paula Machado 1263, Cidade Jardim, ☎ 011/816–4011), which is open Monday and Wednesday–Thursday 7:30 PM–11:30 PM and weekends 2–9. Card-carrying jockey club members get the best seats and have access to the elegant restaurant.

Shopping

People come from all over South America to shop in São Paulo, and shopping is considered an attraction in its own right by many paulistanos. Stores are open weekdays 9–6:30 and Saturday 9–1. A few are open on Sunday (for a list of these shops and their Sunday hours, call ☎ 011/210–4000 or 011/813–3311). Mall hours are generally weekdays 10–10 and Saturday 9 AM–10 PM; during gift-giving holiday seasons malls open on Sunday.

Areas

In **Centro,** Rua do Arouche is noted for leather goods. In **Itaim,** the area around Rua João Cachoeira has evolved from a neighborhood of small clothing factories into a wholesale- and retail-clothing sales district. Several shops on Rua Tabapuã sell small antiques. Also, Rua Dr. Mário Ferraz is stuffed with elegant clothing, gift, and home-decoration stores. **Jardins,** centering on Rua Augusta (which crosses Avenida Paulista) and Rua Oscar Freire, is the most chic area. Double-parked Mercedes-Benzes and BMWs point the way to the city's fanciest stores, which sell leather items, jewelry, gifts, antiques, and art. You'll also find many restaurants and beauty salons. Shops that specialize in high-price European antiques are on or around Rua da Consolação. A slew of lower-price antiques stores line Rua Cardeal Arcoverde in **Pinheiros.**

Department Store
Mappin, one of Brazil's biggest department stores, is especially crowded on Saturday. Lots of *camelôs* (street vendors) offer cassette tapes, T-shirts, and drawings in front of the building. ⊠ *Praça Ramos de Azevedo 131, Centro,* ☎ *011/214–4411. Metrô: Anhangabaú.*

Centers and Malls
Shopping Center Iguatemi. The city's oldest and most sophisticated mall offers the latest in fashion and fast food. Four movie theaters often show American films in English with Portuguese subtitles. The Gero Café, built in the middle of the main hall, has a fine menu. ⊠ *Av. Brigadeiro Faria Lima 2232, Jardim Paulista,* ☎ *011/816–6116.*

Shopping Center Morumbi. Set in the city's fastest-growing area, Morumbi is giving Iguatemi a run for its money. That said, it houses about the same boutiques, record stores, bookstores, and restaurants as Iguatemi, though it has more movie theaters (a total of six). ⊠ *Av. Roque Petroni Jr. 1089, Morumbi,* ☎ *011/553–2444.*

Shopping Paulista. This mall has more than 200 stores and 4 movie theaters and is close to Avenida Paulista. You'll also find a currency exchange office and a tourist information center here. ⊠ *Rua 13 de Maio 1947, Paraíso,* ☎ *011/3178–7300. Metrô: Paraíso.*

Markets
On Sunday, there are **antiques fairs** near the Museu de Arte de São Paulo and (in the afternoon) at the Shopping Center Iguatemi's (☞ Centers and Malls, *above*) parking lot. Many stall owners have shops and hand out business cards so you can browse throughout the week at your leisure. An **arts and crafts fair**—selling jewelry, embroidery, leather goods, toys, clothing, paintings, and musical instruments—takes place Sunday morning in Centro's Praça da República. Many booths move over to the nearby Praça da Liberdade in the afternoon, joining vendors there selling Japanese-style ceramics, wooden sandals, cooking utensils, food, and bonsai trees. **Flea markets**—with second-hand furniture, clothes, and CDs—take place on Saturday at Praça Benedito Calixto in Pinheiros and on Sunday at the Praça Dom Orione in Bela Vista.

Specialty Shops
ANTIQUES

Arte e Companhia. This collective of three dealers sells Latin American and European antiques. ⊠ *Rua Oscar Freire 146, Jardins,* ☎ *011/ 3064–1574.*

Patrimônio. Come here for Brazilian antiques at reasonable prices. It also sells some Indian artifacts as well as modern furnishings crafted from iron. ⊠ *Alameda Ministro Rocha Azevedo 1068, Jardins,* ☎ *011/ 3064–1750.*

Paulo Vasconcelos. Folk art and 18th- and 19th-century Brazilian furniture are among the finds here. ⊠ *Alameda Gabriel Monteiro da Silva 1881, Jardins,* ☎ *011/852–2444.*

Renato Magalhães Gouvêa Escritório de Arte. This shop offers a potpourri of European and Brazilian antiques, modern furnishings, and art. ⊠ *Av. Europa 68, Jardins,* ☎ *011/853–2569.*

ART

Arte Aplicada. For Brazilian paintings, sculptures, and prints, this is the place. ⊠ *Rua Haddock Lobo 1406, Jardins,* ☎ *011/852–5128.*

Camargo Vilaça. The staff here has an eye for the works of up-and-coming Brazilian artists. ⊠ *Rua Fradique Coutinho 1500, Vila Madalena,* ☎ *011/210–7390.*

Espaço Cultural Ena Beçak. Here you can shop for Brazilian prints, sculptures, and paintings and then stop in the café. ⊠ *Rua Oscar Freire 440, Jardins,* ☎ *011/280–7322.*

Galeria Renot. Here you'll find oil paintings by such Brazilian artists as Vicente Rego Monteiro, Di Cavalcanti, Cícero Dias, and Anita Malfatti. ⊠ *Alameda Ministro Rocha Azevedo 1327, Jardins,* ☎ *011/883–5933.*

Galeria São Paulo. This gallery is a leader in contemporary, mainstream art. ⊠ *Rua Estados Unidos 1456, Jardins,* ☎ *011/852–8855.*

Mônica Filgueiras de Almeida. Many a trend has been set at this gallery. ⊠ *Alameda Ministro Rocha Azevedo 927, Jardins,* ☎ *011/282–5292.*

CLOTHING

Alexandre Herchovitch. Senhor Herchovitch is a famous Brazilian designer. His store has prête-à-porter and tailor-made clothes. ⊠ *Alameda Franca 631, Jardins,* ☎ *011/288–8005.*

Anacapri. This shop sells women's underwear, swimsuits, and clothes in large sizes. ⊠ *Rua Juquis 276, Moema,* ☎ *011/532–1154.*

Cori. Everyday outfits with classic lines are the specialty here. ⊠ *Rua Haddock Lobo 1584, Jardins,* ☎ *011/881–5223.*

Ellus. This is a good place to buy men's and women's jeans, sportswear, and street wear. ⊠ *Shopping Eldorado, 3rd Floor, Cerqueira César,* ☎ *011/815–4554.*

Fórum. Although it has a lot of evening attire for young men and women, this shop also sells sportswear and shoes. ⊠ *Rua Oscar Freire 916, Jardins,* ☎ *011/853–6269.*

Le Lis Blanc. This shop is Brazil's exclusive purveyor of the French brand, Vertigo. Look for party dresses in velvet and sheer fabrics. ⊠ *Rua Oscar Freire 809, Jardins,* ☎ *011/883–2549.*

Maria Bonita/Maria Bonita Extra. If you have a little money in your pocket, shop at Maria Bonita, which has elegant women's clothes with terrific lines. At Maria Bonita Extra, the prices are a little lower. ⊠ *Rua Oscar Freire 702, Jardins,* ☎ *011/852–6433.*

Reinaldo Lourenço. The women's clothes here are sophisticated and of a high quality. ⊠ *Rua Bela Cintra 2167, Jardins,* ☎ *011/853–8150.*

Richard's. This store carries one of Brazil's best lines of sportswear. Its collection includes outfits suitable for the beach or the mountains. ⊠ *Alameda Franca 1185, Jardins,* ☎ *011/282–5399. Metrô: Consolação.*

Uma. Young women are intrigued by the unique designs of the swimsuits, dresses, shorts, shirts, and pants sold here. ⊠ *Rua Girassol 273, Vila Madalena,* ☎ *011/813–5559.*

Zoomp. This shop is famous for its jeans and high-quality street wear. Customers from 13 to 35 mix and match the clothes here, creating some unusual combinations. ⊠ *Rua Oscar Freire 995, Jardins,* ☎ *011/3064–1556.*

HANDICRAFTS

Art Índia. This government-run shop sells Indian arts and crafts made by tribes throughout Brazil. ⊠ *Rua Augusta 1371, Loja 119, Cerqueira César,* ☎ *011/283–2102. Metrô: Consolação.*

Casa do Amazonas. As its name suggests, you'll find a wide selection of products from the Amazon in this store. ⊠ *Galeria Metropôle, Av. São Luís 187, Loja 14, Centro,* ☎ *011/258–9727. Metrô: São Luís.*

Galeria de Arte Brasileira. This shop specializes in Brazilian handicrafts. Look for objects made of pau-brasil, hammocks, jewelry, T-shirts, *marajoara* pottery (from the Amazon), and lace. ⊠ *Alameda Lorena 2163, Jardins,* ☎ *011/852–9452.*

JEWELRY

Antônio Bernardo. This store is owned by one of Brazil's top designers. His work includes both modern and classical pieces that use only precious stones. ✉ *Rua Bela Cintra 2063, Jardins,* ☎ *011/883–5034.*
Atelier Cecília Rodrigues. This designer crafts unique pieces of gold and precious stones. ✉ *Rua Horácio Lafer 767, Itaim Bibi,* ☎ *011/829–9394.*
Castro Bernardes. In addition to selling jewelry and precious stones, this store restores old pieces. ✉ *Rua Jerônimo da Veiga 164, 19th floor, Itaim Bibi,* ☎ *011/280–6812.*

São Paulo A to Z

Arriving and Departing

BY AIRPLANE

São Paulo's international airport, **Cumbica** (☎ 011/6445–2945), is in the suburb of Guarulhos, 30 km (19 mi) and a 45-minute drive (longer during rush hour or on rainy days) northeast of Centro. **Aeroporto Congonhas** (☎ 011/536–3555, ext. 195), 14 km (9 mi) south of Centro (a 15- to 30-minute drive, depending on traffic), serves regional airlines, including the Rio–São Paulo shuttle. From June to September, both airports are sometimes fogged in during the early morning, and flights are rerouted to the **Aeroporto Viracopos** (☎ 0192/247–0909) in Campinas; passengers are transported by bus (an hour's ride) to São Paulo.

International airlines serving São Paulo include: **Aerolíneas Argentinas** (☎ 011/214–4233), **Air France** (☎ 011/289–2133 or 011/945–2211), **American Airlines** (☎ 011/214–4000 or 011/258–1244), **British Airways** (☎ 011/259–6144), **Canadian Airlines** (☎ 011/259–9066), **Continental Airlines** (☎ 0800/55–4777), **Delta Airlines** (☎ 0800/22–1121), and **United Airlines** (☎ 011/253–2323).

The domestic carrier **Rio Sul** (011/231–9164) connects São Paulo with most major Brazilian cities daily. **TAM** (0800/12–3100) flies daily to most Brazilian capitals and major cities in São Paulo State. **Transbrasil** (011/231–1988) has daily flights to major U.S. cities, London, and the main Brazilian cities. **Varig** (011/5561–1161) has daily service to many U.S. and Brazilian cities; it also offers regular service to Toronto, London, Sydney, and Auckland. **VASP** (0800/99–8277) serves New York and many Brazilian cities daily, Miami six times a week, Toronto four times a week, and Los Angeles and Sydney three times a week.

From the Airports into Town. EMTU *executivo* **buses** (☎ 011/945–2505)—fancy, green-stripe, "executive" vehicles—shuttle between Cumbica and Congonhas (6 AM–10 PM, every 30 min) as well as between Cumbica and the Tietê bus terminal (5:40 AM–10 PM, every 45 min); the downtown Praça da República (5:30 AM–11 PM, every 30 min); and the Hotel Maksoud Plaza (6:45 AM–11 PM every 35 min), stopping at most major hotels on Avenida Paulista. The cost is $7. **Municipal buses,** with CMTC painted on the side, stop at the airport and go downtown by various routes, such as via Avenida Paulista, to the Praça da Sé and Tietê bus station.

The sleek, blue-and-white, air-conditioned **Guarucoop radio taxis** (☎ 011/208–1881) will take you from Cumbica to downtown for around $40; the fare to town from Congonhas is about $16. *Comum* (regular) taxis also charge $40 from Cumbica and around $12 from Congonhas. **Fleet Car Shuttle** (counter at Cumbica Airport's arrivals Terminal 1, ☎ 011/945–3030), open daily 6 AM–midnight, serves groups of up to 10 people in a van, stopping at one destination of choice. The fee (for the van load) is about $70.

Finally, a travel companion that doesn't snore on the plane or eat all your peanuts.

When traveling, your MCI WorldCom Card is the best way to keep in touch. Our operators speak your language, so they'll be able to connect you back home—no matter where your travels take you. Plus, your MCI WorldCom Card is easy to use, and even earns you frequent flyer miles every time you use it. When you add in our great rates, you get something even more valuable: peace-of-mind. So go ahead. Travel the world. MCI WorldCom just brought it a whole lot closer.

You can even sign up today at www.mci.com/worldphone or ask your operator to make a collect call to 1-410-314-2938.

EASY TO CALL WORLDWIDE

1 Just dial the WorldPhone access number of the country you're calling from.
2 Dial or give the operator your MCI WorldCom Card number.
3 Dial or give the number you're calling.

Argentina	
To call using Telefonica	**0-800-222-6249**
To call using Telecom	**0-800-555-1002**
Brazil	**000-8012**
Mexico	
Avantel	**01-800-021-8000**
Telmex ▲	**001-800-674-7000**
Collect access in Spanish	**980-9-16-1000**
Morocco	**00-211-0012**

For your complete WorldPhone calling guide, dial the WorldPhone access number for the country you're in and ask the operator for Customer Service. In the U.S. call 1-800-431-5402.

▲ When calling from public phones, use phones marked LADATEL.

EARN FREQUENT FLYER MILES

American Airlines
A'Advantage®

Continental Airlines
OnePass

▲ Delta Air Lines
SkyMiles®

◢ MILEAGE PLUS®
United Airlines

U·S AIRWAYS
DIVIDEND MILES

MCI WorldCom, its logo and the names of the products referred to herein are proprietary marks of MCI WorldCom, Inc. All airline names and logos are proprietary marks of the respective airlines. All airline program rules and conditions apply.

The first thing you need overseas is the one thing you forget to pack.

FOREIGN CURRENCY DELIVERED OVERNIGHT

Chase Currency To Go® delivers foreign currency to your home by the next business day*

It's easy—before you travel, call 1-888-CHASE84 for delivery of any of 75 currencies

Delivery is free with orders of $500 or more

Competitive rates—without exchange fees

You don't have to be a Chase customer—you can pay by Visa® or MasterCard®

CHASE

THE RIGHT RELATIONSHIP IS EVERYTHING.®

1•888•CHASE84
www.chase.com

*Orders must be placed before 5 PM ET. $10 delivery fee for orders under $500.
©1999 The Chase Manhattan Corporation. All rights reserved. The Chase Manhattan Bank. Member FDIC.

BY BUS

Combined, São Paulo's four **bus stations** (☎ 011/235–0322 for information on all stations) serve 1,105 destinations. The main station—serving all major Brazilian cities (with trips to Rio every half-hour on the half-hour) as well as Paraguay, Argentina, Uruguay, and Chile—is the **Terminal Tietê** (✉ Av. Cruzeiro do Sul) in the north, on the Marginal Tietê Beltway. **Terminal Bresser** (✉ Rua do Hipódromo), in the eastern district of Brás, serves southern Minas Gerais State and Belo Horizonte. **Terminal Jabaquara** (✉ Rua Jequitibas), near Congonhas airport, serves coastal towns. **Terminal Barra Funda** (✉ Rua Mário de Andrade 664) in the west, near the Memorial da América Latina, has buses to and from western Brazil. All stations have or are close to metrô stops. You can buy tickets at the stations; although those for Rio de Janeiro can be bought a few minutes before departure, it's best to buy tickets in advance for other destinations and during holiday seasons.

BY CAR

The main São Paulo–Rio de Janeiro highway is the Via Dutra (BR 116 North), which has recently been repaved and enlarged in places. The speed limit is 120 kph (74 mph) along most of it, and although it has many tolls, you'll find many call boxes that you can use if your car breaks down. The modern Rodoviária dos Trabalhdores (SP 70) charges reasonable tolls, runs parallel to the Dutra for about a quarter of the way, and is an excellent alternative route. The 429-km (279-mi) trip takes five hours. If you have time, consider the longer, spectacular, coastal Rio–Santos Highway (SP 55 and BR 101). It's an easy two-day drive, and you can stop midway at the colonial city of Parati in Rio de Janeiro State.

Other main highways are the Castelo Branco (SP 280), which links the southwestern part of the state to the city; the Via Anhanguera (SP 330), which originates in the state's rich northern agricultural region, passing through the university town of Campinas; SP 310, which also runs from the farming heartland; BR 116 South, which comes up from Curitiba (a 408 km/265 mi trip); plus the Via Anchieta (SP 150) and the Rodovia Imigrantes (SP 160), parallel roads that run to the coast, each operating one way on weekends and holidays.

Getting Around

BY BUS

There's ample **municipal bus service** (0800/12–3133 transit information), but regular buses (white with a red horizontal stripe) are overcrowded at rush hour and when it rains. Stops are clearly marked, but routes are spelled out only on the buses themselves. The fare is about 60¢. You enter at the front, pay the *cobrador* (fare collector) in the middle, and exit the back. Often the cobrador has no change, and gives out *vale transporte* slips, or fare vouchers (with no expiration time).

The green-and-gray **SPTrans executivo** buses (☎ 158), whose numerical designations all end with the letter *E*, are more spacious and cost around $2 (you pay the driver upon entry). Many *clandestino* (unlicensed, privately run buses) traverse the city. Although not very pleasing to the eye—most are battered, white vehicles that have no signs—it's perfectly fine to take them; they charge the same as SPTrans buses.

BY CAR

Driving isn't recommended in São Paulo because of the heavy traffic (nothing moves at rush hour, especially when it rains), dare-devil drivers, and inadequate parking. If, however, you do opt to drive, there are a few things to keep in mind. Most of São Paulo is between the Rio Tietê and the Rio Pinheiros, which converge in the western part of town. The high-speed routes along these rivers are Marginal Tietê and Marginal Pinheiros. There are also *marginais* (beltways) around the city. Avenida 23 de Maio runs south from Centro and beneath the Parque do Ibirapuera via the Ayrton Senna Tunnel. You can take Avenida Paulista, Avenida Brasil, and Avenida Faria Lima southwest to the Morumbi, Brooklin, Itaim, and Santo Amaro neighborhoods. The Elevado Costa e Silva, also called Minhocão, is an elevated road that connects Centro with Avenida Francisco Matarazzo in the west.

In most commercial neighborhoods you must buy hourly tickets (called Cartão Zona Azul) to park on the street during business hours. Only buy them at newsstands, not from people on the street. Booklets of 20 tickets cost $10. Fill out each ticket—you'll need one for every hour you plan to park—with the car's license plate and the time you initially parked. Leave all tickets in the car's window so that they're visible to the officials from outside. After business hours or at any time near major sights, people may offer to watch your car. Although paying these "caretakers" about $1 is enough to keep your car's paint job intact, to truly ensure its safety opt for a parking lot. Rates are $5–$7 for the first hour and $1–$2 each hour thereafter.

Car rental rates range from $50 to $100 a day. Major rental companies include: **Avis** (⊠ Rua da Consolação 335, Centro, ☏ 011/258–8833), **Hertz** (⊠ Rua da Consolação 439, Centro, ☏ 011/256–9722), or **Localiza** (⊠ Rua da Consolação 419, Centro, ☏ 011/231–3055).

BY METRÔ
The **metrô** (☏ 011/284–8877 for general information) is safe, quick, comfortable, and clean, but unfortunately it doesn't serve many of the city's southern districts. The blue line runs north–south, the orange line runs east–west, and the green line runs under Avenida Paulista from Vila Mariana to the new stations at Sumaré and Vila Madalena, near Avenida Pompéia. The metrô operates daily 5 AM–midnight. Tickets are sold in stations and cost 80¢ one way. (You can get discounts on round-trip fares and when you buy 10 tickets at once; note that ticket sellers aren't required to change large bills.) You insert the ticket into the turnstile at the platform entrance, and it's returned to you only if there's unused fare on it. Transfers within the metrô system are free, and for bus–metrô trips (one bus only), you can buy a *bilhete integração* on buses or at metrô stations for $1.50.

BY TAXI
Most taxis in São Paulo are white. Owner-driven taxis are generally well maintained and reliable as are radio taxis. Fares start at $1.75 and 50¢ for each kilometer (½ mi) or 25¢ for every minute sitting in traffic. After 8 PM fares rise by 20%. You'll also pay a tax if the taxi leaves the city as is the case with trips to Cumbica Airport. Good radio-taxi companies include **Chame Taxi** (☏ 011/865–3033), **Ligue-Taxi** (☏ 011/262–2633), and **Paulista** (☏ 011/846–6555).

Contacts and Resources
BANKS AND CURRENCY EXCHANGE
Avenida Paulista is the home of many banks (generally open 10–4), including **Citibank** (⊠ Av. Paulista 1111, Jardins, ☏ 011/576–1190). For currency exchange services without any extra fees try **Action** (⊠ Guarulhos Airport, TPS2 arrival floor, ☏ 011/6445–4458; ⊠ Rua Melo Alves 357, Jardins, ☏ 011/3064–2910; and ⊠ Shopping Paulista, Rua 13 de Maio 1947, Paraíso, ☏ 011/288–4222). In Centro, you can exchange money at **Banco do Brasil** (⊠ Av. São João 32, ☏ 011/234–1646) and **Banespa** (⊠ Rua Duque de Caxias 200, ☏ 011/222–7722).

Several banks have automatic teller machines (ATMs) that accept international bank cards and dispense reais.

BUSINESS SERVICES

At press time, the **U.S. Commercial Center** (☎ 011/853–2811 for Miguel Pardoezela, Senior Commercial Officer), an arm of the U.S. Department of Commerce, was slated to open a state-of-the-art facility for American businesspeople. It will have fully equipped offices with secretarial support, a library, trade events organizers, meeting rooms, and computer and teleconferencing facilities.

CONSULATES

Australia (✉ Av. Tenente Negrão 140/121, 12th Floor, Itaim Bibi, ☎ 011/829–6281). **Canada** (✉ Av. Paulista 1106, 1st floor, Cerqueira César, ☎ 011/285–5099). **New Zealand** (✉ Rua Pais de Araújo 29, 12th floor, Jardim Europa, ☎ 011/820–5532). **United Kingdom** (✉ Av. Paulista 1938, 17th floor, Cerqueira César, ☎ 011/287–7722). **United States** (✉ Rua Padre João Manoel 933, Jardins, ☎ 011/881–6511).

EMERGENCIES

Ambulance: ☎ 192. **Fire:** ☎ 193. **Hospitals: Albert Einstein** (✉ Av. Albert Einstein 627, Morumbi, ☎ 011/845–1233), **Beneficência Portuguesa** (✉ Rua Maestro Cardim 769, Paraíso, ☎ 011/253–5022), and **Sírio Libanês** (✉ Rua. D. Adma Jafet 91, Bela Vista, ☎ 011/234–8877). **Pharmacies:** The three main pharmacies have more than 20 stores, each open 24 hours. Try: **Droga Raia** (✉ Rua Joaquim Nabuco 84, Brooklin, ☎ 011/240–0584), **Drogaria São Paulo** (✉ Av. Angélica 1465, Higienópolis, ☎ 011/3667–6291), and **Drogasil** (✉ Av. Brigadeiro Faria Lima 2726, Cidade Jardim, ☎ 011/212–6276). **Police (Military):** ☎ 190. **Tourist Police:** The **Delegacia de Turismo** (✉ Av. São Luís 115, Centro, ☎ 011/254–3561 or 011/214–0209) is open weekdays 8–8.

ENGLISH-LANGUAGE BOOKSTORES

Most Avenida Paulista newsstands sell major U.S. and European papers as well as magazines and paperbacks in English. **Livraria Cultura** has a large selection of English books of all types in its store at Conjunto Nacional (✉ Av. Paulista 2073/153, Cerqueira César, ☎ 011/285–4033). **Ática Shopping Cultural** (✉ Rua Pedroso de Morais 858, Pinheiros, ☎ 011/867–0022) sells many international books and periodicals. **Laselva** (✉ Shopping West Plaza, Av. Francisco Matarazzo, Água Branca, ☎ 011/864–0037) usually receives magazines from abroad earlier than other bookstores. **Saraiva**'s (✉ Shopping Eldorado, Av. Rebouças 3970, Pinheiros, ☎ 011/870–5999) megastore also has English-language titles.

HEALTH AND SAFETY

Don't drink tap water in São Paulo. Ask for juice and ice made with bottled water in restaurants and bars. Don't eat barbecued meats sold by street vendors; even those made in some bars are suspect. The city's air pollution might irritate your eyes, especially in July and August (dirty air is held in the city by thermal inversions), so pack eye drops. Stay alert and guard your belongings at all times, especially at major sights. Avoid wearing shorts, expensive running shoes, or flashy jewelry—all of which attract attention. Also beware of the local scam in which one person throws a dark liquid on you and another offers to help you clean up while the first *really* cleans up!

TELEPHONES, THE INTERNET, AND MAIL

Most phone booths operate using prepaid cards, but some still use tokens; both are sold at newsstands. Cards with 20 credits cost $1.17, and each credit allows you to talk for 3 minutes on local calls and 17 seconds on long-distance calls. You can choose your own long-distance company. After dialing 0, dial a two-digit company code (for example, 21 for Embratel or 23 for Bonari), followed by the country code and/or area code and number. For operator assisted (in English) international calls, dial 000111. To make a collect long-distance call (which will cost 40% more than normal calls), dial 9 + the area code and the number. São Paulo's area code is 11.

Internet access is available at many cybercafés (☞ Nightlife, *above*) around town. There's a branch of the **correio** (post office; ⊠ Praça do Correio, ☎ 011/831–5522) in Centro. International couriers include **DHL** (⊠ Rua da Consolação 2721, Jardins, ☎ 011/536–2500) and **FedEx** (⊠ Av. São Luís 187, Loja 43, Centro, ☎ 011/524–7788).

TOUR OPERATORS AND TRAVEL AGENTS

You can hire a bilingual guide through a travel agency or hotel concierge (about $15 an hour with a four-hour minimum). **Gol Tour Viagens e Turismo** (⊠ Av. São Luís 187, Basement, Loja 12, Centro, ☎ 011/256–2388) and **Opcional Tour and Guide Viagens e Turismo** (⊠ Av. Ipiranga 345, 14th floor, suite 1401, Centro, ☎ 011/259–1007) offer custom tours as well as car tours for small groups. A half-day city tour costs about $40 a person (group rate); a night tour—including a samba show, dinner, and drinks—costs around $100; and day trips to the beach cost $80–$90. The English-speaking staff at **Savoy** (⊠ Rua James Watt 142, suite 92, Itaim Bibi, ☎ 011/5507–2064 or 011/5507–2065) specializes in personalized tours.

VISITOR INFORMATION

The most helpful contact is the **São Paulo Convention and Visitors Bureau** (⊠ Rua Dom José de Barros 17, Centro, ☎ 011/255–4600). The sharp, business-minded director, Roberto Gheler, speaks English flawlessly and is extremely knowledgeable.

The branches of the city-operated **Anhembi Turismo e Eventos da Cidade de São Paulo** (⊠ Anhembi Convention Center, Av. Olavo Fontoura 1209, ☎ 011/267–0702; ⊠ Praça da República at Rua 7 de Abril, Centro, ☎ 011/231–2922; ⊠ Av. São Luís at Praça Dom José Gaspar, Centro, ☎ 011/257–3422); ⊠ Av. Paulista, across from MASP, Cerqueira César, ☎ 011/231–2922; ⊠ Av. Brigadeiro Faria Limain, in front of Shopping Center Iguatemi, Jardim Paulista, ☎ 011/211–1277) are open daily 9–6.

The bureaucracy-laden **Secretaria de Esportes e Turismo do Estado de São Paulo** (SEST; ⊠ Praça Antônio Prado 9, Centro, ☎ 011/239–5822), open weekdays 9–5:30, has maps and information about the city and state of São Paulo. SEST also has a booth at the arrivals terminal in Cumbica airport; it's open daily 9 AM–10 PM.

MINAS GERAIS

Updated by
Shane
Christensen

Brazil's central mountainous region is dominated by the state of Minas Gerais, a name (meaning "general mines") inspired by the area's great mineral wealth. In the 18th century, its vast precious-metal reserves made the state, and particularly the city of Ouro Prêto, the de facto capital of the Portuguese colony. That period of gold, diamond, and semiprecious stone trading is memorialized in the historic towns scattered across the mountains and remains a tremendous source of pride for the *mineiros* (inhabitants of the state).

Exploration of Minas Gerais began in the 17th century, when *bandeirantes* (bands of adventurers) from the coastal areas came in search of slaves and gold. Near the town of Vila Rica, they found a black stone

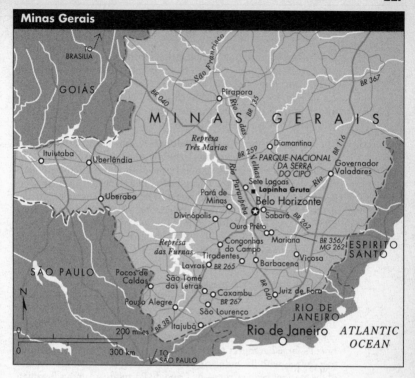

Minas Gerais

that was later verified to be gold (the coloring came from the iron oxide in the soil). Vila Rica thus came to be called Ouro Prêto (Black Gold), and at the beginning of the 18th century, Brazil's first gold rush began. Along with the fortune seekers came Jesuit priests, who were later exiled by the Portuguese (for fear that they would try to manipulate the mineral trade) and replaced by *ordens terceiros* ("third" or lay orders). By the middle of the century, the Gold Towns of Minas were gleaming with new churches built first in the baroque-rococo style of Europe and, later, in a baroque style unique to the region.

Minas was also blessed with a local artistic genius. The son of a Portuguese architect and a former slave, Antônio Francisco Lisboa was born in 1738 in what is today Ouro Prêto. Nicknamed Aleijadinho, "the little cripple," he was left deformed as an adult by an illness. Working in cedarwood and soapstone, Aleijadinho carved the passion of his beliefs in sculptures that grace churches throughout the state.

By the end of the 18th century, the gold began to run out, and Ouro Prêto's population and importance decreased—but only temporarily. Today, Minas is Brazil's second most industrialized state, after São Paulo. The iron that darkened the gold of Ouro Prêto remains an important source of state income, along with steel, coffee, and auto manufacturing. Although some of its once heavily wooded areas have been stripped bare—the heavy price of development—Minas still has diverse and amazingly pristine ecosystems, including Atlantic forests, rain forests, wetlands, and grasslands. The traffic that the mines brought here in the 17th century thrust Brazil into civilization, and now, well into the wake of the gold rush, a steady sense of progress and a compassion for the land remains.

Belo Horizonte

444 km (276 mi) north of Rio, 590 km (366 mi) northeast of São Paulo.

Brazil's first planned state capital, Belo Horizonte (often called the Garden City or just simply "Belo") has tree-lined streets and an intimate small-town atmosphere that belies its size. With a population of almost 2.4 million, it's Brazil's third-largest city. Although it has few tourist attractions, it's the gateway to the region's historic cities, and its citizens are warm, gracious, and helpful.

The well-maintained **Parque Municipal** is in the heart of the business district and close to several hotels. Its tree-lined walks, small lakes, and rustic bridges make it an example of the passion for orderliness that's characteristically mineiro. This same trait has helped make Belo Horizonte one of the cleanest and safest of Brazil's leading cities. Within the park is the **Palácio das Artes** (Palace of the Arts; ⊠ Av. Afonso Pena 1537, ☎ 031/237–7286), a cultural center with a theater; a library; art galleries; exhibition halls; and the Centro de Artesanato Mineiro, with such contemporary Minas handicrafts as carvings of wood and soapstone, pottery, and tapestries—all for sale. Admission is free.

Ironically, though most people come to Belo for the nearby historic region, one of the city's principal attractions is the Pampulha neighborhood, famed for its examples of modern Brazilian architecture. Foremost among these is the **Capela de São Francisco** (Chapel of Saint Francis), completed in 1943 and considered one of the most important works of Brazil's famed architect Oscar Niemeyer. Inside the small but distinctive chapel, with its undulating roof, are frescoes—of St. Francis and of the Stations of the Cross—by Cândido Portinari, a famous Brazilian modernist. To reach the chapel, take a taxi or Bus 2004 (it goes north on Avenida Presidente Antônio Carlos). The chapel is on the edge of an artificial lake a half-hour from downtown; the drive to it is lovely. ⊠ *Av. Otacílio Negrão de Lima, Km 12, Pampulha,* ☎ *031/491–2319.* ⊠ *Admission.* ☉ *Weekdays 8:30–noon and 1:30–6, weekends 9–6.*

Dining

$$$$ ✕ **Vecchio Sogno.** What is widely considered Belo Horizonte's best Ital-
★ ian restaurant attracts a well-heeled clientele. Tuxedo-clad waiters serve selections from the extensive wine list as well as steak, seafood, and pasta dishes. Consider the grilled fillet of lamb with saffron risotto in a mushroom and garlic sauce; the gnocchi *di mare,* made with spinach and potatoes and served with a white-clam and scallop sauce; or the *badejo,* a local white fish baked and dressed in a seafood sauce. Reservations are highly recommended. ⊠ *Rua Martim de Carvalho 75, Santo Agostinho,* ☎ *031/292–5251 or 031/290–7585. AE, DC, MC, V. No lunch Sat. No dinner Sun.*

$$$ ✕ **Amici Miei.** This casual Italian eatery is popular with Brazilians cel-
★ ebrating the end of the workday. The restaurant is often packed both inside and on the large outdoor patio; you may need to wait a minute for the staff to find you a table. Start with the *champignon Recheado* (a large mushroom stuffed with shrimp and prosciutto), followed by *tournedo Amici Miei* (filet mignon wrapped in bacon and marinated in garlic and olive oil). ⊠ *Rua Tome de Souza 1331, Centro,* ☎ *031/ 282–4992. DC, MC, V.*

$$$ ✕ **Chalezinho.** There's only one reason to come here: romance. The
★ dimly lit chalet, with its elegant piano music (accompanied by the occasional saxophone), is a magical retreat in the hills above town. The specialty is fondue; the filet mignon cooked in a bowl of sizzling oil and paired with any one of eight delicious sauces is a treat. Afterward, order a chocolate fondue, which comes with a mouth-watering selec-

tion of fruits waiting to be dipped. When you finish, step outside to the Praça dos Amores (Lovers' Plaza) for a kiss under the moonlit sky. ⊠ *Alameda da Serra 18, Vale do Soreno–Nova Lima,* ☎ *031/286–3155. AE, DC, MC, V. No lunch.*

$$ ✕ **Casa dos Contos.** The menu at this gathering place for local journalists, artists, and intellectuals is unpretentious and varied, ranging from fish and pasta to comida mineira. In keeping with its bohemian clientele, Casa dos Contos serves well past midnight. ⊠ *Rua Rio Grande do Norte 1065, Funcionários,* ☎ *031/222–1070. AE, DC, MC, V.*

$$ ✕ **Restaurante Top Beer.** This trendy restaurant-bar makes an ideal launching pad for your evening. The large outdoor patio offers great people-watching, as students and executives alike plan their night out while sipping caipirinhas. The inside dining room is an inviting tropical enclave, with fountains and trees surrounding the tables. The pasta dishes and grilled steaks are commendable. ⊠ *Rua Tomé de Souza 1121, Savassi,* ☎ *031/221–1116. AE, DC, MC, V.*

$ ✕ **Chico Mineiro.** Dining Minas Gerais–style means ample portions of
★ such hearty dishes as tutu a mineira, the local equivalent of meat and potatoes. Nowhere is it better prepared than at this traditional restaurant in the Savassi neighborhood, home to Belo's liveliest night spots. ⊠ *Rua Alagoas 626, Savassi,* ☎ *031/261–3237. AE, DC, MC, V.*

Lodging

$$$$ ⊞ **Ouro Minas Palace Hotel.** Though not centrally located, this hotel
★ truly deserves a star. Rooms are comfortably decorated and appealing, with large beds and well-appointed bathrooms; minibars and modem hook-ups are standard. The hotel offers numerous amenities uncommon in Belo Horizonte: a pool with waterfalls, a fitness center, tennis courts, and a multilingual staff. ⊠ *Av. Christiano Machado 4001, Ipiranga, 31910-810,* ☎ *031/429–4001,* ℻ *031/429–4002. 343 rooms, 44 suites. Restaurant, bar, café, in-room modem lines, minibars, pool, massage, Turkish bath, 2 tennis courts, health club, business services, car rental. AE, DC, MC, V.*

$$$ ⊞ **Hotel Wimbledon.** An elegant yet warm atmosphere and a central
★ location are two of this hotel's draws. Guest rooms are well decorated, with polished hardwood floors, local artwork, and modern bathrooms; luxury rooms have Jacuzzis. Attentive service makes this hotel feel more like a bed-and-breakfast. There's a rooftop pool and bar—the perfect spot for an afternoon drink. ⊠ *Av. Afonso Pena 772, Centro 30130-002,* ☎ *031/222–6160,* ℻ *031/222–6510. 69 rooms, 1 suite. Restaurant, bar, pool, sauna. AE, DC, MC, V.*

$$$ ⊞ **Merit Plaza.** Located downtown, this hotel offers excellent value, particularly for business travelers in need of modern amenities and a convenient location. Granite covers the contemporary atrium lobby, and guest rooms have sound-proof walls, large beds, well-appointed bathrooms, and phones equipped for computer and fax use. ⊠ *Rua dos Tamoios 341, Centro 30130-002,* ☎ *031/201–9000,* ℻ *031/271–5700. 115 rooms, 2 suites. Restaurant, bar, café, in-room modem lines, business services. AE, DC, MC, V.*

$$$ ⊞ **Othon Palace.** The Othon has the best location of any hotel in Belo Horizonte. Although aging (it opened in 1978), renovations are ongoing, and the level of service remains high. Rooms provide little special character, but are comfortable and enjoy spectacular city views, including the tree-lined Parque Municipal. The rooftop pool and bar is the best in town, and the on-site Restaurante Verandão is excellent. The weekend sees the chef's innovative "soapstone barbecue," where you choose thinly sliced meats to grill on a hot soapstone. Live Brazilian music accompanies dinner nightly. ⊠ *Av. Afonso Pena 1050, Centro 30130-002,* ☎ *031/273–3844,* ℻ *031/212–2318. 266 rooms, 19* *suites. Restaurant, bar, pool, massage, sauna, tennis court, exercise room, concierge floor, business services, meeting rooms. AE, DC, MC, V.*

$$ ☷ **Grandville Hotel.** The lobby of this centrally located hotel, one of the city's older establishments, is often crowded with conventioneers. Rooms are comfortable, if a bit dark; many, however, have the same view of the city and surrounding mountains that you'll find from the small rooftop pool and bar. ⊠ *Rua Espírito Santo 901, Centro 30160-031,* ☎ *0800/31–1188,* 𝔽𝔸𝕏 *031/248–1100. 247 rooms, 8 suites. Restaurant, bar, pool, sauna, exercise room, business services, meeting rooms. AE, DC, MC, V.*

$ ☷ **Palmeiras da Liberdade.** Although it's in the chic Savassi neighborhood, this comfortable hotel is very affordable. Rooms count cable TV and direct-dial phones among their many amenities, all of which make this place a good bet if you lack deep pockets. ⊠ *Rua Sergipe 893, Savassi 30130–171,* ☎ 𝔽𝔸𝕏 *031/261–7422. 62 rooms. Restaurant, bar, air-conditioning, minibars, refrigerators. AE, DC, MC, V.*

Nightlife

For some of Brazil's best cachaças and one of the city's best views, try **Alambique** (⊠ Av. Raja Gabaglia 3200, Chalé 1D, São Bento, ☎ 031/296–7188). The oh-so-chic **Café** (⊠ Rua Cláudio Manoel 583, Funcionários, ☎ 031/261–6019) is open late every night but Monday (when it's closed completely). A traditional bar with live popular Brazilian music is the **Cervejaria Brasil** (⊠ Rua Aimorés 78, Savassi, ☎ 031/225–1099). A popular bar for "GLS" (gays, lesbians, and sympathizers) is **Excess** (⊠ Rua Antonio de Albuquerque 729, Savassi, ☎ 031/227–5133).

Outdoor Activities and Sports

The **Estádio Mineirão** (⊠ Av. Antônio Abrão Carão 1001, Pampulha, ☎ 031/441–6133) is Brazil's third-largest stadium and the home field for Belo's two professional *futebol* (soccer) teams: Atletico Mineiro and Cruzeiro.

Nossa Tropa (☎ 031/9972–8505, 031/9952–7152, or 031/583–0005) arranges day treks on horseback into the mountains surrounding Belo. For amateur spelunkers, the mountains of Minas are replete with caves to be explored, though they must be seen with a guided tour (☞ Tour Operators and Travel Agents in Minas Gerais A to Z, *below*). The **Lapinha Gruta** (☎ 031/681–1958) is only 36 km (22 mi) north of Belo, near the city of Lagoa Santa, on the road leading from Confins airport.

Shopping

On Saturday morning, Avenida Bernardo Monteiro (between Rua Brasil and Rua Otoni) is the site of an **antiques fair and food market,** offering a taste of mineiro cuisine. On Sunday morning, head for the large (nearly 3,000 vendors) **arts-and-crafts fair** in front of the Othon Palace hotel on Avenida Afonso Pena.

Amsterdam Sauer (⊠ Av. Afonso Pena 1050, Centro, ☎ 031/273–3844) is a good place to begin your search for jewelry. **Arte Sacra Antiguidades** (⊠ Rua Alagoas 785, Savassi, ☎ 031/261–7256) offers a fine selection of Minas antiques. The centrally located **Bahia Shopping** (⊠ Rua de Bahia 1022, Centro, ☎ 031/201–7966) is a good place to shop for clothing. Many shops sell designer togs for men and women in Belo Horizonte's most exclusive mall, **BH Shopping** (⊠ BR 040, Belvedere, ☎ 0800/31–9001).

Brasarts (⊠ Rua Curitiba 2325, Lourdes, ☎ 031/291–5220) has a good selection of handicrafts. The **Centro de Artesenato Mineiro** (⊠ Av. Afonso Pena 1537, Parque Municipal, ☎ 031/222–2400), in the Palácio das Artes, offers a wide range of regional crafts.

The **Gem Center** (✉ Av. Afonso Pena 1901, 5th Floor, Centro, ☎ 031/222–8189) is another good bet for jewelry. **H. Stern** (✉ BH Shopping Center, Loja 105–106, BR 040, Belvedere, ☎ 031/286–1568) is one of Brazil's leading names for gems. **Raymundo Vianna** (✉ BH Shopping Center, BR 040, Belvedere, ☎ 031/286–6635; ✉ Rua Bernardo Guimarães 2412, ☎ 031/292–2655) has a fine reputation.

Ouro Prêto

97 km (60 mi) southeast of Belo Horizonte.

The former gold-rush capital is the best place to see the legendary Aleijadinho's artistry. Now a lively university town, it has been preserved as a national monument and a World Heritage Site. The surrounding mountains, the geometric rows of whitewashed buildings, the cobblestone streets and red-tile roofs that climb the hillsides, and the morning mist and evening fog—all give Ouro Prêto an evocative air, as if at any moment it could be transported back three centuries. Nevertheless, a vibrant student population ensures plenty of modern-day activity, and there are many lodging, dining, and shopping options.

In its heyday, Ouro Prêto was one of Brazil's most progressive cities and the birthplace of the colony's first stirrings of independence. A movement called the Inconfidência Mineira was organized to overthrow the Portuguese rulers and establish an independent Brazilian republic. It was to have been led by a resident of Ouro Prêto, Joaquim José da Silva Xavier, a dentist known as Tiradentes (Tooth Puller). But the Minas rebellion never got off the ground. In 1789, word of Tiradentes's intentions reached the capital of Rio de Janeiro; he was hanged, drawn, and quartered, and his followers were either imprisoned or exiled.

Exploring Ouro Prêto

Ouro Prêto has several museums as well as 13 colonial *igrejas* (churches), which are highly representative of mineiro baroque architecture. All the town's sights are within easy walking distance of the central square, Praça Tiradentes, which teems with gossiping students, eager merchants, and curious visitors. From here, the longest walk you'll make takes about 15 minutes. Note that many museums and churches are closed on Monday.

A GOOD WALK

Begin at Praça Tiradentes. Two blocks east stands the distinctive twin-tower **Igreja de São Francisco de Assis.** Two blocks farther east is the **Igreja de Nossa Senhora da Conceição** and its small Aleijadinho museum. From here, head east on Rua da Conceição, which becomes Rua Santa Efigênia to the **Igreja de Santa Efigênia.** Retrace your steps to Praça Tiradentes, and visit the **Museu do Oratório** and its neighboring **Museu da Inconfidência.** Walk north across the plaza to **Museu da Mineralogia e das Pedras,** inside the Escola de Minas.

West of Praça Tiradentes and off Rua Brigadeiro Musqueira is the **Teatro Municipal,** once an opera house. Next door is the **Igreja de Nossa Senhora do Carmo,** with major works by Aleijadinho and Ataíde. Ouro Prêto's original mint, the **Casa dos Contos,** is a short distance northwest on Rua São José. Continuing south on the same street, which becomes Rua Rondolfo Bretas, you'll come to the **Igreja de Nossa Senhora do Pilar** with its rich baroque interior. From here head northwest along Rua Rondolfo Bretas followed by Rua Dr. Getúlio Vargas to the less-ornate but equally intriguing **Igreja de Nossa Senhora do Rosário dos Pretos.**

TIMING

This is an all-day, wear-comfortable-shoes tour. Start out early as some of the churches are only open in the morning. Unless you're an ecclesiastic, plan to spend about 20 minutes in each church, and at least 30–45 minutes in each museum.

SIGHTS TO SEE

Casa dos Contos. The colonial coinage house contains the foundry used to mint the coins of the gold-rush period as well as examples of coins and period furniture. The museum building is considered among the best examples of Brazilian colonial architecture. ⊠ *Rua São José 12,* ☎ *031/ 551–1444.* ☒ *Admission.* ☉ *Tues.–Sat. 12:30–5:30, Sun. 8:30–1:30.*

Igreja de Nossa Senhora do Carmo. Completed in 1772, the impressive Our Lady of Carmel Church contains major works by Aleijadinho and Ataíde. It was originally designed by Aleijadinho's father, himself an architect, but was later modified by the son, who added more baroque elements, including the characteristic soapstone sculptures of angels above the entrance. ⊠ *Praça Tiradentes s/n,* ☎ *031/551–1209.* ☒ *Admission.* ☉ *Tues. and Thurs.–Sun. 1:30–5.*

Igreja de Nossa Senhora da Conceição. The lavishly gilded Our Lady of the Conception Church, completed in 1760, contains the tomb of Aleijadinho as well as a small museum dedicated to the artist. ⊠ *Praça Antônio Dias s/n,* ☎ *031/551–3282.* ☒ *Admission.* ☉ *Tues.–Sun. 8– 11:30 and 1–5.*

Igreja de Nossa Senhora do Pilar. Built around 1711 on the site of an earlier chapel, this is the most richly decorated of Ouro Prêto's churches and one of Brazil's best examples of baroque religious architecture. It's said that 400 pounds of gold leaf were used to cover the interior. ⊠ *Rua Brigador Mosqueira Castilho Barbosa s/n,* ☎ *031/551–4735.* ☒ *Admission.* ☉ *Tues.–Sun. noon–4:30.*

Igreja de Nossa Senhora do Rosário dos Pretos. One of the smaller but more intriguing churches, Our Lady of the Rosary of the Blacks was built by slaves, some of whom bought their freedom with the gold they found in Ouro Prêto. According to legend, the church's interior is bare because the slaves ran out of gold after erecting the baroque building. ⊠ *Largo do Rosário s/n,* ☎ *031/551–1209.* ☒ *Admission.* ☉ *Tues.–Sun. noon–4:30.*

Igreja de Santa Efigênia. This interesting slave church is on a hill east of Praça Tiradentes. Construction lasted 60 years (1730–90) and was funded by Chico-Rei. (This African ruler was captured during Brazil's gold rush and sold to a mine owner in Minas Gerais. Chico eventually earned enough money to buy his freedom—in the days before the Portuguese prohibited such acts—and became a hero among slaves throughout the land.) The clocks on the facade are the city's oldest, and the interior contains cedar sculptures by Francisco Xavier de Brito, Aleijadinho's teacher. ⊠ *Just off Rua de Santa Efigênia,* ☎ *031/551– 5047.* ☒ *Admission.* ☉ *Tues.–Sun. 8–noon.*

★ **Igreja de São Francisco de Assis.** Considered Aleijadinho's masterpiece, this church was begun in 1766 by the Franciscan Third Order and not completed until 1810. In addition to designing the structure, Aleijadinho was responsible for the wood and soapstone sculptures on the portal, high altar, side altars, pulpits, and crossing arch. The panel on the nave ceiling representing the Virgin's glorification was painted by Ataíde. Cherubic faces, garlands of tropical fruits, and allegorical characters are carved into the main altar, and are still covered with their original paint. ⊠ *Largo de Coimbra s/n,* ☎ *031/551–3282.* 🖾 *Admission.* ◷ *Tues.–Sun. 8–11:30, 1:30–4:45.*

★ **Museu da Inconfidência.** A former 18th-century prison as well as the one-time city hall, this museum commemorates the failed Inconfidência Mineira rebellion with many artifacts. Among the displays are furniture, clothing, slaves' manacles, firearms, books, and gravestones, as well as works by Aleijadinho and Ataíde. The museum also holds the remains of the unlucky revolutionaries. ⊠ *Praça Tiradentes 139,* ☎ *031/551–1121.* 🖾 *Admission.* ◷ *Tues.–Sun. noon–5.*

★ **Museu da Mineralogia e das Pedras.** Housed opposite the Museu da Inconfidência in the former governor's palace and inside the current Escola de Minas (School of Mines), the Museum of Minerals and Rocks contains an excellent collection of precious gems (including diamonds), gold, and crystals. The minerals have been organized according to their rarity, color, and crystallization. ⊠ *Praça Tiradentes 20,* ☎ *031/559–1530 or 031/559–1531.* 🖾 *Admission.* ◷ *Weekdays noon–4:45, weekends 9–1.*

Museu do Oratório. This museum established in the old house of the St. Carmel Novitiate celebrates sacred art from the 18th and 19th centuries. Some of the oratories, which reflect ideas of religious beauty from the period, have been displayed at the Louvre. ⊠ *Rua Costa Senna and Rua Antônio Pereira,* ☎ *031/551–5369.* 🖾 *Admission.* ◷ *Daily 9:30–11:50, 1:30–5:30.*

Teatro Municipal. The former opera house, built between 1746 and 1769, still presents shows and plays, making it Latin America's oldest municipal theater still in operation. There's no regular schedule for performances, however; check with the Associação de Guias de Turismo (☞ Visitor Information *in* Minas Gerais A to Z, *below*) for information on events. ⊠ *Rua Brigadeiro Mosqueira s/n,* ☎ *031/551–1544, ext. 224.* 🖾 *Admission.* ◷ *Daily 1–6.*

Dining

$$$ ✕ **Casa do Ouvidor.** Atop a jewelry store in the heart of the historic
★ district, this popular restaurant has garnered several awards for such regional dishes as tutu a mineira, feijão tropeiro, and frango com quiabo. Portions are huge, so come with an empty stomach, and be prepared for a noisy, ever-crowded dining room. ⊠ *Rua Conde de Bobadela 42,* ☎ *031/551–2141. AE, DC, MC, V.*

$$ ✕ **Casa Grande.** Here you can dine with a view of the 18th-century buildings that line Praça Tiradentes. Among the regional dishes are tutu a mineira, frango ao molho pardo, and, for dessert, *dôce de leite com queijo* (fresh white cheese with caramelized milk). ⊠ *Praça Tiradentes 84,* ☎ *031/551–2976. No credit cards.*

$ ✕ **Café Geraes.** This cozy, bi-level café is at the center of Ouro Prêto's
★ artistic and intellectual life. Students sip wine and feast on delicious sandwiches, soups, and other snacks. The pastries and the coffees are equally appealing. ⊠ *Rua Direita 122,* ☎ *031/551–0128 or 031/551–1405. DC, MC.*

$ ✕ **Chafariz.** Regional cuisine is served buffet-style in this informal
★ eatery near the Casa dos Contos. The small, colorful dining room has hardwood floors, wood-beam ceilings, and wood tables draped with blue, green, or white tablecloths. ⊠ *Rua São José 167,* ☎ *031/551–0128. AE, DC, MC.*

Lodging

$$$$ 🏠 **Pousada do Mondego.** This small, intimate inn is next to the Igreja
★ de São Francisco de Assis in a house that dates from 1747. You'll find period furnishings, a colonial ambience, and highly personalized ser-

vice. The hotel also offers two-hour city tours in a minibus from the 1930s, and it has its own antiques store and art gallery. ⊠ *Largo de Coimbra 38, 35400,* ☎ *031/551–2040 or 021/287–3122 ext. 601 (reservations in Rio),* FAX *031/551–3094. 23 rooms. Restaurant, bar, travel services. AE, DC, MC, V.*

$$$$ 🏨 **Solar Nossa Senhora do Rosário.** Superior service and the world-
★ class Le Coq d'Or restaurant are among this hotel's draws. The beau-
tiful 19th-century building feels like a bed-and-breakfast, with elegant yet comfortable decor, quiet floors, and charming guest rooms. When you're not exploring the town, have a swim in the luxurious hilltop pool or stop by the atrium for afternoon tea. The hotel even has its own section of an original mine, discovered during renovations. ⊠ *Rua Dr. Getúlio Vargas 270, 35400,* ☎ *031/551–5200,* FAX *031/551–4288. 28 rooms, 9 suites. Restaurant, bar, pool, sauna, business services, convention center. AE, DC, MC, V.*

$$$ 🏨 **Grande Hotel.** As its name suggests, the Grande is Ouro Prêto's largest hotel (with 35 rooms, it's immense by local standards). It's also the town's premier modernist structure—a curving two-story building on concrete pillars designed by world-acclaimed architect Oscar Niemeyer. Cultural purists and aesthetes, however, consider it an eyesore. ⊠ *Rua Senador Rocha Lagoa 164, 35400,* ☎ FAX *031/551–1488. 35 rooms. Restaurant, bar. AE, DC, MC, V.*

$$$ 🏨 **Luxor Ouro Prêto.** With stone walls that date back 200 years, beau-
tiful wood floors, and gracious antique furnishings, this hotel has the feeling of a 19th-century lodge. The lobby leads to a small, romantic restaurant: typical "mineira" cooking is served to the lucky few tables. Guest rooms enjoy views of the city, and some have original paintings by famous Minas artist Chanina. ⊠ *Rua Dr. Alfredo Baeta 16, 35400,* ☎ FAX *031/551–2244. 16 rooms. Restaurant, bar. AE, DC, MC, V.*

$–$$ 🏨 **Pousada Ouro Prêto.** Popular with backpackers, this pousada has
★ small rooms that are individually decorated with local art. Its open-
air halls have flowers and paintings of Ouro Prêto; the terrace in front of the lobby offers a peaceful view of the city center. The English-speaking staff will do laundry for free. ⊠ *Largo Musicista José dos Anjos Costa 72, 35400,* ☎ FAX *031/551–3081. No credit cards.*

$ 🏨 **Colonial.** Close to the main square, this is a good example of the small, no-frills inns found in most of the historic cities. What you'll get is a very basic, clean room for a low price. Room 1 has a loft and can sleep up to five people. ⊠ *Rua Camilo Veloso 26, 35400,* ☎ *031/ 551–3133,* FAX *031/551–3361. 18 rooms. AE, DC, MC, V.*

Nightlife and the Arts

Even if the food and the barman at **Acoso 85** (⊠ Largo do Rosário, ☎ 031/551–2397) don't impress you, the incredibly high ceilings, stone walls, and medieval ambience will. It's popular with the late-night crowd. **Bardobeco** (⊠ Trv. do Arieira 15, ☎ no phone) is the city's best *cachaçaria,* with more than 40 brands of cachaça, including the owner's own Milagre de Minas. **Fundação das Artes de Ouro Prêto** (FAOP; ⊠ Rua Dr. Getúlio Vargas 185, ☎ 031/551–2014), the local arts foundation, hosts various art and photographic exhibitions throughout the year.

Shopping

At the daily **handicrafts fair,** in front of the Igreja de São Francisco de Assis, vendors sell soapstone and wood carvings, paintings, and other items. The jeweler **Amsterdam Sauer** (☎ 031/551–3383) has a branch in Praça Tiradentes. For authentic Minas antiques as well as handicrafts, visit **Bureau d'Art** (⊠ Largo do Rosário 41). One of the best places in Brazil to purchase gems, especially the rare and beautiful im-
perial topaz, is **Ita Gemas** (⊠ Rua Conde de Bobadela 139, ☎ 031/

551–4895). **Seleiro** (✉ Rua Direita 191, ☏ 031/551–1774) has a good selection of traditional crafts. An excellent store for authenticated gems—including imperial topaz, emeralds, and tourmalines—is **Raymundo Vianna** (✉ Rua Conde de Bobadela 48, ☏ 031/551–2487).

Mariana

11 km (7 mi) east of Ouro Prêto.

The oldest city in Minas Gerais (founded in 1696) is also the birthplace of Aleijadinho's favorite painter, Manuel da Costa Ataíde. Mariana, like Ouro Prêto, has preserved much of the appearance of an 18th-century gold-mining town. Its three principal churches all showcase examples of the art of Ataíde, who intertwined sensual romanticism with religious themes. The faces of his saints and other figures often have mulatto features, reflecting the composition of the area's population at the time. Today, Mariana is most visited for the weekly organ concerts at its cathedral.

The **Catedral Basílica da Sé,** completed in 1760, contains paintings by Ataíde, although it's best known for its 1701 German organ, transported by mule from Rio de Janeiro in 1720. This unique instrument—there are only two of its kind in the world—was a gift from Dom João V. Concerts take place Friday at 11 AM and Sunday at 12:15 PM. ✉ *Praça Cláudio Manoel s/n,* ☏ *031/557–1237.* ▨ *Admission.* ☉ *Tues.– Sun. 8–noon and 2–6:30.*

Behind the cathedral is the **Museu Arquidiocesano,** which claims to have the largest collection of baroque painting and sculpture in the state, including the wood and soapstone works by Aleijadinho and paintings by Ataíde. ✉ *Rua Frei Durão 49,* ☏ *031/557–1237.* ▨ *Admission.* ☉ *Tues.–Sun. noon–1.*

Although the 1793 **Igreja de São Francisco de Assis** (Church of St. Francis) features soapstone pulpits and altars by Aleijadinho, its most impressive works are the sacristy's ceiling panels, which were painted by Ataíde. They depict, in somber tones, the life and death of St. Francis and are considered by many to be the artist's masterpiece. Sadly, however, they've been damaged by termites and water. ✉ *Praça João Pinheiro,* ☏ *no phone.* ▨ *Admission.* ☉ *Daily 8–noon and 1–5.*

The **Igreja da Nossa Senhora do Carmo** (Our Lady of Carmel Church), with works by Ataíde and Aleijadinho, is noteworthy for its impressive facade and sculpted soapstone designs. Ataíde is buried at the rear of the church. ✉ *Praça João Pinheiro,* ☏ *031/557–1635.* ▨ *Admission.* ☉ *Daily 8–5.*

Congonhas do Campo

50 km (31 mi) west of Mariana; 94 km (58 mi) south of Belo Horizonte.

To see Aleijadinho's crowning effort, head to the small Gold Town of Congonhas do Campo. Dominating Congonhas is the hilltop pilgrimage church, **Igreja Bom Jesus do Matosinho,** built in 1757 and the focus of great processions during Holy Week. At the churchyard entrance, you'll see Aleijadinho's 12 life-size Old Testament prophets carved in soapstone, a towering achievement and one of the greatest works of art anywhere from the baroque period. The prophets appear caught in movement, and every facial expression seems marked with the sculptor's own pain during his final years. Leading up to the church on the sloping hillside are 6 chapels, each containing a scene from the Stations of the Cross. The 66 figures in this remarkable procession were carved in cedar by Aleijadinho and painted by Ataíde. ⊠ *Praça da Basílica s/n,* ☎ *031/731–1590.* 🎫 *Admission.* ⊗ *Tues.–Sun. 10–5.*

Tiradentes

129 km (80 mi) south of Congonhas do Campo.

Probably the best historic city to visit after Ouro Prêto, Tiradentes was the birthplace of a martyr who gave it its name (it was formerly called São José del Rei) and retains much of its 18th century charm. Life in this tiny village—nine streets with eight churches set against the backdrop of the Serra de São José—moves slowly. This quality attracts wealthy residents of Belo Horizonte, Rio, and São Paulo, who have sparked a local real estate boom by buying up 18th-century properties as weekend getaways.

Besides the excellent selection of handicrafts—some 20 shops line Rua Direita in the town center—the principal attraction is the **Igreja de Santo Antônio.** Built in 1710, it contains extremely well-preserved, gilded carvings of saints, cherubs, and biblical scenes. The church's soapstone frontispiece—a celebration of baroque architecture—was sculpted by Aleijadinho. ⊠ *Rua Padre Toledo,* ☎ *no phone.* 🎫 *Admission.* ⊗ *Daily 9–noon and 2–5.*

Dining and Lodging

$$ ✕ **Estalagem.** The Estalagem draws rave reviews for its feijão tropeiro
★   and frango ao molho pardo. Although it's small and cozy, its atmosphere is elegant; light music and quiet, attentive service make for a relaxing meal. ⊠ *Rua Gabriel Passos 280,* ☎ *032/355–1144. No credit cards. Closed Mon.*

$$ ✕ **Teatro da Villa.** On the site of an old Greek-style amphitheater, this restaurant offers dinner theater, Tiradentes' style. The menu features international fare, including meat and fish dishes. Most of the performances involve local folk music and dance. ⊠ *Rua do Sol 157,* ☎ *no phone. No credit cards. Closed weekdays.*

$–$$ ✕ **Canto do Chafariz.** This center of regional cuisine is rated tops for its tutu. ⊠ *Largo do Chafariz 37,* ☎ *032/355–1377. Reservations not accepted. No credit cards. Closed Mon.*

$$$$ 🏨 **Solar da Ponte.** In every respect—from the stunning antiques to the
★   comfortable beds to the elegant place settings—this inn is a faithful example of regional style. Breakfast and afternoon tea (included in the rate) are served in the dining room, overlooking well-tended gardens. With advance notice, the English owner and his Brazilian wife can arrange historical, botanical, and ecological tours on foot or horseback. ⊠ *Praça das Mercês s/n 36325,* ☎ *032/355–1255 or 021/287–1592 (reservations in Rio),* 🖷 *032/355–1201. 12 rooms. Bar, dining room, pool, sauna. MC, V.*

$$$ 🏨 **Pousada Alforria.** Alforria enjoys a quiet, peaceful location with a
★   fabulous view of the São José mountains. The light-filled lobby—with its stone floors, high ceilings, and beautiful Brazilian artwork (some of it from Bahia)—leads to a charming breakfast space and courtyard. Rooms have considerable natural light and are individually decorated; mattresses are firm, and bathrooms modern. ⊠ *Rua Custódio Gomes 286, 36325,* ☎ 🖷 *032/355–1536. 9 rooms. Pool. No credit cards.*

$$ 🏨 **Pousada Três Portas.** This pousada is in an adapted colonial house—with hardwood floors and locally made furniture and artwork—in the historic center of Tiradentes. The owner runs a small puppet theater adjacent to the breakfast room. Rooms are clean and modern. ⊠ *Rua Direita 280A, 36325,* ☎ *032/355–1444,* 🖷 *032/355–1184. 8 rooms, 1 suite. Pool, steam room. No credit cards.*

Shopping

Artstones (⊠ Rua Ministro Gabriel Passos 22, ☎ 032/464–4595) carries imperial topaz, emeralds, quartz, and tourmaline, and has some finished jewelry. **Atelier Fernando Pitta** (⊠ Beco da Chácara s/n, ☎ 032/355–1475) is a gallery that's set up like Michelangelo's studio, with wild, abstract variations on religious themes. **Atelier José Damas** (⊠ Rua do Chafariz 130, ☎ 032/9961–0735) belongs to Tiradentes's most famous artist. He paints local scenes—such as a train through the mountains or a dusty afternoon street—on canvas and on stones.

Minas Gerais A to Z

Arriving and Departing

BY AIRPLANE

Belo Horizonte is the gateway to Minas Gerais. **Aeroporto Internacional Tancredo Neves** (☎ 031/689–2700)—also known as Aeroporto Confins—is 39 km (24 mi) north of Belo Horizonte and serves domestic and international flights. Taxis from Confins to downtown cost about $40 and take roughly a half hour. There are also *executivo* (air-conditioned) buses that leave every 45 minutes and cost $11. **Aeroporto Pampulha** (☎ 031/490–2001) is 9 km (5½ mi) northwest of downtown and serves domestic flights. Taxis from here to downtown cost about $10.

Carriers serving the region include **American Airlines** (☎ 0800/12–4001), **TAM** (☎ 031/490–5500), **Transbrasil** (☎ 031/273–6722, 031/689–2480, or 0800/15–1151), **Varig** (☎ 031/339–6000), and **VASP** (☎ 0800/99–8277 or 031/689–5360).

BY BUS

Frequent buses (either air-conditioned executivos or warmer, less comfortable, yet cheaper, coaches) connect Belo Horizonte with Rio ($25–$40; 7 hrs), São Paulo ($25–$50; 9 hrs), and Brasília ($25–$40; 12 hrs). Advance tickets are recommended at holiday times. All buses arrive at and depart from (punctually) the **Rodoviário** (⊠ Av. Afonso Pena at Av. do Contorno, Belo Horizonte, ☎ 031/201–8111 or 031/271–3000).

Bus companies include **Cometa** (☎ 031/201–5611), **Gontijo** (☎ 031/201–6130), **Itapemirim** (☎ 031/271–1027), **Penha** (☎ 031/271–5621), and **Útil** (☎ 031/201–7744).

BY CAR

BR 040 connects Belo Horizonte with Rio (444 km/276 mi) to the southeast and Brasília (741 km/460 mi) to the northwest; BR 381 links the city with São Paulo (586 km/364 mi). The roads are in good condition, although exits aren't always clearly marked.

Getting Around

BY BUS

Belo Horizonte's municipal bus system is safe and runs efficiently, although buses are crowded during rush hour (7–9 and 5–7). Buses are clearly numbered, and you can get route information in the *Guia do Ônibus,* a guide that's available in bookstores. All city buses have a chord to pull or a button to press to request a stop. Fares depend on the distance traveled, but are always less than $1.

Buses are a fabulous way to travel throughout the region. Coaches regularly travel between Belo Horizonte and Ouro Prêto ($7; 2–3 hrs) as well as other historic cities. Companies include **Pássaro Verde** (☎ 031/272–1811) and **Sandra** (☎ 031/201–2927).

BY CAR

Belo Horizonte's rush-hour traffic can be heavy, and parking can be difficult (for on-street parking you need to buy a sticker at a newsstand or bookshop). Narrow cobblestone streets inside the historic cities, however, weren't designed for cars, and some alleys can make for a tight squeeze. Parking isn't a problem in the smaller communities, except during holidays.

The historical cities are, for the most part, connected by fairly decent minor routes to one of the region's main highways. From Belo you can take BR 040 south and BR 356 (it becomes MG 262) east to Ouro Prêto and beyond to Mariana. To reach Tiradentes from Belo, take BR 040 south (Congonhas do Campo is on this route) and then BR 265 west.

Rental cars cost between $20 and $50 per day, depending on whether or not mileage is included. Agencies include **Localiza** (⊠ Aeroporto Confins, Belo Horizonte, ☎ 031/689–2070; ⊠ Rua Bernardo Monteiro 1567, Belo Horizonte, ☎ 0800/99–2000 or 031/247–7957) and **Lokamig** (⊠ Aeroporto Confins, Belo Horizonte, ☎ 031/689–2020; ⊠ Av. Contorno 8639, Belo Horizonte, ☎ 031/335–8977).

BY TAXI
Taxis in Belo Horizonte are white and can be hailed or called. The meter starts at about $1 and costs about 50 cents for every kilometer traveled (slightly higher at night and on weekends). Two reputable companies are **BH Taxi** (☎ 031/215–8081) and **Rádio Taxi** (☎ 0800/31–2288 or 031/421–505).

In the historic towns, it's hard to drive along narrow, cobblestone streets, so taxis aren't abundant. Besides, these towns are small enough to explore on foot.

Contacts and Resources
BANKS AND CURRENCY EXCHANGE
Outside Belo Horizonte, currency exchange can be challenging and/or expensive, so change money before you arrive or plan to do it at your hotel. You can change money at Confins airport weekdays 10–6, and Saturday 10–4 (you're out of luck if you arrive Sunday). **Banco Sudameris** (⊠ Av. João Pinheiro 214, Centro, Belo Horizonte, ☎ 031/277–3134) has good exchange rates. **Banco do Brasil** (⊠ Rua Rio de Janeiro 750, Centro, Belo Horizonte) also offers exchange services, though the rates aren't the best.

CONSULATES
The U.S. has no consulate in Belo Horizonte, but it does have the **U.S. Commercial Service** (⊠ Rua Timbiras, 7th floor, ☎ 031/213–1571), which assists companies that are doing business in Minas Gerais. **British Consulate** (⊠ Rua Inconfidentes 1075, Belo Horizonte, ☎ 031/261–2072).

EMERGENCIES
Ambulance and Police: ☎ 190. **Fire:** ☎ 193. **Hospital: Hospital João XXIII** (⊠ Av. Alfredo Balena 400, Sta. Efigênia, Belo Horizonte, ☎ 031/239–9200). **Pharmacy: Drogaria Araujo** (☎ 031/270–5000) is a 24-hour Belo Horizonte pharmacy that makes deliveries.

HEALTH AND SAFETY
There are no major health concerns in Minas Gerais, although you should drink bottled rather than tap water. Petty crime is an issue in Belo Horizonte, though not as much as it is in Rio or São Paulo. Use common sense: avoid waving your money around or wearing expensive jewelry. The historic cities are among Brazil's safest places.

TELEPHONES, THE INTERNET, AND MAIL
The area code for the region is 031. If you don't want to place long-distance calls from your hotel, you can make them from the *posto tele-*

fônicos (phone offices) found in airports and bus stations throughout Minas. Office hours are generally 7 AM–10 PM. In Belo Horizonte, the main **TELEMIG** (⊠ Av. Afonso Pena 744, Centro) office is open 24 hours. The **main post office** (⊠ Av. Afonso Pena 1270, Centro, Belo Horizonte, ☎ 031/201–9833) is open weekdays 9–7, weekends 9–1. Internet service is slowly making its way to the region and may be available at your hotel's business center. In Belo Horizonte, the **Cybernet Café** (⊠ Av. Cristóvão Columbo 596, ☎ 031/261–5166) lets you hook up for about $10 an hour.

TOUR OPERATORS AND TRAVEL AGENTS

AMETUR (⊠ Rua Alvarenga Peixoto 295/102, Lourdes, Belo Horizonte, ☎ FAX 031/275–2139), the Association of Rural Tourism, is a group of respected, trustworthy ranch owners who have converted their fazendas into accommodations with luxurious, yet down-home, surroundings. You can visit one or more of these ranches, where relaxation, swimming, horseback riding, walks in the woods, and home-cooked meals are the orders of the day.

AMO-TE (⊠ Rua Professor Morais 624, Apartamento 302, Centro, Belo Horizonte, ☎ 031/344–8986), Minas's Association of Ecological Tourism, offers many fascinating tours. **CLN Tourism and Transportation Services** (⊠ Rua Dr. Antônio Ibrahim 103A, Belo Horizonte, ☎ FAX 031/551–6311 or 031/9961–1220) offers exceptional tours of Ouro Prêto and the historic cities.

Sangetur (⊠ Rua Inconfidentes 732, Belo Horizonte, ☎ 031/261–1055) is an all-purpose agency that can help you rent a car, make travel arrangements or hotel reservations, and book city tours. **YTUR Turismo** (⊠ Av. do Contorno 8000, Belo Horizonte, ☎ 031/275–3233) can arrange hotel bookings, transportation plans, and tours of Belo Horizonte and beyond.

VISITOR INFORMATION

In Belo Horizonte **Belotur** (⊠ Rua Pernambuco 284, ☎ 031/277–9797; ⊠ Mercado das Flores at Av. Afonso Pena at Rua da Bahia, Centro, ☎ 031/277–7666; ⊠ Rodoviária, Av. Afonso Pena at Av. do Contorno, Centro, ☎ 031/277–6907; ⊠ Confins airport, ☎ 031/689–2557), the municipal tourist board, is open daily 8 AM–10 PM at the airports and weekdays 8–7 elsewhere.

In Mariana, contact the **Associação de Guias** (⊠ Praça Tancredo Neves s/n, ☎ 031/557–9000) for general information on the city. Its hours are Tuesday–Saturday noon–5:30. The **Associação de Guias** (⊠ Praça Tiradentes 41, ☎ 031/551–2655), formed by Ouro Prêto's professional tour guides, can provide general information on the city weekdays 8–6. Its well-informed, courteous guides also conduct 6- to 7-hour walking tours (in English) of the historic area. Be prepared for some stiff hiking up and down numerous hills. In Tiradentes the **Secretária de Turismo** (⊠ Rua Resende Costa 71, ☎ 032/335–1212) is the best place to go for information weekdays 8–6.

SALVADOR

Updated by Karen Bressler, Marilene Felinto B. de Lima, and Wilma Felinto B. de Lima

The capital of the northeastern state of Bahia is a city of 2 million people, at least 80% of whom are Afro-Brazilian. It captivates visitors with African rhythms that roll forth everywhere—from buses and construction sites to the rehearsals of the Ilê Aiyê percussion group. The scents of coriander, coconut, and palm oil waft around corners that also host white-turbaned women who cook and sell deep-fried spicy shrimp and bean cakes. Baroque church interiors covered with gold leaf hark back to the riches of the Portuguese colonial era, when slaves masked their religious beliefs under a thin Catholic veneer. And partly thanks to modern-day acceptance of those beliefs, Salvador has become the fount of Candomblé, a religion based on personal dialogue with the *orixás,* a family of African deities closely linked to both nature and the Catholic saints.

The influence of Salvador's African heritage on Brazilian music has turned this city into one of the most stirring places to spend Carnaval, the bacchanalian fling that precedes Lent (and only one of more than 20 festivals punctuating the local calendar). As Bahia's distinctive *axé* music has gained popularity around the country, the city has begun to compete with Rio de Janeiro's more traditional celebration. Salvador's Carnaval means dancing night after night in the street to the ear-splitting, bone-rattling music of *trios elétricos* (bands on special sound trucks), and watching the parades of outlandish Carnaval associations. This movable feast formally lasts a week in February or March but begins in spirit at New Year's and continues even into Lent in small towns outside Salvador, with street festivals called *micaretas.*

Exploring Salvador

Salvador was founded on a cliff overlooking Bahia de Todos os Santos, and occupies a triangle that's sided by the bay and the ocean and which comes to a point at the Farol da Barra (Barra Lighthouse). The original city, called the Cidade Histórica (Historical City), is divided into *alta* (upper) and *baixa* (lower) districts and has buildings that date as far back as the 16th century. The Cidade Baixa occupies a space between the cliff's drop-off and the bay; it's a commercial district where you'll find the fully enclosed handicrafts market, the Mercado Modelo, and the port. Sleepy Ilha Itaparica is the largest of the harbor's 38 islands.

The tree-lined Avenida 7 de Setembro runs south through the Vitória neighborhood and down past the Iate Club to the Barra neighborhood, a mix of beach, yuppie bars, good cheap restaurants, low-life cafés, and moderately priced hotels. At the Farol da Barra the city runs east and north again on the oceanside leg of the triangle. The next beaches, Ondina and Rio Vermelho, are home to Salvador's most expensive resorts; the latter is quite bohemian, with some of the city's best bars and music. Going north along the so-called Orla Marítima (a series of connecting avenues running along the coast), there are many restaurants, the cleanest beaches, and, at the city's northernmost point, the Lagoa de Abaeté—a deep, black, freshwater lagoon.

The baroque churches, museums, colonial houses, and narrow, cobbled streets of the Cidade Histórica are best seen on foot. To travel between the Cidade Alta and the Cidade Baixa you can take the room-size Lacerda Elevator or the more utilitarian funicular railway. Inexpensive *comum* (common) taxis are a good way to get around the rest of the city.

Numbers in white bullets in the text correspond to numbers in black bullets in the margins and on the Salvador Cidade Histórico map.

Cidade Alta

A GOOD WALK

Begin your walk at the most famous of the city's 176 churches, the 18th-century baroque **Igreja de São Francisco** ① and its neighboring **Igreja da Ordem Terceira de São Francisco** ②. From here, cross Rua Inácio Accioli (which becomes Rua São Francisco) and head through the Praça Anchieta to Rua da Oração João de Deus and the **Igreja São Domingos** de Gusmão da Ordem Terceira ③. Just beyond this church is the large square called **Terreiro de Jesus** ④. At the Terreiro's northwest end is the 17th-century **Catedral Basílica** ⑤. From the cathedral head up to Rua Francisco Muniz Barreto and take a left onto Rua Alfredo de Brito. Two blocks up this street on your right is the **Fundação Casa de Jorge Amado/Museu da Cidade** ⑥, where you can see memorabilia of the author of such famous titles as *Dona Flor e Seus dos Maridos* (*Dona Flor and Her Two Husbands*), as well as exhibits on the Candomblé religion.

Rua Alfredo de Brito leads into the famed triangular **Largo do Pelourinho** ⑦. To the north stands the baroque **Igreja de Nossa Senhora do Rosário dos Pretos** ⑧. Walk up the hill past ancient pastel-color houses—growing beards of ferns on cornices—and African handicrafts shops and art galleries to the **Igreja e Museu do Convento do Carmo** ⑨, which, though very different from São Francisco, competes with it as the area's most interesting church.

TIMING

Simply walking this route will take about three hours. Pelourinho, with its music, cafés, restaurants, and shops, is a place that can be explored several times over a period of days and yet always seems new.

SIGHTS TO SEE

⑤ **Catedral Basílica.** Hints of Asia permeate this 17th-century masterpiece: Note the intricate ivory and tortoiseshell inlay from Goa on the Japiassu family altar, third on the right as you enter; the Asian facial features and clothing of the figures in the transept altars; and the 16th-century tiles from Macao in the sacristy. A Jesuit who lived in China painted the ceiling over the cathedral entrance. ⊠ *Terreiro de Jesus,* ☏ *no phone.* 🎫 *Free.* ⊙ *Tues.–Sat. 8–11 and 3–6; Sun. 5–6:30.*

⑥ **Fundação Casa de Jorge Amado/Museu da Cidade.** The Jorge Amado House contains the writer's photos, book covers, and a lecture room. Amado lived in the Hotel Pelourinho when it was a student house, and he set many of his books in this part of the city. Next door is the **Museu da Cidade**, with exhibitions of the costumes of the orixas of Candomblé. ⊠ *Corner of Rua Alfredo Brito and Largo do Pelourinho,* ☏ *071/321–0122.* 🎫 *Free.* ⊙ *Fundação: weekdays 9:30 AM–10 PM. Museum: Tues.–Fri. 10–5, weekends 1–5.*

⑨ **Igreja e Museu do Convento do Carmo.** The 17th-century Carmelite Monastery Church and Museum is famous for its restored French organ and carved cedar figure of Christ, the latter kept in the sacristy. Studded with tiny Indian rubies to represent blood, the figure was once carried through the streets in a silver-handled litter during Holy Week, but is now too fragile to be moved. The monastery, which was occupied by the Dutch when they invaded in 1624, features a small church built in 1580 and a chapel with Portuguese *azulejos* (tiles) that recount the story of the Jesuit order. ⊠ *Largo do Carmo s/n,* ☏ *071/242–0182.* 🎫 *Free.* ⊙ *Church: Daily for mass only, 7 AM, but accessible from museum. Museum: Mon.–Sat. 8–noon, 2–6; Sun. 8–noon.*

⑧ **Igreja de Nossa Senhora do Rosário dos Pretos.** Guides tend to skip over the Church of Our Lady of the Rosary of the Blacks, which was built in a baroque style by and for slaves between 1704 and 1796. It's worth a look at the side altars, to see statues of the Catholic church's few black saints. Each has a fascinating story. ⊠ *Ladeira do Pelourinho s/n,* ☏ *no phone.* 🎫 *Free.* ⊙ *Weekdays 8–5, weekends 8–2.*

② **Igreja da Ordem Terceira de São Francisco.** The Church of the Third Order of St. Francis has an 18th-century Spanish plateresque sandstone facade—carved to resemble Spanish silver altars made by beating the

Salvador Cidade Histórico

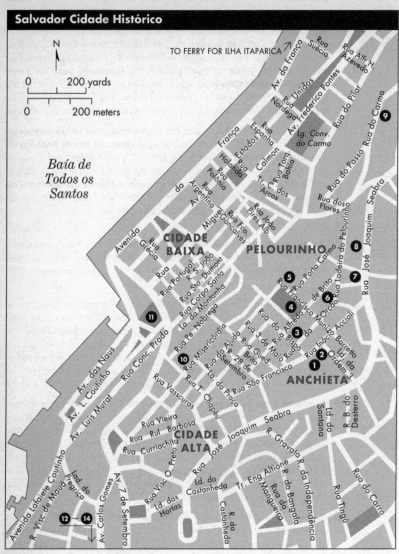

N

| 0 | 200 yards |
| 0 | 200 meters |

TO FERRY FOR ILHA ITAPARICA

Baía de Todos os Santos

CIDADE BAIXA

PELOURINHO

ANCHÍETA

CIDADE ALTA

metal into wooden molds—that's unique in all Brazil. The facade was hidden for decades under a thick coat of plaster, until, the story goes, a drunk electrician went wild with a hammer in the 1930s. ⊠ *Praça Padre Anchieta s/n,* ☎ *071/242–7046.* ⊑ *Free.* ☉ *Mon.–Sat. 8–noon and 2–5; Sun. 8–noon.*

❸ Igreja São Domingos de Gusmão da Ordem Terceira. The baroque Church of the Third Order of St. Dominic (1723) houses a fascinating collection of carved processional saints and other sacred objects. Such sculptures often had hollow interiors used to smuggle gold into Portugal to avoid government taxes. You'll see Asian features and details in the church decoration, evidence of long-ago connections with Portugal's Asian colonies of Goa and Macao. Upstairs are two impressive rooms with carved wooden furniture used for lay brothers' meetings and receptions. ⊠ *Terreiro de Jesus,* ☎ *071/242–4185.* ⊑ *Free.* ☉ *Mon.–Sat. 8–noon and 2–5.*

★ ❶ Igreja de São Francisco. The most famous of the city's churches, the 18th-century baroque Church of St. Francis has an active monastery. Listen for the sound of African drums in the square outside as you appreciate the ceiling painted in 1774 by José Joaquim da Rocha, a mulatto who founded Brazil's first art school. The ornately carved cedar and rosewood interior virtually writhes with images of mermaids, acanthus leaves, and caryatids—all bathed in shimmering gold leaf. Guides will tell you that there's as much as a ton of gold here, but restoration experts say there's actually much less, as the leaf used is just a step up from a powder. A super Sunday morning alternative to crowded beaches is Mass here (9–11, 11–11:45); stay until the end, when the electric lights go off, to catch the wondrous subtlety of gold leaf under natural light. ⊠ *Praça Padre Anchieta,* ☎ *no phone.* ⊑ *Free.* ☉ *Mon.–Sat. 8–noon and 2–5; Sun. 8–noon.*

★ ❼ Largo do Pelourinho. Named for the pillory where slaves were punished, this plaza is now the setting for one of the largest and most charming groupings of Brazilian colonial architecture and a thriving cultural renaissance. There are four public stages in Pelourinho, at least two of which have music nightly, all named after characters in Jorge Amado novels. **Dia & Noite** (☎ 071/322–2525) is the association that organizes the music; they publish a monthly schedule widely available in the area, at most tourist offices, and in hotels.

❹ Terreiro de Jesus. A large square with three churches and a small handicrafts fair, Terreiro de Jesus opens the way to exotic, historic Salvador. Where nobles once strolled under imperial palm trees, protected by their slaves, you'll now see men practicing *capoeira,* a stylized, dancelike foot-fight with African origins, to the thwang of the *berimbau,* a rudimentary but mesmerizing bow-shape musical instrument.

Cidade Baixa and Beyond

You can travel between the Cidade Alta and the Cidade Baixa aboard the popular **Elevador Lacerda** ⑩. Exiting the elevator at the Cidade Baixa, cross the Praça Visconde de Cairú to the **Mercado Modelo** ⑪ for some shopping and some people-watching. From here you have several options. Heading north, away from the ocean and along the bay, you pass the port and the terminal where you can catch a ferry for **Ilha de Itaparica.** Or you can head south by cab to one of several museums: the **Museu de Arte Sacra** ⑫; the **Museu de Arte Moderna da Bahia** ⑬; or the **Museu Carlos Costa Pinto** ⑭, which is in the Vitória neighborhood.

TIMING

You could start late in the morning and make a relaxed day of this tour. Navigating the elevator and the market takes a little more than an hour, though you'll probably want to spend more time browsing. The trip to either Ilha de Itaparica or to one or more of the museums will fill up a leisurely afternoon.

SIGHTS TO SEE

⑩ Elevador Lacerda. Costing about 2¢ and covering 236 ft in a minute, the elevator runs between the Praça Municipal in the Cidade Alta and Praça Visconde de Cairú and the Mercado Modelo. Built in 1872, the elevator ran on steam until its 1930 restoration. Bahians joke that the elevator is the only way to "go up" in life.

OFF THE BEATEN PATH   **ILHA DE ITAPARICA –** Originally settled because of its ample supply of fresh water, Brazil's largest maritime island doesn't have notable beaches, but there are some quiet shady cobbled streets lined with pastel-color colonial homes sure to charm you. As the complete schooner tour can be tiresome, one option is to take it one way, get off at Itaparica, skip the cattle-call lunch, take a taxi to a good restaurant, enjoy a postprandial afternoon stroll, and ride the ferry back to Salvador.

⑪ Mercado Modelo. This enclosed market (closed Sun. afternoon) may not be the cheapest place to buy handicrafts—and you do have to bargain—but it must be experienced. It assaults the senses, with its *cachaça* (a strong Brazilian liquor made from sugarcane), cashew nuts, pepper sauces, cigars, the dried shrimp that are an integral part of Bahian cooking, manioc flour, leather goods, hammocks, lace, musical instruments, African sculptures, and gems. Outside, you'll hear the nasal-voiced *repentistas*, regional folk singers who make up songs on the spot. Notice the blue azulejos on the building with Gothic-style windows, once a sort of chamber of commerce, now a supermarket. Be prepared for extraordinarily persistent salespeople in and around the building. At the rear of the market, boys practice *capoeira* (a sport that's half fighting, half dancing) and sell monkeys; the harbor excursion boats are moored across the way.

⑬ Museu de Arte Moderna da Bahia. A mid-16th-century waterfront mill set between the Cidade Alta and Cidade Baixa houses the Bahian Museum of Modern Art's permanent collection of work by some of Brazil's top modern painters, including Cândido Portinari, Alfredo Volpi, Siron Franco, and Hector Carybé. The museum building is part of a complex that includes the **Solar do Unhão,** a former sugar mill/residential complex that dates from the 18th century. ⊠ *Av. Contorno s/n,* ☎ *071/329–0660.* 🎫 *Free.* ☉ *Tues.–Fri. 1–9, Sat. 11–9, Sun. 2–7.*

⑫ Museu de Arte Sacra. Housed in a former Carmelite monastery near the Cidade Alta, the Sacred Art Museum and its adjoining **Igreja de Santa Teresa** (Church of St. Teresa) are two of the city's best-cared-for repositories of religious objects. An in-house restoration team has worked miracles that bring alive Bahia's 1549–1763 golden age as Brazil's capital and main colonial port. See the silver altar in the church, moved here from the demolished Sé church, and the blue-and-yellow-tiled sacristy replete with a bay view. ⊠ *Rua do Sodré 276,* ☎ *071/243–6310.* 🎫 *Admission.* ☉ *Weekdays 11:30–5:30.*

⑭ Museu Carlos Costa Pinto. The collection is the fruit of one wealthy couple's fascination with art and antiques and a rare example of private support for the arts in Brazil. Among the museum's 3,000 objects fashioned around the world over the last three centuries is Costa Pinto's collection of oversize gold and silver jewelry worn by favored slave women. Here are some prime examples of the *balangandã* (also called the *penca*), a chain of large charms—in the shape of tropical fruits, fish, perhaps a berimbau—worn by slave women around the waist. Prized slaves were initially given the chain and the clasp by their masters, who, over time, continued to reward loyalty and service with gifts of the charms (many jewelry and crafts stores sell replicas of these pieces). The balangandã usually includes a *figa*, a closed fist with a thumb sticking out of the top. According to African legend, the figa can increase warriors' fertility. In Brazil, however, it's considered simply a good-luck charm (in order for it to work, though, it must always be a gift). It's also used as a good-luck gesture, sort of like crossing your fingers. ⊠ *Av. 7 de Setembro 2490,* ☏ *071/336–6081.* ◪ *Admission.* ☉ *Mon. and Wed.– Fri. 2:30–7, weekends 3–6.*

Beaches

Beaches are wall-to-wall people on the weekends, but if you don't mind a crowd it's fun to soak up both sun and beach culture, which includes sand sports, firewater drinks, spicy seafood snacks (don't miss the *acarajé*, a deep-fried bean cake with dried shrimp and sauce) at beachside kiosks, live music, and the briefest of swimwear.

At most local beaches the food and drink kiosks provide chairs and umbrellas free of charge; you pay only for what you consume. Some also offer rudimentary bathroom, changing, and shower facilities free of charge for patrons. Aside from these, there are no functioning bathrooms on the beaches, but some have public showers that run on one-minute tokens costing less than 25¢. Don't leave belongings unattended.

The *jardineira* bus stops at all the beaches along the coast, from downtown north as far as the Stella Maris beach. A more comfortable *ônibus executivo* (executive bus; marked ROTEIRO DAS PRAIAS) runs from Praça da Sé to Flamengo beach, stopping at all the same stops. As a rule, the farther away from the port, the better the beach.

Barra do Jacuípe. A river runs down to the ocean at this long, wide, pristine beach lined with coconut palms, about 40 km (25 mi) north of Salvador. There are beachfront snack bars. The **Santa Maria/Catuense bus company** (☏ 071/359–3474) operates six buses (marked PRAIA DO FORTE) daily that stop at this beach.

Guarajuba. With palm trees and calm waters banked by a reef, this is the nicest beach of them all, though it's 60 km (38 mi) north of Salvador. The bus to Barra do Jacuípe (☞ *above*) continues on to Guarajuba. There are snack kiosks, fishing boats, surfing, dune buggies, and a playground.

Itapuã. Frequented by artist types who live nearby, Itapuã is at the end of the string of beaches that stretch north from Salvador, about a half-hour drive from downtown. Although it's polluted in some places, this beach has a terrific atmosphere. Around K and J streets there are food kiosks, music bars, and amusement park rides, too. A mystical freshwater lagoon, the **Lagoa de Abaeté** lies inland from Itapuã. Set in lush greenery, its black depths provide a startling contrast with the fine white sand of its shores. No one knows the source of these waters, where Bahian women often wash clothes in the morning. City buses going to the lagoon leave from Campo Grande or Estação da Lapa and cost less than 50¢. If you're driving, take the Orla Marítima north out of the city until Itapuã. At the Largo da Sereia (a square with a mermaid statue), follow signs for the lagoon. Tour operators include the lagoon on their beach tours, which cost about $25.

Jaguaribe. This is the "in crowd" hangout, frequented by singles on Saturday and good for surfing, windsurfing, and sailing. There are plenty of snack bars. This beach is just before Piatã (☞ *below*), 16 km (10 mi) north of downtown.

Piatã. Heading north and leaving the more built-up areas of the city behind, the first truly clean beach you'll come to is the wide oceanside Piatã (20 km/13 mi from downtown). Its calm waters and golden sand attract families.

Porto da Barra and Farol da Barra. Some Salvadorans, especially singles, swear by the urban beaches Porto da Barra and Farol da Barra, which are frequented by a colorful mix of people who live nearby and tourists staying at neighboring hotels. Petty thievery is a problem here. There are no bathrooms or kiosks, but you can rent a beach chair for about $1. The corner of Porto da Barra closest to the Grande Hotel da Barra is a gay hangout. Toward the other end, around the corner from the lighthouse, lie the hotel districts of **Ondina** and **Rio Vermelho,** where the beaches intermittently suffer pollution problems.

Stella Maris. The Stella Maris beach (18 km/11 mi north of downtown), *the* beach in Salvador, is popular with surfers and beautiful girls, but it's most famous for its kiosks.

Dining

You can easily find restaurants serving Bahian specialties in Barra, a neighborhood full of bars and sidewalk cafés. There are also many good spots in bohemian Rio Vermelho and a slew of places along the beachfront drive beginning around Jardim de Alah. It's wise to order meat only in *churrascarias* (barbecued-meat restaurants), avoiding it in seafood places.

Brazilian

$$$ ✕ **Casa da Gamboa.** A longtime favorite of Bahian writer Jorge
★ Amado, this is an institution of Bahian cooking. *Casquinha de siri* (breaded crab in the shell) comes as a complimentary starter; then try the *peixe com risoto de ostras* (grilled fish with oyster risotto), followed by the very good traditional desserts. ✉ *Rua João de Deus 32, Pelourinho,* ☎ *071/321–3393. AE, MC, V. No lunch.*

$$$ ✕ **Maria Mata Mouro.** At this intimate restaurant, you almost feel as if you're at a friend's house for dinner. The Bahian food is served with an extra creative twist, and you're assured of a good meal. The *badejo* (grouper) in ginger is delicious. ✉ *Rua Inácio Acciole 8, Pelourinho,* ☎ *071/321–3929. AE, V. Closed Sun.*

$$$ ✕ **Tempero da Dadá.** This is one of the best-loved restaurants in town.
★ The original location, in Federação, where the famous Dadá herself usually cooks, is better-liked, but the newer branch in Pelourinho is just as good. Dadá has been cooking since she was eight, when she stood on stools to get to the stove. Though the house specialty is *bobó de camarão* (shrimp), the grilled fish, the vatapá, and the moquecas are every bit as good. Dadá first started attracting artists and musicians who had heard about her fabulous cooking years ago and just stopped by her home for a meal. On occasion you'll still find local luminaries—like musician Carlinhos Brown—at tables on the veranda. ✉ *R. Teixeira Mendes 55, Federação,* ☎ *071/331–4382. AE, MC, V. Closed Mon.* ✉ *R. Frei Vicente 5, Pelourinho,* ☎ *071/321–5883. AE, MC, V. Closed Mon.*

$$ ✕ **Dona Celina.** This Bahian restaurant in Pelorinho offers alfresco as well as indoor dining, and a good selection of vegetarian dishes. The ambience will charm you. ✉ *Rua Francisco Muniz Barreto 15,* ☎ *071/321–1721. No credit cards.*

$$ ✕ **Uauá.** You'll find cuisine representative of many Brazilian regions here. The clientele, which includes most of the city, are die-hard fans. There are two locations, one in Pelourinho and one at Itapuã Beach. ✉ *R. Gregório de Matos 36, Pelourinho,* ☎ *071/321–3089. AE, DC, MC, V. Closed Mon.* ✉ *Av. Dorival Caymi 46, Itapuã,* ☎ *071/249–9579. AE, DC, MC, V. Closed Mon.*

$ ✕ **Arroz de Hauçá.** Two unemployed brothers convinced their family's 70-year-old cook to go public, and turned their plant-filled house into a restaurant. The restaurant, in turn, put the home-cooked dish it's named for on the map of Bahian cuisine. This hefty plate of rice, in coconut milk and covered with a sauce of shrimp paste and onions, has a circle of fried jerked beef and onions in the middle. And while the *arroz de hauçá* is the star here, you can also find the usual Bahian specialties on the menu. The management doesn't frown on sharing dishes. ⊠ *Rua Sabino Silva 598, Jardim Apipema,* ☎ FAX *071/247–3508. AE, DC, MC, V.*

Eclectic

$$ ✕ **Extudo.** Young professionals and singles jam-pack this bar and restaurant just about every night. Bahian and international dishes include camarão *comodoro,* shrimp and prunes gratinéed in a creamy tomato sauce; Finnegan's steak with black pepper sauce; and *frango flambado,* flambéed chicken. ⊠ *Rua Lídio Mesquita 4, Rio Vermelho,* ☎ *071/334–4669. No credit cards. Closed Mon.*

French

$$$$ ✕ **Chez Bernard.** Discerning *soteropolitanos* (the pompous but nonetheless correct term for natives of the city) say this is undoubtedly the best, as well as one of the oldest, French restaurants in town. There are no particular specialties: everything is worth trying. ⊠ *Gamboa de Cima 11, Aflitos,* ☎ *071/329–5403. AE, V. Closed Sun.*

Seafood

$$$ ✕ **Bargaço.** Typical Bahian food is served in this oversize, brightly lit shed, a 20-minute drive along the beach from downtown, once a must in Salvador that now caters mostly to tour groups. Starters such as *pata de caranguejo* (vinegared crab claw) are hearty and plentiful, but they may do more than take the edge off your appetite for the requisite moqueca de *camarão* (shrimp) or moqueca *de siri mole* (soft-shell crab); try the *cocada baiana* (sugar-caked coconut) for dessert, if you have room. ⊠ *Rua P, Lote 1819, Quadra 43, Jardim Armação, Boca do Rio,* ☎ *071/231–5141 or 071/231–3900. AE, DC, MC.*

$$ ✕ **Frutos do Mar.** This plain, traditional seafood spot in the hopping Barra neighborhood is a favorite among cash-conscious locals for its shrimp moquecas and *ensopados* (catch-of-the-day stews resembling bouillabaisse), which come with a typical, sweet-flavored bean called *feijão de leite.* ⊠ *Rua Marquês de Leão 415, Barra,* ☎ *071/245–6479 or 071/254–6322. AE, DC, MC, V.*

$$ ✕ **Iate Clube da Bahia.** From your captain's chair in this informal air-conditioned yacht club restaurant, set on the cliff between Barra and the Vitória neighborhood, you get a spectacular view of boats bobbing in the bay. You also get honest Continental and Bahian cooking, such as double gratinéed fish and moquecas. ⊠ *Av. 7 de Setembro 3252, Barra,* ☎ *071/336–9011. AE, DC, MC, V. Closed Mon.*

$$ ✕ **Iemanjá.** Probably the best value for regional cooking, Iemanjá is also a place with a bubbly, underwater atmosphere, replete with aquamarine sea-goddess murals and aquariums. The service is somewhat slow and there's no air-conditioning, but most patrons don't seem to mind, concentrating instead on plowing through mountainous portions of moqueca or ensopado. ⊠ *Av. Otávio Mangabeira 929, Jardim Armação,* ☎ *071/231–5770. No credit cards.*

Lodging

There are only a few hotels in the historic Cidade Alta, overlooking the bay. Going south into the Vitória neighborhood along Avenida 7 de Setembro, there are many inexpensive hotels, convenient both to the Barra area beaches and to historic sights. In the yuppie Barra neighborhood, many hotels are within walking distance of cafés, bars, restaurants, and clubs. The resort-hotel district lies farther north, a 20-minute taxi ride from downtown and historic areas, on and around the Ondina and Rio Vermelho beaches.

$$$$ 🏨 **Enseada das Lajes.** Perched on a cliff overlooking the ocean, this ★ hotel is the most exclusive in town, though guests have reported that the standards don't merit the exorbitant rate. Both private and public areas are decorated in antiques, and the hotel is surrounded by gardens that descend to the sea. The owners have a second property by the same name on Ilha de Itaparica. ⊠ *Av. Oceânica 511, Morro da Paciência, Rio Vermelho,* ☎ *071/336–1027,* 🕾 *071/336–0654. 9 rooms. Restaurant, bar, pool. AE, DC, MC.*

$$$$ 🏨 **Transamérica Salvador.** As far as big hotels go, the Transamérica is doubtless among the best. The standard rooms are small but they have terrific views east toward the bay. Although it's in Rio Vermelho, the hotel retains an isolated feel, because it's atop a mountain. Nearby, however, you'll find great restaurants that are open 24 hours. ⊠ *Rua Monte do Conselho 505, Rio Vermelho,* ☎ *071/330–2233,* 🕾 *071/ 330–2200. 202 rooms. Restaurant, bar, pool, tennis court, health club, shops, business services, meeting rooms. AE, DC, MC, V.*

$$$$ 🏨 **Tropical Hotel da Bahia.** Owned by Varig Airlines and often included in package deals, this centrally located hotel is a bit tattered, but practical for those whose priority is Salvador's history and culture, not beach-combing (although there's a free beach shuttle). Some rooms overlook the square where Carnaval begins; the Concha Acústica do Teatro Castro Alves, site of many big musical shows, is within walking distance, and performers there often stay here. ⊠ *Praça Dois de Julho 2, Campo Grande,* ☎ *071/336–0102,* 🕾 *071/336–9725. 282 rooms, 10 suites. Restaurant, bar, coffee shop, 2 pools, massage, sauna, dance club. AE, DC, MC, V.*

$$$ 🏨 **Bahia Othon.** A short drive from most historic sights, nightlife, restaurants, and in-town beaches, this busy modern business and tourist hotel offers an ocean view from all rooms, whose ceramic-tile floors and wood furniture are a bit worn. Top local entertainers often perform at the hotel's outdoor park, and in high season, the staff organizes poolside activities as well as trips to better beaches. ⊠ *Av. Presidente Vargas 2456, Ondina,* ☎ *071/247–1044,* 🕾 *071/245–4877. 300 rooms, 25 suites. Restaurant, bar, coffee shop, pool, sauna, health club, dance club, concierge floor. AE, DC, MC, V.*

$$$ 🏨 **Caesar Towers.** This Caesar has comfortable apartments only 8 km (5 mi) from Centro and 15 km (10 mi) from the best beaches. It's close to Barra district restaurants and bars. ⊠ *Av. Oceânica 1545, Ondina,* ☎ *071/331–8200,* 🕾 *071/237–4668. 120 rooms. Restaurant, coffee shop, pool, sauna, health club, meeting rooms. AE, DC, MC, V.*

$$$ 🏨 **Catussaba Hotel.** Close to the airport and 40 km (25 mi) from the ★ city, this hotel opens directly onto a good swimming beach. All the comfortable, simple rooms have an ocean view, and there's a large, attractive pool area. ⊠ *Alameda Praia de Guarita 101, Alamedas da Praia, Itapuã,* ☎ *071/374–0555,* 🕾 *071/374–4749. 133 rooms. Restaurant, bar, pool, sauna, tennis court, health club, meeting room. AE, MC, V.*

$$$ 🏨 **Fiesta Bahia Hotel.** Though neither on the beach nor close to the historical center, this hotel is a great choice for business travelers. Located in the city's financial district and close to the convention center, the Fiesta offers rooms with direct phone lines, fax and PC terminals, and queen-size beds—amenities that distinguish it from its competitors. ⊠ *Av. Antônio Carlos Magalhães 711, Itaigara,* ☎ *071/352–0000,* 🕾 *071/352–0050. 239 rooms. Restaurant, bar, coffee shop, room service, 2 pools, health club, shops, nightclub, business services. AE, DC, MC, V.*

$$$ ⊞ **Hotel Sofitel Salvador.** Just beyond the city's northern perimeter, this resort and convention hotel near good beaches is a world unto itself, decorated with local art and oversize, old-fashioned farm implements. The green-and-blue-accented rooms all have a view of the spacious grounds and the ocean beyond. Amenities include a gallery, on-site boutiques, crafts demonstrations, and free minibus service to downtown. ⊠ *Rua da Pasárgada s/n, Farol de Itapuãn,* ☎ *071/374–9611, 800/ 763–4835 in U.S.,* ℻ *071/374–6946. 197 rooms, 9 suites. 2 restaurants, 3 bars, room service, 2 pools, beauty salon, massage, 9-hole golf course, 3 tennis courts, health club, boating, shops. AE, DC, MC, V.*

$$$ ⊞ **Ondina Apart-Hotel Residência.** In the resort hotel district, a short drive from the sights, nightlife, and restaurants, this apartment-hotel complex on the beach has simple, modern furniture and kitchenettes. Many businesspeople and families opt for this hotel when they're staying in Salvador for extended periods. ⊠ *Av. Presidente Vargas 2400, Ondina,* ☎ *071/203–8000,* ℻ *071/203–8112. 100 apartments. Restaurant, bar, coffee shop, beauty salon, 2 tennis courts, health club, dance club. AE, DC, MC, V.*

$$ ⊞ **Grande Hotel da Barra.** Near the downtown beaches and convenient to the historic center, the Grande has comfortable, well-maintained rooms with such decorative touches as pink-and-green floral bedspreads, latticework screens, and lots of wood carvings. The front rooms have verandas. Though not all rooms have an ocean view, they do all have VCRs. ⊠ *Av. 7 de Setembro 3564, Porto da Barra,* ☎ *071/ 247–6506,* ℻ *071/264–6011. 112 rooms, 5 suites. Restaurant, bar, pool, beauty salon, sauna. AE, DC, MC, V.*

$$ ⊞ **Hotel Bahia do Sol.** This hotel's low rates and prime location, close to museums and historic sights, may make up for its battered wooden furniture. Front rooms have a partial ocean view, but those in the back are quieter. ⊠ *Av. 7 de Setembro 2009, Vitória,* ☎ *071/336–7211,* ℻ *071/336–7776. 86 rooms, 4 suites. Restaurant, bar, meeting rooms, free parking. AE, DC, MC, V.*

$$ ⊞ **Hotel Catharina Paraguaçu.** The sleeping areas at this intimate,
★ charming hotel—set in a 19th-century mansion—are small but comfortable, and include six split-level suites. It's family-run and in a neighborhood of good restaurants and bars. ⊠ *Rua João Gomes 128, Rio Vermelho,* ☎ ℻ *071/247–1488. 23 rooms, 6 suites. Minibars. MC, V.*

$ ⊞ **Hotel Vila Romana.** On a quiet street minutes from the beach and not far from many upscale bars and cafés, this Bahian version of a Roman palazzo has seen better days. Still, it's favored by many Italian visitors, who don't seem to mind the rudimentary plumbing. Try for one of the back rooms, which are better ventilated. ⊠ *Rua Prof. Leme de Brito 14, Barra,* ☎ *071/336–6522,* ℻ *071/247–6748. 60 rooms, 3 suites. Restaurant, bar, pool. AE, DC, MC, V.*

$ ⊞ **Pousada das Flores.** A great location (within walking distance of
★ Pelourinho), combined with simple elegance conspire to make this one of the city's best budget options. Rooms are large and have high ceilings, a stylish blue and white decor, and hardwood floors. For peace and quiet as well as a view of the ocean, opt for a room on an upper floor. ⊠ *Rua Direita de Santo Antônio 442, Cidade Histórico,* ☎ ℻ *071/243–1836. 6 rooms, 3 suites. AE, DC, MC, V.*

Nightlife and the Arts

Pelourinho has music every night and more bars and clubs than you can count. It's perfectly safe to walk around until late here, as practically every corner has at least one police officer. Activity also centers on the neighborhoods of Barra and Rio Vermelho, and both areas are near many hotels.

Salvador is considered by many artists as a laboratory for the creation of new rhythms and dance steps. As such this city has a lively—almost electric—performing arts scene. See the events calendar published by Bahiatursa or local newspapers for details on live music performances as well as the rehearsal schedules and locations of the *blocos* (Carnaval percussion bands). Gay and lesbian information is available from the **Grupo Gay da Bahia** (⊠ Rua do Sodré 45, ☎ 071/322–2552), which publishes an entertainment guide to Salvador's gay scene, *Guia para Gays,* that costs about $5.

Nightlife

BARS

Good bar bets include **Bambara** (⊠ Av. Otávio Mangabeira, Jardim de Alá, ☎ no phone), which sometimes has live music; **Bananas Beet** (⊠ Rua 3, Jardim Iracema, Patamares, ☎ 071/363–5656); and **Estação do Pelo** (⊠ Rua João de Deus 25, Pelourinho, ☎ no phone), which serves food as well as drink.

DANCE SHOWS

Shows at the **Moenda** (⊠ Jardim Armação, Rua P, Quadra 28, Lote 21, ☎ 071/231–7915 or 071/230–6786) begin daily at 8 PM. There are Afro-Brazilian dinner shows (the shows are much better than the dinners) at the **Solar do Unhão** (⊠ Av. do Contorno s/n, ☎ 071/321–5551), which opens Monday through Saturday at 8 PM. The Afro-Bahian show at the **Teatro Miguel Santana** (⊠ Rua Gregório de Mattos 47, ☎ 071/321–0222) in Pelourinho has the best folkloric dance troupes in town.

NIGHTCLUBS

Many of the best dance clubs are along the beaches of Amaralina and Pituba. Live bands play on stages to dance floors thronging with people all night long. Try **Kalamazoo** (⊠ Av. Otávio Mangabeira s/n, ☎ 071/363–5151), **Queops** (⊠ Hotel Sol Bahia Atlântico, Rua Manoel Antônio Galvão 100, ☎ 071/370–9000), or **Rock in Rio Café** (⊠ Av. Otávio Mangabeira 6000, Boca do Rio, ☎ 071/371–0979).

The Arts

CAPOEIRA REHEARSALS

Capoeira, the hypnotic African sport-cum-dance accompanied by the *berimbau* (a bow-shape musical instrument), can be seen Tuesday, Thursday, and Saturday evenings at 7 at the 17th-century Forte Santo Antônio Além do Carmo, just north of the Museu do Carmo in the Cidade Alta, a 5- to 10-minute taxi ride from downtown. Two schools practice here. The more traditional is the Grupo de Capoeira Angola. Weekday nights are classes; the real show happens on Saturday.

CARNAVAL REHEARSALS

Afro-Brazilian percussion groups begin rehearsals—which are really more like creative jam sessions—for Carnaval around mid-year. **Ilê Aiyê,** which started out as a Carnaval bloco, has turned itself into much more in its 25-year history and now has its own school, promotes the study and practice of African heritage, religion, and history and is involved with many social issues. The work this bloco is undertaking in the name of Afro-Brazilian pride and prosperity is both vast and inspirational. Practices are held every Saturday night at Fort St. Antônio and should not be missed. Olodum, Salvador's most commercial percussion group, has its own venue, the **Casa do Olodum** (⊠ Rua Gregório de Matos 22, Pelourinho, ☎ 071/321–5010).

MUSIC, THEATER, AND DANCE VENUES

Casa do Comércio (⊠ Av. Tancredo Neves 1109, ☎ 071/371–8700) hosts music performances and some theatrical productions. All kinds of musicians play at the **Concha Acústica do Teatro Castro Alves** (✉ Ladeira da Fonte s/n, ☎ 071/247–6414), a band shell. The **Teatro ACBEU** (✉ Av. 7 de Setembro 1883, ☎ 071/247–4395 and 071/336–4411) hosts contemporary and classic music, dance, and theater performances by both Brazilian and international talent. **Teatro Castro Alves** (✉ Ladeira da Fonte s/n, ☎ 071/247–6414) is a top venue for theater, music, and dance. Small theater groups perform at the German-Brazilian Cultural Institute's **Teatro ICBA** (✉ Av. 7 de Setembro 1809, ☎ 071/237–0120), which also screens German films. You can see theatrical, ballet, and musical performances at the **Teatro Iemanjá** (✉ Jardim Armacão s/n, Centro de Convenções).

Outdoor Activities and Sports

Participant Sports

BICYCLING AND RUNNING

For bicycling and running, the best places are **Dique do Tororó** (✉ Entrances at Av. Presidente Costa e Silva and Av. Vasco da Gama, Tororó), a park round a lake; **Jardim dos Namorados** (✉ Av. Otavio Mangabeira, Pituba), a park where you'll find places to rent bikes; there are also volleyball courts and soccer fields; **Parque Metropolitano de Pituaçu** (✉ Facing Praia do Corsário, Pituaçu); and **Parque Jardim de Alá** (✉ between Pituba and Boca do Rio, Costa Azul).

GOLF AND TENNIS

Cajazeira Golfe & Country Club (✉ Av. Genaro Carvalho s/n, Castelo Branco, ☎ 071/246–8007) is an option for golf. **Hotel Sofitel Salvador** (✉ Rua Passárgada s/n, Farol de Itapoã, ☎ 071/374–9611) offers day passes to its golf course and its tennis courts.

SURFING, WINDSURFING, AND SAILING

For surfing, windsurfing, and sailing, contact **Iate Clube da Bahia** (✉ Av. 7 de Setembro, Barra, ☎ 071/336–9011 or 071/336–9693).

Spectator Sport

FUTEBOL

Bahia and Vitória are the two best local teams, and they play year-round (except at Christmastime) Wednesday night and Sunday at 5 PM at the **Estádio da Fonte Nova** (✉ Av. Vale do Nazaré, Dique do Tororó, ☎ 071/243–3322, ext. 237). Tickets are sold at the stadium a day in advance. Avoid sitting behind the goals, where the roughhousing is worst. The best seats are in the *arquibancada superior* (high bleachers).

Shopping

Areas

The city's most traditional shopping area, for a variety of everyday goods at lower prices than in the malls, is **Avenida 7 de Setembro.** For paintings, especially art naïf, visit the many galleries in the Cidade Alta in and around the **Largo do Pelourinho.** For local handicrafts, the **Mercado Modelo** is your best bet.

Centers and Malls

Two big shopping malls have cinemas; restaurants; boutiques that sell locally manufactured clothing; and franchise outlets or branch stores of Rio, São Paulo, and Minas Gerais retailers. **Shopping Center Iguatemi** (✉ Av. Antônio Carlos Magalhães 148), the older and more traditional of the two malls, is near the bus station. **Shopping Barra** (✉ Av. Centenário 2992), in the Barra neighborhood back from the beach, is newer and glitzier. The top hotels provide free transportation to it.

Specialty Stores

ART

Top local artists (many of whom use only first names or nicknames) include Totonho, Calixto, Raimundo Santos, Joailton, Nadinho, Nonato, Maria Adair, Carybé, Mário Cravo, and Jota Cunha. **Atelier Portal da Cor** (⊠ Ladeira do Carmo 31, Pelourinho, ☎ 071/242–9466) is run by a cooperative of local artists.

HANDICRAFTS

The **Casa Santa Barbara** (⊠ Rua Alfredo de Brito, ☎ 071/244–0458) sells Bahian clothing and lacework of top quality, albeit at prices slightly higher than elsewhere. Note that it's closed Saturday afternoon and Sunday. **Kembo** (⊠ Rua João de Deus 21, ☎ 071/322–1379), a shop in Pelourinho, carries handicrafts from many different Brazilian Indian tribes. The owners travel to reservations all over the country and buy from the Pataxós, Kiriri, Tupí, Karajá, Xingú, Waiwai, Tikuna, Caipós, and Yanomami among others.

Salvador has several state-run handicrafts stores, with lower prices and smaller selections. One of the best is the **Instituto Mauá** (⊠ Praça Azevedo Fernandes 2, ☎ 071/235–5440). **Artesanato Fieb-Sesi** (⊠ Rua Borges dos Reis 9, ☎ 071/245–3543) also carries woven and lace goods, musical instruments, sandals, and pottery.

JEWELRY AND GEMSTONES

Salvador has a branch (actually there are several, most of them in malls and major hotels) of the well-known, reputable **H. Stern** (⊠ Largo do Pelourinho, ☎ 071/322–7353) chain. At **Simon** (⊠ Rua Ignácio Accioli, ☎ 071/242–5218), the city's most famous jewelers, you can peer through a window into the room where goldsmiths work.

Salvador A to Z

Arriving and Departing

BY AIRPLANE

The **Aeroporto Deputado Luís Eduardo Magalhães** (☎ 071/204–1010), 37 km (23 mi) northeast of the city, accommodates international and domestic flights. Airlines that serve the city include **Air France** (071/351–6631), **American Airlines** (071/245–0477), **Lufthansa** (071/341–5100), **Rio-Sul** (071/204–1253), **TAM** (071/204–1367), **Transbrasil** (071/377–2467), **Varig** (071/204–1070), and **VASP** (071/377–2495).

From the Airport into Town. Avoid taking comum taxis from the airport; drivers often jack up the fare by refusing or "forgetting" to turn on the meter. Instead opt for a prepaid *cooperativa* (co-op) taxi (they're white with a broad blue stripe); the cost is $30–$45 for the 20- to 30-minute drive downtown. The *ônibus executivo*, an air-conditioned bus, runs daily from 6 AM to 9 PM at no set intervals; it costs about $1.10 and takes about an hour to reach downtown, stopping at hotels along the way. (Drivers don't speak English, but will stop at a specific hotel if shown a written address). Several companies operate these buses, the largest being **Transportes Ondina** (⊠ Av. Vasco da Gama 347, ☎ 071/245–6366). The municipal Circular buses, operated by both Transportes Ondina and **Transportes Rio Vermelho** (⊠ Av. Dorival Caymmi 18270, ☎ 071/377–2587), cost about a quarter and run along the beaches to downtown, ending up at São Joaquim, where ferries depart for Ilha de Itaparica.

BY BUS

You can purchase bus tickets at the **Terminal Rodoviário** (⊠ Av. Antônio Carlos Magalhães, Iguatemi, ☎ 071/358–6633). The **Itapemirim** (☎ 071/358–0037) company has three buses a day to Recife (13 hrs, $35–$45), Fortaleza (19 hrs, $55), and Rio (28 hrs, $80–$155).

BY CAR

Two highways—BR 101 and BR 116—run between Rio de Janeiro and Salvador. If you take the BR 101, get off at the city of Santo Antônio/Nazaré and follow the signs to Itaparica, 61 km (38 mi) away. At Itaparica, you can either take the 45-minute ferry ride to Salvador or continue on BR 101 to its connection with BR 324. If you opt for the BR 116, exit at the city of Feira de Santana, 107 km (67 mi) from Salvador and take the BR 324, which approaches the city from the north. Follow the signs marked IGUATEMI/CENTRO for downtown and nearby destinations.

Getting Around

BY BOAT

Itaparica and the other harbor islands can be reached by taking a ferry or a launch, by hiring a motorized schooner, or by joining a harbor schooner excursion—all departing from the docks behind the Mercado Modelo. Launches cost about $1 and leave every 45 minutes from 7 AM to 6 PM from **Terminal Turístico Marítimo** (⊠ Av. França s/n, ☎ 071/243–0741). The ferry takes passengers and cars and leaves every half hour between 6 AM and 10:30 PM from the **Terminal Ferry-Boat** (⊠ Terminal Marítimo, Av. Oscar Ponte 1051, São Joaquim, ☎ 071/321–7100). The fare is around $1 for passengers, $6–$8 for cars, and takes 45 minutes to cross the bay.

BY BUS AND METRÔ

Buses are crowded, dirty, and dangerous, but they serve most of the city and cost a pittance (50¢). The fancier executivo buses ($1.20) serve tourist areas more completely but have been subject to a spate of robberies. The glass-sided green, yellow, and orange jardineira bus (marked PRAÇA DA SÉ)—which runs from the downtown Praça da Sé to the Stella Maris beach along the beachfront Orla Marítima series of avenues—is fine for getting to the beach.

BY CAR

The dearth of places to park makes rental cars impractical for sightseeing in the Cidade Alta (although the government plans to build more parking areas). Further, many soteropolitanos are reckless drivers (they often ignore even the most basic traffic rules), making driving a dangerous proposition, especially if you don't know your way around. That said, cars are handy for visits to outlying beaches and far-flung attractions. Rental companies include **Avis** (⊠ Av. 7 de Setembro 1796, ☎ 071/237–0155 or 071/377–2276 at the airport), **Hertz** (071/377–3633 at the airport), or **Localiza** (071/377–2272 at the airport).

BY TAXI

Taxis are metered, but you must convert the unit shown on the meter to Brazilian currency using a chart posted on the window. Tipping isn't expected. You can hail a comum taxi (white with a red and blue stripe) on the street (they often line up in front of major hotels) or summon one by phone. If you bargain, a comum taxi can be hired for the day for as little as $50. Try **Ligue Taxi** (☎ 071/358–0733). The more expensive, though usually air-conditioned, *especial* (special) taxis also congregate outside major hotels, though you must generally call for them. Reliable companies include **Coometas** (☎ 071/244–4500) and **Contas** (☎ 071/245–6311).

Contacts and Resources

BANKS AND CURRENCY EXCHANGE

Never change money on the streets, especially in the Cidade Alta. All major banks have exchange facilities, but only in some of their branches. Try **Citibank** (⊠ Rua Miguel Calmon 555, Comércio), which has good rates; **Banco Económico** (⊠ Rua Miguel Calmon 285); and **Banco do Brasil** (⊠ Av. Estados Unidos 561, Comércio), which also offers exchange services at its branches in the Shopping Center Iguatemi and at the airport.

CONSULATES

United Kingdom (Av. Estados Unidos 15, Comércio, 071/243–9222 or 071/243–7399). **United States** (⊠ Rua Pernambuco 568, Pituba, ☎ 071/345–1545).

EMERGENCIES

General emergencies: ☎ 192. **Hospitals: Aliança Hospital** (⊠ Av. Juracy Magalhães Jr. 2096, ☎ 071/350–5600), **Hospital Português** (⊠ Av. Princesa Isabel 2, Santa Isabel, ☎ 071/203–5555), **Hospital Jorge Valente** (⊠ Av. Garibaldi 2135, ☎ 071/203–4333).

Police: The office of the **Delegacia de Proteção do Turista** (☎ 071/320–4103), the tourist police, is down the steps at the back of the Belvedere at the Praça da Sé.

ENGLISH-LANGUAGE BOOKSTORES

Graúna (⊠ Av. 7 de Setembro 1448; ⊠ Rua Barão de Itapoã, Porto da Barra) has many books in English. **Livraria Brandão** (⊠ Rua Rui Barbosa 15B, Centro, ☎ 071/243–5383) sells second-hand books in foreign languages. **Livraria Planeta** (Aeroporto Deputado Luís Eduardo Magalhães) has English-language books, magazines, and newspapers.

HEALTH AND SAFETY

As in any large city, discretion and a low-key approach will more than likely ensure a hassle-free trip to Salvador. Leave valuables at home. Potential thieves are unlikely to know the difference between a real Rolex and a fake one, so it's better not to try to fool anyone. Wear your purse bandolier style (with the strap over one shoulder) and keep your wallet out of easy reach for thieves (a money belt isn't a bad idea). Never leave belongings unattended. Carry only a photocopy of your passport, leaving the original in the hotel safe.

TELEPHONES, INTERNET, AND MAIL

Salvador's area code is 071. The city's main **post office** (☎ 071/243–9383) is in the Praça Inglaterra in the Cidade Baixa. You'll also find branches on the Avenida Princesa Isabel in Barra and the Rua Marques de Caravelas in Ondina, at the Barra and Iguatemi shopping centers, and at the airport. The airport branch is open 24 hours; all others are open weekdays 8–5. All branches offer express-mail service.

TOUR OPERATORS AND TRAVEL AGENTS

The city's large group tours are fairly cursory, and their guides often speak minimal English; such tours are also targeted by hordes of street vendors at almost every stop. Several travel agencies offer half-day minibus tours with hotel pickup and drop-off for about $20–$25. Agencies also offer daylong harbor tours on motorized schooners ($30–$35) and night tours ($40–$45) that include dinner and an Afro-Brazilian music and dance show. A beach tour that includes the Lagoa de Abaeté can be arranged as well, with a car and guide provided for about $30 a head (minimum 2 people).

Another option is a private tour with a Bahiatursa guide (they carry the proper credentials), hired through your hotel, a travel agency, or at a Bahiatursa kiosk (☞ Visitor Information, *below*). Prices vary depending on the size of the group (it costs about $100 for one person, $80 each for two people, and so on) and include a car, which picks you up and drops you off at your hotel. Beware of guides who approach you at church entrances; they overcharge for telling tall tales.

Though it specializes in African heritage tours of Bahia, **Tatur Tours** (✉ Ave. Antônio Carlos Magalhães 2573, Edifício Royal Trade, S. 1308, ☎ 071/358–7216) also offers personalized, special-interest city tours. The staff can also arrange top-notch excursions from Salvador.

Other leading agencies include **Globe Turismo** (✉ Rua Dra. Praguer Fróes 97, ☎ 071/245–9611), **Lilás Viagens e Turismo Ltda.** (✉ Av. Tancredo Neves 274, Bloco B, Centro Empresarial Iguatemi II, ☎ 071/358–7133), and **L. R. Turismo** (✉ Av. Otávio Mangabeira 2365, ☎ 071/248–3333).

VISITOR INFORMATION

The main office of the state tourist board, **Bahiatursa** (✉ Centro de Convenções, Jardim Armação s/n, 41750–270, ☎ 071/370–8400) is far from tourist attractions. However, there are five other conveniently located branches: the **airport** (✉ Aeroporto Internacional, 2 de Julho s/n, ☎ 071/204–1244); the **bus station** (✉ Av. Antônio Carlos Magalhães s/n, Terminal Rodoviário, ☎ 071/358–0871); the **downtown historic center** (✉ Terreiro de Jesus s/n, ☎ 071/321–0388); the **Mercado Modelo** (✉ Praça Visconde de Cairú s/n, ☎ 071/241–0240); and in the **Cidade Alta** (✉ Porto da Barra s/n, ☎ 071/247–3195). All offices are open daily 8–6, except for the main branch, which is open 7–7, and the airport branch, which is open 8:30 AM–10 PM.

Emtursa (✉ Largo do Pelourinho 12, ☎ 071/243–6555 or 071/243–5738; ✉ Trv. da Ajuda 2, 2nd floor, ☎ 071/321–4346 or 071/321–9307), the municipal tourist board, is open weekdays 8–6.

THE AMAZON

Updated by
Brad Weiss

A flight over the Amazon region is unforgettable. The world's largest rain forest seems an endless carpet of green that's sliced only by the curving contours of rivers. Its statistics are as impressive: The region covers more than 10 million square km (4 million square mi) and extends into eight other countries (French Guiana, Suriname, Guyana, Venezuela, Ecuador, Peru, Bolivia, and Colombia). It takes up roughly 40% of Brazil in the states of Acre, Rondônia, Amazonas, Roraima, Pará, Amapá, and Tocantins. The rain forest produces ⅓ of the world's oxygen and is home to ⅕ of its freshwater supply as well as 500,000 catalogued species of plants and animals. Yet it's inhabited by only 16 million people—that's less than the population of metropolitan São Paulo.

Life here centers on the rivers, the largest of which is the Amazon itself. From its source in southern Peru, it runs 6,300 km (3,900 mi) to its Atlantic outflow. It's second in length only to the Nile, and of its hundreds of tributaries, 17 are more than 1,600 km (1,000 mi) long. In places the Amazon is so wide that you can't see the shore, earning it the appellation of Rio Mar (River Sea). Although there has been increasing urbanization, 45% of the Amazon's residents live in rural settlements along the riverbanks.

The Spaniards, including Vincente Pinzon who is credited with having been the first to sail the Amazon in 1500, came in search of gold. Perhaps the most famous voyage was undertaken by Spanish conquistador Francisco de Orellano in 1541. Instead of gold or a lost kingdom, he ran into natives, heat, and disease. When he emerged from the jungle a year later, his crew told a tale of women warriors they called the Amazons (a nod to classical mythology). This captivating story lent the region its name.

Most accounts indicate that early Portuguese contacts with the Indians were relatively peaceful. But it wasn't long before the indigenous populations were devastated. Diseases brought by the Europeans and against which the Indians had no resistance took their toll; attempts to enslave them did the rest. When the Portuguese arrived in Brazil, there were roughly 4.5 million Indians, many of them in the Amazon; today there are just over 300,000 in the nation and fewer than 200,000 in the Amazon. Although the Portuguese conducted expeditions into the Amazon and established forts to protect the territory against other Europeans, they found neither gold nor a viable labor force. Official interest in the region waned until the rubber era of the late 19th century.

Rubber practically transformed Belém and Manaus from outposts to cities. Rubber barons constructed mansions and monuments and brought the most modern trappings of life into the jungle. As money poured in and out of the Amazon, the area attracted a colorful array of explorers, dreamers, and opportunists. The rubber era lasted only into the first two decades of the 20th century. Since then, huge reserves of gold and iron have been discovered. Land-settlement schemes and development projects have followed. Conservation hasn't always been a priority. Vast portions of the "world's lung" have been indiscriminately deforested; tribal lands have again been encroached upon; and industrial by-products have poisoned wildlife and people. Although the Brazilian government has established reserves and made other efforts to preserve the territory, conservationists aren't satisfied. And yet, 500 years after the first Europeans arrived, much of the Amazon has not been thoroughly explored by land. It's still a place where simple pleasures are savored and the mystical is celebrated.

Exploring the Amazon

Although there are regular flights throughout the Amazon, many visitors still opt for the area's primary mode of transportation—boat. The region encompasses hundreds of navigable rivers, but vessels tend to follow only a few well-charted waterways, mainly the Amazon, Negro, Solimões, Madeira, Pará, and Tapajós rivers. A trip along the Amazon itself—especially the 1,602 km (993 mi) three- to five-day journey between Belém and Manaus—is a singular experience. Averaging more than 3 km (2 mi) in width, but reaching up to 48 km (30 mi) in the rainy season, there are many spots where it's impossible to see either bank. At night, the moon and stars are the only sources of light, reinforcing the sense of being in true wilderness. For trip and tour operator options *see* Chapter 2.

Cruises

Whatever your style of travel, your budget, or the length of your stay, there's a boat plying the river to suit your needs. (For Brazilian companies that arrange boat transportation, *see* Tour Operators and Travel Agents *in* the Amazon A to Z *below*). Note that, owing to the dense riverbank vegetation, it's not easy to spot wildlife from a boat. Further, some craft travel far from shore, defeating any chance you have of seeing the flora or the fauna. It's best to plan a boat trip that includes a stop or two, so that you can explore the rain forest.

ENASA BOATS

The state-run Empresa de Navegação da Amazônia S/A (ENASA) has an enormous, first-rate catamaran that travels between Belém and Manaus once or twice a month. All of its 62 cabins have air-conditioning, music, phones, and baths with hot water. Other shipboard amenities include a pool, a bar, and a restaurant that serves regional food. The four- to five-day trip costs roughly $500. Unfortunately, the schedule isn't regular, and you can't make reservations through travel agencies. ENASA has other ships that travel more frequently, but they don't offer the same standard of luxury.

OCEAN-GOING SHIPS

Some cruise ships call at Manaus as part of itineraries that may include stops in Santarém, Rio de Janeiro, and southern Caribbean islands. Most trips take place during the North American winter; they range in length from 11 to 29 days and costs start at $2,500. Several major cruise lines offer such trips, though not every year. Your best bet for arranging one is to contact a travel agent (☞ *also* Arriving and Departing by Boat *in* Brazil A to Z, *below*).

STANDARD RIVERBOATS

If you think that comfort should take a back seat to adventure, consider a leisurely trip by standard double- or triple-decker boats, which carry both freight and passengers. Although you may not get a close-up view of the riverbank, you will get the real feel of life along the river. Frequent stops at small towns are opportunities for interesting interactions and observations.

You might be able to get a cabin, but expect it to be claustrophobic. Cabins cost $100 to $200 between Manaus and Belém. The real adventure, however, is out on the deck, where most passengers sleep in hammocks ($50–$75 between Manaus and Belém), often with little or no space between them. You must bring your own hammock (they're sold onshore for about $15) as well as a few yards of rope to tie it up.

Clusters of booths sell tickets at the docks. Even if you don't speak Portuguese, you can ascertain the necessary information from the signs alongside the booths. Inspect the vessel you will travel on closely (sanitary conditions vary from boat to boat), and, if you plan to sleep in a hammock, board early to secure a good spot (away from the engine and toilets). Travel as light as possible, and keep your gear secure at all times. Bring plenty of sunscreen and insect repellent. Nights can be surprisingly cool, so pack a light blanket. Food is served, but the quality ranges from okay to deplorable. At best, the diet of meat, rice, and beans can become monotonous. Experienced Brazilian travelers bring their own food, bottled water, small stoves, and pans; you can also buy fresh fruit at stops along the way (just be sure to peel or wash it thoroughly with bottled water before eating it).

TOURIST BOATS

Tourist boats, which are used by tour operators and can be hired for private groups, are more comfortable than standard riverboats. They generally travel close to the riverbank and have open upper decks from which you can observe the river and forest. The better tour operators have a regional expert—usually an ecologist or botanist—on board, who's fluent in English. You can either sleep out on the deck in a hammock or in a cabin, which will usually have air-conditioning or a fan. Meals are generally provided.

Belém

On the southern bank of the Rio Guamá, 120 km (74 mi) west of the Atlantic, 2,933 km (1,760 mi) northeast of Rio de Janeiro, 3,250 km (1,950 mi) north of São Paulo.

Belém, the capital of Pará State, is a river port of more than 1.5 million people. The Portuguese settled here in 1616, using it as a gateway to the interior and an outpost to protect the area from invasion by sea. Because of its ocean access, Belém became a major trade center. Like the upriver city of Manaus, it rode the ups and downs of the Amazon booms and busts, alternately bursting with energy and money and slumping into relative obscurity. Its first taste of prosperity was during the rubber era in the late 19th and early 20th centuries. Almost overnight it became an opulent, extravagant city. Architects from Europe were brought in to build churches, civic palaces, theaters, and mansions, often using fine, imported materials. Monuments were erected to honor magnates. When Malaysian rubber supplanted that of Brazil in the 1920s, wood, and later, minerals, provided the impetus for growth.

In the past 20 years, Belém has experienced rapid expansion, pushed by major projects in the surrounding area, including the Tucuruvi hydroelectric dam, Brazil's second-largest, and the development of the Carajás iron-ore mining region. Modern high-rises are replacing the colonial structures. Recently, however, local governments have launched massive campaigns to preserve the city's rich heritage. Several distinctive buildings survive along the downtown streets and around the Praça Frei Caetano Brandão, in the Cidade Velha (Old City). East of here, in the Nazaré neighborhood, colorful colonial structures mingle with new ones housing trendy shops.

Exploring the Cidade Velha

A GOOD WALK

Begin at the **Igreja Nossa Senhora das Mercês,** a large, pink church just northeast of the **Ver-o-Peso** market. Walking southwest through the market, you'll pass the small dock where fishermen unload the day's catch. Turn left on Avenida Portugal (past the municipal clock, crafted in the image of Big Ben), which borders Praça Dom Pedro II. Follow it to the large, baby-blue Palácio Antônio Lemos, which houses the **Museu de Arte de Belém (MABE).** Next door is the even larger, white Palácio Lauro Sodré, in which you'll find the **Museu do Estado do Pará.** Just behind this museum, the golden church, **Igreja de São João Batista,** looms. From here, head back toward Praça Dom Pedro II along Rua Tomásia Perdigão, and turn left onto Travessa Félix Roque. This takes you to the rear of the **Catedral da Sé** (the entrance faces Praça Frei Caetano Brandão). To your right as you exit the cathedral is the **Museu de Arte Sacra,** and just beyond is the **Forte do Castelo.**

TIMING

This tour will take two to three hours—longer if you linger in the museums. It's best to start at 8 AM or 9 AM and finish by lunchtime. Next to the Forte do Castelo is the Círculo Militar restaurant (☞ Dining, *below*), the perfect place to enjoy a meal and the view of Bahía de Guajará (Guajará Bay).

SIGHTS TO SEE

Catedral da Sé. In 1771 Bolognese architect Antônio José Landi, whose work can be seen throughout the city, completed the cathedral's construction on the foundations of an older church. It has an interesting mix of baroque, colonial, and neoclassical styles. Its interior is richly adorned with Carrara marble, and the high altar was a gift from Pope Pius IX. *Praça Frei Caetano Brandão.* 🖾 *Free.* ☉ *Tues.–Fri. 8–noon and 2–5, Sat. 6 PM–8 PM, Sun. 4 PM–9 PM.*

Forte do Castelo. The birthplace of Belém was originally called Forte do Presépio (Fort of the Crèche). It was from here that the Portuguese founders launched their conquests of the Amazon. The fort's role in the region's defense is evidenced by the English- and Portuguese-made cannons. ⊠ *Praça Frei Caetano Brandão.* 🖾 *Free.* ☉ *Daily 8 AM–9 PM.*

Igreja Nossa Senhora das Mercês. Our Lady of Mercy Church is another baroque creation attributed to Antônio Landi. Notable for its pink color and its convex facade, it's part of a complex that includes the Convento dos Mercedários, which has served as a convent and, less mercifully, as a prison. ⊠ *Largo as Mercês.* 🎫 *Free.* ☉ *Mon.–Sat. 8–1.*

Igreja de São João Batista. The prodigious architect Antônio Landi finished the small, octagonal St. John the Baptist Church in 1777. It was completely restored in 1997 and is considered the city's purest example of baroque architecture. ⊠ *Rua Dr. Tomásia Perdigão at Largo de São João.* 🎫 *Free.*

Museu de Arte de Belém (MABE). When you arrive at the Metropolitan Art Museum, don't be surprised if a security guard hands you large, brown, furry objects—these are slippers that you must wear over your shoes to protect the wooden floors. The bottom level has temporary expositions. Shuffle up to the second level and the permanent collection of furniture and paintings that date from the 18th century through the rubber boom. The museum is housed in the recently renovated Palácio Antônio Lemos (circa 1883), a municipal palace built in the Imperial Brazilian style with French influences. ⊠ *Praça Dom Pedro II,* ☏ *091/241–1398.* 🎫 *Free.* ☉ *Tues.–Fri. 10–6, Sat.–Sun. 9–1.*

Museu de Arte Sacra. The first part of a guided Sacred Art Museum tour (call to reserve an English-speaking docent 48 hours in advance) takes you through the early 18th-century, Amazon baroque **Igreja de Santo Alexandre** (St. Alexander Church), which is distinguished by intricate woodwork on its alter and pews. On the second half of the tour, you'll see the museum's collection of religious sculptures and paintings. The first floor has temporary exhibitions, a gift shop, and a café. ⊠ *Praça Frei Caetano Brandão,* ☏ *091/225–1125.* 🎫 *Admission; free on Tues.* ☉ *Tues.–Sun. 10–6.*

Museu do Estado do Pará. The Pará State Museum is in the sumptuous Palácio Lauro Sodré (circa 1771), an Antônio Landi creation with Venetian and Portuguese elements. The first floor hosts consistently outstanding visiting exhibitions; the second floor contains the permanent collection of furniture and paintings. ⊠ *Praça Dom Pedro II,* ☏ *091/225–3853.* 🎫 *Free.* ☉ *Permanent collection: Tues.–Fri. 10–5:45. Temporary exhibits: Tues.–Sun. 10–5:45.*

★ **Ver-o-Peso.** Literally meaning "See the Weight" (a colonial-era sales pitch), this market is a hypnotic confusion of colors and voices. Vendors hawk tropical fruits, "miracle" jungle roots, and charms for the body and soul. There are jars filled with animal eyes, tails, and even heads as well as a variety of herbs—each with its own legendary power. A regional oddity are the sex organs of the river dolphin, supposedly unrivaled cures for romantic problems. In the fish market, you'll get an up close look at pirarucu, the Amazon's most colorful species; the *mero,* which can weigh more than 91 kilos (200 pounds); and the silver-scale *piratema.* Across the street from Ver-o-Peso is the small arched entrance to the municipal meat market. Duck in and glance at the pink and green painted ironwork, imported from Britain and done in a French style. Be sure to visit Ver-o-Peso before noon, which is when most vendors leave, and be careful of pickpockets.

Exploring Nazaré

A GOOD TOUR

Begin at the south end of the **Praça da República.** Across Avenida da Paz is the large, pink **Teatro da Paz.** After leaving the theater, veer left onto Avenida Governador José Malcher; look for the sign for Lá em Casa, one of Belém's best restaurants (☞ Dining, *below*). Just behind it is the elaborate Palacete Bolonha, from which you should continue east along Governador José Malcher (note the burgundy and gold designs painted on the road at several intersections; they're styled after those on marajoara pottery). Turn right onto Travessa Benjamin Constant and right again onto Avenida Nazaré. Just beyond Avenida Generalíssimo Deodoro is the **Basílica de Nazaré.** Continue east three more blocks to the **Museu Emílio Goeldi.** After touring the museum, consider taking a short ($5) taxi ride northeast to the **Bosque Rodrigues Alves,** a chunk of jungle right in the middle of town.

TIMING

It should take about 1½ hours to reach the Museu Emílio Goeldi. Plan to spend an hour or two here owing to the quantity (and quality) of the displays. If you need a break, the museum has a restaurant and a snack bar. Count on at least an hour at Bosque Rodrigues Alves.

SIGHTS TO SEE

★ **Basílica de Nazaré.** It's hard to miss this opulent, Roman-style basilica. Not only does it stand out visually, but in the plaza out front, there's an enormous tree filled with screeching parakeets. It was built in 1908 on the site where a *caboclo* (rural inhabitant) named Placido saw a vision of the Virgin in the early 1700s. The basilica's ornate interior is constructed entirely of European marble and contains elaborate mosaics, detailed stained-glass windows, and intricate bronze doors. In the small, basement-level **Museu do Círio,** displays explain the Círio de Nazaré festival, which is held each October to honor the city's patron saint. ⊠ *Praça Justo Chermont s/n,* ☎ *091/224–9614 for museum.* ☑ *Free to both basilica and museum.* ⊙ *Basilica: Mon. 6–11 and 3–5, Tues.–Sat. 6–11 and 3–7, Sun. 3–7. Museum: weekdays 8–6.*

OFF THE BEATEN PATH

BOSQUE RODRIGUES ALVES – In 1883, this 40-acre plot of rain forest was designated an ecological reserve. Nowadays, you'll find an aquarium and two amusement parks as well as natural caverns, a variety of animals (some in the wild), and mammoth trees. ⊠ *Av. Almirante Barroso,* ☎ *091/226–2308.* ☑ *Admission.* ⊙ *Tues.–Sun. 8–5.*

★ **Museu Emílio Goeldi.** Founded by a naturalist and a group of intellectuals in 1866, this complex contains one of the Amazon's most important research facilities. Its museum has an extensive collection of Indian artifacts, including the distinctive and beautiful pottery of the Marajó Indians, known as marajoara. An adjacent tract of rain forest has reflection pools with giant Victoria Régia water lilies. But the true highlight is the wide collection of Amazon wildlife, including manatees, rare blue alligators, sloths, and various species of monkeys. ⊠ *Av. Magalhães Barata 376,* ☎ *091/249–1233.* ☑ *Admission.* ⊙ *Weekends and Tues.–Thurs. 9–noon and 2–5; Fri. 9–noon.*

Praça da República. Here you'll find a large statue that commemorates the proclamation of the Republic of Brazil, an amphitheater, and several French-style iron kiosks.

Teatro da Paz. Greek-style pillars line the front and sides of this neoclassical theater, which was completed in 1878 and is the third-oldest in Brazil. Inside, note the imported details such as the Italian marble pillars and the French chandeliers. Opera and classical music performances are still held in the theater, which seats more than 800 people. English-speaking guides are available to give 20-minute tours. ☎ *091/224–7355.* ☑ *Admission.* ⊙ *Weekdays 9–noon and 2–5.*

Beaches

The closest ocean beach is **Salinas,** a four-hour drive from Belém. The river beaches are much closer. Depending on the season and time of day, they're either expansive stretches or narrow strips of soft, white sand. Currents are rarely strong, and there's usually a large area of shallow water. Although **Outerio** is an easy half-hour bus ride from town, it's not very scenic; it's also generally crowded and a little dirty.

Most people head for one of the 18 beaches on Ilha Mosqueiro, along the Rio Pará. Connected to the mainland by a large bridge, it's just an hour's drive from the city. Although **Farol** is close to Ilha Mosqueiro's hub, Vila, and is often crowded, it's still pretty. Stands sell fresh fish dishes, and at low tide you can walk to tiny, rocky Ilha do Amor (Love Island). In October, the waves are high enough for river-surfing competitions. **Morubira,** also close to Vila, has beautiful colonial houses and many restaurants and bars.

The water is clear and the shore is clean at **Marahú.** Several stands sell food and drink. The bus from Belém doesn't travel here directly; you have to disembark in Vila and hop another bus. You must also catch a second bus in Vila to reach the aptly named **Paraíso.** It's lined with trees and has soft white sands and clear emerald waters. If you can't bear to leave this paradise at day's end, consider a stay at the Hotel Fazenda Paraíso (☞ Lodging, *below*).

Dining

$$–$$$ ✕ **Au Bon Vivant.** With its soft, blue, neon lighting and abstract art, this French establishment is as chic as it gets in the Amazon. The menu offers a refreshing dose of creativity, which is generally lacking in the region's restaurants. There's also an antipasto bar with premium meats, cheeses, and seafood. ⊠ *Trv. Quintino Bacaiúva 2084, Cremação,* ☎ *091/225–001. AE, DC, MC, V. Closed Mon.*

$$ ✕ **Círculo Militar.** The specialty here, one block from Ver-o-Peso market and near the Forte do Castelo, is fresh fish. Try the *filhote ao leite de coco* (river fish sautéed in a coconut milk). Come for lunch so that you can enjoy the river view. ⊠ *Praça Frei Caetano Brandão s/n, Cidade Velha,* ☎ *091/223–4374. AE, DC, MC, V.*

$$ ✕ **Dom Giuseppe.** From gnocchi to ravioli, the flawless preparation of basics distinguishes this Italian eatery from all the others. Everyone in town knows this, too, so reservations are a good idea, particularly on weekends. Don't leave without ordering a scrumptious *dolce Paula* (an ice cream and brownie dessert). ⊠ *Av. Conselheiro Furtado 1420, Batista Campos,* ☎ *091/241–1146. AE, DC, MC, V.*

$$ ✕ **Lá em Casa.** Not only are the Amazon specialties here superb, but
★ the owner, Dona Ana Maria, has a smile for everyone. Consider trying Belém's premier dish, *pato no tucupi,* duck in a yellow herb sauce made from manioc root and served with the mildly intoxicating *jambu* leaf. The *casquinha de caranqueijo* (stuffed crab shells with coconut sauce) is another good choice, as is the açaí sorbet. There are attractive seating areas indoors (with air-conditioning) and outside on a deck. ⊠ *Av. Governador José Malcher 247, Nazaré,* ☎ *091/223–1212. AE, DC, MC, V.*

$$ ✕ **Miako.** Belém has a large Japanese community (second only to that of São Paulo), so there's no lack of Japanese restaurants. This one, however, is a tried-and-true favorite for its excellent service, attractive wooden decor, and consistently good food. The sushi is terrific. ⊠ *Rua 1 de Março 76, Centro,* ☎ *091/242–2355. AE, DC, MC, V.*

$ ✕ **Casa Portuguesa.** Although it's in the heart of the commercial district, this restaurant does its best to replicate the charm of a Portuguese country home. The specialties are dishes with chicken and, of course, cod. ⊠ *Rua Senador Manoel Barata 897, Centro,* ☎ *091/242–4871. AE, DC, MC, V.*

$ ✕ **Rodeio.** Devoted carnivores take note: there's nothing like a meal in a *churrascaria* after a few days on a riverboat with little to eat but fish and rice. The reasonable fixed-price menu here not only includes as many servings of grilled and roasted meats as you can eat, but also salads and dessert. ⊠ *Trv. Padre Eutíqiu 1308, Batista Campos,* ☎ *091/212–2112. AE, DC, MC, V. No dinner Sun. and Mon.*

Lodging

$$$ 🏨 **Hilton International Belém.** The Hilton's reliability and amenities are topped only by its location right on the Praça da República. Although not very distinguished, the rooms are well equipped and comfortable. Executive rooms have the nicest views as well as access to a lounge with a VCR, a meeting area, and complimentary food and drink. ⊠ *Av. Presidente Vargas 882, Centro 66017–000,* ☎ *091/242–6500 or 800/445–8667 in U.S.,* 𝔽𝔸𝕏 *091/225–2942. 361 rooms. 2 restaurants, 2 bars, pool, beauty salon, sauna, health club, convention center. AE, DC, MC, V.*

$$–$$$ 🏨 **Equatorial Palace.** Its Nazaré location, within walking distance of the port and the Cidade Velha, is the best thing about this hotel. Although it's something of an institution (often featured in package deals) and has a few remnants of a more luxurious past, its rates are hardly consistent with the facilities and services offered. ⊠ *Av. Braz de Aguiar 612, Nazaré 66035–000,* ☎ *091/241–2000,* 𝔽𝔸𝕏 *091/223–5222. 204 rooms, 7 suites. Restaurant, bar, pool. AE, DC, MC, V.*

$$ 🏨 **Hotel Regente.** This hotel offers excellent service and a prime location for a reasonable price. Stained-glass windows and soft leather couches welcome you in the attractive lobby. Rooms on the 12th floor are nicer and more modern than those on other floors, yet cost the same. ⊠ *Av. Governador José Malcher 485, Nazaré 66035–100,* ☎ *091/241–1222,* 𝔽𝔸𝕏 *091/242–0343. 196 rooms, 6 suites. Restaurant, bar, pool. AE, DC, MC, V.*

$$ 🏨 **Itaoca Hotel.** It comes as no surprise that this reasonably priced hotel has the highest occupancy rate in town. Its rooms are extremely comfortable, well equipped, and modern, and most have a fantastic view of the dock area and river. ⊠ *Av. Presidente Vargas 132, Centro 66010–902,* ☎ 𝔽𝔸𝕏 *091/241–3434. 36 rooms. Restaurant, in-room safes, meeting room. AE, DC, MC, V.*

$ 🏨 **Hotel Fazenda Paraíso.** Just a few feet from one of the most beautiful beaches on Ilha Mosqueiro, this hotel is the ideal place to spend a day or two just outside the city. Wooden and brick chalets with red-tile roofs accommodate as many as five people. Similarly designed apartments, which house up to three people, are more economical for singles and couples. The pool is configured in the shape of a clover. Be sure to make reservations as the hotel is very popular on weekends. ⊠ *Beira-Mar, Praia do Paraíso, Ilha Mosqueiro 66915–000,* ☎ *091/772–2444 or 091/228–3950 in Belém. 12 rooms, 10 chalets. Restaurant, pool, horseback riding, beach, boating. AE, DC, MC, V.*

$ 🏨 **Manacá Hotel.** This small, bright-red hotel with a slanted, brown-★ tile roof looks like a cross between a Monopoly hotel piece and a pagoda. With cozy, softly lighted common rooms, it offers more charm than larger places at about a quarter of the price. It's a clean, simple alternative if you can live without a pool or a bar. ⊠ *Trv. Quintino Bocaiuva 1645, Nazaré 66033–620,* ☎ *091/223–3335. AE, DC, MC, V.*

$ 🏨 **Zoghbi Apart Hotel.** The only apartment hotel in town has suites with fully equipped kitchens that are great for families or for those who plan on being in Belém for a while. The already reasonable rate is reduced nearly 50% for stays that exceed 15 days. ⊠ *Rua Ferreira Cantão 100, Centro 66017–110,* ☎ *091/241–1800. 55 apartments. Kitchenettes. V.*

Nightlife

BARS

The clientele at the open-air **Bar do Parque** (⊠ Praça República s/n, ☎ 091/242–8798) consists of a truly interesting cross-section of people, and the view of the Praça da República is beautiful. Popular dock area bars include **Bora Bora** (⊠ Rua Bernal do Couto 38, ☎ 091/241–5848); **Colarinho Branco** (⊠ Av. Visconde de Souza Franco 80, ☎ 091/242–1007); and **Roxy Bar** (⊠ Av. Senador Lemos 231, ☎ 091/224–4514), which tops nearly everyone's list of hip spots.

DANCE AND MUSIC CLUBS

Africa Bar (⊠ Praça Kennedy s/n, next to Paratur, ☎ 091/241–1085) consistently attracts some of the biggest names in Brazilian music. The **Zeppelin Club** (⊠ Av. Senador Lemos 108, ☎ 091/223–8936) is the undisputed king of *boates* (dance clubs) and has prices to match. The cover charge on Friday and Saturday (the only nights the club is open) is about $15. For jazz, try **Zolt** (⊠ Rua Domingos Morreiros 470, ☎ 091/242–5771).

Outdoor Activities and Sports

FISHING

Pará state is renowned for the quality and variety of its fish. For information about fishing trips, contact the **Secretaria de Estado de Ciênicia, Tecnologia e Meio Ambiente** (SECTAM; ⊠ Trv. Lomas Valentinas 2717, ☎ 091/266–5000).

FUTEBOL

Belém's two *futebol* (soccer) teams are Payssandú and Remo—neither of which is currently in the premier league. Still, attending a Brazilian match, regardless of the quality of the team, is a memorable experience. Payssandú plays at **Estádio Leônidas de Castro** (⊠ Av. Almirante Barroso s/n, ☎ 091/241–1726). For Remo games, head to **Estádio Evandro Almeida** (⊠ Av. Almirante Barroso s/n, ☎ 091/223–2847).

JUNGLE AND RIVER EXCURSIONS

On one- to several-day trips from Belém, you can explore the Guamá, Acará, and Mojú rivers. You can also catch a boat in the city at 4:30 AM and be at Ilha dos Papagaios (Parrot Island) by sunrise, when thousands of *papagaios* (parrots) leave in an unforgettable flight. Larger tour operators can make all the necessary arrangements (☞ Tour Operators and Travel Agents *in* the Amazon A to Z, *below*).

As you travel by Jeep along rain forest trails to the **Crocodile Safari Zoo** (☎ 091/222–9102), images of *Jurassic Park* may come to mind. Although the focus at this research station, a half-hour northwest of the city, is crocodiles (more than 500 of them are contained here), it also has a museum with prehistoric fossils and a large collection of shells. There's also river access, so you can take short canoe trips. Call ahead to arrange an afternoon visit accompanied by an English-speaking guide. The cost is roughly $20 per person, including transportation.

Shopping

AREAS AND MALLS

Belém's main shopping street is **Avenida Presidente Vargas,** particularly along the Praça da República. There are also many boutiques and specialty shops in **Nazaré.** To shop in air-conditioning, head for the upscale **Shopping Center Iguatemi** (⊠ Trv. Eutíquio 1078), a mall in the truest sense of the word. In **Icoaraci,** a riverside town 18 km (11 mi) northeast of Belém, shops make and sell marajoara pottery.

Artesanato Paruara (✉ Rua Sezedelo Correo 15, ☎ 091/248–4555) specializes in oils, stones, and other "mystical" items. At **Artindia** (✉ Av. Presidente Vargas 762, Loja 6, ☎ 091/223–6248) you'll find a good selection of jewelry, painted wooden shields, bows and arrows, and other crafts—all handmade by Indians. (Note: Be careful about items that have feathers; some are prohibited by U.S. Customs.) Several places sell marajoara pottery, painted coconut shells, and straw baskets including **Cacique** (✉ Av. Presidente Vargas 692, ☎ 091/242–1144); the small shop at **Paratur** (✉ Praça Kennedy s/n, ☎ 091/224–9633), the state tourist board; and **Vitoria Régia** (✉ Presidente Vargas 552, ☎ 091/241–1113).

Manaus

On the Rio Negro and surrounded by dense jungle; 1,602 km (993 mi) southwest of Belém.

Manaus, the capital of Amazonas state, is a sprawling, hilly city of more than 1 million. Taking its name from the Manaó tribe, which means "Mother of the Gods," the city was founded in 1669. It has long flirted with prosperity. Of all the Amazon cities and towns, Manaus is most identified with the rubber boom. In the late 19th and early 20th centuries, the city supplied the world with 90% of its rubber. The immense wealth that resulted was monopolized by a few rubber barons, never numbering more than 100, who lived in the city, spent enormous sums on ostentatious lifestyles (and structures to match), and dominated the region like feudal lords. *Seringueiros* (rubber tappers) were recruited; a few were Indians, but most were transplants from Brazil's crowded and economically depressed northeast. Thousands flocked to the barons' huge plantations, where they lived virtually as slaves. As work progressed, conflicts erupted between barons and Indians over encroachment on tribal lands. Stories of cruelty abound: One baron is said to have killed more than 40,000 Indians during his 20-year "reign." Another boasted of having slaughtered 300 Indians in a day.

The 25-year rubber era was brought to a close thanks to Englishman Henry A. Wickham, who smuggled rubber-tree seeds out of Brazil in 1876. The seeds were planted in Malaysia, where new trees flourished; within 30 years, Asian rubber ended the Brazilian monopoly. Although several schemes were launched to revitalize the Amazon rubber industry and many seringueiros continued to work independently in the jungles, the high times were over. Manaus entered a depression that lasted until 1967, when it was made a free-trade zone. Its economy was revitalized, and its population jumped from 200,000 to 900,000 in less than 20 years. Today, it's the Amazon's most popular destination, due in large part to the many accessible jungle lodges in the surrounding region. Manaus's principal attractions are its lavish, brightly colored houses and civic buildings—vestiges of an opulent time when the wealthy sent their laundry to be done in Europe and sent for Old World artisans and engineers to build their New World monuments.

Manaus is a fairly spread out city with few true high-rises. Although many hotels and sights are in its Centro (City Center) neighborhood, it lacks a truly concentrated downtown like that found in Belém. Centro isn't particularly large and is set on a slight hill above the river. The biggest problem to getting around town is that many streets don't have signs, especially in the free-trade zone.

Exploring Centro

A GOOD WALK

Begin as early in the day as possible at the **Mercado Adolfo Lisboa.** Exit at its northeast end and continue along the waterfront. You'll pass fishing and trading boats until you reach the Porto Flutuante, the British-made floating dock where most large ships anchor. To the right of the dock, a path runs to the **Alfândega.** Avenida Eduardo Ribeiro continues where the path leaves off; follow it to the municipal clock, on your left, and the stairs that lead to the **Catedral da Nossa Senhora da Conceição.** From here, you can turn right on Avenida 7 de Setembro and visit one of several interesting museums, including the **Palácio Rio Negro** and the **Museu do Índio.**

Alternatively, you can continue north from the cathedral on Avenida Eduardo Ribeiro to the pink **Teatro Amazonas.** Turn right, just before the theater, onto Rua José Clemente and follow it to the plaza dominated by the **Igreja São Sebastião.** From here, head around the other side of the theater, along Rua 10 de Julho, and back onto Avenida Eduardo Riberio to the Praça do Congress. Cross the plaza and Avenida Ramos Ferreira and turn left; follow Ramos Ferreira to the **Praça da Saudade**—a good place to relax, eat, and people-watch.

TIMING

Plan to spend 3–4 hours following the walk from start to finish. The tour that continues to Avenida 7 de Setembro will probably take 1½ hours; if you opt to veer off from the rest of the walk here, count on spending up to 3 hours reaching and visiting the museums.

SIGHTS TO SEE

Alfândega. The Customs House was built by the British in 1902 with bricks imported as ship ballast. It stands alongside the floating dock that was built at the same time to accommodate the annual 40-ft rise and fall of the river. The Customs House is now home to the regional office of the Brazilian tax department; although it's not officially open to the public, the guards may let you in upon request. ⊠ *Rua Marquês de Santa Cruz s/n,* ☎ *092/234–5481.*

Catedral da Nossa Senhora da Conceição. Built originally in 1695 by Carmelite missionaries, the Cathedral of Our Lady of the Immaculate Conception (also called Igreja Matriz) burned down in 1850 and was reconstructed in 1878. It's a simple, predominantly neoclassical structure with a bright, colorful interior. ⊠ *Praça da Matriz,* ☎ *no phone.*

Igreja São Sebastião. Neoclassical St. Sebastian's (circa 1888), with its charcoal-gray color and medieval characteristics, seems foreboding. Its interior, however, is luminous and uplifting, with an abundance of white Italian marble, stunning stained-glass windows, and beautiful ceiling paintings. The church has a tower on only one side. Explanations for this asymmetrical configuration include that the second tower wasn't built due to lack of funds; that it was intentionally not added as a symbolic gesture toward the poor; or that the ship with the materials for its construction sank. ⊠ *Praça São Sebastião,* ☎ *no phone.*

Mercado Adolfo Lisboa. This market, built in 1882, is a wrought-iron replica of the market (now destroyed) in Les Halles in Paris; the ironwork is said to have been designed by Gustave Eiffel himself. Vendors sell Amazon food products and handicrafts daily from around dawn until noon. ⊠ *Rua do Barés 6,* ☎ *092/234–8441.*

Museu do Índio. The Indian Museum was constructed and is maintained by Salesian sisters, an order of nuns with eight missions in the upper Amazon. It displays handicrafts, weapons, ceramics, ritual masks, and clothing from the region's tribes. ⊠ *Rua Duque de Caxias 356,* ☎ *092/ 234–1422.* ☜ *Admission.* ☉ *Weekdays 8:30–11:30 and 2–4:30, Sat. 8:30–11:30.*

Palácio Rio Negro. The extravagant Rio Negro Palace was built at the end of the 19th century as the home of a German rubber baron. Later, it was used as the governor's official residence. Today, it hosts some of the city's finest art exhibits and houses a cultural center. ⊠ *Av. 7 de Setembro 1546,* ☎ *092/622–2834.* ☜ *Free.* ☉ *Tues.–Sun. 3–9.*

Praça da Saudade. This bustling, energetic square is a great place to sit back and soak up the local culture. There's a small amusement park, an amphitheater, and several food stalls that serve such dishes as *vatapá* (shrimp in coconut oil) and *tacacá* (shrimp stew).

★ **Teatro Amazonas.** The city's lavish opera house was completed in 1896 after 15 years. The Italian Renaissance–style interior provides a clear idea of the wealth that marked the Amazon rubber boom: marble doorways from Italy, wrought-iron banisters from England, crystal chandeliers from France, and striking panels of French tiles and Italian frescoes depicting Amazon legends. In April 1997, after a 90-year hiatus, the theater reopened with a two-week long international music festival. Recently, a wide variety of entertainers—from José Carreras to the Spice Girls—have performed here. Half-hour tours are conducted daily between 9 and 4. ⊠ *Praça São Sebastião s/n,* ☎ *092/622–2420.* ☜ *Admission.* ☉ *Mon.–Sat. 9–4.*

Beaches

To reach most Manaus area beaches, catch a boat from the Porto Flutuante. The only day with regularly scheduled trips is Sunday, when boats transport great crowds for about $3 per person. Known to locals as the Copacabana of the Amazon, **Praia do Ponta Negra** is next to the Hotel Tropical (☞ Lodging, *below*), a 20-minute bus ride from Centro. With numerous restaurants, bars, and sports and nightlife facilities, it's busy day and night.

Crescent-shape **Praia da Lua** is 23 km (14 mi) southwest of Manaus. You can only reach it by boat on the Rio Negro, so it's clean and less crowded than other beaches. **Praia do Tupé,** another Rio Negro beach accessible only by boat, is 34 km (20 mi) northwest of Manaus. It's popular with locals and tends to fill up on Sunday and holidays, when a special ship makes the trip from the city.

Dining

$$–$$$ ✕ **La Barca.** You usually have to wait for a table here, a testament to this fish restaurant's popularity. The menu offers many options, but the specialty is pirarucú. Meals are accompanied by live music. ⊠ *Rua Recife 684, Parque 10,* ☎ *092/236–7090. AE, DC, MC, V.*

$$ ✕ **Canto da Paixada.** Few eateries can claim to be fit for a pope; when ★ Pope John Paul II came to Manaus in 1981, this restaurant was chosen to host him. The dining areas aren't elegant, but the fish dishes are outstanding. One platter feeds two. ⊠ *Rua Emilio Moreira 1677, Praça 14,* ☎ *092/234–3021. V. No dinner Sun.*

$$ ✕ **Fiorentina.** The green awning and red-and-white check table cloths hint that this restaurant serves authentic Italian. The pasta dishes are delicious, especially the simple lasagna *fiorentina* (with a marinara and ground-beef sauce). Saturday sees a *feijoada* (black beans, rice, meats, and farofa or farinha) that costs about $10. ⊠ *Praça da Polícia 44, Centro,* ☎ *092/232–1295. AE, DC, MC, V.*

$$ ✕ **Suzuran.** For more than 20 years this festive restaurant has served the town's best Japanese food. If you can't decide between raw fish and your fried favorites, don't. The *suzuran teishoku* contains sushi,

sashimi, tempura, and fried fish. ✉ *Boulevard Álvaro Maia 1683, Adrianópolis,* ☎ *092/234–1693. No credit cards. Closed Tues.*

$ ✕ **Churrascaria Búfalo.** Twelve waiters, each offering a different type
★ of meat, scurry around this large, crowded restaurant. As if all of the delectable meats weren't enough, the table is also set with about 10 side dishes, including two types of manioc root, pickled vegetables, and caramelized bananas. ✉ *Rua Joaquim Nabuco 628–A, Centro,* ☎ *092/ 633–3773. AE, DC, MC, V. No dinner Sun.*

$ ✕ **Coqueiro Verde.** Don't bother asking for a menu—everybody who comes here orders the *carne de sol,* beef cured in the sun for a day or two. This delicious, affordable treat is served with rice, beans, farofa, and salad. All this and you can even pet the restaurant's mascot—a cute, woolly monkey—out in the garden. ✉ *Rua Ramos Ferreira 1920, Centro,* ☎ *092/232–0002. AE, DC, MC, V. No dinner Sun.*

Lodging

Although there are several decent in-town hotels, the jungle lodges—actually small hotels—outside town are far more exciting. They usually have guides on staff and offer treks, alligator "hunts," canoe trips, and opportunities to fish and swim. Many lodges are near the Rio Negro, where mosquitoes aren't a problem because of the water's acidity level. (Price categories for lodges are based on 2 day/1 night packages, which include meals and transportation to and from the lodge.)

HOTELS

$$$$ 🏨 **Tropical.** Nothing in the Amazon can match the majesty of this resort. The sprawling complex is 20 km (12 mi) northwest of downtown and overlooking the Rio Negro, with a short path that leads to the beach. In addition to the on-site zoo, numerous sports facilities, and two gorgeous pools, the Tropical also has its own dock. One drawback here is the staff, whose members aren't always helpful (they can be apathetic). You can book rooms here through Varig Airlines, and if you fly Varig you'll receive a 40% room discount. The on-site Tarumã restaurant is a reliable choice for dinners of regional and international fare. ✉ *Estrada da Ponta Negra s/n, Ponta Negra 69037–060,* ☎ *092/659– 5000,* 🖷 *092/658–5026. 610 rooms. 2 restaurants, bar, coffee shop, in-room safes, 2 pools, sauna, 4 tennis courts, basketball, exercise room, jogging, beach, dock, boating, shops, dance club, recreation room, travel services, helipad. AE, DC, MC, V.*

$$$ 🏨 **Taj Mahal.** When this hotel recently became a member of the Holiday Inn chain, it was a mixed blessing. Meeting the strict new quality standards transformed it into a more modern, more luxurious hotel than before. But much of the original, charming East Indian artwork—some of which you can still see in the lobby—didn't make the cut. Although the Taj Mahal seems more standardized now, it's still a pleasant option with a rooftop pool, a revolving restaurant, and convenient location. Request a room with a river view. ✉ *Av. Getúlio Vargas 741, Centro 69020–020,* ☎ 🖷 *092/633–1010. 144 rooms, 26 suites. Restaurant, bar, pool, beauty salon, massage, sauna, meeting rooms. AE, DC, MC, V.*

$$–$$$ 🏨 **St. Paul.** If you are planning an extended stay, this apartment-hotel (or "flat hotel" as they're called in Brazil) in Centro is your best bet. Accommodations are immaculate and have living rooms and fully equipped, modern kitchens. For stays of more than a week, you can get a discount of as much as 50%. ✉ *Av. Ramos Ferreira 1115, Centro 69010-120,* ☎ *092/622–2131,* 🖷 *092/622–2137. 45 apartments. Pool, sauna, exercise room. AE, DC, MC, V.*

$$ 🏨 **Ana Cássia.** The rooftop pool and most of the rooms at this 10-story hotel offer the city's best river and market views. Entering the lobby—with red leather couches, highly polished green and white floors, and

multiple mirrors—you may feel as if you've stepped into the early '80s. The well-equipped rooms aren't nearly as distinguished. ✉ *Rua dos Andradas 14, Centro 69005–180,* ☎ *092/622–3637,* ℻ *092/622– 4812. 88 rooms, 12 suites. Restaurant, coffee shop, pool, beauty parlor, sauna, meeting room. AE, DC, MC, V.*

$ 🖭 **Central.** Located in the free-trade zone, this hotel is good if you're on a tight budget. Rooms are simple, clean, and have all the standard amenities. ✉ *Rua Dr. Moreira 20, Centro 69005-250,* ☎ *092/622– 2600,* ℻ *092/622–2609. 50 rooms. Minibars. AE, DC, MC, V.*

JUNGLE LODGES

$$$$ 🖭 **Amazon Lodge.** Three hours by boat from Manaus, this lodge consists of rustic, floating cabins with air-conditioning and baths. Because of its remote location, the chances for wildlife spotting are terrific. The English-speaking guides are knowledgeable and friendly. ✉ *Contact Nature Safaris: Conjunto Parque Aripuanã, Rua 12, Casa 02, Planalto, Manaus 69040–180,* ☎ *092/656–5464 or 092/656–3357,* ℻ *092/ 656–6101. 14 rooms. Restaurant, fishing, hiking. No credit cards.*

$$$$ 🖭 **Ariaú Jungle Tower.** This lodge's four-story wooden towers are on
★   stilts and are linked by catwalks. The effect is more dramatic in the rainy season when the river covers the ground below. Although the idea is to make you feel integrated with nature, the size of this complex generally prevents such a sentiment—or much contact with wildlife. The exceptions are the adorable, semi-wild monkeys that often visit and inevitably make mischief. Three hours by boat from Manaus on the Rio Ariaú, the lodge offers excellent food and comfortable rooms. Its most popular accommodation—sought by honeymooners and celebrities—is the Tarzan House in the treetops 100 ft up. ✉ *Mailing address: Rua Silva Ramos 41, Centro, Manaus 69010–180,* ☎ *092/234–7308,* ℻ *092/233–5615. 134 rooms. Restaurant, bar, 2 pools, hiking, dock, fishing, helipad. AE, DC, MC, V.*

$$$$ 🖭 **King's Island.** To reach this ever-so remote lodge you can either spend a week on a boat or 3½ hours on a plane. Your experience here will be very distinct from one at the other lodges, mostly because it's in the São Gabriel da Cachoeira mountains. The area is awash in gorgeous waterfalls and also offers the opportunity to hike in beautiful cloud forests. Exotic-travel enthusiasts will be hard-pressed to find a more fascinating place from which to explore the Amazon. ✉ *Contact Nature Safaris: Conjunto Parque Aripuanã, Rua 12, Casa 02, Planalto, Manaus 69040–180,* ☎ *092/656–5464 or 092/656–3357,* ℻ *092/ 656–6101. 14 rooms. Restaurant, hiking, fishing. No credit cards.*

$$$$ 🖭 **Lago Salvador.** Although it's only a 45-minute boat ride from Man-
★   aus, this lodge still offers a serene, secluded atmosphere. Four cabanas, with three apartments each, are set on the banks of the lake from which the lodge receives its name. The rooms, which have fans and running water, are simple but comfortable. Each cabana has a radio so that you can contact one of the staff members who are on call 24-hours a day to pick you up in a canoe or bring you food. Ask for Cabana 2, which has the nicest facilities. ✉ *Contact Amazônia Expeditions: Tropical Hotel, Estrada da Ponta Negra, Manaus,* ☎ *092/658–4221,* ℻ *092/659–5308. 4 cabanas, each with 3 apartments. Restaurant, room service, hiking, boating. V.*

Nightlife and the Arts

The night-time highlight in Manaus is the Boi-Bumbá. Live, pulsating music is played while men and women in Indian costumes tell stories and perform a fascinating, sensual dance. These performances, and others, are held regularly in the large amphitheater at Ponta Negra Beach. In addition, the Teatro Amazonas still draws some of the biggest names in theater, opera, and classical music.

Many bars and clubs have live music or a DJ. **Coraçao Blue** (⊠ Estrada da Ponta Negra 3701 (Km 6), ☎ 092/984–1391) often has rock bands. Two large clubs in Cachoerinha, **Nostalgia Clube** (⊠ Av. Ajuricaba 800, ☎ 092/233–9460) and **Mixtura Brasileira** (⊠ Av. Ajuricaba, ☎ 092/232–3503), have both live music and a DJ. Another popular, but some-what more high-brow dance club, is the Tropical Hotel's **Estudio Trop-ical** (⊠ Estrada da Ponta Negra s/n, ☎ 092/658–5000), open only on Friday and Saturday.

Outdoor Activities and Sports

FUTEBOL

Manaus's professional soccer teams, Rio Negro and Nacional, play at **Estádio Vivaldo Lima** (⊠ Av. Constantino Nery, ☎ 092/236–1640). A taxi ride to the stadium and tickets should each cost about $10.

JET SKIING

How many of your friends can say they've jet skied in the Amazon? **Clube do Jet** (⊠ Rua Praiana 13, access through Av. do Turismo, ☎ 092/245–1332) rents equipment for about $40 an hour.

JUNGLE AND RIVER EXCURSIONS

The most common excursion is a half- or full-day tourist-boat trip 15 km (9 mi) east of Manaus, where the jet-black water of the Rio Negro flows beside the yellowish-brown water of the Rio Solimões for 6 km (4 mi) before merging into one as the Rio Amazonas. (It's also com-mon to see pink dolphins in this area.) Many of these meeting-of-the-waters treks include motor boat side trips along narrow streams or through bayous. Some also stop at the Parque Ecológico do January, where you can see Amazon birds and a lake filled with giant Victoria Régia water lilies.

Overnight boat trips into the rain forest follow the Rio Negro, exploring flooded woodlands and narrow waterways, and stop for a hike on a trail. At night, guides take you by canoe on an alligator "hunt." They shine flashlights into the alligators' eyes, momentarily transfixing them, after which they grab the reptiles, hold them for photographs, and then release them. Longer trips to the Negro's upper reaches—where the river is narrower and life along the banks easier to observe—are also options. Such trips usually stop at river settlements where you can visit with local families. They can also include jungle treks; fishing (with equipment supplied by boat operators); and a trip to Anavilhanas, the world's largest freshwater archipelago. It contains some 350 islands with amazing Amazon flora. Because of the dense vegetation, however, you won't see much wildlife other than birds and monkeys. To arrange any of these excursions, contact an area tour operator (☞ Tour Op-erators and Travel Agents *in* the Amazon A to Z, *below*).

Shopping

AREAS AND MALLS

If you're not from South America, you probably won't find too much of interest in the free-trade zone. Still, you might want to duck into a couple of the endless shops scattered throughout the downtown dis-trict—just to have a look. The largest, most upscale mall is **Amazonas Shopping** (⊠ Av. Djarma Batista 482, Chapad, ☎ 092/642–3555).

SPECIALTY STORES

You'll find such regional crafts as straw baskets, hats, and jewelry at the **Museu do Índio** (⊠ Rua Duque de Caxias 356, ☎ 092/234–1422), the **Central de Artesanato Branco e Silva** (⊠ Rua Recife 1999, ☎ 092/236–1241), and **Ecoshop** (⊠ Amazonas Shopping, 2nd floor, ☎ 092/642–2026).

The Amazon A to Z

Arriving and Departing

BY AIRPLANE

All flights to Belém are served by **Aeroporto Internacional Val-de-Cans** (⊠ Av. Julio Cesár s/n ☎ 091/257–0522), which is 11 km (7 mi) northwest of the city. **Varig** (☎ 091/224–3344) has three flights a week to and from Miami and daily flights to and from Rio, São Paulo, Brasília, and Manaus. Other domestic carriers fly daily to Rio, São Paulo, Brasília, and Manaus including **TAM** (☎ 092/257–1745), **Transbrasil** (☎ 091/224–3677, and **VASP** (☎ 091/224–5588).

From the Airport in Belém. The easiest route from the airport is south on Avenida Julio Cesár and then west on Avenida Almirante Barroso. The 20-minute taxi ride costs $15. There are also buses; look for those labeled MAREX/PRES. VARGAS (for the Hilton and other hotels), MAREX/PRAÇA KENNEDY (Paratur and the docks), or MAREX/VER-O-PESO (Cidade Velha).

In Manaus, the international **Aeroporto Brigadeiro Eduardo Gomes** (☎ 092/621–1210), 17 km (10 mi) south of downtown, no longer has direct flights to or from the United States. Indirect flights may be cheapest on **LAB** (☎ 092/633–4200) via La Paz or **Aeropostale** (☎ 092/233–7685) via Caracas.

TAM (☎ 092/652–1381), **Transbrasil** (☎ 092/622–1705), **Varig** (☎ 092/622–3161), and **VASP** (☎ 092/622–3470) offer daily flights to and from Santarém, Belém, Brasília, Rio, and São Paulo.

From the Airport in Manaus. The trip to Centro takes about 20 minutes and costs $20–$25 by taxi. A trip on one of the city buses, which depart regularly during the day and early evening, costs less than a dollar.

BY BOAT

Most ships arrive and depart in Belém's general dock area called the escadinha. **ENASA** (⊠ Av. Presidente Vargas 41, ☎ 091/242–3165 or 091/212–2479) ships and standard riverboats head upriver from here to Santarém and Manaus. Many excursions depart from the new tourist-boat terminal 20 minutes south of town on Avenida Alcindo Cacela (Praça Princesa Isabel). If you're bringing a car to the Ilha do Marajó, you must take it on one of the **ferries** (☎ 091/296–7472) that depart from Icoaraci, a town 18 km (11 mi) to the northeast. The docks are quite close to the town center. A taxi ride shouldn't cost more than $5.

In front of the Porto Flutuante in Manaus there's a group of stands where people sell tickets for everything from high-speed cruisers to standard riverboats. **ENASA** (⊠ Rua Marechal Deodoro 61, ☎ 092/633–2307 or 091/633–2563) also has a reservation office in town. The docks are in Centro, so most hotels are quite close. A taxi, if necessary, shouldn't be very expensive.

BY BUS

Belém's bus station, **Rodoviário São Bras** (⊠ Av. Almirante Barroso s/n, Praça Floriano Peixoto), is east of Nazaré. Reservations for buses are rarely needed. **Boa Esperança** (☎ 091/266–0033) makes the 209-km (125-mi) journey to Salinas Beach six times a day. The slow bus (4 hrs) costs $5; the faster bus (3 hrs) costs $7. **Beira-Dão** (☎ 091/226–1162) leaves every half-hour on the 60-km (36-mi), 2-hour, $2 journey to Ilha Mosqueiro. Clearly marked buses to Outeiro Beach and the town of Icoaraci pass the bus station regularly and cost about 50¢.

In Manaus the bus station, **Terminal Rodoviário Huascar Angelim** (⊠ Rua Recife 2784, Flores, ☎ 092/236–2732) is 7 km (4½ mi) north of the center. You'll probably only use it to get to Presidente Figueiredo: take the bus labeled ARUANĀ, which runs regularly and costs $5.

BR 316 begins on the outskirts of Belém and runs eastward toward the coast and then south, connecting the city with Brazil's major north-eastern hubs. To reach the beaches at Ilha Mosqueiro outside Belém, take BR 316 and then head north on PA 391. To reach Salinas Beach, take BR 316 to PA 324 and head north on PA 124. From Manaus, BR 174 runs north to Boa Vista and BR 319 travels south to Porto Velho. Unfortunately, both routes are in terrible condition and are often closed, especially during the rainy season.

Getting Around

BY BUS

Belém's city bus service is safe, efficient, and comprehensive, but a little confusing—ask a local for guidance. You board buses at the rear, where you pay an attendant the equivalent of 50¢ and pass through a turnstile to take your seat.

In Manuas, the city bus system is extensive and fairly easy to use. The fare is about 50¢. Most of the useful buses run along Avenida Floriano Peixoto, including Bus 120, which goes to Ponta Negra and stops near the Tropical Hotel. The Fontur bus, which costs about $5, travels between Centro and the Tropical Hotel several times a day.

BY CAR

Although Belém has the most traffic of any Amazon city and what seems like more than its fair share of one-way streets, in-town driving is relatively easy. Parking is only tricky in a few areas, such as Avenida Presidente Vargas and the escadinha. Rental cars cost between $40 and $70 a day. Several companies have offices at the airport and in town. Try: **Localiza** (⊠ Av. Pedro Álvares Cabral 200, ☎ 091/212–2700) and **Norauto** (⊠ Av. Gentil Bittencourt 2086, ☎ 091/249–4900).

There are no major traffic or parking problems in Manaus. You can rent a car at the airport through **Unidas Rent a Car** (☎ From 092/621–1575).

BY TAXI

There are plenty of taxis in Belém, and they're easy to flag down on the street (you only need call for them at odd hours). All taxis have meters; tips aren't necessary. Reliable companies include **Coopertaxi** (☎ 091/257–1720) and **Taxi Nazaré** (☎ 091/242–7867).

In Manaus taxis, all equipped with meters, are easy to flag down on the streets. At odd hours, you can call **Tucuxi** (☎ 092/622–4040).

Contacts and Resources

BANKS AND CURRENCY EXCHANGE

In Belém an airport branch of the **Banco do Brasil** (☎ 091/257–1983) charges a $20 commission to exchange travelers checks. In town, you'll find the best rates at **Banco Amazônia** (⊠ Av. Presidente Vargas 800, ☎ 091/216–3252), which is open weekdays 10–4. **Casa Francesa Câmbio e Turismo** (⊠ Trv. Padre Prudêncio 40, ☎ 091/241–2716) is one of several exchange houses that offer comparable rates.

At the airport in Manaus, you can exchange money at **Banco do Brasil** and **Banco Real.** In town, you'll probably get the best rates at **Cortez Câmbio** (⊠ Av. 7 de Setembro 1199, ☎ 092/622–4222).

CONSULATES

In Belém: United Kingdom (⊠ Av. Governador José Malcher 815, rooms 410–411, ☎ 091/223–0990 or 091/222—0762), **United States** (⊠ Rua Oswaldo Cruz 165, ☎ 091/223–0613 or 091/223–0810).

In Manaus: United Kingdom (⊠ Rua Poraquê 240, Distrito Industrial, ☎ 092/237–7869 or 092/237–7186), **United States** (⊠ Rua Recife 1010, Adrianópolis, ☎ FAX 092/633–4907).

EMERGENCIES

Ambulance: ☎ 192 in Belém and Manaus. **Fire:** ☎ 193 in Belém or 092/611–5040 in Manaus. **Hospitals: Hospital e Maternidade Dom Luiz I** (⊠ Av. Generalíssimo Deodoro 868, Belém, ☎ 091/241–4144). **Hospital e Pronto Socorro Municipal 28 de Agosto** (⊠ Rua Recife s/n, Adrianópolis, Manaus, ☎ 092/236–0326).

Pharmacies: Big Ben (⊠ Av. Gentil Bittencourt 1548, Belém, ☎ 091/241–3000) has many branches and offers 24-hour delivery service; **Drogaria Angelica** (⊠ Av. Djarma Batista 428, Manaus, ☎ 092/233–6100) offers 24-hour delivery service. **Police:** ☎ 190 in Belém and Manaus.

HEALTH AND SAFETY

Dengue and malaria exist in the Amazon, although they aren't common concerns in the cities. Throughout the region, avoid drinking tap water and using ice made from it. In Belém, watch out for pickpockets at Ver-o-Peso market and avoid walking alone at night, particularly in the Cidade Velha. Manaus also has some crime problems; again solitary night-time walks aren't recommended, especially around the port.

TELEPHONES, THE INTERNET, AND MAIL

The area code for Belém is 091. Public phones, operated with cards (sold in newsstands), are found on many corners. You can make long distance calls at **Telepará** (⊠ Av. Presidente Vargas 610), which is open daily 7 AM–midnight. **Convert** (⊠ Shopping Iguatemi, Trv. Padre Eutíquio 1078, third floor, ☎ 091/250–5566) provides Internet service for $2 an hour and is open daily 10–10. The central branch of the **post office** (⊠ Av. Presidente Vargas 498, ☎ 091/212–1155) is open weekdays 8–noon and 2–6. You can send faxes from here and, as in all Brazilian post offices, SEDEX international courier service is available.

In Manaus, the area code is 092. Public phones, which take cards, are plentiful in Centro but aren't easy to find elsewhere in town. For long distance calls, go to **Telamazon** (⊠ Av. Getúlio Vargas 950, Centro, ☎ 092/621–6339), which is open on weekdays 7–6:30 and Saturday 8–2. **Argo Internet** (⊠ Rua Emílio Moreira 1769, Praça 14, ☎ 092/633–1236) charges $15 per hour to use the Internet. The most central **post office** (⊠ Rua Marechal Deodoro 117, Centro, ☎ 092/622–2181) is open weekdays from 9 to 5 and on Saturday from 9 to 1.

TOUR OPERATORS AND TRAVEL AGENTS

Some of the better operators in Belém are **Amazon Star Tours** (⊠ Rua Henrique Gurjão 236, ☎ 091/212–6244), **Fontenele** (⊠ Av. Assis de Vasconcelos 199, ☎ 091/241–3218), and **Lusotur** (⊠ Equatorial Palace hotel, Av. Braz de Aguiar 612, ☎ 091/241–2000). For excursions as well as help with plane and hotel reservations, contact **Angel Turismo** (⊠ Hilton International Belém, Av. Presidente Vargas 882, Praça da República, ☎ 091/224–2111).

In Manaus, good tour operators include: **Amazônia Expeditions** (⊠ Tropical Hotel, Estrada da Ponta Negra s/n, ☎ 092/658–4221), **Amazon Explorers** (⊠ Rua Nhamundá 21, ☎ 092/633–3319), and **Anaconda Tours** (⊠ Rua Dr. Almínio 36, ☎ 092/233–7642). Another operation, **Tarumã** (⊠ Av. Eduardo Ribeiro 620, ☎ 092/633–3363), can also help with hotel and transportation arrangements.

VISITOR INFORMATION

Belemtur (⊠ Av. Governador José Malcher 592, Nazaré, Belém, ☎ 091/242–0900 or 091/242–0033), the city tourist board, is open weekdays

8–noon and 2–6. Pará State's tourist board, **Paratur** (⊠ Praça Kennedy, on the waterfront, Belém, ☎ 091/223–7029 or 091/212–0669), is open weekdays 8–6. Both agencies are well organized and extremely helpful.

In Manaus, the Amazonas State's tourism authority, the **Secretaria de Estado da Cultura e Turismo** (⊠ Av. 7 de Setembro 1546, Centro, ☎ 092/234–2252), is open weekdays 8–6. The Manaus tourism authority is **Fundação Municipal de Turismo (FUMTUR)** (⊠ Praça Dom Pedro III, Centro, ☎ 092/622–4986 or 092/622–4886); it's open weekdays 8–5.

BRAZIL A TO Z

Arriving and Departing

By Airplane
AIRPORTS

Chicago, Houston, Los Angeles, Miami, and New York are the major gateways for flights to Brazil from the United States and Canada. Several airlines fly directly from London, but there's no direct service from Sydney, Australia or Auckland, New Zealand. The two biggest Brazilian gateways are Rio de Janeiro and São Paulo.

CARRIERS

Major North American carriers serving Brazil include **Air Canada** (☎ 800/776–3000 or 800/361–8620 in Canada), **American Airlines** (☎ 800/433–7300 in North America), **Canadian Airlines** (☎ 800/665–1177 in Canada or 800/426–7000 in the U.S.), **Continental Airlines** (☎ 800/231–0856 in North America), **Delta Airlines** (☎ 800/241–4141 in the U.S.), and **United Airlines** (☎ 800/241–6522 in North America).

From the United Kingdom, **British Airways** (☎ 0345/222–111) has nonstop service from London's Gatwick Airport to Rio and São Paulo. **Continental** (☎ 0800/776464) flies from Gatwick to Newark and on to both Rio and São Paulo.

From Sydney, Australia, you can take **Qantas** (☎ 13–13–13) to Los Angeles, pick up an American Airlines flight to Miami, and then complete your trip to Rio on Varig. **Air New Zealand** (☎ 0800/737–000 or 09/357–8900) offers flights to major Brazilian cities through their partnership with Varig (☞ *below*). Direct flights to Los Angeles—where you transfer to Varig—depart from Auckland once or twice a day.

The Brazilian carrier **Transbrasil** (☎ 800/872–3153) has service from Miami, Orlando, New York, Washington, D.C., Los Angeles and Chicago to its São Paulo hub. **Varig** (☎ 800/468–2744), Brazil's largest international carrier, flies to Rio and São Paulo from Chicago, Los Angeles, Miami and New York as well as to Manaus, Recife, Fortaleza, and Belém from Miami. **Vasp** (☎ 800/732–8271), another Brazilian carrier, flies from Miami, New York, and Los Angeles to São Paulo and Rio and from Miami to Recife and Brasília.

FLYING TIMES

The flying time from New York is 8½ hours to Rio, 9½ hours to São Paulo. From Miami, it's 7 hours to Rio, 8 hours to São Paulo. Most flights from Los Angeles go through Miami, so add 5 hours to the Miami times given; direct flights to São Paulo from Los Angeles take about 11 hours. From London, it's 7 hours to São Paulo. Within Brazil, it's 1 hour from Rio to São Paulo or Belo Horizonte, 2 hours from Rio to Salvador, and 2½ hours from Rio to Belém. From São Paulo it's 4 hours to Manaus and 1½ hours to Iguaçu Falls.

By Boat

Some international cruise lines stop at Brazilian ports during world-wide or South American cruises. Itineraries change from ship to ship, from line to line, and from year to year, so contact a travel agent or the cruise company to get the most recent information. Companies that have included Brazilian ports on their routes include **Cunard** (☎ 800/5–CUNARD), **Holland America Line** (☎ 800/426–0327), **Princess Cruises and Tours** (☎ 800/421–0522), **Radisson Seven Seas Cruises** (☎ 800/285–1835), **Royal Olympic Cruises** (☎ 800/872–6400), **Seabourne Cruise Lines** (☎ 800/929–9595), **Silversea Cruises** (☎ 800/277–6655).

Getting Around

By Airplane

Varig, Vasp, Transbrasil, and TAM provide regular jet service between all of the country's major (and most medium-size) cities. Remote areas are also quite accessible—if you don't mind small planes. The most widely used service is the Ponte Aérea (Air Bridge), the Rio–São Paulo shuttle, which departs every half-hour from 6 AM to 10:30 PM (service switches to every 15 minutes during morning and evening rush hours). It costs $90–$140 each way; reservations aren't necessary.

Although flights in Brazil are extremely expensive, some Brazilian airlines offer 30% discounts for seven-day advance purchases, for travelers over age 60, and for red-eye flights (called *vôo coruja*) between 10 PM and 6 AM. If you plan to travel a lot within Brazil, buy an airpass from Transbrasil or Varig before you leave home (these can only be purchased externally). Varig, which has the better service and flies to more cities, offers three versions: for $490, you get 5 flights within the country over a period of 21 days; for $350, you can travel between 4 destinations in the south, southeast, and central west; $290 buys you 4 flights within the northeast, and you can begin or end your trip in Rio or São Paulo. In high season (Dec.–Feb. and July), prices are higher.

By Bus

The nation's *ônibus* (bus) network is affordable, comprehensive, and efficient—compensating for the lack of trains and the high cost of air travel. Every major city can be reached by bus as can most of the small-to medium-size communities. On well-traveled routes, service is especially frequent and inexpensive. Lengthy bus trips anywhere will involve travel over some bad highways, an unfortunate fact of life in Brazil today. Trips to northern, northeastern, and central Brazil tend to be especially trying; the best paved highways are in the south and southeast.

Buses used for long trips are modern and comfortable (bathrooms and air-conditioning are common amenities), and they stop regularly at reasonably clean roadside cafés. Note that regular buses used for shorter hauls may be labeled AR CONDICIONADO (AIR-CONDITIONED) but often are not. Tickets are sold (expect to pay in cash) at bus-company offices and at city bus terminals. Reservations generally aren't necessary except for trips to resort areas during high season or during major holidays (Christmas, Carnival, etc.) and school-break periods.

By Car

EMERGENCY ASSISTANCE

The **Clube Automótivel do Brasil** (Automobile Club of Brazil; ⌧ Rua do Passeio 90, Rio de Janeiro, RJ, ☎ 021/297–4455) provides emergency assistance to foreign motorists in cities and on highways, but only if they're members of an automobile club in their own nation.

GASOLINE

Gasoline in Brazil costs around $1.30 a liter ($5 a gallon). Unleaded gas is called *especial* and carries the same price. Brazil also has an extensive fleet of ethanol-powered cars. Ethanol fuel is sold at all gas stations, and costs a little less than gasoline. However, such cars get lower mileage, so they offer little advantage over gas-powered cars. Stations are plentiful both within cities and on major highways, and many are open 24 hours a day.

PARKING

In cities, head for a garage or a lot and leave your car with the attendant. Should you find a space on the street, you'll probably have to pay a fee. There are no meters; instead, there's a system involving coupons that allow you to park for a certain time period (usually two hours) and that you post in your car's window. You can buy them from uniformed street-parking attendants or at newsstands.

No-parking zones are marked by a capital letter "E" (which means *estacionamento*, the Portuguese word for "parking") that is crossed out. These zones are, more often than not, filled with cars, which are rarely bothered by the police.

ROAD CONDITIONS

The country's highway department estimates that 40% of the federal highways (including those with either the designation "BR" or a state abbreviation such as "RJ" or "SP"), which constitute 70% of Brazil's total road system, are in a dangerous state of disrepair. Evidence of this is everywhere: potholes, lack of signage, inadequate shoulders, etc. Landslides and flooding after heavy rains are frequent and at times shut down entire stretches of key highways. Increasing traffic adds to the system's woes, as does the fact that neither speed limits nor the most basic rules of safety seem to figure in the national psyche. The worst offenders are bus and truck drivers. For these reasons, if you drive, do so with the utmost caution.

RULES OF THE ROAD

Brazilians drive on the right, and in general, traffic laws are the same as those in the United States. The use of seat belts is mandatory. The national speed limit is 80 kph (48 mph), but is seldom observed. In theory, foreign drivers licenses are acceptable. In practice, however, police (particularly highway police) have been known to claim that driving with a foreign license is a violation in order to shake down drivers for bribes. It's best to get an international driver's license, which is seldom challenged. If you do get a ticket for some sort of violation—real or imagined—don't argue. And plan to spend longer than you want settling it.

Contacts and Resources

Customs and Duties

Formerly strict import controls have been substantially liberalized as part of the Brazilian government's efforts to open up the nation's economy to competition. In addition to personal items, you're now permitted to bring in, duty-free, up to $500 worth of gifts purchased abroad, including up to 2 liters of liquor. If you plan to bring in plants, you may do so only with documentation authenticated by the consular service.

Health and Safety

Plan to drink only bottled water during your stay and check that ice and juice are made with it in restaurants. In addition, be sure to thoroughly wash and/or peel fruit before eating it.

Bichos de pé, parasites found in areas where pigs, chickens, and dogs run free, embed themselves in humans' feet. To avoid these parasites, never walk barefoot in areas where animals are loose.

Sunshine, limes, and skin don't mix well. The oil in lime juice, if left on human skin and exposed to the sun, will burn and scar. If you're using lime and will be exposed to a lot of sun, be sure to wash well with soap and water.

A 1998 publication issued by Brazil's Ministry of Health estimated that there were as many as 500,000 cases of AIDS and HIV in the country. Aside from the obvious safe-sex precautions, keep in mind that Brazil's blood supply isn't, overall, subject to the same intense screening as elsewhere. If you need a transfusion and circumstances permit it, ask that the blood be screened. Insulin-dependent diabetics or those who require injections should take the appropriate supplies with them—syringes, needles, disinfectants—enough to last the trip. In addition, you might want to resist the temptation to get a new tattoo or body piercing while you're in Brazil.

All travelers should have up-to-date tetanus boosters, and a hepatitis A inoculation can prevent one of the most common intestinal infections. If you're heading to tropical regions, you should get yellow fever shots, particularly if you're traveling overland from a yellow-fever country (Peru, Bolivia, etc.). Children must have current inoculations against measles, mumps, rubella, and polio.

In areas with malaria and dengue, which are both carried by mosquitoes, take mosquito nets, wear clothing that covers the body, apply repellent containing DEET, and use a spray against flying insects in living and sleeping areas. In parts of northern Brazil an aggressive strain of malaria has become resistant to chloroquine and may be treated with mefloquine, an expensive alternative whose side effects include everything from headaches, nausea, and dizziness to psychosis, convulsions, and hallucinations.

CRIME
By day, the countryside is quite safe. Although there has been an effort to crack down on tourist-related crime, particularly in Rio, petty street thievery is still prevalent in urban areas. Avoid flashing money around, lock traveler's checks and cash in a hotel safe, and do not wear any jewelry you aren't willing to lose. Watch out for pickpockets, usually young children working in groups. One or more will try to distract you while another grabs a wallet, bag, or camera. Note that Brazilian law requires everyone to carry official identification with them at all times. You should always have a copy (leave the original in the hotel safe) of your passport's data page and the visa stamp.

Language, Culture, and Etiquette
The language in Brazil is Portuguese, not Spanish, and Brazilians will appreciate it if you know the difference. English is spoken among educated Brazilians and, in general, by at least some of the staff at hotels, tour operators, and travel agencies. Store clerks and waiters may have a smattering of English; taxi and bus drivers won't. As in many places throughout the world, you're more likely to find English-speaking locals in major cities than in small towns or the countryside.

Although Brazil is a predominantly Catholic country, in many places there's an anything-goes outlook. As a rule, coastal areas (particularly Rio and parts of the northeast) are considerably less conservative than inland areas and those throughout the south. People dress nicely to enter churches, and hats are frowned upon during mass. Brazilians are a very friendly lot. Don't be afraid to smile in the streets or ask for directions (be aware, however, that a Brazilian may give you false directions before admitting that he or she doesn't know where to point you). The slower pace of life in much of the country reflects an appreciation of family and friendship (as well as a respect for the heat); knowing this will help you understand why things may take a little longer to get done.

Throughout the country, use the "thumbs up" gesture to indicate that something is OK. The gesture created by making a circle with your thumb and index finger and holding your other fingers up in the air has a very rude meaning.

Mail

Post offices are called *correios,* and branches are marked by the name and a logo that looks something like two interlocked fingers; most are open weekdays 8–5 and Saturday until noon. Mailboxes are small yellow boxes marked CORREIOS that sit atop metal pedestals on street corners. Regular airmail from Brazil takes at least 10 or more days to reach the United States, possibly longer to Canada and the United Kingdom, definitely longer to Australia and New Zealand.

POSTAL RATES

Airmail letters, aerograms, and postcards from Brazil to the United States and the United Kingdom cost approximately $1. The country has both national and international express mail services such as Federal Express and DHL. Objects of value—especially currency, checks, or credit cards—should never be sent through the mail.

RECEIVING MAIL

Mail can be addressed to "poste restante" and sent to any major post office. The address must include the postal code (such codes are widely used in this country) for that particular branch. American Express will hold mail for its cardholders.

Money and Expenses

CHANGING MONEY

At press time, the real (plural "reais", though also seen as "reals") was at 2.89 to the pound sterling, 1.82 to the U.S. dollar, 1.20 to the Canadian dollar, 1.17 to the Australia dollar, and 0.95 to the New Zealand dollar.

You can change cash and traveler's checks (well-known names are best) at hotels, banks, *casas de câmbio* (exchange houses), travel agencies, and shops in malls or stores that cater to tourists. The rate for traveler's checks is lower than that for cash, and hotels often change them at a rate that's lower than that available at banks or casas de câmbio. Outside of larger cities, changing money becomes more of a challenge; plan accordingly

Nearly all the nation's major banks have automated teller machines. MasterCard and Cirrus are rarely accepted (some airport Banco Itau ATMs are linked to Cirrus); Visa and Plus cards are. American Express card holders can make withdrawals at most Bradesco ATMs marked 24 HORAS. To be safe, carry a variety of cards.

CURRENCY

One real has 100 centavos (cents). There are notes worth 1, 5, 10, 50, and 100 reais, together with coins worth 1, 5, 10, 25, and 50 centavos, and 1 real, all of which feel and look similar.

FORMS OF PAYMENT

In large cities and leading tourist centers, restaurants, hotels, gas stations, and shops accept major international credit cards. Off the beaten track, you may have more difficulty using them. In addition, many small tradesmen are at a total loss when faced with traveler's checks. Note that some hotels offer discounts for cash payments.

Hotel taxes at press time were roughly 8%; meal taxes, 15.25%; car rental taxes, 12.5%. Taxes on international flights from Brazil aren't always included in your ticket and can run as high as $40; domestic flights may incur a $10 charge. Although U.S. dollars are accepted in some airports, be prepared to pay departure taxes in reais.

At restaurants that add a 10% service charge onto the check, it's customary to give the waiter an additional 5% tip. If there's no service charge, leave 15%. In deluxe hotels, tip porters 50¢ per bag, chambermaids 50¢ per day, $1 for room and valet service. If a taxi driver helps you with your luggage, a per-bag charge of about 35¢ is levied in addition to the fare. In general, tip taxi drivers 10% of the fare.

Tipping in bars and cafés follows the rules of restaurants, although at outdoor bars Brazilians rarely leave a tip if they had only a soft drink or a beer. At airports and at train and bus stations, tip the last porter who puts your bags into the cab (50¢ a bag at airports, 25¢ a bag at bus and train stations). In large cities you will often be accosted on the street by children looking for handouts; 25¢ is an average "tip."

Top hotels in Rio and São Paulo go for more than $200 a night, and meals can—but do not have to—cost as much. Outside Brazil's two largest cities, prices for food and lodging tend to drop considerably. Self-service salad bars where you pay per weight (per kilo) are inexpensive alternatives in all cities and towns, though be sure to choose carefully among them. Taxis can be pricey. City buses, subways, and long-distance buses are all inexpensive; plane fares definitely aren't. For an average week in a Brazilian city, a good strategy is to convert $500 into reais. This provides sufficient cash for most expenses, such as taxis and small purchases and snacks.

Sample Prices. A cup of coffee in São Paulo is $1; bottle of beer or glass of draft, $3; soft drink, $1.50; fresh fruit drink, $2; hamburger, $4–$6; 3-mi taxi ride, $8.

Opening and Closing Times

Banks are, with exceptions, open weekdays 10–4. Office hours are generally 9–5. Within cities and along major highways, many **gas stations** are open 24 hours a day, 7 days a week. In smaller towns, they may only be open during daylight hours Monday–Saturday. Many **museums** are open from 10 or 11 to 5 or 6 (they may stay open later one night a week). Some museums, however, are only open in the afternoon, and many are closed on Monday or Tuesday. Generally, small **shops** are open weekdays from 9 to 6 and on Saturday from 9 to 1 or 2. Centers and malls are often open from 10 to 10. Some centers, malls, and pharmacies are open on Sunday.

New Year's Day (Jan. 1); Epiphany (Jan. 6); Carnaval, the week preceding Ash Wednesday (which falls on March 8 in 2000 and Feb. 28 in 2001), Good Friday (Apr. 21, 2000; Apr. 13, 2001); Easter (Apr. 23, 2000; Apr. 15, 2001), Tiradentes Day (Apr. 21), Labor Day (May 1), Corpus Christi (June 22, 2000; June 14, 2001); Independence Day (Sept. 7); Our Lady of Aparecida Day (Oct. 12); All Souls' Day (Nov. 1); Declaration of the Republic Day (Nov. 15); Christmas (Dec. 25).

Passports and Visas

To enter Brazil, all U.S. citizens, even infants, must have both a passport and a tourist visa (valid for five years). To obtain one, you must submit the following to the Brazilian Embassy or to the nearest consulate: a passport that will be valid for six months past the date of first entry to Brazil; a passport-type photo; a photocopy of your round-trip ticket or a signed letter from a travel agency with confirmed round-trip bookings or proof of your ability to pay for your stay in Brazil; and cash, a money order, or a certified check for $45 (there's also a $10 handling fee if anyone other than the applicant submits the visa).

If you're a business traveler, you may need a business visa (valid for 90 days). It has all the same requirements as a tourist visa, but you'll also need a letter on company letterhead—addressed to the embassy or consulate and signed by an authorized representative (other than you)—stating the nature of your business in Brazil, itinerary, business contacts, dates of arrival and departure, and that the company assumes all financial and moral responsibility while you're in Brazil. The fee is $105 (plus the $10 fee if someone other than you submits the visa). In addition to the forms of payment detailed above, a company check is also acceptable.

Canadian nationals, Australians, and New Zealanders also need visas to enter the country. For Canadians, the fee is US$40; for New Zealanders, US$20; and for Australians, there's no charge. Citizens of the United Kingdom don't need a visa.

In the United States, there are consulates in Atlanta, Boston, Chicago, Houston, Los Angeles, Miami, New York, San Francisco, and San Juan. To get the location of the Brazilian consulate to which you must apply, contact the Brazilian Embassy (☞ Smart Travel Tips A to Z).

Telephones

Public phones are everywhere and are called *orelhões* (big ears) because of their shape. To use them, buy a phone card, *cartão de telefone,* at a *posto telefônico* (phone office), newsstand, or post office. Cards come with a varying number of units (each unit is usually worth a couple minutes), which will determine the price. Buy a couple of cards if you don't think you'll have the chance again soon. Even with a phone card, you may not be able to make long-distance calls from some pay phones—and the logic behind which ones will and which ones won't allow such calls varies from region to region, making it as baffling as it is Brazilian. Phone offices are found at airports, many bus stations, and in downtown neighborhoods of large cities.

COUNTRY & AREA CODES

To call Brazil from overseas, dial the country code, 55, and then the area code, omitting the first 0.

DIRECTORY & OPERATOR INFORMATION

For local directory assistance, dial 102. For directory assistance in another Brazilian city, dial the area code of that city plus 121.

LONG-DISTANCE CALLS

Long-distance calls within and international calls to and from Brazil are extremely expensive. Hotels also add a surcharge, increasing this cost. For operator-assisted international calls, dial 000111. For international information, dial 000333.

With the privatization of the Brazilian telecommunications network, everyone now has a choice of long-distance companies. Hence, to make direct-dial, long-distance calls you must find out which companies serve the area you're calling from and then get their access codes—

the staff at your hotel can help. (Note, however, that some hotels have already made the choice for you, so you may not need an access code when calling from the hotel itself.) For international calls dial 00 + the long-distance company's access code + the country code + the area code and number. For long-distance calls within Brazil dial 0 + the access code + the area code and number. **AT&T** (☎ 800/874–4000), **MCI** (☎ 800/444–4444), and **Sprint** (☎ 800/793–1153) operators are also accessible from Brazil.

Visitor Information

EMBRATUR (www.embratur.gov.br), Brazil's national tourism organization, doesn't have offices overseas, though its Web site is helpful. For information in your home country, your best bet is to contact the Brazilian Embassy or the closest consulate—some of which have Web sites and staff dedicated to promoting tourism. **RioTur** (✉ 3601 Aviation Blvd., suite 2100, Manhattan Beach, CA 90266, ☎ 310/643–2638; ✉ 201 E. 12th St., Suite 509, New York, NY 10003, ☎ 212/375–0801) is a good source for information on the city of Rio. An organization called **Pro-Brazil, Inc.** (✉ 554 5th Ave., 4th floor, New York, NY 10036, ☎ 212/997–4070) represents the Brazilian states of Bahia, Rio, and São Paulo.

When to Go

Throughout Brazil the high tourism season runs from November to April (Brazilian summer), although there are festivals and special events. Carnival, the year's principal festival, occurs during the four days preceding Ash Wednesday, which falls in February or March. For top hotels in Rio and Salvador, the two leading Carnival cities, you must make reservations a year in advance. Hotel rates go up on the average 20% for Carnival, and you should also expect to pay more for taxis, up to double regular fares.

CLIMATE

Seasons below the Equator are the reverse of the north—summer in Brazil runs from December to March and winter from June to September. The rainy season in Brazil occurs during the summer months, but this is rarely a nuisance. Showers can be torrential but usually last no more than an hour or two. In the Amazon, the rainy season (November to May) is more pronounced and is marked by heavy downpours that usually occur twice a day.

Rio de Janeiro is on the Tropic of Capricorn, and its climate is just that—tropical. Summers are hot and humid; winter temperatures are moderate. Along the coast to the northeast, temperatures are slightly higher year-round. In the Amazon, where the equator crosses the country, temperatures in the high 80s to the 90s (30s C) are common throughout the year. Because of their higher altitude, São Paulo and Minas Gerais State are substantially cooler than Rio. Winter temperatures in these regions can fall to the low 40s (5°C–8°C).

The following are the average daily maximum and minimum temperatures for Rio de Janeiro.

Jan.	84F	29C	May	77F	25C	Sept.	75F	24C
	69	21		66	19		66	19
Feb.	85F	29C	June	76F	24C	Oct.	77F	25C
	73	23		64	18		63	17
Mar.	83F	28C	July	75F	24C	Nov.	79F	26C
	72	22		64	18		68	20
Apr.	80F	27C	Aug.	76F	24C	Dec.	82F	28C
	69	21		64	18		71	22

The following are the average daily maximum and minimum temperatures for Salvador.

Jan.	87F	31C	May	80F	27C	Sept.	78F	26C
	76	24		70	21		69	21
Feb.	88F	31C	June	80F	27C	Oct.	80F	27C
	76	24		67	19		69	21
Mar.	87F	31C	July	78F	26C	Nov.	83F	28C
	77	25		66	19		72	22
Apr.	84F	29C	Aug.	80F	27C	Dec.	86F	30C
	73	23		67	19		77	25

FESTIVALS AND SEASONAL EVENTS

Ano Novo (New Year's Eve) followers of Macumba (a spiritualist cult) honor Iemanjá, goddess of the sea, with fireworks, songs, rituals, and offerings along Rio's beaches. In Salvador the **Festival of Iemanjá** is held on the second Sunday of February. Devotees of the Afro-Brazilian Candomblé cult begin singing the sea goddess's praises at the crack of dawn along the beaches. The **Formula I Grand Prix** is held during March in São Paulo. In Salvador, March sees **PanPerc,** a percussion festival in which such music notables as Gilberto Gil and Caetano Veloso perform alongside percussion groups.

The **Festas Juninas** is a cycle of celebrations throughout June honoring various saints. The festivals are particularly noteworthy in Rio de Janeiro State and in several interior regions of the northeast. In São Paulo, the annual **Carlton Dance Festival** starts in June and continues through July. The **Paratins Folk Festival** (June 28–30) takes place 400 km (250 mi) downriver from Manaus and is the Amazon's largest folkloric festival. São Paulo's Museu da Imagem e do Som sponsors the **International Short Film Festival** in August. The month also sees São Paulo's annual, three-day **Free Jazz Festival.** Salvador's **Festin Bahia** is a three-day international music festival held every August or September featuring foreign and local performers.

Ouro Prêto's giant, week-long **Julibeu do Senhor Ben Jesus do Matosinhos** religious festival is held in mid-September. One of Belém's two out-of-season Carnavals, **Paráfolia,** takes place at the end of September. São Paulo's international film festival, **Mostra Internacional de Cinema,** is held in October. The world-renowned biennial art exhibition (South America's largest), the **São Paulo Biennial,** is held from mid-October to mid-December in each even-numbered year in São Paulo's Ibirapuera Park. On the second Sunday in October, thousands of worshipers flock to Belém for the **Círio de Nazaré** processional honoring the city's patron saint. In November Ouro Prêto's **Aleijadinho Week** honors the great 18th-century sculptor, whose work adorns many of the city's churches. The second of Belém's out-of-season Carnavals, **Carnabelém,** takes place in mid-November.

6 CHILE

Bounded by the sea and the sharp spine
of the Andes, Chile makes up in spirit what
it lacks in width. The proximity of active
volcanoes and crumbling glaciers only
increases the lush pleasures of award-
winning vineyards, excellent ski slopes, and
such beachside resorts as Viña del Mar.

Updated by
Charles
Runnette

▌ **LIVE NOW IN A COUNTRY AS SOFT** / as the autumnal flesh of grapes," begins *Country,* a poem by the Chilean poet and Nobel prize-winner Pablo Neruda. With his odes to artichokes, birds, hope, Valparaíso, fish soup, socks, and September, he sang Chile into being and taught us to inhale its sharp salt air or the dry winy bouquet of its Andean peaks before we hold them to our lips and drink them down.

Chile is as luminous and pungent, as rustic and urban, as any of Neruda's poems about it. It encompasses the world's driest desert, a pie slice of Antarctica, the "navel of the universe" (Easter Island), Robinson Crusoe's former haunts, a sophisticated urban landscape, and a temperate southern jungle—all in one slim extension of land squeezed between the Pacific Ocean and the Andes, with a vast and varied human geography to match. In some places the 320-km (200-mi) territorial limit is wider than the country itself, making Chile as much ocean as earth.

From 1973 to 1990, Chile was virtually synonymous with the name of General Augusto Pinochet, who, with U.S. support, led a coup against the elected socialist government in September 1973. His regime's reputation for human-rights violations and violent social conflict discouraged many visitors, but the advent of a civilian, elected government in March 1990 brought considerable improvements. Today the country enjoys considerable social harmony and the most advanced economy in South America.

The first traveler to reach Chile barely gave it a glance: Hernando de Magallanes left his name and little else behind when he journeyed up the southwestern coast in 1520. Diego de Almagro was the first Spaniard to actually explore Chile, in an expedition that would pave the way for cultural domination of the territory and peoples he found here. Setting out from the north in July of 1535, Almagro and a ragged crew of 500 adventurers marched south in search of fame, fortune, and glory. When the band reached the Valley of Aconcagua, they decided that their hopes of mineral riches were far weaker than the fierce Mapuche resistance they encountered there. Later, Pedro de Valdivia traveled south along the Camino del Inca (Road of the Inca) with another gang of adventurers and a sole woman, his lover, Inés de Suárez. Although Pedro de Valdivia is credited with the founding of Santiago in 1541, on more than one occasion Doña Inés saved his neck with her cunning, and even cutthroat, military counsel.

For the next 300 years, Chile's original inhabitants, especially the southern Mapuche, successfully defended a sizable territory and their way of life against Spanish encroachment. Chilean independence from Spain, after a war that lasted from 1810 to 1818, marked the beginning of the end of the Mapuche's independence, as the newly independent nation sought to establish firm control of the whole territory. Their last great rebellion failed in 1881, and soon after, Chilean governments started shipping in German, Swiss, and other European colonists to fill their "empty" lands.

Today's Chileans are a mixture of European and indigenous gene pools, with the lightest hair, skin, and eyes to be found at the top of a hierarchically organized society. Native peoples include about half a million Mapuche living in the region around Temuco; the Aymara, who live in Chile's difficult north, in the world's driest desert; and the Polynesians, who still form the majority of the population of Rapa Nui (Easter Island).

Chile (North)   **Chile (South)**

PERU

Arica

Iquique

BOLIVIA

Pan-American Hwy.

San Pedro
de Atacama

Antofagasta

PACIFIC
OCEAN

Copiapó

ARGENTINA

La Serena

Quintero
Viña del Mar
Valparaíso
Santiago
68

← TO EASTER
ISLAND

Pan-American Hwy.

Concepción

Temuco

Valdivia

N

0   100 miles
0   150 km

Valparaíso
Santiago

Concepción

Temuco

Valdivia
*The Lake
District*
Osorno
Puerto Montt

ARGENTINA

*Isla de
Chiloé*

*Península
Taitao*

*Isla
Wellington*

PACIFIC
OCEAN

**Torres
del Paine
National Park**
Puerto Natales

Punta Arenas

*Penguin
Island*

Estrecho de Magallanes

*Tierra
del
Fuego*

N

0   100 miles
0   150 km

Pleasures and Pastimes

Dining

Kissing her shores from tip to Tierra del Fuego toe, the Pacific Ocean is the breadbasket of Chile's cuisine, proffering delicacies like the conger eel, corvina, sea bass, Antarctic king crab, and *locos* (abalone the size of fat clams). Raw shellfish is a health hazard, but cooked with cheese or white wine, lemon, and fresh coriander, it's an excellent doorway to Chilean cuisine. Awaken your palate with a seafood appetizer, such as *choritos al vapor* (mussels steamed in white wine), *machas à la parmesana* (similar to razor clams but unique to Chile, grilled with tomatoes and parmesan cheese), or *chupo de centolla* (king crab). Simply seasoned grilled fish is a staple Chilean entrée, usually garnished with steamed potatoes or an *ensalada a la chilena* (peeled tomatoes with onions marinated in brine to reduce their acidic flavor). Also worth tasting is the humble *merluza* (hake), which makes a delicious, cheap lunch.

But the Pacífico isn't Chile's only answer to fine dining—European immigrants have influenced a Chilean love for robust country cooking; indeed, many simple country dishes are among the best offerings of Chilean cuisine. *Cazuela,* a superb soup that includes a piece of meat (beef, pork, chicken, or turkey, usually with bone), potatoes, and corn on the cob in a thick, rich squash broth, is a full meal in itself. If your stomach's been upset, a rich chicken cazuela is just the remedy. In summer, *porotos granados,* a thick bean, corn, and squash soup, is the rage with Chileans, as are *humitas,* ground corn seasoned and steamed in its own husk, and *pastel de choclo,* a cornmeal pastry pie that usually contains ground beef, a piece of chicken, and seasonings. Empanadas are the Chilean answer to hamburgers, but as with hamburgers, it's hard to find a good one.

Pork is another Chilean specialty, especially in *arrollados* (a stuffed pork roll encased in pork rind), *costillares* (ribs, often covered in chili, known here as *ají*), *lomo* (roast pork loin), and *pernil* (the whole leg, so make sure you're hungry).

Some Spanish-inspired dishes like *guatitas* (intestines) send Chileans into states of culinary bliss, as do blood sausage, *chunchules* (a spicy stew of beef or pork intestines), and other odds and ends of edible beasts. If you order a *parillada* (a barbecue at your table), ask about the cuts being served so as to avoid those that are too peculiar for your taste.

In southern Chile, the limitations of dining in a small provincial city are compensated for in Punta Arenas by the delights of fresh seafood, especially salmon, king crab, and scallops, along with the local staple, lamb, whose flavor is slightly stronger than in other regions of Chile. Watch out for warnings of red tide, which makes shellfish toxic, but health authorities are strict about monitoring toxin levels, so you're unlikely to have problems.

Chileans know their sweets, with rich kuchen and foamy meringues topping the list of decadence, followed closely by the more popular *alfajor de manjar* (creamy, caramelized sugar smashed between graham wafers and bathed in chocolate). Spring and summer sunshine brings to life an unparalleled Chilean ice cream culture; parlors line almost any pedestrian walkway, and vats filled with artisan creams and exotic fruit flavors will tempt even the most dedicated of dieters.

Prices quoted are per person and include appetizer, main course, and dessert but exclude alcoholic beverages, tax, service charge, and tip. For price charts *see* Dining *in* Smart Travel Tips A to Z.

Lodging

Power and wealth have historically orbited around Chile's capital—Santiago—so it has a wide range of luxury lodging options. In sluggish response to increased tourism, however, novel and new hotels have sprung up in the provinces. In the south you'll find cozy wooden cabins; hot-spring eco-tourist retreats; elaborate hotels designed by Magallenic architects and richly adorned in Patagonian hardwoods; and of course, the always homey and hospitable *residenciales* (bed-and-breakfasts).

Prices quoted are for a double room and include tax and service charge. For price charts *see* Lodging *in* Smart Travel Tips A to Z.

Shopping

Chile is one of only three countries in the world that mine lapis lazuli, so it's worth checking out the workshops and stores along Bellavista Avenue in Santiago. Handicrafts include warm sweaters that are hand-dyed, spun, and knitted in southern Chile (it's cheaper to purchase them there) and ponchos, whose designs vary according to the region; the best are by the Mapuche artisans in and around Temuco and by the Chilote women on the Isla de Chiloé, off the coast from Puerto Montt. Thick wool blankets are woven in Chiloé but are heavy to carry, as are the figures of reddish clay from Pomaire and the famous black clay of Quinchamalí, available at most crafts fairs. Santiago artisans are increasingly sophisticated, and you can find earrings, rings, and necklaces to please virtually every taste. Several towns specialize in wicker, particularly Chimbarongo (about an hour's drive from Santiago) and Chiloé, where baskets and woven effigies of that island's mythical figures abound.

Exploring Chile

When Chileans joke that the Creator made their nation of the universe's leftovers, they are only partly in jest. Chile's thin ribbon of territory comprises some of nature's most spectacular anomalies: the looming Andes impose the country's eastern boundaries, stretching from the desolate Atacama Desert to the archipelagos and fjords of forbidding Magallenes, where the concept of the final frontier is still fresh in the hearts of its inhabitants. Farther north and just above Puerto Montt lies the Alpine land of lakes, with its distinctively German and Swiss cultural enclaves. The central Maipo Valley, fertile home of Chile's famous vineyards and fruit fields, also houses the frenzy of cosmopolitan Santiago.

West of the capital is the resort town of Viña del Mar, in close proximity to Valparaíso, a rustic port city. For those with more time on their hands, Rapa Nui (Easter Island) and its mystic Polynesian histories lie some 3,700 km (2,300 mi) west of Valparaíso, in the middle of the Pacific Ocean.

Great Itineraries

IF YOU HAVE 5 DAYS

Take at least two days to explore and enjoy **Santiago,** Chile's capital and largest city. A fun and worthwhile day trip is the **Maipo Canyon** and the village of San Alfonso; skiers may want to opt for a day in one of the **Andean ski resorts.** On your fourth day, hop a bus to **Valparaíso** in the morning, meandering among this port city's picturesque hills and many elevators. Plan to spend the night in **Viña del Mar,** awaking to explore beachfront Avenida San Martín and Viña's glittery cafés and restaurants before heading back to Santiago to catch your flight home.

Spend your first four days following the tour above. On the fifth day, however, fly south to **Puerto Montt** and rent a car to explore the **Lake Llanquihue** area. Days six and seven may be spent around the lake, choosing from Puerto Montt, **Puerto Varas, Frutillar,** or **Puerto Octay** for lodging, and heading north to **Valdivia** on your eighth day. After a boat tour of Valdivia's Spanish fortresses, plan to spend the night in one of the **Lake District's** many hot springs. Between soaking in the springs and exploring the district's three national parks, take at least two full days to enjoy this pristine area. Spend your eleventh day in **Temuco,** exploring Chile's Mapuche territory, before flying back to Santiago and home.

Follow the tours above, but begin exploring the **Lake District** in **Temuco,** gradually making your way south to **Lake Llanquihue** and **Puerto Montt.** Take a morning flight from Puerto Montt to **Punta Arenas** for a spectacular view of frosted Andes glaciers crumbling into an aquamarine ocean. Spend your first day exploring Punta Arenas, and visit **Penguin Island** your second day. On day three, head for **Puerto Natales** and the **Torres del Paine National Park,** where you'll need at least three days to wander through the wonders of the park's granite spires and awesome wildlife. Give yourself another full day in Puerto Natales for a day-long boat ride to view glaciers. Arrange to fly back to Punta Arenas, from where you'll make another short hop to Ushuaia, on the Argentine half of **Tierra del Fuego** (☞ Patagonia *in* Chapter 3). Between the Tierra del Fuego National Park and Haberton Ranch, you'll need three days in **Argentina.** From Ushuaia, make your way back to Punta Arenas and fly to Santiago.

SANTIAGO

A curious mixture of modern skyscrapers, 19th-century European architecture, and Spanish colonial convention, Santiago's architecture reflects the fact that the city is really a universe composed of multiple worlds. The population is almost 6 million; nevertheless, residents are always likely to bump into an acquaintance along the city center's overcrowded streets and bustling walkways, since they're concentrated in a small area around the Ahumada and Huérfanos pedestrian malls. The Paseo Ahumada stretches northward from the Avenida Libertador Bernardo O'Higgins to the Plaza de Armas and is bisected halfway by Paseo Huérfanos. Modern stores and banks stretch out for blocks around the Plaza de Armas, which is full of colorful gardens and fountains. The parks, the food, and a relaxed attitude toward time enchant visitors, as do dancing and nightlife, which begin at 10 PM and continue most of the night.

Exploring Santiago

Santiaguinos orient themselves along an east–west axis, with the Cordillera (the Andes mountain range) to the east and the coastal mountains to the west. Santiago itself nestles in the valley between them and is cut into approximately equal halves north and south by the Mapocho River. The Avenida Libertador Bernardo O'Higgins, commonly known as the Alameda, is laid out over what was once the southern arm of the Mapocho River, from east to west. Plaza Baquedano, better known as Plaza Italia, is Santiago's figurative belly button, and has become a semi-permeable boundary between east-side *cuicos* (a pejorative term for the rich) and western *rotos* (an equally derisive name for the Santiaguino poor). East of Plaza Italia the Alameda becomes

Providencia, an upscale shopping district; farther east and northward it's called Apoquindo; and yet farther along it turns into Las Condes and is the address of some of the city's fanciest houses.

The city center is to the south of the Mapocho, radiating out on a grid pattern from the central square known as the Plaza de Armas. The Central Market is on the river's south side, about three blocks north of the plaza; the Vega, a cheaper, more colorful version of the market, is across the river. The General Cemetery is about five minutes' drive north from the Vega, and the Bellavista area—full of restaurants, clubs, and art galleries—is about five minutes' drive east of the Vega. The Parque O'Higgins is about 20 minutes' drive south of downtown, or about 10 minutes by metro.

Much of Santiago is best explored on foot; use the metro and an occasional taxi to manage larger distances. However, a combination of the metro and taxis is probably the quickest, most comfortable, and most economical way to get around. You'll probably want the rented car or taxi to get to the *barrio alto* (upper-class neighborhoods) or take a general tour of the city.

Numbers in white bullets in the text correspond to numbers in black bullets in the margins and on the Sanitago map.

Downtown

A GOOD WALK

If you really want to get to know Santiago, start at the city's heart, the central **Plaza de Armas** ①, between Estado, Catedral, and Compañía streets and four blocks north of the Universidad de Chile metro station. At one time the highest court in colonial Chile, the Real Audiencia building is just across Catedral Street and home to the **Museo Histórico Nacional** ②. To the east of the museum is the pastel pink **Correo Central** ③. **La Catedral** ④, twice destroyed by earthquakes and once by fire before its final 18th-century neoclassical construction in stone, is on the west end of the plaza. A motley assortment of commercial arcades completes the fringes of the square and adds a special touch of modernity that is likely to bring a neoliberal capitalist smile to the average Chilean face.

Just south of the square and a little east on Merced Street, you'll find the **Casa Colorada** ⑤. The **Museo Precolombino** ⑥ is one block west of the Plaza de Armas on the corner of Compañía and Bandera streets. Just across the street from the Pre-Columbian Museum are Chile's lordly **Tribunales de Justicia** ⑦. North of the Tribunals of Justice and encompassing an entire city block are the **Ex Congreso Nacional** ⑧ and its gated gardens. A bench in the Congress' gardens is a good spot to take a moment's refuge from the hustle and bustle of Santiago Centro.

Walk two blocks south on Morandé and find yourself at the Agustinas–Morandé corner of the **Plaza de la Constitución** ⑨. Across the plaza, it's a step to the **Palacio de la Moneda** ⑩ and the main nerve center of the Chilean state. Five blocks east and one block south, just across Avenida Libertador Bernardo O'Higgins, are the **Museo Colonial** ⑪ and the **Iglesia San Francisco** ⑫. The slopes of **Cerro Santa Lucía** ⑬ rise above the Iglesia San Francisco, but take care getting there. To avoid jaywalking across that sea of crazy drivers speeding down the Avenida O'Higgins, cross underground via the Santa Lucia metro station. Walk around the **Biblioteca Nacional,** and then head east through Vicuña Mackenna Plaza; the main entrance to Cerro Santa Lucia is on the corner of Santa Lucia and Avenida O'Higgins.

TIMING

The walk alone, without climbing Cerro Santa Lucia, should take about an hour. Combined with museums, a rest here and there, and a climb, this itinerary could take the better part of a day. Plan to leave plenty of daylight for Cerro Santa Lucia, as the hill is not a safe place around sunset. In the winter months Santa Lucia is best visited in the early morning, when air pollution is at a minimum. Each museum will take about 45 minutes, but allot more time according to your interests.

SIGHTS TO SEE

⑤ Casa Colorada. This red-washed, colonial former residence, aptly named the Red House, was once the home of Mateo de Toro y Zambrano, the most prosperous Santiaguino businessman of the 18th century, and is today one of the best-preserved colonial structures in all of Santiago. The Santiago Museum, modest but informative, is an excellent place to dive into the history of the foundation of Santiago through the time of the republic. For an explanation of the exhibits, ask for a guidebook in English. ☒ *Merced 860, Santiago Centro,* ☎ *2/633–0723.* ☒ *Admission every day but Sun.* ☉ *Tues.–Fri. 10–6, Sat. 10–5, Sun. 11–2.*

④ La Catedral. In 1541, Pedro de Valdivia declared that a house of God would be constructed at this site. The first adobe structure burnt to the ground, and it was destroyed twice again by the earthquakes of 1647 and 1730. The neoclassical Cathedral standing today was finally finished in 1789 by the Italian architect Joaquín Toesca. ☒ *Northwest corner, Plaza de Armas,* ☎ *2/696–2777.* ☉ *Mon.–Sat. 11, 12:30, and 7:30; Sun. 10, 11, and noon.*

⑬ Cerro Santa Lucia. The mazelike park of St. Lucí Hill is a notorious hangout for park-bench smoochers, people-watchers, vendors, and the occasional mugger. A gallery and art fair at the base of the hill are excellent places to buy Aymara, Rapa Nui, and Mapuche crafts. Walking up the hill takes about 30 minutes along a spiral maze of interconnected paths, plazas, and fountains. An elevator, on the north end of the hill at Huérfanos and Santa Lucia, climbs halfway to the summit; beware of its erratic scheduling. The crow's nest, reached via a series of steep and slippery stone steps, affords an excellent 360-degree view of the entire city. ☉ *9 AM–9 PM.*

③ Correo Central. Housed in what was formerly the site of the colonial Government Palace, a recent face-lift to this main post office has made waiting in long lines to mail a letter aesthetically tolerable. The Central Post Office is next door to the National History Museum (☞ *below*). ☒ *Plaza de Armas,* ☎ *2/699–4531.* ☉ *Weekdays 8–7, Sat. 8–2.*

⑧ Ex Congreso Nacional. Built on the site of an old church and named for the former Old National Congress (the building was nonfunctional during the dictatorship; congress was moved to Valparaíso in 1990), it now houses the offices of the Ministry of Foreign Affairs in its palatial baroque interior. The original structure, the Iglesia de la Compañía de Jesús (the Church of the Society of Jesus), was destroyed by a fire in the last century; 2,000 members of Santiago's families perished. Inside the peaceful gated gardens is the **Virgin Statue,** a monument commemorating the church fire.

⑫ Iglesia San Francisco. Surviving all of Santiago's successive earthquakes, the massive, earth-toned St. Francis Church remains the last trace of Santiago's 16th-century colonial architecture. Visible on the main altar is the image of the Virgen del Socorro (Virgin of Assistance) that Pedro de Valdivia carried to protect and guide him on his conquest. ☒ *Londres 4,* ☎ *2/638–3238.* ☉ *Mass Tues.–Sat. 8, 10, noon, and 7:30, Sun. 9, 10, 11, noon, 1, and 7:30.*

Exploring

Santiago

KEY

❶ Exploring Sights

① Hotels and
Restaurants

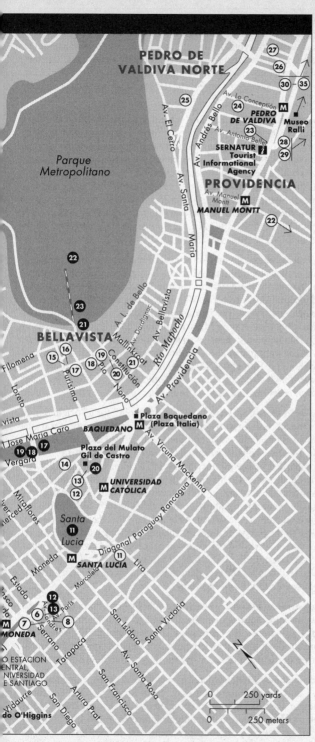

⑪ **Museo Colonial.** Home of the best collection of 17th-century colonial paintings found on the continent, the Colonial Museum has 54 large-scale canvases portraying the life and times of St. Francis and a plethora of religious imagery. Most pieces are labeled with English translations, and a small exhibit is devoted to the poet Gabriela Mistral (1889–1957). ⊠ *Londres 4, Santiago Centro*, ☎ *2/638–3238.* ☜ *Admission.* ☉ *Tues.–Sat. 10–1:30 and 3–6, Sun. 10–2.*

❷ **Museo Histórico Nacional.** The Natural History Museum building dates from 1804, but the exhibits offer little substantive information, especially for those unfamiliar with Chilean history. For example, the museum marks 300 years of native resistance to Spanish and Chilean invasions with a pen-and-ink sketch titled *La Pacificación de la Araucanía* (The Pacification of the Araucanian Territories), and it reduces most major historical events to the uniform worn by such-and-such a general or the bed that X slept in every night. ⊠ *Plaza de Armas 951, Santiago Centro*, ☎ *2/638–1411.* ☜ *Admission every day but Sun.* ☉ *Tues.–Sat. 10–5:30, Sun. 10–1:30.*

★ ❻ **Museo Precolombino.** If you plan to visit only one museum in Santiago, it should be the Pre-Columbian Museum. It contains a well-endowed collection of artifacts of Central and South America's indigenous peoples housed in a beautifully restored colonial building that once served as the Royal Customs House. The permanent collection includes textiles and ceramics from what is now Mexico southward, including Chile. As in most Chilean museums, there isn't a lot of information with the displays, so you might want to call ahead of time for an expert guide or rent a set of headphones (p500, about $1) from the library for an electronic tour. ⊠ *Bandera 361, Santiago Centro*, ☎ *2/695–3851 or 2/695-3627.* ☜ *Admission every day but Sun.* ☉ *Tues.–Sat. 10–6, Sun. 10–2.*

❿ **Palacio de la Moneda.** Literally named "the coin" for its original purpose as the Spanish Crown's mint, the Government Palace is a traditional Spanish colonial–style complex, with a neoclassical design by Joaquín Toesca. The palace housed Chilean presidents until 1958 and was bombarded by the military in the 1973 coup, when Salvador Allende heroically defended his presidency with a Soviet-issue submachine gun. A historical haze still clouds the real cause of Allende's death— some say he went down fighting, others claim he took his own life before Pinochet entered the palace. Although La Moneda was once easily accessible to the public, technocratic paper shuffling has turned a simple tour into a week-long application process. Speak with a guard if you're interested. In the latter half of the 20th-century it has become a Chilean tradition for the president to reside in his own home. ⊠ *Moneda between Teatinos and Morandé.*

❶ **Plaza de Armas.** A bronze well in the center of Arms Plaza once served as the main water source for colonial Santiago. Its distinctive fountains and gardens—closed for renovations through mid-2000—reveal the Chileans' pride of place. You can pick up a game of chess in the southern corner of the plaza or enjoy live music on Thursdays and Sundays.

❾ **Plaza de la Constitución.** Bordered by a collection of governmental ministries, Constitution Square houses the heart of Santiago's civic center. Adorning it are three monuments to: Diego Portales, organizer of the Chilean republic; Don Eduardo Frei, president from 1964 to 1970 and father of the second post-coup president; and Jorge Alessandri. The plaza also serves as the roof of the underground bunker Pinochet had installed when he did his famous "redecorating" of La Moneda. Four pillars in the corners of the square serve as ventilation ducts for the bunker. Locals joke that these monoliths represent the four founding members of the military junta—they're made of stone, full of hot air, and no one knows their real function.

❼ Tribunales de Justicia. During the military government, the Courts of Justice was the site of many a human-rights demonstration, as it is still today. In front of the building, perhaps in irony, is a monument celebrating justice and the promulgation of Chile's civil code. ✉ *Plaza Montt Varas, public entrance at Bandera 344.* ☉ *Mar.–Nov., weekdays 1–6:30; Dec.–Feb., Mon. 1–6:30 and Tues.–Fri. 8–1.*

The Market Area

A GOOD WALK

Walk four blocks north from Plaza de Armas to the **Mercado Central** ⑭. Cross the Mapocho River and then head north on Avenida La Paz to find the **Pérgola de las Flores** flower market ⑮. If the Central Market feels more like a roadside attraction than a functional market, turn east on Artesanos and walk until you see the lime-green entrance to **Mercado Vega Chica** ⑯; to the north is the **Vega Central de Santiago.** Across Recoleta Avenue, east of the Vega, is Santiago's **Patronato** area, with bargains on clothes, sheets, and towels.

TIMING

Walking the market circuit should take about an hour. Be aware that both the Vega Chica and the Vega Central are in a crowded commercial sector of Santiago—keep an eye on your personal belongings!

SIGHTS TO SEE

⑭ Mercado Central. The structure housing the Central Market was prefabricated in England and erected in Chile between 1868 and 1872. It has the lofty wrought-iron ceiling of a Victorian train station and soars above a matchless selection of marvelous sea creatures. Depending on the season, you might see the delicate beak of *picorocos,* the world's only edible barnacle; the orange stars of sea urchins in their prickly shells; or shadowy pails full of succulent bullfrogs. You can find a cheap, filling meal at most of the stands along the south end of the market. ✉ *Ismael Valdés Vergara, 900 block.* ☉ *Sun.–Thurs. 7–4, Fri. and Sat. 7 AM–8 PM.*

Patronato. Once the exclusive preserve of Chileans of Arab origin, this traditional textile neighborhood is now home to more and more Korean-owned shops. If you continue eastward along Antonia López de Bello, you'll pass the storefront shops in old Arab-style mansions built by families who made their fortunes in textiles. Keep walking, and you come to the spirited bohemian neighborhood of Bellavista.

⑮ Pérgola de las Flores. The Trellis of Flowers market is the source of the complex wreaths and flower arrangements made mostly for visitors to the two cemeteries in the area. *Pérgola de las Flores,* a famous Chilean musical, is based on the conflict that arose in the 1930s when the mayor of Santiago wanted to remove the market. Practice your Spanish with one of the chatty florists and learn all about it. ✉ *Corner of Av. La Paz and Artesanos.*

⑯ Vega Central and Vega Chica. From fruit to furniture, meat to machinery, the Central and Small Vega markets have it all. Alongside the more ordinary items, like pet food and pickles, you can also find rare delicacies like exotic mushrooms and piñones, Chile's giant pine nuts found on monkey puzzle trees. If you're undaunted by the Vega Chica, try a truly typical Chilean meal in one of the many *picadas* (eateries) dotting the fringes of the market. ✉ *Antonia López de Bello, 700 block.*

Around Parque Forestal

A GOOD WALK

Santiago's green and grassy **Parque Forestal** ⑰ begins near Mercado Central and runs parallel to the Mapocho for several blocks. Strolling east through the Parque Forestal will bring you to the **Museo de Bellas Artes** ⑱ and the adjacent **Museo de Arte Contemporáneo** ⑲ and finally back to the bustle of Plaza Italia. Just south of the park, near the corner of Merced and Victorino Lastarria streets, you'll find the Plaza del Mulato Gil de Castro, a pleasant little nook with a handful of art galleries, cafés, and the **Museo Arqueológico** ⑳.

TIMING

A quick but pleasant jaunt, it will take no more than a half hour to walk. The Archeology Museum will take approximately 30 minutes, but give the Fine Arts Museum at least an hour.

SIGHTS TO SEE

⑳ **Museo Arqueológico.** Some 3,000 pieces with English explanations blow a breath of life back into the fading Mapuche, Aymara, Fueguino, Huilliche, and Pehuenche cultures. The little Archaeological Museum is devoted specifically to indigenous Chile. After taking in the museum, browse one of the bookstores in the Plaza del Mulato Gil de Castro or relax a bit in one of the quiet cafés. ⊠ *Victorino Lastarria 307, 2nd Floor (in the Plaza del Mulato Gil de Castro), Santiago Centro.* ☒ *Free.* ☼ *Weekdays 10–2 and 3:30–5:30; Sat. 10–2.*

⑲ **Museo de Arte Contemporáneo.** In the west wing of the Museo de Bellas Artes, through a separate entrance on the opposite side of the building, the airy Contemporary Arts Museum has a collection of predominantly Latin American contemporary paintings and sculpture. Look for the Botero sculpture out front. *In Parque Forestal, near the intersection of Ismael Valdéz Vergara and Mosqueto, Santiago Centro,* ☎ *2/639–6488.* ☒ *Admission.* ☼ *Tues.–Sat. 11–7, Sun. 11–2.*

⑱ **Museo de Bellas Artes.** The Fine Arts Museum is packed with paintings, drawings, and sculpture by 16th- to 20th-century Chilean and European artists. Originally built to house the school of fine arts, the museum has an impressive glass-domed ceiling that illuminates the main hall in bright white light. A movie theater on the second floor shows clips on featured artists. ⊠ *José Miguel de la Barra and Loreto, Santiago Centro,* ☎ *2/633–0655.* ☒ *Admission every day but Sun.* ☼ *Tues.–Sun. 10–7.*

⑰ **Parque Forestal.** After beating back the swelling edges of the Mapocho with an 1891 canal project, Santiago inherited a thin strip of land that it didn't quite know what to do with. The area quickly filled with squatters and the city's refuse. At the turn of the century Enrique Cousiño reclaimed the strip and initiated the Forest Park. The eastern tip, near Plaza Italia, is distinguished by the Wagnerian-scale **Fuente Alemana** (German Fountain). Donated by the Germanic community of Santiago, the fountain commemorates the hundredth anniversary of Chilean Independence.

Bellavista

A GOOD WALK

The heart of Bellavista is at Pío Nono and Antonia López de Bello streets. Heading north along Constitución and then left on Fernando Márquez de la Plata Street, you'll find the house Pablo Neruda designed, **La Chascona** ㉑. One of Bellavista's main attractions is the Parque Metropolitano, at the north end of Pío Nono Street, which covers the entirety of Santiago's highest hill, **Cerro San Cristóbal** ㉒. Halfway up the hill is the **Jardín Zoológico de Santiago** ㉓. After making the summit you can ride the skyline in a lift, which will let you out at either Tupahue

Station (for access to the eastern half of Metropolitan Park and the Museo de Vino [Wine Museum]) or Pedro de Valdivia Norte (just seven blocks north of metro station Pedro de Valdivia along Pedro de Valdivia Street).

TIMING

This route is best done in the morning, before Santiago is hidden under a haze of smog. Give yourself an hour to wander through Bellavista, and at least one more to climb Cerro San Cristóbal. Pack a picnic for the summit, or dine out at Tupahue station. If you decide to watch the sunset from the hill, avoid walking back down alone since the area is not well patrolled and muggings have been reported.

SIGHTS TO SEE

Bellavista. This trendy neighborhood has streets lined with acacia trees, small cafés, restaurants, and one-story homes painted in pinks, aquamarines, and blues.

㉑ La Chascona. This house designed by Pablo Neruda was named the "Woman with the Tousled Hair" after Mathilde Urratia, the lover with whom he lived his final years. Visits, by appointment only, allow you to step into the extraordinary mind of the poet who has been called an "organic architect": winding this way and that around the hillside is a path through the garden, leading to a library stuffed with books, a bedroom in a tower, and a secret passageway—all filled with the collections of butterflies, books, seashells, bowsprits, wine glasses, and other odd objects that inspired Neruda's poetry. ⊠ *Fernando Márquez de la Plata 0192, Bellavista,* ☎ *2/777–8741.* ⊡ *Admission.* ☉ *Tues.– Sun. 10–1 and 3–6.*

㉒ Cerro San Cristóbal. St. Christopher's Hill is perhaps *the* tourist attraction in Santiago. You can walk up—it's a steep but enjoyable one-hour climb—or take the funicular or an open bus to the summit, which is crowned by a huge white statue of the Virgin Mary and a fabulous view of the entire city. Once at the summit, buy a lift ticket to explore the other half of the park at Tupahue Station and the **Museo Enoteca.** Hardly a fully fledged museum, it offers wine tasting for a nominal fee. ⊠ *Cerro San Cristóbal,* ☎ *2/777–6666 for park administration, 2/737–6669 for lift and funicular information.* ⊡ *Free (park); fee for round-trip lift.* ☉ *Park: Daily 8:30 AM–10 PM. Lift service: Mon. noon–8, Tues.– Fri. 10:30–8, weekends 10:30–8:30.*

㉓ Jardín Zoológico de Santiago. The Santiago Zoo is a good place to see examples of many Chilean species, some nearly extinct, that you might not otherwise encounter. Be careful: Some of the cages aren't properly protected, and the animals can bite. ⊡ *Admission.* ☉ *Oct.–Mar., Tues.–Sun. 9–7; Apr.–Sept., Tues.–Sun. 10–6.*

Parks, Gardens, and Cemeteries

OFF THE BEATEN PATH

CEMENTERIO GENERAL – It may be unusual as far as tourist attractions go, but this cemetery at the end of Avenida la Paz, a short taxi ride northwest from the Cerro San Cristóbal or downtown, is a fine source of insights into traditional Chilean society. You pass through the lofty stone arches of the main General Cemetery entrance and find yourself among marble mausoleums, the squat mansions belonging to Chile's wealthy families. The cemetery has well-maintained gardens, neat roads and walkways, stained-glass windows, and religious icons. The 8- or 10- story "niches" farther along—literally concrete shelves housing thousands of coffins—resemble middle-class apartment buildings; their inhabitants lie here until the "rent" runs out and they're evicted. As you're walking through Santiago's burial grounds, look for **Salvador Al-**

lende's resting spot. If you're traveling during September, the cemetery is not a safe place to visit around the 11th, as it is an emotionally charged reminder of a problematic past.

OFF THE
BEATEN PATH

PARQUE BERNARDO O'HIGGINS – Named for Chile's national liberator who led rebel troops to victory against the Spanish, this park has an open area complete with swimming pools, paved marching grounds for military parades, and lots of space to fly kites. Street vendors sell *volantines* (kites) and string outside the park year-round; high winds make September and early October the prime kite-flying season. **El Pueblito,** an adobe village with restaurants, museums, and crafts stands, is to the left of the park's main entrance and a popular destination for family entertainment. ⊠ *Metro station Parque O'Higgins, Santiago Centro,* ☎ *2/556–1927.* ☒ *Free.* ⊙ *Daily 9–7.*

Dining

Since the mid-'80s, restaurants have blossomed in Santiago, particularly in the Bellavista and Providencia neighborhoods. Many specialize in "international cuisine," a term that can mean just about anything, from lasagna to sushi to fiery Szechuan beef. The authenticity of ethnic cuisine is relative, and even the most exotic of foreign foods have been given a Chilean flavor.

Chilean

$$$ ✕ **Balthazar.** Contemporary cuisine with a Chilean twist is served in this carefully restored old adobe stable. In the center of the small dining room, a rough-hewn wooden trestle table groans with a buffet of exquisite, inventive salads and hors d'oeuvres that borrow from Indonesian, Japanese, Chinese, Arab, and other flavorings. The scallops and stuffed trout with olive sauce are superb. ⊠ *Av. las Condes 10690,* ☎ *2/215–1090. AE, DC, MC, V. Closed Sun.*

$$ ✕ **Torres.** Fronting on the Avenida Libertador Bernardo O'Higgins, this claims to be the oldest surviving restaurant in the downtown area. The huge shiny wooden bar, old fans, and light fixtures take you back to the era of President Barros. Specialties are classic Chilean dishes and sandwiches, making it a perfect lunch spot. On Thursday through Saturday nights, tangos and boleros are performed. ⊠ *Av. Libertador Bernardo O'Higgins 1570,* ☎ *2/698–6220. AE. Closed Sun.*

$ ✕ **Pica Isidro.** Don Isidro was here on the outskirts of Bellavista long before the neighborhood even dreamed of its present dining chic-dom. His *picada* specializes in seafood and has 27 different classes of wine to accompany such favorites as *jardín de mariscos* (a shellfish stew) or *choritos al vapor* (mussels steamed in white wine). Don Isidro swears he's open 24 hours, 365 days of the year, but outside of regular business hours call ahead of time just to be certain. ⊠ *Purísima 269, Bellavista,* ☎ *2/737–3645. No credit cards.*

$ ✕ **Plaza Blue.** Washed in saffron and sky blues, the main dining room of this restaurant is a plaza in miniature. Live Latin music accompanies standard but solid Chilean fare on weekends, when students and young hipsters flock to this area. Try the *omelette al langostino* (crawfish omelet) or the *reineta a la plancha* (grilled mackerel). ⊠ *Pío Nono 185, Bellavista,* ☎ *2/732–3870. No credit cards. Closed Sun.*

$ ✕ **Restorán Don Peyo.** For first-rate Chilean food at reasonable prices,
★ Don Peyo's is hard to beat. With squat ceilings and patched stucco walls, what this place lacks in aesthetics it makes up for in flavor. The hot sauce and the garlic and avocado spreads in themselves warrant a visit, but the beef dishes—especially the *plateada,* a Chilean version of roast

beef—are what put this restaurant on the map. A mixed group of working- and middle-class Chileans enjoys a night out here in a family atmosphere. ⊠ *Av. Grecia 448 and Lo Encalada 465, Ñuñoa,* ☎ *2/ 274–0764. AE, DC, MC, V. Closed Sun.*

$ ✕ **El Venezia.** Long before the Bellavista neighborhood became fash-
★ ionable, this tacky, bare-bones restaurant was where TV stars and publicists rubbed elbows with the people of the street. The beer is icy, the waiters are simpático, and the food is abundant and well prepared. There's no fish on Monday, but the *congrío frito* (fried conger eel, really a fish), available the rest of the week, is delicious, as are the *costillar de chancho* (pork ribs), the filet mignon, and the roast or stewed chicken. ⊠ *Pío Nono 200,* ☎ *2/737–0900. AE, DC, MC, V.*

French

$$ ✕ **Les Assassins.** The immediate impression on entering this neighborhood institution is of a rather somber bistro with an odd jumble of fittings and fixtures. However, the atmosphere and service are friendly and the Provence-influenced food is first-rate. The steak au poivre and crêpes suzette would make even a Frenchman's eyes water. If you want to practice your Spanish, there's always a line of talkative locals in the cozy ground-floor bar. ⊠ *Merced 297–B,* ☎ *2/638–4280. AE, DC, MC, V. Closed Sun.*

Indian

$$$ ✕ **Taj Mahal.** Adorned with colored silks and characteristic handicrafts, this restaurant offers a spicy change from the often bland Chilean cuisine. The curries aren't as fiery as you'd expect, but the flavors of the traditional tandoori cooking are as authentic as you'll find this far from India. ⊠ *Av. Isadora Goyenechea 3215, Las Condes,* ☎ *2/232–3606. AE, DC, MC, V.*

Japanese

$$ ✕ **Japón.** Take off your shoes, settle onto a cushion, and prepare for an authentic taste of the rising sun. Frequented by Santiago's small but growing Japanese community, this restaurant, just off of Plaza Italia, offers a first-rate sushi bar and three cozy dining rooms. The most patient waiters in town—Yes sir, raw fish sir—provide a friendly and linguistically tolerant atmosphere. The *unagi* (eel) is fantastic, the ramen a meal in itself. ⊠ *Marcoleta 39, Santiago Centro,* ☎ *2/222–4517. AE, DC, MC, V.*

Mexican

$$$ ✕ **Santa Fe.** Brightly decorated in blues, pinks, and ochers, this Tex-Mex restaurant is always packed with Santiago's flashy Yuppies. If you're over 6 feet tall, you'll feel cramped in the main dining room, but it's worth squeezing in for the fajitas (with seafood or meat fillings), frozen margaritas, and authentic guacamoles. Don't come if you want a quiet, romantic dinner, as it's always noisy. ⊠ *Av. Las Condes 10690, Las Condes,* ☎ *2/215–1091. AE, DC, MC, V.*

Peruvian

$$ ✕ **Cocoa.** Although they are probably the two smallest restaurants in Santiago, what these spots lack in size, they make up for in delicious Peruvian cuisine. The *pisco* sours (lemon, egg white, sugar, and pisco—an Andean liquor, distilled from grapes) and ceviche (seafood marinated in lemon juice, wine, and seasonings) are the best in town. Other choices change regularly and are simply read out by the owner. The desserts are all homemade, and the cheesecakes and *suspiro limeño* (a rich meringue-topped lemon dish) are now being supplied to other area establishments. ⊠ *José Victorino Lastarria 297, Santiago Centro,* ☎ *2/632–1272; Antonia Lope de Bello 60, Bellavista,* ☎ *2/735-0634. AE. Closed Sun.*

Seafood

$$$$ ✕ **Aquí Está Coco.** The best fish and shellfish in Santiago are served
★ up in comfortable surroundings decorated with a nautical theme; the
walls are covered with flotsam and jetsam from Chilean beaches. Ask
your waiter what's best each day. This is a good place to try Chile's
famous machas, here served à la parmesana (with tomatoes and parmesan cheese), or corvina, one of Chile's tastiest fish, offered with a
choice of various butters and sauces. Also noteworthy is the wine list;
this is one of the few restaurants in Santiago that serves export-qual-
ity Chilean wines. ⊠ *La Concepción 236, Providencia,* ☎ *2/205–*
5985 or 2/251–5751. Weekend reservations essential. AE, DC, MC,
V. Closed Sun.

$$$ ✕ **Azul Profundo.** This less formal restaurant serves fish without all of
★ the sauces that are so common in Chile. For a taste of some truly de-
licious grilled fish try the *lata,* a piece of salmon that comes to the table
still sizzling and served with just tomatoes and onions. Popular as this
restaurant is with the young, attractive, and wealthy Chilenos who enjoy
"slumming it" in Bellavista, you must reserve in advance for a chance
of getting a table. ⊠ *Constitucíon 111, Providencia,* ☎ *2/738–0288.*
Weekend reservations essential. AE. Closed Sun.

$$ ✕ **Todo Fresca.** As the name suggests, all the seafood served here is fresh—
and, as if to prove that fact, much of the menu's offerings are on dis-
play as you walk in the door. This new addition to the Bellavista
restaurant scene is known for its Peruvian-style seafood and multitiered
dining room. ⊠ *Antonio Lopez de Bello 61, Bellavista,* ☎ *2/735–0988.*
AE, DC, MC, V. Closed Sun.

$ ✕ **Donde Augusto.** Situated inside the bustling Central Market, Donde
Augusto offers the best values on seafood in town. If you don't mind
informal service and the odd tear in the tablecloths, you can dine on
delicious *erizos* (sea urchin), *locos,* or ceviche. Placido Domingo eats
here on every visit to Chile. If you can't get a table, try one of the many
stalls in the fish market; it may not look especially clean, but the seafood
is the freshest in Santiago. ⊠ *Mercado Central, Santiago Centro,* ☎ *2/*
672–2829. Reservations not accepted. AE, DC, MC, V. No dinner.

Spanish

$$ ✕ **La Esquina al Jerez.** This noisy establishment with hams hanging
★ from the rafters specializes in food from Spain, or the *madre patria*
(mother country), as many Chileans still call it. The mixed shellfish hors
d'oeuvres are tasty and a bit on the hot side. If you want to try *callos*
(beef stomach lining boiled and then sautéed in oil with chorizo, red
pepper, garlic, and red wine), a Spanish delicacy, this is the place to do
it. ⊠ *Dardignac 0192, Bellavista,* ☎ *2/777–4407. Weekend reserva-*
tions essential. AE, DC, MC, V. Closed Sun.

Thai

$$$ ✕ **Anakena.** This bright, spacious Thai establishment, with a large out-
★ door area overlooking an oasislike pool, serves some of the finest spicy
food in Santiago. It also offers a unique way of ordering your food:
As in a market, you choose which piece of fish or meat you want and
then tell the chef whether you want it cooked in the traditional wok
or on the grill. ⊠ *Hyatt Regency, Av. Presidente Kennedy 4601, Las*
Condes, ☎ *2/218–1234. AE, DC, MC, V.*

Vegetarian

$$ ✕ **Café el Patio.** Hidden in the back of quaint Galería del Patio, this
café doubles as a bar at night. The chef uses all organically grown pro-
duce, half of which is farmed by the owners themselves. The chef's salad,
with lettuce, tomato, Gruyére, and hearts of palm, is exquisite. The
menu also includes a handful of dishes with an Oriental flair. ⊠ *Prov-*

idencia 1670, local 8 of Galería del Patio, Providencia, ☎ *2/236–1251. AE, DC, MC, V. Closed Sun.*

$$ ✕ **El Huerto.** In the heart of Providencia, this vegetarian restaurant and café has become a hangout for young, trendy Santiaguinos. The natural foods it offers are made with a wide range of fresh vegetables (organic when possible), tofu, and dairy products. Simple dishes like stir-fried veggies with saffron rice and pancakes stuffed with asparagus and mushrooms are full of flavor, but it is the soups and freshly squeezed juices that score highest. Besides lunch and dinner, afternoon tea is also served. ⊠ *Orrego Luco 054, Providencia,* ☎ *2/233–2690. AE, DC, MC, V. No lunch Sun.*

¢ ✕ **Govinda's.** Cheap but hearty vegetarian food is prepared here by Santiaguino Hari Krishnas. Card tables and lawn chairs are the extent of the decor, but the fresh juices and homemade bread are delicious. Try the yogurt with mixed fruit and honey for dessert. ⊠ *Av. Compañía 1489, Santiago Centro,* ☎ *2/673–0892. No credit cards.* ☉ *Lunch only Mon.–Fri. Closed weekends.*

Lodging

In Santiago, accommodations range from five-star international hotels to comfortable, inexpensive residenciales, the Chilean equivalent of bed-and-breakfasts. It's wise to reserve well in advance during the peak seasons (Jan.–Feb. and July–Aug.).

$$$$ ▦ **Carrera.** Recent renovations have maintained the traditional atmosphere of Santiago's oldest hotel yet have added up-to-date amenities, including many for businesspeople. An executive floor offers butler service and a private bar. The flavor is distinctly English, with chintz bedspreads, hunting prints, and floral upholstery on the comfortable armchairs. Try for a room on the plaza; interior rooms tend to be dark. ⊠ *Teatinos 180, behind the Moneda,* ☎ *2/698–2011,* ℻ *2/672–1083. 325 rooms, 30 suites. 2 restaurants, bar, pool, health club, business services, meeting rooms. AE, DC, MC, V.*

$$$$ ▦ **Hotel Kennedy.** This tall glass structure may seem imposing, but small details—such as phones in bathrooms and beautiful vases atop wardrobes—show the care that has gone into providing amenities. Bilingual secretarial services and an elegant board room are among the pluses available for visiting executives. The Aquarium restaurant has a first-rate French chef, five-star international cuisine, and a cellar of excellent Chilean export wines. ⊠ *Av. Presidente Kennedy 4570,* ☎ *2/ 219–4000,* ℻ *2/290–8100. 133 rooms, 10 suites. Restaurant, bar, pool, beauty salon, exercise room, business services, travel services. AE, DC, MC, V.*

$$$$ ▦ **Hotel Plaza San Francisco.** Facing the historic Iglesia San Francisco ★ in downtown Santiago, this executive-oriented hotel has cozy rooms with large beds, reproduction antique furniture, and marble-trim baths. The Bristol restaurant is equally impressive, with heavy wooden trim, richly colored wallpapers, and bronze lamps that create a slightly nautical feeling. The chef, Guillermo Rodríguez, has won the most important annual gastronomic competition in Chile four times, more than anyone in the country, and is the chef of the Chilean President. And while the lovely rooms, central location, and fantastic restaurant are all tremendous draws, the real reason to choose this hotel is for its helpful, professional staff. ⊠ *Av. Libertador Bernardo O'Higgins 816,* ☎ *2/639–3832,* ℻ *2/639–7826. 160 rooms, 20 suites. Restaurant, bar, in-room modem lines, in-room VCRs, indoor pool, health club, business services. AE, DC, MC, V.*

$$$$ 🏨 **Hyatt Regency.** Far from downtown in the wealthy residential area known as Las Condes, the Hyatt Regency compensates for its out-of-the-way location with first-class accommodations. The building is an architectural wonder, with rooms curving around a 24-story central shaft lined with windows; each room has an excellent view and many have terraces. The four-story executive suites have private dining and games areas. The health club is large, and its windows overlook a kidney-shape pool complete with waterfall. ✉ *Av. Presidente Kennedy 4601, Las Condes,* ☎ *2/218–1234,* FAX *2/218–2513. 310 rooms, 10 suites. 2 restaurants, bar, in-room VCRs, pool, health club, baby-sitting, business services. AE, DC, MC, V.*

$$$$ 🏨 **Santiago Park Plaza.** Elegant English-style furniture, deep burgundy and cream decorations, and receptionists sitting behind individual mahogany desks set the mood in this self-proclaimed "classic European-style" hotel. The refined atmosphere extends to the adjoining Park Lane restaurant, whose chef masterfully combines international and Chilean cuisine. The glass-roof pool and spa area on the top floor offer great views of the city. ✉ *Av. Ricardo Lyon 207, Providencia,* ☎ *2/233–6363,* FAX *2/233–6668. 104 rooms, 6 suites. Restaurant, bar, indoor pool, sauna, exercise room, business services. AE, DC, MC, V.*

$$$$ 🏨 **Sheraton Santiago and San Cristóbal Tower.** This complex is, in ef-
★ fect, two distinct hotels that share a lobby and various services. The Sheraton is a standard luxury hotel with all the amenities and extras that you would expect. The adjoining super luxurious 25-story, $50 million San Cristóbal Tower is in a class all its own. Finished in 1998, this new property has quickly established itself as the favorite of business travelers and foreign dignitaries, who value its efficiency, impeccable service, and elegance. Rooms are tastefully decorated in soft cream tones and come equipped with a stereo, VCR, and CD player, plus an assortment of pillows. But pampering is not all that goes on at the San Cristóbal Tower—the attentive staff at the business center provide guests with Internet access, executive meeting rooms, and fax and printing services. ✉ *Av. Santa María, Providencia,* ☎ *2/233–5000,* FAX *2/234-1732. 379 rooms, 14 suites in the Sheraton; 139 rooms, 12 suites in the Tower. Restaurant, bar, in-room safes, minibars, 2 pools, sauna, exercise room, laundry service, business services, convention center, travel services. AE, DC, MC, V.*

$$$ 🏨 **Hotel Bonaparte.** Designed in the style of a small French château, this charming hotel on the quieter part of the tree-lined Avenida Ricardo Lyon deserves more than it receives. The rooms with the most light are on the top floor, but all are tastefully decorated and have large bathrooms. On the ground floor there's a small restaurant and a cozy lounge with a bar to one side. ✉ *Av. Ricardo Lyon 1229,* ☎ *2/274–0621,* FAX *2/204–8907. 25 rooms, 2 suites. Restaurant, lobby lounge, pool. AE, DC, MC, V.*

$$ 🏨 **Acacias de Vitacura.** The rooms here are modest, with thick gray carpets, textured wallpaper, and printed bedspreads in quiet colors, but the owner's eclectic collection of old carriages and Asian handicrafts gives this hotel personality, as does its extraordinary location in the midst of a lush garden and towering eucalyptus and acacia trees, some more than 100 years old. The hotel is quite a distance from the city center (about 30 minutes by bus), in the wealthy shopping and residential area of Vitacura, in the northwest section of Santiago. ✉ *El Manantial 1781,* ☎ *2/211–8601,* FAX *2/212–7858. 36 rooms, 2 suites. Dining room, minibars, pool, meeting rooms. AE, DC, MC, V.*

$$ 🏨 **Foresta.** This seven-story hotel across the street from Santa Lucía hill, on the edge of Santiago's city center, feels like an elegant old home. Guest rooms have floral wallpaper and antique furnishings, accented by bronze and marble. Rooms on the upper floors overlooking the hill are best. A rooftop restaurant, bar, and street-level piano bar are also on site. ✉ *Victoria Subercaseaux 353*, ☎ ℻ *2/639–6261. 35 rooms, 8 suites. Restaurant, bar, piano bar. AE, DC, MC, V.*

$$ 🏨 **Hotel Majestic.** Towering white pillars, peaked archways, and glittery brass ornaments complete the decor of this Indian-inspired hotel. Even though the bright, nondescript rooms have "soundproof" windows, ask for one off the street and away from the restaurant. A warm staff and its relatively central location make the Majestic a comfortable and accommodating choice. ✉ *Santo Domingo 1526, Santiago Centro*, ☎ *2/695–8366*, ℻ *2/697–4051. 50 rooms. Restaurant, bar, café, in-room safes, minibars, pool. AE, DC, MC, V.*

$$ 🏨 **Hotel Orly.** Country manor furnishings, pine floors, and wood windows make this hotel as sweet as it is comfortable. The Orly combines **★** all the amenities of luxury with family friendliness, a helpful staff, and a posh location. Cafetto, the downstairs café and restaurant, has some of the finest coffee drinks in town. The Orly beats the quality of the corporate hotels for half the price, and it's just a few short blocks from the Pedro de Valdivia metro stop. ✉ *Av. Pedro de Valdivia 027, Providencia*, ☎ *2/231–8947*, ℻ *2/252–0051. 24 rooms, 2 suites. Restaurant, café, in-room safes, minibars, bicycles. AE, DC, MC, V.*

$ 🏨 **Apart-Hotel Marqués del Forestal.** A good alternative for families or groups, these small apartments for four people cost less than $80. Rooms are furnished simply in pinks and browns, with sofa beds and double beds and kitchenettes. It's near the Central Market and overlooks Forest Park. ✉ *Ismael Valdés Vergara 740, Santiago Centro*, ☎ *2/633–3462*, ℻ *2/639–4157. 14 apartments with shower. Bar, kitchenettes. AE, DC, MC, V.*

$ 🏨 **Hotel Los Arcos.** Off of Plaza Brasíl in little-explored historic Santiago, this simple hotel has become a haven for young foreigners. Rooms are bare but clean, and some have windows that overlook an interior courtyard and café. Three rooms have small lofts. ✉ *Agustinas 2173, Santiago Centro*, ☎ *2/699–0998 or 2/696–5602*, ℻ *2/699–7998. 21 rooms. Café. DC, MC, V.*

$ 🏨 **Hotel Vegas.** The open-beam architecture of this 1920s building, adorned with wood paneling, photos of Santiago in the '30s, and a boar's head in the lobby, give the Hotel Vegas a cozy, hunting-cabin charm. Rooms are clean with tacky carpeting and lots of windows (ask for a room with a view of the street), and some even come with cribs. ✉ *Londres 49, Londres/París*, ☎ *2/632–2498 or 2/632–2514*, ℻ *2/632–5084. 20 rooms. Bar, café, room service, laundry service. AE, DC, MC, V.*

$ 🏨 **Residencial Londres.** Built in the 1920s, this inexpensive hotel in the **★** picturesque Londres/París neighborhood is behind the San Francisco Church and a stone's throw from the city's center. Rooms are spacious, with high ceilings, wood floors, detailed moldings, and tiled (if somewhat moldy) bathrooms. The best rooms have stone balconies overlooking this charmingly atypical neighborhood. The hosts are friendly and helpful to visitors. ✉ *Londres 54, Londres/París*, ☎ *2/638–2215. 27 rooms. No credit cards.*

Nightlife and the Arts

Nightlife

After years of curfews under the military government, Santiago is slowly developing an active nightlife, with good food, music, theater, dancing, and comedy as the main activities.

COMEDY

If you understand Spanish, look out for Chile's best, most intelligent humorist, **Coco Legrand,** who has his own theater called **Circus OK** (✉ Providencia 1176, Providencia, ☎ 2/235–1822).

DRINKING AND DANCING

There are bars and pubs all over Santiago, but two streets in particular have such a concentration of establishments that they become virtual street parties on the weekend. Try pub crawling with all the young, well-heeled locals on Avenida Suecia, between Providencia and Andrés Bello; or, if you're looking for something a little more bohemian, head for Pío Nono, Bellavista's main strip. Santiago's colorful club scene continues to flourish despite the fact that traditionalism and strict morality are still very much in force. If you look around a bit, you're bound to find something to suit your fancy.

Bunker (⊠ Bombero Nuñez 159, ☎ 2/737–1716), part of Santiago's small but vivacious gay underground, has a funky drag show with the wittiest MC in town. Cages, lit from below, line the large dance floor. Whatever your sexual orientation, the Bunker is a blast.

Cimarrón (⊠ Av. Irarrázabal 1730, Nuñoa, ☎ 2/225–1627), with salsa and tango classes on Wednesday and Thursday nights, is the perfect spot to teach those hips how to shake to a tropical beat. On Fridays and Saturdays this *salsoteca* comes alive with sensuous salsa, merengue, boleros, and milonga.

The Oz (⊠ Chucre Mansur 6, Bellavista, ☎ 2/737–7066), the best of the expensive spots, plays a good mix of techno, hip-hop, and jazz-funk. A huge stairway leads down from the upper bar to a wide dance area, so if you want to make a show of yourself, this is the place to do it.

FILM

Santiago has more than 40 cinemas. Movie listings are posted in *El Mercurio,* the country's largest daily newspaper. Box-office prices range from p1,500 to p3,000, and admission is half price on Wednesdays. Many art cinemas tend to prefer international films over the Hollywood hits. **Biógrafo** (⊠ José Victorino Lastarria 181, Santiago Centro, ☎ 2/633–4435), **Centro de Extensión Universidad Católica** (⊠ Av. Libertador Bernardo O'Higgins 390, Santiago Centro, ☎ 2/635–1994), and **Cine Arte Normandie** (⊠ Av. Tarapacá 1181, Santiago Centro, ☎ 2/697–2979) are the most popular.

LATE-NIGHT DINING

There are good after-hours restaurants throughout most of the city, particularly in Bellavista, Providencia, and Las Condes.

From the entrance, **Casa de Cena** (⊠ Almirante Simpson 20, Santiago Centro, ☎ 2/635–4418) looks like an average hole in the wall, but this is one of those irresistible dives. Most nights a band wanders through the labyrinth of wood-paneled rooms singing Chilean folk songs while the waiters listen to endless stories from their inebriated regulars. Whether you're looking for food, drink or just some late-night entertainment, Casa de Cena is sure to meet your post meridiem needs.

The **Libro Café and Tasca Mediterránea** duo (⊠ Purísima 165, Bellavista, ☎ 2/735–0928) is a late-night haunt for artists, intellectuals, and students. If you just want to *picar* (nibble), head to the café for a *tortilla malageña* and a carafe of house red. The Tasca, next door, will satisfy a larger appetite.

The **Phone Box** (⊠ Av. Providencia 1670, local 1, Providencia, ☎ 2/235–9972) is a typically British pub, serving favorites like steak-and-kidney pie. Check out the menu—the owner has put together a list of funny bastardizations of the English language.

Prosit (⊠ Plaza Baquedano 13, ☎ 2/222–7582) is a Chilean-style Denny's-till-dawn hangout. This no-frills diner, with standard Chilean grub, attracts all types of nocturnal critters and characters.

The Arts

MUSIC

Good Chilean music is hard to find these days, but the **Teatro Municipal** (⊠ San Antonio at Agustinas, Santiago Centro, ☎ 2/633–2549), Santiago's 19th-century theater, presents excellent classical concerts, opera, and ballet by national and international groups throughout the March–December season.

THEATER

Provided that you understand Spanish, you can enjoy Chilean theater, which is among the best in Latin America. Long-respected ICTUS performs in the **Teatro la Comedia** (⊠ Merced 349, Santiago Centro, ☎ 2/639–1523). **Teatro la Feria** (⊠ Crucero Exeter 0250, Bellavista, ☎ 2/737–7371) mounts Chilean versions of English comedies. **El Conventillo** (⊠ Bellavista 173, ☎ 2/777–4164) produces a mixed offering of Latin American humor and drama.

Outdoor Activities and Sports

Horse Racing

Horse racing is popular at every level of society. There are two large hippodromes in Santiago. The **Club Hípico** (⊠ Blanco Encalada 2540, ☎ 2/683–6535) has racing weekend and Wednesday afternoons. At the **Hipódromo Chile** (⊠ Hipódromo Chile 1715, Independencia, ☎ 2/736–9276), post times tend to be earlier.

Skiing

While the Northern Hemisphere swelters, it's Chile's peak snow season, and three ski resorts operate a mere 45 minutes from Santiago. For more details, *see* Andean Ski Resorts *in* Side Trips from Santiago, *below.*

Soccer

Chile's most popular and most absorbing spectator sport is soccer, but a close second is watching the endless battles and bickering that go on among owners, players, and trainers whenever things aren't going well. The venue is the **Estadio Nacional** (⊠ Av. Grecia 2001, ☎ 2/238–8102); the season is March through December; and matches are on weekends and some Wednesdays, mostly at 4. Even if you're not a soccer fan, the Estadio National is worth a commemorative visit—it was here that the military junta corralled and killed thousands of supporters of the left in 1973, including Chilean folk singer Victor Jara. To assure he would never again provoke Chileans with his music, Jara's hands were mutilated before his murder.

Shopping

Centers

Santiago now has plenty of places where an A-to-Z of brand names sits under the same roof. **Alto Las Condes Shopping Center** (⊠ Av. Presidente Kennedy 9001, ☎ 2/229–1383) contains the aptly named Jumbo supermarket, where the staff wears roller skates to restock the aisles. It has a wide range of Chilean export wines. To get there, take metro line 1 to Escuela Militar station, and hop any bus that says LAS CONDES. **Parque Arauco** (⊠ Av. Kennedy 5413, ☎ 2/242–0600) is a typical North American–style shopping center, with an eclectic mix of department and boutique stores. Three large department stores—Falabella, Almacenes París, and Ripley—offer everything from perfume to plates. There's even a McDonald's for those who have acute bouts of homesickness. From Escuela Militar take any of the blue PARQUE ARAUCO metrobuses. The new **Mall del Centro** (⊠ At the corner of Puente and Rosas) is a smaller version of Parque Arauco, with a more central location.

Markets

Los Graneros del Alba is a crafts "village" with a wonderful display of cockatoos, exotic chickens, and other live birds. It's a nice place to visit, especially on weekends, when traveling musicians and performers add live entertainment to an already interesting mix of handicrafts and antiques. ⌧ *Av. Apoquindo 8600, beside the Iglesia los Domínicos.* ⊙ *Tues.–Sun. 10:30–8.*

There's a **permanent crafts fair** in Bellavista in the evenings, in the Domingo Gómez Park near the Law School on Pío Nono, just across the river from Plaza Baquedano. More vendors gather on weekends to display their handicrafts. Another crafts center is just across the Avenida Libertador Bernardo O'Higgins from Cerro Santa Lucia. For other spots to buy handcrafted articles, check with the Servicio Nacional de Turismo (known in Chile by the acronym SERNATUR, ☞ Santiago A to Z, *below*) to learn where local crafts fairs are currently operating.

Specialty Shops

WINE AND LIQUOR

If you want to take home some Chilean wine, you can choose from almost the entire export range at **La Vinoteca** (⌧ Isidora Goynechea 3520, Las Condes, ☎ 2/334–1987), which has its own sommelier—and he speaks English. **The Wine House** (⌧ Av. El Bosque N 0500, Providencia, ☎ 2/207–3520) has a wide selection of Chilean wines, including many that are usually exported. If you're looking for a particular wine, the best deal is to visit the vineyard; most will sell and ship cases directly to your home.

Side Trips from Santiago

Santiago offers many interesting excursions, most of which can be taken by bus. The most diversified is a visit to the Cajón del Maipo, or Maipo Canyon, deep in the Andes, an outing that can include a soak in a natural hot spring, visits to interesting mountain villages where low adobe houses line the road, and a drive through the stark but majestic landscape. If you're a snow-sports enthusiast and visit during the winter months, the Andes hold other opportunities—three major ski resorts less than an hour from the city.

Andean Ski Resorts

Between June and October, as the winter smog shrouds Santiago, the majestic Andes become both a clean-air refuge and home to some of the Southern Hemisphere's best winter-sports facilities. Most of Chile's ski resorts are in the high Cordillera close to the capital, and with the top elevations at the majority of ski areas extending to 3,300 m (11,000 ft), you can expect long runs and deep, dry snow. Most of the recent investment has gone into the higher-altitude Valle Nevado, where snowboarding, heli-skiing, and para-gliding are also available to those with enough money and nerves. Despite millions of dollars being invested over the last decade, however, the Chilean ski industry is still very underdeveloped, with frustratingly slow lifts and often far from luxurious facilities. The majority of the accommodations are either apartments or apart-hotels, and it's essential to book early. It is also not uncommon for the road up to the resorts (which still has no safety barriers) to be closed, even after the lightest of snowfalls.

THE RESORTS

Peak season is July–August; during this time you can expect to pay around $60 a day for a ski pass covering the first three resorts listed here, all of which are interconnected.

Farellones–Colorado. This 2,190-m (7,300-ft) area has nine lifts. ✉ *Centro de Ski, Av. Apoquindo 4900, local 48, Las Condes,* ☎ *2/246–3344 or 2/220–9501,* 🖷 *2/206–4078.*

La Parva. The snow is skiable as early as May at this 2,400-m (8,000-ft) spot with 16 lifts. ✉ *Av. Concepción 266, office 301, Providencia, Santiago,* ☎ *2/264–1466 or 2/220–9530,* 🖷 *2/264–1569 or 2/220–8510.*

Valle Nevado. This ski area has 25 runs and eight lifts. ✉ *Gertrudis Echeñique 441,* ☎ *2/206–0027,* 🖷 *2/208–0695.*

OFF THE BEATEN PATH	**PORTILLO –** Not connected to the others, this luxurious hotel and ski resort is 145 km (90 mi) northeast of Santiago. Opened in the 1930s, it is a beautiful ski area with 12 lifts, nestled in a valley set around Lake Inca. ✉ *Renato Sánchez 4270,* ☎ *2/263–0606,* 🖷 *2/263–0595.*

Maipo Canyon

The landscape of the Maipo Canyon is so diverse that you can spend an hour, an afternoon, or several days on this excursion. A narrow road winds its way up into the Andes mountain range along the route of the Maipo River, which supplies most of Santiago's drinking water. As you drive along the river, you'll see massive mountains of sedimentary rock, heaved up and thrown sideways, as if ready for a geology lesson. On a sunny day, colors are subtle but glowing, ranging from oranges and reds to ochers, buffs, beiges, and elusive greens and browns. Small mountain villages lie along the road. At the far end of the canyon, if you reach it, you'll find yourself in an austere moonscape of blue and gray rocks, where hot springs spill from the earth and the mountains display shades of violet and purple.

Any of the small towns you pass is worth a visit. Most have small cafés offering basic Chilean meals at reasonable prices; groceries are available, but you're better off buying lunch supplies in Santiago. Near the village of **El Manzano** is a picnic area where you can have an *asado* (barbecue) and spend the day enjoying the sun and fresh air. The canyon's main town, **San José de Maipo,** an hour's journey from the bus terminal in Santiago's Parque Bernardo O'Higgins, is another nice place to stop for refreshment, stretch your legs, and generally get a sense of small-town mountain life.

Five km (3 mi) farther along is **San Alfonso,** a small but extraordinary village where the traditional landowning family went hippie, producing fantastic houses that look as if they've been stolen from a fairy tale. One of their creations, the **Cascada de las Ánimas** (Waterfall of the Spirits) is off to the right of the highway, straddling the Maipo River. It has a circular outdoor swimming pool, a jealously protected wildland park, and lovely cabins that can be rented at reasonable prices; you must, however, book well ahead in the busy season. The family also organizes daily and overnight trips on horseback high up into the Andes. The guides are excellent. About 15 minutes farther up the road is the abandoned mining town of **El Volcán,** where you can visit the old abandoned copper-mine shafts and peer into the decaying, cramped miners' quarters.

If you really want to make a day of it, don't settle for the temptations of the low-level mountain villages: Instead, push on up the canyon, past San Alfonso and El Volcán, and take the gravel road into the mountains. The landscape becomes harsher and more majestic as green slopes give way to drier and barer mountain cliffs. Here you'll see layer on layer of sedimentary rock, packed with fossils from the time when this whole area was under the ocean. There are hot springs at **Baños Morales,** but if you're driving and have the time, take the right fork onward and upward to Los Valdés, stopping for refreshment or a filling lunch or tea at the **Refugio Alemán** (☎ 2/220–7610); it's well worth staying the night here (one night's spartan accommodations and three meals cost just over $50, but you're really paying for the location).

Eleven km (7 mi) from the refugio, along a difficult road through an impressive, rocky moonscape of mauves, grays, and steely blues, are the isolated and picturesque **Baños de Colina** hot springs. These huge natural bowls, scooped out of the mountain edge and overflowing with hot water, are well worth the trip. Here you can slip into a bathing suit (in your car—there are no changing rooms) and choose the pool that has the temperature most to your liking. Let your body float gently in the mineral-rich waters, and enjoy the view down the valley as your fellow soakers give one another medical advice, trade salt and lemons to suck on, and chat about the medicinal properties of these waters.

DINING AND LODGING

$$ ✕🏨 **Hostería los Ciervos.** At this pleasant hostelry you can have a filling lunch of hot Chilean dishes like pork and pot roast or of such typical summer foods as porotos granados or pastel de choclo. There are nine simple guest rooms, plus a small outdoor pool for guests. ✉ *Av. Argentina 711, San Alfonso,* ☎ FAX *2/861–1581. 9 rooms. Restaurant, outdoor pool. AE, MC, V.*

Santiago A to Z

Arriving and Departing
BY AIRPLANE
Santiago's new **Comodoro Arturo Merino Benítez International Airport** (☎ 2/220–7610) is about 30 minutes' drive west of the city, alongside the rather dilapidated old terminal, which now services domestic flights. The new facility is an efficient and beautifully designed metal-and-glass structure that contains far better facilities than its predecessor.

Among the U.S. carriers that serve Santiago, Continental has a daily non-stop flight from New York. American serves Santiago from Dallas and Miami, while United has a daily non-stop from Miami. Lan-Chile flies nonstop to Santiago from both Miami and Los Angeles. From London, the British Airways' flight that stops in Buenos Aires is the best bet. You can get from the airport to Santiago by taxi for less than p10,000, or you can spend only p1,000 and get into town via **Buses Tour Express** (☎ 2/671–7380). **Delfos** (☎ 2/226–6020), **Navett** (☎ 2/695–6868), and **Transfer** (☎ 2/777–7707) will shuttle you from the airport to any address within the city for less than p5,000. There is no metro connection.

BY BUS
Terminal Santiago (✉ Av. Libertador Bernardo O'Higgins 3848, Universidad de Santiago metro station, ☎ 2/779–1385) handles southern and coastal traffic. **Terminal Los Héroes** (✉ Tucapel Jiménez 21, ☎ 2/696–9076, 2/696–9080, or 2/696–9082) handles some northern and southern traffic. **Terminal Alameda** (✉ Av. Libertador Bernardo O'Higgins 3714, Universidad de Santiago metro station, ☎ 2/776–1038) handles some coastal and southern traffic. (☞ Chile A to Z, *below,* for phone numbers of individual lines.)

Skitotal (✉ Av. Apoquindo 4900, local 39, ☎ FAX 2/246–0156) runs a bus service to all of the Andean ski resorts except Portillo. It departs from the Skitotal office at 8:45; a round-trip ticket is $13. Also available for hire are ski-taxis—$90 a day with driver included—and minibuses ($125) that hold up to 12 people. **Manzur Expediciones** (⊠ Sótero del Río 475, suite 507, Santiago, Baquedano station, ☎ 2/777–4284, FAX 2/643–5651) runs a bus service to Portillo on Wednesday, Saturday, and Sunday that leaves at 8:30 and returns at 5.

BY CAR
If you're coming into Santiago from the north, you'll probably arrive via the Pan-American Highway, also called Highway 5; from Viña or Valparaíso, Highway 68; from the south, the Pan-American Highway South, still Highway 5; from the Andes (Argentina) Highway 57. Route 78 brings you into Santiago from San Antonio and other coastal towns.

BY TRAIN
The Central Station is **Estación Central** (⊠ Av. Libertador Bernardo O'Higgins 853, Santiago Centro, ☎ 2/689–1825). It has its own metro stop of the same name.

Getting Around
BY AIRPLANE
The major cities in Chile are served by LanChile and Avant. If you have a limited amount of time in Chile you could either book a Chile Pass from LanChile in advance of your trip or visit a Santiago travel agent and purchase a ticket once you've arrived. A one-way ticket from Santiago to Puerto Montt costs about p45,000 ($95) and from Santiago to Punta Arenas it's about p76,000 ($155).

BY BUS
Buses have improved but are still fast, reckless, and unreliable; because bus service is private, with employees earning only commission, bus drivers almost invariably say they go where you want to go, whether they do or not. Bus fare is usually 150–250 pesos (less than 50¢), paid upon boarding, and drivers can usually change up to a 1,000-peso bill.

Terminal Alameda (⊠ Av. Libertador Bernardo O'Higgins 3750, Universidad de Santiago metro station, ☎ 2/776–1038) handles traffic for Pullman (☎ 2/776–2426) and Tur Bus (☎ 2/270–7500) buses. **Terminal Los Héroes** (⊠ Tucapel Jiménez 21, Los Héroes metro station, ☎ 2/696–9087) handles Flota Barrios (☎ 2/696–9311), Tas-Choapa (☎ 2/697–0062), and Cruz del Sur (☎ 2/696–9324); **Terminal Santiago** (⊠ Av. Libertador Bernardo O'Higgins 3848, Universidad de Santiago metro station, ☎ 2/779–1385) handles another 20 or so smaller bus companies; and **Terminal Torres de Tajamar** (⊠ Av. Providencia 1072) handles Varmontt (☎ 2/231–3505) and Jac (☎ 2/235–2484).

Bus service to Maipo Canyon is cheap (less than $10 for a round-trip ticket to Refugio Alamán) and frequent. Only the 7:30 AM bus, however, goes all the way up to Baños Colina and the Refugio, approximately a two-hour trip. It leaves from the Buses Manzur office on Ramón Carnícier, near the Plaza Italia. For all other buses that run throughout the day to Maipo Canyon take the Santiago metro southern line to the Parque Bernardo O'Higgins stop. The Santiago–Cajón del Maipo bus terminal is across the street and 50 yards north of Parque O'Higgins's main entrance. Within half an hour you'll have started the climb through the canyon; sit on the right side of the bus for a good view of the river.

BY CAR
You can rent a car in the airport from **Hertz** (☎ 2/601–0477), **Budget** (☎ 2/601–9421), or **Avis** (☎ 2/690–1382).

Drivers in Santiago don't respect traffic signs, lights, or lines on the road, and rush hour means wall-to-wall cars lined up along major and minor thoroughfares. However, a rented car or taxi is still your best bet for an overview of the city or for enjoying short drives into the surrounding countryside. Between May and August, roads, underpasses, and parks can flood when it rains, and they can become very dangerous, especially for drivers who don't know their way around. Avoid driving if it has been raining for several hours. Keep in mind that the speed limit in the city is 50 km/h (31 mph) unless otherwise posted.

It takes about two hours to reach the three main Andean ski resorts, which lie 30–35 mi from Santiago. If you intend to drive, make sure you have either a four-wheel-drive vehicle or snow chains. There's a police checkpoint before the road starts to climb up into the Andes, and they will not let you pass if you don't have chains. In any case, be warned—the road is narrow, dangerous, and full of Chileans who think they're Ayrton Senna, the former Formula One racing car champion (who, ironically, was tragically killed during a race in 1995).

To reach the resorts, get onto Avenida Presidente Kennedy or Avenida las Condes and drive east toward the Andes. Follow the signs for Farellones. The three resorts are well signposted once you get into the mountains. Portillo is much farther away from Santiago and in a different direction than the other resorts. If you are thinking of driving yourself, you should get a good map and call the hotel ahead of time to find out about the road conditions.

For Maipo Canyon, from Plaza Italia turn south on Ramón Carnícer (one block east of Vicuña MacKenna) to Grecia, and left (east) on Grecia to Avenida José Alessandri; turn right and continue southward to the Rotonda Departamental, a large traffic circle. There you can take Camino Las Vizcachas, following it south into the canyon as far as you choose to go.

BY METRO

Santiago's metro is best for reaching downtown, or anywhere along its east–west axis. It is modern, comfortable, cheap, and safe; make it the backbone of your explorations. Every station has a clear map of all three lines, with adjoining streets. The Universidad de Chile stop on line 1 is the main station for the city center; the Escuela Militar is the upper-class end of the city; and Pudahuel is the poorer, less developed area. Buy tickets in the glass booths at the stations; a *boleto inteligente* (value ticket)—good for up to 10 journeys at any time of day and valid on all three metro lines—is cheapest at about $4.

BY TAXI

Taxi drivers aren't as honest as they used to be, but taxis, especially when combined with the metro for large distances, are a reasonable alternative for most transportation needs. With some 50,000 taxis in Santiago, you can flag one down on most streets; the average ride costs around $8 (more for designated airport taxis). Radio-dispatched cabs—from **Andes Pacífico** (☎ 2/225–3064 or 2/204–0104) or **Las Condes** (☎ 2/211–4470)—are slightly more expensive but will pick you up at your door.

Most individual taxi drivers are willing to be hired for the day. To increase your bargaining power, head for the taxi stand at Huérfanos and MacIver streets in the heart of downtown, where you can talk to more than one driver.

Contacts and Resources

BANKS AND CURRENCY EXCHANGE

Banks in Chile are open weekdays 9–2 and bureau de change offices are open weekdays 9–2 and 3–6. There are many places to exchange money in Santiago, including the **American Express Bank** (⊠ Av. Augustinas 1360, ☎ 2/672–2156) and **Citibank** (⊠ Paseo Ahumada 40, ☎ 2/338–5000), the latter of which probably has the most ATMs in town. The Citibank ATMs are in English and work with all PLUS and CIRRUS cards; some local bank ATMs only work with CIRRUS. The airport also has reasonable exchange rates, and two ATMs are located on the second level.

BUSINESS SERVICES

The large hotels in Santiago have business centers for guests. Otherwise, try the **HQ Centro de Negocios** agency (⊠ Av. Huérfanos 835, 21st floor, ☎ 2/644–4833), which provides secretarial and translation services and rents offices.

EMERGENCIES

Police: ☎ 133. **Fire:** ☎ 132. **Hospitals:** Clínica Alemana (⊠ Av. Vitacura 5951, ☎ 2/212–9700). Clínica Vitacura (⊠ Av. Presidente Kennedy 3210, ☎ 2/228–9043).

ENGLISH-LANGUAGE BOOKSTORES

The **Instituto Chileno-Norteamericano de Cultura** (⊠ Moneda 1467, Santiago Centro, ☎ 2/696–3215) has a nonlending library, as well as English-language periodicals. **Larraín Hudson Ltda.** (⊠ Av. Providencia 1652, local 5, Providencia, ☎ 2/235–1205) sells secondhand English books. **Librería Inglesa** (⊠ Av. Pedro de Valdivia 47, Providencia, ☎ 2/231–6270) has new books at high prices. For popular newspapers and magazines in English (from weeks ago), check the kiosks on Paseo Ahumada.

TELEPHONES, THE INTERNET, MAIL

If you plan to use a pay phone in the street you'll need to buy a phone card at a newsstand. The tricky bit is to be sure you buy a card that works with the phone you want to use (for an Entel phone you need an Entel phone card; you'll need a CTC card for a CTC phone). Your best bet is to use one of the many phone company offices that have booths where you can sit to make all of your calls and then pay at the end. Two such offices in the center of the city are **Entel** at Huérfanos 1133 and **CTC** at Moneda 1151.

In Santiago there are two Internet cafés where you can order a cup of Joe and check your E-mail account. Close to the Plaza Italia and open every day of the week is **Café Virtual** (⊠ 145 Alameda, Centro, ☎ 2/638–6846), which has more than 10 computer terminals. **Café Internet Cybercenter** (⊠ 170 General Holley, Providencia, ☎ 2/231–4207), in a more upscale part of town, is open Mon.–Sat., 10–10.

The main post office (Correo Central) (☞ Santiago, *above*) is located on the north end of the Plaza de Armas. Another branch is in Providencia (⊠ Av. Providecia 1466). For overnight mail, try **Federal Express** (⊠ San Camilo 190 or Providecia 1951) or **DHL** (⊠ Huérfanos 1109).

TOUR OPERATORS AND TRAVEL AGENCIES

Adventure. Altué Expediciones (⊠ Encomenderos 83, ☎ 2/232–1103, FAX 2/233–6799) and **Cascada Expediciones** (⊠ Orrego Luco 019, 2nd floor, ☎ 2/234–2274, FAX 2/233–9768) offer adventure trips such as rafting on wild rivers and hiking to the mouths of volcanoes.

Orientation. SERNATUR (☞ Visitor Information, *below*,) maintains a register of experienced individual tour guides who, for a half-day fee (around $35 per group), will take you on a personalized tour of Santiago and the surrounding area. These guides can greatly enrich visits to Santiago's less documented museums, for example, by providing background knowledge that is not generally available to the public.

Other operators include **Turismo Cocha** (⊠ El Bosque Norte 0430, ☎ 2/230–1000, FAX 2/203–5110) and **Chilean Travel Services** (⊠ Antonio Bellet 77, Office 101, Providencia, ☎ 2/251–0400, FAX 2/251–0426), who handle tours of both Santiago and the rest of Chile. Another agency offering individualized tours is **Sportstour** (⊠ Moneda 970, 14th floor, ☏ 2/549–5200, ⅎᴬˣ 2/698–2981).

Winery. Agencia Chile-Andino (☏ 2/744–3630, ⅎᴬˣ 2/362–1996) runs half- and full-day tours of Chile's vineyards and wineries. Short tours are based around some of the oldest wineries, such as Viña Cousiño Macul and Viña Santa Rita, whose beautiful old family houses and private gardens are close to the capital. Longer tours will take you to some of the newer boutique wineries to the south and to the home of Chile's best white wines, the Casablanca Valley.

VISITOR INFORMATION
SERNATUR (⊠ Av. Providencia 1550, Providencia, ☏ 2/236–1416, ⅎᴬˣ 2/251–8469) is the national tourist service. The office is between the metro stops Manuel Montt and Pedro de Valdivia and is open daily from 9 AM–10 PM.

VALPARAÍSO AND VIÑA DEL MAR

Twin cities could hardly differ more than these, side by side on Chile's Pacific coast, just over an hour and a half's drive from Santiago. Valparaíso (population 275,000) is a working port complete with naval installations, sailors' bars, and bordellos as well as the winding, hilly streets, and colorful houses that have made it a classic setting for travel posters. Viña del Mar (literally, "the Sea's Vineyard"), with a population of 300,000, is an international showcase, with beautifully kept gardens, expensive hotels, stylish restaurants, and a luxury casino. There is cheap, regular bus and train service between the two. If you want to lie on the beach, arrange to stay overnight in Viña. It's lively, crowded, fashionable, and somewhat expensive, with plenty of nightlife in its central cafés. But if you want to watch the workings of a busy international port, check out Valparaíso; there are plenty of good walks, most of which converge upon Plaza Victoria.

Valparaíso

120 km (75 mi) northwest of Santiago on Rte. 68.

The most pleasant way to see ships loading and unloading their cargo at the port is to take an hour-long **motorboat tour** around the harbor from the **Muelle Prat** (Prat Dock) in Valparaíso—a private boat costs about $12 and can take up to 10 people. The dock, which has permanent crafts kiosks, is between the historic buildings of the Dirección Nacional de Aduana (National Customs House) and the Estación Puerto del Ferrocarril (Port Railway Station). Frequent trains (30 per day) run along the scenic coastline between Valparaíso's Muelle Prat and downtown Viña del Mar.

Seven blocks west of the dock in Valparaíso is the 19th-century customs building; next to it is the **Ascensor Artillería**, a cable car that will pull you uphill to the **Paseo 21 de Mayo**, a wide cliff's-edge balcony surrounded by well-tended gardens and tall, old trees, from which you can survey the port and a goodly portion of Valparaíso. Here, you are in the **Cerro Playa Ancha** (Wide Beach Hill), one of Valparaíso's nicest neighborhoods. Near the top of the cable car is a large neoclassical mansion that until recently housed the Naval School and still belongs to the navy. Avid picture-takers should be careful, because much of Valparaíso Harbor is considered part of the naval base, and photography is prohibited. In this same building is the **Museo Naval y Marítimo** (Naval and Maritime Museum), which offers historical information on the port and displays of the ships and forts that once defended it. ⊠ *Paseo 21 de Mayo, Cerro Astillería,* ☎ *32/283749.* 🎫 *Admission.* ☉ *Tues.–Sun. 10–5:30.*

Take the cable car back down the hill, then head down the first street on your right, Bustamante Street. Here, in Valparaíso's oldest neighborhood, you'll see the **Plaza e Iglesia de la Matriz** (Plaza and Church of la Matriz), built in 1842, which contains a 17th-century carving of Jesus on the cross donated by the king and queen of Spain.

If you'd like to see a sampling of the sort of wall murals that have made several Latin American artists famous, head down Bustamante Street to **Plaza Victoria** (Victory Square) to visit Valparaíso's **Museo a Cielo Abierto** (Open-Air Museum). Start from the Plaza Victoria and follow along Molina Street to Aldunate Street, then right one block to Huito, toward the hill, where there's a long, long stairway and the first of 17 murals painted by Chile's most important painters. As the name suggests, the exposition takes the form of colorful murals painted on the walls that line the many stairs, walkways, and streets leading up and down Valparaíso's crowded hillsides. An easier route to the Open-Air Museum is to take the **Ascensor Espíritu Santo** (Holy Spirit Elevator), from Calle Aldunate, near the bottom of the hill, up and then walk down through the museum. ⊠ *Aldunate 1560,* ☎ *no phone.* 🎫 *Admission.* ☉ *Daily 7 AM–11 PM.*

★ **La Sebastiana,** yet another of Pablo Neruda's houses, is nestled in the hills just above the Museo a Cielo Abierto. You can begin the climb from the top of the Open-Air Museum or start out from Edwards Street in Plaza Victoria. Follow Edwards towards the bottom of Cerro Florida (Florida Hill), where it turns into Ferrari. It's a short but grueling hike (25 minutes) to the entrance to Plaza Sebastiana, but Neruda's third house makes the climb worthwhile. Washed in sky-blue and pink "so that the walls might begin to dance," the three floors of La Sebastiana are crammed with odds and ends—boats, bottles, cups, and saucers— from the poet's past. A maze of twisting stairwells leads up to the library and study, from where you can marvel at the Océano Pacífico as Neruda so often did in his poetry. ⊠ *Ferrari 692, Cerro Florida,* ☎ *32/256606.* 🎫 *Admission.* ☉ *Tues.–Sun. 10:30–2:30, 3:30–6.*

Dining

$$$ ✕ **Bote Salvavidas.** This restaurant at the end of Prat Dock in Valparaíso
★ offers the best view of the harbor and, naturally, specializes in seafood. Fish dishes—such as panfried conger eel with sea urchin sauce, and *sopa Salvavidas* (fish soup with mussels and clams in a paprika-flavored broth)—are among the popular specialties that are served in the simple plant-filled dining room. ⊠ *Muelle Prat,* ☎ *32/251477. AE, DC, MC, V.*

$$ ✕ **Bar Inglés.** The "English Bar" has the longest bar in Valpo and incorporates Dutch lamps and American oak furnishings as part of its effort to imitate an English country pub. The specialty is international cooking, particularly hot and cold soups, beef, and shellfish baked with cheese, sautéed with garlic, or dipped in mayonnaise; also try such imaginative vegetable dishes as an artichoke, mushroom, and asparagus combination. ⊠ *Cochrane 851,* ☎ *32/214625. No credit cards. Closed weekends and holidays.*

$$ ✕ **Café Turri.** Set among other large mansion houses on Concepción Hill, this 19th-century property commands one of the best views of Valparaíso and offers some of the finest seafood. The corvina in almond sauce alone is worth driving to the coast for, and the *tortilla de erizos* (Spanish-style omelet filled with local sea urchin) is far tastier than it sounds. ⊠ *Templeman 147, Paseo Gervasoni,* ☎ *32/259198. AE, DC, MC, V.*

$ ✕ **Winnipeg.** An eclectic smattering of posters from someone's European vacation, exposed-beam architecture, and a lonely beach-cruiser bicycle match the mixed crowd of tourists and Valparisian artists that frequent this café, restaurant, and cultural center. Full meals are served, as well as tapas, cocktails, and coffees. There is an art cinema next door, and the Winnipeg is open until the wee hours on weekends, making it a pleasant atmosphere for a rest after a bout with Valparaíso's disco circuit. ⊠ *Esmeralda 1083, 2 piso,* ☎ *32/254844. No credit cards.*

Nightlife

To bump elbows and bottoms with Valparaíso's young and spirited Bohemian crowd, venture up to **Plazuela Ecuador,** just five blocks west of Plaza Victoria. Here you can find the whole sleazy-to-snazzy gamut of bars, clubs, and discos. None of them have phones, but they are all in and around the small square, and are easy to find. Live jazz on weekends can be found at **La Curva** bar and disco. **L'O Devi** has a downstairs bar with live music and an upstairs disco with a bumping techno beat.

Outdoor Activities and Sports

BOATING

Ship owners and operators at the **Prat Dock** rent out their boats or take passengers on ocean excursions.

GOLF

Golf can be played at the 18-hole **Granadillas Country Club** (☎ 32/689527) just north of downtown Viña in the Santa Inés section of town.

Viña del Mar

130 km (85 mi) northwest of Santiago, 10 km (6 mi) north of Valparaíso on Rte. 68.

Viña del Mar's central square, **Plaza José Francisco Vergara,** with its majestic palms and in-line skaters, butts up against Avenida Valparaíso, the city's main artery and tourist thoroughfare. A horse and buggy tour ($12.50 for 30 minutes) will trot you past some of Viña's mansions from the last century. Or, take a waterfront stroll along Avenida San Martín and see the glitter of the present era.

Viña has one of Chile's best botanical gardens, the **Quinta Vergara,** which includes its own palace, the **Museo de las Bellas Artes** (Fine Arts Museum), a fine arts school, and a large, open-air theater famous for an international music festival held every February. Fine Arts Museum: ⊠ *Errázuriz 563,* ☎ *32/684137.* 🎫 *Admission.* ☉ *Tues.–Sun. 10–2 and 3–6; park daily 7:30–6, until 8 Jan.–Feb.*

Dining and Lodging

$$$ ✕ **Cap Ducal.** This ship-shaped restaurant rises from the sea and affords excellent views of the shore and the horizon. The creative kitchen specializes in European-style cooking as well as its own inventions, including a popular eel stew and grilled fish in a spicy herb sauce. ⊠ *Av. Marina 51,* ☎ *32/626655. AE, DC, MC, V.*

$$$ ✕ **Delicias del Mar.** Don't be fooled by the Marilyn Monroe photos—
★ this nationally renowned restaurant's Basque-style seafood is tasty, even though the decor may not be. The grilled sea bass, bathed in a shrimp and mushroom cognac sauce, is fantastic, as are the machas *curadas* (steamed with dill and parmesan cheese). Top it off with one of Delicias' fine desserts and you'll know why owner and chef Raúl Madinagoitía cooks on television. Chef Madinagoitía is also a partner in Vinoteca, the speciality wine shops in Viña and Santiago, so oenophiles should note the excellent wine list. ⊠ *San Martín 459,* ☎ *32/901837. AE, DC, MC, V.*

CHILEAN WINES

CHILEAN WINES HAVE COME A long way in the last decade. Although many vineyards in the valleys around Santiago have been producing wine for over 100 years—some with French vinestocks that date back to the middle of the 19th century—Chilean wines were only really introduced to the world when California wines priced themselves out of the "high quality yet inexpensive" category. It was in the 1980s that the ever-expanding global gourmand culture dubbed Chilean Merlots and Cabernet Sauvignons a great value. Since that time, the Chilean wineries have been furiously working to keep pace with the broadening international demand while steadily trying to improve their product so that their wines can break through into the "world-class" category.

An oft-repeated curious fact about wine business in Chile is that the best is made almost exclusively for the export market. It's not just that the domestic market for wine is somewhat small, but more importantly that up until recently the average Chilean had little interest in wines except the traditional oxidized whites and aged reds. Though a wine culture is slowly developing in Chile, the big vintners are still concentrating their energy on the crucial international market. To that end, the best wineries are modernizing the growing and fermenting methods (with investment and consulting help from French and Californian oenological experts) to produce wines that are better suited for the European and North American markets. These changes have paid off in recent years with improved overall quality of the Chilean wines. In fact, a small number of Chilean vintners are already turning out a few truly first-rate wines, including Concha y Toro's Don Melchor Reserve, Santa Rita's Casa Real, and Veramonte's Primus.

It is important to point out, though, that not all Chileans are the wine neophytes they are frequently made out to be. Of late, many well-heeled residents of the bigger cities have become interested in the celebrated European-style wines that are a source of national pride. Wines basically created for the export market can now be found on lists in Santiago's best restaurants alongside the more traditional-style Chilean wines. One of the 15 sommeliers in all of Santiago, Alejandro Farais of the Bristol restaurant in the Hotel San Francisco, recommends four very specific showcase wines he believes are some of the best in Chile: Carmen's tropical fruity Sauvignon Blanc ('98); Casa Blanca's sweet and bitter Chardonnay ('97); Santa Maria's luxuriously smooth Reserve Merlot ('96); and San Pedro's berry-flavored Cabo de Hornos Cabernet Sauvignon ('96).

As a general rule, Merlots or Chardonnays in Chile are more likely to be the export-style, fruity, fresh wines that Americans and Europeans enjoy. The Chilean Sauvignon Blanc on a wine list will probably be a domestic-style wine, liable to be more interesting than actually tasty to most Americans. Cabernet Sauvignon is Chile's best wine, and while the quality will vary according to the price, you are prone to get the very best wine. When you're considering these different varietals, keep the name of Chile's largest winery and the biggest exporter, Concha y Toro, in mind. It has a number of different labels (some made exclusively for the domestic market) that usually offer good value, from the affordable and popular Casillero del Diablo label to the higher priced, export-oriented Trio wines. Other reliable wineries that are strong in the domestic market include Errazuriz, Santa Carolina, and Santa Rita. Also, be on the lookout for the smaller Casa Lapostolle boutique winery, whose wines (particularly reds) are highly regarded but not widely available.

—By Charles Runnette

$$$ ✕ **La Fontana.** Inside the Viña del Mar Casino, this elegant Italian restaurant is decorated with views of Venice and the characteristic bougainvilleas of Viña. It offers a complete fish and shellfish menu, but it's the pasta and risotto dishes that have built its reputation. After a plate of fettuccine with fresh salmon and caviar, you'll feel ready to gamble the night away. ⊠ *San Martín 199,* ☏ *32/689200. AE, DC, MC, V.*

$$$$ 🏨 **Hotel Gala.** A recent Viña addition, this 14-story luxury hotel offers panoramic views of the city and bay, modern rooms (some with terraces) with fax and personal computer connections, and a multifunctional, state-of-the-art convention center. ⊠ *Arlegui 273,* ☏ *32/686688,* 🅵🅰🆇 *32/689568. 64 rooms, 13 suites. Restaurant, bar, in-room data ports, minibars, pool, massage, sauna, business services, convention center, meeting rooms. AE, DC, MC, V.*

$$$ 🏨 **Hotel Alcazar.** This recently remodeled hotel has a very no-nonsense feel. The rooms are standard issue and the staff is helpful, but not as fluent in English as they claim. The reason to choose this hotel is for the charming cabins in a lush courtyard. Accessible from the street (through a passageway), the cabins are cheaper than the rooms in the hotel and give you the feeling of staying in your own little beach house, though not right at the beach. ⊠ *Alvarez 646,* ☏ *32/685112,* 🅵🅰🆇 *32/884245. 52 rooms, 22 cabins. Restaurant, bar, minibars, meeting rooms. AE, DC, MC, V.*

$$$ 🏨 **Hotel O'Higgins.** Dominating one side of the main square in Viña del Mar, this grand seaside hotel was built in 1935 and has huge rooms with high ceilings. Many parts of the hotel are in need of renovation, but if you don't mind the occasional faded curtain and worn carpet, it offers ample space, charm, and traditional service. ⊠ *Plaza Vergara,* ☏ *32/882016,* 🅵🅰🆇 *32/883537. 262 rooms, 2 suites. Restaurant, bar, pool, dance club, business services. AE, DC, MC, V.*

$$ 🏨 **Magno Hotel.** This modern, centrally located hotel opened in late 1998. The rooms are small, but they have double-glazed windows to keep out the street noise. ⊠ *Arlegui 372,* ☏ *32/881172,* 🅵🅰🆇 *32/993316. 26 rooms. Bar, free parking. AE, DC, MC, V.*

$ 🏨 **Hotel Rokamar.** This centrally located hotel, on the main road to town, is an excellent alternative to some of Viña's overpriced, run-down options. Three floors of rooms spiral around a wood-paneled lobby with a raulí-wood reception desk and a very friendly staff. Off-season rates are often negotiable. ⊠ *Viana 107,* ☏ 🅵🅰🆇 *32/690019. 24 rooms, 2 suites. Breakfast room, free parking. AE, DC, MC, V.*

Nightlife and the Arts

Viña's artistic activities and nightlife vary considerably according to the season, with the most glittering attractions concentrated in the summer months, January and February. Check the newspapers (including Santiago's) for listings.

Blues & Booze (⊠ Muelle Vergara, ☏ 32/688256) is the hot new club out on a pier past Acapulco beach. Live bands perform throughout the week; happy hour is 8–10 PM.

The James-Bond-in-the-'70s style **Casino** (⊠ Av. San Martín 199, ☏ 32/689200) has a restaurant, disco, cabaret, and—of course—games of the roulette and blackjack sort. It's open nightly until the wee hours; formal dress is encouraged in the game rooms. The p3,000 cover charge includes a free drink.

Cocodrilo (⊠ Av. Borgon 13101, Reñaca, ☏ 32/831158), a miniature castle perched on the cliff between Viña and Reñaca, is always packed on the weekends and often stays open until 8 AM. Thick stone walls, a catacomblike dance floor, and bartenders who mix Chile's best *caipirinahs*—Brazil's national drink, made with lime, ice, sugar, and *cachaça* (Brazilian rum)—make it a unique and atmospheric night out.

Outdoor Activities and Sports

BEACHES

Follow Viña's Avenida Pedro Montt until you reach a large, solar-powered clock, consisting of continually replanted flowers and two large working hands. Across from the clock you'll find **Playa Los Marineros** (Sailors' Beach). This is followed by a long stretch of coastline that belongs to the navy (off-limits to the public) that ends at **Playa Las Salinas** (Las Salinas Beach), a sheltered area packed with sun-loving crowds in summer. Quieter seaside areas lie to the north: **Concón,** 8 km (5 mi) up the coast; **Quintero,** 18 km (11 mi); **Maitencillo,** 65 km (40 mi); and **Papeete,** 88 km (55 mi).

Pollution is a problem around Viña and up the coast, in addition to strong currents, undertow, and sudden, large waves. A red flag indicates you should definitely not swim at a specific beach, although you'll probably see people in the water anyway. The Humboldt Current, which flows northward up the coast of Chile, brings cold water to almost all the country's beaches. If you plan to windsurf or surf, you'll need a wet suit.

WATER SPORTS

Faenas Marítimos Cristóbal Colón (☎ 32/246286) offers skin diving, scuba diving, gear rental, boat trips, and fishing for tuna, corvina, sea bass, and conger eel.

Shopping

The **Feria Internacional de Artesanía** (International Crafts Fair) sets up in the Quinta Vergara from mid-January through early February. Outdoor stalls feature weaving, leather crafts, jewelry, paintings, ceramics, and toys. For more information, contact the Viña del Mar Tourist Office (☎ 32/269332).

Valparaíso and Viña del Mar A to Z

Arriving and Departing

BY BUS

There's excellent, continual bus service between Santiago and Valparaíso/Viña. Take the metro to the Universidad de Santiago station, south side exit, and check out the **Terminal Alameda** (✉ Av. Libertador Bernardo O'Higgins 3714, Universidad de Santiago metro station, ☎ 2/776–1038) or the main **Terminal Santiago** (✉ Av. Libertador Bernardo O'Higgins 3848, ☎ 2/779–1385) just a block westward for regular service.

Contacts and Resources

BANKS AND CURRENCY EXCHANGE

In Viña, a local branch of **Citibank** (✉ 1 Norte 633) will exchange money and traveler's checks and has a 24-hour ATM. For bureau de change only, try one of the many cambios on Av. Arlegui, such as **Afex** (✉ Arlegui 641). In Valparaíso the banks and exchange bureaus are all located in the center of town along Prat and Esmerelda, including **Citibank** (✉ Av. Esmerelda 932) and **Cambios Gema** (✉ Av. Esmerelda 940).

EMERGENCIES

Police: ☎ 133. **Fire:** ☎ 132.

TELEPHONES, THE INTERNET, MAIL

Entel (✉ Av. Valparaíso 510, local 10) and **CTC** (✉ Av. Valparaíso 628) both have offices in Viña. In Valparaíso CTC is at the southeast corner of Plaza de la Victoria. Check with the tourist offices in Viña or Valparaíso for an up-to-date list of Internet cafés. The post office in Viña is at the corner of Arlegui and Av. Libertad near the Tourist Information office. Valparaíso's main post office is at the southeast corner of Plaza Sotomayor; another is south of Plaza de la Victoria on Av. Edwards. **DHL** (✉ Plaza Sotomayor 55) in Valparaíso is open weekdays 9–7, Sat. 9–6.

Contact **Chilean Travel Services** (✉ Antonio Bellet 77, Office 101, ☎ 2/251–0400), **Turismo Cocha** (✉ El Bosque Norte 0430, ☎ 2/230–1000) in Santiago, or **Centro de Turismo** (✉ Arlegui and Liberdad, north of the Plaza Vergara, ☎ 32/883154) in Viña. Each has a very helpful staff and can arrange tours.

SERNATUR (✉ Av. Valparaíso 507, Office 305, Viña del Mar, ☎ 32/882285). The **Viña del Mar Centro de Turismo** (☞ Tour Operators and Travel Agents, *above*) has a helpful staff, lots of brochures, and better maps.

THE LAKE DISTRICT

If you've never flirted with a volcano, Chile's Lake District is the place to start. As you travel along roads bordered by grazing cattle or through dense native forests of *alerce* and *raulí* trees, the broad, snow-capped shoulders of volcanoes emerge, mysteriously disappear, then materialize again, peeping through trees or towering over lake-lined valleys. The sometimes difficult journey along narrow mountain roads that wind through breathtaking passes is almost inevitably rewarded by a clear mountain lake, vibrant and blue. Often, there are hot springs in which tired travelers can soak stiff muscles.

Your best route is to start in Temuco and work your way south through the Valdivia–Villarica area to Lake Llanquihue and Puerto Montt, a journey of about 340 km (212 mi). You'll find information about these destinations following the general Lake District information immediately below.

Unlike that of Chile's fertile Central Valley region between Santiago and Temuco, weather can be a major factor in your seeing and enjoying the Lake District. The summer (December–early March) offers the most likelihood of sunshine, although if you're prepared for rain, a few showers probably won't bother you.

Temuco

675 km (405 mi) south of Santiago.

In addition to its claim as the fastest growing city in Chile, Temuco is home to a large population of Mapuche, one of Latin America's hardiest groups of indigenous peoples. Many Mapuche sell their products in Temuco, and the **Mercado Municipal** (Municipal Market) is one of the best places to find traditional woolen ponchos, pullovers, and blankets. ✉ *Manuel Rodríguez 960.* ☉ *Mon.–Sat. 8–6, Sun. 8:30–3.*

The **Museo Araucano** (Araucanian Museum) covers some aspects of Mapuche history, along with a general history of the area. It has an odd array of poorly labeled artifacts and relics, including musical instruments, utensils, and Mapuche jewelry. Sadly, the museum falls short of documenting the complexities and richness of one of the few living Chilean subcultures. Although much official rhetoric tries to reduce the colonization of this area to a process called the "Pacificación de la Araucanía" ("The Pacification of the Araucanian Territories"), which took place in the 1880s, in reality the Mapuche successfully fought

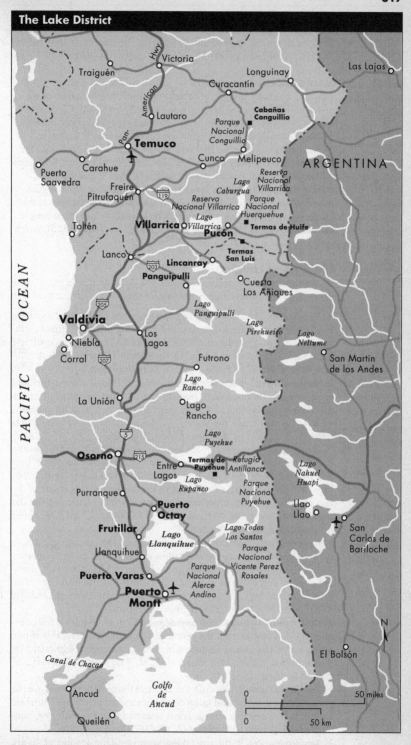

The Lake District

Traiguén

Victoria

Longuinay

Las Lajas

Curacantín

American Hwy

Lautaro

Cabañas Conguillio

Parque Nacional Conguillio

ARGENTINA

Temuco

Cunco

Melipeuco

Par-

Carahue

Puerto Saavedra

Freire

Pitrufaquén

Lago Caburgua

Reserva Nacional Villarrica

119

Reserva Nacional Villarrica

Parque Nacional Huerquehue

Toltén

Villarrica

Lago Villarrica

Termas de Huife

Pucón

Lanco

Termas San Luis

Lincanray

203

Cuesta Los Añiques

Panguipulli

Lago Panguipulli

205

Lago Pirehueico

Lago Neltume

Valdivia

Los Lagos

San Martin de los Andes

Niebla

207

Futrono

Corral

Lago Ranco

La Unión

Lago Rancho

5

Lago Puyehue

Osorno

215

Termas de Puyehue

Refugio Antillanca

Lago Nahuel Huapi

Entre Lagos

Lago Rupanco

Parque Nacional Puyehue

Purranque

Llao Llao

Puerto Octay

San Carlos de Bariloche

Frutillar

Lago Todos Los Santos

Lago Llanquihue

Parque Nacional Vicente Perez Rosales

Llanquihue

Puerto Varas

Parque Nacional Alerce Andino

Puerto Montt

N

El Bolsón

PACIFIC OCEAN

Canal de Chacao

Golfo de Ancud

Ancud

0   50 miles

Queilén

0   50 km

off the Spanish and defended a huge tract of territory for the better part of three centuries before finally facing defeat by the Chilean army, fresh from war with Peru and Bolivia. ⊠ *Av. Alemania 084,* ☎ *45/ 211108.* ☒ *Admission.* ☉ *Mon.– Fri. 9–5, Sat. 11–4:45.*

<table>
<tr><td>OFF THE
BEATEN PATH</td><td>**PARQUE NACIONAL CONGUILLÍO** – If you have time and a car, a visit to this park makes for an unforgettable experience. In the shadow of the active Volcán Llaima (which erupted as recently as 1994), Conguillío National Park is home to thousands of araucaria pines, often known as monkey puzzle trees. Heavy snow can cut off the area in winter, so November to March is the best time to visit. To get to the park, take the Pan-American Highway north out of Temuco as far as Lautero, then head 54 km (34 mi) east to the town of Curacautín, then follow the signs. **CONAF** (⊠ Av. Bilbao 931, Temuco, ☎ 45/236312 or 45/238900) provides maps and information, and in summer, organizes hikes to the Sierra Nevada. The only accommodation available close to the park is **Cabañas Conguillío** (⊠ Temuco, ☎ 45/213291 or 45/214363), which rents four-person cabins for about $75 a night.</td></tr>
</table>

Dining and Lodging

Establishments come and go frequently in this region, and many close down after the peak summer and winter seasons.

$$ ✕ **La Estancia.** North of the city, this restaurant offers good southern
★ beef in the form of steaks, roasts, and barbecues in a traditional country atmosphere. Cured hams hang from the ceiling, and the walls are decorated with reindeer heads. ⊠ *Rudecindo Ortega 02340-A Interior,* ☎ *45/220287. AE, DC, MC, V. No dinner Sun.*

$$ ✕ **Grill de la Piscina Municipal.** In summer, this spot at the municipal swimming pool is an excellent place to stop for lunch, especially if you're traveling with children. You can savor a good meal and the pleasant view while they enjoy the water. ⊠ *Av. Pablo Neruda 01080,* ☎ *45/ 248189. No credit cards. Closed Mon. in winter.*

$$ ✕ **La Pampa.** Frequented by the wealthy professionals of this bustling city, this upscale modern steak house serves huge, delicious cuts of beef and the best papas fritas in Temuco. While most Chilean restaurants love to douse any kind of meat with a creamy sauce, this is one of the few exceptions: a restaurant that serves meat without anything but the simplest of seasonings. ⊠ *Caupolicán 0155,* ☎ *45/329999. Weekend reservations essential. DC, MC, V.*

$ ✕ **Bavaria.** Part of a national chain, this café and restaurant offers three types of parrilladas and the most unusual vegetarian pizza you'll ever experience—two kinds of cheese, green beans, pickles, tomatoes, olives, red pepper, and oregano all on a cakey crust. Bavaria also has coffee drinks, sweets, and all the other traditional Chilean staples. ⊠ *Manuel Rodríguez 1075,* ☎ *45/215569. No credit cards.*

$ ✕ **Café Artesanía Raíces Indoamericanas.** Though the city is full of reminders that it was once the center of Mapuche territory, this is one of the few restaurants in Temuco where you can sample traditional Mapuche dishes. ⊠ *Manuel Montt 645,* ☎ *45/232434. DC, MC, V. Closed Sunday.*

$ ✕ **Confitería Central.** Hot coffee drinks and homemade pastries are the specialties of this café and salón de té, but sandwiches, simple lunches, and ice cream are also served. Fresh empanadas are available on Sundays and holidays. ⊠ *Bulnes 442,* ☎ *45/210083. DC, MC, V.*

$ ✕ **Temuco Market.** In the central market around the produce stalls are small stands and kitchens offering such typical Chilean meals as cazuela, fried fish, winter fish soup, and other seasonal fare such as empanadas and pastel de choclo. ⊠ *Manuel Rodríguez 960,* ☎ *no phone.*

In case you want to see the world.

At American Express, we're here to make your journey
a smooth one. So we have over 1,700 travel service locations in over 130 countries ready to help. What else
would you expect from the world's largest travel agency?

do more

Travel

In case you want to be welcomed there.

We're here to see that you're always welcomed at establishments everywhere. That's why millions of people carry the American Express® Card – for peace of mind, confidence, and security, around the world or just around the corner.

do more

Cards

In case you're running low.

We're here to help with more than 190,000 Express Cash locations around the world. In order to enroll, just call American Express at 1 800 CASH-NOW before you start your vacation.

do more AMERICAN EXPRESS

Express Cash

And in case you'd rather be safe than sorry.

We're here with American Express® Travelers Cheques. They're the safe way to carry money on your vacation, because if they're ever lost or stolen you can get a refund, practically anywhere or anytime. To find the nearest place to buy Travelers Cheques, call 1 800 495-1153. Another way we help you do more.

do more

Travelers Cheques

$$$ ✕🏨 **Hotel de la Frontera.** Remodeled in 1996, this hotel's refurbished rooms are modern and comfortable with neutral decor; they have double-paned windows to keep out the street noise. If you're traveling on a tight budget, the hotel also offers its older rooms for half price. La Taberna, the downstairs restaurant, has excellent international dining, as well as a live orchestra and dancing on weekends. ✉ *Bulnes 733–726,* ☎ *45/200400,* FAX *45/200401 or 45/200402. 60 rooms, 2 suites. Restaurant, bar, minibars, indoor pool, convention center, meeting rooms. AE, DC, MC, V.*

$ ✕🏨 **Hotel Continental.** The oldest hotel in all of Chile, the Continental was founded in 1890 and has lodged a slew of historical Chilean personalities, including Pablo Neruda and Salvador Allende. Checkered in black and white tile, the lobby is adorned with cracked leather furniture, antique bronze lamps, and worked *alerce* (Chilean redwood) and raulí trim. Rooms have hardwood floors and lofty ceilings, and are tastefully painted in ash-blue and cream tones. In honor of the Alzuget family, which has run the establishment for 70 years, the restaurant serves very good French cuisine. Every town has its lodging gem—in Temuco it's the Continental. ✉ *Antonio Varas 708,* ☎ *45/238973,* FAX *45/233830. 40 rooms. Restaurant, bar. AE, DC, MC, V.*

$$$ 🏨 **Hotel Terraverde.** A recent addition to the Panamericana chain, this hotel combines all the comforts of modern amenities with a hunting lodge decor. Most of the rooms have a view of Ñielol Hill and all have light carpeting, floral patterned bedspreads, and black-trimmed furnishings. ✉ *Av. Prat 0220,* ☎ *45/239999, 2/696–6826 in Santiago;* FAX *45/239455, 2/672–0316 in Santiago. 74 rooms, 10 suites. Restaurant, piano bar, in-room safes, minibars, no-smoking rooms, pool, convention center, meeting rooms. AE, DC, MC, V.*

$ 🏨 **Hotel Espelette.** Simple but serviceable, this two-story hotel rents rooms with or without private bathrooms. The downstairs rooms are large and airy with nondescript furnishings. Soft beds compensate for hard pillows the size of watermelons. ✉ *Claro Solar 492,* ☎ FAX *45/234805. 17 rooms, 10 with bath. Breakfast room. DC, MC, V.*

Pucón and Villarrica

112 km (70 mi) south of Temuco.

One of the loveliest, least spoiled areas of the southern Andes, here towering volcanoes shoot off wisps of vapor during the day and glow orange through the clear nights, while roses and natural hot springs flourish in rural and wild settings. The ideal way to travel is by car, spending the night in a local hot-springs resort or camping out. Wherever you sleep, step out at night to enjoy the southern sky, full of stars and constellations unfamiliar to those who live north of the equator.

The town of Pucón, on the southern shore of Lake Villarrica, is a small, rural supply center most of the year. However, during the summer holiday and winter skiing seasons it becomes a trendy resort crowded with wealthy, fashionable Chileans who come to enjoy their luxurious vacation homes, stroll along the main strip, try the fantastic adventure sports activities in the area, and flock to the major nightspots.

Villarrica, like its sister town of Pucón, offers little to the visitor during the off-season, but attracts Chile's jet set who come for the skiing in winter and the pleasant weather during the summer. Although the town has no sights per se, two stunning national parks lie nearby.

Villarrica National Park, between Villarrica and Pucón, offers skiing, hiking, hot springs—and a volcano. You don't need to have any climbing experience to reach the 3,116-m (9,350-ft) summit of Volcán Villarrica, but a guide is essential. Travel agencies such as **Expediciones Trancura** (✉ O'Higgins 211, Pucón, ☎ 45/441189) and **Sol Y Nieve** (✉ Corner of O'Higgins and Lincoyan, ☎ 45/441070) will lease equipment and guides for less than $60 per person. It's a steep uphill walk to the snow line, and then crampons and ice axes are needed. Your reward for the six-hour climb is a rare view of an active crater, which continues to release clouds of sulfur gases and mini-explosions of lava, as well as superb views of the nearby inactive volcanoes, Quetrupillán and Lanín.

Unless you're an expert driver with a four-wheel-drive vehicle, **Huerque-hue National Park** is accessible only during the summer. However, it's worth a visit for the two-hour hike from the ranger station near the entrance. You head up into the high Andes through groves of arau-caria pine to three startling lagoons with panoramic views of the whole area, including the distant Villarrica Volcano. Contact SERNATUR in Temuco (☞ Visitor Information, *below*); the national forestry service CONAF (☎ 45/236312 or 45/238900), which administers the parks; or the rangers in the parks themselves for trail information.

Gardeners will appreciate the pleasant hamlet of **Panguipulli**, 49 km (30 mi) east of the Pan-American Highway, on the shores of epony-mous Lake Panguipulli. Although it's a pleasant place to stop for lunch and a swim on the beach, it's most noteworthy in spring and summer, when roads, houses, public squares, and private gardens seem to stag-ger under a display of roses of all sizes, scents, and colors.

The resort town of **Licanray** on Lake Calafquén has modern hotels and hostels, supermarkets, dance halls, restaurants, and some of the best beaches in the southern lakes. You can rent rowboats and sailboats along the shore.

Dining and Lodging
The Lake District is littered with lodging options, ranging from tradi-tional hotels to more swanky spa resorts. Cabanas and cabins invari-ably accompany hot-spring sites; full room and board, as well as soaking privileges, usually are included in the price of a night's stay.

$$ ✕ **Café 2001.** For a thick, filling sandwich and an espresso or cappuccino made from freshly ground beans, topped off with a freshly baked kuchen, this is the place to stop in Villarrica. Pull up around a table up front, or slip into one of the quieter booths by the fireplace in the back. The "Lomito Completo" sandwich—with a slice of pork, avo-cado, sauerkraut, tomato, and mayonnaise—is one of the best in the south. ✉ *Camilio Henríquez 379,* ☎ *45/411470. AE, DC, MC, V.*

$$ ✕ **En Alta Mar.** The best seafood in Pucón is served in this trailerlike structure with the ubiquitous nautical theme that is altogether over-done in Chile. ✉ *Fresia and Urrutia,* ☎ *45/442294. AE. Closed Sun.*

$$$$ ▥ **Gran Hotel Pucón.** Leveled by fire and rebuilt a decade ago, this im-posing Pucón hotel has somewhat drab rooms, but its location along one end of Lake Villarrica provides access to the beach and a good view of the water. ✉ *Clemente Holtzapfel 190,* ☎ ℻ *45/441001, 2/232-6008 in Santiago. 145 rooms. 2 restaurants, bar, 3 pools, massage, sauna, squash. AE, DC, MC, V.*

$$$$ ▥ **Hotel Antumalal.** Perched atop a cliff overlooking Lake Villarrica, this
★   Frank Lloyd Wright–inspired, 1950s masterpiece is easily one of the best hotels in Chile. A small, family-run hotel in Pucón with the atmosphere of a country inn, the property's rooms are done with fireplaces and have complimentary room service. The grounds are spectacularly landscaped with waterfalls, walking paths, and scenic overlooks. If you tire of re-laxing on the wisteria-shaded deck with a refreshing pisco sour, just ask owner Rony Pollak to arrange an adventure for you: favorites include

fly-fishing, white-water rafting, and volcano cave tours. ⊠ *Casilla 84, Pucón,* ☎ *45/441011,* FAX *45/441013. 18 rooms, 2 suites. Restaurant, bar, pool, travel services. AE, DC, MC, V.*

$$$$ 🏨 **Hotel Del Lago.** A vision of glass, brass, and blond wood, this glitzy new hotel in Pucón is a little short on charm but has everything else you could hope for in deluxe accommodations. It's best known as "the Casino" for its Las Vegas–style ground floor, complete with rows of one-arm bandits and tables for everything from roulette to poker. The beige-tone rooms are modern, with the usual amenities one would expect of a hotel in this price category. ⊠ *Miguel Ansorena, corner of Pedro de Valdivia,* ☎ *45/291000, 2/245–6005 in Santiago,* FAX *45/291200. 81 rooms, 2 suites. Restaurant, bar, snack bar, minibars, 2 pools, massage, sauna, exercise room, casino, business center, meeting rooms. AE, DC, MC, V.*

$$$$ 🏨 **Termas de Huife.** This resort offers thermal baths and two hot pools made of natural stones beside an icy mountain stream. For an additional fee, you can enjoy an individual bath, a massage, or both. The resort includes a few luxury cabins, all of which have their own enormous tubs, which you can fill with water from the hot springs. For those just visiting for the day, there's a country house past the spa where, for a modest fee, you can relax in hot pools in a more private setting. The resort is 33 km (20 mi) from Pucón on the road to Caburga. ⊠ *Casilla 18,* ☎ FAX *45/441222. 10 cabins. Restaurant, bar, minibars. AE, DC, MC, V.*

$$$ 🏨 **Hotel Gudenschwager.** Once a fishing lodge, this attractive three-story building in Pucón, covered with the wooden shakes typical of southern Chile, has a view of a corner of the lake and a comfortable country atmosphere. ⊠ *Pedro de Valdivia 12,* ☎ FAX *45/441156. 20 rooms, 1 suite. Restaurant. DC, MC, V.*

$$$ 🏨 **Termas de San Luis.** The hot springs are the main attraction of this Pucón hideaway, but you can also rent a large cabin that will sleep up to six people. Rates include all meals and free use of the baths. ⊠ *Camillo Henríquez 301,* ☎ *63/412880 or 63/411388. 8 cabins. No credit cards.*

$$ 🏨 **Del Volcan Apart Hotel.** Overlooking the center of Pucón, this new chalet-style apart-hotel is a great value. Some of the bigger suites feature balconies and can sleep up to six people. In keeping with the *Mitteleuropa* vibe, the furnishings look like they come straight from Germany, with checked fabrics covering the well-fluffed duvets. ⊠ *Fresia 420,* ☎ FAX *45/442053. 28 apartments. In-room safes, kitchenettes, free parking. AE, DC, MC, V.*

¢ 🏨 **école!** Part youth hostel, part hotel, this friendly Pucón hostería with a beach-house vibe has one room with a private bath; the rest have shared facilities. Day hikes and volcano, horseback riding, and hot spring expeditions can be arranged. Even if you're not staying here, the vegetarian food in the restaurant is worth a try. ⊠ *General Urrutia 592,* ☎ FAX *45/441675. 15 rooms, 1 with bath. Restaurant, travel services. DC, MC, V.*

CAMPGROUNDS

The **Volcán Villarrica–Sector Rucapillán** camping area is in the lap of the Villarrica Volcano and in the midst of a wood of *coigüe,* Chile's massive red oaks. For more information, contact SERNATUR in Temuco (☞ Visitor Information, *below*).

Outdoor Activities and Sports

Pucón is the major departure point for adventure sports in the region, and there's plenty to choose from: river rafting, skiing, trekking, horseback riding, fishing, and biking. On the mellower side, the region's volcanic activity has given rise to a number of hot springs; for more information, *see* Dining and Lodging, *above*.

BEACHES AND WATER SPORTS

The entire Lake District is full of beaches offering every kind of water sport and comfort imaginable, except perhaps solitude. **Licanray** and **Lake Villarrica** offer the most in the way of water-skiing, motorboat rental, and more sophisticated water sports. **Lake Tinquilco** in Huerquehue National Park is quieter and more isolated; here you can rent a rowboat and tow a fishing line through the depths. The beaches along **Lake Panguipulli** are clean and comfortable. There is some concern about possible pollution of Lake Villarrica, but nearby **Lake Caburgua** remains crystalline and is slightly warmer for swimming, thanks to volcanic activity in the surrounding region.

BICYCLING

Dozens of shops along the main road (O'Higgins) in Pucón offer mountain-bike rentals during the summer.

SKIING

The popular Villarrica–Pucón ski area is in Villarrica National Park, in the lap of the Villarrica Volcano. Villarrica is one of the best-equipped ski areas in southern Chile, with 15 runs, three rope tows, and three double-chair tows. Information about the **Centro de Esquí** can be obtained via the Gran Hotel Pucón (☞ *above*).

TREKKING

Both Huerquehue and Villarrica parks have well-marked hiking trails that zigzag past open fields and massive Chilean oak trees, with views of lakes and volcanoes occasionally appearing as you walk uphill. Try the visitor centers in the parks or SERNATUR in Temuco (☞ Visitor Information, *below*) or CONAF (☞ Temuco, *above*) for more information.

Southern Chile has several of the country's most beautiful national parks, including **Conguillío,** near Melipeuco, **Villarrica,** near the town of Villarrica, and **Huerquehue,** near Pucón. All provide sites for camping, as well as well-marked hiking trails of differing degrees of difficulty. All also provide necessary information at their ranger stations, but not all have telephones. Contact CONAF (☞ Temuco, *above*), or **SERNATUR** in Santiago (☎ 2/236–1416) or in the town nearest the park.

WHITE-WATER RAFTING

Pucón is the center for rafting expeditions in the Lake District. **Cascada Expediciones** (✉ Orrego Luco 054, 2nd floor, ☎ 2/234–2274, FAX 2/233–9768) out of Santiago organizes white-water trips in the region. William Hatcher of **Sol Y Nieve** (✉ O'Higgins at the corner of Lincoyan, ☎ FAX 45/441070) has the best reputation in the Pucón area; he is a local celebrity of sorts, who offers the most reliable service. Other small companies in Pucón offer similar services for marginally less money in summer. They usually set up shop along the main street, complete with photographic displays and other information on prices and services.

Valdivia

145 km (90 mi) southwest of Pucón.

One of Chile's oldest and most beautiful cities gracefully combines an architecture of wooden, shake-covered houses with the style of the well-to-do German settlers who colonized the area in the late 1800s. Situated between two rivers and near the coast, this university town offers fine evening walks along the waterfront and restaurants that serve fresh fish and seafood and tasty kuchen. The region has many cattle ranches and farms, and native communities make a hardscrabble subsistence on the less fertile grounds. Valdivia is also an excellent base for day trips throughout the area or a good starting point for a journey northeast into the Andes.

For an historic overview of the region, start with a visit to the **Museo Histórico de Valdivia,** on the campus of the Austral University. The valuable collection focuses on the German immigrants and the city's colonial period, during which it was settled by the Spanish, burned by the Mapuche, and invaded by Dutch corsairs. ⊠ *Los Laureles, Isla Teja,* ☎ *63/212872.* ⊡ *Admission.* ☉ *Call for hrs.*

The **Botanic Gardens,** north and west of the university campus, is a fine place to walk, whatever the weather, although it's particularly enjoyable in spring and summer. ⊠ *Isla Teja,* ☎ *63/216964.* ⊡ *Admission.*

Dining and Lodging

Lodging options in Valdivia are generally expensive and run-of-the-mill at best, with a couple of notable exceptions. The residenciales and hostels at least offer mediocrity at more reasonable prices.

$$$ ✕ **Camino de Luna Restaurant.** This unusual restaurant floats on the river near the Pedro de Valdivia bridge in Valdivia. Specialties are beef and seafood; the conger eel served with a cheese-and-tomato sauce is particularly good. Most tables are by the windows and offer views of the river, Teja Island, and Valdivia. ⊠ *Costanera s/n,* ☎ *63/213788. AE, DC, MC, V.*

$$$ ✕ **New Orleans.** Very little about this place resembles New Orleans, but the Caipirinhas are terrific, and the tastiest dish, *locos al limo* (Chilean abalone in lemon sauce), is one of the best things to eat in all of Valdivia. ⊠ *Esmeralda 682,* ☎ *63/218771. AE, DC, MC, V. Closed Sun.*

$$ ✕ **La Calesa.** If you're looking for a break from Chilean food, try this Peruvian restaurant near the center of town. More hot spices and peppers are used in Peruvian dishes, particularly the stews; an example here is *Ají* (chicken stew served with cheese, milk, and peppers). ⊠ *Yungay 735,* ☎ *63/225467. AE, DC, MC, V. Closed Sun. No lunch Sat.*

$$ ✕ **La Cerveceria.** On the road to Niebla, this restaurant and "beer museum" are attached to the brewery for one of Chile's most celebrated beers, Kunstmann. Along with the typical Chilean fare, La Cervercería serves wurst and sauerkraut and, of course, giant chilled mugs of their refreshing beer. ⊠ *Casilla 1441,* ☎ *63/292969. DC, MC, V.*

$$ ✕ **Salón de Té Entrelagos.** Swanky Entrelagos caters to a Valdivian executive class. The specialties are sandwiches such as the Isla Teja—a grilled chicken sandwich with tomato, artichoke hearts, asparagus, olives, and red pepper—decadent crepes, and sweet-tooth goodies. ⊠ *Pérez Rosales 622,* ☎ *63/212047. No credit cards.*

$ ✕ **Café Haussmann.** Valdivia was the center of German and Swiss immigration at the turn of the century, and this is one place to enjoy the fruits of that exchange: excellent *crudos* (steak tartare) and German-style sandwiches, with delicious kuchen for dessert. ⊠ *Libertador Bernardo O'Higgins 394,* ☎ *63/213878. No credit cards. Closed Mar. 15–Apr. 15.*

$ ✕ **Café Paula.** This café is part of a chain famous for ice cream and pastries, but the Valdivia branch also offers sandwiches and full meals. ⊠ *Vicente Pérez 633,* ☎ *63/212328. DC, MC, V.*

$$$ ⊞ **Hotel Nagulián.** A bit out of town, this riverside hotel has more charm than most, as well as a garden with a pool to sit around and relax while you watch the boats pass by along the river. Ask for a room in the newer building; rooms have balconies and are generally more spacious. ⊠ *General Lagos 1927,* ☎ *63/212851,* ℻ *63/219130. 29 rooms, 3 suites. Restaurant, bar, pool, dock, baby-sitting, free parking. AE, DC, MC, V.*

$$$ ⊞ **Hotel Pedro de Valdivia.** Valdivia's pink palace is large, old, elegant,
★ and—unlike most hotels here—quite wonderful. With pleasant views of the Río Calle Calle and the city, this centrally located gem is most notable for its excellent service. The rooms are comfortable and decked

in beige; some have small terraces. ⊠ *Carampagne 190,* ☎ *63/212931, 2/639–3832 in Santiago,* ℻ *63/203888. 77 rooms, 5 suites, 7 apartments. Restaurant, bar, pool, meeting rooms, airport shuttle, free parking. AE, DC, MC, V.*

$$$ 🏨 **Hotel Puerta del Sur.** Solid services and sound infrastructure are the pluses of this hotel, which strays far from the lavish pampering one might expect of its rating. Spacious rooms are decorated in soft lavender tones; all have views of the river. ⊠ *Los Lingues 950, Isla Teja,* ☎ *63/224500, 2/633–5101 in Santiago,* ℻ *63/211046, 2/633–6541 in Santiago. 40 rooms, 2 suites. Restaurant, 2 bars, in-room safes, pool, outdoor hot tub, sauna, tennis court, volleyball, dock, meeting rooms, travel services. AE, DC, MC, V.*

$$ 🏨 **Hostal Centro Torreón.** Originally constructed in 1916 for a family of German settlers, this hostel offers basic lodging inside one of Valdivia's more architecturally appealing homes. A stairway of *pellín* oak twists up to the luminous second-story rooms, all of which have suffered a bout of tacky renovation. José Retamales Prelle, the hotel's amiable proprietor, gives discounts to Hosteling International members. ⊠ *Pérez Rosales 783 Interior,* ☎ *63/212622,* ℻ *63/203217. 13 rooms. Breakfast room, café, travel services. DC, MC, V.*

$$ 🏨 **Hotel Isla Teja.** Situated on the island floating among three of Valdivia's rivers, and close to the Botanic Gardens, this affordable hotel doubles as student housing for the Austral University. Semi-separate from students' quarters, the guest rooms are quiet and comfortable, with modern amenities. ⊠ *Las Encinas 220, Isla Teja,* ☎ *63/215015,* ℻ *63/214911. 95 rooms. Restaurant, bar, meeting rooms, travel services, free parking. AE, DC, MC, V.*

CAMPGROUNDS

Most of the camping around Valdivia is along the rivers and relatively expensive. **Complejo Turístico Isla Teja** (⊠ Los Robles and Los Cipreses, Isla Teja, ☎ ℻ 63/213584) on Teja Island, with an attractive view of the river, has campsites ($15 for two people) with electricity and hot showers. Contact SERNATUR (☞ Visitor Information *in* The Lake District A to Z, *below*) for more camping information.

Outdoor Activities and Sports

BEACHES

The ocean beaches, 43 km (27 mi) from Valdivia, make a good day trip from the city. The road is paved as far as **Niebla;** from there, drive along ocean cliffs toward **Los Molinos** beach, **San Ignacio** beach, or past the villages of Loncollén and Calfuco to the village and beach of **Curiñanco.**

Lake Llanquihue

190 km (118 mi) southeast of Valdivia.

Three charming small towns ring the western shore of Lake Llanquihue, which lies just east of the Pan-American Highway heading down into Puerto Montt. As they are not spoiled by the trappings of tourism, you may want to stop by on your way to Puerto Montt, which lies just south.

Puerto Octay, 79 km (50 mi) north of Puerto Montt along the western side of the lake, is the northernmost town. It has a spectacular view of the Osorno and Calbuco volcanoes. The small **Museo El Colono** displays farm machinery and other mementos of the town's turn-of-the-century settlers. ⊠ *Independencia 591,* ☎ *no phone.* 🎫 *Free.* ⊙ *Mon.–Sat. 9:30–1 and 3–7.*

Halfway down the western edge of the lake lies the small colonial town of **Frutillar** (actually two joined hamlets, Frutillar Alto and Frutillar Bajo), with its perfectly preserved German architecture. You can take a step into the past by visiting the beautifully landscaped, open-air **Museo de la Colonización Alemana,** a short walk up Arturo Prat from the lake. Besides displays of the 19th-century agricultural and household implements, there are full-scale reconstructions of buildings—a smithy and barn, among others—used by the original German settlers. ⊠ *Museum of German Colonization,* ☎ *no phone.* ☏ *Admission.* ⊙ *Dec.–Mar., Mon.–Sun. 10–2 and 3–8; Apr.–Nov., Mon.–Sun. 10–2 and 3–6.*

Each January and February, the town hosts the **Semanas Musicales de Frutillar** (☎ 65/421698), an excellent series of classical and jazz concerts in an idyllic outdoor setting.

Just 27 km (16 mi) south of Frutillar is **Puerto Varas,** a small, sleepy resort town with northern European influences. It's known for its stunning rose arbors, which are in full bloom from December to March. A wealthy Puerto Montt business class has settled here, stimulating a wide variety of tourist services. Often described as the Lucerne of Chile, you'll find cozy cafés, homemade ice cream, and affordable restaurants.

Dining and Lodging

$$ ✕🖫 **Hotel Salzburg.** This minivillage on the north edge of town consists of wooden cabins, all commanding excellent views of the lake. The staff can organize fishing trips, and the restaurant features some of the best smoked salmon in the area. ⊠ *Costanera Norte, Frutillar Bajo,* ☎ *65/421589,* 🖷 *65/421599. 31 rooms, 9 cabins, 5 bungalows. Restaurant, bar, pool, sauna, mountain bikes, travel services. AE, DC, MC, V.*

$$$ 🖫 **Hotel Colonos del Sur.** Alerce and pine dominate the decor at this time-worn, four-story waterfront hotel. Rooms are unremarkable, but the vista is magnificent. ⊠ *Del Salvador 24, Puerto Varas,* ☎ *65/233369,* 🖷 *65/232080. 54 rooms, 2 suites. Restaurant, bar, indoor pool, sauna, meeting rooms. AE, DC, MC, V.*

$$–$$$ 🖫 **Hotel Cabañas del Lago.** The rooms in this recently remodeled hotel are comfortable, and most have lovely views of the lake and Osorno Volcano, but the cabins are what make this spot special. With capacity for five, each A-frame has its own woodstove and full kitchen; hidden amongst carefully tended gardens and paths, they are decorated with lace curtains, pine paneling, and floral patterned bedding. ⊠ *Klenner 195, Puerto Varas,* ☎ *65/232291,* 🖷 *65/232707. 63 rooms, 21 cabins, 2 suites. Restaurant, bar, indoor pool, massage, sauna, billiards, baby-sitting, children's programs (ages 5–12), meeting rooms. AE, DC, MC, V.*

$$–$$$ 🖫 **Termas de Puyehue.** Probably Chile's most famous hot springs resort, this massive compound is set on the edge of Puyehue National Park. Part of the hotel burned in the 1950s, but it's still a grandiose lodge with skiing, indoor thermal baths, horseback riding, boating, sport fishing, and a conference center. To reach the springs, head west out of Osorno, which is halfway between Valdivia and Puerto Montt. ⊠ *Termas de Puyehue Hotel, on Lake Puyehue,* ☎ *64/232157; 2/231–3417 or 2/293–6000 in Santiago,* 🖷 *64/371383; 2/231–3582 in Santiago. 80 rooms, 5 suites. 3 restaurants, 2 pools, mineral baths, meeting rooms, travel services. AE, DC, MC, V.*

Puerto Montt

20 km (12 mi) south of Lake Llanquihue.

For most of Chile's history, Puerto Montt has been the end of the line, whether you were traveling by railway, dirt road, or highway. Now the Austral Highway carries on southward, but for most intents and purposes, Puerto Montt remains the last significant outpost of civilization, a small provincial city that is the hub of local fishing, textile, and tourist activity. Today the town consists of low clapboard and wooden houses perched on hills above the ocean, with four- to six-story office buildings and stores, most built earlier this century. If it's a warm, sunny day, head east along the shoreline to **Pelluco** or one of the other beaches. If you're more interested in getting to know the area generally, drive along the shoreline through the city for a good view of the surrounding hillsides and the relatively protected stretch of ocean on which the city stands.

The **Museo Juan Pablo II** east of the bus terminal has a collection of crafts and relics from one of Chile's strongest regional cultures, that of the Archipelago of Chiloé. Historical photos at the Juan Pablo II Museum give a sense of the area's slow and often difficult growth and the impact of the 1960 earthquake, which virtually destroyed the port. ⊠ *Between Av. Costandera and Av. Diego Portales, east of the bus terminal,* ☎ *no phone.* ☞ *Admission.* ☉ *Mon.–Sun. 9–7.*

A few kilometers west of downtown along the Costadera (Coast Road) is the **Caleta Angelmó,** Puerto Montt's fishing cove. From here you can get a good view of Tenglo Island, which protects a busy port serving small fishing boats, large ferries, and cruisers carrying travelers and cargo southward through the straits and fjords that form much of Chile's shoreline. On weekdays you'll notice the water traffic from many of the outlying islands—small launches and fishing boats that arrive early in the morning and leave in the afternoon. The **fish market** offers one of the most varied selections of seafood in all of Chile (☞ Dining, *below*).

An excellent selection of handicrafts sold at the best prices in Chile can be found in the **Feria Artesanal** (Crafts Fair). Baskets, Chilote ponchos, mythical Chilote figures woven from different kinds of grasses and straws, and warm sweaters of raw, hand-spun, and hand-dyed wool are all offered. Most of the people selling here are intermediaries, and many of the styles have been adapted to buyers' tastes, but if you look carefully you'll also see the less commercial, more authentic offerings. Dickering over prices is expected. ⊠ *On Coast Rd., near Angelmó Fishing Cove.*

Dining and Lodging

$$$ ✕ **Balzac.** One of Puerto Montt's finest, Balzac specializes in seafood
★   prepared with a French flair. Try the *Jaiba de Chardonnay* (baked stew of king crab, parmesan cheese, and white wine). The owner's father—an endearing gentleman and a rich source of local Chilote history—passes his time downstairs chewing the fat with friends and making visitors feel at home. ⊠ *San Martín 244,* ☎ *65/259495. AE.*

$$$ ✕ **Merlin.** Often called the best restaurant in southern Chile, the Merlin features a variety of local fresh fish and vegetables combined in unique ways. Specialities are razor clams with vegetable strips in a curry vinaigrette, and beef tenderloin in a barnacle morel-mushroom sauce. For dessert, look for peaches packed with an almond cream, served with espresso amaretto and vanilla ice-cream. ⊠ *Walker Martínez 584,* ☎ *65/233105. AE, DC, MC, V. No lunch.*

$$ ✕ **Restaurant Kiel.** Hospitable German-born proprietor Helga Birkir stands guard at this Chileo-Teutonic seafood restaurant on the coast west of Puerto Montt. Her stunning garden makes lunch here a particular delight. *Camino Chinquihue km 8, Chinquihue,* ☎ *65/255010. AE.*

$–$$ ✕ **Angelmó Market.** A variety of small kitchens offer *mariscal* (raw shellfish soup) and *caldillo* (hot soup), as well as machas, *ostiones* (scallops), and *almejas* (clams) à la parmesana. Separate tables and counters are located at each kitchen in this enclosed market, which is 7 km (4 mi) west of Puerto Montt along the Costandera. ⊠ *Angelmó Fishing Cove,* ☎ *no phone. No credit cards.*

$–$$ ✕ **Café Restaurant Amsel.** Serving breakfast, lunch, and dinner, this two-story café has a variety of inexpensive meat and seafood dishes, in addition to sandwiches and an extensive vegetarian selection. This is a good spot to socialize over a well-brewed cortado or cappuccino when the weather proves unfriendly. ✉ *Diego Portales and Pedro Montt,* ☎ *65/253941. DC, MC, V.*

$ ✕ **Café Central.** This old-style café in the heart of Puerto Montt has been remodeled but retains the spirit of the 1920s and 1930s. It's a good place for a filling afternoon tea, with its menu of creamy coffees, ice cream, sandwiches, and pastries. ✉ *Rancagua 117,* ☎ *65/254721. No credit cards.*

$$$ 🏨 **O'Grimm.** The rooms in this four-story hotel in the center of Puerto Montt are decorated in pastel grays, roses, greens, and golds. ✉ *Guillermo Gallardo 211,* ☎ *65/252845,* 𝖥𝖠𝖷 *65/258600. 27 rooms, 1 suite. Restaurant, bar, minibars, laundry service. AE, DC, MC, V.*

$$$ 🏨 **Viento Sur.** This remodeled old Victorian house sits on its hill like a castle, giving a majestic view of the city and the sea. Rooms are comfortably furnished with generous use of native Chilean woods; suites have hot tubs. The restaurant serves excellent Chilean seafood. ✉ *Ejército 200,* ☎ *65/258700,* 𝖥𝖠𝖷 *65/258701. 27 rooms, 2 suites. Restaurant, bar, sauna, laundry services. AE, DC, MC, V.*

$$$ 🏨 **Vincente Pérez Rosales.** The grandest of Puerto Montt hotels, this Alpine lodge is right in the middle of town facing the bay. After a much-needed recent renovation, it has been restored to its 1960s Gstaad-by-the-sea glory. Be sure to ask for a room with a view of the water—but not on the top floor as the ceilings are a bit low. ✉ *Antonio Varas 447,* ☎ *65/252571,* 𝖥𝖠𝖷 *65/255473. 81 rooms, 2 suites. Restaurant, bar, in-room safes, minibars, meeting room. AE, DC, MC, V.*

$$–$$$ 🏨 **Don Luis Gran Hotel.** The rooms are comfortable, clean, and modern, and there's a small salon for breakfast, which is included in the rate. ✉ *Urmeneta and Quillota,* ☎ *65/259001,* 𝖥𝖠𝖷 *65/259005. 60 rooms, 1 suite. Restaurant, bar. AE, DC, MC, V.*

$$ 🏨 **Hotel Burg.** Rooms in this waterfront hotel are bright and cheery, with tongue-and-groove wood paneling and cushy beds. The fifth floor offers the best views of the bay and includes rooms with high ceilings. ✉ *Diego Portales and Pedro Montt,* ☎ *65/253941,* 𝖥𝖠𝖷 *65/253813. 30 rooms, 1 suite. Restaurant, bar, room service, laundry service. DC, MC, V.*

CAMPGROUNDS

Campgrounds around Puerto Montt all charge around $15 (p8,000) per vehicle per night, but offer various comfort levels and views. **Chinquihue** (✉ Costandera, ☎ 65/262950), 7 km (4½ mi) west of Angelmó Fishing Cove, has bathrooms, showers, and attractive views of the beach. **El Ciervo** (✉ Costandera, ☎ 65/255271), 1 km (½ mi) west of Angelmó, offers 20 sites with electrical hookups, general lighting, hot showers, and boat rental. **Los Alamos** (✉ Costandera, ☎ 65/264666), 11 km (7 mi) west of Angelmó, has fine views of the Reloncaví Strait and Tenglo Island and offers electricity, roofed sites, general lighting, water, bathrooms, hot showers, a dock and launching area, a play area and sports field, and boat rentals. **Paredes** (✉ Costandera, ☎ 65/258394), 6 km (4 mi) west of Angelmó, is short on shade but has a pretty beach, hot showers, a soccer field, and a playground.

Outdoor Activities and Sports

BEACHES

For ocean beaches, Puerto Montt and the coast west of Valdivia are the best choices. Puerto Montt's main beach is 3 km (2 mi) east of town along the shoreline, in the village of **Pelluco,** which offers several restaurants specializing in seafood, a few bars, a disco, and a scenic lookout point. If your idea of a good beach is something a little more peaceful and solitary, head west past Angelmó on the road to Chinquihue, and choose from beaches at camping sites at El Ciervo and Chinquihue (☞ Campgrounds, *above*). Be careful: In recent years, many beaches have been polluted owing to developing industry in the region.

The Lake District A to Z

Arriving and Departing

BY AIRPLANE

The three main airports serving the lake district are **Manquehue Airport** in Temuco (☎ 45/337703 and 45/337880), **Pichoy Airport** in Valdivia (☎ 63/272225 and 63/272236), and **Tepual Airport** in Puerto Montt (☎ 65/253144 and 65/254689).

LanChile, Ladeco, and Avant all have flights from Santiago to—and between—the main cities within the Lake District, including **Temuco** (LanChile ☎ 45/211339, Ladeco ☎ 45/214325, Avant ☎ 45/270670); **Valdivia** (LanChile ☎ 63/213042, Ladeco ☎ 63/213392, Avant ☎ 63/251431); and **Puerto Montt** (LanChile ☎ 65/253141, Ladeco ☎ 65/252090, Avant ☎ 65/258277). **A.L.T.A. Airlines** (⊠ Las Urbinas 30, Providencia, ☎ 2/244–1781 in Santiago) runs twin-prop planes between most Chilean destinations, including **Temuco** (☎ 45/213090), **Valdivia** (☎ 63/228150), and **Puerto Montt** (☎ 65/268646)(☞ Getting Around *in* Chile A to Z, *below*).

BY CAR

Although it's useful to rent a car once you've reached the Lake District, it will be easier on your nerves if you skip driving down on the Pan-American Highway and fly or take the train to your first Lake District destination.

BY TRAIN

Chile's **State Railway Company** (☎ 2/689–6070, 2/632–2802, or 2/228–2983 in Santiago; 45/233522 in Temuco; 63/214978 in Valdivia; 65/232210 in Puerto Varas) has frequent service southward from Santiago, usually several times a day, particularly in the peak period during the summer. The journey to Temuco, at the northern limit of the Lake District, takes about 11½ hours; to Puerto Varas, at the southernmost end of the line, is a 20-hour trip. If you prefer to rent a vehicle in Santiago, you can use the auto-train service from there to Temuco or Puerto Montt, but it's probably cheaper to rent a car in Temuco or Puerto Montt (☞ Getting Around *in* Chile A to Z, *below*).

Getting Around

BY BUS

There are two levels of service within the region: regular intercity buses provided by companies based primarily in Santiago, and local buses that bump between Lake District cities and the small towns that adjoin them; both services are reasonably priced. Three of the most reliable companies are **Buses JAC** (☎ 2/776–1582), **Varmontt** (☎ 2/231–3505), and **Fenix** (☎ 2/696–9089); all numbers are for Santiago.

In Temuco, there's no central bus terminal, but several companies are close together along Vicuña MacKenna and Lagos: **Cruz del Sur** (⊠ Vicuña MacKenna 671, ☎ 45/210701), **Buses JAC** (⊠ Vicuña MacKenna 798, ☎ 45/210313), and **Tur Bus** (⊠ Lagos 538, ☎ 45/239190). Both Puerto Montt and Valdivia have their own **bus terminals,** where most bus companies' offices are concentrated (**Valdivia's bus terminal:** ⊠ Anfión Muñoz 360, ☎ 63/212212; **Puerto Montt's bus terminal:** ⊠ Avenida Diego Portales, ☎ no phone); each bus line has its own phone number, listed in the local phone book's Yellow Pages.

You'll see a lot more of the Lake District if you have a vehicle. A few rental-car companies like Hertz will allow you to hire a car in Temuco and return it to any of their other offices in the south, so you can even avoid the inconvenience of retracing your steps.

Once you're this far south, driving is much easier because there's far less traffic, even on the Pan-American Highway. However, many of the mountain roads you must follow are gravel at best, so a four-wheel-drive vehicle is ideal. It's 112 km (70 mi) from Temuco to Pucón; 163 km (101 mi) from Temuco to Valdivia; and 210 km (130 mi) from Valdivia to Puerto Montt.

Rentals are available through **Automóvil Club de Chile** (Puerto Montt ☎ 65/254776, 45/248903 in Temuco), **Autovald** (Puerto Montt ☎ 65/256355), **Avis** (Puerto Montt ☎ 65/253307, 45/238013 in Temuco), **First** (Temuco ☎ 45/233890), **Hertz** (Puerto Montt ☎ 65/259585, 45/235385 in Temuco, 63/218316 in Valdivia), as well as a few local travel agencies; a few of the latter include a return service.

Contacts and Resources

BANKS AND CURRENCY EXCHANGE

All of the major cities in the Lake District have several banks with ATMs and currency exchange offices that accept cash and traveler's checks. Banco Santander, Banco de Chile, and Banco de Credito have the most reliable ATMs, and the district's three main airports have ATMs and cambios. Many larger hotels will also exchange money and traveler's checks for a nominal fee.

EMERGENCIES

Police: ☎ 133. **Fire:** ☎ 132. **General emergency:** ☎ 133. **Hospitals:** Hospital Regional (Valdivia) (⌗ Av. Bueras 1003, ☎ 63/214066). Hospital Regional (Temuco) (⌗ Av. Manuel Montt 115, ☎ 45/212525). Clínica Alemana (Puerto Varas) (⌗ Dr. Bader 810, ☎ 65/232336).

TELEPHONES, THE INTERNET, MAIL

Entel and CTC have offices throughout the region; both can place calls and send faxes. You can check E-mail at hotels in the larger towns and cities, but don't expect a fast connection. Internet centers include **Cyber Centro** in Puerto Varas (⌗ Av. Gramado, at Av. San Jose, ☎ 65/311901), which is open every day of the week, and **Internet Centro** in Valdivia (⌗ 236 Av. Letelier, room 202, ☎ 63/294300), which is open Mon.–Sat. 11–8. Puerto Montt's post office (⌗ Av. Rancagua 126) is around the corner from the Plaza de Armas. Temuco's post office (⌗ Av. Diego Portales, at Av. Prat) is next to the Telex Chile office. In Valdivia the main post office (⌗ Av. O'Higgins 575) faces the Plaza de la República. None of the U.S.-based international express mail services have drop-off locations in the Lake District.

TOUR OPERATORS AND TRAVEL AGENTS

Around Puerto Montt. You can arrange a boat ride through the Port Authority in Angelmó or by talking directly with the owner or captain of one of the boats. Rates are $3 per passenger per hour, with group discounts available; touring the channel around Angelmó takes about two hours, and an excursion to the small fishing village and port of Calbuco will take about three. You can spend the day in Calbuco, then return by the same boat or take a bus back along the main road to Puerto Montt for a different view.

To the San Rafael Glacier. If you have a limited amount of time, and want to experience the power and beauty of Chilean Patagonia, a cruise down the coast south of Puerto Montt will give you a unique perspective of the rugged coastline, fjords, and glaciers. **Turismo Skorpios** (✉ Angelmó 1660, ☎ 65/252996, FAX 65/258315; ✉ Augusto Leguía Norte 118, Las Condes, Santiago, ☎ 2/231–1030, FAX 2/232–2269) runs a six-day cruise that visits the historic city of Castro on Chiloé, remote villages in the Guaitecas and Chonos archipelagoes, and 200-ft-high ice spires at the San Rafael Glacier. High-season prices (Dec.–Feb.) vary from $850 for a single cabin to $3,730 for a honeymoon suite.

Fishing. Trout (brown, rainbow, steelhead, and sea), salmon (ketta, coho, chinook, salar, sakura, and king), perch, and smelt are among the popular sport fish in Chile; many areas within the Lake District were first developed as fishing resorts. However, the restocking programs were suspended and good fishing is now harder to find. To fish the rivers and lakes of Chile, you must get a permit from the National Fisheries Service, known as **SERNAP** (✉ San Antonio 427, Office 801, Santiago, ☎ 2/632–4765, FAX 2/632–1918). The permit is personal and valid throughout Chile. If you're fishing on private property and the landowner is nearby, be sure to get his or her permission. SERNAP is a good source of information on what's biting and where; also check with local tourist offices. SERNATUR publishes a brochure in English called "Lakes and Fishing," and it provides location-specific details of the fishing rules, creel limits, and the like. **APSA** travel agency (✉ Matías Cousiño 82, Office 1104, ☎ 2/632–7215, FAX 2/696–6319) specializes in fishing trips in Chilean Patagonia. Valdivia-based tour operator **Jumping Chile** also organizes marvelous fly fishing trips for two–six people in the rivers near Puerto Montt (✉ ☎ 63/253377). For further information on fishing tours, see Chapter 2.

River Tours. Several companies in Valdivia offer boat rides along the rivers. **H. E. Tours** (☎ 63/210533) offers an island lunch tour, and **Catamarán Extasis** (☎ 63/212464) runs a popular romantic dinner cruise. Most of the companies are on Avenida Prat along the Calle Calle River. There are regular launches from the Puerto Fluvial (close to the SERNATUR office at Prat 555) to the 17th-century Spanish forts at Fuerte de Corral, Fuerte Castillo de Armagos, and Isla Mancera. Check boats for life jackets and an inflatable raft; there have been some serious boating accidents.

VISITOR INFORMATION

Puerto Montt SERNATUR (✉ Edificio Intendencia, 2nd floor, ☎ 65/254580). **Puerto Varas OFITUR** (✉ San Francisco 441, ☎ 65/233315). **Temuco SERNATUR** (✉ Bulnes 586, ☎ 45/211969). **Valdivia SERNATUR** (✉ Prat 555, ☎ 63/215739, FAX 63/213596).

PUNTA ARENAS

Navigating the icy strait that today bears his name, Hernando de Magallanes first wandered these waters in 1520, "discovering" what is now Punta Arenas and Chile's southernmost region. A geographic choke point between the oceans of the Old and New Worlds, this area quickly became a stomping ground for European explorers, pirates, adventurers, and entrepreneurs; characters such as Sir Francis Drake and Charles Darwin were drawn to these shores. Steam navigation intensified Punta Arena's commercial importance, leading to the city's short-lived age of splendor from 1892 to 1920. European settlers founded enormous sheep ranches, prospected precious metals, and managed to combine the extremes of Patagonian solitude with every imaginable luxury imported from Europe. But even the brightest of shiny things fade—the opening of the Panama Canal all but bumped Punta Arenas off the map, and by 1920 many of the founding families decided to move on.

The capital of Chile's Magallanes region, Punta Arenas is 3,141 km (1,960 mi) from Santiago and light-years away in attitude. The city looks like it's about to be swept into the Strait of Magellan, and on a windy day it feels that way, too. The houses are mostly made of sheets of tin with colorful tin roofs, best appreciated when seen from above. Although the general view of the city may not be particularly attractive, look for details: the pink-and-white house on a corner, the bay window full of plants, a garden overflowing with flowers. Today's residents share this extraordinary natural landscape with penguins, the llama-like guanacos, and other wildlife.

Well connected with the entire southern continent, Punta Arenas is an excellent hub from which to base your Patagonian travels. Transportation services—both by land and air—link Punta Arenas with hard-to-get-to Argentine destinations, such as El Calafate, Glacier National Park, and Ushuaia (☞ Patagonia *in* Chapter 3). In general, tourist services in the entire region are expensive, although you'll find exceptions. If you make the effort to come south, bring extra funds so you can really travel and enjoy some of the once-in-a-lifetime experiences that the region offers. You'll probably want to spend a day or so visiting Punta Arenas itself, particularly the museums, which offer valuable background information on this extraordinary area. Punta Arenas is also South America's major jumping-off point for cruises and flights to Antarctica (☞ Chapter 2).

Exploring Punta Arenas

A Good Walk

Start from the central square, **Plaza Muñoz Gamero,** where you'll find the **Club de la Unión** and the **Museo Regional de Magallanes.** Climb Calle Fagnano about four blocks to reach the **Mirador Cerro la Cruz.** After admiring the vast expanse of the strait, retrace your steps one block to Avenida España and turn left, walking three blocks through a primarily residential area to reach Avenida Colón. Follow the narrow park running down the middle of Colón three blocks east to Calle Bories, then turn left and walk four more blocks to reach the **Museo Salesiano de Mayorino Borgatello.** Bories turns into Avenida Manuel Bulnes, and the main entrance to the **Cementerio** is about four blocks up, where Romulo Correa crosses Bulnes. After a stroll through Punta Arenas's historical burial grounds, walk back towards the city center along store- and restaurant-lined Bories or Hernando Magallanes. You can also follow Colón all the way down to the oceanfront and enjoy a windy, invigorating walk along the edge of the strait.

TIMING

The walk itself will take at least 1½ hours; exploring the cemetery and museums will take the better part of a day. Keeping in mind that the Salesiano Museum has erratic hours and officially closes from noon to 3, get an early start. Club de la Unión can only be visited on Tuesday and Thursday afternoons.

SIGHTS TO SEE

Cementerio. The fascinating history of this area is chiseled in tombstone at the Punta Arenas Cemetery. Ornate mausoleums honoring the original pioneering families are scattered along sculpted cypress-lined paths. In a quirky effort to recognize Punta Arenas's indigenous past, there is a **shrine to the unknown native** in the northern part of the cemetery, where the remains of the last Selk'nam are buried. Local legend says that rubbing the statue's left knee brings luck and good favors.

Club de la Unión. Located in the former mansion of Sara Braun, the Union Club building was constructed in 1895 and entirely adorned with imported European furnishings. It has been completely restored and today is a social club and part of the José Noguiera Hotel and Restaurant. ⊠ *Av. Bories at Av. Waldo Seguel,* ☎ *no phone.* ⊡ *Admission.* ⊙ *Tues. and Thurs. 4–6.*

Mirador Cerro La Cruz. From the Hill of the Cross Lookout you have a truly breathtaking view of the city's colorful roofs, orderly streets, and the Strait of Magellan.

★ **Museo Regional de Magallanes.** Housed in what was once the mansion of the powerful Braun-Menéndez family, the Regional Magellan Museum provides an intriguing glimpse of a wealthy provincial family's pretensions at the beginning of this century. Lavish Carrara marble hearths, English bath fixtures, and Cordovan leather walls complete the original furnishings. The museum also has an excellent series of displays depicting Punta Arenas's past, from the moment of European contact to the opening of the Panama Canal. ⊠ *Magallanes 949,* ☎ *61/244216.* ⊡ *Admission.* ⊙ *Tues.–Sun. 11–5; 11–1 in winter.*

Museo Salesiano de Mayorino Borgatello. Commonly referred to as the Salesianos, the Mayorino Borgatello Museum is operated by the Salesian religious order, which came to Punta Arenas in the 19th century, ostensibly to bring God to the native people and help them integrate into Chilean society. The adventurous Italian clergy, most of whom spoke no Spanish, proved to be daring explorers; they traveled throughout the region, collecting artifacts as well as native survivors, who were "relocated" to a camp on Dawson Island, across the Magellan Strait, where they died by the hundreds. (The island was used as a prison camp by the military government after the 1973 coup.) The museum contains an extraordinary collection of everything from skulls and native crafts to stuffed animals (some with sensational birth defects, such as a two-headed lamb). ⊠ *Av. Bulnes 398,* ☎ *61/241096.* ⊡ *Admission.* ⊙ *Daily 10–noon, 3–6.*

Plaza Muñoz Gamero. A canopy of conifers shades Muñoz Gamero Square, which is hemmed in by regional government buildings and splendid baroque mansions from the last century. A bronze sculpture commemorating the voyage of Hernando de Magallanes pokes through the trees and dominates the center of the plaza. Local wisdom has it that a kiss on the Selk'nam's toe, at the base of the monument, will bring you back to Punta Arenas.

Dining

$$$ ✕ **Los Navegantes.** This restaurant in the Hotel Los Navegantes (☞ Lodging, *below*) serves delicious grilled salmon and roast lamb, with shellfish appetizers, in a simple but comfortable dining room with a bright garden at one end. ⊠ *José Menéndez 647,* ☎ *61/244677. AE, DC, MC, V.*

$$$ ✕ **El Remezón.** Exquisite meals are hard to find this far south, but El ★ Remezón is the exception. Run by José Miguel, this cheerful little restaurant is set up to make you feel like you've been invited to dine at a friend's house—if only all your friends could cook so well. The deliciously seasoned fish and meats are prepared with ingredients used by the natives of this area. It's a bit of out of town, but the terrific food, great atmosphere, and potent pisco sours make it worth the walk. ⊠ *21 de Mayo 1469,* ☎ *61/241029. AE.*

$$$ ✕ **Sotito's.** East of the city center, this seafood restaurant serves some of the best king crab in the area. Don't let the half-empty room up front full of foreigners fool you; locals love this place—they're just all sitting in the back room where they can smoke. ⊠ *O'Higgins 1138,* ☎ *61/243565. AE, DC, MC, V.*

$$ ✕ **Restaurant Asturias.** Rough-hewn beams, stark white stucco walls, and landscape reprints of Oviedo and Gijón complete the decor of this Asturian restaurant. The *salmón papillote* (salmon poached in white wine with cured ham, cream cheese, and tomatoes) combines smoky aromas with flavors from the sea. Try the *cordero asado a la española* for a distinctive taste of Patagonian lamb. ✉ *Lautaro Navarro 967,* ☎ *61/243763. AE, DC, MC, V.*

$–$$ ✕ **Calipso.** This tearoom and bar offers cable television, good espresso, fresh pastries, moderately priced sandwiches, and more expensive salmon and crab dinners. The proprietors also run a side business arranging tours to Penguin Island and Fort Bulnes. ✉ *Bories 817,* ☎ *61/ 241782. DC, MC, V.*

$ ✕ **La Mamá.** Massive plates of lovingly prepared pasta in a cozy atmosphere have made this restaurant popular with tourists and locals alike. A bulletin board in the corner is plastered with raving compliments from every corner of the globe. ✉ *Armando Sanhueza 720,* ☎ *61/225127. Reservations not accepted. No credit cards.*

$ ✕ **El Quijote.** The best café in town, this place has delicious sandwiches, soups, and a variety of meat and seafood dishes. Espresso drinks are served, as well as a creative range of shakes. ✉ *Lautaro Navarro 1087,* ☎ *61/241225. AE, DC, MC, V.*

Lodging

$$$$ 🏨 **Cabo de Hornos.** This massive, eight-story building along the central square affords dazzling views of the city and strait. The lobby and most of the rooms have all the details you would expect of a luxury hotel—fresh paint, sound business services, beautiful furnishings, and a fine restaurant. ✉ *Plaza Muñoz Gamero 1025,* ☎ FAX *61/242134. 100 rooms, 1 suite. Restaurant, bar, minibars, sauna, baby-sitting, convention center, travel services. AE, DC, MC, V.*

$$$$ 🏨 **José Nogueira.** A national monument and the oldest of the 19th-
★ century mansions, this hotel is the finest Punta Arenas has to offer. The place is delightfully comfortable and beautifully designed: Public rooms are decorated with richly textured striped wallpaper, pillars of polished wood, marble floors, and lots of bronze details. Guest rooms are on the small side, but they have high ceilings, thick carpets, antique-style wood furniture, and ceramic-tile bathrooms. The suites have hot tubs. ✉ *Bories 959,* ☎ *61/248840,* FAX *61/248832. 25 rooms, 3 suites. Restaurant, bar, laundry service. AE, DC, MC, V.*

$$$–$$$$ 🏨 **Hotel Isla Rey Jorge.** One block from the plaza, this intimate hotel has become a popular choice with foreign travelers for its impeccable service and charming English decor. The well-lit guest rooms have lofty wood windows and are decorated in mint greens and burgundy. Fourth-floor rooms have vaulted ceilings and views of the strait. Richly toned *linga* and *coigüé* woodwork continues down into the ever-popular basement pub, El Galeón. ✉ *21 de Mayo 1243,* ☎ FAX *61/248220. 25 rooms, 4 suites. Restaurant, bar, travel services. AE, DC, MC, V.*

$$$ 🏨 **Hotel Finis Terrae.** This modern, oversized A-frame hotel has the standard amenities of a Best Western–affiliate property. The lack of character in the rooms and lobby is compensated for in the spectacular views from the top-floor restaurant and bar. ✉ *Colón 766,* ☎ *61/228200,* FAX *61/248124. 66 rooms, 4 suites. Restaurant, bar, minibars, airport shuttle. AE, DC, MC, V.*

$$$ 🏨 **Hotel Los Navegantes.** This comfortable, unpretentious hotel has spacious double rooms with gray-and-pink carpets and colorful paisley bedspreads. The price includes a substantial, American-style breakfast, and transportation from the airport. ✉ *José Menéndez 647,* ☎

61/244677, FAX 61/247545. *50 rooms, 2 suites. Restaurant, bar, in-room safes, minibars, travel services. AE, DC, MC, V.*

$$ ⌂ **Apart-Hotel Colonizadores.** A block from the water, this hotel includes apartments with living rooms, dining rooms, and kitchens, making them as spacious as they are comfortable. This is an affordable option for families and groups. ⊠ *Av. Colón 1106,* ☎ *61/243578,* FAX *61/244499. 5 apartments. Kitchenettes, refrigerators, laundry service. AE, DC, MC, V.*

$$ ⌂ **Hostal Carpa Manzano.** This comfortable establishment is decorated in warm pastel colors, with wicker furniture and low four-poster beds. It's central and has a friendly, helpful proprietor. ⊠ *Lautaro Navarro 336,* ☎ *61/242296,* FAX *61/248864. 10 rooms. Snack bar, room service. DC, MC, V.*

$$ ⌂ **Hostal de la Avenida.** The rooms of this homey residencial all over-
★ look a garden that is lovingly tended by its owner, a local of Yugoslav origin. ⊠ *Av. Colón 534,* ☎ *61/247532. 7 rooms. Breakfast room. AE, DC, MC, V.*

$$ ⌂ **Hotel Condor de Plata.** The idiosyncratic decor includes scale models and photographs of old-fashioned airplanes that once traveled to the Magellan region. Rooms are small, carpeted, and colored in neutral browns and beiges; cable TV is available. ⊠ *Av. Colón 556,* ☎ *61/247987,* FAX *61/241149. 14 rooms. Bar, cafeteria, minibars, in-room safes, laundry service. AE, DC, MC, V.*

$ ⌂ **Residencial Sonia Kuscevic.** Doña Kuscevic owns and operates the only Punta Arenas inn affiliated with Hosteling International. The small, clean rooms all have private bathrooms, mountains of warm blankets, and gas heaters. Breakfast is included and discounts are available for students. ⊠ *Pasaje Darwin 175, off Angamos between Chiloé and Sanhueza,* ☎ FAX *61/248543. 5 rooms. Breakfast room, lounge. No credit cards.*

Shopping

The most popular shopping area in the city is the Zona Franca just north of town.

Side Trips from Punta Arenas

Penguin Island

Penguin Island, a half-day trip from Punta Arenas by boat, provides an extraordinary opportunity for visitors to see penguins in their natural habitat. The island is a reserve where the birds are free to reproduce and raise their young with full protection from hunters.

Torres del Paine National Park

A trip to Torres del Paine National Park offers a once-in-a-lifetime opportunity to view nature at its finest: The spectacular towering mountains that give the park its name are surrounded by sparkling turquoise lakes, some touched by the icy-blue sculptures of icebergs and glaciers. Some 12 million years ago, lava flows pushed through the thick sedimentary crust that covered this area, cooling to form granite mass. Glaciers then swept through the park, grinding away all but the ash-gray granite spires seen today. Mother Nature continues to favor this part of her kingdom, blessing it with the most provocative sunset pyrotechnics she ever dares to display. You'll see much of the typical wildlife of the region, including foxes, falcons, flamingos, condors, guanacos (a woolly, graceful version of the llama), and *ñandús* (rhea), along with a wide variety of other birds, wildflowers, and berries.

Plan to spend an extra day in **Puerto Natales**, the largest town near the park, and take the daylong boat ride to view glaciers on the *21 de Mayo* cutter (⊠ Eberhard 554, Puerto Natales, ☎ FAX 61/411978; ✉

$45). Arrange a bag or box lunch and take warm clothes. The trip takes you through canals lined with sheer rock walls, past a cormorant nesting area and a seal colony, and on to the glaciers, one of which you can visit on foot. On your way back to port, you can sip on a pisco or whiskey chilled with glacier ice.

DINING AND LODGING

$$ ✕ **Don Alvarito.** A quirky clash of ambience mixes fine dining service with diner decor. If you can stand the fluorescent lighting, Don Alvarito has carefully prepared scallops and filet mignon in simple, tasty sauces, as well as a wide variety of other options. ⊠ *Blanco Encalada 915, Puerto Natales,* ☎ *61/411187. No credit cards.*

$ ✕ **Café Melissa.** Quick and simple sandwiches with the best espresso in town, Café Melissa also has pastries and cakes. ⊠ *Blanco Encalada 258, Puerto Natales,* ☎ *61/411944. No credit cards.*

$ ✕ **Don Pepe.** During the winter months this restaurant, part of the Hotel Glaciares (☞ Lodging, *below*), doubles as a popular karaoke gathering; during summer months it's a tourist favorite for its creative seafood sauces. Try the May-May (a crab and cream sauce) salmon, a house specialty. ⊠ *Ladrilleros 172, Puerto Natales,* ☎ *61/412189. DC, MC, V.*

$$$$ 🏨 **Hotel Salto Chico–Explora.** On the southeast corner of Lago Pehoé,
★ this eco-hotel is a deluxe alternative to roughing it in the park. As the name suggests, the focus of this hotel is on exploring the local environment, and bookings must be for a minimum of four days (sufficient time for you to become acquainted with nature). The interior is Scandinavian in style, with local woods used for ceilings, floors, and furniture. No expense has been spared, with bed linen from Barcelona, china from England, and wicker furniture from Chimbarongo. Every day, the hotel offers five different types of exploration, depending on the weather conditions and guests' interests. Prices start at around $1,100 for a three-night stay; this includes transportation to and from Punta Arenas, all meals, and daily excursions with bilingual guides. The owners have recently opened another Explora at San Pedro de Atacama, in the heart of the Atacama Desert. ⊠ *Américo Vespucio Sur 80, 5th floor, Las Condes, Santiago,* ☎ *2/206–6060 (reservations),* FAX *2/228–4655, or 800/858–0855 in the U.S. 26 rooms, 4 suites. Restaurant, bar, pool, outdoor hot tub, massage, sauna, exercise room, hiking, horseback riding, boating, recreation room, library, baby-sitting, laundry service, business services, meeting rooms. AE, DC, MC, V.*

$$$ 🏨 **Hostería Pehoé.** Right on Lake Pehoé, this neglected *hostería* offers spectacular views. Its somewhat cramped rooms are rather expensive, but they include a large, American-style breakfast. Book well in advance. ⊠ *Lago Pehoé,* ☎ *61/411390 at the park, 61/244506 in Puerto Natales. 31 rooms. Restaurant, bar. AE, MC, V. Closed May–mid-Sept.*

$$$ 🏨 **Hotel CostAustralis.** Dominating the waterfront, this is Puerto Natales' newest and finest lodging option. Half of the hotel has a majestic view of the gulf and snow-capped peaks of Torres del Paine. Designed by a local Magallanes architect, rooms have wood paneled entryways and Venetian and Czech furnishings. ⊠ *Corner of Pedro Montt and Bulnes, Puerto Natales,* ☎ *61/412000,* FAX *61/411881. 50 rooms, 2 suites. Restaurant, bar, café, in-room safes, minibars, travel services. AE, DC, MC, V.*

$$ 🏨 **Hotel Captain Eberhardt.** Also on the waterfront, this clean and comfortable establishment combines the amenities of a hotel with the charm and gracious staff of a hosteria. ⊠ *Pedro Montt 58, Puerto Natales,* ☎ *61/411208,* FAX *61/411209. 45 rooms. Restaurant, bar. AE, DC, MC, V.*

$$ 🏨 **Hotel Glaciares.** A homey choice in Puerto Natales, this establishment also offers tours of the park in its own private fleet of minivans. All rooms have scarlet carpet, cable TV, and some have partial views

of the Gulf of Almirante Montt. ⊠ *Eberhard 104, Puerto Natales,* ☎ *61/412758,* ☎ FAX *61/412189. 15 rooms. Restaurant, laundry service, travel services. DC, MC, V.*

CAMPGROUNDS

Backpackers from every corner of the globe come to experience the truly awesome wonders of Torres del Paine. A thorough exploration of the park's perimeter can be done in about 10 days, but a number of shorter routes are available, too. Trails are dotted with well marked campgrounds and refuges; some have kitchen and shower facilities. For camping and general park information, call **CONAF** or **SERNATUR** (☞ Tour Operators and Travel Agents *in* Punta Arenas A to Z, *below*). **Fronteriza** (⊠ Eberhard 230, Puerto Natales, ☎ 61/410595) rents camping gear, but you should plan to bring your own as prices are high and the selection is limited.

Punta Arenas A to Z

Arriving and Departing

BY AIRPLANE

Aerovías DAP (⊠ Luís Thayer Ojeda 0172, Santiago, ☎ 2/334–9672, FAX 2/334–5843; ⊠ O'Higgins 891, Punta Arenas, ☎ 61/200202 or 61/200203, FAX 61/225804) offers regular flights to the entire region, including Puerto Williams, Porvenir, and Ushuaia, Argentina. DAP is also the only airline with regular flights to the Malvinas/Falkland Islands. South of Santiago, **Avant** (⊠ Bucarest 214, Providencia, Santiago, ☎ 2/335–3077; ⊠ Roca 924, Punta Arenas, ☎ 61/228312) provides frequent regional flights, including 737 jet service from Puerto Montt to Punta Arenas. Avant's fares are often cheaper than LanChile and Ladeco, but they don't have ticket offices outside South America. Both **LanChile** and **Ladeco** have regular flights; if you don't have a Visit Chile pass (☞ Getting Around *in* Chile A to Z, *below*), try for a reduced fare seat. These must be booked at least two to three months in advance, especially if you plan to travel during the peak season in January and February, when the weather in Punta Arenas is at its best. Your best bet is to use a travel agency such as **Sportstour** (⊠ Moneda 970, 14th floor, Santiago, ☎ 2/549–5200, FAX 2/698–2981), since travel agents can work the occasional miracle of getting cheaper seats at the last minute.

For aerial exploration of Torres del Paine National Park and helicopter ski-drops, **Aerovías DAP** offers an extensive charter service (☞ Arriving and Departing By Plane *in* Punta Arenas A to Z, *above*).

BY BOAT

Navimag (⊠ El Bosque N 0440, 11th floor, Santiago, ☎ 2/442–3120, FAX 2/203–5025 and ⊠ Independencia 840, 2nd floor, Punta Arenas, ☎ 61/224256, FAX 61/225804) offers cruises from Puerto Montt down Chile's west coast. For the truly adventurous wishing to avoid commercial tours, the Chilean Navy makes frequent cruises from Punta Arenas to Antarctica. Embarkation times all depend upon military whim, making reservations an impossibility and the length of any cruise subject to change. Accommodations are a far cry from luxurious—sometimes cargo containers converted into cabins—but prices are affordable. For more information, walk down to the port and ask to speak directly with a Navy captain.

BY BUS

Only **Turibus** (⊠ Errázuriz 932, Punta Arenas, ☎ FAX 61/225315, ☎ 2/779–1377 in Santiago) runs the 48-hour route between Santiago and Punta Arenas, departing from the **Terminal Santiago** (⊠ Av. Libertador Bernardo O'Higgins 3848, ☎ 2/779–1385).

The best way to visit Torres del Paine National Park, which is 400 km (250 mi) from Punta Arenas along a road that is gravel for the last 145 km (90 mi), is by bus. **Buses Fernández** (✉ Armando Sanhueza 745, Punta Arenas, ☎ FAX 61/242313; ✉ Eberhard 555, Puerto Natales, ☎ 61/411392) and **Bus Sur** (✉ Corner of Av. Colón and Magallanes, Punta Arenas, ☎ 61/244464 or ✉ Baquedano 534, Puerto Natales, ☎ FAX 61/411325) run a daily bus service between Punta Arenas and Puerto Natales; be sure to book and arrive early or you may not get on. **Andescape** (✉ Pedro Montt 308, Puerto Natales, ☎ FAX 61/412592), **Turismo Zaahj** (✉ Arturo Prat 236, Puerto Natales, ☎ FAX 61/411355), and **Bus Sur** have daily bus service from Puerto Natales to the park.

BY CAR

It's an exhausting four- or five-day drive to Punta Arenas from Santiago. The prettiest route is via the Pan-American Highway south as far as Osorno, then eastward through the mountains via Paso Puyehue to Bariloche, Argentina. From there drive south through the Argentine National Parks (Nahuel Huapi, Los Alerces) to the town of Comodoro Rivadavia, 1,200 km (750 mi) from Osorno on Argentina's Atlantic coast. At Comodoro Rivadavia, drive south to Río Gallegos, 1,916 km (1,200 mi) from Osorno, and on to Punta Arenas. Some sections of the route are unpaved. Punta Arenas is about 2,230 km (1,400 mi) from Osorno.

Getting Around

Punta Arenas is a small, walkable city, with most of its main attractions concentrated around the central square. Tourist agencies and even cafés offer day trips to Penguin Island and Fort Bulnes, and there is regular bus service to Puerto Natales and the Torres del Paine National Park, so you can get to most places whether you've got a vehicle or not. To really explore the surrounding region, however, you may find a car worth the expense.

To avoid a guided tour of Torres del Paine National Park, **Andes Patagónicos Expeditions** (☞ Tour Operators and Travel Agents, *below*) offers rental cars; rates are high by U.S. standards.

Contacts and Resources

EMERGENCIES

Police: ☎ 133. **Fire:** ☎ 132. **General emergency:** ☎ 133.

VISITOR INFORMATION

CONAF (☎ 61/691931) is the place to go for general information on the national parks and camping. **Oficina Austro Chile** (✉ Colón and Magallanes, kiosk in the park strip, ☎ 61/223798) can also help with travel details. **SERNATUR** has a main office (✉ Croatia 833, ☎ FAX 61/241330) and a branch in the square (✉ Plaza Muñoz Gamero, ☎ 61/221644) of Punta Arenas, as well as an office in Puerto Natales (✉ Corner of Pedro Montt and Phillipi, ☎ 61/412125).

EASTER ISLAND

Rapa Nui, known to most as Easter Island, is one of the world's most persistent mysteries. Only 166 square km (50 sq mi) in size, its mixed European-Chilean-Polynesian population recalls its history in a series of often contradictory stories. The landscape itself, formed by the action of a now-dormant volcano, is characterized by the idyllic palm-lined beaches of golden sand and low rocky mountains typical of most South Pacific islands. One small town on the southwest tip of this inverted triangle, Hanga Roa, houses the island's 3,000 permanent residents, and rough dirt roads trace the footsteps of the ancient and modern peoples who have used, and often abused, their island home. Huge stone statues known as *moai* are scattered all over the island, attesting to the skills of the craftspeople who carved, moved, and erected these imposing creatures, some more than 68 ft tall.

Conflicting theories battle to explain how Easter Island was first settled. Anthropologist Thor Heyerdahl argued that similarities between customs in parts of Peru and Easter Island indicate that native peoples from the South American mainland first settled the island. However, the dominant theory is that the island was first occupied by a thriving Polynesian culture that at its height had a population of 15,000 and developed a sophisticated system of beliefs expressed by the island's massive stone moai. Archaeologists believe the island's population experienced a crisis toward the end of the 16th century, possibly due to overpopulation, and after a lengthy period of violent conflicts, a new culture developed.

In 1870 a ship raced westward and claimed the island for Chile, before France could do so, and in 1888 Easter Island formally became part of Chile. Until 1952 the owners of a private sheep ranch ran the island as their own, shutting inhabitants up in the main town of Hanga Roa. Today the main activities of the town's inhabitants, 70% of whom are of native origin, include servicing a growing tourism industry and conducting scientific excavations and studies, along with more traditional pursuits such as agriculture, fishing, and handicrafts produced in the form of wood carvings of ancient figures, necklaces, and other pieces worked in shells and coral. Count on spending at least one-and-a-half to two days here; you'll need four to five days to see the entire island without feeling rushed.

Hanga Roa

In the town of **Hanga Roa** itself, it's well worth visiting the **church**, where traditional Catholic figures are rendered by island carvers with surprising results. The noon service on Sunday is usually in the island's indigenous language, and the songs have a distinctly Polynesian rhythm and flavor. There's also a modest **museum** with shells, carvings, and other interesting pieces on view just outside town near the **Tahai** archaeological site, which is on the coast. A pleasant half-day walk along the dirt road to Tahai will take you through a coastal landscape dotted with buried and broken moai; you'll pass the **plaza** that once served as a ceremonial meeting place, near which religious and social leaders built their boat-shape residences, or *hare paenga* (meaning "the foundations of one who remains visible").

Elsewhere on the Island

Take a day trip to **Orongo,** the small village south of Hanga Roa that has been re-created by Chile's National Parks division to provide insight into the mysteries of a culture that left 150 carvings behind on cliffs. Nearby is the **Rano Kau Volcano,** a ceremonial crater a mile wide that is decorated with characteristic petroglyphs. Bring solid, comfortable walking shoes appropriate for stony roads and some climbing, along with a light rain jacket and a flashlight for exploring caves. It's also worth driving across to the northeast shore of the island for a day at Anakena Beach, where natural caves that you can explore on your own once sheltered the island's earliest residents.

Easter Island A to Z

Arriving and Departing

The only way to reach Easter Island, which lies 3,700 km (2,300 mi) west of Chile, is by plane. The airport is a few minutes southwest of

Hanga Roa. Service is via **LanChile** (☎ 2/687–2323 in Santiago, 800/ 735–5526 in the U.S.). Round-trip fare from Santiago is about $850, but a good travel agent should be able to get a better deal if you plan ahead. One such agency in Santiago that specializes in Easter Island is the appropriately named, **Rapa Nui** (✉ Huerfanos 1160, Suite 912, ☎ 2/672–1050, ℻ 2/672–3428).

Getting Around

BY CAR

You can rent a Jeep from **Viajes Kia Koe** (✉ Policarpo, ☎ 32/100282), or from **Hertz** (✉ Across the street from the airport, ☎ 32/100654, 2/ 235–9666 in Santiago); count on spending about $75 per day. Boats are available for rental in the caleta (fishing village) near Hanga Roa. You can rent a horse to explore the island, without guides, for less than $50 a day near the **Hotu Matua Hotel** (✉ Av. Pont, ☎ 32/100242, 2/ 635–3275 in Santiago).

Contacts and Resources

EMERGENCIES

Police: ☎ 133. **Fire:** ☎ 132. **General emergency:** ☎ 133.

TELEPHONES, THE INTERNET, MAIL

Calling Easter Island can be exasperating; prefix codes are frequently changing and busy signals are usual. To call, dial your choice of carriers followed by 32 and then the number. Alternatively, **Entel** has a fax number for all hotel reservations on the island (℻ 32/100105).

TOUR OPERATORS

Hanga Roa Hotel (✉ Av. Pont, ☎ 32/223229 or 2/633–5334 in Santiago) offers full-day ($45 per person) and half-day ($20) tours of the island. You can also arrange for a skin-diving tour in the caleta near Hanga Roa.

CHILE A TO Z

Arriving and Departing

By Airplane

Chile's new international airport terminal is about 30 minutes' drive west of Santiago, alongside the rather dilapidated old terminal which now services domestic flights. You can get from the airport to Santiago by taxi for less than $20, via **Buses Tour Express** (☎ 2/671–7380) for p1,000. **Delfos** (☎ 2/226–6020), **Navett** (☎ 2/695–6868), and **Transfer** (☎ 2/777–7707) will shuttle you from the airport to any address within the city for less than p4,000. You can rent a car in the airport from **Avis** (☎ 2/601–9966), **Budget** (☎ 2/601–9421), or **Hertz** (☎ 2/601–9262). There is no subway connection.

CARRIERS

U.S. carriers that serve Chile include American Airlines, Continental Airlines, and United Airlines.

LanChile (☎ 800/735–5526) flies to Santiago from Miami, Los Angeles, New York, and Sydney. **Aero Peru** (☎ 800/777-7717) also serves Chile.

FLYING TIMES

Flying times to Santiago are 13 hours from New York, 10 hours from Miami, and 9 hours from Los Angeles.

By Car

You can cross into Chile from Peru at the northern town of Arica. It is not recommended to drive from Argentina, as it involves crossing the Andes, where roads are often closed.

Getting Around

By Airplane

Flying around Chile is fast and comfortable. The advantage of flying is that you avoid the dangers of the Chilean highways; the disadvantage is that you miss the landscape, but you can compensate for this by renting a car and exploring locally.

Excellent-value air-travel packages are available, but only for purchase outside Chile. Chile's main airline, **LanChile** (in North America ☎ 800/735–5526, 2/687–2323 in Chile, ℻ 2/632–9334) offers a Visit Chile pass. These passes, which you must buy before arriving in Chile, allow you three flights north or south of Santiago (excluding Easter Island) for around $350. You can add up to three more flights (segments) for $80 each. The price for the Visit Chile Pass goes down considerably if you are arriving in Santiago on LanChile. **Aerovías DAP** (in Santiago, ⊠ Luís Thayer Ojeda 0172, ☎ 2/334–9672, ℻ 2/334–5843; in **Punta Arenas**: ⊠ O'Higgins 891, ☎ 61/223340, ℻ 61/221693) has extensive charter service within the Magallanes region. **ALTA Airlines** (⊠ Las Urbinas 30, Santiago, ☎ 2/334–5872) specializes in regional flights, connecting 23 Chilean cities with its frequent and affordable service. **Avant** (in Santiago, ⊠ Bucarest 214, Providencia, ☎ 2/335–3077; ⊠ Roca 924, Punta Arenas, ☎ 61/228312) has frequent regional flights both north and south of Santiago, most of which are far below LanChile and Ladeco's prices.

By Bus

Bus travel in Chile is relatively cheap and safe, provided you use one of the better lines. Luxury bus travel between cities costs about one-third the plane fare and is more comfortable, with wide, reclining seats with footrests, drinks, music, movies, and meals or snacks. Intercity bus service is a comfortable, safe, and reasonably priced alternative for getting around Chile. The most luxurious and expensive service offered by most bus companies is known as *salón cama*.

Fenix (☎ 2/696–9089, ℻ 2/779–1149) and **Varmontt** (☎ 2/231–3505, ℻ 2/555–8372) offer both luxury and regular service to many points between Santiago and Puerto Montt, as well as farther south. **Tramaca** (☎ 2/235–1695, ℻ 2/236–3300) runs a widespread service to the north. You can often negotiate a cheaper fare with roaming vendors during a stroll through the relevant bus terminal. Most individual bus companies are difficult to phone; your best bet is to check schedules and purchase tickets personally. Buses can fill quickly on holiday weekends and over Christmas and Easter, so plan accordingly.

By Car

Your own driver's license and an International Driving Permit make it legal for you to drive, but your stay in Chile will probably be more pleasant if you avoid using a car or if you use one with great prudence.

EMERGENCY ASSISTANCE

The Automóvil Club de Chile (⊠ Av. Vitacura 8620, Santiago, ☎ 2/212–5702, ℻ 2/211–9208) offers low-cost road service and towing in and around the main cities to members of the Automobile Association of America (AAA).

GASOLINE

Gasoline prices range from 55¢ per liter for 84 octane to 60¢ per liter for 93 and unleaded and 46¢ per liter for diesel. Prices increase the farther you travel from Santiago. There are plenty of gas stations on main routes, but they're more sparsely spread on the northern half of the Chilean Pan-American. If you plan to cross the Atacama Desert, make sure your car is topped up with fuel and water.

Roads are hopelessly overcrowded, especially in Santiago. The main national thoroughfare is the *Panamericana,* the Pan-American Highway, which begins on the Chile–Peru border and extends south through Santiago and on to Puerto Montt and beyond. It is also known as Route 5.

RULES OF THE ROAD

Chilean drivers are wild and reckless and tend to make up the rules as they go along. Foreign insurance may cover the basic costs of an accident, but if you're in an accident that kills or cripples someone, you can be sued, and a Chilean court may award damages far beyond your ability to pay. Local insurance is provided by rental car agencies. Speed limits are usually 100 kph (62 mph) on highways and 50 kph (31 mph) in cities, with the Pan-American being well monitored by police speed traps. Should you be stopped, never attempt to bribe the carabineros.

By Train

Good train service is a thing of the past in Chile; the only real advantage of trains now is that they allow travelers to avoid the Pan-American Highway. Accommodations include sleeper cars, salón, economy, and, for some destinations, first and second classes. There are daily departures from Santiago for most places in southern Chile, but be prepared for a painfully slow journey (Santiago–Puerto Montt takes 20 hours) with frequent delays. There is no northbound service from Santiago. **Reservations** are recommended; make them at the train station itself (☎ 2/689–1825), in the city center (☎ 2/632–2801), or in the Escuela Militar metro station (☎ 2/228–2983).

You can take advantage of an **excellent train service** that carries you and your vehicle between Santiago and southern Chile. Round-trip prices from Santiago to Temuco are $275 to transport your car, plus $180 for a private cabin for two or $100 for two coach seats. The rates are slightly less if you only go as far as Concepción. The trip must be booked well in advance, particularly if you intend to travel during the peak season; tickets must be paid for when you make a reservation (☎ 2/689–1825).

Contacts and Resources

Customs and Duties

ON ARRIVAL

You may bring into Chile up to 400 cigarettes, 400 grams of tobacco, 50 cigars, two open bottles of perfume, 2 liters of alcoholic beverages, and gifts. On arrival, you will be given a flimsy, minute piece of paper that is your three-month tourist visa. This has to be handed in when you leave; because getting a new one involves waiting in many lines and a lot of bureaucracy, put it somewhere safe.

ON DEPARTURE

Visitors, although seldom questioned, are prohibited by regulation from leaving with handicrafts and souvenirs worth more than $500 total. You will be charged an $18 airport tax upon departure.

Electricity

The electric current in Chile is 220 v/50hz.

Embassies

American (✉ Av. Andrés Bello 2800, Providencia, ☎ 2/232–2600). **British** (✉ Av. El Bosque N 0125, p. 3, Providencia, Santiago, ☎ 2/231–3737). **Canadian** (✉ Nueva Tajamar 481, p. 12 Torre Norte, Las Condes, Santiago, ☎ 2/362–9600).

Health and Safety

FOOD AND DRINK

From a health standpoint, Chile is one of the safer countries in which to travel. The cholera epidemic that swept the continent in the early 1990s has been effectively controlled here. Restaurants are not allowed to serve raw salads and seafood, which represent the prime sources of the bacteria that produce not only cholera but also typhoid fever, hepatitis, and gastroenteritis in general. Avoid raw vegetables unless you know they've been thoroughly washed and disinfected. Be wary of strawberries and other unpeeled ground fruits and vegetables for the same reason, because many farm fields are irrigated with barely treated sewage. When purchasing ice cream, pastries, and other sweet items, buy in locales with proper refrigeration. Avoid luncheon meats, except good-quality ham, because these are a prime source of bacterial infections, especially in summer. Almost all drinking water receives proper treatment and is unlikely to produce health problems. Mineral water is good and comes in carbonated and noncarbonated incarnations, but you'll probably do all right with tap water.

Should you need medical aid, the best facilities tend to be in the private hospitals in Santiago (☞ Santiago A to Z, *above*).

OTHER PRECAUTIONS

Santiago's city center and most areas frequented by tourists are generally safe, provided you dress down, don't wear flashy jewelry, and don't ever handle money in public. It's a good idea to keep your money in a pocket rather than a wallet, which is easier to steal. On buses and in crowded areas, hold purses or handbags close to the body; thieves use knives to slice the bottom of a bag and catch the contents as they fall out. In Santiago, areas in which to be particularly cautious include Bellavista, where recent increases in car theft have affected restaurant trade; pedestrian walkways such as Paseo Huérfanos in the downtown district; and around Santa Lucia at night. The poor residential areas of Santiago, known as *poblaciones,* which ring most neighborhoods and commercial centers, have an interesting history and informed, opinionated people, but you need a knowledgeable guide to visit them safely. Chilean men are more subtle in their machismo than men in other South American countries, but it's still a strong aspect of the culture, and foreign women are considered fair game. Men are apt to misinterpret a casual, informal attitude and take advantage.

Language, Culture, and Etiquette

Chile's official language is Spanish, and you'd be wise to learn at least a few words and carry a good phrase book. Chilean Spanish, often recognized as one of the most bastardized forms of the language, is fast, slurred, clipped, and chock-full of colloquialisms, presenting the foreigner with an often frustrating cross-cultural experience. However, receptionists at most upscale hotels speak English, as do many taxi drivers and salespeople.

Mail

POSTAL RATES

Postage on regular letters and postcards to Canada and the United States costs about 60¢. The postage to Britain is about 70¢. The postal system is efficient and, on average, letters take 5–7 days to reach the United States or Europe.

Money Matters

CURRENCY

Exchange rates fluctuate constantly, so check your local newspaper for the most current information; at press time there were approximately

330 Chilean pesos to the Canadian dollar, 485 pesos to the U.S. dollar, and 785 pesos to the pound sterling. Chilean coins come in units of 1, 5, 10, 50, and 100 pesos; bills are issued in 500, 1,000, 5,000, and 10,000 pesos.

Credit cards and traveler's checks are accepted in resorts and in a large number of shops and restaurants in major cities, though you should always carry some pesos with you. Once you stray from the tourist establishments, you can only pay with cash pesos or occasionally credit cards. Besides banks, many travel agencies will change money at competitive rates; most charge a small commission on traveler's checks.

SERVICE CHARGES, TAXES, AND TIPPING

An 18% value-added tax (VAT, called IVA here) is added to the cost of most goods and services in Chile; often you won't notice because it's included in the price quoted. When it's not, the seller gives you the price, plus IVA. At many hotels you may receive an exemption from the IVA if you pay in American dollars or traveler's checks; some also offer this service if you use an American Express credit card.

The usual tip in restaurants is 10%, more if you really liked the service. City taxi drivers don't usually expect a tip, because most own their cabs. If you hire a taxi to take you around a city, you should consider giving a good tip.

WHAT IT WILL COST

Sample Prices: A cup of coffee, $1; bottle of beer, $3; soft drink, $1; bottle of house wine, $10; ham-and-cheese sandwich, $3; 1-mi taxi ride, $2; city bus ride, 50¢; museum entrance, $2.

Opening and Closing Times

Bank hours are weekdays 9–2. Most **museums** are closed on Monday, as are theaters. Otherwise, museum hours tend to coincide with shopping hours. **Stores** generally are open weekdays 10–7 and on Saturday until 2. In small towns, stores close for lunch between about 1 and 3 or 4.

NATIONAL HOLIDAYS

New Year's Day (Jan. 1); Good Friday (2000: Apr. 23; 2001: Apr. 15); Labor Day (May 1); Day of Naval Glories (May 21); Corpus Christi (in June); Feast of St. Peter and St. Paul (June 29); Anniversary of Coup (Sept. 11); Independence Celebrations (Sept. 18–19); Discovery of the Americas (Oct. 12); Day of the Dead (Nov. 1); Immaculate Conception (Dec. 8); Christmas (Dec. 25).

Many shops and services are open as normal on these days, but transportation is always heavily booked up on and around the holidays.

Passports and Visas

Travelers with U.S., Canadian, or British passports do not require special visas. Upon arrival in Chile, U.S. citizens will pay $45 for an entry card that is good for as long as your passport is valid; Canadians will pay $55. As you approach Santiago by plane, you'll receive a tourist card valid for 90 days, which will be stamped by immigration officers. Don't lose it. You will face considerable difficulties if you cannot produce your original card upon departure.

Telephones and the Internet

Chileans are generally very aware of the Internet, but it is not as widely used as in the United States, which may be partly due to the sluggish connection speeds. Only the most expensive hotels have business centers with access to the Internet-linked computer terminals. If your hotel doesn't, just ask at the front desk or at any **SERNATUR** office; they will direct you to one of the mounting number of little cyber-shops where travelers can check their E-mail. There is at least one such shop in every town; connection fees are generally $1 for a half hour. If you're planning to bring a laptop into the country, check the manual first to see if it requires a converter. Newer laptops will only require an adapter plug. Chile uses the same phone plugs as the United States, so plan accordingly if you'll be using a modem.

LOCAL CALLS

A 100-peso piece is required to make a local call in a public phone booth, usually allowing about 2 minutes of conversation. Prefix codes and multicarrier numbers are not needed for local dialing. Some public phones, called "intelligent" phones, allow you to insert varying amounts of money and make several calls in succession, provided you don't hang up in between: There's a special button to push that cuts off one call and starts another. The intelligent phones also include English-language instructions. Most city areas have standing phone booths, but phones are also found at restaurants, calling centers, and even newsstands. You may have to wait several seconds after picking up the receiver before a steady humming sound signals that you may dial. After dialing, you'll hear a characteristic beep-beep repeatedly as your call goes through; then there's a pause, followed by a long tone signaling that the other phone is ringing. A busy sound is similar but repeats itself with no pause in between.

LONG-DISTANCE AND INTERNATIONAL CALLS

If you plan to call abroad while in Chile, it's in your best interest to buy a local phone card (sold in varying amounts at kiosks and calling centers) or use a calling center. To dial an international number directly from a private phone, you first dial the number of the carrier you want to use (**Transam**, dial 113; **Entel**, dial 123; **CTC**, dial 188; **Chilesat**, dial 171; **Bellsouth**, dial 181), then dial 0, followed by the country code, the area or city code, and the phone number. Price differences among carriers can be large; to verify rates, dial the carrier's number, followed by 123.

For long-distance operator service, you must still choose one of the carrier codes before dialing, followed by 122. **AT&T** (☎ 800/800–311), **MCI** (☎ 800/207–300 on a CTC phone or 800/360–180 on an Entel phone), and **Sprint** (☎ 800/360–777) have direct calling programs.

Reduced rates to most places apply after 8 PM on weekdays, 2 PM on Saturdays, and on Sunday and holidays. Most hotels charge extra for long-distance calls made from your room.

When to Go

Chile's seasons are the reverse of North America's—that is, June–August is Chile's winter. Tourism peaks during the hot summer months of January and February, except in Santiago, which tends to empty as most Santiaguinos head for the coast. Though prices are at their highest, it's worth braving the summer heat if you're interested in lying on the beach or enjoying the many concerts, folklore festivals, and outdoor theater performances offered during this period.

If you're heading for the Lake District or Patagonia and want good weather without the crowds, the shoulder seasons of December and March are the months to come; those planning to visit the Atacama Desert should arrive in late spring, preferably in November, when temperatures are bearable and air clarity is at its peak. In spring Santiago blooms, and the fragrance of the flowers will distract even the most avid workaholic. A second tourist season occurs in the Chilean winter, as skiers flock to Chile's mountaintops for some of the world's best skiing, available at the height of northern summers. Winter smog is a good reason to stay away from Santiago during July and August, unless you're coming for a ski holiday and won't be spending much time in the city.

CLIMATE

Chile's climate is agreeable and, given the country's enormous length, varied. The north enjoys the extremes of desert weather, with hot, dry days and freezing nights, except on the coast, where the ocean moderates, providing a mild climate year-round. Santiago has hot summers, cool springs and falls, and very gray, smoggy winters. Farther south, in the Lake District, you should be prepared for hot days, cold nights, and rainstorms. And even farther south, in Punta Arenas, summer temperatures are seldom higher than 20°C (68°F), and you'll contend with snow and icy winds in winter.

The following are the average daily maximum and minimum temperatures for Santiago.

Jan.	85F	29C	May	65F	18C	Sept.	66F	19C
	53	12		41	5		42	6
Feb.	84F	29C	June	58F	14C	Oct.	72F	22C
	52	11		37	3		45	7
Mar.	80F	27C	July	59F	15C	Nov.	78F	26C
	49	9		37	3		48	9
Apr.	74F	23C	Aug.	62F	17C	Dec.	83F	28C
	54	7		39	4		51	11

The following are the average daily maximum and minimum temperatures for Punta Arenas.

Jan.	58F	14C	May	45F	7C	Sept.	46F	8C
	45	7		35	2		35	2
Feb.	58F	14C	June	41F	5C	Oct.	51F	11C
	44	7		33	1		38	3
Mar.	54F	12C	July	40F	4C	Nov.	54F	12C
	41	5		31	0		40	4
Apr.	50F	10C	Aug.	42F	6C	Dec.	57F	14C
	39	4		33	1		43	6

FESTIVALS AND SEASONAL EVENTS

The **Festival Foclórico** (Folklore Festival) is held in Santiago during the fourth week of January. Every February Valdivia has its week-long **Semana Correaleña,** a favorite celebration for those living in the Lake District with fireworks and festivities on the rivers around the city. September 18 is National Independence Day and **Fiestas Patrias** (patriotic festivals) take place all over the country, but there's extra fun around Rancagua, with hard-fought rodeo competitions.

Wine fanciers may want to coordinate their trip with one of two food-and-wine fairs that are run annually in Santiago. **ExpoGourmand** (☎ 2/204–7766, FAX 2/223–2307), organized by the magazine *Gourmand,* is a gastronomic feast of wine tastings, cooking demonstrations, and stalls displaying local cuisines. The event runs over four days, during September. In November, the Chilean wine industry shows off the fruits of its hard labor at the annual **Feria International de Vino del Hemisferio Sur;** information can be obtained from Santiago International Fair (☎ 2/553–2838, ext. 224, FAX 2/533–1667).

The **Feast of the Virgin of Andacollo,** patron saint of miners, is honored on December 8th in this northern town near La Serena. In Santiago during the second week of December is the **International Artisans' Fair.**

7 COLOMBIA

Scattered from the valleys of the Andes
to the coastal plains, Colombia's cities
have nurtured customs and ways of life as
disparate as their elevations. The Old World
formality of high Bogotá and the tropical
Caribbean flair of sea-level Cartagena
yield distinct varieties of the music, cuisine,
costumes, dialects, and attitudes that make
Colombia so alluring.

Updated by
Mick Elmore

COLOMBIA IS BLESSED. Its regal location on the continent's northern tip makes it the only South American country that fringes both the Atlantic and Pacific oceans. It's rich in emeralds, coffee, and, increasingly, oil. And, because it's on the equator, it's one of the lushest countries in terms of tropical flora and wildlife. You can jump on a plane and, less than an hour later, find yourself in a different dramatic setting—be it the cobblestone streets of a weathered colonial port, the stalls of a crowded market where Chibcha Indian merchants still speak the tongues of their ancestors, or at the base of snow-covered volcanoes rising sharply from a steamy coastal plain.

Bogotá, Colombia's sprawling capital of more than 6 million people, stands at the end of a vast plateau in the eastern Andes. The metropolis extends north through tidy brick suburbs, south to shantytowns, and west through industrial parks and modern suburban developments. Poverty and drug-related violence are facts of life here, but rarely covered in the international press are Bogotá's elegant shopping streets; grand high-rises; the colonial old-city neighborhood of La Candelaria; and chic Zona Rosa nightclubs, where young, stylish *bogotaños* (as inhabitants of Bogotá are called) exit with the sunrise.

Colombia's western half, traversed by the central Andean ridge, the Cordillera Central, is where most of the country's 39 million people live. As you ascend the mighty Andes, subtropical valleys give way to rigid, fern-carpeted mountains where ever-present mists are brightened only by votive candles placed by truck drivers at roadside shrines. West of Bogotá, quiet Indian villages hug the hillsides en route to Medellín, home to the eponymous drug cartel. Despite its notorious reputation, Medellín is a pleasant, relatively safe, modern city surrounded by velvety green hills and miles of lush farmland. South of the city, the Pan-American Highway meanders through dramatic mountain landscapes before reaching Cali and colonial Popayán, famous across the continent for its Holy Week festival.

If you equate vacationing with lounging in the sun, the beaches of San Andrés and Providencia islands are Colombia's most compelling. Undeterred by the 640-km (400-mi) trip from the mainland, Colombians escape to the resort islands for weekends of swimming, sunbathing, shopping, and sipping rum at thatched waterfront bars. Back on the mainland, Cartagena, widely revered as the most striking colonial city in South America, makes an excellent base for forays along the Caribbean coast.

Before the arrival of the Spanish, Colombia was sparsely inhabited by indigenous tribes. In the high basins of the Andes, the most powerful of these tribes was the Chibcha, whose master goldsmiths may have sparked the El Dorado (The Golden One) myth with their exquisite creations and their tradition of anointing a chief each year by rolling him in gold dust. The Chibchas had given up this custom long before the first Europeans landed on Colombian shores, but the legend lingered and drove a host of New World adventurers in search of gilded cities.

The Spanish settled parts of Panama as early as 1510. But it wasn't until Rodrigo de Bastidas founded the Colombian port of Santa Marta, in 1525, that a permanent settlement was established in what is today Colombia. Soon after, explorers like Gonzalo Jiménez de Quesada plundered and pillaged their way inland. Quesada reached what is now

Colombia

Bogotá in 1535 and, after quickly dispatching the local Chibcha Indians, established a Spanish settlement.

Despite their near extinction, Colombia's Indians have left a lasting mark on the country. The extraordinary carved stones at San Agustín, in southwestern Colombia, speak of Indian empires once rich in gold, emeralds, and the technological skills necessary to erect temples to now long-forgotten gods. In the Andes and on the coastal plains, you'll find modern descendants of these lost tribes living a simple, traditional life somewhat unchanged since Columbus presumptuously claimed Colombia in the name of King Ferdinand of Spain.

Visitors to Colombia today don't get around by bus or rental car. Although buses are available and car rental agencies operate in the bigger cities, it's currently not a safe way to explore. For more information about transportation risks and alternative travel options, *see* Getting Around *in* Colombia A to Z, *below*.

Pleasures and Pastimes

Beaches

The country's favorite beaches have always been those on the Caribbean islands of San Andrés and Providencia. Cartagena's beach is also popular (a euphemism for crowded), but it doesn't compare with the sun-swathed northeastern stretches, especially those beyond Santa Marta, where the forest-cloaked mountains of Tayrona National Park rise dramatically behind sun worshipers.

Colonial Charm

Cartagena, the crown jewel of Colombia's colonial heritage, is one of the most historically important and beautiful cities of the Americas. The mountain-valley city of Popayán is an impressive urban reproduction of the nation's true colonial past. The city was painstakingly restored after an earthquake in 1983 nearly demolished it. Bogotá's Candelaria neighborhood is another haven of colonial architecture, with massive churches and former mansions that now house hotels, museums, and restaurants.

Dining

From the hearty soups served in the highlands to the seafood dishes along the Caribbean coast, you'll find distinctive regional menus here. Beef is popular everywhere—as steaks or in shish kebabs or stews—as is chicken, which is usually roasted over a fire of *guisado,* (coffee wood) and served in a mildly spiced sauce. Bogotá's most traditional dish is *ajiaco,* a thick chicken and potato soup garnished with capers, sour cream, and avocado. On the Caribbean coast, you're more likely to dip your spoon into a *cazuela de mariscos,* a seafood soup with cassava. Also popular is *sancocho de sábalo,* fish prepared in coconut milk with strips of potato, plantain banana, and yucca. On San Andrés and Providencia islands, the local favorite is *rendón,* a fish-and-snail soup slowly cooked in coconut milk with yucca, plantain, breadfruit, and dumplings.

Colombians are fond of bread, particularly dinner rolls, pastries, and deep-fried empanadas: be sure to try *mogollas,* whole-wheat muffins with raisin-flavored centers; *roscones,* sugar-sprinkled pastries filled with guava jelly; and *buñelos,* little balls of cheese bread, which go particularly well with a cup of Colombia's famous coffee. Popular for dessert are *obleas,* giant wafers frosted with sugar-and-milk paste.

Colombians don't necessarily drink wine with dinner, although they're fond of two reasonable national offerings: Santo Tomás, a full-bodied red wine, and the Chianti-like Vino Moriles.

Restaurants in many cities often close for a few hours between lunch and dinner (roughly 3 to 6). To prevent imminent hunger, plan your mealtimes in advance. Appropriate attire in restaurants is comparable to U.S. or European standards—dressy for the more formal, expensive places, and casual everywhere else. For price categories, *see* Dining *in* Smart Travel Tips A to Z.

Lodging

Top-end, modern hotels usually have prices and standards comparable to those in North America, although, outside of Bogotá, in such tourist meccas as Cartagena and San Andrés, hotel rates are surprisingly low. Consider staying at a small, locally owned hotel; and not because the big hotels are completely booked for conventions, but rather to better experience Colombian hospitality and atmosphere. For price categories, *see* Lodging *in* Smart Travel Tips A to Z.

Pre-Columbian Treasures

Several archaeological sites and an array of collected artifacts testify to the cultural richness that thrived in the country before European domination. The enigmatic statues of San Agustín, the painted tombs of Tierradentro, and the remote ruins of La Ciudad Perdida may be off the beaten track, but they merit the time and effort it takes to visit them. Or, for a quick and easy sojourn into Colombia's distant past, duck into Bogotá's Museo de Oro to see the world's largest collection of pre-Columbian gold pieces; it's just one of many Colombian museums that exhibits the treasures of lost cultures.

Exploring Colombia

The extremes of Colombia's varied topography are epitomized by the Andean highlands with temperate Bogotá, and the truly tropical Caribbean, which comprises the islands, coast, and hinterlands near Cartagena. The cities of Medellín and Cali, and the countryside surrounding them, lie somewhere between those two contrasting areas, with Medellín being slightly more Caribbean, and Cali more Andean.

Great Itineraries

Commonly those who travel to Colombia on business disembark in Bogotá, the modern capital and financial center; most vacationers see only historic Cartagena and the Caribbean coast. Yet a complete experience of Colombia must include a visit to colonial Popayán and a stop in nearby Cali to enjoy the café culture.

IF YOU HAVE 5 DAYS

If you start in **Bogotá,** you'll want to spend a day or two exploring the historic Candelaria district and visiting museums. However, don't wait too long to jump on a flight to **Cartagena,** which offers more than you could possibly see in a day. If you can drag yourself away from the colonial splendors you'll face a choice: a stay at a Caribbean resort, with a trip up the coast to **Santa Marta** and its beaches, or a flight to **Popayán** for a day in that southwestern city.

IF YOU HAVE 10 DAYS

Spend your first two days in **Bogotá,** admiring its many museums and monuments. On day three, fly to **Popayán** for a day and night in this city surrounded by snowcapped volcanoes. Via the nearby city of **Cali,** fly to **Cartagena,** where you can spend a couple of days exploring the walled city and fortresses, and take a one-day excursion to the Islas del Rosario. For your last two days head up the coast to **Santa Marta** and kick back on the beaches before returning by plane to Bogotá.

IF YOU HAVE 14 DAYS OR MORE

Spend up to four days enjoying the sights of **Bogotá** including an excursion to nearby **Tunja,** the colonial capital of Boyacá province. Then head to **Popayán,** where you can spend a day wandering the cobblestone streets before heading for the countryside destinations of **Silvia** and **Puracé National Park.** Archaeology buffs will want to spend more time here, perhaps making the long journey to **San Agustín.** From Popayán, it's a three-hour drive north to **Cali,** the air-travel hub of the southwest, where you can spend a night just outside the city at a traditional hacienda. Unless business brings you to **Medellín** first, fly from Cali to **Cartagena** for two days in this old port town. From here, head up the coast to the beaches of **Santa Marta,** or fly to either **San Andrés** or **Providencia** for a couple of nights before returning to Bogotá.

BOGOTÁ

Like many old colonial cities, Santa Fé de Bogotá, as it's officially named, is a city of contrasts. Elegant shopping centers coexist with makeshift open-air bargaining markets; mansions in the city's north, with shanties on the surrounding hills; and futuristic glass towers, with colonial churches. Simultaneous displays of ostentatious wealth and shocking poverty have existed here for centuries. In the neighborhood of La Candelaria, a rich assemblage of colonial mansions grandly conceived by the Spanish were built by Indian slaves and financed by plundered gold.

Bogotá, a city of more than 6 million people, has grown 20-fold in the past 50 years. It suffers the growing pains typical of any modern city, and a few uniquely its own: a collapsed transportation system, chronic air pollution, squalid shantytowns, rampant petty-crimes, a scurrilous drug trade, and occasional acts of guerrilla terrorism. However, plans to create jobs and expand Colombian tourism are in the works, and while neither can remedy the country's safety issues, they may help to alleviate some conditions that contribute to crime. Also, in an unprecedented gesture, President Andrés Pastrana met with guerrilla leaders to discuss a plan for peace. Although it hasn't brought about immediate progress, this direction seems to indicate an active desire for peace and reconciliation.

Spanish conquistadors built their South American cities in magnificent locations, and Bogotá, which stands on a high plain in the eastern Andes, is no exception. During his disastrous search for the legendary El Dorado, Gonzalo Jiménez de Quesada, the Spanish explorer on whom Cervantes reputedly modeled Don Quixote, was struck by the area's natural splendor and its potential for colonization. Though it's a mere 1,288 km (800 mi) from the equator, Bogotá's 2,593-m (8,500-ft) altitude lends it a refreshing climate. Jiménez de Quesada discovered one of South America's most advanced pre-Columbian peoples, the Muisca or Chibcha. Despite their great skills as goldsmiths, the Chibcha were no match for the Spaniards: On August 6, 1538, Quesada christened his new conquest Santa Fé de Bogotá, on the site of the razed Chibcha village of Bacatá.

Bogotá rapidly became an important administrative center and in 1740 was crowned the capital of the Viceroyalty of New Granada, an area comprising modern Colombia, Venezuela, Panama, and Ecuador. With its new important status, grand civic and religious buildings began to spring up, often with the hand-carved ceilings and sculpted doorways that were the hallmark of New Granada architecture. Nevertheless, by 1900 Bogotá was still only a city of 100,000. It was not until the 1940s that rapid industrialization and the consequent peasant migration to urban centers spurred Bogotá's exponential growth.

Exploring Bogotá

Numbers in white bullets in the text correspond to numbers in black bullets in the margins and on the Bogotá map.

At the foot of Monserrate Peak is Bogotá's oldest neighborhood, La Candelaria, which is packed with colonial mansions (some of which are now museums) and exquisite churches. To the north is the downtown area, which although seedy has a handful of fairly decent bars and restaurants (most are in La Macarena). Farther uptown and marked by towering office buildings is the Centro Internacional, the city's financial center. This modern development, built largely in the 1970s and now rather dated, is fringed by the Parque de la Independencia, a welcome area of green. The city becomes more stylish north of Calle 72 (Av. Chile), and 10 blocks farther in this direction is the leafy Zona Rosa, a popular boutique- and nightclub-filled district. As you tour the city, keep in mind that *carreras* (roads) run north–south and *calles* (streets) run east–west.

A Good Walk (or Two)

Begin your walk at **Plaza de Bolívar** ①, a historic square surrounded by stately buildings: to the east is the graceful Catedral Primada de Colombia, which is next door to the late-17th-century Capilla del Sagrario; to the north stands the Palacio de Justicia, rebuilt following its occupation by guerrillas in November 1985. And, at the plaza's southern end, the national Congress convenes in the grand 19th-century Capitolio Nacional. Cross Carrera 8, which runs along the square's western edge, and walk one block south to the **Iglesia Museo Santa Clara** ②. Continue south on Carrera 8, passing the main entrance of the **Palacio de Nariño** ③, on your left, to the **Museo de Artes y Tradiciones Populares** ④. From here, head two blocks east along Calle 7, and turn left on Carrera 6, where, one block north and on your left, you'll find the entrance to the **Museo Arqueológico** ⑤.

The Museo Arqueológico marks the proper entrance of La Candelaria, a historic neighborhood with colonial Spanish architecture and narrow streets. From the museum walk two blocks north to the **Museo de Arte Colonial** ⑥. Continue north to the corner, walk east one block, then turn left onto Carrera 5, and continue north another block to the **Casa de la Moneda** ⑦, the former mint. The modern building across the street is the **Biblioteca Luis Angel Arango** ⑧. Walk three blocks east to Carrera 2, turn left and walk two blocks to **La Plaza del Chorro del Quevedo** ⑨. From here, head downhill five blocks on Calle 13, and turn right onto Carrera 7. Walk two blocks to the **Iglesia de San Francisco** ⑩, continuing north a block farther to the **Iglesia de la Tercera Orden** ⑪. Across Carrera 7 from La Tercera, behind a small plaza, is a modern building that holds the **Museo de Oro** ⑫. If you're up for a walk of more than a kilometer, you can follow busy Avenida Jiménez east to the **Quinta de Bolívar** just below the cable car stop to the top of **Cerro de Monserrate.**

On another day, visit the compact Centro Internacional. Start your walk in the morning at the large, redbrick **Plaza de Toros Santamaría** ⑬, just north of Parque de la Independencia, at Calle 27. When you're done watching the bullfighters, head north to Calle 28 and Carrera 7, for the **Museo Nacional** ⑭, which resembles an ancient fortress. From here, turn left on Carrera 7, and walk three blocks south to the **Iglesia San Diego** ⑮. Cross Carrera 7 and walk south for two long blocks to Calle 24; turn left and walk up the block to **Museo de Arte Moderno** ⑯. On another day, plan an excursion to the former provincial capital of **Tunja.**

TIMING AND PRECAUTIONS

Take two days to see the sights on this tour, visiting Plaza de Bolívar and La Candelaria in one day, and Centro Internacional on another. Because you'll pass so many museums in La Candelaria, a good strategy is to start early in the day, paying only a quick visit to the sights, and returning to those that pique your interest. Note that many museums are closed on Monday. The altitude can wear you out, so allow yourself a leisurely pace on this 4 km (2.5 mi) walk—a sweep of the neighborhood may take four hours. A walk in Centro Internacional can easily be completed in a few hours. Mornings are best for glimpsing the bullfighters.

Be careful not to wander too far off track, since there are dangerous neighborhoods east of La Candelaria, above Carrera 2 and south of Calle 7. Also, avoid Plaza de Bolívar, La Candelaria, and El Centro after dark and on Sunday, when few people are about. Leave your valuables and documents in your hotel, take only the money you'll need for the day, and try to keep your camera out of sight.

SIGHTS TO SEE

⑧ ★ Biblioteca Luis Angel Arango. The Luis Angel Arango Cultural Center houses several museums, the most interesting of which is the **Museo de Arte Religioso** (Museum of Religious Art), with changing exhibits of colonial religious art. Don't miss its two spectacular gold processional crosses, the Tunja and the Lechuga; the latter is encrusted with 1,600 emeralds. ✉ *Calle 11 No. 4–92,* ☎ *091/286–4610.* ☞ *Free.* ☉ *Tues.–Sun.*

⑦ Casa de la Moneda. Colombia's former national mint has coins whose gold content was secretly reduced by the king of Spain, slugs made by revolutionaries from empty cartridges, and currency minted for use exclusively in Colombia's former leper colonies. ✉ *Calle 11 No. 4–93,* ☎ *091/343–1331.* ☞ *Admission.*

OFF THE BEATEN PATH

CERRO DE MONSERRATE – Although dense smog often obscures the skyline, the view of chaotic Bogotá stretching to the horizon from Monserrate Peak is still breathtaking. The panorama extends from the Río Bogotá to the colonial city, whose red Spanish tiles make it easy to spot, especially in the early morning when the sky is most clear. A *teleférico* (cable car) runs every half hour from Monserrate Station near Quinta de Bolívar to the peak weekdays 10–midnight and Sunday 10–4. The trip takes 15 minutes. Although an hour-long trek up a winding footpath will also get you to the top, attempt this only on Sunday, when the path is fairly busy; weekday robberies are all too common.

★ ② Iglesia Museo Santa Clara. The simple, unadorned facade of the 17th-century Church and Museum of Saint Clara gives no hint of the dazzling frescoes and wall reliefs—the work of nuns once cloistered here—that bathe the interior walls. The small museum has paintings and sculpture by various 17th-century artists. ✉ *Carrera 8 No. 8–91,* ☎ *091/337–6762 or 091/282–8759.* ☞ *Admission.* ☉ *Weekdays 9–1, 2–5; Sat. 9–4.*

⑮ Iglesia San Diego. This simple two-aisle church built by Franciscan monks in the early 17th century once stood on a quiet hacienda on the outskirts of colonial Bogotá; today trees and pastures have been replaced by the towering offices of Bogotá's "little Manhattan," the Centro Internacional. Both the church and its beautiful statue of the Virgin of the Fields, with her crown of intricate gold and silver filigree work, are a homage to the city's bucolic past. You can visit only during prayer services. ✉ *Carrera 7 No. 26–37,* ☎ *091/341–2476.* ☞ *Free.* ☉ *Sun.–Fri. 8, noon, 6, 6:30, 7, 7:30.*

⑩ Iglesia de San Francisco. The 16th-century Church of Saint Francis is famous for its fabulous Mudéjar interior, carved with intricate linear designs borrowed from Islamic tradition. Its huge gilded altar is shaped like an amphitheater and has shell-top niches. ✉ *Av. Jiménez at Carrera 7.*

⑪ Iglesia de la Tercera Orden. The altar's mahogany carvings at the Church of the Third Order are lauded as the most beautiful in Bogotá. A local myth claims that the completion of the altar so exhausted sculptor Pablo Caballero that he died a madman. ✉ *Carrera 7 at Calle 16.*

Bogotá

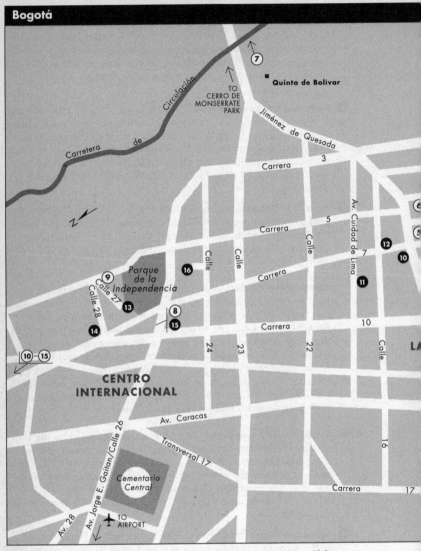

Exploring

Biblioteca Luis Angel Arango, **8**

Casa de la Moneda, **7**

Iglesia Museo Santa Clara, **2**

Iglesia San Diego, **15**

Iglesia de San Francisco, **10**

Iglesia de la Tercera Órden, **11**

Museo Arqueológico, **5**

Museo de Arte Colonial, **6**

Museo de Arte Moderno, **16**

Museo de Artes y Tradiciones Populares, **4**

Museo Nacional, **14**

Museo de Oro, **12**

Palacio de Nariño, **3**

Plaza de Bolívar, **1**

La Plaza del Chorro del Quevedo, **9**

Plaza de Toros Santamaría, **13**

Dining

Carbón de Palo, **11**

Casa Medina, **10**

Casa San Isidro, **7**

El Patio, **9**

La Fragata, **13**

Restaurante SEAP, **3**

Romana Cafetería, **5**

Lodging

Bogotá Royal, **12**

Hostería de la
Candelaria, **1**

Hotel Ambala, **4**

Hotel Internacional, **6**

Hotel de la Opera, **2**

Hotel Tequendama, **8**

Las Terrazas, **15**

Los Urapanes, **14**

⑤ Museo Arqueológico. This magnificent mansion, now the Museum of Archaeology, once belonged to the Marquís of San Jorge, a colonial viceroy famous for his cruelty. Today it displays a large collection of pre-Columbian ceramics. ⊠ *Carrera 6 No. 7–43,* ☎ *091/282–0940.* 🖃 *Admission.* ☉ *Tues.–Sat. 8–12 and 1–4:30; Sun. 10–1.*

⑥ Museo de Arte Colonial. In 1999, renovations helped to preserve this 17th-century Andalusian-style mansion, home of the Museum of Colonial Art. In its substantial collection are paintings by Vasquez and Figueroa, 17th- and 18th-century furniture, and precious metalwork. ⊠ *Carrera 6 No. 9–77,* ☎ *091/287–9113.* 🖃 *Admission.* ☉ *Tues.–Sun.*

⑯ Museo de Arte Moderno. The large windows in the beautifully designed Museum of Modern Art create a marvelous sense of interior spaciousness. Here, you can peruse the strong permanent collection of contemporary Colombian art; the changing exhibits of works by national and international artists; and the bookstore, which stocks a range of (rather pricey) English-language titles on Colombian and international painters. ⊠ *Calle 24 No. 6–00,* ☎ *091/283–3109.* 🖃 *Admission.* ☉ *Tues.–Sun.*

④ Museo de Artes y Tradiciones Populares. A former Augustinian cloister that dates from 1583, the Museum of Folk Art and Traditions is one of Bogotá's oldest surviving buildings and is undergoing an extensive renovation. Much of the building is closed until 2002, but a completed section has a range of contemporary crafts made by Indian artisans from across the country. Also open are a crafts shop and a good restaurant specializing in traditional Andean cooking. ⊠ *Carrera 8 No. 7–21,* ☎ *091/342–1266.* 🖃 *Admission.* ☉ *Tues.–Sat.*

⑭ Museo Nacional. The striking building that houses the National Museum was designed by the English architect Thomas Reed and was a prison until 1946; some parts of it, particularly the narrow top-floor galleries, still have a sinister air. Pre-Columbian artifacts through contemporary art are on display. Noteworthy are works by such well-known 19th- and 20th-century Colombian artists as Enrique Grau, Alejandro Obregón, Fernando Botero, and Andrés Santamaría. ⊠ *Carrera 7 No. 28–66, between Calles 28 and 29,* ☎ *091/334–8366.* 🖃 *Admission.* ☉ *Tues.–Sun.*

★ ⑫ Museo de Oro. Bogotá's phenomenal Gold Museum contains a comprehensive collection of pre-Columbian gold artifacts. The museum's more than 36,000 pieces (in weight alone worth $200 million) were culled over the centuries—often by force—from indigenous cultures, including the Muisca, Nariño, Calima, and Sinú. Don't dismiss these as merely primitive; these works represent virtually all the techniques of modern goldsmithing today. Most of the gold, and perhaps the largest uncut emerald in the world, is in the top-floor strong room. Tours in English are at 10:15 AM, and individual English audio tours are available for $2.50. ⊠ *Carrera 6A No. 15–82,* ☎ *091/342–1111, ext. 1417 or 1224.* 🖃 *Admission.* ☉ *Tues.–Sun.*

③ Palacio de Nariño. The Presidential Palace had to be rebuilt in 1949 following its destruction during the Bogotazo, a popular uprising sparked by Liberal populist Gaitán's assassination. Although it's not open to the public, outside the guard is changed ceremoniously each day at 5 PM. ⊠ *Carrera 7 between Calles 7 and 8.*

① Plaza de Bolívar. This large plaza surrounded by stately structures marks the spot where Bogotá was formally founded in the presence of Spanish potentates several centuries ago. Today it's popular with photographers snapping pictures, unemployed men intermittently snoozing and chatting, street theater groups performing for a peso, and children who never seem to grow bored with chasing pigeons.

On the plaza's east side, the **Catedral Primada de Colombia** (The Cathedral of the Primate of Colombia) was completed three centuries after construction began in 1565 due to a series of misfortunes—including the disastrous earthquake of 1785. Its French baroque facade is made from locally mined sandstone, and the large windows give the immense interior a light, airy feel, even on one of Bogotá's many gray rainy-season days. The ornate altar with gold leaf over heavily carved wood contrasts with the lack of ornamentation elsewhere. In one of the side chapels lies Quesada's tomb. It's open Monday through Saturday. Next door is the exquisite baldachino altar in **Capilla del Sagrario**, open daily, a smaller version of that found at St. Peter's in Rome. The Sanctuary Chapel also has a splendid collection of paintings, including works by the Taller de Figueroa and Gregorio Vasquez. The Capitolio Nacional and the Palacio de Justicia are not open to the public. ⊠ *Between Carreras 7 and 8 at Calle 10.*

⑨ La Plaza del Chorro del Quevedo. This is where Quesada and his soldiers celebrated the founding of Bogotá on August 6, 1538. A small fountain here recalls the "Chorro del Quevedo," the brook where the conquistadors quenched their thirst and that today has been prosaically confined to subterranean drainage pipes. ⊠ *Carrera 2 at Calle 13.*

⑬ Plaza de Toros Santamaría. Bogotá's bullring was designed by Rogelio Salmona in a traditional Andalusian style. For a free peek, the best time to visit is in the morning, when you may see young *toreros* (bullfighters) polishing their skills. Bullfighting season is January through February, but small fights are held throughout the year. Check with your hotel for a schedule. The **Museo Taurino** here has exhibits devoted to the sport. ⊠ *Carrera 7 at Calle 26,* ☎ *no phone.* ⊡ *Admission.* ☉ *Mon.–Sat. mornings.*

OFF THE
BEATEN PATH

QUINTA DE BOLÍVAR – Simón Bolívar, the revolutionary hero who drove the Spanish from the northern half of the continent, passed the last years of his life in this rustic house with his mistress, Manuela Saenz. Built in 1800, it was donated to Bolívar in 1820 for his services to the fledgling republic. The house has a distinct Spanish flavor and a lovely garden. García Márquez's befitting novel, *The General in His Labyrinth* (1989), portrays Bolívar's final years. ⊠ *Calle 20 No. 2–91,* ☎ *091/284–6819.* ⊡ *Admission.* ☉ *Tues.–Sun.*

TUNJA – The capital of Boyacá province was founded in 1539 by Captain Gonzalo Suárez Rendón. Although modern Tunja is infested with industrial complexes and shantytowns, the historic center retains some of its original colonial character, with its stately churches and pre-republic mansions. Be sure to visit **Casa del Fundador Suárez Rendón** (⊠ Plaza Bolívar), with a small museum devoted to Tunja's founder. **Casa de Don Juan de Vargas** (⊠ Calle 20 near Carrera 8; closed Mon.) exhibits colonial artwork. Don Juan was a scribe, and his large library of art books probably inspired the imagery on the ceiling frescoes. Tunja lies 137 km (85 mi) northeast of Bogotá. Buses depart regularly from Bogotá's Terminal de Transporte, and the three- to four-hour ride costs less than $4 each way.

Dining

Bogotá's phone book lists more than 1,000 restaurants, and the best offer first-class service and outstanding Colombian cuisine. The most traditional recipes aim to fill the belly and ward off the cold. Soups, such as ajiaco and *puchero* (with chicken, pork, beef, potato, yucca, cabbage, corn, and plantain and accompanied by rice and avocado) are common on local menus. Bogotaños like to start the day off with *santafereño*, a steaming cup of chocolate accompanied by a slab of cheese—you melt the cheese in the chocolate. Lunch is generally served between noon and 2. Restaurants open for dinner around 7, and the more expensive ones stay open until after midnight.

Colombian

$$ ✕ Carbón de Palo. Bogotá's premier grilled-meat restaurant is a favorite north-end meeting place of senior politicians and plutocrats. The menu is dominated by grilled steak, chicken, and pork—but excellent salads are served with great aplomb. Choose a seat in the delightful indoor patio full of hanging plants. On weekends, musicians serenade you with traditional Colombian music. ⊠ *Calle 106 No. A–60A,* ☎ *091/214–5482. AE, DC, MC, V.*

$$ ✕ Restaurante SEAP. This lovely colonial mansion just steps from the
★ Plaza de Bolívar dates from 1650 and is now owned by a local non-profit organization, the Sociedad Economica de Amigos del Pais, comprised of liberal-minded politicians and citizens. (Conservatives are also welcome.) SEAP's clientele and elegant dining rooms make it a bit formal for a lunch-only place: politicians and businessmen regularly fill the tables that overlook a small courtyard and a garden shaded by large trees. The menu has such Colombian favorites as cazuela de mariscos or *sobrebarriga en salsa* (flank steak in red sauce), and typical desserts such as *cuajada con melao* (white cheese in sweet sauce). ⊠ *Calle 11 No. 6–42,* ☎ *091/336–5849. DC, MC, V. Closed Sun. No dinner.*

Eclectic

$–$$ ✕ Romana Cafetería. This Candalaria spot is particularly good for a breakfast of Colombian hot chocolate with cheese and bread. Later in the day, pasta dishes are a solid choice. ⊠ *Av. Jiménez No. 6–65,* ☎ *091/334–8135. DC, MC, V. Closed Sun.*

French

$$$$ ✕ Casa Medina. Chef José Ovalle prepares such outstanding French
★ dishes as medallions of trout smothered in fennel and onion or coquilles St. Jacques (scallops) with asparagus. Each of the elegant dining rooms evokes a different European country, strewn as they are with Old World antiques imported by aristocratic Bogotaño families. ⊠ *Carrera 7 No. 69A–22,* ☎ *091/217–0288. AE, DC, MC, V.*

Italian

$–$$ ✕ El Patio. None of the cutlery or plates match, and the small dining room is a little cramped. But this simply adds to the restaurant's eccentric charm as does its location a couple blocks from the bullring, in the bohemian La Macarena neighborhood. Try one of the masterful salads or the veal parmigiana. ⊠ *Carrera 4A No. 27–86,* ☎ *091/ 282–6141. V. Closed Sun.*

Seafood

$$$$ ✕ Casa San Isidro. This French seafood restaurant with white-glove
★ service is worth the trip for the setting alone. Perched 2,000 ft (610 m) over Bogotá and accessed by teleférico, you'll dine fireside to the tunes of a grand piano. Fortunately, the food also warrants a visit. Try the San Isidro lobster with squid and shrimp. Isidro also has a choice of good wines from nearly 10 countries. But be sure to leave by midnight, Cinderella, when the last cable car returns to the streets below. ⊠ *Cerro de Monserrate,* ☎ *091/281–9270 or 091/281–9309. AE, DC, MC, V. Closed Sun.*

$$$$ ✕ **La Fragata.** With its slowly revolving dining room, this is probably the most striking of the capital's Fragata chain restaurants. Somehow the dimly lit, dark-oak interior successfully conveys the atmosphere of a 19th-century frigate. The lobster, crab, red snapper, and locally caught rainbow trout are satisfying but slightly overshadowed by the service and presentation. ⊠ *Calle 100 No. 8A–55, 12th floor,* ☎ *091/616–7461. AE, MC, V. Closed Sun.*

Lodging

Bogotá's better hotels are in the wealthy northern districts—undoubtedly among the most alluring parts of the city, and also the safest (there are security guards quite literally on every corner). If you want to soak up the color of the picturesque Old City, or are on a tight budget, book a room in La Candelaria. No matter where you stay, avoid wandering the streets at night.

$$$$ 🏨 **Bogotá Royal.** In addition to modern rooms—with good views, sofas, and cable TV—the Royal has a business center and a small health club. It's in Bogotá's World Trade Center in the north end of town, a short taxi ride from the airport and many offices, but it's far from most museums and other attractions. ⊠ *Av. 100 No. 8A–01,* ☎ *091/218–9810,* FAX *091/218–3261. 143 rooms. 2 restaurants, 2 bars, sauna, exercise room. AE, DC, MC, V.*

$$$$ 🏨 **Hotel Tequendama.** One of Bogotá's oldest and most refined hotels is now part of the Inter-Continental chain. Its medium-size rooms lack real character, but they have impressive city views. The hotel is in the Centro International, conveniently close to the Candelaria district and most downtown offices. ⊠ *Carrera 10 No. 26–21,* ☎ *091/286–1111,* FAX *091/282–2860. 650 rooms. 3 restaurants, 2 bars, room service, beauty salon, sauna, exercise room, casino. AE, DC, MC, V.*

$$$–$$$$ 🏨 **Los Urapanes.** At this intimate hotel in the heart of the leafy Zona
★ Rosa, you stay in modest but luxurious suites with full room service and a minibar. The adjoining restaurant is popular for its exquisitely presented Colombian and international cuisine. ⊠ *Carrera 13 No. 83–19,* ☎ *091/218–1188,* FAX *091/218–1242. 32 rooms. Restaurant, bar, minibars, room service. AE, DC, MC, V.*

$$$ 🏨 **Hotel de la Opera.** This colonial building in La Candelaria was ren-
★ ovated and opened in 1998 as an elegant hotel. The tile and polished hardwood floors are remarkable, and the furniture is imported from Italy as is the cuisine at the hotel's restaurant, La Scala. In-room phones and remote-control TVs with lots of channels work flawlessly. The service is particularly attentive. ⊠ *Calle 10 No. 5–72,* ☎ *091/336–2066,* FAX *091/337–4617. 28 rooms. Restaurant, minibars, room service. AE, DC, MC, V.*

$$ 🏨 **Hostería de la Candelaria.** Easily the city's most charming hotel, this
★ friendly lodging occupies two colonial houses. Rooms—which open onto lovely courtyards—have thick adobe walls, high ceilings, antiques, and small baths. The Cafe de Rosita here serves an excellent lunch special that's usually a traditional Colombian dish; it's closed evenings and Monday. ⊠ *Calle 9 No. 3–11,* ☎ *091/342–1727,* FAX *091/352–0173. 14 rooms. Restaurant. No credit cards.*

$$ 🏨 **Las Terrazas.** Although it's downtown, this small hotel has a rustic
★ appeal because it's built into the hillside overlooking the city. The scrupulously clean rooms have good views of downtown and come in various sizes. A respectable adjoining restaurant serves Bogotá specialties as well as standard international fare. ⊠ *Calle 54A No. 3–12,* ☎ *091/255–5400 or 091/255–5966,* FAX *091/255–6834. 33 rooms. Restaurant, room service. AE, DC, MC, V.*

¢–$ ⊞ **Hotel Ambala.** Rooms in this small, economy inn are cramped, but they're clean and comfortable. They also have plenty of amenities for the money: firm beds, phones, TVs, and lots of hot water. Rooms on the street are brighter, but can be noisy. ⊠ *Carrera 5 No. 13–46,* ☎ *091/341–2376,* FAX *091/286–3693. 30 rooms. No credit cards.*

¢ ⊞ **Hotel Internacional.** If you're on a tight budget, this north-end Candelaria hotel is a good bet. Worn rugs distract from the high ceilings, but rooms are clean, and most have private bathrooms with hot water. Useful maps line the lobby walls. ⊠ *Carrera 5 No. 14–45,* ☎ *091/341–3151. 18 rooms, 12 with bath. No credit cards.*

Nightlife and the Arts

Nightlife

Bogotá's deserved reputation for random violence and muggings hasn't put a damper on its ebullient nightlife, which often lasts well beyond sunrise. The two main partying areas are the Zona Rosa, between Calles 81 and 84 and Carreras 11 and 15, and La Calera in the city's affluent north end. Downtown, at the intersection of Carrera 5 and Calle 27, there's also a handful of popular salsa bars. Zona Rosa and La Calera are full of security guards and are quite safe. Less so is the lively, bohemian downtown district, La Macarena, though you should travel by taxi and avoid wandering alone or aimlessly anywhere.

BARS AND NIGHTCLUBS

Arcanos, in the Normandia neighborhood (⊠ Ave. Boyaca No. 48–49, ☎ 091/251–7726), has live acoustic Latin folk music most evenings, and there's no cover. **Charlotte's** (⊠ Calle 82 No. 12–51, ☎ 091/257–3508) is a busy Zona Rosa nightclub, with an outdoor dance floor and blazing log fires to keep you warm. **Coconuts** (⊠ Calle 82 No. 12–50, ☎ 091/257–2006), on the edge of Zona Rosa, is really a restaurant impersonating a nightclub—the huge patio overlooking the street is a popular spot for drinks and chitchat.

The Arts

THEATERS

Bogotá has a lively theater scene, though you must understand Spanish to appreciate it. **Teatro la Candelaria** (⊠ Calle 12 No. 2–59, ☎ 091/281–4814) has been producing experimental theater for more than a decade. **Teatro Nacional** (⊠ Calle 71 No. 10–25, ☎ 091/217–6663) puts on musicals and popular comedies. Tickets can be purchased in advance at the box office.

Outdoor Activities and Sports

Bullfighting

Bullfights are held every Sunday in January and February and at least once a month the rest of the year at the **Plaza de Santamaría,** near Parque de la Independencia. Tickets can be bought on site just before the fight—prices range from affordable to hundreds of dollars for some fights.

Soccer

Soccer or *futbol* matches are held on most Sundays at 3:45 PM and Wednesdays at 8 PM at the **Estadio Municipal** (Municipal Stadium, ⊠ Calle 63 at Carrera 50), near the Hipódromo del Techo. **El Campín** stadium (⊠ Carrera 30, between Calles 53 and 63), named for the neighborhood in which it's located, also hosts matches. There's no need to book ahead except when there's a match between the two most popular local teams—Santa Fé and Millionarios. Tickets are cheap and can be purchased just before a match.

Shopping

Bogotá's shops and markets stock all types of leather and pure wool goods appropriate for life on the high plains. Handwoven *ruanas* (ponchos) are particularly popular; the oil in the wool makes them almost impervious to rain. Colombian artisans also have a way with straw: *toquilla,* a tough native fiber, is used to make a dizzying variety of hats, shoes, handbags, and even umbrellas.

Markets

In the warren of stalls at the daily **Pasaje Rivas** market (⊠ Carrera 10 at Calle 10) look for bargain-priced ponchos, blankets, leather goods, and crafts. The **Mercado de Pulgas,** a weekly flea market that sprawls northward along Carrera 3 from Calle 19, is a good place for bargain hunting on Sunday. Consider taking a taxi, and don't linger after dark: the surrounding neighborhood has an unsavory reputation.

Shopping Center

The massive **Unicentro Shopping Center** (⊠ Av. 15 No. 123–30, ☎ 091/ 213–8800) in Bogotá's affluent north is one of South America's largest air-conditioned malls and has a huge selection of shops.

Specialty Shops

ANTIQUES

Antiques shops are found mainly in the northern districts of Chapinero and Chicó. One of the best is **Medina's** (⊠ Carrera 7 at Calle 50). **Maria Cancino** (⊠ Calle 63 No. 9–54, ☎ 091/249–5454) is good for both Colombian antiques and European pieces. A good bet for quality antiques is **Jaime Botero's** (⊠ Calle 10 No. 2–57, ☎ 091/342–9070), in the 17th-century La Toma de Agua building in La Candelaria.

EMERALDS

Seventy percent of the world's emerald supply is mined in Colombia, but, unless you know how to spot a fake, you should buy only from reputable dealers, who provide certificates of authenticity. The bright, meadow-green Colombian emerald is the second most valuable variety next to the darker, Old India emerald, which are no longer culled and can only be found in museums or private collections. Value depends on weight, color, clarity, brilliance, and cut, with octagonal cuts being the most valuable. If you're really serious about emeralds start at the **Emerald Trade Center** on the corner of Avenida Jimeneæz and Carrera 5. Inside are nearly 50 reputable dealers and jewelry shops. There are also countless jewelry shops south of the center mostly along Carreras 6 and 7. **Kawai** (⊠ Calle 100 No. 8A–37, ☎ 1/618–3070) is an established north-end jeweler. **H. Stern** (⊠ Tequendama Hotel, Carrera 10 No. 26–2, ☎ 1/283–2819) sells gold and gems.

HANDICRAFTS

In the cloister of Las Aquas, a neighborhood just off La Candelaria, at the base of Monserrate, **Artesanías de Colombia** (⊠ Carrera 3 No. 18–60, ☎ 091/286–1766) stocks an excellent variety of high-quality, handmade crafts—from straw umbrellas to handwoven ponchos. The shop at the **Museo de Artes y Tradiciones Populares** (⊠ Carrera 8 No. 7–21, ☎ 091/342–1266) carries many hand-made items.

POTTERY

Pottery can be found in many Centro Internacional shops. **Precolombianos San Diego** (⊠ Carrera 10 No. 26–50, ☎ 091/342–3200), near the Hotel Tequendama, sells reproductions of pre-Columbian ceramic pieces and other artifacts.

Bogotá A to Z

Arriving and Departing

BY AIRPLANE

Aeropuerto El Dorado (☎ 091/413–9500), a 20-minute taxi ride northwest of downtown, is served by American, Continental, and Copa (Panama), as well as all major domestic carriers, including Avianca, Intercontinental de Aviación, Aces, AIRES, and SAM.

BY BUS

The massive **Terminal de Transportes** (✉ Calle 33B No. 69–13, ☎ 091/295–1100) looks more like an airport than a bus station. It's served by all major bus companies (and plenty of thieves, so watch your bags). Buses depart for other major cities about every hour. For Quito or Caracas, departures are usually daily and often require a connection near the border. To reach the station, take a taxi from downtown for around $6. **Copetrán** (☎ 091/263–2102) is a dependable carrier for coastal destinations. For Medellín and Cali, you can contact **Flota Magdalena** (☎ 091/295–0651), **Flota La Macarena** (☎ 091/295–0539 or 091/295–1602), or **Expresso Bolívariano** (☎ 091/261–0988).

Getting Around

Although other options exist, taxis or hired cars with drivers are recommended for getting around Bogotá safely.

BY BUS

Buses, mainly noisy, ancient, and driven at top speed, are divided into two categories: *busetas,* which cost 450 pesos (30¢) per ride, and the larger and more comfortable *ejecutivos,* which cost 800 pesos (60¢) per ride. Buses 7, 13, and 15 cross the city from north to south along carreras of the same numbers.

BY CAR

Before you rent a car, you should consider whether it's absolutely necessary. Cars, which indicate wealth, may put you at risk and be a source of anxiety rather than a convenience. It may be more useful to take taxis or hire a driver for a day of sightseeing.

The main international car-rental companies in Bogotá include **Avis** (✉ El Dorado airport, ☎ 091/414–8278; ✉ Av. 15 No. 101–45, ☎ 091/610–4455), **Hertz** (✉ El Dorado airport, ☎ 091/413–9302; ✉ Av. 15 No. 107–24, ☎ 091/214–9745), and **National** (✉ Carrera 15 No. 93–47, ☎ 091/621–1173 or 091/620–0055).

BY COLECTIVO

A *colectivo* is a small bus that is often able to get through traffic jams better than a regular bus. They travel the same routes as buses, and cost the same as ejecutivos, but are a good deal more cramped.

BY TAXI

Taxis are required by law to have meters—make sure they're used. The minimum charge is 700 pesos (45¢), plus 10 pesos per 260 ft (80 m). Fares increase by 30% after dark; a list of surcharges should be displayed. Taxis with bilingual drivers can be hired by the hour or for a full day at the Hotel Tequendama (☞ Lodging, *above*).

Contacts and Resources

BANKS AND CURRENCY EXCHANGE

Your hotel is probably the most convenient place to exchange money, although **Banco de la República** (✉ Carrera 7 No. 14–78) is open weekdays 9 to 3 and takes a slightly lower cut. Several banks on Carrera 10, near the Hotel Tequendama, will also exchange money.

Ambulance: Cruz Roja (Red Cross) ☎ 132. **Police:** ☎ 156 or call the tourist police (✉ Carrera 13 No. 26–62, ☎ 286–8111, ext. 376 or 337–4413, ext. 112). **Hospitals and pharmacies:** Clinica San Pedro Claver (✉ Calle 24 No. 29–61, ☎ 268–9000).

MAIL
Stamps are sold at stores and hotels. The **post office** (✉ Carrera 7 No. 16–36) is open roughly 9 to noon and 2 to 5.

TOUR OPERATOR
The **Tierra Mar y Aire** (✉ Carrera 10 No. 27–91, Local 1–26, ☎ 091/283–2955) travel agency, which is also the American Express office, has day and night bus tours of Bogotá, for about $25 per person. It's closed weekends. ☞ For trips to Colombia's islands, *see* Carnaval Tours *in* San Andrés and Providencia A to Z, *below*.

VISITOR INFORMATION
The **Corporación Nacional de Turismo** (✉ Edificio del Centro de Comercio International, Calle 28 No. 13A–15, ground floor, Local 4, ☎ 091/284–3761) has information on hotels, restaurants, and sights. For maps and general information visit **Fondo de Promocísion Turistica** (✉ Calle 90 No. 18–35, ☎ 091/616–6874).

MEDELLÍN

Nestled in the narrow Aburrá Valley, this northwestern city of 2 million is the capital of Antioquia Province. In this fertile, mountainous region, the adobe walls and barrel tiles of traditional farm houses dot the lush landscape.

Successful coffee and textile industries have enabled Medellín to prosper; today it's the second-largest city in Colombia and a busy Latin American convention center. It's modern and relatively affluent, with wide, tree-lined boulevards, plenty of skyscrapers, three respected universities, and a hard-working middle class. And, unlike Bogotá, it enjoys a spring-like climate year-round. But Medellín is also home to thousands of impoverished citizens, whose shanties appear on the city's edges, and the eponymous drug cartel led, until recently, by the notorious kingpin, Pablo Escobar. Although local and international intervention has lessened the drug mafia and their trading practices, the city remains violent and unpredictable. Exercise caution when touring Medellín day or night, and always stick to central areas.

Exploring Medellín

Medellín is Colombia's main industrial beehive, but don't expect a sooty city full of smoking chimneys: the factories are well out of town. Deep-green mountains that rise sharply around the city provide a bold backdrop to the glass-and-concrete towers of its elegant financial district. Poor neighborhoods climb the surrounding city slopes and should be avoided because of the gangs that lurk here. Yet, well-developed tourist facilities in the city proper testify to the region's relative economic strength. When visiting sights, remember that calles run east–west and carreras, north–south.

A Good Walk

Begin downtown at **Parque de Bolívar,** to the north of which stands the massive **Catedral Basilica Metropolitana.** Walk south from the park along the Pasaje Junin pedestrian mall to Calle 51, turn right and walk a block to **Parque Berrío.** Two blocks farther west on Calle 51 is the 18th-century **Ermita de la Veracruz,** next to which is the **Museo**

de Antioquia. From here, hail a taxi (and rest your feet) to the peak of Cerro Nutibara (Nutibara Hill) for an excellent view of downtown. At the very top is **Pueblito Paisa** and the surrounding **Parque de las Esculturas.** Have your taxi wait while you explore, then take it to the **Museo El Castillo,** in the affluent El Poblado neighborhood, which also has some of the city's best restaurants. Finish your tour at the **Jardín Botánico Joaquín Antonio Uribe,** also accessible by taxi.

TIMING AND PRECAUTIONS

Your walking tour of the downtown sites could be completed in less than a half hour, not including forays into the churches and the Museo de Antioquia. Visits to farther flung attractions take several hours, including taxi trips. Visiting everything on this tour will take a full day. Only attempt this tour during the day, and take precautions before you embark to reduce your risk of being robbed or confronted.

Sights to See

Catedral Basílica Metropolitana. The Metropolitan Cathedral, whose ornate coffee-color facade overlooks the Parque de Bolívar, is among Medellín's most striking buildings. Designed by the French architect Charles Carré and built in 1875, it's South America's largest cathedral and the third-largest brick building in the world. ⊠ *Carrera 49 No. 44–56.* ☺ *Free.* ☺ *Tues.–Sun.*

Ermita de la Veracruz. Distinguishing the temperate interior of the Veracruz Hermitage are its white walls and columns with gilded capitals. Just off a picturesque plaza, it's also a quiet escape from Medellín's noisy streets. ⊠ *Carrera 52 at Calle 51.* ☺ *Free.*

Jardín Botánico Joaquín Antonio Uribe. The botanical gardens have more than 500 native plant species, an aviary with strikingly colored tropical birds, and a huge greenhouse teeming with orchids. ⊠ *Carrera 52 No. 73–298,* ☎ *094/233–7025.* ☺ *Admission.* ☺ *Daily 9–5.*

Museo de Antioquia. The Antioquia Provincial Museum contains the world's largest collection of paintings and sculptures by Fernando Botero (1932–) and other well-known Colombian artists. Thematically, Botero's artwork interprets pre-Columbian history from a distinctly Latin-American standpoint—Colombians affectionately refer to him as "the man who paints fat people." Although his work is known internationally, its appeal and access to "ordinary people" is always an important component. ⊠ *Carrera 52A No. 51A–29,* ☎ *094/251–3636.* ☺ *Admission.* ☺ *Tues.–Sat.*

Museo El Castillo. The 1930s Gothic-inspired Castle Museum, whose beautiful French-style gardens comprise sweeping lawns and exuberant flower beds, was once the home of a powerful Medellín family. On display is their furniture and art collected from around the world. ⊠ *Calle 9 Sur No. 32–269,* ☎ *094/266–0900.* ☺ *Admission.* ☺ *Daily 9–noon, 2–5.*

Parque Berrío. This small cement plaza is overwhelmed by the city's elevated modern metro, the only one of its kind in Colombia. Nearby is the colonial church of **Nuestra Señora de la Candelaria.** To the south, the Banco de la República building stands next to a huge female torso sculpted by Fernando Botero, who wanted to make his work publicly accessible. On the bank's other side, a bronze fountain and marble monument honor Atanasio Girardot, an 18th-century champion for Colombian independence. ⊠ *Carrera 50, between Calles 50 and 51.*

Parque de Bolívar. Despite its central location this shady park has a generous amount of open space. In the evenings, it's popular with young people, who congregate on the steps of the nearby cathedral.

Parque de las Esculturas. This small Sculpture Park near Nutibara Hill's peak is a maze of paths dotted with modern and traditional sculptures by Latin American artists.

Pueblito Paisa. As you enter this reproduction of an old-time Antioquian village, you'll see a traditional town square with a small church, town hall, barbershop, school, and village store. For your present needs, it also has a small restaurant and several souvenir shops.

OFF THE
BEATEN PATH

SANTA FÉ DE ANTIOQUIA – Eighty km (50 mi) northwest of Medellín is the province's former capital, Santa Fé de Antioquia. Founded in 1541, the town is now a well-preserved colonial showpiece, with cobbled streets and old whitewashed houses. It's particularly well known for its *orfebrería* (gold work). Visit the workshops on Carrera 10 between the cathedral and the Bogotá River. There are daily buses from Medellín's Terminal de Transporte, although a taxi can be hired to take up to four people for about $50 round-trip.

Dining

Traditional Antioquian cooking means hearty peasant fare—plenty of meat, beans, rice, and potatoes. But Medellín is full of high-quality restaurants where you'll find a range of cuisines. On the first Saturday of every month, the **Parque de las Delicias** (⊠ Carrera 73 and Av. 39D) is packed with food stalls selling everything from *obleas* (thin jam-filled waffles) to *lechona* (roast stuffed pork).

Colombian

$$ ★ × **El Hato Viejo.** Large portions draw locals to this second story restaurant, just a block from the Parque de Bolívar. Waiters in Panama hats serve you on a plant-filled balcony or in the large dining room with terracotta floors. Try the *sopa de guineo* (plantain soup) before sinking your teeth into *lomito* (tenderloin) or *langostinos* (lobsters). Finish your feast with *brevas con queso* (figs with white cheese). (El Hato Viejo has another location at the Inter-Continental Hotel, *see* Lodging, *below*). ⊠ *Pasaje Junin No. 52–170,* ☎ *094/251-2196. AE, DC, MC, V.*

$ × **Aguas Claras.** Here you can experience a variety of Colombian dishes in one meal. The hearty *plato típico* is a sampling of 10 different items, including four kinds of meat. The lighter *plato del cura* (priest's plate) is a complete meal of soup, beef, rice, and bread for about $5. The nicest tables are on the balcony, which overlooks the popular Pasaje Junin shopping mall. ⊠ *Pasaje Junin No. 52–141,* ☎ *094/231–6642. AE, DC, MC, V.*

International

$$$–$$$$ × **Las Cuatro Estaciones.** Medellín's most popular restaurant combines first-rate food and service with decor that borders on the tacky. Choose one of four thematic dining rooms—decorated in Colombian, European, Asian, and Spanish styles—then keep your eyes on your plate and concentrate on the meal at hand. The house specialties are seafood and paella. ⊠ *Calle 16 No. 43–79, El Poblado,* ☎ *094/266–7120. AE, DC, MC, V.*

Lodging

There are some high-quality hotels downtown, near most of the city's attractions, but you should avoid walking around here at night.

$$$$ 🏨 **Inter-Continental.** This modern hotel in the hills outside Medellín has spectacular city views and all the services you would expect from an upscale international chain. It's about 20 minutes by taxi from the

city center and 40 minutes from the airport. ✉ *Variante Las Palmas,* ☎ *094/266–0680, 800/327–0200 in the U.S.,* ☏ *094/266–1548. 294 rooms. 2 restaurants, bar, pool, massage, sauna, tennis court, exercise room, casino, dance club. AE, DC, MC, V.*

$$–$$$ ⌶ **Hotel Nutibara.** The Nutibara is a stylish 1940s-era building replete with a casino and heated indoor pool. Rooms in the newer Residencias building across the street have less personality, but cost half of those in the main building. From the hotel's downtown location, it's a short taxi ride to restaurants and bars. ✉ *Calle 52A No. 50–46,* ☎ *094/511–5111,* ☏ *094/231–3713. 90 rooms. Restaurant, bar, café, pool, hot tub, casino, dance club. AE, DC, MC, V.*

$ ⌶ **La Bella Villa.** Just a few blocks from Parque de Bolívar, this hotel has five floors of modern (circa 1993) rooms with white tile floors, small bathrooms, cable TV, and tacky pictures. All rooms surround a covered courtyard. ✉ *Calle 53 No. 50–28,* ☎ *094/511–0144,* ☏ *094/512–9477. 50 rooms. Restaurant, sauna. DC, MC, V.*

Shopping

Medellín's **Centro Commercial San Diego** mall (✉ Calle 12 No. 30–5) has crafts, jewelry, and clothing shops. You'll find souvenir shops at **Pueblito Paisa,** atop Cerro Nutibara. Check the outdoor-market stalls on **Pasaje Junin,** just south of Parque de Bolívar, for handicrafts. For Antioquian crafts, visit the **open-air crafts market,** held on the first Saturday of every month at the Parque de Bolívar.

Medellín A to Z

Arriving and Departing

BY AIRPLANE

Medellín's **Aeropuerto Jose Maria Córdoba,** (☎ 094/562–2885), 38 km (24 mi) southeast of the city, is served by **Aces** (☎ 094/261–2020), **Avianca** (☎ 094/251–2093), **COPA** (☎ 094/511–4660), and **SAM** (☎ 094/251–5544). The flight to Bogotá takes 45 minutes and costs about $165; to Cali, it's 50 minutes and costs about $110; to Cartagena, it's an hour and 15 minutes and costs about $190.

From the Airport. From the airport to downtown, it's about $12 for a taxi, and $3 for a colectivo. Tickets are sold at the central booth, and there's a stop outside each airport exit. The trip takes 45 minutes.

BY BUS

Medellín has two bus stations: the **Terminal de Transporte del Notre,** (☎ 094/230–8514), for buses to Bogotá and the Caribbean coast, and the **Terminal de Transporte del Sur** (☎ 094/361–1499), for buses to Cali and Ecuador. Both terminals are large and modern with shops, cafés, and information desks. It's a 10-hour ride to Bogotá, 9 hours to Cali, and 13 hours to Cartagena.

BY CAR

Car travel is not particularly safe, but if you must drive, note the following. A paved, two-lane highway connects Bogotá and Medellín via Manizales and Honda. The 560-km (347-mi) journey takes about nine hours. West of Bogotá, the Pan-American Highway descends into the stifling heat of the Tierras Calientes, or hot lands, of the Magdalena Valley. Continuing southwest, the landscape becomes mountainous as you approach the Andean Cordillera Central and Medellín. Although this is one of Colombia's major cocaine routes, the road is generally well patrolled. Watch for landslides in wet weather, and expect detours and potholes on the Honda–Medellín leg.

Getting Around

Medellín has an excellent transportation system, comprising buses, colectivos, and a modern **Metro,** an elevated train opened in 1995 with two lines: one running north–south, the other east–west. There are also plenty of taxis that are easily hailed, which charge about $3 to either of the bus stations.

Contacts and Resources

BANKS AND CURRENCY EXCHANGE

Banco de la República (⊠ Parque Berrio, near the intersection of Carrera 50 and Calle 50) is open 9–3.

EMERGENCIES

Ambulance: Cruz Roja (Red Cross) ☎ 125. **Police:** ☎ 156 or call local information ☎ 113 and ask for emergency assistance. **Hospitals and pharmacies:** Clinica Medellín (⊠ Calle 53 No. 38–46, ☎ 511–6044) or Hospital Pablo Tobón Uribe (⊠ Calle 78B No. 69–240, ☎ 441–5252).

MAIL

Post office: ⊠ Carrera 52 No. 51A–01.

TOUR OPERATORS

You can arrange local, private tours with **Tierra Mar Aire** (⊠ Calle 52 No. 43–124, ☎ 094/512–0922), which is also the American Express office. Or, call **Abanico Tours** (⊠ Calle 48D No. 65A–46, ☎ 094/230–3222) and talk with Ana Olavia about a personalized tour.

VISITOR INFORMATION

The **Oficina de Turismo** (⊠ Calle 57 No. 45–129, ☎ 094/254–0800) has a good city map but little else.

THE SOUTHWEST

Tucked in the fertile Valle de Cauca (Cauca Valley), Cali is a lively provincial capital and an important agricultural center. Visitors come for its Indian markets, its colonial architecture, and, more recently, for its burgeoning café culture. Farther south, where the Pan-American Highway climbs into the Andes, is Popayán—a city which approximates Cartagena in its colonial appeal. The highland region surrounding Popayán has traditional indigenous communities, snowcapped volcanoes, and two important pre-Columbian sites.

Cali

Cali is the economic center of Valle Province, responsible for a hefty portion of the country's sugar, coffee, and maize exports. The city's elevation of 915 m (3,000 ft) contributes to the year-round spring-like temperature and the tropical vegetation that encroaches upon Cali's shantytown outskirts. Within the rapidly expanding city (it has grown fourfold in the past 40 years) you'll find many green areas, a small colonial quarter, and the muddy Río Cali. Its tree-lined avenues and lazy open-air cafés make it an attractive stop, particularly during the Christmas–New Year *feria,* when the city unapologetically devotes itself to merrymaking. Like Medellín, however, Cali is still a difficult city to enjoy wholeheartedly; the prevalence of violence and crime require you to be cautious at all times.

A Good Walk

Begin your tour at **Paseo de Bolívar,** a large park on the Río Cali's north bank. Cross the bridge, over this muddy river, to the **Iglesia de la Ermita** on the other side. From here, continue one block south on Calle 11 to the **Plaza de Caicedo,** which is surrounded by such monuments as the **Catedral Metropolitana** and the **Palacio Nacional.** From the cathedral, walk south one block on Calle 11, turn right on Carrera 6, and walk one block west to the church of **San Francisco.** Follow Carrera 6 two blocks west to Calle 7, turn right, and walk two blocks north to the church of **La Merced** and two nearby museums: **Museo Arqueológico La Merced** and **Museo de Arte Colonial.** For a panoramic city view, take a taxi to the top of the **Cerro de los Cristales.**

TIMING AND PRECAUTIONS

This short walk could easily be completed in the course of a morning or afternoon. Some of the buildings are closed Monday or weekends. Take safety precautions before venturing out.

Sights to See

Catedral Metropolitana. Though construction began in 1772, it was interrupted during the war for independence, and consequently wasn't completed until 1841. The pale interior of this massive temple is complemented by its marble columns and brilliantly gilded main altar. ⊠ *Calle 11 No. 5–53.* ☜ *Free.* ☉ *Tues.–Sun.*

Cerro de los Cristales. Crystal Hill is a popular lookout point (1,421 m; 4,660 ft) on Cali's west end that affords a spectacular city view. The monumental statue of Christ (26 m; 85 ft tall) here is visible for miles around. To get here, take a taxi from downtown and have it wait for you (about $9 round-trip). Don't go if it's getting dark.

Iglesia de la Ermita. A small, white-and-blue, neo-Gothic creation, built between 1930 and 1948, Hermitage Church has for some reason become a symbol of Cali, commonly seen on postcards. ⊠ *Av. Colombia at Calle 13.* ☜ *Free.* ☉ *Sun.*

La Merced. The Church of Grace was completed in 1680 and stands on the site where the city's founders celebrated their first mass in 1536. It's Cali's oldest church. ⊠ *Carrera 4 at Calle 7.* ☜ *Admission.* ☉ *Tues.–Sat.*

Museo Arqueológico La Merced. Next door to La Merced, this archaeological museum displays regional pre-Columbian pottery and a scale-model reproduction of Cali. ⊠ *Carrera 4 No. 6–59,* ☎ *092/881–3229.* ☜ *Admission.* ☉ *Mon.–Sat.*

Museo de Arte Colonial. This small colonial art museum has mostly religious pieces, including Colombia's most complete collection of paintings by Gregorio Vazquez and sculptures by Pablo Ceballos, two colonial-era artists whose work is displayed in churches across Colombia. The entrance is around the corner from La Merced. ⊠ *Carrera 3 and Calle 7,* ☎ *092/880–4737.* ☜ *Admission.* ☉ *Mon.–Sat.*

Palacio Nacional. Intricately carved doors under equally ornate arches adorn the National Palace on Plaza de Caicedo's east side. This neoclassical government building also has a small **museo** that commemorates 300 years of growing and processing sugarcane, for which Cali and Valle de Cauca are famous. ⊠ *Carrera 4 at Calle 12.* ☜ *Free.* ☉ *Weekdays.*

Paseo de Bolívar. Tropical trees shade this large park on the Río Cali's north bank. The modern buildings to the west of the park house municipal offices and are collectively known as the CAM, a term also used by locals to identify the park. ⊠ *Av. 6 and Río Cali.*

Plaza de Caicedo. In the middle of this shady city-center park is a statue of Joaquín Caicedo y Cuero, the 18th-century patriot who liberated Cali from the Spanish. ⊠ *Carrera 4 between Calles 11 and 12.*

San Francisco. This large, redbrick church and adjacent Franciscan monastery date from the early 19th century. Note the Moorish architecture; in fact, the church's brick **Torre Mudéjar** (Moorish Tower), is considered one of the finest examples of Spanish-Moorish art in South America. ⊠ *Carrera 6 between Calles 9 and 10.* 🎫 *Free.* ☉ *Tues.–Sun.*

Dining and Lodging

$$$ ✕ **Mi Tierra.** The city's most popular Colombian restaurant is in a colonial-style building on the Río Cali's north side. Food is served upstairs, and the ground floor has a colorful bar. The menu favors such grilled dishes as the *brocheta mi tierra,* a beef, chicken, and shrimp shish kebab. ⊠ *Av. 8 No. 10N–18,* ☎ *092/668–2686. AE, DC, MC, V.*

$ ✕ **Obelisco Plaza.** Although you can eat inside, many prefer the tables across the street, beside the banks of the Río Cali. Waiters literally risk their lives crossing the busy Avenida Colombia to deliver drinks and meals. The specialties include bite-size empanadas and *chuzos* (shish kebabs), but they also serve pizza and pastas. Because this is a popular night spot, tables can fill up early. ⊠ *Av. Colombia No. 4,* ☎ *092/ 883–6133. DC, MC, V. No lunch.*

$$$ ✕🏠 **Don Jaime.** This intimate 30-room hotel provides more personalized attention than its larger corporate rivals without sacrificing any such luxuries as cable TV and air-conditioning. A popular café here overlooks busy Avenida 6, and the hotel restaurant is among the best in Cali. ⊠ *Av. 6 No. 15N–25,* ☎ *092/667–2828 or 092/667–8287,* FAX *092/668–7098. 30 rooms, 25 with bath. Restaurant, bar, café, room service. AE, DC, MC, V.*

$$$$ 🏠 **Dann Carlton.** Overlooking an attractive residential quarter near the Río Cali, the towers of this luxury hotel have appealing, carpeted rooms with city views, sofas, cable TV, and large tiled baths. On balmy days, you can cool off in the fourth-floor swimming pool. ⊠ *Av. Colombia 1–60,* ☎ *092/893–3000,* FAX *092/893–4000. 198 rooms. 2 restaurants, bar, minibars, pool, sauna, exercise room. AE, DC, MC, V.*

$$ 🏠 **Hotel La Merced.** A namesake and neighbor of Cali's oldest church, this hotel bears a quintessential colonial entryway—the lobby has high ceilings, tile floors, and colonial-style furnishings. Rooms are modern, with ceiling fans and TVs, although more economical yet somewhat dated rooms are also available. ⊠ *Calle 7 No. 1–65,* ☎ *092/882–4053,* FAX *092/884–6330. 60 rooms. Restaurant, bar, pool, sauna. AE, DC, MC, V.*

Shopping

The region's crafts include hand-carved, hardwood bowls and serving utensils, finely embroidered blouses and dresses, and handwoven ponchos and *chumbes,* long multicolored woolen strips used for belts. Try **Artesanías Pancandé** (⊠ Av. 6 No. 17, ☎ 092/668–6373) or **San Alejo** (⊠ Calle 2 No. 2–43, ☎ 092/885–8700). Both are open roughly 9 to 5.

Palmira

42 km (26 mi) northeast of Cali.

You can hire a horse-drawn carriage for a tour of this beautifully preserved colonial village, which is graced by the soaring 279-ft tower of its 17th-century cathedral.

At the lovely, restored **Hacienda El Paraíso**—on the Via Palmira, 40-minutes from Cali—you can see how the Colombian aristocracy lived during the early part of the 18th century. The farmhouse is furnished with antiques and surrounded by well tended gardens. ⊠ *Via Palmira, turn right at Amaime,* ☎ *no phone.* 🎫 *Admission.* ☉ *Tues.–Sun.*

At the open-air **Museo de la Caña de Azucar** (Sugarcane Museum), guided tours (in Spanish) are given every 30 minutes. The museum consists of an 18th-century *ingenio* (sugar processing plant) and a hacienda, just south of the Hacienda El Paraíso, *above*. ⊠ *Via Palmira.* ⊠ *Admission.* ☉ *Tues.–Sun.*

Buga

50 km (31 mi) north of Palmira.

Buga is somewhat of a national monument, with its preserved 17th- and 18th-century buildings. You can easily visit such notable sights as the Iglesia de San Francisco, the Catedral de San Pedro, and the Basilica del Señor de los Milagros, since they're all within four blocks of Buga's peaceful main square.

Popayán

130 km (81 mi) south of Cali.

Founded in 1537 by Sebastián de Belalcázar, Popayán quickly became an important administrative center of the Viceroyalty of New Granada because of its position on the Cartagena–Quito gold route. Although the town was largely destroyed by an earthquake on Good Friday, 1983, its colonial buildings have been painstakingly rebuilt, and most of its monuments are in excellent condition. Hotel rooms must be booked months ahead of time for Holy Week (Palm Sunday through Easter Sunday), when the streets are filled with colorful religious processions.

A Good Walk

Begin at the **Puente del Humilladero.** Walk south to Calle 3, turn left and walk a block to the **Casa Mosquiera,** which is across from the Casa Caldas, home of the local tourist office. From here, walk one block south to the **Iglesia de Santo Domingo,** then half a block east on Calle 4 to the **Museo de Arte Religioso.** After visiting the museum, walk west to the shady **Plaza Central.** Cross the park to Calle 5, and walk another block west to the **Iglesia de San Jose.** Continue west to the next corner, turn right on Carrera 9, and walk one block north to the **Iglesia de San Francisco.**

TIMING AND PRECAUTIONS

This short walk can be completed in a few hours but won't be very interesting on a Monday, since many of the buildings will be closed. And here, more than most places, you'll notice a general placidity and calmness, so it's relaxing to stroll through the town, marveling at the colonial buildings. While Popayán has seen less violence than other Colombian cities, you should not let your guard down here. Take the precautions that you would anywhere else.

Sights to See

Casa Mosquiera. One of Popayán's founding families once owned this now-restored colonial house and the religious art on display here. Across the street, in a similar building, is the Casa Caldas, the local tourist office, where you can pick up a city map. ⊠ *Calle 3 No. 5–14,* ☎ *no phone.* ⊠ *Admission.* ☉ *Tues.–Sun.*

★ **Iglesia de San Francisco.** Popayán's most important colonial church is in remarkable condition, thanks to extensive renovation following the 1983 quake. The church's bright interior has gilded wooden altars, and its tower holds a 3-ton bell. ⊠ *Calle 4 at Carrera 9.* ⊠ *Free.* ☉ *Tues.–Sun.*

Iglesia de San José. This bright-yellow, 18th-century church is one of Popayán's most attractive, but unfortunately it's only open for masses. You can ask around town or at your hotel for times. ⊠ *Calle 5 at Carrera 8.* ☞ *Free.*

Iglesia de Santo Domingo. After an earthquake destroyed the town's original Dominican chapel, which dated from 1574, this church was built in 1741. It's notable for the stonework around its doorway, which depicts exotic flowers and animals, and for the silver Virgin behind its altar, brought from Spain in 1588. Next door, what was once a monastery now houses a regional university. ⊠ *Calle 4 at Carrera 5.* ☞ *Free.* ☉ *Tues.–Sun.*

Museo de Arte Religioso. The Museum of Religious Art is in a lovely colonial mansion and has predominately paintings, but also some valuable gold and silver work. ⊠ *Calle 4 No. 4–56,* ☎ *no phone.* ☞ *Admission.* ☉ *Tues.–Sun.*

Plaza Central. This large plaza, shaded by tall palms and pines, is also called Plaza Caldas, after Martin Caldas, the independence fighter whose statue is here. The city's cathedral, completed in 1906, is to the south; to the east is the 18th-century clock tower.

Puente del Humilladero. The long brick bridge that spans the Molino River was built at the end of the 18th century, as was the smaller bridge to its right.

Dining and Lodging

$ ✕ **Restaurante Italiano.** The decor isn't memorable, but the food is great at this small bilevel restaurant catercorner to the San Francisco church. It has a good selection of pizzas, pastas, salads, and excellent *cremas* (cream soups). ⊠ *Calle 4 No. 8–85,* ☎ *092/824–0607. No credit cards.*

$$ 🏨 **Hotel Camino Real.** Built in 1591 as a women's college, this renovated colonial building off the central square has tile floors and old—though well-kept—wooden furniture. Rooms, most of which overlook a patio, have modern conveniences and big bathrooms. The first-floor restaurant serves Colombian and European food. ⊠ *Calle 5 No. 5–59,* ☎ *092/ 824–1254,* FAX *092/824–0816. 28 rooms. Restaurant. AE, DC, MC, V.*

$$ 🏨 **Hotel Monasterio.** Rooms in this restored 18th-century Franciscan ★ monastery surround a lovely courtyard with a large fountain. The extensive grounds have well-tended gardens and views of the adjacent San Francisco church. Rooms are large, with high ceilings, colonial-style furnishings, and tiled baths. ⊠ *Calle 4, between Carreras 9 and 10,* ☎ *092/824–3491,* FAX *092/824–4065. 48 rooms. Restaurant, bar, pool. AE, DC MC, V.*

¢ 🏨 **Casa Familiar el Descanso.** This small pensión, down the hill from ★ the tourist office, is quite a bargain. Rooms are simple but clean and share bathrooms off the central hallway. Complimentary breakfasts are served in a bright sitting area, and owner, Haydee de Varela, is a wealth of information. ⊠ *Carrera 5 No. 2–41,* ☎ *092/824–0019. 6 rooms, share 2 baths. No credit cards.*

Silvia

50 km (31 mi) northeast of Popayán.

Silvia is famous for its Tuesday market, when Gaumbiano Indians descend upon the town from surrounding villages to sell their wares. The Gaumbiano have preserved many of their centuries-old customs, such as a fondness for black bowler hats and bright purple skirts, an ensemble worn by both women and men. On Tuesday, Silvia's central square is crammed with such local products as corn, Andean tubers, and heavy wool ponchos. On other days, you can inquire in town about renting horses or obtaining a guide for a hike to one of the nearby indigenous communities.

Puracé National Park

50 km (31 mi) east of Popayán.

If you're a nature lover or a dedicated hiker, visit this protected area in one of Colombia's most spectacular mountain regions. The park ranges from 1,890 m (6,202 ft) to almost 4,804 m (15,750 ft) and is the source of several large rivers. The most popular area, **Pilimbala**, is 2 km (1 mi) off the road to La Plata, where a youth hostel provides the perfect base for ascents of the Puracé Volcano. Guided tours can be arranged through Corporacion de Turismo del Cauca in Popayán, *see below*. The community of **San Juan**, 13 km (8 mi) east of the park, has hot springs and the Cascada del Bedón waterfall.

Tierradentro

113 km (68 mi) northeast of Popayán.

One of the country's preeminent pre-Columbian sites, Tierradentro is near the community of San Andrés Pisimbalá. You can visit its intricately painted underground tombs, and it also has some stone carvings and an interesting church. Because there's limited bus service from Popayán, it's best to arrange a tour or drive here. Because it's nearly a five-hour journey from Popayán on a bad road, it's likely a worthwhile journey only for true archaeology lovers.

San Agustín

303 km (180 mi) southeast of Popayán.

At first glance San Agustín's mysterious statues look strikingly similar to the megaliths of Chile's Easter Island. Some archaeologists have linked these larger-than-life stone figures to the Maya, but it's likely they're the work of a pre-Columbian tribe that flourished in the first through eighth centuries and was decimated by disease and simply vanished shortly after the Europeans arrived. The closest town to San Agustín is **Pitalito,** where you'll find hotels, restaurants, car-rental agencies, and taxis. From Popayán it's a six-hour drive on roads only slightly better than those to Tierradentro.

Lodging

$$ 🏨 **Hotel Osoguaico.** The closest accommodations to the ruins has plainly furnished and clean rooms. Insist on one with hot water. *1.5 km (1 mi) west of the archaeological park,* ☎ *098/837–3069. Restaurant. No credit cards.*

The Southwest A to Z

Arriving and Departing

BY AIRPLANE

Most domestic carriers have regular flights between Bogotá, Cartagena, or Medellín and Cali's **Aeropuerto Alfonso Bonilla Aragón** (☎ 0928/442–2624), 20 km (12 mi) northeast of the city. International carriers based in Cali are **Avianca** (☎ 0928/667–6886), which has daily flights to New York, Miami, and Panama, and **Copa** (☎ 0928/659–2399), which flies to Panama and Miami several times a week.

From the tiny **Aeropuerto Popayán** (it's behind the bus terminal), there are two daily flights from Bogotá. **Avianca** (✉ Calle 4 No. 7–

58, Popayán, ☎ 0928/244020) makes the one-hour afternoon flight and **Intercontinental de Aviación** (✉ Carrera 7 No. 4–28, Popayán, ☎ 0928/241861) flies in the morning. Both use turbo-prop aircraft and cost about $70 each way.

From the Airport: Taxis into Cali cost about $10; minibuses that connect the airport and bus terminal about 20 minutes away depart every 10 minutes and cost $1. Taxis are about $3 to most Popayán hotels.

BY BUS

It's about a 10-hour trip from Bogotá and Medellín to Cali. Buses travel between each of the three cities about once every hour. Popayán is about three hours from Cali, and buses leave every 20 minutes from Cali's bus terminal. The tourist office in Popayán (☞ *below*) has information about bus trips to outlying attractions.

BY CAR

For safety reasons, driving is not recommended between cities. But if you must, you should know that the highway between Bogotá and Cali is poor, although it's fully paved. The 680-km (422-mi) journey takes around 10 hours, and, being one of Colombia's major routes, it's relatively safe. Cars can be rented in Cali from **Avis** (☎ 0928/883–6027) or **Hertz** (☎ 0928/882–2428); if you plan to drive to Puracé or Tierradentro, you'll want a four-wheel-drive vehicle. There are no car rental agencies in Popayán.

Contacts and Resources

BANKS AND CURRENCY EXCHANGE

Banco de la República (✉ Calle 11 No. 4–14) is open 9–3.

EMERGENCIES

Ambulance: Cruz Roja (Red Cross) ☎ 132.

Police: ☎ 156 or call local information ☎ 113 and ask for emergency assistance.

Hospitals and pharmacies: In Cali, **Clínica de Occident** (✉ Calle 18N No. 5–34, ☎ 660–3000) or **Clínica Santiago de Cali** (✉ Avenida 4 No. 21–54, ☎ 660–0303). In Popayán, **Hospital Universitario San José** (✉ Carrera 6, Calle 9N, ☎ 234–508).

MAIL

Post office: In Cali, ✉ Calle 12N No. 2N–33. In Popayán, ✉ Carrera 7, between Calles 5 and 6.

VISITOR INFORMATION

Contact the **Corporacion Regional de Turismo del Valle de Cauca** (✉ Av. 4N No. 4N–10, Cali, ☎ 0928/660–5000). **Viajes Oganesoff** (✉ Inter-Continental Hotel, ☎ 0928/667–3131) arranges tours from Cali. In Popayán contact **Corporacion de Turismo del Cauca** (✉ Casa de Caldas, Calle 3 No. 4–70, ☎ 0928/242251).

THE CARIBBEAN COAST

A world away and lost to another time, it seems, is Colombia's sultry Caribbean coast, a self-contained region linked to Bogotá and the interior only by the national flag, the milky Río Magdalena, and a couple of snaking highways. The local *costeño* people project an air of gaiety unseen in the capital, driven by salsa and the accordion-heavy *vallenato* music, a regional specialty. Despite the strength-sapping heat and Carnival-like atmosphere, the Caribbean coast has nurtured Colombia's best-known writers and artists, including novelist Gabriel García Márquez and painter Alejandro Obregón.

Toward the western end of the 1,600-km (992-mi) Caribbean shoreline is Cartagena, Colombia's greatest colonial attraction. With its barrel-tile roofs and wooden balconies, Cartagena's Ciudad Amurallada, as the old city is called, often looks more Spanish than Spain, but the feeling is tropical, Creole, and altogether more exotic. The nearby Rosario Islands beckon snorkelers and scuba divers, as does the enchanting colonial port of Mompós.

Northeast of Cartagena is Barranquilla—a relatively uneventful city that comes alive during its Ash Wednesday carnival. Farther east, past mangrove-encircled lagoons, is the old port town of Santa Marta. Some of the country's finest beaches stretch eastward from here, toward the magnificent Parque Nacional Tayrona. Beyond Tayrona's deserted beaches is the snowcapped Sierra Nevada, whose rain-forested slopes harbor the mysterious Ciudad Perdida (Lost City), a remote archaeological site.

Cartagena

When founded in 1533 by Pedro de Heredia, Cartagena was the only port on mainland South America. Gold and silver, mined in the interior and looted from Indians, passed through here en route to Spain, making Cartagena an obvious target for pirates. The most destructive of these was Sir Francis Drake, who in 1586 torched 200 houses, destroyed the cathedral, and made off for England with more than 100,000 gold ducats. Cartagena's magnificent walls and countless fortresses grew in response to these raids, and also to safeguard the most important African slave market in the New World. The Ciudad Amurallada attracts many to Cartagena, but it actually comprises a small section of this city of half a million. Most of Cartagena's hotels and restaurants are in the Bocagrande district: an elongated peninsula where high-rises overlook a long, gray-sand beach.

A Good Walk

Begin in the Ciudad Amurallada, on Calle de la Factoria, at the ocher-painted **Casa de Marqués Valdehoyos.** Walk one block south to the **Plaza Santo Domingo.** Continue south one block, past pricey antiques stores, and turn left onto Calle Inquisición and follow it to the end of the block and the **Plaza de Bolívar.** To your left stands the whitewashed Palacio de la Inquisición; directly opposite is the Museo del Oro y Arqueología. Two blocks south is **San Pedro Claver,** a convent. From here, walk northeast (across the Plazas de la Aduana and los Coches) and turn left onto Calle de las Carretas, which you should follow north three long blocks to the Plaza Fernandez de Madrid. This garden square marks the beginning of the old city's **Barrio San Diego,** where you can shop for crafts. From here, hail a taxi for a 5-minute ride to the impregnable **Castillo de San Felipe de Barajas.** When you've explored the fort, take a taxi up **Cerro de la Popa,** a 153 m (500-ft) hill crowned by a 17th-century monastery. On another day, the desolate town of **Mompós** is a worthwhile day-trip destination for its especially well-preserved colonial character.

TIMING AND PRECAUTIONS

Spend the morning in the walled city, lunch here or nearby, and take the afternoon to visit San Felipe and Cerro de la Popa. Because many sights are closed by 6 PM, you'll want to do the tour by day, but be sure to tour the Ciudad Amurallada at night by horse-drawn carriage (☞ Nightlife, *below*), to admire its floodlighted monuments.

Sights to See

Barrio San Diego. The seldom-visited streets of this enchanting north-end district are lined with squat colonial mansions brightly painted in white, ocher, and electric blue. Geraniums cascade over balconies, and open doorways reveal hidden, luxurious courtyards. Zigzagging toward the sea on Calle del Jardin, then Calle de las Bovedas, you arrive at the **Bóvedas** (Vaults), an arcaded row of 18th-century strong rooms, along the northern wall, now occupied by the city's best crafts shops. After you've loaded up on hats, hammocks, and leather goods, take a stroll along the nearby city walls and watch as the setting sun reddens the Caribbean.

Casa de Marqués Valdehoyos. Although scantily furnished, this elegant house exudes a powerful aroma of well-to-do colonial life (the sturdy mansion and its shady courtyard, low arches, and elaborate wooden balconies are the product of the marqués's slave-trade fortune). The tourist office inside provides useful maps. ⊠ *Calle Factoría No. 36–57,* ☎ *095/664–6567.* ☒ *Free.* ☉ *Daily 8–noon, 2–6.*

Castillo de San Felipe de Barajas. Designed by Antonio de Arévalo in 1639, San Felipe Fort's steep-angled redbrick and concrete battlements were arranged so that, if part of the castle fell into the wrong hands—which it never did—defenders in one part of the fort could fire on invaders in another. A maze of tunnels, minimally lit today to allow for spooky exploration, still connects vital points of the fort. ⊠ *Southeast of Ciudad Amurallada, between Calle 30 and Avenida Pedro San Felipe,* ☎ *095/666–4790.* ☒ *Admission.* ☉ *Daily 8–5:30.*

★ **Cerro de la Popa.** For the best views of Cartagena, the vista from Stern Hill is spectacular, especially around sunset. Because of its strategic location, the 17th-century monastery here intermittently served as a fortress during the colonial era. It now houses a colonial museum and a chapel dedicated to the Virgin de la Candelaria, Cartagena's patron saint. ⊠ *3 km (2 mi) southeast of Ciudad Amarallada,* ☎ *no phone.* ☒ *Admission.* ☉ *Daily 9–6.*

OFF THE BEATEN PATH	**MOMPÓS –** Founded in 1537 on the eastern branch of the Río Magdalena, Mompós was a key trading point between the Caribbean and the interior for more than two centuries. However, in the 18th century, the Magdalena's current shifted toward the western branch, leaving Mompós stranded on what has become an unnavigable channel. Although the commercial vibrancy of the town quickly dissipated, its colonial architecture remains: Mompós's parallel streets, curved so as to thwart cannonball volleys, are lined with squat mansions guarded by intricate iron grilles, and several old churches. Simón Bolívar once stayed at the **Casa Bolivariana** (⊠ Calle Media), open Monday to Saturday. Of the town's various churches, the **Iglesia de Santa Bárbara** is the most interesting because of its Moorish bell tower.

Plaza de Bolívar. Every Colombian city has a central plaza that goes by this name. Here it's a popular, shady place from which to admire Cartagena's 16th-century **cathedral,** to the northeast, with its colorful bell tower and 20th-century dome. Inside is a massive gilded altar. To the east, the **Museo del Oro y Arqueología** (Gold and Archaeological Museum), open weekdays 8:30–noon and 2–6, has an assortment of gold ornaments and pottery culled from the Zinús, an indigenous tribe who lived here 2,000 years ago. On the plaza's west side, a baroque limestone doorway marks the entrance to the **Palacio de la Inquisición** (Palace of the Inquisition), the headquarters of the repressive arbiters of political and spiritual orthodoxy, who once exercised jurisdiction over Colombia, Ecuador, Venezuela, Central America, and the Caribbean. The ground-floor rooms contain implements of torture—racks and thumbscrews, to name but two—and architectural models of bygone Cartagena. It's open daily 8–11:30 and 2–5. The museum and palace charge a small admission. ⊠ *Carrera San Pedro Claver and Calle Baloco.*

Plaza Santo Domingo. The eponymous church looming over the plaza is the city's oldest; built in 1539, it has a simple whitewashed interior, bare limestone pillars, a raised choir, and an adjacent cloistered seminary. Local lore says the bell tower's twisted profile is the work of the Devil, who, dispirited at having failed to destroy it, threw himself into the plaza's well. At night the area fills up with tables from surrounding bars and restaurants, and becomes the place to see and be seen. ⊠ *Calle Santo Domingo and Carrera Santo Domingo.*

San Pedro Claver. San Pedro was a Spanish monk who devotedly ministered to African slaves until his death in 1654 (in 1888 he was made the New World's first saint). You can visit his dim, cell-like bedroom and the infirmary where he died from Parkinson's disease. His body rests in a glass coffin beneath the altar of the adjoining church. ⊠ *Plaza San Pedro Claver.* ⊡ *Free.* ☉ *Daily 9–6.*

Dining

Seafood is the regional specialty, as is *arroz con coco* (rice cooked in coconut milk) and sancocho. Tropical *jugos* (juices) are an excellent companion to *carimañolas* (stuffed yucca), *arepas de huevo* (egg-filled pancakes), and *butifarras* (small meatballs).

$$$$ ✕ **Club de Pesca.** Time slips gently by at this 18th-century fortress, which overlooks a modern marina. It's easy to linger on the waterfront terrace, in the shade of a giant fig tree, especially when you're savoring one of the delicate specialties, such as snapper with lemon, soy, tahini, and mint. ⊠ *Take the bay shore road southeast from the convention center for 2 km (1 mi); Fuerte de San Sebastián del Pastelillo, Manga,* ☎ *095/660–4594. AE, DC, MC, V.*

$$$ ✕ **Paco's.** Heavy beams, rough terra-cotta walls, chunky wooden benches, and tunes from an aging Cuban band (Wed.–Sat.) are the hallmarks of this downtown eatery. Drop by for a drink and tapas, or try the more substantial langostinos *a la sifú* (fried in batter). You can sit inside or out on the plaza. ⊠ *Plaza Santo Domingo,* ☎ *095/664–4294. AE, DC, MC, V.*

$$$ ✕ **La Vitrola.** This friendly restaurant on a quiet Ciudad Amurallada
★   corner is the result of a New Yorker's love affair with the Caribbean; everything from the menu to the music reflects that romance. You can begin with ceviche *catalina* (fish and octopus marinated in lime juice), then try a *zarzuela de mariscos* (seafood casserole), or perhaps *corvina con salsa de cebollin y jenibre* (sea bass with scallion-ginger sauce). Ceiling fans, historic photos, and live Cuban music complete the ambience. ⊠ *Calle Baloco, near Carrera Santo Domingo,* ☎ *095/664–8243. AE, DC, MC, V.*

$$ ✕ **Café de la Plaza.** Of the seven cafés with tables spilling out onto the Plaza Santo Domingo, this popular café has particularly good food and generous portions. The menu is predominantly Italian, with a good selection of pastas, salads, and sandwiches. They also serve breakfast. ⊠ *Plaza Santo Domingo,* ☎ *no phone. DC, MC, V. Closed Sun.*

$$ ✕ **Café San Pedro.** Although they serve Colombian fare, the international dishes including Thai, Italian, and Japanese make this a good lunch or dinner choice. You can also come simply for a drink and watch the activity on the plaza from one of the tables here or inside. ⊠ *Plaza San Pedro. DC, MC, V. Closed Sun.*

Lodging

Make your hotel reservations well in advance for Holy Week and June through December. Be aware that prices are typically inflated during these times.

$$$$ ⊡ **Hilton.** Every spacious room at this hotel on the tip of the Bocagrande peninsula has a sea-facing balcony, but those overlooking the terrace, its leafy gardens, and its three pools have the best views. A path from the hotel leads to a private beach lined with palms, magnolias, and thatched oyster bars. ⊠ *Av. Almirante Brión, El Laguito,* ☎ *095/ 665–0666, 800/445–8667 in the U.S.,* FAX *095/665–2211. 289 rooms, 5 suites. 2 restaurants, 2 bars, 3 pools, massage, sauna, tennis court, exercise room, waterskiing, casino. AE, DC, MC, V.*

$$$$ ⊡ **Santa Clara.** This Ciudad Amurallada hotel managed by Hotel Sof-
★ itel delivers one of Colombia's best lodging experiences. The lobby, restaurants, conference rooms, and suites are housed in the 17th-cen-tury convent that was featured in García Márquez's novel, *Of Love and Other Demons.* Beyond the arched porticos and lush courtyard is a new wing that has guest rooms and a pool. You can also book here for the hotel's private-island lodge on the Islas del Rosario. ⊠ *Calle del Torno,* ☎ *095/664–6070, 800/221–4542 in the U.S.,* FAX *095/664– 7010. 144 rooms, 18 suites. 3 restaurants, bar, pool, massage, sauna, steam room, exercise room. AE, DC, MC, V.*

$$$$ ⊡ **Santa Teresa.** Another tastefully decorated hotel in a former con-
★ vent (☞ *above*), rooms have marble floors, large baths, and lots of char-acter. The rooftop pool and restaurant have great views of the Caribbean and surrounding Ciudad Amurallada. ⊠ *Plaza Santa Teresa,* ☎ *095/ 664–9494,* FAX *095/664–9447. 70 rooms, 21 suites. 2 restaurants, bar, pool. AE, DC, MC, V.*

$$$–$$$$ ⊡ **Caribe.** The oldest hotel on Bocagrande, this is one of the few beachfront lodges that offers any atmosphere. Bedrooms in the refur-bished old building have heaps more charm than those in the modern wings, though they can be a bit noisy on weekends. Behind the hotel, giant ficus trees shade a large pool; only a narrow lane separates the hotel from the beach. ⊠ *Carrera 1A No. 2–87, Bocagrande,* ☎ *095/ 665–0155,* FAX *095/665–4970. 363 rooms. 2 restaurants, bar, pool, mas-sage, sauna, tennis court, exercise room, casino. AE, DC, MC, V.*

$–$$ ⊡ **Casa Grande.** An original Bocagrande beach house, now dwarfed by skyscrapers, Casa Grande is a pleasant, quiet lodging option. Rooms vary in style and price: the nicest are those in the old house; those off the garden have sloped wooden roofs with ceiling fans and are a good value. ⊠ *Carrera 1 No. 9–128,* ☎ *095/665–3943,* FAX *095/665–6806. 30 rooms. Restaurant, bar. AE, DC, MC, V.*

$ ⊡ **Las Tres Banderas.** In the historic San Diego neighborhood, this at-
★ tractive little 19th-century hotel is an inexpensive, yet attractive op-tion. Rooms border a narrow courtyard, and combine colonial ambience with such modern amenities as orthopedic mattresses, air-condition-ing, and TV. The hotel also has a lodge on the Islas del Rosario. ⊠ *Calle Cochera del Hobo No. 38–66,* ☎ *095/660–0160;* ☎ *514/274– 5565 in Canada. 8 rooms. No credit cards.*

Nightlife

You can dance the night away to Latin rhythms or take a romantic ride through the Ciudad Amurallada in a horse-drawn *coche* (carriage), which you can hire in front of the Caribe or Santa Teresa hotels. A rowdier option is a *rumba en chiva,* which is popular with Colombians and consists of a bar-hopping city tour in a colorful bus complete with live music (☞ Tour Operators, *below*). The most popular night spot in the Ciudad Amurallada is **Plaza Santo Domingo,** where several restaurants have outdoor seating. Also, you'll notice that many Colombians party on **Bocagrande's beaches.** Vendors rent plastic chairs and sell cold beer, and roving trios play vallenato, the typical regional music. Or, for some-thing a little less intoxicating, on Friday at 5PM, you can watch a brass band play at the Parque Simón Bolívar. It lasts less than an hour.

BARS AND CLUBS

The largest of the Bocagrande dance clubs is **La Escollera** (⊠ Carrera 1 at Calle 5, ☎ 095/665–3030), a two-story wooden building that resembles a ship. **Mr. Barbilla** (⊠ Av. del Arsenal No. 893, ☎ 095/664–7005) is a busy bar with good food and a Cuban band on weekends.

Outdoor Activities and Sports

BEACHES

For white sand and palm trees, your best bet is **Playa Blanca,** about 15 minutes away by boat. Or you can take a boat to the **Islas del Rosario,** a verdant archipelago surrounded by aquamarine waters and coral reefs one hour away. All boats leave from Cartagena's Muelle de los Pegasos, a pier, flanked by statues of two flying horses, beside the convention center. Trips with Ecobuzos (☞ *below*) cost about $30, including lunch, and leave between 6 AM and 8 AM, but plenty of freelancers (a.k.a. men with boats) along the pier will also offer to be your guide anytime.

FISHING

The **Club de Pesca** in Manga (⊠ Calle 24 at Carrera 17, ☎ 095/660–4593) can arrange sportfishing charters.

SCUBA DIVING

The **Caribe Dive Shop** (☎ 095/665–0813) at the Caribe Hotel (☞ Lodging, *above*) organizes snorkeling trips to the Islas del Rosario and scuba diving at underwater wrecks. From their concrete building on the waterfront, **Ecobuzos** (⊠ Avenida Venezuela, ☎ 095/665–5449) arranges snorkeling and scuba excursions to the Islas del Rosario. Most travel agencies in Cartagena also arrange day trips to the Islas del Rosario (☞ Tour Operators, *below*).

Shopping

Las Bóvedas, a series of large, arched vaults in the Ciudad Amurallada's northwest corner, now houses about two dozen shops with the best selection of local crafts. If you're looking for emeralds, visit the jewelry shops on or near Calle Pantaleón, beside the cathedral.

En Route   If you're taking the coastal road to Santa Marta, 115 km (71 mi) northeast of Cartagena you'll pass Barranquilla, worth visiting only for Carnival, the week leading up to Ash Wednesday, when its dusty streets are overcome by costumed dancers, salsa bands, and crazed drunks swilling *aguardiente* (firewater), or to see the national soccer stadium where Colombia's team practices and international matches are held.

Santa Marta

237 km (147 mi) northeast of Cartagena.

Santa Marta lies at the foot of the snowcapped Sierra Nevada, the world's highest coastal range. The mountains are largely protected within Parque Nacional Tayrona (Tayrona National Park), and hidden on their slopes are the pre-Columbian ruins of La Ciudad Perdida.

Although Santa Marta is the oldest surviving Hispanic town in Colombia (it was founded in 1525), modern industry and architecture largely obscure its colonial heritage. Today the city's 200,000 inhabitants rely heavily on the deep-water port where banana boats lie anchored in thick clusters. Most of the cargo, of course, is legitimate, but Santa Marta also handles more contraband than any other Colombian port. In the 1970s, that meant mostly Sierra Nevada–cultivated marijuana; today, U.S.-solicited cocaine reigns supreme. Santa Marta is mostly nonchalant and friendly, but inquisitiveness in this feral, fascinating city is unwise; some of its residents carry weapons as a matter of course.

The **Museo Arqueológico Tayrona,** in a handsome, erstwhile customs house on the main square, has a small collection of Tayrona gold and pottery and a model of La Ciudad Perdida. It's well worth a look *before* you head there. ⊠ *Calle 14 at Carrera 2,* ☎ *no phone.* ☞ *Admission.* ☉ *Open weekdays.*

On the seafront, flag down a taxi and ask to be let off at the **Quinta de San Pedro Alejandrino,** 20 minutes away. This pleasant honey-color hacienda is where Simón Bolívar died in 1830, ironically enough as a guest of a Spanish royalist. On the grounds are a huge gleaming monument to the liberator and a helpful pictorial history of his life. ⊠ *Mamatoco.* ☞ *Admission.* ☉ *Wed.–Mon. 9:30–4:30.*

Dining and Lodging

$$$ ✕▥ **La Sierra.** Situated in El Rodadero, a resort area 5 km (3 mi) from Santa Marta, this modern, 10-story hotel has large rooms with balconies, air-conditioning, and TVs. You can ask for one facing the ocean. The restaurant serves an international menu, with seating indoors or on a street-side patio. ⊠ *Carrera 1 No. 9–47, El Rodadero,* ☎ *095/422–7960,* FAX *095/422–8198. 73 rooms. Restaurant, bar. AE, DC, MC, V.*

$ ▥ **Hotel Panamerican.** Despite its austere concrete-block appearance, this friendly hotel has a friendly, efficient staff and huge, bright bedrooms with TVs and phones. Sea-facing rooms with a balcony are best; you can have air-conditioning for a small charge but it's scarcely needed with the sea breeze. ⊠ *Carrera 1A No. 18–23, Santa Marta,* ☎ *095/421–1238. 46 rooms. Restaurant, café. AE, DC, MC, V.*

¢ ▥ **Tayrona Hotel.** For those on a budget, this two-story colonial-style building across from the black-sand beach, is your best bet (and as good as many that cost more). Rooms have firm beds, TVs and fans, and big bathrooms with hot water. There's also a good, outdoor restaurant in front. ⊠ *Carrera 1 No. 11–21, Santa Marta,* ☎ *095/421–2408. 24 rooms. Restaurant. No credit cards.*

Outdoor Activities and Sports

BEACHES

The beaches at Santa Marta and the nearby fishing village of Taganga are dirty; but just south is **El Rodadero,** a white-sand beach with excellent lodging facilities (☞ Dining and Lodging, *above*).

TREKKING

The Sierra Nevada has some outstanding hiking and climbing that includes Pueblito, a historic town with *caminos de piedra* (avenues of stone), La Ciudad Perdida, and the 5,774-m (18,930-ft) summit of Pico Colón. The latter two require fit, well-organized, and experienced guides and hikers, as well as equipment and time—this is no casual hike. Low-elevation hikes, however, can be arranged with ease (☞ Visitor Information *and* Tour Operators, *below*).

Shopping

A block from the Hotel Panamerican, the **Almacenes Típicos El Tiburón** (⊠ Carrera 2A No. 18–09, Santa Marta) sells Colombian crafts. They also have a store in El Rodadero's Edificio Liberador on Calle 8.

Parque Nacional Tayrona

38 km (24 mi) east of Santa Marta.

Parque Nacional Tayrona has steep, jungle-clad slopes, ancient ruins, palm-fringed beaches, and coral reefs, all accessible from the Santa Marta–Riohacha Highway. (A taxi from Santa Marta costs about $20 round-trip.)

At **Arrecifes**, a 45-minute walk west of the parking lot along a slippery jungle trail, you can take nourishment at the rustic bars and restaurants with the hippies who inhabit the beautiful beaches nearby. Note that swimming here and at Cañaveral (☞ *below*) is extremely dangerous due to riptides, and, yes, sharks. **Pueblito**, an ancient Tayrona village that's being excavated, is a two-hour uphill hike from Arrecifes; along the path you'll find a few basic camping areas. On a clear day, you can see the snow-covered Sierra Nevada from Pueblito.

The park's eastern sector around **Cañaveral** is far more lush than the west, and the final few kilometers to Cañaveral's beach weave through damp jungle before arriving at a parking lot and restaurant. Get your bearings from the spectacular *mirador* (lookout), a 10-minute walk east of the restaurant, then descend to inspect the giant sculptured monoliths on the beach, which lend something of a Planet-of-the-Apes look to the scenery.

You can stay overnight in Parque Tayrona in Cañaveral's "Eco-habs," circular thatched huts (about $10 per person) with paneled interiors, firm beds, cotton sheets, and balconies with 360° views. You can (and should) reserve an Eco-hab in Santa Marta through TURCOL (☞ Tour Operators, *below*).

Outdoor Activities and Sports

BEACHES

Spectacular and deserted white-sand strands lie on Parque Tayrona's outskirts. Swimming here is extremely dangerous, however, due to riptides and sharks. Drownings are *very* common.

La Ciudad Perdida

142 km (88 mi) southeast of Santa Marta.

When *guaqueros* (treasure hunters) stumbled upon La Ciudad Perdida in 1975, they discovered one of the Americas' largest pre-Columbian citadels ever. Dating from sometime between AD 500 and 700, it's anchored on the rugged northern Sierra Nevada slopes at 1,200 m (3,937 ft) and can only be reached by means of a six-day guided trek or a three-hour helicopter ride. Both can be arranged from Santa Marta (☞ Tour Operators, *below*).

The Caribbean Coast A to Z

Arriving and Departing

BY AIRPLANE

There are daily flights between Bogotá, Cali, Medellín, and Cartagena's international **Aeropuerto Rafael Nuñez** (☎ 095/666–1308 or 095/666–0134), 3 km (2 mi) east of downtown. There are daily flights between Bogotá and Santa Marta's **Aeropuerto Simón Bolívar** (☎ 095/421–8480), 20 km (12 mi) and an $8 taxi ride from the city center. Carriers include **Aces** (Cartagena, ☎ 095/664–6858), **Avianca** (Cartagena, ☎ 095/665–5504; Santa Marta, ☎ 0954/210–276 or 0954/210–278), and **Intercontinental** (Cartagena, ☎ 095/666–2995).

BY BUS

Expresso Brasilia (✉ Cartagena, ☎ 095/666–1692; ✉ Santa Marta, ☎ 095/420–8612) regularly connects Cartagena with Bogotá (24 hrs), Barranquilla (2 hrs), and Santa Marta (4 hrs); and Santa Marta with Barranquilla (2 hrs), Cartagena (4 hrs), and Bogotá (20 hrs). There are six trips daily between Cartagena and Magangué, where a *chalupa* (river launch) makes the short trip to Mompós. The bus ride is four hours each way. **La Costeña** (✉ Cartagena, ☎ 095/664–058; ✉ Santa Marta, ☎ 095/420–9044) regularly connects Barranquilla, Cartagena, and Santa Marta, with departures every 20 minutes or so between 6 AM and 4 PM.

BY CAR

Traveling from Bogotá and the interior is laborious; the drive between Bogotá and Cartagena, for example, takes 20 hours on the Pan-American Highway. The Darien Gap, a swath of jungle on the Panama/Colombia border, makes driving to or from Panama impossible—you must put your vehicle on a cargo ship in Panama or Miami, which can be quite expensive. Avoid driving at night, and inquire about the safety of your route before heading out. Ambushes are not uncommon, especially on the road between Bucaramanga and Santa Marta.

Contacts and Resources

BANKS AND CURRENCY EXCHANGE

Banco de la Republica (✉ Calle 14, at Carrera 1C, Santa Marta; Plaza de Bolívar, Cartagena) is open 9–3.

EMERGENCIES

Ambulance: Cruz Roja (Red Cross) ☎ 132.

Police: ☎ 156 or call local information ☎ 113 and ask for emergency assistance.

Hospitals and pharmacies: In Cartagena, **Hospital de Bocagrande** (✉ Calle 5, Carrera 6, Bocagrande, ☎ 665–5270). In Santa Marta, **Clinica El Prado** (✉ Carrera 5, Calle 26, ☎ 213–598).

MAIL

In Cartagena, the **post office** (✉ Plaza de los Coches, off Avenida Venezuela) is open from 9 to 3, but you can also send mail from any of the Avianca Airlines offices, which are open until 5. The Santa Marta post office (✉ Carrera 3 No. 17–26) keeps similar hours.

TOUR OPERATORS

In Cartagena **Tesoro Tours** (✉ Av. San Martín No. 6–129, Bocagrande, ☎ 095/665–4713) arranges city tours for $12 per person and day and overnight tours to Mompós from about $20 per person. **TMA** (✉ Carerra 4 No. 196, Bocagrande, ☎ 095/665–1062) books city tours, rumba en chiva tours, and trips to the Islas del Rosario. Trips by boat to the Islas del Rosario depart daily at 8 AM from the Muelle de los Pegasos, a pier next to the convention center, and return by 4 PM. Trips can be booked through **Caliente Tours** (☎ 095/665–5346), **Media Maranja** (☎ 095/666–4606), or **Raphael Pérez** (☎ 095/660–4214).

In Santa Marta **TMA** (✉ Calle 15 No. 2–60, Edificio Bolívar, ☎ 095/421–4190) has city tours plus treks to Pueblito, La Ciudad Perdida, and Parque Tayrona. Through **TURCOL** (Turismo Colombiano; ✉ Carerra 1C No. 20–15, Santa Marta, ☎ 095/421–2256) you can reserve a Tayrona Eco-hab or just browse the information.

VISITOR INFORMATION

Cartagena's **Oficina de Turismo** (✉ Aeropuerto Rafael Nuñez Airport, ☎ 095/664–7015 or 095/664–8078) and **Casa del Marqués Valdehoyos** (✉ Calle de la Factoría No. 36–57, Cartagena, ☎ 095/664–6567) are open roughly 9 to 1 and 2 to 5.

The Santa Marta **Oficina de Turismo** (✉ Calle 10 No. 3–10, El Rodadero, ☎ 095/422–9483) has maps and can recommend a guide but is often closed.

SAN ANDRÉS AND PROVIDENCIA

The resort islands of San Andrés and Providencia lie 640 km (400 mi) northwest of the Caribbean coast, closer to Nicaragua than Colombia. Christopher Columbus was the first European to set foot on the islands during his fourth voyage to the New World. They were later settled by English pilgrims (who landed in their vessel, the *Seaflower*, at the same time pilgrims landed at Plymouth Rock) and then by Jamaican cotton growers. Today the islands' roughly 60,000 residents speak an English patois and Spanish. Frequent air service and San Andrés's duty-free status mean both islands now receive a steady stream of visitors, mostly well-to-do Colombians, who dive and snorkel between bouts of sunbathing and shopping. Moreover, the islands are a welcome escape from the troubles at home, as they've experienced much less crime than continental Colombia.

San Andrés

645 km (400 mi) off Colombia's Caribbean coast.

The island's duty-free status is responsible for the bland boutiques in the concrete jungle of **El Centro,** San Andrés's commercial center. Come for the surrounding coral cays and reefs, and not the shopping. Diving is a big draw here, as is angling for sailfish, bonito, and marlin; you can organize a diving trip or rent snorkeling gear from **Aquamarina** (⊠ *Av. Colombia, next to El Aquamarina hotel,* ☎ 09851/26649).

San Andrés is only 13 km (8 mi) long; it's easy to explore by bicycle or motor scooter, which you can rent from one of the shops along Avenida Colombia in El Centro. Tour the coastal road and visit **Cueva Morgan,** a small beachfront settlement where the pirate Henry Morgan reputedly stashed his loot after pillaging coastal Cuba and Panama in the 1670s. Beach bums should head for **Johnny Cay** or **San Luis,** the island's two most popular strands.

Dining and Lodging

The absence of fresh water on San Andrés explains why many hotels have saltwater showers. Those listed below have either fresh- or desalinated-water showers.

$$$$ ✕☰ **Maryland.** Small chintzy rooms open onto a seafront balcony—the architectural norm around here. The airport is nearby. ⊠ *Av. Colombia 9–38,* ☎ FAX *09851/24825. 65 rooms. Restaurant, bar, pool, hot tub. AE, DC, MC, V.*

$$–$$$ ✕☰ **El Aquarium.** Large, fan-cooled rooms occupy 15 towers that overlook the sea. Rooms have stucco walls, terra-cotta floors, and tile baths. ⊠ *Av. Colombia 1–19, Punta Hansa,* ☎ 09851/23117, FAX *09851/26938. 250 rooms. 2 restaurants, 2 bars, saltwater pool. AE, DC, MC, V.*

$$ ✕☰ **Lord Pierre Hotel.** This beachfront hotel has a wide, private pier for sunbathing and is near the commercial center for convenient shopping. Rooms are medium size with big beds and bamboo furniture. ⊠ *Av. Colombia N1B–106,* ☎ 09851/27541, FAX *09851/25666. 58 rooms, 2 suites. Restaurant, café, bar, pool. AE, DC, MC, V.*

Providencia

90 km (56 mi) northwest of San Andrés.

Volcanic in origin, tiny Providencia Island (it's a mere 7 km/4.5 mi long and 4 km/2.5 mi wide) has rugged hills, abundant fresh water, and much less development than San Andrés. Its lack of real commerce or industry makes it a quiet, easygoing Caribbean retreat. On the west coast is **Aquadulce,** the island's largest town, where you can rent bicycles and motor scooters or join a boat tour of the surrounding islets. Smaller **Santa Isabel,** on the island's northern tip, is the governmental center, and although it has a few restaurants, it's less-populated by visitors. The best beaches are to the south, in Manzanillo and South West Bay; Crab Cay is best for snorkeling. Choose a clear day to hike up the 305-m (1,000-ft) summit of **El Pico,** which has superb views of the island's turquoise seashore and necklace of coral cays; it's a 90-minute trek each way from Casa Baja, the village at the bottom.

Dining and Lodging

$ ✕⌂ **Cabañas El Paraíso.** These wooden cabins on Aquadulce's beach have clean and simple rooms with ocean views. Adjoining the complex is a no-frills but dependable restaurant. You can reserve a room through Islatur (☞ Visitor Information, *below*). ✉ *Aquadulce,* ☎ *09851/24127. 15 rooms. Restaurant, fans. No credit cards.*

San Andrés and Providencia A to Z

Arriving and Departing

BY AIRPLANE

Aeropuerto Sesquicentenario is a short taxi ride from most San Andrés hotels and is regularly served by **Aces,** in Bogotá, ☎ 091/341–8499 or 091/336–0300; **Avianca,** ☎ 9851/23307; **Intercontinental,** ☎ 9851/26115 or 9851/6270; and **Satena,** ☎ 9851/29393. The 90-minute flight from Bogotá costs about $180 each way; the one-hour flight from Cartagena, about $130 each way. SAM also links San Andrés with Providencia Island three times daily for about $80 round-trip.

BY BOAT

There are no passenger boats from the Colombian mainland to the island or between the islands.

Contacts and Resources

BANKS AND CURRENCY EXCHANGE

In San Andrés, U.S. currency is accepted by some stores in addition to pesos, and credit card advances on MasterCard and Visa are available at many banks. Traveler's checks can be cashed at banks and some hotels. Bring pesos with you to Providencia; here you'll have a hard time changing traveler's checks or exchanging foreign currency. **Banco de la República** (Avenida Colon, between Costa Rica and Avenida Providencia, San Andrés Town) is open 9 to 3.

EMERGENCIES

Ambulance: In San Andrés, **Cruz Roja** (Red Cross) ☎ 512–7333. For the **police,** call local information ☎ 113 and ask for emergency assistance or ☎ 09851/24390. In Providencia, call ☎ 11 for emergencies. **Hospitals and pharmacies:** In San Andrés, **Hospital** (✉ Avenida Providencia, ☎ 23–057). In Providencia, **Hospital** (☎ 48–119).

MAIL

In San Andrés, the **post office** (✉ Avenida Duarte Blum, between Avenida 20 de Julio and Avenida Colombia) is open 9 to 3.

TELEPHONES

The area code for the islands is 09851.

TOUR OPERATORS

In Bogotá **Carnaval Tours** (✉ Carrera 5 No. 14–55, ☎ 091/286–1129) specializes package tours to San Andrés and Providencia, starting at about $200 round-trip from Bogotá.

VISITOR INFORMATION

On San Andrés visit **Oficina de Turismo** (✉ Aeropuerto Sesquicente-nario, ☎ 09851/6110; ✉ Av. Colombia, ☎ 09851/24230) or, for tours, call **Islatur** (✉ Hotel Cacique Toné, Av. Colombia, ☎ 098/512–4127, ℻ 098/512–4256).

COLOMBIA A TO Z

Arriving and Departing

By Airplane

AIRPORTS

International airports in Barranquilla, Bogotá, Cali, Cartagena, Medel-lín, and San Andrés regularly serve destinations in the U.S. and Eu-rope. As a safety precaution, you may be asked to arrive at the airport as early as 3 hours before your departure time.

CARRIERS

U.S. carriers serving Colombia include **American Airlines** (☎ 091/413–9595 or 091/285–1111 for reservations), which flies from Miami; and **Continental Airlines** (☎ 091/312–2565), which flies from Hous-ton. European carriers include **British Airways** (☎ 091/218–0200); **Air France** (☎ 091/413–9500 or 091/254–8990 for reservations); and **Al-italia** (☎ 091/285–7305).

Aces (☎ 091/336–0300 in Bogotá; 094/261–2020 in Medellín) serves Bogotá and Medellín from Miami. **Avianca** (☎ 091/341–5497 or 091/282–2341 in Bogotá; 0928/667–6886 or 0928/667–4141 in Cali; 095/665–5504 in Cartagena), Colombia's national carrier, serves Barran-quilla, Bogotá, Cali, and Cartagena from Los Angeles, Miami, and New York; and, in Europe, from Frankfurt, London, Madrid, and Paris. It also has regular flights from Colombia to other South American cities. **Copa** (☎ 094/358–4261 or 094/358–9479 in Bogotá; 092/659–2399 in Cali; 095/664–4526 or 095/664–8289 in Cartagena; 094/511–4660 in Medellín) has regular service from Miami to Barranquilla, Bogotá, Cali, Cartagena, and Medellín, via Panama City. **Mexicana** (☎ 094/413–9500 or 094/610–7258) flies from Mexico City to Bogotá about once a month.

FLYING TIMES

Flights from Houston to Bogotá take five hours; flights from Miami are less than three hours.

By Boat

A daily ferry makes the four-hour trip between Panama's Puerto Obaldía and the Colombian port of Turbo.

Getting Around

Wherever possible, avoid taking buses or driving a car in Colombia, especially for out-of-town excursions. Information for these types of travel is available, but not recommended. When traveling from one Colombian city to another, fly, take an organized tour through a tour-company, or hire a driver through your hotel.

Even as a passenger, avoid driving at night because of the risk of am-bush by guerrillas or dangerous thugs impersonating them. (The road from Bucaramanga to Santa Marta, for example, should be especially avoided). Keep your car doors locked and windows rolled up at all times.

By Airplane

Regular flights connect all major Colombian cities. Since the country is fairly large—almost twice the size of Texas—it's more practical to fly, especially between the Caribbean coast and Medellín, Bogotá, or Cali. Avianca, the oldest airline in the Americas and the second-oldest in the world, sells a Discover Colombia air pass, which includes three intra-country flights, not including San Andrés and Providencia islands, for $100, and five flights for $180. The air pass can only be purchased outside Colombia and all flights must be reserved in advance.

There are daily flights between most major cities, and many smaller destinations with **Aces** (✉ Carrera 10 No. 27–51, Office 201, Bogotá, ☎ 091/341–8499 or 091/336–0300), **AIRES** (✉ Av. 13 No. 79–56, Bogotá, ☎ 091/610–9653 or 091/611–2629), **Avianca** (✉ Carrera 7 No. 16–36, Bogotá, ☎ 091/341–5497 or 091/282–2341), **Intercontinental de Aviación** (✉ Carrera 10 No. 28–31, Bogotá, ☎ 091/413–5666 or 091/284–0177), **SAM** (✉ Carrera 13A No. 93–36, Bogotá, ☎ 091/266–9600), and **Satena** (✉ Carrera 10A No. 27–51, Suite 211, Bogotá, ☎ 091/284–9332 or, for reservations, 091/423–8500).

By Bus

The U.S. Department of State strongly warns against traveling by bus in Colombia due to the risk of theft, druggings, and violence. If you must take the bus, be absolutely self-protective and discreet. Avoid the very basic *corriente* (standard) service; opt for a first-class bus (variously called *pullman, metropolitano, de lujo,* or *directo*) or a deluxe bus with air-conditioning (called *thermo* or *climatizado*), which only run between Bogotá, Medellín, Cali, and the Caribbean coast. You'll pay $2–$5 per 100 km (62 mi). These buses have toilets, and, on longer trips, they show movies and stop for meals.

By Car

EMERGENCY ASSISTANCE

In an emergency contact **Policia Vial** (☎ 091/247–1151), who have a mobile workshop for fixing breakdowns. If you rent a car, it's a good idea to affiliate yourself with the **Automóvil Club de Colombia** (✉ Diagonal 187 No. 41–85, Bogotá, ☎ 091/677–5966), who will tow your car to a mechanic if they can't fix it themselves.

GASOLINE

Gasoline comes in two grades: *premium* (95 octane), available only in large cities for about $1.60 per U.S. gallon; and *corriente* (84 octane), sometimes called "regular," which costs around $1.20 per U.S. gallon and is available throughout the country. Although, for safety reasons, and to avoid getting fined for running out of gas, you should consider bringing a gallon along with you.

RENTALS

Car rentals in Colombia are very expensive: $450–$800 per week. You'll need a credit card, passport, and driver's license. You may be better off hiring your own car and driver; inquire at your hotel. In Bogotá, *see* Hotel Tequendama, *above.*

ROAD CONDITIONS

Driving in Colombia is not recommended—carjackings are common enough to supercede poor road conditions as most threatening. Reduce the risk of becoming a target for your car and rent a taxi for excursions. If you must drive, beware the crumbling, narrow, and winding roads. During rainy season, roads can turn to mud or, like bridges, wash out completely. And bring a good map as signs are irregularly posted. Night driving is strongly discouraged. Tolls (up to $1.50, payable only in pesos) are common; motorcycles are usually exempt. Where possible, leave your car in an attended parking lot, especially at night.

RULES OF THE ROAD

The rules and courtesies you may be familiar with at home, such as speed limits and yielding to pedestrians, often aren't followed here. If you plan to drive here, get an international license *before* you leave home. National driver's licenses are accepted but must be accompanied by an official translation, which is a bureaucratic time-waster. Police checkpoints are common, and you should make sure your documents are always at hand. Note that roadblocks set up by military groups are often designed to exact money and automobiles from drivers. Highway speed limits are typically 100 kph. There's an automatic fine for running out of gasoline on the road.

Contacts and Resources

Customs and Duties

ON ARRIVAL

The duty-free allowance per person is 200 cigarettes, 50 cigars, up to 250 grams of tobacco, and two bottles of either wine or spirits. You can bring electronic equipment, such as video cameras and laptops, as long as they bear clear signs of use, although it's not recommended that you bring valuables with you.

ON DEPARTURE

If you have purchased any gold, platinum, or emerald articles, you must present a proof of purchase. There's no limit on the amount of money you can bring in or out of the country. Colonial objects can be taken out of the country without hindrance, but exporting pre-Columbian artifacts is against the law. Expect to pay an airport tax of $17, $30 for stays longer than 60 days.

Electricity

The electrical current in Colombia is 120 volts AC, just like in North America. Sockets take two-prong plugs.

Embassies

United States (✉ Calle 22D Bis No. 47–51, Bogotá, ☎ 091/315–0811, FAX 091/315–219697). Upon arrival in Colombia, it's recommended that U.S. citizens register with the Consular Section of the embassy. **United Kingdom** (✉ Calle 9 No. 76–49, 9th floor, Bogotá, ☎ 091/317–6690). **Canada** (✉ Calle 76 No. 11–52, Bogotá, ☎ 091/313–1355).There's no embassy for citizens of **Australia**, but in an emergency Australians can call a representative at ☎ 091/249–9829, or the nearest embassy in Caracas, Venezuela, ☎ 0091/582/263–4033. Citizens of **New Zealand** are represented by the United Kingdom.

Emergencies

Police (☎ 156). **Ambulance** (☎ 125).

Health and Safety

CRIME

Violence perpetrated by drug cartels and guerrilla groups are a fact of life in Colombia, but if you're discreet, alert, and take precautions—leave jewelry in your hotel safe, know your surroundings, conceal your camera, carry money not just in your wallet or money belt but maybe also in a shoe—you'll be less likely to run into problems. And, if a curfew is in effect—most likely it will be from dusk to dawn—be sure to obey it.

In downtown Bogotá and other large cities, don't be duped by plain-clothes "policemen" demanding to register your money—they are almost certainly thieves. In case of such confrontations, you may want to hand over a "disposable" $20 bill to extricate yourself quickly. Avoid black market money-changers or any dubious transaction aimed at getting a better rate of exchange. Watch your possessions carefully in airports and public places. Have nothing to do with drug dealers, especially because many of them freelance as police informers. Possession of cocaine or marijuana can lead to a long sentence in an unpleasant Colombian jail. Don't accept gifts of food, drink, cigarettes, or chewing gum from strangers; there have been reports of travelers being drugged and relieved of their valuables in this way.

Although its reputation has been marred by Medellín's and Cali's drug cartels, Colombia is hardly a war zone. To be sure, you'll regularly see machine-gun-toting soldiers, but for destinations in this chapter, there's a fairly established "gringo trail," and thousands visit each year without mishap. Before you go, consult the U.S. Department of State Travel Advisory (☎ 202/647–4000, www.travel.state.gov/colombia.html).

FOOD AND DRINK

Don't drink the water or fountain soft drinks, and ask for your beverages *sin hielo* (without ice). The water in Bogotá and Medellín is heavily chlorinated and may be safe enough to drink, but it's best to simply rely on bottled, purified water everywhere. Also avoid eating unpeeled fruit, uncooked vegetables, and salads.

SHOTS AND MEDICATIONS

Colombia's pharmacies are well stocked, although you should bring some basic supplies to combat diarrhea, just in case. Some people experience dizziness and headaches upon arrival in Bogotá because of the thin mountain air. You should avoid alcohol until you acclimatize, get extra sleep (at lower altitudes than during waking hours if possible), and drink a lot of water and juice to keep hydrated. A local remedy *mate de coca* (tea made from coca leaves) helps alleviate some symptoms, as does aspirin. See a doctor and descend to a lower elevation, even if it's just to the hotel lobby, if you experience vomiting, breathlessness, or disorientation. Immunizations against the following diseases are recommended at least three months in advance of your trip: hepatitis A (and hepatitis B, if you're being extra careful), tetanus-diphtheria, typhoid, and yellow fever. The decision whether or not to take malaria-preventing pills should be made after you've talked with your doctor.

Language, Culture, and Etiquette

Spanish is the official language, although you may overhear some of the roughly 90 Indian languages that are also spoken. English is widely understood on San Andrés and Providencia islands and is commonly spoken in the major cities' resort hotels and restaurants.

Mail

All international airmail is handled by Avianca, Colombia's largest airline. Airmail post offices are normally next to the airline's offices and are open weekdays 7:30–6, Saturday 8–noon. You can also use Colombia's postal service, although mail will take longer, and business hours are shorter, usually 9 to 3. For post office locations, *see* Mail *in* each city section.

POSTAL RATES

Airmail service costs about 80¢ to the United States and $1 to Europe and is relatively reliable, taking about 7–14 days.

RECEIVING MAIL

Avianca holds letters for up to 30 days, and you'll need your passport to claim them from the *poste restante* desk.

WRITING TO COLOMBIA

Letters should be sent to poste restante, Correo Aéreo Avianca, followed by the city and province name. If you have American Express traveler's checks or credit cards, you can have mail sent to you at their offices.

Money Matters

You can use credit cards and traveler's checks in the bigger, international hotels and in the shops and restaurants of major cities, though you should always carry some pesos with you. (Master Card and Visa are more commonly accepted than American Express or Diner's Club.) Elsewhere credit cards are only occasionally accepted, and you'll be expected to pay with cash.

U.S. currency and traveler's checks can be exchanged for a small fee in big hotels, travel agencies, and money exchange offices (less reliably British, Canadian, Australian, and New Zealand currencies or traveler's checks). You'll get a better rate at the banks, which, unfortunately, have very limited hours; mornings are your best bet. Credit cards give the most stable and highest rate of exchange, so you should use them for cash advances as much as possible. Either way, keep your exchange receipts to protect yourself against fraud. When departing, you can convert unused pesos into U.S. dollars (up to $60) at the airport's casa de cambio.

CURRENCY

Colombia's monetary unit is the peso, which has lost so much value it's no longer divided into centavos. Peso bills are circulated in the following denominations: 2,000, 5,000, 10,000, and 20,000. Peso coins come in denominations of 50, 100, 200, 500 and 1,000. At press time the official exchange rate was about 1,680 pesos to the U.S. dollar, 2,690 pesos to the pound sterling, 1,150 to the Canadian dollar, 1,105 pesos to the Australian dollar, and 916 pesos to the New Zealand dollar.

SERVICE CHARGES, TAXES, AND TIPPING

Throughout Colombia, hotels add 16% to your bill, and there's a 15% value-added tax (IVA) added to almost everything. Taxi drivers don't expect tips. Porters at airports and hotels are usually given 300 pesos for each piece of luggage. In many restaurants, bars, and cafés, a 10% service charge is automatically added to the bill; if not, a 10% tip is expected. Leave hotel maids the equivalent of a few dollars when departing, and tip clerks as you would a porter.

WHAT IT WILL COST

Bogotá, Cali, Cartagena, and San Andrés are the most expensive destinations; but, even then, you'll find first-class accommodations for $50 per night. The least-expensive areas are coastal and mountain villages, where you'll part with $2 for a meal and $5 for accommodation.

Sample Prices: cup of coffee, 50¢; bottle of beer, $1; bottle of wine in a restaurant, $15–$20; bottle of wine in store, $7–$10; 1-mi taxi ride, $2; city bus ride, 60¢; theater or cinema ticket, $2.

Opening and Closing Times

Banks are generally open weekdays 9–3 (until 3:30 on Friday), with a couple of hours off for lunch. In Bogotá many banks close an hour earlier. On the last working day of the month, banks are only open in the early morning, though in Bogotá they're open until noon. Most **museums** are open roughly from 9 to 1 and 2 to 5, and tend to be closed on Monday. **Shops** and stores are open roughly 9 to 5, though a majority close daily for lunch between 12:30 and 2 PM. Most are also closed on Sunday.

The Circumcision of Our Lord (Jan. 1); Epiphany (Jan. 6); St. Joseph's Day (Mar. 21); Holy Week (Palm Sunday through Easter Sunday): Palm Sunday, Maundy Thursday, and Good Friday (Apr. 16, 20 and 21 in 2000; Apr. 8, 12 and 13 in 2001), Easter (Apr. 23 in 2000; Apr. 15 in 2001); Labor Day (May 1); Ascension Day (June 2 in 2000; May 25 in 2001); Corpus Christi (June 22 in 2000; June 10 in 2001); Sts. Peter and Paul's Day (July 4); Independence Day (July 20); Battle of Boyacá (Aug. 7); Assumption Day (Aug. 15); Discovery of America (Oct. 12); All Saints' Day (Nov. 1); Independence of Cartagena (Nov. 14); Immaculate Conception (Dec. 8); Christmas (Dec. 25).

Passports and Visas

Citizens from Australia, Canada, the United States, the United Kingdom, and New Zealand need only a valid passport to enter Colombia for up to 30 days; tourist visas aren't required.

Telephones

CALLS TO COLOMBIA

Colombia's country code is 57. When dialing Colombia internationally, drop the 0 from the in-country area code.

LOCAL CALLS

Direct dialing is available almost everywhere (exceptions include some places in the Andes and along the Caribbean coast, where you'll do best to visit a Telecom office). Public telephones are common in large cities but are scarce everywhere else; they accept 100- and 500-peso coins. If you don't have access to a phone, there's also a Telecom office in nearly every town where you can make calls.

For directory assistance (in Spanish) within Colombia, dial **113.**

LONG-DISTANCE AND INTERNATIONAL CALLS

When dialing long distance from within Colombia, dial 009, the area code, and then the number. Direct-dial international calls are best made from a Telecom office, where you must leave a deposit of $5–$10 before dialing, or from your hotel, where the rate will be *substantially* more. The average rate per minute to the United States is $6; from a hotel, it's about $10. Or, for inter-city calls, use the blue-and-yellow or red long-distance booths marked *larga distancia* (which only accept 500-peso coins).

Access Codes: To make credit card and collect calls through an **AT&T** operator, dial 980–11–0011. For **MCI,** dial 980–16–0001. For **Sprint,** dial 980–13–0010.

Visitor Information

Colombian Embassy: 2118 Leroy Place NW, Washington, DC, 20008, ☎ 202/387–8338, ℻ 202/232–8643 or 202/387–0176.

When to Go

December through February are the best (read: driest) months to visit Colombia. These are the peak-season months when hotel prices are highest. Colombians also travel during these sometimes hot and humid months. While visiting during a festival will add an exciting cultural edge to your trip, you'll experience inflated prices and often overwhelming crowds.

CLIMATE

Colombia is often perceived as a steamy tropical country, but its climate varies greatly with altitude. Along the Caribbean coast temperatures are an average of 82°F (28°C); in high-Andes Bogotá, it's a chilly 54°F (12°C) and frequently overcast. The valley cities of Medellín and Cali have pleasant weather, with average temperatures somewhere between those of Bogotá and the coast.

Seasons don't really exist in Colombia, but rainfall and brisk winter-like weather is common October to November and April to June. Rainfall is rarely excessive and is only a problem if you plan to travel off the beaten track on Colombia's rough-paved mountain roads. The dry season usually runs December to March in mountainous areas, mid-December to April and July to September in low-lying coastal regions.

The following are the average monthly maximum and minimum temperatures for Bogotá.

Jan.	67F	19C	May	66F	19C	Sept.	66F	19C
	48	9		51	10		49	9
Feb.	68F	20C	June	65F	18C	Oct.	66F	19C
	49	9		51	10		50	10
Mar.	67F	19C	July	64F	18C	Nov.	66F	19C
	50	10		50	10		50	10
Apr.	67F	19C	Aug.	65F	18C	Dec.	66F	19C
	51	10		50	10		49	9

FESTIVALS AND SEASONAL EVENTS

In Popayán, the **Black and White Carnival** held on January 5 and 6 celebrates the racial diversity of the three wise men with bodypainting and dancing.

Carnival season (March) is particularly festive in Barranquilla. In April, **Holy Week,** Palm Sunday through Easter Sunday, processions fill the colonial towns of Popayán and Mompós.

The **flower festival** is held in Medellín in late May or early June. The **Folklore Festival** is held in Ibagué, usually during the last week in June.

In early November, Cartagena's **Reinado Nacional de la Belleza** features beauty contests and a full week of merrymaking that celebrates the city's independence. Once a sugar harvest celebration, Cali's popular **feria** is now a party for its own sake, running from December 25 to January 1.

8   ECUADOR

A patchwork of highland and jungle,
this tiny nation is home to colonial
cities preserved from the days of the
conquistadors, snowcapped volcanoes
quilted with green, terraced plots, and the
flora and fauna of the Amazon Basin—
natural wonders that change the very way
we see ourselves and the world.

Updated
by Shane
Christensen

SANDWICHED BETWEEN PERU AND COLOMBIA, Ecuador is often overlooked as a mere stepping-stone to the more famous Galápagos Islands. Yet mainland Ecuador, an increasingly popular destination for ecotourism, is an adventurer's paradise that should not be missed. The growing market for adventure travel is reminiscent of Costa Rica a decade ago, and visitors can choose from a wide variety of stimulating activities: white-water rafting along wild rivers, trekking and mountaineering on some of the world's highest volcanic peaks, and horseback riding and mountain biking through lush subtropical valleys. Dedicated birders will spot many of Ecuador's more than 1,500 indigenous and migratory species—from toucans and tanagers to macaws and parrots—in cloud forests, tropical dry forests, and, of course, the rain forests of the Amazon Basin.

Traversing the entire country from north to south, the rugged Andes embrace a series of fertile, high-altitude valleys easily accessed from the Pan-American Highway. Most travelers to Ecuador begin or end their trip in the highlands with a visit to Quito, which, at 2,907 m (9,530 ft) above sea level, is South America's second-highest capital city. Quito is a pleasant mixture of modern and colonial sights: You'll find art galleries and stylish cafés in the New City, while the historic Old City has striking colonial architecture protected by the United Nations Educational, Scientific, and Cultural Organization (UNESCO).

South of Quito, the Pan-American Highway winds past the country's tallest volcanoes (which are best visited from towns such as Baños and Riobamba), eventually arriving at the tranquil city of Cuenca. In addition to being a pleasant town packed with impressive architecture, Cuenca lies near the country's most important Inca site.

West of Quito towers the recently active Pichincha Volcano, beyond which the Andes plunge toward the coast. Although tourist infrastructure along Ecuador's Pacific coast is spotty, Machalilla National Park is beginning to draw both development and adventurous tourists to the central coast. Guayaquil, South America's busiest port, attracts more foreign business than tourism; although it's noisy and neglected-looking, the city still has its share of excellent restaurants and first-class hotels.

More impressive is Ecuador's upper Amazon Basin, El Oriente, which comprises one-third of the country's landmass but has only about 4% of its population. There are endless waterways to explore, many species of wildlife to discover, and little-known Indian cultures to encounter deep within Ecuador's enigmatic rain forest. Border wars with Peru, the most substantive in 1942, have reduced Ecuador's portion of El Oriente by half—a fact that Ecuadoran mapmakers have yet to accept. Despite this, tourists have little to fear in the Oriente, and recent improvements in relations with Peru may lead to new border openings.

Ecuador's most touristed area is the Galápagos Islands, separated from the mainland by 960 km (600 mi) of Pacific Ocean. This barren, volcanic archipelago is inhabited not only by giant tortoises and spiny marine iguanas but also by modern Robinson Crusoes who have traded creature comforts for an island existence in shorts and sandals. Tour the islands by boat, swimming with sea lions and snorkeling or diving in waters rich with marine life, and you, too, may understand why locals willingly accept a lack of modernization in exchange for life in what's known as Darwin's "living laboratory of evolution."

In some senses, Ecuador still feels isolated from the rest of the world. The land is pristine and the people largely untainted by Western cyni-

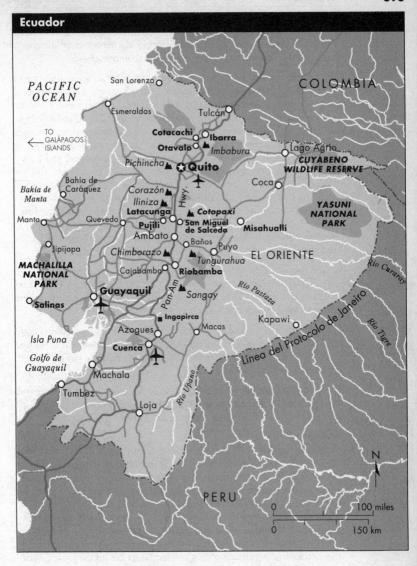

cism. The country's majestic, varied landscapes are home to indigenous peoples who have lived off the earth for generations with comparatively little contact with the West. In rural Ecuador, in particular, the people seem good-natured, trustworthy, and excited to meet foreigners. Confronted by this sincere enthusiasm, travelers have little choice but to give Ecuador a special place in their hearts. From the sleek ships touring the Galápagos to the rattling *collectivos* hurtling down mountain passes, from the fierce volcanic peaks to the impenetrable cloud forest, and from the cosmopolitan *Quiteños* to the beautiful *indígenas*, Ecuador is a land of irresistible contrasts and unparalleled natural beauty.

Pleasures and Pastimes

Dining

In the major cities you can enjoy international or traditional Ecuadoran dishes at pleasingly low prices, although wines and most hard liquors are imported and can double the tab. The main meal of the day is lunch, *el almuerzo,* which typically consists of a meat or fish plate accompanied by rice and fried potatoes, and a small salad. Time to relax or sleep after such a large meal is essential. Seafood is a mainstay on the coast, though even Quito menus feature fresh fish and seafood.

For the adventurous carnivore, there are succulent suckling piglets and guinea pigs (called *cuy*), often roasted—teeth, paws, and all—over a charcoal fire. *Seco de chivo* is a fully garnished lamb stew. *Humitas* are sweet corn tamales eaten by tradition-minded Ecuadorans only in the late afternoon, generally with black coffee. Other Andean favorites include *llapingachos* (mashed cheese and potato pancakes) and *locro de queso,* a milk-based soup that contains corn, potatoes, and a garnish of fresh avocado. An Ecuadoran specialty is ceviche, fish or seafood marinated in lime juice and seasoned with onion, tomato, chili peppers, and cilantro and often served with *cangil* (popcorn). *Churrasco* is a steak fillet with a fried egg, usually accompanied by rice and salad. Typical coastal cuisine is based around *arroz con menestra,* huge portions of white rice served with either black beans or lentils and *patacones,* green bananas fried in oil, smashed, and refried.

Cafeterias and inexpensive restaurants often are open throughout the day. Better restaurants open for lunch between noon and 4 PM, then reopen for dinner at 7 PM and serve until 10 PM, or as late as midnight in Guayaquil. Many restaurants close on Sunday.

While most $$$ and $$$$ restaurants do not actually require a coat and tie, Ecuadorans who spend that amount on dinner *do* dress up. You may feel uncomfortably shabby, or be spurned by your waiter, if you do not follow suit.

Prices quoted are per person and include appetizer, main course, and dessert but exclude alcoholic beverages, tax, service charge, and tip. For price categories *see* Dining *in* Smart Travel Tips A to Z.

Lodging

Accommodations range from the modern luxury hotels of the main cities, where guests can easily imagine they're in Miami, to centuries-old haciendas that have been converted to *hosterías* (country inns), where you might sometimes feel as if you've slipped into another century. While the highland hotels offer exposure to local history and culture, those in the tropical forests of the Oriente, Pacific coast, and Galápagos Islands provide close contact with nature at its best. Unless you stay in the most expensive hotels, you'll find the rates refreshing; most middle- and lower-range hotels offer remarkable services for the price. Check-out time is 1 PM at most hotels and breakfast is not usually included in the rate.

Prices quoted are for a double room and include a 20% tax and service charge. For price categories, *see* Lodging *in* Smart Travel Tips A to Z.

The Creatures of the World

There are few places on Earth that offer the kind of close contact with nature that the Galápagos Islands are famous for, but there are other spots in Ecuador where the animal-watching is nothing less than spectacular. The isolated national parks of the Oriente protect important expanses of the tropical rain forest and Amazon tributaries that are inhabited by anacondas, howler monkeys, anteaters, pink river dolphins, and hundreds of birds. The highland forests are also home to an array of avian species—ranging from delicate hummingbirds to the mighty condor—while the pastures that surround those forests offer close encounters with llamas, alpacas, and other Andean ungulates.

Shopping

Market day, which begins early Saturday morning in villages across Ecuador, is also social day. This is when indigenous people descend from the surrounding mountains into the city valleys—where the wealthy landowners historically lived—to sell fruits, vegetables, meats, textiles, and anything else they grow or make. This is where you can buy ponchos and Panama hats, beads and handmade jewelry. Among the most interesting sights is the slaughterhouse—typically watched over by a statue of the Virgin Mary—where beef, lamb, pork, and fish are sliced from whole carcasses. Unfortunately, sanitary conditions are often lacking and you're best off purchasing only fruits that can be peeled.

Browsing and bartering at one of the country's outdoor markets is a must for all but the most avowed shopping haters. The popular wares of Ecuador include colorful wool sweaters and jackets, wood statues, handwoven bags, belts, ponchos, llama-skin rugs, jewelry, and Panama hats, which are produced in Ecuador. Weekly markets are a tradition in the Andes region, where Indians in colorful regional dress arrive from the countryside on foot, horseback, bus, burro, or in fancy new pickup trucks. Bargaining is an indispensable yet polite ritual. Mild curiosity, with a slightly shocked look when the price is offered, begins the process. A counteroffer of half the asking price is usual, and the norm is to agree on about 75% of the original asking price.

Exploring Ecuador

The Pan-American Highway runs north–south through the heart of the Ecuadoran highlands, passing near most of the country's important towns and cities and some of its most spectacular scenery. This makes the majority of the country's attractions easy to reach by land, although inexpensive flights among Quito, Cuenca, and Guayaquil make air travel convenient for at least part of any itinerary. Air travel is essential for visiting the Galápagos Islands and much of the Oriente; the flight to Galápagos is the only relatively expensive trip in Ecuador. Although you could easily explore much of the highlands and Pacific lowlands on your own, packaged tours are definitely the best option for visiting the Galápagos Islands and Amazon Basin.

Great Itineraries

You could spend a month exploring Ecuador, but a minimum of 10 days is needed to truly sample the country's varied attractions. The three major regions—the highlands, the Oriente, and the Galápagos Islands—each require a minimum of three days, and deserve much more than that, while visits to the Pacific coast and other areas off the beaten track will require you to extend your stay further.

IF YOU HAVE 5 DAYS

Most trips to Ecuador begin and end in **Quito,** which has an extensive, well-preserved colonial sector, a good selection of museums, and some other interesting attractions close by. After two nights in the capital you'll either want to head for **Imbabura Province** to the north, or the **central highlands** to the south for a couple of days amid the volcanoes and market towns before returning to Quito. It is best to schedule a trip to Imbabura around the famous **Otavalo Saturday market.** Travelers whose port of entry is **Guayaquil** will want to head to **Cuenca,** where they can spend a few days exploring that colonial city and surroundings, or to the Pacific coast for deep-sea fishing, whale-watching, or simply lounging on the beach.

After a day or two exploring the capital, head either north or south, to **Imbabura Province** or the **central highlands,** respectively, and spend a couple of nights in one of the market towns or nearby colonial hosterías. Return to **Quito** for a flight to the **Galápagos,** where you should really spend a minimum of three days. You may prefer to skip the islands and make your way slowly south through the highlands, loitering in **Baños** and **Cuenca** both of which lie near impressive natural areas. If you don't loiter too much in the highlands, you can fly from Cuenca to Guayaquil and make a quick visit to coastal **Machalilla National Park** before flying back to Quito.

After you explore **Quito** at a leisurely pace for three or four days, head north to **Imbabura Province,** where the market towns are complemented by verdant volcanoes and mountain lakes. After two days or so head south overland into the central highlands. Three days should cover the highlands (which you can explore on horseback, mountain bike, or in a rubber raft), and from **Baños** you can travel by land into **the Oriente** for a couple of days in the bosom of nature itself. Take a quick flight to the colonial city of **Cuenca,** which, in addition to being Ecuador's most attractive town, has enough natural and cultural attractions nearby to keep you busy for several days. Finish up with a short flight from Cuenca to **Guayaquil,** which not only lies near the Pacific beaches, but is connected to the **Galápagos Islands** via daily flights. The Galápagos require a minimum of three days to visit and are connected to Quito via daily flights.

QUITO

More than a simple stopping-off point on the way to the Galápagos Islands, Quito is an engaging city and an excellent base for excursions into the nearby central highland and Imbabura regions. Ecuador's capital is scenically situated in a long, narrow valley at the foot of the restless Pichincha Volcano. Rugged, dark-green mountains surround the city, providing the sort of photogenic backdrop you might not expect in a sprawling metropolis of 1.2 million people. Quito lies only 24 km (15 mi) south of the equator, but because of its altitude it has a mild climate all year. Quiteños are fond of saying that their city gives you four seasons in one day—a statement supported by the springlike mornings, summery afternoons, autumnal evenings, and wintery nights.

After the weather, Quito's other surprise is its preserved, vibrant Old City, a maze of colonial mansions, cathedrals, and crowded cobblestone streets. UNESCO has declared the Old City a World Heritage Site, banning the destruction of colonial buildings and limiting new construction, which is why Quito's colonial sector is one of the best preserved in South America. Exploring the Old City's cobbled streets, plazas, and churches is the high point of any stay in Quito. Nonetheless, after a morning in the crowded Old City, the relative tranquillity of the New City—with its outdoor cafés, galleries, and smart shops—is a welcome change of pace.

Exploring Quito

Numbers in white bullets in the text correspond to numbers in black bullets in the margins and on the Quito map.

The Old City

The oldest part of Quito was founded in 1534 by Spanish explorer Sebastián de Benalcázar on the site of the ancient Indian town of Shyris.

The original colonial town was bordered by its four most important monasteries: San Francisco, La Merced, San Agustín, and Santo Domingo. Today, informal markets and street vendors still crowd the cobbled routes that run between those ancient monuments, while the interiors of the churches and monasteries are quiet, timeless refuges.

A GOOD WALK

Begin your walk at the regal **Plaza de la Independencia** ①, also known as the Plaza Grande. Free English-speaking guides wearing blue uniforms are available each day from 9–1 and will answer tourist questions and help direct you. **La Catedral** ② flanks the square on the south. Adjoining La Catedral to the right is elegant **La Iglesia Parroquial del Sagrario** ③. After you inspect these colonial sights, walk one block east from the plaza's northeast corner to **La Iglesia de San Agustín** ④. Return to the Plaza Grande from San Agustín, then continue west three more blocks to the crowded plaza and sober baroque facade of **La Iglesia de la Merced** ⑤, one block north of which is the **Museo de Arte Colonial** ⑥. After you explore this museum, head three blocks south to the rather barren Plaza San Francisco, which is dominated by **La Iglesia de San Francisco** ⑦, Quito's largest colonial building and the first church built in the Americas. There's a museum in the adjacent monastery. Typically, there are also guides standing in the plaza who will happily speak about Quito, the old city, and artwork inside the church free of charge. One block east of the plaza's northeast corner is **La Compañía de Jesús** ⑧, whose magnificently sculpted stone facade has won it a reputation as one of the most beautiful religious structures in the Americas. Another block to the east lies **La Casa de Sucre** ⑨, a lovely colonial mansion housing a small museum. One block to the east and south is **La Iglesia de Santo Domingo** ⑩, the last of the Old City's major churches. From here you can walk three blocks north and three blocks west back to the Plaza Grande, or grab a taxi to the top of **El Panecillo** ⑪—a hill that offers a great view of Quito—or back to the New City.

TIMING

This walk should take no more than a few hours, unless you spend a long time in the churches and museums. Most of the churches are open for limited hours, and you'll be able to see the interiors better if you take this walk during the morning or late afternoon. Once evening approaches, however, it's best to leave the Old City, which has a chronic crime problem. It is also safer to do the walk on weekdays, when there are more people on the streets; nonetheless, you should be careful in crowds, where bag slashers and pickpockets thrive. When you explore the Old City, leave your valuables and important documents in your hotel, and keep close tabs on whatever you do bring with you.

SIGHTS TO SEE

⑨ La Casa de Sucre. The restored home of Field Marshal Antonio José de Sucre displays 19th-century furniture and clothing, as well as photographs, historical documents, and letters. ⊠ *Calle Venezuela 573, at Calle Sucre,* ☎ *02/512860.* ☞ *Admission.* ☉ *Tues.–Sat. 8:30–12:30 and 1:30–4.*

② La Catedral. The city's cathedral houses the tomb of Quito's liberator, Field Marshal Antonio José de Sucre. The exceptional sculpting abilities of Manuel Chili Caspicara can be appreciated in the 18th-century tableau *The Holy Shroud,* which hangs behind the choir, and in the intricate designs of the rococo Chapel of St. Ann in the right aisle. ⊠ *Plaza de la Independencia.* ☞ *Free.* ☉ *Mon.–Sat. 8–10 and 2–4.*

★ **⑧ La Compañía de Jesús.** The high central nave and the delicacy of its Arab-inspired, gilded plasterwork give the Church of the Company of

398

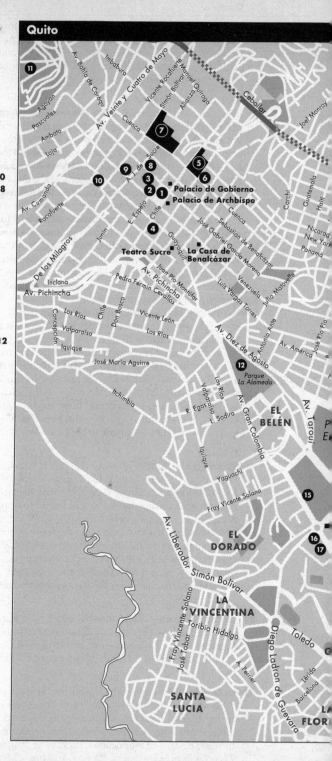

Quito

KEY

AE — American Express Office

1 — Exploring Sights

① — Hotels and Restaurants

Dining
La Canoa Manabita, **9**
Il Grillo, **12**
The Magic Bean, **8**
Pizzeria Le Arcate, **4**
La Querencia, **17**
Il Risotto, **6**
La Ronda, **16**
La Terraza del Tártaro, **5**

Lodging
Apart-Hotel Antinea, **10**
Café Cultura, **2**
Hilton Colón Quito, **1**
Hotel Ambassador, **15**
Hotel Sebastián, **13**
Hotel Sierra Madre, **3**
La Posada del Maple, **11**
Mansion del Angel, **7**
Oro Verde Swissôtel, **14**

Jesus a sumptuous, almost sinfully rich appearance. Indeed, almost 1½ tons of gold were poured into the ceilings, walls, pulpits, and altars during its 170 years of construction (1605–1775). At the center of the main altar is a statue of the Quiteña saint Mariana de Jesús; her remains are entombed at the foot of the altar. ⊠ *Calle García Moreno at Calle Sucre.* ▱ *Free.* ☉ *Daily 9:30–11 and 1–6.*

⑤ La Iglesia de la Merced. The Church of Mercy's beautiful, light-filled interior contains a brilliant statue of the Virgin of Mercy, located above the main altar. It was sculpted to honor a Virgin who supposedly intervened to save Quito from a series of 18th-century earthquakes and volcanic eruptions. The church's 47-m (153-ft) tower houses the city's largest bell. The adjoining convent, shown by appointment only, features a rich collection of colonial paintings and sculptures. ⊠ *Calle Chile at Calle Cuenca.* ▱ *Free.* ☉ *Mon.–Sat. 3–8.*

③ La Iglesia Parroquial del Sagrario. The Cathedral Chapel is noted for its beautiful facade in sculpted stone, large gilded altar, and colorful interior, which includes a lovely 18th-century painting of eight archangels covering the cupola. ⊠ *Main entrance at Calle García Moreno and Calle Espejo.* ▱ *Free.* ☉ *Mon.–Sat. 8–11 and 1–6.*

④ La Iglesia de San Agustín. In 1809, Ecuador's declaration of independence was signed in the Church of St. Augustine, and many of the soldiers who fought the Spanish crown are buried here. The gilded crucifix on the main altar offers an impressive example of School of Quito art, a baroque style that combines Spanish and Indian artistic themes. The main alter also displays paintings by Miguel de Santiago about Saint Augustine's life, while more paintings of St. Augustine crowd the side aisles. ⊠ *Calle Chile at Calle Guayaquil.* ▱ *Free.* ☉ *Daily 9–1 and 3–6.*

★ **⑦ La Iglesia de San Francisco.** Established by Franciscan monks in 1536 and said to be the first church built in the Americas, the Church of San Francisco was named for the patron saint of the city. The twin towers, destroyed by an eruption of Pichincha Volcano in 1582, were rebuilt at half their original size, contributing to the facade's uninspiring appearance. Inside, however, you will find the first New World example of an interior entirely covered with sculpted, gilded, and painted wood. Stationed at the main altar is Bernardo de Legarda's famed 18th-century sculpture, *Virgin of the Apocalypse of the Immaculate Conception.* The monastery at the north end of the complex now houses a museum of religious colonial art. The entrance fee includes a guided tour. ⊠ *Plaza San Francisco,* ☎ *02/211124.* ▱ *Church: free; museum: admission.* ☉ *Mon.–Sat. 9–11 and 3–6.*

⑩ La Iglesia de Santo Domingo. The interior of the colonial Church of Santo Domingo may not be as impressive as the Old City's other temples, but it does feature an eye-catching clock tour and some interesting statues, including the Virgen del Rosario. The adjacent Dominican monastery also holds a small museum of religious art and a verdant courtyard. ⊠ *Calle Flores at Rocafuerte.* ▱ *Free.* ☉ *Mon.–Fri. 3–5.*

⑥ Museo de Arte Colonial. The Museum of Colonial Art, housed in a restored 17th-century colonial mansion, includes colonial furniture and 16th- to 18th-century sculpture and paintings by Miguel de Santiago and various members of the School of Quito. The amusing *Vices and Virtues of the European Countries* is a series of 12 allegorical 18th-century paintings by colonial masters Samaniego and Rodríguez. ⊠ *Cuenca 901, at Calle Mejía,* ☎ *02/212297.* ▱ *Admission.* ☉ *Tues.–Fri. 10–6, Sat. 10–2.*

⑪ **El Panecillo.** "The bread roll" is a rounded hill that affords a marvelous view of the city and surrounding countryside. At the top stands the monumental cast-aluminum statue of the city's protectress, the Virgin of Quito—a copy of Bernardo de Legarda's famous 18th-century sculpture *Virgin of the Apocalypse of the Immaculate Conception,* on display in the Church of San Francisco. A long flight of stairs at the foot of Calle García Moreno climbs to the top of El Panecillo; muggers regularly lie in wait for tourists here, however, which is why we recommend hiring a taxi to take you up, wait for you, and bring you back to the city ($6–$8 round-trip with the wait).

❶ **Plaza de la Independencia.** Also known as La Plaza Grande, the city's main square is a charming plaza shaded by palms and pines, where tourists and locals alike enjoy the Andean sunshine, a shoe shine, and local flavor. The white, neoclassical **Palacio de Gobierno** (Government Palace), built in the 19th century, occupies the west side of the plaza. The portico gracing the plaza's northern end, once the archbishop's palace, now holds a variety of stores and businesses, including several souvenir and sweets shops. A free English-speaking guide service is offered from 9–1; look for smiling Ecuadorans in blue uniforms.

The New City

A GOOD WALK

Start your walk in the triangular **Parque La Alameda** ⑫, at the southern extreme of the New City. The narrow end of the triangle points south, but you should walk several blocks north, to the larger **Parque El Ejido** ⑬. Across the street from the northeast corner of the Parque El Ejido stands **La Casa de la Cultura,** a round, mirrored building that houses both the **Museo del Banco Central** ⑭ and the **Museo de Arte Moderno** ⑮. Just to the east is a large, colonial building, on the third floor of which is the **Museo Arqueológico Weilbauer** ⑯. From here walk north along Avenida 12 de Octubre until you enter the campus of the Universidad Católica; ask to be pointed to the **Museo Jijón Caamaño** ⑰ on the third floor of the *biblioteca* (library). Leaving the campus, continue north about five blocks along Avenida 12 de Octubre to the Centro Cultural Abya Yala, which holds the **Museo Amazónico** ⑱. From here, take a 15-minute taxi-ride to the residential neighborhood of Bellavista and the **Museo Guayasamin** ⑲, which is dedicated to Ecuador's most famous living artist.

TIMING

Because the New City holds more museums, it tends to take longer to explore than the Old City. You could easily complete this walk in the course of a morning or afternoon, but you'd have to move pretty quickly through the museums. A better recommendation is dedicating a day to the walk or spreading it over two days and combining it with a walk in the Old City.

SIGHTS TO SEE

⑱ **Museo Amazónico.** The Amazon Museum houses an impressive collection of artifacts and utilitarian items from different Amazonian cultures, including cooking pots, bowls, jewelry, hunting implements, stuffed jungle animals, and shrunken heads. The bookstore on the first floor has a superb collection of books about Latin American culture and its indigenous peoples, most of them in Spanish. ⊠ *Av. 12 de Octubre 1430, at Wilson,* ☎ *02/506247.* ⌨ *Admission.* ☉ *Daily 10–4.*

★ ⑯ **Museo Arqueológico Weilbauer.** The Weilbauer Archaeology Museum offers free English-language tours of its extensive and impressive collection of pre-Columbian ceramics and other artifacts. The building that houses the collection dates from the colonial era, and once served as the U.S. embassy. ⊠ *Av. Patria at Av. 12 de Octubre*, ☎ *02/230577.* ☎ *Free.* ⊘ *Weekdays 9–4.*

⑮ **Museo de Arte Moderno.** Exhibits at the Museum of Modern Art include two stories of contemporary Ecuadoran and indigenous works, such as paintings by Eduardo Kingman and Oswaldo Guayasamín, religious and children's art, and an excellent collection of pre-Columbian and colonial musical instruments. ⊠ *Across from Biblioteca, southern entrance of La Casa de la Cultura,* ☎ *02/223392.* ☎ *Admission.* ⊘ *Tues.–Fri. 10–6 and Sat. 10–2.*

★ ⑭ **Museo del Banco Central.** The Central Bank Museum, Quito's most modern, features an astonishing collection of pre-Columbian archeology and Incan ruins. Brightly lit cases containing sculptures from different Ecuadoran regions stand next to large-scale dioramas detailing the minutiae of pre-Columbian life. The first floor includes an unparalleled collection of gold artifacts; journey upstairs to an exhibit of excellent religious colonial paintings and sculptures. Up one flight more, you'll find an impressive collection of modern and contemporary Ecuadoran paintings. This museum shouldn't be missed. ⊠ *Av. Patria at Av. 6 de Diciembre (northern side of La Casa de la Cultura),* ☎ *02/ 223258.* ☎ *Admission.* ⊘ *Tues.–Fri. 9–5, Weekends 10–3.*

⑲ **Museo Guayasamín.** One of Ecuador's most famous living artists, Guayasamín, has a workshop and beautiful museum in the residential neighborhood of Bellavista. On display are pre-Columbian ceramics, colonial sculptures and paintings, and a permanent exhibit of paintings. Original works by Guayasamín, as well as prints, posters, and T-shirts, are sold in the gift shop. ⊠ *Calle José Bosmediano 543, at José Carbo,* ☎ *02/446455.* ☎ *Free.* ⊘ *Mon.–Fri. 9:30–1 and 3–6:30, Sat. 9:30–1.*

⑰ **Museo de Jijón Caamaño.** Located on the third floor of the Universidad Católica (Catholic University), the museum contains a large collection of colonial art, with paintings and sculptures from some of the masters of the School of Quito. There is also a small collection of Ecuadoran and Peruvian archaeological finds. Well-informed docents lead free English-language tours. ⊠ *Av. 12 de Octubre at Calle Roca,* ☎ *02/529250, ext. 1317.* ☎ *Free.* ⊘ *Weekdays 9–4.*

⑫ **Parque La Alameda.** The elongated triangle of La Alameda Park lies between the Old and New cities, near the **Asamblea Legislativa,** a large, modern building that houses the nation's congress. At the center of the park stands **El Observatorio,** the oldest astronomical observatory in South America rendered useless by the city's lights. A monument to Simón Bolívar dominates the southern apex of the triangle.

⑬ **Parque El Ejido.** One of the larger parks in Quito, El Ejido is popular for its extensive playgrounds and *ecuavoli* (three-person volleyball) courts. Theater groups regularly hold impromptu performances here, and there are often open-air art exhibitions on Saturdays. As pleasant as it is by day, El Ejido should be avoided once the sun goes down.

OFF THE BEATEN PATH
GUÁPULO – Nestled in a secluded valley below the Hotel Quito, the village of Guápulo is a preserved pocket of colonial architecture only 2 km (1 mi) from Quito's New City. The settlement, with narrow cobblestone lanes lined with traditional, two-story white houses trimmed in blue, grew up around its impressive 17th-century church, **El Santuario de Guápulo.** The Guápulo Sanctuary contains pieces by some of Quito's most exceptional sculptors and painters; the paintings in the central nave are the work of Miguel de Santiago, and the side altar and pulpit—completed in 1716 and considered masterpieces of colonial art—were carved by Juan Bautista Menacho. ☎ *Free.* ⊘ *Mon.–Sat. 8–11 and 3–6.*

If you visit in early September, you can help celebrate Guápulo's annual festival, with food and drink and marching bands. To reach Guápulo, walk downhill via the steep staircase directly behind the Hotel Intercontinental Quito. To return, make the uphill trek back the same way or take a taxi for about $2.

Dining

Quito's better restaurants are in the New City. Even at the most tony establishments, formal attire is more of a guideline than a requirement. Many restaurants close between 3 and 7 PM, and all day on Sunday.

Ecuadoran

$$ ✕ **La Querencia.** Appreciate the excellent views of Quito from the rus
★ tic fireside dining room, or eat in the serene outdoor garden, the perfect place to linger over a meal. La Querencia is best known for its superb Ecuadoran dishes; try the *seco de chivo* (lamb stewed with fruit), or langostinos flambéed in cognac. On a slow night, friendly waiters can be heard singing alongside soft Ecuadoran music as they roam the restaurant. ✉ *Av. Eloy Alfaro 2530, at Calle Catalina Aldaz,* ☎ *02/461664 or 02/446654. AE, DC, MC, V. No dinner Sun.*

$$ ✕ **La Ronda.** During the day businesspeople gather in what looks to be a Bavarian lodge for traditional Ecuadoran meals. Among the best dishes are *cazuela de mariscos,* a seafood casserole soup, and pernil (roast pork) with llapingachos, peanut sauce, and avocado. During the week, dinners are accompanied by folkloric guitar music, and folk dancing follows dinner on Sundays. ✉ *Calle Bello Horizonte 400, at Calle Almagro,* ☎ *02/540459 or 02/545176. AE, DC, MC, V.*

¢ ✕ **La Canoa Manabita.** Virtually unknown to tourists despite its lo
★ cation in the Mariscal district, this no-frills eatery serves exquisite Ecuadoran seafood lunches. Try the *viche,* a hearty fish and peanut soup with corn on the cob and plantain dumplings, or *corbina menestra* (served with rice, lentils, and patacones). ✉ *Calle Calama 231, at Calle Almagro,* ☎ *02/525353. DC. Closed Mon. No dinner.*

International

$$ ✕ **La Terraza del Tártaro.** In the heart of the New City, this longtime Quito favorite is known for its reliable service and delicious yet simply prepared meats. The penthouse restaurant atop the Edificio Amazonas (Amazon Building) is cheered by a blazing fire at night, when low lighting draws attention to the brilliantly lit city below. ✉ *Calle Veintimilla 1106, at Av. Amazonas,* ☎ *02/527987. AE, DC, MC, V. Closed Sun.*

$ ✕ **The Magic Bean.** It's not magic but the powerful spell cast by qual
★ ity food draws travelers, expatriates, and locals to "the Bean" to socialize over healthy salads and do business over cappuccinos or cocktails. Blackberry pancakes and bagels light up the morning, while the lunch and dinner menu emphasizes salads, soups, personal-size pizzas, sandwiches, and shish kebabs. The atmosphere is casual and the service friendly; solo diners will feel very comfortable here. The Magic Bean also has live music some nights. ✉ *Calle Foch 681, at Calle J. L. Mera,* ☎ *02/566181. AE, DC, MC, V.*

Italian

$$$ ✕ **Il Risotto.** Considered the finest Italian restaurant in Quito, Il Risotto
★ is small and romantic—in the heart of the Mariscal District. The two-level dining room charms you with candlelit tables and fresh roses; the walls have prints of northern Italy and programs from Milan's *Teatro alla Scala.* Begin your meal with *insalata del pescatore* (shellfish salad), followed by three fresh lobsters on a bed of pasta *pomodoro* (in chunks

of tomatoes), or a chicken roll with spinach and ricotta cheese. The portions are large, the service excellent, and the desserts marvelous: consider the crêpes suzette with Grand Marnier or the tiramisu with decadent chocolate and cognac. ⊠ *Pinto 209, at Almagro,* ☎ *02/ 220400. DC, MC, V. Closed Mon.*

$$ ✕ **Pizzeria Le Arcate.** This trendy pizzeria attracts well-heeled foreign and Ecuadoran patrons who come to choose from 59 types of individual thin-crust pizzas. The attractive, emerald-colored dining room, with inlaid wood floors, Romanesque columns, and an arched foyer, buzzes with international conversations. Crowds reach their peak around 10 PM. In addition to pizzas, a variety of pasta, fish, and meat dishes are available. ⊠ *Baquedano 358, at Juan León Mera,* ☎ *02/ 237659. DC, MC, V. Closed Mon.*

$–$$ ✕ **Il Grillo.** This attractive restaurant in a house across the street from the Parque Gabriela Mistral is relatively new, but is already one of the city's most popular eateries. The decor is simple, but the fresh pasta, pizza, and salads keep it packed during peak dining hours. If the homemade gnocchi, ravioli, or tortellini don't strike your fancy, try the langostino bisque. ⊠ *Calle Baquirizo at Calle Almagro,* ☎ *02/225531. AE, DC, MC, V. Closed Mon.*

Lodging

Accommodations in the nation's capital range from expensive modern hotels with business services, restaurants, and sports facilities to smaller family-run inns with more personal attention and favorable prices. Almost all the luxury hotels are in the New City, but the best deals are in the pleasant Mariscal neighborhood. Less expensive hotels often lack air-conditioning and heating, although Quito's moderate climate means this usually isn't a worry.

$$$$ ⊞ **Hilton Colón Quito.** This large, modern hotel in the heart of the New City has an excellent location across from El Ejido Park. The marble lobby is a bit sterile, but it holds numerous shops and on-site services. Rooms are functional but nondescript; those on the lower floors can be noisy because of street traffic. ⊠ *Av. Amazonas at Av. Patria,* ☎ *02/560666, 800/445–8667 in the U.S.,* 𝖥𝖠𝖷 *02/563903. 415 rooms. 2 restaurants, bar, pool, sauna, steam room, exercise room, casino, business services, travel services. AE, DC, MC, V.*

$$$$ ⊞ **Oro Verde Swissôtel.** Originally the Hotel Oro Verde, the Swissô-
★ tel remains one of Quito's most luxurious and expensive high-rise hotels. A spacious atrium lobby overlooks the central pool area and garden. Rooms feature beautiful dark wood furnishings and modern screen prints; those on the upper floors enjoy impressive city views. The hotel's four restaurants—French, Italian, international, and Japanese—have excellent reputations. ⊠ *Av. 12 de Octubre 1820, at Calle Cordero,* ☎ *02/567600, 800/223–6800 in the U.S.;* 𝖥𝖠𝖷 *02/ 568080. 193 rooms, 48 suites. 4 restaurants, bar, indoor-outdoor pool, sauna, steam room, exercise room, racquetball, squash, casino, business services. AE, MC, V.*

$$$ ⊞ **Hotel Sebastián.** This attractive eight-story hotel is ideally situated in the Mariscal district near shops and restaurants. Comfortable, carpeted rooms have tasteful pastel color schemes and handsomely framed watercolors. Suites cost slightly more than the regular rooms. ⊠ *Calle Almagro 822, at Calle Cordero,* ☎ *02/222400 or 02/222300,* 𝖥𝖠𝖷 *02/ 222500. 49 rooms, 7 suites. Restaurant, bar, convention center. AE, DC, MC, V.*

$$$ ⊞ **Mansion del Angel.** Opened in 1998, this exclusive boutique hotel
★ offers Quito's most luxurious accommodations. The contrast between

the bustling streets outside and the subdued, refined interior is striking: this turn-of-the-century mansion has lavish baroque furnishings, immaculately decorated rooms with four-poster beds, and quiet respectful service. A full American breakfast, served in the elegant living room parlor or on the Mediterranean-style terrace, is included. Great museums, restaurants, and folklore shops are nearby. ⊠ *Wilson E5-29, at Juan León Mera , ☎ 02/557721, 800/327–3573 in the U.S., ℻ 02/ 237819. 10 rooms. No credit cards.*

$$ ▦ **Café Cultura.** Attention to detail makes this self-assured, anglophone hotel—formerly the Center for Arts and Culture of the French Embassy—stand out from the competition. The wood-beamed lobby glows from a fire in the stone-trimmed hearth, and the mezzanine above leads to the inn's comfortable guest rooms (some with fireplaces). Outside, the quiet garden is perfect for soaking up the equatorial sunshine. A popular café off the lobby serves breakfast and lunch. ⊠ *Calle Robles at Calle Reina Victoria, ☎ 02/504078 and 02/564956, ℻ 02/ 224271. 21 rooms, 3 suites. Café. AE, DC, MC, V.*

$$ ▦ **Hotel Sierra Madre.** This handsomely restored Spanish villa offers moderate accommodations in Quito's popular Mariscal district. A charming mix of European and traditional Ecuadoran furnishings highlights the decor. Five of the guest rooms have private terraces with views of Quito and the surrounding Andean mountains. On the first floor, a sunny Mediterranean restaurant features a buffet breakfast and commendable Peruvian dishes. ⊠ *Veintimilla 464, at Luis Tamayo, ☎ 02/505687, 800/327–3573 in the U.S., ℻ 02/505715. 16 rooms. Restaurant, bar. AE, DC, MC, V.*

$–$$ ▦ **Apart-Hotel Antinea.** Once you check into one of the spacious apart-
★ ments in this charming inn, you may never want to check out. These two former homes on a shady side street in the Mariscal area have been divided into a variety of simple but elegant rooms, half of which are spacious apartments with well-stocked kitchenettes. Most rooms open onto a patio or garden, several have balconies, and one has a fireplace. The small restaurant has seating inside or on a patio. ⊠ *Calle Juan Rodríguez 175, at Calle Almagro, ☎ 02/506839 or 02/506838, ℻ 02/ 504404. 7 rooms, 8 apartments. Restaurant. AE, DC, MC, V.*

$ ▦ **Hotel Ambassador.** Centrally located in the New City, the Ambassador is an older hotel that may have seen better days, but is nevertheless quite a bargain. The bar consists of several elegant sitting rooms, one of which has a fireplace, and the rooms are large and comfortable, if a bit threadbare. ⊠ *Av. 9 de Octubre at Av. Colón, ☎ 02/ 561777, ℻ 02/503712. 60 rooms. Restaurant, bar. AE, DC, MC, V.*

¢ ▦ **La Posada del Maple.** It's the air of easy camaraderie (and not the small, plain rooms) that lures everyone from seasoned travelers to Peace Corps volunteers to this friendly, inexpensive bed-and-breakfast. The price includes a hearty American-style breakfast and kitchen privileges. ⊠ *Calle Juan Rodríguez 148, near Av. 6 de Diciembre, ☎ 02/ 544507. 13 rooms. Restaurant. AE, MC, V.*

Nightlife and the Arts

Nightlife

As with cultural events, the number of bars and dance clubs has boomed in the past few years, and there are now plenty of *salsatecas* (for lovers of salsa music) and discotheques. At the *peñas* (clubs where traditional Andean musicians perform), you can hear traditional Ecuadoran music and drink late into the night with locals. Bars usually open in the late afternoon, while dance clubs and peñas open around 10 PM; all close around 2 AM. Cover charges for the latter two range from free to $10; most peñas are closed Sunday through Thursday.

BARS AND CAFÉS

The tranquil **Bangalo Salon de Te** (⊠ Foch 451, between Almagro and 6 de Diciembre, ☏ 02/501332) features a blazing fireplace and non-stop Brazilian music. **El Pobre Diablo** (⊠ Calle Santa María 338, at Calle J. L. Mera, ☏ 02/224982) is a gathering place for local artists and young intellectuals. At **Ghoz** (⊠ Calle La Niña 425, at Calle Reina Victoria) you can eat Swiss food and play darts, pool, or board games while listening to high-decibel rock and salsa music. **Papillón** (⊠ Calle Santa María at Calle Almagro, ☏ 02/228251) blasts pop and techno music, which draws young foreigners and Ecuadorans. A young party-going crowd is found at **Tijuana** (⊠ Reina Victoria and Santa Maria, ☏ 02/238324). **Veradero** (⊠ Calle Reina Victoria at Calle La Pinta) plays live Latin music on Wednesday, Friday, and Saturday; it fills up with locals early on weekends.

DANCE CLUBS

Cali Salsateca (⊠ Calle Almagro 1268, at Av. Orellana) is a popular weekend spot that plays mostly Latin music and only admits couples. Locals have been coming to **Salsateca Seseribó** (⊠ Calle Veintimilla 325, at Av. 12 de Octubre) for years to dance cumbia, salsa, and merengue.

PEÑAS

If you're looking for a peña in the Old City, try **La Taberna Quito Colonial** (⊠ Calle Marabí at Calle Vargas, ☏ 02/283102). One of the New City's most established peñas is the **Ñuncanchi Peña** (⊠ Av. Universitaria 496, at Calle Armero, ☏ 02/540967). **Peña Pacha Camac** (⊠ Calle Jorge Washington 530, at Calle J. L. Mera, ☏ 02/234855) is a small place in the Mariscal neighborhood.

The Arts

Quito's arts scene has grown significantly in the last few years. Check the national paper *El Universo,* local newspapers *El Comercio* and *Hoy,* and English-language newspapers *Inside Ecuador* and *Q* (sold in bookstores and at newsstands) for information about theater, concerts, and art expositions.

CONCERTS

Classical and folkloric concerts are sometimes held at the **Corporación Financiera Nacional** (National Financial Corporation; ⊠ Calle J. L. Mera, behind Hotel Colón, ☏ 02/561026) and also at other venues throughout the city. Check the sources listed above for information.

DANCE

Jacchigua (National Folkloric Ballet) performs Wednesday and Friday at 7:30 PM in the **San Gabriel Theater** (⊠ Av. América at Calle Mariana de Jesús, ☏ 02/506650, ext. 131). Tickets cost $14–$20 and can be purchased in advance at the theater or through Metropolitan Touring (☞ Tour Operators *in* Quito A to Z, *below*).

FILM

Cinemas in Quito often show American films in English with Spanish subtitles. For strictly English-language or art films, try **The British Council** (⊠ Av. Amazonas at La Niña, ☏ 02/225421); the cinema at **La Casa de la Cultura** (House of Culture; ⊠ Av. Patria at Av. 12 de Octubre, ☏ 02/565808); and **La Casa del Lado** (House Nearby; ⊠ Calle Valladolid 1018, at Calle Cordero, ☏ 02/226398). **Multicines** (⊠ Amazonas and Naciones Unidas, ☏ 02/259677) shows films in Spanish and English.

Outdoor Activities and Sports

Bullfighting

The only regularly scheduled bullfights are held during the week-long Fiestas de Quito, in early December. Hotels sometimes will purchase tickets for guests with room reservations. The **bullring** is at ⊠ Avenida Amazonas and Calle Ascaray.

Soccer

Games are held during the season (Mar.–Dec.) at around noon on Sunday, with an occasional Saturday game, at the **Estadio Olímpico "Atahualpa"** (Atahualpa Olympic Stadium; ⊠ Av. 6 de Diciembre and Av. Naciones Unidas, ☎ 02/247510). Tickets, which cost $2.50–$10, generally must be purchased at the stadium, though try asking your hotel concierge first.

Shopping

Quito's best shopping area is the New City's Mariscal district—bounded by Avenidas Amazonas, 6 de Diciembre, Patria, and Colón—which has a tightly packed collection of boutiques and crafts stands. The specialty and crafts stores are reasonably priced, and although they don't rival the outlying Indian markets for bargains, the quality of the merchandise is often superior. Look for brightly painted balsa-wood birds made in the Amazon region and cedar statues from highland villages. Wool and cotton sweaters, shawls, and tapestries vary in quality and price, as do items made of leather. Stores throughout Quito are generally closed Saturday afternoon and Sunday.

Handicrafts

Casa Indo Andina (⊠ Calle Roca 606, at Calle J. L. Mera) sells top-of-the-line items, including original and reproduced religious art and silver- and bronze-gilded frames; there are also alpaca wool sweaters from Peru, reproductions of pre-Columbian ceramic ware, and a showy collection of silver jewelry. **El Centro Artesanal** (⊠ Calle J. L. Mera 804, ☎ 02/548235) specializes in hand-knit apparel. The most extensive collection of shops is found at Quito's modern shopping mall, **El Jardin** (⊠ Amazonas and La Républica, ☎ 02/466570). **Galería Latina** (⊠ Calle J. L. Mera 833, ☎ 02/221098) offers an enormous variety of sterling silver jewelry, woven rugs, ceramic figures, and antiques. In addition to its regional crafts, **La Bodega** (⊠ Calle J. L. Mera 614, ☎ 02/225844) has an extensive collection of hand-knit wool and cotton sweaters. **Olga Fisch's Folklore** (⊠ Av. Colón 260, ☎ 02/563085) is one of Quito's more expensive boutiques; it specializes in handwoven rugs and tapestries designed by the late owner and inspired by indigenous motifs.

Markets

You can lose yourself among the stalls at the **Mercado de Santa Clara**, in the New City at the corner of Calle Versalles and Calle Marchena. At this traditional neighborhood market, you'll find fruits and vegetables piled high in pleasing geometrical arrangements, bundles of dried and fresh herbs, grains, and huge bunches of freshly cut flowers. You can listen to a musician play soulful accordion tunes, or you can light a candle to the Virgin Mary at the neon shrine tucked between the vendors' stalls.

Side Trips from Quito

Cotopaxi

Massive, snowcapped Cotopaxi Volcano, 67 km (42 mi) southeast of Quito, is one of Ecuador's most impressive landmarks. At 5,897 m (19,347 ft) above sea level, Cotopaxi is not only the country's second highest mountain, it is also the highest active volcano in the world. Although mountaineers risk their lives to reach Cotopaxi's icy summit, you need risk little more than a slight case of altitude sickness to wander around its lower slopes, which are protected within Cotopaxi National Park.

Once inside the park, the drive towards Cotopaxi is unforgettable. As you make your way to higher altitudes, you are likely to spot California red pine, llamas, white tail deer, Andean condors, sparrow hawks, black frogs, and wild horses. Fewer animals roam the semi-arid plains of the "paramo" zone, extending from 3,200 to 4,800 m (10,496–15,744 ft). There are no trees here—only small plants and scrubland that have adapted to the harsh environment. Above the paramo zone lies the permafrost zone, where giant glaciers extend across the volcano's summit. Cotopaxi is most impressive at dawn, when sunlight sprinkles rays across the surface of the glaciers and casts shadows on the surrounding mountains.

A tour operator with a four-wheel-drive vehicle can take you to the base of the volcano, located at 4,800 m (15,744 ft). If you're not suffering from the altitude, it is possible to climb about 1,000 ft to the refugio, where simple dormitory accommodations serve as a base for eager climbers. From here, you'll need at least six hours and mountain climbing equipment—including ice picks—to climb to the glacier-covered summit. The crater has a circumference of 800 m (2,624 ft) and is covered by snow. In case you're considering the sanity of a climb, the last major eruption took place in 1877, with lava currents reaching the Pacific 200 km (124 mi) away. Admission to the park is $10, and it's open daily, 7 AM to 3 PM.

LODGING

$ ▥ **Hostería La Estación.** Owned by the same family for four generations, this picturesque bed-and-breakfast is settled amid a fantastic mountain panorama. The A-frame log house has touches of rustic elegance everywhere, with Ecuadoran antiques, courtyard fountains, and fresh flowers filling its corners. Individually decorated rooms have private baths and breathtaking views. The gracious owners welcome you into their home as if family, preparing homemade Ecuadoran cuisine and arranging day hikes to Cotopaxi and El Corazon mountains. The hosteriá is a half hour from the entrance to Cotopaxi National Park near the small village of Machachi. ✉ *Machachi,* ☎ *02/309246. 10 rooms. Restaurant, hiking. No credit cards.*

Equatorial Monument

La Mitad del Mundo (the Middle of the World) monument, 26 km (16 mi) north of Quito, marks the spot that in 1736 the French Geodesic Mission determined to be the exact latitudinal center of the Earth. Visitors today may have less scientific interest, but nonetheless seem to enjoy themselves as they leap back and forth between the Northern and Southern hemispheres or have their photograph taken as they straddle the equator (latitude 0° 00′ 00″).

The monument proper—a 33-ft-tall trapezoidal stone—is not particularly attractive, but beneath it lies an informative ethnographic museum with displays on Ecuador's diverse cultural groups. Although the explanatory text is in Spanish only, the exhibits themselves prove interesting to most English speakers. Sunday is a good time to visit the monument, when there is a folkloric program with music, dancing, and mimes. ☎ *02/527077.* ▣ *Free.* ☉ *Daily 10–6.*

Papallacta Hot Springs

A stunning drive over the eastern range of the Andes brings you to the edges of the Amazon jungle and to the natural hot springs of Papallacta, 65 km (40 mi) east of Quito. A mile beyond the small town you'll find the **Termas de Papallacta,** with eight thermal baths and two cold crystalline pools. It's a beautiful setting, and on a clear day you can see the snowcapped peak of Antisana Volcano. The hot springs are open 6 AM–10 PM, and the site includes dormlike accommodations, a restaurant, and changing facilities.

Pasochoa Forest

Pasochoa Forest, 38 km (24 mi) from Quito, is a protected area administered by **Fundación Natura** (Nature Foundation; ☎ 02/447341 or 02/246072), a private conservation organization dedicated to preserving the remaining 988 acres of high Andean forest that once covered the region. Nearly 100 species of birds have been identified here, including hummingbirds, honeycreepers, and tanagers. There are many walking trails, from short loops to all-day hikes; the trail to the summit (13,800 ft) is popular but rigorous, and you should take drinking water and snacks. Guides can be hired through Fundación Natura. Camping is permitted within the park, and there are picnic areas with spigots and latrines. Fires are not permitted, however, and you should bring all of your own supplies. The best way to get to the park is through a Quito-based tour operator, although buses stop a few kilometers from the entrance, from where you can hitch or hike the rest of the way. The park fee is $7 for day use, $12 for a multiday camping permit.

Quito A to Z

Arriving and Departing

BY AIRPLANE

Quito's international gateway is **Aeropuerto Mariscal Sucre** (☎ 02/430555 or 02/241580), 10 km (6 mi) north of the city center. American Airlines (☎ 02/260900), Continental (☎ 02/557170), and SAN/Saeta (☎ 02/502707 or 02/502712) each have a daily flight—American and Saeta from Miami and Continental from Houston. Travelers from the U.K. could connect with American Airlines via Virgin Atlantic, Continental, or British Airways. Connecting with American via Quantas is the best bet for travelers from Australia and New Zealand.

Ecuador's major domestic carriers, Saeta/SAN and TAME, fly daily from Quito to Guayaquil (45 minutes) and Cuenca (50 minutes) for $50–$100 (TAME is usually less expensive than SAN). Those flying Saeta internationally may book two internal flights on SAN for a reduced fee; if you book a ticket to the Galápagos, you will be allowed a free stopover in Quito or Guayaquil.

Taxis in Quito use meters, but those leaving the airport are exempt. Agree on a price before you enter a cab. You should pay about $7 to the Old City and $5 to the New City (a bit more during rush hour).

BY TRAIN

For information on the sporadic service of the Quito–Riobamba line, contact its operator, **Metropolitan Touring** (☞ Tour Operators, *below*). The train—which usually runs Tuesday, Thursday, and Saturday—has a Pullman coach and an open-sided car that's often crowded with farmers, their produce, and sometimes small farm animals. You can embark at the Quito **train station** (⊠ Av. Maldonado at Calle Sincholagua, Quito, ☎ 02/656142).

Getting Around

It's roughly 3 km (2 mi) from the center of the Old City to the beginning of the New City at Avenida Amazonas. Sights in the Old City are relatively easy to explore on foot, but the New City—apart from the Mariscal, Colón, and La Floresta districts—is larger and best conquered by cab.

BY BUS

Quito's buses are inexpensive (about 10¢) and run frequently during the day, but due to heavy crowds during the morning and afternoon rush it's best to walk or hail a taxi. Clearly marked *Ejecutivo* buses cost 20¢ and guarantee seating, making them the more comfortable option. Slightly more expensive, but faster, is the new *trole* (trolley bus), which runs through the center of town along Avenida 10 de Agosto in the New City, switching over to Calle Guayaquil in the Old City.

For Cotopaxi, buses to Ambato, which leave from Quito's **Terminal Terrestre** every 30 minutes, will drop you off in Lasso, about 10 km (6 mi) from the park entrance. The 30-km (18-mi) ride takes just under an hour and costs less than $2. Most Quito tour operators offer day trips to the park for around $40; park admission is $10.

To reach the Equatorial Monument, buses marked Mitad del Mundo depart every 20 minutes from the New City at the intersection of Avenida de las Américas and Avenida P. Guerrera; the 75-minute ride costs less than $1. Most Quito-based tour operators offer half-day tours for $10–$20 per person.

Direct buses travel every hour to the Papallacta Hot Springs, though you may have to pay the entire Quito–Tena fare, which is nonetheless under $3.

There are no direct buses to Pasochoa; your best bet is taking a bus from Quito's La Marin square to Amaguaña, and asking the bus driver to drop you off when you're about 7 km (4½ mi) away. From there you can either walk or hire a pickup truck to take you the rest of the way.

BY CAR

Quito is on the Pan-American Highway, a twisty, 269-km (167 mi) drive of four hours from Tulcán, on the Colombian border. However, driving in the region is generally not recommended because of the lack of clearly marked signs and the danger of theft.

BY TAXI

Taxis are ubiquitous and inexpensive, which makes them an ideal form of transportation. Agree on a price beforehand if the driver says the meter is not working. Standard crosstown fare is less than $5, much less if you stay within the Old or New City, and tipping is not expected. You might pay a maximum $2 surcharge after dark. **Tele Taxi** (☎ 02/411119 or 02/411120) and **City-Taxi** (☎ 02/633333) are reliable cab services that will send a driver to your door and arrange city tours for less than $10 per hour.

For $5–$8, you can hire a taxi in Lasso to take you to Cotopaxi and either wait for you or return later to pick you up. If you drive, head south on the Pan-American Highway and watch for the turnoff to the park on your left, about 65 km (41 mi) south of Quito, shortly before you reach Lasso. A taxi will take up to four people to the Equatorial Monument for $30, which includes the wait while you visit the monument and museum. For about $60 you can hire a taxi to take you to the Papallacta Hot Springs, wait for an hour or two, and then return you to Quito. You can hire a taxi for the day to reach Pasochoa—the going rate is around $30.

Contacts and Resources

BANKS AND CURRENCY EXCHANGE

American Express (⊠ Amazonas 339 and Jorge Washington, 5th floor, ☎ 02/560488). **Western Union** (⊠ Republica 396 and Almagro, ☎ 02/502194).

BUSINESS SERVICES

Most major hotels have business centers with copy machines, computers, faxes, modem lines, and other services. Some establishments also allow non-guests to use these facilities for a fee. If you need to send or receive a fax, you can also do so through the **post office** (⊠ Elroy Alfaro 354 and 9 de Octubre, ☉ Mon.–Fri. 7:30–5:45, Sat. 8–11:45).

EMERGENCIES

For an **ambulance,** ☎ 131; **fire,** ☎ 102; **police,** ☎ 101; **general emergency,** ☎ 111. **Hospital/Hospitals: Hospital Voz Andes** (⊠ Juan Villalengue 267 and 10 de Agosto, ☎ 02/241540), **Hospital Metropolitano** (⊠ Mariana de Jesus and Occidental, ☎ 02/431520). **Medical Assistance:** ☎ 131. **Pharmacies: Farmacia Americana No.1** (⊠ Av. Colon 112, ☎ 02/237677), **Farmacia Fybeca No. 1** (⊠ Av. 6 de Diciembre 2077, ☎ 02/231263). **Police:** ☎ 101.

ENGLISH-LANGUAGE BOOKSTORES

LibriMundi (⊠ Calle J. L. Mera 851, ☎ 02/234971).

TELEPHONES, INTERNET, AND MAIL

EMETEL is the national phone system for local, national, and international calls. Although you can wait in line to make a call at EMETEL offices, it's far easier to use the phones in your hotel.

Internet service is now in Ecuador, although the only reliable service is through the business centers at Quito's major hotels.

For courier service, contact **DHL International** (⊠ 433 Republica at Almagro).

TOUR OPERATORS AND TRAVEL AGENTS

Guided, English-language tours cost $10–$25 per person and cover Quito's principal sights in about three hours. There are dozens of tour companies in the Mariscal neighborhood, especially along Avenida Amazonas. One of the best operators is **Angermeyer's Enchanted Excursions** (⊠ Foch 769, at Amazonas, ☎ 02/569960, FAX 02/569956), which organizes biking expeditions, horseback riding, hiking trips, train journeys, and river and coastal canoe rides. **Metropolitan Touring** (⊠ Av. República de El Salvador 970, ☎ 02/464780, 800/527–2500 in the U.S.; FAX 02/464702, 214/783–1286 in the U.S.), the king of Ecuadoran tourism, can arrange everything from a Galápagos cruise to a custom adventure vacation. **Kleintours** (⊠ Av. de los Shyris 1000, at Calle Holanda, ☎ 02/430345) is another well-established travel coordinator. **Safari** (⊠ Calle Calama 380, at Calle J. L. Mera, ☎ 02/223381, FAX 02/220426) offers a variety of mountain biking and trekking excursions to the volcanoes and protected areas around Quito.

VISITOR INFORMATION

The **tourist office** (⊠ Av. Eloy Alfaro 1214, at Calle Carlos Tovar, ☎ 02/228304 or 02/228305), run by Ecuador's Ministerio de Turismo, provides maps and brochures and is open weekdays 8:30–5. **LibriMundi** (⊠ Calle J. L. Mera 851, ☎ 02/504209) is a large bookstore that carries maps and tourism-related publications, among other things. For members, the **South American Explorers Club** (⊠ Jorge Washington 311, at Leonidas Plaza, ☎ 02/225228, 607/277–0488 in the U.S.) has an information board and travel library; it can also put members in touch with reliable guides for a variety of activities.

IMBABURA PROVINCE

When the Spanish conquered the territory north of Quito—called Imbabura after the 4,630-m (15,190-ft) volcano of the same name—they introduced sheep to the indigenous people of the region. Over time the mountain-dwelling *otavaleños* became expert wool weavers and dyers; even today you may find craftspeople who painstakingly collect and prepare their own natural dyes, despite the increasing popularity of modern synthetic colors. Traditional dyeing methods may be declining, yet the otavaleños themselves proudly retain many of the old customs, including their manner of dress. The women are striking in their embroidered, ruffle-and-lace, white blouses, straight blue wraparound skirts, black or blue head cloths, and row upon row of beaded gold necklaces. The men, extremely handsome with their beige felt hats and long, braided hair, are most often seen in Western attire, although some of the older men still wear the traditional calf-length white pants, white shirt, and dark blue poncho.

Many small weaving villages dot the green and gold valleys of Imbabura, and every weekend artisans make the trek to Otavalo—the largest and most prosperous of these crafts towns—for its fabulously colorful market. Otavalo's Plaza de Ponchos and adjacent streets fill up each Saturday with merchants selling weavings, rugs, ponchos, colorful cotton and wool sweaters, jewelry, and antiques. At a nearby street market, locals shop for *alpargatas* (rope-soled sandals) and medicinal herbs; just outside town, livestock dealers do a brisk business in squealing pigs, cackling hens, and colossal guinea pigs. Such smaller villages as Cotacachi (famous for its leather) and San Antonio de Ibarra (known for its woodwork) host their own colorful markets, though none on such a grand scale as the Saturday market in Otavalo.

Otavalo

113 km (70 mi) north of Quito.

Otavalo is in the rugged lake district nearly 2,602 m (8,530 ft) above sea level. Days in this high-altitude valley—a patchwork of small gardens, cerulean lakes, and plowed and fallow fields—are often sunny and warm. Over the land rise the craggy peaks of three now extinct volcanoes—Imbabura, Cotacachi, and Cayambe, Ecuador's third-tallest mountain. Villagers trudge along the road carrying huge burdens or prodding their laden burros to do the same; come Thursday or Friday, there is a good chance they're headed for Otavalo's famous Saturday market, held at the **Plaza de Ponchos.** Although tourist-oriented, the market is still a remarkable event, where beautiful, self-assured otavaleñas crowd the stalls and stands that surround the plaza, selling piles of wool and cotton sweaters; traditional and modern ponchos; tapestries, rugs, and wall hangings; antiques; and sterling silver and *alpaca* (nickel silver) jewelry imbedded with Andean jade, lapis lazuli, and other semiprecious stones.

Near the corner of Calles Modesto Jaramillo and García Moreno locals shop for embroidered blouses, alpargatas, and herbs to cure ailments and attract lovers. The produce market held simultaneously at the Plaza 24 de Mayo does an equally brisk business; so, too, does the animal market at the Plaza San Juan, where people from both town and the surrounding countryside—many colorfully dressed in traditional clothing—bargain for cows, pigs, and other livestock. The animal market begins at 5:30 AM, and most sellers are packing to go by 11 AM. The Plaza de Ponchos market doesn't reach full swing until 7 or

8 AM and lasts until about 2 or 3 PM; a secondary market is held on Wednesday, and some vendors appear every day of the week.

Dining and Lodging

Lodging reservations are essential on Friday nights, when tourists fill the region's hotels and hosterías in anticipation of Otavalo's Saturday market.

$ ✕ **SISA.** This two-story cultural complex consists of an intimate restaurant on the second floor that serves Ecuadoran and international cuisine, a ground-floor coffee bar, and an excellent bookstore. The restaurant presents live folk music during Friday dinners and weekend lunches and dinners. ⊠ *Calle Abdón Calderón 409,* ☎ *06/920154. AE, DC, MC, V.*

¢–$ ✕ **Mi Otavalito.** One block from the Plaza de Ponchos, this small, Indian-owned restaurant has a simple menu that includes fresh trout and pepper steak. Seating is available on an interior patio or in the narrow dining room. The daily lunch specials are a great deal. ⊠ *Calle Sucre at Calle Morales,* ☎ *06/922105. No credit cards.*

$ ✕🛏 **Ali Shungu.** In Quichua, *Ali Shungu* means "good heart," and the American owners of this colorful hotel go out of their way to make their guests feel at home. The spacious bedrooms with terra-cotta floors and local weavings surround an enclosed garden, beyond which Imbabura Volcano can be seen. Two giant suites are ideal for families. The light-filled restaurant has wholesome dishes like vegetarian lasagna and deep-dish chicken pie served with organically grown vegetables. The hotel also offers shuttle service between Quito and Otavalo. ⊠ *Calle Quito at Calle Miguel Egas,* ☎ *06/920750. 16 rooms, 2 suites. Restaurant, bicycles. No credit cards.*

Nightlife and the Arts

During the week things are very quiet in Otavalo (some would say downright dull), but the town has a reasonable selection of peñas which open only weekend nights. One is **Amauta,** which has two locations. ⊠ *Jaramillo and Salinas, and Jaramillo and Morales,* ☎ *06/920967.* ☯ *Open Fri. and Sat. after 8 PM.* 🎟 *Nominal cover charge.*

Lago San Pablo

8 km (5 mi) southeast of Otavalo.

Easily accessible from Otavalo is the large, deep, blue lake called Lago San Pablo, which lies at the base of the massive 4,630-m (15,190-ft) Imbabura Volcano. Although the scenery is spectacular, the village of San Pablo—a collection of adobe buildings on the lake's shore—is a typical highland town. Lodges on or near the lake are much nicer than those in Otavalo proper. Buses run between Otavalo and San Pablo about every 15 minutes, or you can take a taxi for around $3.

Dining and Lodging

$$$ ✕🛏 **Hostería Cusín.** This restored colonial hacienda on the edge of the
★ town of San Pablo is one of the country's most charming inns. Rooms have colonial-style furniture, and many have fireplaces and windows that look out onto the colorful gardens. The main buildings, which date from the 17th century, hold the restaurant, bar, and sitting rooms, all of which are furnished with antiques. ⊠ *San Pablo,* ☎ *06/918013, 800/ 683–8148 in the U.S.;* 🖷 *06/918003, 617/924–2158 in the U.S. 40 rooms. Restaurant, bar, horseback riding, mountain bikes. DC, MC, V.*

$$$ ✕🛏 **Hostería Puerto Lago.** A gorgeous panorama of volcanic peaks forms the backdrop of this lakeside country inn, just a few miles southeast of Otavalo. The view from the restaurant, built out over the lake, is enough to warrant a meal here: try the panfried trout, served head and

all. Bungalow-style rooms are spacious, with redbrick walls, wood-beamed ceilings, simple Ecuadoran decor, and cozy fireplaces. The hotel rents rowboats and kayaks, and offers several excursions a day on a festive pontoon boat with a bar and live music. Breakfast and dinner are included. ✉ *Pan-American Hwy. S, Km 5½,* ☎ *06/920920,* FAX *06/920900. 23 rooms, 3 suites. Restaurant, bar, boating, waterskiing. AE, MC, V.*

Outdoor Activities and Sports

HORSEBACK RIDING

IntiExpress (✉ Calle Sucre at Morales, Otavalo, ☎ FAX 06/920737) arranges single and multiday horseback trips to local villages and to natural mineral springs. Hostería Cusín (☞ above), in San Pablo, specializes in horseback riding, and offers guests a series of tours ranging from two hours to five days.

Cotacachi

15 km (9 mi) north of Otavalo.

Though famous for its leather products and the nearby lake of Cuicocha, Cotacachi is actually a very attractive, traditional town well worth a visit. It's a quiet place that sees few tourists—most of whom simply pass through on their way to the lake—with a small central plaza where children play and old men sit and gossip. A few blocks away, Calle 10 de Agosto is lined with shops selling an array of locally produced leather jackets, skirts, shoes, purses, belts, wallets, and luggage of respectable quality at amazingly low prices.

Dining and Lodging

$$$$ ✕🏨 **Hostería La Mirage.** Peaceful, elegant, and idyllic, La Mirage is
★ an oasis of European culture in the midst of the highlands. Trickling fountains and shaded courtyards wind through flower-filled gardens to beautifully decorated casitas and suites. Rooms have handcrafted furniture, extensive windows, wood-burning fireplaces, and well-appointed bathrooms. While you're off at dinner, discreet staff members slip in to build a fire and place hot water bottles at the foot of your bed—an example of the outstanding service provided throughout your stay. La Mirage's sophisticated restaurant serves international and Ecuadoran cuisine; come morning, you may indulge in breakfast in bed (included). ✉ *Av. 10 de Agosto,* ☎ *06/915237, 800/327–3573 in the U.S.;* FAX *06/915065. 23 rooms. Restaurant, bar, pool, spa, steam room, tennis court, horseback riding. DC, MC, V.*

$ ✕🏨 **Hostería Mesón de las Flores.** This two-story, postcolonial building by the town church is an inexpensive and authentically Ecuadoran lodging option. Most rooms are on the second floor surrounding a courtyard restaurant, and have small balconies and soft beds. A spacious suite on the third floor is a great deal for a couple. ✉ *Calle García Moreno at Calle Sucre,* ☎ *06/916009,* FAX *06/915828. 18 rooms. Restaurant, bar. AE, DC, MC, V.*

Laguna de Cuicocha

18 km (11 mi) west of Cotacachi.

Mile-wide Laguna de Cuicocha (Cuicocha Lake) is an oblong lake cradled in a crater on the lower flanks of Cotacachi Volcano. A well-marked hiking trail heads up the crater's rim into an ecological reserve, which affords fantastic views of the lake below and distant Imbabura and Cayambe volcanoes. Within the lake lie two vegetation-covered volcanic islands, which can be visited on inexpensive boat tours. The restaurant **Cuicocha** (☎ 09/722718), perched over the edge of the lake, enjoys a great view; boat trips can be arranged from here. Taxis and pickup trucks near the bus station in Cotacachi will make the trip to the lake for $5–$8.

Ibarra

25 km (16 mi) north of Otavalo.

Ibarra, capital of Imbabura Province, is a pleasant colonial city, but most tourists stop first at **San Antonio de Ibarra,** on the Pan-American Highway a few miles before the capital. San Antonio is the "Cotacachi of wood carvings"; the stores that surround its central plaza sell variations on identical woodworking themes. Religious statuary of cedar or walnut—priced anywhere from a few dollars to several hundred dollars—is ubiquitous; pieces with more bawdy or whimsical themes are also available.

Dining and Lodging

$$ ✕⌂ **Hostería Chorlaví.** Wide, shaded verandas; thick, whitewashed
★ walls; and spacious, antiques-furnished rooms make this inn a favorite weekend retreat for Ecuadorans and tourists alike. The restaurant emphasizes fresh fish and typical Andean dishes, all served on a flower-filled patio where live folk music accompanies weekend lunches. Rooms in the old building are lovely, though they can be loud on weekends; more private rooms in a new building in back all have fireplaces. ⌂ *Pan-American Hwy. S, 4 km (2½ mi) south of Ibarra,* ☎ *06/955777 or 06/955775,* ℻ *06/932224. 51 rooms. Restaurant, pool, hot tub, sauna, steam room, tennis court, basketball, squash, volleyball. AE, DC, MC, V.*

Imbabura Province A to Z

Arriving and Departing

BY BUS

From Quito's Terminal Terrestre, buses depart every 30 minutes for Ibarra (2½ hours) and Otavalo (2 hours); round-trip fare is less than $5. **Transportes Otavalo** (☎ 02/570271) deposits passengers in Otavalo's center. **Flota Imbabura** (☎ 02/572657) has direct service to Ibarra, but for Otavalo they drop you a few blocks outside of town.

BY CAR

Driving a car in Quito and its surroundings is difficult at best. Many roads are unmarked, road conditions are often poor, and there are better ways of traveling through the city and its outskirts. Taxis are very inexpensive, and there are numerous tour operators that can arrange for a car with a driver. If you do decide to drive yourself, however, make sure to get very specific directions from the rental agency for the places that you want to visit, and ask for the best they have.

Otavalo is just off the Pan-American Highway, 113 km (70 mi) north of Quito.

BY TAXI

For around $50, taxis that carry up to four passengers can be hired in Quito for a daylong trip to Otavalo and the surrounding countryside or other towns. The more expansive hotels listed above will arrange transportation to and from your hotel in Quito.

Getting Around

Buses run among Imbabura's major towns about every 15 minutes. A taxi ride between Otavalo and Ibarra costs about $6.

Contacts and Resources

BANKS AND CURRENCY EXCHANGE

Bring all the local currency you'll need when traveling to small towns, since exchange houses are few and far between. Most hotels can change traveler's checks; however, credit cards are usually not accepted.

Try **Casa de Cambio Otavalo** (✉ Jaramillo, near Quiroga) to change money in Otavalo.

EMERGENCIES

Ambulance: ☎ 131. **Fire:** ☎ 102. **Police:** ☎ 101. **General emergency:** ☎ 111.

TOUR OPERATORS AND TRAVEL AGENTS

Diceny Viajes (✉ Sucre 1014, Otavalo, ☎ FAX 06/921217), owned and operated by indigenous people, offers a variety of trekking and horseback excursions to the area around Otavalo. **IntiExpress** (✉ Calle Sucre at Morales, Otavalo, ☎ 06/920737) offers a good selection of day trips to highland lakes and Indian villages. Most operators in Quito offer one- and two-day tours, which typically include visits to several weaving villages and sometimes overnights at hosterías. **Metropolitan Touring** (☞ Tour Operators and Travel Agents *in* Quito A to Z, *above*) has daily departures. **Safari** (☞ Tour Operators *in* Quito A to Z, *above*) offers tailor-made excursions.

VISITOR INFORMATION

There's a **tourist office** (✉ Av. Olmedo 956 at Velasco, ☎ FAX 06/958547) in Ibarra open weekdays 8:30 until 5.

THE CENTRAL HIGHLANDS

South of Quito the Andes rise sharply on either side of the Pan-American Highway, creating a narrow corridor of fertile, high-elevation valleys that are home to nearly half of Ecuador's population. Along this 175-km (109-mi) stretch between Quito and Riobamba are seven of Ecuador's 10 tallest volcanoes. Alexander von Humboldt, the German scientist who explored the area in 1802, was so impressed by the landscape that he coined a sobriquet still used today: the Avenue of the Volcanoes.

Latacunga, a few hours south of Quito, is an excellent base for visiting the area's colorful market villages, including Saquisilí, Pujilí, and San Miguel de Salcedo. Among the central highlands' most popular destinations is Baños, a sleepy tourist town surrounded by a wealth of natural attractions. Die-hard cyclists should contemplate the 65-km (40-mi) downhill ride from Baños to Puyo (you and your cycle can return to Baños by bus). Riobamba, the pleasant, unruffled capital of Chimborazo Province, is an excellent stop on any tour of the Central Highlands, since it is the point of departure for the famous train trip past the Nariz del Diablo (Devil's Nose)—a 305-m (1,000-ft) drop that the narrow-gauge train negotiates via an ingenious system of hairpin turns, span bridges, and tunnels.

Latacunga

96 km (58 mi) south of Quito.

With its 40,000 inhabitants, Latacunga represents a slice of real Ecuadoran life. While this "Ecuadoran reality check" may or may not interest the typical tourist, Latacunga is an excellent base from which to explore some of the central highlands markets and mountaintops.

The capital of Cotopaxi Province, Latacunga has been rebuilt three times in the wake of massive eruptions of Cotopaxi, the volcano whose perfect, snow-covered cone dominates the city. Latacunga's main plaza, **Parque Vicente León,** is dominated by juniper trees trimmed in an assortment of geometric shapes. At the Saturday market held on **Plaza San Sebastián,** most of the goods for sale are geared for locals—fruits and vegetables, plastic ware, and medicinal herbs. Still, you may find *shigras*, the colorful, handwoven hemp bags used by indigenous people.

Dining and Lodging

The region has several hosterías with comfortable, homespun rooms. These former haciendas are, logically, found outside the cities and towns, so count on country solitude if you choose one.

$$$$ ✕🏨 **Hacienda San Agustín de Callo.** More a historic monument than a hotel, San Agustín has been inhabited for more than five centuries. Once an Inca fortress, it became an Augustinian monastery after the Spanish conquest and now belongs to a prestigious Ecuadoran family. Two original Inca rooms have survived the centuries and are used as the chapel and the dining room—where guests enjoy outstanding Ecuadoran cuisine and five-star service (two meals are included). *National Geographic* archaeologists have continued to discover Inca ruins throughout the property; you can even request a guest room with Inca stone walls. And as if all the history and ambience weren't enough, San Agustín sits just a few miles from Cotopaxi National Park, offering a front-row view of that impressive peak, as well as excellent horseback riding, trout fishing, mountain biking, and trekking. The hacienda is 5 km (3 mi) from Lasso; you will need a taxi or a four-wheel-drive vehicle to get here. ✉ *San Agustín,* ☎ *02/242508 or 02/ 269884 in Quito,* ☎ FAX *03/719160. 4 rooms, 1 suite, 1 casita. Restaurant, horseback riding. MC, V.*

$$ ✕🏨 **La Ciénega.** This former hacienda, 20 km (12 mi) north of Latacunga, has been owned by the descendants of the Marqués de Maenza since colonial days. The country-style furnishings in the main salon are elegant, though the room decorations are more functional than inspired. The lovely ornamental gardens behind the hotel give way to open fields; in the distance, the huge cone of Cotopaxi can be seen. The restaurant serves respectable Ecuadoran cuisine. ✉ *Pan-American Hwy. S, Km 72, Lasso,* ☎ *03/719093, 02/549126 for reservations;* FAX *03/ 719182, 02/228820 for reservations. 33 rooms, 2 suites. Restaurant, bar, horseback riding. DC, MC, V.*

Pujilí

10 km (6 mi) west of Latacunga.

In the tiny mountain village of Pujilí, colorful markets are held on Sunday and, with much less ado, on Wednesday. Few tourists find their way to Pujilí—so instead of sunburned gringos, you'll see locals in bright turquoise or carmine red ponchos and miniature fedoras buying and selling produce, pottery, and costume jewelry.

Saquisilí

13 km (8 mi) northwest of Latacunga.

Indigenous people in regional dress fill all eight of the village's dusty plazas during the Thursday market, where you can pick through piles of traditional wares—including grotesque, painted wooden masks of animals and devils.

San Miguel de Salcedo

14 km (9 mi) south of Latacunga.

This interesting, accessible market town on the Pan-American Highway has pleasant streets and plazas that make it appealing on any day. However, it's most interesting to plan your visit around the Sunday market or the smaller one held on Thursday. Taxis between Latacunga and Pujilí, Saquisilí, and Salcedo cost less than $10 each way.

Baños

180 km (113 mi) south of Quito, 84 km (53 mi) southeast of Latacunga.

At the base of Tungurahua Volcano and surrounded by lush mountains, tumbling waterfalls, and natural hot springs, Baños is one of Ecuador's top tourist spots. Quiteños have been soaking in the curative thermal springs here for decades, although foreign visitors may feel squeamish about entering the brownish waters. The city's real appeal—as Baños tourist operators will attest—lies in the abundant hiking trails, whitewater rafting rivers, and horseback excursions possible in the surrounding highlands.

In the heart of town, the twin spires of **La Iglesia de la Virgen del Agua Santa** (the Church of the Virgin of Holy Water) rise above the tree-lined plaza. The church, whose black-and-white facade is slightly startling, was built to honor Baños's miracle-working Virgin; the huge paintings inside are testimonials from her many exultant beneficiaries. A few blocks away, on a dead-end street, is the small but interesting **Museo Huillancuna,** a private museum that has exhibits on pre-Columbian ceramics, Andean musical instruments, and local history. ⊠ *Pasaje Velasco Ibarra and Av. Montalvo,* ☎ *03/740973.* ☞ *Admission.* ☉ *Dawn–dusk.*

Baños means "baths" in Spanish, and there are several thermal springs in town, but the best is a series of pools called **El Salado** (the Salty), 2 km (1 mi) outside town on Vía al Salado, off the main road to Ambato. Its six man-made pools overflow with brownish mineral water of various temperatures and are adjoined by a refreshing, fast-moving stream. The pools are drained and refilled each morning at dawn. ☞ *Admission.* ☉ *Dawn–dusk.*

Dining and Lodging

$ ✕ **El Higuerón.** This small, charming restaurant hidden by bougainvillea and flowering vines serves tasty salads, sandwiches, pastas, and casseroles. Wood tables and sunny windows make for a colorful meal, and there are a few inviting tables on the outdoor patio. The owner, William Navarette, is among the region's most knowledgeable mountaineers. ⊠ *Calle 12 de Noviembre 270,* ☎ *03/740910. MC, V. Closed Wed.*

$$$ ✕▥ **Luna Runtún.** Perched high over Baños on the slopes of Tungurahua
  ★ Volcano, Luna Runtún is owned and managed by a Swiss/Ecuadoran couple; the hotel combines colonial-style architecture and gorgeous scenery with the attention to detail you would expect from a European hotel. Rooms have terra-cotta floors, whitewashed walls decorated with works by local artists, and lots of windows that overlook the hotel's gardens and the verdant slopes beyond. Deluxe rooms with porches and breathtaking views of Baños Valley are well worth the extra money. The attractive restaurant has plenty of windows, so you don't lose sight of the view, and it serves an inventive selection of Continental cuisine; breakfast and dinner are included in the price of the room. ⊠ *Runtún, 6 km*

(4 mi) from Baños, ☎ *03/740882 or 03/740883;* FAX *03/740376. 33 rooms, 1 suite. Restaurant, bar, horseback riding. AE, DC, MC, V.*

¢–$ ✕☒ **Le Petit Auberge and Restaurant.** After establishing a reputation
★ as one of this town's best restaurants, Le Petit recently expanded to include an inexpensive hotel, all set back from the street in a shady garden. Attractive rooms have hardwood floors, white stuccoed walls, and balconies; six have fireplaces. The restaurant serves excellent French cuisine, with a menu that includes crepes, vegetarian rata-touille, chateaubriand, and fondues. ✉ *Av. 16 de Diciembre at Calle Montalvo,* ☎ *03/740936. 12 rooms. V. Restaurant closed Mon.*

$$ ☒ **Hotel Sangay.** This family-oriented hotel across the street from the municipal baths has three different kinds of rooms: those in the old building, which are the best deal; larger *cabañas* (cabins) behind the pool; and executive rooms, which are spacious and have balconies with views of the Waterfall of the Virgin across the road. The second-floor restaurant also enjoys a nice view, and serves a complimentary Con-tinental breakfast. ✉ *Plazoleta Ayora 101,* ☎ *03/740490,* FAX *03/740056. 70 rooms. Restaurant, bar, pool, 2 hot tubs, sauna, steam room, tennis court, squash. AE, DC, MC, V.*

¢–$ ☒ **Hosteria Monte Selva.** Four three-room brick bungalows are on a lush hillside at the edge of town. Each room has several beds and a small bathroom; outer quarters have views of Baños. At the foot of the hill is a swimming pool, a sauna, and a little restaurant, all of which are surrounded by foliage. ✉ *Calle Halflants, near Calle Montalvo,* ☎ FAX *03/740244. 12 rooms. Restaurant, bar, pool, hot tub, sauna, steam room. DC, MC, V.*

Outdoor Activities and Sports

BICYCLING

AUCA (✉ Calle Maldonado and Calle Oriente, ☎ 03/740637) orga-nizes bicycle tours through the highlands, as well as canoeing expedi-tions through the jungle. Mountain bikes can be rented inexpensively at **Bill Mountain** (✉ Calle Ambato at Calle Maldonado, ☎ 03/740221), which also offers bicycling tours along the road from Baños to Puyo, winding its way through subtropical jungle and past thundering wa-terfalls. You can also do the five-hour, 65-km (40-mi) downhill ride to Puyo on your own and then board a bus in Puyo, bike and all, for the return trip to Baños.

HORSEBACK RIDING

Many excellent day trips or overnight horseback excursions are accessible from Baños, and there are at least a dozen tour operators that offer trips. **Caballos con José** (✉ Calle Maldonado, near Calle Martínez, ☎ FAX 03/740929) is a reliable operation that offers tours lasting from two hours to several nights. **Huillacuna Tours** (✉ Calle Santa Clara 206, ☎ 03/740187) runs half- and full-day tours to Runtún, as well as overnight trips. **Rio Loco** (✉ Calle Maldonado and Calle Martinez, ☎ 03/740929) offers a variety of excursions outside Baños; the Swiss owner is very helpful.

RAFTING

White-water rafting trips on the Patate and Pastaza rivers are avail-able out of Baños. The Class III Patate is a good trip for beginners, while the Pastaza is a more challenging, four-hour trip that flows through some spectacular jungle. Trips can be booked through **Geo-tours** (✉ Calle Maldonado at Calle Espejo, ☎ 03/740332). The local rafting outfitter is **Rio Loco** (☎ 03/740929).

Shopping

Like any respectable tourist town, Baños has no shortage of shopping opportunities. Most of the things for sale come from other parts of

Ecuador, but there are a few interesting local crafts that can be purchased from the people who produce them. Look for brightly colored, handmade wooden toucans, parrots, turtles, and other tropical creatures. **Recuerdos** (⊠ Calle Maldonado near Calle Montalvo) sells brightly painted balsa-wood statues of parrots and other birds made in a workshop behind the store. **El Cade** (⊠ Calle Maldonado 681), near the bus station, makes and sells a variety of items carved from the seed of the tagua palm, also known as vegetal ivory.

Riobamba

105 km (63 mi) south of Latacunga.

Three of Ecuador's most formidable peaks—Chimborazo, Altar, and Tungurahua—are visible from Riobamba, a pleasant, high-altitude town with wide, tree-lined streets and some well-preserved colonial architecture. Most travelers who head to Riobamba do so because it is the starting point for the train trip to Durán (near Guayaquil), which winds its way through some spectacularly narrow gorges past the Devil's Nose. Most people ride the train only as far as Bucay, after which the terrain is flat and uninteresting; from here you can catch a bus back to Riobamba or on to Guayaquil.

There are good buys at the tourist-oriented Saturday market held in the **Parque de la Concepción** (Park of the Conception; ⊠ Calle Orozco at Calle Colón); look for embroidered belts, hand-knit sweaters and weavings, shigras, and locally produced clothing and jewelry. Across the street from the market, the **Museo de Arte Religioso** (Museum of Religious Art), housed in the beautifully restored **Iglesia de la Concepción** (Church of the Conception) has an impressive collection of colonial art. ⊠ *Calle Argentina,* ☎ *03/952212.* ⊡ *Admission.* ☉ *Tues.–Sat.*

The hill at the center of the **Parque 21 de Abril** (⊠ Calle Argentina), on the north side of town, affords an excellent view of the city and, on clear days, several snowcapped volcanoes. The mural below the lookout depicts the city's history.

Dining and Lodging

$$ ⊞ **Abras Pungo.** Reminiscent of a mountaineer's lodge, Abras Pungo is among the most practical accommodations in the Central Highlands. Each of the clean, comfortable rooms is named after a different mountain peak; several overlook the surrounding hills. Horses, stabled on site, are available for day treks. The owner, Marco Cruz, is a famous mountaineer who can provide information on the best hikes in the region. ⊠ *3½ mi from Riobamba on road to Guano, Box 0601425,* ☎ *03/940820,* ⅀ *03/940819. 18 rooms, 2 suites. Restaurant, bar, hiking, horseback riding. AE, DC, MC, V.*

$$ ✕⊞ **Hostería El Troje.** Riobamba's premier sleeping stopover lies out-
★ side of town. Most of the spacious rooms have a fireplace. When there are enough guests, the hotel puts on a show with folk music and dancing before dinner. The owner is one of the most famous mountain climbers in Ecuador. ⊠ *4½ km (3 mi) southeast of town on minor road to Chambo, Box 50,* ☎ ⅀ *03/960826 or 03/964572. 48 rooms. Restaurant, bar, pool, basketball, playground. AE, DC, MC, V.*

¢ ✕⊞ **Hostel Montecarlo.** This charming, turn-of-the-century house, with its fern-filled central courtyard, is conveniently located mid-city. Its elegant yet homelike restaurant, around the corner from the hotel, is first-rate. ⊠ *Av. 10 de Agosto 2541,* ☎ ⅀ *03/960557. 18 rooms. Restaurant, cafeteria. MC, V.*

The Central Highlands A to Z

Arriving and Departing

BY BUS

From Quito there are frequent buses to Latacunga (2 hours), Baños (3½ hours), and Riobamba (4 hours). All cost less than $5 each way. Local buses connect Latacunga with Pujilí, Saquisilí, and San Miguel de Salcedo.

BY CAR

Latacunga lies just off the Pan-American Highway, 89 km (55 mi) south of Quito. The nearby villages of Pujilí, San Miguel de Salcedo, and Saquisilí are accessed via unpaved but hard-packed roads. Baños is 40 km (25 mi) east of Ambato on the road to Puyo. Riobamba is nestled along the Pan-American Highway 188 km (117 mi) south of Quito.

BY TAXI

You can take a taxi from any major city to reach the central highlands. However, when you do so, you must also pay for the driver's return fare back to the city regardless of whether he waits for you or just drops you off at a site. You can also ask the driver to accompany you on your travels as a private chauffeur—but you must pay for his food and lodging as well as the cab fare. This is a popular and inexpensive way to take side trips around Quito; the fare to Baños, for example, would cost around $100.

Getting Around

Although it's possible to rent a car to drive around the region, it isn't recommended, as roads are often unmarked and unpaved. It is better to either hire a car with a driver, so you can sit back and enjoy the scenery while still being in charge, or to take one of the many buses that run from Quito.

Contacts and Resources

BANKS AND CURRENCY EXCHANGE

Traveler's checks and credit cards aren't usually accepted in this region, and money changers are few and far between. Bring all of the cash that you'll need; your hotel can probably change more if necessary, but not always at the best rates.

EMERGENCIES

Ambulance: ☎ 131. **Fire:** ☎ 102. **Police:** ☎ 101. **General emergency:** ☎ 111. Riobamba's **hospital:** (⊠ Olmedo 11-01, ☎ 03/961705).

TOUR OPERATORS AND TRAVEL AGENTS

Metropolitan Touring (☞ Tour Operators and Travel Agents *in* Quito A to Z, *above*) has tours of the region that include the rail trip down the Devil's Nose, either in a private caboose or an autoferro. **Safari** (☞ Tour Operators and Travel Agents *in* Quito A to Z, *above*) specializes in smaller, off-the-beaten-track excursions that often include trekking or mountain biking.

VISITOR INFORMATION

Baños. The local hotel association has an information office in front of the Hostel Banana (⊠ Calle 12 de Noviembre 500, ☎ 03/740309). There is also tourist information at the bus station. **Riobamba.** The **tourist office** (⊠ 2072 Av. 15 de Junio, at 10 de Agusto, ☎ 03/941213) is open Monday–Saturday.

EL ORIENTE

The Ecuadoran Amazon, called El Oriente (literally, The East), accounts for roughly one-third of Ecuador's landmass but just 4% of its population. One of the world's biodiversity hot spots, it is home to hundreds of colorful bird species, including massive macaws, toucans, and the prehistoric-looking hoatzin. Jaguars, pumas, tapir, and peccaries are present but elusive; pink river dolphins are frequently sighted, however, as are many species of monkey, including the howler, woolly, squirrel, spider, and tamarin. An abundance of insects thrives under the jungle canopy, including workaholic leaf-cutter ants, society spiders, and enormous, electric blue morpho butterflies. Myriad plant species coexist, and in some cases even cooperate, with the jungle animals. The giant kapok tree, El Oriente's tallest species, soars to nearly 60 m (200 ft) above the jungle floor. Creeping vines cascade from strangler figs, which in turn envelop other species.

In this exuberant world, eight different indigenous peoples continue, to varying degrees, to live their traditional lifestyles. Indeed, one group still lives a nomadic life and hostilely repels any attempts at rapprochement by outsiders. Others, however, including the Cofán and the Siecoya of Cuyabeno Reserve and the Huaorani who live in and around Yasuni National Park, allow tourist groups to visit and share their tremendous knowledge of plants and animals.

Trips to El Oriente are best planned with a tour operator, which will usually arrange all details of transportation, lodging, and exploring. Independent travel is possible, but it is difficult and not recommended. Tours to both Cuyabeno and Yasuni, which are dominated by primary rain forest, offer the best possibilities for viewing wildlife. At a minimum, you should allow four days for a trip to the jungle.

Misahuallí

228 km (143 mi) southeast of Quito.

The jungle around the town of Misahuallí is popular, especially among backpackers, for its accessibility and economic tour prices; heavy colonization in the area, however, means there is little in the way of wildlife here. **The Butterfly Lodge** (✉ Av. Río Coca 1734, Quito, ☎ 02/253267, FAX 02/253266 for reservations), formerly known as Cabañas Alinahui, downstream from Misahuallí on the shores of the Napo River, offers a taste of the Amazon for those who haven't time for a more extensive trek. The comfortable lodge is affiliated with **Jatun Sacha,** a biological research station dedicated to conservation, education, and study of the rain forest.

Cuyabeno Wildlife Reserve

72 km (45 mi) east of Lago Agrio.

This 642,000-acre wildlife reserve, with over 500 bird species, is reached via a short flight from Quito to Lago Agrio, on the headwaters of the Aguarico River. Once you head east from Lago Agrio things start to get wild, and traveling on your own can be extremely difficult. Virtually the only way to visit this area is on some sort of tour. **Metropolitan Touring** (☞ Tour Operators and Travel Agents *in* Quito A to Z, *above*) has three options for exploring the Cuyabeno area, all of which combine nature observation and visits to traditional Cofán communities. Ask about staying a night on the **Flotel Orellana,** a floating hotel built to cruise the Aguarico River. **Emerald Forest Expedition** (✉ Av. Amazonas 1023, at Calle Pinto, Quito, ☎ 02/526403, FAX 02/

541543) has several options for exploring the area south of Cuyabeno, based on either camping or staying in a jungle lodge. **Safari** (☞ Tour Operators and Travel Agents *in* Quito A to Z, *above*) runs cultural trekking trips with the Huaorani.

Macas

246 km (154 mi) northeast of Cuenca.

The pleasant town of Macas is the gateway to the southern Oriente, which is more heavily settled and has less primary rain forest than the northern sector. Nonetheless, there is still spectacular rain forest to be found here. A trip with **Ecotrek** (✉ Calle Larga 7–108, Cuenca, ☎ 07/834677 or 07/842531, Ⅲ 07/835387; ☞ Chapter 2 for U.S. representative, Southwind Adventures) will put you in contact with the Shuar people who live to the east of Macas, around the missionary town of Miazal. Also out of Macas, **Remote Odysseys Worldwide** (also known as ROW) leads five-day white-water rafting trips on the scenic Upano River (☞ White-Water Rafting and Kayaking *in* Chapter 2). **Emerald Forest Expeditions** (☞ *above*) has cultural tours that facilitate living with the Shuar Indians.

Kapawi

184 km (115 mi) east of Macas.

One of the most remote corners of Ecuador, this eastern jungle region near the Peru border is the territory of the Achuar Indians. Kapawi is actually the name of one of the Achuar villages and of the nearby ecological reserve managed by the Indians. The Guayaquil-based ecotourism company **Canodros** (✉ Calle L. Urdaneta at Av. del Ejército, ☎ 04/285711, ⅢX 04/287651) runs a lodge in the area that, according to an agreement signed with Achuar leaders, will belong to the Achuar in the year 2011. The Kapawi Ecolodge consists of typical Achuar huts—no nails were used in construction—equipped with modern amenities like electric lights (solar-powered) and private baths. Canodros offers all-inclusive packages lasting four to eight days, which are not only excellent trips for seeing wildlife but also allow contact with the Achuar.

El Oriente A to Z

Arriving and Departing

BY AIRPLANE
Coca, Lago Agrio (officially known as Nuevo Loja), and Macas are just 40 minutes and $60 (one-way) from Quito on TAME Airline (☎ 02/509382 or 02/509385). Coca and Lago Agrio are served Monday–Saturday; Macas on Monday, Wednesday, and Friday. There are also several small charter companies that specialize in jungle towns and other remote destinations; these are considerably more expensive than scheduled flights.

BY BUS
From Quito to Lago Agrio takes 8 hours by bus; Quito to Coca takes 9 hours. Cuenca to Macas takes 10–12 hours and costs $7 each way.

BY CAR
The long land trip through lush cloud forests of giant tree ferns, orchids, and bromeliads is a beautiful opportunity to see transitional zones between the Andes and the rain forest. The Quito–Lago Agrio trip takes six hours by car; Quito–Coca takes eight hours. Misahuallí can be reached from Quito via Baeza and Tena or via Baños; both journeys take five–six hours by car. Since Macas is so remote, and the road some-

times becomes impassable, it is advisable to fly there. No roads pass near Kapawi.

BY TAXI

Taxis from Quito can be hired to reach the main towns of El Oriente; it's just a matter of negotiating the price. Remember, if you want a chauffeur type of deal, you'll have to pay his room and board along the way in addition to the fare.

Getting Around

Most travel within El Oriente is by canoe. Driving is not recommended.

Contacts and Resources

BANKS AND CURRENCY EXCHANGE

It is difficult to change money in this remote region. Bring all of the local currency that you will need.

EMERGENCIES

Fire: ☎ 06/830119. **Police:** ☎ 06/830222. Lago Agrio **hospital:** ☎ 06/830250.

TOUR OPERATORS

In Coca, **Ejarsytur** (☎ 06/880251) offers a variety of travel services and tours. **Expeditiones Dayuma** (✉ Dayuma Hotel, Misahuallí, ☎ 06/571513) can assist with travel plans.

VISITOR INFORMATION

A tourist office is occasionally open in Coca at the dock on the Rió Napo.

CUENCA

Cuenca is a walker's—and shopper's—paradise, where the cobblestone streets are lined with restored colonial and postcolonial mansions, their iron-grill balconies filled with potted plants. Old men gossip in the many plazas, oblivious to the call of scruffy shoe-shine boys, while cars and taxis trundle by in a relaxed manner unknown to Quito or Guayaquil. One of Ecuador's most visitor-friendly cities, Cuenca was isolated for centuries from the country's more cosmopolitan centers; paved roads were not laid from Cuenca to Guayaquil and Quito until the 1960s. It's not surprising that the *cuencanos* have, over the years, developed a stubborn pride in themselves and their workmanship. Cuenca is among Ecuador's leaders in cottage industries, producing fine ceramics, textiles, jewelry, and Panama hats.

On market days—Thursday and Sunday—hundreds of townspeople and *indígenas* from surrounding towns throng Cuenca's open-air plazas to buy and sell crafts and household items. The *cholas cuencanas* dress for the day in their finest straw hats. These female descendants of mixed Spanish and Cañari couples, famed for their beauty, are striking in their colorful *polleras*—gathered wool skirts in violet, emerald green, rose red, or marigold—and satiny, peasant-style polka blouses.

Exploring Cuenca

A Good Walk

In the heart of Cuenca's compact Old City lies the shaded **Parque Abdón Calderón.** The grand facade and periwinkle-blue domes of Cuenca's **Catedral de la Inmaculada,** also known as the New Cathedral, tower over the park's western edge. Opposite the New Cathedral sits the small, unimposing **Sagrario,** the Old Cathedral. Walk two blocks east of El Sagrario, then turn right on Calle Hermano Miguel and walk 1½ blocks south to the entrance for the **Museo de las Conceptas.** Stop in at the **tourist office** next door. Return to Parque Calderón and continue west along the edge of the New Cathedral to the small plaza on your left. There you'll find a colorful flower market and the church/nunnery, **Carmen de la Asunción.** Turn left at the corner and head one block south, past the crowds and stalls that occupy the Plaza de San Francisco, to the tan-and-white **Iglesia de San Francisco.** Walk back to Carmen de la Asunción, turn left, and walk west for five blocks along Calle Mariscal Sucre to the **Museo de Arte Moderno,** which overlooks the plaza and church of San Sebastián. If you still have energy, walk behind the museum and head southeast to the Riobamba River, which flows along the southern edge of the Old City. Follow the river east, crossing a bridge at some point for better views. When you reach the bridge at Avenida Huayna-Capac, cross the river again and walk one block north to the modern **Banco Central,** which houses the **Museo del Banco Central.**

TIMING

This walk takes three or four hours, unless you spend a long time in the museums; note that these are closed on Sundays. It's worthwhile to stretch it out a bit to include lunch, since most of the restaurants listed below are around the center of town.

Sights to See

Carmen de la Asunción. The stone carvings that surround the doorway are a good example of Spanish Baroque design, while the church's interior is typically ostentatious—especially noteworthy is the gold-covered pulpit encrusted with mirrors. The flower market held on the plaza outside is in full blossom every day until sunset. ⊠ *Calle Mariscal Sucre at Calle Padre Aguirre.* ☒ *Free.* ☉ *Daily 6 AM–8 PM.*

★ **Catedral de la Inmaculada.** The little light that enters through the miniature stained-glass windows of the New Cathedral becomes diffused and golden, casting a pale glow over the thick brick walls. The heavy atmosphere of the church, which was built in fits and starts between 1886 and 1967, is lightened somewhat by pillars of Ecuadoran marble and Italian marble floors. ⊠ *Parque Abdón Calderón,* ☏ *07/842097.* ☒ *Free.* ☉ *Daily 6:30–4:30.*

El Sagrario. Also called the Old Cathedral, the church was begun in 1557, the year the city was founded. Unfortunately, the church is closed for renovation until 2001. ⊠ *Parque Calderón.*

Iglesia de San Francisco. Built in the 1920s, the Church of San Francisco is famous for its soaring steeple and intricately carved, gold-drenched main altar, which contrasts nicely with the church's pale interior. ⊠ *Av. Gran Colombia at Calle Padre Aguirre.* ☒ *Free.* ☉ *Mon.–Wed. 7:30–8:15 AM, Thurs.–Sat. 6:30–7:15 AM, Sun. 7:30–9:30 AM and 4–5 PM.*

Museo de Arte Moderno. The Museum of Modern Art, housed in a colonial building, always has several interesting, well-presented exhibitions of local artists, though its permanent collection consists mainly of dark, bleak paintings by anonymous colonial masters. ⊠ *Calle Mariscal Sucre at Calle Coronel Talbot,* ☏ *07/831027.* ☒ *Free.* ☉ *Weekdays 9–1 and 3–7, weekends 10–1.*

Museo del Banco Central. The concrete-and-glass Central Bank Museum houses an ethnographic and archaeological museum, in addition to exhibits of colonial and postcolonial art. Near the river behind the museum is a small archaeological site under excavation. ⊠ *Calle Larga at Av. Huayna-Capac,* ☏ *07/831255, ext. 234.* ☒ *Admission.* ☉ *Weekdays 9–6, Sat. 9–1.*

Museo de las Conceptas. In the 16th century one of Cuenca's leading citizens, Doña Ordóñez, donated her house (which filled an entire city block) to the Catholic church, whereupon it became the cloistered convent of the Order of the Immaculate Conception. Four centuries later, part of this spacious and well-preserved edifice houses the Museum of the Conception, which contains an impressive collection of religious art from the 16th to 19th centuries. ⊠ *Calle Hermano Miguel 6–33, between Calles Juan Jaramillo and Presidente Córdova,* ☎ *07/830625.* 🎟 *Admission.* ⊙ *Mon. 2:30–5:30, Tues.–Fri. 9–7:30, Sat. 10–1.*

Parque Abdón Calderón. Surrounded by beautiful colonial architecture, Cuenca's central square sparkles with activity. Manicured trees look over dignified patriarchs, gossiping mothers, frolicking children, and vendors selling their wares. The park is dominated by the pale rose Catedral de la Inmaculada towering over its western edge.

Plaza de San Francisco. The plaza is filled with locals hawking a variety of shoes, sweaters, lipstick, shampoo, and bric-a-brac. Under the northern colonnade, Indian merchants sell wares that are of more interest to travelers, mainly colorful ponchos, hand-knit sweaters, and woven wall hangings. You should avoid this plaza at night.

Dining

Though Cuenca suffers a dearth of bars and restaurants—cuencanos are a stay-at-home lot and tourism is still relatively new—the city does have a few excellent eateries. Most restaurants, outside of the major hotels, are closed Sunday.

Contemporary

$$ ✕ **Villa Rosa.** Cuenca's best international restaurant is perfectly en-
★ sconced inside a meticulously restored postcolonial house. Soft music floats through several tastefully decorated salons to the upper balcony, where an open fireplace blazes. Try the grilled trout with almonds and, for dessert, the fruit-and-chocolate fondue. ⊠ *Av. Gran Colombia 1222,* ☎ *07/837944. DC, MC, V. Closed weekends.*

Ecuadoran

$$ ✕ **El Jardin.** One of Cuenca's more elegant restaurants, El Jardin attracts a sophisticated dinner crowd and many repeat visitors. Hand-painted menus list a variety of steak and seafood dishes, and the grilled lobster is an inexpensive treat. Relaxed, friendly service complements the Ecuadoran decor. Consider a fine Chilean wine with your meal. ⊠ *Presidente Cordova 7–23,* ☎ *07/831120. AE, DC, MC, V.*

$$ ✕ **Los Capulíes.** Los Capulíes is Cuenca's most charming restaurant.
★ Refined service and carefully prepared Ecuadoran dishes make this an excellent dinner choice; the dining room's abundant greenery, hand-woven textiles, and trickling fountains add to the enchanting atmosphere. Start with a delicately sweetened empanada, followed by the *plato tipico cuencano*—a sampler dish of llapingachos, grilled pork, *mote pillo* (boiled corn mixed with onions and eggs), sweet sausages, and a tamale. For dessert, try *moras con crema* (blackberries with cream) accompanied by a warm glass of *canelazo* (a sweet liquor combining sugar cane, cinnamon, and bitter orange with the rumlike *zhumir*). Live Andean music is presented weekends evenings. ⊠ *Calle Borrero at Calle Córdova,* ☎ *07/832339. AE, DC, MC, V.*

$$ ✕ **Montebello.** This beautiful, new Mediterranean-style restaurant and bar in Mirador de Turi affords panoramic views of Cuenca. White and purple tables and chairs contribute to the modern decor; request a window table at night. Meat dishes are featured, and the *parillada Montebello*—a casserole of pork, beef, chicken, sausage, and rice—is among the best selections. You'll need a taxi to get here; the driver will know the way to the restaurant. ⊠ *Mirador de Turi,* ☎ *07/883403 or 07/ 843079. AE, V. Closed Mon.–Wed.*

¢–$ ✕ **Raymipampa.** A convenient location next to the New Cathedral has
★ a lot to do with this casual restaurant's popularity, but the food and prices alone are enough to make it a hit. An extensive menu includes a variety of crepes and ceviches, and such Ecuadoran favorites as *locro de queso* (a milk-based potato soup garnished with avocado and cheese). ⊠ *Calle Benigno Malo 859,* ☎ *07/834159. AE, DC, MC, V.*

Mexican

$ ✕ **El Pedregal Azteca.** Savory Mexican food may prove a welcome alternative to local cuisine, but beware the deadly margaritas. Try the *chile relleno* (breaded, deep-fried chili pepper stuffed with cheese), or the specialty of the house, *carne asada a la tampiqueña* (beef grilled with salt and lemon). There is live music and two-for-one margaritas on weekends. ⊠ *Av. Gran Colombia 1029, at Calle Padre Aguirre,* ☎ *07/823652. DC, MC, V. Closed Sun.*

Lodging

Cuenca's accommodations may not rival those in the rest of the country, but the rates are remarkably low.

$$$ ☷ **Hotel Oro Verde.** This classy, Swiss-run hotel caters mainly to inter-
★ national business travelers and tour groups. The rooms shine with dark, polished wood; special touches include extra-large closets, electric heaters, and bathtubs. A 2-km (1-mi) taxi ride from the town center, the hotel overlooks a man-made lagoon, beyond which flows the Tomebamba River. The restaurant is famous for its fish; try the trout marinated in brandy. ⊠ *Av. Ordóñez Lazo,* ☎ *07/831200, 800/447– 7462 in the U.S.;* ℻ *07/832849. 80 rooms, 2 suites. Restaurant, bar, coffee shop, pool, sauna, steam room, airport shuttle. AE, DC, MC, V.*

$$ ☷ **Hotel Crespo.** This intimate hotel overlooking the Tomebamba River on the southern edge of town combines comfort with a friendly, unpretentious setting. The restaurant and about one-third of the rooms have good views of the river. Numerous sitting and reading rooms give the Crespo a familiar, homey atmosphere. ⊠ *Calle Larga 793,* ☎ *07/842571,* ℻ *07/839473. 37 rooms, 3 suites. Restaurant, bar. AE, DC, MC, V.*

$ ☷ **Hotel Inca Real.** This friendly, sunny hotel—a restored colonial home—has cozy rooms grouped around three enclosed courtyards. Though small, the rooms are neat and cheerfully furnished in bright blue and white. Original art and unique glass lighting highlight the decor. ⊠ *Calle General Torres 840, between Calles Sucre and Bolívar,* ☎ *07/ 823636,* ℻ *07/840699. 30 rooms. Restaurant, bar, meeting room. AE, DC, MC, V.*

$ ☷ **Las Casas de Guapdondélig.** This quiet, family-run inn occupies three former homes in a residential neighborhood on the south side of the city, one block from the Mercado 12 de Abril. It's popular with families and students, who enjoy the indoor pool, complimentary Continental breakfast, and other amenities. Rooms are simple, with floral patterns. From time to time, live folkloric music accompanies dinner in the restaurant. ⊠ *Calle Guapdondélig at Calle J. Roldos,* ☎ ℻ *07/861917. 22 rooms. Restaurant, bar, pool, sauna, steam room. AE, DC, MC, V.*

¢ ☷ **Posada del Sol.** Occupying an attractive, 19th-century corner build-
★ ing, this hotel is a bargain. Carpeted rooms are tastefully decorated; several have small balconies. There's a fireplace on the second floor, and a small, covered courtyard where complimentary Continental breakfast is served. The owner can arrange trekking and horseback tours of Cajas National Park and nearby wilderness areas. The restaurant

serves mostly vegetarian dishes. ⊠ *Calle Bolívar 5–03, at Calle Mariano Cueva,* ☎ *07/838695,* 𝖥𝖠𝖷 *07/838995. 11 rooms. DC, MC, V.*

Nightlife and the Arts

Cuenca is not about nightlife. Locals usually stay home during the week and sally forth on Friday and Saturday nights to have dinner and drinks, or maybe to see a movie or a play.

Nightlife

La Cantina (⊠ Calle Presidente Borrero at Calle Córdova) is an attractive little bar next to Los Capulíes, which features live Latin music on weekend nights. **Wunderbar Café** (⊠ Calle Hermano Miguel at Calle Larga, ☎ 07/831274) is an intimate, German-owned bar popular with young people. It's in an old building on the Escalinata, the wide stairs leading down to the river. For dancing, check out **El Conquistador** (⊠ Av. Gran Colombia 665, ☎ 07/831788).

The Arts

Theater is sometimes performed at **La Casa de la Cultura** (⊠ Calle Luis Cordero 718, ☎ 07/828175), and movies are shown most nights at 9. For information regarding other events, look in the daily newspaper, *El Mercurio,* or contact **La Fundación Paul Rivet** (⊠ Av. Solano and 10 de Agosto, ☎ 07/885951), which distributes a monthly newsletter of cultural events.

Shopping

Cuenca is among Ecuador's leaders in cottage industries, producing fine ceramics, textiles, silver and gold jewelry, and leather. Among its most important products is the Panama hat, whose name sticks in the collective craw of proud Ecuadorans. (These finely made straw hats—also known as *toquilla* hats—are named for the country to which they were first exported en masse, hence the Panama sobriquet.)

Concuero (⊠ Calle Mariscal Lamar 1137) sells good-quality leather jackets, shoes, wallets, and handbags. **Fundación Jorge Moscoso** (⊠ Calle Presidente Córdova 614) has a limited but precious collection of antiques; well-made, modern, regional indigenous clothing; and a small archaeological museum. **Kinara** (⊠ Calle Mariscal Sucre 770) stocks stylish gold and silver jewelry, women's hats, and jackets and shawls made of traditional ikat textiles, where the threads are knotted and dyed prior to weaving. **Señor Ortega** (⊠ Av. Gil Ramirez Davalos 3–86, the road to the airport, ☎ 07/823429) has one of Ecuador's most extensive selections of Panama hats. If you don't see what you want in the store, ask for a tour of the adjacent factory where the famous hats are made.

Side Trips from Cuenca

Mirador de Turi

For a fantastic view of Cuenca by night or day, hike 3 km (2 mi) south or take a taxi to the lookout point at the tiny village of Turi, where there is also a photogenic, mural-covered church. Walk along Turi's main street and you'll soon find yourself in green, sometimes burnt-brown, hills where stucco and adobe farmhouses punctuate cornfields and potato patches. Many of Cuenca's wealthiest homes stand in this area.

Ingapirca

Long before the Inca invasion of Ecuador in the latter half of the 15th century, the fierce and industrious Cañari people ruled Guapdondélig

("Plain as Wide and Beautiful as the Sky"), their name for the fertile highlands surrounding Cuenca. Yet while Ingapirca, 70 km (42 mi) north of Cuenca, was an important religious and political center to the Cañari, the site is better remembered for its **Inca ruins:** After the Inca king Tupac-Yupanqui conquered the Cañari, he added his own temples and monuments to the site. (*Ingapirca* literally means *Wall of the Inca.*) The mortarless, stone-built structures are thought to be Cañari temples to the moon, while the elliptical building at the center is acknowledged to be the conquering Incas' vast temple to the sun. There is also a museum, and an excellent restaurant ½ km (¼ mi) away serves luscious local dishes. ⊡ *Admission.* ☉ *Daily; museum Tues.–Sat.*

El Cajas Recreational Area

Thirty-two kilometers (20 miles) west of Cuenca are the wild, cold, cloudy moors of El Cajas, where the average elevation is 10,500 ft. The rugged terrain is the legacy left by glaciers as they retreated some 5 million years ago. Today the nearly 70,000 acres of moors are home to Andean condors, hawks, and the elusive gray-breasted mountain toucan, as well as wolves, gazelle, and white-tailed deer. Fishers appreciate the abundant trout in many of the area's 230 lakes.

El Cajas is best explored with an accomplished guide, because visitors can easily become disoriented in the stark landscape. An experienced guide will point out the unique páramo (high barren plain) vegetation and set up camp each evening. If you don't want to take a tour, try to hike with a local who knows the area, or take your compass. In any case, go prepared for strong sun, cold wind, and the possibility of rain. Sunglasses and sunscreen are also recommended. There is a park station near the entrance where one can sometimes sleep for a small fee, although if the accommodations are full you'll have to make other plans. Camping is permitted throughout the park—pay the nominal charge at the ranger station—but is advised only for well-equipped, experienced campers.

Gualaceo and Chordeleg

Thirty-eight kilometers (24 miles) east of Cuenca lies the market and weaving town of Gualaceo, a cozy hamlet that seems plucked from another time. It has many well-preserved, postcolonial buildings, and throngs of well-dressed Cañari women in polleras and jaunty straw or felt hats gather around the main square, particularly on market day. At the Sunday market, locals buy and sell plastics, costume jewelry, clothing, and other necessities, as well as a wide variety of produce and cooked foods. The town is best known for producing the traditional Azuay shawl, the *macana.* The ikat weaving style is thought to have originated in Polynesia. Try to visit during one of Gualaceo's major festivals—in early March there's the annual Peach Festival, and the religious Festival of St. James is celebrated on June 25.

Just a few miles from Gualaceo is the silver- and gold-mining town of Chordeleg. Some complain that the quality of the gold and silver filigree jewelry has diminished, but it's still quite remarkable, and there are good bargains. Ikat weavings, embroidered clothing, pottery, and Panama hats—as well as mountains of jewelry—are sold in the little shops that surround the tree-shaded plaza.

Cuenca A to Z

Arriving and Departing

BY AIRPLANE

Cuenca's **Aeropuerto Mariscal Lamar** (⊠ Av. España, ☎ 07/862203) is 2 km (1 mi) from the city center, past the bus terminal. A cab from the airport to downtown costs around $3. **SAN/Saeta** (☎ 07/831850, 07/800239 airport) and **TAME** (☎ 07/827609, 07/862193 airport) fly twice daily between Quito and Cuenca. The 40-minute flight costs approximately $60. On weekdays only, TAME makes the 30-minute flight between Guayaquil and Cuenca for roughly $40.

BY BUS

From Cuenca's **Terminal Terrestre** (⊠ Av. España), 1½ km (1 mi) from the town center, there are daily departures to Quito (10 hours) and Guayaquil (five–six hours), both priced under $7.

BY CAR

Cuenca is 472 km (293 mi) south of Quito via the Pan-American Highway. The drives from Quito (eight hours) and Guayaquil (four hours) both have fantastic scenery: The former takes you along the Avenue of the Volcanoes, while the latter climbs through subtropical lowlands before beginning a dizzying mountain ascent—2,490 m (8,300 ft) in just over 240 km (150 mi). Although there are sufficient services along the way, road conditions south of Riobamba and continuing to Cuenca remain poor in the aftermath of El Niño.

Getting Around

Cuenca's center is small and extremely easy to negotiate on foot. Most of its churches, museums, and shops are within a six-block radius of the main plaza, Parque Calderón. Taxis do not use meters, so agree on a price beforehand. Most trips cost less than $2.

BY BUS

You can reach El Cajas Recreational Area by bus, which leaves between 6 and 6:30 AM only, from the Church of San Sebastián (⊠ Corner of Calles Bolívar and Colonel Talbot). Be forewarned: Weekend trips can be crowded, the bus ride takes nearly two hours, and you may have to stand. The only bus back returns at *about* 3 PM; check with the driver, and whatever you do, don't miss it! An alternative is to take a taxi and arrange to be picked up later in the afternoon. Considering the difficulties involved, those truly interested in bird-watching and incredible, albeit stark, landscapes should seriously consider a guided excursion. Approximately $40 will pay for a taxi and driver for the day, and a couple of dollars will take you all the way there and back by bus.

Buses from Cuenca's Terminal Terrestre leave throughout the day for Gualaceo and Chordeleg and cost less than $1. The trip takes 45 minutes.

Guided tours of Ingapirca can be arranged through most Cuenca-based operators for about $40 per person, including lunch. Try to book a tour that makes several stops along the way—in, for example, Azogues—the center of Ecuador's Panama hat industry and the site of a colorful Saturday market—or tiny Cañar, which has a small Sunday market. Alternatively, you can hire a taxi for the day for $20–$40.

BY TAXI

To reach Mirador de Turi, either hike south (and uphill) for several miles along Avenida Fray Vicente Solano, or take a taxi (less than $3). Since taxis can be few and far between in Turi, you may want to plan to walk back down or pay your driver to wait.

Contacts and Resources

BANKS AND CURRENCY EXCHANGE

Traveler's checks and credit cards are accepted at many establishments in this region. You can change money at **Banco del Pacifico** (⊠ Malo 975, at Gran Columbia).

EMERGENCIES
Ambulance: ☎ 131. **Fire:** ☎ 102. **Police:** ☎ 101. **General emergency:** ☎ 111. **Clínica Santa Ana:** (24-hour emergency service) ⊠ Av. Manuel J. Calle 1-104, ☎ 07/814068.

TELEPHONES, INTERNET, AND MAIL
Phone calls are best made from hotels or from the **EMETEL** office (⊠ Benigno Malo and Sucre).

TOUR OPERATORS
Metropolitan Touring (⊠ Mariscal Sucre 662, ☎ 07/831185). **EcoTrek** (⊠ Calle Larga 7108 and Cordero, ☎ 07/842531). **Seitur** (⊠ Gran Colombia 20–109, ☎ 07/842007).

VISITOR INFORMATION
The tourist office (⊠ Calle Hermano Miguel 686, at Calle Presidente Córdova, ☎ 07/839337 or 07/839338) is open weekdays 8:30–5.

GUAYAQUIL AND THE COAST

Guayaquil, the capital of Guayas Province, is South America's busiest Pacific port and Ecuador's largest city, with a population of more than 2 million people. Although the people are friendly and hospitable, the city itself is not terribly attractive, and much of the downtown area suffers a serious crime problem. Still, if business takes you to Guayaquil, or if you end up spending a night or two there during your travels, you need only be careful to enjoy your stay. The city has first-rate restaurants, decent nightlife, and a couple of good museums. The Malecón—the shady park that stretches along the waterfront—is a pleasant area during the day, and the lively Urdesa district has enough restaurants, bars, and discotheques to liven up your nights.

The nearby Pacific coast is something else entirely. During the hot and stifling rainy season, usually December to April, Guayaquil becomes particularly unbearable, and *guayaquileños* head en masse for the beach city of Salinas, about 145 km (90 mi) west. Here the blue waters of the Pacific Ocean teem with sailfish, albacore, wahoo, dolphin, and black, blue, and striped marlin, providing a year-round lure for sport fishermen. Some 100 km (62 mi) north are Puerto López and Machalilla National Park. Ecuador's newest park is attracting more visitors than ever to observe the rare flora and fauna—and to lounge on the beaches—of the central coast.

Guayaquil

250 km (156 mi) southwest of Quito.

A walk along the **Malecón,** Guayaquil's waterfront promenade, is pleasant any time of day, but is most beautiful first thing in the morning or around sunset. Small fishing trawlers and the occasional indigenous dugout add a dash of life to this otherwise busy commercial waterway. Overlooking the river at the foot of Avenida 9 de Octubre, the impressive stone monument **La Rotunda** commemorates the historic meeting in 1822 between Ecuador's venerated liberator, Simón Bolívar, and Argentine general San Martín, who liberated Chile and Peru. The **Clock Tower,** an unusual structure with plenty of Moorish influence, is one of the city's principal landmarks.

The **Museo Nahim Isaias** (⊠ Calle Clemente Ballén at Calle Pichincha, ☎ 04/329099; closed Sun.) is a small museum just a couple of blocks from the Malecón that has both pre-Columbian and colonial exhibits. The **Archaeological Museum of the Banco del Pacífico** (⊠ Calle

P. Ycaza 113, at Calle Pichincha, ☎ 04/566010 or 04/563744), open Tuesday–Friday 10–6, presents a rotating schedule of archaeological exhibits in addition to displays of colonial and 19th-century South American art.

Dining and Lodging

The majority of Guayaquil's nicer restaurants are clustered in the Urdesa district, north of downtown, where you'll also find some of the city's most popular bars and dance clubs. Many restaurants close daily between 4:30 and 7:30, then reopen for dinner, which people tend to eat around 9 or 10 PM.

$$$ ✕ **El Caracol Azul.** This downtown restaurant specializes in seafood prepared Peruvian style and is popular with business executives. The interior of the ordinary cement building is surprisingly attractive, with paintings by local artists and a plant-covered bar beneath a skylight. Start off with *chicharrón de calamar* (deep-fried squid) or corbina ceviche, then move on to a langostino *picante* (in a spicy cream sauce). ⊠ *Av. 9 de Octubre at Calle Los Ríos,* ☎ *04/280361. AE, DC, MC, V. Closed Sun.*

$$$ ✕ **Trattoria da Enrico.** Tiny shuttered windows set into thick whitewashed
★ walls, and a profusion of plants and bottles of wine, reflect this restaurant's Mediterranean influence. A dining room in back features a fountain wall covered with plants and a ceiling aquarium. After a prosciutto and melon appetizer, try some homemade pasta or chicken with sour cream, vodka, and mushroom sauce. ⊠ *Calle Bálsamos 504, at Calle Ebanos,* ☎ *04/387079. DC, MC, V. Closed Tues.*

$–$$ ✕ **La Parrillada del Ñato.** With several long grills and large dining rooms, this South American barbecue appears to have been designed to feed an army. It's a good thing, too, because legions of hungry carnivores fill the restaurant seven days a week to feast on racks of ribs, succulent steaks, and an array of other tasty meat dishes. ⊠ *Av. V. E. Estrada 1219, at Calle Costañera,* ☎ *04/387098. AE, DC, MC, V.*

$$$$ ✕▥ **Oro Verde.** On the west end of downtown, this modern, luxury hotel is a world apart from the slightly seedy neighborhood it inhabits. Like all the hotels in the chain, this Oro Verde has a luxurious lobby, sports facilities, several excellent restaurants, and fully equipped, modern rooms, which makes it the choice of traveling executives. ⊠ *Av. 9 de Octubre at Calle García Moreno,* ☎ *04/327999, 800/447–7462 in the U.S.;* ℻ *04/329690. 192 rooms, 62 suites. 4 restaurants, bar, pool, sauna, steam room, exercise room, casino, business services, car rental. AE, DC, MC, V.*

$$$ ✕▥ **Gran Hotel Guayaquil.** This 22-year-old hotel has become one of Guayaquil's landmarks. Near the Malecón and most other downtown attractions, it shares a city block with Guayaquil's cathedral. Small, comfortable rooms have tiled baths, large windows, and cable TV. The 24-hour coffee shop specializes in Ecuadoran food, and the gourmet 1822 Restaurant serves higher-class fare. ⊠ *Calle Boyaca at Av. 10 de Agosto,* ☎ *04/329690, 800/334–3782 in the U.S.;* ℻ *04/327251. 170 rooms, 10 suites. 3 restaurants, coffee shop, pool, sauna, steam room, exercise room, business services, travel services. AE, DC, MC, V.*

$$$$ ▥ **Hilton Colón Guayaquil.** This new Hilton, just outside the city cen-
★ ter, is a giant complex with a 10-story atrium lobby. Guest rooms are modern and spacious, delivering all the amenities you'd expect from a large American chain. There's a well-equipped health club, as well as a beautiful pool area wrapped in palm trees. A variety of business and travel services are offered on site. The hotel is 1.5 km (1 mi) from the airport on Av. Francisco de Orellana. ⊠ *Box 0904662,* ☎ *04/68900, 800/445–8667 in the U.S.,* ℻ *04/689149. 273 rooms, 19 suites. 3 restau-*

rants, bar, pool, beauty salon, health club, business services, travel services, airport shuttle, car rental. AE, DC, MC, V.

$ ⊞ **Hotel del Rey.** This pleasant, mid-size hotel several blocks from Parque Guayaquil is a favorite of visiting soccer players. The well-kept rooms are on the small side, but this is one of the few moderately priced hotels in town that has exercise facilities. Continental breakfast is included. ⊠ *Calle Aguirre at Calle Andrés Marín,* ☎ *04/453037 or 04/ 452053,* FAX *04/453351. 47 rooms. Restaurant, bar, sauna, exercise room. DC, MC, V.*

Salinas

141 km (88 mi) west of Guayaquil.

Guayaquileños flock to Salinas's long, if sometimes dirty, sand beach on holidays and during the hot and humid rainy season (many restaurants and hotels are closed June through September). For tourists, deep-sea fishing is the main draw here. The continental shelf drops sharply to the ocean floor just 19 km (12 mi) offshore, providing a fertile feeding ground for Pacific sailfish, swordfish, amberjack, tuna, sailfish, grouper, and shark, as well as striped, blue, and black marlin. The biggest catches are made November through May, but fishing continues year-round. **PescaTours** (Guayaquil, ☎ 04/443365, FAX 04/443142; Salinas, ☎ 04/772391) organizes daylong charters for two to six people for around $250. Taxis will take you from Guayaquil to Salinas for less than $10 each way.

Dining and Lodging

$$$ ⊞ **Hotel Calypso.** The best hotel in Salinas is actually a time-share, which means it can be tough to get a room here during the last two weeks in December or during Holy Week (Easter week). Most rooms have ocean views; all have tile floors and kitchenettes. Master suites, with two bedrooms, are a good deal. ⊠ *Calle Malecón at Capitanía del Puerto,* ☎ *04/772425 or 04/772435,* FAX *04/773533. 38 rooms, 10 suites. AE, DC, MC, V.*

Machalilla National Park and Environs

167 km (104 mi) northwest of Guayaquil.

In the extreme southwest corner of the state of Manabí is the 136,850-acre Machalilla National Park, created in 1979 to halt the destruction of Ecuador's remaining tropical dry forests. Unlike the lush greenery associated with rain forests, typical dry-forest vegetation includes *kapok* (silk-cotton) trees, prickly pear cactus, strangler fig, and laurel. The $20 entrance fee is good for five days and includes access to the offshore **Isla de la Plata** (Silver Island), a 3,000-acre seabird sanctuary where red-footed, blue-footed, and masked boobies can be observed. The waters that surround the island teem with flying fish, dolphins, and, from July through October, whales. Both the park and the island are most accessible from the small town of Puerto López, which is home to both the **National Park Visitor Center** (⊠ Catercorner from church, ☎ 05/604170, ☉ open daily 7–5) and most of the area's visitor services.

Puerto López

Visitors come to Puerto López for the beaches, but swimmers should be aware that riptides are common in this area, especially when the ocean is rough. Although the water is swimmable year-round, it is warmest during the rainy summer months (December to May).

Dining and Lodging

$ ✕ **Carmita's Restaurant.** Among the best fish restaurants along the coast,
★   Doña Carmita and her sister have the seafood business down pat. The
signature dish at this simple beachfront eatery is the zesty *pescado al
vapor con vegetales* (lemony fish soup with vegetables). A wide variety of drinks, including German and Chilean wines and liqueurs, is available. ⊠ *Calle Malecón s/n*, ☎ *05/604148 or 05/604149. V.*

$ ✕ **Delfín Mágico.** This simple cabana in Salango, halfway between Puerto
López and Atamari, is built in the traditional style of the area, with
open sides and a thatch roof. It's the food (and not the sometimes slow
service) that makes this restaurant magic. Try such regional favorites
as pescado *en salsa de maní* (in peanut sauce) or shrimp in garlic butter. ⊠ *Salango*, ☎ *no phone. No credit cards.*

$$$ ✕🏨 **Hotel Atamari.** This isolated resort is perched atop a rocky promon-
★   tory 28 km (17 mi) south of Puerto López, well away from civiliza-
tion. Bougainvillea, papayas, and palms grow among the white A-frame,
thatch-roof cottages, which have simple wooden interiors and ocean
views. Each cottage accommodates two to four guests. Trails lead to
a private beach where hundreds of birds and butterflies hover. The out-
door restaurant serves international cuisine, with an emphasis on
seafood. Although taxis are available, it may be easier (albeit more ex-
pensive) to have the hotel arrange transportation to and from Puerto
Lópex or Guayaquil. ⊠ *Sector Ayampe*, ☎ *09/446933.* ⊠ *Reserva-
tions: Box 17-12-91, Quito,* ☎ *02/227896 or 02/228470,* 𝖥𝖠𝖷 *02/
508369. 8 cottages, 4 suites. Restaurant, pool. AE, DC, MC, V.*

$ ✕🏨 **Alandaluz.** The two- and three-story, split-bamboo, thatch-roof
cabanas at this laid-back hotel face several miles of blond-sand beaches
frequented by fishing enthusiasts and Alandaluz's languid guests.
About 15 minutes south of Puerto López, near the village of Puerto
Rico, this relaxed hotel is a favorite among ecotourists who appreci-
ate nature more than extensive amenities. Many travelers come for a
night and end up spending a week, lounging in hammocks and talk-
ing travel at the friendly, open-air bar. The restaurant emphasizes veg-
etarian fare. ⊠ *Baqueadano 330, Quito,* ☎ 𝖥𝖠𝖷 *05/604103 (Puerto López
reservations);* ☎ *02/505084 (Quito reservations);* 𝖥𝖠𝖷 *02/543042. 38
rooms. Restaurant, bar. No credit cards.*

Outdoor Activities and Sports

FISHING

Manta Raya (☎ 05/604167, 02/467980 in Quito; 𝖥𝖠𝖷 02/437645) ar-
ranges fishing charters ($570 per day for up to 20 passengers) with
advance notification. Most experienced fishers will be happier if they
bring their own equipment; otherwise, gear of dubious quality can be
rounded up by the agency. In the Ecuadoran Pacific, blue marlin is the
fish of choice.

HORSEBACK RIDING AND TREKKING

Trips to beautiful Los Frailes Cove can be arranged through **Pacarina**
(⊠ Puerto López, ☎ 𝖥𝖠𝖷 05/604173) or at Alandaluz (☞ Dining and
Lodging, above) for less than $5 for a half-day trip. Pacarina also ar-
ranges overnight camping trips within Machalilla National Park. An
excursion popular with birders is the seven-hour hike from Agua
Blanca to San Sebastián, which passes through dry forest to cloud for-
est to, finally, tropical rain forest—each climate with its own distinct
species of flora and fauna. After a night camping outside San Se-
bastián, you can return to Agua Blanca on foot or by horse. The fee
for horses (including guide service), for this or other excursions in the
area, is less than $7 per day.

Guayaquil and the Coast A to Z

Arriving and Departing

BY AIRPLANE

Guayaquil's domestic and international airport, **Aeropuerto Simón Bolívar** (⊠ Av. de las Américas, ☎ 04/290005), is 6 km (4 mi) north of the city center; taxis to downtown cost less than $4. From Guayaquil, **TAME** (☎ 04/565806) and **SAN/Saeta** (☎ 04/200600) each have a daily 40-minute flight to Quito ($100), and TAME has one 30-minute flight each weekday to Cuenca ($50). For the Galápagos, SAN flies five times a week to San Cristóbal Island and TAME flies daily to Baltra; both three-hour flights are $320–$350 round-trip.

BY BUS

Guayaquil is 10 hours by bus from Quito, and around five hours from Cuenca. Both trips run daily and cost less than $5. The city's main bus station, Terminal Terrestre, is just north of the airport.

To get to Machalilla and Puerto López from Guayaquil, take the bus from Terminal Terrestre to Jipijapa and change buses at the CITM bus station (one block from the main square, on Calle Sucre). Catch a bus heading south toward La Libertad and get off in Machalilla, Puerto López, Salango, or Ayambe (about four hours). You'll have to tell the driver where you want to disembark, as there are no scheduled stops. A longer route takes you along the coast from Guayaquil via La Libertad (5½ hours), passing the above-named towns in reverse order. Both journeys cost less than $5.

BY CAR

From Riobamba drive southwest through Cajabamba and El Triunfo. From Quito, drive west along a narrow paved road over the Cordillera mountains, descending through stunning subtropical landscapes to Santo Domingo de los Colorados on the way to Quevedo and Babahoyo. The drive from Quito, 416 km (259 mi) east, lasts about eight hours; however, the trip is difficult in bad weather or after severe rains.

Getting Around

The most pleasant neighborhood for strolling in Guayaquil is Urdesa; the adjacent areas of La Garzota and Nueva Kennedy also have numerous bars, cafés, and restaurants. The Parque Centenario lies at the heart of the city at Calle 6 de Marzo and Calle Velez, and Avenida 9 de Octubre—the main financial and shopping street—runs roughly west–east on either side. The area south of Parque Centenario is unsafe for walking, even during the day. Taxis throughout the city are inexpensive, but most do not use meters; be prepared to haggle a bit. The average trip should cost $3.

Contacts and Resources

BANKS AND CURRENCY EXCHANGE

Banco del Pacífico (⊠ Fco. P. Ycaza 200, ☎ 04/311744). **Citibank** (⊠ Av. 9 de Octubre and Lorenzo de Garaicoa, ☎ 04/563650).

EMERGENCIES

Ambulance: ☎ 131. **Fire:** ☎ 102. **Police:** ☎ 101. **General emergency:** ☎ 111. **Clínica Kennedy** (⊠ Av. El Periodista, ☎ 04/286963).

ENGLISH-LANGUAGE BOOKSTORES

Librería Científica (⊠ Luque 225 and Chile).

TELEPHONES, INTERNET, AND MAIL

It's easiest to make phone calls and send and receive mail at your hotel. To make calls, you can also try **EMETEL** (⊠ Pedro Carbo y Aguirre and L. Urdaneta 426).

TOUR OPERATORS
Spanish-speaking guides can be hired at the park visitor center for less than $10 a day for up to 10 persons. Non-Spanish speakers may arrange guided tours through **Manta Raya** (☎ 05/604167, 02/467980 in Quito; FAX 02/437645), on the Malecón, which runs through the center of town.

VISITOR INFORMATION
The tourist office (✉ P. Icaza 203 and Pichincha, 4th floor, ☎ 04/561281) is open weekdays 8:30–5.

THE GALÁPAGOS ISLANDS

A zoologist's dream, the Galápagos Islands afford a once-in-a-lifetime chance to visit some of the world's most unique animals in their natural habitat. From the moment you step onto land, you're confronted by sea lions basking in the sun, lava lizards darting between rocks, and frigates swooping overhead. Among the highlights are red-footed and masked boobies, Darwin's finches, giant tortoises, and lava lizards. Other endemic species include the mangrove finch, dark-rumped petrel, penguin, and cormorant.

It is possible that indigenous coastal tribes were the first to discover the remote Galápagos Islands—the chain of rocky, highly active volcanic islands that lie roughly 1,000 km (620 mi) off the coast of Ecuador; at least some think this is the explanation for legends among Ecuador's coastal peoples referring to "a land of fire across the sea." Less dramatic, perhaps, and certainly better documented, was the arrival of Fray Tomás de Berlanga, the Bishop of Panama, in 1535. His ship was becalmed on a fact-finding mission to Peru and eventually drifted on strong currents to the Galápagos. Centuries later, English pirates used the remote Galápagos as a place to rest and recoup after plundering the Ecuadoran and Peruvian coast. Many of the islands received their English names—some of which are still in use—during the patriotic tenure of these scurrilous buccaneers.

Charles Darwin, the most famous visitor to the Galápagos, found inspiration for his ground-breaking treatise, *The Origin of Species,* among the strange and marvelous island creatures. Yet the islands attracted only adventure seekers and recluses until well into the 20th century. Tourism began in a limited fashion after the Ecuadoran government declared the islands a national park in 1959. Not even five decades later, the Galápagos must cope with 100,000 yearly visitors.

The delicate balance that exists on the Galápagos is difficult to overstate. Ecologists are concerned that the steadily increasing number of tourists will prove destructive to this unique, irreplaceable environment. The islands are particularly threatened by introduced animals like goats, cats, pigs, dogs, and rats, which interrupt the islands' natural food chain. While more than 250,000 giant tortoises once roamed the islands, there are fewer than 15,000 today due to human hunting and newly introduced predators. Yet people are not the only ones to blame: El Niño currents in 1998 raised water temperatures as high as 40°C (104°F), killing thousands of fish and destroying the food source for marine birds. The Charles Darwin Research Center based on Santa Cruz works to mitigate the effects of man-made and natural disasters and is dedicated to conserving the fragile Galápagos ecosystem.

The best months to visit the Galápagos are generally May–June and November–December. Among the 13 principal islands, Santa Cruz and San Cristóbal are the most developed, each with a population of

The Galápagos Islands

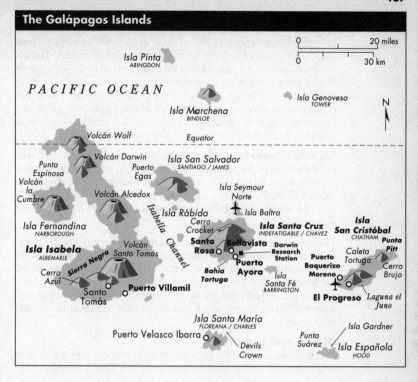

roughly 6,000 year-round residents. Of the two, Santa Cruz has more allure for visitors, with its dozen or so hotels, restaurants, and boutiques. The archipelago's four populated islands can be visited on a limited basis without guides, but the uninhabited islands can be seen only with a guide licensed through the Galápagos National Park Service. Visitors commonly book their own airfare and prearrange a one- to two-week package that includes guided visits to islands like Española and Isabela. A cruise of 10 days or longer is needed to reach the more remote northern islands or to climb either of Isabela's two accessible volcanic craters.

Santa Cruz

Overlooking Academy Bay on the island's southern shore is **Puerto Ayora,** a relatively developed town with hotels, souvenir shops, restaurants, and even a few clubs. Follow the main road east from Puerto Ayora to the **Charles Darwin Research Station** and its Van Straelen Visitor Center, which has an informative exhibit explaining the basics of Galápagos geology, weather patterns, volcanology, and ecology. Self-guided trails lead to the station's giant tortoise pens, where you can see the only tortoises you're likely to encounter during your visit. ☎ 05/526146 or 05/526147.

Bahía Tortuga (Turtle Bay), 3 km (2 mi) southwest of Puerto Ayora, has a long, white-sand beach where marine iguanas sometimes strut along the water's edge. There are no facilities along the water, but if you walk from town (take the road to Bellavista and turn left past the bank) you'll pass a soda and beer stand at the top of a lava-rock staircase. Marine turtles drag their bulky shells up the beach to lay eggs between November and February, with baby turtles hatching from June to July.

Near the small village of **Bellavista** you can explore amazing underground lava tubes. Los túneles, as they're known on the island, were created when flowing lava cooled more quickly on the surface, forming a crust that enclosed a labyrinth of tall, empty chambers. The underground tunnels are nearly a mile long, and you can easily walk upright as you grope through the caverns with the aid of a flashlight. To reach the tunnels from Puerto Ayora go north on the road to Bellavista; turn right (east) at the cross street and walk about a mile until you find a farm with a sign that announces LOS TÚNELES. A small entrance fee is collected by the farm owners, who also provide flashlights.

The road to **Santa Rosa,** 13 km (8 mi) beyond Bellavista, is lined with giant elephant grass, avocado and papaya trees, and boughs of yellow trumpet vines, all of which are in marked contrast to the dry, cactus-spotted lowlands. About 2 km (1 mi) beyond Santa Rosa look for a pair of giant sinkholes called **Los Gemelos** (The Twins), one on either side of the road.

The unattended **National Park Tortoise Reserve** is one of the few places in the archipelago where you can view giant Galápagos turtles in the wild. An unmarked track leads to the reserve from Santa Rosa. Along the way keep alert for Galápagos hawks, Darwin finches, and short-eared owls. In Santa Rosa, a small restaurant across from the church sometimes rents horses, which you are allowed to ride inside the tortoise reserve.

Dining and Lodging

Island restaurants and lodgings can be quite rustic. Many hotels have only cold running water, and rooms often lack electrical outlets.

$$ ✕ **Four Lanterns.** Most diners sit around long tables on the lantern-lit
★ outdoor patio, enjoying lasagna, gnocchi, cannelloni, or pizza with friends. The Italian proprietress takes pride in her culinary creations—her signature dish is fettuccine *mare e monte* (with mushrooms and shrimp). An accepted piece of local wisdom: Everyone eventually ends up at the Four Lanterns. ⊠ *Av. Charles Darwin, Puerto Ayora,* ☎ *no phone. No credit cards. No lunch.*

$$ ✕ **La Garrapata.** This popular restaurant, which translates as "The Tick," is run by the offspring of one of Galápagos's pioneer families. It attracts both tourists and locals to its exclusively outdoor tables. The menu, which features seafood, also includes chicken and pasta. Next door is the popular discotheque, La Panga, where salsa and club music are mixed until the lights shut down or the last patron leaves. ⊠ *Av. Charles Darwin, Puerto Ayora,* ☎ *05/526266. MC, V. Closed Sun.*

$$ ✕ **La Tolda Azul.** This is the first restaurant you'll find as you step off the boat in port Ayora. The small outdoor patio, usually filled with lonesome landlubbers, has nine tables with red tablecloths and hanging lamps. The seafood menu offers a wonderful selection of lobster dishes served in large portions; also recommended are the grilled steaks. ⊠ *Muelle Municipal,* ☎ *05/526565. MC.*

$$ ✕ **Narwahl.** Set in the lush highlands of Santa Cruz, with a gorgeous view of the island on a clear day, this hideaway eatery has set meals that include a welcome cocktail, soup or salad, and a dependably good entrée of chicken, fish, or beef (vegetarian entrées are available with advance notification). ⊠ *Road to Santa Rosa,* ☎ *no phone. No credit cards.*

$$$ ⌷ **Hotel Galápagos.** This casual, comfortable hotel—drenched in bougainvillea and other flowering plants—is a short walk to Puerto Ayora and the Darwin Research Station. On 5 acres of waterfront, the hotel looks over cruise ships bobbing in the port. Ocean-view rooms have cement floors covered by palm-frond mats; the seaside lounge has hammocks, bookshelves, and a self-serve bar. The restaurant serves

healthy international dishes, although meals for nonguests are by previous arrangement only. The hotel also arranges scuba-diving excursions and day trips to surrounding islands. ⊠ *Av. Charles Darwin, Puerto Ayora,* ☎ FAX *05/526296 or 05/526330. 14 rooms. Restaurant, bar, scuba diving. MC.*

$ ⊞ **Gran Hotel Fiesta.** This Mediterranean-style complex is administered by the former mayor of Santa Cruz. Simple, clean rooms have fans and bathrooms with cold water. Each of the six three-person cabins has a separate dining room and small refrigerator. The hotel is a five-minute walk from the village center and very peaceful at night. ⊠ *Las Ninfas, Puerto Ayora,* ☎ *05/526440, 02/509654 in Quito. 14 rooms, 6 cabins. Restaurant. No credit cards.*

San Cristóbal

Puerto Baquerizo Moreno is the capital of Galápagos Province and the largest town on San Cristóbal, though with only a few hotels and restaurants it is less tourist-oriented than Puerto Ayora. Still, Puerto Moreno's harbor provides anchorage for numerous tour boats, and there is some good trekking in the area. Two km (1 mi) east of the port is **Frigatebird Hill,** where both great and magnificent frigate birds—two species of black seabirds famed for their courtship displays—make their nests. On a clear day there are sweeping views of the bay.

El Progreso, one of San Cristóbal's first colonies, is a small village about 8 km (5 mi) east of Puerto Moreno at the end of one of the island's few roads (buses connect the two towns twice daily). You can rent a Jeep in town and explore the shores of **Laguna el Junco,** one of the archipelago's few permanent freshwater lakes, 10 km (6 mi) east.

Punta Pitt, at the northeastern tip of the island, is the only place in the Galápagos where you can view three species of boobies—masked, blue-footed, and red-footed—nesting together, as well as frigate birds, storm petrels, and swallow-tailed gulls. The site is accessible by motor launch from Puerto Moreno; inquire at your hotel for details.

Dining and Lodging

$$ ✕⊞ **Hostal Orca.** In the tiny village of San Cristóbal, Hostal Orca is a small, comfortable hotel situated on the beach. Second-floor rooms have balconies overlooking the bay, and the lively restaurant also enjoys an ocean view. ⊠ *Quito Cordero 1313 and Mera, Quito,* ☎ FAX *05/520233, 02/230552 in Quito. 20 rooms. Restaurant, bar. MC.*

Isabela

Although Isabela is the largest island in the archipelago, no tour boats are based here and its infrastructure is extremely limited. The key reasons to visit the island are the giant tortoises, large marine iguanas, and volcanoes. The few hotels are very basic, with intermittent hot water, and there are only two restaurants. Sleepy **Puerto Villamil,** founded in 1897 as a center for extracting lime, is the focus of the island's scant tourist trade. Nearby are several lagoons where flamingos and migrant birds can be viewed up close, as well as sand-and-lava beaches with large populations of herons, egrets, and other birds.

Isabela's active volcano, 1,346-m (4,488-ft) **Sierra Negra,** can be climbed with local guides based in Puerto Villamil or Santo Tomás, a rural village 18 km (11 mi) northwest. From Santo Tomás you can also hire horses for the 9-km (5½-mi) trek to the volcano's rim. The view from here is awe-inspiring: The volcano's caldera—roughly 10 km (6 mi) in diameter—is the largest in the Galápagos and the second-largest in the world. A more ambitious climb, which requires adequate planning and equipment, is **Volcán Alcedox** (3,600 ft). The site can be reached only by boat, after which a 10-km (6-mi) trail climbs over rough terrain. Your rewards: stunning vistas and the opportunity to view the archipelago's largest population of Galápagos tortoises.

The Galápagos Islands A to Z

Arriving and Departing

BY AIRPLANE

Santa Cruz. TAME flies once daily from Quito, via Guayaquil, to Baltra, a tiny island just north of Santa Cruz. The flight takes roughly three hours and costs $350–$400 round-trip. To reach Puerto Ayora, on Santa Cruz, take a TAME bus to the ferry and, once across the channel, hop on any bus for the 30-minute trip across the island.

San Cristóbal. SAN/Saeta has one flight per day, five days a week, from Quito and Guayaquil to San Cristóbal Island. If you buy an international ticket to the Galápagos with Saeta, you can arrange a free stopover in Quito or Guayaquil (30 days maximum).

Note: All foreign visitors who enter the Galápagos must pay the National Park Service $100 in American cash—not traveler's checks—and the bills must be clean, without markings or tears. The money is earmarked for training guides and rangers, as well as for funding conservation efforts in Ecuador's national parks.

Getting Around

Limited inter-island transportation is available by boat with the municipal agency **INGALA** (☎ 05/525149 or 05/526151), on Santa Cruz Island on the road to Bellavista. Currently there is one trip per week from Santa Cruz to Floreana and Isabela islands, and there are two boats per week between Santa Cruz and San Cristóbal. Each trip costs approximately $45.

Contacts and Resources

BANKS AND CURRENCY EXCHANGE

Tour boats usually accept payments in dollars or travelers checks. For the islands, you should bring local currency. On Puerto Ayora, you can change money at **Banco del Pacifico** (✉ Av. Charles Darwin).

EMERGENCIES

Ambulance: ☎ 131. **Fire:** ☎ 102. **Police:** ☎ 101. **General emergency:** ☎ 111.

TELEPHONES, INTERNET, AND MAIL

Although telephone lines now connect the Galápagos with mainland Ecuador, phone service is poor.

TOUR OPERATORS

Boat Tours. For tours of the Galápagos, you can choose from luxury, tourist, and economy boats. Although they're the cheapest, economy vessels (typically converted fishing trawlers) are often poorly maintained and accompanied by auxiliary guides who need a refresher course in English. It's better to stick with tourist-class or luxury vessels, which generally offer three-, four-, and seven-night tours for $100–$275 per day. You dine and sleep on board, and much of the sailing is done at night to maximize time spent touring the islands. Most of these vessels employ naturalist guides who are knowledgeable in biology and related sciences, and who speak at least two languages. At least once a day you will have an opportunity to swim or snorkel, and the luxury boats usually offer scuba diving.

If you're hoping to save money, you can wait until you arrive on the islands and try to bargain for a cheaper fare. Boat operators of all vessel classes come to the airport selling last-minute fares (tourist class might only cost $65 per day, for example). The risk of doing this, however, is that you might not find an available boat during peak seasons, leaving you dry-docked.

Cruise Ships. Two cruise ships currently operating in the Galápagos can be booked through **Metropolitan Touring** (☞ Tour Operators *in* Quito A to Z, *above*): the *Santa Cruz*, which carries up to 90 passengers (the largest allowed in the Galápagos) and departs from Baltra; and the more luxurious (and expensive) *Isabela II,* which sleeps 38 passengers in larger cabins.

Yachts and Motor Sailers. Luxurious 6- to 40-person yachts can be booked for individual travelers (FIT) or as private charters. You may save money by booking directly with operators within Ecuador; contact **Metropolitan Touring** (☞ Tour Operators *in* Quito A to Z, *above*), **Angermeyer's Enchanted Excursions** (☞ Tour operators *in* Quito A to Z, *above*), or **Quasar Naútica** (⊠ Av. Los Shyris at Gaspar de Villarroel, Edificio Autocom, 3rd Floor, Quito, ☎ 02/446996, 800/247–2925 in the U.S.; ℻ 02/257822, 813/637–9876 in the U.S.).

Land-Based Tours. If you don't relish three to seven nights aboard a ship, consider Metropolitan Touring's land-and-sea Delfín package. The three-, four-, or seven-night itineraries combine lodging at the comfortable Hotel Delfín on Santa Cruz, with daily island excursions on the 36-passenger *Delfín II.* All but the most queasy landlubber should seriously consider a ship-based package, however, which allows you to see more of the islands and their wildlife.

VISITOR INFORMATION

Tour reservations are typically booked through agencies in Quito, Guayaquil, or the United States. **The tourist office** (⊠ Av. Charles Darwin, Santa Cruz Island, ☎ 05/526174) offers limited information about tours and guides.

ECUADOR A TO Z

Arriving and Departing

By Airplane

AIRPORTS

International airports are on the outskirts of Quito, **Aeropuerto Mariscal Sucre** (⊠ Av. 10 de Agosto, ☎ 02/430555); Guayaquil, **Aeropuerto Simón Bolívar** (⊠ Av. de las Américas, ☎ 04/282100); and Cuenca, **Aeropuerto Mariscal Lamar** (⊠ Av. España, ☎ 07/862203).

CARRIERS

U.S. carriers that serve Ecuador include **American Airlines** (☎ 02/260900 in Quito, 04/564111 in Guayaquil), which flies from Miami to Quito and Guayaquil, and **Continental Airlines** (☎ 02/261503 in Quito, 04/567241 in Guayaquil), which flies from Houston to and from Guayaquil and Quito.

Aero Peru (☎ 02/561699 in Quito; 800/777–7717 in the U.S.), whose international service has been indefinitely discontinued, may again have service to Ecuador via Quito.

Saeta (☎ 02/254510 in Quito, 04/201516 in Guayaquil, 800/827–2382 in the U.S.) serves the Ecuadoran cities of Quito and Guayaquil from Miami, Los Angeles, and New York, with connections to the Galápagos Islands. With the purchase of a round-trip international flight to the Galápagos, the airline offers a stopover in Quito or Guayaquil at no additional charge, or two internal flights at a discounted rate.

FLYING TIMES

Flights that originate in Houston fly to Quito in six hours; those that originate in Miami fly to Quito in four and a half hours and to Guayaquil in four and a half hours.

By Bus

Major bus companies in Colombia and Peru offer direct service to Quito, Cuenca, and Guayaquil. For direct tickets to major cities in those countries, contact **Panamerican Internacional** (✉ *Av. Colón at Calle Reina Victoria, Quito,* ☎ *02/557133*).

By Car

The Darien Gap, an interruption in the Pan-American Highway between Panama and Colombia, makes it impossible to drive straight to Ecuador from North America. There are good roads that lead into the country from both Colombia and Peru, but you won't be able to cross either of those borders in a rental car.

Getting Around

By Airplane

Ecuador's principal domestic carriers are **Saeta/SAN** (✉ Av. Colón at Av. Amazonas, Quito, ☎ 02/564969 or 02/502706) and **TAME** (✉ Av. Amazonas 1354, at Av. Colón, ☎ 02/509382 or 02/509385). Both fly regularly among Quito, Guayaquil, and Cuenca, and between Quito or Guayaquil and Baltra, in the Galápagos Islands ($350–$400).

By Bus

Buses run frequently throughout the country and are extremely cheap: The two-hour Quito–Otavalo bus ride costs $2; the 10-hour Quito–Guayaquil ride, about $8. Sadly, crime is on the rise, so keep a close eye on your valuables. Though it costs more, you're better off using a private bus company such as **Reytur** (✉ Calle Gangotena 158, Quito, ☎ 02/565299 or 02/546674), or the better-regarded **Panamerican Internacional** (✉ Av. Colón at Reina Victoria, Quito, ☎ 02/557133). Such buses travel among major cities like Quito, Baños, and Guayaquil and are equipped with air-conditioning, toilets, and VCRs.

By Car

Renting a car in Ecuador is difficult and expensive, and driving is generally not recommended. Rentals are more expensive than in the U.S. or Europe, and hefty deposits are required. Traffic in the major cities is heavy and parking is often nonexistent. In rural areas, road conditions are typically poor, especially in bad weather, and there are few directional signs. In most parts of the country, a four-wheel-drive vehicle is required.

EMERGENCY ASSISTANCE

No emergency roadside service exists, although passing motorists will frequently stop to help a disabled vehicle, and your rental agency should provide you with emergency numbers and a list of garages.

GASOLINE

Regular leaded gas, called "extra," costs about $1.25 per U.S. gallon; higher-octane, unleaded "super," roughly $1.50 a gallon.

PARKING

Park your car at your hotel rather than leaving it on the street, where it is susceptible to theft. Smaller hotels are less likely to have private parking than more expensive chains.

RENTAL AGENCIES

Car rental offices outside Quito, Guayaquil, and Cuenca are virtually nonexistent. In Quito, the most reliable agency is **Budget** (⊠ Av. Amazonas 1408, at Av. Colón, ☎ 02/545761, 02/459052 at the airport). Other Quito-based agencies include **Avis** (⊠ Av. Amazonas Oe3-22,, ☎ 02/550243, 02/440270 at the airport) and **Hertz** (⊠ Av. Amazonas at Río Arajuno, ☎ 02/254257). If you rent a car, make sure to check your headlight alignment, tires, spare tire, and jack, and inquire about deductibles for damage and theft, which can be quite high.

RENTAL RATES

Renting a car in Ecuador is not cheap. The weekly rates can run higher than $300 for a small car, and close to $375 for a four-wheel-drive model, including mileage, insurance, and taxes.

ROAD CONDITIONS

The Pan-American Highway runs the length of the country, entering from Colombia in the north, passing through Quito and the major cities of the Andes, and continuing south into Peru. The highway is usually in fair condition except during the rainy season, when potholes multiply. The coast road is incomplete in some areas, requiring inland detours; a four-wheel-drive vehicle is essential for most of the Oriente and any climbs to the base of the Cotopaxi volcano.

RULES OF THE ROAD

On the narrow mountain roads, bus drivers are notorious for passing on curves and for making other dangerous maneuvers. Road signage is poor, especially outside the major cities.

By Taxi

Taxis are a safe, convenient, and economical way to travel in Ecuador— they may even be a better option than renting a car. It often costs less to take a taxi for major distances in Ecuador than it would to take a bus comparative distances in North America or Western Europe. It's easy to negotiate a rate with a driver beforehand for a half- or full-day trip to your destination. A three-hour taxi ride on the Ecuadoran Coast, for example, only costs about $20.

By Train

Ecuador's railroad network presently operates in chunks and slices, and by no means services the entire country. Only three lines exist, and service is regularly disrupted due to flood damage and repairs. There is daily rail service ($3 one-way) between Ibarra, capital of Imbabura, and San Lorenzo, on the northern coast. For information on train service and a variety of one- to three-night tours, contact **Metropolitan Touring** (☞ Arriving and Departing By Train and Tour Operators *in* Quito A to Z, *above*). Trains depart from the Quito **train station** (⊠ Av. Maldonado at Calle Sincholagua, ☎ 02/656144). The most popular train runs most days from Riobamba to Durán, on the coast, winding its way down narrow valleys past the Devil's Nose.

Contacts and Resources

Customs and Duties

ON ARRIVAL

You can import 1 liter of spirits, 300 cigarettes or 50 cigars, and reasonable amounts of perfumes, gifts, and personal effects. Do not bring firearms, ammunition, drugs, fresh or dried meats, or plants and vegetables into the country. There is a $100 fee to visit the Galápagos Islands, payable only in U.S. dollars and in cash (clean, unmarked bills).

A $25 airport departure tax, must be paid in U.S. cash dollars or Ecuadoran sucres.

Electricity
In Ecuador, the electric current is 110 volts; 2-pronged plugs are used. Areas outside of major cities are subject to frequent power surges.

Embassies
American (⊠ Av. 12 de Octubre at Av. Patria, Quito, ☎ 02/562890). **British** (⊠ Calle González Suárez 111, Quito, ☎ 02/560670). **Canadian** (⊠ Av. 6 de Diciembre 2816, at Calle J. Ortón, Quito, ☎ 02/543214).

Emergencies
For an **ambulance,** dial 131; for **police,** dial 101.

Health and Safety

CRIME

Although political turmoil and violence are not a part of the Ecuadoran landscape, pickpockets and purse slashers are a growing problem. Leave your valuable jewelry at home, keep a good grip on cameras and day packs, and avoid displaying cash. Use extra caution in all crowded metropolitan areas. In Quito be especially wary in the streets and plazas of the Old City, where pickpockets and bag slashers lurk, and on the stairs and road leading to El Panecillo, where muggers lie in wait. In Guayaquil, don't wander around the historic Las Peñas area or the southern half of downtown. Also, keep an eye on your belongings when traveling anywhere by bus.

FOOD AND DRINK

Cholera and dysentery are not serious problems in Ecuador. Nevertheless, drink only bottled water to reduce the risk of contracting intestinal parasites, and avoid ice and uncooked or unpeeled vegetables and fruits that have been washed in tap water. Excluding the best hotels, you should always brush your teeth with bottled water.

OTHER PRECAUTIONS

Consider malaria pills if you're traveling to the rain forest, to the northern coast around Esmeraldas, or to the regions surrounding Guayaquil. In the Galápagos, the most serious threat you'll face is sunburn—do not underestimate the intensity of the equatorial sun. Those prone to seasickness should bring pills or patches if planning a ship-based tour of the archipelago.

Language, Culture, Etiquette
Ecuador's two official languages are Spanish and Quechua, the language of the Inca and still spoken by indigenous peoples in both the highlands and the Oriente. English is the lingua franca of tourism, and you will find many young Ecuadorans in travel-related fields who speak excellent English. In rural areas you may have to struggle along in Spanish.

Mail
Post offices throughout the country keep fairly standard hours: weekdays 9–5. First-class mail costs about 60¢ to the United States, 70¢ to Europe. The casualty rate for letters and postcards is surprisingly low, and you can expect most to reach international destinations within two weeks.

RECEIVING MAIL

Travelers can receive mail Post Restante at any post office; letters and packages can be picked up during office hours. The **American Express** office in Quito (⊠ Amazonas 399) will also hold mail.

Money Matters
CURRENCY
Ecuador's unit of currency, the sucre, is named for its revered liberator, Field Marshal Antonio José de Sucre. Owing to inflation, bills under 100 sucres are rarely seen; the usual denominations are 100, 500, 1,000, 5,000, 10,000, 20,000, and 50,000 sucres. Coins are frequently used, and come in denominations of 50, 100, 500, and 1,000 sucres. At press time (winter 1999), the exchange rate was 6,600 sucres to the U.S. dollar and 10,000 sucres to the pound sterling. Prices, unless otherwise noted, are listed in U.S. dollars.

You can change money quickly at the many exchange houses in larger cities and get the same rate as at a bank. While U.S. dollars are accepted in payment at larger hotels and restaurants and by dollar-wise locals, you should carry sucres when traveling to smaller towns and the Galápagos Islands. Visa, Diners Club, MasterCard, and American Express cards are widely accepted.

SERVICE CHARGES, TAXES, AND TIPPING
A few businesses add a surcharge of 3% to 10% on credit-card purchases. Most hotels and restaurants add 20% to your bill, half of which is for taxes and half is a service charge. Some include this government tax when they quote prices; others do not, so be sure to inquire.

A tip of 5%–10% is appropriate for waiters in expensive restaurants. (A 10% surcharge added to your bill is supposed to go toward service, although whether waiters actually receive this gratuity is questionable.) Taxi drivers are not tipped. Porters and bellhops receive the equivalent of 50¢ per bag. Naturalists and other expert guides expect $4–$8 per person per day, drivers about $2 per person per day.

WHAT IT WILL COST
Many items—from taxi fares to textiles to ceramic tea sets—are very inexpensive by Western standards. You can gorge yourself at even the most elegant restaurants and still struggle to spend $20 for dinner. Accommodations ranging from simple and clean to downright charming cost $10–$30 per person, though international chain hotels charge $70–$200 per night for a comfortable yet generic double room. Tourist facilities are sometimes scarce outside the major cities, but when you do find them they will fall inevitably into the "bargain" category.

Sample Prices: A cup of coffee, 25¢; a 750-milliliter bottle of beer at a restaurant, $1.50; a soft drink, 50¢; a bottle of wine, $8; a sandwich, $2; a 1-mi taxi ride, 50¢; a city bus ride, 10¢; museum entrance, $1.

Opening and Closing Times
Office hours in the public sector are from 8:30–5. **Banks** are open weekdays from 9–6, weekends from 9–1. Exchange houses, which are much more efficient and less crowded, are open from 9 until 3 to 5:30. Hours at **museums** vary, and be aware that descriptions and printed materials are almost without exception in Spanish; some museums, however, have English-speaking docents. Traditional hours for **shops** are 9–1 and 3–6. Tourist-related shops generally don't close for lunch, but many are closed Saturday afternoon and all day Sunday.

NATIONAL HOLIDAYS
New Year's Day (Jan. 1); Easter (2000: Apr. 24; 2001: Apr. 15); Labor Day (May 1); Battle of Pichincha (May 24); Simón Bolívar's birthday (July 24); Independence Day (Aug. 10); Columbus Day (Oct. 12); All Souls' Day (Nov. 2); Christmas (Dec. 25).

Passports and Visas

Only a valid passport is required for U.S., Canadian, and British citizens for stays of up to 90 days.

Telephones

LOCAL CALLS

To call Ecuador from overseas, dial the country code, 593, and then the number listed in this guide without the initial 0. The 0 that begins every number listed above is dialed only when calling long distance from within the country.

LOCAL CALLS

Coin-operated pay phones have become nearly obsolete. Those few in existence require a 1,000-sucre coin or a token purchased at a newsstand or nearby shop. Some stores sell local calls just as they sell candy bars, at about 25¢ for a brief call; look for a sign in the window that announces TELÉFONO or LLAMADAS. Telephone cards are commonly used and can be purchased in most stores. Another alternative is **ANDINATEL,** Ecuador's communications agency, known as EMETEL in the highlands and as PACIFICTEL on the coast, which also has fax services. Offices are in every city and many small towns; most are open daily 8 AM–9:30 PM.

Directory assistance is available in Spanish by dialing 104.

LONG-DISTANCE AND INTERNATIONAL CALLS

To make collect or credit-card calls through an English-speaking **AT&T** operator, dial 999–119. To reach an **MCI** operator, dial ☎ 999–170. To contact **Sprint,** dial ☎ 999–171. These calls are usually free, but some hotels charge for the service. Calls made through hotels are subject to a 20% surcharge. You can also call direct or collect from any EMETEL office. Most hotels and tour operators now have faxes.

Visitor Information

Contact the Ecuadoran embassy in the following countries: **Canada** (✉ 50 O'Connor St., Suite 1311, Ottawa, Ontario K1P6L2, ☎ 613/563–8206); **U.K.** (✉ 3 Hans Crescent, Flat 3B, London SW1X OLS, ☎ 44171/584–1367); **U.S.** (✉ 2535 15th St. NW, Washington, DC 20009, ☎ 202/234–7200).

When to Go

You may want to plan your trip around one of the country's many festivals. If snorkeling or diving in the Galápagos is on your itinerary, shoot for the hotter, albeit wetter, winter months. The high season revolves around holidays, especially Christmas, New Year's, Carnival, and Easter week. During these peak periods hotel rooms become scarce and prices jump noticeably.

CLIMATE

Ecuador's climate is strongly influenced by ocean currents, trade winds, and altitude, which make generalization difficult. One constant is the rainy season, which lasts from December to May and occasionally precipitates landslides or power outages. Weather in Quito is similar year-round, with warm sunny days giving way to very cool nights. On the coast, the rainy season is hot and muggy, especially in Guayaquil; the rest of the year the coast is much cooler and drier than might be expected on the equator. In the Galápagos, the weather is generally hot and humid from January through April, with frequent afternoon showers. Cooler temperatures prevail the rest of the year, creating *garua*, a fine, light mist. The seas are roughest in September and October, when many Galápagos tour boats head for dry dock.

The following are the average daily maximum and minimum temperatures for Quito.

Jan.	69F	20C	**May**	69F	20C	**Sept.**	72F	22C
	46	8		47	8		45	7
Feb.	69F	20C	**June**	70F	21C	**Oct.**	70F	21C
	47	81		46	8		46	8
Mar.	69F	20C	**July**	71F	22C	**Nov.**	70F	21C
	47	8		44	7		46	8
Apr.	69F	20C	**Aug.**	71F	22C	**Dec.**	70F	21C
	47	8		44	7		46	8

FESTIVALS AND SEASONAL EVENTS

Galápagos Days, celebrating the islands' statehood, is held on the second week in February and features parades and all-out revelry throughout the inhabited islands. During **Carnival** Ecuadorans douse one another (and tourists!) with buckets of water, water balloons, and squirt guns. Carnival motivates festivities in Cotopaxi Province—local dances and fairs are held in Saquisilí, Pujilí, Latacunga, and Salcedo.

Corpus Christi is observed in many mountain towns with fireworks, bands, and dances, while **La Fiesta de San Juan** (Feast of St. John) enlivens highland towns around Otavalo, particularly Otón, on June 24.

Otavaleños give thanks to the Earth for its bounty during **La Fiesta de Yamor** (Festival of Yamor), celebrated the first two weeks in September. In Latacunga, September 24 is the **Fiesta de la Mamá Negra,** which honors Our Lady of Mercy with lively processions and dancers in disguise.

The **Fiestas de Quito** (Quito Festivals) are vigorously celebrated in the first week in December with bullfights, exhibitions, and outdoor concerts.

9   PARAGUAY

History is perceptible in Paraguay: In
Asunción, the plazas buzz with Guaraní, a
native language unique to this quiet inland
country, and, to the south, the well-preserved
ruins of 17th-century Jesuit missions mark the
land's colonial past.

Updated by
Tom Samiljan

VIEWED BY EVEN SEASONED TRAVELERS as a curious footnote to South America's more glamorous regions, Paraguay remains a largely unknown entity. Isolated by more than three decades of authoritarian rule under General Alfredo Stroessner, whose regime was toppled in a 1989 coup, the country was left behind while neighboring Brazil and Argentina made rapid economic progress. As recently as March 1999, the assassination of former vice president Luis María Argaña demonstrated how uncertain democracy remains here. In addition to the country's political troubles, its landlocked location has inhibited outside investment. The economic consequence for visitors is that institutions and services catering to their needs are still rare: museums are run-down, maintained more by enthusiasm than government funds, the highway system is primitive, and good hotels are rare.

But the advantages to this less-than-perfect infrastructure are evident. Paraguay has not entered the rat race, and many comment on the easy pace of life and the Old World courtesies of the people. Crowds are seldom a problem, and both the wild countryside and places of historic interest—restored Jesuit missions and, in the capital, Asunción, well-preserved examples of both Spanish colonial and 19th-century architecture—can be explored easily.

A visit to the tranquil southern region of the *ruinas Jesuiticas* (Jesuit ruins) transports you to a time when missionaries worked the fields alongside their Guaraní converts. Nature lovers can explore the subtropical jungle of the northeast—home to parrots, macaws, and toucans, as well as the fast-disappearing jaguar—or observe varied and abundant bird life in the Paraná plateau swamps. Some of the world's best fishing is had in rivers teeming with giant catfish. Anglers can test their skills as clouds of snowy egrets take flight and monkeys swing through riverside trees. Vultures, kites, and eagles soar over the sunscorched plains of the Chaco, an arid scrubland that covers half of Paraguay and is one of the most sparsely populated spots on earth, with less than one inhabitant for each of its 250,000 sq km (97,500 sq mi).

More than a quarter of Paraguay's 4.9 million people live in greater Asunción, and most of the rest live in or around the numerous small towns to the east. Guaraní and Spanish are the official languages, reflecting a society in which about 80% of the population is mestizo, Spanish and Indian descent. Although nearly everybody speaks Guaraní, only about half the population speaks Spanish as well (some say that while Spanish is the language of business, the soft-toned Guaraní is the language of love). Paraguay also has a fairly large and influential German community—one reason for the high quality of the local beer.

The driving forces of the Paraguayan economy are largely agriculturally based products. Since 1927, when the first Mennonite settlers arrived from Canada, 2.5 million acres of the Chaco's inhospitable scrub have been turned into fertile farmland, supplying more than half of Paraguay's dairy produce. Industry is still in its infancy. After an economic boom in the 1970s, fueled by the construction of the Itaipú Dam with Brazil, Paraguay's economic growth has slowed to a trickle, the most important factor being the success or failure of the cotton and soybean harvests.

But Paraguay faces an even greater challenge. Although press and individual freedoms have been fully restored, and free elections have been held, vestiges of the past remain. Widespread corruption and smuggling (especially in the tri-border area around Ciudad de Este) continue

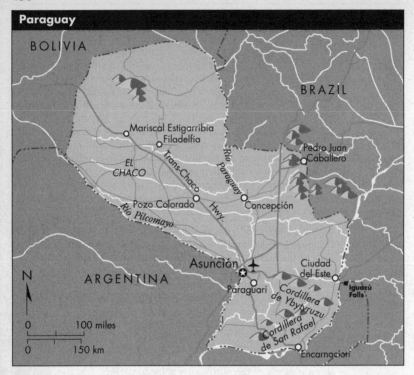

Paraguay

to create instability and undermine the rule of law. It remains to be seen whether Paraguay's still-fragile democracy can withstand and eventually wrest control of these problems.

Pleasures and Pastimes

Baroque and Colonial Architecture

Asunción's colonial structures are worth a look, but Paraguay's most interesting architectural attractions are the ruins of some 30 Jesuit missions in the southeast. Although Spanish missionaries came to what is now Paraguay as early as 1588, what largely remain are traces of 17th century *reducciones* (mission villages), where the indigenous and nomadic Guaraní people were organized into self-sufficient farming and Christian communities.

Dining

Asunción has plenty of excellent restaurants, bars, and cafés, but outside the capital and other major cities, the choices drop dramatically. Visitors traveling along the highways will find a few good roadside restaurants serving grilled meat, fish, and fast food. Paraguayan portions tend to be generous; don't hesitate to share a dish.

A staple of Paraguayan dining is *parrillada*, a mixed grill of barbecued meats including blood sausages and organ meats, served in large portions at restaurants called *parrillas* (grills). Beef is the mainstay, but pork, chicken, and fish are also common. Usual accompaniments are salad (Paraguay's tomatoes are incredibly flavorful) and boiled *manioc*, a white, fibrous root with a bland taste. Hearts of palm are considered a delicacy and are served with salad at most good restaurants. *Sopa paraguaya*, a kind of corn bread made with *queso fresco* (a type of cheese), eggs, and onions; or *chipá-guazú*, a similar dish in which roughly ground corn is substituted for cornmeal, may also accompany meat dishes. *Chipá,* bread made from corn flour, ground manioc, and sometimes cheese, is sold everywhere and is best eaten hot. *Puchero* is a meat, sausage, vegetable, and chick-pea stew that's eaten in the cooler months. *Bori-bori* is a hearty soup with bits of meat, vegetables, and balls molded from cheese and corn.

Cafés and bars usually sell quickly prepared, mostly fried or grilled snacks. The most popular is *milanesa,* thin slices of batter-fried beef, chicken breast, pork, or fish. Other favorites are empanadas, an envelope of pastry filled with beef, pork, chicken, corn, or cheese; *croquetas,* sausage-shaped minced meat or poultry, rolled in bread crumbs, then deep fried; and the *mixto,* a ham and cheese sandwich. Many cafés have a dish of the day—*plato del día*—on the menu. Pasta dishes are also common.

Paraguay's rivers abound with edible fish, like the *surubí,* a giant fast-water catfish, and *dorado,* a ferocious, salmonlike predator. These are prepared in a variety of ways; try *milanesa de surubí* (battered and deep-fried fillets of fish) and plain grilled dorado. A soup made from the fish's head and other leftovers is surprisingly delicious.

Typical desserts include *dulce de leche,* a pudding made from slow-cooking milk and sugar; papaya preserved in syrup; and such fresh fruits as pineapple, banana, mango, and melon.

Few Paraguayans are seen without their *guampa,* a drinking vessel made of cow's horn, metal, or wood, from which they sip *tereré,* a cold infusion made from *yerba maté* tea. Maté is drunk hot throughout South America, but the cold version, often mixed with medicinal herbs, is more common here. Paraguayan pilsner beers, particularly the Baviera brand, are quite good. Beer on tap is known as *chopp* (pronounced "shop"). Choose beer over the local wine whenever possible. In Asunción, society women fill the top hotels' tables for afternoon tea, and baby showers and parties for brides-to-be often take the form of teas. Espresso and often filter coffee is served demitasse except at breakfast.

Since restaurants sometimes close between meals, it's important to plan when to eat. Lunch can begin at 11:30, but 12:30 is more typical. Some restaurants stop serving lunch as early as 2. Dinner is often available at 7 PM, with restaurants staying open until 11. More sophisticated dining spots open at 8 PM and serve until shortly after midnight. On weekends and special occasions, dinner hours are extended. Café hours are generally 7 AM–10 PM.

Prices quoted are per person and include appetizer, main course, and dessert but exclude alcoholic beverages, tax, service charge, and tip. For price categories, *see* Dining *in* Smart Travel Tips A to Z.

Fishing

Paraguayans claim to have some of the best fishing in the world. Anglers come chiefly to catch dorado, spectacular fighters that leap high into the air when hooked, and surubí, giant fast-water catfish that take off like an express train if caught. Dorado are generally between 4 and 12 kg (9 and 27 lbs), although they have been known to weigh up to 18 kg (40 lbs). Surubí that weigh as much as 20 kg (44 lbs) are not uncommon, while monsters of more than 40 kg (90 lbs) are occasionally caught. The best spots for anglers are in the Southwest: Ayolas, on the Paraná River, about 350 km (220 mi) from Asunción, and Villa Florida, on the Tebicuary River.

Handicrafts

The best-known local craft is the delicate *ñandutí,* a type of spiderweb lacework. Designs represent plants, animals, or scenes from local legends, and, although traditionally made with white silk or cotton thread, colored threads are now worked in. Both this and *ao p'oí,* a type of embroidery, are incorporated into tablecloths and place mats. Wood carvings, intricately decorated gourds, and figurines—including nativity figures—are reasonably priced mementos. Rustic leather items, such as suitcases, knapsacks, and briefcases, are long-lasting and only a fraction of the price of Argentine leather goods. Plain white or colorful woven hammocks are another good buy.

Lodging

Paraguay's lodging situation is pretty bleak. A superior hotel here is comparable to an average chain property in North America, and you should expect it to be overpriced. Be sure to ask for an air-conditioned room in summer, and don't be surprised to find yourself surrounded by dated furniture.

Outside Asunción, hotels are few and far between, as many villages are just a few hundred yards long and consist of little more than a handful of houses, a couple of general stores, a bakery, and, sometimes, a gas station. In some budget hotels, showers are warmed by electric heaters built into the shower head. On no account should the apparatus be touched, even if it doesn't appear to be working; the wiring could be live and highly dangerous, especially if the floor is wet.

Prices quoted are for a double room and include tax and service charge. For price categories, *see* Lodging *in* Smart Travel Tips A to Z.

Exploring Paraguay

Paraguay is divided into two distinct regions, separated by the Río Paraguay. The southeast region is distinguished by a subtropical climate, thick jungles, and numerous rivers. It contains 40% of the country's territory and 98% of its population. Asunción, Ciudad del Este, Encarnación, and the Jesuit missions are all in the east. Paraguay is also an inexpensive gateway to Iguazú Falls (☞ Chapter 3), which can be reached from Ciudad del Este, directly east of Asunción, at the tri-border frontier where Paraguay, Argentina, and Brazil meet.

Paraguay's northwest, known as El Chaco, is a sparsely populated and largely unexplored expanse. This vast and desolate Paraguayan pampa is used for lumber and cattle raising.

Great Itineraries

Try to combine a visit here with a trip to Iguazú Falls (☞ Iguazú Falls *in* Chapter 3). If you only have one day in Paraguay, visit Asunción's historical and archaeological sites. If you have longer, visit the capital's beautiful surroundings, and then head southeast to some of South America's most impressive Jesuit ruins.

IF YOU HAVE 3 DAYS

Explore **Asunción**'s tree-lined streets and colonial plazas, absorbing the city's mestizo heritage. Many of the capital's most interesting sights, including the cathedral and the Palacio de Gobierno (the seat of the Presidency), surround El Paraguayo Independiente, which runs west from Plaza Independencia to the port. Once you've explored Asunción, venture outside the city to **San Bernadino,** a rustic lakeside resort, which also makes a good day trip. A number of smaller towns en route offer chances to buy indigenous handicrafts.

IF YOU HAVE 5–7 DAYS

After two or three days in **Asunción** and relaxing in **San Bernadino,** head south to Paraguay's greatest attraction, the well-preserved ruins of dozens of 17th-century Jesuit missions. Some Asunción tour operators offer a one-day marathon regional tour. However, since it's a five-hour journey from Asunción, you should allow at least two or three days for the round-trip—plus an additional day or two if you're an angler here to sample the region's famous streams—with overnight stays in **Villa Florida** or **Encarnación.** Once in the area, focus on the towns of **Jesús, San Cosme, Damián,** and **Trinidad.** If you have time, head to Ciudad del Este and cross the border to see **Iguazú Falls** (☞ Iguazú Falls *in* Chapter 3); then either return to Asunción via Route 2, a 327-km (204-mi) journey, or continue on to Brazil or Argentina.

ASUNCIÓN

Like most Latin American cities, Asunción suffers from haphazard development and an inadequate infrastructure. During the day the *zona centro* (city center) is packed. Street vendors crowd sidewalks, and traffic hurtles by. Drivers play a dangerous game of chicken at every intersection, and crossing the street becomes a terrifying experience as buses bear down on pedestrians with seemingly murderous intent.

But take a step back, and you'll see another side of the city that was once the colonial capital of southern South America. On the drive from the airport, the taxi whisks by the magnificent mansions lining Avenida Mariscal López—a furtive glimpse through a doorway reveals a peaceful patio reminiscent of those in southern Spain. Remnants of Asunción's prosperous past can also be detected in the delicately decorated facade and balconies of belle epoque buildings that have survived the vagaries of fashion; although, in some instances, they've yielded to commercialism, letting the ground floor to fast-food joints and their blaring neon signs. Alongside the money changers and peddlers of fake Rolex watches who patrol the streets and plazas, Indian women sell bundles of herbs and roots—centuries-old remedies for every bodily ailment. Contrasting with the hustle and bustle of the commercial center just 100 meters away, the pristine columned Government and Legislative palaces overlook the Bay of Asunción, as cool river breezes rustle through jacaranda and flame trees in the nearby riverside park.

During the day rich and poor rub shoulders, air-conditioned sedans jostling at crossroads with packed buses. At night the wealthy drive to their elegant suburban homes, while street vendors lug their unsold wares back to the reclaimed swampland of La Chacarita shantytown just below the Legislative Palace. Yet, despite the chasm between the classes, visitors need not be overly concerned with theft and violence. Rich or poor, the Asunceño is invariably courteous and helpful.

Exploring Asunción

The city is built on a rise overlooking a large bay, to the northwest, formed by the Río Paraguay. The zona centro runs south–southeast from the bay for about 10 blocks to Teniente Fariña, and it stretches 17 blocks from Colón in the west to Estados Unidos in the east. Most hotels, restaurants, shops, and offices can be found in this rectangle. Asunción's streets follow a grid; downtown they are narrow and generally have one-way traffic. Three downtown squares, each with its own personality, provide cool resting places in the shade of jacaranda trees—Plaza de los Héroes, Plaza de la Democracia, and Plaza Uruguaya.

A Good Walk

Begin your walk on the northwest corner of **Plaza de los Héroes** ①, at the pink-domed **Panteón Nacional de los Héroes** ②. Walk two blocks west on Palma, which runs along the north edge of the square, and turn right onto 14 de Mayo to find **Casa de la Independencia** ③. Two blocks farther north on 14 de Mayo, at El Paraguayo Independiente, is **Casa de los Diputados** ④. For a look at Paraguay's capitol, head two blocks west on El Paraguayo Independiente, which runs west toward the port; here you'll find the neoclassical, horseshoe-shape **Palacio de Gobierno** ⑤, which is not open to the public.

From the palace, retrace your steps to Avenida Republica and turn left. Walk east for three blocks to Plaza Independencia, around which most of Asunción's important public buildings lie. Facing the square from the north is the **Palacio Legislativo** ⑥, and on the southeast corner is the **Catedral Metropolitana** ⑦. Behind the cathedral toward the river is the neighborhood known as **La Chacarita** ⑧. From the cathedral, walk two blocks east on Mariscal López and then two blocks south on Iturbe to the **Museo de Bellas Artes** ⑨. Then head east down Estigarribia to **Plaza Uruguaya** ⑩. If Asunción's crowds and pollution start to wear on you, take a walk across this plaza at dusk, when the shrill voices of creepers and critters hidden in the trees will remind you that, despite the city, you're deep in a South American jungle, surrounded by wildlife.

Save an afternoon for a trip to the **Parque y Museo de Historia Natural** ⑪. It's about a 15-minute taxi or bus ride from *zona centro* (city center). Don't miss taking a peek inside the **Gran Hotel del Paraguay** ⑫, about 20 blocks from downtown, or stopping in for a drink.

TIMING

Asunción is a small capital city, so its zona centro can be explored in a day, and many of the attractions are free. Expect unbearably hot temperatures October through March, when you should plan outdoor activities only in the early morning and evening. The rest of the year, Asunción has a pleasant springlike climate.

SIGHTS TO SEE

❹ **Casa de los Diputados.** Once the military college and until recently a museum housing military artifacts, the Spanish Colonial-style building, formerly the Casa de la Cultura, now contains offices for members of the national congress. ⊠ *14 de Mayo at El Paraguayo Independiente*, ☎ *021/445–212.* 🎫 *Free.* ☉ *Weekdays 7:30–noon and 1:30–6, weekends 8–noon.*

❸ **Casa de la Independencia.** This late-18th-century house may have a rather typical appearance with whitewashed walls, brick floors, and a patio, but it was once the secret meeting place of revolutionaries plotting to break away from Spain. Relics from the May 1811 revolution, which achieved Paraguay's independence, are now displayed here. ⊠ *14 de Mayo at Presidente Franco*, ☎ *021/493–918.* 🎫 *Free.* ☉ *Tues.– Fri. 7–noon and 2:30–6:30, weekends 8–noon.*

❼ **Catedral Metropolitana.** Inside the Metropolitan Cathedral, which dates from 1687, are an enormous gilded altar and many 18th- and 19th-century religious statues and paintings. ⊠ *Plaza Independencia*, ☎ *021/449–512.* 🎫 *Free.*

❽ **La Chacarita.** Paraguay is perhaps the poorest of South American countries, as a stroll through the city's shantytown illustrates. In the narrow, unpaved streets that wind between rickety tin, wood, and bare-brick huts, barefoot children play while chickens peck amid the garbage. La Chacarita now has running water and its own school and is steadily establishing itself as a permanent community. It's also slowly becoming urbanized with the installation of electricity and a sewage system. If the majority of your time in Asunción has been in luxury hotels and restaurants and gleaming high-rises, it's worth taking a quick and casual look during the day. It's also one of the few ways to get close to Asunción's waterfront.

⑫ **Gran Hotel del Paraguay.** This well-preserved mansion has an illustrious past as the former home of Madame Elisa Lynch, the Irish mistress of Solano López, the somewhat licentious Paraguayan dictator (1862–1870) often likened to Napoléon. Now the oldest hotel in Asunción, and not quite where the action is, it's nonetheless surrounded by verandas and lush, carefully tended tropical gardens. Go inside to see the collection of 19th-century furniture and paintings and to have a cocktail at the bar. ⊠ *Calle de la Residenta 902,* ☎ *021/200–051.*

❾ **Museo de Bellas Artes.** Learn something about Paraguayan art and art history at the Museum of Fine Arts, which has a collection of paintings and sculpture by both Paraguayan and South American artists. Some of Paraguay's most important documents are found in the museum's archive. ⊠ *Mariscal Estigarribia at Iturbe,* ☎ *021/447–716.* ▨ *Free.* ⊙ *Tues.–Fri. 7–7, weekends 8–noon.*

❺ **Palacio de Gobierno.** The horseshoe-shape Government Palace is an elegant building overlooking the bay, with verandas and wide spiral staircases. It's only open to the public on special occasions. ⊠ *El Paraguayo Independiente and Ayolas.*

❻ **Palacio Legislativo.** Paraguay's constitution was proclaimed on the first floor of the Legislative Palace in 1870, and the national congress continues to meet here today. The second floor was added in 1857, destroying the original symmetry of the single-story Jesuit design. Debates of both senators and deputies, in Spanish, are open to the public. ⊠ *Plaza Independencia,* ☎ *021/441–077 or 021/441–078.* ▨ *Free.* ⊙ *Weekday mornings only.*

❷ **Panteón Nacional de los Héroes.** Modeled after Les Invalides in Paris, the National Pantheon of Heroes memorializes the servicemen who died in Paraguay's major wars: the War of the Triple Alliance (1865–70) against Brazil, Uruguay, and Argentina, in which 80% of Paraguay's male population perished and nearly half the country's territory was lost; and the Chaco War (1929–35) against Bolivia. The Panteón, guarded around the clock by two grenadiers, also houses the remains of President Carlos Antonio López (who commissioned many of Asunción's public buildings during his administration, from 1841 until his death in 1862) and those of his son, Mariscal Francisco Solano López, the most venerated hero of the Triple Alliance War, who became president just like his father. Paraguay's commander in the Chaco War, José Felix Estigarribia, is also buried here, along with the remains of two unknown soldiers. ⊠ *Plaza de los Héroes,* ☎ *no phone.* ▨ *Free.*

⑪ **Parque y Museo de Historia Natural.** The government has recently improved maintenance at this park and botanical gardens (a trend that's catching on in other parts of the country as well). Lingering upkeep problems aside, the park has much to offer including a grand array of plants, a small zoo, an 18-hole golf course, and a campsite. You'll also find a fine example of a Paraguayan country house, which was once the home of President Francisco Solano López (he owned the grounds as well) and is now a museum with exhibits on Paraguayan wildlife, ethnology, and history. ⊠ *Gral Artigas and Primer Presidente,* ☎ *021/ 425–680.* ▨ *Admission.* ⊙ *Weekdays 8–11 and 2:30–5.*

❶ **Plaza de los Héroes.** Since the subtleties of Paraguayan life are laid bare in its busy plazas, this is a good place to rest in the shade and people-watch. Guaraní sell feather headdresses and bows and arrows, artisans put their wares on display, and traveling salesmen hawk anything from patent cures to miracle knife sharpeners. You can also climb onto a high chair for a shoe shine or have your picture taken with an old

Río Paraguay

Puerto Asunción ■
Aduana

Paraguayo Independiente

Av. República

Benjamín Constant

Casa
Viola

Casa
de la
Cultura

Presidente Franco

Correo

Dirección
Turismo

Palma

Ayolas

Estrella

Juan. E. O'Leary

15 de Agosto

14 de Mayo

Alberdi

Oliva

Colón

Montevideo

Gen. Díaz

Haedo

Humaitá

KEY

❶ Exploring Sights

① Hotels and Restaurants

Piribebuy

Exploring

Casa de los
Diputados, **4**

Casa de la
Independencia, **3**

Catedral
Metropolitana, **7**

La Chacarita, **8**

Gran Hotel del
Paraguay, **12**

Museo de Bellas
Artes, **9**

Palacio de
Gobierno, **5**

Palacio Legislativo, **6**

Panteón Nacional de
los Héroes, **2**

Parque y Museo de
Historia Natural, **11**

Plaza de los
Héroes, **1**

Plaza Uruguaya, **10**

Dining

Il Capo, **13**

La Cascada, **6**

Chez Takao, **16**

Churrasquaria
Acuarela, **17**

Delicias Café Bar, **4**

Mburicaó, **20**

Oliver's, **8**

La Paraguayita, **19**

La Pérgola Jardin, **14**

Peter's Restaurant en
Casapueblo, **18**

La Preferida, **15**

Talleyrand, **16**

Tio Lucas, **9**

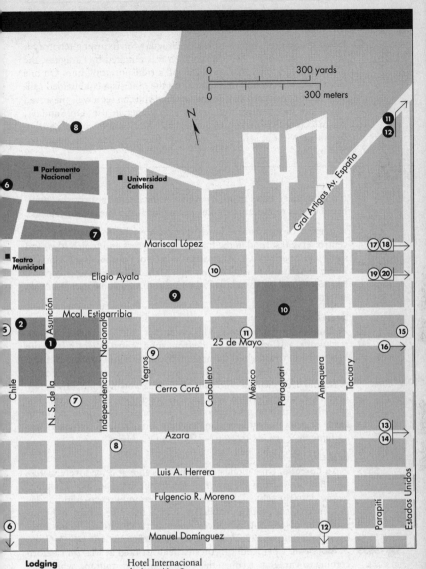

Lodging

Hotel Asunción Palace, **1**

Hotel Casino Yacht y Golf Club Paraguayo, **12**

Hotel Cecilia, **15**

Hotel Chaco, **10**

Hotel Continental, **3**

Hotel Excelsior, **6**

Hotel Guaraní, **7**

Hotel Internacional de Asunción, **2**

Hotel Presidente, **8**

Hotel Renacimiento, **5**

Sabe Center Hotel, **11**

box camera. On public holidays the square is often the scene of live music and folk-dance performances. ⊠ *Mcal. Estigarribia, at Chile.*

⑩ **Plaza Uruguaya.** Named to honor Uruguay for returning territory it seized in the bloody 1870 war, which was initiated by Paraguay, the plaza is both a busy market place and a transportation hub. On one side is a covered book market and on the other is a colonnaded **railway station**, built in 1861. In the terminal you can see a well-preserved old steam locomotive, the *Sapucaí,* no longer in use. On Sundays, steam locomotives make an all-day trip to the artisan town of Areguá—but those without sentiment for steam trains can take the hour-long trip by bus.

Dining

For its small size and relative poverty, Asunción has a surprising number of decent restaurants serving international and Paraguayan cuisine.

A number of inexpensive lunch spots scattered throughout the zona centro serve fast food in the form of hamburgers and french fries, and some local specialties. Locals particularly favor **Pancholo's** (⊠ Mariscal López at Salaskín; Brasilia at Santiago; Mariscal López at Convención), **Bar San Miguel** (⊠ España at Padre Cardoso), and **San Roque** (⊠ Ayala at Tacuari).

Brazilian

$$ ✕ **Churrasquaria Acuarela.** This enormous, 1,300-seat *rodízio*-style
★ restaurant, a 10-minute taxi ride from zona centro, might just be the best value in town, charging around $13 for all you can eat. Waiters traverse the dining room with skewers of grilled sausage, chicken, pork, and beef, slicing it onto your plate, while you intermittently mosey over to the buffet laden with salads, vegetables, and desserts. For something different, ask for *cupim,* a cut of meat taken from the hump of the Brahma-like cattle bred in Paraguay and Brazil. ⊠ *Mariscal López at Teniente Zotti,* ☎ *021/601–750. AE, DC, MC, V.*

Eclectic

$$$$ ✕ **La Cascada.** Dine alongside Asunción's elite and the lovely waterfall that flows from the foyer of the Hotel Excelsior (☞ Lodging, *below*) into the refined, lower-level dining room. French- and Italian-influenced dishes with an emphasis on local fish, like surubí in shrimp sauce, are tasty—but overpriced in comparison with the many zona centro alternatives. ⊠ *Chile 980,* ☎ *021/495–632. AE, DC, MC, V.*

$$$–$$$$ ✕ **Mburicaó.** Chef Rodolfo Angenscheidt worked at Maxim's before coming to Paraguay to open this contemporary restaurant, which has become a favorite of business people. Specialties include innovative takes on South American and Continental favorites, including fresh Patagonian truffle risotto and surubí with mozzarella and tomato in puffed pastry. The airy dining room overlooks a lush patio through floor-to-ceiling windows. ⊠ *Prof. A. González Riobbó 737, at Chaco Boreal,* ☎ *021/660–048. AE, DC, MC, V.*

$$–$$$ ✕ **Peter's Restaurant en Casapueblo.** On weekday evenings, the Con-
★ tinental three-course prix fixe menu here is the best (and most mouth-watering) deal in town. A traditionalist, German emigre chef Peter Stenger uses natural ingredients, as in his fresh tomato soup with cheese and the filet mignon medallions on a bed of julienned seasonal vegetables. Pastas, crepes, steaks, and chicken dishes are also served. The adjacent pub and disco attracts large crowds on weekends. Stenger also runs Stenger's Restaurant at Perón and Félix Bogado. ⊠ *Mariscal López at Mayor Rivarola,* ☎ *021/610–447 or 021/609–663. AE, DC, MC, V. Closed Sun.*

$$$ ✕ **La Pérgola Jardin.** Smoky floor-to-ceiling mirrors, modern black-lacquer furniture, and live sax and piano make this restaurant one of Asunción's most sophisticated dining spots. The service is efficient and friendly, and the menu, which changes weekly, is contemporary (warning—the hot *pan de queso*, small cheese-flavored rolls that come in the bread basket, are irresistible). ✉ *Peru 240,* ☎ *021/210–219, 021/214–014, or 021/214–015. Weekend reservations essential. AE, DC, MC, V.*

$$$ ✕ **Talleyrand.** Specialties at this local chain include duck à l'orange, sirloin steak, and surubí. The soft green color scheme and the hunting prints lend the dining rooms a refined colonial ambience, although this is somewhat compromised by the oversized modern china, which clashes with the decor. Talleyrand also has locations at Brasilia 808 and Shopping del Sol. ✉ *Estigarribia 932,* ☎ *021/441–163 or 021/445–246. Weekend reservations essential. AE, DC, MC, V. Closed Sun.*

$$ ✕ **Oliver's.** This favorite executive lunchtime meeting place at the Hotel Presidente (☞ Lodging, *below*) has a midday and evening buffet. You can choose from a range of all-you-can-eat hot dishes, such as goulash, pasta with mushrooms and cream sauce, and cold cuts, or order chateaubriand Oliver and other Continental dishes from an à la carte menu. ✉ *Azara 128,* ☎ *021/494–931 or 021/494–932. AE, DC, MC, V.*

Italian

$$$ ✕ **Il Capo.** Just opposite La Pérgola Jardin (☞ *above*), this small and simple 15-table eatery has whitewashed and brick walls, wooden beams, and tile floors. The homemade pastas, like lasagna *con camarones* (with shrimp) and *melanzana alla parmegiana* (gratinéed eggplant with tomato and Parmesan), are excellent and the Italian wine list is reasonably priced. ✉ *Peru 291,* ☎ *021/213–022 or 021/204–401. AE, DC, MC, V.*

$$ ✕ **Delicias Café Bar.** This old colonial building is now a no-frills Italian restaurant and café. Try the Waldorf salad, beef Stroganoff, or a pasta dish. Or, just pull up to one of the café's marble-top tables for coffee. ✉ *Estrella at 14 de Mayo,* ☎ *021/449–295 or 021/440–819. No credit cards. Closed Sun.*

$ ✕ **Tio Lucas.** A glossy cream-and-black decor with matching Thonet bentwood chairs gives this corner bar-restaurant a crisp, modern look. The specialty here is pizza. ✉ *25 de Mayo at Yegros,* ☎ *no phone. No credit cards. Closed Sun. and bank holidays.*

Japanese

$$$$ ✕ **Chez Takao.** A sushi bar (and an oversized Johnnie Walker case) is
★ the center of things at this intimate Japanese restaurant, where a devoted clientele comes for the delicious sashimi, sushi, and tempura. Several "chef's suggestions" also allow you to combine dishes, including grilled steak or chicken. The attentive staff works hard to ensure satisfaction. ✉ *San Martín,* ☎ *021/611–416 or 021/607–736. AE, DC, MC, V.*

Paraguayan

$$$ ✕ **La Preferida.** Rub shoulders with politicians and diplomats in the Hotel Cecilia (☞ Lodging, *below*), where the Austrian owners have fine-tuned the service to a pace of friendly efficiency. The two dining areas (one of which is no-smoking at peak hours) are set with crisp, floral linen tablecloths and classic silver and glassware. Among the house specialties are a surubí *ahumado* (smoked) appetizer; the mild curry surubí; and *lomo de cerdo à la pimienta* (peppered pork tenderloin)—ask for it if it's not on the menu. An American-style brunch is served Sundays. ✉ *25 de Mayo 1005,* ☎ *021/210–641. AE, DC, MC, V.*

$$ ✕ **La Paraguayita.** With its shady dining terrace, this is the best of a
★ host of grills on Avenida Brasilia. Huge portions of perfectly cooked beef and pork come with wonderful sopa paraguaya and chipá-guazú. The chorizo sausages make a good starter, especially when dunked in

tangy *criollo*, an onion, tomato, and garlic sauce. ⊠ *Brasilia at Siria,* ☎ *021/204–497. DC, MC, V.*

Lodging

Accommodations in Asunción are limited to mostly mediocre hotels, which vary from modest, no-nonsense establishments costing less than $20 a night to the luxury Hotel Casino Yacht y Golf Club Paraguayo resort (☞ *below*), which charges about $200 a night. Air-conditioned rooms are generally available at all but the cheapest hotels and are recommended in summer.

$$$$ ⊞ **Hotel Casino Yacht y Golf Club Paraguayo.** Although it may once have been one of South America's finest hotels, this riverside resort 13 km (8 mi) southeast of Asunción is now rather unspectacular and rundown in places. You'll have a lot of recreational options here though, including water sports, fishing, golf, and tennis. Some of the rooms, which are decorated with leather furniture, open onto verdant patios where hummingbirds nest in the foliage. ⊠ *Av. del Yacht 11, Lambaré (mailing address:* ⊠ *Box 1795, Asunción),* ☎ *021/906–121 or 021/906–117,* FAX *021/906–120. 128 rooms, 5 suites. 4 restaurants, bar, 2 snack bars, air-conditioning, minibars, pool, beauty salon, 18-hole golf course, 18 tennis courts, health club, squash, windsurfing, boating, jet skiing, casino, laundry service, airport shuttle. AE, DC, MC, V.*

$$$$ ⊞ **Hotel Excelsior.** Regency-style wallpaper, antique and reproduction dark-wood furniture, and Oriental rugs make the Excelsior one of the city's most elegant hotels, although some of the guest rooms are starting to show signs of wear and tear. A disco here means your nightlife is close by, and the three-story Excelsior Mall is across the street. ⊠ *Chile 980,* ☎ *021/495–632 or 021/495–636,* FAX *021/496–748. 128 rooms, 12 suites. 2 restaurants, bar, breakfast room, pub, air-conditioning, in-room modem lines, room service, pool, beauty salon, tennis court, health club, laundry service, business services, meeting rooms, airport shuttle. AE, DC, MC, V.*

$$$$ ⊞ **Hotel Guaraní.** In 1957, the Guaraní, on the Plaza de los Héroes, was Paraguay's first high-rise building and luxury hotel. Although the hotel holds a special place in Asunción's development, it's much less grand today. A new management staff promises to revamp the hotel, but this has yet to be realized, so let this hotel be your backup to more solid lodging choices. ⊠ *Oliva and Independencia Nacional,* ☎ *021/ 491–131, 800/448–8355 in the U.S. 168 rooms, 28 suites. Restaurant, bar, air-conditioning, pool, beauty salon, sauna. AE, DC, MC, V.*

$$$ ⊞ **Hotel Cecilia.** Priding itself on personalized attention, the Cecilia has established a devoted international clientele. The double rooms are large, though slightly austere; the single rooms are quite small, and the air conditioners are so perilously close to the bed that they blast your sleeping body with an icy wind. The sixth-floor pool and terrace has a terrific bay view. Adjacent to the hotel, you'll find an excellent deli and pastry shop. ⊠ *Estados Unidos 341,* ☎ *021/210–365,* FAX *021/497– 111. 50 rooms. Restaurant, bar, air-conditioning, pool, sauna, exercise room. AE, DC, MC, V.*

$$$ ⊞ **Hotel Chaco.** This comfortable if rather unremarkably decorated hotel has large carpeted rooms with pink bathrooms (although beds are small), good breakfasts (which are included in the rate), and friendly, attentive service. ⊠ *Caballero 285,* ☎ *021/492–066,* FAX *021/444–223. 72 rooms. Restaurant, bar, pool, laundry service. AE, DC, MC, V.*

$$$ ⊞ **Sabe Center Hotel.** The eight-year-old Sabe avoids the shabbiness
★   that too often besets its competition, although it suffers from trying just a bit too hard to impress: in a generically modern, small-scale building, a giant chandelier shimmers above Oriental rugs and marble lobby

floors. Rooms are less regal, but modern. A breakfast buffet is included. ✉ *25 de Mayo at Mexico,* ☎ *021/450–094 through 021/450–098,* FAX *021/450–101. 98 rooms. 2 restaurants, bar. AE, DC, MC, V.*

$$ 🏨 **Hotel Continental.** Pale blue hallways give way to austere but clean rooms, some of which have bay views. A rooftop terrace has great views of the city and the bay. On weekends, the hotel's second-floor karaoke bar fills up with local crooners. The hotel's French restaurant is recommended by locals. ✉ *Estrella and 15 de Agosto,* ☎ *021/493–760,* FAX *021/496–176. 66 rooms, 9 suites. Restaurant, bar, pool, sauna, exercise room. AE, DC, MC, V.*

$$ 🏨 **Hotel Internacional de Asunción.** An abundance of plants and floral arrangements greets you in the reception area of this modern, 15-floor high-rise hotel. The sleek lobby has a small snack bar, an executive bar, and two computer terminals with free Internet access. Many of the small rooms, which are redecorated every year, have views of the bay, alarm clocks, and cable TV, a rarity in these parts. ✉ *Ayolas 520, at Oliva,* ☎ *021/494–114,* FAX *021/494–383. 80 rooms, 20 suites. Restaurant, bar, snack bar, air-conditioning, pool, sauna, exercise room, business services, meeting rooms. AE, DC, MC, V.*

$$ 🏨 **Hotel Presidente.** This small, comfortable hotel, centrally located ★ two blocks from the Plaza de los Héroes, has conveniences usually reserved for more expensive establishments. All rooms have modern bathrooms, direct-dial phones, and cable TV. Business travelers have access to fax machines and computers. Oliver's restaurant (☞ Dining, *above*), next to the plant-filled lobby, draws an executive crowd. ✉ *Azara 128,* ☎ *021/494–931 or 021/494–932,* FAX *021/444–057. 54 rooms, 5 suites. Restaurant, air-conditioning, minibars, business services. AE, DC, MC, V.*

$$ 🏨 **Hotel Renacimiento.** Little remains of the original Belle Epoque interior of this converted building on the Plaza de los Héroes, and the heavy wooden furniture and low ceilings make the rooms and hallways seem cramped. Service is friendly, but only the budget-conscious should consider staying here. Still, the location is unbeatable. ✉ *Chile 388,* ☎ *021/445–165,* FAX *021/496–500. 40 rooms. AE, DC, MC, V.*

$ 🏨 **Hotel Asunción Palace.** Built 150 years ago as a private residence and now a historic site, this beaux arts–style hotel is, for all its charm, noisy and rather shabby. However, all the sparsely furnished rooms have air-conditioning and private bathrooms, making it a good value. ✉ *Colón 415,* ☎ *021/492–152,* FAX *021/492–153. 41 rooms. Restaurant. AE.*

Nightlife and the Arts

Asunción's free weekly arts and nightlife Spanish newsletter, *Fin de Semana,* has cinema and theater listings and is widely available in hotels and restaurants. The Friday editions of Asunción's daily newspapers, particularly *Última hora,* also have excellent weekend arts and entertainment sections.

The Arts

Paraguay is renown for its contribution to harp music—classical, contemporary classical, and Latin American popular—and folk dancing. Traditional dances include the polka; the *chamamé,* danced in pairs to the accordion; and *la danza de las botellas,* literally "dance of the bottles," a mixture of grace and balance in which a female dancer moves in time to the music while stacking six empty wine bottles on her head.

You can catch harp music and folk dances at **Jardín de la Cerveza** (✉ Avs. Argentina and Castillo, ☎ 021/600–752). Although the club prefers that you eat something while watching the show, it's not mandatory, and, given the mixed quality of the food, you're better eating elsewhere.

Nightlife

BARS AND DANCE CLUBS

Asunción doesn't have much nightlife when compared with other Latin American capitals, especially during the week. However, the scene picks up Thursday through Saturday nights when locals dress up. In fact, tennis shoes, jeans, and T-shirts are not permitted. Most places have a small cover charge.

Faces (✉ Brasilia 786, ☎ 021/205–901) is a good place to talk and have a drink. You can nibble on snack food and partake of Paraguayan pilsner at such trendy, youthful hot spots as **Tequila Rock** (✉ Brasilia at Amistad), **Mouse Cantina** (✉ Brasilia at Patria), and **Café Bohemia** (✉ España and San Rafael). The streetside café and nautical-theme tavern at **La Chopería del Puerto** (✉ Palma 1028 at Garibaldi, ☎ 021/445–590) is open 24-hours.

The most popular pub and disco is **Casapueblo** (✉ Mariscal López and Mayor Rivaroli, ☎ 021/611–081), with modern and Latin music. **Chaco's Pub** (✉ Republica Argentina 1035, ☎ 021/603–199) spins international disco music. Asunción's elite boogie the night away at **Coyote** (✉ Sucre 1655 at San Martín, ☎ 021/662–816) and **Caracol** (✉ Avenida Perón and Felicidad).

CASINO

If you're over 21, you can try your luck at slot machines, roulette, baccarat, and blackjack at the **Hotel Casino Yacht y Golf Club Paraguayo** (✉ Av. del Yacht 11, Lambaré, ☎ 021/906–043), which is about 13 km (8 mi) outside of town. Table bets range from $5 to $2,000. The casino is open 9 PM–6 AM.

CYBERCAFES

Internet access in Paraguay is very expensive, but many hotels have service in their business centers or lobbies. You can often find free Internet terminals in shopping malls (☞ *below*). And, around the corner from the Gran Hotel del Paraguay, **El Cielo Cibercafe** (✉ Avenida Perú, ☎ 021/214–606) serves snacks and coffee and has about a half dozen PC terminals with Internet connections and printers.

Outdoor Activities and Sports

Soccer

Soccer (*futbol*) is Paraguay's main sport. The most important teams are Cerro Porteño and Olimpia. Matches are played on Sunday, with the best first-division games held at the Defensores del Chaco stadium in the suburb of Sajonia. Local newspapers publish current game schedules and ticket information.

Tennis

South American tennis tournaments, including zone matches of the Davis Cup, are held at the **Hotel Casino Yacht y Golf Club Paraguayo** (✉ Av. del Yacht 11, Lambaré, ☎ 021/906–043). If you're not a guest here, you can book a court at the **Club Internacional de Tenis** (✉ Mademoiselles Lynch and Lilio, ☎ 021/671–912).

Shopping

The best shopping in Asunción falls into two very distinct categories: handicrafts and electronics. Prices for both are among the lowest in South America, and hard bargaining can make them even cheaper.

Crafts Shops

One of the best shops for lacework is **Ao P'oí Raity** (✉ F. R. Moreno 155, ☎ 021/494–475). **Folklore** (✉ Mariscal Estigarribia at Iturbe, ☎

021/450–148) sells carved wood, as well as ceramics, filigree jewelry, and lacework. For leather goods try **Casa Vera** (⊠ Mariscal Estigarribia 470, ☎ 021/445–868). **Overall** (⊠ Mariscal Estigarribia 399, ☎ 021/448–657) is a well-known store for lace.

Consider taking a drive out to Luque, a settlement of craftspeople near the international airport, where you can purchase Paraguayan harps, guitars, and fine silver filigree jewelry. **Constancio Sanabria** (⊠ Av. Aviadores del Chaco 2852, ☎ 021/662–408), in Luque, is highly recommended for musical instruments.

Markets and Shopping Districts

The **Mercado 4,** on Avenida Pettirossi, is a crowded street market that overflows onto several blocks, its stalls laden with produce, cheap clothing, hammocks, and clucking, caged chickens. Get an early start as tables are set up before dawn, but also because the heat and crowds can be suffocating. The market is open all day, every day, except Sunday afternoons.

A wide range of handicrafts is sold in the area bordered by Palma, Estrella, Colón, and **Plaza de los Héroes** (☞ Sights to See, *above*). Bargains are sold on the sidewalks, but for quality goods stick to the specialty stores. Hundreds of small stores here sell imported watches, electronics, cameras, pens, and athletic shoes. Watch out for fake perfumes and whiskeys.

Shopping Malls

For department-store items, try the three-story **Excelsior Mall** (⊠ Chile, across from Hotel Excelsior, ☎ 021/443–015). **Shopping del Sol** (⊠ Av. Aviadores del Chaco and Prof. D. E. Gonzàlez, ☎ 021/611–780) also has a cinema and a children's game area. **Mariscal López Shopping** (⊠ Quesada 5050, ☎ 021/611–272) has clothing, book and record stores, and computer terminals with free Internet access.

Side Trip from Asunción

San Bernardino

46 km (29 mi) from Asunción. Leave the center of Asunción by Avenida Pettirossi and, where it ends, take the left fork along Avenida Eusebio Ayala, which becomes Route 1. Pass through San Lorenzo and follow the signs to Route 2. Take Route 2 to Ypacaraí, 35 km (22 mi) from Asunción, where a turnoff to the left skirts the lake to San Bernardino.

The popular holiday resort of San Bernardino, on the shores of Lake Ypacaraí, makes an excellent day trip from the capital. From December to March, it's packed with middle- and upper-class weekenders and families who come for the good restaurants, the clear, dark blue waters ringed by clean, white sand, and for the water-sports—boats, jet skis, and windsurfing equipment can be rented at the public beaches near the cloverleaf or the Condovac Hotel.

The town of **Areguá,** across the lake, is a quieter alternative to San Bernardino, which once drew wealthy families and artisans. Clay pots and other ceramics are still handmade here. It can be reached by bus or by train from the capital.

En Route Looping back toward Asunción, the road passes through **Caacupé,** a town considered the country's Catholic capital, where the *Día de la Nuestra Senõra de Los Milagros* (Day of Our Lady of the Miracles) is celebrated on December 8. Thousands make a pilgrimage to the basilica here, which was consecrated by the Pope in 1988.

DINING AND LODGING

$$ ✕🏨 **Pueblo Hotel.** The tranquility of the surrounding trees and nearby lake is a welcoming change from the noise and crowds of Asunción.

Rooms are simple but comfortable, with TVs, full bathrooms, and views of the lake. Try the restaurant for lunch, where you can order locally prepared surubí, sopa paraguaya, and bori-bori. ✉ *Calle 5 at Av. Mbocayá,* ☏ ℻ *0512/2195. 12 rooms, 6 suites. Restaurant, air-conditioning, minibars, pool. AE, MC, V.*

$ ✕🔲 **Hotel del Lago.** This low-key, lakeside, Spanish-style hotel has simple, clean rooms with comfortable beds, but no televisions. The small rustic restaurant has colonial-style furniture and a view of the water. The forte is the roast beef or pork, cooked in a wood-fired oven and served with sopa paraguaya. ✉ *Caballero at Teniente Weiler,* ☏ *0512/ 2201. 25 rooms. Restaurant, pool. DC, MC, V.*

Asunción A to Z

Arriving and Departing

BY AIRPLANE

Aeropuerto Internacional Silvio Pettirossi (☏ 021/206–195 through 021/ 206–199) is 15 km (9 mi) from zona centro.

Between the Airport and Zona Centro: Taxis are the most practical means of getting to town, and they charge a fixed rate of about $18; if you're worried about getting taken, the airport transportation information desk can tell you the going rate beforehand. They can also arrange for an *omnibus special* whenever there are six or more passengers. This costs $5 per person and will take you to any address in central Asunción. Less conveniently, bus 30A leaves from the tollbooths on the road into the airport (about 200 yards from the terminal) and departs for downtown Asunción every 15 minutes; the fare is about 30¢. When making your lodging arrangements, you should ask if the hotel has pick-up service. Some hotels have minivans that meet each international flight.

For information on international and domestic carriers and flights *see* Paraguay A to Z, *below.*

BY BUS

All intercity services leave from **Terminal de Omnibus Asunción** (✉ España, at Fernando de la Mora, ☏ 021/551–740 or 021/551–764). The major bus companies **La Encarnación** (☏ 021/551–745), **Pluma** (☏ 021/ 445–024), and **Rápido Yguazú** (☏ 021/551–618 and 021/551–601) also have some information on Plaza Uruguaya.

BY CAR

There are three major roads to Asunción. From the east via the town of Luque, take Avenida Mariscal López or Aviadores del Chaco (which branches off Mariscal López) or Avenida Pettirossi, which is a direct route. However, Pettirossi passes through suburban shopping areas and frequently becomes jammed with traffic. From the north, the Trans-Chaco Highway (Route 9) runs through Villa Presidente Hayes, joins with Puerto Falcon (across from the Argentine border town of Clorinda), and then crosses the Puente Remanso bridge, 12 mi from Asunción. The Trans-Chaco Highway continues northwest and runs into Avenida Primer Presidente. Turn right for a few hundred yards and then left onto General Artigas. The route is clearly marked. Leaving Asunción, you can take Avenida Pettirossi and then the left fork onto Avenida Eusebio Ayala, which becomes Route 1.

The 29-mi route to San Bernardino is somewhat circuitous, but a tour operator (☞ *below*) can provide a car and driver for between $35 and $50 per person, depending on the number of passengers (sharing a car is cheaper, of course). There's also a bus that leaves from the central bus station (it reads SAN BERNARDINO in the front window). It makes a lot of stops but costs only a dollar. The visitor's center also has bus trip information.

Getting Around

Most of Asunción's sights can easily be seen on foot, although you should leave valuables in your hotel's safe. Unless you plan to travel out of town, avoid renting a car—driving in Asunción can be nerve-racking, and taxis are plentiful.

BY BUS

Ever since the old, yellow trams were removed, Asunción's bus service has improved. New local buses run every eight minutes. The fare is about 10¢. As in all big cities, watch your belongings carefully.

BY CAR

Driving in Asunción is not recommended. Frequent rainstorms, aggressive bus drivers, confusing routes, and never-ending road construction make even Paraguayans (who rarely follow traffic rules) nervous. Taxis and car services are quite reasonable and will get you where you need to go. ☞ For rental car information *see* Getting Around *in* Paraguay A to Z.

BY TAXI

Taxis are inexpensive and can range from a modern Mercedes to a rattly Volkswagen Beetle. You can hail them, go to one of the 70 taxi stands around the city, or stroll by one of the main hotels where they often wait. A 30% surcharge is added after dark, but make sure your driver turns the meter on or you risk being charged an outrageous fare. It can also be difficult to find a taxi at night, so it's perfectly acceptable to ask your hotel or restaurant to call one. If you haven't rented a car, excursions or longer rides that involve waiting time can almost always be bargained.

Contacts and Resources

BANKS AND CURRENCY EXCHANGE

U.S. dollars are easiest to change and get a better exchange rate than traveler's checks. Rates for other currencies might not reflect their true international value. It's most convenient to change money either at the *casas de cambio* (exchange houses) or at major hotels, which have a slightly lower rate than casas de cambio. Banks are inefficient and their exchange rates are less competitive than the casas de cambio. (The bank at the Asunción airport, however, changes money at competitive rates.) There are several casas de cambio along Calle Palma and around the main square in Asunción that accept both cash and traveler's checks; no commission is charged. The **American Express** office (⊠ Yegros 690, ☎ 021/490–111) has decent rates; other good bets are **Citibank** (Chile at Estrella, ☎ 021/494–951), which may also have an ATM that takes your card, and **La Moneda** (25 de Mayo 127, ☎ 021/494–724).

EMBASSIES AND CONSULATES

American (⊠ Av. Mariscal López 1776, ☎ 021/213–717), open weekdays 7–5, passports 7–10:30 AM only. **British** (⊠ Presidente Franco 706, at O'Leary, ☎ 021/444–472, 021/496–067, or 021/496–068), open weekdays 8–3. **Canadian** (⊠ Benjamin Constant at Colón, ☎ 021/449–505 or 021/227–207), open weekdays 8–4.

EMERGENCIES

Ambulance: ☎ 204–800 or 290–336. **Police:** ☎ 130. **Fire:** ☎ 420–035. **Towing:** ☎ 293–493.

In a medical emergency go to the emergency room of the nearest hospital. **Hospitals: Hospital Privado Francés** ⊠ Brasilia at Insaurralde, ☎ 021/295-250; **Hospital Privado Migone** ⊠ Pdte. E. Ayalya, Curupayty, ☎ 021/498–200; **Hospital Privado Bautista** ⊠ Argentina, Campos Cervera, ☎ 021/600–171.

HEALTH AND SAFETY

Asunción has escaped the crime typical of Mexico City and Bogotá, although women may feel less comfortable than men when exploring. For further information, *see* Smart Travel Tips A to Z at the front of this guide.

TOUR OPERATORS

Guided city tours and side trips to Areguá and other destinations start at $10 and $35, respectively, at **Lions Tour** (⊠ Alberdi 454, 1st Floor, ☎ 021/490–278 or 021/490–591), **VIP's Tour** (⊠ Mexico 782, ☎ 021/497-117), and, the American Express affiliate, **Inter Express** (⊠ Yegros 690, ☎ 021/495–112).

TELEPHONES, THE INTERNET, MAIL

Since there are so few public phones here and those that exist are only good for local calls, you might want to head directly for the main **AN-TELCO** office (⊠ Gral. Diaz and Alberti, ☎ 021/444–075) to make a call. Asunción's cybercafés come and go, but you can check your E-mail at several hotels or at the Internet service kiosks in the city's malls. For postal service, go to the **Dirección General de Correos** (⊠ Alberdi and Benjamin Constant, ☎ 021/498–1120). For further information on international mail and telephone service, *see* Paraguay A to Z, *below*.

VISITOR INFORMATION

The helpful staff at **Dirección de Turismo** has lodging and sightseeing information. Stop in during regular hours for pamphlets and maps or go upstairs for detailed information and advice weekdays 7–1. ⊠ *Palma 468 and 14 de Mayo*, ☎ *021/491–230 and 021/441–530*, 𝙁𝘼𝙓 *021/491–230.* ☉ *Weekdays 7–7, Sat. 8–11.*

Lions Tour (☞ Tour Operators, *above*) has a desk at the airport with country-wide transportation, hotel, and tour information. The desk is open when international flights arrive. Most hotels also provide pamphlets and maps, give advice, arrange tours, and hire cars.

SOUTHERN PARAGUAY AND THE JESUIT MISSION RUINS

The 405-km (253-mi) drive from Asunción to Jesús takes in seven 17th-century Jesuit missions and affords glimpses of Paraguayan rural life amidst a variety of landscapes. The missions date from as far back as 1609, when the newly formed Society of Jesus was granted permission to organize the nomadic Guaraní people, threatened by slave traders from Brazil, into stable, self-sufficient communities based on agriculture and Christianity. Each mission, called a *reducción* (literally, "reduction"), had a population of about 3,000 Guaraní under the charge of two or three priests who taught agricultural and such other practical skills as stonemasonry and metalwork. The reduction was based around a large, central plaza with a church, an adjacent bell tower, the priests' living quarters, and usually a school. The Guaraní's houses were built in rows spreading back from the central square. The main buildings were most often constructed of red sandstone blocks, with terra-cotta-tile, semicircular cantilever roofs that formed wide verandas.

Under the Jesuits, the Guaraní embraced Christianity but they also proved to be sensitive artists—excelling at wood carving, pottery, and calligraphy—and particularly fine musicians. Performing mainly in church choirs and orchestras, they were able to adapt the complex European baroque counterpoint to their own traditional musical styles. The colonial experiment, however, was so successful that the Spanish monarchs became jealous of the Jesuits' power and banned them from

The Jesuit Mission Towns

the South American continent in 1766. The 100,000 Guaraní soon returned to their old way of life and the missions fell into disrepair.

Itá

37 km (23 mi) south of Asunción. Take Route 1 southeast from Asunción, past San Lorenzo, and continue southeast toward Encarnación to Itá.

As you approach Itá, a state-run handicraft exhibition on the roadside has local ceramics and hammocks for sale. After Itá the countryside opens up into fruit orchards, sugarcane fields, and maize plantations. On February 3, the town comes alive, celebrating the Feast of San Blas, the patron saint of Paraguay, with singing, dancing, a parade, and horse racing.

Yaguarón

11 km (7 mi) south of Itá.

Once the center of the Franciscan missions, Yaguarón has a restored 17th-century church. Inside are brightly colored wooden sculptures by Guaraní artists.

Villa Florida

130 km (80 mi) south on Route 1 from Yaguarón.

The hilly and fertile farm land gives way to rolling grasslands as you approach Villa Florida, the grazing grounds of white Brahma-like Nelore cattle. Cowboys in wide-brim hats tend the herds on horses saddled in sheepskin, while sheep and goats stealthily graze on hibiscus- and bougainvillea-filled gardens outside tiny, rustic cottages along the **Tebicuary River**. The river once marked the western border of the Jesuit mission area and now has popular beaches; anglers know it well as a prime spot for catching dorado and surubí. The town is not particularly pretty, but there are magnificent sunsets over the water and a complement of hotels and restaurants.

Dining and Lodging

$$ ✕ 🍽 **Centu Cué.** Bungalows scattered along the Tebicuary River banks
★ make up this isolated lodge frequented mainly by anglers and wildlife observers. It has an ideal fishing spot, but lounging on the private beach or having a swim are also respectable activities here. At the nautically furnished riverside restaurant, mounted heads of enormous fish and photos of proud fishermen with their catches may mock your day's accomplishments. And what else would you eat here but dorado or surubí, grilled or in a casserole, caught just a few yards from the table? ⊠ *7 km (4½ mi) off Rte. 1 junction at km 163, Desvío, ☎ 083/219. 30 rooms. Restaurant, horseback riding, fishing. No credit cards.*

$$ ✕ 🍽 **Hotel Nacional de Turismo.** Spanish colonial-style rooms with heavy wooden furniture, all open onto a shady central courtyard. The service is very friendly, and special camping areas near the river have been set aside for fishing enthusiasts. The restaurant serves a wide variety of grilled meats and poultry; a must is the milanesa, made with freshly caught surubí. The chef is highly obliging, and, with reasonable notice, will prepare special orders. ⊠ *Rte. 1, km 162, ☎ 083/207. 20 rooms, 1 suite. Restaurant, cafeteria, pool, fishing. AE, DC, MC, V.*

Outdoor Activities and Sports

FISHING

Arrangements for boat charters, guides, and bait can be made through the **Hotel Nacional de Turismo** (☞ *above*). Anglers should bring their own medium-weight rod, line, and lures suitable for trolling, spinning, and live baiting. **Hotel Centu Cué** (☞ *above*), 7 km (4½ mi) from Rte 1, at km 163, has one of the river's best fishing spots, but you must be a guest to fish here. The hotel sells fishing supplies.

San Miguel

17 km (11 mi) south on Route 1 from Villa Florida.

Throughout San Miguel, handwoven woolen blankets, rugs, and ponchos hang outside houses for sale. A few miles farther on is the Jesuit town of San Juan Batista, which is known for its cobblestone streets and sidewalks and quaint homes.

Santa María de Fe

20 km (16 mi) south of San Miguel on Route 1, take a left onto a dirt road leading to Santa María de Fe.

Nearly 7,000 Guaraní lived here in the early 18th century, and some of the original albeit restored houses remain. The **Santa María de Fe Museum** has some 70 Guaraní carvings and statues, the latter that represent the life of Jesus. (If the door is locked, you may have to ask around for the priest to gain admission.)

San Ignacio

18 km (11 mi) south of Santa Maria on Route 1.

★ The Jesuits established Paraguay's first mission here, and today the **Museo de San Ignacio** displays the country's best collection of Guaraní wood carvings and other period artifacts, like gilded pulpits, door panels, and statues. A statue of St. Paul signaling new lands to be evangelized particularly stands out; at his feet are carved a number of faces, most with Guaraní features. The building itself, with its thick adobe walls, is believed to be the oldest in Paraguay, dating from 1609. ⊠ *Rte. 1 (look for the sign)*, ☎ *no phone.* ⊡ *Free.* ☉ *Mon.–Sat., 8* AM*–11* AM *and 2* PM*–5* PM.

Santa Rosa

19 km (12 mi) east of San Ignacio on Route 1.

The ringing of bells from the red sandstone bell tower, built in 1698, can still be heard in the town of Santa Rosa. Nearby, in the small Loreto museum, you can see frescoes of Jesuit religious imagery, part of the Capilla de Nuestra Señora de Loreto church's old altar, and a group of centuries-old carvings representing the Annunciation.

San Cosme y Damián

95 km (59 mi) southeast of Santa Rosa on Route 1.

The vegetation thickens as Route 1 nears the Paraná Valley; just before Coronel Bogado, a 25-km (15-mi) paved highway leads to the village of San Cosme y Damián, near the banks of the Paraná River. Follow the signs along a dirt track to the red sandstone mission buildings, still functioning as a Jesuit school. Many original Guaraní houses are still in use.

Encarnación

27 km (17 mi) southeast of San Cosme y Damián on Route 1; 370 km (230 mi) from Asunción.

Linked by bridge to the Argentine town of Posadas, Encarnación is otherwise a somewhat dreary border town, whose muddy streets are lined with shops selling cheap imported goods. However, it's a good place to stop and eat or sleep.

Dining and Lodging

\$\$ ✕⊞ **Cristal.** Built in 1988, four blocks from the downtown bus terminal, this nine-story hotel has rooms with modern wooden furniture, green carpets and drapes, and original paintings. The restaurant fills up at lunch with local businesspeople and serves contemporary and local fish dishes. ⊠ *Mariscal Estigarribia 1157*, ☎ *071/202–371*, ℻ *071/202–372. 75 rooms. Restaurant, pool. No credit cards.*

\$\$ ✕⊞ **Novotel.** Amid spacious gardens with sports facilities and a playground, this French-owned chain hotel is a quiet 3 km (2 mi) away from the highway and town. The decor throughout is modern, and rooms have direct-dial phones, modem outlets, and color TVs. The restaurant's menu has Paraguayan specialties, like milanesas, sopa paraguaya, and cassava. From town, you can take a taxi or bus 3. ⊠ *Rte. 1, km 361, Villa Quiteria*, ☎ *071/204–131*, ℻ *071/204–224. 102 bedrooms, 4 suites. Restaurant, bar, air-conditioning, minibars, room service, pool, tennis court, soccer, volleyball. AE, DC, MC, V.*

Trinidad

28 km (17 mi) northeast of Encarnación.

Trinidad has the area's most impressive Jesuit ruins, superior even to those of Argentina and Brazil, yet restoration projects are frequently suspended while the government searches for funding. The red sandstone reduction, built between 1712 and 1764, stands on a slight rise in an open field, enabling its full size to be appreciated. After the expulsion of the Jesuits, much of it was destroyed by an unscrupulous, temporary official who ripped out stones to build his own residence, causing the structure to collapse. Many of the church walls and arches remain intact, however, even though the church is open to the elements. Note the elaborately carved doors and wall friezes depicting angels playing the clavichord, harp, and other musical instruments. The pulpit, made from thousands of pieces of stone, depicts the Evangelists. The only building with a roof is the sacristy, with intricate relief work above the main entrance. Also surviving are the school and cloister foundations and a sandstone tower.

Dining and Lodging

$$ ✕🏨 **Tirol de Paraguay.** Built on a hillside, 25 km (16 mi) from Encarnación, you can come here for the spectacular views of the verdant, rolling countryside or to take the waters. Rustic rooms with red brick and white walls are furnished with sturdy dark wooden furniture and have views of the lush vegetation outside. Accommodations are in single-story bungalows that surround four swimming pools fed by natural springs, which are said to have therapeutic properties. Rates include all meals. ⊠ *Off Rte. 6 at km 20, 8 km (5 mi) from Trinidad, Capitán Miranda,* ☎ *071/202–388,* 📠 *071/205–555. 56 rooms. Air-conditioning, fans, 4 pools. AE, MC, V.*

Jesús

38 km (24 mi) north of Encarnación, 10 km (6 mi) north of Trinidad.

The Jesuits were expelled from South America before they could finish the unique hilltop church they were building—its Moorish-style arches distinguish it from the other missions of that time. It's just off Route 6.

Southern Paraguay and the Jesuit Ruins A to Z

Arriving and Departing

BY BUS

Service between Asunción and Encarnación is frequent, and the five-hour trip costs $10. You can get off the bus along Route 1 to visit the Jesuit missions and then flag down another, which will stop unless full. **Rapido Iguazú** (☎ 021/551–601) runs between Asunción and Encarnación. From here, service on to Ciudad del Este (3 hrs) costs $7 one-way. **La Encarnaceña** (☎ 071/203–448) has routes between Asunción and Encarnación; between Encarnación and Ciudad del Este; and local service to the Trinidad and Jesús ruins.

BY CAR

Route 1 runs from Asunción to Encarnación; from Encarnación Route 6 stretches northeast to Ciudad del Este, 280 km (175 mi) away, to the Brazil and Argentine border near Iguazú Falls. The missions are all on or just off Route 1 or Route 6. A bridge links Encarnación with the Argentine town of Posadas.

Contacts and Resources

BANKS AND CURRENCY EXCHANGE

In Encarnación, try **Guarani Cambios** (⊠ Mariscal Estigarribia 307, ☎ 071/204301) or **Banco Regional** (⊠ Carlos A. López 533, ☎ 071/204–746).

In Ciudad del Este, **Yguazú Cambios** (⊠ Av. Mons. Rodríguez y Piribebuy, ☎ 061/501–612) exchanges U.S. currency.

EMERGENCIES

In an emergency, call the **police** ☎ 441–111 or an **ambulance** ☎ 204–800.

For medical care in Encarnación, try **Instituto Medico Privado** (⊠ J.L. Mallorquin 1629, ☎ 071/3615) and, in Ciudad del Este, **Clinica Medica San Jose** (⊠ Av. Sauce, ☎ 061/62730).

TOUR OPERATORS

In Ciudad del Este, **ASPRA** (071/62709) and **RYSA** (⊠ Encomiendas, ☎ 071/203–316) arrange tours to the missions.

VISITOR INFORMATION

The **Secretaria Nacional de Turismo** (⊠ Monseñor Wiessen and Mariscal Estigarribia, ☎ 071/205–326) in Encarnación is usually open weekdays 8–noon.

PARAGUAY A TO Z

Arriving and Departing

By Airplane

AIRPORT

Several international airlines, most of them South American, serve Asunción's **Aeropuerto Internacional Silvio Pettirossi** (☎ 021/206–195 through 021/206–199). The airport departure tax is $18.

CARRIERS

The only U.S. carrier serving Paraguay is **American Airlines** (☎ 021/443–330), which flies from Miami to Asunción via São Paulo. **TAM Mercosur** (☎ 021/491–040) flies to Miami via São Paolo. Other carriers that serve Asunción include **Aerolíneas Argentinas** (☎ 021/491–011), **Iberia** (☎ 021/214–246), **Lloyd Aéreo Boliviano (LAB)** (☎ 021/441–586), and **Varig** (☎ 021/448–777).

FLYING TIMES

It's approximately 12½ hours from Miami to Asunción, including a two-hour stopover in São Paulo.

Getting Around

In Paraguay a street can go by several names at different points along its course, which frequently causes the street numbers to run out of sequence. (Sometimes there are no street numbers at all.) Therefore, addresses are often listed as the intersection of two streets, as in "Ayolas con Brasil" or "Ayolas y Brasil."

By Airplane

Paraguay's domestic carrier Aerolineas Paraguayas (ARPA) has almost-daily service between Asunción and the major interior cities. The one-hour flight to Ciudad del Este from Asunción costs $91, while the nearly two-hour flight to Pedro Juan Caballero, on the northeastern border with Brazil, costs $82 one way. **ARPA** (⊠ Oliva 761, ☎ 021/491–040) is the national carrier, which is affiliated with the privatized **TAM Mercosur. Paraguayo SRL** (⊠ Próceres de Mayo 783, ☎ 021/206–300) is a one-hour air taxi to the northeast jungle, including the Cerro Corá National Park, that operates out of Asunción.

By Bus

Intercity buses are inexpensive, fast, and reliable. Long-distance buses—some air-conditioned, with reclining seats and movies—race between the major centers, while bone-shaking local buses, known as *colectivos,* rattle between villages and along city streets. The 370-km (230-mi) journey from Asunción to Encarnación takes about five hours by bus and costs $10; the 330-km (205-mi) trip from Asunción to Ciudad del Este also takes five hours and costs about $7. For the names and telephone numbers of the companies serving each route, call Asunción's **main bus terminal** (☎ 021/551–732 and 021/551–764) or *see* Getting Around *in* Asunción A to Z.

By Car

Since driver's education courses are not required here, motorists tend to completely ignore traffic laws. Night driving may be particularly dangerous, and there's no national roadside emergency-assistance organization to call for help. If you plan to see the Jesuit towns to the south, consider going on a tour.

GASOLINE

Distances between gas stations can be long, so you should top off your tank regularly. Stations are normally open until midnight. Normal and super grades of gasoline are available and both cost under a $1/liter.

MAPS

For road maps, try **Instituto Geográfico Militar** (⊠ Artigas, at Perú, Asunción, ☎ 021/204–969), although you might have an easier time getting them from the **Touring y Automovil Club** (⊠ Brazil at 25 de Mayo, Asunción, ☎ 021/210–550).

RENTAL AGENCIES

You'll get the best rates in Asunción at **Only Rent a Car** (⊠ airport, ☎ 021/206–195, ext. 112; ⊠ 15 de Agosto 472, Asunción, ☎ 021/492–731). **Hertz** (⊠ airport, ☎ 021/206–196 or 021/206–199; ⊠ Av. Eusebio Ayala, km 4.5, Asunción, ☎ 021/605–708 or 021/503–921) also has chauffeur-driven vehicles. **National** (⊠ Yegros 501, Asunción, ☎ 021/491–848, 021/492–157, or 021/491–379) and **Touring Cars** (⊠ airport, ☎ 021/206–195, ext. 24; ⊠ Iturbe 682, Asunción, ☎ 021/447–945) are reputable international companies.

ROAD CONDITIONS

Paraguay has few paved roads. Two main roads leave Asunción to the east, one cutting south to Encarnación and the other heading to Ciudad del Este and Iguazú Falls. To the northwest is the Trans-Chaco Highway, which when completed will link Paraguay with Bolivia. At press time, the road was paved as far as Mariscal Estigarribia, some 600 mi (372 mi) from Asunción. The main, paved highways have tolls, approximately $1 per car.

With a few exceptions, most roads outside of Asunción are unpaved, dangerously riddled with potholes, or closed altogether because of flooding. Beware of animals that wander onto the highways, particularly at night. On weekends and around public holidays, access roads into and out of the capital can be jammed with traffic.

RULES OF THE ROAD

Your home driver's license is accepted here and, like virtually everywhere else, wearing your seat belt is mandatory. The highway speed limit is 80 kph (50 mph), although this is widely disregarded, and 40 kph (25 mph) in urban areas. Care should be taken at intersections in Asunción, as drivers rarely offer to give way.

Contacts and Resources

Customs and Duties

Non-residents may bring any personal use items, plus 1 liter of spirits or two bottles of wine and 400 cigarettes. Sums of more than $10,000 may not be taken into or out of Paraguay.

Electricity

The electrical current is 220 volts AC, and wall outlets take a continental-type plug, with two round prongs.

Health and Safety

Crime is supposedly rising in Paraguay, although you may not see any foul play on your trip. Instances of carjackings and robbery at gunpoint have been documented, however, as has the pilfering of checked luggage. Border towns, such as Ciudad del Este, are reputedly more troublesome than others.

In hotels, be on the lookout for faulty water-heating showerheads, which may be extremely dangerous, especially when broken, as live wires and wet environments are a fatal combination. If you're at all uncertain about your shower's safety, make bathing arrangements elsewhere. Outside of Asunción, mosquitoes and snakes can be a problem. Bring plenty of mosquito repellent—you might need to use it in hotels without air-conditioning—and, if you're cautious, a snake-bite kit.

FOOD AND DRINK

Although tap water is safe to drink in Asunción, it's advisable to drink *agua purificada* (purified water) everywhere. *Agua con gas* and *agua sin gas* are the respective terms for water with and without carbonation.

Language

Paraguayans are extremely polite, friendly and approachable. If you speak some Spanish, do not hesitate to use it. English is spoken in the more expensive hotels and many restaurants have multilingual menus. Outside the main cities, it's unusual to find anyone who speaks anything but Spanish or Guaraní. There are some immigrant communities where German is spoken; some Mennonites speak Plattdeutsch, a German dialect.

English newspapers are occasionally available at hotels. Local newspapers are *Ultima Hora, Noticias, ABC Color,* and *Eldia y la Nacion.*

Mail

Postal codes are not used consistently here. You can buy stamps and send mail from the *oficinas de correos* (post offices), which are scattered about town, the main post office (☞ *below*), or most major hotels. Documents and anything else of value (or valuable-looking) should be sent via a courier service, such as **DHL International** (✉ Haedo 105, Asunción, ☎ 021/496–683) or **World Courier** (✉ Haedo 179, 14th Floor, Asunción, ☎ 021/448–289).

POSTAL RATES

Airmail letters to North America and Europe cost about 25¢ and 45¢, respectively, and take about two weeks.

RECEIVING MAIL

You can have mail sent to the main post office, **Dirección Nacional de Correo** (✉ Poste Restante, Alberdi 130 y Bejamín Constant, Asunción, ☎ 021/498–112), where it'll be held for collection on production of identity. **American Express** (✉ Yegros 690, Asunción, ☎ 021/490–111) will hold members' mail for free at their Inter-Express office.

Money Matters

COSTS

Quality accommodations with private bathroom and air-conditioning can be found for $60–$120 per night for two people, including breakfast. A well-prepared three-course meal without alcohol in a good restaurant runs around $12, plus tip. Shoe and luggage repairs and laundry and dry cleaning services are cheaper here than elsewhere in South America.

Sample Prices: Espresso, around 60¢; a pint of beer in a bar, $1.50; hamburger and french fries, $2; local bus ride, 30¢; 1-mi taxi ride, $1.

CURRENCY

The Paraguayan guaraní (G) comes in bills of 500, 1,000, 5,000, 10,000, 50,000, and 100,000 guaraníes, with coins in units of 10, 50, 100, and 500 guaraníes. At press time the exchange rate was about 2,253 guaraníes to the Canadian dollar, 3,295 guaraníes to the U.S. dollar, and 5,340 guaraníes to the pound sterling.

As it's impossible to change guaraníes outside Paraguay, you should exchange them before leaving. The currency's steady devaluation means it's not worth saving for a future visit.

SERVICE CHARGES, TAXES, AND TIPPING

A 10% non-refundable value-added tax, known as IVA, is charged on all goods and services. It's included in dinner and drink prices, but it's added to hotel bills, so watch for double-billing: IVA shouldn't be added to food-related bills charged to your room.

An appropriate tip is 10% of the restaurant bill, more if the service is exceptionally good. This applies to upscale discos and bars, but in cheaper, less fashionable places, round up the bill to the nearest thousand guaraníes. Round up taxi fares to the nearest 500 G, give porters around 50¢ per bag, and 50¢ for doormen who hail you a taxi. Leave the chambermaid $2 per day and $5–$10 after a week's stay. Gas-station attendants are tipped up to 30¢ for full service. Give ushers and checkroom and rest-room attendants 10¢–30¢.

Opening and Closing Times

Siestas, generally between noon and 3:30, are taken to beat the heat. Nearly everything closes, except for department stores and the odd café.

Most **banks** are open weekdays 8:45–3. Asunción airport's bank is open daily 9–6. **Casas de cambio** are open weekdays 8:30–1 and 2:30–6; Saturdays 8:30–1. **Museum** hours vary, but most are open weekdays 8–noon and 4–6 and Saturday morning. Public **offices** operate weekdays 7–1 (post offices are open 7–noon and 2:30–7:30), and businesses are open around 7:30 or 8 until midday, and then reopen from 3 to 6. Most **stores** open weekdays at around 7:30 AM, close for the siesta between 12:30 and 3:30, and then reopen until around 8. Grocery stores, bakeries, and other food shops open between 7 and 8, close at noon, and reopen around 3 until around 7 PM. Department stores and shopping centers are open weekdays 8–7:30.

NATIONAL HOLIDAYS

New Year's Day (Jan. 1); Feast of San Blas (Feb. 3); Heroes Day (Mar. 1); Holy Week (Palm Sunday through Easter Sunday): Palm Sunday, Maundy Thursday, and Good Friday (Apr. 16, 20 and 21 in 2000; Apr. 8, 12 and 13 in 2001), Easter (Apr. 23 in 2000; Apr. 15 in 2001); Labor Day (May 1); Independence Day (May 15); Armistice of Chaco War (June 12); Founding of Asunción (Aug. 15); Immaculate Conception (Dec. 8); Christmas (Dec. 25).

Passports and Visas

U.S. and U.K. citizens with passports don't need visas for non-business related stays up to 90 days. Canadians need a visa from the **Embassy of Paraguay** (⊠ 151 Slater St., Suite 401, Ottawa, K1P 5H3, ☎ 613/567–1283 or 613/567–1005, FAX 613/567–1679). There's no fee, but your application must be accompanied by a bank statement, photo, and, possibly, your return ticket. Australian and Irish citizens also need a visa.

Telephones

CALLS TO PARAGUAY

Paraguay's country code is 595. To call Paraguay, dial the country code, then the area code, omitting the first 0.

For local operator assistance, dial 010. For directory assistance, dial 112. For the international operator, dial 0010.

LOCAL CALLS

Pay phones, good for local calls only, are few and far between. They take tokens called *fichas* (approximately 10¢) as well as pre-paid phone cards, both of which can be purchased at tobacco kiosks, bars, and post offices. The cost of a three-minute local call is 9¢.

For cellular phone rental, call **Celular** (✉ Av. Gral Genes 1170 at Calle Bulnes, Asunción, ☎ 021/600–605).

LONG-DISTANCE AND INTERNATIONAL CALLS

Long-distance and international calls cannot be made from public phones, except at ANTELCO telephone offices or some roadside service stations that have their own mini-ANTELCO office. Fortunately, even the tiniest village has an ANTELCO. International calls can be made directly by dialing 002 followed by the country code and local number. Calls to the United States cost about $2.85 per minute during peak hours, $2.50 off-peak. Lines can become congested at peak hours, and, if you're calling from a hotel, be sure to hang up before 20 seconds have elapsed if there's no answer; otherwise, you'll be charged for a three-minute call.

Access Codes: To make credit card and collect calls through an **AT&T** operator, dial 008–11–800. For **MCI,** dial 008–12–800. For **Sprint,** dial 008–13–800.

When to Go

Traveling can be uncomfortable here October to March, when it's extremely hot. Many Paraguayans go on vacation December to February, which is considered low season for the country's hotels. Year-round reservations in Asunción are necessary, however, where space in high-quality hotels is always limited.

CLIMATE

The wettest months are December to April, the driest June, July, and August. Rainfalls year-round in Asunción and the southeast frequently take the form of torrential cloudbursts that can turn streets into torrents of muddy red water. Temperatures are high most of the year, so make sure that your hotel rooms have air-conditioning or fans. In the summer months (Oct.–Mar.), the heat is so intense that it's advisable not to plan activities between midday and 4 PM, which is easy to manage given the siesta.

The following are the average daily maximum and minimum temperatures for Asunción.

Jan.	93F	34C	May	77F	25C	Sept.	80F	27C
	72	22		55	14		60	16
Feb.	93F	34C	June	72F	22C	Oct.	84F	29C
	72	22		55	13		62	17
Mar.	91F	33C	July	75F	24C	Nov.	88F	31C
	70	21		57	14		66	19
Apr.	82F	28C	Aug.	77F	25C	Dec.	91F	33C
	64	18		57	14		70	21

FESTIVALS AND SEASONAL EVENTS

The town of Itá celebrates the **Feast of San Blas** (Feb. 3), the patron saint of Paraguay, with folk dancing, popular music, and horse racing. On December 7, **Immaculate Conception,** and December 8, the **Día de la Nuestra Senõra de Los Milagros** (Day of Our Lady of the Miracles) is celebrated in the town of Caacupé, where an effigy of Mary is paraded through the streets, followed by folk dancing and music.

10 PERU

Bordered on the east by the Amazon rain forest, its center split by the Andes and its western coastline fringed by the Pacific, Peru is a natural wonderland that picks up the heartbeats of adventurers. Outside major cities, much of the country seems caught in an ancient time warp. Famed Machu Picchu, the lost city of the Incas, is only one of innumerable pre-Columbian sites.

Updated by
Joan Gonzalez

OFTEN THE FIRST THING THAT COMES TO mind when Peru is mentioned is Machu Picchu, the great stone sanctuary built high in the Andes mountains more than 100 years before the arrival of Spanish conquistadors. This incredible structure—and its magnificent backdrop—are perfect examples of how "The Land of the Inca" is a nation of extraordinary beauty and myriad attractions, both geographic and archaeological. Its many historical sites are scattered among markedly different regions, each with its own character.

Although Peru is considered an Andean nation, it is in fact 57% jungle. Its vast and still largely pristine Amazon Basin rain forests end only 250 km (155 mi) from the coast. From here, the Andes pierce the heavens, forming an impenetrable barrier of snowcapped peaks, high plateaus, and intermontane valleys. Beyond them to the west, an utterly barren strip of coastal desert stretches north–south for 2,000 km (1,240 mi), broken by dozens of fertile but narrow river valleys.

The Costa, the arid desert coast, is the setting for the Nazca lines, a mystery etched in the sand centuries before the Inca civilization appeared. North of Lima, ruins of vast, ancient cities and adobe pyramids linger like echoes of the sophisticated Moche and Chimú societies that thrived in the desert oases as early as 200BC. In the Sierra is the monumental city of Cuzco, once the capital of the Tawantinsuyo (the name of the Inca empire in the native tongue, Quecha), later a Spanish colonial city, and today a mestizo (mixed-blood) city where Spanish and Indian heritages jostle for space. Spanish culture maintains a tighter hold in the colonial city of Arequipa, while the nearby Colca Canyon, the deepest canyon on earth, is crisscrossed with Inca and pre-Inca agricultural terraces.

In Peru's Amazon Basin, known as the Selva (jungle), lies the tropical rain forest and the gateway city of Iquitos. The region's marvels include the Canopy Walkway in the northeast, which takes the visitor among the treetops of one of the world's last frontiers. Farther south are the jungles of the *departamento* (province) of Madre de Dios (aptly named Mother of God): remote, nearly untouched, but accessible to the adventurous. In the highland jungles, which Peruvians call the Ceja de Selva (Eyebrow of the Jungle), is the famous "lost city of the Incas," Machu Picchu. Its vertiginous setting and stunning architecture make it a centerpiece of humanity's archaeological record and one of the true wonders of the world.

As a nation and a people, Peru has a strong character, not unlike the national drink, *pisco,* a heady grape brandy distilled in the coastal valleys south of Lima. As pronounced as it is, however, the Peruvian personality is heterogeneous, perhaps the product of such markedly different terrains and climates. The people of the Andes, often called *serranos,* tend to be introverted, especially in dealings with outsiders, with a sharp sense of identity and a melancholic side best expressed in their haunting music. Quite the opposite are the friendly and more lighthearted inhabitants of the Costa and the Selva. The *costeño* is quick with a joke but, like his beloved cuisine, *comida criolla* (Creole food), has a piquant, teasing side to his nature.

Since before recorded history, Peru's inhabitants have shown a fierce determination to tame their environment. The results of their efforts can be seen in the agricultural terraces that still lace the highlands and in the elaborate irrigation systems that watered the desert a thousand years ago. Today, this nation of 22 million has had to focus that de-

WITHOUT KODAK MAX
photos taken on 100 speed film

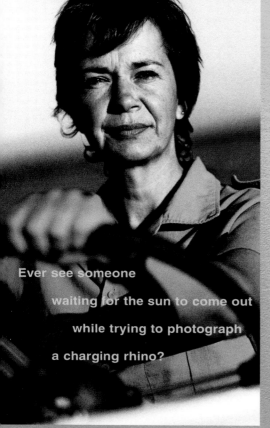

Ever see someone

waiting for the sun to come out

while trying to photograph

a charging rhino?

New!
Kodak Max film:

Now with better color,
Kodak's maximum
versatility film gives
you great pictures in
sunlight, low light,
action or still.

WITH KODAK MAX
photos taken on Kodak Max 400 film

It's all you need
to know about film.

www.kodak.com

Distinctive guides packed with up-to-date expert advice and smart choices for every type of traveler.

Fodor's. For the world of ways you travel.

termination on a fight for survival. For the past three genera⌁ lions of *campesinos* (peasants) have left the countryside for th⌁ They have built homes on rocky hillsides and sand dunes, princ⌁ on the outskirts of Lima, and are struggling to make a place for the⌁ selves by working in small factories and workshops and on the streets as vendors.

Unfortunately, Peru did not enjoy the vigorous industrialization process that would have rewarded its migrating campesinos with the jobs and comforts associated with modern urban life. The country's resulting mix of deep economic crisis, poverty, and frustration erupted into political violence, most intensely at the end of the 1980s and the beginning of the 1990s. It finally ended in 1992 and 1994 with the capture of the top leaders of the most brutal rebel group, the Marxist-Leninist Sendero Luminosa (Shining Path), who had killed an estimated 30,000 people.

Today Peru is still striving for economic prosperity, hoping to achieve it through privatization, encouraging foreign investment, and increasing exports. The return of high-volume tourism is also expected to help bring about economic recovery.

Pleasures and Pastimes

Ancient Cities
Although Peru is most famous for the ancient city of Machu Picchu, there are extensive ruins of ancient cities throughout the country. Five km (3 mi) from Trujillo is Chán Chán, the largest adobe city in the world. Near Chachapoyas is Kuelap, called "The City of the Cloud People" because of the white skin of its former inhabitants. Other impressive ruins nearby are Gran Vilaya, and Gran Pajaten in the Río Abiseo National Park.

Crafts
Lovely, handmade crafts are sold everywhere from busy street corners to sleepy villages. Specialties include jewelry made with native silver and precious stones, ceramics, leather goods, and alpaca knits.

Dining
From the Amazon to the desert to the Andes, your journey of food will be as varied as the landscapes you'll encounter, but all have one thing in common: the use of a small, thin *ají* pepper. The use of hot peppers is common in Latin America, especially Mexico, but Peruvian chefs strip the pepper of its veins and seeds and soak it or boil it in water to cool it down while retaining the flavor.

Peruvian cuisine is hard to define, as it has evolved from pre-Inca and Spanish colonial times, and has been influenced by African, European, and Oriental cooking. Fresh seafood is found everywhere, including shrimp, lobster, corvina (a delicious sea bass), trout from mountain lakes, six-ft paiche (found in jungle lakes), dorado, and piranha (good but bony). Some of Peru's best dishes include *ceviche* (marinated raw fish with onions and peppers, served as an appetizer); *aji de galina* (chicken in a cream sauce); *lomo saltado* (sautéed beef with onions and peppers, served with fried potatoes and rice); *pachamanca* (a meat and vegetable stew); *anticuchos* (a shish kebab of marinated beef hearts); and *choclo* (Peru's corn-on-the-cob). For dessert, try *Suspiro a la Limeña* (a rich, sweet pudding) and *mazamorra morada* (a purple, fruity pudding). The best ethnic cooking in Peru is Chinese, known as *chifa*.

Both Peru and Ecuador claim to have given the world the potato, and hundreds of varieties are grown here. Among the tastier recipes are *papa*

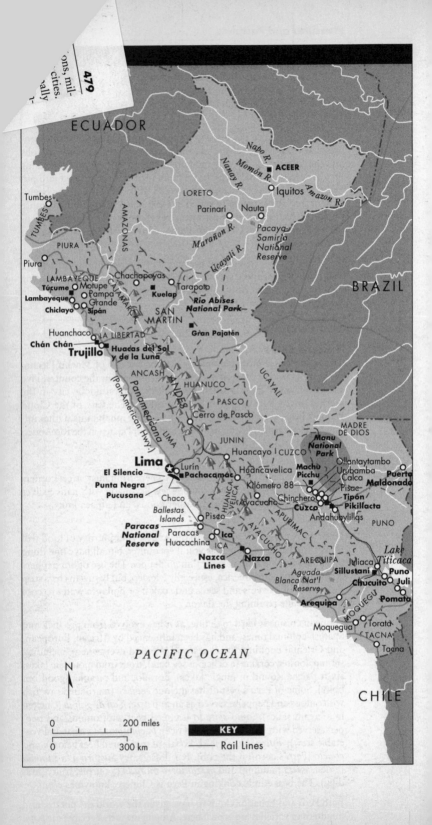

ons, mil-
cities.
ally
i-

ECUADOR

Tumbes

Piura

BRAZIL

PIURA

AMAZONAS

LORETO

Nabo R.

Nancy R.

Momón R.

ACEER

Iquitos

Amazon R.

Parinari

Nauta

Marañón R.

Ucayali R.

Pacaya-
Samiria
National
Reserve

TUMBES

Chachapoyas

Tarapoto

LAMBAYEQUE

Túcume

Lambayeque

Chiclayo

Motupe

Pampa
Grande

Sipán

Kuélap

CAJAMARCA

SAN
MARTIN

Río Abises
National Park

Huanchaco

Chán Chán

Trujillo

LA LIBERTAD

Huacas del Sol
y de la Luna

Gran Pajatén

ANCASH

ANDES

(Panamericana)

(Pan-American Hwy.)

HUANUCO

PASCO

UCAYALI

Cerro de Pasco

LIMA

JUNIN

Huancayo

MADRE
DE DIOS

Manu
National
Park

CUZCO

Lima

El Silencio

Punta Negra

Pucusana

Lurín

Pachacamác

Chaco

Ballestas
Islands

Paracas
National
Reserve

Paracas

Huacachina

Pisco

Ica

ICA

Huancavelica

HUANCA-
VELICA

Kilómetro 88

Chinchero

Ayacucho

AYACUCHO

APURIMAC

Machu
Picchu

Ollantaytambo

Urubamba

Calca

Pisac

Cuzco

Tipón

Pikillacta

Andahuaylillas

Puerto
Maldonado

PUNO

Nazca
Lines

Nazca

AREQUIPA

Aguada
Blanca Nat'l
Reserve

Lake
Titicaca

Juliaca

Sillustani

Chucuito

Puno

Juli

Pomata

Arequipa

MOQUEGUA

Torata

Moquegua

TACNA

Tacna

CHILE

PACIFIC OCEAN

N

0   200 miles

0   300 km

KEY

—— Rail Lines

a la huancaina (potatoes in spicy cheese sauce), *ocopa* (in spicy peanut sauce), and *carapulcra* (a stew of dried potatoes served over rice). Peru has wonderful fruit, such as *chirimoya* (custard apple) and *tuna* (cactus fruit).

Peru's national drink is the Pisco Sour, made from distilled grape liquor. Peruvian beers are not bad. In Lima, try Cristal and the slightly more upscale Pilsen Callao, both produced by the same brewing group. In the south it's Arequipeña, from Arequipa; Cusqueña, from Cuzco; and San Juan beer in Iquitos. Tacama's Blanco de Blancos is considered the country's best wine.

The cost and quality of dining out in Peru can vary widely, but a modest restaurant that looks clean may serve as splendid a meal as one with snazzier decor. Most smaller restaurants offer a lunchtime *menú*, a prix-fixe meal ($2–$5) that consists of an appetizer, a main dish, dessert, and a beverage. Peru is also full of cafés, many with a selection of delicious pastries. Food at bars is usually limited to snacks and sandwiches.

Top-notch restaurants serve lunch and dinner, but most Peruvians think of lunch as the main meal of the day, and many restaurants open only for lunch. Served between 1 and 3, lunch is traditionally followed by a siesta, though the custom has largely died out. Dinner can be anything from a light snack to another full meal. Peruvians tend to dine late, between 7 and 11 PM. Cafés are open from 10 AM to 10 PM or later; bars open at around 6 PM but don't become lively until 10 or 11.

Peruvians dress quite informally when they dine out, and often a sport jacket is sufficient for men even at very expensive restaurants. A smart pair of slacks or a skirt is always appropriate for women. Shorts are frowned upon everywhere except at the beach, and T-shirts should be worn only in very modest restaurants.

Meals are subject to an 18% sales tax, which should be included in the bill. Better restaurants also include a 10% service charge. Prices quoted are per person and include appetizer, main course, and dessert but exclude alcoholic beverages, tax, service charge, and tip. For price categories, *see* Dining *in* Smart Travel Tips A to Z.

Lodging

Accommodations in Peru range from bare-bones rooms with shared bathrooms to luxury hotels. They come with names such as *hostal, pensión, residencial,* and *hotel,* and though the implication is that the last is more upscale, this is not always the case. Many budget hotels and hostels now offer not only TV in the rooms but also cable, and may have such amenities as airport shuttle and free breakfast. Rooms are more scarce during the high season (June through September), and if you're planning to visit during a festival, it's best to reserve in advance.

Camping in Peru is limited to some beaches (where Peruvians camp in large groups for protection) and as part of mountain and jungle treks. The only legal campsites are in some national parks, such as Manu National Park (☞ Madre de Dios, *below*). Camping is pretty much required for those hiking the Inca Trail, but be careful and try to stay with a group.

Hotels usually charge an 18% tax and occasionally service charges of up to 13%. A Continental breakfast is often but not always included in the room rate; the most expensive hotels are least likely to include breakfast. Prices quoted are for a double room and include tax and service charge. For price categories, *see* Lodging *in* Smart Travel Tips A to Z.

Exploring Peru

Peru can be divided roughly into three major geographical areas. The arid coastal desert extends the full length of the country. Within this narrow stretch are the Nazca lines, a coastal marine park teeming with wildlife, verdant oases, rocky hills, and desert. Running through the country like a spine, separating desert from jungle, are the majestic Andes, with their green valleys, snowcapped peaks, rivers, and hidden ruins. To the east lies the world's widest river, the Amazon, and Peru's thick chunk of jungle basin.

Great Itineraries

Peru offers a diverse combination of tours. The best advice: Plan a flexible itinerary with your travel agent, or with an agency in Peru, allowing for unexpected obstacles or detours you may want to make along the way.

IF YOU HAVE 7 DAYS

Arrive in **Lima,** spend the night, and take your first full day to explore the city's museums and markets. The next morning, fly to **Cuzco** and take an easy afternoon tour of city and nearby ruins. Spend the night, then take the morning train to **Machu Picchu,** where you can discover Peru's ancient past. Spend the night and return to Cuzco late the next afternoon. The next day, you can either shop, tour more nearby ruins, or both. Spend the night and take a morning flight back to Lima, where you can make an afternoon souvenir-scouting trip before returning home.

IF YOU HAVE 10 DAYS

Follow the same itinerary as the seven-day tour, but after visiting **Machu Picchu** you can return to **Cuzco** and take the train or fly to **Puno** on **Lake Titicaca.** Spend three nights and two full days exploring this beautiful high-altitude region before returning to Lima. Alternatively, you could fly to **Iquitos** or **Puerto Maldonado** and spend three nights and two full days discovering the Amazon region.

IF YOU HAVE 14 DAYS

Enter through Lima and begin the seven-day itinerary, but take an extra day to explore the environs of **Cuzco.** Spend the night, then take the train or fly to **Puno** on **Lake Titicaca,** where you can spend two nights and a full day. From here, fly to the colonial town of **Arequipa** and take the day to explore the town, spend the night, and head for **Colca Canyon.** Overnight here, then return to Arequipa and take the next three days to explore **Paracas National Reserve** or **Nazca** (and the Nazca lines)—or both—before returning to Lima.

LIMA

Founded along the banks of the Rimac River by Francisco Pizarro in 1535, for 300 years Lima was the capital of Spain's South American empire, and it is still the country's capital today. The "City of Kings" has a vice-regal history that lingers on in its sophistication, the decaying beauty of its boulevards, and the liveliness of its intellectual life. Over the past 30 years, however, Lima has lost much of its elite character as Peru's rural population, recognizing that the bulk of the country's resources were concentrated in this city of 7 million, migrated here in hopes of finding jobs, homes, and education.

Exploring Lima

The majority of the city's most splendid buildings and museums are in the *centro* (downtown), around the Plaza Mayor. From here, the main roads lead like spokes of a wheel to Lima's most important districts, through working-class neighborhoods like Brena, Rimac, and La Victoria to the huge shantytowns that ring the city and to upscale seafront residential neighborhoods like Miraflores and San Isidro. There are also posh neighborhoods like La Molina in the foothills of the Andes, where Lima's wealthiest live among watered lawns behind guarded gates and high walls. From central Lima west to the sea, the city is flat, but the Peruvian coast is so narrow that the barren Andean piedmont juts spiky hills into the sky just 10 minutes east of the city center. Most parks begin on downtown's western fringe, and become more frequent as you near the sea.

Walking is your best bet within a neighborhood, but you will need to take a taxi or bus between them. While many businesses, shops, and restaurants have relocated to the upscale San Isidro and Miraflores districts, you can easily and safely (especially in the daytime) walk to the main plaza from the downtown hotels. If you prefer accommodations in one of the districts, they are only about a 15-minute ($2) taxi ride away.

Visitors should plan to spend a day or two seeing the downtown area, with an additional one or two days devoted to the museums, which are south of downtown. Take time to wander through Barranco, once a seaside vacation spot for people who lived in downtown Lima. The café scene is lively here, attracting artists and intellectuals.

Numbers in white bullets in the text correspond to numbers in black bullets in the margins and on the Lima map.

Centro

A GOOD WALK

Many of Lima's most interesting historical sites are contained in the centro, within walking distance of the **Plaza Mayor** ①. Across the plaza is the 20th-century neocolonial **Municipalidad** ②. The imposing **Palacio de Gobierno** ③ is on the north side of the plaza, and **La Catedral** ④ is to the east. Walk four blocks southeast and you can explore one of the more gruesome aspects of Peru's history in the **Museo de la Inquisición** ⑤. Three blocks northeast and two blocks northwest is the **Iglesia de San Francisco** ⑥, one of Lima's most interesting churches. Two blocks further northwest is the **Casa Aliaga** ⑦. From here, you can walk to the northwest corner, take a left, and cross the street to reach the **Iglesia de Santo Domingo** ⑧; it's just one block off Plaza Mayor if you'd like to stop your tour here. Otherwise, continue three more blocks northwest to reach **Santuario de Santa Rosa de Lima** ⑨. Head southwest along Avenida Tacna toward the **Iglesia de las Nazarenas** ⑩. From here, five blocks along Jirón Huancavelica, is the **Iglesia de la Merced** ⑪. Head southwest to the end of the block, cross the street, and on the right side you'll find **La Casa de Riva Agüero** ⑫. The **Iglesia de Jesús María** ⑬ is two blocks farther southwest. Walk a block southeast on Jirón Puno and take a right for a block on Jirón de la Unión to reach the **Plaza San Martín** ⑭. Near the "entrance" to the centro, where the expressway to Miraflores and Barranco begins, you'll find the **Museo de Arte Nacional** ⑮.

TIMING

An unhurried visit to the centro's main attractions takes a day, with at least an hour devoted to both the Museo de Arte Nacional and the Museo de la Inquisición. Don't miss the 45-minute guided tour of San Francisco church and its underground catacombs. Also, spend some time just sitting on the Cathedral steps, as the locals do.

SIGHTS TO SEE

❼ **Casa Aliaga.** Said to be the oldest colonial mansion in South America, the Aliaga House has been owned and occupied by the same family

484

Plaza Bolivar

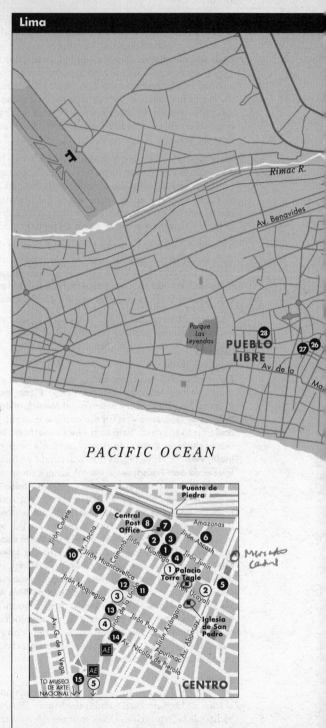

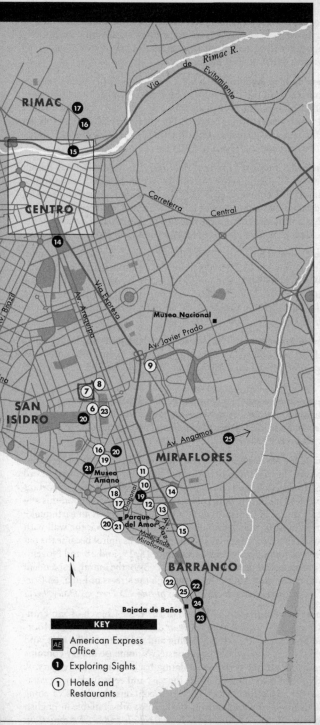

Dining

Alfresco, **1, 21**

Bircher-Benner, **12**

Las Brujas de Cachiche, **17**

Haití, **10**

La Costa Verde, **22**

L'eau Vive, **2**

Lung Fung, **9**

Matsuei, **8**

Las Mesitas, **26**

Il Postino, **11**

El Rincón Gaucho, **15**

La Rosa Náutica, **20**

La Tiendecita Blanca, **19**

Trattoria don Vito, **14**

Lodging

Los Delfines, **19**

Gran Hotel Bolívar, **4**

Hostal la Castellana, **13**

Hotel Antigua Miraflores, **18**

Hotel Sheraton & Casino, **5**

Kamaná Hotel, **3**

Miraflores Park Plaza, **16**

Posada del Inca, **6**

Sonesta Lima Hotel El Olívar, **23**

Swissôtel, **7**

since Francisco Pizarro granted the land to Jerónimo de Aliaga in 1535. Its elaborate rooms are decorated with colonial furnishings. Unfortunately, visitors must arrange tours in advance exclusively through Lima Tours (☞ *Tour Operators in Lima A to Z, below*). ⊠ *Unión 224,* ☎ *01/427–7736.*

⑫ **La Casa de Riva Agüero.** Ornately carved wooden terraces overlook the courtyards of the Riva Agüero House's typical colonial mansion; balconies have *celosías* (intricate wood screens through which ladies could watch passersby unobserved). An interesting museum of folk art is on the patio. ⊠ *Camaná 459,* ☎ *01/427–7678.* 🖾 *Free.* ⊙ *Tues.– Fri. 10–12:30 and 2–7:30, Sat. 9–1.*

④ **La Catedral.** Completed in the 17th century, the Cathedral was rebuilt after the 1746 earthquake nearly destroyed it. In addition to impressive baroque decoration, especially the intricately carved choir stalls, the Cathedral has a museum of religious art and artifacts whose highlight is a coffin said to hold the remains of Pizarro. ⊠ *East side of the Plaza Mayor,* ☎ *01/431–7056.* 🖾 *Admission.* ⊙ *Mon.–Sat. 10–5.*

Correo Central. The Central Post Office's spectacular, light-pink building, inaugurated in 1897, looks more like a church than Lima's postal hub. Within you'll find a gamut of services, from postcard sales to phone and fax to a café. There is also a tiny museum of stamps, the **Museo Postal y Filatélico.** ⊠ *Conde de Superunda, between Unión and Camaná,* ⊙ *Mon.–Fri. 8:30–6, Sat. 9–1.*

⑬ **Iglesia de Jesús María.** The simple Church of Jesus and Mary dates from 1659 and became a Capuchin monastery in the 18th century. ⊠ *Corner of Camaná and Moquegua,* ☎ *01/427–6809.* 🖾 *Free.* ⊙ *Daily 9–7.*

⑪ **Iglesia de la Merced.** The Church of Mercy, with its colonial facade and peaceful cloisters, was begun by Hernando Pizarro (Francisco's brother) in 1535. ⊠ *Corner of Unión and Miro Quesada,* ☎ *01/427– 8199.* 🖾 *Free.* ⊙ *Daily 9–7.*

⑩ **Iglesia de las Nazarenas.** The 18th-century Church of the Nazarenes has become the repository of the icon of the **Señor de los Milagros,** Lord of the Miracles, the patron of Lima's most passionate and important religious festival. In the mid-1600s, a black freeman living on this site painted a mural of Christ on the wall of his hut. When an earthquake destroyed most of the surrounding shantytown in 1655, the wall with the mural remained standing, and the miraculous mural became the patron icon of Lima. Every year on October 18, 19, and 28 and November 1, purple-robed devotees carry an oil copy of the mural, resplendent in a gold frame atop a silver litter, through the streets of Lima. ⊠ *Corner of Tacna and Huancavelica,* ☎ *no phone.* 🖾 *Free.* ⊙ *Daily 9–7.*

⑥ **Iglesia de San Francisco.** Completed in 1674, the Church of San Francisco is famed for its beautiful *mudejar* decoration (a hybrid of Moorish and Spanish styles) on its vaulting and columns, Seville tiles, and paneled ceilings. The adjoining monastery's immense library contains thousands of antique texts, some dating back to the 17th century. A guided tour of the church includes the vast and eerie underlying catacombs—the city's first cemetery, which contains the bones of some 25,000 dead—discovered only in 1951. Tours are available in English throughout the day. ⊠ *Ancash 471,* ☎ *01/427–1381.* 🖾 *Admission.* ⊙ *Daily 9:30–5.*

✓ **Iglesia de San Pedro.** One of the finest examples of early colonial religious architecture in Peru, San Pedro Jesuit Church was built in 1638. The interior is richly appointed with gilded altars, Moorish-style wood carvings in the choir and vestry, and glazed, decorated tiles through-out. ⊠ *Corner of Ucayali and Azángaro,* ☎ *01/428–3010.* ☒ *Free.* ☉ *Daily 8–12:30 and 5–8:30.*

❽ **Iglesia de Santo Domingo.** The late-16th-century church holds the tombs of two venerated Peruvian saints, Rosa de Lima and Martín de Porres. ⊠ *1st block of Camaná,* ☎ *01/427–6793.* ☒ *Admission.* ☉ *Daily 3–6.*

❷ **Municipalidad.** Inaugurated in 1944, the City Hall was built follow-ing the basic elements of colonial design. On the south side, ground level, is the Lima Municipal Tourist Office and a small art gallery, the **Galería Pancho Fierro.** Guided tours of the interior reveal a magnifi-cent collection of Peruvian art and old photos. For tours, you need a minimum of five people and proper attire; no jeans, shorts, or tennis shoes. ⊠ *West side of the Plaza Mayor,* ☎ *01/427–6080.* ☒ *Admis-sion.* ☉ *Municipalidad: Mon.–Fri. 9–1 and 2–4; Galeri: Daily 10–5.*

❻ **Museo de Arte Nacional.** The National Art Museum chronicles four centuries of Peruvian art and design. Highlights are 2,000-year-old weav-ings from Paracas and paintings from the Cuzco School. ⊠ *Colón 125,* ☎ *01/423–4732.* ☒ *Admission.* ☉ *Tues.–Sun. 10–1 and 2–5.*

❺ **Museo de la Inquisición.** This museum is housed in the building that was the Spanish Inquisition's headquarters in South America from 1570 to 1820. You can visit the original dungeons and torture chambers, where stomach-churning, life-size exhibits illustrate methods of extracting information from the accused. ⊠ *Junín 548,* ☎ *01/428–7980.* ☒ *Ad-mission.* ☉ *Mon.–Sat. 10–1 and 2–5.*

❸ **Palacio de Gobierno.** Completed in 1938, the Government Palace is the official residence of the president; it also houses his offices and those of his staff. It was built on the site of Francisco Pizarro's palace, where he was murdered in 1541. An equestrian statue of the conquistador watches over the palace from across the street. The changing of the palace guard takes place daily at noon. Free tours are available only by prearrangement. ⊠ *Plaza Mayor,* ☎ *01/426–7020.*

Palacio Torre Tagle. The city's most elegant colonial mansion was built in 1735. Because the Foreign Ministry has offices here, visits by the public are limited to the patio and courtyard, but even that peek re-veals tiled ceilings, carved columns, and a 16th-century carriage com-plete with portable commode. ⊠ *Ucayali 363,* ☎ *01/427–3860.* ☒ *Free.* ☉ *Weekdays 9–5.*

❶ **Plaza Mayor.** Formerly known as the Plaza de Armas, this vast square that once formed the nucleus of power in Spanish colonial Peru was remodeled in traditional colonial style and renamed in 1997 to reflect the name originally given by Pizarro to the main plaza in 1535.

❹ **Plaza San Martín.** Facing the bustling plaza are elegant 1920s build-ings such as the **Gran Hotel Bolívar,** a pleasant place to stop for tea or a sandwich, and the exclusive **Club Nacional.** The plaza itself is a stage for a wild variety of street performers, from magicians and co-medians to hawkers of modern-day snake medicine.

❾ **Santuario de Santa Rosa de Lima.** Within the small, simple, 17th-cen-tury Sanctuary of Saint Rosa of Lima, the tiny adobe cell that was Santa Rosa's hermitage keeps alive the memory of the first saint in the West-ern Hemisphere. The church also houses the **Museo Etnográfico,** where ethnographic exhibits detail the lives of Peru's jungle peoples. ⊠ *1st block of Tacna,* ☎ *01/425–0143.* ☉ *Sanctuary: seasonally.*

Rimac

An extension of the colonial center, the district of Rimac has declined into a somewhat rough neighborhood, especially at night. Daytime tours of the area's residential neighborhoods, however, reveal some of the oldest and most interesting architecture in the city. Rather than go on your own, it is a good idea to either take a tour or hire a taxi.

A GOOD WALK

Just stroll the centro to Rimac across the historic **Puente de Piedra** ⑯. A few blocks from the bridge is the **Alameda de los Descalzos** ⑰. Stroll down this sadly deteriorated lovers' lane to the **Convento de los Descalzos** ⑱.

TIMING

Depending on your enthusiasm for architecture, a brief stroll through Rimac can be completed in a few hours. It's a good way to pass a lazy Sunday afternoon.

SIGHTS TO SEE

⑰ **Alameda de los Descalzos.** The tree-lined courtship walk along the Promenade of the Barefoot Friars is graced by 12 marble statues that represent the signs of the zodiac.

⑱ **Convento de los Descalzos.** The 16th-century Franciscan Monastery of the Barefoot Friars has four main cloisters and two lavish chapels. In one chapel a baroque altar gleams with gold leaf. The kitchen still contains antique wine-making equipment, and there's also a fine collection of colonial paintings. English-speaking guides are available. ⊠ *Alameda de los Descalzos,* ☎ *01/481–0441.* 🎟 *Admission.* ☉ *Daily 9:30–1 and 3–6.*

⑯ **Puente de Piedra.** Across the often arid Rimac River from the Government Palace, Rimac is linked to the center by this 17th-century stone bridge, whose builders strengthened their mortar with thousands of egg whites.

Miraflores

An upscale residential district, the seaside suburb of Miraflores is an attractive place to stroll and window-shop among chic fashion boutiques, art galleries, and crafts stores. Some of Lima's swankiest hotels and restaurants are here.

A GOOD WALK

The heart of Miraflores is a roughly triangular area around the **Parque Miraflores** ⑲, which lies between Larco and Diagonal. If you continue down either, you'll come to the **Malecón,** a cliff-top road that looks out over the Pacific. Turning left or right, you'll pass small parks and the houses and apartments of the well-to-do. It's an especially lovely area during a summer sunset. A walk down Larco will also bring you to the **Huaca Puellna** ⑳ and, seven blocks away, the **Museo Amano** ㉑ both of which are open only during the day.

TIMING

The best time to stroll Miraflores may be late afternoon, when locals are off work and in a good mood. About a half hour of walking leads from the Parque Miraflores to the Malecón, where you'll want to spend another hour strolling and looking over the cliff at the ocean. Take a taxi or walk back along Larco Herrera and browse the shops, many of which stay open late. Be sure to stop again in the middle of the Parque Miraflores at the artisans' market 5–10:30 PM.

20 **Huaca Puellna.** This posh neighborhood is the setting for an enormous pre-Inca *huaca* (religious site), also known as the Huaca Juliana. A museum, crafts gallery, and restaurant (with folk music on Sundays at 7 PM) are also on the premises. ⊠ *Corner of Larco Herrera and Elías Aguirre.* ☑ *Admission.* ⊙ *Daily 9–5.*

21 **Museo Amano.** This museum displays a fine private collection of pre-Columbian ceramics and weavings by the Chancay culture, a small central-coastal state around present-day Lima that flourished between AD 1000 and AD 1500. ⊠ *Retiro 160,* ☎ *01/441–2909.* ☑ *Free.* ⊙ *Weekdays; tours by appointment only.*

19 **Parque Miraflores.** This park has a lively crafts fair daily 5–10:30 PM; frequent open-air concerts are also held here. It's a great place to sit and people-watch in one of the cafés or eat ice cream at the colorful D'Onofrio parlor on the east side.

Barranco

A sort of artists' quarter filled with galleries, cafés, and nightclubs, this funky seafront district has a scenic Malecón (coastal road) and winding, tree-lined streets.

Above the Bajada de Baños, a cobblestone street lined with wonderful old houses that leads down to the ocean, is Lima's own Bridge of Sighs, the **Puente de los Suspiros** ㉒. A few blocks south along the seafront is the **Museo Pedro de Osma** ㉓. The **Parque Municipal** ㉔ is one block from the Puente de los Suspiros. Continuing around the park you'll find **La Santicima Cruz,** an old Catholic church. In back of the church is the **Cafe Las Mesitas,** which is a great place for a dessert break.

23 **Museo Pedro de Osma.** This important museum has a fine collection of colonial paintings, sculpture, and silver. ⊠ *Malecón Pedro de Osma 423,* ☎ *01/467–0141.* ☑ *Admission.* ⊙ *Tues.–Sun. 10–1:30 and 2:30–6.*

24 **Parque Municipal.** This is one of the best places in Lima to just sit and watch Peruvians at their best—relaxing with friends, their children playing about them. Surrounding the park and on Barranco's lanes are several trendy bars and cafés (☞ Nightlife and the Arts, *below*).

22 **Puente de los Suspiros.** The Bridge of Sighs is a secluded lover's lane filled with flowering trees. The walkway leads under a wooden bridge and down a cliff that overlooks the ocean.

Museums Around Town

A number of Lima's best museums are in outlying neighborhoods.

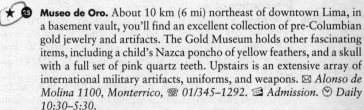

25 **Museo de Oro.** About 10 km (6 mi) northeast of downtown Lima, in a basement vault, you'll find an excellent collection of pre-Columbian gold jewelry and artifacts. The Gold Museum holds other fascinating items, including a child's Nazca poncho of yellow feathers, and a skull with a full set of pink quartz teeth. Upstairs is an extensive array of international military artifacts, uniforms, and weapons. ⊠ *Alonso de Molina 1100, Monterrico,* ☎ *01/345–1292.* ☑ *Admission.* ⊙ *Daily 10:30–5:30.*

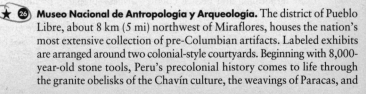

26 **Museo Nacional de Antropología y Arqueología.** The district of Pueblo Libre, about 8 km (5 mi) northwest of Miraflores, houses the nation's most extensive collection of pre-Columbian artifacts. Labeled exhibits are arranged around two colonial-style courtyards. Beginning with 8,000-year-old stone tools, Peru's precolonial history comes to life through the granite obelisks of the Chavín culture, the weavings of Paracas, and the ceramics of such civilizations as the Nazca, Moche, Chimú, and Inca. ⊠ *Plaza Bolívar, Pueblo Libre,* ☎ *01/463–5070.* ▨ *Admission.* ◷ *Daily 9–5.*

㉗ **Museo de Historia Nacional.** The National History Museum displays a collection of period clothing, furniture, and other items that date mainly from Peru's early 19th-century War of Independence. ⊠ *Plaza Bolívar, Pueblo Libre,* ☎ *01/463–5070.* ▨ *Admission.* ◷ *Daily 9–5.*

★ ㉘ **Museo Rafael Larco Herrera.** This museum in Pueblo Libre contains the world's largest private collection of pre-Columbian art pieces in gold, silver, and semiprecious stones. The famous erotic ceramic collection shows that Peru's ancient artists were surprisingly explicit and uninhibited. ⊠ *Plaza Bolívar 1515, Pueblo Libre,* ☎ *01/461–1835.* ▨ *Admission.* ◷ *Mon.–Sat. 9–6, Sun. 9–1.*

Dining

Whether you want *comida criolla* (spiced meat, fish, or poultry dishes, often with onions and prepared fried, stewed, or simmered with rice), the fresh bounty of the Pacific Ocean, or something more ethnic—chifa is a favorite here—Lima won't disappoint you. For dessert or after-dinner coffee, visit one of Lima's cafés. These gathering spots play an important role in the city's social and intellectual life, especially among the middle-class 30s–50s set. The best café action is between 5 and 7 PM and after 10.

Cafés

$$ ✕ **La Tiendecita Blanca.** Excellent pastries, a baby grand piano for ambience, and shelves full of confections lure foreigners and locals to this European-style café in Miraflores. ⊠ *Larco Herrera 111,* ☎ *01/445–9797. AE, DC, MC, V.*

$ ✕ **Haití.** This landmark sidewalk café in Miraflores is a favorite hangout for Lima's aging artists and intellectuals. Stick to the sandwiches, coffee, and beer. ⊠ *Diagonal 160,* ☎ *01/447–5052. AE, DC, MC, V.*

$ ✕ **Las Mesitas.** An old-fashioned Limeño café with tables of wrought
★ iron and marble, this romantic spot ½ block north of the Parque Municipal in Barranco is a magnet for fans of traditional sweets. The mazamorra morada, a sweet pudding of cornmeal and candied fruit, is heavenly. ⊠ *Grau 323,* ☎ *01/477–4199. V.*

Chinese

$$–$$$ ✕ **Lung Fung.** This spectacular chifa in San Isidro has interior Chinese
★ gardens complete with tiny bridges and ponds. Try the *kam-lu wantan* (fried wontons with shrimp and sweet-and-sour sauce). ⊠ *República de Panamá 3165,* ☎ *01/441–8817. AE, DC, MC, V.*

International

$$$$ ✕ **Matsuei.** Sushi chefs shout out a Japanese welcome in unison as you enter this cozy restaurant in San Isidro, which specializes in excellent sushi, sashimi, and other dishes. It's widely considered the best Japanese restaurant in town. ⊠ *Manuel Bañon 260,* ☎ *01/422–4323. AE, DC, MC, V.*

$$–$$$ ✕ **L'eau Vive.** The setting is an old colonial mansion across from the Torre Tagle Palace in central Lima, and the specialties are excellent international and French country dishes—prepared by nuns. Fittingly, the *Ave Maria* is performed each night at 10, and diners are urged to sing along with the pros. Profits from the restaurant are given to the poor. ⊠ *Ucayali 370,* ☎ *01/427–5612. AE, MC, V. Closed Sundays and holidays.*

$$–$$$ ✕ **Trattoria don Vito.** There are countless varieties of pasta at this
★ friendly Miraflores restaurant, which also serves mouthwatering pizzas and desserts, flambéed at your table. ✉ *Martín Dulanto 111,* ☎
01/445–8156. AE, DC, MC, V.

$$ ✕ **Il Postino.** Within this early 1900s home tucked away on a side street
in Miraflores, chefs Flavio and Domenico Gallotta serve up delicious
pasta dishes in a friendly and personal manner. In addition to the
exquisite handmade pastas, excellent steaks are also served. ✉ *Calle
Colina 401,* ☎ *01/446–8381. AE, MC, V. Closed Sun. and Mon.*

Peruvian

$$–$$$ ✕ **Las Brujas de Cachiche.** This upscale spot is in a pleasant location over-
looking a secluded park on a Miraflores backstreet. The specialty here
is creole cuisine. ✉ *Bolognesi 460,* ☎ *01/444–5310. AE, DC, MC, V.*

Seafood

$$$$ ✕ **La Costa Verde.** This Barranco restaurant's relaxing atmosphere, high-
★ lighted by sweeping Pacific sunset views, is just one of the reasons it's
considered among the best in town. Highlights include fresh lobster,
an excellent Sunday buffet, and good Pisco Sours. La Costa Verde also
has the only disco in the ocean-front neighborhood. ✉ *Barranquito
Beach,* ☎ *01/477–2424. AE, MC, V.*

$$$$ ✕ **La Rosa Náutica.** One of Miraflores's loveliest restaurants is set in
a Victorian-style pink-and-green rotunda at the end of a pier, perched
over the Pacific Ocean. Dishes include scallops grilled with Parmesan
cheese and *corvina* (sea bass). For dessert, try the crepes *Suchard,*
filled with ice cream and topped with hot-fudge sauce. ✉ *Espigón 4,
Costa Verde,* ☎ *01/447–0057. AE, DC, MC, V.*

$$ ✕ **Alfresco.** This is one of Lima's largest restaurant chains specializ-
★ ing in seafood. Modern decor enhances the taste of excellent ceviche,
available here at reasonable prices. ✉ *Carabaya 445; Malecón Balta
790, Miraflores; Santa Luisa 295, San Isidro,* ☎ *Lima, 01/445–4311;
Miraflores, 01/444–7962; Santa Luisa, San Isidro, 01/422–8915 or 01/
440–5099. AE, DC, MC, V.*

Steak House

$$–$$$ ✕ **El Rincón Gaucho.** Nestled on a Miraflores hillside above the ocean,
in a rustic setting of rough-hewn wood ceilings, cowhides hanging on
the walls, and other such touches, this steak house serves tender Argentine beef. The best bet is the *parrillada,* a mixed grill of steaks, beef-
heart kebabs, kidney, liver, pork chops, chicken legs, and blood pudding;
the order for two will feed three or four people. ✉ *Parque Salazar,* ☎
01/447–4778. AE, DC, MC, V.

Vegetarian

¢ ✕ **Bircher-Benner.** In a colonial-style house amid gardens on a quiet
street in Miraflores, choose from a wide variety of meatless international and Creole dishes. The salads are excellent, as is the soy-pro-
tein *cau-cau.* ✉ *Schell 598,* ☎ *01/444–4250. AE, V.*

Lodging

Although Lima has an abundance of hotels, rates are relatively high
here—it helps to book through a tour operator. The more expensive
establishments tend to have the best rooms with the most amenities,
but these can be overpriced, yet the least expensive hotels can be run-
down and noisy. The strong competition for tourists and business
travelers, therefore, has led mid-range hotels and hostels to provide the
best value and service—and often the most interesting ambience. Many
offer complimentary breakfasts, airport shuttles, cable TV, and direct
phone lines. As downtown Lima has become safer, older hotels that

are within walking distance of the main attractions have been refurbished and are again a viable place to stay. Most of the new hotels are located along the ocean in the Miraflores and San Isidro districts, 15–20 minutes from downtown by taxi.

$$$$ 🏨 **Los Delfines.** First impressions of this luxury hotel come at the entrance, where a large tank that extends all the way into the lobby bar is home to a pair of dolphins. Although rooms here are on the small side, they're comfortably furnished. On site is the Knossos gourmet restaurant, complete with Hindu decor; soft piano music entertains both guests and dolphins in the bar. A convenient location in San Isidro and golf privileges at the Lima Golf Club are additional draws to stay. ⊠ *Los Eucaliptos 555,* ☎ *01/211–9000,* ℻ *01/211–9002. 207 rooms, 24 suites. Restaurant, bar, coffee shop, pool, health club, casino. AE, MC, V.*

$$$$ 🏨 **Hotel Sheraton & Casino.** The most luxurious of the downtown hotels has three executive floors and the largest casino in Peru. Rooms are decorated in subdued colors and surround an open atrium. This is a good location for business travelers, with eight large meeting rooms and a business center that includes computers for guests. However, the hotel is also a favorite with tourists, as its location offers direct access to the expressway leading to San Isidro and Miraflores and it's within walking distance of Lima's historical district. ⊠ *Paseo de la República 170,* ☎ *01/315–5000,* ℻ *01/315–5015. 438 rooms, 10 suites. 3 restaurants, bar, coffee shop, pool, tennis court, casino. AE, DC, MC, V.*

$$$$ 🏨 **Miraflores Park Plaza.** This luxury, all-suites hotel has windows with spectacular views of the Pacific ocean all around, while paintings by Peruvian artists brighten the rest of the walls. Cuisine and decor of the dining establishments on site cover the world: French, Italian, and Peruvian dishes in the Ambrosia restaurant; international cuisine in the Park Café; and a cozy, classic English theme in the Dr. Jekyll and Mr. Hyde bar. ⊠ *Av. Malecon de la Reserva 1035,* ☎ *01/242–3000,* ℻ *01/242–3393. 81 suites. 2 restaurants, 2 bars, pool, health club. AE, MC, V.*

$$$$ 🏨 **Sonesta Lima Hotel El Olívar.** Located along what was once an olive
★ grove—the park still has the original olive press—in one of Lima's most beautiful parks, this luxurious hotel is just the place to relax in San Isidro. The beauty and tranquility of the natural setting is continued indoors, where green plants thrive in the lobby and restaurants. The La Botija Cafe has an excellent breakfast fruit bar; seafood and a salad bar are featured at later meals. Refined Italian cuisine is served along with soft piano music in the I Vitrali restaurant, where diners have a view of the park. The Ichi Ban Bar completes the international dining offerings with its vast selection of sushi. ⊠ *Pancho Fierro 194,* ☎ *01/221–2121,* ℻ *01/221–2141. 134 rooms, 11 suites. 3 restaurants, bar, pool, business services. AE, DC, MC, V.*

$$$$ 🏨 **Swissôtel.** This deluxe hotel, which opened in 1996, is renowned
★ for its outstanding service. A convenient location in the commercial area of San Isidro is another draw for travelers who enjoy relaxing in
— contemporary elegance. ⊠ *Via Central 150, Centro Empresarial Real,* ☎ *01/421–9888,* ℻ *01/421–4360. 244 rooms, 48 suites. 2 restaurants, bar, café, pool, tennis court, health club. AE, DC, MC, V.*

$$$ 🏨 **Gran Hotel Bolívar.** Although this decades-old institution on the Plaza San Martín is being remodeled, it retains the timeless grandeur of the days when Hemingway stayed here; look for the magnificent stained-glass dome over the rotunda lobby. Rooms are on the plain side, though, with the staid look of old English decor. The English Pub, which is also being refurbished, has the best Pisco Sours in town. ⊠ *Plaza San Martín,* ☎ *01/428–7672,* ℻ *01/428–7674. 272 rooms, 5 suites. 2 restaurants, bar. AE, DC, MC, V.*

$$ ⊞ **Hostal La Castellana.** A favorite with foreign visitors, this neo-colonial hotel in Miraflores is built around a sunlit courtyard. Rooms have whitewashed walls, wood-shuttered windows, and industrial carpeting. Reservations should be made at least a month in advance. ⊠ *Grimaldo del Solar 222,* ☎ *01/444–4662,* FAX *01/446–8030. 29 rooms. Restaurant. AE, DC, MC, V.*

$$ ⊞ **Hotel Antigua Miraflores.** This small, elegant hotel, built in a cen-
★ tury-old mansion, has impeccable, friendly service and close proximity to downtown Miraflores. The colorful art that adorns the lobby and rooms is for sale. ⊠ *Grau 350 (5th block of Pardo),* ☎ *01/241–6116,* FAX *01/241–6115. 15 rooms. Restaurant, bar. AE, DC, MC, V.*

$$ ⊞ **Posada del Inca.** With parks, shops, restaurants, and nightclubs within walking distance, this San Isidro hotel is a good value. This is also an excellent choice for those who use wheelchairs, as ramps allow guests to freely move through the halls. Suites have kitchenettes, and a buffet breakfast is included. The hotel is conveniently located close to downtown and 20 minutes from the airport. ⊠ *Av. Libertadores 490,* ☎ *01/222–4373,* FAX *01/222–4370. 45 rooms, 5 suites. Restaurant, bar. AE, DC, MC, V.*

$ ⊞ **Kamaná Hotel.** One of the best values in downtown Lima, this hotel
★ combines excellent service with tasteful room decor using colorful local textiles. Though street-side rooms are nicer, choose a room away from the street if traffic noise bothers you. ⊠ *Camaná 547,* ☎ *01/426–7204,* FAX *01/426–0790. 44 rooms. Restaurant, bar. AE, DC, MC, V.*

Nightlife and the Arts

Nightlife

The most popular nightlife in Lima is at *peñas,* bars that offer Creole music (romantic ballads and waltzes that combine native Peruvian, black, and Spanish influences) or folk music, and occasionally jazz. This scene centers on Barranco, especially around the municipal square. Most peñas exact a cover charge and are open from around 9 or 10 PM until the wee hours of the morning.

For details on nightlife in Lima, look for *The Lima Herald,* published in English and available at newsstands on Fridays. Also check with *The Lima Times,* a small, monthly English newspaper with travel information. *El Comercio,* a Spanish daily paper, carries a complete listing of events. Ask at your hotel for the free *Peru Guide,* which is full of current information on restaurants, hotels, and things to see.

BARS

Amnesia is the trendiest of the bars that line Sánchez Carrión Boulevard, a pedestrian street off one corner of Barranco's municipal square. ⊠ *Bul. Sánchez Carrión 153,* ☎ *01/477–9577. Closed Sun.–Wed.*
El Ekeko, an artsy bar, has a bookshop attached. Different musical groups play each night, covering the gamut of genres from Calypso to jazz. ⊠ *Grau 266,* ☎ *01/477–5823. Closed Sun.*
La Noche, at the far end of Sánchez Carrión Boulevard, is the quintessential Barranco bar, offering videos and artistic events from time to time and a youthful, noisy atmosphere all the time. ⊠ *Bolognesi 307, Barranco,* ☎ *01/477–4154. Closed Sun.*

PEÑAS CRIOLLAS

Los Balcones (⊠ Grau, in front of the Parque Municipal, Barranco, ☎ no phone) specializes in música negra, the black variant of música criolla.
Manos Morenos (⊠ Pedro de Osma 409, Barranco, ☎ 01/467–0421) is probably the most upmarket of the peñas, with a $15 cover charge and a menu that features typical (expensive) Peruvian dishes. The atmosphere tends to be rather staid, however, in comparison with

other peñas. **Sachún** (✉ Ejército 657, Miraflores, ☎ 01/441–0123) is one of middle-class Lima's favorite spots for dancing and drinking; it's closed on Sunday.

FOLK-MUSIC PEÑA

La Estación de Barranco (✉ Pedro de Osma 112, Barranco, ☎ 01/467–8804) in an old train station, is frequented by locals and tourists, except on Sundays, when it's closed.

DANCE CLUBS

Casually elegant women (21 and up) and men (24 and up) dance in the oceanfront **Costa Verde Pub Discoteque** (✉ Playa Barranquito, Barranco, ☎ 01/441-3367) Thursday–Saturday from 10 PM to 5 AM. Make a reservation and put on your best duds for a night at **Zoe,** (✉ Pasaje Tello 181, ☎ 01/444–3056) a dance club, bar, and lounge, near Parque Kennedy in Miraflores. It's open from Thursday to Saturday; happy hour is from 9 PM–11 PM.

The Arts

GALLERIES

Miraflores is full of art galleries that show the works of Peruvian and occasionally foreign artists. The **Alliance Française** (✉ Arequipa 4595, Miraflores, ☎ 01/241–7014) puts on a variety of shows. **Formas** (✉ Larco Herrera 1150, Miraflores, ☎ 01/446–1313) is a private gallery with works for sale by contemporary Peruvian artists. The **Galería Municipal de Miraflores** (✉ Corner of Larco Herrera and Diez Canseco, ☎ 01/444–0540, ext. 16) sponsors exhibitions of sculpture, photography, and paintings. Another private gallery selling local works is **Trapecio** (✉ Larco Herrera 743, Mezzanine 2, Miraflores, ☎ 01/444–0842).

MUSIC AND THEATER

Lima does not often attract the top-notch musicians and theatrical performances of Buenos Aires or Mexico City. However, there are a number of venues where you can catch performances of classical and popular (including Latin American) music.

From April through November, the **Auditoria de Santa Ursula** (✉ Santo Toribio, San Isidro, ☎ 01/440–7474) hosts classical-music concerts by international performers; the shows are usually sponsored by the Sociedad Filarmónica (✉ Porta 170, Office 301, Miraflores, ☎ 01/445–7395). The **Centro Cultural Juan Parra del Riego** (✉ Pedro de Osma 135, Barranco, ☎ 01/477–4506) holds Peruvian and Latin American music performances. The **Centro Cultural Ricardo Palma,** in the Municipalidad de Miraflores (✉ Larco Herrera 770, ☎ 01/446–3959), sponsors cultural events throughout the week, including cinema, poetry, and music recitals.

The **Instituto Cultural Peruano Norteamericano** (✉ Corner of Angamos and Arequipa, Miraflores, ☎ 01/446–0381) offers a range of cultural events, including theater, jazz, classical, and folk music.

Outdoor Activities and Sports

Beaches

The coast south of Lima is strung with beaches—a bit arid by foreign standards but often backed with massive, glistening sand dunes. The ocean is rough and cold; lifeguards, as well as such amenities as bathrooms and changing rooms, are nonexistent. At most beaches, however, you will find kiosks with cold drinks and fresh seafood. Two of the most popular beaches are El Silencio, 42 km (26 mi) from Lima, and Punta Negra, 50 km (31 mi) away. Continue south and you'll reach Pucusana, a cliff-top fishing village 60 km (37 mi) from Lima. The beaches are all off the Pan-American Highway out of Lima; exits are well marked.

Whatever you do, and no matter how many local people you see doing it, *do not* swim at the beaches in Lima itself. The Peruvian Ministry of Health and the municipality of Lima regularly warn people that the beaches are highly contaminated; however, a clean-up is in progress. The beaches south of the city are not polluted.

Bullfighting

Bullfighting in Peru, which takes place in October and November, is Spanish style (that is, the bull is killed) and is quite popular. The spectacle takes place at the **Plaza de Acho** (⊠ Cajamarca, Block 5, ☎ 01/482–3360) in Rimac. The **Museo Taurino** (⊠ Cajamarca, Block 5, ☎ 01/482–3360), which has bullfighting artifacts and paintings by Goya, is next door. It's open Monday through Saturday 9 to 4.

Soccer

Peru's leading teams are Alianza, Universitario, Sport Boys, and Cristal. Games are played year-round at the **Estadio Nacional** (⊠ Calle José Díz, ☎ 01/433–6366).

Shopping

Areas and Malls

On Avenida La Paz in Miraflores, crafts, jewelry, and antiques stores abound. The block-long, cobblestone, pedestrian-only street of **El Suche** has a wide variety of sweaters and crafts. The newest shopping center is the **Jockey Plaza,** in the Monterrico (Surco) district, which has cinemas, fast-food restaurants, and exclusive shops.

Specialty Shops

CLOTHING

Alpaca III (⊠ Camino Real Shopping Center, Level C, Shop 36, San Isidro, ☎ 01/441–9294) specializes in alpaca-wool outfits.

HANDICRAFTS

One of the better shops for Peruvian crafts is **Antisuyo** (⊠ Tacna 460, Miraflores, ☎ 01/447–2557), which sells only traditional goods from many Peruvian cultures. **Artesanías del Perú** (⊠ Jorge Basadre 610, San Isidro, ☎ 01/440–1925) and **Kuntur Huasi** (⊠ Ocharán 182, below 2nd block of Benavides, Miraflores, ☎ 01/444–0557) both sell traditional and modern crafts, including alpaca and leather goods, ceramics, and paintings. **Las Pallas** (⊠ Cajamarca 212, parallel to 6th block of Grau, Barranco, ☎ 01/477–4629) specializes in traditional, original, and antique crafts. The store is closed on Sundays; on other days, just knock.

FABRIC

Silvania Prints (⊠ Diez Canseco 376, Miraflores; Conquistadores 915, San Isidro, ☎ Miraflores, no phone; San Isidro, 01/422–6440) sells colorful Peruvian designs created in 1956 by Silvia Lawson. These were inspired by Peru's archaeological treasures and contemporary Indian crafts, and they are printed by hand on pima cotton. You can buy fabric by the meter, along with clothing, scarves, purses, and tablecloths.

JEWELRY

Branches of the Brazilian firm **H. Stern Jewelers,** which carries upscale gold and silver jewelry with Peruvian designs, are in the Hotel El Olívar (⊠ Pancho Fierro 194, ☎ 01/221–2121), the Miraflores César's Hotel (⊠ Av. La Paz, at Av. Canseco, ☎ 01/444–2121), the Sheraton (⊠ Paseo la Republica 170, ☎ 01/433–3320), and the Museo del Oro (⊠ Av. Alonso de Molina 1100, ☎ 01/345–1292). Local silver designer and manufacturer **Dellapina** (⊠ Chacas 264, Breña, ☎ 01/424–6016) schedules "silver tours" of its factory.

Lima A to Z

Arriving and Departing

BY AIRPLANE

Jorge Chávez International Airport (☎ 01/575–1712) is 10 km (6 mi) north and a 20–30 minute drive from downtown Lima or the residencial and hotel districts of Miraflores and San Isidro. After collecting your bags and before exiting into the terminal, there are desks where you can purchase an "official" $20 taxi ticket. The vehicles are in excellent condition and drivers often even wear suits. If you choose to brave bargaining for a taxi outside—albeit at half the cost of an official taxi—set the price before you get in, as there are no meters. Those on tours can arrange airport transfers with the tour operator. *See* Peru A to Z, *below,* for information on international arrivals and departures and on domestic carriers and flights.

BY BUS

Current bus schedules and information about advance purchases are best obtained by calling or inquiring at your hotel or travel agency. In a pinch, taxi drivers usually know embarkation points. Lima's bus stations include **Cruz del Sur** (⊠ Jirón Quilca 531, ☎ 01/424–1005 or 01/424–0589), **Ormeño** (⊠ Javier Prado Este 1059, ☎ 01/472–1710; Carlos Zavala 177, ☎ 01/427–5679), and **Tepsa** (⊠ Paseo de la República 129, ☎ 01/427–5642).

BY CAR

Driving in Lima is not recommended, but if you are determined to do so, Lima is on the Transcontinental Carretera Panamericana (Pan-American Highway). Panamericana Norte (north) becomes the ring road known as the Vía de Evitamiento, which hits a large and well-marked cloverleaf at Avenida Javier Prado. Javier Prado leading west will take you into San Isidro; from there it is easy and safe to get to Miraflores and the beach area of Barranco, where visitors are more likely to stay.

From Panamericana Sur (south), you can get off onto Avenida Benavides heading east, which takes you directly to Miraflores, or again, onto Javier Prado. If you are crazy enough to drive into the center of Lima, go past the Javier Prado cloverleaf to Evitamiento. Once you cross the Rimac River you will be north of the center, and there are several bridges (Ricardo Palma, Santa Rosa) that cross back down into the center. Paseo de la Republica is a wide expressway that leads from downtown, in front of the Sheraton Hotel, all the way to the ocean, with exits for San Isidro, Miraflores, and Barranco.

Getting Around

BY BUS

Regular buses, the school bus-size *micros,* and the van-size *combis,* offer frequent service, are inexpensive ($1–$1.50 for any distance), and stop at almost every corner. You must flag them down, but it is often difficult to tell where they are going. Ask before you board. One local who provides safe, hourly transportation is Luis Calderón Orrego (☎ 01/940–7603)

BY CAR

Lima's main streets are in good condition, but heavy traffic and the scarcity of traffic lights make driving a harrowing experience. If you must drive, park in a lot to protect the car against theft, or hire a child who offers *"cuidar su carro"* (to look after your car). Pay him or her 50¢–$1 when you return and find your car intact.

Most rental-car agencies also offer the services of a driver, a good solution for those who want the freedom of a car without the driving responsibility. Agencies with 24-hour service at the Lima airport include **Avis** (☎ airport 01/575–1637, Miraflores 01/446–3156), **Budget** (☎ airport 01/575–1674, Miraflores 01/444–4546, San Isidro 01/442–8703), **Hertz** (☎ airport 01/575–1590 or 01/575–0912, ext. 4154; San Isidro 01/442–4475), and **National** (☎ airport 01/575–1111, Lima 01/433–3750, San Isidro 01/222–1010).

BY TAXI

Reliable taxi service from Lima's major hotels is about double what you will pay in the streets. It's best to ask the fare first, but if you don't, the yellow cabs seem to be consistent, charging between $1.50 and $2 between Lima centro and the districts. Besides the address, try to have some point of reference to where you're going, because you can't count on drivers knowing the location of a particular street.

Radio taxi fares are not negotiable. Local radio-cab companies include **Taxi Fono** (☎ 01/422–6565), **Taxi Metro** (☎ 01/437–3689), and **Taxi Seguro** (☎ 01/438–7210).

Contacts and Resources

BANKS AND CURRENCY EXCHANGE

Money changers congregate around Plaza San Martin in front of the Gran Hotel Bolivar. It is safest to change money in banks, hotels or money-changing houses, but if you do change on the street, check their figures. ATMs are now quite common in banks, even in small towns, but try to use the ATM during banking hours—there have been reports of a counterfeit bill or two spilling out of the machine. **Banco Latino** (✉ Main office: Av. Paseo de la Republica 3505, San Isidro, ☎ 01/422–1290) has branches all over Lima with ATM machines; call for hours. On Avenida Jose Pardo, a main commercial street in Miraflores, there's a bank on nearly every block.

When changing money, you will usually be asked to show your passport. Changing houses include **Universal Money Exchange** (✉ Av. Jose Pardo 620, Of. 6, Pardo Shopping Center, ☎ 01/446–1409), which is open weekdays 9–6 and Saturdays 9–1. **P & P, S.A.** in Miraflores (✉ Benavides 735, ☎ 01/444–2404) is open weekdays 9:30–5; the Lima branch (✉ Av. La Colmena 805, ☎ 01/428–8877) is open weekdays 9:30–5 and Saturdays 10–1; and the Monterrico branch (✉ Jockey Plaza Mall, ☎ 01/437–0004) is open Monday through Saturday 9:30–10 and Sundays and holidays 11–10. The American Express office (✉ Belén 1040, ☎ 01/330–4482 or 01/330–4485) is in central Lima.

EMERGENCIES

General emergencies: ☎ 011/5114. **Hospital:** Clinica Anglo-Americana (24 hrs) ✉ Alfredo Salazar, San Isidro, ☎ 01/221–3656. **Pharmacy:** Farmacia Deza ✉ Av. Conquistadores 144, San Isidro, ☎ 01/441–5860. **Tourist Police:** ☎ 01/225–8698 or 01/225–8699.

ENGLISH-LANGUAGE BOOKSTORES

On Barranco's main plaza, **Ekeko** (✉ Av. Grau 266, ☎ 01/247–3148) is a café, bar, and restaurant with a good selection of books. At night it's called **El Portal de Barranco** and turns into a cultural center.

The *Lima Herald* is an English-language newspaper published every Friday. There are a variety of English-language guides and maps for sale throughout the city.

TELEPHONES, THE INTERNET, AND MAIL

Peruvian coins are used in public phones, but you can also make local or international calls with phone cards. **Telefónica del Perú** (✉ main office: Jr. Carabaya 933, Plaza San Martin, ☎ 01/433–1616) has branches throughout the city where you can purchase phone cards.

Most major or luxury hotels have room connections for laptop computers, as well as business offices with computers for guest use. Even many small hotels will send E-mail messages, usually for a fee. Internet services are available by the hour at the **Phantom Café** (✉ Avenida Diagonal 344, Miraflores, ☎ 01/242–7949), which is open Mondays 6–11 PM and Tuesday through Sunday 11 AM–midnight. **Cinco Continentes** (✉ Calle Los Canarios 110, La Molina,☎ 01/348–0792) is open daily from 8 AM–11 PM. **Cybersandeg** (✉ De la Union St. 853, downtown, ☎ FAX 01/427–1695) is open Monday through Saturday 8:30 AM–10 PM and Sundays 10:30–6. The cost per hour is usually $1–$2.

As for sending mail, Lima's main post office (✉ Av. Conde de Superunda, ☎ 01/427–8531) is a large pink building on the street behind the Government Palace, just off Plaza Mayor; it's open Monday through Saturday 8–8 and Sundays 9–1. The branch at the Jorge Cháez International Airport is open 24 hours. There are also branches in Miraflores (✉ Av. Petit Thouars 5201, ☎ 01/445–0697) and San Isidro (✉ Av. Libertadores 325, ☎ 01/440–0797). For overnight and international mail, Miraflores has **DHL** (✉ Av. Los Castanos 225, Miraflores, ☎ 01/221–2474), open weekdays 8–9, Saturday 9–5, and Sunday 9–1; **Federal Express** (✉ Av. Jorge Chávez 481; and **UPS** (✉ Av. Pasaje Tello 241, ☎ 01/447–2222), open weekdays 9–6 and Saturday 9–1.

TOUR OPERATORS

Two recommended agencies in Lima are **Coltur** (✉ Av. José Pardo, Miraflores, ☎ 01/241–5551) and **Condor Travel** (✉ Av. Mayor Amando Blondet 249, San Isidro, ☎ 01/442–3000). **Lima Tours** (✉ Belén 1040, Box 4340, ☎ 01/424–5110) arranges bus tours that include access to some of Lima's finest colonial mansions. **Peru Chasquitur S.A.** (✉ Mariano de los Santos 183, San Isidro, ☎ 01/441–1279, 800/327–3573 in the U.S.), who take their name from the *chasquis,* relay runners who carried messages on the royal roads for the Incas, arrange tours throughout the country. **Receptour** (✉ Av. Alvarez Calderón 155, San Isidro, ☎ 01/221–3341) conducts excursions throughout Peru. Other notable operators are **Setours S.A.** (✉ Comandante Espinar 229, Miraflores, ☎ 01/447–1190) and **Solmartour S.A.** (✉ Av. Grau 300, Miraflores, ☎ 01/444–1313).

VISITOR INFORMATION

PromPerú (✉ Calle Uno Oeste, Edificio Mitinci, 14th floor, San Isidro, ☎ 01/224–3126, www.peruonline.net) is the organization for tourism promotion and planning; English- and Spanish-language information and current literature are available. Note: Visitors must show a photo ID at the gate for a tag (passports are preferred). **Trafico** (www.traficoperu.com) provides an excellent information directory for sites, restaurants, and hotels throughout Peru.

THE NORTH COAST

More than a thousand years ago, long before the Inca empire raised its great stone fortresses and built Machu Picchu in the southern Andes, civilizations flourished in the desert and fertile river valleys of Peru's north coast. Many of their carefully planned irrigation systems that turned the desert into productive agricultural land are still in use today. These early cultures are often referred to as the *Moche* or *Mochica,* a derivative of *Muchik,* an ancient language spoken on the north coast.

The Spanish who settled these lands built their own cities—Trujillo, Chiclayo, and Lambayeque, among others—neglecting the spectacular agricultural and architectural achievements of earlier days. Although voracious looters, or *huaqueros,* have stolen many of the gold, silver, and ceramic treasures left in the ruins, modern archaeologists sifting through the sand still occasionally make miraculous finds. The tomb of the Lord of Sipán, discovered intact in 1987, is the most famous example.

Trujillo

561 km (350 mi) northwest of Lima on the Pan-American Highway.

A lively metropolis that vies with Arequipa for the title of Peru's "Second City," Trujillo was founded in 1534 by the Spanish, who named it in honor of conquistador Francisco Pizarro's Spanish hometown. More than any other city in Peru, Trujillo maintains much of its colonial charm, especially within the confines of Avenida España, which encircles the heart of the city, replacing a 30-ft-high wall erected in 1687 to protect it from pirates. A piece of the wall still stands at the corner of Estete and España.

Trujillo is also considered the cultural capital of Peru, with its many festivals, including the National *Marinera* (dance) Competition, an international ballet festival, the *Caballos de Paso* (Peruvian Pace Horse), a contemporary art biennial, and the Totora raft exhibition.

The heart of the city is the broad **Plaza de Armas,** fronted by the 17th-century cathedral and surrounded by the *casonas* (colonial mansions) that are Trujillo's architectural glory.

Like most of the restored colonial museums in Trujillo, **Casa Urquiaga** was saved by a bank whose offices now occupy part of the building. You can visit this early 19th-century mansion on the Plaza de Armas, with its baroque patio and fine collection of furniture, mirrors, paintings, and pre-Columbian ceramics. ✉ *Pizarro 446,* ☎ *044/245382.* ☜ *Free.* ◷ *Mon.–Sat. 9–1 and 5–7.*

A block away is the **Casa del Mayorazgo de Facala,** built in 1709. Constructed of thick adobe and covered with white stucco, this is a classic example of Trujillo colonial architecture. The open courtyard is surrounded by cedar columns and holds a colonial carriage. Notable features inside the house are the Moorish-style carved-wood ceiling and the upstairs balcony, with its celosías. ✉ *Banco Wiese, Pizarro 314,* ☎ *044/256600.* ☜ *Free.* ◷ *Mon.–Sat. 9–1 and 5–7.*

Trujillo declared its independence from Spain on December 29, 1820, in the nearby **Casa de la Emancipación** (Emancipation House), which has an interesting scale model of colonial, walled Trujillo. ✉ *Pizarro 610,* ☎ *044/246061.* ☜ *Free.* ◷ *Mon.–Sat. 9–1 and 5–7.*

Another colonial home open for visits is the **Palacio Iturregui** (✉ Pizarro 688), sometimes described as the most beautiful neoclassical home in South America. **Casa Bracamonte** (✉ Independencia 441) is where the general who procured Trujillo's independence lived.

El Carmen Church and Monastery, built in 1725, displays valuable altarpieces and colonial art. Nearby is the **Pinacoteca,** an art museum with paintings brought from Ecuador in the 17th century. ✉ *Av. Colon, at Av. Bolivar.* ☜ *Admission.* ◷ *Museum: Mon.–Sat. 9–1.*

The **Archaeological Museum of the National University of Trujillo,** in an old colonial home, has been expanded and contains artifacts recovered from tombs. ⊠ *Jr. Ayacucho and Jr. Junín 682.* 🖾 *Admission.* ⊘ *Daily 8–1.*

Most travelers who visit this splendid Spanish-colonial city, however, come to marvel not at the works of Spain but at those built nearby by the Moche and Chimú—gigantic temple pyramids and a sprawling city made solely of mud.

On the Pan-American Highway, 10 km (6 mi) southeast of Trujillo, several notable ruins stand across the Moche river in **Campiña de Moche.** Although monument-building city-states existed in the environs of present-day Trujillo more than a thousand years before Christ, Moche was the first to spread its influence over much of the north coast. Their capital city and two enormous adobe pyramids were built around AD 100, but their influence continued for 600 more years.

The **Huaca del Sol** (Pyramid of the Sun) stands over 130 ft high and measures 1,105 ft by 520 ft—and is only half as big as it once was. At least 140 million bricks went into building this, the largest extant adobe-brick structure in the New World. Scattered around the pyramid's base are "signature bricks," with distinctive hand, finger, and foot marks that identify the community whose labor produced the bricks for their Moche lords. Archaeologists believe that the pyramid served as an imperial palace and mausoleum, a center of political and religious power. Once a stronghold of untold treasures, it has been stripped clean over the centuries by huaqueros. So great were its riches that in 1610 the Spanish diverted the Moche River to wash away the pyramid's base and lay bare the bounty within.

The smaller **Huaca de la Luna** stands southward across a 1,635-ft-wide plain that once held a bustling royal city. This Pyramid of the Moon is painted with anthropomorphic and zoomorphic reliefs. If you visit on a weekday with a guide, you may be allowed to observe archaeologists as they uncover multicolored murals and friezes. A small tourist center is at the entrance. 🖾 *Admission.* ⊘ *8–1.*

In the northern sector of the city, the privately owned **Museo Cassinelli** is in, of all places, the basement of a gas station. Among the most spectacular objects in the 2,800-piece collection, which covers pre-Columbian ceramics that date from 1200 BC through the Inca period, are realistic Moche portrait vases with surprisingly sensitive renderings of individuals. ⊠ *Av. Nicolás de Piérola 607,* 🖀 *044/232312.* 🖾 *Admission.* ⊘ *Mon.–Sat. 9–1 and 3:30–6:30.*

Three hundred years after the Moche civilization faded, a new empire, the Chimú, arose in its place. Although much less famous than the Inca empire, which conquered it in 1470, the Chimú empire, called Chimor, was the second-largest in pre-Columbian South American history. It stretched along 1,000 km (620 mi) of Pacific coastline, from Chillón, just north of present-day Lima, to Tumbes, on the border with Ecuador.

Chán Chán, Chimor's huge, adobe-brick capital city whose ruins lie 5 km (3 mi) west of Trujillo, has been called the largest mud city in the world. It once held boulevards, aqueducts, gardens, palaces, and some 10,000 dwellings. Within the city were nine royal compounds, one of which, the Tschudi (named for a 19th-century Swiss explorer of the ruins), has been partially restored and opened to the public. Although wind, huaqueros, and the occasional rain storm have damaged the city, its size—20 square km (8 square mi)—still impresses, and the walls are studded with adobe friezes. If you don't have a guide, you can hire one at the entrance to the site for a few dollars. ⊠ *Carretera Huanchaco,* 🖀 *no phone.* 🖾 *Admission.* ⊘ *Daily 9–5.*

Two km (1¼ mi) west of Trujillo is the Chimú **Huaca Esmeralda** (Emerald Pyramid). Like other pyramids on the north coast, this ancient temple mound served as a religious ceremonial center and burial site for the priest-kings. The highlights of the ruins are the two stepped platforms and unrestored friezes of the fish, seabirds, waves, and fishing nets that were central to the life of the Chimú. ⊠ *Av. Mansiche exit, Pan-American Hwy. N,* ☎ *no phone.* ☒ *Admission.* ☉ *Daily 9–5.*

Jarringly out of place in an urban setting north of Trujillo's center is the restored **Huaca El Dragón** (Pyramid of the Dragon), also known as the Huaca Arcoiris (Rainbow Pyramid). This early Chimú walled temple pyramid is decorated with the repeating figure of a mythical creature who looks like a cross between a giant serpent or dragon and a rainbow. ⊠ *Pan-American Hwy. N, La Esperanza district,* ☎ *no phone.* ☒ *Admission.* ☉ *Daily 8–5.*

OFF THE BEATEN PATH

EL BRUJO COMPLEX – Near the mouth of the Chicama river, 35 km (22 mi) northeast of Trujillo, archaeologists are at work on the El Brujo Complex, one of the latest Chimú sites to be discovered. They have unearthed some striking raised murals, many of which bear their original bright colors. The complex is called *El Brujo* (the witch man) because it was once used by the witches of Chicama and shows evidence of human sacrifice. ☒ Admission.

Dining and Lodging

Trujillanos are big on fish dishes. Ceviches of fish or shellfish are extremely popular, as is *causa,* a cold casserole of mashed potatoes molded around a filling of fish, ají, and onions and topped with olives and slices of hard-boiled egg. *Cabrito al horno* (roast kid), *seco de cabrito* (stewed kid), and *shámbar,* a bean stew, are other local specialties. Restaurants in Trujillo tend to be casual, making up for their lack of decorative pizzazz with outstanding seafood and comida criolla. Bringing picnic food bought in Trujillo for trips to isolated sites like Chán Chán is a good idea. Buy fresh food in the market in the sixth block of Gamarra; other foodstuffs are available in the bodegas in downtown Trujillo.

If you plan to visit Trujillo during the local festivals in January and October (☞ *Peru A to Z, below*), be sure to make hotel reservations at least a month in advance.

$$$ ✕ **Las Bóvedas.** This quiet, elegant restaurant in the Hotel Libertador
★ (☞ *below*) has a vaulted brick ceiling—a *bóveda* is a vaulted chamber—and arched, plant-filled wall niches. The house specialty is the local delicacy *shámbar,* a thick soup made with beans, split peas, wheat grains, bacon, and pork and garnished with *canchita* (semipopped corn) and ground hot-pepper sauce. ⊠ *Independencia 485,* ☎ *044/232741. AE, DC, MC, V.*

$$ ✕ **Club Colonial.** French and creole dishes, featuring the fruits of the sea, are expertly prepared in this old colonial *casona* across from the Plaza de Armas. ⊠ *Av. Grau 272, Huanchaco,* ☎ *035/1703. MC, V.*

$$ ✕ **De Marco.** Right on the street, this noisy but cheery spot, popular
★ with locals and tourists for its excellent comida criolla and Italian dishes (don't miss the homemade gelato), has paneled walls decorated with original local art. Try the *tacu tacu,* a typical coastal dish of rice and beans, with seco de cabrito. ⊠ *Pizarro 725,* ☎ *044/234251. MC, V.*

$$ ✕ **El Mochica.** Set in an old casona, in a long, open hall with white-washed walls and chandeliers, this seafood restaurant has a down-at-the-heels flair. A typical meal starts with an industrial-size portion of spicy, fresh ceviche de lenguado, followed by a *picante* (seafood sauce

served over rice) of *camarones* (shrimp) or other *mariscos* (shellfish). ⊠ *Bolívar 462,* ☎ *044/252457. No credit cards. No dinner.*

$ ✕ **Lucho Del Mar.** This informal, lively restaurant on Huanchaco Beach can be noisy, especially if there's a large party on the mezzanine, but the view of the ocean is superb and it's right in the center of the action. Dishes are typical of Huanchaco, with lots of seafood concoctions. ⊠ *Av. Victor Larco 600,* ☎ *044/461460. MC, V.*

$ ✕ **Il Valentino.** This cozy spot cooks up pizza to satisfy every taste and also serves excellent pasta and garlic bread. ⊠ *Orbegoso 224,* ☎ *044/ 246643. MC, V.*

$ ✕🏨 **Hostal Bracamonte.** Across the wide boulevard from the Huanchaco beach, this pleasant hotel has a pool, beautiful landscaping, and a small restaurant serving, among other things, home-baked pies. ⊠ *Jr. Los Olivos 503,* ☎ *044/461162,* ꜰꜲꭗ *044/1266. 25 rooms. Restaurant, bar, cafeteria. AE, MC, V.*

$$$ 🏨 **Gran Hotel El Golf.** This attractive, low-level building curves around a large pool and is surrounded by landscaped gardens. The hotel is conveniently located 10 minutes from the center of town and 15 minutes from the airport. ⊠ *Los Cocoteros 500, Urb. El Golf,* ☎ *044/282515,* ꜰꜲꭗ *044/282231. 118 rooms, 4 suites. Restaurant, piano bar, 9-hole golf course, tennis court. AE, MC, V.*

$$$ 🏨 **Hotel Libertador.** The former Hotel de Turistas on the Plaza de
★ Armas has been splendidly renovated to blend modern comfort and colonial elegance. The patio pool, surrounded by a hummingbird-filled garden, is especially delightful. Rooms are decorated with modern paintings that interpret pre-Columbian designs, locally tooled leather and wood, and wrought-iron wall lamps. ⊠ *Independencia 485,* ☎ *044/232741,* ꜰꜲꭗ *044/235641. 75 rooms. Restaurant, bar, café, pool, sauna. AE, DC, MC, V.*

$$ 🏨 **Los Conquistadores.** This all-suites hotel near the Plaza de Armas is a good value, with an American breakfast included in the rate. Suites are large, and the decor is modern and comfortable. ⊠ *Diego de Almagro 586,* ☎ *044/244505,* ꜰꜲꭗ *044/235917. 50 suites. Restaurant, bar, sauna. AE, MC, V.*

$$ 🏨 **Hotel Los Jardines.** Though an inconvenient 10 minutes by taxi from the Plaza de Armas, this "garden hotel" in the northern district of Los Jardines lives up to its name: Each room is a simple, uncarpeted bungalow with a big picture window that looks out on gardens and trees. ⊠ *Av. América Norte 1245,* ☎ *044/222258,* ꜰꜲꭗ *044/254721. 60 rooms. Restaurant, bar, pool, tennis court. AE, DC, V.*

$ 🏨 **Pullman Hotel.** Located in Trujillo's original center on a cobblestone arcade, this spotless hotel has a small travel agency and offers free entry to a club on nearby Huanchaco Beach. ⊠ *Pizarro 879,* ☎ *044/203624,* ☎ ꜰꜲꭗ *044/205448. 42 rooms. Restaurant, bar. AE, DC, MC, V.*

Nightlife and the Arts

NIGHTLIFE

Two popular bars that offer Creole folk peñas into the wee hours are **Canana** (⊠ San Martín 791, ☎ 044/232503) and **Luna Rota** (⊠ Av. América Sur 2119, ☎ 044/228877). The area around the Central Market, on the sixth block of Gamarra, is full of movie theaters.

THE ARTS

Local newspapers, such as *La Industria,* have listings of cultural events at the **Instituto Cultural Peruano Norteamericano** (⊠ Corner of Húsares de Junín and Venezuela, ☎ 044/232512) and the **Alliance Française** (⊠ San Martín 858, ☎ 044/231232).

Outdoor Activities and Sports

BEACHES

Peru's beaches are all on the Pacific Ocean, which means water can be on the chilly side—it's warmest between December and April. Cool temperatures don't deter surfers, however, or the cowboys who race in their *caballitos de mar* (little sea-horse boats; they're made from bundles of totora reeds). **Huanchaco Beach,** 15 km (9 mi) from Trujillo, has a long, protected cove, and is a pleasant, laid-back, beach town where many Peruvians spend their summer holidays.

Shopping

Throughout Trujillo you may be approached by vendors who offer cheap *huacos,* usually hollow ceramic figurines, vases, or bowls. It is illegal to export genuine pre-Columbian artifacts, but anything offered you is probably not authentic. Stands at the Huaca El Dragón and Chán Chán offer more expensive imitations.

A good place for ceramic and apparel bargains is along Avenida España, especially where it intersects with Junín. Stalls display the locally made leather goods for which Trujillo is nationally famous, particularly shoes, bags, and coats. Don't hesitate to haggle. For made-to-order boots or leather belts, check out **Creaciones Cerna** (⊠ Jr. Bolognese 567, ☎ 044/205679). A daily market with all sorts of souvenirs thrives on Huanchaco Beach.

Chiclayo

219 km (131 mi) north of Trujillo.

A lively commercial center, Chiclayo is both prosperous and easygoing. It is not as big as Trujillo, nor does it have as much preserved colonial architecture, but it is surrounded by pre-Columbian sites. The Moche and Chimú both had major administrative and religious centers in the area, as did a third culture, the Lambayeque (Sicán), which flourished from about AD 700 until Chimor conquered it, around 1370.

A minor tourism boom was set off in 1987 with the discovery of the unlooted tomb of the Lord of Sipán. Chiclayo now provides a comfortable base from which to visit the tomb and other archaeological sites, as well as the famed Brüning Museum, all of which are in such nearby towns as Sipán and Lambayeque (☞ *below*).

Dining and Lodging

Chiclayo is most famous for a pastry called the "king kong" (sometimes bastardized into *kinkón*), a large, round, crumbly cookie with *manjar blanco*—a very sweet filling made of sweetened or condensed milk and cinnamon boiled down until it is very thick and caramel-color—in the center. Another local specialty is *pescado seco* (dried fish, often a ray), used in stews or fried.

$$$ ✕ **Restaurante Típico Fiestas.** The decor might seem garish at this restaurant in the Tres de Octubre district, but the main attraction is the chef, whose showcases of *comida norteña* (typical food of northern Peru) in Lima have earned him kudos. ⊠ *Salaverry 1820,* ☎ *074/ 228441. MC, V. No dinner.*

$$ ✕ **Las Tinajas.** A woven-cane roof, wicker chairs, and ceiling fans give this simple restaurant a tropical flair. The seafood is top-notch. ⊠ *Elías Aguirre 952,* ☎ *no phone. No credit cards. No dinner.*

$ ✕ **Charro Panzón.** Salsa replaces ají at this cute restaurant, where the Mexican owner cooks delicious (but heavy) flautas, tacos, and parrilla *à la Mexicana.* You'll enjoy the homemade tortillas. ⊠ *Virgilio D'Allorso 15–2 (across from Hotel Sipán),* ☎ *074/227342. V.*

$$ \quad \boxed{\text{I}} \text{ **Garza Hotel.** A pleasant poolside patio and bar, very friendly staff,}$$
★ and a central location make this hotel one of the nicest in Chiclayo. The restaurant, with stucco walls, a fireplace, and brass chandeliers, serves excellent regional cuisine. ⊠ *Bolognesi 756,* ☎ *074/228172,* FAX *074/228171. 71 rooms. Restaurant, pool. AE, DC, MC, V.*

$$ \text{ **Gran Hotel Chiclayo.** Extensive remodeling has given this luxury busi-}$$
ness hotel a new shine. The amenities, central location, and competitive prices make it excellent for tourists, too. ⊠ *Federico Villareal 115,* ☎ *074/234911,* FAX *074/223961. 129 rooms, 16 suites. 2 restaurants, bar, pool, beauty salon, casino. AE, DC, MC, V.*

$ 🖫 **Inca Hotel.** Although the outside is nothing to stare at, the rooms are clean, with indoor-outdoor carpets and ceiling fans. Rooms that don't face the street have less light but are quieter. ⊠ *Luis Gonzales 622,* ☎ *074/235931,* FAX *074/227651. 69 rooms. Restaurant, casino. AE, DC, MC, V.*

Nightlife and the Arts

NIGHTLIFE

The most popular spot in town for Creole peñas is **El Señorío.** ⊠ *Balta and Manuel María Izaga,* ☎ *no phone.* ☉ *Peñas nightly at 10:30.*

Shopping

Chiclayo's Central Market on Avenida Balta is famed for its colorful mix of fresh food and live animals, ceramics, weavings, and a variety of herbs and charms from local *curanderos* (folk healers). If the subject interests you, ask at one of the stalls for an evening session with a local shaman.

Sipán

35 km (21 mi) south of Chiclayo.

The Moche **Tomb of the Lord of Sipán**—saved from huaqueros in 1987 by renowned Peruvian archaeologist Walter Alva in a dramatic last-minute rescue—stands in the Huaca Rajada, a pyramid near the town of Sipán. The trip out takes you past sugar plantations and through the fertile valley of Chancay to a huge, fissured mud hill that is actually the Huaca Rajada. The smaller hill beside it is part of the pyramid, once connected to the bigger one by a platform. The three major tombs in the smaller mound date from about AD 290 and earlier, and together form one of the most complete archaeological finds in the Western Hemisphere.

The most extravagant funerary objects were found in the tomb of the so-called Lord of Sipán, now filled with replicas placed exactly where the original objects were discovered. The originals are now on permanent display in the Museo Brüning in Lambayeque (☞ *below*). The dig at the complex is ongoing, and other tombs continue to be excavated. ☎ *No phone.* 🎫 *Admission.*

A 15-minute drive east from Sipán is the 8th-century Moche capital **Pampa Grande,** a 6-square-km (2½-square-mi) archaeological complex that contains one of the largest pyramids ever built in the Andes, the 178-ft-high **Huaca Fortaleza** (Pyramid of Strength). Pampa Grande marked the final years of the Moche empire, and for unknown reasons the city was put to the torch and abandoned near the beginning of the 9th century. ☎ *No phone.* 🎫 *Admission.*

Túcume

35 km (21 mi) northwest of Chiclayo.

With the decline of the Moche civilization, legend has it that a lord called Naymlap arrived in the Lambayeque Valley, accompanied by his wife and retinue and a fleet of balsa boats. Naymlap and his 12 sons founded the Lambayeque dynasty, whose cities included the immense pyramid complex of Túcume. Here, from the heights of the natural rock hill **El Purgatorio,** you can see 26 giant adobe pyramids and dozens of smaller ones spread across a desert sprinkled with hardy little algarobo (mezquite) trees. Norwegian explorer Thor Heyerdahl, of *Kon-Tiki* fame, has built a home here and directs excavations of the pyramids. ☎ *No phone.* 🖾 *Admission.*

Lambayeque

12 km (7 mi) north of Chiclayo.

The Moche, Lambayeque, and other pre-Inca cultures, including the Cupisnique, Chavín, Moche, Chimú, and Sicán, are explored at the
★ **Museo Brüning** in Lambayeque. Directed by Walter Alva, it is one of the finest archaeological collections in Peru. Among the highlights are the Sipán treasures; a group of ceramic frogs from 1200 BC; a small gold statue of a woman known as the *Venus de Frías,* 100 BC–AD 300; and Moche and Sicán ceramics. The museum has excellent interpretive displays, but the legends are in Spanish. ⊠ *Huamachuco and Atahualpa,* ☎ *074/282110.* 🖾 *Admission.* ⊘ *Mon.–Fri. 8:30 AM–6:30 PM; weekends and holidays 9–6.*

The North Coast A to Z

Arriving and Departing

BY AIRPLANE

AeroContinente (☎ 01/242–4242 in Lima, 044/244042 in Trujillo, 074/229916 in Chiclayo, 877/359–7378 in the U.S.) has daily flights to Trujillo and Chiclayo.

BY BUS

Cruz del Sur (⊠ Jirón Quilca 531, ☎ 01/424–1005), **Ormeño** (⊠ Javier Prado Este 1059 or Carlos Zavala 177, Lima, ☎ 01/427–5679), and **Tepsa** (⊠ Paseo de la República 129, Lima, ☎ 01/427–5642) have bus service from Lima to Trujillo and Chiclayo. **Expreso de Chiclayo** (⊠ Grau 653, Lima, ☎ 01/428–5072) has service from Lima to Chiclayo. When planning your trip, call, check with a local travel agency, or have your hotel call for up-to-date bus schedules.

BY CAR

The major highway that serves the north coast—and the only route from Lima—is the Pan-American Highway.

Getting Around

BY BUS

Always ask for information on which buses and bus stations are the best for where you're going, and where the best places are to catch a *collectivo* or *combi*—not all stations are in safe areas. **Emtrafesa** (⊠ Av. Miraflores 127, Trujillo, ☎ 044/24–3981; ⊠ Av. Colón, at Av. Bolognesi, Chiclayo, ☎ 074/23–4291) plies between Trujillo and Chiclayo, a three- to four-hour trip. Two main bus terminals in Trujillo are **Oltursa** (⊠ Av. del Ejército 342, ☎ 044/26–3055) and **Expreso Cruz del Sur** (⊠ Av. del Ejército 285, ☎ 044/26–1801).

BY CAR

Hiring a driver and guide through a reputable travel agency or tour operator such as **Trujillo Tours** (☞ Tour Operators and Travel Agents, *below*) is an efficient way to see the ruins around Trujillo; some of the sites are isolated, and one can easily get lost on the unnamed little back roads that lead to them.

BY TAXI

Taxis are a good way to get wherever you're going around Trujillo. The average fare from the city center to the airport or Huanchaco Beach is $3.50.

Contacts and Resources

BANKS AND CURRENCY EXCHANGE

Banks are usually open weekdays 9–1 and 4–6:30 and Saturdays 9–noon. There is an ATM in the **Banco de Lima** (✉ Av. Jiron Pizarro, at Av. Orbegoso, ☎ 044/26–1030). **Banco Wiese** (✉ Av. Pizarro 314, ☎ 044/25–6600), in an old mansion, is a place to cash traveler's checks and get cash with a MasterCard. For cash with an American Express card, try **Banco de Credito** (✉ Av. Gamarra 562, ☎ 044/24–2360). On the corner of Pizarro and Gamarra, **Banco Internacional del Peru - Interbanc** (✉ Av. Pizarro, at Av. Gamarra, ☎ 044/25–7506) gives cash on Visa cards.

EMERGENCIES

General emergency: ☎ 105. **Hospitals:** Hospital and Clinic Av. Mansiche 702. **Hospital Regional** ☎ 044/232861. **Peruvian Americana Clinic** ☎ 044/231261. **Pharmacy:** Av. Mansiche 864, ☎ 044/232281. **Police:** ☎ 044/233181.

ENGLISH-LANGUAGE BOOKSTORES

Two bookstores that sell books and magazines in English are **Libreria Peruana** (✉ Jr. Pizarro 505, ☎ 044/23–2521), open daily 9–1 and 4:30–9, and **Libreria Ideal** (✉ Jr. Orbegoso 548, ☎ 044/20–1976), open daily 9–9:30. Both are near the Plaza de Armas.

TELEPHONES, THE INTERNET, MAIL

National or international calls can be made from your hotel or from public phones using phone cards or coins. For phone calls or faxes, go to the central office of **Telefónica del Peru** (✉ Av. Bolivar 658). Mail can be sent or received at the **Post Office** (✉ Av. Independencia 286, ☎ 044/24–5941). For sending packages, try **DHL** (✉ Av. Pizarro 318, Of. 103, ☎ 044/23–3630).

TOUR OPERATORS AND TRAVEL AGENTS

Condor Travel (✉ Av. Pizarro 576, ☎ 044/24–4658) offers tours to the ruins and nearby areas. **Trujillo Tours** (✉ Diego de Almagro 301, ☎ 044/23–3091) organizes tours to the ruins around Trujillo.

You can hire English- and Spanish-speaking private guides through both the **POLTUR** (Tourism Police) and **CARETUR** (Tourism Chamber) offices (☞ Visitor Information, *below*). Guides normally charge around $15–$20 for a day-long tour, excluding transportation and entrance fees to museums and ruins, and will tailor tours to suit your interests. These guides normally utilize cheap public buses or taxis, so costs are minimal. For very thorough tours, contact Clara Bravo and her husband Michael White, two **English-speaking guides** (✉ Huayna Capac 542, ☎ 044/24–3347, FAX 044/24–8644), with excellent information about the community and the nearby ruins.

VISITOR INFORMATION

Chiclayo: POLTUR (✉ Saenz Peña 830, ☎ no phone), **Indiana Tours** (✉ Colón 556, Chiclayo, ☎ 074/242287, FAX 074/240833), and **Sipan Tours** (✉ Manuel M. Izaga 399, Chiclayo, ☎ 074/208816) have details on and arrange tours and guides for the ruins outside Chiclayo.

Trujillo: POLTUR (✉ Independencia 630, ☎ no phone), **CARETUR** (✉ Independencia 628, ☎ 044/258216), **Touring and Automobile Club** (✉ Argentina 258, Urbanización El Recreo, ☎ 04/423–2635), and **Trujillo Tours** (☞ *above*) provide information and organize tours and guides for the ruins outside Trujillo.

THE SOUTH

Traveling south out of Lima, the Pan-American highway cuts through the desert with an occasional view of the Pacific Ocean. At first you might think it a wasteland, but then a sudden patch of green appears— a thriving farm, a field of cotton, a patch of date palms. Add water to the desert and anything will grow. The highway leads to Pisco, which is mainly a jumping-off point for the Paracas National Reserve (☞ *below*) and Chaco, where boats depart for the Ballestas Islands (☞ *below*).The Paracas Peninsula is around 245 km (152 mi) from Lima. If you're driving, you can take a short detour to one of the seaside resorts or stop at San Vincente de Cañete, at Km 144, capital of an oasis in the valley of the Cañete River. You won't miss much if you skip Pisco and stop overnight at Paracas instead, or even continue to Ica. For Pisco or Paracas, turn off the highway at Km 232. The best place to stay is the **Hotel Paracas** (☞ Paracas National Reserve, *below*) on the bay, but if you choose to spend the night in Pisco, you can pick one of two equally featureless hotels within a couple of blocks of each other.

Paracas National Reserve

15 km (10 mi) south of Pisco.

The Paracas National Reserve, founded in 1975, was the first marine conservation center in Peru. Although some of the park is on the desert sands, the rest is in the ocean surrounding the Ballestas Islands. A fault discovered on the ocean floor here is the point where two currents— "El Niño, warm waters coming from the north, and cold waters from the south—merge, creating an ideal condition for the plankton and phytoplankton that feed an abundance of fish species. The reserve also has one of the highest concentrations of marine birds in the world.

Besides wildlife areas and beaches, the park encompasses two fishing villages and a small port, Puerto General San Martín. The mainland portion of the reserve is best explored by car in a half-day tour (from $6 to $20, depending on the agency), or by taxi (about $20). Many people explore here in the afternoon after visiting the islands early in the morning. Mainland tours usually include about an hour to lounge on one of the beaches, and can be booked at the same time as tours to the Ballestas Islands.

At the Paracas Reserve office you will find maps and the **Julio Tello Museum,** devoted to natural history and archaeology. Humans have lived in the area for thousands of years, and the Paracas culture, which produced some of the most exquisite and colorful woven textiles in pre-Columbian America, reached its height between 700 BC and AD 100. The finest examples of Paracas textiles are in the Museo Histórico Regional in Ica (☞ *below*) and the Museo de Antropología de Arqueología in Lima (☞ Sights to See *in* Lima, *above*).

Adjacent to the museum are the **flamingo colonies** (best seen in June and July). Though hard to detect from a distance, a ½-km (¼-mi) walk will take you within viewing distance of the magnificent birds (ask a museum staff member to point them out).

Twelve km (8 mi) from the museum is the **Mirador de Lobos** (Wolf Lookout), a cliff that overlooks a sea lion colony. Just before the cliff are beaches that can be reached on foot, but don't swim alone—there are no lifeguards on duty.

Offshore lie the **Ballestas Islands**, also part of the reserve. Here seals and sea lions stake a noisy claim to the beaches below rocky outcrops white with guano of thousands of sea birds. Pelicans, boobies, terns, cormorants, and even the small Peruvian penguins vie for nesting space on the rocks in a flapping, rowdy mass of feathers. Tourists are not allowed on the islands, which are knee-deep in bird guano, but your boat will be surrounded by friendly sea lions. Most hotels in Pisco and Paracas provide information about tours to the islands. The usual length of tours is two hours ($10–$15); most leave at 8 or 10 AM.

Dining and Lodging

At Chaco, just before the national reserve and the starting point for most cruises to the Ballestas Islands, the seafront is lined with simple fish restaurants. The food is excellent, prices are cheap, and portions are enormous.

$$ ✕⌂ **Hotel Paracas.** This resort near the entrance to the Paracas National Reserve has flower-bedecked bungalows with terraces that overlook the bay. The restaurant is excellent but expensive. The hotel can arrange for fishing trips in Paracas Bay (no license required), where mackerel is the most likely catch, including transportation, a hook, and a roll of fishing line—more sophisticated tackle is unavailable. ⊠ *Av. Paracas 173,* ☎ *034/221736; 01/446–5079 or 01/446–5138 in Lima,* 🅵🅰🆇 *034/225379; 01/447–6548 in Lima. 105 rooms. Restaurant, bar, pool, miniature golf, tennis court, boating, travel services. AE, DC, MC, V.*

$ ⌂ **Hostal El Mirador.** Cement walls and linoleum floors give this place little charm, but the owner is helpful, the rooms are clean, and the setting overlooks the Bahía de Paracas. ⊠ *Ribera del Mar (entrance to Chaco),* ☎ *034/665842; 01/432–5757 in Lima,* 🅵🅰🆇 *01/432–0109 in Lima. 35 rooms. Restaurant, bar, pool. V.*

Outdoor Activities and Sports

BEACHES

The Paracas National Reserve has lovely, if isolated, beaches. There are no lifeguards, so only strong swimmers should swim outside the sheltered bays. There are also jellyfish in these waters. The beaches are often deserted but are becoming popular with limeños on weekends, especially in summer. Try not to go alone. Get a map from the reserve office before you try **La Mina** or **Yumaque** beaches, or the longer, straighter beach at **Arquillo.**

BICYCLING

Although some of the roads are in poor shape, they are largely free of traffic, which makes the reserve one of the few suitable bicycling spots along the Peruvian coast. A map of the reserve is available in the park office. The prevailing northerly winds, especially in the afternoon, can make the outward trip rough going but the return a breeze. The **Viento Sur** agency at the Hotel Paracas (☞ *above*) rents mountain bikes.

Ica

56 km (35 mi) southeast of Paracas.

Ica is a fertile patch of green in the middle of mountains of sand dunes where the sun is constantly shining. It is best known as the center for Peru's wine and pisco production, and as a base for visiting the Lines of Nazca and the Paracas National Reserve. It was the seat of the Nazca culture, noted for its 3rd- to 8th-century weavings and ceramics. The Spaniards brought date palms and grape vines to Ica in the 16th and 17th centuries, and Ica became famous for its gracious lifestyle and its high-stepping *caballos de paso* (Peruvian-bred, smooth-gaited horses).

Ica is in the heart of **Peruvian wine country.** Chilean and Argentine wines generally outstrip Peruvian wines in quality and price, but some of the finer Peruvian labels hold their own in competition, and Peruvians disparage Chile's attempts to produce pisco. The winery most convenient to visit is the **Bodega Vista Alegre** (✉ La Tinguiña, Km 2, ☎ 034/231432), about 3 km (2 mi) outside of town. Eight km (5 mi) farther is the **Bodega Tacama** (✉ La Tinguiña, Km 10, ☎ 034/231422), which produces some of Peru's best wines; try the Blanco de Blancos. About 24 km (15 mi) south of Ica, the **Bodega Ocucaje** (✉ Pan-American Hwy. S, Km 336, ☎ 034/220215, 01/440–7977 in Lima) is attached to a tourist center, principally comprised of a hotel and restaurant. At all bodegas you can see wine presses and cellars and taste samples. The **Bodega El Carmen** has an old press made from a tree trunk, where wine was once made by stomping on the grapes. Old-time workers still claim this method made the purest wine.

★ Ica's **Museo Histórico Regional** is a small but important museum that covers a thousand years of pre-Columbian history and possesses some splendid Paracas textiles, still colorful despite the passage of centuries. From the Nazca culture, which developed in the Nazca, Pisco, and Ica Valleys between 200 BC and 600 AD, a remarkable ceramic sculpture shows a pregnant princess pointing at her belly—and in profile shows the fetus in her womb. There is also an interesting exhibit comparing ancient diseases with those of today. ✉ Ayabaca s/n, ☎ 034/23–4383. 🎟 Admission. ⊙ Mon.–Sat. 9–6:30, Sun. 9–2.

Dining and Lodging

If you plan to visit Ica during the Vendimia, the wine harvest festival in March, be sure to reserve a hotel room at least a month in advance. One treat available only during the festival is *cachina,* a partially fermented wine.

$$ ✕ **El Otro Peñoncito.** This friendly, relaxed restaurant serves Peruvian and international cuisine. The fettuccine *con ajo* (with garlic), with a spicy sauce similar to that used in the traditional papa a la huancaina, is intriguing. ✉ Bolívar 255, ☎ 034/233921. DC, MC, V.

$ ✕ **Tacuba.** This small, stylish café has an unbeatable burger special and excellent breakfasts. It also delivers to your hotel (minimum order S/11). ✉ Lima 446, ☎ 034/214295. V.

$$ ✕🏨 **Hotel Las Dunas.** A cluster of whitewashed buildings amid sand
★ dunes, this colonial-style resort is a favorite getaway for Peruvian families. All rooms are spacious and have balconies that overlook lush lawns—the suites, with their sunny, built-in courtyards and whirlpools, are outstanding. Dine poolside or in the gazebo on such dishes as flounder with seafood sauce or a spicy lomo saltado of steak, tomatoes, potatoes, and onions. Flights over the Nazca lines leave from the hotel's airstrip ($130). ✉ La Angostura 400, ☎ 034/256224; 01/442–3090 in Lima, 𝖥𝖠𝖷 034/256231; 01/442–4180 in Lima. 109 rooms. Restaurant, bar, cafeteria, 2 pools, sauna, 9-hole golf course, tennis court, exercise room, horseback riding, dance club. AE, DC, MC, V.

$ 🏨 **El Carmelo Hotel & Hacienda.** At this colonial-style, slate-roof hotel 5 km (3 mi) from downtown Ica, rooms are in several buildings around a flower-filled courtyard. An inviting garden house has wicker furniture and a 19th-century wine press. ✉ Pan-American Hwy., Km 301, ☎ 034/232191, 𝖥𝖠𝖷 034/263–4556. 40 rooms. Restaurant, bar, pool. DC, V.

$ 🏨 **Hostal Olimpia.** This spotless, friendly, budget hotel near the Plaza de Armas is a good place to camp out for a single night, though rooms might be too small for some travelers. Even the shared bathrooms are sparkling clean. ✉ Lima 446, ☎ 034/234731, 𝖥𝖠𝖷 034/225894. 20 rooms with shared baths. AE, MC, V.

Nightlife and the Arts

Ica is a quiet town. For any nightlife, ask the locals or inquire at your hotel to see if there's anything special happening.

Shopping

For wines or pisco, buy either in the bodegas themselves, where the wines are slightly discounted, or in the liquor stores clustered around the Plaza de Armas. Look for Tacama's Blanco de Blancos and Occucaje's rich red Fond du Cave.

Huacachina

5 km (3 mi) southwest of Ica.

A 10-minute drive from downtown Ica will take you to the oasis of Huacachina, a green gem nestled amid towering sand dunes. In the 1920s, wealthy Peruvians flocked to this resort beneath the palm trees that crowd the shores of a lagoon. After decades of decline, the resort is on the upswing. Locals come regularly to take a refreshing dip, or even to ski down nearby sand dunes on locally rented "sandboards." Don't swim alone, however—the lagoon's soft, sandy bottom reportedly makes swimming hazardous.

Lodging

$$ 🏨 **Hotel Mossone.** Set in a century-old mansion that was a plush re-
★ sort hotel in the 1920s and was fully restored in 1989, this hotel is a soothing trip back in time. The rooms are built around an interior garden patio. Dining is on a veranda that overlooks the Huacachina Lagoon. Come for lunch or dinner if you can't spend the night; the comida criolla is excellent, especially the papa a la huancaina. Weekday rates are reduced. ⊠ *Balneario de Huacachina,* ☎ *034/213630; 01/442–3090 in Lima,* 📠 *034/236137. 53 rooms. Restaurant, bar, pool. AE, DC, MC, V.*

Nazca

120 km (75 mi) southeast of Ica.

Nazca has one of the world's great archaeological mysteries: the glyphs known as the Nazca lines, drawn on the rock-strewn Pampa de San José, 20 km (12 mi) north of the city. Ranging from straight lines to geometric forms to stylized human and animal shapes, these giant markings—the straight lines vary in length from ½ km to 8 km (⅓ mi to 5 mi)—have stirred the popular imagination for decades.

Although theories about the origin of the Nazca lines include extraterrestrial intervention, two main schools of thought prevail in the archaeological community. One—propounded by German mathematician Maria Reiche, who came from Germany to Peru in 1932 as a governess and dedicated her life to studying and preserving the lines—suggests that they were part of an immense astronomical calendar noting the rainy season in the highlands (where Nazca's water supply originates) and seasonal changes in the region's climate. The other theory suggests that the lines were physically and ritually related to the flow of water from the mountains to and across the Nazca plain. What is clear is that between BC 1900 and AD 660, the Nazca people etched the lines through the desert's dark surface layer into underlying, lighter-color soil and then outlined them with stones. The most famous drawings are in the shapes of animals, such as the 150-ft-long spider and the 300-ft-long monkey.

The best way to see the lines is from the air, in one of the many small planes that offer 45-minute overflights from the Nazca airport for approximately $50–$60 per person, though fare wars among airlines allow travelers to bargain for prices upon arrival in Nazca. Eager tour guides waiting at the bus stop book overflights for as low as $35 that include visits to a fascinating local cemetery where mummified remains were left exposed by looters, and small, family-run gold and ceramics factories.

Overflights are not recommended for anyone prone to airsickness. In addition to turbulence, the small planes make continuous tight turns over the lines. Early morning is best, when there is less wind, and as a precaution, do not eat or drink anything for an hour prior to the flight. Local flights can be booked at hotels, travel agencies, or at the airlines' headquarters (☞ The South A to Z, *below*).

Dining and Lodging

¢ ✕ **La Taberna.** With a ceiling fan over the bar and live music most Saturdays, this popular criollo restaurant is so laid-back that guests sign their names on the walls. ⊠ *Lima 321,* ☎ *034/522322. AE, MC, V.*

$$ ⊞ **Hotel de la Borda.** Surrounded by cotton fields in an 80-year-old hacienda, this somewhat isolated, old-fashioned hotel 1½ km (1 mi) from Nazca airport offers a taste of coastal farm life. Rooms are set around a huge garden. Recreational options include horseback riding and excursions in a Jeep or by mountain bike. ⊠ *Pan-American Hwy. S, Km 447,* ☎ *01/440–8430 in Lima,* ☎ FAX *034/522576. 39 rooms. Restaurant, pool. DC, MC, V.*

$$ ⊞ **Hotel Maison Suisse.** Conveniently located by the airport, this hotel has gardens and comfortable, if somewhat graceless, rooms with old-fashioned wood furniture. The suites have hot tubs. ⊠ *Pan-American Hwy. S, Km 445,* ☎ *01/242–6615 in Lima,* ☎ FAX *034/52–2434. 32 rooms, 6 suites. Restaurant, pool. AE, DC, MC, V.*

$$ ⊞ **Hotel Nazca Lines.** Rooms are laid out around a courtyard oasis and
★ decorated with wrought-iron headboards and charcoal drawings; many rooms have a sun porch beside a sunken garden. Meals are served on a tiled walkway beside the courtyard. Flight tickets for the Nazca lines are sold here. ⊠ *Jirón Bolognesi,* ☎ *034/522293, 01/442–3090 in Lima,* FAX *034/522112. 34 rooms. Restaurant, bar, pool, tennis court. AE, DC, MC, V.*

Arequipa

1,000 km (625 mi) southeast of Lima.

With its bright, clean image and palm trees, Arequipa is reminiscent of a city along Spain's Costa del Sol. Dubbed the "Independent Republic of Arequipa," Arequipeños love their city and are highly resentful of the notion that Peruvian life begins and ends in Lima.

An area prone to earthquakes, the fertile oasis that is now Arequipa was occupied long before the Inca period. Founded in 1540 by the Spanish in the shadow of the snowcapped El Misti Volcano, it is now a thriving city of 1 million that has preserved the best of its forefathers' traditions. At 7,500 ft above sea level, Arequipa enjoys constant sunshine, warm days (averaging 23°C, or 73°F), and comfortable nights (14°C, or 57°F).

Arequipeños call their home "the white city" because of the grayish-white local volcanic rock, *sillar,* used to construct most of its colonial buildings and churches. The city's crowning glory is the **Convento de la Santa Catalina,** a miniature walled town founded in 1579 a few blocks from what is now downtown's Plaza de Armas. It was closed to the public for 400 years, but 20 nuns and three novices live there today; at the Dominican convent's height, there were 400 women residents—

nuns, slaves, and servants. Once inside its high walls, the nuns never left the five-acre convent. Novices had to pay to join the convent, and nuns were separated according to how much they had paid—the higher the "contribution," the more luxurious the cell. Nuns (or their slaves) prepared their own food in the tiny kitchens each cell included. It's a good idea to hire a guide at the entrance (tip about $2.50), but leave some time to wander the twisting streets on your own. Also take time to try the nuns' famous *torta de naranja* (orange cake) or another pastry in the small cafeteria midway through. ⊠ *Corner of Santa Catalina and Ugarte,* ☎ *054/229798.* ☞ *Admission.* ⊙ *Daily 9–4.*

The colonial aristocracy left its mark in the fine mansions of downtown Arequipa, many of which you may enter through high, arched portals. Tall gateways were a 17th-century status symbol, designed to allow the passage of an armored knight on horseback bearing an upright lance. Two particularly striking mansions are open to the public. A block from the Plaza de Armas is **Casa Ricketts** (⊠ San Francisco 108, ☎ 054/215060), once the archbishop's palace. Today it is owned by Banco Continental and contains a small museum that displays colonial paintings, costumes, and furniture. **Casa del Moral** (⊠ Corner of Moral and Bolívar, ☎ 054/213171), a block from Santa Catalina, has a stunning sillar portal carved in a mestizo design (or baroque mestizo, which blends indigenous and Spanish motifs) that combines puma heads with snakes emerging from their mouths and a Spanish coat of arms.

Just off the Plaza de Armas, **La Compañía** (The Society) church consists of a fine series of buildings in traditional Arequipa style. The 1525 church is well worth seeing, and once inside you should also visit the **St. Ignatius** chapel and the former church sacristy, covered from floor to dome with 17th-century paintings from the Cuzco School. The former monastery, now converted into shops, contains two cloisters with carved-stone pillars. They may be entered from General Morán or Palacio Viejo. ⊠ *Corner of General Morán and Alvarez Tomás,* ☎ *no phone.* ☞ *Admission (chapel).* ⊙ *Daily 8–11:30 and 5–8.*

Another religious center is **Monesterio de la Recoleta,** across the Chili River from the city's colonial center. Founded in 1648, the Franciscan monastery comprises a huge ancient library, a museum of the Amazon, a colonial-art collection, and, of course, cloisters and cells. Guides are available (tip about $2). ⊠ *Recoleta 117,* ☎ *054/270966.* ☞ *Admission.* ⊙ *Mon.–Sat. 9–noon and 3–5.*

OFF THE BEATEN PATH

YANAHUARA AND CAYMA – From Recoleta you can take a pleasant stroll through two colonial suburbs. Yanahuara, within walking distance of the city center and home to many *picantería,* casual restaurants open only for lunch (☞ Dining and Lodging, *below*), has an overlook with a stunning view of the city and El Misti Volcano. Uphill from Yanahuara is Cayma, whose 16th-century church is an outstanding example of local colonial architecture. Built of sillar and decorated with mestizo ornamentation, the church, like most of those in Arequipa, avoids the cluttered ostentation typical of colonial churches in other Peruvian cities.

Dining and Lodging

Arequipa's cuisine is a special version of comida criolla. Perhaps the most famous dish is *rocoto relleno*—a very hot pepper, large and red, stuffed with a mixture of meat, onions, and raisins and then baked. The dish may bring tears to your eyes. Comida Arequipeña, however, is not always spicy. There are also rich, succulent stews, like *adobo,* a beef stew particularly popular as a cure for hangovers. Try at least to sample the *cuy* (guinea pig), an Andean staple. You'll find comida arequipeña served at picanterías.

\$\$ ✕ Sambambaias. In a leafy suburb a 10-minute walk from the center
★ of town, this restaurant has pink decor, mirrors, and a pianist that may
all strike you as charming or horribly kitsch, depending on your tastes.
The food is basically international and the service is excellent. ✉ *Luna
Pizarro 304, Vallecito,* ☎ *054/223657. AE, DC, MC, V.*

\$\$ ✕ Tradición Arequipeña. Just outside town, in the Paucarpata district,
this restaurant offers the same traditional dishes and music as the picanterías, served in more comfortable surroundings. Sample the cuy,
served in quite a surprising way! ✉ *Dolores 111,* ☎ *054/426467. AE,
DC, MC, V.*

\$ ✕ El Balcón. On a balcony above the Plaza de Armas, this restaurant
offers international fare that matches the wonderful view. Prices are
surprisingly reasonable for the location. It's also one of the city's few
restaurants open on Sunday. ✉ *Portal San Agustín 111,* ☎ *054/
213473. MC, V.*

\$ ✕ Le Bistrot. The crepes and salads are outstanding at this chic café/bar
connected to the Alianza Francesa. Students often gather here to play
chess, people-watch, and polish their French. ✉ *Santa Catalina 208,*
☎ *054/215579. MC, V. Closed Sun.*

\$ ✕ La Canasta. A bread-lover's dream, this bakery/café offers typical
fresh breads, such as *pan de yema* (regional version of brioche) and
pan de tres cachets (croissant filled with *dulce de leche*), which can be
savored with coffee in a quiet courtyard. ✉ *Jerusalén 115,* ☎ *054/
214900. AE, DC, MC, V. Closed Sun.*

\$\$ ✕🏨 La Posada del Puente. This delightful 22-room hotel with an ex-
★ cellent restaurant is located in a scenic area close to the historical, financial, and commercial areas. It has beautiful gardens and a view of
the Chili River and Misti volcano. The restaurant has excellent pastas
and a fine selection of Peruvian and Chilean wines. ✉ *Bolognesi 101,*
☎ *054/253132. 22 rooms. Restaurant, bar. AE, DC, MC, V.*

\$\$\$ 🏨 Hotel Libertador. This neoclassical luxury hotel is conveniently lo-
★ cated within walking distance of the Plaza de Armas on a sprawling,
flower-filled lawn. The 1940 colonial-style keeps its theme with colonial furniture, and renovations have made it one of the most beautiful hotels in Arequipa. The outdoor swimming pool in the back looks
out at the Misti Volcano. ✉ *Plaza Bolívar, Selva Alegre,* ☎ *054/
215110,* ℻ *054/241933. 92 rooms, 6 suites. Restaurant, bar, pool, exercise room. AE, DC, MC, V.*

\$\$ 🏨 Hostal A'Grada. One of the newest hotels on the Plaza de Armas,
this tiny hostal offers clean, quiet, modern rooms in a colonial setting,
with a balcony restaurant that overlooks the central square. ✉ *Portal
de San Agustín 113,* ☎ *054/219859,* ℻ *054/237334. 9 rooms. Restaurant. AE, DC, MC, V.*

\$\$ 🏨 La Posada del Monasterio. Across from the Santa Catalina Monastery
near the Plaza de Armas, this elegant hotel's courtyard, reception, and
lounge areas are authentically colonial, while the rooms are clean and
modern. Service is outstanding. ✉ *Santa Catalina 300,* ☎ ℻ *054/
215705. 52 rooms. Café. AE, DC, MC, V.*

\$ 🏨 La Casa de Melgar. One of the most unusual hotels in Peru, this fam-
★ ily-owned, colonial hostal has magnificent double rooms with towering sillar ceilings—the suite has an original cookstove. Since there are
no TVs or phones, a night here transports you back in time. Showers
are piping hot, and prices are unbeatable. ✉ *Melgar 108,* ☎ *054/222459.
20 rooms, 1 suite. Cafeteria. No credit cards.*

$ 🏨 **La Casa de Mi Abuela.** A ramshackle complex of houses turned into a hotel, "My Grandmother's House" has lovely gardens and homey, wood-paneled rooms with worn easy chairs. Some even have a small kitchen. Popular with the younger crowd, the hotel is six blocks from the Plaza de Armas. ✉ *Jerusalén 606,* ☎ *054/241206,* 𝔽𝔸𝕏 *054/242761. 32 rooms. Cafeteria, pool, playground. MC, V.*

Nightlife and the Arts

The **Instituto Cultural Peruano Norteamericano** (✉ Melgar 109, ☎ 054/243201) hosts evening concerts of traditional and classical music. The **Alianza Francesa** (✉ Santa Catalina 208, ☎ 054/215579, 𝔽𝔸𝕏 054/218406) schedules concerts and cultural events. An excellent folkloric show begins nightly at 8 PM at **Las Quenas** restaurant (✉ Santa Catalina 302, ☎ 054/281115 or 054/215468). For nightly live blues, try the **BLUES Card Club** (✉ San Francisco 319, ☎ 054/283387).

Shopping

The Plaza San Francisco is the site of a year-round **crafts fair,** commonly known as *el fierro,* open daily until about 8 PM. Jewelry and knick-knacks made of Arequipa agate, as well as local crafts (Arequipa is known for its leather work and alpaca textiles), are sold at boutiques behind the cathedral, on the narrow, pedestrians-only **Pasaje Catedral.** For high-quality, reasonably priced jewelry of silver and inlaid stone, stop at **L. Paulet** (✉ General Morán 118, ☎ 054/287786. **Alpaca 21** (✉ Jerusalén 115, ☎ 054/213425) sells high-quality clothing and accessories. The Ibérica brand of chocolates and sweets, made and widely available locally, is one of the best in Peru. Arequipa is also a good place to buy antiques; try the shops on Jerusalén street.

Colca Canyon

150 km (93 mi) north of Arequipa.

About five hours of rough driving from Arequipa takes you through the Reserva Nacional de Aguada Blanca (Aguada Blanca National Reserve), where herds of graceful, long-necked vicuñas graze, to the magnificent Colca Canyon, which slices a green and fertile trough through rocky, barren mountains. Said to be the deepest canyon in the world, twice as deep as the Grand Canyon, Colca Canyon is a rare blend of natural and man-made beauty.

Once you arrive, be on the lookout for immense Andean condors; the best place to spot them is from the **Cruz del Condor** overlook in mid-canyon. Colca Canyon is also the site of a vast, pre-Columbian agricultural terracing network. Colca's complex of agricultural terraces is, in its way, as impressive as Machu Picchu—especially since, 450 years after the Spanish conquest, they are still in use (the crops are corn and the indigenous, high-protein grains *quinoa* and *kiwicha*). In the canyon's unspoiled Andean villages, people of the Collaguas and Cabana tribes still wear their traditional costumes and embroidered hats. Full-day tours to the Colca Canyon are available; however, if possible, you should spend at least one night.

Dining and Lodging

For a taste of real life in the country, you can stay with families in the villages of Chivay, Coporaque, Ichupampa, and Madrigal, about 200 km (124 mi) from Arequipa. The homestay experience offers a chance to visit ruins with those who know local history, as well as to participate in daily work and festivities. You can make home-stay arrangements with tour operators in Arequipa (☞ The South A to Z, *below*). The cost is about $5 a day for meals and lodging.

$$–$$$ ✕🗔 **Colca Lodge.** Located between the towns of Yanque and Ichupampa, this hotel offers daily excursions into the canyon on foot, horseback, or bicycle, on-site hot springs, and the ultimate in rustic comfort. ✉ *Reservations: Zela 212, Arequipa,* ☎ *054/245199,* 𝖥𝖠𝖷 *054/242088. Restaurant. AE, MC, V.*

$ ✕🗔 **Rumi Llaqta.** This small hotel in Chivay has the feel of a Swiss ski lodge, with comfortable cabins made of stone (the hotel's name means "city of stone"). The restaurant is excellent. ✉ *Huayna Capac, Chivay,* ☎ *054/241974. 28 rooms. Restaurant. No credit cards.*

Outdoor Activities and Sports

TREKKING

Colca Canyon offers spectacular scenery for trekking, especially around Misma Mountain, the source of the Amazon. Most tour agencies in Arequipa, including **G.A. Travel Expert, Condor Travel Arequipa,** and **Transcontinental Tours** (☞ The South A to Z, *below*) can arrange treks.

WHITE-WATER RAFTING

The **Majes River,** which runs through Colca Canyon, is too rough to raft in the central part of the valley. Between January and March, however, the river above Chivay offers excellent conditions. **Transcontinental Tours** (☞ The South A to Z, *below*) can outfit these trips. Below Colca Canyon, toward Camaná, the conditions are once again superb for rafting. **Majes Tours** (✉ Villa Flórida B-7, Cerro Colorado, Arequipa, ☎ 054/255819) outfits trips down this part of the river and offers accommodations at a rustic lodge on the river in Ongoro.

The South A to Z

Arriving and Departing

BY AIRPLANE

Aero Continente (☎ 01/242–4242) has daily round-trip flights from Lima to Arequipa, as does **Lan Peru** (☎ 01/215–1800; 0–801–1-1526 toll-free; 800/526–4246 in the U.S. Airlines with flights from Lima to Ica and Nazca, with 45-minute overflights of the Nazca Lines, are **Aero-Condor** (☎ 01/442–5615) and **Aeroico** (☎ 01/242–6661).

BY BUS

There is good, comfortable bus service throughout the region. From Lima to Pisco, it's 237 km (147 mi), from Lima to Ica it's 303 km (188 mi), from Lima to Nazca it's 443 km (275 mi), and from Lima to Arequipa it's 1,009 km (627 mi). The longest stretch, from Nazca to Arequipa, is 566 km (351 mi) and a 10-hour bus trip. Delays due to mud slides or sand drifts are common. Because bus service and routing are subject to frequent changes, check with your hotel or a Peruvian travel agency for up-to-date information.

Ormeño (✉ Av. Carlos Zavala 177, ☎ 01/427–5679 or ✉ Av. Javier Prado Este 1059, Lima, ☎ 01/427–5679) has excellent buses and a new Royal Class service on many of their routes. **Cruz del Sur** (✉ Jirón Quilca 531, Lima, ☎ 01/427–1311) is another good company to try.

Getting Around

BY AIRPLANE

Aero Continente has daily round-trip flights from Lima, Juliaca (1 hour from Puno), and Cuzco to the Arequipa airport, **Rodríguez Ballón** (☎ 054/443464), 7 km (4½ mi) from town.

It's possible to fly over the Nazca lines in smaller passenger planes that originate in Lima, Pisco, Ica, and Nazca. **Aero Condor** (☎ 034/522424) in Nazca has 45-minute local overflights for around $55, as well as overflights that originate in **Lima** (✉ Juan de Arona 781, San Isidro,

☎ 01/442–5663) and Ica (Hotel Las Dunas, ☞ Dining and Lodging *in* Ica, *above*). The airline also charters special itineraries.

Aero Nazca offers flights from Pisco that can be booked at its offices in the Hotel Paracas (☞ Dining and Lodging *in* Paracas National Park, *above*), and flights from Nazca sold through local travel agencies. **Aero Paracas** offers flights that originate in Lima (⊠ Santa Fe 270, Higuereta, ☎ 01/271–6941), **Pisco** (⊠ Hotel Paracas, ☞ Dining and Lodging *in* Paracas National Park, *above*), and **Nazca** (⊠ Nazca airport, ☎ 034/522688).

Aero Ica (⊠ Hotel Maison Suisse, Nazca, ☞ Dining and Lodging *in* Nazca, *above*; ⊠ Tudela and Varela 150, Lima, ☎ 01/440–1030) offers overflights that originate in Nazca. Though prices fluctuate, approximate costs are $210 from Lima, $130 from Pisco and Ica, and $40 from the Nazca airport. Some travelers shorten their journey south by stopping in Nazca and continuing their trip by land. Because no scheduled flights over the Nazca lines originate in Arequipa, travelers must first go by land to Nazca (unless you charter a flight), and schedule an overflight heading north.

BY BUS

Because bus service and routing are subject to frequent changes, check with your hotel or a Peruvian travel agency for up-to-date information.

BY CAR

Depending on your appreciation of desert scenery, the trip south from Lima via the Pan-American Highway may strike you as starkly beautiful or monotonous. Either way, the government has invested heavily in road repairs and the highway is in generally good condition. The most recommended self-drive route is between Lima, Pisco, Ica, and Nazca; without stops, Lima to Ica is about 4 hours. Rental agencies should provide maps, details on road conditions, and emergency phone numbers.

The **Touring and Automobile Club of Peru** (⊠ Goyeneche 313, ☎ 054/215640; J. M. Manzanilla 523, Ica, ☎ 034/235061) can provide maps and details on drive routes.

BY TRAIN

Four times a week, **ENAFER** runs a night train (10 hours) between Arequipa (⊠ Corner Tacna and Arica 200, ☎ 054/215350) and Puno. Be sure to request the safer, more comfortable Pullman class, which costs about $20. For current schedule information, check with ENAFER or any travel agency. This isn't really recommended except for the adventurous. There is no train service between Lima and the south coast.

Contacts and Resources

BANKS AND CURRENCY EXCHANGE

In Arequipa, **Banco de Crédito** (⊠ Av. San Juan de Dios y General Morán, ☎ 054/22–2112) and **Arequipa Inversiones S.A.** (⊠ Jerusalén 109–C, ☎ 054/23–8033) are options for changing money. In Ica, try **Banco de Crédito** (⊠ Av. Grau 105, ☎ 054/23–5959). In Nazca, there's **Interbanc** (⊠ Av. Arica 359, ☎ 054/2465).

EMERGENCIES

Hospital: Regional Honorio Delgado Hospital ⊠ Av. Carrión, ☎ 054/238465. **Pharmacy:** Farmacia Libertad ⊠ Av. Piérola 108. **Tourist Police** (Arequipa): ⊠ Jerusaléhot linen 315-A, ☎ 054/239888. **Traveler complaint hot line** (24 hrs): ☎ 01/224–7888 in Lima; 0-800-4-2579 toll-free.

The best place for sending mail is Arequipa's **post office** (✉ Calle Moral 118, ☎ 054/422896). You can send courier packages with **DHL** in Arequipa (✉ Av. Santa Catalina 115, ☎ 054/234288), Ica (✉ Av. San Martin 398, ☎ 054/234549), and Nazca (✉ Jr. Fermín del Castillo 379, ☎ 054/52-2016).

TOUR OPERATORS

Most Lima travel agencies offer three- to seven-day minivan tours of Paracas, Ica, and Nazca. Some include Arequipa on the overland tour, but check the total time you'll spend in the bus (the trip south is quite long, especially if continuing to Arequipa) before booking.

Operators that offer overland trips from Lima to southern Peru include **Explorandes** (✉ San Fernando 320, Lima, ☎ 01/442–1738 or 01/445–0532, FAX 01/445–4686), **Hirca Travel** (✉ Bellavista 518, Miraflores Lima, ☎ 01/242–0275), **Lima Tours** (✉ Belen 1040, Lima, ☎ 01/424–5110), **Peru Chasquitur** (✉ Mariano de los Santos 183, San Isidro, Lima ☎ 01/441–1279), or **Receptour** (✉ Av. Alvarez Calderon 155, Suite 304, San Isidro, Lima, ☎ 01/221–3341).

Arequipa and Colca Canyon: Condor Travel Arequipa (✉ Av. Puente Bolognesi 120, Arequipa, ☎ 054/218362) and **G.A. Travel Expert** (✉ Santa Catalina 312, Arequipa, ☎ 054/247722) can help with trips to area sites. **Lima Tours Arequipa** (✉ Santa Catalina 120, ☎ 054/242271, FAX 054/241654) offers an excellent orientation tour of the city. **Santa Catalina Tours** (✉ Jerusalén 400–D, ☎ FAX 054/216991) has overnight trips for about $30 per person. Though buses can be cramped and are prone to flat tires, the guides and overnight lodging are commendable. **Transcontinental Tours** (✉ Puente Bolognesi 132, Arequipa, ☎ 054/213843, FAX 054/218608) conducts more expensive overnight trips in spacious buses with excellent guides and lodging.

Ica: Costa Linda (✉ Prolongación Ayabaca 509, ☎ FAX 034/234251, 01/451–1733 in Lima) and **Pelican Travel Service** (✉ Independencia 156, Galerías Siesta, ☎ FAX 034/225211) offer tours of the city and can arrange trips to Paracas and to the Nazca lines.

Nazca: Information and tours of the pre-Columbian ruins in the area are available from **Alegría Tours** (✉ *Lima 168, Nazca,* ☎ FAX *034/522444).*

Pisco: Guided tours of Paracas National Park and trips to the Ballestas Islands (☞ Exploring, *above*) are run by **Ballestas Travel Service** (✉ San Francisco 249, ☎ 034/53–3095, 01/221–5773 in Lima).

VISITOR INFORMATION

Arequipa: Oficina de Información Turística (✉ Portal de la Municipalidad 112, Plaza de Armas, ☎ 054/21–1021).

Colca Canyon: Basic information about the canyon is provided by the **Tourism Police** in Chivay (✉ Portal de la Municipalidad, Chivay, ☎ no phone). For information on the **Reserva Nacional de Aguada Blanca,** contact the Dirección de Areas Protegidas, **INRENA,** in Lima (✉ Petirrojos 355, Urbanización El Palomar, San Isidro, ☎ 01/441–0425, FAX 01/441–4606).

Paracas: For information on Paracas National Park, contact the Dirección de Areas Protegidas, **INRENA** (☞ *above*).

PUNO AND LAKE TITICACA

Legend has it that Manco Capac and Mama Ocllo, founders of the Inca empire, emerged from the waters of Lake Titicaca. Indeed, as one watches the mysterious play of light on the water and the shadows on the mountains the myths seem tangible. This is the altiplano of Peru, the high plains, where the earth has been raised so close to the sky that the atmosphere takes on a luminous quality. Don't forget, too, that at 3,827 m (12,550 ft) above sea level, Puno will be a challenge to your cardiorespiratory system, so take it easy your first full day there (☞ Health and Safety *in* Peru A to Z, *below*).

Puno

975 km (609 mi) southeast of Lima.

Puno, the capital of the province of the same name, is the folklore capital of Peru. Traits of the Aymara, Quechua, and Spanish cultures who settled on the shores of the lake are evident in the art, music, dance, and dress of the city's inhabitants, who call themselves the "Children of the Sacred Lake." Much of the city's character comes from the on-going practice of ancient traditions: Every month there is a special observance, a parade, a festival, or a celebration. Also, each Sunday at 11 AM at the Plaza de Armas, a patriotic ceremony with bands and high-stepping young men in military uniforms takes place.

Puno is a small town, with a small-town friendliness. Most sites are between Pino Park and the Plaza de Armas, and restaurants and shops line pedestrian-only Jirón Lima, which connects the two. This is a place to enjoy wandering—and there is plenty to see and do in the surrounding areas.

Dining and Lodging

Puno has many small, informal restaurants, especially along Jr. Lima and in some of the hotels. On the menu are typical Peruvian dishes, grilled chicken, pizza, and best of all, fresh *trucha* (trout) and pejerrey from the lake. As for hotels, not all are adequately heated; especially during the winter, ask when you register if there's an electric space heater in your room. Prices can rise as much as 30% during the most popular festivals in February and November—reserve at least a month ahead if you're visiting then. Those on a budget can bargain for a room in a hostal. Most hotels in the small towns outside Puno are run-down and not recommended.

$ ✗ **Apu Salkantay.** This small restaurant on Jr. Lima has fresh food made with natural ingredients; music is nightly from 8 PM. ⊠ *Lima 341,* ☎ *054/623312. MC, V.*

$ ✗ **La Casona.** Larger than it looks from the street, this is a very nice restaurant decorated with antique irons. Eating areas are separated into rooms to create a more intimate atmosphere. ⊠ *Av. Lima 128,* ☎ *054/351106. MC, V.*

$ ✗ **Don Piero.** This clean, colorful restaurant, which proudly displays its local culinary awards, has hunting trophies on the walls and a life-size cutout of Marilyn Monroe to welcome guests at the door. Barbecued chicken and fresh fish (pejerrey and trucha) are house specialties. Local musical groups entertain nightly. ⊠ *Lima 364,* ☎ *054/351766. MC, V.*

$$$ 🏨 **Libertador Hotel Isla Esteves.** This newly remodeled hotel, 5 km (3 mi) from Puno, is now the area's most luxurious. On an island connected by a causeway, it features views of the lake and a look-out point where you can sit and enjoy the sunrise or sunset. All rooms are heated. The hotel is a $3 taxi ride from town. ⊠ *Isla Esteves,* ☎ *054/367780,*

FAX *054/367879. 126 rooms, 11 suites. Restaurant, bar, dance club. AE, DC, MC, V.*

$$ 🏨 **Qelgatani.** This excellent new hotel is on a quiet street two blocks from Jr. Lima. The large rooms have space heaters and sizable baths, and breakfast is included. Local tours and luxury bus trips to Cuzco and Bolivia can be arranged. ⊠ *Tarapaca 355,* ☎ *054/366172,* FAX *054/351052. 14 rooms. Restaurant, coffee shop, travel services. AE, MC, V.*

$ 🏨 **Hostel Italia.** This hotel with an interior garden and rooftop sun terrace has a restaurant that's considered one of the best. The rooms are simple but comfortable, with parquet floors and wood furniture; those on the fourth floor have a view of the lake. ⊠ *Teodoro Valcarcel 122,* ☎ *054/352521,* FAX *054/352131. 30 rooms. Restaurant. MC, V.*

$ 🏨 **Pukara.** On a quiet side street near Jr. Lima, this friendly hostel has private baths and cable TV. ⊠ *Libertad 328,* ☎ FAX *054/368448. 10 rooms. MC, V.*

Nightlife and the Arts

Folk music and dancing are popular in Puno, especially at festival time (☞ When to Go *in* Peru A to Z, *below*). For entertainment closer to the center of town, browse the myriad restaurants and bars along busy Jirón Lima. The **Apu Salkantay Café Internet Bar** (☎ 054/ 351962)—the restaurant of the same name is just down the street— also has a disco, as well as nightly folk music and excellent Pisco Sours. **Casa de Abuelo** (⊠ Tarapaca 395, ☎ 054/368448) has music and folklore dances 8–11 PM Tuesday through Saturday. The $5 admission includes pisco or beer.

Outdoor Activities and Sports

FISHING

Lake Titicaca is stocked with trout and has such native fish as pejerrey (which are bringing the trout to near extinction). There are no tackle shops in Puno, but if you've brought your own fishing gear, you might consider hiring a boatman at the Puno dock, especially on Sunday when everyone goes fishing. An alternative is to contact **Pesquera los Andes** (⊠ Lambayeque 154, ☎ 054/369510).

TREKKING

Consult the local tourism office (☞ Puno A to Z, *below*) about safe mainland treks. One hike out of Puno leads up the road to Juliaca (the continuation of Avenida La Torre). After about 2 km (1 mi) a dirt road that leads to the right is marked with a sign to **Huerta Huaraya,** a peasant community on the lakefront. The walk there is an easy and beautiful one that takes about an hour.

Shopping

Model reed boats, small stone carvings, and sheep-, llama-, and alpaca-wool articles are among the local crafts sold at the **public market** in Puno, near the train station on Calle Cahuide. In fact, some of Peru's highest-quality alpaca sweaters are sold here at excellent prices—don't be fooled by the market's shabby appearance (but do watch your valuables). The government-run **Artesanías Puno** (⊠ Lima 549, ☎ 054/ 351261) sells a modest selection of locally made alpaca items in addition to high-quality alpaca cloth in earth tones. The owners of Apu Salkantay (☞ Dining and Lodging, *above*) also run an artisan shop across the street, and sell books and paintings.

Lake Titicaca

Divided by the border between Peru and Bolivia, Lake Titicaca draws visitors both for its scenery and for the vivid Quechua and Aymara cultures that still thrive on its shores. Surrounded by high, barren mountains, the lake is truly an inland sea, whose opposite shores are often beyond view. Some 3,827 m (12,500 ft) above sea level—and 8,288 square km (3,200 square mi) and 274 m (900 ft) deep—Lake Titicaca is the largest lake in South America and the highest navigable lake in the world. The Bayhía de Puno, separated from the lake proper by the two jutting peninsulas of Capaschica and Chucuito, is home to both the floating Uros Islands and to surface plants that blossom due to water pollution. The lakeshores are lush with totora reeds—valuable as building materials, cattle fodder, and, in times of famine, human food.

The Floating Islands

The most famous excursion from Puno is a trip to the Uros "floating islands," 8–24 km (5–15 mi) offshore. These man-made islands of woven totora reed provide a fascinating look at a form of human habitation evolved over centuries. At the same time, the visit is a bit sad, with adults and runny-nosed children trying to sell you miniature reed boats and weavings. You can walk around the springy, moist islands, hire an islander to take you for a ride in one of his or her reed boats, see the islanders—Uro peoples who have intermarried with the Aymara—weaving and drying fish in the sun, and marvel at the microwave telephone stations on the islands of Torani Pata and Balsero.

Taquile and Amantani

These two lake islands are around an hour by launch from Puno. Unlike the floating islands, which are in the Bay of Puno, Taquile and Amantani are in Lake Titicaca proper and are surrounded by a vast, oceanlike panorama. The proud, Quechua-speaking people of Taquile, where the hills are topped with Inca and Tiahuanaco ruins, weave some of Peru's loveliest textiles. They still wear traditional dress and have successfully maintained the strong community ties and cooperative lifestyle of their ancestors, though there are signs that the island may be losing its unspoiled character under the weight of tourism. Amantani, also with pre-Columbian ruins, has a larger, mainly agricultural population, whose traditional way of life has therefore stood up better to outside pressure.

For a day visit to the islands, it is best to take one of the agency tours, which leaves at around 7:30 AM and includes a visit to one of the floating islands. If you want to make an overnight stay on Taquile or Amantani (which is recommended), travel instead on the slower local ferry, since there are sometimes problems with the agency services if you try to break your trip and continue the next day. The overnight stay costs about $4, and you stay in a local home. Nights can be cold and blankets inadequate, so you may wish to bring a sleeping bag. Bring your own water or water-purification tablets.

Outdoor Activities and Sports

Short hikes can be made to hilltop Inca and pre-Inca Tiahuanaco ruins on the island of Taquile. The island people can give you directions.

Shopping

On Taquile, two **cooperative stores** on the main square sell weavings and the elegantly embroidered clothing the islanders wear. Because the local culture is cooperative, buying crafts anywhere other than the stores is discouraged, as it disrupts equal distribution of wealth among this society. Giving monetary handouts also is discouraged here.

Chucuito

20 km (12 mi) southeast of Puno.

Chucuito is surrounded by hillsides crisscrossed with agricultural terraces. Be sure to take a look at the stone sundial that graces its main plaza, as well as at the local lakefront cottage industry: making reed boats for use on Titicaca.

Juli

60 km (37 mi) south of Chucuito.

Juli is considered a sort of altiplano Rome because of its disproportionate number of churches. The village, which may have been an important Aymara religious center (whose hold over popular devotion the Spanish Jesuits wanted to transfer to Catholicism), became a Jesuit base in the altiplano.

San Juan de Letran is now a museum that displays 17th-century paintings chronicling the lives of John the Baptist and St. Teresa, among other artworks. It's across the street from **Parque Pino** and is one of the first things you see when you enter Puno from the airport. The **Iglesia Nuestra Señora de la Asunción** is on the Plaza de Armas and has lovely murals and a large courtyard.

Pomata

20 km (12 mi) south of Juli.

The mestizo baroque carvings and alabaster windows of the church of **Santiago Apostle** are spectacular. They were built with beautifully carved pink granite, with altars covered in gold leaf.

Sillustani

30 km (19 mi) northwest of Puno.

High on a hauntingly beautiful peninsula in Lake Umayo is the necropolis of Sillustani. Twenty-eight stone burial towers represent a city of the dead that both predated and coincided with the Inca empire. The proper name for the tower is an *ayawasi* (home of the dead), but they are generally referred to as *chullpas,* which are actually the shrouds used to cover the mummies that were deposited inside. This was the land of the Aymara-speaking Colla people, and the precision of their masonry rivals that of the Inca.

Sillustani's mystique is heightened by the view it provides over Lake Umayo and its mesa-shape island, El Sombrero, as well as by the utter silence that prevails, broken only by the wind over the water and the cries of lake birds. On your way to the chullpas, keep an eye out for shepherds watching over their sheep and alpacas.

Most of the chullpas date from the 14th and 15th centuries, but some were erected as early as AD 900. The tallest, known as the Lizard because of a carving on one of its massive stones, has a circumference of 28 ft and is 39 ft high. To fully appreciate Sillustani, it is necessary to make the long climb to the top; fortunately, the steps are wide and it's an easy climb.

Note: You will be besieged at the site by young Indian girls selling necklaces that are interesting, attractive, and inexpensive. This is good way to contribute to their economy. Also—although you won't be asked to do so—if you take photos of Indian mothers, children, and pet alpacas, a donation of a couple of soles will be much appreciated.

The iron ship **El Yavari,** built in England in 1862 and currently undergoing restoration, sits in Puno's port, 1 km (½ mi) east of the Plaza de Armas. Inside, are a museum and bar, and future plans include day and night excursions on Lake Titicaca. ☎ *054/369329.* 🎟 *Free.* ⊙ *8–5.*

Puno and Lake Titicaca A to Z

Arriving and Departing

BY AIRPLANE

Aero Continente has daily flights from Lima, Arequipa, and Cuzco to the **Aeropuerto Manco Capac** (☎ 054/321821) in Juliaca, a commercial and industrial center 50 km (31 mi) north of Puno. Travel and tour operators usually arrange for airport transfers to your hotel; alternatively, you can take a taxi (about $20) to Puno or share a minibus ($2).

BY BOAT

There is no direct service across Lake Titicaca between Bolivia and Puno. You can, however, go by bus and catamaran or hydrofoil from Puno to La Paz, Bolivia. Both trips start from Puno with a three-hour bus ride to Copacabana, where passengers have lunch. The hovercraft takes 2½ hours to cross the lake to Huatajata, Bolivia; the catamaran takes 6 hours. Travelers continue by bus to La Paz, although, if crossing by hydrofoil, you can overnight at the Inca Utama hotel in the Andean Cultural Complex or at La Posada del Inca; both are on Lake Titicaca.

You can buy combined tickets for the bus/catamaran trip from **Transturin** (✉ Jirón Libertad 176, Puno, ☎ 054/352771). Coming from Bolivia, **Crillón Tours** (✉ Av. Camacho 1223, La Paz, ☎ 02/374566) runs the bus/hydrofoil trip for about the same amount. You can also contact **Rey Tours** (☞ Tour Operators, *below*).

BY TRAIN

An **ENAFER** night train runs directly between Arequipa and Puno (✉ La Torre 224, ☎ 054/351233) four times a week; the trip takes about 10 hours. Travel the more comfortable and safe Pullman class—the cars are locked, so you can sleep peacefully. Some travelers might be dismayed by the rough ride and lack of scenery; air travel between these cities is a quicker and affordable option.

The daytime train between Puno and Cuzco chugs high across the altiplano, revealing its haunting landscapes. At the highest point, 13,200 ft, the train stops for photo-taking. It runs four times a week and takes 12 hours, with a 45-minute stop in Juliaca; watch your belongings during the layover, as the train station is notorious for its thieves. Never travel in first or second class, as thievery in both is rampant. Take the Tourismo Inca class, which offers full meals, sandwiches, and beverages (including beer and Pisco Sours), comfortable seats, and tables.

Getting Around

Puno is really a walking town, although for excursions outside the lakeshore you will need a car. You can also sign on for a tour, hire a private guide through a travel agency, or hire a taxi for about $30 a day. Cabs are not metered, so settle the price before you climb in.

Contacts and Resources

BANKS AND CURRENCY EXCHANGE

Banco de Crédito (✉ Jr. Lima 516, ☎ 054/352119) will change money and travelers checks.

EMERGENCIES
Hospitals: Hospital Regional Manuel Nuñez Butron ✉ Av. el Sol 1022, ☎ 054/353780. **Clínica Los Pinos** ✉ Pasaje los Pinos, ☎ 054/351071. **Doctor:** Dr. Edy Mercado, ☎ 054/622020 **Police:** ☎ 105.

ENGLISH-LANGUAGE BOOKSTORES
Along the pedestrian-only Jr. Lima, between Pino Park and the Plaza de Armas, gift shops sell books, newspapers, and magazines.

TELEPHONES, THE INTERNET, MAIL
Telefónica del Perú (✉ Jr. Lima, ☎ 054/36–9180) is a good place to make calls. International fax service, E-mail, and photocopying are available at a store along the same street between Pino Park and Av. Libertad. You can send or receive E-mail for around $2. The **post office** (✉ Av. Moquegua 269) is two blocks from the Plaza de Armas. **DHL** courier service (✉ Av. Lambayeque 175, ☎ 054/352001) is also available.

TOUR OPERATORS AND TRAVEL AGENTS
The excursion to the Floating Islands, which lasts three to four hours, can be arranged through **Rey Tours** (✉ Tarapaca(ac) 399, Puno, ☎ 054/352061). **Turpuno** (✉ Lambayeque 175, ☎ FAX 054/351431), **Grace Tours** (✉ Lima 385, ☎ FAX 054/355721), and **Kontiki Tours** (✉ Melgar 188, ☎ FAX 054/353473) can also arrange trips.

Most tours depart between 7:30 and 9 AM, as the lake can become choppy in the afternoon. You also can take the local boat at the Puno dock for about the same price as a tour, although boats usually don't depart until there are at least 10 passengers.

VISITOR INFORMATION
Touring and Automobile Club of Peru (✉ Dos de Mayo 67, Puno, ☎ FAX 054/723121). **Información Turística** (✉ Lima 582 and Ayacucho 682, ☎ 054/351261).

CUZCO AND ENVIRONS

In a fertile valley in the Andes mountains, 3,490 m (11,444 ft) above sea level and an hour by air from Lima, is Cuzco, the southern capital of the Inca empire. The presence not far from Cuzco of Pikillacta, a pre-Inca city of the Wari culture, which existed from AD 600 to 1000, is an indication that this territory, like most of Peru, was the site of sophisticated civilizations long before the Inca appeared on the scene—an event, according to Inca lore, that occurred around AD 1100. While the name *Inca* originally applied only to the royal family, in particular the emperors (e.g., Inca Pachacuti), today it describes the people as a whole. The Inca language was Quechua in this empire they called Tawantinsuyo.

Today Cuzco is a city of terra-cotta roofs and cobblestone streets, where the blending of the Inca and Spanish cultures has emerged into a distinct local style. Also known as the archaeological capital of the Americas, Cuzco reflects the image of a highly developed and intelligent ancient civilization. The city has existed for nine centuries, first as the capital of the Inca empire, then as the new settlement of the conquering colonial Spanish, and finally as home to the mestizo culture of today. The later Spanish architecture appears sloppy compared with precise stonework visible in the city's early walls and foundations.

Too often Cuzco and Machu Picchu are sold as a three-day/two-night package, which is a shame. Cuzco is a destination in its own right, not just an embarkation point for the trek to Machu Picchu. The ruins should also be appreciated and absorbed on their own, and require more than the three or four hours spent at the site during a typical day tour. You should plan a minimum of five days in Cuzco, with at least one night in Machu Picchu.

Exploring Cuzco

To visit the region's most important historical sites (not including Machu Picchu), you must purchase a *boleto turístico,* or tourist ticket, ($11, $5 for students with an international student ID), a combined ticket for admittance to 14 sites in and around Cuzco. In Cuzco, the **Dirección Regional de Turismo** (⊠ Portal Mantas 188, ☎ 084/263176) sells the ticket, as do **Coricancha, Santa Catalina,** and the **cathedral.**

Numbers in white bullets in the text correspond to numbers in black bullets in the margins and on the Cuzco map.

A Good Walk

Most of Cuzco's main attractions lie within its historic center, whose heart is the **Plaza de Armas** ①. In the eastern corner of the Plaza de Armas, you can still see remnants of an Inca wall, part of the **Acllahuasi** (House of the Chosen Women). The palace of the great Inca (Emperor) Pachacuti, who turned the Inca kingdom into an empire, once stood on what is now the western corner of the plaza. The **Catedral** ② sits on the northeast side. Nearly rivaling the cathedral in stature is **La Iglesia de La Compañía** ③, on the corner diagonally across the plaza. As you face the cathedral you will see to the right a steep, narrow street, Triunfo, now rebaptized with its original Quechua name of Sunturwasi. One block up on the right, where the street name changes to Hatunrumiyoc, stands what is believed to have been the **Palacio de Inca Roca** ④. Today, the colonial building that rests on the Inca foundations is home to the **Museo de Arte Religioso** ⑤. The street leads up to a steep, cobblestone hill known as the Cuesta de San Blas, the entry into the traditional artists' quarter of **San Blas.** Continue on the same street for one block to reach the **Plazoleta de San Blas** ⑥. Also on the square is the **Galería Mendívil** ⑦. The work of contemporary ceramicist Edilberto Mérida is shown a block away at the **Galería Mérida** ⑧.

Starting again from the Plaza de Armas, left of the cathedral, the street named Cuesta del Almirante will take you to a beautiful colonial mansion, the **Palacio del Almirante,** which today houses Cuzco's **Museo Arqueológico** ⑨. To the left of the modern fountain in the **Plazuela del Tricentenario,** in front of the mansion, is a 656-ft-long walkway with a fine view of the Plaza de Armas and central Cuzco. Once again starting from the Plaza de Armas, follow the street named Santa Catalina Angosta along the Inca wall of the Acllahuasi to the **Convento de Santa Catalina** ⑩. A few blocks away is one of the most splendid examples of Inca architecture, the Temple of the Sun, known as **Coricancha** ⑪, with a colonial church superimposed on it. West of the Plaza de Armas, along the Calle del Medio, is the Plaza Kusipata, still commonly referred to by its former name, Plaza Regocijo. Beyond it is the **Casa de Garcilaso** ⑫. Walk down Heladeros to Mantas to reach the church and monastery of **La Merced** ⑬. Follow Mantas to the **Plaza y Iglesia de San Francisco** ⑭. From here, through the attractive Arco Santa Clara, a colonial archway, Cuzco's public market area begins. Ahead are the churches of **Santa Clara** ⑮ and **San Pedro** ⑯.

TIMING

The city is compact, so you can visit most sites in a day. However, to fully enjoy Cuzco—and to adjust to the high altitude—you need at least two days.

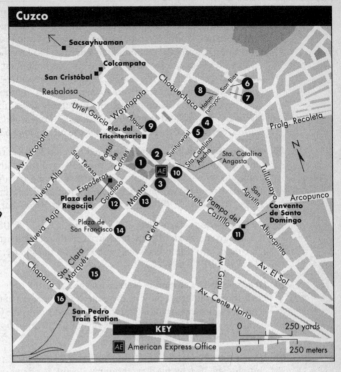

Sights to See

⑫ Casa de Garcilaso. This is the colonial childhood home of Inca Garcilaso de la Vega, the famous chronicler of the Spanish conquest who was the illegitimate son of one of Pizarro's captains and an Inca princess. The mansion, with its cobblestone courtyard, now houses the **Museo de Historia Regional**, which displays a collection of Cuzco School paintings and Inca mummies, ceramics, metal objects, and other artifacts. ⊠ *Corner of Heladeros and Garcilaso,* ☎ *084/223245.* 🎟 *Admission.* ☉ *Mon.–Sat. 8–6:30.*

★ ② Catedral. The baroque cathedral is where the palace of the Inca Wirachocha is believed to have been. Construction began in 1550 and ended a century later. It is considered one of the most splendid Spanish colonial churches in the Americas. Within its high walls are some of the best examples of the Cuzco School of painting (which added Andean motifs to its basically European style), including a painting of the Last Supper with a local specialty, cuy, as the main dish. Other highlights include a massive, solid-silver altar and the enormous 1659 María Angola bell, the largest in South America, which hangs in one of the towers. The cedar choir has carved rows of saints, popes, and bishops, all in stunning detail down to their delicately articulated hands. *Av. Santa Catalina Angosta,* ☎ *no phone.* 🎟 *Admission.* ☉ *Mon.–Sat 10–11:30 and 2:30–5:30.*

⑩ Convento de Santa Catalina. Still an active convent, Santa Catalina has a church with high and low choirs and a museum that displays religious art. ⊠ *Santa Catalina Angosta,* ☎ *no phone.* 🎟 *Museum: Admission.* ☉ *Mon.–Thurs. and Sat. 9–5:30, Fri. 9–3.*

★ ⑪ Coricancha. The Temple of the Sun was built to honor the Tawantinsuyos' most important divinity and served as the central seat of government and the repository of the realm's gold treasure. Terraces that face it were once filled with life-size gold and silver statues of plants and animals. In the 16th century, above its looted ruins, the Spanish constructed the convent of **Santo Domingo** using stones from the temple. An ingenious restoration to recover both buildings after the 1953 earthquake allows visitors the chance to see how the convent was built on and around the walls and chambers of the temple. In the Inca structures left exposed, one can admire the mortarless masonry, earthquake-proof trapezoidal doorways, curved retaining wall, and exquisite carving that exemplify the Incas' artistic and engineering skills. ⊠ *Pampa del Castillo and Santo Domingo,* ☎ *no phone.* 🔳 *Admission.* 🕙 *Mon.–Sat. 8–5:30.*

❼ **Galería Mendívil.** Set in the home of a famous 20th-century Peruvian religious artist, Hilario Mendívil, this gallery displays the sculptures of the Virgin with the elongated necks that are the artist's trademark. The artist's sons have continued the tradition since their father's death. ⊠ *San Blas 634,* ☎ *084/22–6506.* 🔳 *Free.* 🕙 *Mon.–Sat. 8–5:30.*

❽ **Galería Mérida.** The gallery (⊠ Carmen Alto 133, ☎ 08/422–1714) is home to the work of contemporary ceramicist Edilberto Mérida; if it's closed, you'll find his works at a shop on the square. ⊠ *Plazoleta San Blas 120,* ☎ *084/221714.*

❸ **La Iglesia de La Compañía.** Named for the Company of Jesus, the powerful Jesuit order that built it, the church was finished in the late 17th century. Note the outstanding carved facade and, inside, the Cuzco School paintings of the life of St. Ignatius of Loyola. ☎ *no phone.* 🔳 *Free.* 🕙 *Daily 7–11:30 and 6–7:30.*

⓰ **Iglesia San Pedro.** Stones from Inca ruins were used to build this church. The nearby market, though colorful, is not particularly recommended for tourists—leave important belongings in your hotel room. ⊠ *Corner of Santa Clara and Chaparro,* ☎ *no phone.* 🔳 *Free.* 🕙 *Mon.–Sat. 7–11:30 and 6–7:30; market open daily.*

⓯ **Iglesia Santa Clara.** The altar in this oldest cloistered convent in Peru is decorated with thousands of mirrors. ⊠ *Santa Clara,* ☎ *no phone.* 🔳 *Free.* 🕙 *Daily 7–11:30 and 6–7:30.*

⓭ **La Merced.** Rebuilt in the 17th century, the Monastery of Grace's cloister—surrounded by two stories of portals and graced with a colonial fountain, gardens, and benches—is decorated with a spectacular series of murals that depict the life of the founder of the Mercedarian order, St. Peter of Nolasco. A small but impressive museum of the convent's treasures displays, among other objects, the **Custodia,** a solid gold monstrance encrusted with hundreds of precious stones. ⊠ *Mantas.* 🔳 *Admission.* 🕙 *Church, daily 7–8 AM and 6–8 PM; museum, Mon.–Sat. 8–noon and 2–5.*

❾ **Museo Arqueológico.** Among the displays of pre-Inca and Inca objects is a collection of Wari art, turquoise figures from Pikillata. ⊠ *Corner of Ataúd and Córdoba de Tucumán,* ☎ *084/237380.* 🔳 *Admission.* 🕙 *Weekdays 8–6, Sat. 8–2.*

❺ **Museo de Arte Religioso.** A highlight of the collection of religious art is a 17th-century series of paintings that depict the city's Corpus Christi procession. ⊠ *Corner of Hatunrumiyoc and Herejes,* ☎ *084/222781.* 🔳 *Admission.* 🕙 *Mon.–Sat. 8–11:30 and 3–5:30.*

❹ **Palacio de Inca Roca.** Inca Roca lived in the 13th or 14th century. Halfway along the palace's side wall, nestled amid other stones in perfect harmony, is the famous **12-angled stone,** an example of the Incas' masterful masonry. Ask one of the shop owners along the street to point it out. ⊠ *Hatun Rumeyoc.*

❶ **Plaza de Armas.** The imposing plaza is a direct descendant of imperial Cuzco's central square, which the Incas called the Huacaypata and which extended beyond the area covered by the present-day square to as far as the Plaza del Regocijo.

⓮ **Plaza y Iglesia de San Francisco.** The plaza, though unimpressive, has an intriguing garden of native plants. The church has two sepulchers with arrangements of bones and skulls, some pinned to the wall to spell out morbid sayings.

❻ **Plazoleta de San Blas.** The little square in San Blas is home to a simple adobe church that holds one of the jewels of colonial art in the Americas—the **pulpit of San Blas,** an intricately carved 17th-century wooden pulpit dominated by the figure of Christ triumphant. ☎ *No phone.* ✉ *Admission.* ☉ *Mon.–Sat. 10–11:30 and 2–5:30.*

San Blas. Cuzco's traditional old quarter is one of the city's most picturesque districts. Recently restored, its whitewashed adobe homes with bright blue doors shine anew. The *Cuesta de San Blas* (San Blas Hill), one of the main entrances into the area, is sprinkled with galleries that sell paintings in the religious Cuzco School style of the 16th through 18th centuries. Many of the stone streets are built as stairs or slopes (not for cars) and have religious motifs carved into them.

OFF THE
BEATEN PATH

COLCAMPATA – For the energetic, the 15-minute walk to Colcampata offers a tour through colonial neighborhoods to the heights above the city. Following Procuradores from the Plaza de Armas to Waynapata and then Resbalosa, you'll come to a steep cobblestone staircase with a wonderful view of La Compañía. Continuing to climb, you'll find the church of San Cristóbal, which is of little intrinsic interest but affords another magnificent panorama of the city. The church stands atop Colcampata, believed to have been the palace of the first Inca, Manco Capac. The Inca wall to the right of the church has 11 niches in which soldiers may once have stood guard. Farther up the road, the lane on the left leads to a post-conquest Inca gateway beside a magnificent Spanish mansion.

Dining

Cuzco has a variety of restaurants. There are excellent places with international menus, especially Italian, while other eateries serve local delicacies such as cuy, often served in a hot sauce, and *chicharrón,* fried pork or chicken.

$$ ✕ **Mesón de Espaderos.** You'll drink in history as you dine on a rustic, second-floor terrace above the Plaza de Armas. The steaks and parrilladas are the best in Cuzco; the parrillada for one person is more than enough for two. ✉ *Espaderos 105,* ☎ *084/235307. AE, MC, V.*

$$ ✕ **El Paititi.** On the Plaza de Armas, this tourist-oriented restaurant has good fish, especially the grilled or fried trout, and tasty pizzas. Additional lures are live folk-music shows nightly and a free Pisco Sour for all diners. ✉ *Portal de Carrizos 270,* ☎ *084/252686. AE, MC, V.*

$$ ✕ **La Retama.** Exposed Inca stone walls, a cartwheel chandelier, and a nightly folk-music show make for a charming ambience. The fish dishes are delicious—try the trout in fennel cream sauce. ✉ *Pampa del Castillo 315,* ☎ *084/225911. AE, DC, MC, V.*

$ ✕ **El Arriero.** This is another tourist-oriented restaurant, but its specialty is steak cooked before your eyes on the grill. Folk-music shows start at 8 PM, and diners receive a free Pisco Sour. ✉ *Portal de Harinas 195, Plaza de Armas,* ☎ *084/252533. AE, DC, MC, V.*

$ ✕ **El Ayllu.** This café on the Plaza de Armas serves hearty breakfasts accompanied by a big glass mug of *café con leche* (coffee with steamed milk) and mouthwatering pastries, including a scrumptious apple strudel. ✉ *Portal de Carnes 208,* ☎ *084/232357. No credit cards.*

$ ✕ **Bagdad Café.** The two main things going for this café are the location on a balcony above the Plaza de Armas and the delicious pizzas, cooked in a clay oven. Nightly music adds to the already lively atmosphere. ✉ *Portal Carnes 216,* ☎ *084/239949. V.*

$ ✕ **Café Varayoc.** Perfect for a midday snack, this café with exposed wooden beams and whitewashed walls serves good pastries and huge glass mugs of *mate de coca* (coca tea) with fresh leaves floating in them. A popular place with artsy types. ✉ *Corner of Espaderos and Regocijo,* ☎ *084/232404. No credit cards.*

$ ✕ **Chez Maggy.** If you're cold and tired, you can warm up in front of
★ the open brick ovens that produce the café's great pizzas and calzones. The atmosphere is casual and friendly; seating is at two long wooden communal tables. ✉ *Procuradores 365,* ☎ *084/234861. AE, V.*

$ ✕ **Govinda.** This vegetarian restaurant run by Peruvian Hare Krishnas has appropriately austere benches and Hindu decoration and background music. The breakfast of juice, yogurt, fresh fruit, and granola is especially good. ✉ *Espaderos between the Plazas de Armas and Regocijo,* ☎ *084/25–2723. No credit cards.*

$ ✕ **Al Grano.** This small restaurant off the Plaza de Armas specializes in Asian rice plates. It offers a fantastic selection of affordable dishes from Thailand, Malaysia, Sri Lanka, and Indonesia. ✉ *Santa Catalina and Ancha 398,* ☎ *no phone. No credit cards.*

$ ✕ **Pucara.** This is the best restaurant in Cuzco for local specialties and
★ it's always busy. The lunch specials are ample and reasonably priced. The ají de gallina is outstanding (but heavy). On the lighter side, the fish dishes are served with a colorful assortment of vegetables. The homemade truffles are the perfect dessert. ✉ *Plateros 309, next to Plaza de Armas,* ☎ *084/222027. AE, MC, V.*

Lodging

Accommodations are just as varied as Cuzco's restaurants, and bargaining is expected. Although Cuzco is cold, most hotels provide enough extra blankets, and the most expensive have central heating. If you visit during June, the time of the Corpus Christi and Inti Raymi festivals, you must reserve a room as far in advance as possible. Prices are likely to be higher then as well.

The Association of Family Lodgings has a listing of 192 rooms in 32 houses in Cuzco and the Sacred Valley that are near archaeological sites, historical monuments, natural attractions, and Quechuas settlements. There are three categories: *Inti,* which has a private bathroom; *Quilla,* which shares a bathroom with another room; and *Chaska,* which shares a bathroom with the family. Breakfast is included, and lunch and dinner are also available. For prices and reservations, contact **AMPEEH-CUSCO** (☞ Tour Operators, *below*).

$$ ✕🏠 **Hostel Turquesa.** This country house 21 km (13 mi) from Ollantaytambo has verdant gardens and comfortable rooms. It is very popular with travelers and has a self-service restaurant frequented by tour groups. ✉ *Vía Cuzco, Km 69, Urubamba,* ☎ *084/221174. 42 rooms. Restaurant, pool. AE, DC, MC, V.*

$$$$ 🏠 **Hotel Libertador.** This hotel opposite Coriacancha near the Plaza de Armas was once the home of Francisco Pizarro, the first governor of Peru. Rooms, decorated in Peruvian colonial style with views of patio gardens, have central heating. ✉ *Plaza Santo Domingo 259,* ☎ *084/*

231961, ⊠ *084/233152. 130 rooms, 13 suites. Restaurant, bar, café. AE, DC, MC, V.*

$$$$ ⊡ **Monasterio de Cuzco.** One of Peru's loveliest hotels is a restored sem-
★ inary, considered a national historic monument. Planners managed to retain the austere beauty of the complex, keeping rooms simple and elegant. At night the view of the stars from the hotel's main courtyard, soft lighting, and sounds from the fountain are truly serene. ⊠ *Palacio 136,* ☎ *084/240696, 01/221–0826 in Lima,* ⊠ *084/23–7111, 01/440–6197 in Lima. 123 rooms, 17 suites. Restaurant, bar, café. AE, DC, MC, V.*

$$$ ⊡ **Holiday Inn Cuzco.** Despite the boring Holiday Inn reputation, rooms at this hotel are comfortable, warm, and quiet. The hotel's colonial facade is in keeping with the surroundings, and it's just six blocks from the Plaza de Armas. ⊠ *El Sol 602,* ☎ *084/226207, 01/224–0263 in Lima,* ⊠ *084/224457, 01/224–8581 in Lima. 45 rooms. Restaurant, bar. AE, DC, MC, V.*

$$$ ⊡ **Hotel Picoaga.** The front half of this hotel consists of a colonial build-ing with rooms arranged around an attractive courtyard. Behind it is a modern wing with a restaurant that overlooks the Plaza de Armas. The rooms are worn, but the colonial setting is attractive. ⊠ *Santa Teresa 344,* ☎ *084/252330,* ⊠ *084/221246. 70 rooms. Restaurant, bar, casino. AE, DC, MC, V.*

$$ ⊡ **Hostel Colonial Palace.** Built inside the 17th-century Convent of Santa Teresa, about a block from the Casa del Marqués de Valleumbroso, this friendly hotel has simply furnished but worn rooms with either French doors or picture windows, laid out around a lovely brownstone patio. Space heaters are available. ⊠ *Quera 270,* ☎ *084/232151,* ⊠ *084/232329. 38 rooms, 32 with bath. Restaurant. AE, V.*

$$ ⊡ **Hotel Royal Inka II.** The facade is colonial, but the rooms inside this hotel are modern, clean, and spacious, each with heaters and attrac-tive wood-frame windows. There's an enormous, colorful mosaic that represents the area's history in the main courtyard. ⊠ *Santa Teresa 335,* ☎ *084/222284, 800/664–1819 in the U.S.,* ⊠ *084/234221. 45 rooms. Restaurant, bar, hot tub, sauna. AE, DC, MC, V.*

$$ ⊡ **Posada del Inca.** In the heart of the Sacred Valley, this 300-year-old
★ former convent has gardens, cobblestone walkways, a church, and a public museum with extensive holdings of pre-Inca and Inca ceram-ics. The colonial-style guest rooms, with brick-tile floors, unstained wood ceilings, and carved-wood headboards, have balconies that overlook the gardens or the terraced hillsides. The restaurant has excellent fare, including a popular Sunday lunch buffet. Bring warm clothing, as rooms can be cold. ⊠ *Plaza Manco II, Yucay,* ☎ ⊠ *084/201107, 01/422–4345 in Lima. 65 rooms. Restaurant, bar. AE, MC, V.*

$$ ⊡ **San Agustin Urubamba.** This peaceful hotel is located in the Urubamba valley. Rates include a continental breakfast. ⊠ *Hwy. Cuzco–Urubamba, Km 69,* ☎ *084/201025, 01/424–9438 in Lima,* ⊠ *01/424–7102 in Lima. 26 rooms. Restaurant, bar.*

$ ⊡ **Hostel Centenario.** Just four blocks from the Plaza de Armas, this hostel is modern, clean, and friendly, with an endless supply of hot water in the showers. ⊠ *Centenario 689,* ☎ *084/224235,* ⊠ *084/231681. 22 rooms. Restaurant. AE, MC, V.*

$ ⊡ **Hostel Loreto.** In a colonial building with an attractive sunlit court-yard, this tiny establishment features four rooms with an original Inca wall. Those without the wall are nothing special, however. ⊠ *Loreto 115,* ☎ *084/226352. 9 rooms. No credit cards.*

$ ⊡ **Hostel Pascana.** This small, quiet hostel faces an Inca wall near the Temple of the Sun. The rooms are sunny and there is plenty of hot water. ⊠ *Calle Awaqpinta 539,* ☎ *no phone. 6 rooms. Laundry service. No credit cards.*

$ 🏠 **Hostel Tika Wasi.** On a lovely, winding street in the San Blas neighborhood, the Tika Wasi has a flower-filled garden. The suite provides an excellent view of the entire city. ⊠ *Tandapata 491, San Blas,* ☎ 𝖥𝖠𝖷 *084/231609. 20 rooms. Café. AE, MC, V.*

Nightlife and the Arts

Cuzco is full of bars and discos where you can listen to live folk music or recorded pop dance tunes. Several restaurants have shows that feature local folk dancing and music (☞ Dining, *above*).

El Muki (⊠ Santa Catalina Angosta 114, ☎ no phone) is like a little cave, popular with the younger crowd. A favorite gringo bar, **Kamikase** (⊠ Above the Café Varayoc, Regocijo, ☎ 084/233865), plays disco and has live folk music. For a beer and a game of darts, try **Cross Keys** (⊠ Portal de Confiturías 233, Plaza de Armas, 2nd floor, ☎ no phone), a British-style pub.

Outdoor Activities and Sports

Fishing
The rainbow trout in the Vilcanota and Urubamba rivers make the towns of Urubamba and Yucay popular fishing spots. There are no tackle shops; most locals just use hand lines—very successfully!

Trekking
The stunning Inca Trail runs from outside Cuzco to Machu Picchu. For more information, *see* The Inca Trail *in* Machu Picchu, *below.*

White-Water Rafting
The Cuzco region offers some of the best rafting in Peru, east of the highlands where the rivers rapidly drop toward the Amazon Basin. Many adventure-travel agencies (☞ Tour Operators, *below*) in Cuzco offer rafting trips on the Vilcanota River, known as the Urubamba River after it passes Huambutío.

Shopping

Cuzco is full of opportunities to shop for both traditional crafts and artwork and more modern handmade items, especially clothing made of alpaca, llama, or sheep wool. Vendors will approach you relentlessly on the **Plaza de Armas,** and if you keep your eyes open and bargain hard, you may find attractive sweaters. Three **enclosed crafts markets** are good bets for bargains: the **Feria Inca** (⊠ Corner of San Andrés and Quera); a fair at **Loreto 208,** on the passage beside La Compañía; and **Galería Portada del Sol** (⊠ Triunfo 376).

Triunfo is lined with crafts shops as far as San Blas. One of the best, **Taller Maxi** (⊠ Triunfo 393, ☎ no phone), sells dolls in historical and local costumes (you can also have them custom made), *retablos* (dioramas) that show Cuzco's most popular sites, and alpaca jackets decorated with local weavings. A nonprofit cooperative store, **Antisuyo** (⊠ Triunfo 387, ☎ 084/227778), sells high-quality crafts from all over Peru. Religious art, including icons and elaborately costumed statues of the Virgin Mary by a famous family of local artists, is sold at the shop at the **Galería Mendívil** (⊠ Plazoleta San Blas, ☎ 084/226506). Also in San Blas, the **Galería Mérida** (⊠ Carmen Alto 133, ☎ 08/4221714) sells the much-imitated ceramics of Edilberto Mérida.

Outside of Cuzco, both Pisac and Chinchero hold Sunday **markets** that sell, in addition to foodstuffs and household goods, a wide variety of crafts, including woolens, weavings, ceramics, and painted leather masks. Pisac has a smaller market on Tuesdays and Thursdays.

Side Trips from Cuzco

Cuzco is the gateway to some of Peru's greatest historical areas and monuments, such as Sacsayhuaman, on a hill that overlooks the city, and the Sacred Valley, an Inca breadbasket for centuries, still marked with the footprints of its imperial past.

Sacsayhuaman and Environs

Dominating a hilltop 2 km (1 mi) north of the city is the massive complex of Sacsayhuaman, perhaps the most important Inca monument after Machu Picchu. Built of stones of astonishing size and weight—the largest is 361 tons—the center seems to have served both religious and military ends, with zigzag walls and cross-fire parapets that allowed defenders to rain destruction on attackers from two sides. Today only ruins remain of the original fortress city, which the Spanish tore down after crushing Manco Inca's rebellion in 1536 and then ransacked for years as a source of construction materials for the new Spanish city at Cuzco. Sacsayhuaman is a half-hour walk to the northern edge of Cuzco. As the walk is uphill, it's easier to book a tour or take a taxi. ☎ *No phone.* ✉ *Admission.*

Smaller archaeological sites around Sacsayhuaman include **Qenco,** 2 km (1 mi) away, a huaca with a small amphitheater where the mummies of nobles and priests were kept and brought out on sunny days for ritualistic worship. Continue 6 km (4 mi) to reach **Puka Pukara,** which some archaeologists believe was a fort and others claim was an inn and storage place used by the Inca nobility. Nearby **Tambomachay** is a huaca built on a natural spring. Perhaps a place where water, which the Incas considered a source of life, was worshiped, the huaca is almost certain to have been the scene of sacred ablutions and purifying ceremonies.

Valley of Cuzco

Along the highway that runs southeast of Cuzco to Sicuani are a number of lesser-known pre-Columbian sites. Despite the fact that they are easy to visit in one day by car, you may find that you have these magnificent ruins all to yourself, for they are off the traditional two-day Cuzco–Machu Picchu tourist circuit.

Tipón, 23 km (14 mi) southeast of Cuzco, is one of the best surviving examples of Inca land and water management. It consists of a series of terraces crisscrossed by aqueducts and irrigation channels that edge up a narrow pass in the mountains. One theory is that the Incas used Tipón as an agricultural station to develop special crop strains. Unfortunately, the rough dirt track that leads to the complex is in wretched condition. If you visit, either walk up (about two hours each way) or go in a four-wheel-drive (about 45 minutes to the site and 30 minutes back).

Nine km (5½ mi) down the highway from the Tipón turnoff stand the haunting ruins of **Pikillacta,** a vast city from the pre-Inca Wari culture, which existed between AD 600 and 1000. Like other Andean cultures, the Wari empire—which at its height stretched from near Cajamarca to the border of the Tiahuanaco empire based around Lake Titicaca—had a genius for farming in a harsh environment and built sophisticated urban centers such as Pikillacta. Wari's capital was at Ayacucho, but little is known about the empire. The rough ruins, once enclosed by a defensive wall whose remains are still evident, confirm the Incas' superiority in architecture and masonry. They are spread over several acres and include many two-story buildings. At the thatch-roofed excavation sites you can see uncovered walls that show the city's stones were once covered with plaster and whitewashed. Across the road lies a beautiful lagoon, **Lago de Lucre.**

Continuing 8 km (5 mi) along the same highway, you'll come to the small town of **Andahuaylillas,** whose main attraction is a small 16th-century church on the plaza. The contrast between the simple exterior and the rich, expressive, colonial baroque art inside is notable. The gilt that once covered the church walls is still evident.

Sacred Valley of the Incas

In the time of the Tawantinsuyo, this area's pleasant climate, fertile soil, and proximity to Cuzco made it a favorite with the Inca nobles, many of whom are believed to have had private country homes here. Today Inca remains lie throughout the length of the valley, which is filled with agricultural terraces and dominated by the archaeological remains of Pisac and Ollantaytambo.

The Sacred Valley of the Incas, along the Urubamba River, is traditionally held to begin at Pisac, about 30 km (18 mi) northeast of Cuzco. The valley "ends" 60 km (36 mi) northwest of Pisac at Ollantaytambo, where the cliffs that flank the river grow closer together, the valley narrows, and the agriculturally rich floodplain thins to a gorge as the Urubamba begins its abrupt descent toward the Amazon Basin. (Machu Picchu is farther downriver, among the cloud forests on the Andean slopes above the Amazon jungle.)

At the valley's southern extreme, amid rugged sandstone cliffs, is **Huambutío,** a launching point for raft trips (☞ Outdoor Activities and Sports, *above*). The road from Cuzco meets the valley at a better-known point, **Pisac.** Pisac has two parts: the colonial town, which holds a popular Sunday market (☞ Shopping, *above*), and the Inca ruins up on a mountain. From the market area you can rent a horse to ride up to the ruins, hike, or take a taxi up the winding but well-maintained road. Archaeologists think there was a fortress here to defend the empire from the fierce Antis (jungle peoples). The terraces and irrigation systems also support the theory that it was a refuge in times of siege. The fortress is a masterpiece of Inca engineering, with narrow trails that wind tortuously among and through solid rock. On non-market days (Monday, Wednesday, and Friday), you may find yourself practically alone on the series of paths in the mountains that lead you among the ruins, through caves, and past the largest known Inca cemetery (the Inca buried their dead in tombs high on the cliffs). Another Sunday attraction takes place in Pisac's simple **stone church,** where a Quechua mass is held, with the indigenous *varayocs* (mayors) attending in full ceremonial regalia.

From Pisac the valley road passes through the quiet colonial towns of **Calca, Yucay,** and **Urubamba** and, 60 km (37 mi) from Pisac, ends at **Ollantaytambo,** a well-preserved Inca site. The fortress of Ollantaytambo, a formidable stone structure that climbs massive terraces to the top of a peak, was the valley's main defense against the Antis and was the site of the Incas' greatest victory against the Spanish during the wars of conquest. Below the fortress lies a complete Inca town, also called Ollantaytambo, still inhabited and with its original architecture and layout preserved.

To return to Cuzco, take the road from Urubamba that climbs the valley wall to the town of **Chinchero.** Apparently one of the valley's major Inca cities, Chinchero has a colonial church that was built on top of the remains of an Inca palace, as well as immense agricultural terraces. A colorful Sunday market is frequented by tourists and locals.

Cuzco A to Z

Arriving and Departing

BY AIRPLANE

Aero Continente (☎ 01/242–4260) has flights to Cuzco's **Aeropuerto Velasco Astete** (☎ 084/222611) from Lima, Arequipa and (Puno) Juliaca. The airport is 3 km (2 mi) from the city.

BY BUS

The bus trip from Lima to Cuzco via Arequipa is rough and recommended only for the adventurous. Ditto for the road trip from Pisco through Ayacucho, which runs right through the adobe Colorado ruins. **Rey Tours** (☞ Tour Operators *in* Puno and Lake Titicaca A to Z, *above*) coordinates comfortable six-hour bus tours between Puno and Cuzco. In Cuzco, **Cruz del Sur** (⊠ Pachacutec 510, ☎ 084/221909) and **Ormeño** (⊠ Tupac Amaru 114B, ☎ 084/228712) have bus services to Lima via Arequipa.

BY CAR

Although one can drive from Lima to Cuzco, poor road conditions and security problems make it highly inadvisable (☞ Health and Safety *in* Peru A to Z, *below*).

BY TRAIN

There are four trains a week between Cuzco and Puno, a scenic but rough ride, with connections to Arequipa. Always travel in turismo (Pullman) class, rather than first or second class, where thieves abound. The Puno train arrives and departs from the **Wanchaq station** on Pachacutec (☎ 084/238722).

Getting Around

BY CAR OR TAXI

To visit areas such as Pikillacta, Chinchero, or the Sacred Valley, you must go by car. For about $50 a day you can hire a taxi, either on the street or by phone.

ON FOOT

In compact downtown Cuzco, the best way to get around is on foot. If you are in good health, you may want to make the hike to Sacsayhuaman, on the northern outskirts of Cuzco. Remember that at 11,444 ft above sea level, Cuzco will be almost as much a challenge to your cardiorespiratory system as Puno, so you should take it just as gently your first full day in town (☞ Health and Safety *in* Peru A to Z, *below*).

Contacts and Resources

BANKS AND CURRENCY EXCHANGE

Cash usually works better than traveler's checks in Cuzco, but there are three banks where you can exchange money and get money on credit cards: **Banco de Créadito** (⊠ Av. El Sol 189), **Banco Latino** (⊠ Av. Almagro 125, ☎ 084/244945), and **Banco Wiese** (⊠ Calle Maruri 315). **American Express** (⊠ Portal de Harinas 177, Main Square, ☎ 084/235241) has an office in town, as does **Diners Club** (⊠ Av. El Sol 615, ☎ 084/234051).

EMERGENCIES

Hospital: Hospital Regional ⊠ Av. de la Cultura. Most hotels have oxygen available for anyone having trouble with the altitude.

TELEPHONES, THE INTERNET, MAIL

In Cuzco, the **post office** (⊠ Av. del Sol) is open Monday through Saturday 7:30–8 and Sunday 8–2. For courier items, try **DHL** (⊠ Portal de Harinas 177, ☎ 084/223874).

Travel agencies that offer tours of Cuzco and the surrounding area are **Cruz del Sur** (✉ Pachacutec 510, ☎ 084/221909), **Lima Tours** (✉ Portal de Harinas 177, Plaza de Armas, ☎ 084/228431), **Ormeño** (✉ Tupac Amaru 114B, ☎ 084/228712), and **Peru Chasquitur** (✉ Av El Sol 346, Centro Commercial Ollanta, ☎ 084/241280).

Tour operators in Cuzco that offer guided treks along the Inca Trail are **Explorandes** (✉ Jirón Sucre J8, Urbanización Huancaro, ☎ 084/238380, 🖷 084/233784), **Hirca Travel** (✉ Retiro 128, Oficina 100, ☎ 084/225384, 🖷 084/234147); and **Peruvian Andean Treks** (✉ Pardo 705, ☎ 084/225701, 🖷 084/238911). The last offers probably the most complete range of expeditions in the area around Cuzco.

The **Dirección Regional de Turismo** (✉ Portal Mantas 188, ☎ 084/263176) and the tourist **information booth** at the airport (☎ no phone) are open every day and provide information about the city and surrounding attractions. For information and prices at area home-stays, contact **AMPEEH-CUSCO** (✉ Calle San Agustin 415, ☎ 🖷 084/229227).

To better understand and appreciate Cuzco, two books are indispensable: Peter Frost's *Exploring Cusco* and John Hemming's *Conquest of the Incas*. Both are available at bookstores in town.

MACHU PICCHU

This mystical city, a three-hour train ride from Cuzco, is the most important archaeological site in South America, and its beauty is so spectacular that the disappointed visitor is rare indeed. Its attraction lies in the exquisite architecture and synergism of the Incas' massive stone structures, and in the formidable backdrop of steep sugarloaf hills, with winding Urubamba River far below.

Ever since American explorer Hiram Bingham "discovered" the city in 1911, there have been debates over Machu Picchu's original function. What *is* clear is that it was an Inca religious center and small city of some 200 homes and 1,000 residents, with agricultural terraces to supply the population's needs and a strategic setting that overlooked but could not be seen from the valley floor. Exactly when Machu Picchu was built is not known, but one theory suggests that it was a country estate of Inca Pachacuti, which means its golden age was in the mid-15th century. The site's belated discovery has led some academics to conclude that the Incas abandoned Machu Picchu before the Spanish conquest. Whatever the reason, this "lost city of the Incas" was missed by the ravaging conquistadors and survived untouched until the beginning of the 19th century.

You should plan at least a two-day visit to Machu Picchu, staying either at the hotel at the entrance to the ruins or one below. If you have only time for a day trip, you'll have just a few hours at the ruins, so bring a lunch with you; if you line up in the cafeteria you'll have even less time, as you must leave no later than 3:15 PM to catch the train back to Cuzco. On the other hand, if you stay overnight, you'll be able to wander the ruins after most tourists have gone. You'll also have time for a soak in the thermal baths in the village of Aguas Calientes, 1½ km (1 mi) from the Puente Ruinas train station, where the bus departs for the 30-minute zigzag climb to the ruins.

After you enter the ruins through the terraces at the agricultural sector, you come to a series of 16 small, ritual baths linked to the Inca worship of water. Beyond them is the round **Temple of the Sun.** Here, on June 22 (the date of the winter solstice in the southern hemisphere, when the sun is farthest from the equator), the light shines through a small, trapezoid-shaped window and casts light into the middle of a large, flat granite stone presumed to be an Inca calendar. A stone staircase leads to the **Temple of the Three Windows**—one entire wall is built from a single massive rock with trapezoidal windows cut into it. The **Principal Temple** is so dubbed because its masonry is among Machu Picchu's best. Onward is a hillock that leads to the famous **Intihuatana,** the "Hitching Post of the Sun." Every important Inca center had one of these vertical stone columns (called gnomons), but their function is a mystery. Across and around a grassy plaza are many more buildings and huts. ⊠ *Admission (reduction on 2nd-day ticket with 1st-day stub).* ⊘ *Daily 7–6.*

Several trails lead from the site to surrounding ruins. A 45-minute walk southeast of the main complex is **Intipunku,** the Sun Gate, a small ruin in a pass through which you can see the sun rise at different times of the year. It is also the gateway to the Inca Trail (☞ *below*). A two- or three-hour hike beyond the Intipunku along the Inca Trail will bring you to the ruins of **Huiñay Huayna,** a complex that climbs a steep mountain slope and includes an interesting set of ritual baths.

From the cemetery at Machu Picchu, a 30-minute walk along a narrow path leads to yet another example of the Incas' ingenuity and engineering skills: the **Inca Bridge,** built rock by rock up a hair-raising stone escarpment. The **Huayna Picchu** trail, which follows an ancient Inca path, leads up the sugarloaf hill in front of Machu Picchu for an exhilarating, if challenging, trek. Climbers must register at the entrance to the path behind **La Roca Sagrada** (The Sacred Rock), where locals often pray. At the top and scattered along the way are Inca ruins and the **Temple of the Moon.** The walk up and back takes at least two hours—more if you stay on the summit to enjoy the sun and drink in the marvelous view of Machu Picchu. Bring insect repellent; the gnats can be ferocious.

Dining and Lodging

$$$$ ✕⊡ **Hotel Machu Picchu Ruinas.** This comfortable, conveniently located establishment is the only hotel at the entrance to the ruins. You'll have the ruins to yourself after the majority of tourists depart each afternoon, as well as the experience of watching the sun rise over Machu Picchu. The restaurant has an international menu. Reservations are difficult to obtain; your best bet is to book early and through a travel agency. ⊠ *Machu Picchu,* ☎ *084/240696, 01/221–0826 in Lima,* 🕿 *084/ 237111, 01/440–6197 in Lima. 32 rooms. Restaurant, bar. AE, DC, MC, V.*

$$$–$$$$ ✕⊡ **Machu Picchu Pueblo Hotel.** This eco-friendly hotel is set in a high
★ tropical cloud forest just off the twisting road leading up to the ruins. The stone bungalows have cathedral ceilings, exposed beams, and an atmosphere of rustic elegance. Activities include a one-day trek of the Inca Trail, bird watching excursions, trout fishing, and orchid tours. Dining is first-rate—try the *crema de choclo* (corn chowder). ⊠ *Aguas Calientes,* ☎ *084/211032; Cuzco reservations,* ⊠ *Procuradores 48,* ☎ *084/232161,* 🕿 *084/223769; Lima reservations,* ⊠ *Andalucía 174, Miraflores,* ☎ *01/446–7775,* 🕿 *01/445–5598. 26 rooms. Restaurant, bar, pool, travel services. AE, MC, V.*

THE INCA TRAIL

HE INCAS TRAVELED THEIR empire via carefully built and well-maintained paths. The Inca Trail, a 50-km (31-mi) section of the road that probably went from Cuzco to Machu Picchu, connects the Sacred Valley and Machu Picchu. Hiram Bingham "rediscovered" the trail in 1915, although research has shown that parts of it were used during the colonial and early republican eras. Now a famous trekking route, the trail begins three hours by train outside of Cuzco at a place called **Kilómetro** 88 (here you sign in and pay a $15 fee, which covers one day in Machu Picchu). Still largely paved with stones, the Inca Trail takes you past ruins and through stunning scenery that starts in the thin air of the highlands and ends in **Machu Picchu**'s cloud forests.

The best (but also the most crowded) months to make the three- to five-day trek are May–September (July is coldest); rainy weather is more likely in April and October and a certainty the rest of the year. This is the principal South American hiking destination, and conservation has become a problem. At press time authorities were considering issuing permits to walk the trail, so check before you set out.

If you've never backpacked, get professional advice or first try a short trip near home. If you don't hire a guide (☞ Tour Operators *in* Cuzco, *above*), do not go with fewer than four people; there have been armed thefts on the trail, although they are not common. You must be in decent shape—even if you hire porters—as the trail is often steep and climbs to over 13,775 ft. You must be in *excellent* shape if you plan to carry your own pack. Also, the trail is occasionally narrow and hair-raising, so go only if you can handle heights.

Your gear should include: sturdy hiking boots; a waterproof tent with fly; a sleeping bag; clothing for cold, rainy weather; a hat; sunblock; mosquito repellent; all the food you need; water and water-purification tablets; matches; a flashlight; a towel; and plastic bags (so you can carry all your garbage off the trail with you). Toilet paper is another essential on this rustic trail with few comfort stations; just be sure to bury your waste off the trail. Avoid lighting fires, camping in the ruins, or cutting flowers and vegetation. There are seven well-spaced, designated campsites along the trail, and you should camp there only. You'll find a bed for the night at a badly maintained hotel at Wiñay-Wayna, 7 km (4½ mi) from Machu Picchu.

A sine qua non companion for the trip is Peter Frost's book *Exploring Cusco*, which includes maps, detailed descriptions, and heartening comments for those long, steep hauls. The best source for other maps is the **South American Explorers Club** (☞ Health and Safety *in* Peru A to Z, *below*).

Machu Picchu A to Z

Arriving and Departing

BY HELICOPTER

Helicuzco (✉ Portal de Comercio 195, Plaza de Armas, or ✉ Triunfo 379, Cuzco, ☎ 084/234181 or 084/227283) has daily flights to Machu Picchu for $82 one-way and $165 round-trip. These take about 25 minutes, leaving at 8:45 AM and returning at 3:30 PM. The company also organizes charter flights to destinations like the Sacred Valley. Flights may be canceled if there are not enough passengers.

BY TRAIN

The quickest way to get from Cuzco to Machu Picchu by train is the *autovagón* (tourist train car), which has comfortable compartments with toilets, onboard attendants, and snacks for sale. It leaves Cuzco daily at 6 AM and arrives at Machu Picchu at 9:25; it then returns in the afternoon at 3:30 and arrives back at Cuzco at 6:30. The price of a round-trip ticket is $55. Another train, also for tourists, leaves Cuzco at 6:25 AM and arrives in Machu Picchu at 10, then returns in the afternoon at 4, arriving in Cuzco at 8; however, trips may be canceled in low season. Three classes of tickets, with comfort depending on price, are Coche Inka ($45), Pullman ($34), and Expreso ($20). Both trains are clean and safe. Purchase tickets daily between 8 and 6 directly at the **San Pedro station** (☎ 084/23–3551) in front of the main city market or through a travel agency, which costs slightly more.

The first stop in the area, which has signs that say MACHUPICCHU, is actually Aguas Calientes, the small town at the foot of the mountain. *Don't get off here!* A few minutes later, the train stops at a station labeled PUENTE RUINAS; disembark here and get in line for the buses to the ruins; it's also the final stop for those staying at the Peru Hotel, Machu Picchu Ruins.

Local trains to Quillabamba, which stop at Machu Picchu, leave twice daily from San Pedro station. Although they cost considerably less than the tourist train, local trains take longer and the risk of theft is much greater. They do, however, stop at Kilómetro 88, where Inca Trail (☞ *above*) hikers begin their trek; the tourist train does not.

Contacts and Resources

BANKS AND CURRENCY EXCHANGE

There is very little to spend money on in Machu Picchu, except for meals in the hotels—and most accept credit cards. However, take cash in soles with you to buy souvenirs.

TELEPHONES, THE INTERNET, MAIL

International direct dialing is available at the Machu Picchu Ruinas Hotel at the ruins and the Machu Picchu Pueblo Hotel near the railroad station.

MADRE DE DIOS

The national parks, reserves, and other undeveloped areas of Madre de Dios are among the most biologically diverse in the world—sheltering some 15,000 plant, 1,000 bird, and 200 mammal species—and offer a rare opportunity to see birds and large mammals, such as tapirs and jaguars. Groups such as the Nature Conservancy and Conservation International view the province as one of the world's natural arks, a place where the rain forest has a chance for survival.

Two areas of Madre de Dios are of special interest. One is around the city of Puerto Maldonado, including the Tambopata–Candamo Reserve;

easily accessible, it offers lodges amid primary rain forest and excellent birding. Manu National Park, though more difficult to reach, provides unparalleled occasions for observing wildlife in one of the largest virgin rain forests in the New World. Both areas are best visited between May and October, the dry months; the lodges, however, are open year-round.

During the dry season, especially July, sudden *friajes* (cold fronts) bring rain and cold weather to Madre de Dios, so be prepared for the worst. Temperatures can drop from 32°C (90°F) to 10°C (50°F) overnight, so bring at least one jacket or warm sweater. No matter when you travel, bring a rain jacket or poncho and perhaps rain pants, since rain may come at any time, with or without friajes.

For more information about Madre de Dios and the southern Peruvian rain forest, contact the **Conservation Association of the Southern Rain Forest** (☞ Madre de Dios A to Z, *below*).

Puerto Maldonado

500 km (305 mi) east of Cuzco.

Puerto Maldonado lies at the meeting point of the Madre de Dios and Tambopata rivers. It is a rough-and-tumble town whose main attraction is the **municipal market,** where you can buy freshly harvested *castañas* (Brazil nuts) very cheaply. (Buying them also gives the local people an economic incentive to protect the rain forest and the majestic castaña trees.) Maldonado is a convenient jumping-off point for visiting the rain forest, which you can do in one of two ways. The safest and most comfortable way is to spend a few days in one of the area's jungle lodges (☞ Dining and Lodging, *below*). More adventurous travelers may choose to hire a **private guide,** who generally provides camping equipment and handles details like stocking food and hiring a boat. One guide is particularly recommended: Orlando Carlton James (☞ Madre de Dios A to Z, *below*).

Up the Tambopata River from Maldonado is the **Tambopata–Candamo Reserve,** a 3.8-million-acre "reserved zone" in which only environment-friendly activities—such as ecotourism, rubber cultivation, and Brazil-nut harvesting—are permitted. The area holds world records in the number of bird and butterfly species recorded by scientists, and is the site of a *colpa* (clay lick) visited daily by hundreds of parrots and macaws.

Dining and Lodging

The listings below are all jungle lodges, which provide rustic but more than adequate accommodations in wooden huts raised on stilts, with mosquito netting in the windows and no electricity. Price ratings are based on package rates, which include transportation and meals.

$$–$$$ ✕🖼 **Cuzco Amazónico.** A 45-minute boat ride downriver from Puerto Maldonado on the Madre de Dios River, this is the most accessible of the jungle lodges. Each of its private bungalows, set amid trees beside the river, has a flush toilet, a shower, and a porch hammock. Because the lodge is relatively close to Puerto Maldonado, large mammals are rare, but visitors often see smaller ones, such as anteaters and agoutis. Opportunities for wildlife-viewing include a day trip to Lago Sandoval, where birds abound and, on very rare occasions, the giant Amazon river otter may be seen. The typical jungle dinner—fried bananas, *pacamoto* (fish or chicken cooked inside bamboo over coals), and fresh papaya for dessert—is very good. ⊠ *Reservations: Andalucía 174, Miraflores, Lima,* ☎ *01/446–2775,* ℻ *01/445–5598;* ⊠ *Procuradores 48, Cuzco,* ☎ *084/232161. AE, MC, V.*

$$–$$$ ✕🖭 **Explorer's Inn.** At this lodge about three hours up the Tambopata River from Puerto Maldonado, you may see monkeys in the surrounding forest. In addition to four-bedroom bungalows, each with private flush toilet and shower, it has a small library, a specimen collection, and interpretive displays about the rain forest. Foreign and Peruvian researchers are always on hand to serve as guides for the nature walks. Wildlife-viewing includes a night trip on the Tambopata River, with a chance to see small caimans. If you plan to stay at the inn during the rainy season, coordinate your visit well in advance; boats will not make the run to the inn for just one passenger. ✉ *Reservations through Peruvian Safaris, Garcilaso de la Vega 1334, Lima,* ☎ *01/431–6330,* 🅕🅐🅧 *01/432–8866;* ✉ *Plateros 329, Cuzco,* ☎ *084/236919. 30 rooms. AE, MC, V.*

$$ ✕🖭 **Tambopata Jungle Lodge.** A little farther up the river from the Ex-
★ plorer's Inn (☞ *above*), a 3½-hour boat ride from Puerto Maldonado, this lodge offers a chance to observe birds, butterflies, and some mammals on two- to five-night excursions that include visits to the *cocha* (oxbow) lakes. Four bungalows have two double rooms each, and two bungalows have two quad rooms each; every room has a private bathroom. ✉ *Reservations through Peruvian Andean Treks, Pardo 705, Cuzco,* ☎ *084/225701,* 🅕🅐🅧 *084/238911. 8 double rooms, 4 quad rooms. Restaurant, bar. AE, MC, V.*

$$ ✕🖭 **Tambopata Research Center.** Four hours upriver from the Tambopata
★ Jungle Lodge (☞ *above*), this lodge has the most pristine setting of any in the area and thus offers the best chance to see wildlife, including monkeys and the hundreds of macaws and parrots that put on a colorful show each morning at the nearby clay lick. It is, however, the most primitive of the lodges, consisting of a raised, roofed platform divided into cubicles where guests sleep on netting-enclosed mattresses; an open dining area; and latrines and showers. A unique on-site research project on macaws allows visitors to interact with wild but hand-reared macaws. A four- or five-day package that combines this with the Tambopata Jungle Lodge (☞ *above*) is available. ✉ *Reservations: Rainforest Expeditions, Galeón 120, Chacarilla del Estanque, San Borja, Lima,* ☎ *01/ 435–3510,* 🅕🅐🅧 *01/447–2497; in the U.S., Wildland Adventures,* ✉ *3516 N.E. 155th St., Seattle, WA 98155,* ☎ *206/365–0686 or 800/345–4453,* 🅕🅐🅧 *206/363–6615. 13 rooms. Restaurant, bar. MC, V.*

Manu National Park

50 km (30 mi) northeast of Cuzco.

This national park the size of Massachusetts encompasses more than 4.5 million acres of pristine wilderness, ranging in altitude from almost 12,000 ft down through cloud forest and into a seemingly endless lowland tropical rain forest at less than 1,000 ft. Not surprisingly, this geographical variety shelters a stunning biodiversity. Birds include macaws, toucans, roseate spoonbills, and 5-ft-tall wood storks. The park's 13 monkey species observe visitors with curiosity. White caimans sun themselves lazily on sandy riverbanks while the larger black ones lurk in the oxbow lakes. Giant river otters and elusive big cats, such as jaguars and ocelots, sometimes make fleeting appearances.

To enter the park you need permission from park authorities. Entry costs $25. We strongly recommend that you travel with a reputable tour operator or guide (☞ Tour Operators, *below*), who will take care of getting the proper authorization and have great respect for the park's wildlife.

Manu Nature Tours, which owns the park's only lodge (☞ Dining and Lodging, *below*), offers two basic programs. The eight-day program takes guests into the park by land and river and out by river and charter plane. Mountain biking and white-water rafting on the Quosñipata River, in the park's highland region, are options. The more expensive four-day program uses charter flights to enter and leave the park.

If you wish to travel alone, you must send a written request to the **Dirección de Areas Protegidas y Fauna Silvestre** (☞ Madre de Dios A to Z, *below*). These offices also can supply information about the park.

Dining and Lodging

JUNGLE LODGE

¢ ✕🏠 **Manu Lodge.** Set deep in the park, on a 2-km-long (1-mi-long) oxbow lake called Cocha Juárez, this is the park's only lodge, a rustic building with a two-story dining area. Guests have access to three habitats: the cochas, the river, and a trail network that spans 10 square km (4 square mi) of rain forest. The lodge also has tree-climbing equipment to lift visitors up onto canopy platforms for viewing denizens of the treetops. ⊠ *Reservations: Sol 582, Cuzco,* ☎ *084/224384,* FAX *084/234793; Centro Comercial Plaza Conquistadores,* ⊠ *Conquistadores 396, San Isidro, Lima,* ☎ FAX *01/442–8980; in the U.S., Wildland Adventures,* ⊠ *3516 N.E. 155th St., Seattle, WA 98155,* ☎ *206/365–0686 or 800/ 345–4453,* FAX *206/363–6615. 12 rooms. Restaurant, bar. MC, V.*

CAMPING

Those who wish to combine a lodge visit with some camping might contact one of the agencies that conduct camping trips in the park. They usually provide all equipment (unless you specifically request a very low-budget version of the trek) and food, but you must bring your own sleeping bag. One of the most experienced guide services, the Cuzco-based **Manu Expeditions** (⊠ Procuradores 50, ☎ 084/226671, FAX 084/ 236706), offers park camping trips that last five to nine days. Another reliable agency, **Hirca** (⊠ Bellavista 518, Miraflores, ☎ FAX 01/447–3807; ⊠ Retiro 128, Oficina 100, Cuzco, ☎ 084/225384, FAX 084/234147), operates five- and nine-day full-service treks into Manu.

Madre de Dios A to Z

Arriving and Departing

BY AIRPLANE

Starting in Lima and stopping in Cuzco, **Aero Continente** has daily flights to **Aeropuerto Padre Aldamiz** (☎ 084/575133), 5 km (3 mi) from Puerto Maldonado.

BY BUS

A long, rough, jungle road leads to Puerto Maldonado from Cuzco, but it is a grueling two- to three-day truck ride. The overland trip from Cuzco to Manu, 12 hours over rugged terrain, is via a road called the Carretera a Shintuya, which plunges spectacularly from the *páramo* (highlands) down into the cloud forests at Atalaya. Here or at Shintuya, farther downriver, you take a boat along the Alto Madre de Dios River deep into the rain forest and Manu National Park. Except for the adventurous, however, the only recommended way to reach Puerto Maldonado is to fly.

Contacts and Resources

BANKS AND CURRENCY EXCHANGE

Since trips into this jungle area are usually package deals and prepaid, there should be no need for anything but small cash. Don't count on lodges to cash traveler's checks or accept credit cards.

EMERGENCIES

When staying at jungle lodges, minor emergencies are handled by the camp caretakers. For serious emergencies, the camp must contact medical services in Puerto Maldonado or Cuzco. Bring all necessary medical items with you before you arrive, and have extras on hand in case you're delayed in the area.

VISITOR INFORMATION

The **Conservation Association of the Southern Rain Forest** (✉ Asociación para la Conservación de la Selva Sur, Attn: Daniel Blanco, Portal los Panes 123, Oficina 305, Plaza de Armas, Apartado 1002, Cuzco, ☎ FAX 084/240911) has details about parks in the region. **Dirección de Areas Protegidas y Fauna Silvestre**, INRENA (✉ Petirrojos 355, Urbanización El Palomar, San Isidro, Lima, ☎ 01/441–0425, FAX 01/441–4606; ✉ Urbanización Mariscal Gamarra 4-C, Apartado 1057, Cuzco, ☎ 084/223633) offers information about Manu National Park.

IQUITOS AND ENVIRONS

Founded by Jesuit priests in the late 1500s, Iquitos was once called the "Pearl of the Amazon." It isn't quite that lustrous today, but it's still a pleasant, friendly town on the banks of the Amazon River in Peru's northeastern jungle. Motor scooters outnumber cars and the typical family transportation is a three-wheeler with a canvas top. When the river is high, the picturesque waterfront district of Belén actually floats; when the river is low, Belén is about a half mile out, and it rises and falls from season to season by as much as 50 ft. While the main reason to drop into town is to explore the surrounding rain forest, given a chance, Iquitos will grow on you as you become accustomed to the hot, humid climate and relaxed, easy ways of its citizens. A revamped river walk is the popular place for an evening stroll, followed by entertainment in the new riverside plaza.

Iquitos

1,150 km (719 mi) northeast of Lima.

Iquitos enjoyed its greatest importance as a port around the turn of the century, during the rubber boom. Some of the wealth of that time can still be detected in the imported tiles that face many buildings along the riverbank, notably the former **Hotel Palacio** (Putumayo and Malecón Tarapacá), now converted into an army barracks and looking a little worn around the edges. A smaller oil boom during the 1970s gave the city a burst of modern growth. Today, with a population of roughly 280,000, it is still the biggest city in the Peruvian jungle, and though mainly a local port, it is navigable for oceangoing ships coming from the Atlantic Ocean.

Dining and Lodging

$$$ ✕ **Maloca.** This most elegant of Iquitos's restaurants is housed in a lovely building encrusted with colorful *azulejos* (glazed tiles). The international fare is varied, though dishes made with local ingredients are particularly good. ✉ *Sargento Lores 170*, ☎ 094/233126, FAX 094/242143. *AE, DC, MC, V.*

$ ✕ **La Casa de Jaime.** This laid-back restaurant, along the riverfront
★ on the beautifully restored Malecón Maldonado, is the perfect place to people-watch. Try the mouthwatering *lanza de pescado* (catfish kebabs) topped with melted water buffalo–milk mozzarella. ✉ *Malecón Maldonado 177*, ☎ 094/239456. *MC, V.*

$ ✕ **El Meson.** Recently relocated on the river walk, this restaurant provides ample meals. Try the delicious paiche, a giant fish found in jungle lakes. ⊠ *Av. Malecón Maldonado 153,* ☎ *094/231857. AE, MC, V.*

$$ 🖭 **Hotel Dorado.** A small pool, pleasant patio, and a waterfall complement this elegant hotel. ⊠ *Napo 362,* ☎ *094/237326,* 🖷 *094/232203. 50 suites. Restaurant, bar, pool. AE, DC, V.*

$$ 🖭 **Victoria Regia Hotel.** This modern, airy building offers rooms dressed
★   in cool colors that line a courtyard containing a small swimming pool.
    ⊠ *Ricardo Palma 252,* ☎ *094/231983,* 🖷 *094/232499. 42 rooms.
    Restaurant, bar, pool. AE, DC, V.*

Shopping

There are many stores and souvenir stands along the Malecon and the streets leading off the Plaza de Armas. Look for pottery, painted cloth from Pucalpa, and jungle items such as preserved pirañhas, seed necklaces, fish and animal teeth, blow guns, spears, and balsa-wood parrots.

Into the Jungle

About 50 km (31 mi) from Iquitos, the jungle can more precisely be called primary rain forest, where there has been no regular logging or farming, only hunting and gathering. Sadly, even this light touch has had an effect, and hunting has all but eliminated large animals from accessible areas around Iquitos. However, visitors are likely to see birds, large blue morpho butterflies, monkeys, pink freshwater dolphins, and caimans along the Amazon River and its tributaries. There are three ways to visit the rain forest: a river cruise, which usually will include meals and may include guided trail walks; a jungle camping trip; or a stay at a jungle lodge. Most lodge packages include river transportation and meals.

Dining and Lodging

Explorama Tours (☞ Iquitos A to Z, *below*) owns a primitive camp and four lodges in the Amazon, and the company is one of the sponsors of the spectacular ACEER Canopy Walkway (☞ *below*). Transportation to the lodges is via a *palmcari* (large wooden boat with a thatched roof) with very small rest-room facilities on board. The Explorama lodges are the Explorama Inn and the adjoining new Ceiba Tops, the Explorama Lodge, and the Explornapo. Explorama Tours also takes bookings for ACEER, the Amazon Center for Environmental Education and Research (⊠ Av. de la Marina 350, Box 446, Iquitos, ☎ 094/252530; 800/707–5275 in the U.S.), which is within walking distance of the Explorama lodge.

$$$$ ✕🖭 **Explorama Inn.** Only 40 km (24 mi) downriver from Iquitos, this establishment has individual palm-thatch cottages along the Amazon river. Rooms have fans, electricity, and private baths with running water and showers. Travelers gather at the comfortable lounge and dining area. There is easy access to jungle trails, and macaws are regular guests. *26 cottages. Restaurant, bar. No credit cards.*

$$$ ✕🖭 **ACEER.** The Amazon Center for Environmental Education and Research, an education-and-research post open to scientists and visitors, has basic facilities. ACEER features the most important attraction in the Iquitos region: the **Canopy Walkway,** the only such facility in the Americas. *20 rooms. Restaurant, hiking. No credit cards.*

$$ ✕🖭 **Explornapo.** This camp is set deep in the middle of a reserve, 70
★   km (43 mi) up the Napo River, 1½ hours by boat from the Yanamono area. Twenty rooms, separate shower facilities, a hammock house, and a screened dining room are all part of the renovated facilities. It will

take some backpacking to get there. Guided nature walks in the forest are offered. *20 rooms. Dining room. No credit cards.*

Other Lodges

$$ ✕⊡ **Amazon Lodge.** Only an hour by speedboat downriver from Iquitos, this lodge has primitive (no electricity) yet comfortable bungalows. Activities include guided jungle walks and visits to Yagua Indian villages. *⊠ Receptour: Alvarez Calderón 155, San Isidro Lima, ☎ 01/221–3341, FAX 01/221–0974. 45 rooms with private bath/shower. No credit cards.*

$$ ✕⊡ **Casa de la Loma.** Two American nurses who have a history of working with humanitarian and volunteer groups run this lodge that sits on a hill overlooking the Amazon River in Pevas. Located 56 km (90 mi) downriver from Iquitos, Pevas is the oldest town in the Peruvian Amazon. Interesting trips are arranged into the primary and secondary rain forest and to visit Indian villages. The lodge is used to support a free clinic run by the nurses. Pevas is reached by scheduled, rest room–equipped speedboats from Iquitos (3 ½ hours). *⊠ P.O. Box 555 Iquitos, ☎ 800/966–6539 in the U.S., FAX 094/221184. 45 rooms with private bath/shower. No credit cards.*

$$ ✕⊡ **Yacumama Lodge.** Located on the Yarapa River, a tributary of the Amazon, this well-constructed, beautiful lodge is 145 km (90 mi) upriver from Iquitos, three to four hours by speedboat. It was designed to have the least impact possible on the ecosystem, and although rooms don't have private facilities, there are two large, modern buildings with showers and flush toilets (separate for men and women) and a screened hammock house. Pink river dolphins are often seen in the area. *⊠ Explorandes: San Fernando 520, Miraflores, Lima, ☎ 01/445–0532 in Lima, FAX 01/445–4686 in Lima. 15 bungalows. Restaurant, bar. No credit cards.*

Outdoor Activities and Sports

RIVER CRUISES

Amazon Tours and Cruises (⊠ Requeña 336, Iquitos, ☎ 094/233931, FAX 094/231265; in the U.S., ⊠ 8700 W. Flagler St., Suite 190, Miami, FL 33174, ☎ 305/227–2266 or 800/423–2791, FAX 305/227–1880) arranges jungle expeditions and specializes in river cruises ($$$), using boats of 8, 10, 13, and 21 cabins. The longest and most comprehensive cruise includes a six-day round-trip on the Amazon River between Iquitos and Leticia, Colombia (where Peru, Brazil, and Colombia meet), with weekly departures on the *M/V Rio Amazonas* or the *M/V Arca,* and a 10-day run from Iquitos to Manaus, Brazil, on the *M/F Marcelito.* The *Marcelito* departs once a month from Iquitos to Manaus. Both the *Rio Amazonas* and the *Marcelito* have comfortable, air-conditioned cabins with private facilities. The boats stop at various points for guided nature tours and to visit villages along the river. The company also has three smaller boats, the *M/V Amazon Explorer, M/V Delfin,* and *M/V Amazon Discoverer,* which can travel up the tributaries on special expeditions or charters.

TSANZA Adventures has an eight-day kayaking or canoeing adventure downriver from Iquitos on the Amazon, Nanay, Napo, and Sucusari rivers. Participants camp in villages and stay in jungle lodges. Top equipment and guides who grew up paddling these rivers make this a fascinating journey. Beginners receive instruction and practice time on the Nanay River before starting out. Paddlers return upriver to Iquitos by speedboat. ⊠ Jr. Arica 1041, ☎ 094/23–5374 in Iquitos, 800/831–3014 in the U.S.

Iquitos and Environs A to Z

Arriving and Departing

BY AIRPLANE

From Lima, **AeroContinente** (☎ 094/243489 in Iquitos, 01/242–4260 in Lima, 877/359–7378 in the U.S.) has several flights a day to Iquitos. **TANS** (☎ 094/234632 in Iquitos, 01/575–3842 in Lima) has two flights a day between Iquitos and Lima.

Contacts and Resources

BANKS AND CURRENCY EXCHANGE

There are three banks in Iquitos where money can be changed or traveler's checks cashed: **Banco de Crédito** (✉ Av. Putumayo 201, ☎ 094/233838), **Banco Latino** (✉ Av. Próspero 330, ☎ 094/241421), and **Banco Wiese** (✉ Av. Própero 278, ☎ 094/232350).

EMERGENCIES

Hospitals: Hospital Regional de Iquitos ✉ Av. 28 de Jukio, Cuadra 15, ☎ 094/252004 or 94/251882. Clinica Adventista Anna Stahl ✉ Av. de la Marina 285, ☎ 094/252518 or 094/252535. **Tourism Police:** ☎ 094/237067. The best source of help is at the desk of the lodge where you are staying or from the tour operator who is handling your trip.

ENGLISH-LANGUAGE BOOKSTORES

For leisure reading it's best to bring your own paperback books. Occasionally you may find a book or two in one of the lodges that a previous guest left behind. Limited information in English can be found at **Infotur Iquitos Peru** (✉ Av. Távara 436, ☎ 094/238523).

TELEPHONES, THE INTERNET, MAIL

Public telephone service in Iquitos is very good, with direct-dial options and phone cards or coins. However, at jungle lodges and camps, communication is by radio. Some Iquitos hotels, travel agencies, and tour operators have Internet service. Iquitos also has a **post office** (✉ Av. Arica 402, ☎ 094/23–1915) but there is no mail service from the lodges.

TOUR OPERATORS AND TRAVEL AGENTS

Amazon Tours & Cruises (✉ Av. Requena 336, Iquitos, ☎ 094/233931 in Iquitos, 800/423–2791 in the U.S. and Canada) arranges river trips, hotel and jungle lodge accommodations, and tours to other areas of Peru. **Emily Tours** (✉ Jr. Progreso 268–270, ☎ 094/23–5273) arranges tours in Peru and airline tickets. **Explorama Tours** (✉ Av. de la Marina 350, Box 446, Iquitos, ☎ 094/252530, 800/223–6764 in the U.S.) can plan river trips and journeys into the rain forest. **Paseos Amazonicos** operates rain forest tours and has a jungle lodge, Amazonas Sinchicuy, near Iquitos ✉ Calle Pevas 246, ☎ 094/23–3110, FAX 094/23–1618. **Turismo Pacifico Iquitos** (✉ Calle Ricardo Palma 180, ☎ 094/231627) arranges tours and airline tickets. **TSANZA Adventures** (✉ Jr. Arica 1041, ☎ 094/235374 in Iquitos, 800/831–3014 in the U.S.) has kayak and canoe trips on the Amazon, mountain biking trips in Manu National Park, and white-water expeditions and motorcycle trips along the Pacific coast.

VISITOR INFORMATION

A **tourist information office** is in downtown Iquitos (✉ Av. Arica 122, ☎ 094/238523) and at the airport (☎ 094/231591).

PERU A TO Z

Arriving and Departing

By Airplane

AIRPORT

Lima's **Jorge Chávez International Airport** (☎ 01/575–1712) is the major international point of entry.

CARRIERS

Airlines that serve Peru from the U.S. include **American** (☎ 01/211–7000), **Continental** (☎ 01/221–4340), **Delta** (☎ 01/440–4328), **Lan Chile** (☎ 01/241–5522), and **United** (☎ 01/421–3334).

FLYING TIMES

Check with your travel agent or individual airlines for flight schedules, which are subject to seasonal schedule changes and rerouting. Approximate flying times to Lima from the U.S. are: New York, 7 ½ hours; Atlanta and Houston, 6 ½ hours; and Miami, 5 ½ hours. From London, connections are best through Miami, or on a nonstop flight via Madrid on Iberia Airlines. Connections from Australia or New Zealand can be made through Los Angeles.

By Bus

Unless you're traveling in a group on a comfortable, long-distance bus chartered by a reputable tour operator, travel between Colombia, Ecuador, Peru, and Chile is not recommended. Petty theft is common at bus stations, and even the Pan American Highway is not always in the best condition, especially during the December–March rainy season.

By Car

Travel by car between countries is definitely not recommended, although some highway segments in Peru are considered safe, especially between Lima and Ica/Nazca—provided you don't travel at night.

By Boat

Travel across Lake Titicaca from Peru to Bolivia is usually by a bus/hydrofoil or bus/catamaran combination, going by bus from Puno to Copacabana, Bolivia. then by hydrofoil to the harbor at Huatajata. You can continue by bus to La Paz, Bolivia, or overnight at a hotel on Lake Titicaca.

Getting Around

Though most people associate Peru with verdant mountains, the country also contains the endless Amazon jungles to the east and a vast, coastal desert. Thanks to modern transport, all of these regions are within two hours of one another by plane and can easily be visited by other modes of travel within the span of an average-length vacation.

By Airplane

The major carriers in Peru that offer regularly scheduled flights to major cities and towns are **Aero Continente** (☎ 01/242–4242, 877/359–7378 in the U.S.) and **Lan-Peru** (☎ 01/215–1800, 800/735–5526 in the U.S.), a new domestic carrier owned in part by Lan Chile.

A few smaller airlines and charters also operate within the country, but offer less regular and reliable service and have been known to vanish as quickly as they started. One of the best, **Aero Condor** (✉ San Juan de Arona 781, San Isidro, Lima, ☎ 01/441–1354) offers charter flights throughout the country on a variety of airplanes and can always be counted on for flights to the Nazca Lines.

When purchasing your international ticket, be sure to ask about special discount coupons available for flights within Peru in conjunction with your international flight.

By Boat

Passenger boats are the most important means of transportation in the jungle. If you visit a jungle lodge, your hosts will probably pick you up in an outboard-powered canoe. Larger boats make 4- to 10-day cruises on the Amazon from Iquitos. In smaller towns throughout the jungle, you can arrange private river excursions by hiring a *peke-peke,* a wooden longboat that has a small motor, may or may not have a roof, and is slower and cheaper than a boat with an outboard motor. On Lake Titicaca, small boats offer taxi service to the floating Uros Islands and the larger island of Taquile.

By Bus

The intercity bus system in Peru is extensive, and fares are usually very cheap. Beware, however, of the informal, "pirate" bus lines, whose safety records are abysmal. Some of the better lines are **Cruz del Sur** (☎ 01/ 427–1311), **Ormeño** (☎ 01/427–5679), and **Tepsa** (☎ 01/427–5642). All three offer regular and first-class service. The regular second-class buses (*servicio normal*) tend to be overcrowded and uncomfortable, while the more expensive first-class service is safer, more comfortable, and much more likely to arrive on schedule.

Alternative forms of public transportation are the *collectivos,* small vans or large cars that cover the same routes as the buses. They charge about twice as much but are usually much faster. The catch is that they don't leave until they fill up. Collectivos are organized by *comités* (groups of drivers who cover a given route) and usually cover specific regions. You will find them listed in the yellow pages of the telephone directory under "Transportes Terrestres," or ask at your hotel desk for a comité that will take you where you want to go.

For longer bus trips you may wish to bring bottled water, snacks, and toilet paper. If you are traveling into the Sierra, take warm clothing or a blanket. You can buy bus tickets through a travel agent. Whenever possible, travel and arrive at your destination during daytime. For caveats on where not to travel by bus, *see* Health and Safety, *below.*

By Car

Since taxis and public transportation are inexpensive, driving is not recommended. If you do drive, remember that most Peruvians see traffic laws as suggestions rather than commands. Outside cities, drive only during daylight hours, fill your gas tank whenever possible, make sure your spare tire is in good repair, and carry planks to help you out of soft spots on or off the road.

The major highways in Peru are the Panamericana (Pan-American Highway), which runs along the entire coast of Peru, and the Carretera Central, which runs from Lima to Huancayo and from there to the central jungle. Most highways have no names or numbers; they are referred to by destination, e.g., "the highway to Arequipa." You can purchase good maps from the **Touring and Automobile Club of Peru** (✉ César Vallejo 699, Lince, Lima, ☎ 01/221–2432). Members of the American Automobile Association (AAA) and affiliates can get these maps at members' prices.

EMERGENCY ASSISTANCE

The **Touring and Automobile Club of Peru** (☞ *above*) will provide 24-hour emergency road service for members of AAA and affiliates upon presentation of their membership cards.

GASOLINE

Gas costs around $2 a gallon. Stations on the highway are widely spaced, and most close at 11 PM.

PARKING

Parking lots that charge about $1 an hour are common and provide the best security. Parking on the street costs between 25¢ and 50¢; you should tip someone to watch your car.

ROAD CONDITIONS

Conditions have improved markedly on the Pan-American Highway and the Carretera Central due to a multimillion-dollar government road-improvement drive. Elsewhere, including all of Lima, roads tend to be littered with potholes, and farther afield conditions degenerate rapidly. Security on some highways is also a serious problem (☞ Health and Safety, *below*). Signs outside Lima are relatively rare, except at major turnoffs, and lighting is nonexistent. In Lima vehicular chaos quite literally rules, while traffic in other major cities is only slightly better.

RULES OF THE ROAD

You can drive in Peru with a foreign license for up to six months, after which you will need an international driver's license. Driving is on the right, passing on the left. Speed limits are 25 kph–35 kph (15 mph–20 mph) in residential areas, 85 kph–100 kph (50 mph–60 mph) on highways. Traffic tickets range from a minimum of $4 to a maximum of $40. The police and military routinely do vehicle spot checks, sometimes for reasons of security, and drivers with their documents in order (driver's license, car registration, and, for foreigners, valid passport) are waved on. Peruvian law makes it a crime to drive while intoxicated, although many Peruvians ignore that prohibition. If you are caught driving while under the influence, you will either pay a hefty bribe or spend the night in jail.

By Train

Trains in Peru are operated by **ENAFER** (☎ 01/427–6620), the government-owned railway company. For reasons of safety, only three routes are recommended for tourists: the Cuzco–Machu Picchu–Quillabamba line; the Puno–Juliaca–Cuzco line; and the Arequipa–Juliaca–Puno line, which, because it's a night train, carries a warning because of the possibility of theft. Tickets can be purchased either at train stations or through travel agencies; first-class tickets should be bought in advance.

Except on the Cuzco–Machu Picchu tourist train, railway travel in Peru tends to be somewhat slow, and theft is very common. Food and drinks are often not available on board, and although vendors clamber aboard at every stop or will sell you food from the station platform, you are advised to bring food and bottled water with you. If you are traveling via Puno or La Oroya, bring a blanket, a sleeping bag, or warm clothes, as it can get very cold at high altitudes.

Contacts and Resources

Customs and Duties

ON ARRIVAL

You may bring into Peru up to $1,000 worth of goods and gifts, which are taxed 20% (excluding personal and work items); everything thereafter is taxed at a flat rate of 25%. You may also bring a total of three liters of liquor; jewelry or perfume worth less than $300; and 20 packs of cigarettes or 50 cigars.

Airport taxes are $25 for international and $4 for domestic flights. Be sure to keep your white entry paper that you filled out before arrival, as you will need it to check out of the country.

Electricity

Electric current is 220 volts, 60 cycles. An adapter is needed for appliances requiring 110 voltage. Adapters can usually be purchased in luggage stores.

Embassies and Consulates

American (⊠ Encalada, Cuadra 16, Monterrico, Lima, ☎ 01/434–3000). **British** (⊠ Edificio El Pacifico, Arequipa, 5th block, Plaza Washington, Lima, ☎ 01/433–4738 or 01/433–4839). **Canadian** (⊠ F. Gerdes 130, Miraflores, Lima, ☎ 01/444–4015). **New Zealand** (⊠ Av. Natalio Sánchez 125, Floor 12, Plaza Washington, Lima, ☎ 01/433–4738). Note that Australia does not have diplomatic representation in Peru.

Health and Safety

FOOD AND DRINK

In 1991 an epidemic of cholera, a potentially deadly illness that causes severe diarrhea and vomiting, swept Peru. The number of cases reported in subsequent years has dropped dramatically, but you should still take care. Even Peruvians tell you to stick to bottled water and beverages. Anything raw merits caution, including ceviche, sold on the street or at piers, although in a good restaurant it should be safe. Ceviche made from deep-sea fish such as corvina, cojinova, or lenguado is unlikely to have cholera. In restaurants, avoid salads and fruits that you can't peel. In Lima you can buy solutions, such as Zonalin, to disinfect fresh fruit and vegetables. Remember also that it is just as important to watch where you eat as what you eat. Food from street stalls, for instance, is notorious for causing stomach problems, while a clean, well-kept restaurant is much safer.

Immunizations can help with some types of food- and water-borne diseases, such as hepatitis A, which is common in Peru. Check with health authorities about which vaccinations they feel are necessary and which are only recommendations. Other possibilities include vaccinations for typhoid, polio, and tetanus-diphtheria. If you intend to travel in the jungle, you'll need a yellow fever vaccination and malaria prophylactics.

OTHER PRECAUTIONS

Soroche (altitude sickness) hits most visitors to sky-high cities such as Cuzco and Puno, but with care its symptoms remain mild. Headache, shortness of breath, and insomnia are common. When you visit areas at least 10,000 ft above sea level, always rest a few hours before you go out to explore, and take it easy on your first day. Avoid heavy foods, alcohol, and cigarettes, and drink plenty of liquids. To fight soroche, Peruvians swear by mate de coca.

As for crime, all the areas covered in this chapter are basically safe for tourists, and most visitors enjoy their time in Peru without major mishaps. By staying alert and using your common sense, you should be able to avoid problems. Wherever you travel in Peru, your best safeguard is to use a reputable travel agency. Their knowledge and experience should keep you out of unsafe areas and can also help you avoid some of the headaches you may encounter if you are trying to do it all on your own in a foreign country.

Petty crime is common throughout Peru. Urban bus and train stations, some train routes, and markets are sometimes the scenes of purse and camera snatching and backpack slashing. Also, streets in most Peruvian cities are not well lit, so stay in safe areas at night. Your best bet is to travel during the day, avoid wearing flashy jewelry or watches, stay out of dark and empty streets, leave your valuables in a safe deposit box at your hotel, and keep a firm grip on your belongings. A common diversionary tactic of thieves is to squirt you with liquid or spill food on you and then offer to help clean up—while an accomplice takes your purse or wallet—so don't be fooled into letting your guard down.

In general, air travel is safe everywhere, while long-distance overland travel can be dangerous in places, especially at night because of the possibility of bandits. Before traveling to the Apurímac, Huancavelica, Pasco, Ucayali, Huánuco, and San Martín provinces, check for travel warnings. In the last two, *under no circumstances* should you visit the drug-ridden Huallaga Valley.

Language, Culture, and Etiquette

Spanish is Peru's national language, but many indigenous languages also enjoy official status. Many Peruvians speak Quechua, the language of the Incas, as their first language, but most speak Spanish as well. Other native languages include the Tiahuanaco language, Aymara, which is spoken around Lake Titicaca, and several linguistic groups in the jungle. Wealthier Peruvians and those who work with tourists often speak English, but they are the exception. If you speak any Spanish at all, by all means use it. Your hosts will appreciate the effort, and any laughter that greets your words will be good-natured rather than mocking.

A word on spelling: Since the Incas had no writing system, Quechua developed as an oral language. With European colonization, words and place names were transcribed to conform to Spanish pronunciations. Eventually, the whole language was transcribed, and in many cases words lost their correct pronunciations. During the past 30 years, however, national pride and a new sensitivity to the country's indigenous roots have led Peruvians to try to recover consistent, linguistically correct transcriptions of Quechua words. As you travel, you may come across different spellings and pronunciations of the same name. An example is the city non–Latin Americans know as Cuzco. The city government uses "Qosqo" as the official spelling, though most Peruvians still use the "Cusco" spelling. To avoid confusion, the "Cuzco" spelling is used throughout this chapter. Note, however, that Peruvians may prefer the Quechuan pronunciations and linguistically correct transcriptions.

Peru is one of South America's most hospitable nations. Even in the overburdened metropolis of Lima, people are happy to give directions, chat, and ask a question you'll hear a lot in Peru, *De dónde vienes?* (Where are you from?). Peruvians are quite knowledgeable and proud of the history of their country. Don't be surprised if your best source of information isn't your tour guide, but your taxi driver. Women usually greet each other with a single kiss on the cheek; men shake hands.

Mail

Note that, except in Lima, Peru does not have postal codes.

POSTAL RATES

Airmail letters and postcards sent within the Americas cost S/2.70 ($1) for less than 20 grams; anything sent from Peru to the U.S., Canada, the U.K., Australia, or New Zealand costs S/3.30 ($1.30). Airmail packages sent within and outside the Americas cost an average of $30 per kilogram first-class, and $12 for second-class. Bring packages to the post office unsealed, and be prepared to wrap them in white burlap and sew them shut after you show the contents to postal workers. Mail theft is occasionally a problem.

RECEIVING MAIL

If you don't know where you will be staying in advance, you can have mail sent to you (mark the letters POSTE RESTANTE) at the following addresses: ⊠ A/C Correo Central, Pasaje Piura, Lima 1; ⊠ Correo de Miraflores, Petit Thouars 5201, Lima 18. If you or the sender are an American Express cardholder you can receive mail at the Lima American Express office (⊠ Belén 1040); South American Explorer Club members can receive mail at their club houses in Lima (⊠ Av. Republica de Portugal 146, ☏ FAX 01/425–0142) and Cuzco (⊠ Av. del Sol 930, ☏ no phone). They will also forward mail for club members.

WRITING TO PERU

Postal service has improved to Peru, but outside the main cities service can still be slow.

Money and Expenses

CURRENCY

Peru's national currency is the nuevo sol (S/), or new sun, which is divided into 100 céntimos. Bills are issued in denominations of 5, 10, 20, 50, and 100 soles. Coins are 1, 5, 10, 20, and 50 céntimos, and 1, 2, and 5 soles.

At press time, the exchange rate was S/3.10 to the U.S. dollar, S/2.27 to the Canadian dollar, S/4 to the pound sterling, S/.456 to the Australian dollar, and S/1.78 to the New Zealand dollar. The Peruvian currency is volatile, however, and the economy is dollarized—that is, when the number of soles per dollar increases, so do the prices in soles (though prices in dollars may remain unchanged). Therefore, all prices in this chapter are given in dollars, a more stable indicator.

You can safely exchange money in a bank, at your hotel, or from *casas de cambio* (exchange houses)—but never on the street. Traveler's checks are accepted at casas de cambio, banks, and big hotels. The rate is usually the same as for cash, but many banks have a ceiling on how much they will exchange at one time. Stores, smaller hotels, and restaurants rarely accept traveler's checks. Major credit cards, especially Visa, are accepted in most tourist-oriented hotels, restaurants, and shops.

SERVICE CHARGES, TAXES, AND TIPPING

Peru's economy has stabilized after the chaos of the '80s and '90s, but although the basics are reasonably cheap, anything that might loosely be called a luxury tends to be moderately expensive in South American terms. An 18% sales tax, known as *impuesto general a las ventas,* or IGV, is levied on everything except items bought at open-air markets and from street vendors. It is usually included in the advertised price of merchandise and should be with food and drink.

Restaurants have been ordered to publish their prices, including taxes and a 10% service charge that is sometimes added on, but they do not always do so. They are also prone to levy a cover charge for anything from live entertainment to serving you a roll with your meal. It is best to check before you order. Hotel bills may also have taxes and a 10% service charge added on.

If a 13% service charge has been included, only a nominal tip is expected (2%–5% of the pre-tax bill); otherwise 5%–10% is sufficient in most restaurants. Porters in hotels and airports expect 50¢–$1 per bag. There is no need to tip taxi drivers. At bars, tip 20–50 céntimos for a beer, more for a mixed drink. Bathroom attendants get 20 céntimos; gas station attendants, 50 céntimos for extra services such as adding air to your tires or oil. Tour guides and tour bus drivers should get 5–10 soles each per day.

Airport taxes are $25 for international and $4 for domestic flights.

Sample Prices. In Lima: cup of coffee, $1; bottle of beer, $2; Pisco Sour, $2–$5; soft drink, 90¢; chicken and avocado sandwich, $3; 2-km (1-mi) taxi ride, $1.35; museum entrance, free-$6.

Opening and Closing Times

Opening hours vary among **banks,** with most of the larger ones closing for a couple of hours at lunchtime and reopening until as late as 6 PM. Some banks are open on Saturday morning. The hours for **churches** are irregular. Some are open to visitors only in the early morning, while others have hours similar to those of museums, except that they are also open Sunday. Most **museums** are open Monday–Saturday 9–6. Some close at lunch, usually between 1 and 3 or 4 PM. **Stores** are generally open Monday–Saturday 10–8. Many smaller stores close for two hours at lunchtime and on Saturday are open in the morning only.

NATIONAL HOLIDAYS
New Year's Day (Jan. 1); Easter holiday, which begins midday on Maundy Thursday and continues through Easter Monday (Apr. 24, 2000, Apr. 16, 2001; Labor Day (May 1); St. Peter and St. Paul Day (June 29); Independence Day (July 28); St. Rosa of Lima Day (Aug. 30); Battle of Angamos Day, which commemorates a battle with Chile in the War of the Pacific, 1879–81 (Oct. 8); All Saints' Day (Nov. 1); Immaculate Conception (Dec. 8); Christmas (Dec. 25).

Passports and Visas

Visitors from the United States, Canada, the United Kingdom, Australia, and New Zealand require only a valid passport and return ticket to be issued a 60-day visa at their point of entry into Peru. For safety reasons, travelers are advised to carry a copy of their passport while exploring, leaving the original in a secure place in the hotel room.

Telephones and the Internet

CALLS TO PERU
It is much easier to get through to Peru with their updated phone system. To call Peru direct, dial 011 followed by the country code (51), then the city code, and the number of the party you are calling.

LOCAL CALLS
Telefónica del Peru, the newly privatized and merged telephone company, has invested a hefty sum in Peru's new phone system. Now, "intelligent" pay phones require a coin or "CPT" card instead of the old, tedious token system. Unless you're making tons of calls, using coins is much easier than fumbling with the cards, which don't always work and must be purchased in special outlets. With the new phones, coins are deposited before dialing and register a credit in a small window. Local calls cost approximately S/50 for the first minute. For information inside Peru, dial 103.

LONG-DISTANCE AND INTERNATIONAL CALLS
To call another area in Peru, first dial 0 and then the area code. International calls are easy to make from Lima and the coast, at times difficult in the highlands, and sometimes impossible in the jungle (except for Iquitos). Hotels add hefty surcharges to international calls made from guest rooms, so you may want to call from the telephone company's calling centers or try to find a newer pay phone from which you can make international calls. Calls to the United States cost approximately $2 per minute.

To dial direct, dial 00, then 1 for the United States and Canada or 44 for the United Kingdom. To make an operator-assisted international call, dial 108. To reach an **AT&T** operator, dial 171. For **MCI,** dial 190. For **Sprint,** dial 176.

THE INTERNET
E-mail has come to Peru in full force. Even along Jr. Lima in Puno on Lake Titicaca you can stop in a small shop and send an E-mail message back home for $2 or receive one for $4. A bank of computers in the coffee shop at Lima airport's international departure area lets you send E-mail for $2. Many hotels have equally inexpensive services for guests.

Visitor Information

The **South American Explorers Club** (⊠ República de Portugal 146, Breña, Lima, ☎ 01/425–0142; 126 Indian Creek Rd., Ithaca, NY 14850, ☎ 800/274–0568 in the U.S.) provides excellent maps and information on destinations throughout the country. The **Citizens' Emergency Center** (☎ 202/647–5225) at the U.S. State Department Bureau of Consular Affairs publishes travel advisories available by fax (☞ U.S. Government Travel Briefings *in* Smart Travel Tips A to Z).

When to Go

The tourist season in Peru runs from May through September, which corresponds to the dry season in the Sierra and Selva. The best time to visit is May through July, when the cool, misty weather is just beginning on the Costa, and the highlands are dressed in bright green under crystalline blue skies. June brings major festivals to Cuzco, such as Inti Raymi (the Inca festival of the sun) and Corpus Christi. Other important festival months are February, which means Carnival throughout Peru and the Virgen de la Candelaria (Candlemas) celebrations in Puno, and October, when chanting, purple-clad devotees of El Señor de los Milagros (the Lord of the Miracles) fill the streets of Lima.

CLIMATE
When it's dry in the Sierra and the Selva, it's wet on the Costa, and vice versa. The Selva is hot and humid year-round, with endless rain between January and April. Friajes from Patagonia occasionally sweep through the southern rain forests of Madre de Dios, but the average daily minimum and maximum temperatures in the Selva are 20°C (69°F) and 32°C (90°F).

In the Sierra expect rain between October and April, and especially January through March. The rest of the year the weather is dry and the temperatures fickle. The sun can be hot, but in the shade it's refreshingly cool. Nights are chilly, and the temperature may drop to freezing. Temperatures during Cuzco's dry months average 0°C (32°F)–22°C (71°F).

It never rains in the coastal desert, but a dank, heavy fog called the garua, coats Lima from June through December. Outside Lima, coastal weather is clearer and warm.

The following are average daily maximum and minimum temperatures for Lima.

Jan.	27C	81F	May	25C	77F	Sept.	19C	66F
	21	70		19	66		15	59
Feb.	28C	82F	June	23C	73F	Oct.	21C	70F
	21	70		17	63		16	61
Mar.	29C	84F	July	18C	64F	Nov.	23C	73F
	23	73		15	59		17	63
Apr.	27C	81F	Aug.	18C	64F	Dec.	24C	75F
	22	72		15	59		18	64

In early January, dancing and parades for the **Festival of the Magi** take place in Puno, Cuzco, and nearby Ollantaytambo. During the last week of January, artists perform the most spectacular and seductive of the coastal Creole dances at the **National Festival and Competition of La Marinera** in Trujillo. The town's **National Marinera Competition,** which takes place in January, celebrates a romantic local dance performed to the accompaniment of guitars and the cajón, a boxlike, wood percussion instrument. In Puno, **Candlemas** takes place in early February and lasts a week; parades and traditional dances are held. Nearby Acora holds a traditional dance festival the same week. Also in February, the religious **Cruz de Chalpón** (or **Cruz de Motupe**) festival takes place in Motupe, 80 km (48 mi) northwest of Chiclayo on the Pan-American Highway.

Carnival is celebrated throughout Peru. In Lima and many other cities, the party has degenerated into a water fight—people throw buckets of water and water balloons—but Carnival in Cajamarca and Puno remains a colorful affair, with parades and dancing in the streets. **Carnaval Huanchaquero** in Trujillo takes place on Huanchaco Beach Feb. 25–27. Early March sees the **Vendimia Festival** in Ica, a celebration of the region's vineyards, with wine tastings and dances. On **Good Friday** there's a procession in Puno. On **Easter Monday** a Cuzco procession honors the Lord of the Earthquakes.

Festivals of the Cross take place around Lake Titicaca in early May. Trujillo's **Festival of the Sea,** which includes a surfboard competition, happens on Huanchaco Beach in mid-May. In celebration of **Corpus Christi,** statues of saints from all of Cuzco's churches are taken in procession to the cathedral. The **Festival of Inti Raymi** (Inca Sun Festival) takes place outside Cuzco on June 24. The Incas' winter solstice is commemorated with music, dancing, and a special procession. **St. Peter and St. Paul Day,** June 29, also called Pope's Day, is celebrated in honor of the pope.

The little town of Monsefu, 12 km (7 mi) south of Chiclayo on the Pan-American Highway, holds an annual **FEXTICUM** crafts fair July 27–29; **St. Rosa of Lima Day** is celebrated in the capital; and a parade is held in Arequipa for the **Day of the Campesino.** Torchlit all-night processions highlight Ica's **festivals of the Señor de Luren** (Holy Week and the third Monday of October). During Trujillo's **Spring Festival** in October, dancing, parades, and exhibitions of the stunning Peruvian *caballos de paso* dressage welcome spring. In late October, **Our Lord of the Miracles** is celebrated with processions in many cities, but the biggest celebration is in Lima; throughout October devotees wear purple. The **bullfight season** (late October to early November) is on in the capital's ring.

Throughout Peru, people carry food, drink, and flowers to the local cemetery on **All Saints'** and **All Souls' Days** (November 1–2). November 4–5, **Puno Days,** commemorate the legendary emergence of Manco Capac and Mamá Ocllo, founders of the Inca empire, from Lake Titicaca. The highlight is a stupendous procession with masked dancers.

11 URUGUAY

Aside from the sparkling resorts along its coast, gently rolling hills and grasslands are the hallmarks of Uruguay, but its people—well-educated yet unpretentious, industrious yet relaxed—are the most remarkable aspect of the country for many travelers.

URUGUAY HAS LONG BEEN CONSIDERED the most European of South American countries. Its population is almost all of European descent—largely Spanish, Portuguese, and Italian—and the influence of these cultures is readily apparent in Uruguay's architecture and outlook. Even the country's "traditional cuisine" brings to mind pasta, paella, and slabs of succulent steak.

Updated by
Tom Samiljan

Uruguay's original inhabitants, the seminomadic Charrúas Indians, were driven out first by the Portuguese, who settled the town of Colonia in 1680, and by the Spanish, who in 1726 established a fortress at Montevideo. In 1811, José Gervasio Artigas, captain of the Spanish forces in Uruguay, mobilized Creoles and locals to fight against the heavy-handed influence of Buenos Aires. Though Artigas's bid for Uruguayan independence was unsuccessful, Uruguay finally became an autonomous state in 1825. On July 18, 1830—a date that gives the name to many a street in Uruguay—the country's first constitution was framed.

Following a period of civil war, José Batlle y Ordóñez was elected president in 1903. Under his guidance, Uruguay became the first Latin American country to grant voting rights to women and the first country to sever relations between church and state—a striking maneuver considering the Catholic Church's strong influence on the continent. Since then, except for a brief period from 1973 (when the military staged a coup) until 1985 (when free elections were once again held), Uruguay has been one of the strongest democracies in South America.

With the continent's highest literacy rate (94%), Uruguay rightfully takes pride in its great number of outstanding artists. Local theaters and galleries are full of works by masters such as José Belloni (1880–1965), the internationally famed sculptor; Joaquín Torres-García (1874–1949), the founder of Uruguay's Constructivist movement; and Pedro Figari (1861–1938) and Pedro Blanes Viale (1879–1926), both of whom influenced a generation of Uruguayan painters. As in Argentina, the legendary gaucho is Uruguay's most potent cultural fixture, and it is difficult to pass a day without some reference to these cowboys who once roamed the country singing their melancholy ballads. (Remnants of the gaucho lifestyle may still be seen on active ranches, or *estancias,* throughout the country.)

Uruguay attracts internationally known artists who perform during the Montevideo opera season or cavort in the resort city of Punta del Este during the Southern Hemisphere summer. Montevideo's lively Carnival, the annual celebration that marks the beginning of Lent, attracts its fair share of celebrants and performers from across the continent, though you will probably want to plan your trip around the weeklong festival if large crowds, strained facilities, and high prices are not on your itinerary.

Pleasures and Pastimes

Carnival

Almost every town in Uruguay celebrates Carnival, the weeklong festival that coincides with the beginning of Lent. The whole country participates in the *comparsas,* which involve dancing, drinking, eating, and general merriment. Montevideo's famous *llamadas* are the most typical and popular. In the border towns to the north such as Melo, Carnival has a more Brazilian flavor, with music and almost nonstop dancing. Unlike the more renowned festivities in Rio, however,

Uruguay

Uruguayan Carnival is very safe, and visitors are encouraged to participate as much as possible; if dancing is not your thing, you can buy a seat, which costs US$3.

Criollas

Also known as *Jineteadas,* these Uruguayan-style rodeos are held throughout the country, although the most spectacular is held in Montevideo's El Prado every Easter, when gauchos from all over the country come to display their superb control over the particularly wild horses that fight to throw their riders. If you visit an estancia, ask the owner to take you to a criolla; they are usually held weekends or on feast days. Gauchos are extremely proud of their skill and will often be more than pleased to display their talents for visitors.

Dining

Except in coastal fishing villages, beef is the staple of the Uruguayan diet. It is cheap, abundant, and often grilled in a style known as *parrilla,* borrowed directly from the gauchos (a meal in a *parrillada,* a Uruguayan steak house, is not to be missed). Beef is also made into sausages such as chorizo and *salchicha,* or it's combined with ham, cheese, bacon, and peppers to make *matambre.* Seafood can be delicious but expensive; popular among Uruguayans are *raya a la manteca negra* (ray in blackened butter), *lenguado* (flounder), *merluza* (hake), and *calamar* (squid). If you are not up to a full meal, try Uruguay's national sandwich, the *chivito,* a steak sandwich smothered with all varieties of sauces and condiments; a popular version is *à la Canadiense* (with cheese and Canadian bacon). Uruguayan wines under the Santa Rosa and Calvinor labels, a step up from table wine, are available in most restaurants.

Lunch is served between noon and 3; restaurants begin to fill around 12:30 and are packed by 1:30. Dinner is served late: Many restaurants do not even open until 8 PM and are rarely crowded before 10 PM. Most pubs and *confiterías* (cafés) are open all day. Formal dress is rarely, if ever, required. Smart sportswear is accepted at even the nicest establishments.

Prices quoted are per person and include appetizer, main course, and dessert but exclude alcoholic beverages, tax, service charge, and tip. For price categories *see* Dining *in* Smart Travel Tips A to Z.

Lodging

ESTANCIAS

Estancias are becoming a popular tourist experience and offer a superb opportunity to see Uruguay as it once was. Many of these working country ranches have added horseback riding, nature tours (Uruguay is in the migration path of four major bird groups), and other delights to their overnight packages. Because of the range of activities, accommodations, and pricing, visits are best booked in advance and through an agency that specializes in estancias. (☞ Estancias in the Uruguayan Countryside *in* Side Trips from Montevideo, *below*.)

HOSTERÍAS

Hosterías are country inns that not only offer modest rooms, but are open for tea and dinner as well. Menus tend to be limited, though the food served is unfailingly hearty. Outside the cities hosterías are likely to be charming, but rustic.

HOTELS AND RESORTS

Uruguayan resorts are generally clean, comfortable, and well equipped to deal with foreign travelers. Many quote rates that include one or two meals a day, so be sure to ask when making a reservation. Summer in Uruguay can be onerous without air-conditioning, and many hotels are not yet equipped with that luxury; be sure to inquire. You can save up to 30% in the same hotel by requesting a *habitacion turística*, usually a bit plainer, smaller, and without a view, but with the same standards of cleanliness and service.

For price categories, *see* Lodging *in* Smart Travel Tips A to Z.

Religious Processions

Uruguayans are renowned throughout Latin America for their piety, and Uruguay's religious processions are worthy of interest for the intensity of their participants. One of the most important is the Procession of Verdun in the department of Lavalleja. Every April 19th since 1901, thousands of believers climb a hill to thank the Virgin of the Immaculate Conception—who is believed to have appeared here. What is truly remarkable is that they climb the hill on their knees, and many arrive bleeding at the summit. The Festival of San Cono, which takes place every June 3 throughout the department of Florida, also attracts thousands of worshipers, who come to pray at the icon of the Italian saint. Brought here by the region's first Italian settlers in 1885, the icon is believed to have the power to perform miracles.

Soccer

"Other countries have their history," Helenio Herrera, Uruguay's most famous soccer coach once said, "we have our football." Indeed, soccer—*fútbol* here—is played *everywhere:* In every public square, on every street . . . literally anywhere there is a space, you will find men—young and old—playing it with passion and often a lot of skill, while their families and friends look on in support. To get an inkling of how passionately the game is followed here, try to attend a *clássico*, a match between Montevideo's two great rival professional teams, Nacional and

Peñarol, played amid the screams and encouragement of fanatical supporters at the capital's Estadio Centenario.

Exploring Uruguay

One of the smallest countries in South America, Uruguay might be described as a lonely nation buffeted by the sea, surrounded by vast amounts of farmland and gently rolling hills (nothing in the country is more than 2,000 ft in elevation). In sparsely developed Uruguay, all roads lead to the capital, Montevideo, which has the country's largest university, half the newspapers (with 90% of the circulation), half the doctors, and almost half the population. Montevideo's only cosmopolitan rival is Punta del Este, one of a handful of Atlantic Ocean resorts popular with well-heeled Brazilians and Argentines who can afford the region's high-priced variety of fun (mornings and afternoons at Gucci, evenings at heady bars and discos).

Great Itineraries

IF YOU HAVE 5 DAYS

Start your visit in **Montevideo** (everybody arrives in Montevideo, unless you're traveling by hydrofoil from Argentina) with a three-hour tour of the city. If you can, have lunch at the **Mercado del Puerto.** If you still have the energy, attend a tango show at **Cafe Sorocabana** or **Casa de Becho.** On the morning of your second day, depart by bus for **Punta del Este.** The two-hour ride should whet your appetite for a seafood lunch at one of Punta's many restaurants. If you don't suffer from seasickness, take the four-hour excursion to **Seawolf Island** in the afternoon. On the morning of the third day take a city tour of Punta del Este; if you're traveling by car, you can see all the major sights in one day. During your exploration you might well chance upon an invitation to one of the many chic summer parties thrown by the Brazilian and Argentine vacationers who overrun Punta during the high season; if not, enjoy the summer breeze on your post-dinner stroll. On the fourth day, travel back to Montevideo and on to **Colonia del Sacramento,** where you can wander around the settlement or arrange for an organized tour. Overnight in Colonia and return to Montevideo on the fifth day.

IF YOU HAVE MORE THAN 5 DAYS

Follow the itinerary described above. On the fifth day, return to Montevideo and organize a stay in an estancia (although arrangements should be made before or as soon as you first arrive in Montevideo). Although off the beaten path, the estancia experience is unique in that it affords the opportunity to experience Uruguayan rural life in modern comfort: most of the estancias included in this chapter offer such amenities as fine dining, swimming pools, and other comforts for when you tire of living the life of a cowboy. Spend as much time as you like in the countryside before returning to Montevideo.

MONTEVIDEO

Uruguay's capital and only major city, Montevideo has its share of glitzy shopping avenues and modern mid-rise office buildings. But few visitors come here specifically in search of big-city pleasures—Buenos Aires is where Montevideans themselves go when they need a dose of urban stimulation. This city of 1.5 million can be underwhelming if you let it, so turn your attention to the simpler things: walking down a quiet lane under a canopy of lavender-flower jacaranda trees, or wandering through a warren of vendors hawking crafts and caramelized peanuts. Here, your best memories are apt to be the result of serendipity.

Legend has it that Montevideo gained its name when a Portuguese explorer first laid eyes on the 435-ft-tall El Cerro hill at the mouth of the harbor and uttered the words *"monte vide eu"* (I see a hill). Built along the eastern bank of the Río de la Plata (River Plate), Montevideo takes full advantage of its scenic locale. When the weather is good, La Rambla, a waterfront avenue that links Ciudad Vieja (Old City) with the eastern suburbs, is packed with fishermen, ice cream vendors, sun worshipers, and joggers. Around sunset, volleyball and soccer matches smooth the way for hand-in-hand strolls and music—perhaps from a street musician playing tangos on his accordion.

Exploring Montevideo

Modern Montevideo expanded outward from the peninsular Ciudad Vieja, which is still noted for its narrow streets and elegant colonial architecture. The El Prado district, an exclusive enclave a few miles north of the city center, also retains the look and attitude of colonial Montevideo with its lavish mansions and grand parks. Bear in mind that these magnificent mansions were once summer homes for aristocratic Uruguayans who spent most of the year elsewhere, and you'll get some idea of the wealth this small country once enjoyed.

Numbers in white bullets in the text correspond to numbers in black bullets in the margins and on the Montevideo map.

Ciudad Vieja

A GOOD WALK

Begin at the Plaza Independencia, which marks the eastern border of the Old City and is where modern mid-rises begin to outnumber the city's colonial and republican artifacts. On the east side is the **Palacio Salvo** ①. The **Palacio Estevez** ② is on the south side of the plaza and the **Teatro Solís** ③ is a short walk east. A few blocks west in the center of the Old City is **Plaza Matriz** ④ and facing the plaza is the modest **El Cabildo** ⑤. On the opposite side of the square sits the oldest public building in Montevideo, **Catedral Matriz** ⑥. Calle Rincón marks the commercial and financial heart of the Old City; banks with names both familiar and obscure are cheek by jowl with art galleries and antiques dealers. At the corner of Calles Rincón and Misiones looms the **Casa de Rivera** ⑦. Turn left and walk southwest for two blocks on Washington, cross to the Plaza Zabala, and then continue north two blocks to reach the **Casa de Lavalleja** ⑧.

TIMING

This walk should take three or four hours. Ciudad Vieja is best visited in the morning, before noon, as it can get very crowded in the afternoon. The Cabildo is only open for visits from 4 PM to 8 PM, daily.

SIGHTS TO SEE

⑧ **Casa de Lavalleja.** The Lavalleja House was built in the early 18th century and later became the home of General Juan A. Lavalleja, who distinguished himself in Uruguay's war for independence from Spain (1825–28). Donated to the state in 1940 and incorporated into the National History Museum system, this pristine colonial home now displays period manuscripts and historical memorabilia. ⊠ *Calle Zabala 1469,* ☎ *2/915–1028.* ☞ *Free.* ☉ *Tues.–Fri. 1:30–6:30, Sun. and national holidays 2:30–6:30.*

⑦ **Casa de Rivera.** Once the home of General Fructuso Rivera, Uruguay's first president, and acquired by the government in 1942, the Rivera House currently contains a branch of the National History Museum. Exhibits inside document the development of Uruguay from the colo-

Montevideo

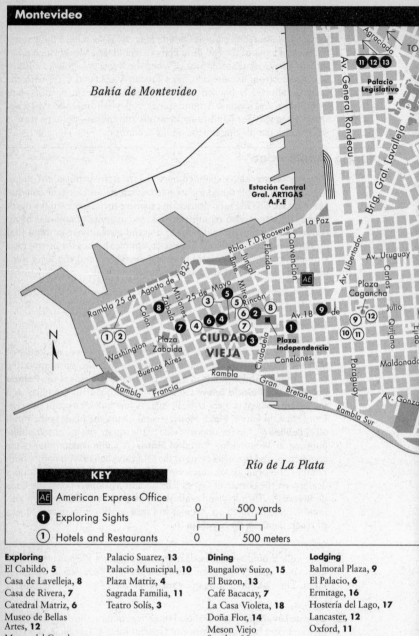

Bahía de Montevideo

Estación Central
Gral. ARTIGAS
A.F.E

Palacio
Legislativo

KEY

|AE| American Express Office
1 Exploring Sights
(1) Hotels and Restaurants

0   500 yards

0   500 meters

Río de La Plata

Exploring
El Cabildo, **5**
Casa de Lavelleja, **8**
Casa de Rivera, **7**
Catedral Matriz, **6**
Museo de Bellas
Artes, **12**
Museo del Gaucho y
la Moneda, **9**
Palacio Estevez, **2**
Palacio Salvo, **1**

Palacio Suarez, **13**
Palacio Municipal, **10**
Plaza Matriz, **4**
Sagrada Familia, **11**
Teatro Solís, **3**

Dining
Bungalow Suizo, **15**
El Buzon, **13**
Café Bacacay, **7**
La Casa Violeta, **18**
Doña Flor, **14**
Meson Viejo
Sancho, **10**
Olivier, **3**
La Pasiva, **4**
La Proa, **1**
Río Alegre, **2**

Lodging
Balmoral Plaza, **9**
El Palacio, **6**
Ermitage, **16**
Hostería del Lago, **17**
Lancaster, **12**
Oxford, **11**
Plaza Fuerte Hotel, **5**
Radisson Victoria
Plaza, **8**

nial period through the 1930s. ☒ *Calle Rincón 437,* ☏ *2/915–1051.* ☑ *Free.* ☉ *Tues.–Fri. 1:30–6:30, Sun. and national holidays 2:30–6:30.*

❻ Catedral Matriz. The oldest public building in Montevideo has a distinctive pair of dome-capped bell towers guarding the plaza like sentinels. Except for small touches such as its stained glass and its domed sanctuary, the Matriz Cathedral is most notable as the final resting place of Uruguay's most important political and military figures. ☒ *Calle Sarandí at Calle Ituzaingó.* ☑ *Free.* ☉ *Weekdays 8–8.*

❺ El Cabildo. The old City Hall is where the Uruguayan constitution was signed in 1830. This two-story colonial edifice now houses an impressive collection of paintings, antiques, and costumes, plus rotating history exhibits. English-speaking guides are available. ☒ *Calle Juan Carlos Gómez at Calle Sarandí,* ☏ *2/915–9685.* ☑ *Free.* ☉ *Daily 4–8.*

❷ Palacio Estevez. On the south side of Plaza Independencia, Estevez Palace was acquired by the government in 1878 and is used by the president on occasion for ceremonial purposes.

❶ Palacio Salvo. When it was built in 1927, the 26-story Salvo Palace was the tallest building in South America; today this commercial office block is still the tallest building in Montevideo.

Palacio Taranco. Built in 1908 atop the rubble of Uruguay's first theater, the Taranco Palace is representative of the French-inspired architectural styles favored in turn-of-the-century Montevideo. Today it has been converted into a cultural center filled with period furniture, statuary, draperies, clocks, and portrait paintings. ☒ *Calle 25 de Mayo 376,* ☏ *2/915–1101.* ☑ *Free.* ☉ *Tues.–Sun. 10–6.*

Plaza Independencia. Portions of Independence Square were once occupied by the *Ciudadela* (Citadel), a military fortification built originally by the Spanish but deemed militarily useless and destroyed in 1833. In the center stands a 30-ton statue of General Gervasio Artigas, the "father" of Uruguay and the founder of its 19th-century independence movement. At the base of the monument, two flights of polished granite stairs lead to the tomb where Artigas's remains are interred; a spotlight at night ensures that the general's urn is never in the dark.

❹ Plaza Matriz. Officially, Matriz Square is called Plaza Constitución, but nobody calls it that. The cantilever fountain in the center of the square was installed in 1871 to commemorate the inauguration of the city's water system.

❸ Teatro Solís. Completed in 1856 and named in honor of the discoverer of the Río de la Plata, Juan Diaz de Solís, the Solís Theater is famed for its acoustics. It is still the most important theater in Montevideo, as well as the site of numerous national and international cultural events. Unfortunately, it's currently closed for restoration. Sharing the building is the **Museo Nacional de Historia Natural** (National Museum of Natural History), with rotating history exhibits in addition to a few antiques and republican-era paintings. ☒ *Calle Buenos Aires 652,* ☏ *2/916–0908.* ☑ *Free.* ☉ *Call for hrs.*

Avenida 18 de Julio

Montevideo's main street has everything—shops and museums, cafés and plazas, bustling markets, and chrome-and-steel financial towers. It runs east from Plaza Independencia, away from the Old City.

A GOOD WALK

Walk east from Plaza Independencia along Avenida 18 de Julio; three blocks up the street is the **Museo del Gaucho y la Moneda** ⑨. Four blocks past Plaza Cagancha is the **Palacio Municipal** ⑩.

TIMING

It's a ½ hour walk from Plaza Independencia to the Palacio Munici-pal. To visit both sights on this tour, allow another 1½ hours for both. If shopping is your main interest, however, you may want to devote an entire afternoon to browsing and buying along the avenida.

SIGHTS TO SEE

★ ❾ **Museo del Gaucho y la Moneda.** The Gaucho and Coin Museum is in a lush 19th-century rococo mansion near Calle Julio Herrera y Obes, four blocks east of the plaza. Articles from everyday life, from tradi-tional gaucho garb to the detailed silver work on the cups used for *mate* (an indigenous herb from which tea is brewed), make this the city's best museum. Ancient South American and European coins are on the first floor, and other floors house paraphernalia associated with Uruguay's cowboys. English tours are available with two days' notice. ✉ *Av. 18 de Julio 998,* ☎ *2/900–8764.* ✆ *Free.* ⊙ *Tues.–Sun. 4–7.*

❿ **Palacio Municipal.** In its basement, the City Hall houses the **Biblioteca de Historia del Arte** (Library of Art History) and the **Museo de His-toria del Arte** (Museum of Art History). Bypass the library's large aca-demic holding and spend some time browsing the museum's small collection of pre-Columbian and colonial artifacts. At the Calle Sori-ano entrance you can take an elevator to the building's 26th-floor ob-servation deck for a panoramic view of the city. ✉ *Calle Ejido 1326,* ☎ *2/908–9252, ext. 500.* ✆ *Museum and library free, observation deck admission.* ⊙ *Weekday hours vary, observation deck 1 PM–11 PM.*

El Prado

A GOOD WALK

The El Prado district lies roughly 6 km (4 mi) north of Plaza Inde-pendencia and the Old City. You could make the long uphill walk along the busy Avenida Agraciada, but most prefer to take a taxi to the diminu-tive **Sagrada Familia** ⑪ (Holy Family) chapel. Calle Luis Alberto de Herrera cuts to the heart of the district, past numerous 18th- and 19th-century mansions. In many instances, estate grounds have been sold off and used for the later—and frankly bland—constructions that now occupy portions of this stretch. Breaking the tedium is the **Museo de Bellas Artes** ⑫. Enter the vast Parque El Prado, the district's name-sake, at Rambla Costanera and work your way toward **Avenida Buschental.** Avenida 19 de Abril eventually leads to Avenida Agraci-ada and the **Palacio Suarez** ⑬.

TIMING

This walk should take about two hours. Allow an hour for a visit to the Museo de Bellas Artes. It is pleasant to walk along Buschental and 19 de Abril streets in fall and spring, when the trees are in full color.

SIGHTS TO SEE

Avenida Buschental. This street meanders past the park's famous rose garden and into a neighborhood of imposing colonial mansions. Near the intersection of Calle Ruiz and Avenida 19 de Abril, look for some of El Prado's most splendid colonial homes; many have been immac-ulately restored, and several house private international foundations.

⑫ **Museo de Bellas Artes.** The Museum of Fine Arts, known locally as the Blanes Museum, is housed in an elegant colonial mansion that once belonged to Uruguay's foremost 19th-century painter, Juan Manuel Blanes. Although he was entirely self-taught and did not begin paint-ing until he was in his fifties, his realistic portrayals of gauchos and the Uruguayan countryside compose the core of the museum's other-wise bland collection. ✉ *Av. Millán 4015,* ☎ *2/336–2248.* ✆ *Free.* ⊙ *Tues.–Sun. 1–7.*

⑬ **Palacio Suarez.** The Presidential Palace is the president of Uruguay's official residence. The magnificent complex is closed to the public, but it can still be appreciated from the street. ⊠ *Av. Agraciada 3423.*

⑪ **Sagrada Familia.** Too tiny to need flying buttresses, the ornately Gothic Holy Family Church is complete in all other respects; a troop of gargoyles peers down at you, and the finely wrought stained-glass windows become radiant when backlit by the sun. ⊠ *Calle Luis Alberto de Herrera 4246,* ☎ *2/203–6824.* 🎟 *Free.* ☉ *Masses: Mon.–Sat. 6:30 PM–8 PM; Sun. from 9 AM–12:30 PM and 6:30 PM–8 PM.*

OFF THE
BEATEN PATH

MUSEO NACIONAL DE ARTES VISUALES – Parque Rodo has a little something for everyone—two amusement parks, a number of decent eateries, and the fascinating National Museum of Visual Arts, which recently hosted exhibits from as far afield as China and Poland. Between December 5 and January 6, Parque Rodo is also the site of Montevideo's best *feria artesanal* (crafts fair). ⊠ *Av. T. Giribaldi at Av. J. Herrera y Reisig,* ☎ *2/711–6054.* 🎟 *Free.* ☉ *Wed.–Sun. 4–8.*

PALACIO LEGISLATIVO – Almost 50 different types of native marble were used in the construction of the Legislative Palace, the seat of Uruguay's bicameral legislature. Free Spanish-language tours are available when the congress is in session; passes are available inside at the information desk. ⊠ *Av. Agraciada at Av. Flores,* ☎ *2/200–1334.* 🎟 *Free.* ☉ *Weekdays.*

Dining

Menus do not vary much in Montevideo—meat is king—so the food may not provide a distraction from the blinding light: even the toniest restaurant in Montevideo is brightly illuminated. For a light meal try one of the city's ubiquitous parrilladas, informal and often family-operated steak houses.

French

$$$$ ✕ **Doña Flor.** Housed in a renovated turn-of-the-century home in Punta Carretas, a nearby suburb of Montevideo (take a cab for less than $8), this quiet, elegant restaurant offers a diverse menu heavily indebted to the French (the pâté is rich as butter and twice as smooth). The house specialty is green lasagna with salmon. ⊠ *Bul. Artigas 1034, Punta Carretas,* ☎ *2/708–5751. Lunch reservations essential. AE, D, MC, V. Closed Dec. 20–Easter.*

$$$$ ✕ **Olivier.** Stone walls and cozy French provincial decor set the mood
★ in the intimate split-level dining room of one of Montevideo's finest restaurants, which occupies a renovated colonial home in the Old City. French chef Olivier Horion prepares an exquisite pâté de foie gras, and you shouldn't pass up his rabbit marinated in white wine and served with olives and salted potatoes. The desserts are delicately decorated and superb. The restaurant is always open for lunch, and special dinners are held on various days throughout the month. ⊠ *Calle Juan Carlos Gómez 1420,* ☎ *2/915–0617. AE, D, MC, V.*

Swiss

$$$$ ✕ **Bungalow Suizo.** This small restaurant makes you feel as though you are dining at the informal but refined home of a good friend. The split-level dining area is subdued and intimate, with private tables tucked into quiet corners. Fondue is the specialty of the house, supplemented by various cuts of beef. ⊠ *Calle Sol 150,* ☎ *2/601–1073. MC, V. Closed Sun. and Dec.–Apr. No lunch.*

Uruguayan

$$$-$$$$ ✕ **Meson Viejo Sancho.** What draws the posttheater crowds to this friendly but essentially nondescript downtown restaurant are gargantuan portions of smoked pork chops and *papas* Suez (fried potatoes). ⊠ *Calle San José 1229,* ☎ *2/900–4063. MC. Closed Sun.*

$$ ✕ **El Buzon.** This unassuming restaurant-cum-bar serves excellent pastas and parrilla. The *pollo Deschuesado* (boneless breast of chicken) is really something. For dessert try the *charlot* (vanilla ice cream with chocolate cream). ⊠ *Calle Hocquard 1801,* ☎ *2/200–9781. MC, V. No dinner Sun.*

$$ ✕ **La Casa Violeta.** A wide assortment of all-you-can-eat meats and a good selection of salads are the specialties at this restaurant, located in a beautiful house in the Carrasco neighborhood. Try the espeto corrido. ⊠ *Pedro Murillo 6566, Carrasco,* ☎ *2/600–1979. AE, DC, MC, V. Closed Mon. No dinner Tues.–Fri.*

$$ ✕ **La Proa.** In front of the Mercado del Puerto, the Old City's best food
★ plaza, this restaurant offers excellent dining in a lively outdoor atmosphere. The proprietor, Darwin, loves to talk about the artistry of refined cooking—he recommends his beef in prune sauce, "like Chaplin ate"—but most Montevideans come to La Proa because it's the best parrillada in the city. ⊠ *Calle Pérez Castellano at Calle Yacaré,* ☎ *2/916–2575. AE, D, MC, V.*

$ ✕ **Café Bacacay.** This small and smartly designed restaurant in front of Theater Solís has a European atmosphere and a wide selection of international dishes. Regina, the owner, takes special care in preparing the excellent salads. Try the Bacacay salad or the Sarandí salad. Otherwise, you can try the *plato del día* (plate of the day). ⊠ *Bacacay 1310, at Buenos Aires, Ciudad Vieja,* ☎ *2/916–6074. No credit cards. Closed Sun.*

$ ✕ **La Pasiva.** This popular *chopperia* (beer house), part of a local chain, is a late-night favorite. The specialties are ice-cold beer and uncomplicated bar food; try the chivitos. ⊠ *Calle Sarandí at Calle J.C. Gómez,* ☎ *no phones. Reservations not accepted. No credit cards.*

$ ✕ **Río Alegre.** Pepe, the proprietor of this intimate but lively restaurant, will stuff you full of homemade chorizo sausage and grilled provolone sprinkled with oregano. For a main course, *asado de tira* (short ribs) or *filete a la pimienta* (pepper steak) are good choices. ⊠ *Calle Pérez Castellano at Calle Piedras, in the Mercado del Puerto, local (stall) 033,* ☎ *2/915–6504. Reservations not accepted. V. No dinner.*

Lodging

Many downtown hotels are grouped around Plaza Bolívar and Plaza Libertad. In the weeks before and after Carnival in February, hotel rooms become scarce; be sure to book well in advance and be prepared to pay handsomely for even low-end rooms.

$$$-$$$$ 🏨 **Hostería del Lago.** Set among a huge slice of parkland in Carrasco,
★ 12 km (7 mi) from downtown, this white Spanish colonial hotel offers a relaxed atmosphere, a private lakefront beach, and a friendly multilingual staff. The suite-size rooms are split-level and fully carpeted; all have views of the lake. ⊠ *Av. Arizona 9637, Carrasco,* ☎ *2/601–2210,* FAX *2/601–2880. 70 rooms. Restaurant, room service, pool, tennis court, horseback riding, playground, airport shuttle. AE, D, MC, V.*

$$$-$$$$ 🏨 **Plaza Fuerte Hotel.** This renovated turn-of-the-century hotel is in
★ the heart of the Old City. While the rooms tend to be very small, they're quite stylish and immaculate. Each has a distinct look—themes range from "Zen" and "Pompeii" to an updated colonial style in the Del Virrey Room—rendered by a different interior designer. Wrought iron, flowing draperies, glass walls, and French windows are common touches.

Most rooms are bi-level to accommodate complete baths, and some have hot tubs. Landmark-preservation laws forbid changes to the hotel's public areas, so the lobby is virtually nonexistent—as it was in 1913—but abundant art, the original elevator, and elegant common sitting areas convey fin de siècle luxury. ⊠ *Bartolomé Mitre 1361, at Calle Sarandí,* ☏ *2/915–9563,* 𝖥𝖠𝖷 *2/915–9569. 24 rooms. Restaurant, bar, breakfast room, tea shop, minibars, no-smoking rooms, room service, laundry service. AE, D, MC, V.*

\$\$\$–\$\$\$\$ 🏨 **Radisson Victoria Plaza.** This property now comprises an old and a new Victoria: both dominate the best view of Montevideo and the rococo kitsch of Plaza Independencia. The newer wing, a luxurious glass-and-brick contemporary structure, is Montevideo's only internationally recognized five-star hotel, and it is where every famous person and president who visits the country stays. ⊠ *Plaza Independencia 759,* ☏ *2/902–0237,* 𝖥𝖠𝖷 *2/902–1628. 190 rooms, 64 suites. 2 restaurants, bar, coffee shop, minibars, room service, pool, exercise room, squash, airport shuttle. AE, D, MC, V.*

\$\$ 🏨 **Balmoral Plaza.** The lobby and accommodations are contemporary, bright, large, and quiet (double-pane windows nearly eliminate city noise)—a wonderful respite from noise and bustle of the Plaza Cagancha outside. A gracious multilingual staff and convenient downtown location make the Balmoral a favorite with business travelers. ⊠ *Plaza Cagancha 1126,* ☏ *2/902–2393,* 𝖥𝖠𝖷 *2/902–2288. 93 rooms, 4 suites. Restaurant, 2 bars, minibars, room service, sauna, exercise room, laundry service, meeting rooms. AE, D, MC, V.*

\$\$ 🏨 **Ermitage.** This unprepossessing, sandstone-fronted building over-
★ looks Plaza Tomas Gomensoro and the beach. The Ermitage has developed a loyal core of long-term residential guests, giving it a pleasant homey feeling; patrons visit over a drink or sit and play cards in the huge wood-paneled lobby. Rooms are furnished with 1920s furniture and light fixtures, reminiscent of kinder and gentler times. ⊠ *Calle Juan Benito Blanco 783,* ☏ *2/710–4021 or 2/711–7447,* 𝖥𝖠𝖷 *2/710–4312. 90 rooms. Restaurant. AE, D, MC, V.*

\$\$ 🏨 **Oxford.** Glass walls, broad windows, and mirrors that date from a recent renovation give the small lobby an open but intimate feel, much like the hotel itself. The rooms are immaculately clean, the staff friendly and heroically helpful. Despite its downtown location, street noise is not a problem. ⊠ *Calle Paraguay 1286,* ☏ *2/902–0046,* 𝖥𝖠𝖷 *2/902–3792. 64 rooms, 2 suites. Bar, in-room safes, minibars, business services. AE, D, MC, V.*

\$ 🏨 **El Palacio.** This no-frills place is comfortable and extremely well located. The rooms are all furnished with antiques, and each has its own balcony overlooking the Old City. ⊠ *Calle Bartolomé Mitre 1364,* ☏ *2/916–3612. 14 rooms. No credit cards.*

\$ 🏨 **Lancaster.** Hidden away in a corner of Plaza Cagancha, near the bus terminal, the Lancaster might be past its glory days, but no one has told either the staff or loyal patrons. The rooms are sunny and large, with full-length French doors that open over the plaza. ⊠ *Plaza Cagancha 1334,* ☏ *2/902–0029 or 2/902–1054,* 𝖥𝖠𝖷 *2/908–1117. 78 rooms. Bar, cafeteria, laundry service. AE, D, MC, V.*

Nightlife and the Arts

Nightlife

Montevideo has all kinds of nightlife if you know where to find it. There are quiet late-night bars as well as hip-hopping clubs and folk music shows. The entertainment and cultural pages of local papers are the best sources of information; particularly useful is the *Guía del Ocio,* a magazine inserted into the Friday edition of *El Pais.* With few exceptions bars and clubs come to life around 1 AM and do not close until it is time for breakfast.

DANCE CLUBS

You can hear live music and dance to house hits at **Mariachi** (⊠ Gabriel Pereira 2964, ☎ 2/709–1600). **Milenio** (⊠ 25 de Mayo and Ciudadela) is popular with the MTV generation. Twentysomethings also flock to **XYZ** (⊠ Jackson 1072), which comprises nine separate bars. **New York** (⊠ Calle Mar Artico 1227, ☎ 2/600–0444) draws an older crowd. The retro set flocks to **Aquellos Años** (⊠ Calle Beyrouth 1405), which features music from the '50s and '60s.

PUBS

Amarcor (⊠ Calle Julio Herrera y Obes 1231, ☎ 2/900–1207) is popular with young Montevidean artists, actors, and intellectuals. Also try **Perdidos en la noche** (⊠ Calle Yaguarón 1099, ☎ 2/902–6733). **Riff Gallery Pub** (⊠ Bul. España 2511, ☎ no phone) is the only bar in the city devoted to jazz, with live shows on Thursday and Saturday.

TANGO SHOWS

Although you need reservations for most tango shows, they are not blatantly geared to tourists. The weekend shows at **La Vieja Cumparsita** (⊠ Calle Carlos Gardel 1181, ☎ 2/901–6245) feature a tango and candombe—dance and music associated with Carnival. **Cafe Sorocabana** (⊠ Peatonal Yi 1377, ☎ 2/900–8710) has tango shows on Friday and Saturday. **La Casa de Becho** (⊠ New York 1415, ☎ 2/400–2717), the house where Mattos Rodríguez, the composer of "La Cumparsita," lived, has weekend shows for a younger crowd.

The Arts

Closed for renovations, the **Teatro Solís** (⊠ Calle Buenos Aires 678, ☎ 2/915–1968) normally hosts symphonies, ballet, and opera between May and November. **SODRE,** the Servicio Oficial de Difusió Radio Elétrica (Official Radio Service; ⊠ Av. 18 de Julio 930, ☎ 2/901–2850) has a season of classical concerts that runs from May to November. A number of binational centers such as the **Alliance Française** (⊠ Calle Soriano 1176, ☎ 2/900–8084), the **Instituto Goethe** (Goethe Institute; ⊠ Calle Canelones 1524, ☎ 2/409–3499), and the U.S.-sponsored **Alianza Artigas-Washington** (⊠ Calle Paraguay 1217, ☎ 2/900–2721) host plays and concerts by foreign talent.

Shopping

Centers

There are three major shopping centers in Montevideo, offering everything from imported designer-label clothing to gourmet foods to art supplies. The original, called **Montevideo Shopping Center** (⊠ Av. Luis Alberto de Herrera and Calle General Galarza, ☎ 2/622–1005), is near Parque Rodo. **Portones de Carrasco** (⊠ Avs. Bolívia and Italia, ☎ 2/601–1733) is in the suburb of Carrasco. **Punta Carretas Shopping Center** (⊠ Calles Ellauri and Solano ☎ 2/701–0598) is housed in a former prison, of which a portion is preserved and open to the public.

Markets

Weekend *ferias* (open-air markets) are probably the best forum for leisurely browsing among a warren of crafts stalls. Government regulations dictate that all ferias must close for the day in the early afternoon, so arrive around 10 AM. **Feria Tristán Narvaja** was started more than 50 years ago by Italian immigrants and nowadays is Montevideo's premier Sunday attraction. The Saturday morning feria at **Plaza Biarritz** in Pocitos, a nearby suburb, features foodstuffs, *artesanía* (crafts), clothes, and some antiques. At **Plaza Cagancha,** between Avenida 18 de Julio and Calle Rondeau, there is a daily crafts market. It is now part of a larger artisan market at Calle San José and Aquiles Lanza.

Specialty Shops

ANTIQUES

Calle Tristán Narvaja north of Avenida 18 de Julio is packed with antiques shops. **El Rincón** (⊠ Calle Tristán Narvaja 1747, ☎ 2/400–2283) is one of the area's best antiques dealers. In the Old City, Calle Bartolomé Mitre and Calle Rincón are also lined with antiques stores. You can get good deals from the vendors on the streets surrounding the Tristán Narvaja Market on Sundays.

GEMSTONES AND JEWELRY

Gemas de América (⊠ Av. 18 de Julio 948, ☎ 2/902–2572) carries amethyst and topaz jewelry, agate slices, and elaborate objects made of gemstones. **Amatistas Del Uruguay** (⊠ Calle P. Sarandí 604, ☎ 2/916–6456) also specializes in agates, as well as amethyst, topaz, and other gemstone jewelry. **La Limeña** (⊠ Calle Buenos Aires 542, ☎ no phone) has good prices on unset stones.

HANDICRAFTS

Manos de Uruguay (⊠ Calle Reconquista 602; ⊠ Calle San José 111; ⊠ Montevideo Shopping Center [☞ *above*], ☎ no phone) has three locations with a wide selection of woolen wear and locally produced ceramics. **Ema Camuso** (⊠ Av. 8 de Octubre 2574, ☎ no phone) offers a sophisticated and sporty line of hand-knit sweaters for export, all permanently on sale at factory prices. The **Louvre** (⊠ Calle Sarandí 652, ☎ no phone), an antiques store, is the only source for handmade and painted trinket boxes—the perfect *recuerdos* (souvenir).

LEATHER

Shops near Plaza Independencia specialize in hand-tailored nutria coats and jackets. **Peleteria Holandesa** (⊠ Calle Colonia 894, ☎ 2/901–5438) carries a wide array of leather clothing. **Péndola** (⊠ Calle San José 1087, ☎ 2/900–1524) also has a particularly good selection of different leather apparel. Also try **Casa Mario** (⊠ Calle Piedras 639, ☎ 2/916–2356). Custom-made boots are available from **Damino Botas** (⊠ Calle Rivera 2747, ☎ 2/709–7823).

Side Trips from Montevideo

Colonia de Sacramento

Originally a Portuguese settlement founded in the 17th century, Colonia del Sacramento is the small but lovely *barrio histórico* (historic district) of greater Colonia. The city's **tourist office** (⊠ Av. General Flores 499, ☎ 522/2182) stocks maps, but everything here is within walking distance. Start at the municipal museum, housed in the two-story **Casa de Brown** (Brown House; ⊠ Calle San Francisco, ☎ no phone), with a collection of colonial artifacts and documents. The city's oldest church, **La Vieja Iglesia** (⊠ Calle 18 de Julio), dates from 1680. The impressive **Callejón de Suspiros** (Street of Sighs) is lined with single-story colonial homes covered with bougainvillea.

Dining and Lodging

$$ × **Restaurant Pulpería de los Faroles.** The specialties at this old, stone, colonial house are *lomo a los faroles* (beef with beans) and its fantastic selection of pastas. ⊠ *Calle Misiones de los Tapes y del Comercio 101,* ☎ *522/5399. AE, MC, V. Closed Mon.–Wed.*

$$$ ⊡ **Hotel Plaza Mayor.** This renovated hotel in the historic district is an experience in colonial lodging. The simple, clean rooms, many with high ceilings and beveled-glass doors, overlook a peaceful garden. ⊠

Calle Del Comercio 111, ☎ *522/3193. 8 rooms. Breakfast room, minibars, room service. AE, D, MC, V.*

Estancias in the Uruguayan Countryside

One of the nicest ways to experience Uruguay's vast unspoiled countryside is to stay at an estancia. These large ranches usually raise cattle or sheep for the country's most-prized export goods—wool, beef, and leather. Although some now exist solely to host tourists, most are fully working ranches that cultivate nearly all the food consumed by visitors—from milk and honey to vegetables and the obvious meat. Guests may meet the *estancieros* (ranchers) and stay in quarters that date from the colonial period. For most visitors, however, the highlight is accompanying the gauchos, Uruguay's cowboys, while they herd cattle, shear sheep, tend farm animals, assist at calvings, or simply sit around a fire roasting up some farm-fresh sausages for lunch.

Accommodations range from the comfortable to the most luxurious, and meals are generally included. Some estancias have built swimming pools and tennis courts; most offer guests a chance to roam their vast estates on horseback and to fish, boat, and swim in local rivers, lakes, or swimming holes. Still, the most important thing to do when visiting an estancia is to relax, eat well, and breathe the fresh air of the open Uruguayan range.

Estancias

$$ ✕⌂ **Estancia San Pedro del Timote.** Originally established in 1854, this massive estate in the department of Florida was once the biggest farm in Uruguay. Completely renovated in 1997, it combines the true feeling of an old estancia with all the comforts of the modern world (minus TVs). Arched walkways surround a lush garden, the outdoor pool, and a tennis court; inside, colorful tiled floors and antique wooden furniture adorn the library, salons, and rooms of San Pedro. In addition to the usual walks in the country, rodeos, and gaucho activities, San Pedro offers an extensive spa program. ⊠ *Book through Estancias Gauchas (☞ Tour Operators and Travel Agencies in Montevideo A to Z, below),* ☎ FAX *2/711–1531 in Montevideo. 20 rooms. Breakfast room, pool, spa, tennis court, library, meeting rooms. AE, D, MC, V.*

Montevideo A to Z

Arriving and Departing

BY AIRPLANE

Uruguay's principal airport, **Carrasco International Airport** (☎ 2/601–1991), is 24 km (15 mi) east of Montevideo. It is regularly served by several airlines including **American** (☎ 2/916–7138 or 2/916–7139), **PLUNA-Varig** (☎ 2/902–0273, 2/902–3906, or 2/902–1414), and **United Airlines** (☎ 2/902–4630 or 2/902–5932). Getting from the airport to your hotel is as easy as hailing a cab (about $35 to downtown). There's also an airport bus to Plaza Independencia ($5), which you can pick up out in front of the small airport.

BY BUS

Montevideo's new, central, state-of-the-art bus terminal, **Tres Cruces** (⊠ Bul. General Artigas 1825, at Calle Galicia, ☎ 2/401–8998), makes taking the bus an easy option. Buses depart here for all cities in Uruguay as well as Argentina, Brazil, Paraguay, and Chile. Carriers offering frequent service at Tres Cruces are: **CITA** (☎ 2/402–5425), which serves San José, Canelones, Florida, Rocha, and Cerro Largo; **COIT** (☎ 2/401–5628), which serves Asuncíon, Paraguay; **COPSA** (☎ 2/409–9855), which serves Canelones and Punte del Este–Maldonado; **COT** (☎ 2/409–

4949); **EGA** (☎ 2/402–5164), which serves Chile; **Rutas del Sol** (☎ 2/
402–5451), which serves Rocha, Maldonado, and Lavalleja; **Rutas
del Plata** (☎ 2/402–5129), which serves Río Branco; and **TTL** (☎ 2/
401–1410), which serves Porto Allegre and Sáo Paolo, Brazil.

BY CAR

Coming from Brazil, take Route 1 west, which eventually becomes La
Rambla, Montevideo's riverside thoroughfare; turn north on Calle
Ciudadela to reach Plaza Independencia. Route 1 also connects Mon-
tevideo with Colonia.

BY FERRY

Buquebus (✉ Calle Río Negro 1400, ☎ 2/902–0170, 2/903–2109, or
2/902–0671, FAX 2/901–2555) has hydrofoil service between Montevideo
and Buenos Aires. Fares are around $75 round-trip. Including board-
ing and customs at either end, the journey takes roughly 3½ hours.

Getting Around

BY BUS

Montevideo's public buses crisscross the entire city 24 hours a day and
offer a great alternative to the difficult task of obtaining a taxi during
peak hours, but they are only for the adventurous who are willing to
learn the system. It takes some extra effort on your part to find out
exactly where buses stop and where to get off, but you don't need exact
change, and the price—for any trip within Montevideo—is only 50¢.

Colonia is 242 km (150 mi) west of Montevideo and serviced daily by
bus from Montevideo; contact **COT** (✉ Tres Cruces bus terminal, Montevideo, ☎ 2/409–4949) or **TURIL** (✉ Tres Cruces bus terminal, Montevideo, ☎ 2/402–1990). The three-hour ride costs less than $15.

BY TAXI

All cabs have meters and the initial fare is roughly 65¢ at flag fall and
40¢ per ⅓ km. You can hail taxis on the street with ease or call one of
the radio-dispatched cab companies: **Radio Taxi Carrasco** (☎ 2/600–
0416), **Radio Taxi La Española** (☎ 2/401–5151), and **TeleTaxi** (☎ 2/
487–4956 or 2/487–2525).

ON FOOT

Distances between Montevideo's districts can be quite far for all but
the most determined walkers, so consider taking a bus or cab between
most destinations. A revitalization of the Old City has made it safer
to walk at night, but as in any large city, you should always be extra
cautious after dark. Most of Montevideo's residents stay up quite late,
so the streets are usually full of people until 1 AM.

Contacts and Resources

BANKS AND CURRENCY EXCHANGE

Cambio Matriz (✉ Av. Rincón 487, ☎ 2/915–0800) is a convenient
place to change money. **Bancomat** and **Redbrou** machines accept ATM
cards on the CIRRUS network; you can withdraw both dollars and
Uruguayan pesos.

BUSINESS SERVICES

Almost every large hotel in Montevideo has some type of office for business services. Some include computers and Internet access as well as
photocopying and fax machines.

EMERGENCIES

Ambulance: ☎ 105. **Fire:** ☎ 104. **Police:** ☎ 109. **Pharmacy** (24-hours):
☎ 0900-2020.

The best place to find English–language print media is in one of the shops at the major hotels.

HEALTH AND SAFETY

Although Montevideo doesn't have the crime problems of other large cities in South America, it is advisable to watch your wallet in crowded markets and to avoid walking down deserted streets at night. Also, the city bus authority discourages getting on empty buses at night, as foreigners can be targets for robbery.

TELEPHONES, THE INTERNET, AND MAIL

Telephone service in the city is dependable most of the time. As for E-mail and Internet access, your best bet is from the major hotels. You might find a cybercafé or two, although they tend to come and go quickly. Ask at your hotel to see what's available.

The main branches of the **Post Office** (✉ Av. Ejido 1322, ☎ 2/900–4038 and ✉ Av. Mercedes 929, ☎ 2/900–4366) are the most reliable places to send and receive mail. A general number (☎ 0800–2108) is also available to help customers find the addresses of other post office locations. Both Federal Express and DHL have offices in Montevideo (☞ Mail in Uruguay A to Z, *below*).

TOUR OPERATORS AND TRAVEL AGENTS

Viajes Buemes (✉ Av. Colonia 979, ☎ 2/902–1050, FAX 2/902–1791) organizes half-day, English-language bus tours. Passengers are collected from the major hotels starting at 9 AM. On Friday and Saturday nights the "Montevideo by Night" tour includes an abbreviated city tour, dinner and a tango show at Casa de Becho, and a casino visit.

Cecilia Regules Viajes (✉ Bacacay 1334, Local C, ☎ 2/916–3011 or 2/915–7308, FAX 2/916–3012), a travel agency with English-speaking agents, can arrange everything from city tours and excursions to the country to departing flights; one division of the agency, Estancias Gauchas, books popular packages at more than 100 working ranches in the countryside. They can also book estancia packages that include stays in Montevideo. You can also contact **Free Way** (✉ Colonia 994, ☎ 2/908931 or 2/900–8933) for walking tours, city tours, and other excursions.

Full-day tours of Colonia del Sacramento with an English-speaking guide are offered by **J. P. Santos Travel Agency** (✉ Calle Colonia 951, Montevideo, ☎ 2/902–0397).

VISITOR INFORMATION

Ministerio de Turismo (✉ Calle Colonia 1021, ☎ 2/900–1078 or 2/901–4340, FAX 2/901–6907), with additional offices at Carrasco Airport and Terminal Tres Cruces, has city maps and other basic information; hours are from 9–6.

PUNTA DEL ESTE

Despite being a mere two hours down the pike from Montevideo, Uruguay's highly touted Punta del Este is definitely a world apart. Punta del Este (shortened to "Punta" by locals) and the handful of surrounding beachfront communities are famous as jet-set resorts and sites of countless international festivals and conferences—the sort of places where lounging on white sand and browsing designer boutiques constitute the day's most demanding activities.

Punta is not for everyone: The resort's colonial architecture has been largely replaced with high-rise hotels and apartments, and those striking mansions you see hidden among tall pines on the beach house well-to-do Argentines, Brazilians, and Europeans, not museums. Still, Punta is justly revered for its long stretches of white-sand beach and elegant shopping avenues. For thousands of younger South Americans it is also *the* place (excluding Rio, of course) to let your hair down and watch the sunrise from the balcony of an all-night disco.

Punta is underwhelming in the low season—the buildings are shuttered against the elements, their tenants gone elsewhere. On January 1 the city comes alive, lured out of dormancy by the smell of tourist dollars. Plan on a visit in either December or March (except during Holy Week, when prices skyrocket). During these two months the weather is superb, with an average daily temperature of 75°F, and the beaches are not unbearably crowded.

Piriápolis

98 km (61 mi) east of Montevideo.

First established as a private residence by a Uruguayan developer more than a century ago, Piriápolis is nowadays a laid-back beachfront enclave that lacks the sophistication—and the extortionate prices—of nearby Punta del Este. Piriápolis has plenty of stores and restaurants, a casino, and the grand Hotel Argentino, built in the old European tradition with spas and thermal pools (and an ice-skating rink!). **Punta Fría and Playa Grande** are the town's best beaches, with white sand and large summertime crowds.

Punta Ballena

25 km (15 mi) east of Piriápolis, 10 km (6 mi) west of Punta del Este.

Built on a bluff overlooking the ocean, Punta Ballena is almost impossible to see from the main road—no cause for complaint from the resort's wealthy patrons. The main draw here is **Casa Pueblo,** an exclusive artists' community perched at the tip of a rocky point with tremendous views of the Atlantic. Casa Pueblo is a showpiece that fits no known architectural definition: Entirely of white stucco and adorned with strange projections and even stranger appurtenances, it can best be described as Dali meets Disney. Inside is an art gallery with a warren of rooms showcasing Picasso-derivative art, a restaurant, and an aloof hotel. Inland, the **Arboretum Lussich** is a huge parkland that perfumes the air with the scent of eucalyptus.

Punta del Este

10 km (6 mi) east of Punta Ballena, 138 km (86 mi) east of Montevideo.

The resort town of Punta del Este, which also lends its name to the broader region encompassing Punta Ballena and La Barra de Maldonado, has long been a favorite spot for sunseekers escaping the Northern Hemisphere winter. In Punta proper—the peninsular resort bounded by Playa Mansa (Mansa Beach) and Playa Brava (Brava Beach)—beach bumming is the prime activity. In fact, if you are not into eating, drinking, and worshiping the sun, about the only other attractions are the gypsies hustling tourists on Calle Gorlero, and the artisans' feria at Plaza Artigas. This colorful crafts market is held at the intersection of El Ra-manso and El Corral and is open weekends 5 PM–midnight; between Christmas and Holy Week, it's open daily 6 PM–1 AM.

Punta is circled by **Rambla Artigas,** the main coastal road that leads past residential neighborhoods and pristine stretches of beach. **Calle Gorlero,** Punta's main commercial strip, runs north–south through the heart of the peninsula and is fronted with cafés, restaurants, and elegant shopping boutiques bearing names such as Yves St. Laurent and Gucci.

Dining

Restaurants come and go with seasonal regularity in Punta del Este. The better restaurants reopen from year to year, often transferring their operations to Montevideo during the low season and returning to Punta around Christmastime. Year-round options—none of them spectacular—are generally along Punta's Calle Gorlero; they tend to be moderately priced and serve meat rather than seafood.

$$$$ ✕ **La Bourgogne.** A shaded terra-cotta terrace gives way to an arch-win-
★ dowed breezeway, while the intimate reception area opens onto a large split-level dining room where antique sideboards serve as "stations." The food, served by impeccably clad waiters who go about their business with cordial authority, is prepared with only the finest and freshest of ingredients; the breads are baked on the premises (an adjoining bakery sells them by the loaf), and the herbs and berries are grown in the backyard garden. Start your meal with the gourmet salad, then try the plaice with pink peppercorns. The desserts are sublime, and the sampler is a good way to try them all. ⊠ *Av. del Mar at Calle P. Sierra,* ☎ 42/82007. *Reservations essential. MC. Closed Holy Week–Dec. 25.*

$$$ ✕ **Andrés.** Operated by a father and son, both of whom answer to Andrés, this unassuming restaurant on the Rambla offers fine dining at relatively moderate prices. Most of the tables are outdoors under a canopy, so you can appreciate the excellent service while also enjoying the sea breeze. The fish *Andrés* (seasonally available fish in a white wine and tomato sauce), spinach soufflé or cheese soufflé, and grilled meats are recommended. ⊠ *Parada 1, Edificio Vaguardia,* ☎ 42/81804. *AE, MC, V. Closed Mon.–Wed. Apr.–Nov.*

$$$ ✕ **Citrus.** This restaurant in La Barra, the trendiest spot in Punta, is owned by chef Alejandra, an Argentine-American who brought her Latino–Californian nouvelle cuisine from Los Angeles, where her fans included the likes of Spielberg and Streisand. The warm chicken salad and grilled swordfish with a ginger citrus sauce are specialties. ⊠ *Ruta 10, between Calles 9 and 10, La Barra,* ☎ 42/70530. *Reservations essential. No credit cards. Closed Apr.–Dec. 14. No lunch.*

$$$ ✕ **Yacht Club Uruguayo.** Long a favorite with locals, this small eatery has a great view of the Isla Gorriti across the water. The menu includes a bit of everything, but the specialty of the house is seafood; perennial favorites are *brotola a la* Roquefort (baked hake) and *pulpo* Provençal, likely the most tender octopus you have ever eaten. ⊠ *Rambla Artigas between Calles 6 and 8,* ☎ 42/41056. *AE, D, MC, V.*

$$ ✕ **Restaurante Ciclista.** This no-frills restaurant serves the best inexpensive meals in Punta. The *tortilla de papas* (potato pancake) is extremely hearty, as are the pastas. The homemade soups are another popular lure. ⊠ *Calle 20 at Calle 27,* ☎ 42/40007. *AE, D, MC, V.*

Lodging

There are numerous hotels in and around Punta del Este, running the architectural gamut from wonderfully modern to bland ho-hum. Except during the high season many rooms are empty and often stay that way for months at a time; but during January and February, Punta teems with sunbathers and pleasure seekers, and rooms are extremely difficult to come by, so book well in advance.

$$$$ 🏨 **L'Auberge.** In the heart of the Parque del Golf neighborhood, Punta's chicest, the small lobby of this renovated hotel is bursting with antiques and cozy sofas. An 18th-century crenellated water tower, which contains guest rooms, rises from the hotel's double-winged chalet. Rooms are tastefully adorned with beautiful antiques; some even have working fireplaces. The property is landscaped with a rolling lawn and a lovely terraced flower garden; some of Punta del Este's finest beaches are just a few blocks away, but the secluded grounds create a world apart from the busy and often crowded beach. ⊠ *Barrio Parque del Golf,* ☎ *42/82601,* 🏷 *42/83408. 40 rooms. Restaurant, bar, breakfast room, pool, hot tub. AE, D, MC, V.*

$$$$ 🏨 **Conrad Resort & Casino Punta del Este.** This huge resort has given Punta del Este an incredible new look. Spectacularly lit fountains and gardens, an abundant use of marble, and stunning art by Uruguayan painter Carlos Páez Vilaró make this one of Punta's most extraordinary hotels. Every room has a terrace with views of La Brava and La Mansa beaches. Unique to most of the region's hotels, two of the floors cater to nonsmokers. There are two ballrooms and a casino to rival some of Las Vegas's best. ⊠ *Calle Biarritz y Bulevar Artigas at Parada 4 de la Mansa,* ☎ *42/91111,* 🏷 *42/91361. 278 rooms, 24 suites. Restaurant, bar, no-smoking floors, pool, business services. AE, D, MC, V.*

$$$ 🏨 **Palace Hotel.** The Palace occupies a central position on the Gorlero ★ shopping avenue inside one of Punta's oldest structures—a three-story Spanish colonial masterpiece complete with an airy interior courtyard. The restaurant has one of the largest wine cellars in the country. ⊠ *Calle Gorlero at Calle 11,* ☎ *42/41919 or 42/41418,* 🏷 *42/44695. 47 rooms. Restaurant, bar, breakfast room, room service. AE, D, MC, V.*

$$ 🏨 **Hotel Salzburg.** This charming hotel occupies a white-stucco, three-story chalet with polished slate floors and exposed beams. Its rooms are blessed with ceiling fans, modern bathrooms, and fine views framed by flower-filled window boxes. ⊠ *Calle Pedragosa Sierra at El Havre,* ☎ *42/88851. 14 rooms. Bar, cafeteria. No credit cards.*

Nightlife

The very name Punta del Este is synonymous with high-paced evenings in bars and nightclubs that start as late as 1 AM and only reach a fever pitch around sunrise. Most are open during the high season only and have a cover charge—sometimes as much as $30 per person.

DANCE CLUBS

Hop in a cab and head for **Gitane La Plage** (⊠ Rambla Brava, Parada 12, ☎ no phone), which is located on the road towards La Barra. The club is right on Playa Brava and has two dance floors, both of which feature booming house music. In La Barra, **Space** (⊠ Central La Barra, ☎ no phone) occupies an enormous warehouse bursting with five different bars. All taxi drivers are familiar with the area.

Outdoor Activities and Sports

Equipment rental, especially for water sports, is not an idea whose time has come in Punta del Este, despite the many surf shops that have sprung up over the last few years.

GOLF

There are two golf clubs in Maldonado. Greens fees average $70 for 18 holes. Contact Punta's **Club de Golf** (☎ 42/82127) or Punta Ballena's **Club de Lago** (☎ 42/78423).

HORSEBACK RIDING

Mosey over to **Club Hípico Parque Burnett** (☎ 42/30765), an equestrian center on the distant outskirts of Punta in Pinares, for an afternoon of trail riding.

Estancias Gauchas (☞ Tour Operators and Travel Agents *in* Montevideo A to Z, *above*) offers various options not farther than 60 km (40 mi) from Punta del Este, where you can ride and observe the Gaucho life.

POLO

From December 15th to February 28th there are several polo tournaments in Punta del Este, the most famous of which are the **Medellín Polo Cup** and the **José Ignacio Tournament,** attended by some of the best players from South America and Europe.

La Barra de Maldonado

5 km (3 mi) east of Punta del Este.

Gaily painted buildings give La Barra a carnivalesque atmosphere, but this small resort also has some of the area's cleanest and finest beaches. From Punta you can walk along the beach and cross over to La Barra on a cement camelback bridge. Just before you reach La Barra, at Parada (bus stop) 17, is Playa Verde, one such beach. In town, you'll find a handful of antiques dealers, surf shops, and pubs that are offer an afternoon's diversion—it's also where Punta's young people come to do their eating, dancing, and drinking. Once you move off Calle No. 7 (also called Del Encuentro), La Barra's principal thoroughfare, there's nothing notable except the ocean.

Dining and Lodging

$$$$
★
✕🎍 **La Posta del Cangrejo.** From its stylish lobby to its relaxed lounge and restaurant, this hotel takes an informal approach to luxury. The Mediterranean theme—red tile floors and white stucco walls—complements the impeccably decorated guest rooms; each is furnished with hand-stenciled antiques and canopied beds and has views of either the beach or the small country garden. The staff is warm, accommodating, and inordinately fond of their hotel. The adjoining seafood restaurant is equally outstanding. ⊠ *La Barra de Maldonado,* ☎ 42/70021 or 42/70271, 🆋 42/70173. *29 rooms. Restaurant, bar, breakfast room, air-conditioning, in-room safes, pool, laundry service. AE, D, MC, V.*

Punta del Este A to Z

Arriving and Departing

Consider a package tour from Montevideo regardless of the length of your stay. There is much to see and do in nearby Punta Ballena and La Barra, and travel plans will be more difficult, not to mention costly, to arrange once you're in Punta.

BY AIRPLANE

All international commercial flights land at Montevideo's **Carrasco International Airport** (☎ 2/601–1991), about 24 km (15 mi) east of downtown. A small airport in Punta del Este, **El Jaquel** (☎ 42/84513) is used for private jets and commuter flights to and from Buenos Aires. There is no air service between Montevideo and Punta del Este's **Aeropuerto Internacional de Laguna del Sauce** (also known as Aeropuerto Carlos Curbelo; ⊠ Camino del Placer, ☎ 42/59777), on the northern edge of the city. However, **PLUNA-Varig** (☎ 42/45292), **Aerolíneas Argentinas** (☎ 42/44343), and **LAPA** (☎ 42/90840) fly regularly between Buenos Aires and Punta. The flight takes 30 minutes and costs about $60 each way.

BY BUS

Many bus lines travel daily between Montevideo and Piriápolis, with ongoing service to Punta del Este's **Terminal Playa Brava** (⊠ Rambla

Artigas and Calle Inzaurraga). It is best to check with Montevideo's Tres Cruces bus terminal about departure times (☞ Arriving and Departing By Bus *in* Montevideo A to Z, *above*). In Punta del Este, you can call **COPSA** (☎ 42/89205) or **COT** (☎ 42/86810).

BY CAR

From Montevideo follow Interbalnearia (Rte. 1) east to the Route 93 turnoff. The road is well maintained and marked, and the trip takes about 1½ hours.

Contacts and Resources

BANKS AND CURRENCY EXCHANGE

Discount Bank (✉ Av. Gorlero 903) and the **American Express** office (✉ Av. Gorlero 644, ☎ 42/42555) are convenient places to change money. **Bancomat** and **Redbrou** machines accept ATM cards on the CIRRUS network; you can withdraw both dollars and Uruguayan pesos.

BUSINESS SERVICES

Some of the larger hotels have business service offices with computers, fax machines, and other equipment.

EMERGENCIES

Ambulance: ☎ 105. **Fire:** ☎ 104. **Hospital:** Calle Ventura Alegre, ☎ 42/25889. **Police:** ☎ 109. **Pharmacies:** La Barra, Ruta 10, Km 160, ☎ 42/45326 (24 hours); Campus, Av. Gorlero 920, ☎ 42/44444.

ENGLISH-LANGUAGE BOOKSTORES

The only places to pick up English-language publications are at the larger hotels and street kiosks.

TELEPHONES, THE INTERNET, AND MAIL

Calls can be made from public or hotel phones; service is usually reliable. The **Cybermix** (✉ Av. Gorlero and Calle 30, ☎ 42/47158) is a cybercafé that offers E-mail and Internet services. Sending and receiving mail is most convenient through the main **Post Office** (✉ Av. Gorlero and Calle 17, ☎ 42/40103).

TOUR OPERATORS AND TRAVEL AGENTS

The **Piriápolis Tourist Office** (✉ Rambla de los Argentinos 1348, ☎ 43/22560) can provide hotel listings and maps for the town.

For package tours to Punta Ballena and La Barra, contact **Cecilia Regules Viajes** (✉ Calle Bacacay 1334, Local C, ☎ 2/915–7308 or 2/916–3011, FAX 2/916–3012). Travel agencies on Calle Gorlero can assist with hotel bookings, onward travel plans, and excursions. The **Centro de Hoteles y Restaurantes** (✉ Plaza Artigas, on Av. Gorlero between Calle 25 and Calle 23, ☎ 42/40512) and the **Centro de Informes** (✉ Gorlero 688, ☎ 42/41218 or 42/41227) also provide tourist information.

VISITOR INFORMATION

Liga de Fomento (✉ Calle 31 and Calle Rambla, ☎ 42/44069; or ✉ Plaza Artigas, ☎ 42/46510 or 42/46511).

URUGUAY A TO Z

Arriving and Departing

By Airplane

AIRPORTS

All international commercial flights land at Montevideo's **Carrasco International Airport** (☎ 2/601–1991), about 24 km (15 mi) east of downtown. A small airport in Punta del Este, **El Jaquel** (☎ 42/84513) is used for private jets and commuter flights to and from Buenos Aires.

CARRIERS

Uruguay's national airline, **PLUNA-Varig** (⊠ Calle Colonia 1001, Montevideo, ☎ 2/903–0273 or 2/902–1414), flies daily to Uruguay from major cities throughout South America. U.S. carriers serving Uruguay include American Airlines and United Airlines.

FLYING TIMES

All Montevideo-bound flights are routed through Buenos Aires, São Paulo, or Rio de Janeiro. Flying times to Montevideo are 1 hour from Buenos Aires, 2 hours from São Paulo, and 2½ hours from Rio.

By Car

From Argentina, you can transport your car across the Río de la Plata by ferry (☞ *below*). Alternatively, you can cross the Argentina–Uruguay border in three places: Puerto Unzue-Fray Bentos, Colon-Paysandu, or Concordia-Salto. From Brazil, you can cross the border either at Chuy, the Río Branco, Rivera, or via the bridge at Quarai-Artigas.

By Hydrofoil and Ferry

Hydrofoils and ferries cross the Río de la Plata between Buenos Aires and Uruguay several times daily. They travel either directly to Montevideo or to Colonia, where you can get a bus to Montevideo and Punta del Este. The best companies are **Aliscafos** and **Buquebus** (⊠ Av. Córdoba and Madero, ☎ 1/313–4444), in the same office. **Ferry Lineas Argentina** and **Ferry Tur** (⊠ Florida 780, ☎ 1/322–8421 or 1/394–8424) also share an office.

Getting Around

By Bus

You can go almost anywhere in Uruguay by bus. Some border on the luxurious, with air-conditioning, video players, rest rooms, and snack service. Departures are frequent and fares low—Montevideo to Punta del Este, for example, costs $12 round-trip. Most companies are based in Montevideo and depart from its new state-of-the-art Tres Cruces terminal. Dependable carriers include COT, TTL, and Rutas (☞ Arriving and Departing By Bus *in* Montevideo A to Z, *above*).

By Car

EMERGENCY ASSISTANCE

For roadside assistance, contact the **Automovil Club Uruguayo** (⊠ Libertador 1532, Montevideo, ☎ 2/902–5792; ⊠ 3 de Febrero y Roosevelt, Punta del Este, ☎ 42/20156). They will help even if you are not a member, but expect to pay $35 to enroll on the spot.

GASOLINE

Shell, Esso, Texaco, and ANCAP (the national petroleum company) service stations throughout Uruguay are open Monday–Saturday until 9 PM or so. The ANCAP station at Carrasco Airport is open daily 6 AM–11 PM.

RENTAL AGENCIES

Special rates or package deals are virtually nonexistent in Uruguay, and rental rates are higher than in the United States because of the value-added tax (IVA). For an economy-size car, expect to pay around $45 per day, plus 22¢ per km; you'll pay upwards of $385 per week with unlimited mileage. In Montevideo, contact the following: **Avis** (⊠ Aquiles Lanza between Calle Paysandú and Calle Uruguay, ☎ 2/902–0127 or 2/903–0303); **Budget** (⊠ Calle Mercedes 935, ☎ 2/901–6363); or **Class** (⊠ Hotel Victoria Plaza, Room 105, Plaza Independencia 759, ☎ 2/902–0237).

ROAD CONDITIONS

Roads between Montevideo and Punta del Este are quite good, as are the handful of main highways. Deeper into the Uruguayan countryside, roads are usually surfaced with gravel. If you want to drive to areas off the main highways, it's best to plan for extra travel time; if possible, speak with locals about current road conditions before setting off. On the up side, country roads have very little traffic and, in some places, spectacular scenery and a chance to see traditional Uruguayan gauchos.

RULES OF THE ROAD

Uruguayans tend to drive carefully, but visitors from Argentina have the reputation of driving with wild abandon. Since almost all roads have only two lanes, keep a close eye out for passing vehicles.

Contacts and Resources

Customs and Duties

ON ARRIVAL

You may bring up to 400 cigarettes, 50 cigars or 500 grams of loose tobacco, and 2 liters of alcoholic beverages. Live animals, vegetable products, and products that originate from plant or animal products are not allowed into Uruguay. There is no limit on the amount of currency you can bring into the country.

Electricity

Uruguay runs on 220-volt power. The two-pronged plugs, such as those used in continental Europe, are standard here.

Embassies

American (✉ Lauro Müller, No. 1776 (on the Rambla), Montevideo, ☎ 2/203–6061, FAX 2/408–7777), open weekdays 9–1, 2–5. **British** (✉ Marco Bruto, No. 1073, ☎ 2/622–3630, FAX 2/622–7815), open weekdays 9–1, 2–5:15. **Canadian**: The nearest Canadian embassy is in Buenos Aires.

Health and Safety

FOOD AND DRINK

Cholera is almost unheard of in Uruguay, but you should still eat fresh fruit and salads with caution. Also avoid tap water, because many pipes in older buildings are made of lead. Almost everyone drinks locally bottled *agua mineral* (mineral water), which is available with or without carbonation (*con gas* or *sin gas*, respectively).

OTHER PRECAUTIONS

Pickpockets are your biggest threat in the larger cities in Uruguay. Street crime has risen dramatically in recent years, particularly in Montevideo, so keep a vigilant eye on your purse or wallet. Crime at the swank Punta del Este resorts is not a serious problem and in the countryside it is practically nonexistent.

Language, Culture, and Etiquette

Spanish is the official language of Uruguay, though some descendants of early Italian and British settlers speak the language of their forefathers. Many Uruguayans speak at least a little English.

As for etiquette, there are no obvious taboos to be aware of. You will find that the majority of Uruguayans are quite considerate, helpful, and easygoing. The best way to get along in the country is simply to observe and show respect for the culture.

Mail

Because of frequent strikes by Uruguayan postal workers, it is best to check with locals as to whether the postal system is running efficiently at the time of your visit. If the postal service is working, be prepared to pay for the privilege—it costs nearly $1.80 to send a standard-size piece of international mail. Anything sensitive should be sent via a courier service such as **Federal Express** (✉ Calle Juncal 1351, Montevideo, ☏ 2/ 915–6627) or **DHL** (✉ Calle Zabala 1377, Montevideo, ☏ 2/916–0217).

POSTAL RATES

The postal rates to countries outside of Uruguay range from 11–25 pesos.

RECEIVING MAIL

The most reliable places to receive mail are the main post offices or American Express offices.

WRITING TO URUGUAY

To send a letter to Uruguay, simply give the name, address, and city on the letter or package. No specific postal codes are required.

Money Matters

CURRENCY

On March 1, 1993, the Uruguayan government changed the monetary system from Nuevos Pesos (N$) to Pesos Uruguayos. The latter is officially designated NP$, but more often you will see prices listed with a simple dollar sign ($) or ($U). For the moment, Nuevos Pesos coins and bills are still in use and are convertible to Pesos Uruguayos by dropping the last three zeros on a given bill (N$l,000 = NP$1). Prices everywhere are quoted in Pesos Uruguayos even though you may pay with Pesos Nuevos. Currently the Pesos Uruguayos currency is available in the following denominations: $10, $20, $50, 100, $200, $500, and $1,000.

All banks and exchange houses, which are plentiful in Montevideo, will change traveler's checks and cash. Most banks will also process cash advances from major credit cards; expect a 5%–10% surcharge on all credit-card charges, however.

At press time the exchange rate was 10.79 Uruguayan pesos to the U.S. dollar, 6.96 pesos to the Canadian dollar, 17.57 pesos to the pound sterling, and 6.26 pesos to the Australian dollar. Rates escalate almost daily to keep pace with Uruguay's inflation. In this chapter all prices are listed in U.S. dollars unless otherwise noted.

SERVICE CHARGES, TAXES, AND TIPPING

In restaurants a flat 10% tip is considered adequate. For any other services, from tours and valet service to taxi rides, a tip of $5–$10 is the norm. For taxis, round off the fare to the next highest peso. Throughout the country a value-added tax (called IVA) of 14% is added to hotel and restaurant bills. Almost all other goods and services carry a 23% IVA charge.

WHAT IT WILL COST

Once one of the best bargain spots in the Southern Hemisphere, Uruguay can no longer boast about its low prices. The inflation rate rises daily; many services, especially those catering to tourists, now quote prices exclusively in U.S. dollars. Although you will need to keep some pesos for taxis and small purchases, it is best to convert dollars to pesos only as needed. You can also save a substantial amount by visiting in the low season: Prices on everything from hotels to meals can literally double during January and February, particularly in Punta del Este.

Sample Prices: Cup of coffee, $1.80; bottle of beer, $3; soft drink, $2; bottle of house wine, $5; sandwich, $4; ½-mi taxi ride, $1–4; city bus ride, 50¢; museum entrance, free.

Opening and Closing Times

In Montevideo, banks are open weekdays 1–5 PM. In outlying areas banks are usually open during the morning only. Money changers are open during regular business hours (9–5:30). Some are open later and on Saturdays and Sunday mornings. Many shops stay open throughout the day (9–7), especially in Montevideo and Punta del Este, where they may also remain open until late in the evening. In smaller cities, it is common for shops to close at midday for an hour or two.

NATIONAL HOLIDAYS

New Year's Day (Jan. 1); Three Kings' Day (Jan. 6); Maundy Thursday and Good Friday (Apr. 23–24, 2000; Apr. 14–15, 2001); Disembarkation of the 33 Exiles (Apr. 19); Labor Day (May 1); Battle of Las Piedras (May 18); Artigas's Birthday (June 19); Constitution Day (July 18); Independence Day (Aug. 25); Columbus Day (Oct. 12); All Souls' Day (Nov. 2); Christmas (Dec. 25).

Passports and Visas

U.S. and British citizens need only a valid passport for stays of up to 90 days in Uruguay. Canadian citizens further require a tourist visa (C$37.50), available from the **Consulate of Uruguay** (✉ 30 Albert St., Suite 1905, Ottawa, Ontario K1P 5G4, ☎ 613/234–2937).

Telephones

CALLS TO URUGUAY

To call Uruguay from overseas, dial the country code, 598, and then the area code.

LOCAL CALLS

You may have to check several public telephones in downtown Montevideo before you find one that is in working order. To place a call you need a magnetic phone card. These are used in place of coins and are available in the following denominations: $5, $25, $47, $83, $140, $203, and $316. Unless you're planning on calling outside of Montevideo, the $5 card should be sufficient for about 10 local calls. Phone cards can be purchased at telecentros, kiosks, and small stores near public phones. Cellular phones can be rented from **Moviecom** (☎ 0800–2611) for about $7 per day; local cellular rates are around $.55 per minute. For assisted local calls and directory information, dial 0009.

LONG-DISTANCE AND INTERNATIONAL CALLS

You'll need a magnetic phone card if you are dialing from a pay phone. International calls can also be made—for a much higher price—through *telecentro* offices of **ANTEL** (✉ Calle Fernández Crespo 1534, Calle San José 1102, and Calle Rincón 501, Montevideo, ☎ 02/901–1685), the national telecommunications company, which offers direct-dial services.

For assisted long-distance within Uruguay, dial 0007; for assisted international calls, dial 0008. English-speaking operators are available from **AT&T** (☎ 000410), **MCI Worldcom** (☎ 000412), and **Sprint** (☎ 000417). Canadian operators (☎ 000419) are also available.

When to Go

The finest weather falls between mid-October and late March, when the temperature is pleasantly warm, the whole country is in bloom, and prices will not yet have inflated with the annual influx of Argentines and jet-setters. However, unless you are prepared to tangle with the tsunami of tourists that overwhelms Punta del Este in January and February, late spring (Oct.–Dec.) is the most appealing season to lounge on the beach in Punta.

CLIMATE

Uruguay's climate has four distinct but mild seasons. Summer (Jan.–Mar.) can be hot and humid, with temperatures as high as 90°F. Fall (Apr.–June) is marked by warm days and evenings cool enough for a light sweater. Winter (July–Sept.) is cold and rainy with average temperatures generally below 50°F. Although it seldom reaches the freezing point here, the wind off the water can provide a chill factor that feels like Chicago in late November. Spring (Oct.–Dec.) is much like the fall, except that the trees will be sprouting, rather than dropping, their leaves.

The following are average daily maximum and minimum temperatures for Montevideo.

Jan.	83F	28C	May	64F	18C	Sept.	63F	17C
	62	17		48	9		46	8
Feb.	82F	28C	June	59F	15C	Oct.	68F	20C
	61	16		43	6		49	10
Mar.	78F	25C	July	58F	14C	Nov.	74F	23C
	59	15		43	6		54	12
Apr.	71F	22C	Aug.	59F	15C	Dec.	79F	21C
	53	12		43	6		59	15

FESTIVALS AND SEASONAL EVENTS

An annual citywide celebration of **Carnival** overtakes Montevideo with parades, dancing in the streets, and general all-hours revelry. **Semana Criolla,** celebrated the week before Easter Sunday at the Prado and Parque Roosevelt in Carrasco (a suburb of Montevideo), provides an excellent opportunity to observe traditional gaucho activities. Montevideo holds an annual **cattle fair** in August.

12 VENEZUELA

The two faces of Venezuela's cities gaze in opposite directions—one romantically toward a colonial past of cobblestone streets and tiled roofs, the other hungrily toward a future of glass, steel, and neon. Exploring the remainder of the country, you'll encounter diverse and mystical landscapes, from the jungles of Amazonas, to the snowcapped heights of the Andes, to the black lagoons and pink-sand beaches of Canaima National Park.

Updated by
Corey Nettles

JUST A FEW HOURS FROM THE SOUTHEASTERN United States, Venezuela is perhaps the most accessible South American nation for North American travelers. For hundreds of years it was one of the poorest and most neglected backwaters on the continent, lacking the consolation of the gigantic pre-Columbian civilizations and the archeological riches of Ecuador and Peru. Then in the 1920s huge deposits of oil were discovered and Venezuela became one of the founding members of OPEC. During the past 50 years, the urban centers of Venezuela have blossomed into cities that rival the largest and most cosmopolitan of the United States, and the country continues to grow with the energetic impatience of its youthful population (70% are under 35 years). An oil boom in the 1970s gave birth to many of the country's gargantuan cultural centers, apartment towers, and commercial complexes—the most numerous of which are found in Caracas, the capital city.

For natural wonders of all kinds, this country is a land of superlatives. Venezuela enjoys South America's longest Caribbean coastline, with 2,750 km (1,700 mi) of pristine white sand beaches lapped by warm turquoise waters. Isla Margarita is an island destination popular with sun-seeking European tourists, while the tiny keys of Archipelago los Roques—which make up one of Venezuela's 43 national parks—offer an enchanting fishing village, mangroves, and arguably the most spectacular snorkeling and scuba diving in the Caribbean. From the Andean city of Mérida, the world's longest and highest cable car carries passengers to the foot of glacier-topped Pico Bolívar. Returning to the valley, you'll pass through the dramatic beauty of the highlands and many cozy mountain villages dotting the length of the Trans-Andina Highway. Los Llanos, vast savannas which cover the central part of the country, are home to multitudes of wildlife and brilliantly colored tropical birds, including the rare jabiru stork. In the southeast, awesome table-top mountains called *tepuis* tower over the high-elevation grasslands of Canaima National Park. Here, the world's highest waterfall, Angel Falls, plummets over 807 m (2,647 ft), in a bizarre landscape of black lagoons, pink sand beaches, and unique plant life.

Pleasures and Pastimes

Bird-Watching

With more than 1,300 species of birds, Venezuela is one of the world's top destinations for avid ornithologists. In the Llanos, you will be awed by immense flocks of roseate spoonbills, giant egrets, green ibis, scarlet ibis, and jabiru storks. Hoatzin (primitive birds whose chicks have finger-like claws on their wings) live in the brush that crowds the rivers crisscrossing the plains. In the Andean foothills, you may catch a glimpse of the brilliant red cock-of-the-rock, and in higher altitudes witness the magnificent soaring flight of Andean condors. Henry Pittier National Park (about one hour west of Caracas) protects a cloud forest that is renowned for its remarkable variety of bird life; more than half of Venezuela's species have been found here, including the spectacular golden tanager and long-tailed sylph. On the Caribbean coast, numerous lagoons shelter flocks of pink flamingos.

Dining

Venezuela's larger cities boast a wide variety of restaurants: from Spanish *tascas* (Spanish-style casual restaurants with bars) and French bistros to Japanese sushi bars. But while you're here, you'll want to sample Venezuela's own unique cuisine. The national dish, *pabellón criollo,* consists of shredded beef or fish served with rice, black beans

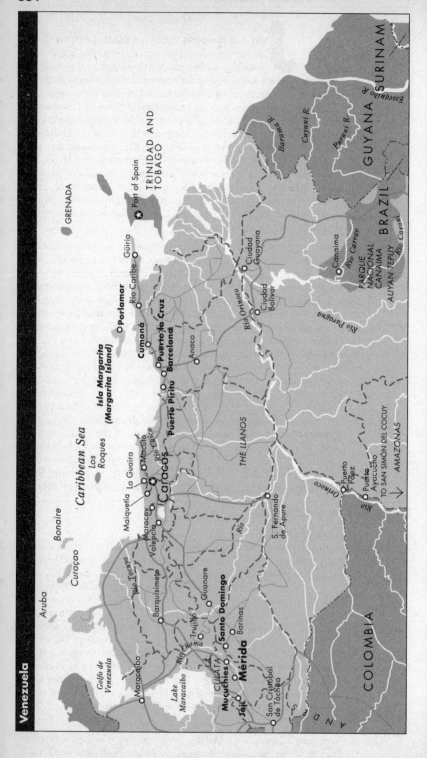

(*caraotas*), fried plantains (*tostones*), and local white cheeses such as *queso de mano.* Venezuelans like beef, and restaurants that specialize in grilled meats (called *pardilleras* or *churrasquerías*) are popular with locals.

Excellent fish and shellfish dominate in the coastal areas and on Isla Margarita, including grouper, snapper, mackerel, tuna, swordfish, lobster, crab, shrimp, and clams. In the Andean regions, treat yourself to rainbow trout. If you visit during the Christmas season, try the holiday specialty called *hallaca,* a tamale-like combination of chicken, corn, olives, and pork, all wrapped in aromatic banana leaves.

Don't leave Venezuela without sampling at least one of these scrumptious, typical desserts: *bien me sabe* (coconut cake), *torta de guanábana* (soursop cake), *merengón de nispero* (medlar meringue cake), and the always popular *cascos de guayaba,* (guava shells served with white cheese). Beer, whiskey, and rum are the favored libations among locals. French wines tend to be expensive, and old vintages suffer because of the preservatives used to withstand the tropics. More moderately priced are the light Italian reds Valpolicella and Bardolino, the Italian whites Pinot Grigio and Verdicchio, and Chile's Santa Carolina and Cousinho Macul, both white and red. Venezuela also produces some surprisingly good domestic wines, such as Viña Altagracia from the Lara State in the northwest region of the country.

Lunch, the main meal of the day, begins at noon and lasts until about 3. Dinner is taken between 7 and 10 PM; don't count on being served much past 10:30 PM, except in the Las Mercedes district of Caracas, where some restaurants remain open until midnight. Some restaurants offer a prix-fixe meal at lunchtime known as the *menu ejecutivo.* This includes a *primero* (appetizer of soup or salad); a *segundo,* the main course; and *postre* (dessert). Espresso or *guayoyo,* a watery, American-style coffee, is included.

High-end restaurants frequently have dress codes, so inquire when making reservations. Pack a coat and tie or cocktail dress if you plan to dine or dance in elegance. For most other dining establishments, a woman can't go wrong in an informal dress nor a man in a collared shirt with optional tie.

Prices quoted are per person and include appetizer, main course, and dessert but exclude alcoholic beverages, tax, service charge, and tip. For price categories, *see* Dining *in* Smart Travel Tips A to Z.

Diving and Snorkeling

The Caribbean reefs of Venezuela are swarming with colorful fish and invertebrates, and represent one of the most sensational and unspoiled wonders of the country. Los Roques National Park is a diver's paradise, with its dramatic drop-offs, submarine caves, and wide stretches of living coral. Experts say that the diving here rivals that of anywhere in the Caribbean.

Fishing

Los Roques is one of the top bone fishing destinations in the world, and many visitors come to Venezuela specifically to cast for this quick-running sport fish. You can catch *pavon,* huge peacock bass, in the Llanos and in the Orinoco River, where you may also enjoy the added thrill of angling for feisty piranha. Trout fishing is a popular diversion in the Andes, where local tour operators host a variety of expeditions to well-stocked, scenic lakes.

Lodging

Venezuela offers lodging options to suit almost every price range and comfort level—from the resort citadels of Caracas to the colorful, three-room posadas of the Gran Roque. Take in a view of the Andes from the window of a restored 17th-century monastery, or from the cobble-stone courtyard of a renovated coffee hacienda nestled in the cloud forest above Mérida. In the Llanos, you can stay on a working cattle ranch or in the guest facilities of a biological field station. Those who seek adventure by day and comfort by night will relish the prime location and amenities offered by the Aerotuy camp in the Canaima area.

Luxury hotels, common in large cities and resort areas, are rated within Venezuela on a scale of one to five stars; the latter rating, however, is not always indicative of superior quality. Still, most five-star hotels are reasonably modern and feature such facilities as car rental offices, swimming pools and tennis courts, souvenir shops, clothing and jewelry boutiques, restaurants, bars, and dance clubs. Three- and four-star hotels usually offer a smattering of these. Water shortages and cutoffs are common even in the big cities, though resort hotels often have their own auxiliary supplies and thus are immune to the problem. Keep in mind that even modest accommodations are at inflated prices in Caracas and such resort areas as Isla Margarita.

Posadas, the local version of pensions, are found mostly in beach areas and the Andes; these typically offer accommodation plus meals. Luxury hotels rarely include meals when quoting room rates. Note: Room prices jump 10%–20% during holiday periods, particularly during Christmas and Carnival.

Prices quoted are for a double room and include tax and service charge. For price categories, *see* Lodging *in* Smart Travel Tips A to Z.

Shopping

Caracas is infested with hip clothing boutiques and shoe stores; the selection is interesting and the atmosphere fun, but prices are generally high. The Mérida region offers folkloric items, particularly pottery and wood carvings. Isla Margarita is a duty-free extravaganza where you'll find European clothing and leather goods, liquor, tobacco, and perfume. Hammocks are another favorite Margarita purchase, well known for their fine craftsmanship and immense size. Although bargaining is not acceptable in city stores, prices at outdoor markets—and sometimes in smaller towns and villages—are negotiable.

Wilderness Expeditions

Venezuela boasts grandiose natural monuments and some of the world's largest parks, which cover 15% of the country's landmass. True adventurers can take a boat ride through the remote headwaters of the Orinoco in Venezuela's Amazonas region, a national park that harbors more than 48,000 square km (30,000 square mi) of protected areas. Those who prefer cooler climes can jump from a mountain top and paraglide over deep, forest-carpeted canyons in the Venezuelan Andes or mountain-bike to remote mountain villages still inaccessible by car. Perhaps the most incredible destinations for the avid explorer are the Gran Sabana and Canaima national parks, where some of the most surreal landscapes on earth can be found. Here, tepuis rise above a high grassland characterized by bizarre plant life, black rivers, and powerful yellow waterfalls. Pemón Indians lead excursions to the top of the tepuis—most notably Roraima on the border with Guayana. Each tepuy has its own endemic flora, fauna, and strangely beautiful terrain at the summit. These same geological formations inspired Sir Arthur Conan Doyle's *Lost World*.

Exploring Venezuela

Venezuela has an astonishing variety of landscapes. Caracas, the capital, is a cosmopolitan if somewhat chaotic city, with its fair share of urban glories and woes. Sun-seeking travelers should head to the turquoise waters of the country's Caribbean coast and Isla Margarita. Mérida and the Andean towns feature the country's most charming and reasonably priced hotels and restaurants, against the sublime backdrop of the mountains. Elsewhere in Venezuela, the adventurous explorer can marvel at the multitudes of wildlife of the expansive Llanos, the majesty of Angel Falls, and the lush jungle of Amazonas.

Great Itineraries

Remember that the *second* largest of Venezuela's 43 national parks is the size of Belgium, and you'll quickly realize that this is not a small country. Each far-flung region offers something unique and spectacular; nonetheless, with careful planning, many of the country's high points can be experienced even during a short trip. Maximize a short or limited visit by contacting a tour operator—an agent can arrange for guides, charter flights, and ideal accommodations.

IF YOU HAVE 4–5 DAYS

If your port of entry is **Isla Margarita,** you'll want to spend a couple of days there enjoying the water sports and lively, beach town atmosphere before flying south to **Canaima National Park.** Two days in this region will allow sufficient time to splash in the waterfalls, hike in the shadow of the majestic tepuis, and fly over the famed **Angel Falls.** From Canaima, try a one- or two-day visit to the paradisal archipelago **Los Roques.** Pristine beaches, crystal blue water, a picturesque fishing village, and some of the best snorkeling, scuba diving, and bone fishing in the Caribbean await.

If you enter the country through **Caracas** you'll want to spend a day or two experiencing the capital's museums, historical sites, and fabulous dining scene. Next head to the **Llanos,** the vast grasslands, which offer the best wildlife panoramas this side of the Serengeti. Two full days of exploring the region by Jeep or canoe will introduce you to capybara, alligator, and hundreds of species of wildly colored tropical birds. Before departing Venezuela, spend a day in Los Roques.

IF YOU HAVE 6–9 DAYS

With a bit more time to play with, add an Andean adventure to one of the itineraries listed above. Leave the Llanos for the city of **Barinas,** then spend a couple of days winding your way along the magical Trans-Andina Highway towards **Mérida.** Here, you should take a day to ride the world's longest cable car to the glaciers of Pico Bolívar. You could also try one or more of the outstanding hiking, fishing, and horseback riding excursions in the area.

IF YOU HAVE 10–14 DAYS

With an extra few days you may want to follow the Caracas, Llanos, and Andes itinerary with a two-day scenic drive along the Caribbean coast to check out beach towns all the way to **Puerto La Cruz**—the home of Venezuela's favorite nightclub scene. Take a two-hour ferry trip to **Isla Margarita** from Puerto La Cruz. Spend at least two days lounging on the beaches and then continue by plane to the **Gran Sabana/Canaima** region for two days of exploring. Other enticing options include a visit to **Puerto Ayacucho** in Las Amazonas, or a stay in the Aerotuy camp Boca de Tigre in the **Orinoco Delta.**

CARACAS

On a wall facing the Plaza el Venelozano, the Libertador is quoted as follows: SI SE OPONE LA NATURALEZA LUCHAREMOS CONTRA ELLA Y LA HAREMOS QUE NOS OBEDEZCA (If nature is opposed, we'll struggle against her and make her obey us). Nowhere in Venezuela is the seriousness of Bolivar's threat more apparent than in Caracas itself. Whether gazing at the city's terrific, undeniable skyline from the 17th-story window of a high-rise hotel or strolling in the shadows of looming concrete edifices, one wistfully dreams of what Caracas might have been had its sudden growth spurt occurred during any other architectural moment than the 1970s. Recklessly ostentatious and desperate in its quest for modernity, Caracas has sacrificed charm, elegance, and grace for all of the generic trappings of an urban center.

What redeems Caracas is the Caraqueños themselves: a diverse, young, and lively population that colors the grimy streets of the capital with laughter, music, and unrestrained enthusiasm. The sophisticated tastes of the nearly 5 million inhabitants demand the endless parades of boutiques and fine restaurants that crowd upscale commercial areas. In the gargantuan cultural center of Bellas Artes, museums and concert halls erupt with the artistic accomplishments of Venezuela's past and present. Hip, fast-paced, and altogether cosmopolitan, Caraqueños still manage to retain a warmth and amiability you may not expect to encounter so consistently in a city this vast.

Although Caracas is a sprawling metropolis, its places of interest can be explored comfortably in a day or two. Worldly museums and cultural centers, lively bars, and refined dining establishments are all interconnected by the city's clean, efficient subway system. The weather, too, facilitates exploring: At 3,000 ft above sea level, Caracas has one of the world's most comfortable climates, with an average daily temperature of 75°F. Be advised, however, that Caracas well deserves its reputation as a dangerous city, and all types of criminal activity are on the constant rise. Even residents do not go unescorted after 9 PM, and taxis are recommended as the safest means of transportation after dark.

Exploring Caracas

Caracas can be divided into four principal areas of interest: the downtown El Centro district and its monument-packed Plaza Bolívar; Parque Central and the surrounding Bellas Artes cultural district; Las Mercedes and the Bulevar Sabana Grande, with its many boutiques and restaurants; and the residential, very wealthy suburbs of Altamira and La Castellana. These districts are all connected with El Centro by subway. Taxis are a convenient but costly option for traversing the city.

Numbers in the white bullets in the text correspond to numbers in black bullets in the margins and on the Caracas map.

El Centro

A GOOD WALK

Take the metro to El Capitolio to reach the historic heart of Caracas, **El Centro** ①. From street level it's a short walk to **Plaza Bolívar** ②, where you'll find the **Palacio de Gobernación** ③, the **Catedral Metropolitana de Caracas** ④, and the adjacent **Museo Sacro de Caracas** ⑤. On the southern side of the plaza is the **Concejo Municipal** ⑥, across the street from **El Capitolio Nacional** ⑦. Continue south to the end of the block to the beautiful **Iglesia de San Francisco** ⑧. Two blocks east of Plaza Bolívar and beside the tree-lined Plaza El Venezolano are the **Museo Bolívar** ⑨ and the **Casa Natal** ⑩, Bolívar's childhood home. Five blocks north of Plaza Bolívar is the awesome **Panteón Nacional** ⑪.

TIMING

Unless you have a particular passion for history (or Bolívar), you'll need only about two hours to experience this district. With the exception of the Panteón, which is a 15-minute stroll from Plaza Bolívar, all of the buildings are within a five- to 10-minute walking radius; a satisfying exploration requires no more than 20 minutes at each. Museums tend to be more crowded on the weekends and are closed on Mondays. While this area is safe for exploring in the day, after dusk it has a decidedly seedy edge to it.

SIGHTS TO SEE

⑩ Casa Natal. The house where Simón Bolívar was born on July 24, 1783, is a pilgrimage site for Venezuelans, but holds little of general interest. Notice the monumental paintings by Tito Salas, with themes focusing on various aspects of Bolívar's early life, and respect the reverent silence with which most visitors peruse the furniture of the beloved Libertador. ✉ *Av. Universidad, at Av. Norte 1,* ☎ *02/541–2563.* 🎟 *Admission.* ⊙ *Tues.–Fri. 9–noon, 2:30–5; weekends 10–1, 2:30–5.*

⑦ El Capitolio Nacional. Venezuela's congress is housed in the National Capital, formerly the site of the 17th-century convent of the Sisters of the Conception. In 1874, President Guzmán Blanco ordered the disbanding of all convents, razed the building, and began constructing the Federal and Legislative palaces. Take note of the ancient, gnarled tree surrounded by a chicken-wire fence in front of the building; it's commonly believed throughout Caracas to magically grant wishes. ✉ *Av. Norte 2, at Av. Oeste 2.* 🎟 *Free.* ⊙ *Daily 9–12:30, 3–5.*

④ Catedral Metropolitana de Caracas. Completed in 1674, the handsome Metropolitan Cathedral of Caracas is the only church in the city whose original colonial facade is unaltered. The main altar is a magnificent baroque creation gilded with more than 300 pounds of gold leaf. ✉ *Plaza Bolívar,* ☎ *02/862–1518.* 🎟 *Free.* ⊙ *Tues.–Sun. 8–1, 3–6.*

⑥ Concejo Municipal. The Municipal Council palace is considered the cradle of Venezuelan nationhood: On July 5, 1811, the National Congress met inside and approved the Declaration of Independence. Nowadays, the building houses the **Museo Criollo,** which exhibits a permanent collection of works by noted Venezuelan painter Emilio Boggio (1857–1920) and scale-model miniatures by Raúl Santana that depict every imaginable aspect of Venezuela's early culture. ✉ *Plaza Bolívar,* ☎ *02/545–6706.* 🎟 *Palace and museum free.* ⊙ *Palace and museum Tues.–Fri. 9–11, 2:30–4:30; Sat. 10:30–4.*

★ ⑧ Iglesia de San Francisco. Designed in 1593, and the site of Bolívar's massive funeral, St. Francis Church is filled with richly gilded altars and remains the loveliest example of colonial architecture in Caracas. ✉ *Av. Bolsa at Av. San Francisco,* ☎ *02/484–5172.* 🎟 *Free.* ⊙ *Daily 7–noon, 3–6.*

⑨ Museo Bolívar. The museum features documents and historical paraphernalia related to Simón Bolívar and Venezuela's War of Independence against Spain. ✉ *Av. San Jacinto at Av. Norte,* ☎ *02/545–9828.* 🎟 *Admission.* ⊙ *Tues.–Fri. 9–noon, 2:30–5; weekends 10–1, 2:30–5.*

★ ⑤ Museo Sacro de Caracas. The Museum of Religious Art of Caracas, a former sacristy and ecclesiastical prison built in 1844, now houses beautiful religious statues and sumptuous costumes from the colonial era. Especially noteworthy in the first salon is the silver canopy made for Our Lady of the Rosary, and downstairs you'll find an intriguing common grave, or ossuary, where remains of the religious are interred in sealed niches. ✉ *Plaza Bolívar,* ☎ *02/545–9829.* 🎟 *Admission.* ⊙ *Tues.–Sun. 10–5.*

Caracas

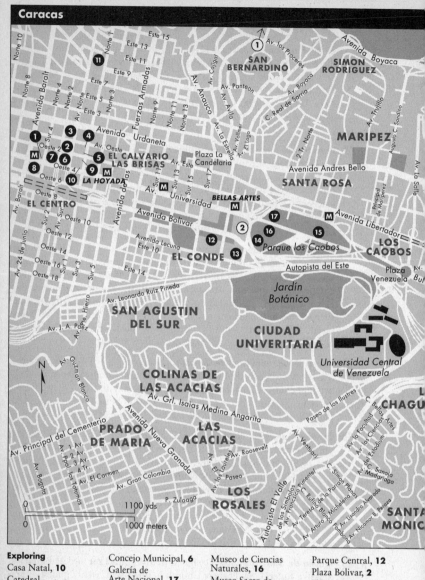

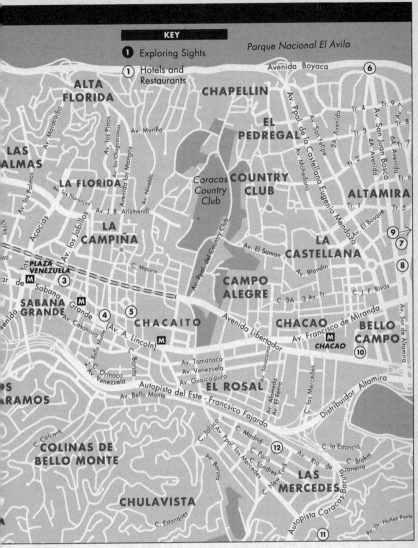

Dining
Café L'Attico, **8**
Da Guido, **3**
Lasserre, **9**
Mi Tasca, **4**
Taiko, **12**
Tarzilandia, **6**

Lodging
Caracas Hilton International, **2**
Continental Altamira, **7**
Hotel Avila, **1**
Savoy, **5**
Shelter Suites, **10**

Tamanaco Inter-Continental, **11**

❸ **Palacio de Gobernación.** The art deco–style Government Palace, built in 1935, now houses political offices and a ground-floor salon with rotating exhibits of international and Venezuelan art. ⊠ *Plaza Bolívar,* ☎ *02/811.111.* 🎫 *Free.* ☉ *Tues.–Sat. 10–6*

⓫ **Panteón Nacional.** The national mausoleum is perhaps the city's most striking monument. An exquisite marble interior honors the remains of 138 Venezuelan political and historical figures, including those of Simón Bolívar. The walls and ceilings are graced with murals depicting some of the most famous battles against the Spanish for independence. ⊠ *Av. Norte,* ☎ *02/693–0629.* 🎫 *Free.* ☉ *Tues.–Fri. 9–noon, 2:30–5; weekends 10–noon, 3–5.*

❷ **Plaza Bolívar.** The pleasant shady square has wooden benches, flocks of pigeons, and an imposing equestrian statue of its namesake, Simón Bolívar, dubbed "El Libertador" in 1813 for his leadership in the struggle against Spanish rule in South America.

Bellas Artes
A GOOD WALK

Begin your walk at the Bellas Artes metro stop. When you reach street level, look for the two tall, glass towers to the south. Walk toward the towers, and you'll reach a gargantuan cement complex known as the **Parque Central** ⑫. In the eastern end of this complex, you'll encounter the **Museo de Arte Contemporaneo de Sofía Imber** ⑬, and crossing the pedestrian bridge will bring you to the **Teresa Carreño Complejo Cultural** ⑭. A short stroll north brings you to the entrance of the immense **Parque Caobo** ⑮, where you'll find the **Museo de Ciencias Naturales** ⑯ and the **Galería de Arte Nacional** ⑰.

TIMING

Visiting all of the sights of Bellas Artes will take a full morning or afternoon. Allow an hour and a half to visit the museums of Parque Central, and at least 15 minutes to walk leisurely through the Teresa Carreño Complejo Cultural, checking out its underground bookstore and coffee shop. Proceed toward Parque Caobo and spend about an hour viewing the displays at the science and art museums there. A 20-minute walk through the park will take you all the way to Plaza Venezuela. On Saturdays and Sundays, the museums are filled with locals, and these are the best days to enjoy people-watching in the park. All museums are closed on Monday.

SIGHTS TO SEE

⓱ **Galería de Arte Nacional.** The National Art Gallery, which houses art from all periods in Venezuela's history, shares a building with the **Museo de Bellas Artes.** The latter exhibits a hodgepodge of works: Chinese ceramics, diverse Egyptian pieces, a hall dedicated to Cubism, and rotating exhibitions of modern international art. ⊠ *Plaza Morelos,* ☎ *Gallery: 02/578–1818; museum: 02/571–1819.* 🎫 *Gallery and museum free.* ☉ *Gallery and museum Tues.–Fri. 9–5, weekends 10–5.*

⓭ **Museo de Arte Contemporaneo de Sofía Imber.** The Sofía Imber Contemporary Art Museum contains one of the most complete collections of modern art in South America, including works by numerous Venezuelan artists and a permanent exhibition of engravings by Pablo Picasso. ⊠ *Parque Central,* ☎ *02/573–7289 or 02/573–0075.* 🎫 *Free.* ☉ *Tues.–Sun. 10–6.*

⓰ **Museo de Ciencias Naturales.** The Museum of Natural Science includes archaeological, botanical, and zoological exhibits. The pre-Columbian displays are particularly noteworthy. ⊠ *Plaza Morales.* 🎫 *Free.* ☉ *Tues.–Fri. 9–noon, 3–4:30; weekends 10–5.*

⑭ Teresa Carreño Complejo Cultural. World-class ballet, opera, and classical concerts are regularly presented at the Teresa Carreño Cultural Complex's **Teatro Teresa Carreño** (☞ Nightlife and the Arts, *below*). Hanging from the theater roof is the kinetic sculpture Yellow Pendants by Venezuelan artist Jesús Soto. Adjacent to the complex is the **Teatro Ateneo de Caracas** (☞ Nightlife and the Arts, *below*), home of a popular movie theater, a bookstore, and the biannual International Theater Festival. ⊠ *Plaza Morelos, Parque Los Caobos.*

Sabana Grande and Las Mercedes

A GOOD WALK

Begin your walk at the eastern end of the **Bulevar de Sabana Grande.** Explore the large **Central Comercial Chacaíto,** where you can shop or people-watch, before continuing east into the **El Rosal** district. Hop in a cab for **Las Mercedes.**

TIMING

You may spend no more than an afternoon visiting the Central Comercial and the El Rosal district. If you can, try to visit Las Mercedes in the late afternoon or early evening, so that the art galleries are still open and the restaurants and clubs are beginning to ply their nightly trade.

SIGHTS TO SEE

Bulevar de Sabana Grande. Sometimes called Avenida Abraham Lincoln, this is a festive promenade where visitors and Caraqueños converge on weekends to sip a *marrón grande* (large coffee) at the famous Gran Café, browse among the troop of street stalls, or take in the fleeting panorama of street musicians, mime groups, comics, and flame-swallowers performing for rapt crowds. Pickpockets are also attracted by all the crowds, so be sure to keep an eye on your belongings while strolling. Sabana Grande is flanked by Avenida Casanova and Avenida Francisco Solano, which are both lined with numerous restaurants and affordable hotels.

Central Comercial Chacaíto. The far eastern end of Bulevar Sabana Grande is anchored by the Central Comercial Chacaíto, a large, aging shopping complex that has been supplanted by the bigger, glitzier shopping meccas of CCCT and Sambil (☞ Shopping, *below*). The nearby Chacaíto metro stop opens onto a relaxed square, Plaza Chacaíto, fronted by fast-food eateries and cafés.

Las Mercedes. Considered one of Caracas's most chic districts, Las Mercedes flaunts its discos, boutiques, art galleries, and innumerable restaurants, which are strewn throughout the side streets. At the end of the main strip, Avenida Principal de las Mercedes, is the large Paseo de las Mercedes shopping mall.

El Rosal. East of Chacaíto is the lively El Rosal district, noted for its covey of nightspots along Avenida Tamanaco.

Altamira and La Castellana

These very safe and decidedly upscale neighborhoods are two of the few areas in Caracas that aren't abandoned to an eerie, unsettling silence as soon as the sun goes down. On the contrary, the streets and parks are crowded with families, couples, and fashionable young Caraqueños taking advantage of the area's great restaurants and nightspots. The districts can be reached by subway (Altamira stop), or on foot from Chacaíto along Avenida Francisco Miranda. Elegant restaurants line La Castellana's main thoroughfare as it funnels onto the district's main square, Plaza La Castellana.

OFF THE
BEATEN PATH

PARQUE NACIONAL EL ÁVILA – This gigantic, lush, mountainous park borders the north of the city, offering an escape from the hectic pace of Caracas. The cable car leading from the top of the mountain down to the beach is now defunct; you can climb to the summit, however, via the many well-marked hiking trails that crisscross the park. There is direct access here from the Altamira section of the city, at the end of the Av. San Juan Basco at the Decima (10th) Transversal, and at other points off the Avenida Boyaca.

Dining

Caracas has one of the busiest and most varied restaurant scenes in Latin America, from the tables of fine French restaurants to the long lines at McDonald's counters. Although dining out in Caracas is more expensive than in the rest of the country, the variety of restaurants is impressive. Many restaurants vanish as quickly as they appear along the streets of the capital; however, there are a few dozen establishments that have endured the whims of fashion. To dine on the cutting edge, consult the information desk of your hotel, or ask residents for their recommendations. Dressy sportswear is appropriate for most restaurants, but always inquire about a dress code when making reservations.

Continental

$$ ✗ **Café L'Attico.** With dimmed lights glimmering on brass bar rails, this time-honored Caracas institution echoes the atmosphere of a neighborhood Bostonian pub. Strategically placed large-screen TVs categorize L'Attico as a sports bar, but the large menu of freshly prepared specialties gives it a flavor that is altogether more sophisticated. Don't miss their Sunday brunch featuring Belgian waffles, eggs Benedict, and quiches that are out of this world. ⊠ *Av. Luis Roche at 1a Transversal, Altamira,* ☎ *02/265–8555. AE, D, MC, V.*

French

$$$$ ✗ **Lasserre.** For more than 30 years Venezuelans have enjoyed the finest in classical French food at Lasserre. Owner Tito (he goes only by his first name) offers his "talking menu" and rolls out the superb game, fish, poultry, and meat entrées. House specialties include the hard-to-find *lapa,* a small tropical boar cooked to perfection in a rich red-wine sauce, and *pabon,* an exquisite freshwater peacock bass. The Grand Marnier soufflé, which must be ordered in advance, is a great finishing touch, and the wine cellar is top-class. ⊠ *Av. Tercera, between 2a and 3a Transversals, Los Palos Grandes,* ☎ *02/283–4558 or 02/283–3079. AE, D, MC, V. Closed Sun.*

Italian

$$ ✗ **Da Guido.** This casual, family-style restaurant with hams hanging from the ceiling and colorful murals depicting the Italian countryside was voted best Italian restaurant in Caracas by locals who enjoy its classic dishes and great prices. Owner Eliseo Peserico and his friendly waiters have been serving up delicious veal *parmigiana,* gnocchi, ravioli, and fettuccine for more than 30 years. ⊠ *Av. Mariscal Francisco Solano 8, Sabana Grande,* ☎ *02/763–0937. AE, MC, V.*

Japanese

$$$ ✗ **Taiko.** In the ultra-hip Las Mercedes neighborhood, this chic restaurant serves excellent Japanese dishes ranging from hibachi-grilled meats and seafood, udon noodle soups, and lightly fried *tempura* to fresh sushi and sashimi. The modern, industrial decor is softened by touches of wood, rock, and the pleasant buzz of happy diners. ⊠ *Calle La Trinidad, near Calle Madrid,* ☎ *02/993–5647. AE, MC, V.*

Spanish

$ ✕ **Mi Tasca.** Sabana Grande is crowded with the shady storefronts of intimate tascas; one worth seeking out is this friendly, neighborhood meeting place where families, young couples, and guffawing old gentlemen convene for great food and rowdy conversation. Spanish in ambience, Mi Tasca offers an enormous selection of weekly specials, often including the excellent *calamares en su tinta* (squid served in its ink). ✉ *Av. Solano, Sabana Grande,* ☎ *02/718362. AE, D, MC, V. Closed Mon.*

Venezuelan

$$ ✕ **Tarzilandia.** Lush tropical vegetation, parrots, tree frogs, and tur-
★ tles crawling around in the garden have all been a part of the experience at this Caracas landmark since it opened in 1950. The unique menu features exotic Venezuelan dishes such as turtle pie, shrimp mixed with tropical fruit, and delectable grilled steaks and seafood. As a closer, diners often indulge in mango flambé à la mode. ✉ *Av. San Juan de Bosco at Decima Transversal, Altamira,* ☎ *02/261–8419 or 02/261–0628. AE, MC, V. Closed Mon.*

Lodging

Most of Caracas's best hotels are a few kilometers east of downtown in the refined Bellas Artes, Las Mercedes, and Altamira districts. Although security-minded visitors may feel more comfortable in established hotels such as the Hilton, Caracas does offer a few alternative lodging options that are easier on the budget. The Sabana Grande district is considered especially desirable for more adventurous travelers; you can pick and choose from the many budget-price pensions crowding the lively Avenida Casanova and Avenida Francisco Solano. Unfortunately, as with dining, prices for hotels are inflated compared with the rest of the country.

$$$$ 🏨 **Caracas Hilton International.** In the Bellas Artes cultural district, this mammoth complex has long been the primary destination of international businesspeople. Although rooms suffer from a bland, international style of decoration, the hotel's advantages include a convenient location and panoramic views of the nearby Parque Los Caobos. This huge complex feels like a small city unto itself. ✉ *Av. México at Calle Sur 25, near Bellas Artes metro,* ☎ *02/503–5000, 800/221–2424 in the U.S.;* FAX *02/503–5003. 820 rooms, 27 suites. 5 restaurants, 2 bars, room service, 2 pools, beauty salon, massage, sauna, 2 tennis courts, health club, business services. AE, D, MC, V.*

$$$$ 🏨 **Hotel Avila.** This serene hotel, built by Nelson Rockefeller in 1942,
★ is surrounded by gardens and so bedecked with flowers and vines that you may gratefully forget you're in Caracas. All of the spacious rooms have balconies, many of which command a resplendent view of Mt. Avila. The poolside dining area is attractively furnished with white wicker. This is the most charming hotel in the city—and just a quick taxi ride from downtown. ✉ *Av. Jorge Washington, San Bernardino,* ☎ *02/555–3000 or 02/551–5128,* FAX *02/552–3021. 113 rooms. Restaurant, pool, 7 tennis courts, health club, playground, travel services. AE, D, MC, V.*

$$$$ 🏨 **Tamanaco Inter-Continental.** The oldest of the city's top hotels sits on a hill in the south-central part of the city, near the restaurant-filled Las Mercedes district. Both the old and newer wings offer large rooms, many with a clear view of Mt. Avila. Facilities include a gigantic swimming pool and a modern health club. The El Punto bar is one of the city's most popular watering holes. ✉ *Av. Principal de las Mercedes,* ☎ *02/909–7111, 800/327–0200 in the U.S.;* FAX *02/909–7165. 537 rooms, 23 suites. 4 restaurants, 3 bars, minibars, pool, 3 tennis courts,*

health club, sauna, jogging, car rental, business services, travel services. AE, D, MC, V.

$$$ 🖭 **Continental Altamira.** Within walking distance of the Plaza Altamira metro station, the Centro Plaza shopping center, and the Altamira restaurant sector, this modern hotel is a favorite of those who demand reasonable prices and a great location. Rooms are amply sized, and the majority have balconies with views of tree-lined Avenida San Juan Bosco and Mt. Avila. ⊠ *Av. San Juan Bosco, Altamira,* ☎ *02/261–0644 or 02/261–9091,* ᶠᴬˣ *02/261–0131. 80 rooms, 4 suites. Restaurant, pool. AE, D, MC, V.*

$$ 🖭 **Savoy.** At this Sabana Grande budget hotel, service and style are not sacrificed for price. After tackling the nearby restaurants, bars, and shops, you can relax in the Savoy's small patio restaurant or retire to your comfortable, quiet room. The atmosphere is casual and not particularly fancy, but the friendly environment facilitates meeting fellow travelers. ⊠ *Av. Francisco Solano López at 2da Av. Las Delicias (near Chacaito metro), Sabana Grande,* ☎ *02/762–1971 or 02/762–1979,* ᶠᴬˣ *02/762–2792. 95 rooms. Restaurant. AE, D, MC, V.*

$$ 🖭 **Shelter Suites.** This modern hotel, tastefully decorated in muted colors, is conveniently located near the Chacao metro stop and across the street from the Sambil shopping and entertainment complex. Relax in your spacious room with a view of Mt. Avila, or in the bar with nightly live music. Many rooms feature balconies and jacuzzi baths. ⊠ *Av. Libertador, Chacao,* ☎ *02/265–3860 or 02/265–3866,* ᶠᴬˣ *02/265–7861. 79 rooms. Restaurant, bar, conference room. AE, MC, V.*

Nightlife and the Arts

Nightlife

Caracas sleeps only on Monday nights; beginning on Tuesday the intensity of the capital's partying gradually increases, peaking on Saturday when the whole population seems to be out on the town with buckets of red paint. As in much of Latin America, the nightlife doesn't really get swinging until after midnight. **Las Mercedes,** reminiscent of Mexico City's Zona Rosa, is packed with street cafés, fast-food outlets, restaurants, and dance clubs; the district is especially energetic on Fridays and Saturdays. Although Caracas is a casual sort of town, clubs typically require that men wear jackets.

BARS

In the El Rosal district, **Juan Sebastian Bar** (⊠ Av. Venezuela at Calle Mohedano, ☎ 02/951–0595) is a distinguished yet swinging bar and restaurant that features live jazz and dancing with no cover charge. In Las Mercedes, **Weekends** (⊠ Av. San Juan Bosco at La Segunda Transversal, ☎ 02/261–3839) is a popular sports bar that has live music, pool tables, and Tex-Mex food.

CYBERCAFÉ

Take care of all your Web surfing, computer printing, and photocopying (including high-quality color and laser) while you enjoy a coffee and snack at the **CyberCafé Madrid** (⊠ Centro Sambil, Nivel Acuario, Plaza del Arte, ☎ 02/267–1866), located in the massive Sambil shopping complex.

DANCE CLUBS

Unlike their North American counterparts, Caraqueños start dancing the salsa and merengue at a tender age, and the proliferation of dance clubs and music venues testifies to this abiding passion. The most popular Brazilian nightclub in Caracas is **Aquarela Brasilera** (⊠ Calle Humboldt, La Cha-guarmos, ☎ 02/661–5897), which features live Brazilian music nightly and occasional belly dancing. **El Sarao** (⊠ Centro Comercial Bello Campo, on lower level at Av. Francisco de Miranda, ☎ 02/261–4303) features live merengue, salsa, and tambores (drum) bands nightly. Two excellent spots for salsa in Sabana Grande, both with packed dance floors and hot live music are **El Maní Es Así** (⊠ Calle El Cristo at Av. Francisco Solano López, ☎ 02/763–0523) and **La Cibeles** (⊠ Sabana Grande Blvd. near Sabana Grande Metro stop, ☎ 02/763–6807).

The Arts

Professional theater, as well as classical and popular music concerts, are popular nighttime diversions. For current listings, pick up a copy of the English-language newspaper *Daily Journal,* available at most newsstands.

MUSIC

On the campus of Universidad Central, **Aula Magna** (☎ 02/578–1132) features Sunday concerts at 11 AM by the Venezuelan Symphony Orchestra (except Aug. and Sept.) and acoustic "clouds" by Alexander Calder, who helped design the Aula Magna. The **Teatro Ateneo de Caracas** (⊠ Plaza Morelos, ☎ 02/571–3664) hosts chamber music and operatic concerts between September and April. The Venezuelan Symphony Orchestra regularly plays at the **Teatro Teresa Carreño** (⊠ Plaza Los Cabos, ☎ 02/571–7279).

THEATER

The **Teatro Municipal** (⊠ Esquina Municipal, ☎ 02/415385) and **Teatro Nacional** (⊠ Av. Lacuna, ☎ 02/482–5424) feature active programs of dance, music, and cultural events. Traveling by taxi is a good idea because neither theater is in the best neighborhood.

Outdoor Activities and Sports

On a continent where soccer is nearly a religion, Venezuela's obsession with baseball is a notable exception. The popularity of the sport is due in a large part to the thriving professional winter league, where North American players such as Johnny Bench, Pete Rose, and Darryl Strawberry have all honed their skills. The **Universidad Central** stadium (⊠ Ciudad Universitaria, ☎ 02/572–2211) is the most accessible venue for either baseball or soccer, depending on the season.

Horse Racing

This sport's popularity is evidenced by the number of betting booths in Caracas, as well as all the radios and televisions tuned in to broadcasts from the beautiful **La Rinconada** racetrack (☎ 02/681–0513) in the suburb of El Valle. To participate in the fun and the wagers, take a taxi ($5 from downtown) any Saturday or Sunday between noon and 6 PM; admission is less than $1, and there are betting windows manned by English-speakers.

Shopping

Thanks to shopping habits developed during the oil-bonanza years, as well as to European and U.S. influence, Caraqueños are quite style-conscious; hence, the city's numerous modern shopping centers. Leather goods—including shoes, handbags, and luggage—may be the best bargains in Caracas, but don't expect a great steal in the wake of skyrocketing inflation. Although bartering is unacceptable in most shops, you can haggle with street vendors and at modest establishments.

Markets

The most popular open markets are the Mercadito de Chacao, held one block from Avenida Francisco de Miranda in the Chacao district, and Mercado Guacaipuro, three blocks from the Caracas Hilton on the corner of Avenidas Andrés Bello and Libertador. The best bargains for trinkets and artwork are found on the streets, in Sabana Grande, and at Plaza Morelos.

Shopping Centers

Caracas has two of the most gargantuan shopping and entertainment centers on the continent. **Centro Sambil** (⊠ Av. Libertador, Metro Chacao, ☎ 02/266–5047), the largest mall in South America, is a five-level city packed with more than 500 shops, restaurants, cinemas, and amusement park rides. The **Central Comercial Ciudad Tamanaco or CCCT** (⊠ Calle La Estancia, ☎ 02/717435), east of Las Mercedes in the suburb of Chuao, attracts crowds with its upstairs cinemas, fast-food restaurants, and swanky boutiques. Nearby is the multistory mall **Central Comercial Chacaíto** (⊠ Chacaíto metro, Av. Francisco de Miranda, ☎ 02/959–2169). Las Mercedes has its own shopping complex, **Paseo de las Mercedes** (⊠ Av. Principal de las Mercedes, near the Tamanaco Inter-Continental, ☎ 02/917242).

Shopping Districts

In the downtown area, next to **Avenida Urdaneta,** you can find excellent shoe and leather shops owned by artisans who manufacture their own products. Three-kilometer-long (two-mile-long) **Bulevar Sabana Grande** is closed to traffic and has more than 300 shops. The **Las Mercedes** sector features a 10-block cluster of fancy shops and fashionable restaurants, but avoid its main strip, Avenida Principal de las Mercedes, which has an overwhelming though essentially bland collection of chintzy clothing stores and neon-lit trinket shops.

Specialty Shops

CRAFTS AND TAPESTRIES

For the best selection of crafts—and the kind of exquisite souvenirs you simply must take back home—take a taxi (approximately $25) to **El Hatillo,** a restored colonial village on the southern outskirts of town. Its finely preserved streets and quaint 17th-century buildings house dozens of tiny handicraft shops, boutiques, and fancy restaurants, and it's well worth the 30-minute trip.

GEMS AND GOLD

Inside the CCCT shopping center (☞ *above*) in Chuao is **Muzo Gemologists** (⊠ CCCT shopping center, Chacaíto, 3rd floor, ☎ 02/959–3995), which has displays of gemstones, crystals, and rough stones. Another reputable gem dealer in the CCCT is **Diamoro** (⊠ CCCT shopping center, Chacaíto, 3rd floor, ☎ 02/955–0988). **H. Stern,** one of South America's largest gem dealers, sells all grades of gems at outlets in the Hotel Tamanaco Inter-Continental (☎ 02/927313) and the **Caracas Hilton International** (☎ 02/571–0520).

Side Trips from Caracas

El Litoral District

Lively beach towns such as Caraballeda, Macuto, Catia La Mar, and La Guaira are good bets for visitors who need an escape from urban Caracas without the hassle and expense of renting a car. They are also good for overnight stays when you need quick morning access to Caracas's airport in the nearby coastal town of Maiquetía. All are in the El Litoral district, a 30- to 45-minute trip by subway or bus from downtown Caracas, and offer sunbathing and the opportunity to indulge in fresh fish at a dozen oceanfront restaurants. The beach next to the Sheraton Macuto hotel in Caraballeda is particularly popular.

$$$$ 🏨 **Puerto Viejo Hotel and Marina.** This luxury resort offers the convenience of a location five minutes from the airport. All the spacious suites overlook the ocean and a private marina below; several have jacuzzis and terraces. ⊠ *Av. Principal de Puerto Viejo, Catia La Mar,* ☎ *031/524–044,* 🆊 *031/521–311. 107 suites. Restaurant, bar, 3 pools, health club, tennis court, volleyball, shops, meeting rooms. AE, D, MC, V.*

$$$$ 🏨 **Sheraton Macuto Resort.** Guests can take advantage of a wide range of sports facilities; rental equipment is available for waterskiing, sailing, surfing, windsurfing, and some of the finest deep-sea fishing in the Caribbean. ⊠ *Calle Comercio, Urb. Caribe, Caraballeda, Box 65, La Guaira,* ☎ *031/944–300, 800/325–3535 in the U.S.,* 🆊 *031/944318. 493 rooms. 3 restaurants, 2 bars, room service, 2 pools, sauna, 2 tennis courts, bowling, health club, jogging, volleyball, business services, meeting rooms. AE, D, MC, V.*

Colonia Tovar

Colonia Tovar, roughly 65 km (40 mi) from Caracas, was colonized by German immigrants in 1843 and today remains as authentically German as anything you'll find in the Black Forest. Some of the townsfolk are naturally blond, and given the cooler climate and chalet accommodations, one quickly forgets that this high-altitude and sometimes breezy mountain retreat is in a steamy tropical country. The real joy is to hike in the hills surrounding Tovar, or to spend an evening in one of the village's jovial chalets, chomping on sausage and other hearty German foods.

Los Roques National Park

Envision yourself on the pristine, white-sand beach of a tiny coralline island, surrounded by clear turquoise water. Just beneath the surface, thriving coral reefs host graceful anemone, tube worms, and more than 300 radiant species of fish. You conclude a full day of snorkeling, kayaking, and sunbathing on the deck of a luxurious catamaran, and return to your room at a colorful posada in a tiny fishing village. What may be more difficult to imagine is that this vision of paradise comes to life after a mere 30-minute flight north of Caracas.

Archipelago Los Roques is a favorite destination for Venezuelans seeking the genuine delights of a Caribbean holiday; nevertheless, don't expect high-rise hotels and overwhelming crowds of sun-worshipers. As a national park, Los Roques is subject to strict federal regulations that limit the number of visitors and the amount of tourist activity, and prohibit any new construction on the islands. Every structure is original to the fishing village of 450 that grew up on Gran Roque before the archipelago became a national park, but almost all have been extensively remodeled and meticulously maintained as posadas.

Approximately 60 adorable, independently owned posadas line the sandy streets of Gran Roque (there is only one automobile on the island), all of which have two to six rooms with private or shared bath and a common dining area. Except during the high season, you should have no difficulty finding lodging on the island, so take your time visiting a number of posadas before choosing one that suits your fancy. Intense competition keeps quality exceptionally high and prices at around $70 per person for lodging, breakfast, and dinner, or $110 per person for lodging, all meals, and a full day of organized excursions.

Linea Turisticas Aerotuy is the only major airline and tour company that operates posadas on Gran Roque. After the quick flight in a prop-plane from Caracas or Isla Margarita, you can retire to a room in one of the island's posadas. Breakfast and dinner buffets are served in the beach-front restaurant, but lunch is usually had on board one of LTA's lux-urious catamarans, which tour the wonders of the archipelago (free snorkeling equipment and kayaks are available). Guests interested in bone fishing may take excursions aboard *peñeros* (typical fisherman boats). Diving expeditions, likewise, are available for certified divers, as are scuba certification classes. All excursions are led by highly trained, multilingual guides who take great strides to accommodate the needs of every guest (and children are more than welcome). Two-day, one-night LTA packages, including round-trip airfare, lodging, meals, and guided excursions, begin at $350 per couple. Reservations are re-quired (☎ 02/761–6247 or 02/761–6231, ⅎ푨Ⅹ 02/762–5254).

Caracas A to Z

Arriving and Departing

BY AIRPLANE

The **Simón Bolívar International Airport** (☎ 031/355–1060 or 031/355–2598), in the coastal suburb of Maiquetía, is served by domestic car-riers and a number of well-known foreign carriers such as **American Airlines** (☎ 02/209–8111), **British Airways** (☎ 02/266–6133), **Conti-nental Airlines** (☎ 800/35926), and **United Airlines** (☎ 02/278–4545). Most domestic flights within Venezuela either originate or stop over in Caracas's airport in Maiquetía on the way to their final destination. Venezuela has many domestic airlines serving the country and other routes in South America. A couple of the major ones include **Avensa** (☎ 800/28367 or 02/561–3366), which has routes to Miami, New York, Mérida, Porlamar, Canaima, and Ciudad Bolivar, and **Avior** (☎ 800/28467), which specializes in flights to and from the eastern part of the country. Other reputable domestic airlines with offices in Caracas in-clude **Aeropostal** (☎ 800/28466), **Aeroejecutivos** (☎ 02/993–5493), and **Aserca** (☎ 800/88356).

Aerotuy (☎ 02/761–6247 or 02/761–6231, ⅎ푨Ⅹ 02/762–5254) departs from Caracas and Porlamar daily to Los Roques. Round-trip airfare ranges between $75 and $110.

Upon landing at Simón Bolívar International Airport, visitors are is-sued their mandatory (though free) tourist visa, valid for a stay of up to three months. Cab fare for the 30- to 45-minute trip to downtown Caracas costs about $25–$30 (☞ By Taxi, *below*). A more economi-cal option is to climb aboard a public bus parked directly outside the domestic terminal (accessible 7AM to 9 PM from the international ter-minal via a free shuttle bus); for $2 the public bus will transport you to various downtown destinations, including the Gato Negro metro stop, making a final stop at Parque Central near the Caracas Hilton and Bellas Artes metro stop.

BY BUS

There are two inconveniently located and slightly unsavory public bus terminals that serve Caracas. For travel to destinations west of the city, buses leave from **Terminal del Occidente. Terminal del Oriente** serves destinations to the eastern part of the country. Far more convenient and safely located—and definitely worth the slightly higher prices—**Aeroexpresos Ejecutivos** (✉ Av. Principal Bello Campo, ☎ 02/266–3601 or 02/266–1295) offers luxury nonstop service to many Venezue-lan cities, and all buses depart from the company's own clean, quiet terminal in the Bello Campo district.

Getting Around

Downtown Caracas is immense, but the areas of general interest can be accessed by taxi and subway or explored on foot during the day. Most districts, excluding the Altamira and La Castellana areas, are not safe for wandering at night.

BY BUS

Clean, air-conditioned Metrobuses leave all metro stops for areas outside the reach of the subway system. The cost is about 50¢. If your ticket is used within four hours of purchase, it's also valid for a one-way ride on the metro. Additional smaller public buses called *carritos* connect all parts of the city, but they can be crowded and slow during rush-hour traffic.

BY CAR

Heavy traffic, a lack of parking, and the city's baffling layout combine to render Caracas a driving nightmare for visitors. Don't even consider renting a car to explore the city.

To reach El Litoral, follow signs to the airport and La Guaira and then continue east along the same highway.

BY METRO

Caracas's excellent, safe metro system traverses the city from east (Palo Verde) to west (Propatria), with connecting north–south lines from El Capitolio and Plaza Venezuela. The most convenient downtown stops for visitors are Bellas Artes, Plaza Venezuela, Altamira, and El Capitolio. One-way fare is Bs 260, and tickets can be purchased in all stations. If you plan to use the metro frequently, opt for the convenience of a *multi abono* card (Bs 2,500), valid for 10 rides, or the *multi abono integrado* card (Bs 3,500), valid for 10 metro rides and 10 metrobus rides. Purchasing these cards saves you the time and hassle of waiting in potentially long lines for individual tickets. The metro operates daily 5:30 AM–11 PM.

For El Litoral, take the subway to Gato Negro, and at street level climb aboard any of the vans or buses marked LA GUAIRA or MACUTO.

BY TAXI

Don't be surprised if your driver cuts corners, ignores stop signs, and blows right through red lights as he maneuvers through downtown traffic. Legitimate, licensed taxis have yellow license plates that say *libre* and secured signs on the roof, while *pirata* (pirate) varieties have signs that are obviously detachable. If you're leaving a hotel or restaurant, inquire at the establishment about the going rate for taxi fares between there and your destination; this information will be your bargaining chip when a taxi driver tries to rip you off. Always negotiate price with the driver before you get in, as meters are completely disregarded. Fares jump as much as 50% at night, on weekends, and when you are arriving or departing from luxury hotels.

If you're headed for El Litoral, a taxi from Caracas to Macuto will cost about $25. For Colonia Tovar, check with your hotel or the tourist office for information about frequent full-day tours—there is no direct public transportation to the village, though you can take a public bus as far as Junquito and then hire a cab for the remaining 40-minute drive ($20).

Contacts and Resources

BANKS AND CURRENCY EXCHANGE

Banks often won't exchange money, and it can take a long time to execute the transaction when they do. You'll be able to exchange dollars at all the larger hotels, but usually at lower rates than the exchange offices.

Italcambio is a reputable *casa de cambio* (currency exchange office) with good exchange rates and several convenient locations in Caracas. The agency also has windows at the domestic and international airport terminals, with hours corresponding to flight arrivals and departures. ⊠ *Edificio Belmont, P.B., Av. Luis Roche near Altamira Metro stop,* ☎ *City office: 02/263–7110; airport: 031/551–080 or 031/551–081.* ⊙ *Mon.–Fri. 8:30–5, Sat. 8:30–noon.*

Another option is to use your ATM card to withdraw bolívars at **Banco Unión** branches. There are many offices in Caracas, including one in the Sabana Grande district (Av. Abraham Lincoln, Torre Lincoln, ☎ 02/781–4897) and one in the Bellas Artes district near the Hilton (Av. Lecuna, Parque Central, Edificio Tacagua, ☎ 02/573–4964).

Other currency exchange outlets include **American Express** (⊠ Torre Consolidado, Av. Blandín, Edificio "Anexo," ☎ 02/206–0333) and **Thomas Cook Travel Agency** (⊠ Maso Tours, Av. Francisco de Miranda, Torre Provincial B, 11th Floor, Chacao, ☎ 02/264–6466).

EMERGENCIES
Ambulance: ☎ 02/545–4545. **Doctor** (24-hr): ☎ 02/483–7021. **Fire:** ☎ 166. **General emergency:** ☎ 171. **Police:** ☎ 169.

Venezuela's socialized medical system allows for free treatment of visitors as well as residents in all public hospitals and clinics. A reputable private clinic with an English-speaking staff is the **Clínica El Ávila** (⊠ Av. San Juan Bosco at 6a Transversal, Altamira, ☎ 02/208–1001).

Pharmacies in different neighborhoods take turns staying open all night; you can spot them by the sign *turno,* or consult local newspapers for lists of open *farmacias* (pharmacies). If you have an ongoing medical problem, contact your embassy to obtain a list of doctors and clinics specializing in your area of need.

ENGLISH-LANGUAGE BOOKSTORES
The American Bookshop (⊠ Edificio Belveder, Av. San Juan Bosco, between 1a and 2a Transversal, Plaza Altamira Norte, ☎ 02/263–5455) carries new and used books of all kinds, including books about Venezuela.

TELEPHONES, THE INTERNET, MAIL
You can make long-distance calls with a credit card at the state telephone company **CANTV** (⊠ Centro Sambil, Nivel Acuario, Chacao, ☎ 02/263–7783) or by using a prepaid phone card in pay phones. The cards are sold in 2,000, 3,000 and 5,000 bolívar credit amounts at CANTV offices, newsstands, kiosks, and some pharmacies.

You can access the Internet at the business centers in luxury hotels, or at the **CyberCafé Madrid** (☞ Nightlife and the Arts, *above*).

A main branch of the post office, **Ipostel** (⊠ Edificio Sur, Centro Simón Bolívar, ⊙ weekdays 8–6, Sat. 8–2) is near the Capitolo metro stop. A more reliable way to send anything is by private, overnight service. **DHL** (⊠ Final Av. Principal de Los Ruices, Edificio DHL, ☎ 02/235–9080) has several service centers, including one in the Hotel Tamanaco Inter-Continental (☎ 02/909–8226).

TOUR OPERATORS AND TRAVEL AGENTS
A larger hotel will either organize guided tours of the city or have an office of a local tour operator near the lobby area; contact the concierge or a travel agency. The Caracas **American Express** office (☞ *above*) has travel services in addition to money exchange. Two very reputable tour operators in Caracas who can put together soft to hard adventure tours throughout the region and the country are **Orinoco Tours** (⊠

Edificio Galerías Bolívar, Piso 7, Oficina 75-A, Boulevard de Sabana Grande, ☎ 02/761–7712) and **Turven** (✉ Edificio Unión, Piso 1, Local 13, Boulevard de Sabana Grande, ☎ 02/951–1032).

VISITOR INFORMATION

Corporturismo has two offices: at Parque Central (✉ Torre Oeste, 37th Floor, ☎ 02/507–8607 or 02/507–8612, FAX 02/573–8983) and at Simón Bolívar International Airport (☎ 031/551–060 or 031/552–598). Corporturismo also has a special branch called **Unatur** (✉ Torre Oeste, 35th Floor, ☎ 02/507–8607) staffed with tourist-friendly, English-speaking representatives.

THE CARIBBEAN COAST

The Route of the Sun is what Venezuelans call the 563-km (350-mi) stretch of highway that parallels the coast from Caracas to Puerto La Cruz and Cumaná. Fueled by a surge of tourism in the 1980s, major resorts and condominiums have blossomed along the sweeping sandy shores of this coastline, contributing to weekend bottlenecks along the arterial Autopista del Oriente (Eastern Highway, also known as Hwy. 9). Still, the coast also comprises unspoiled lagoons and rugged peninsulas, as well as many isolated beaches scarcely touched by tourism.

Río Chico

167 km (103 mi) east of Caracas.

The attraction here is **Playa Colada,** Río Chico's well-kept beach, lined with palm-thatched restaurants, lively bars, and umbrella-shaded tables. Follow the signs to **Parque Nacional Laguna de Tacarigua,** about 18 km (11 mi) northeast of Playa Colada. At the park's entrance is a fishing dock with an open-sided, very rustic bar where you can drink and dance with local beachgoers. In the late afternoon, the surrounding mangrove forest comes alive as thousands of white herons and scarlet ibis return home and settle down for the night.

Puerto Píritu

110 km (70 mi) east of Río Chico.

In this sleepy village at the edge of the sea the streets are lined with preserved colonial mansions fronting wooden grills, carved eaves, and somber color schemes. The highlight, though, is Píritu's beach: For nearly 2 km (1 mi), the bright blue Caribbean laps a wide ribbon of clean white sand. Restaurants, bars, and hotels are clustered at regular intervals along Píritu's shoreline drive, Boulevard Fernández Padilla.

Barcelona

41 km (25 mi) east of Puerto Píritu.

The capital of Anzótegui State is the site of the region's largest airport. On the corner of Plaza Boyacá, the city's tree-lined main square, it's hard to miss **Iglesia de San Cristóbal,** a stunning two-story church built in 1748.

Even more impressive than the town's church is the adjacent **Palacio del Gobierno** (Palace of the Government), built in 1671 and home today to the **Museo de la Tradición,** which has rotating exhibits of colonial and religious art. ✉ *Plaza Boyacá,* ☎ *081/773–481.* 🎟 *Palace and museum free.* ☉ *Palace and museum daily 9–12:30 and 3–5.*

Puerto La Cruz

40 km (24.5 mi) east of Barcelona.

Puerto La Cruz, the region's main tourist hub, is heavily industrialized, but its expanding marinas and canals are being transformed into attractive Newport Beach–style waterways lined with town houses and expensive villas. Although Puerto La Cruz's own beach is dirty and unswimmable, this city's primary attraction is as a jumping-off point for ferries to Isla Margarita and for excursions to nearby islands and the beautiful Mochima National Park. Visitors flock to the maze of shops on the waterfront **Paseo Colón,** a busy thoroughfare that borders downtown along the beach. During the day, the Paseo and its casual restaurants and bars are packed. At night, the crowds move to the bars and dance clubs in town. The ferry terminal for Isla Margarita is at the western end of Paseo Colón. At the eastern end you'll find boats that shuttle beachgoers between Puerto La Cruz and the small islands visible in the bay, and to Mochima Park. Expect to pay $8–$24 for round-trip service.

Dining and Lodging

Hotels on the Caribbean Coast will add a 10% surcharge to your bill unless you have a Venezuelan passport. Reservations are a must on holidays and summer weekends.

$$ ✕ **Porto Vecchio.** This Italian restaurant is regarded as the best in eastern Venezuela. A lively clientele drops in from the paseo walk for delicious veal and the excellent house-specialty pastas with fish and shellfish. ⊠ *Paseo Colón 117, at Calle Boyacá,* ☎ *081/652–047. AE, D, MC, V.*

$$$ ⬚ **Gran Hotel Hesperia Puerto La Cruz.** This comfortable hotel at the end of the Paseo Colón is near the marina, where the boats take off for day trips to the islands. Spacious rooms overlook the lush gardens and pool bordering the marina. At press time, the hotel was planning a luxurious renovation by the Spanish-owned Hesperia Group. ⊠ *Paseo Colón, Puerto La Cruz 6023,* ☎ *081/653–611, or 1800/62747 in Venezuela, 800/558–6625 in the U.S.,* 𝐅𝐀𝐗 *081/674401. 220 rooms. 2 restaurants, bar, pool, dive shop, snorkeling, boating, meeting rooms, travel services, car rental. AE, D, MC, V.*

$$$ ⬚ **Hotel Punta Palma.** Built at the end of the long curve of the bay of Puerto La Cruz, this hotel has an enviable view of the city and the port from its idyllic El Morro location. Most of its pastel rooms have balconies and overlook the fine swimming pool, the small private beach, and the marina. ⊠ *Prolongación Av. La Península, Cerro El Morro,* ☎ *081/811–211,* 𝐅𝐀𝐗 *081/818–277. 154 rooms, 27 suites. 2 restaurants, 2 bars, pool, 4 tennis courts, dock, meeting rooms, car rental. AE, D, MC, V.*

$$ ⬚ **Hotel Caribbean Inn.** This modern hotel is an exceptional value for this price range. Only two blocks from the beach and near all the shops and restaurants, it features stylish, air-conditioned rooms in pastel colors, with breakfast and a welcome cocktail included. ⊠ *Calle Freitas at Calle Libertad,* ☎ *081/647–292 or 081/672–811,* 𝐅𝐀𝐗 *081/672–857. 102 rooms. Restaurant, bar, pool, meeting room. AE, D, MC, V.*

Nightlife

You won't have to look far to find bars and dance clubs in Puerto La Cruz: All are either on Paseo Colón or adjacent side streets. A popular addition to the nightlife scene is **Harry's Pub** (⊠ Calle Bolívar 53, ☎ 081/653–605), a casual, vibrant watering hole with an interesting mix of young locals and seasoned wayfarers.

Outdoor Activities and Sports

For a small fee, resort hotels sometimes allow nonguests to use tennis courts, weight rooms, and spa facilities.

FISHING

Boat owners throughout the region will take you surf or lagoon fishing in their small, wooden, open-top peñeros. The price will reflect your ability to bargain; the going rate is about $5 per person, including basic equipment, for a half-day excursion. **Amerinda Tours** (☞ *below*) charters deep-sea boats for serious anglers. The friendly, multilingual staff at **Macite Turismo** (⊠ Centro Comercial Paseo Mar, Calle Sucre at Paseo Colón, ☎ 081/655703) has $140 full-day packages to Tortuga Island for barracuda fishing, including meals and transport.

SNORKELING, DIVING, AND SAILING

Explosub (⊠ Gran Hotel Hesperia Puerto La Cruz, Paseo Colón, ☎ 081/673–256) offers scuba diving, snorkeling, and excursions to the islands and to Mochima. You can become certified through them if you are not already an experienced diver.

In El Morro, near Puerto La Cruz, **Odisea** (⊠ Hotel Doral Beach, ☎ 081/812–222) rents sailboats, windsurfers, and pedal boats. In Puerto La Cruz proper, you can rent sailboats from **Amerinda Tours** (⊠ Hotel Caribbean Inn, ☎ 081/670–693).

Mochima

50 km (30 mi) east of Puerto La Cruz.

Beyond the town of Santa Fe, you'll pass the turnoff for Mochima, the launching point for boat trips to the tranquil beaches of **Parque Mochima,** which encompasses hundreds of small islands and sand spits just offshore. Contract a *peñero* (boatman) to take you to any of the nearby beaches, where you can spend a relaxing morning or afternoon bathing and eating fresh fish. The going round-trip rate is $7–$10 per person.

Cumaná

75 km (47 mi) east of Puerto La Cruz.

The capital of Sucre State, Cumaná is the oldest European settlement on South America's mainland, dating from 1521. Most of Cumaná's colonial mansions and buildings are within walking distance of the central **Plaza Bolívar.** One block south, the **Ateneo de Cumaná** (⊠ Calle Antonio, ☎ 093/311–284) hosts dance and opera evenings in addition to periodic exhibits of contemporary and colonial art. Overlooking Cumaná from its hilltop perch, **Castillo de San Antonio de la Eminencia** is one of two forts commissioned in the 1680s to protect what was at the time the world's largest salt deposit. The four-point fort was built entirely of coral and outfitted with 16 guns, much like its companion, **Castillo de Santiago de Araya,** on the rugged, treeless Araya Peninsula. Car and passenger ferries leave daily from Cumaná's harbor for the Araya Peninsula; the crossing takes 90 minutes.

It's estimated that **Cueva del Guácharo,** Venezuela's largest cave, has at least 9 km (5½ mi) of subterranean passageways. You are led into the dank, eerie caverns in groups by a guide who totes a kerosene lantern so as not to upset the light-sensitive guácharos—nocturnal, fruit-eating birds. Visitors are not allowed to bring anything inside, including purses, flashlights, food, or cameras. To reach the cave from Cumaná, take Highway 9 south toward Caribe for about 65 km (40 mi) and follow the signs. Macite Tours (☞ Outdoor Activities and Sports *in*

Puerto La Cruz, *above*) has a full-day, meals-inclusive excursion to the cave for $60. ⊠ *Parque Nacional El Guácharo,* ☎ 081/784–445. 🖃 *Admission.* ⊙ *Daily 8–4.*

Dining and Lodging

$$$ ✕🖬 **Hotel Los Bordones.** This hotel on the outskirts of town has a relaxed, family-friendly atmosphere that attracts more Venezuelans than not. When you're not frolicking in the pool, you can enjoy the nearly secluded beach just a pebble's throw away. An on-site travel office can arrange snorkeling and windsurfing jaunts. Polinesia, the popular on-site restaurant, is considered the best in town for fresh seafood. ⊠ *Av. Universidad,* ☎ 093/513–111. ﬀ *093/515–377. 114 rooms, 3 suites. 3 restaurants, pool, 2 tennis courts, travel services, car rental. AE, D, MC, V.*

$$ ✕🖬 **Gran Hotel.** This plain and functional hotel is in the center of town, opposite the entrance to the Universidad del Oriente. Most rooms are equipped with private bathrooms, air-conditioning, and TVs. The hotel restaurant is quite respectable. ⊠ *Av. Universidad,* ☎ 093/653–711 or 093/653–811. 50 rooms. Restaurant. AE, D, MC, V.*

$$$$ 🖬 **Cumanagoto Hesperia.** Exquisite attention to detail and style set this
★ place above even the most luxurious hotels in Venezuela. Large wrought-iron perches holding colorful macaws border the open-air, Mediterranean style lobby, which has a terra-cotta floor and plenty of Old World charm. The large rooms have terraces overlooking the beautiful pools and surrounding gardens below; these are just a step away from the beach. ⊠ *Final Av. Universidad, 6101 Cumaná,* ☎ 093/301–400, ﬀ *093/521–877. 150 rooms, 12 suites. 4 restaurants, 2 bars, 2 pools, beauty salon, massage, sauna, golf course, casino. AE, D, MC, V.*

The Caribbean Coast A to Z

Arriving and Departing

BY AIRPLANE

Avensa (☎ 800/28367), **Aserca** (☎ 800/88356), **Avior** (☎ 800/28467), and **Laser** (☎ 800/52737) fly daily from Simón Bolívar International Airport in the Caracas suburb of Maiquetía to the coastal towns of Barcelona and Cumaná. There is no airport in Puerto La Cruz.

BY BUS

There are daily buses from Caracas to Barcelona, Puerto La Cruz, and Cumaná; one-way fare for each is about $15. You can also take local buses to any of the smaller towns such as Río Chico or Puerto Píritu along the way. Reservations are suggested and should be made up to 24 hours in advance; contact **Aeroexpresos Ejecutivos** (⊠ Av. Principal de Bello Campo, ☎ 02/266–3601).

Por puesto taxis or buses are another option. These carry up to 15 people and travel set routes between the Terminal de Oriente in Caracas and the Caribbean Coast. Drivers shout the names of cities they serve and leave the terminal when their vehicles are full. Por puestos do not accept reservations, and the rates are fixed; expect to pay $20 between Caracas and Puerto La Cruz, and about $6 between Puerto La Cruz and Cumaná.

BY CAR

The often congested Autopista del Oriente (Hwy. 9) joins Caracas with Barcelona, Puerto La Cruz, and Cumaná; the highway has all road-side services because it is the major artery for coastal cities. Inside the airport terminals are dozens of car rental agencies. Rates are high (an economy car rents for as much as $70 per day) but you can always count on cheap gas—a fill-up costs less than $4.

Both **Gran Cacique**(✉ Terminal Los Cocos, Puerto La Cruz, ☎ 081/630–935 or Terminal Puerto Sucre, Cumaná, ☎ 093/320–011) and **Conferry**(✉ Terminal Los Cocos, Puerto La Cruz, ☎ 081/677–847 or Terminal Puerto Sucre, Cumaná, ☎ 093/311–462) take passengers up to six times daily from Puerto La Cruz and Cumaná to Isla Margarita. For vehicles, **Naviarca** (☎ 093/26230) operates between Cumaná and Isla Margarita twice daily; **Conferry** also carries cars to Margarita from both Puerto La Cruz and Cumaná.

Purchase tickets at least two hours in advance for all ferries, particularly on weekends and holidays. Crossings take from two to four hours and cost $10–$25 per passenger and $20–$40 per car.

BY TAXI

You will find taxis waiting at the bus stations and airports in Barcelona, Puerto La Cruz, and Cumaná. A taxi between the Barcelona airport and Puerto La Cruz costs about $25; a taxi between Cumaná's airport and hotels should be about $15.

Getting Around

A rental car is a nice option for this part of the country, where you will be able to pull off and check out the beautiful beaches at your leisure along the coastal route. Otherwise, buses connect the region very efficiently and inexpensively. Taxis are plentiful (except during the holiday crushes of Carnaval, Easter, and Christmas), but the costs will add up if you rely on them exclusively to transport you between cities.

Contacts and Resources

BANKS AND CURRENCY EXCHANGE

You can use your ATM card to get bolívars at the downtown branch of **Banco Unión** (✉ Calle Libertad at Calle Freites, Edificio Banco, ☎ 081/649–857) in Puerto La Cruz.

EMERGENCIES

General emergency: ☎ 171.

TELEPHONES, THE INTERNET, MAIL

In Puerto La Cruz, the **Ipostel** office (Calle Freites, at Calle Libertad), and the public phone offices of **CANTV**(Calle Freites, at Calle Bolívar) are conveniently located a block from the beach boardwalk.

TOUR OPERATORS AND TRAVEL AGENTS

In Puerto La Cruz, **Macite Turismo** (✉ Centro Commercial Paseo Mar, Calle Sucre at Paseo Colón, ☎ 081/655–703) can arrange for local fishing and boating expeditions, as well as more far-flung tours to Canaima, the Orinoco River Delta, Los Roques, and more.

VISITOR INFORMATION

Barcelona: CORANZTUR (✉ Av. 5 de Julio, Palacio de Gobierno, ☎ 081/743–355). **Cumaná**: Información Turística (✉ Calle Sucre 49, ☎ 093/322–403). **Puerto La Cruz**: CORANZTUR (✉ Paseo Colón at Calle Maneiro, ☎ 081/688–170).

ISLA MARGARITA

Tourists regard Isla Margarita as a sea-and-sun playground, but most Venezuelans know it better as a duty-free place to shop. Margarita is no quaint little island, nor is it especially inexpensive: A recent building boom produced plenty of high-rise hotels and upscale shopping centers. Still, the island has many charms, chief among them its palm-lined beaches, 16th-century forts, and two national parks blessed with mangroves and semi-tropical mountains.

Isla Margarita can be reached by plane from Caracas or by ferry from Puerto La Cruz or Cumaná. It is divided into two sections that are connected by a narrow spit of sand; the bulk of its 200,000 residents live on the more developed eastern half. Cars are the most convenient way to get around and can be rented at the airport; however, taxis and por puesto buses connect Margarita's larger towns with one another and with the beach.

Porlamar

Founded in 1536, Porlamar is the commercial heart of Margarita; its streets have been packed with shops and hotels ever since the area was granted free-port status by the government in 1973. There are relatively few historic sights here, though—perhaps the reason why the most popular pastimes are shopping, sunbathing, and eating.

Dining and Lodging

With the expansion of tourist facilities, new restaurants are always appearing in Margarita, turning the island into a dining delight. The dress code is always casual. Thanks to Margarita's free-port status (which means that duties are not charged on goods), wine is quite inexpensive. As on the Caribbean coast, hotels add a 10% surcharge to your bill unless you have a Venezuelan passport. Reserve ahead during peak seasons.

$$–$$$ ✕ **Cocody.** A variety of international and French dishes has made this restaurant on the road to El Morro beach one of the most select eateries on the island. Particularly tasty is the excellent local seafood, often served with savory sauces—try the bisque or the grilled fish platter with a selection from the impressive wine list. The elegant atmosphere is enhanced by the open-air terrace dining under palms and overlooking the beach. ⊠ *Av. Raúl Leoni,* ☎ *095/618–431. AE, MC, V.*

$$ ✕ **Bahia.** The dining area's large bay windows afford striking views
★   of the beach—part of the reason for Bahia's genuine popularity among locals. Other reasons are warm service, strolling musicians, and delicious, Spanish-influenced seafood. Wade into an appetizer of octopus before moving on to the jumbo shrimp bathed in cream and topped with cheese; in season, try the fresh lobster. ⊠ *Av. Raúl Leoni,* ☎ *095/614–156. AE, MC, V.*

$$ ✕ **Lucky.** Tired of fish? Try this lovely Chinese restaurant featuring Cantonese specialties, many vegetable dishes, and a savory Peking duck. ⊠ *Av. Santiago Mariño,* ☎ *095/642–991. AE, MC, V.*

$$ ✕ **Sevillana's.** This pleasant Spanish restaurant specializes in local fish and shellfish dishes—the paella is particularly good. The colonial-style decor, all leather and bulky wood furnishings, is complemented by the ever-present sound of flamenco music, either from the owner's large taped collection, or from one of the two live shows presented nightly at 9 and 11:30. ⊠ *Av. Bolívar, Bella Vista district,* ☎ *095/638–258. AE, MC, V.*

$$$ 🏨 **Margarita Hilton International.** Close to the beach and only 10 minutes from the city of Porlamar, the Hilton offers a great location as well as attractive amenities. The upper-floor rooms are spacious with balconies overlooking the sea, but you may spend most of your time lying by the lovely pool or taking advantage of the lighted tennis courts and water-sports facilities. ⊠ *Calle Los Uveros, Costa Azul,* ☎ *095/623–333, 800/221–2424 in the U.S.,* 🖷 *095/620–810. 269 rooms, 11 suites. 3 restaurants, lobby lounge, room service, pool, barbershop, beauty salon, massage, sauna, 2 tennis courts, health club, snorkeling, boating, jet skiing, parasailing, waterskiing, dance club, baby-sitting, business services, meeting rooms, airport shuttle, car rental. AE, D, MC, V.*

$ 🏨 **Hotel Maria Luisa.** The moderately sized but well-kept and comfortable guest rooms are only one reason this hotel is such an excellent value and is popular with Venezuelans. Note also the intimate poolside patio and prime location near restaurants, nightlife, and the beach. ⊠ *Av. Raúl Leoni,* ☎ *095/610–564 or 095/637–940,* 🆇 *095/635–979. 98 rooms. Restaurant, snack bar, pool. AE, MC, V.*

Nightlife

Nightspots are tucked behind Avenida Santiago Mariño in Porlamar. Don't miss the **Mosquito Coast Bar & Grill** (⊠ Paseo Guaranguao, ☎ 095/613–524), a moderately priced bar and dance club behind the Bella Vista hotel that offers good Tex-Mex food with open-air dining, great atmosphere, and rowdy fun; it's extremely popular with young Venezuelans. If you're seeking a more sedate evening, the low lights and sultry looks of **Piano Blanco** (⊠ Calle Jesús María Patiño, ☎ 095/640–236), also in Porlamar, create the perfect atmosphere for unwinding and enjoying an evening of tranquil jazz.

Shopping

Although Venezuelans have long regarded Isla Margarita as a shopper's paradise, foreigners may be less impressed by the selection and prices. Porlamar offers a good selection of local crafts, designer clothing, and electronic goods. Shops are concentrated around Porlamar's Plaza Bolívar, east along Calle Igualdad to the intersection of Avenida Santiago Marino, and up to Avenida 4 de Mayo, where serious, expensive shopping begins.

El Valle

5 km (3 mi) north of Porlamar.

Margarita's first capital was founded in 1529. Today it is a center for souvenirs and crafts, from hammocks to rag dolls. A point of pilgrimage for islanders—especially on September 8, the Virgin of El Valle's feast day—is the **Santuario de la Virgin del Valle,** a pink twin-towered edifice on El Valle's main plaza.

La Asunción

5 km (3 mi) north of El Valle.

The mountains of **El Copey National Park** allow striking views of the island before the road slowly descends to La Asunción, the modern capital of Margarita Island. Built in 1568, the **Catedral Nuestra Señora** (Church of Our Lady) stands prominently on La Asunción's main plaza and is one of the earliest examples of colonial architecture in Venezuela. Of particular note is its square, three-tiered tower—the country's only surviving example of a colonial church tower. Overlooking the main square, the **Castillo de Santa Rosa** (🆓 Free), open daily, is a handsomely restored fort built in 1681, offering panoramic views of the island.

Pampatar

10 km (6 mi) north of Porlamar.

The coastal village of Pampatar is a popular anchoring spot for yachts. Strategically placed above the harbor is the impressive **Castillo de San Carlos de Borromeo,** a brawny fort built wholly of coral rock between 1664 and 1684 (🆓 Free), open daily. The adjacent 17th-century church, **Iglesia Santisimo Cristo,** features a flat-faced bell tower accessed by an outside staircase—an architectural detail common only on Isla Margarita.

Lodging

$$$ 🏨 **Flamingo Beach Hotel.** A glass elevator climbs to rooms with views of the sea and, in many instances, the island itself. Although the pink-accented decor is a bit dated, it matches the hotel's festive party atmosphere. Sumptuous breakfast and dinner buffets are served on a deck overlooking the nearby beach and tennis courts. ⊠ *Calle El Cristo, Sector La Caranta,* ☎ *095/624–822, 800/221–5333 in U.S.;* FAX *095/622–672, 305/599–1946 in the U.S. 158 rooms. Restaurant, bar, pool, tennis court, beach, snorkeling, windsurfing, boating. AE, MC, V.*

$$$ 🏨 **Margarita Laguna Mar.** This sprawling hotel with several wings, a waterskiing lagoon, many swimming pools—including a water slide and children's pool—and a beach, offers all you could ask for in the way of water facilities. Meals are included, with dining options ranging from a poolside cafeteria to a fine formal restaurant. ⊠ *Vía Agua de Vaca, Guacuco Beach,* ☎ *095/620–711, 800/858–2258 in the U.S.,* FAX *095/621–045, 305/460–8961 in the U.S. 287 rooms, 119 suites. 3 restaurants, 2 bars, cafeteria, 9 pools, 6 tennis courts, beach, windsurfing, jet skiing. AE, D, MC, V.*

OFF THE   **PARQUE NACIONAL LAGUNA DE LA RESTINGA –** This unique, mangrove-
BEATEN PATH lined nature reserve, 36 km (22 mi) west of Porlamar, is reached via the road to Boca del Río. For $7–$12 per person, boatmen will give you a tour of the park's lagoons, which shelter more than 100 species of birds. The boatmen can also bring you straight to a 29-km- (18-mi-) long beach, where you'll find palm-thatched restaurants and a few crafts stands. Boats depart from the El Indio dock behind the park information center. ☎ 095/42995. 🎫 Free. 🕐 Daily, 8–5.

Playa El Agua

16 km (10 mi) north of Pampatar.

Near Margarita's northern tip, Playa El Agua is rightly famous for its fine sand, coconut palms, and quiet restaurants.

Lodging

$$–$$$ 🏨 **Miragua Village.** White-walled, thatched-roof rooms and individ-
★   ual, semi-detached cottages surround palm-filled plazas and gardens at this enchanting hotel, across the street from Playa El Agua. Airy rooms have bamboo furniture, and breakfast is included in the price. All-inclusive packages are available. ⊠ *Av. Playa El Agua,* ☎ *095/490–923 or 095/491–823,* FAX *095/490–509. 58 rooms, 7 suites. Restaurant, bar, pool, shops, recreation room, car rental. AE, D, MC, V.*

Pedro González

15 km (9 mi) west of Playa El Agua.

This small fishing village on the tranquil, less commercialized western side of the island is a 10-minute walk from the pristine, palm-lined beaches of Puerto Cruz and Puerto Viejo.

Lodging

$$$$ 🏨 **Isla Bonita Hotel.** Quiet beaches, a secluded location, and the only 18-hole golf course on the island are great reasons to stay at this resort. The soaring atrium in the lobby evokes the feeling of a Spanish plaza, and the spacious rooms are tastefully decorated in warm tones. The sumptuous breakfast buffet is free for guests, as is the daily shuttle service to Porlamar. ⊠ *Playas Puerto Viejo and Puerto Cruz,* ☎ *095/657–111,* FAX *095/657–211. 312 rooms, 7 suites. 4 restaurants, 3*

bars, 2 pools, spa, 18-hole golf course, 2 tennis courts, health club, shops, meeting rooms, car rental. AE, D, MC, V.

Isla Margarita A to Z

Arriving and Departing

BY AIRPLANE

Aeropostal (☎ 800/28466) flies directly from New York and Miami to Margarita; **Avensa** (☎ 800/28367) and **Aserca** (☎ 800/88356) operate routes from Miami only. Most major domestic carriers also have daily service from Maiquetía, Cumaná, Valencia, and Maracaibo to Isla Margarita's **Aeropuerto Internacional del Caribe** (☎ 095/691438), 29 km (18 mi) south of Porlamar. A one-way domestic ticket from Caracas costs less than $75.

BY BUS

Unión Conductores de Margarita in Caracas (✉ Terminal de Oriente, ☎ 02/541–0035) and Porlamar (✉ Calle Maneiro, ☎ 095/637987) have bus-ferry packages from Caracas to Isla Margarita, a 12-hour trip that costs less than $20.

BY FERRY

Conferry (✉ Av. La Acacias at Av. Casanova, Caracas, ☎ 02/781–9711 or 02/782–8544) shuttles passengers and up to 150 cars six times daily from **Puerto La Cruz** (✉ Terminal Los Cocos, ☎ 081/677–847) to Punta de Piedras, 25 km (16 mi) west of Porlamar on Margarita Island. It also offers twice-daily service from **Cumaná** (✉ Terminal Puerto Sucre, ☎ 093/311–462). **Naviarca** (☎ 093/26230) carries up to 60 cars on its daily ferry from Cumaná to Punta de Piedras.

Purchase tickets at least two hours in advance for all ferries, particularly on weekends and holidays. The crossings take from two to four hours and cost about $20–$40 per car and $10–$25 per passenger.

Getting Around

You may want to consider renting a car to explore Isla Margarita to take advantage of more secluded stretches of sand still found off the beaten track. The highways are generally in good condition and the distances between towns are never far. Two reliable companies include **Hertz** (Aeropuerto del Caribe, ☎ 095/691237) at the airport, or **Beach Car Rental** (Calle Tubores, ☎ 095/617753) in Porlamar. Otherwise, there are buses connecting all parts of the island, and taxis are numerous at the airport and any areas catering to tourists.

Contacts and Resources

BANKS AND CURRENCY EXCHANGE

In Porlamar there is a convenient downtown branch of **Banco Unión** (✉ Av. 4 de Mayo, Edificio Banco Unión, ☎ 095/658–631) for cash withdrawals with your ATM card.

EMERGENCIES

General emergency: ☎ 171. In Porlamar, the **Ambulatorio San Francisco** (✉ Av. 4 de Mayo, ☎ 095/611481) is a centrally located clinic.

VISITOR INFORMATION

Corporación de Turismo (✉ Aeropuerto del Caribe, ☎ 095/691–438; ✉ Centro Artesanal Gilberto Machini, Vía Pampatar, Los Robles, ☎ 095/624–194).

MÉRIDA AND THE ANDES

As you leave behind the subtropical lowlands and begin your ascent of the Andes, the changes are swift and unmistakable. Thatched farms give way to tile-roof hamlets clinging to hillsides. At 3,300 m (10,000 ft) the rugged mountain landscape includes stone-strewn fields sprouting wheat and coffee. Wind your way past the sensational views along the **Trans-Andina Highway,** through lovely mountain villages, and into the fascinating environment of the páramo, the arid region above the timber line. After reaching an altitude of 3,983 m (13,146 ft) at Paso Pico El Aguila, the highway descends towards the capital city of Mérida, passing through the picturesque towns of Apartaderos, San Raphael de Mucuchíes, and Mucuchíes. The villages along the road and Mérida itself are filled with the warm, family-style lodges called *posadas,* similar to bed & breakfasts, and a delightful change of pace from more impersonal hotels. Unless you can bear pressing your nose longingly against a bus window as you zoom past these marvelous sights, consider arranging an excursion through a tour operator or renting a car for your magical drive through the Venezuelan Andes. Mérida also serves as an excellent jumping-off point to explore the wildlife wonders of **The Llanos** grasslands (☞ Elsewhere in Venezuela, *below*).

Mérida

622 km (422 mi) southwest of Caracas.

Mérida rests in the heart of the Andes, cradled in a valley by the two arms of the mountain chain; yet this is anything but a sleepy Andean town. Spectacular views of the mountains and lingering colonial architecture set the scene for a city whose spirit is decidedly intellectual, young, and bohemian. Home of one of Venezuela's largest and finest universities, Mérida has all the pleasures of an academic center, including excellent bookstores, lively coffeehouses, and an artistic life that ranges from refined and traditional to wildly spontaneous. For the traveler overwhelmed by Caracas, Mérida has a welcoming exuberance. Its streets may be safely explored on foot or by automobile, its inhabitants are famed for their warmth and hospitality, and a delightful variety of affordable accommodations are available both within and around the city.

Founded in 1558, Mérida grew up around the **Plaza Bolívar,** a lively center that attracts artisans hawking their wares by day, and flocks of young lovers by night. Fronting it is the embellished baroque facade of Mérida's **Catedral Metropolitana.** Construction on the cathedral began in 1787 and wasn't completed until 1958, but with its ornate zoomorphic and geometric designs, the cathedral stands today as one of Venezuela's most striking. ⊠ *Plaza Bolívar.* ☜ *Free.*

Dedicated to the artist responsible for the famous stone chapel of San Raphael, the **Casa de Cultura Juan Felix Sánchez** (Juan Felix Sánchez Cultural House) hosts dynamic exhibitions of paintings, sculpture, ceramics, and woodwork by regional artists. This restored colonial house is found on Plaza Bolívar, opposite the cathedral. ⊠ *Plaza Bolívar,* ☎ *074/526–101.* ☜ *Free.* ☉ *Weekdays 8:30–noon and 2:30–6:30, weekends 9–5.*

Mérida's **Museo de Arte Colonial** (Colonial Art Museum) houses a rich collection of religious art culled from the 16th to 19th centuries. ⊠ *Av. 4, at Calle 20,* ☎ *074/527–860.* ☜ *Admission.* ☉ *Tues.–Fri. 8–noon and 2–6, weekends 8:30–12:30.*

The **Museo Arqueológico** (Archaeological Museum) has the region's finest collection of anthropomorphic figurines, ceramics, and tools from the pre-Hispanic cultures that once dominated the Andes. ✉ *Av. 3, Edificio Rectorado,* ☎ *074/402–344.* 🎟 *Admission.* ⊙ *Tues.–Fri. 8–11:30 and 4–5:30, weekends 1–6.*

On **Parque Reloj de Beethoven,** there's a well-known clock that ushers in the hour with music from the great composer. The adjacent **Museo de Arte Moderno** (Modern Art Museum) contains an excellent permanent collection of works by some of Venezuela's most heralded contemporary painters. ✉ *Centro Cultural Tulio Febres Cordero, Av. 2 at Calle 21,* ☎ *074/529–664.* 🎟 *Free.* ⊙ *Weekdays 9–noon and 3–6, weekends 10–5.*

At least once during your sojourn in Mérida, pause, catch your breath, and enjoy a scoop of *chicharrón* (fried pork skin) ice cream at **Heladería Coromoto.** Proprietor Manuel Da S. Oliviera holds a proud place in the Guinness Book of World Records for producing the most flavors of ice cream (725 and counting). Dare your companions to sample the black bean or smoked trout, and order for yourself a cone topped with rose petal, ginger, or strawberry ice cream. ✉ *Av. 3, No. 28–75,* ☎ *074/523–525.* ⊙ *Tues.–Sun. 2–10.*

Parque Las Heroínas contains the substation of Mérida's **Teleférico,** the longest mountain cable car in the world and one of the city's most popular attractions. Built in the 1960s by French engineers, the Teleférico ascends in four breathtaking stages to 4,737-m (15,633-ft) Pico Espejo, which is nearly 272 m (900 ft) taller than Switzerland's Matterhorn. The first car heads up around 7 AM, the last around 1 PM. Take an early morning trip to allow yourself plenty of time to enjoy the view; if you forget to bring a picnic, there are pleasant snack bars in each station. Purchase tickets early for the 90-minute trip from the Teleférico office on Calle 25. ☎ *074/525–080.* 🎟 *Admission.* ⊙ *Wed.–Sun., Tues. during holidays.*

OFF THE
BEATEN PATH

LOS NEVADOS – From Lomas Redonda station, the second-highest point served by the Teleférico, you can hire mules or horses for a four- to five-hour guided descent to Los Nevados, a secluded mountain village that was once a garrison for Spanish conquistadors. The first leg of the journey involves a sharp ascent through the Bosque de los Coloraditos, and then begins the descent to Los Nevados along a boulder-strewn path best negotiated on donkey or mule. Bone-weary and winded, you finally come upon the red-tile outline of Los Nevados, where you can find unpretentious accommodations in local posadas (pensions) with open-air courtyards.

Dining and Lodging

Room rates in Mérida and the Andes are generally reasonable and of better quality than elsewhere in the country, although lodging may be difficult to find during Christmas, Carnaval, and Easter. Book ahead whenever possible.

$$–$$$ ✕ **Mirame Lindo.** This relaxed, intimate restaurant inside the Chama Hotel is noted for its succulent Basque cuisine. The exquisitely prepared gourmet specialties include peppers stuffed with fish, *pargo a la champagne* (snapper in champagne), and *muslo de pollo al ron* (chicken drumstick in rum). ✉ *Calle 29 at Av. 4,* ☎ *074/529–437. AE, V.*

$$ ✕ **El Oso Polar.** A quick cab ride from the center of town will get you
★ to one of Mérida's most popular and Venezuela's most unusual restaurants. Graffiti and theater posters adorn the walls, as El Oso Polar attracts a clientele as varied and appealing as the menu. Try the *pollo durazno* (chicken with apricot and yogurt sauce) or the spinach and

cheese souffle. ⊠ *Pedgregosa Alta at La Gran Parada,* ☎ *no phone.* *No credit cards. Closed Mon.*

$$$ 🏨 **Hotel Belensate.** About 10 minutes' drive west of downtown, this
★ beautiful hotel pampers guests with spacious rooms, lush gardens, a gorgeous Romanesque swimming pool, and open-air dining. The atmosphere is a perfect mix of Andean hospitality in Mediterranean-style surroundings. ⊠ *Urbanización La Hacienda,* ☎ *074/663–722,* FAX *074/661–255 or 074/662–823. 84 rooms, 7 cabins. Restaurant, bar, pool, travel services, meeting rooms. AE, D, MC, V.*

$$ 🏨 **El Tisure.** From the window of your simply elegant room, you may be able to glimpse the dome of the Catedral Metropolitana three blocks away. In addition to a superb location, El Tisure offers a whirlpool bath in every room, central air-conditioning, and a private parking lot. ⊠ *Av. 4 Bolívar 17–47,* ☎ *074/526–072,* FAX *074/626–061. 33 rooms. Restaurant, bar, dance club. AE, D, MC, V.*

$ 🏨 **Posada Luz Caraballo.** Facing the leafy, quiet Plaza Sucre (Milla), this homey posada is a wonderful budget option. The simple yet cheerful rooms all have heaters, private bathrooms, and cozy plaid blankets, and the lobby lounge features a fireplace for cold mountain nights. ⊠ *Av. 2 Lora 13–80,* ☎ *074/525–441. 40 rooms. Restaurant. No credit cards.*

Nightlife and the Arts

In the Andes, hotels and inns are often the only choice for after-dark excitement; many have informal bars and regularly host live folkloric bands, particularly on weekends. In Mérida, the dance club **Birosca Tasca** (⊠ Calle 24 at Av. 2) swings into the wee hours with live salsa, rock, and Brazilian music.

Outdoor Activities and Sports

BICYCLING

Lost World Adventures (☎ 800/999–0558 or 404/919–5820), in cooperation with the local tour company **Promociones Montaña Adventure** (⊠ Av. Las Americas, Edificio Las Americas, ☎ FAX 074/661–448), arranges multiday excursions to El Tisure, the secluded village of Los Nevados, and along Paso Pico El Aguila. Bilingual guides, food, and bicycling equipment are provided.

FISHING

Around Mérida, the mountains are liberally sprinkled with small lakes and lagoons regularly stocked with rainbow and brown trout. In remote reaches, hooking a 15-pound trout is not inconceivable. Jeeps, horses, and mules can be rented for the sometimes arduous journey into the heart of the mountains. Lost World Adventures (☞ *above*) arranges guided fishing trips in season (March 30–September 30).

TREKKING

Mérida is the base for three- to seven-day treks (Grade 1–4) in the Andes. Operators typically provide bilingual guides and all necessary equipment, as well as transportation to and from the sights and food and accommodations along the way. Contact Lost World Adventures (☞ *above*), or try **Alpi Tour** (⊠ Av. Sucre, Centro Parque Boyaca, Piso 1, Oficina 2, Caracas, ☎ 02/284–1433) or **Paramo Tours** (⊠ Centro Commercial Oasis, Piso 2, Viaducto Campo Elias, Mérida, ☎ 074/448–855).

Shopping

Mercado Principal de Mérida. The 433 stalls of this market offer a giddy array of flowers, food, clothing, and *recuerdos* (souvenirs). Begin your morning by sampling traditional, Andean fast-food on the first floor: *pasteles* (pocket-like pastries) filled with pork, chicken, or beef accompanied by a Vitamina Andina—a sweet, milky breakfast drink not unlike a vanilla milk shake. You might want to take home a *cuatro* (traditional four-string guitar) or a mounted calf's head from any of the dozens of handicraft shops that crowd the top two floors. Quality varies among the artesania stalls, but excellent, original arts and crafts by local artists are always available at the gallery **La Calle Mayor** (☎ 074/527–552, ◷ daily 8–1) on the third floor. Six different kitchens serve the common dining area on the top floor, all providing large, tasty meals for just a few dollars. ✉ *Av. Las Americas at the Viaducto Miranda bridge.* ◷ *Daily.*

Mucuchíes

52 km (30 mi) east of Mérida.

East of Mérida, the Trans-Andina Highway brings you to the Mucuchíes region, where the starkly beautiful landscape—scrub-filled fields and barren hillsides—includes half a dozen lakes. This is the "place of cold" in Indian dialect; you'll see the prefix *mucu*—meaning "place of"—beginning the names of many Andean villages here. The town of San Rafael de Mucuchíes is the home of the famous Capilla de Juan Félix Sanchez, also known as the stone chapel. Señor Sanchez, an iconoclastic local artist who was greatly loved in this region, single-handedly constructed this beautiful building to honor the Virgin of Coromoto.

Dining and Lodging

The road to Mucuchíes is a spectacular one-hour drive from Mérida and offers two exceptional lodging options, both of which are splendid alternatives to staying in a Mérida hotel.

$$$ ✕☷ **Hotel Carillon.** This attractive hotel grew up beside its parent restaurant, a sumptuously decorated dining establishment serving French cuisine so superb that even Caraqueños think it worth the long trip to the Andes. The Carillon looks as though it was born with the mountains, resting against the hillside and draped with flowering gardens. Enormous, bilevel suites feature whirlpool baths, inlaid hardwood floors, and elegantly carved furniture made on the premises in the woodcrafter/artesania shop. ✉ *Trans-Andina Hwy.,* ☎ *074/820160. 22 rooms. Restaurant, room service, recreation room, meeting room. AE, D, MC, V.*

$$ ☷ **Cabañas Xinia y Peter.** This tranquil refuge off the Trans-Andina Highway—1 km (½ mi) before Tabay on the way to Mucuchíes, 11 km (7 mi) past Mérida—is lovingly run by a couple who make you feel right at home. Every detail is perfect, from the gourmet meals and craftsman furnishings of the fully equipped cabins with kitchens to the fresh flowers, candles, and thick comforters in the bedrooms. The staff provides warm personal attention and can arrange for horseback, fishing, and hiking tours. Reservations are required for the rooms and at the restaurant. ✉ *La Mucuy Baja 5116 Tabay,* ☎ *014/742–166,* FAX *074/830–214. 4 cabins. Restaurant. No credit cards.*

Santo Domingo

86 km (50 mi) east of Mucuchíes.

The road to Santo Domingo passes through barren, austere mountain terrain and the town of Apartaderos, famous for its delicious cured hams. This is the Andean páramo, an arid, eerily beautiful region above the timberline where the most typical vegetation is the *frailejon* (espeletia), a grayish-green plant whose leaves are covered by velvety hairs that protect it from the harsh ultraviolet rays penetrating the thin mountain air. Sharp, craggy peaks pierce the skies above cold, blue, glacial lagoons that reflect the flight of soaring Andean condors. Those interested in intimately exploring this rugged landscape should contact **Lost World Adventures** (☞ Bicycling *in* Outdoor Activities and Sports, *above*) to custom-design tours by car, by bike, or on foot.

Dining and Lodging

$$$ ✕🏨 **La Trucha Azul.** The soothing sounds of rushing water from the fountains and small rivers on the grounds, the graceful plazas surrounding red-tiled buildings with panoramic views, and the other touches of Andean charm make this a special place. Most of the stylish rooms have fireplaces and wood beams. The elegant restaurant with whitewashed walls and dark wood furnishings serves excellent local trout. ⊠ *Trans-Andina Hwy., Santo Domingo*, ☎ *073/88066 or 073/88079*, 🖷 *073/88067. 50 rooms. Restaurant, bar, café, dance club, recreation room, playground. AE, D, MC, V.*

$$$ 🏨 **Los Frailes.** The most popular destination for Venezuelan honey-
★ mooners, Los Frailes overflows with colonial charm from the bell tower to the courtyard fountain. Each room in this converted 17th-century monastery is uniquely and exquisitely decorated; the attention to detail is also evident in the dining area and Spanish-style bar. After a full day of fishing or horseback riding to nearby lakes, curl up by the fireplace on one of the wide, comfortable couches. The hotel is located 70 km (44 mi) northeast of Mérida, between Apartaderos and Santo Domingo. ⊠ *Trans-Andina Hwy., Santo Domingo*, ☎ *074/63773, 02/907–8031 in Caracas, or 800/606–9111 in the U.S.*, 🖷 *02/907–8140, 305/751–3315 in the U.S. 48 rooms. Restaurant, bar. AE, D, MC, V.*

Shopping

Roadside stands in the Andes are polluted with trinkets, most of which come from Ecuador, Peru, and even Guatemala. However, if you're seeking folkloric art that is genuinely Venezuelan, visit **La Casa Del Páramo** in Apartaderos. Wood carvings, pottery, furniture, tile mosaics, candles, stained glass, and hand-painted clothing—all bearing the signatures of their artists—are attractively displayed in the rooms surrounding the shop's lovely courtyard garden. You'll be delighted by the quality of the merchandise and the reasonable prices. ⊠ *San Isidro 29*, ☎ 🖷 *074/880–132.* ☉ *Daily. MC, V.*

Paso Pico El Aguila

Leaving Apartaderos, follow the Trans-Andina Highway 10 km (6 mi) toward Valera to experience the incredible views from Paso Pico El Aguila, a 4,242-m (14,000-ft) pass and Venezuela's highest roadway. Paso Pico El Aguila marks the spot where Bolívar and his army actually crossed the Andes in 1813 on their way to fight the Spanish in Colombia. A café serving steaming cups of *calentado* (a regional drink made with liquors and herbs) and fresh trout is near the statue commemorating the triumphant crossing.

OFF THE   **MUCUBAJÍ –** Containing five beautiful lakes and several waterfalls, this
BEATEN PATH   section of Sierra Nevada National Park is aptly named the "place of water," and is an ideal area in which to get to know the páramo. The well-designed and informative displays of the Mucubají visitors' center—although, unfortunately, offering only Spanish text—introduce guests to the flora and fauna of the region. Travel on foot or horseback along the clearly marked scenic trails to lakes, waterfalls, and Pico Mucuñuque, which rests at an elevation of 4,600 m (13,800 ft). While you're enjoying the mountain air, remember that there isn't much of it: Keep your pace slow and take time to smell the frailejones. You'll find Mucubají just 2 km from Apartaderos on the road to Barinas.

Jají

35 km (22 mi) west of Mérida.

Tiny Jají, west of Mérida on the Azulita Road, bedazzles with white-washed walls, fountains, and flowers. Founded in the late 16th century, Jají received a government makeover in the 1960s, when its colonial buildings were restored to promote tourism.

Lodging

$$ 🏨 **Hostería Hacienda El Carmen.** This family-owned, century-old cof-
★ fee hacienda 2 km (1 mi) west of Jají, nestled in a cloud forest and beautifully renovated to accommodate tourists, is in itself worth the one-hour drive from Mérida. Fronted by cobblestone patios, the open-air dining room serves delicious grilled meats and, naturally, some of the best coffee around. Adding to its charm, Hacienda El Carmen is still a working plantation where, at certain times of the year, visitors can watch coffee beans being picked and then processed by antique machines. Reservations are required. ⊠ *Aldea La Playa,* ☎ *014/974–1760,* FAX *074/635–852. 18 rooms. Restaurant, hiking, horseback riding, recreation room. AE, MC, V.*

El Valle

10 km (7 mi) northeast of Mérida.

The hills to the northeast of Mérida that form the gentle, verdant La Culata Valley gradually become steeper as you climb ever higher. The drive offers stunning views and one of the most luxurious lodging experiences in the Andes.

Lodging

$$$$ ✕🏨 **Estancia San Francisco.** Wake up to the sound of a rushing river,
★ singing birds, and incredible mountain vistas. Here, you can catch trout in a private lagoon and have the restaurant chef cook it up for dinner with freshly baked wheat flour *arepas* (a thin, biscuit-like bread). From the down pillows and comforters, cushy bathrobes, and wood beam ceilings to the fireplaces in the gracious bar and lounge areas, this deluxe mountain retreat is worth every bolívar. All the suites have two levels and feature spectacular views; the three-bedroom chalets are even more luxurious, with fireplaces, and kitchens. ⊠ *Carretera Via La Culata, km 10, Sector Alto Viento, Mérida,* ☎ *074/448338 or 014/974–3000,* FAX *014/974–4000. 20 suites, 6 chalets. Restaurant, bar, horseback riding, fishing, bicycles, recreation room, laundry services. AE, D, MC, V.*

Mérida and the Andes A to Z

Arriving and Departing

BY AIRPLANE

Mérida's **Carnevali Airport** (☎ 074/639–330), five minutes by taxi from the city center, is served daily by domestic carriers such as **Avensa** (☎ 800/28367), **Avior** (☎ 800/28467), **LAI** (☎ 074/634072), and **Air Venezuela** (☎ 074/630597). One-way tickets from Caracas cost less than $60.

BY BUS

There are morning and evening departures to Mérida's **Antonio Paredes** bus terminal (Av. Las Americas, ☎ 074/661–193) from Caracas's Terminal de Occidente. The 10- to 13-hour trip costs less than $25. Purchase your ticket at least a day in advance from **Expreso Alianza** (☎ 02/541–1975) or **Expreso Mérida** (☎ 02/541–1975) at the terminal.

BY CAR

The spectacular 12-hour journey from Caracas begins on Highway 51 west to Valencia. From here, follow the road to Barinas, where the ascent of the Andes begins via the Trans-Andina Highway.

Getting Around

BY BUS

Por puesto buses leave Mérida's bus terminal daily, covering all the smaller mountain towns along the Trans-Andina Highway, such as Jají, Apartaderos, and Mucuchíes.

BY CAR

The Trans-Andina Highway is one of the most scenic routes in the country, with wonderful towns and posadas along the way—which is why this is a region that you might want to explore with a car. Both **Budget** (☎ 800/28343 or 074/631758 and **Davila** (☎ 074/634510) rent cars from their Mérida airport locations.

Contacts and Resources

BANKS AND CURRENCY EXCHANGE

Use your ATM card for cash withdrawals in Mérida at **Banco Unión** (✉ Av. Bolívar and Calle 4, ☎ 074/527218).

EMERGENCIES

General emergency: ☎ 171.

ENGLISH-LANGUAGE BOOKSTORES

Because it's a university town, Mérida has many bookstores with a great selection of titles in English.

TOUR OPERATORS AND TRAVEL AGENTS

From tours of the Andes to three-night explorations of the wildlife of the Llanos, **Natoura Adventure Tours** (✉ Calle 24, ☎ 074/524216) is a reputable Mérida-based outfit.

VISITOR INFORMATION

Corporación Merideña de Turismo (CORMETUR; ✉ Av. Urdaneta at Calle 45, ☎ 074/630814, 074/635918, or 800/63743, FAX 074/632782).

ELSEWHERE IN VENEZUELA

The Llanos

A broad grassland called the Llanos covers almost one-third of Venezuela's total area, and is an alluring destination for those interested in wildlife or adventure. The Llanos has two very distinct seasons, both of which offer opportunities to see a wide variety of animals and birds. From May to November, the plains are inundated with water and crisscrossed by powerful rivers, forcing land animals to scramble for high ground as the rains unleash their full fury. This is the best time to observe large river otters, and to see flocks of parrots and troops of monkeys gather in the small patches of gallery forest. In August, you may also see egrets and other large wading birds make their nests on branches above the water, as caimans gather underneath to snatch hapless fledglings.

With the end of the rainy season in December, the landscape begins a dramatic transformation. Standing water quickly evaporates in the heat of the tropical sun, revealing the bright greens, yellows, and golds of the grasses. By the end of the dry season in April, the mighty rivers have become trickles, and only a few pools remain, where capybaras, speckled caimans, and huge flocks of waterfowl gather. At this time of year, you can view giant anteaters lumbering across the expanse punctuated by knee-high termite mounds, or behold the splendor of hundreds of brilliantly colored scarlet ibis flying low over the plains.

The Llanos is considered by many to be the cultural heart of Venezuela. Here, most people lead a quiet, simple lifestyle on broad cattle ranches called *hatos* and continue to ride the open range, milk cows, and make fresh cheeses. The traditional music of Venezuela, *joropo,* was born in the Llanos, and local festivals ring with its lilting sound.

Dining and Lodging

As the Llanos becomes a more popular ecotourism destination, more hatos are developing and improving facilities to accommodate tourists. Well-known and established ranches like Hato El Frío and Hato El Cedral are approaching luxurious, with amenities such as air-conditioning, recreation facilities, and television. Hato Piñero, on the other hand, welcomes visitors to a working biological field station. Three- to seven-day packages cost upward of $150 per person per day, which includes transfers to and from the hato, three meals a day, and treks with experienced guides. Aventura San Leonardo, a newer hato, has a prime riverside location and amenities such as a pool to make up for its rather spartan cabins, all of which have private baths and electricity. For additional information and reservations on the above hatos, contact **Orinoco Tours** (☎ 02/761–8431 or 02/762–7662) in Caracas, **Lost World Adventures** (☎ 800/999–0558 or 404/373–5820 in the U.S.), or **Turven Tour Express** (☎ 02/264–6466) in Caracas.

Canaima National Park

Here, in Venezuela's remote southeast, is a surreal landscape of pink beaches and black lagoons, where giant waterfalls plunge from the summits of prehistoric table-top mountains, formations that harbor some of the most unusual life on earth. A trip to Venezuela is not complete without a visit to this grassland, whose mist-enshrouded plateaus inspired Sir Arthur Conan Doyle's *Lost World*. This unique region is protected by Canaima National Park, which covers an area the size of Belgium. Most of the park is untouched by tourists, and currently there are only two main gateways. The settlement of Canaima is at the northwestern edge of the park, a small collection of expensive posadas that surround a black lagoon in an area accessible only by plane. Nearby Angel Falls, the world's tallest waterfall, plummets 807 m (2,647 ft)—more than twice the height of the Empire State Building—from atop the giant Auyantepuy mesa. The falls were named after the U.S. pilot Jimmy Angel, who crash-landed on Auyantepuy's vast surface in 1937 while in search of gold.

The eastern half of the park is crossed by a road, and this region is referred to as the Gran Sabana. Three- to four-day excursions to the Gran Sabana are made in four-wheel-drive vehicles and will carry you to waterfalls, Indian villages, and vantage points that provide breathtaking views of the tepuis. These round-trip excursions generally begin in Ciudad Bolívar or Ciudad Guayana, working slowly south toward Santa Elena de Uairén. The especially adventurous can hire a Pemón guide and scale a large tepuy called Roraima, an undertaking that requires a minimum of five days. At the top, you'll be surrounded by a marvelous lunar landscape, not unlike the unearthly world of a science fiction movie.

Dining and Lodging

Camps throughout the region generally offer packages that include food, lodging, and a variety of excursions.

$$$$ ✕▥ **Arekuna.** Removed from the hectic hub of tourist activity that ex-
★ plodes daily at Canaima lagoon, the Arekuna—a self-contained luxury camp—rests on the bank of the Caroni River, just outside the park
boundaries. After a full day of land and water excursions, enjoy a glorious sunset from the hilltop dining area before retiring to a stylish
cabaña, where the attention to detail is evident in the hand-painted sinks
and the curious figures carved into the walls. All of the building materials are produced locally and the entire camp is powered by solar
energy. Most importantly, the hotel is staffed by extremely personable,
multilingual guides who create a fun, informative atmosphere. Packages for this 90-person facility, including round-trip airfare, lodging,
meals, and guided excursions, start at $375 per couple. ☎ 02/761–
6247 or 02/761–6231, ⨳ 02/762–5254 for reservations.

$$ ✕▥ **Campamento Tomas Bernal.** This option is for more rugged, ad-
venturous travelers who can only tolerate guided excursions for a lim-
ited time. Although accommodations are plain—hammocks with
mosquito netting in a common room—and the food mediocre, this camp
is surrounded by numerous trails that can be explored independently
during the dry season. Packages including lodging, meals, and orga-
nized excursions run $90 per person for 1 night/2 days. ✉ *Orinoco
Tours in Caracas,* ☎ 02/762–7662, ⨳ 02/761–6801.

Amazonas Territory

Venezuela's largest region is Amazonas, an ironic name given that vir-
tually the entire area lies within the watershed of the mighty Orinoco
River and not the Amazon itself. Amazonas contains two gargantuan
national parks which together cover an area of almost 48,000 square
km (30,000 square mi), feature varied flora and fauna, and comprise
the homeland of many native peoples, most notably the Yanomami.
Tourist facilities in this vast area are limited to a small number of lodges
and posadas that are connected to the outside world through the re-
gion's only sizable town, Puerto Ayacucho.

Dining and Lodging

Yutajé Camp. This camp in the Manapiare Valley, just east of Puerto
Ayacucho, appeals to families who prefer beds, baths, cabins, and sit-
down meals. Built and run year-round by José Raggi, the camp has a
5,000-ft airstrip and accommodations for about 30. During the day
you'll probably find yourself trekking through the jungle in search of
howler monkeys, or floating down a river in search of waterfalls. A
three-day, two-night package from Caracas, including air and meals,
runs about $450 per person. ✉ *Alpi Tours, Av. Sucre, Centro Parque
Boyacá, Torre Centro, 1st floor, Office 11, Los Dos Caminos, Cara-
cas,* ☎ 582/283–1433, ⨳ 582/285–6067.

Elsewhere in Venezuela A to Z

Arriving and Departing

BY AIRPLANE

To reach the Llanos region, you can fly daily on Avensa or Avior to
San Fernando de Apure, Barinas, and Guanare. Round-trip tickets cost
roughly $170. Avensa and Aerotuy regularly fly to Canaima from
Ciudad Bolívar ($110 each way) and from the Caracas suburb of Mai-
quetía ($180 each way). Weather permitting, all flights to Canaima fly
over Angel Falls. To reach Amazonas, you can fly daily on Avensa from

Caracas's Simón Bolívar International Airport (San Fernando de Apure) to Puerto Ayacucho ($80–$100 one-way), the region's only tourist hub. Aerotuy flies once weekly to Puerto Ayacucho from Ciudad Bolívar (Ciacara).

Cities such as Barinas and San Fernando de Apure in the Llanos are accessible by bus from Caracas and other major cities. The Amazonas region is not readily accessible by bus (you can get to Puerto Ayacucho from Caracas via San Fernando de Apure, but it's at least a 16-hour trip), so most visitors fly into the region instead. There is no land access to Canaima.

Getting Around

From Canaima, Avensa and Aerotuy can arrange boat trips to Angel Falls and Kavac Falls for $120–$180 per person. In Amazonas, launches from the docks in Puerto Ayacucho cross over to Colombia and return again for less than $15, an inexpensive way to spend a day cruising the river.

Contacts and Resources

BANKS AND CURRENCY EXCHANGE

You should be able to exchange money if necessary in Barinas, Ciudad Bolívar, or Puerto Ayacucho, but keep in mind that you will be away from cities and banks on tours of Amazonas, the Llanos, and Canaima. Try to make any financial transactions before you leave.

EMERGENCIES

General emergency: ☎ 171.

TOUR OPERATORS AND TRAVEL AGENTS

In Caracas, **Orinoco Tours** (☎ 02/762–7662) organizes relaxed, three-day Amazonas adventures based at the Tucan lodge. **Selva Tours** (☎ 048/22122) arranges one- to four-day Amazonas river treks as well as overnight stays at jungle lodges near San Juan de Manapiare. **Alechiven** (☎ 041/211828) runs Amazonas river tours from Puerto Ayacucho to San Simón de Cucuy. **Alpi Tours** (☎ 02/283–1433) organizes group packages from Caracas to the Yutajé hotel in Amazonas for about $450 per person. The price includes three days, two nights, and full meals.

VISITOR INFORMATION

CORBATUR (✉ Av. Marquez del Pumar, 5–42, Barinas, ☎ 073/27091), **CADETUR** (✉ Av. Río Negro, Edificio Sede de la Gobernación, Puerto Ayacucho, ☎ 048/21033), or **CIAT** (✉ Av. Bolívar, Qta. Yeita 59, Ciudad Bolívar, ☎ 085/21613).

VENEZUELA A TO Z

Arriving and Departing

By Airplane

CARRIERS

Major U.S. carriers serving Venezuela include **American Airlines** (☎ 800/433–7300) , **Continental** (☎ 800/231–0856), **Delta** (☎ 800/241–4141), and **United Airlines** (☎ 800/241–6522). **Avensa** (☎ 800/428–3672) flies from Miami to Caracas, Valencia, Maracaibo, and Porlamar. **Aeropostal** (☎ 305/591–2282) runs from Miami to Caracas.

Aeroperu (☎ 800/777–7717) also serves the country.

Flying Times. Flying times to Caracas are five hours from New York, three hours from Miami, and eight hours from Los Angeles (flights are through Miami).

By Boat

Ferries run between the Caribbean port of Güiria at the easternmost tip of Venezuela and the islands of Trinidad, St. Vincent, Barbados, and St. Lucia; the whole trip takes about a week. From Güiria to Port of Spain, Trinidad, the trip takes about seven hours and costs around $60 one way.

By Bus

You can enter Venezuela from Colombia at four crossings; the safest, most convenient connects the towns of Cúcuta and San Antonio de Táchira, about six hours south of Mérida. Buses connect Manaus, Brazil, to Santa Elena de Uairén, a trip that takes six hours and costs $15.

Getting Around

By Airplane

Venezuela is served by its own international carriers—Avensa, Aeropostal, and Aserca—as well as by a number of primarily domestic regional carriers, including **Aerotuy** (⊠ Av. Abraham Lincoln, Bulevar de Sabana Grande 174, Ed. Gran Sabana Caracas, ☎ 02/717–375 or 02/716–397), **Air Valencia** (⊠ J. D. Valencia Caracas, ☎ 041/320–705), **Avior** (⊠ Aeropuerto Nacional Simón Bolívar, ☎ 031/552–767 or 02/238–4622), and **Laser** (⊠ Av. Principal La Castellana at Primera Transversal, La Castellana, Caracas, ☎ 02/263–4227 and 02/263–4047).

By Bus

Almost all of Venezuela can be traversed by bus, the least expensive and often most agreeable way to see the country. Companies such as **Aeroexpressos Ejecutivos** (⊠ Av. Principal de Bello Campo, ☎ 02/266–3601) offer *servicio especial* (special service)—equipped with air-conditioning and videotape players—including routes from the capital to Mérida, Valencia, Puerto La Cruz, Ciudad Guayana (Puerto Ordaz), and Maracaibo.

Making sense of Caracas's two public bus terminals is not always easy. The best bet are the private carriers, usually referred to as *rápidos* (expresses), which also depart from the terminals. Private companies typically accept reservations and offer comforts such as assigned seats, air-conditioning, toilets, and on-board attendants. Two dependable carriers are **Expresos del Oriente** (⊠ Terminal de Oriente, ☎ 02/462–5371) and **Expresos Alianza** (⊠ Terminal de Occidente, ☎ 02/620–546).

By Car

EMERGENCY ASSISTANCE

The major rental agencies will tow your car in an emergency. Towing services can be found under *grúas* in the phone book.

GASOLINE

At 10¢ per liter of 95-octane gas (about 45¢ a gallon), leaded-gas prices are among the cheapest in the world; unleaded gas is not used in Venezuela. The national oil company, Petroleos de Venezuela (PDV), operates 24-hour stations on main highways, some of which have credit-card pumps. Shell, Texaco, and others also have stations.

PARKING

Car theft is a problem in Venezuela, so never leave anything of value in your car, and park in enclosed or guarded parking lots when possible. Although it is wise to be vigilant everywhere, this is more of an issue in Caracas and other major urban centers.

RENTAL AGENCIES

The major rental companies are well represented in Venezuela, as are a few local, lesser-known agencies. It's a good idea to obtain liability and collision insurance, and be sure to get an air-conditioned vehicle, particularly if you'll be visiting the coast or Isla Margarita.

In Caracas, contact **Budget** (☎ 02/283–4778 or 800/28343) or **Hertz** (☎ 02/952–1603 or 800/43781). On Isla Margarita, contact **Budget** (☎ 095/691047 or 800/28343) or **Hertz** (☎ 095/971976 or 800/43781). In Mérida, contact **Budget** (☎ 074/631–768 or 800/28343).

RENTAL RATES

Fees are rising swiftly with inflation. At the moment, the cheapest rental costs about $70 per day including free mileage; dole out an additional $25 for tax and insurance.

ROAD CONDITIONS

Although the Venezuelan highway system cannot be compared to those of developed nations, more than 80% of the country's roads are paved and provide easy access to the most popular tourist attractions.

RULES OF THE ROAD

Travel by day whenever possible; driving at night can be hazardous because of poor lighting and the sometimes erratic behavior of truck and bus drivers. Stopping in the middle of nowhere at night is not safe. Venezuelans often drive as if the traffic rules are merely suggestions they'd rather ignore; consequently, it's important to drive defensively and, if possible, avoid taking a car into Caracas at all. City traffic is aggressive: Watch out for impatient drivers who disregard red lights and other traffic signs.

Contacts and Resources

Customs and Duties

Persons entering Venezuela may bring in duty-free up to 400 cigarettes and 50 cigars, 2 liters of liquor, and new goods such as video cameras and electronics up to $1,500 in value if declared and accompanied by receipts. Plants, fresh fruit, dairy products, and pork are prohibited.

ON DEPARTURE

The airport departure tax for international flights leaving Venezuela is about $20.

Electricity

Venezuela operates on a 110 volt, 60-cycle system, with a single-phase AC current.

Embassies

American (✉ Calle F at Calle Suapure, Colinas de Valle Arriba, ☎ 02/977–0553 or 02/977–2011). **Australian** (✉ Qta. Yolanda and Av. Luis Roche, between 6a and 7a Transversals, Altamira, ☎ 02/263–4033). **British** (✉ Edificio Las Mercedes, Av. La Estancia, Chuao, ☎ 02/993–4111 or 993–5280). **Canadian** (✉ Complejo Gerencial Mohedano, Calle Los Chaguaramos, La Castellana, ☎ 02/264–0833 or 02/263–4666).

Health and Safety

FOOD AND DRINK

Fresh fruit and salads do not pose health risks in Caracas, nor do other dishes at any respectable restaurant; it is not advisable, however, to eat food cooked at street stands. In the interior, avoid fruits and vegetables, raw fish, and tap water because of cholera epidemics in Brazil and traces of cholera in Venezuela. Throughout the country, bottled water is cheap and readily available. Bottled beer and soft drinks are equally safe.

OTHER PRECAUTIONS

Caraqueños are particularly paranoid about crime, and the warning words of concerned locals combined with the obnoxious assortment of security devices employed by homes and businesses can spook any visitor. Use common sense. The vast slums that surround Caracas should always be avoided, and don't wander aimlessly or wear expensive jewelry after dark in the downtown areas of any city. If you're planning a late dinner or an evening at a dance club, take a taxi, preferably one from the hotel taxi line. Petty theft and pickpocketing are on the rise; you're most vulnerable in busy marketplaces and in crowded subway and bus stations.

Language, Culture, and Etiquette

Spanish is the official language of Venezuela, but many words in common usage are unique to the country, especially regarding foods. For instance, Venezuelans call a banana a *cambur;* a watermelon a *patia;* a papaya a *lechosa;* and a passion fruit a *parchita.*

When meeting someone for the first time, a handshake is an acceptable gesture of greeting or farewell. At subsequent meetings, women exchange kisses on both cheeks with each other and with men.

Mail

POSTAL RATES

The state-owned postal service, **Ipostel,** is slow and not very reliable (it can take up to a month between Venezuela and the U.S. or Europe—if it arrives at all). This is partly due to the confusing address system, where actual street numbers aren't very common. It costs 30¢ to send a letter domestically and 90¢ internationally. One of the main Ipostel offices in Caracas is in the Edificio Sur Centro Simón Bolívar, near the Capitolio metro stop; it's open weekdays 8–6, Saturday 8–2. If you have something important to send or to receive, you are better off with a private courier service.

WRITING TO VENEZUELA

Venezuela's mail system is unreliable, due in part to the lack of numerical addresses and the fact that zip codes are not commonly used. For any correspondence that is essential or time sensitive, it's best to fax, E-mail, or use a private courier service.

Money Matters

Blessed with vast reserves of oil, Venezuela rode a tidal wave of prosperity in the 1970s, but dramatic devaluations of the bolívar in 1983 and 1994 have led to massive inflation and unemployment. Still, Venezuela's standard of living is one of the highest in South America, and although the country's reputation continues to suffer from bad press—concerning everything from widespread corruption to a high crime rate to money laundering—Caracas maintains one of the busiest international airports on the continent. Two coup attempts in 1992 marred Venezuela's reputation as South America's most enduring democratic state, but in the 1998 free elections, the leader of the attempted coups, Hugo Chavez, was swept into office with strong popular support for his promises of fairer wealth distribution.

CURRENCY

The bolívar is the official unit of currency. Bolívars (Bs) come in bills of Bs 5, 10, 20, 50, 100, 500, 1,000, 2,000, 5,000, and 10,000. Coins include the Bs 1, 2, and 5, but you rarely see these. The exchange rate is not fixed, but lingers around Bs 614 to the U.S. dollar, Bs 415 to the Canadian dollar, Bs 984 to the British pound, Bs 398 to the Australian dollar, and Bs 322 to the New Zealand dollar.

U.S. dollars, British pounds, and some European currencies can be exchanged in city or airport exchange offices, hotels, and banks, but U.S. dollars are your best option, as you can change them everywhere and the rates are often more favorable than with other currencies. Bolívars can be acquired quickly and at the best exchange rate by using an ATM or credit card at a Banco Union automated teller machine; most major cards are accepted, and Banco Union has locations in almost every city. Italcambio is a reputable chain of currency exchange offices with booths in international airport terminals and major cities.

Repurchasing dollars and other currencies is a complicated process. Visitors are advised to change into bolívars only what is strictly necessary and use a credit card whenever possible for purchases, in restaurants, and at hotels.

In major cities, credit cards and traveler's checks are generally accepted at hotels, restaurants, and some shops; however, carrying cash is advisable when travelling in more remote areas.

SERVICE CHARGES, TAXES, AND TIPPING

At hotels, foreigners must pay a 10% "tourist tax." Venezuela has a 16.5% sales tax, which is added to the price of all articles except basic foodstuffs and medicine. Restaurants inevitably add 10% to the bill for service; you are expected to tip an additional 10%. Tipping hotel porters, hairdressers, and guides from Bs 500 up to 10% is customary. Taxi drivers do not expect a tip unless they carry suitcases. The airport departure tax for international flights is about $20.

WHAT IT WILL COST

Travelers holding U.S. and strong West European currencies should find some hotels and most transportation relatively inexpensive, although the prices are inordinately inflated in Caracas and on Isla Margarita. The best hotels cost up to $250 per double, the less accommodating and spartan as little as $20–25. Going to the theater can cost from $4 to $60 for special shows or featured artists. Movies are still a bargain at $3. Nightlife ranges greatly in price; some of the best clubs charge upward of $5 for a hard-liquor drink. You will find the best prices and bargains outside the major cities and resorts.

Sample Prices. Cup of coffee, 50¢–$2.50; bottle of beer, 75¢–$2; soft drink, 50¢–90¢; bottle of wine, $4 (at a liquor store); sandwich, $2–5; crosstown taxi ride, $4; city bus ride, 50¢; museum entrance, free–$2.

Opening and Closing Times

Banks are open weekdays 8:30–3:30. Watch for special bank holidays—which are numerous—when all branches are closed. Most **museums** are open 9–noon and 2–5, Tuesday through Sunday. **Stores** are open weekdays 9–1 and 3–7:30; on Saturday, they tend to stay open all day, from 9 to 7. On Sunday, most shops are closed.

NATIONAL HOLIDAYS

New Year's Day (Jan. 1); Carnival, the week before Ash Wednesday; Easter Thursday and Good Friday; Proclamation of Independence Day (Apr. 19); Labor Day (May 1); Battle of Carabobo (June 24); Independence Day (July 5); Simón Bolívar's birthday (July 24); Christmas Eve and Day (December 24–25).

Passports and Visas

Australian, British, Canadian, and U.S. citizens who fly directly to Venezuela are issued 90-day tourist visas, free of charge, immediately upon arrival. If you arrive by car or bus, you may end up paying $3–$5 at the Venezuelan border. For additional information, contact the

Consulate of Venezuela (⊠ 7 E. 51st St., New York, NY 10022, ☎ 212/826–1660).

Student and Youth Travel

The International Youth Hostel Federation has recently opened an office in Venezuela. Although the country doesn't have an extensive network of youth hostels at this point, this organization will issue hostel cards and give information about budget accommodations and student discounts. ⊠ *Av Lecuna, Parque Central, Edificio Tajamar, Oficina 107, Caracas,* ☎ *02/576–4493.*

Telephones

CALLS TO VENEZUELA

To call Venezuela from overseas, dial the country code, 58, and then the area code, omitting the first 0. Have patience, as the lines to reach the country are frequently busy.

LOCAL CALLS

A three-minute local call costs Bs 10. Public pay phones accept phone cards, available in denominations of Bs 2,000, Bs 3,000, and Bs 5,000 at kiosks and newsstands marked TARJETA INTELLIGENTE (smart card). To speak with a local directory operator, dial 103.

LONG-DISTANCE AND INTERNATIONAL CALLS

International calls are extremely expensive: The average international rate per minute is $3.50 to the United States and $10 to Europe. Hotels typically add 40% to the CANTV rate, so avoid calling from your room; call from a CANTV office, where you can pay with a credit card, or use a phone card at a pay phone.

You can reach an English-speaking long-distance operator by dialing 122. To use a calling card or credit card, or to place a collect call, contact **AT&T** in the U.S. by dialing 800/11–120, or 800/11–100 in Canada, at any public phone. To reach **MCI,** dial 800/11–140. To reach **Sprint,** dial 800/11–110.

Visitor Information

Venezuelan Tourism Association (⊠ Box 3010, Sausalito, CA 94966, ☎ 415/331–0100, FAX 415/332–9197). You can also contact the Venezuelan Embassy's Web site at www.embavenez-us.org.

When to Go

The most popular time to visit is between December and April, during Venezuela's dry season. During peak holiday periods, such as Christmas, Carnival in February, and Easter, an influx of tourists pushes prices higher and makes it more difficult to find accommodations. During the rainy season from May to October—when there is still plenty of good weather—crowds are rare and hotel prices drop significantly.

CLIMATE

Caracas and much of Venezuela boast a year-round mild climate, temperatures ranging between 65°F and 75°F during the day and rarely dropping below 55°F at night. Expect it to be somewhat chillier in the higher altitudes of the Andes, so bring a sweater. Some coastal areas are hotter and more humid, but you can usually depend on a cool breeze blowing in off the ocean.

The following are the daily maximum and minimum temperatures for Caracas.

Jan.	79F	26C	May	81F	27C	Sept.	82F	28C
	60	16		66	19		64	18
Feb.	80F	27C	June	80F	27C	Oct.	81F	27C
	62	17		65	18		64	18
Mar.	81F	27C	July	80F	27C	Nov.	82F	28C
	62	17		65	18		62	17
Apr.	80F	27C	Aug.	84F	29C	Dec.	80F	27C
	64	18		65	18		61	16

FESTIVALS AND SEASONAL EVENTS

During February's **Carnival** the entire country goes on a Mardi Gras–like binge; in Caracas, nearly everyone vacates the city and heads for the beach. Also in February, Mérida celebrates its **Feria del Sol** (Festival of the Sun) with bullfights and open-air salsa and merengue performances.

The German-colonized town of Colonia Tovar hosts a **Chamber Music Festival** in March. Of Venezuela's important cultural events, the most famous is Caracas's biannual **International Theater Festival,** held every even-numbered year in April. El Hatillo hosts an annual **music festival** in late October or early November with classical and pop performances. On September 24, Jají celebrates the **Feast of St. Michael the Archangel** with music, dance, and much fanfare.

PORTUGUESE VOCABULARY

Words and Phrases

English	Portuguese	Pronunciation
Basics		
Yes/no	Sim/Não	**see**ing/nown
Please	Por favor	pohr fah-**vohr**
May I?	Posso?	**poh**-sso
Thank you (very much)	(Muito) obrigado	(**moo**yn-too) o-bree **gah**-doh
You're welcome	De nada	day **nah**-dah
Excuse me	Com licença	con lee-**ssehn**-ssah
Pardon me/what did you say?	Desculpe/O que disse?	des-**kool**-peh/o.k. **dih**-say?
Could you tell me?	Poderia me dizer?	po-day-**ree**-ah mee dee-**zehrr**?
I'm sorry	Sinto muito	**seen**-too **moo**yn-too
Good morning!	Bom dia!	bohn **dee**-ah
Good afternoon!	Boa tarde!	**boh**-ah **tahr**-dee
Good evening!	Boa noite!	**boh**-ah **noh**ee-tee
Goodbye!	Adeus!/Até logo!	ah-**deh**oos/ah-**teh loh**-go
Mr./Mrs.	Senhor/Senhora	sen-**yor**/sen-**yohr**-ah
Miss	Senhorita	sen-yo-**ri**-tah
Pleased to meet you	Muito prazer	**moo**yn-too prah-**zehr**
How are you?	Como vai?	**koh**-mo **vah**-ee
Very well, thank you	Muito bem, obrigado	**moo**yn-too **beh**-in o-bree-**gah**-doh
And you?	E o(a) Senhor(a)?	eh oh sen-**yor**(**yohr**-ah)
Hello (on the telephone)	Alô	ah-**low**

Numbers

1	um/uma	oom/**oom**-ah
2	dois	**doh**ees
3	três	**treh**ys
4	quatro	**kwa**-troh
5	cinco	**seen**-koh
6	seis	**seh**ys
7	sete	**seh**-tee
8	oito	**oh**ee-too
9	nove	**noh**-vee
10	dez	**deh**-ees
11	onze	**ohn**-zee
12	doze	**doh**-zee
13	treze	**treh**-zee

14	quatorze	kwa-**tohr**-zee
15	quinze	**keen**-zee
16	dezesseis	deh-zeh-**sehys**
17	dezessete	deh-zeh-**seh**-tee
18	dezoito	deh-**zoh**ee-toh
19	dezenove	deh-zeh-**noh**-vee
20	vinte	**veen**-tee
21	vinte e um	**veen**-tee eh **oom**
30	trinta	**treen**-tah
32	trinta e dois	**treen**-ta eh **doh**ees
40	quarenta	kwa-**rehn**-ta
43	quarenta e três	kwa-**rehn**-ta e **treh**ys
50	cinquenta	seen-**kwehn**-tah
54	cinquenta e quatro	seen-**kwehn**-tah e **kwa**-troh
60	sessenta	seh-**sehn**-tah
65	sessenta e cinco	seh-**sehn**-tah e **seen**-ko
70	setenta	seh-**tehn**-tah
76	setenta e seis	seh-**tehn**-ta e **sehys**
80	oitenta	ohee-**tehn**-ta
87	oitenta e sete	ohee-**tehn**-ta e **seh**-tee
90	noventa	noh-**vehn**-ta
98	noventa e oito	noh-**vehn**-ta e **oh**ee-too
100	cem	**seh**-ing
101	cento e um	**sehn**-too e **oom**
200	duzentos	doo-**zehn**-tohss
500	quinhentos	key-**nyehn**-tohss
700	setecentos	seh-teh-**sehn**-tohss
900	novecentos	noh-veh-**sehn**-tohss
1,000	mil	meel
2,000	dois mil	**doh**ees meel
1,000,000	um milhão	oom mee-lee-**ahon**

Colors

black	preto	**preh**-toh
blue	azul	a-**zool**
brown	marrom	mah-**hohm**
green	verde	**vehr**-deh
pink	rosa	**roh**-zah
purple	roxo	**roh**-choh
orange	laranja	lah-**rahn**-jah
red	vermelho	vehr-**meh**-lyoh
white	branco	**brahn**-coh
yellow	amarelo	ah-mah-**reh**-loh

Days of the Week

Sunday	Domingo	doh-**meehn**-goh
Monday	Segunda-feira	seh-**goon**-dah **fey**-rah
Tuesday	Terça-feira	**tehr**-sah **fey**-rah
Wednesday	Quarta-feira	**kwahr**-tah **fey**-rah
Thursday	Quinta-feira	**keen**-tah **fey**-rah

| Friday | Sexta-feira | **sehss**-tah **fey**-rah |
| Saturday | Sábado | **sah**-bah-doh |

Months

January	Janeiro	jah-**ney**-roh
February	Fevereiro	feh-veh-**rey**-roh
March	Março	**mahr**-soh
April	Abril	ah-**bree**l
May	Maio	**my**-oh
June	Junho	gy**oo**-nyoh
July	Julho	gy**oo**-lyoh
August	Agosto	ah-**ghost**-toh
September	Setembro	seh-**tehm**-broh
October	Outubro	owe-**too**-broh
November	Novembro	noh-**vehm**-broh
December	Dezembro	deh-**zehm**-broh

Useful Phrases

Do you speak English?	O Senhor fala inglês?	oh sen-**yor fah**-lah een-**glehs**?
I don't speak Portuguese.	Não falo português.	nown **fah**-loh pohr-too-**ghehs**
I don't understand (you)	Não lhe entendo	nown ly**eh** ehn-**tehn**-doh
I understand	Eu entendo	**eh**-oo ehn-**tehn**-doh
I don't know	Não sei	nown say
I am American/ British	Sou americano (americana)/inglês (inglêsa)	sow a-meh-ree-**cah**-noh (a-meh-ree-**cah**-nah)/een-**glehs** (een-**gleh**-sa)
What's your name?	Como se chama?	**koh**-moh seh **shah**-mah
My name is . . .	Meu nome é . . .	mehw **noh**-meh eh
What time is it?	Que horas são?	keh **oh**-rahss **sa**-ohn
It is one, two, three . . . o'clock	É uma/Saõ duas, três . . . hora/ horas	eh **oom**-ah/**sa**-ohn oo**mah**, **doo**-ahss, **trehy**s **oh**-rah/**oh**-rahs
Yes, please/No, thank you	Sim por favor/ Não obrigado	seing pohr fah-**vohr**/ nown o-bree-**gah**-doh
How?	Como?	**koh**-moh
When?	Quando?	**kwahn**-doh
This/Next week	Esta/Próxima semana	**ehss**-tah/**proh**-see-mah seh-**mah**-nah
This/Next month	Este/Próximo mêz	**ehss**-teh/**proh**-see-moh mehz
This/Next year	Este/Próximo ano	**ehss**-teh/**proh**-see-moh **ah**-noh
Yesterday/today tomorrow	Ontem/hoje amanhã	**ohn**-tehn/**oh**-jeh/ ah-mah-**nyan**
This morning/ afternoon	Esta manhã/ tarde	**ehss**-tah mah-**nyan** / **tahr**-deh
Tonight	Hoje a noite	**oh**-jeh ah **noh**ee-tee

What?	O que?	oh **keh**
What is it?	O que é isso?	oh **keh** eh **ee**-soh
Why?	Por quê?	pohr-**keh**
Who?	Quem?	**keh**-in
Where is . . . ?	Onde é . . . ?	**ohn**-deh eh
the train station?	a estação de trem?	ah es-tah-**sah**-on deh train
the subway station?	a estação de metrô?	ah es-tah-**sah**-on deh meh-**tro**
the bus stop?	a parada do ônibus?	ah pah-**rah**-dah doh **oh**-nee-boos
the post office?	o correio?	oh coh-**hay**-yoh
the bank?	o banco?	oh **bahn**-koh
the hotel?	o hotel . . . ?	oh oh-**tell**
the cashier?	o caixa?	oh **kahy**-shah
the museum?	o museo . . . ?	oh moo-**zeh**-oh
the hospital?	o hospital?	oh ohss-pee-**tal**
the elevator?	o elevador?	oh eh-leh-vah-**dohr**
the bathroom?	o banheiro?	oh bahn-**yey**-roh
the beach?	a praia de . . . ?	ah **prahy**-yah deh
Here/there	Aqui/ali	ah-**kee**/ah-**lee**
Open/closed	Aberto/fechado	ah-**behr**-toh/feh-**shah**-doh
Left/right	Esquerda/direita	ehs-**kehr**-dah/dee-**ray**-tah
Straight ahead	Em frente	ehyn **frehn**-teh
Is it near/far?	É perto/longe?	eh **pehr**-toh/**lohn**-jeh
I'd like to buy . . .	Gostaria de comprar . . .	gohs-tah-**ree**-ah deh cohm-**prahr** . . .
a bathing suit	um maiô	oom mahy-**owe**
a dictionary	um dicionário	oom dee-seeoh-**nah**-reeoh
a hat	um chapéu	oom shah-**peh**oo
a magazine	uma revista	**oo**mah heh-**vees**-tah
a map	um mapa	oom **mah**-pah
a postcard	cartão postal	kahr-**town** pohs-**tahl**
sunglasses	óculos escuros	**ah**-koo-loss ehs-**koo**-rohs
suntan lotion	um óleo de bronzear	oom **oh**-lyoh deh brohn-zeh-**ahr**
a ticket	um bilhete	oom bee-lyeh-teh
cigarettes	cigarros	see-**gah**-hose
envelopes	envelopes	eyn-veh-**loh**-pehs
matches	fósforos	**fohs**-foh-rohss
paper	papel	pah-**pehl**
sandals	sandália	sahn-**dah**-leeah
soap	sabonete	sah-bow-**neh**-teh
How much is it?	Quanto custa?	**kwahn**-too **koos**-tah
It's expensive/cheap	Está caro/barato	ehss-**tah** kah-roh / bah-**rah**-toh
A little/a lot	Um pouco/muito	oom **pohw**-koh/**moo**yn-too

More/less	Mais/menos	**mah**-ees /**meh**-nohss
Enough/too much/too little	Suficiente/ demais/ muito pouco	soo-fee-see-**ehn**-teh/ deh-**mah**-ees/ **moo**yn-toh **pohw**-koh
Telephone	Telefone	teh-leh-**foh**-neh
Telegram	Telegrama	teh-leh-**grah**-mah
I am ill.	Estou doente.	ehss-**tow** doh-**ehn**-teh
Please call a doctor.	Por favor chame um médico.	pohr fah-**vohr shah**-meh oom **meh**-dee-koh
Help!	Socorro!	soh-**koh**-ho
Help me!	Me ajude!	mee ah-**jyew**-deh
Fire!	Incêndio!	een-**sehn**-deeoh
Caution!/Look out!/ Be careful!	Cuidado!	kooy-**dah**-doh

On the Road

Avenue	Avenida	ah-veh-**nee**-dah
Highway	Estrada	ehss-**trah**-dah
Port	Porto	**pohr**-toh
Service station	Posto de gasolina	**pohs**-toh deh gah-zoh-**lee**-nah
Street	Rua	**who**-ah
Toll	Pedagio	peh-**dah**-jyoh
Waterfront promenade	Beiramar/ orla	behy-rah-**mahrr**/ **ohr**-lah
Wharf	Cais	**kah**-ees

In Town

Block	Quarteirão	kwahr-tehy-**rah**-on
Cathedral	Catedral	kah-teh-**drahl**
Church/temple	Igreja	ee-**greh**-jyah
City hall	Prefeitura	preh-fehy-**too**-rah
Door/gate	Porta/portão	**pohr**-tah/porh-**tah**-on
Entrance/exit	Entrada/ saída	ehn-**trah**-dah/ sah-**ee**-dah
Market	Mercado/feira	mehr-**kah**-doh/ **fey**-rah
Neighborhood	Bairro	**buy**-ho
Rustic bar	Lanchonete	lahn-shoh-**neh**-teh
Shop	Loja	**loh**-jyah
Square	Praça	**prah**-ssah

Dining Out

| A bottle of . . . | Uma garrafa de . . . | **oo**mah gah-**hah**-fah deh |
| A cup of . . . | Uma xícara de . . . | **oo**mah **shee**-kah-rah deh |

A glass of . . .	Um copo de . . .	oom **koh**-poh deh
Ashtray	Um cinzeiro	oom seen-**zeh**y-roh
Bill/check	A conta	ah **kohn**-tah
Bread	Pão	**pah**-on
Breakfast	Café da manhã	kah-**feh** dah mah-**nyan**
Butter	A manteiga	ah mahn-**tehy**-gah
Cheers!	Saúde!	sah-**oo**-deh
Cocktail	Um aperitivo	oom ah-peh-ree-**tee**-voh
Dinner	O jantar	oh **jyahn**-tahr
Dish	Um prato	oom **prah**-toh
Enjoy!	Bom apetite!	bohm ah-peh-**tee**-teh
Fork	Um garfo	**gahr**-foh
Fruit	Fruta	**froo**-tah
Is the tip included?	A gorjeta esta incluída?	ah gohr-**jyeh**-tah ehss-**tah** een-clue-**ee**-dah
Juice	Um suco	oom **soo**-koh
Knife	Uma faca	**oo**mah **fah**-kah
Lunch	O almoço	oh ahl-**moh**-ssoh
Menu	Menu/ cardápio	me-**noo** / kahr-**dah**-peeoh
Mineral water	Água mineral	**ah**-gooah mee-neh-**rahl**
Napkin	Guardanapo	gooahr-dah-**nah**-poh
No smoking	Não fumante	nown foo-**mahn**-teh
Pepper	Pimenta	pee-**mehn**-tah
Please give me	Por favor me dê	pohr fah-**vohr** mee **deh**
Salt	Sal	sahl
Smoking	Fumante	foo-**mahn**-teh
Spoon	Uma colher	**oo**mah koh-ly**ehr**
Sugar	Açúcar	ah-**soo**-kahr
Waiter!	Garçon!	gahr-**sohn**
Water	Água	**ah**-gooah
Wine	Vinho	**vee**-nyoh

SPANISH VOCABULARY

Words and Phrases

	English	Spanish	Pronunciation
Basics			
	Yes/no	Sí/no	see/no
	Please	Por favor	pore fah-**vore**
	May I?	¿Me permite?	may pair-**mee**-tay
	Thank you (very much)	(Muchas) gracias	(**moo**-chas) **grah**-see-as
	You're welcome	De nada	day **nah**-dah
	Excuse me	Con permiso	con pair-**mee**-so
	Pardon me	¿Perdón?	pair-**dohn**
	Could you tell me?	¿Podría decirme?	po-dree-ah deh-**seer**-meh
	I'm sorry	Lo siento	lo see-**en**-to
	Good morning!	¡Buenos días!	**bway**-nohs **dee**-ahs
	Good afternoon!	¡Buenas tardes!	**bway**-nahs **tar**-dess
	Good evening!	¡Buenas noches!	**bway**-nahs **no**-chess
	Goodbye!	¡Adiós!/¡Hasta luego!	ah-dee-**ohss/ah** -stah-**lwe**-go
	Mr./Mrs.	Señor/Señora	sen-**yor**/sen-**yohr**-ah
	Miss	Señorita	sen-yo-**ree**-tah
	Pleased to meet you	Mucho gusto	**moo**-cho **goose**-to
	How are you?	¿Cómo está usted?	**ko**-mo es-**tah** oo-**sted**
	Very well, thank you.	Muy bien, gracias.	**moo**-ee bee-**en**, **grah**-see-as
	And you?	¿Y usted?	ee oos-**ted**
	Hello (on the telephone)	Diga	**dee**-gah
Numbers			
	1	un, uno	oon, **oo**-no
	2	dos	dos
	3	tres	tress
	4	cuatro	**kwah**-tro
	5	cinco	**sink**-oh
	6	seis	saice
	7	siete	see-**et**-eh
	8	ocho	**o**-cho
	9	nueve	new-**eh**-vey
	10	diez	dee-**es**
	11	once	**ohn**-seh
	12	doce	**doh**-seh
	13	trece	**treh**-seh
	14	catorce	ka-**tohr**-seh

15	quince	**keen**-seh
16	dieciséis	dee-**es**-ee-**saice**
17	diecisiete	dee-**es**-ee-see-**et**-eh
18	dieciocho	dee-**es**-ee-**o**-cho
19	diecinueve	**dee-es**-ee-new-**ev**-ah
20	veinte	**vain**-teh
21	veinte y uno/veintiuno	**vain**-te-**oo**-noh
30	treinta	**train**-tah
32	treinta y dos	train-tay-**dohs**
40	cuarenta	kwah-**ren**-tah
43	cuarenta y tres	kwah-**ren**-tay-**tress**
50	cincuenta	seen-**kwen**-tah
54	cincuenta y cuatro	seen-**kwen**-tay **kwah**-tro
60	sesenta	sess-**en**-tah
65	sesenta y cinco	sess-**en**-tay **seen**-ko
70	setenta	set-**en**-tah
76	setenta y seis	set-**en**-tay **saice**
80	ochenta	oh-**chen**-tah
87	ochenta y siete	oh-**chen**-tay see-**yet**-eh
90	noventa	no-**ven**-tah
98	noventa y ocho	no-**ven**-tah-**o**-choh
100	cien	see-**en**
101	ciento uno	see-**en**-toh **oo**-noh
200	doscientos	doh-see-**en**-tohss
500	quinientos	keen-**yen**-tohss
700	setecientos	set-eh-see-**en**-tohss
900	novecientos	no-veh-see-**en**-tohss
1,000	mil	meel
2,000	dos mil	dohs meel
1,000,000	un millón	oon meel-**yohn**

Colors

black	negro	**neh**-groh
blue	azul	ah-**sool**
brown	café	kah-**feh**
green	verde	**ver**-deh
pink	rosa	**ro**-sah
purple	morado	mo-**rah**-doh
orange	naranja	na-**rahn**-hah
red	rojo	**roh**-hoh
white	blanco	**blahn**-koh
yellow	amarillo	ah-mah-**ree**-yoh

Days of the Week

Sunday	domingo	doe-**meen**-goh
Monday	lunes	**loo**-ness
Tuesday	martes	**mahr**-tess
Wednesday	miércoles	me-**air**-koh-less
Thursday	jueves	hoo-**ev**-ess

Friday	viernes	vee-**air**-ness
Saturday	sábado	**sah**-bah-doh

Months

January	enero	eh-**neh**-roh
February	febrero	feh-**breh**-roh
March	marzo	**mahr**-soh
April	abril	ah-**breel**
May	mayo	**my**-oh
June	junio	**hoo**-nee-oh
July	julio	**hoo**-lee-yoh
August	agosto	ah-**ghost**-toh
September	septiembre	sep-tee-**em**-breh
October	octubre	oak-**too**-breh
November	noviembre	no-vee-**em**-breh
December	diciembre	dee-see-**em**-breh

Useful Phrases

Do you speak English?	¿Habla usted inglés?	**ah**-blah oos-**ted** in-**glehs**
I don't speak Spanish	No hablo español	no **ah**-bloh es-pahn-**yol**
I don't understand (you)	No entiendo	no en-tee-**en**-doh
I understand (you)	Entiendo	en-tee-**en**-doh
I don't know	No sé	no seh
I am American/British	Soy americano (americana)/inglés(a)	soy ah-meh-ree-**kah**-no (ah-meh-ree-**kah**-nah)/ in-**glehs** (ah)
What's your name?	¿Cómo se llama usted?	koh-mo seh **yah**-mah oos-**ted**
My name is . . .	Me llamo . . .	may **yah**-moh
What time is it?	¿Qué hora es?	keh **o**-rah es
It is one, two, three . . . o'clock.	Es la una. . . . Son las dos, tres	es la **oo**-nah/sohn lahs dohs, tress
Yes, please/No, thank you	Sí, por favor/No, gracias	**see** pohr fah-**vor**/no **grah**-see-us
How?	¿Cómo?	**koh**-mo
When?	¿Cuándo?	**kwahn**-doh
This/Next week	Esta semana/la semana que entra	**es**-teh seh-**mah**-nah/lah seh-**mah**-nah keh **en**-trah
This/Next month	Este mes/el próximo mes	**es**-teh mehs/el **proke**-see-mo mehs
This/Next year	Este año/el año que viene	**es**-teh **ahn**-yo/el **ahn**-yo keh vee-**yen**-ay
Yesterday/today/tomorrow	Ayer/hoy/mañana	ah-**yehr**/oy/mahn-**yah**-nah
This morning/afternoon	Esta mañana/tarde	**es**-tah mahn-**yah**-nah/**tar**-deh

Tonight	Esta noche	**es**-tah **no**-cheh
What?	¿Qué?	keh
What is it?	¿Qué es esto?	keh es **es**-toh
Why?	¿Por qué?	pore **keh**
Who?	¿Quién?	kee-**yen**
Where is . . . ?	¿Dónde está . . . ?	**dohn**-deh es-**tah**
the train station?	la estación del tren?	la es-tah-see-**on** del **train**
the subway station?	la estación del Tren subterráneo?	la es-ta-see-**on** del trehn soob-tair-**ron**-a-o
the bus stop?	la parada del autobus?	la pah-**rah**-dah del oh-toh-**boos**
the post office?	la oficina de correos?	la oh-fee-**see**-nah deh koh-**reh**-os
the bank?	el banco?	el **bahn**-koh
the hotel?	el hotel?	el oh-**tel**
the store?	la tienda?	la tee-**en**-dah
the cashier?	la caja?	la **kah**-hah
the museum?	el museo?	el moo-**seh**-oh
the hospital?	el hospital?	el ohss-pee-**tal**
the elevator?	el ascensor?	el ah-**sen**-sohr
the bathroom?	el baño?	el **bahn**-yoh
Here/there	Aquí/allá	ah-**key**/ah-**yah**
Open/closed	Abierto/cerrado	ah-bee-**er**-toh/ ser-**ah**-doh
Left/right	Izquierda/derecha	iss-key-**er**-dah/ dare-**eh**-chah
Straight ahead	Derecho	dare-**eh**-choh
Is it near/far?	¿Está cerca/lejos?	es-**tah sehr**-kah/ **leh**-hoss
I'd like . . .	Quisiera . . .	kee-see-ehr-ah
a room	un cuarto/una habitación	oon **kwahr**-toh/ **oo**-nah ah-bee-tah-see-**on**
the key	la llave	lah **yah**-veh
a newspaper	un periódico	oon pehr-ee-**oh**-dee-koh
a stamp	un sello de correo	oon **seh**-yo deh koh-**reh**-oh
I'd like to buy . . .	Quisiera comprar . . .	kee-see-**ehr**-ah kohm-**prahr**
cigarettes	cigarrillos	ce-ga-**ree**-yohs
matches	cerillos	ser-**ee**-ohs
a dictionary	un diccionario	oon deek-see-oh-**nah**-ree-oh
soap	jabón	hah-**bohn**
sunglasses	gafas de sol	**ga**-fahs deh sohl
suntan lotion	loción bronceadora	loh-see-**ohn** brohn-seh-ah-**do**-rah
a map	un mapa	oon **mah**-pah
a magazine	una revista	**oon**-ah reh-**veess**-tah

paper	papel	pah-**pel**
envelopes	sobres	**so**-brehs
a postcard	una tarjeta postal	**oon**-ah tar-**het**-ah post-**ahl**
How much is it?	¿Cuánto cuesta?	**kwahn**-toh **kwes**-tah
It's expensive/ cheap	Está caro/barato	es-**tah kah**-roh/ bah-**rah**-toh
A little/a lot	Un poquito/ mucho	oon poh-**kee**-toh/ **moo**-choh
More/less	Más/menos	mahss/**men**-ohss
Enough/too much/too little	Suficiente/ demasiado/ muy poco	soo-fee-see-**en**-teh/ deh-mah-see-**ah**-doh/**moo**-ee poh-koh
Telephone	Teléfono	tel-**ef**-oh-no
Telegram	Telegrama	teh-leh-**grah**-mah
I am ill	Estoy enfermo(a)	es-**toy** en-**fehr**-moh(mah)
Please call a doctor	Por favor llame a un medico	pohr fah-**vor ya**-meh ah oon **med**-ee-koh
Help!	¡Auxilio! ¡Ayuda! ¡Socorro!	owk-**see**-lee-oh/ ah-**yoo**-dah/ soh-**kohr**-roh
Fire!	¡Incendio!	en-**sen**-dee-oo
Caution!/Look out!	¡Cuidado!	kwee-**dah**-doh

On the Road

Avenue	Avenida	ah-ven-**ee**-dah
Broad, tree-lined boulevard	Bulevar	boo-leh-**var**
Fertile plain	Vega	**veh**-gah
Highway	Carretera	car-reh-**ter**-ah
Mountain pass, Street	Puerto Calle	poo-**ehr**-toh **cah**-yeh
Waterfront promenade	Rambla	**rahm**-blah
Wharf	Embarcadero	em-bar-cah-**deh**-ro

In Town

Cathedral	Catedral	cah-teh-**dral**
Church	Templo/Iglesia	**tem**-plo/ee-**glehs**-see-ah
City hall	Casa de gobierno	kah-sah deh go-bee-**ehr**-no
Door, gate	Puerta portón	poo-**ehr**-tah por-**ton**
Entrance/exit	Entrada/salida	en-**trah**-dah/sah-**lee**-dah
Inn, rustic bar, or restaurant	Taverna	tah-**vehr**-nah
Main square	Plaza principal	plah-thah prin-see-**pahl**

Market	Mercado	mer-**kah**-doh
Neighborhood	Barrio	**bahr**-ree-o
Traffic circle	Glorieta	glor-ee-**eh**-tah
Wine cellar, wine bar, or wine shop	Bodega	boh-**deh**-gah

Dining Out

A bottle of . . .	Una botella de . . .	**oo**-nah bo-**teh**-yah deh
A cup of . . .	Una taza de . . .	**oo**-nah **tah**-thah deh
A glass of . . .	Un vaso de . . .	oon **vah**-so deh
Ashtray	Un cenicero	oon sen-ee-**seh**-roh
Bill/check	La cuenta	lah **kwen**-tah
Bread	El pan	el pahn
Breakfast	El desayuno	el deh-sah-**yoon**-oh
Butter	La mantequilla	lah man-teh-**key**-yah
Cheers!	¡Salud!	sah-**lood**
Cocktail	Un aperitivo	oon ah-pehr-ee-**tee**-voh
Dinner	La cena	lah **seh**-nah
Dish	Un plato	oon **plah**-toh
Menu of the day	Menú del día	meh-**noo** del **dee**-ah
Enjoy!	¡Buen provecho!	bwehn pro-**veh**-cho
Fixed-price menu	Menú fijo o turistico	meh-**noo fee**-hoh oh too-**ree**-stee-coh
Fork	El tenedor	el ten-eh-**dor**
Is the tip included?	¿Está incluida la propina?	es-**tah** in-cloo-**ee**-dah lah pro-**pee**-nah
Knife	El cuchillo	el koo-**chee**-yo
Large portion of savory snacks	Raciónes	rah-see-**oh**-nehs
Lunch	La comida	lah koh-**mee**-dah
Menu	La carta, el menú	lah **cart**-ah, el meh-**noo**
Napkin	La servilleta	lah sehr-vee-**yet**-ah
Pepper	La pimienta	lah pee-me-**en**-tah
Please give me	Por favor déme	pore fah-**vor deh**-meh
Salt	La sal	lah sahl
Savory snacks	Tapas	**tah**-pahs
Spoon	Una cuchara	**oo**-nah koo-**chah**-rah
Sugar	El azúcar	el ah-**thu**-kar
Waiter!/Waitress!	¡Por favor Señor/Señorita!	pohr fah-**vor** sen-**yor**/sen-yor-ee-tah

INDEX

N

L@@king © FOR A great place to go?

We know just the place. In fact, it attracts more than 125,000 visitors a day, making it one of the world's most popular travel destinations. It's previewtravel.com, the Web's comprehensive resource for travelers. It gives you access to over 500 airlines, 25,000 hotels, rental cars, cruises, vacation packages and support from travel experts 24 hours a day. Plus great information from Fodor's travel guides and travelers just like you. All of which makes previewtravel.com quite a find.

Preview Travel has everything you need to plan & book your next trip.

air, car & hotel reservations

vacation packages & cruises

destination planning & travel tips

24-hour customer service

previewtravel.com

preview travel

aol keyword: previewtravel

www.previewtravel.com